Energy use in the United States by state and region

A statistical compendium of 1972 consumption, prices and expenditures

IRVING HOCH

RESEARCH PAPER R-9

RESOURCES FOR THE FUTURE / WASHINGTON, D.C.

Resources for the Future is a nonprofit organization for research and education in the development, conservation, and use of natural resources and the improvement of the quality of the environment. It was established in 1952 with the cooperation of the Ford Foundation. Grants for research are accepted from government and private sources only if they meet the conditions of a policy established by the Board of Directors of Resources for the Future. The policy states that RFF shall be solely responsible for the conduct of the research and free to make the research results available to the public. Part of the work of Resources for the Future is carried out by its resident staff; part is supported by grants to universities and other nonprofit organizations. Unless otherwise stated, interpretations and conclusions in RFF publications are those of the authors; the organization takes responsibility for the selection of significant subjects for study, the competence of the researchers, and their freedom of inquiry.

Library of Congress Catalog Card Number 78-4358
ISBN 0-8018-2123-1

Published April 1978. $15.00.

Second Printing, January 1979

Table of Contents

List of Tables, Grouped By Topic

Appendix Tables: Detailed Information on Energy Quantities,
Prices and Expenditures by State and Region

Acknowledgments

Sylvia Steadham typed the text of this report in its several stages from draft manuscript to completed text, and also typed the headings for the tables. The tables, per se, were generated on the Brookings Institution computer and terminals employing library computer programs and several computer programs written for this project by Judith Drake. In addition, Mrs. Drake helped in developing the source data for this project.

A number of individuals and agencies also helped in the development of source data, as indicated by citations in the text; specific mention should be made of Flora Stetson of RFF; Lulie Crump, James Diehl and Leonard Fanelli of the Bureau of Mines; and the statistical office of the American Petroleum Institute, who afforded access to trade publications.

William Watson of RFF and Sylvia Harbin, Jane Middlebrooks, Mimi Schade, James Selario and Richard Thomas of the Brookings Computer Center staff were helpful in the technical phase of performing the calculations and printing the tables.

Herbert Morton made a number of useful suggestions on the organization of the report and the presentation of the results, and was relied on for his advice throughout the project. Joan Tron advised on preparing the manuscript for press.

Jack Alterman, Joel Darmstadter and Kenneth Frederick reviewed the report and made a number of helpful critical comments which led to some important revisions and extensions incorporated in the final draft of the report.

PART I

Substantive Results

Chapter 1

Overview

Purpose and Uses

This report contains a compendium of statistics on U.S. energy use by
state and region in 1972, some applications of those statistics in describing
the role of energy in subnational economies, and some critical evaluations
of the adequacy of those statistics. The work was carried out because of
a discerned need to develop information on subnational energy use. Energy
problems and conflicts often involve geography, and shifts in energy relationships are likely to have considerable impact on state and regional
economies. But these topics seldom can be addressed in depth because of
limitations of data, particularly price and expenditures data. This report
attempts to start a remedial process, by developing and presenting such data
for the benchmark year of 1972, thus demonstrating that the job can be done,
at least in terms of a useful first approximation. In addition, the compre-
hensive nature of the report, which includes a discussion of source data gaps
and conflicts, should be of help in any successive closer approximations and
in the extension of coverage to later years.

In addition to the systematic presentation of expenditures and price
data to parallel data on consumption of BTU, a major contribution of the
report is its estimated distribution of energy use by sectors (household,
business and government sectors), thus recasting energy statistics into
a form consistent with national and regional income accounting, and with

input-output analysis. As an elaboration of this classification process, concentric levels of use are identified, beginning with use by final demand sectors (household and government), expanding to use by "customers" (final demand plus business use exclusive of energy used in energy production) and concluding with all use (including energy used in energy production).

As a compendium of statistics, this report should be of use as a source book for those needing a datum or a data series on a particular form of energy use by locale, including the United States, since national values appear for all series. The text discusses major patterns observed in the data, and such may be a useful descriptive narrative for those interested in the role of energy in state and regional economies. The critical evaluations of the adequacy of statistics may be of use to professional practitioners, both in flagging pitfalls and in indicating where investments might be made in improved statistics. Finally, the data here can be drawn on for analysis and for applications to policy questions. Some examples are presented in text in the form of equations relating energy use per capita or per worker to price, income, climate and region.

Organization and Content

This report presents information on energy consumption, expenditures and prices using three systems of classification, respectively involving energy source, function and sector. The energy source classification includes petroleum products, natural gas, electricity, coal, hydroelectric power and nuclear power, with the last three sources often combined into one category. Petroleum products, in turn, are subclassified into gasoline, heating fuels, non-gasoline transportation fuels and products employed in industrial processing, energy production and miscellaneous uses. The categories in the

functional classification are residential, commercial, industrial, transportation, electric utility use, non-electric utility energy production
and municipal-institutional use. The sector classification consists of
household, business, federal government, and state and local government
use.

Quantity consumed and expenditures data are presented in the form of
amounts of use, per capita levels of use and various indexes and fractions
of use relative to national or total levels. Price data appear in the form
of prices for specific "key" products, average costs per unit borne by
consumers for groups of products (equal to expenditures divided by corresponding quantities), and price indexes, obtained by weighting state prices
by U.S. quantity weights.

All of the energy use statistics are for 1972, seen as a useful base
year because 1973 was the year in which OPEC carried out its massive price
increases. Admittedly, 1972 may now seem a distant period, but this judgement can go too far. There is always a lag of several years before data
become available, so that 1972 is not so long ago in terms of the ability
to carry out data manipulations and analysis. Further, massive energy
price increases at the producer level are much less massive at the retail
level, where other costs comprise a major part of the total; in addition,
as of 1978, much of the relative price increase in energy had been dissi-
pated by increases in the general price level, so that 1978 conditions are
not as different from those of 1972 as is commonly perceived. Despite this
deemphasis of the difference between periods, it seems obvious that the
development of similar information for a more recent year, or years, would
be of considerable use in comparative analysis and policy. The present report

may be of help in furnishing methods and sources useful in the development
of such data, as well as in furnishing some of the base statistics for
the comparisons.

The report appears in two major parts. Part I presents information
at a more aggregate level than does Part II, and it focuses on questions
involving subject matter. It presents the final results of what was often
an involved estimating process, and is primarily concerned with the meaning
and interpretation of those results.

In contrast, Part II presents more detailed information and focuses
on questions of method. It contains detailed information on the estimating
process and documentation of the data sources drawn upon in developing the
results, organized as a set of appendixes plus supporting materials.

In both parts, the presentation follows the same basic pattern. The
text of a section (a chapter or an appendix) is presented, in turn followed
by the set of tables discussed in that section, with the tables presenting
information on state and regional energy use in terms of quantities consumed,
expenditures and prices. Those major tables are numbered, with the numbers
in consecutive order in Part I, and keyed to appendix designation and sub-
section in the appendixes; tables presented in text for purposes of documentation or interpretation are not numbered.

In Part I, the present overview chapter brings together information
on all energy use by combining data on specific energy sources that are
covered in subsequent chapters. Thus, Chapter 2 is devoted to petroleum
product use, Chapter 3 to natural gas, Chapter 4 to electricity and Chapter 5
to coal, hydroelectric power and nuclear power. Chapter 6, which concludes
Part I, reviews the estimating process, carries out some comparative analyses

and makes some suggestions for future research. Part II is the under-
girding for Part I. Thus, the chapters on specific energy sources in
Part I draw on underlying information appearing in the appendixes of Part II,
where appendixes A through E present detailed information on petroleum
products, and F through I cover natural gas, electricity, coal and hydropower
plus nuclear power, respectively. Hence, the order of presentation essentially reverses the flow of the work as it was carried out, with initial
"basic" components reported on last (in the appendixes), intermediate stages
and components reported on in the later chapters of Part I, and the ultimate
aggregation discussed in this initial chapter of Part I. Then, a retro-
spective review of the work of the appendixes is employed in Chapter 6 to
critically appraise source data and to suggest likely data improvements.

Part II also presents supporting materials in the form of tables of
basic scale factors, a list of references, and a detailed set of source notes.
The tables of scale factors include 1972 population data and energy unit
conversion factors, showing BTU per physical unit, such as BTU per barrel
of distillate fuel oil. (The BTU is the standard unit employed in measuring
energy quantities, and it equals the amount of energy required to raise the
temperature of water one degree fahrenheit. A gallon of gasoline contains
138,700 BTU.) The list of references covers citations employed in Part II;
since many of the references in Part II were cited on numerous occasions
at various points in the appendixes, a specialized reference system using
that list was employed for ease of exposition. The set of source notes
shows how each table was derived, so that all data can be traced back to
underlying sources. The source notes cover both Parts I and II and show how
initial tables in a chapter or an appendix were derived from previous tables

or data, and then how those tables were operated on to yield succeeding tables. Thus, the initial tables in Chapter 1 were derived by bringing together corresponding information from Chapters 2, 3, 4 and 5, which in turn were derived from a set of "ultimate" estimates in the appendixes. Initial tables of state levels of use were summed to yield regional totals, or were divided by corresponding population figures to yield per capita results. The ultimate estimates in the appendixes were developed from raw source data through what was often an involved estimating process, described in detail in the appendixes and in step-by-step fashion in the source notes. A narrative summary, focusing on data gaps and conflicts, appears in Chapter 6. An even shorter summary is presented next to sketch in some of the fundamental procedures and philosophy employed in developing the tables. The cost in possible repetition seems outweighed by the benefit of giving the reader a general understanding of the estimating process at an early stage. The discussion includes some comparison and reconciliation of U.S. totals obtained here with corresponding Bureau of Mines data.

Procedures and Philosophy

Primary reliance was placed on Bureau of Mines series for raw source data on quantities for petroleum products, natural gas and coal. The Edison Electric Institute _Yearbook_ was the primary source for quantities of electricity, hydroelectric power and nuclear power.

The Bureau of Mines data series were compared and combined with a number of other series, obtained primarily from the Federal Highway Administration and a confidential source in the case of petroleum products, the American Gas Association in the case of natural gas, and the National Coal Association in the case of coal. When comparisons revealed data problems,

procedures were developed to fill in gaps or resolve conflicts by drawing
on data from other agencies and associations, and by applying internal
evidence. In a number of cases, conflicts were resolved by averaging or
splicing the alternative series.

Primary data on hydroelectric and nuclear power consisted of electric
power generated, and this was converted to "fossil fuel-equivalent" input,
with a small ex post adjustment for efficiency differences.

A key element of the estimating process was that of building upward from
specific uses to ever more aggregated quantities; in practice, checks were
employed at every stage of the combination process. The penultimate check
is contained in the table on the next page, which compares results in this
study to Bureau of Mines data on U.S. consumption by energy source.

In its series on petroleum consumption the Bureau of Mines (BOM) includes
"raw materials," amounting to about 10 percent of total BTU, and a trivial
amount under the heading of "miscellaneous and unaccounted for." Asphalt
and road oil accounts for about a third of the raw material BTU, and the
remainder is catalogued under special napthas, lubes and waxes, petroleum
coke and petrochemical feedstock offtake.[1] Such uses as petrochemical inputs
were considered to be non-energy consumption, and hence, were treated as
outside the scope of the present study. With the elimination of raw materials
and the miscellaneous-unaccounted for category, the BOM fuel and power BTU
total corresponds closely to the U.S. petroleum total here, the difference
reflecting those cases where a BOM series was combined with a series from
another source. Such combination usually yielded a small change in the total
for the specific consumption category.

---

[1]U.S. Bureau of Mines, Minerals Yearbook, 1973, Vol. I, table 22, 43.

Comparison of U.S. Energy Consumption, 1972, Bureau of Mines
    Versus This Study

Energy Source	Trillion BTU	
	BOM	This Study
Petroleum (and Natural Gas Liquids)		[a]
Total	(32,966)	——
Fuel and Power	29,454	29,404
Raw Material	(3,428)	——
Miscellaneous and unaccounted for	(84)	——
Natural Gas, dry	23,035	22,952
Electricity	5,988	5,383
Coal: Anthracite, Bituminous & Lignite	12,423	12,331
Hydroelectric Power	2,946	2,611
Nuclear Power	576	511
Total (including petroleum fuel and power only, and electricity)	74,422[b]	73,192

Sources: U.S. Bureau of Mines, Minerals Yearbook, 1973, Vol. I,
Tables 17, 18 and 22, pages 37-39, 43; this study, Tables 3, H.1.5,
and I.1.5.

[a] ——: treated as outside scope of present study.

[b] Total using this study accounting convention. The Bureau of
Mines follows the convention of listing "total gross energy inputs"
as excluding electricity but including all petroleum products, with
a 1972 total of 71,946 trillion BTU; then a net energy figure is
obtained by adding utility electricity distributed of 5,988 trillion
BTU, and subtracting inputs into electricity generation by utilities
of 18,543 trillion BTU, yielding a net total of 59,391 trillion BTU
(71,946 + 5,988 - 18,543 = 59,391). This process of accounting
for "conversion losses" in the generation of electricity contrasts
with the "double-counting" approach advocated and employed here,
as being consistent with an input-output framework of analysis.

The small differences in the respective natural gas and coal totals between the BOM and this study are explained in like fashion.

The differences between the BOM and this study in totals for electricity, hydroelectric power and nuclear power BTU all stem from a common source, though the rationales for those differences vary. In all three cases, the amount shown here is about 90 percent of the BOM amount, because the BOM employed data on electricity at point of generation,[2] while the present study used Edison Electric Institute data on electricity use at point of consumption, the 10 percent difference between the two accounted for primarily by trans-mission losses. It is possible to view transmission losses as a form of consumption, but in the case of electricity, use as registered at the point of consumption was consistent with both the general accounting scheme adopted, and with data in other sources, so that approach was adhered to as the accounting convention here. Applied to hydroelectric and nuclear power, how-ever, this approach appears to go too far, yielding an apparent 10 percent underestimate; but it seems reasonable to argue that the differential repre-sents efficiency differences, so that the estimates are defensible, after all. (In any event, the effect on totals and distribution of use is quite minor.) This argument is developed in detail in chapter 5 and appendix I.

Given the closeness of the components, it is not surprising that the BOM total and that of this study are quite close, with most of the difference accounted for by the electricity transmission loss convention. With that eliminated, the difference between totals is under one half of one percent.

---

[2]FPC data as listed in Edison Electric Institute, Statistical Yearbook of the Electric Utility Industry for 1972, table 225, 33.

The treatment of electricity yields another source of accounting difference between the BOM data and that shown here. The BOM total of 74,422 trillion BTU which is shown here was obtained following the present study's accounting convention of including both electricity use and the fuel inputs involved in generating that electricity as part of the same total. This "double-counting" approach contrasts with the BOM "conversion loss" approach, in which either the fuel inputs appear and electricity is excluded, or electricity appears and fuel inputs are excluded. The rationale for double-counting is presented in a later section of this chapter as part of an extended discussion of accounting conventions and use by sector.

Much of the work on energy quantities involved estimating use by sector, since such data are not directly available in published series. In this process, an operation applied to all of the energy sources was the allocation of commercial use between business, federal government and state and local government use. As a first step, commercial use was distributed among hospitals, schools, offices, retail stores, and all other commercial uses. This was done by applying regional proportions for each category of commercial use, based on data for each source in an Arthur D. Little study,[3] and then disaggregating from regional to state use levels by applying state scale factors derived from several sources. Next, use by each commercial category was distributed to sectors, based on an estimated distribution for each state, again applying data from a number of sources. Retail trade and all other commercial use were assumed to be entirely business sector use, while the other categories had some use in each of the three sectors of

---

[3] Arthur D. Little, Inc., for Federal Energy Administration, Project Independence, Energy Conservation, Vol. I, Residential and Commercial Use Patterns, 1970-1990, Washington, D.C., 1974.

interest. As a last step, use for an individual sector was aggregated;
for example, state and local government hospital use, school use and office
use were collected together and summed to obtain a state and local government
total.

Some related allocation procedures were necessary in the cases of
petroleum heating fuels and natural gas. For the former, industrial and
residential use were distinguished as functional categories separate from
commercial use, and levels of use for all the functional categories were
estimated by state; then, each functional category was distributed between
sectors, and sector totals were obtained. For the latter, data in the Little
study led to an initial redistribution of commercial use, with a part allocated to residential use (to account for multifamily apartment building use)
and another part allocated to industrial use, before the remaining "net"
commercial use was distributed between sectors.

In the work on quantities, a Bureau of Mines study by Crump and Readling[4]
was of considerable help; it was a major source for the scale factors converting physical units to BTU, it served as a source of raw data for coal
use and industrial use of hydroelectric power, and it furnished some comparative data in the analysis of natural gas quantities.

Given the development of estimates of quantities, the next step in the
estimation process was the development of data on prices and expenditures.

For energy sources other than petroleum, this next step was fairly
straightforward. Expenditures were directly available for natural gas from
series published by the American Gas Association and the Bureau of Mines,

---

[4]Lulie H. Crump and Charles L. Readling, Fuel and Energy Data, United
States by State and Region, U.S. Bureau of Mines Information Circular,
8647, 1974.

and for electricity from series published by the Edison Electric Institute.
Division by corresponding quantities gave prices. Prices for coal used by
electric utilities were obtained by combining data from the Edison Electric
Institute and the National Coal Association; then scale factors, based on
a scattering of data from several sources, were applied to estimate coal
prices in other uses. Here, prices times quantities yielded expenditures.
Finally, a fuel-equivalent price was estimated for hydroelectric and nuclear
power on the basis of the price of the cheapest available alternative fuels.
Admittedly, this "shadow price" is an upper bound, but that difficulty yielded
the rationale for a downward quantity adjustment.[5]

In contrast to the other energy sources, petroleum posed great difficulty
because price data were limited and scattered, and expenditures series were
not available (apparently such data either did not exist or were not publicly
distributed). The problem was solved by tapping a large number of sources
to develop a set of "patchwork" series for each of a number of products.
Major sources utilized were Platt's trade publications, The Oil and Gas
Journal, reports by Foster Associates, and a National Coal Association price
series on petroleum products used by electric utilities. It turned out
that petroleum product prices displayed relatively modest variation by
locale, but showed much more variation by level of use (from the retail
level to the wholesale or producer level) and between products. When the
petroleum price series had been developed for each of the major products,
multiplication by corresponding quantities yielded expenditure estimates.

---

[5]The issue is discussed at several points; as noted above, chapter 5
and appendix I cover the issue at some length.

Combining all of the underlying estimates, estimated 1972 U.S.
expenditures and cost per million BTU emerge as follows:

	1972 U.S. Expenditures in Million Dollars	Average Cost Per Million BTU
Petroleum Products	53,833.90	1.831
Natural Gas	14,161.10	0.617
Electricity	27,921.07	5.187
Coal	5,069.97	0.411
Hydroelectric Power	809.48	0.310
Nuclear Power	249.85	0.489
Total	102,045.37	1.394

Accounting Conventions and Use by Sector

As noted earlier, distinguishing use by sectors is seen as a major
contribution of this study, because that breakdown conforms to standard
accounting practice in economic analysis. Such a breakdown is usually not
available in energy use series, and such seems a major drawback to their
application; for example, a combined residential-commercial category is
often employed, so that household and business use can not be distinguished.
But a sectoral classification is important for applications involving national,
regional and state income accounting and in the construction of input-
output tables. The identification of levels of final demand (household
and government use) is crucial in both applications.

An additional accounting convention employed here was the distinction
of two categories of business use: (1) Energy used to produce energy, with
electric utility use of fuel a major component, but also including refinery

and oil and gas field use of fuel. (Such minor items as oil company use of electricity do not appear here, either because of data limitations or because the use involved seemed relatively insignificant.) (2) All other business use, labeled "net business use." This convention permits the identification of successively broader groupings of consumption beginning with final demand (households and government use, only); expanding to "customer" use of energy, encompassing net business use with final demand; and finally, all use of energy, including energy used in energy production. The concentric sets of levels of consumption should "solve" double-counting problems by treating the counting as a matter of convenience, depending on the purposes served. This approach corresponds to the accounting scheme used in input-output tables; given shipments by an industry to final demand, to all other industries and to itself, output totals can be presented in progressively more inclusive form.

In an earlier comparison of data, it was noted that the Bureau of Mines followed the convention of listing "total gross energy inputs" as excluding electricity but including fuel inputs employed in electricity generation, while a net energy figure is obtained by including electricity and excluding the inputs used in its generation. The rationale is the avoidance of double-counting, but the convention seems cumbersome at best, and somewhat misleading at worst. It seems misleading because there is no attempt to eliminate the "double-counting" inherent in other energy production use of energy, and because its categories do not correspond very well to energy consumer decision processes.

To expand on these points, note first that other energy production use of energy is of fairly substantial magnitude, estimated here as amounting

to .065 of total U.S. BTU in 1972, in contrast to electric utility use of
.247 of U.S. BTU in that year. (And the .065 estimate is liable to involve
some understatement.) Electricity appears to be treated as a special case
because of the magnitude of "conversion losses," since electricity BTU is
equal to only about one-third of the BTU content of the fuel used to produce
it. Such treatment, although appealing intuitively, may be hard to defend
on logical grounds. Consumers at every level, from retail to producer,
make their energy consumption decisions by treating electricity as an
energy source that may compete with other energy sources. The accounting
conventions employed in the present study seem consistent with such decision-
making. The Bureau of Mines accounting conventions may well be viewed as
a partial response to the problem of level of use (final demand versus
customer versus all use), and, of course, it is argued here that a full
response is preferable.

Levels of U.S. Use and Cross-tabulations of That Use

U.S. totals were obtained for every major series developed in this
report and such data should be of use in their own right, particularly when
employed to give tabulations of use cross-classified by energy source,
function and sector. Those tabulations follow in the form of four tables.
The first cross-classifies sector use by source and the second cross-
classifies sector use by function, with both quantities consumed and expenditures shown in each table. The third and fourth tables show three-way
classifications of sector use by function and energy source, with consumption covered in the third table and expenditures in the fourth.

Cross Classification Of Sector Use By Source

Sector	Petroleum Products	Natural Gas	Electricity	Coal	Hydro-Electric Power	Nuclear Power	Total, All Sources
Consumption in Trillion BTU							
Household	12,584.38	5,702.70	1,744.98	308.20	—	—	20,340.35
Business	15,241.68	16,523.57	3,175.17	12,022.67	2,611.44	510.59	50,085.13
Federal Government	1,033.66	45.10	79.36	—	—	—	1,158.12
State & Local Government	544.57	680.29	383.64	—	—	—	1,608.50
Total	29,404.28	22,951.76	5,383.15	12,330.87	2,611.44	510.59	73,192.09
Expenditures in Million Dollars							
Household	31,776.52	6,685.51	11,729.83	400.74	—	—	50,592.61
Business	20,176.85	6,968.69	13,381.86	4,669.23	809.48	249.85	46,255.95
Federal Government	995.72	29.39	360.87	—	—	—	1,385.98
State & Local Government	884.81	477.50	2,448.51	—	—	—	3,810.82
Total	53,833.90	14,161.10	27,921.07	5,069.97	809.48	249.85	102,045.37
Sources: T indicates table number in text	T.83,T.84, T.85,T.86	T.130	T.150	T.170	T.173	T.173	T.3,T.13, T.21 (checks)

—: no entry

Cross Classification of Sector Use by Function

| | Residential | Commercial | Industrial | Transportation | Energy Production | | Municipal Institutional | All Use |
					Non-Electric Utility	Electric Utility		
Consumption in Trillion BTU								
Household	11,811.76	—	—	8,528.59	—	—	—	20,340.35
Business	—	2,819.81	17,177.13	7,342.78	4,725.62	18,019.79	—	50,085.13
Federal Government	—	78.35	20.43	1,003.33	—	—	56.01	1,158.12
State and Local Government	—	917.68	33.68	194.61	—	—	462.53	1,608.50
Total	11,811.76	3,815.83	17,231.23	17,069.31	4,725.62	18,019.79	518.55	73,192.09
Expenditures in Million Dollars								
Household	25,506.79	—	—	25,085.81	—	—	—	50,592.61
Business	—	8,146.03	14,949.94	13,989.70	1,802.05	7,368.22	—	46,255.95
Federal Government	—	203.60	7.41	964.02	—	—	210.96	1,385.98
State and Local Government	—	2,269.16	14.32	511.25	—	—	1,016.09	3,810.82
Total	25,506.79	10,618.80	14,971.67	40,550.78	1,802.05	7,368.22	1,227.05	102,045.37

Data Sources: as shown in tables on sector use by function and energy source

Sector BTU Use by Function and Energy Source

Consumption in Trillion BTU

	Residential	Commercial	Industrial	Transportation	Energy Production Non-Electric Utility	Electric Utility	Municipal Institutional	All Use
Petroleum Products								
Household	4,055.79	—	—	8,528.59	—	—	—	12,584.38
Business	—	1,132.19	1,947.92	7,327.63	1,759.73	3,074.21	—	15,241.68
Federal Government	—	30.33	—	1,003.33	—	—	—	1,033.66
State & Local Govt.	—	349.96	—	194.61	—	—	—	544.57
Natural Gas								
Household	5,702.80	—	—	—	—	—	—	5,702.80
Business	—	708.50	8,769.49	—	2,948.34	4,097.24	—	16,523.57
Federal Government	—	24.68	20.43	—	—	—	—	45.10
State & Local Govt.	—	317.02	33.68	—	—	—	329.59	680.29
Electricity								
Household	1,744.98	—	—	—	—	—	—	1,744.98
Business	—	960.62	2,181.86	15.15	17.55	—	—	3,175.17
Federal Government	—	23.35	—	—	—	—	56.01	79.36
State & Local Govt.	—	250.70	—	—	—	—	132.94	383.64
Coal								
Household	308.20	—	—	—	—	—	—	308.20
Business	—	18.50	4,245.87	—	—	7,758.29	—	12,022.67
Hydroelectric Power								
Business	—	—	31.99	—	—	2,579.45	—	2,611.44
Nuclear Power								
Business	—	—	—	—	—	510.59	—	510.59
Total	11,811.76	3,815.83	17,231.23	17,069.31	4,725.62	18,019.79	518.55	73,192.09

Data Sources: T shows table number; Petroleum products: T.83, T.84, T.85, T.86; Natural Gas: T.122, T.123, T.124; Electricity: T.150, T.150, T.G.1.11 (appendix G); Coal: T.170; Hydroelectric & nuclear power: T.173; Check: T.37.

Sector Expenditures by Function and Energy Source

Expenditures in Million Dollars

	Residential	Commercial	Industrial	Transportation	Energy Production Non-Electric Utility	Energy Production Electric Utility	Municipal Institutional	All Use
Petroleum Products								
Household	6,690.71	—	—	25,085.81	—	—	—	31,776.52
Business		1,218.61	1,963.71	13,904.40	1,058.34	2,031.79	—	20,176.85
Federal Government		31.71		964.02	—	—	—	995.72
State & Local Govt.		373.56		511.25	—	—	—	884.81
Natural Gas								
Household	6,685.51	—	—		—	—	—	6,685.51
Business		638.36	4,270.54	—	705.81	1,353.98	—	6,968.69
Federal Government		21.98	7.41	—	—	—	—	29.39
State & Local Govt.		279.23	14.32	—	—	—	183.95	477.50
Electricity								
Household	11,729.83	—	—		—	—	—	11,729.83
Business		6,274.77	6,983.89	85.30	37.90	—	—	13,381.86
Federal Government		149.91	—	—	—	—	210.96	360.87
State & Local Govt.		1,616.37	—	—	—	—	832.14	2,448.51
Coal								
Household	400.74	—	—	—	—	—	—	400.74
Business		14.29	1,721.89	—	—	2,933.05	—	4,669.23
Hydroelectric Power								
Business		—	9.91	—	—	799.56	—	809.48
Nuclear Power								
Business		—	—	—	—	249.85	—	249.85
Total	25,506.79	10,618.80	14,971.67	40,550.78	1,802.05	7,368.22	1,227.05	102,045.37

Data Sources: T shows table number – Petroleum products: T.83, T.84, T.85, T.86; Natural gas: T.122, T.123, T.124; Electricity: T.150, T.151, T.G.3.8 (appendix G); Coal: T.170; Hydroelectric & nuclear power: T.173; check: T.37.

Sources for entries appear at the foot of each table; most of the source data appears in Part I of the report, but in a few cases, data were drawn from Part II. As a general rule, a fair amount of aggregation occurs in Part I for all three of the basic classifications (energy source, sector and function), so that readers interested in finely detailed information will sometimes have to turn to Part II. For example, military use, if wanted as a separate category, could be developed by combining entries from several of the tables in Part II.

Some detailed discussion of the major relationships embodied in these cross-tabulations is deferred to subsequent sections of this chapter, which consider patterns of use for all energy sources combined by drawing on the tables appearing at the end of the chapter. Although the focus of those sections is on regional and state relationships, some U.S. use data are presented for purposes of comparison. Several key U.S. relationships, however, may be noted at this point.

For the United States in 1972, total energy consumed by all sectors was estimated as 73,192 trillion BTU, at a cost of 102.045 billion dollars, while corresponding household energy use was 20,340 trillion BTU at a cost of 50.593 billion dollars. Hence, the household sector used roughly one quarter of the BTU and paid half the cost of energy. The dollar magnitudes compare to 1972 gross national product of 1,158.0 billion dollars and personal income of 949.9 billion dollars.[6] Household spending on energy as a fraction of personal income thus was .054.

---

[6]*Survey of Current Business*, Oct. 1974, 14.

The distribution of energy consumption and expenditures over all sectors were:

	BTU Consumed	Expenditures
Households	.278	.496
Business	.684	.453
Federal government	.016	.014
State and local government	.022	.037
	1.000	1.000

The business BTU fraction of .684 consisted of .311 in energy production and .374 in "net" business use; corresponding fractions of .090 and .363 held for the .453 fraction of total expenditures in business use. The government share of energy use was about four percent of consumption and five percent of expenditures.

Roughly 60 percent of household consumption of BTU was for residential use, with the remaining 40 percent in transportation use, but expenditures on the two functions were roughly equal, indicating the effect of higher prices for transportation use. The leading functional category for the business sector was industrial use, that for state and local government was commercial use, and that for the federal government was transportation (which includes military use).

Coal, hydroelectric power and nuclear power are specialized to the production of electricity, which is the exclusive use of the last energy source, and the preponderant use of hydropower. In BTU terms, the industrial function accounted for the greatest use of both natural gas and electricity, equalling roughly 40 percent of use in each case. In expenditure terms, however, residential use accounted for the greatest share of the total, amounting to 47 percent of natural gas and 42 percent of electricity. Transportation accounted for roughly 60 percent of BTU, and for 75 percent of expenditures on petroleum products.

Essentially all energy in transportation use is furnished by petroleum products, with a miniscule share furnished by electricity and no use attributed to coal. The table on the next page cross-tabulates transportation use by sector, fuel source, and mode of transportation. The preponderance of the highway mode is evident, since it accounts for 80 percent of transportation BTU and 90 percent of expenditures.

Regression Equations

The present report is an exercise in descriptive statistics, but the data developed here may have some major future applications in statistical inference. In particular, it will be a fairly straightforward procedure to fit statistical demand curves using that data, developing relationships both for energy use by specific source and for energy use by all sources. Applying regression analysis, the usual confidence intervals can be constructed and tests of hypotheses carried out for various demand elasticities. Some preliminary analyses have, in fact, been carried out and are discussed in some detail in Chapter 6. Results can be summarized here as follows. For specific energy sources, residential consumption of energy per capita and industrial consumption of energy per worker in manufactures were related to a number of explanatory variables by regression analysis. Results squared well with expectations: the price elasticity for a given source

Transportation Use by Sector, Fuel Type and Transportation Mode

Transpor-tation Mode	Gasoline				Other Petroleum Products			Electricity	All Sources And Sectors
	Household	Business	Federal Govt.	State & Local Govt.	House-hold	Business	Federal Govt.	Busi-ness	
Consumption in Trillion BTU									
Highway	8,405.54	3,438.82	127.97	190.68	—	1,189.23	117.59	—	13,469.83
Aviation	16.86	35.40	31.49	3.93	—	1,519.75	571.47	—	2,178.90
Marine	85.81	—	—	—	20.37	610.11	154.81	—	871.10
Railroad	—	—	—	—	—	534.32	—	15.15	549.47
Sector Total	8,508.21	3,474.22	159.46	194.61	20.37	3,853.41	843.87	15.15	17,069.71
Expenditures In Million Dollars									
Highway	24,827.13	9,192.65	251.28	503.18	—	2,502.09	104.73	—	37,381.06
Aviation	48.10	78.33	48.40	8.07	—	1,307.27	474.77	—	1,964.94
Marine	186.85	—	—	—	23.73	401.45	84.84	—	696.87
Railroad	—	—	—	—	—	422.61	—	85.30	507.91
Sector Total	25,062.08	9,270.98	299.68	511.25	23.73	4,633.42	664.34	85.30	40,550.78

Sources: T.83, T.A.1.7, T.A.3.4, T.85, T.D.1.8, T.D.1.10, T.151, T.D.1.13, T.D.3.5, T.D.3.6

—: indicates no use in category.

was always negative and almost always statistically significant, and the cross-elasticities for competitive sources were usually positive. In residential use, income elasticity was positive and close to one, and the effect of climate fit expectations and was statistically significant for all energy sources. In addition, some regional differences occurred, but were not particularly pronounced.

Explicitly, the following own price elasticity and cross price elasticities were estimated from logarithmic consumption relationships in which a large number of other explanatory variables appeared (Tables 193 and 195).

Residential Use Per Capita

Price Elasticity	Petroleum Product Use	Natural Gas Use	Electricity Use
Own Price Elasticity	− 0.661	− 1.886*	− 1.244*
Competitive Product Price Elasticities	a		
Petroleum products	——	− 0.989	− 0.008
Natural gas	1.707*	——	0.185*
Electricity	0.469	1.111*	——

Industrial Use Per Worker in Manufactures

Price Elasticity	Petroleum Product Use	Natural Gas Use	Electricity Use	Coal & Hydropower Use
Own Price Elasticity	− 2.924*	− 1.977*	− 0.800*	− 0.434
Competitive Product Price Elasticities	a			
Petroleum products	——	1.684	2.991*	− 6.295
Natural gas	0.963*	——	0.016	0.824
Electricity	0.340	0.409	——	0.430
Coal	0.322	0.009	− 0.511	——

a —— indicates accounted for as own price elasticity.

* indicates statistical significance at 10% level.

Regional and State Relationships

Definition of Regions

The remainder of this chapter examines the tables of descriptive
statistics on all energy use which appear at the conclusion of the chapter.
Although some U.S. data are presented, the focus of the discussion is on
regional and state relationships, where regions are defined as corresponding
to the nine Census Bureau divisions: New England, Middle Atlantic, East
North Central, West North Central, South Atlantic, East South Central,
West South Central, Rocky Mountain and Far West. The geographic represen-
tation of those divisions and the major Census regions in which they fall
(Northeast, North Central, South and West) appears in the figure on the
next page.

Some Central Findings

Some of the central findings of this report are summarized in the
following table. First for households and then for all sectors, the table
shows per capita consumption, per capita expenditures and price indexes
(based on U.S. quantity weights) for all energy use.

There are pronounced geographic patterns in both household and all
sector use. In household use, expenditures per capita follow a descending
course in a southwestward direction, reflecting the influence of both climate
and price. The BTU consumption pattern is less regular, although there is
clearly a marked differential between major Census regions, with the North's
per capita consumption about 30 percent above that in the South and West
(110 relative to 85), with the Rocky Mountain area in-between. Price
indexes might be characterized as showing less variation between regions
than consumption; the Northeast's price index is about 10 percent above the

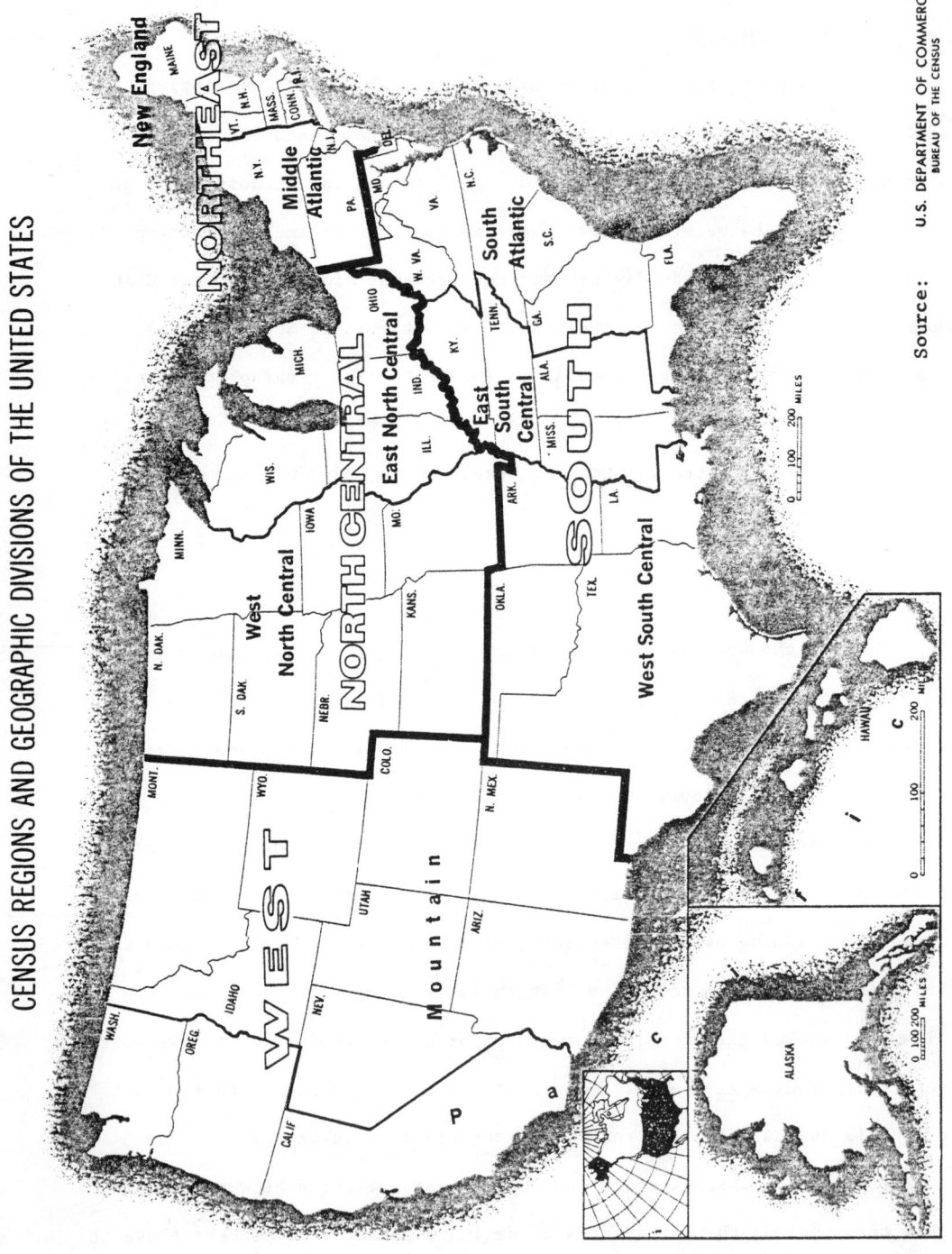

CENSUS REGIONS AND GEOGRAPHIC DIVISIONS OF THE UNITED STATES

Source: U.S. DEPARTMENT OF COMMERCE
BUREAU OF THE CENSUS

U.S. average, and the South Central region's is about 10 percent below
that average, with the remaining regions' indexes falling within 5 percent
of the U.S. value of 100. It is the common perception that the Northeast
energy price position is severely disadvantaged, but these data suggest the
perception may be somewhat overdrawn. Nevertheless, the totality of
regional price and quantity differentials lend some weight to the speculation
that higher energy prices have speeded up the shift of population from the
Northeast and North Central regions to the "sun-belt" states of the South
and West.

	HOUSEHOLD USE			ALL SECTOR USE		
	Per Capita Consumption & Expenditures		Price Indexes	Per Capita Consumption & Expenditures		Price Indexes
	Million BTU	$	U.S.=100	Million BTU	$	U.S.=100
New England	116.1	297.0	113.7	270.1	514.1	120.5
Mid Atlantic	103.2	256.7	109.6	291.2	484.9	112.7
East North Central	112.5	256.6	97.4	369.6	512.6	100.9
West North Central	104.4	244.9	96.0	336.8	482.0	98.7
South Atlantic	82.4	238.1	101.4	299.8	480.2	101.0
East South Central	85.1	223.7	92.6	385.8	483.2	90.9
West South Central	88.6	222.9	89.5	565.4	519.3	82.6
Rocky Mountain	95.5	232.0	98.6	403.6	514.0	94.0
Far West	86.9	211.5	97.3	322.9	443.2	90.7
United States	97.7	243.0	100.0	351.5	490.1	100.0
Source: (T=table)	T.24	T.24	T.74	T.24	T.24	T.74

For all sector use, the regional differentials in price indexes
seem somewhat more pronounced, and the range in per capita use of BTU is
certainly more pronounced than the corresponding series in household use.
Essentially the same pattern holds when use is restricted to "customer"
use, excluding energy production use (see Table 30). It seems plausible
that some of the use level variations have occurred in response to the
price index differences. There is some suggestion of unitary price elasticity
with per capita BTU consumption in the West South Central region 2.1 times
that in New England, while those regions have essentially the same expenditures. When the comparison is restricted to consumption by customers only
(excluding energy production), a ratio of 1.65 holds for per capita BTU use
in the highest use region relative to the corresponding amount in the lowest
use region, and again the expenditures are about the same (Table 30). This
evidence reinforces the regression results which suggest considerable price
elasticity.

At the state level, million BTU per capita in household use ranges
from a low of 40.3 for Hawaii to a high of 152.3 for Wyoming. For all use,
the range is 219.2 for Vermont to 999.0 for Wyoming. In household expenditures per capita, Vermont becomes the highest state with $354, while Hawaii
remains the lowest with $168. For all use per capita, Alaska is highest
with $855 and California is lowest with $428. Hawaii has the highest price
index in both household and all sector use, with values of 145.1 and 147.2
respectively, while the lowest price indexes are Tennessee's 85.9 in household
use, and Washington's 79.4 in all use.

Let us now consider the regional and state data in some detail.

Topical Coverage

There are 74 tables following the text of this chapter, with the first 62 presenting information on quantities consumed in BTU units, and on expenditures in dollars. The remaining tables present price information. Within that classification, use is further classified, not only by energy source, but by sector and function. For the consumption and expenditure data, Tables 1 through 18 show use by energy source, Tables 19 through 34 show use by sector, and Tables 35 through 62 show use by function. The use statistics typically appear in sets of three tables, with the first showing quantities consumed by state, the second showing expenditures by state, and the third showing both quantities and expenditures by region. For each group, the tables will be discussed by showing the organization scheme for the group, summarizing some of the key findings and then presenting a more detailed set of findings. Readers interested only in a summary of results may wish to skim or skip that last detailed discussion for each group.

Use By Energy Source

Organization

To recapitulate: specific sources of energy are classified under the headings of petroleum products; natural gas; electricity; coal, hydroelectric power and nuclear power (sometimes referred to as "coal, etc." for economy of exposition), and the total from all sources. (The aggregate for coal, etc. is disaggregated to its components in Chapter 5 and in Appendixes H and I.)

Use by specific source of energy is first shown for all sectors combined and then for the household sector, only. The following cross-classification shows eontent coverage by table number:

	Amounts of Use	Per Capita Use	Fraction of Use
All Sectors	1, 2, 3	4, 5, 6	7, 8, 9
Households	10, 11, 12	13, 14, 15	16, 17, 18

Key Findings

The U.S. distributions of consumption and expenditures by source, for all sectors, were:

	% BTU	% Expenditures
Petroleum products	40.2	52.7
Natural gas	31.4	13.9
Electricity	7.3	27.4
Coal, hydro, nuclear power	21.1	6.0
Total	100.0	100.0

For households, the distributions were:

	% BTU	% Expenditures
Petroleum products	61.9	62.8
Natural gas	28.0	13.2
Electricity	8.6	23.2
Coal, hydro, nuclear power	1.5	0.8
Total	100.0	100.0

Differences in percentage between BTU and expenditures reflect price differences. As noted above, the cost of electricity per BTU is relatively high because of conversion losses in generating electricity. Much of the price differential between petroleum and natural gas can be attributed to taxes on gasoline and other fuels used in transportation.

Some specialization of use of energy source by region is manifest. New England is heavily dependent on petroleum products for all sector use (80% of total BTU) and household use (82%). The East North Central region relies heavily on natural gas for household use (38%) while the West South Central region relies on that source for all sector use (66%) - primarily for energy production and for industrial use. Electricity as a fraction of all BTU attains its peak value in the East South Central region (with 10% for all sector use and 15% for household use), no doubt reflecting use in the TVA region.

Peak per capita use by source for both BTU and expenditures occurs in Alaska for petroleum products, in Louisiana for natural gas, and in West Virginia for coal. For per capita electricity use, Washington leads in BTU and Delaware in expenditures.

Some Additional Detail

The East North Central region (comprising the Great Lakes States) is the largest consumer of energy in terms of both BTU and expenditures for all sources combined, its share of energy expenditures amounting to 20 percent of the U.S. total for both households and all use.

In terms of BTU from all sources, the largest state consumers of energy are Texas, California and New York, with 6851, 5846 and 4536 trillion BTU, respectively. Those states also have the highest expenditures on energy, but the order here is California, New York and Texas, with 8.75, 8.32 and 6.13 billion dollars, respectively (from Tables 1 and 2).

Of course, population level is a major determinant of total use, and such can obscure some comparisons, leading to the need for per capita information.

At the state level, for all sources, quantities and expenditures per capita are distributed as follows:

Million BTU Per Capita		Dollars Per Capita	
Level of use	No. of Cases	Level of use	No. of Cases
200 - < 250	4	425 - < 450	1
250 - < 300	13	450 - < 475	14
300 - < 400	19	475 - < 500	14
400 - < 600	11	500 - < 550	15
600 - ≤ 1000	4	600 - ≤ 900	4
Total	51	Total	51

Neither distribution shows great symmetry, for there is a peaking at the lower end of the range covered, and a scattering of cases at the upper end of the range.

States with greatest BTU consumed per capita (in millions) for all sources in all use are Wyoming (999), Louisiana (727), Alaska (658) and West Virginia (617). States with least BTU per capita (again in millions) are Vermont (219), Rhode Island (221), the District of Columbia (232) and New York (247). In dollar terms, highest levels per capita occur for Alaska ($855), Wyoming ($830), Nevada ($659) and Delaware ($654); lowest levels hold for California ($428), North Dakota ($452), and Colorado and New York (both at $453).

For all sectors, maximum and minimum use for specific sources occurs in the following states:

Source	Million BTU Per Capita	Dollars Per Capita
Maximum Use		
Petroleum products	Alaska (348)	Alaska (539)
Natural gas	Louisiana (534)	Louisiana (168)
Electricity	Washington (55)	Delaware (193)
Coal, etc.	West Virginia (402)	West Virginia (147)
Minimum Use		
Petroleum products	West Virginia (78)	West Virginia (192)
Natural gas	Hawaii (0)	Hawaii (0)
Electricity	Alaska (13)	Utah (98)
Coal, etc.	Rhode Island (0.3)	Hawaii (0.1)

Peak use by households occurs for specific sources in the following states:

Source	Million BTU Per Capita	Dollars Per Capita
Petroleum products	Vermont (118)	Vermont (272)
Natural gas	Wyoming (67)	Illinois (53)
Electricity	Washington (18.6)	Florida (83)
Coal	Pennsylvania (5.6)	Pennsylvania (7)

Although there is specialization by energy source between states and regions, this seems more pronounced for all sector use than it is for households, where petroleum always plays a major if not dominant role. In household use, petroleum products--which average 60 percent of total BTU for the U.S.--account for a minimum of 44 percent of all BTU (in West Virginia), and for less than 50 percent in only three other states (Illinois, Ohio and Kansas, all with 47 percent).

In contrast, for all sector BTU use, petroleum products--which average 40 percent of U.S. use--account for less than 30 percent of state use in 12 states (Table 7), and range from 13 percent in West Virginia to 89 percent in Maine. In part, the difference reflects the much greater non-household reliance on coal, hydropower and nuclear power, which are primarily inputs for industrial and electric utility production, with use varying considerably between states and regions. Similarly, natural gas is a major fuel for industrial and electric utility use in the West South Central region. It is also possible that non-household use is more responsive to price differences (has greater price elasticity of demand) than household use of energy. Some evidence on this hypothesis is presented in Chapter 6.

Use By Sector

Organization

Use by sector is shown for the "basic" sectors: households, business, federal government and state and local government, and is also shown for sectoral class of users, involving concentric levels of use, beginning with sales to final demand, expanding to cover sales to "customers" (final demand plus non-energy producing business use) and then to total use, including

energy used in energy production.   The following cross-classification shows
content coverage by table number:

	Amounts of use	Per capita use	Fraction of use
Four "basic" sectors	19, 20, 21	22, 23, 24	31, 32, 33
Sectoral class of user (concentric levels)	25, 26, 27	28, 29, 30	————

The final table in this group (Table 34) shows energy expenditures as
a fraction of income, by state.

Key Findings

On a per capita basis, these U.S. averages were obtained:

	Million BTU	Dollars
Households	97.7	243.0
Business	240.5	222.1
Federal government	5.6	6.7
State and local government	7.7	18.3
Total	351.5	490.1

The following table expands on the summary discussion of per capita
use of energy presented earlier by showing per capita indexes of household

use, all other sector use and total use for BTU and dollars per capita.
(Indexes were obtained by dividing by the U.S. value and then multiplying
the result by 100.)

Region	Indexes of Per Capita Use, U.S. = 100					
	BTU Consumed			Dollars Spent		
	House-hold Use	Other Sector Use	Total Use	House-hold Use	Other Sector Use	Total Use
New England	118.85	60.67	76.84	122.24	87.85	104.90
Mid Atlantic	105.66	74.06	82.85	105.66	92.35	98.95
East North Central	115.20	101.27	105.14	105.63	103.58	104.59
West North Central	106.85	91.58	95.82	100.81	95.94	98.35
South Atlantic	84.36	85.65	85.29	98.01	97.97	97.99
East South Central	87.12	118.46	109.75	92.08	104.99	98.59
West South Central	90.68	187.85	160.85	91.73	119.98	105.97
Rocky Mountain	97.77	121.40	114.83	95.49	114.12	104.88
Far West	88.94	92.99	91.87	87.04	93.78	90.44
United States	100.00	100.00	100.00	100.00	100.00	100.00

Source: Derived from Table 6 and Table 15.

Concentric levels of use, by sectoral class, had these national values:

	Trillion BTU	Billion Dollars
Final Demand	23,107	$ 55,789
Customers (non-energy producers)	50,447	92,875
All Use	73,192	102,045

It was noted earlier that household spending on energy as a fraction
of personal income was .054. Corresponding regional values[7] were:

New England	.0621
Mid Atlantic	.0510
East North Central	.0540
West North Central	.0567
South Atlantic	.0557
East South Central	.0634
West South Central	.0573
Rocky Mountain	.0551
Far West	.0429
United States	.0536

The East South Central region has the highest ratio, and Mississippi,
with a ratio of .0737 has the highest state value within that region,
suggesting the high ratio reflects low levels of per capita income.
Climate seems a major factor explaining the ratio; for individual states
(Table 34), Hawaii (.0329) and California (.0412) had the lowest ratios,
and Vermont (.0912), Maine (.0811), New Hampshire (.0764) and Wyoming
(.0701) had the highest. The Alaska ratio was only .0523, but this appears
to occur because a large part of motor vehicle transportation in that state
is military transportation, with costs alloted to the federal government,
rather than the household sector. (See Tables 100 and 107 in Chapter 2.)

---

[7] Regional income data were obtained from Survey of Current Business,
August 1974, Table 2, 33.

Some Additional Detail

In earlier discussion, it was shown that household energy use per capita ranged from 82.4 million BTU in the South Atlantic region to 116.1 million BTU in New England, while expenditures ranged from $212 in the Far West to $297 in New England. At the state level, household energy use per capita ranges from 40 million BTU in Hawaii to 132 million BTU in Vermont, with corresponding expenditures of $168 versus $354 per capita. State quantities used and expenditures per capita are distributed as follows:

Million BTU Per Capita		Dollars Per Capita	
Level Of Use	No. of Cases	Level Of Use	No. of Cases
< 80	5	< 200	3
80 - < 90	13	200 - < 230	14
90 - < 105	18	230 - < 260	22
105 - < 115	8	260 - < 300	9
115 - < 125	5	≥ 300	3
≥ 125	2		
Total	51	Total	51

These distributions seem more symmetric than those for the all sector data, relative to the respective average values of 97.7 and 243.0 (Table 15).

Business use had maximum per capita values of 460.9 million BTU and $272.6 in the West South Central region, and minimums of 138.2 million BTU and $189.3 in New England (Table 24). The pattern for "net" business

use in large measure paralleled that for all business use, although magnitudes

were considerably lower (Table 30). At the state level, Wyoming had

highest per capita consumption of 820.9 million BTU and expenditures of

$492.9, while Vermont had the lowest per capita consumption of 81.2

million BTU and Rhode Island the lowest expenditures of $151. Again, the

net business use pattern was quite similar to that for all business use.

For the federal government, the extremes were minimums of 2.1 million BTU

and $3.0 per capita in the West North Central region, and maximums of 12.3

million BTU and $13.2 in the Far West. Both North Central regions (East

and West) had federal expenditure levels about half the national average,

considerably below those for the other regions of the country. (The data

on federal spending might be drawn on in the debate over putative "dispari-

ties" in federal spending between states and regions, but many of the differ-

ences can be attributed to the location of military facilities, including

naval bases, whose location may be hard to debate.) For state and local

government, minimum levels occurred for the East South Central region,

with 5.9 million BTU and $13.7, and maximums occurred for the Rocky Mountain

region, with 12.5 million BTU and $21.1, per capita. At the state level,

Alaska led other jurisdictions in federal use by a wide margin, with 73.0

million BTU and 98.5 dollars per capita. Surprisingly, the District of

Columbia federal levels were below several other states, as well. Its

per capita BTU of 16.3 was below that of Maine (26.5), Virginia (19.9),

and Rhode Island (17.9), and its expenditures of $25.5 per capita were

exceeded by those of Maine ($29.4). Maximum per capita use by state and

local government also occurred in Alaska, for both BTU and expenditures

(31.4 million BTU and $38.4, respectively).

Use By Function

Organization

Data on use by function appears in Tables 35 through 62, with major functions listed under these use classifications: residential, commercial, industrial, transportation, energy production, and municipal-institutional. Energy production use is subclassified into non-electric utility and electric utility use. The following cross-classification shows content coverage by table number:

	Amounts Of Use	Per Capita Use	Per Capita Use In Index Number Terms	Fraction Of Total
Major Functions	35, 36, 37	38, 39, 40	41, 42, 43	——
Functional Use By Fuel Category				
Residential	——	44, 45, 46	——	——
Commercial	——	47, 48, 49	——	——
Industrial	——	50, 51, 52	——	58, 59
Transportation	——	53, 54, 55	——	60, 61
Electric Utility (regional data)	——	56	——	62
Municipal-institutional (regional data)	——	57	——	——

The first nine tables in this grouping present information on all of the major functions. Then, the remaining tables show more detail for the most important of the specific functions, with coverage for the residential, commercial, industrial and transportation functions presented in terms of both state and regional data, while coverage for electric utility and municipal-institutional use is limited to regional data. (Readers interested in the categories not given detailed treatment here will find the data of interest in the remainder of this report.)

Key Findings

For the United States, the percentage distribution of use by major function, in terms of quantity consumed versus expenditures, were as follows (from Table 40):

Use	Percent of Use	
	Quantity Consumed	Expenditures
Residential	16.14	25.00
Commercial	5.21	10.41
Industrial	23.54	14.67
Transportation	23.32	39.73
Energy		
Non-electric utility	6.46	1.77
Electric utility	24.62	7.22
Municipal-Institutional	0.71	1.20
Total	100.00	100.00

There are some marked differences in percentages between quantities and expenditures, reflecting price differences between functions. Such price differences reflect differences in price per BTU between energy sources and regions, and differences in the price of a given energy source depending on level of consumption, ranging from producer level through various wholesale levels to the retail level.

The effects of climate, and to some extent, regional price differences are even more pronounced for residential use than for household use, which is not too surprising since both quantities and prices for household use of gasoline involve less variation by locale than do quantities and prices for residential use of energy. Thus, regional indexes of residential use per capita are:

Indexes of Per Capita Residential Use

	Quantities	Expenditures
New England	132.3	141.3
Mid Atlantic	119.0	118.5
East North Central	124.6	108.5
West North Central	112.6	105.9
South Atlantic	67.8	87.7
East South Central	78.0	84.9
West South Central	79.3	85.2
Rocky Mountain	94.9	90.2
Far West	80.1	75.4
United States	100.0	100.0

Considerably different patterns of per capita use between regions hold for the other major functions. The least variation occurs in transportation use, with per capita indexes of BTU consumed ranging from a low of 81.2 (Mid Atlantic) to a high of 122.1 (West South Central and Far West), and with per capita indexes of expenditures ranging from 84.6 (Mid Atlantic) to 120.3 (Rocky Mountain). In contrast, energy production per capita for non-electric utilities shows extreme variation, and industrial use shows considerable variation between regions. The ranges for these respective uses were as follows:

	Percentage of U.S. Average	
Energy Production:	Quantities	Expenditures
(non-electric utilities)		
Minimum	8.4	18.8
	(New England)	(New England)
Maximum	536.4	401.1
	(West South Central)	(West South Central)
Industrial Use		
Minimum	40.6	63.7
	(New England)	(Far West)
Maximum	203.5	135.6
	(West South Central)	(East North Central)

For the United States, major functional categories of use show the following percentage distributions of energy furnished by source:

	Petroleum Products	Natural Gas	Elec- tricity	Coal, Hydro, & Nuclear Power	Total
Quantities Consumed (Percent of Total)					
residential	34.3	48.3	14.8	2.6	100.0
commercial	39.6	27.5	32.4	0.5	100.0
industrial	11.3	51.2	12.7	24.8	100.0
transportation	99.9	——	0.1	——	100.0
electric utility	17.1	22.7	——	60.2	100.0
Expenditures (Percent of Total)					
residential	26.2	26.2	46.0	1.6	100.0
commercial	15.3	8.9	75.7	0.1	100.0
industrial	13.1	28.7	46.6	11.6	100.0
transportation	99.9	——	0.1	——	100.0
electric utility	27.6	18.4	——	54.0	100.0

In terms of BTU consumed, natural gas is the major energy source in both residential and industrial use; petroleum plays that role in commercial use and accounts for essentially all of transportation consumption; and coal, etc. furnishes more than half of electric utility use. In expenditure terms, electricity accounts for roughly half of residential and industrial expenditures, and for three quarters of expenditures on commercial use. Disaggregating the coal, etc. category in electric utility use, these percentages hold for the components:

	Percent of Electric Utility Use	
	Quantities Consumed	Expenditures
Coal	43.1	39.8
Hydropower	14.3	10.8
Nuclear power	2.8	3.4
Total	60.2	54.0

Major functions vary somewhat in their patterns of regional speciali-zation by energy source of BTU. The basic pattern is for petroleum to serve as the leading energy source in the Northeast, with natural gas the leading source in the rest of the country for residential, commercial and industrial use, and with coal the leading source in the rest of the country for electric utility use. The basic pattern can be discerned in the following listing of leading energy source by region, which also shows occasional shifts and exceptions to that basic pattern.

<u>Leading Energy Source of BTU</u>

Region	FUNCTION			
	Residential	Commercial	Industrial	Electric Utility
New England	Pet	Pet	Pet	Pet
Mid Atlantic	Pet	Pet	Coal, etc.	Pet
East North Central	NG	Pet	NG	Coal
West North Central	Pet	Pet	NG	Coal
South Atlantic	NG	Elec	NG	Coal
East South Central	NG	NG	NG	Coal
West South Central	NG	Elec	NG	NG
Rocky Mountain	NG	NG	NG	Coal
Far West	NG	Elec	NG	Hydro
United States	NG	Pet	NG	Coal

Pet: petroleum products; NG: natural gas; Elec: electricity; Coal, etc: Coal, hydro and nuclear power; hydro: hydropower.

Some Additional Detail

The following table shows leading state consumers for each function, both for quantities and expenditures. In most cases, the leading state consumed roughly 10 percent of the U.S. total for both quantities and expenditures. Non-electric utility energy production was an exception, with use by Texas accounting for a third of BTU and a quarter of expenditures.

Leading State Consumers By Function

Use By Function	Quantities			Expenditures		
	U.S. Total	Amount In Leading State	Leading State	U.S. Total	Amount In Leading State	Leading State
	Trillion BTU			Million Dollars		
Residential	11811	1205	N.Y.	25507	2615	N.Y.
Commercial	3816	404	N.Y.	10619	1198	N.Y.
Industrial	17231	1928	Tex.	14972	1345	Penn.
Transportation	17069	2023	Calif.	40551	4184	Calif.
Energy Production						
Non-electric utility	4726	1553	Tex.	1802	439	Tex.
Electric utility	18020	1376	Tex.	7368	664	N.Y.
Municipal-Industrial	519	60	Tex.	1227	228	N.Y.
All Use	73192	6851	Tex.	102045	8748	Calif.

The table on the following page shows state maximum and minimum per capita consumption levels by function, both for BTU and expenditures. Those extreme values are expressed as a percentage of the respective U.S. average level, and the average levels (in BTU and dollars per capita) are also listed. There is considerable spread in use levels for most functions. In the BTU comparisons, the ratio of maximum to minimum is on the order of ten to one (or more) for all functions except transportation and all use, with ratios of around five to one. The expenditures spread is less pronounced, yet some marked differences occur between extreme values. The transportation ratio falls to three to one, while the all use ratio falls to two to one.

For residential, commercial and industrial consumption of BTU per capita, states with maximum consumption of energy from a specific energy

Extreme Levels of Use By Function and State

Use By Function	Quantities Per Capita					Expenditures Per Capita				
	U.S. Average (Million BTU)	Percent of U.S. Average Max.	Min.	State Max.	Min.	U.S. Average ($)	Percent of U.S. Average Max.	Min.	State Max.	Min.
Residential	56.7	186.8	17.6	Wyo.	Hawaii	122.5	165.8	54.1	Vt.	Hawaii
Commercial	18.3	421.5	41.2	D.C.	Hawaii	51.0	315.8	41.1	D.C.	Tenn.
Industrial	82.8	346.9	11.2	La.	D.C.	71.9	215.4	15.1	Del.	D.C.
Transportation	82.0	311.9	56.3	Alaska	D.C.	194.7	205.1	66.9	Alaska	D.C.
Energy Production										
Non-electric utility	22.7	769.3	3.5	La.	Me.	8.7	682.8	6.9	Wyo.	N.Y.
Electric utility	86.5	344.6	20.6	Wyo.	R.I.	35.4	258.5	33.4	W.Va.	R.I.
Municipal-Institutional	2.5	901.8	9.1	Alaska	Del.	5.9	305.9	33.8	Alaska	Ala.
All Use	351.5	284.2	62.4	Wyo.	Vt.	490.1	174.4	87.5	Alaska	Calif.

Sources: Tables 40, 41 and 42.

source are shown in the following list:

Maximum Consumption Per Capita By State For Specific Energy Source

Use by Major Function	Petroleum Products		Natural Gas		Electricity		Coal, etc.	
	Million BTU	State	Million BTU	State	Million BTU	State	Million BTU	State
Residential	72.0	Vt.	66.7	Wyo.	18.6	Wash.	5.6	Pa.
Commercial	50.2	D.C.	27.9	Wyo.	14.8	D.C.	5.4	Mont.
Industrial	61.2	Me.	259.4	La.	28.1	Tenn.	143.4	W.Va.

Some of the high use rates for the District of Columbia occur because of a net inflow of commuting workers, so that population measured by residence understates the "proper" population (some combination of daytime, workforce population and night time residential population). A similar problem occurs for Nevada, with large numbers of tourists augmenting the resident population.

Regional specialization in use by energy source seems particularly pronounced for industrial and electric utility use (Tables 58, 59 and 62). Thus, consider BTU from each source as a fraction of total electric utility use in terms of the U.S. level versus the maximum and minimum regional values for that fraction:

BTU by Source as Fraction of Electric Utility Use

	U.S. Fraction	Maximum Fraction	Minimum Fraction	Region Of Maximum	Region Of Minimum
Petroleum Products	.171	.755	.016	NE	ESC
Natural Gas	.227	.944	.012	WSC	NE
Coal	.431	.826	.003	ENC	FW
Hydro Power	.143	.569	.012	FW	ENC
Nuclear Power	.028	.123	.000	NE	ESC, WSC, RM

NE: New England; ENC: East North Central; ESC: East South Central; WSC: West South Central; RM: Rocky Mountain; and FW: Far West

The range for these cases seems quite pronounced. Regions not appearing at any of the extremes include the Middle Atlantic, West North Central and South Atlantic regions, suggesting a pattern of use deviating less from the average than those of the other regions.

Prices

Organization

Price information is presented in two basic forms: (1) as an expression of average costs actually paid, obtained by dividing expenditures by quantities for given locales (states or regions) and (2) as weighted prices and price indexes. Weighted prices are obtained by multiplying prices for individual components of an aggregate by U.S. quantity weights. Division of such weighted prices by corresponding U.S. average prices, and scaling by 100, yields price indexes. Such, in fact, is the standard procedure in index number construction.

The presentation of tables in this section is organized as follows, showing table numbers within the cross classification:

	Average Costs	Weighted Prices & Price Indexes
Sector	63, 64	—
Function	65, 66	—
Energy Source:		
Non-Petroleum	—	67
Petroleum	—	68, 69, 70
All Sources	—	71, 72
All Use	—	73, 74

Additional information on prices appears in the individual chapters on specific energy source (chapters 2 through 5).

Key Findings

Energy prices in the sense of average costs borne by consumers are
shown for sectors by state in Table 63, and by region in Table 64, while
corresponding prices by function appear for states in Table 65, and
for regions in Table 66. In all of these tables, entries were obtained
by dividing the expenditures of a given sector or function by the corresponding quantities consumed within each geographic unit. For all use,
the average 1972 cost of energy in dollars per million BTU was $1.39 for the
nation, with the following U.S. averages for individual sectoral and functional
use:

Sector	Price In Dollars Per Million BTU	Function	Price In Dollars Per Million BTU
Household	$2.49	Residential	$2.16
Federal Govt.	1.20	Commercial	2.78
State & Local Govt.	2.37	Industrial	0.87
Business Use	0.92	Transportation	2.38
All Sectors	1.39	Energy Production	
		Non-Electric Utility Use	0.38
		Electric Utility Use	0.41
		Municipal-Institutional	2.37
		All Functions	1.39

Average cost in all use ranged from $0.92 in the West South Central
region to $1.90 in New England. Much of this differential between regional
prices is explained by differences in mix of products consumed, including
differences in level of use, ranging from producer to retail level. The
mix phenomenon partially explains the apparently anomalous result of
relatively low prices for household use of energy in New England and the
Mid Atlantic regions (Table 64). Although there is a wide-spread impression

that those regions have energy prices considerably above average, they
consume relatively more lower priced products than occurs nationally,
e.g., relatively more petroleum heating fuels and less gasoline for
passenger cars.

The following table summarizes price information by regions for
households and all use, showing average consumer costs and weighted prices
as percentages of the corresponding U.S. average price. Residential use
comprises a subclass of household use, and price indexes for that category
also appear.

The weighted prices seem much more consistent with the conventional
image of regional price patterns than do the average consumer costs. For
the former set, New England and the Mid Atlantic regions stand out, with
prices clearly above average, while the West South Central region has
prices clearly below average. Yet, though the weighted price differentials
are clear-cut, they seem relatively modest when contrasted with the conventional image of a marked divergence of prices in the Northeast from those
in the rest of the country. For all use, New England's price index is
20 percent above the nation's, and the Mid Atlantic's is 13 percent above;
the household differentials are even smaller, at 14 and 10 percent, respectively. At the other extreme, the West South Central price indexes are
17 and 10 percent below the national level for all use and household use,
respectively.

Hence, the Northeast does not seem as disadvantaged as the conventional
perception (and rhetoric) might lead one to believe.

Price Indexes Comparing Consumer Costs to Weighted Prices

	Household and Residential			All Use	
	Prices As Average Consumer Costs		Weighted Prices	Prices As Average Consumer Costs	Weighted Prices
	Household	Resi-dential	Household		
New England	102.9	106.9	113.7	136.5	120.5
Mid Atlantic	100.0	99.6	109.6	119.4	112.7
East North Central	91.7	87.1	97.4	99.5	100.9
West North Central	94.4	94.1	96.0	102.7	98.7
South Atlantic	116.2	129.3	101.4	114.9	101.0
East South Central	105.7	108.8	92.6	89.8	90.9
West South Central	101.2	107.5	89.5	65.9	82.5
Rocky Mountain	97.7	95.0	98.6	91.3	94.0
Far West	97.9	94.1	97.3	98.5	90.7
United States	100.0	100.0	100.0	100.0	100.0

Sources: Tables 64, 66, 71 and 72.

The point at issue becomes even stronger when it is made explicit that a measured price index involves some overstatement of "true" differentials because substitution possibilities and effects are not fully accounted for by the index.[8]

An intuitively obvious example of the difficulty is apparent when a locale is faced with a very high price for a commodity that is widely used elsewhere, and accordingly, consumes little or nothing of it, making do with substitutes, instead. The use of national quantity weights can than raise that locale's price index substantially.

[8] See N. Laviatan and D. Patinkin "On The Economic Theory Of Price Indexes." Economic Development and Cultural Change, April, 1961, 502-536.

The regional comparisons shown above drew on weighted prices and corresponding price indexes that are developed and presented in Tables 67 through 74. Table 67 shows state prices for natural gas, electricity and coal, etc., for household use and for all use. The household price was obtained directly as the cost for the specific energy source in residential use. The price for all use is the weighted price obtained by applying U.S. quantity weights. Formally, for a specific energy source:

$$WP_i = \sum_j P_{ij}(Q_{0j}/Q_0)$$

where:

WP_i is the weighted price for all use in state i, i = 1, 2, ..., 51
(including the District of Columbia)

P_{ij} is the price of specific use component j in state i

Q_{0j} is the U.S. quantity consumed of component j, where $Q_{0j} = \sum_i Q_{ij}$, and

Q_{ij} is quantity of use component j consumed in state i

Q_0 is the total quantity consumed (for the given energy source),
with $Q_0 = \sum_j Q_{0j}$

The corresponding price index is found by forming

$$IP_i = \frac{\sum_j P_{ij}(Q_{0j}/Q_0)}{\sum_j P_{0j}(Q_{0j}/Q_0)} = \frac{\sum_j P_{ij}Q_{0j}}{\sum_j P_{0j}Q_{0j}}$$

where:

IP_i is the price index for all use in state i and

P_{0j} is the average U.S. price for use j, where

$$P_{0j} = \frac{\sum_i P_{ij} Q_{ij}}{\sum_i Q_{ij}}$$

The entries in Table 67 were obtained from Tables 144, 166 and 191, which respectively list price information on natural gas, electricity and coal, etc. Besides household prices and weighted prices for all use, those tables also show prices for all use in terms of average costs borne by consumers in each state. Details on development of weighted prices and price indexes for the non-petroleum sources are given in the attendant discussions of the source tables.

Table 68 shows state weighted prices for petroleum products in terms of household use, non-household use and all use. Table 113 in Chapter 2 shows the corresponding average costs borne by consumers. Tables 69 and 70 show the component prices used in obtaining the entries in Table 68.

The national weights for the components were as follows:

Household Use	U.S. Quantity Weights
Passenger car and motorcycle gasoline	.66793
All other transportation use	.00978
All other petroleum products	.32229
	1.00000

Non-household Use	
Gasoline	.22761
All other transportation fuels, (non gasoline)	.27927
Heating fuels	.09101
All other, except use by electric utilities	.21934
Electric utility use	.18277
	1.00000

The all use weighted price was obtained by weighting the household and non-household use prices by .42798 and .57202, respectively, equal to their national shares of total petroleum product use.

Tables 71 and 72 present regional weighted prices and price indexes for the four individual energy sources, and for all energy use (all sources combined), with Table 71 covering household use and Table 72 covering all use (all sector and all function use of energy from specific sources and from all sources). The individual energy source data and corresponding average costs paid by consumers appear in Table 115 for petroleum products, Table 145 for natural gas, Table 167 for electricity, and Table 192 for coal, etc. Regional prices for a given source were obtained by weighting each price for states in the region by the fraction expressing the ratio of the state population to the regional population. Alternative weighting schemes are possible, of course, but the approach used here can be defended as expressing the price facing the "average" consumer in the region. A "difficulty" here is that when the regional prices are weighted by their share of U.S. population, the U.S. weighted price obtained generally will not equal the original average price (the P_{0j} in the mathematical derivation). However, this appears to be a general problem of index numbers. Thus, weighting by share of energy quantities consumed, rather than by share of population, would seem a plausible altern-ative. However, inspection of the mathematical formulae involved, and construction of some simple numerical examples show that the U.S. weighted price under the alternative approach also will generally diverge from the original average price.

The price indexes for the individual sources were combined into an "all energy" index by weighting by their respective fraction of U.S. total BTU consumed. These were the weights employed.

	Household	All Use
Petroleum	.61869	.40174
Natural Gas	.28037	.31358
Electricity	.08579	.07355
Coal, etc.	.01515	.21113
	1.00000	1.00000

Results appear as the last columns of Tables 71 and 72, covering all energy use for households and all uses, respectively. Division by the U.S. average and scaling by 100 yields the price indexes shown in those tables.

Table 73 presents state weighted prices for all energy sources combined, for household and all use. Table 73 applies the quantity weights for individual sources to the state data of Tables 67 and 68 to obtain the weighted prices shown; division by the U.S. average, and scaling, yields the corresponding indexes.

Finally, Table 74 obtains regional values from Table 73 by applying the fractions of state populations to regional population as weights for specific regions. Results for indexes presented in Table 74 show slight deviations from corresponding results shown in Tables 71 and 72 because of round-off differences, which occurred because the two sets of numbers were constructed in reverse order.

As indicated above, U.S. average prices appearing in Tables 71, 72, and 74 were obtained by weighting the individual state price indexes by the fraction expressing the ratio of the state population to the U.S. population, and, as a result, the average U.S. prices in those tables differ somewhat from the average costs paid by consumers. The comparative values are:

	Costs Paid by Consumers	Population Weighted Price Indexes
Households	$2.487	$2.587
All Use	1.394	1.479

Differences are not particularly pronounced.

States with highest price indexes for all use were Hawaii, Alaska, Maine, and Massachusetts. States with lowest price indexes for all use were Washington, Texas, Louisiana, Oregon and Montana. Indexes for household use were well correlated with those for all use, although there were some shifts in order between the two sets, and Tennessee replaced Montana as fifth lowest in rank. Specifically, these were the extreme values of the indexes, arranged in order of value for all use:

	Household Use	All Use
Hawaii	145.1	147.2
Alaska	120.7	126.0
Maine	122.1	124.3
Massachusetts	113.7	120.7
Tennessee	85.9	87.7
Montana	93.1	85.4
Oregon	88.7	82.9
Louisiana	89.9	82.3
Texas	87.7	80.1
Washington	86.3	79.4

Some Additional Detail

The distribution of prices in the sense of average cost per unit paid by consumers has considerably more spread (or variance) than that of weighted prices. Such is not surprising, since variation in quantity is removed in the construction of weighted prices. The distributions of prices for total energy consumed by households and in all use are as follows:

Dollars per million Btu	Number of Cases Households		Dollars per million Btu	Number of Cases All Use	
	Average Costs	Weighted Prices		Average Costs	Weighted Prices
< 2.0	1	0	< 1.0	6	0
2.0 - < 2.2	2	0	1.0 - < 1.3	9	8
2.2 - < 2.4	13	9	1.3 - < 1.6	18	31
2.4 - < 2.7	22	29	1.6 - < 1.9	12	11
2.7 - < 3.1	11	10	1.9 - < 2.4	5	1
3.1 - < 4.0	1	3	≥ 2.4	1	0
≥ 4.0	1	0			
	51	51		51	51

The variation in average costs for all use appears greater than that for households, but the distributions of weighted costs seem quite similar for the two categories.

The table on the following page shows the range of average cost per million BTU for sectors and functions, and the states having the extreme values for each category.

Extreme Values In Average Cost by Sector and Function

Use By Sector	Cost Per Million BTU		State With:	
	Minimum Price	Maximum Price	Minimum Price	Maximum Price
Household Use	$1.97	4.18	Wyo.	Hawaii
Federal Government Use	0.80	3.59	R.I.	Vt.
State and Local Government Use	1.04	5.89	N.Mex.	Hawaii
Business Use	0.51	1.91	La.	Vt.
All Use	0.75	2.42	La.	Vt.
Use By Function				
Residential Use	1.60	6.60	Wyo.	Hawaii
Commercial Use	1.74	5.39	Wyo.	Hawaii
Industrial Use	0.46	3.05	La.	Hawaii
Transportation Use	1.56	3.06	Alaska	Vt.
Energy Use				
Non-Electric Utility Use	0.18	1.20	N.Mex.	Vt.
Electric Utility Use	0.18	0.87	Wash.	Hawaii
Municipal-Institutional Use	0.65	16.00	N.Mex.	Del.

The range of weighted prices for household use and for all use, respectively, are shown in the table on the following page.

Extreme values seem easy to explain in most of the cases. Alaska or Hawaii have the maximums for all cases, at least in part reflecting a high general price level which in turn reflects high transportation costs of

imports.[9] Low prices for Washington and Tennessee reflect massive federal
power projects in those states (the Bonneville Power Authority and the TVA)
that have very low electricity rates, and low prices for Texas and Wyoming
probably reflect their energy supplying status. But the North Dakota, New
Mexico and Oklahoma results shown probably reflect some relatively minor
differentials that are given great (and presumably excessive) weight by the
estimating procedure. Despite this occasional "outlyer" problem, the bulk
of the weighted price entries appear to give a realistic picture of state
price differentials, with considerable consistency among states in a region,
and reasonable extreme values within regions.

	Weighted Price Per Million BTU		State With:	
Household Use	Minimum Price	Maximum Price	Minimum Price	Maximum Price
Petroleum Products	2.28	3.52	N. Dak.	Hawaii
Natural Gas	0.72	3.00	Wyo.	Hawaii
Electricity	3.08	9.77	Wash.	Alaska
Coal, Etc.	0.91	1.94	Okla.	Alaska
All Sources	2.22	3.75	Tenn.	Hawaii
All Use				
Petroleum Products	1.68	2.36	Texas	Hawaii
Natural Gas	0.39	2.00	Wyo.	Hawaii
Electricity	2.28	8.05	Wash.	Alaska
Coal, Etc.	0.18	1.94	N. Mex.	Alaska
All Sources	1.17	2.18	Wash.	Hawaii

---

[9]Hawaii is shown with no natural gas use in the tables of energy
consumption, but a price estimate for natural gas was necessary if a
weighted price for Hawaii were to be constructed. The estimate was based
on American Gas Association (AGA) data, which showed some very low per
capita use at very high prices. The AGA data covers natural gas plus
other gas (presumably manufactured or imported liquified gas) and the
Hawaiian use appears to involve other gas. The price was accepted as a
reasonable figure for natural gas in Hawaii. See Chapter 3 and Appendix F
of Part II for additional detail.

Table 1

Consumption Of Energy In Trillion BTU, 1972, By State

All Sector Energy Use By Energy Source

REGION AND STATE	PETROLEUM PRODUCTS	NATURAL GAS	ELECTRICITY	COAL, HYDROPOWER & NUCLEAR POWER	TOTAL, ALL SOURCES
NEW ENGLAND:					
CONNECTICUT	595.036	70.703	61.897	82.422	810.058
MAINE	311.701	1.699	19.353	17.808	350.561
MASSACHUSETTS	1303.448	160.369	95.594	27.841	1587.252
NEW HAMPSHIRE	143.371	8.898	15.166	38.626	206.062
RHODE ISLAND	174.456	24.574	15.333	0.244	214.608
VERMONT	75.418	3.831	10.280	11.321	100.849
MID ATLANTIC:					
NEW JERSEY	1445.057	333.813	144.389	74.605	1997.864
NEW YORK	2798.659	728.428	319.889	688.981	4535.957
PENNSYLVANIA	1572.422	843.794	285.888	1719.364	4421.469
EAST NORTH CENTRAL:					
ILLINOIS	1447.476	1219.689	261.264	1029.443	3957.871
INDIANA	749.833	576.881	142.369	1098.051	2567.134
MICHIGAN	1017.076	932.837	208.698	884.110	3042.722
OHIO	1030.115	1200.253	330.558	1599.659	4160.585
WISCONSIN	487.673	364.380	95.372	398.881	1346.307
WEST NORTH CENTRAL:					
IOWA	319.783	369.682	59.038	164.937	913.439
KANSAS	293.740	686.835	52.978	14.077	1047.630
MINNESOTA	522.415	388.393	78.626	225.571	1215.005
MISSOURI	546.389	429.885	99.395	351.403	1427.072
NEBRASKA	195.869	238.322	32.527	45.967	512.684
NORTH DAKOTA	89.907	36.725	10.372	125.861	262.866
SOUTH DAKOTA	90.542	35.051	10.598	82.211	218.401
SOUTH ATLANTIC:					
DELAWARE	130.060	25.373	17.657	49.152	222.243
DISTRICT OF COLUMBIA	119.153	31.389	17.091	7.174	174.806
FLORIDA	1249.844	308.399	201.659	129.553	1889.455
GEORGIA	601.289	337.914	125.797	284.427	1349.426
MARYLAND	629.963	182.995	89.224	227.349	1129.531
NORTH CAROLINA	661.841	183.249	153.738	543.986	1542.814
SOUTH CAROLINA	311.131	162.723	90.558	248.033	812.446
VIRGINIA	844.537	163.713	113.323	219.947	1341.520
WEST VIRGINIA	140.670	191.686	53.544	721.696	1107.596
EAST SOUTH CENTRAL:					
ALABAMA	368.893	287.100	133.798	706.261	1496.052
KENTUCKY	340.420	259.547	134.136	629.070	1363.172
MISSISSIPPI	288.704	387.436	56.731	74.550	807.421
TENNESSEE	400.549	283.755	198.838	525.144	1408.285
WEST SOUTH CENTRAL:					
ARKANSAS	274.682	317.641	51.620	17.028	660.972
LOUISIANA	598.326	1996.015	119.127	4.200	2717.668
OKLAHOMA	337.016	649.910	64.947	16.010	1067.883
TEXAS	1871.249	4531.777	384.956	63.471	6851.452
ROCKY MOUNTAIN:					
ARIZONA	212.153	241.355	57.397	74.552	585.458
COLORADO	280.221	301.651	42.640	136.973	761.486
IDAHO	98.441	60.085	38.139	78.545	275.210
MONTANA	125.803	87.021	31.360	115.811	359.995
NEVADA	85.621	75.223	22.519	49.693	233.056
NEW MEXICO	154.376	311.896	19.994	139.312	625.579
UTAH	169.268	116.399	20.974	91.266	397.907
WYOMING	98.543	128.728	11.976	106.419	345.666
FAR WEST:					
ALASKA	113.117	75.031	4.364	21.310	213.822
CALIFORNIA	2684.897	2303.562	476.247	382.192	5846.898
HAWAII	215.584	0.000	15.528	0.211	231.322
OREGON	307.526	115.327	96.792	352.306	871.949
WASHINGTON	480.018	179.823	188.892	755.873	1604.605

Table 2

Expenditures On Energy In Million Dollars, 1972, By State

All Sector Energy Use By Energy Source

REGION AND STATE	PETROLEUM PRODUCTS	NATURAL GAS	ELECTRICITY	COAL, HYDROPOWER & NUCLEAR POWER	TOTAL, ALL SOURCES
NEW ENGLAND:					
CONNECTICUT	963.263	120.367	442.520	51.677	1577.827
MAINE	470.778	4.156	123.193	6.345	604.472
MASSACHUSETTS	1903.561	296.566	744.413	16.717	2961.257
NEW HAMPSHIRE	264.234	14.070	98.520	18.442	395.267
RHODE ISLAND	282.004	42.988	115.200	0.185	440.377
VERMONT	165.368	3.950	67.324	7.190	243.833
MID ATLANTIC:					
NEW JERSEY	2241.077	476.213	1039.173	51.546	3808.009
NEW YORK	4570.820	930.111	2423.865	392.871	8317.667
PENNSYLVANIA	2832.628	812.581	1712.746	758.916	6116.870
EAST NORTH CENTRAL:					
ILLINOIS	2687.243	1012.625	1614.555	441.257	5755.680
INDIANA	1452.391	442.077	741.723	379.719	3015.910
MICHIGAN	2098.398	775.079	1179.740	420.730	4473.947
OHIO	2364.585	984.458	1538.210	649.023	5536.276
WISCONSIN	1029.591	306.246	581.257	209.753	2126.848
WEST NORTH CENTRAL:					
IOWA	738.618	243.542	382.381	67.374	1431.915
KANSAS	542.522	279.266	288.069	4.989	1114.846
MINNESOTA	1007.481	294.540	485.145	102.773	1889.939
MISSOURI	1155.197	324.285	615.018	110.044	2204.544
NEBRASKA	424.923	135.672	175.019	20.258	755.872
NORTH DAKOTA	160.840	23.306	72.042	30.330	286.518
SOUTH DAKOTA	187.778	26.627	74.142	37.398	325.945
SOUTH ATLANTIC:					
DELAWARE	208.950	26.729	110.139	27.686	373.504
DISTRICT OF COLUMBIA	179.572	41.254	117.937	4.480	343.244
FLORIDA	2023.912	172.554	1158.503	55.742	3410.711
GEORGIA	1266.304	243.319	615.506	128.118	2253.247
MARYLAND	1066.487	214.268	543.178	126.495	1950.429
NORTH CAROLINA	1434.361	143.711	694.216	251.726	2524.014
SOUTH CAROLINA	694.289	113.747	375.469	124.018	1307.523
VIRGINIA	1342.604	166.754	569.719	106.992	2186.069
WEST VIRGINIA	345.161	128.545	241.554	264.508	979.767
EAST SOUTH CENTRAL:					
ALABAMA	849.528	170.589	495.417	271.476	1787.010
KENTUCKY	779.974	167.028	450.981	185.799	1583.782
MISSISSIPPI	621.020	156.578	275.086	29.461	1082.146
TENNESSEE	935.497	172.661	598.648	196.134	1902.940
WEST SOUTH CENTRAL:					
ARKANSAS	582.977	135.203	255.447	6.661	980.288
LOUISIANA	884.866	626.454	512.075	0.939	2024.335
OKLAHOMA	676.328	216.423	343.212	3.847	1239.811
TEXAS	3128.134	1334.448	1656.982	14.056	6133.620
ROCKY MOUNTAIN:					
ARIZONA	490.756	129.463	315.548	23.728	959.496
COLORADO	614.451	159.818	252.897	43.320	1070.486
IDAHO	217.387	45.008	119.373	15.420	397.188
MONTANA	225.303	49.892	92.331	32.798	400.324
NEVADA	194.697	48.348	92.583	15.751	351.378
NEW MEXICO	329.440	112.043	114.942	21.117	577.542
UTAH	305.253	73.557	110.274	31.199	520.282
WYOMING	162.573	46.999	56.226	21.665	287.463
FAR WEST:					
ALASKA	175.283	46.271	40.959	15.283	277.796
CALIFORNIA	4755.864	1440.401	2414.283	137.379	8747.927
HAWAII	301.749	0.000	108.497	0.112	410.358
OREGON	599.762	96.797	278.154	62.371	1037.083
WASHINGTON	898.114	133.514	396.679	133.478	1561.785

Table 3

Consumption Of Energy In Trillion BTU And Expenditures On
    Energy In Million Dollars, 1972, By Region

All Sector Energy Use By Energy Source

REGION	PETROLEUM PRODUCTS	NATURAL GAS	ELECTRICITY	COAL HYDROPOWER & NUCLEAR POWER	TOTAL, ALL SOURCES
Consumption In Trillion BTU					
NEW ENGLAND	2603.43	270.07	217.62	178.26	3269.39
MID ATLANTIC	5816.14	1906.04	750.17	2482.95	10955.29
EAST NORTH CENTRAL	4732.17	4294.04	1038.26	5010.14	15074.62
WEST NORTH CENTRAL	2058.65	2184.89	343.53	1010.03	5597.10
SOUTH ATLANTIC	4688.49	1587.44	862.59	2431.32	9569.84
EAST SOUTH CENTRAL	1398.57	1217.84	523.50	1935.02	5074.93
WEST SOUTH CENTRAL	3081.27	7495.34	620.65	100.71	11297.98
ROCKY MOUNTAIN	1224.43	1322.36	245.00	792.57	3584.36
FAR WEST	3801.14	2673.74	781.82	1511.89	8768.60
TOTAL	29404.28	22951.76	5383.15	15452.90	73192.09
Expenditures In Million Dollars					
NEW ENGLAND	4049.21	482.10	1591.17	100.56	6223.03
MID ATLANTIC	9644.53	2218.90	5175.78	1203.33	18242.55
EAST NORTH CENTRAL	9632.21	3520.49	5655.49	2100.48	20908.66
WEST NORTH CENTRAL	4217.36	1327.24	2091.82	373.17	8009.58
SOUTH ATLANTIC	8561.64	1250.88	4426.22	1089.77	15328.51
EAST SOUTH CENTRAL	3186.02	666.86	1820.13	682.87	6355.88
WEST SOUTH CENTRAL	5272.31	2312.53	2767.72	25.50	10378.05
ROCKY MOUNTAIN	2539.86	665.13	1154.17	205.00	4564.16
FAR WEST	6730.77	1716.98	3238.57	348.62	12034.95
TOTAL	53833.90	14161.10	27921.07	6129.30	102045.37

Table 4

Consumption Of Energy In Million BTU Per Capita, 1972, By State

All Sector Energy Use By Energy Source

REGION AND STATE	PETROLEUM PRODUCTS	NATURAL GAS	ELECTRICITY	COAL, HYDROPOWER & NUCLEAR POWER	TOTAL, ALL SOURCES
NEW ENGLAND:					
CONNECTICUT	193.194	22.956	20.096	26.760	263.006
MAINE	303.802	1.656	18.862	17.357	341.678
MASSACHUSETTS	224.888	27.669	16.493	4.804	273.853
NEW HAMPSHIRE	185.234	11.497	19.595	49.905	266.230
RHODE ISLAND	180.037	25.360	15.824	0.252	221.474
VERMONT	163.952	8.327	22.349	24.610	219.238
MID ATLANTIC:					
NEW JERSEY	196.633	45.423	19.647	10.152	271.855
NEW YORK	152.374	39.660	17.416	37.512	246.962
PENNSYLVANIA	132.081	70.877	24.014	144.424	371.396
EAST NORTH CENTRAL:					
ILLINOIS	128.733	108.475	23.236	91.555	351.998
INDIANA	141.853	109.134	26.933	207.728	485.648
MICHIGAN	112.845	103.499	23.155	98.093	337.593
OHIO	96.075	111.943	30.830	149.194	388.042
WISCONSIN	107.749	80.508	21.072	88.131	297.461
WEST NORTH CENTRAL:					
IOWA	110.882	128.184	20.471	57.190	316.727
KANSAS	129.515	302.837	23.359	6.207	461.918
MINNESOTA	134.747	100.179	20.280	58.182	313.388
MISSOURI	115.102	90.559	20.938	74.026	300.626
NEBRASKA	128.186	155.970	21.287	30.083	335.526
NORTH DAKOTA	141.809	57.926	16.360	198.519	414.615
SOUTH DAKOTA	133.150	51.545	15.585	120.899	321.179
SOUTH ATLANTIC:					
DELAWARE	227.777	44.437	30.923	86.081	389.218
DISTRICT OF COLUMBIA	158.447	41.740	22.727	9.540	232.455
FLORIDA	170.116	41.976	27.448	17.633	257.174
GEORGIA	127.042	71.395	26.579	60.094	285.110
MARYLAND	155.623	45.206	22.041	56.163	279.034
NORTH CAROLINA	126.765	35.099	29.446	104.192	295.502
SOUTH CAROLINA	115.749	60.537	33.690	92.274	302.249
VIRGINIA	177.238	34.357	23.782	46.159	281.536
WEST VIRGINIA	78.367	106.789	29.830	402.059	617.045
EAST SOUTH CENTRAL:					
ALABAMA	104.769	81.539	38.000	200.585	424.894
KENTUCKY	102.970	78.508	40.574	190.281	412.333
MISSISSIPPI	127.971	171.736	25.147	33.045	357.899
TENNESSEE	98.367	69.684	48.830	128.965	345.846
WEST SOUTH CENTRAL:					
ARKANSAS	136.794	158.188	25.707	8.480	329.169
LOUISIANA	160.066	533.979	31.869	1.124	727.038
OKLAHOMA	127.997	246.832	24.667	6.081	405.577
TEXAS	161.259	390.536	33.174	5.470	590.439
ROCKY MOUNTAIN:					
ARIZONA	108.076	122.952	29.239	37.979	298.246
COLORADO	118.537	127.602	18.037	57.941	322.117
IDAHO	130.385	79.582	50.516	104.033	364.516
MONTANA	175.703	121.538	43.798	161.748	502.786
NEVADA	160.641	141.131	42.250	93.233	437.254
NEW MEXICO	143.473	289.866	18.582	129.472	581.393
UTAH	150.193	103.282	18.610	80.982	353.067
WYOMING	284.807	372.046	34.613	307.569	999.036
FAR WEST:					
ALASKA	348.054	230.864	13.427	65.570	657.915
CALIFORNIA	131.542	112.859	23.333	18.725	286.458
HAWAII	264.196	0.000	19.029	0.258	283.483
OREGON	140.744	52.781	44.298	161.238	399.061
WASHINGTON	140.438	52.611	55.264	221.145	469.457

Table 5

Expenditures On Energy In Dollars Per Capita, 1972, By State

All Sector Energy Use By Energy Source

REGION AND STATE	PETROLEUM PRODUCTS	NATURAL GAS	ELECTRICITY	COAL, HYDROPOWER & NUCLEAR POWER	TOTAL, ALL SOURCES
NEW ENGLAND:					
CONNECTICUT	312.748	39.080	143.675	16.778	512.281
MAINE	458.848	4.051	120.071	6.185	589.154
MASSACHUSETTS	328.427	51.167	128.436	2.884	510.914
NEW HAMPSHIRE	341.388	18.178	127.287	23.827	510.680
RHODE ISLAND	291.026	44.363	118.885	0.191	454.466
VERMONT	359.496	8.587	146.357	15.631	530.071
MID ATLANTIC:					
NEW JERSEY	304.950	64.800	141.403	7.014	518.167
NEW YORK	248.860	50.640	131.968	21.390	452.859
PENNSYLVANIA	237.936	68.255	143.868	63.748	513.807
EAST NORTH CENTRAL:					
ILLINOIS	238.993	90.059	143.593	39.244	511.889
INDIANA	274.762	83.632	140.318	71.835	570.547
MICHIGAN	232.819	85.996	130.893	46.680	496.388
OHIO	220.536	91.817	143.463	60.532	516.347
WISCONSIN	227.484	67.664	128.426	46.344	469.918
WEST NORTH CENTRAL:					
IOWA	256.109	84.446	132.587	23.361	496.503
KANSAS	239.207	123.133	127.015	2.200	491.555
MINNESOTA	259.861	75.971	125.134	26.508	487.475
MISSOURI	243.353	68.314	129.559	23.182	464.408
NEBRASKA	278.091	88.791	114.541	13.258	494.680
NORTH DAKOTA	253.691	36.760	113.631	47.839	451.921
SOUTH DAKOTA	276.144	39.157	109.032	54.997	479.331
SOUTH ATLANTIC:					
DELAWARE	365.937	46.812	192.888	48.486	654.123
DISTRICT OF COLUMBIA	238.793	54.860	156.831	5.958	456.441
FLORIDA	275.475	23.486	157.684	7.587	464.232
GEORGIA	267.548	51.409	130.046	27.069	476.072
MARYLAND	263.460	52.932	134.184	31.249	481.825
NORTH CAROLINA	274.729	27.526	132.966	48.214	483.435
SOUTH CAROLINA	258.292	42.317	139.683	46.137	486.430
VIRGINIA	281.764	34.996	119.563	22.454	458.776
WEST VIRGINIA	192.290	71.613	134.570	147.358	545.831
EAST SOUTH CENTRAL:					
ALABAMA	241.275	48.449	140.703	77.102	507.529
KENTUCKY	235.927	50.523	136.413	56.201	479.063
MISSISSIPPI	275.275	69.405	121.935	13.059	479.674
TENNESSEE	229.739	42.402	147.016	48.166	467.323
WEST SOUTH CENTRAL:					
ARKANSAS	290.327	67.332	127.215	3.317	488.191
LOUISIANA	236.722	167.591	136.992	0.251	541.556
OKLAHOMA	256.866	82.196	130.350	1.461	470.874
TEXAS	269.574	114.999	142.794	1.211	528.578
ROCKY MOUNTAIN:					
ARIZONA	250.003	65.952	160.748	12.088	488.790
COLORADO	259.920	67.605	106.978	18.325	452.828
IDAHO	287.930	59.613	158.110	20.424	526.077
MONTANA	314.668	69.682	128.954	45.807	559.111
NEVADA	365.285	90.709	173.702	29.551	659.246
NEW MEXICO	306.171	104.129	106.823	19.625	536.749
UTAH	270.854	65.268	97.847	27.683	461.652
WYOMING	469.865	135.836	162.503	62.615	830.818
FAR WEST:					
ALASKA	539.334	142.371	126.028	47.025	854.758
CALIFORNIA	233.005	70.570	118.283	6.731	428.589
HAWAII	369.790	0.000	132.962	0.138	502.890
OREGON	274.491	44.301	127.302	28.545	474.638
WASHINGTON	262.760	39.062	116.056	39.051	456.929

Table 6

Consumption Of Energy In Million BTU Per Capita And Expenditures On Energy
   In Dollars Per Capita, 1972, By Region

All Sector Energy Use By Energy Source

REGION	PETROLEUM PRODUCTS	NATURAL GAS	ELECTRICITY	COAL, HYDROPOWER & NUCLEAR POWER	TOTAL, ALL SOURCES
Consumption In Million BTU Per Capita					
NEW ENGLAND	215.071	22.311	17.978	14.726	270.086
MID ATLANTIC	154.598	50.664	19.940	65.999	291.201
EAST NORTH CENTRAL	116.010	105.269	25.453	122.825	369.557
WEST NORTH CENTRAL	123.880	131.478	20.672	60.779	336.809
SOUTH ATLANTIC	146.882	49.732	27.024	76.169	299.807
EAST SOUTH CENTRAL	106.314	92.576	39.795	147.094	385.780
WEST SOUTH CENTRAL	154.195	375.086	31.059	5.040	565.379
ROCKY MOUNTAIN	137.886	148.914	27.590	89.254	403.644
FAR WEST	139.979	98.462	28.791	55.676	322.909
UNITED STATES	141.212	110.224	25.852	74.211	351.500
Expenditures In Dollars Per Capita					
NEW ENGLAND	334.507	39.826	131.447	8.307	514.088
MID ATLANTIC	256.360	58.980	137.577	31.986	484.903
EAST NORTH CENTRAL	236.136	86.305	138.645	51.494	512.580
WEST NORTH CENTRAL	253.783	79.868	125.877	22.455	481.982
SOUTH ATLANTIC	268.222	39.188	138.666	34.140	480.216
EAST SOUTH CENTRAL	242.191	50.692	138.360	51.910	483.153
WEST SOUTH CENTRAL	263.840	115.725	138.504	1.276	519.344
ROCKY MOUNTAIN	286.020	74.902	129.975	23.085	513.982
FAR WEST	247.865	63.229	119.262	12.838	443.195
UNITED STATES	258.533	68.008	134.089	29.435	490.066

Table 7

Consumption Of Energy As Fraction Of Total Consumption (BTU), 1972, By State

All Sector Energy Use By Energy Source

REGION AND STATE	PETROLEUM PRODUCTS	NATURAL GAS	ELECTRICITY	COAL, HYDROPOWER & NUCLEAR POWER
NEW ENGLAND:				
CONNECTICUT	0.7346	0.0873	0.0764	0.1017
MAINE	0.8891	0.0048	0.0552	0.0508
MASSACHUSETTS	0.8212	0.1010	0.0602	0.0175
NEW HAMPSHIRE	0.6958	0.0432	0.0736	0.1874
RHODE ISLAND	0.8129	0.1145	0.0714	0.0011
VERMONT	0.7478	0.0380	0.1019	0.1123
MID ATLANTIC:				
NEW JERSEY	0.7233	0.1671	0.0723	0.0373
NEW YORK	0.6170	0.1606	0.0705	0.1519
PENNSYLVANIA	0.3556	0.1908	0.0647	0.3889
EAST NORTH CENTRAL:				
ILLINOIS	0.3657	0.3082	0.0660	0.2601
INDIANA	0.2921	0.2247	0.0555	0.4277
MICHIGAN	0.3343	0.3066	0.0686	0.2906
OHIO	0.2476	0.2885	0.0794	0.3845
WISCONSIN	0.3622	0.2707	0.0708	0.2963
WEST NORTH CENTRAL:				
IOWA	0.3501	0.4047	0.0646	0.1806
KANSAS	0.2804	0.6556	0.0506	0.0134
MINNESOTA	0.4300	0.3197	0.0647	0.1857
MISSOURI	0.3829	0.3012	0.0696	0.2462
NEBRASKA	0.3820	0.4649	0.0634	0.0897
NORTH DAKOTA	0.3420	0.1397	0.0395	0.4788
SOUTH DAKOTA	0.4146	0.1605	0.0485	0.3764
SOUTH ATLANTIC:				
DELAWARE	0.5852	0.1142	0.0794	0.2212
DISTRICT OF COLUMBIA	0.6816	0.1796	0.0978	0.0410
FLORIDA	0.6615	0.1632	0.1067	0.0686
GEORGIA	0.4456	0.2504	0.0932	0.2108
MARYLAND	0.5577	0.1620	0.0790	0.2013
NORTH CAROLINA	0.4290	0.1188	0.0996	0.3526
SOUTH CAROLINA	0.3830	0.2003	0.1115	0.3053
VIRGINIA	0.6295	0.1220	0.0845	0.1640
WEST VIRGINIA	0.1270	0.1731	0.0483	0.6516
EAST SOUTH CENTRAL:				
ALABAMA	0.2466	0.1919	0.0894	0.4721
KENTUCKY	0.2497	0.1904	0.0984	0.4615
MISSISSIPPI	0.3576	0.4798	0.0703	0.0923
TENNESSEE	0.2844	0.2015	0.1412	0.3729
WEST SOUTH CENTRAL:				
ARKANSAS	0.4156	0.4806	0.0781	0.0258
LOUISIANA	0.2202	0.7345	0.0438	0.0015
OKLAHOMA	0.3156	0.6086	0.0608	0.0150
TEXAS	0.2731	0.6614	0.0562	0.0093
ROCKY MOUNTAIN:				
ARIZONA	0.3624	0.4122	0.0980	0.1273
COLORADO	0.3680	0.3961	0.0560	0.1799
IDAHO	0.3577	0.2183	0.1386	0.2854
MONTANA	0.3495	0.2417	0.0871	0.3217
NEVADA	0.3674	0.3228	0.0966	0.2132
NEW MEXICO	0.2468	0.4986	0.0320	0.2227
UTAH	0.4254	0.2925	0.0527	0.2294
WYOMING	0.2851	0.3724	0.0346	0.3079
FAR WEST:				
ALASKA	0.5290	0.3509	0.0204	0.0997
CALIFORNIA	0.4592	0.3940	0.0815	0.0654
HAWAII	0.9320	0.0000	0.0671	0.0009
OREGON	0.3527	0.1323	0.1110	0.4040
WASHINGTON	0.2992	0.1121	0.1177	0.4711

Table 8

Expenditures On Energy As Fraction Of Total Expenditures, 1972, By State

All Sector Energy Use By Energy Source

REGION AND STATE	PETROLEUM PRODUCTS	NATURAL GAS	ELECTRICITY	COAL, HYDROPOWER & NUCLEAR POWER
NEW ENGLAND:				
CONNECTICUT	0.6105	0.0763	0.2805	0.0328
MAINE	0.7788	0.0069	0.2038	0.0105
MASSACHUSETTS	0.6428	0.1001	0.2514	0.0056
NEW HAMPSHIRE	0.6685	0.0356	0.2492	0.0467
RHODE ISLAND	0.6404	0.0976	0.2616	0.0004
VERMONT	0.6782	0.0162	0.2761	0.0295
MID ATLANTIC:				
NEW JERSEY	0.5885	0.1251	0.2729	0.0135
NEW YORK	0.5495	0.1118	0.2914	0.0472
PENNSYLVANIA	0.4631	0.1328	0.2800	0.1241
EAST NORTH CENTRAL:				
ILLINOIS	0.4669	0.1759	0.2805	0.0767
INDIANA	0.4816	0.1466	0.2459	0.1259
MICHIGAN	0.4690	0.1732	0.2637	0.0940
OHIO	0.4271	0.1778	0.2778	0.1172
WISCONSIN	0.4841	0.1440	0.2733	0.0986
WEST NORTH CENTRAL:				
IOWA	0.5158	0.1701	0.2670	0.0471
KANSAS	0.4866	0.2505	0.2584	0.0045
MINNESOTA	0.5331	0.1558	0.2567	0.0544
MISSOURI	0.5240	0.1471	0.2790	0.0499
NEBRASKA	0.5622	0.1795	0.2315	0.0268
NORTH DAKOTA	0.5614	0.0813	0.2514	0.1059
SOUTH DAKOTA	0.5761	0.0817	0.2275	0.1147
SOUTH ATLANTIC:				
DELAWARE	0.5594	0.0716	0.2949	0.0741
DISTRICT OF COLUMBIA	0.5232	0.1202	0.3436	0.0131
FLORIDA	0.5934	0.0506	0.3397	0.0163
GEORGIA	0.5620	0.1080	0.2732	0.0569
MARYLAND	0.5468	0.1099	0.2785	0.0649
NORTH CAROLINA	0.5683	0.0569	0.2750	0.0997
SOUTH CAROLINA	0.5310	0.0870	0.2872	0.0948
VIRGINIA	0.6142	0.0763	0.2606	0.0489
WEST VIRGINIA	0.3523	0.1312	0.2465	0.2700
EAST SOUTH CENTRAL:				
ALABAMA	0.4754	0.0955	0.2772	0.1519
KENTUCKY	0.4925	0.1055	0.2847	0.1173
MISSISSIPPI	0.5739	0.1447	0.2542	0.0272
TENNESSEE	0.4916	0.0907	0.3146	0.1031
WEST SOUTH CENTRAL:				
ARKANSAS	0.5947	0.1379	0.2606	0.0068
LOUISIANA	0.4371	0.3095	0.2530	0.0005
OKLAHOMA	0.5455	0.1746	0.2768	0.0031
TEXAS	0.5100	0.2176	0.2701	0.0023
ROCKY MOUNTAIN:				
ARIZONA	0.5115	0.1349	0.3289	0.0247
COLORADO	0.5740	0.1493	0.2362	0.0405
IDAHO	0.5473	0.1133	0.3005	0.0388
MONTANA	0.5628	0.1246	0.2306	0.0819
NEVADA	0.5541	0.1376	0.2635	0.0448
NEW MEXICO	0.5704	0.1940	0.1990	0.0366
UTAH	0.5867	0.1414	0.2120	0.0600
WYOMING	0.5655	0.1635	0.1956	0.0754
FAR WEST:				
ALASKA	0.6310	0.1666	0.1474	0.0550
CALIFORNIA	0.5437	0.1647	0.2760	0.0157
HAWAII	0.7353	0.0000	0.2644	0.0003
OREGON	0.5783	0.0933	0.2682	0.0601
WASHINGTON	0.5751	0.0855	0.2540	0.0855

Table 9

Consumption And Expenditures On Energy As A Fraction Of Total Use, 1972, By Region

All Sector Energy Use By Energy Source

REGION	PETROLEUM PRODUCTS	NATURAL GAS	ELECTRICITY	COAL, HYDROPOWER & NUCLEAR POWER
Consumption As Fraction Of Total Consumption (BTU)				
NEW ENGLAND	0.7963	0.0826	0.0666	0.0545
MID ATLANTIC	0.5309	0.1740	0.0685	0.2266
EAST NORTH CENTRAL	0.3139	0.2849	0.0689	0.3324
WEST NORTH CENTRAL	0.3678	0.3904	0.0614	0.1805
SOUTH ATLANTIC	0.4899	0.1659	0.0901	0.2541
EAST SOUTH CENTRAL	0.2756	0.2400	0.1032	0.3813
WEST SOUTH CENTRAL	0.2727	0.6634	0.0549	0.0089
ROCKY MOUNTAIN	0.3416	0.3689	0.0684	0.2211
FAR WEST	0.4335	0.3049	0.0892	0.1724
UNITED STATES	0.4017	0.3136	0.0735	0.2111
Expenditures As Fraction Of Total Expenditures				
NEW ENGLAND	0.6507	0.0775	0.2557	0.0162
MID ATLANTIC	0.5287	0.1216	0.2837	0.0660
EAST NORTH CENTRAL	0.4607	0.1684	0.2705	0.1005
WEST NORTH CENTRAL	0.5265	0.1657	0.2612	0.0466
SOUTH ATLANTIC	0.5585	0.0816	0.2888	0.0711
EAST SOUTH CENTRAL	0.5013	0.1049	0.2864	0.1074
WEST SOUTH CENTRAL	0.5080	0.2228	0.2667	0.0025
ROCKY MOUNTAIN	0.5565	0.1457	0.2529	0.0449
FAR WEST	0.5593	0.1427	0.2691	0.0290
UNITED STATES	0.5275	0.1388	0.2736	0.0601

Table 10

Consumption Of Energy In Trillion BTU, 1972, By State

Household Energy Use By Energy Source

REGION AND STATE	PETROLEUM PRODUCTS	NATURAL GAS	ELECTRICITY	COAL, HYDROPOWER & NUCLEAR POWER	TOTAL ALL SOURCES
NEW ENGLAND:					
CONNECTICUT	253.206	39.149	24.502	0.100	316.956
MAINE	113.674	0.988	7.223	0.100	121.986
MASSACHUSETTS	566.744	100.339	35.584	0.950	703.617
NEW HAMPSHIRE	84.617	5.225	6.421	0.300	96.563
RHODE ISLAND	84.873	14.985	5.384	0.050	105.292
VERMONT	54.438	1.398	4.869	0.200	60.905
MID ATLANTIC:					
NEW JERSEY	631.232	176.201	46.192	3.500	857.125
NEW YORK	1230.643	439.558	93.782	13.350	1777.333
PENNSYLVANIA	750.979	345.351	85.143	67.100	1248.573
EAST NORTH CENTRAL:					
ILLINOIS	606.270	557.791	77.405	39.150	1280.616
INDIANA	343.527	180.273	45.499	23.750	593.049
MICHIGAN	573.555	381.629	65.012	18.750	1038.947
OHIO	568.649	518.040	81.656	35.650	1203.994
WISCONSIN	299.500	115.894	36.607	21.500	473.501
WEST NORTH CENTRAL:					
IOWA	172.556	102.310	23.911	2.100	300.877
KANSAS	110.501	104.257	18.282	0.500	233.539
MINNESOTA	266.073	119.955	29.831	8.450	424.309
MISSOURI	270.376	173.903	37.430	2.600	484.309
NEBRASKA	89.136	64.159	13.088	1.000	167.383
NORTH DAKOTA	36.224	11.899	5.104	1.600	54.828
SOUTH DAKOTA	47.306	14.200	5.674	2.000	69.181
SOUTH ATLANTIC:					
DELAWARE	47.306	9.047	4.422	0.650	61.424
DISTRICT OF COLUMBIA	37.076	18.302	5.033	0.100	60.511
FLORIDA	412.996	23.323	98.194	0.700	535.213
GEORGIA	264.095	91.655	47.533	1.000	404.283
MARYLAND	241.598	82.486	26.218	1.950	352.251
NORTH CAROLINA	339.708	35.656	54.544	10.100	440.008
SOUTH CAROLINA	158.019	21.962	26.829	5.800	212.609
VIRGINIA	297.754	61.913	43.220	11.400	414.287
WEST VIRGINIA	67.263	61.900	13.245	7.400	149.808
EAST SOUTH CENTRAL:					
ALABAMA	182.217	56.392	42.142	1.800	282.551
KENTUCKY	164.875	89.254	30.868	8.700	293.697
MISSISSIPPI	130.170	40.919	21.953	1.600	194.642
TENNESSEE	208.713	57.454	70.192	12.300	348.659
WEST SOUTH CENTRAL:					
ARKANSAS	119.241	48.245	16.896	0.000	184.382
LOUISIANA	163.159	87.167	37.095	0.000	287.420
OKLAHOMA	146.836	81.660	23.959	0.000	252.455
TEXAS	668.337	257.612	119.782	0.100	1045.831
ROCKY MOUNTAIN:					
ARIZONA	89.711	39.113	18.671	0.000	147.494
COLORADO	126.147	91.991	13.856	0.600	232.594
IDAHO	51.787	12.134	9.663	0.000	73.584
MONTANA	38.521	25.416	5.835	0.400	70.171
NEVADA	35.730	11.062	8.039	0.000	54.831
NEW MEXICO	60.972	38.398	5.268	0.000	104.638
UTAH	57.789	47.131	6.688	0.500	112.107
WYOMING	27.215	23.065	2.300	0.100	52.679
FAR WEST:					
ALASKA	23.328	9.331	1.918	0.100	34.676
CALIFORNIA	910.425	736.134	136.019	0.000	1782.578
HAWAII	27.834	0.000	5.084	0.000	32.918
OREGON	140.394	28.210	37.235	0.100	205.939
WASHINGTON	191.081	48.367	63.678	0.100	303.227

Table 11

Expenditures On Energy In Million Dollars, 1972, By State

Household Energy Use By Energy Source

REGION AND STATE	PETROLEUM PRODUCTS	NATURAL GAS	ELECTRICITY	COAL, HYDROPOWER & NUCLEAR POWER	TOTAL, ALL SOURCES
NEW ENGLAND:					
CONNECTICUT	605.777	78.664	200.493	0.162	885.096
MAINE	246.561	2.948	57.742	0.155	307.406
MASSACHUSETTS	1186.561	220.654	321.822	1.316	1730.353
NEW HAMPSHIRE	186.688	10.066	50.243	0.396	247.393
RHODE ISLAND	182.803	29.897	49.191	0.071	261.962
VERMONT	125.351	2.389	34.928	0.311	162.978
MID ATLANTIC:					
NEW JERSEY	1399.451	335.374	414.898	5.683	2155.406
NEW YORK	2900.959	677.329	895.238	19.189	4492.715
PENNSYLVANIA	1789.162	446.158	691.009	83.519	3009.848
EAST NORTH CENTRAL:					
ILLINOIS	1615.789	601.595	644.784	52.457	2914.625
INDIANA	847.325	201.882	303.987	28.419	1381.613
MICHIGAN	1395.467	408.961	461.322	24.938	2290.687
OHIO	1602.343	529.024	568.960	45.275	2745.602
WISCONSIN	700.015	149.404	256.539	30.152	1136.109
WEST NORTH CENTRAL:					
IOWA	442.820	110.882	187.588	2.843	744.134
KANSAS	279.257	76.119	126.880	0.568	482.824
MINNESOTA	615.324	143.716	222.627	12.377	994.044
MISSOURI	695.733	186.015	286.116	3.043	1170.907
NEBRASKA	230.587	61.726	86.002	1.341	379.656
NORTH DAKOTA	77.045	12.677	38.874	2.290	130.886
SOUTH DAKOTA	106.747	15.615	42.281	3.087	167.730
SOUTH ATLANTIC:					
DELAWARE	116.781	14.985	39.343	0.948	172.057
DISTRICT OF COLUMBIA	95.528	26.887	36.902	0.156	159.473
FLORIDA	1151.440	47.209	609.606	0.939	1809.194
GEORGIA	737.850	110.417	266.073	1.350	1115.690
MARYLAND	624.705	132.130	202.722	2.848	962.405
NORTH CAROLINA	879.500	48.610	325.452	13.496	1267.058
SOUTH CAROLINA	430.713	34.081	165.716	7.924	638.434
VIRGINIA	748.123	94.463	266.591	14.753	1123.930
WEST VIRGINIA	196.328	57.854	89.888	8.891	352.961
EAST SOUTH CENTRAL:					
ALABAMA	519.505	68.560	205.947	2.245	796.257
KENTUCKY	465.304	80.894	159.439	9.952	715.589
MISSISSIPPI	358.514	42.971	126.438	1.927	529.851
TENNESSEE	569.084	57.232	259.821	15.216	901.354
WEST SOUTH CENTRAL:					
ARKANSAS	314.923	39.572	113.642	0.000	468.136
LOUISIANA	423.559	76.917	236.994	0.000	737.470
OKLAHOMA	371.541	70.560	168.668	0.000	610.769
TEXAS	1658.380	250.412	728.228	0.141	2637.162
ROCKY MOUNTAIN:					
ARIZONA	259.673	44.619	130.208	0.000	434.499
COLORADO	354.932	73.157	105.670	0.699	534.459
IDAHO	125.123	17.020	45.328	0.000	187.471
MONTANA	97.777	23.559	36.880	0.612	158.827
NEVADA	105.406	14.918	36.746	0.000	157.070
NEW MEXICO	166.837	34.260	42.085	0.000	243.182
UTAH	151.485	45.004	43.944	0.542	240.975
WYOMING	70.226	16.616	16.738	0.123	103.703
FAR WEST:					
ALASKA	55.415	14.001	18.725	0.194	88.335
CALIFORNIA	2567.077	737.945	932.442	0.000	4237.465
HAWAII	95.135	0.000	42.317	0.000	137.452
OREGON	351.326	44.480	139.451	0.094	535.351
WASHINGTON	482.569	65.084	196.305	0.094	744.053

Table 12

Consumption Of Energy In Trillion BTU And Expenditures On Energy
In Million Dollars, 1972, By Region

Household Energy Use By Energy Source

REGION	PETROLEUM PRODUCTS	NATURAL GAS	ELECTRICITY	COAL, HYDROPOWER & NUCLEAR POWER	TOTAL, ALL SOURCES
Consumption In Trillion BTU					
NEW ENGLAND	1157.55	162.08	83.98	1.70	1405.32
MID ATLANTIC	2612.85	961.11	225.12	83.95	3883.03
EAST NORTH CENTRAL	2391.50	1753.63	306.18	138.80	4590.11
WEST NORTH CENTRAL	992.17	590.68	133.32	18.25	1734.43
SOUTH ATLANTIC	1865.81	406.24	319.24	39.10	2630.39
EAST SOUTH CENTRAL	685.98	244.02	165.16	24.40	1119.55
WEST SOUTH CENTRAL	1097.57	474.68	197.73	0.10	1770.09
ROCKY MOUNTAIN	487.87	288.31	70.32	1.60	848.10
FAR WEST	1293.06	822.04	243.93	0.30	2359.34
TOTAL	12584.38	5702.80	1744.98	308.20	20340.35
Expenditures In Million Dollars					
NEW ENGLAND	2533.74	344.62	714.42	2.41	3595.19
MID ATLANTIC	6089.57	1458.86	2001.14	108.39	9657.97
EAST NORTH CENTRAL	6160.94	1890.87	2235.59	181.24	10468.64
WEST NORTH CENTRAL	2447.51	606.75	990.37	25.55	4070.18
SOUTH ATLANTIC	4980.97	566.64	2002.29	51.31	7601.20
EAST SOUTH CENTRAL	1912.41	249.66	751.65	29.34	2943.05
WEST SOUTH CENTRAL	2768.40	437.46	1247.53	0.14	4453.54
ROCKY MOUNTAIN	1331.46	269.15	457.60	1.98	2060.19
FAR WEST	3551.52	861.51	1329.24	0.38	5742.66
TOTAL	31776.52	6685.51	11729.83	400.74	50592.61

Table 13

Consumption Of Energy In Million BTU Per Capita, 1972, By State

Household Use Of Energy By Energy Source

REGION	PETROLEUM PRODUCTS	NATURAL GAS	ELECTRICITY	COAL, HYDROPOWER & NUCLEAR POWER	TOTAL, ALL SOURCES
NEW ENGLAND:					
CONNECTICUT	82.210	12.711	7.955	0.032	102.908
MAINE	110.794	0.963	7.040	0.097	118.895
MASSACHUSETTS	97.782	17.312	6.139	0.164	121.397
NEW HAMPSHIRE	109.325	6.750	8.296	0.388	124.759
RHODE ISLAND	87.588	15.464	5.556	0.052	108.660
VERMONT	118.344	3.038	10.585	0.435	132.402
MID ATLANTIC:					
NEW JERSEY	85.894	23.976	6.285	0.476	116.632
NEW YORK	67.003	23.932	5.106	0.727	96.768
PENNSYLVANIA	63.081	29.009	7.152	5.636	104.878
EAST NORTH CENTRAL:					
ILLINOIS	53.919	49.608	6.884	3.482	113.893
INDIANA	64.988	34.104	8.607	4.493	112.192
MICHIGAN	63.636	42.342	7.213	2.080	115.272
OHIO	53.036	48.316	7.616	3.325	112.292
WISCONSIN	66.173	25.606	8.088	4.750	104.618
WEST NORTH CENTRAL:					
IOWA	59.832	35.475	8.291	0.728	104.326
KANSAS	48.722	45.968	8.061	0.220	102.971
MINNESOTA	68.629	30.940	7.694	2.180	109.443
MISSOURI	56.957	36.634	7.885	0.548	102.024
NEBRASKA	58.335	41.989	8.566	0.654	109.544
NORTH DAKOTA	57.135	18.769	8.051	2.524	86.479
SOUTH DAKOTA	69.568	20.883	8.344	2.941	101.736
SOUTH ATLANTIC:					
DELAWARE	82.847	15.843	7.744	1.138	107.573
DISTRICT OF COLUMBIA	49.303	24.338	6.692	0.133	80.467
FLORIDA	56.213	3.174	13.365	0.095	72.848
GEORGIA	55.799	19.365	10.043	0.211	85.418
MARYLAND	59.683	20.377	6.477	0.482	87.019
NORTH CAROLINA	65.066	6.829	10.447	1.934	84.277
SOUTH CAROLINA	58.787	8.170	9.981	2.158	79.096
VIRGINIA	62.488	12.993	9.070	2.392	86.944
WEST VIRGINIA	37.472	34.485	7.379	4.123	83.459
EAST SOUTH CENTRAL:					
ALABAMA	51.751	16.016	11.969	0.511	80.247
KENTUCKY	49.872	26.997	9.337	2.632	88.838
MISSISSIPPI	57.700	18.138	9.731	0.709	86.277
TENNESSEE	51.256	14.110	17.238	3.021	85.623
WEST SOUTH CENTRAL:					
ARKANSAS	59.383	24.026	8.414	0.000	91.824
LOUISIANA	43.649	23.319	9.924	0.000	76.891
OKLAHOMA	55.768	31.014	9.100	0.000	95.881
TEXAS	57.595	22.200	10.322	0.009	90.127
ROCKY MOUNTAIN:					
ARIZONA	45.701	19.925	9.511	0.000	75.137
COLORADO	53.362	38.913	5.861	0.254	98.390
IDAHO	68.592	16.072	12.798	0.000	97.462
MONTANA	53.800	35.497	8.149	0.559	98.005
NEVADA	67.035	20.755	15.082	0.000	102.872
NEW MEXICO	56.666	35.686	4.896	0.000	97.247
UTAH	51.277	41.820	5.934	0.444	99.474
WYOMING	78.655	66.661	6.647	0.289	152.251
FAR WEST:					
ALASKA	71.779	28.710	5.900	0.308	106.696
CALIFORNIA	44.605	36.066	6.664	0.000	87.334
HAWAII	34.111	0.000	6.230	0.000	40.341
OREGON	64.254	12.911	17.041	0.046	94.251
WASHINGTON	55.904	14.151	18.630	0.029	88.715

Table 14

Expenditures On Energy In Dollars Per Capita, 1972, By State

Household Use Of Energy By Energy Source

REGION	PETROLEUM PRODUCTS	NATURAL GAS	ELECTRICITY	COAL, HYDROPOWER & NUCLEAR POWER[a]	TOTAL, ALL SOURCES
NEW ENGLAND:					
CONNECTICUT	196.681	25.540	65.095	0.053	287.369
MAINE	240.313	2.873	56.279	0.151	299.616
MASSACHUSETTS	204.721	38.070	55.525	0.227	298.543
NEW HAMPSHIRE	241.199	13.006	64.913	0.511	319.629
RHODE ISLAND	188.652	30.853	50.765	0.073	270.343
VERMONT	272.501	5.192	75.930	0.676	354.300
MID ATLANTIC:					
NEW JERSEY	190.427	45.635	56.456	0.773	293.292
NEW YORK	157.944	36.877	48.742	1.045	244.608
PENNSYLVANIA	150.287	37.477	58.044	7.015	252.822
EAST NORTH CENTRAL:					
ILLINOIS	143.702	53.504	57.345	4.665	259.216
INDIANA	160.296	38.192	57.508	5.376	261.372
MICHIGAN	154.828	45.375	51.184	2.767	254.154
OHIO	149.444	49.340	53.065	4.223	256.072
WISCONSIN	154.665	33.010	56.681	6.662	251.018
WEST NORTH CENTRAL:					
IOWA	153.544	38.447	65.044	0.986	258.021
KANSAS	123.129	33.562	55.944	0.250	212.885
MINNESOTA	158.711	37.069	57.422	3.192	256.395
MISSOURI	146.563	39.186	60.273	0.641	246.663
NEBRASKA	150.908	40.396	56.284	0.878	248.466
NORTH DAKOTA	121.522	19.995	61.315	3.612	206.444
SOUTH DAKOTA	156.980	22.964	62.178	4.540	246.662
SOUTH ATLANTIC:					
DELAWARE	204.520	26.243	68.902	1.661	301.325
DISTRICT OF COLUMBIA	127.032	35.755	49.072	0.207	212.065
FLORIDA	156.722	6.426	82.973	0.128	246.249
GEORGIA	155.895	23.329	56.217	0.285	235.726
MARYLAND	154.324	32.641	50.080	0.703	237.748
NORTH CAROLINA	168.454	9.311	62.335	2.585	242.685
SOUTH CAROLINA	160.235	12.679	61.650	2.948	237.513
VIRGINIA	157.004	19.824	55.948	3.096	235.872
WEST VIRGINIA	109.375	32.230	50.077	4.953	196.636
EAST SOUTH CENTRAL:					
ALABAMA	147.545	19.472	58.491	0.638	226.145
KENTUCKY	140.745	24.469	48.227	3.010	216.452
MISSISSIPPI	158.916	19.047	56.045	0.854	234.863
TENNESSEE	139.755	14.055	63.807	3.737	221.354
WEST SOUTH CENTRAL:					
ARKANSAS	156.834	19.707	56.595	0.000	233.136
LOUISIANA	113.312	20.577	63.401	0.000	197.290
OKLAHOMA	141.109	26.798	64.059	0.000	231.967
TEXAS	142.915	21.580	62.757	0.012	227.263
ROCKY MOUNTAIN:					
ARIZONA	132.284	22.730	66.331	0.000	221.345
COLORADO	150.141	30.946	44.700	0.296	226.082
IDAHO	165.726	22.543	60.037	0.000	248.305
MONTANA	136.560	32.903	51.508	0.855	221.826
NEVADA	197.761	27.988	68.942	0.000	294.691
NEW MEXICO	155.053	31.840	39.112	0.000	226.006
UTAH	134.414	39.933	38.992	0.481	213.820
WYOMING	202.966	48.025	48.376	0.355	299.721
FAR WEST:					
ALASKA	170.507	43.080	57.615	0.598	271.800
CALIFORNIA	125.769	36.154	45.683	0.000	207.607
HAWAII	116.587	0.000	51.859	0.000	168.446
OREGON	160.790	20.357	63.822	0.043	245.012
WASHINGTON	141.185	19.042	57.433	0.028	217.687

[a] Coal only in household use

Table 15

Consumption Of Energy In Million BTU Per Capita And Expenditures On Energy
     In Dollars Per Capita, 1972, By Region

Household Use Of Energy By Energy Source

REGION	PETROLEUM PRODUCTS	NATURAL GAS	ELECTRICITY	COAL, HYDROPOWER & NUCLEAR POWER [a]	TOTAL
Consumption In Million BTU Per Capita					
NEW ENGLAND	95.626	13.390	6.938	0.140	116.094
MID ATLANTIC	69.452	25.547	5.984	2.231	103.214
EAST NORTH CENTRAL	58.628	42.991	7.506	3.403	112.527
WEST NORTH CENTRAL	59.705	35.545	8.023	1.098	104.370
SOUTH ATLANTIC	58.453	12.727	10.001	1.225	82.406
EAST SOUTH CENTRAL	52.146	18.550	12.555	1.855	85.104
WEST SOUTH CENTRAL	54.925	23.754	9.895	0.005	88.580
ROCKY MOUNTAIN	54.941	32.467	7.919	0.180	95.507
FAR WEST	47.618	30.272	8.983	0.011	86.884
UNITED STATES	60.436	27.387	8.380	1.480	97.683
Expenditures In Dollars Per Capita					
NEW ENGLAND	209.314	28.469	59.019	0.199	297.000
MID ATLANTIC	161.866	38.778	53.192	2.881	256.718
EAST NORTH CENTRAL	151.037	46.355	54.806	4.443	256.641
WEST NORTH CENTRAL	147.281	36.512	59.596	1.537	244.926
SOUTH ATLANTIC	156.045	17.752	62.728	1.607	238.133
EAST SOUTH CENTRAL	145.375	18.978	57.138	2.230	223.721
WEST SOUTH CENTRAL	138.538	21.892	62.430	0.007	222.866
ROCKY MOUNTAIN	149.939	30.310	51.531	0.222	232.003
FAR WEST	130.787	31.726	48.950	0.014	211.477
UNITED STATES	152.604	32.107	56.332	1.925	242.967

[a] Coal only in household use.

Table 16

Consumption Of Energy By Source As Fraction Of Total Consumption (BTU), 1972, By State

Household Use Of Energy By Energy Source

REGION AND STATE	PETROLEUM PRODUCTS	NATURAL GAS	ELECTRICITY	COAL, HYDROPOWER & NUCLEAR POWER[a]
NEW ENGLAND:				
CONNECTICUT	0.7989	0.1235	0.0773	0.0003
MAINE	0.9319	0.0081	0.0592	0.0008
MASSACHUSETTS	0.8055	0.1426	0.0506	0.0014
NEW HAMPSHIRE	0.8763	0.0541	0.0665	0.0031
RHODE ISLAND	0.8061	0.1423	0.0511	0.0005
VERMONT	0.8938	0.0229	0.0799	0.0033
MID ATLANTIC:				
NEW JERSEY	0.7365	0.2056	0.0539	0.0041
NEW YORK	0.6924	0.2473	0.0528	0.0075
PENNSYLVANIA	0.6015	0.2766	0.0682	0.0537
EAST NORTH CENTRAL:				
ILLINOIS	0.4734	0.4356	0.0604	0.0306
INDIANA	0.5793	0.3040	0.0767	0.0400
MICHIGAN	0.5521	0.3673	0.0626	0.0180
OHIO	0.4723	0.4303	0.0678	0.0296
WISCONSIN	0.6325	0.2448	0.0773	0.0454
WEST NORTH CENTRAL:				
IOWA	0.5735	0.3400	0.0795	0.0070
KANSAS	0.4732	0.4464	0.0783	0.0021
MINNESOTA	0.6271	0.2827	0.0703	0.0199
MISSOURI	0.5583	0.3591	0.0773	0.0054
NEBRASKA	0.5325	0.3833	0.0782	0.0060
NORTH DAKOTA	0.6607	0.2170	0.0931	0.0292
SOUTH DAKOTA	0.6838	0.2053	0.0820	0.0289
SOUTH ATLANTIC:				
DELAWARE	0.7701	0.1473	0.0720	0.0106
DISTRICT OF COLUMBIA	0.6127	0.3025	0.0832	0.0017
FLORIDA	0.7716	0.0436	0.1835	0.0013
GEORGIA	0.6532	0.2267	0.1176	0.0025
MARYLAND	0.6859	0.2342	0.0744	0.0055
NORTH CAROLINA	0.7720	0.0810	0.1240	0.0230
SOUTH CAROLINA	0.7432	0.1033	0.1262	0.0273
VIRGINIA	0.7187	0.1494	0.1043	0.0275
WEST VIRGINIA	0.4490	0.4132	0.0884	0.0494
EAST SOUTH CENTRAL:				
ALABAMA	0.6449	0.1996	0.1491	0.0064
KENTUCKY	0.5614	0.3039	0.1051	0.0296
MISSISSIPPI	0.6688	0.2102	0.1128	0.0082
TENNESSEE	0.5986	0.1648	0.2013	0.0353
WEST SOUTH CENTRAL:				
ARKANSAS	0.6467	0.2617	0.0916	0.0000
LOUISIANA	0.5677	0.3033	0.1291	0.0000
OKLAHOMA	0.5816	0.3235	0.0949	0.0000
TEXAS	0.6390	0.2463	0.1145	0.0001
ROCKY MOUNTAIN:				
ARIZONA	0.6082	0.2652	0.1266	0.0000
COLORADO	0.5423	0.3955	0.0596	0.0026
IDAHO	0.7038	0.1649	0.1313	0.0000
MONTANA	0.5490	0.3622	0.0831	0.0057
NEVADA	0.6516	0.2018	0.1466	0.0000
NEW MEXICO	0.5827	0.3670	0.0503	0.0000
UTAH	0.5155	0.4204	0.0597	0.0045
WYOMING	0.5166	0.4378	0.0437	0.0019
FAR WEST:				
ALASKA	0.6727	0.2691	0.0553	0.0029
CALIFORNIA	0.5107	0.4130	0.0763	0.0000
HAWAII	0.8456	0.0000	0.1544	0.0000
OREGON	0.6817	0.1370	0.1808	0.0005
WASHINGTON	0.6302	0.1595	0.2100	0.0003

[a] Coal only in household use.

Table 17

Expenditures On Energy As A Fraction Of Total Use, 1972, By State

Household Energy Use By Energy Source

REGION And STATE	PETROLEUM PRODUCTS	NATURAL GAS	ELECTRICITY	COAL, HYDROPOWER & NUCLEAR POWER a/
NEW ENGLAND:				
CONNECTICUT	0.6844	0.0889	0.2265	0.0002
MAINE	0.8021	0.0096	0.1878	0.0005
MASSACHUSETTS	0.6857	0.1275	0.1860	0.0008
NEW HAMPSHIRE	0.7546	0.0407	0.2031	0.0016
RHODE ISLAND	0.6978	0.1141	0.1878	0.0003
VERMONT	0.7691	0.0147	0.2143	0.0019
MID ATLANTIC:				
NEW JERSEY	0.6493	0.1556	0.1925	0.0026
NEW YORK	0.6457	0.1508	0.1993	0.0043
PENNSYLVANIA	0.5944	0.1482	0.2296	0.0277
EAST NORTH CENTRAL:				
ILLINOIS	0.5544	0.2064	0.2212	0.0180
INDIANA	0.6133	0.1461	0.2200	0.0206
MICHIGAN	0.6092	0.1785	0.2014	0.0109
OHIO	0.5836	0.1927	0.2072	0.0165
WISCONSIN	0.6162	0.1315	0.2258	0.0265
WEST NORTH CENTRAL:				
IOWA	0.5951	0.1490	0.2521	0.0038
KANSAS	0.5784	0.1577	0.2628	0.0012
MINNESOTA	0.6190	0.1446	0.2240	0.0125
MISSOURI	0.5942	0.1589	0.2444	0.0026
NEBRASKA	0.6074	0.1626	0.2265	0.0035
NORTH DAKOTA	0.5886	0.0969	0.2970	0.0175
SOUTH DAKOTA	0.6364	0.0931	0.2521	0.0184
SOUTH ATLANTIC:				
DELAWARE	0.6787	0.0871	0.2287	0.0055
DISTRICT OF COLUMBIA	0.5990	0.1686	0.2314	0.0010
FLORIDA	0.6364	0.0261	0.3369	0.0005
GEORGIA	0.6613	0.0990	0.2385	0.0012
MARYLAND	0.6491	0.1373	0.2106	0.0030
NORTH CAROLINA	0.6941	0.0384	0.2569	0.0107
SOUTH CAROLINA	0.6746	0.0534	0.2596	0.0124
VIRGINIA	0.6656	0.0840	0.2372	0.0131
WEST VIRGINIA	0.5562	0.1639	0.2547	0.0252
EAST SOUTH CENTRAL:				
ALABAMA	0.6524	0.0861	0.2586	0.0028
KENTUCKY	0.6502	0.1130	0.2228	0.0139
MISSISSIPPI	0.6766	0.0811	0.2386	0.0036
TENNESSEE	0.6314	0.0635	0.2883	0.0169
WEST SOUTH CENTRAL:				
ARKANSAS	0.6727	0.0845	0.2428	0.0000
LOUISIANA	0.5743	0.1043	0.3214	0.0000
OKLAHOMA	0.6083	0.1155	0.2762	0.0000
TEXAS	0.6289	0.0950	0.2761	0.0001
ROCKY MOUNTAIN:				
ARIZONA	0.5976	0.1027	0.2997	0.0000
COLORADO	0.6641	0.1369	0.1977	0.0013
IDAHO	0.6674	0.0908	0.2418	0.0000
MONTANA	0.6156	0.1483	0.2322	0.0039
NEVADA	0.6711	0.0950	0.2339	0.0000
NEW MEXICO	0.6861	0.1409	0.1731	0.0000
UTAH	0.6286	0.1868	0.1824	0.0022
WYOMING	0.6772	0.1602	0.1614	0.0012
FAR WEST:				
ALASKA	0.6273	0.1585	0.2120	0.0022
CALIFORNIA	0.6058	0.1741	0.2200	0.0000
HAWAII	0.6921	0.0000	0.3079	0.0000
OREGON	0.6563	0.0831	0.2605	0.0002
WASHINGTON	0.6486	0.0875	0.2638	0.0001

a/ Coal only in household use

Table 18

Consumption And Expenditures On Energy As A Fraction Of Total Use, 1972, By Region

Household Energy Use By Energy Source

REGION	PETROLEUM PRODUCTS	NATURAL GAS	ELECTRICITY	COAL, HYDROPOWER NUCLEAR POWER a/
NEW ENGLAND	0.8237	0.1153	0.0598	0.0012
MID ATLANTIC	0.6729	0.2475	0.0580	0.0216
EAST NORTH CENTRAL	0.5210	0.3820	0.0667	0.0302
WEST NORTH CENTRAL	0.5720	0.3406	0.0769	0.0105
SOUTH ATLANTIC	0.7093	0.1544	0.1214	0.0149
EAST SOUTH CENTRAL	0.6127	0.2180	0.1475	0.0218
WEST SOUTH CENTRAL	0.6201	0.2682	0.1117	0.0001
ROCKY MOUNTAIN	0.5753	0.3399	0.0829	0.0019
FAR WEST	0.5481	0.3484	0.1034	0.0001
UNITED STATES	0.6187	0.2804	0.0858	0.0152
NEW ENGLAND	0.7048	0.0959	0.1987	0.0007
MID ATLANTIC	0.6305	0.1511	0.2072	0.0112
EAST NORTH CENTRAL	0.5885	0.1806	0.2136	0.0173
WEST NORTH CENTRAL	0.6013	0.1491	0.2433	0.0063
SOUTH ATLANTIC	0.6553	0.0745	0.2634	0.0067
EAST SOUTH CENTRAL	0.6498	0.0848	0.2554	0.0100
WEST SOUTH CENTRAL	0.6216	0.0982	0.2801	0.0000
ROCKY MOUNTAIN	0.6463	0.1306	0.2221	0.0010
FAR WEST	0.6184	0.1500	0.2315	0.0001
UNITED STATES	0.6281	0.1321	0.2318	0.0079

a/ Coal only in household use

Table 19

Consumption of Energy In Trillion BTU, 1972, By State

Use By Sector

REGION AND STATE	HOUSEHOLD USE	BUSINESS USE	FEDERAL GOVERNMENT USE	STATE & LOCAL GOVERNMENT USE	ALL USE
NEW ENGLAND:					
CONNECTICUT	316.956	466.844	8.100	18.158	810.058
MAINE	121.986	193.402	27.167	8.007	350.561
MASSACHUSETTS	703.617	786.886	38.304	58.444	1587.253
NEW HAMPSHIRE	96.563	103.192	1.689	4.617	206.062
RHODE ISLAND	105.292	85.000	17.317	6.999	214.608
VERMONT	60.905	37.355	0.411	2.178	100.849
MID ATLANTIC:					
NEW JERSEY	857.125	1053.815	45.482	41.442	1997.864
NEW YORK	1777.333	2515.358	86.379	156.886	4535.957
PENNSYLVANIA	1248.573	3083.882	31.744	57.271	4421.469
EAST NORTH CENTRAL:					
ILLINOIS	1280.616	2561.291	30.639	85.324	3957.871
INDIANA	593.049	1930.963	4.295	38.826	2567.134
MICHIGAN	1038.946	1898.615	36.137	69.024	3042.722
OHIO	1203.994	2872.569	11.347	72.675	4160.585
WISCONSIN	473.501	836.001	9.122	27.683	1346.307
WEST NORTH CENTRAL:					
IOWA	300.877	588.227	1.716	22.620	913.439
KANSAS	233.539	781.848	9.992	22.253	1047.631
MINNESOTA	424.309	729.170	12.547	48.979	1215.005
MISSOURI	484.309	896.354	4.862	41.547	1427.072
NEBRASKA	167.383	320.720	4.016	20.565	512.684
NORTH DAKOTA	54.828	201.743	1.355	4.940	262.866
SOUTH DAKOTA	69.181	141.986	0.903	6.331	218.401
SOUTH ATLANTIC:					
DELAWARE	61.424	155.579	1.415	3.825	222.243
DISTRICT OF COLUMBIA	60.511	87.759	12.235	14.301	174.806
FLORIDA	535.213	1270.139	20.470	63.634	1889.455
GEORGIA	404.283	901.293	12.244	31.607	1349.426
MARYLAND	352.251	715.144	33.636	28.499	1129.531
NORTH CAROLINA	440.008	1048.712	16.614	37.481	1542.814
SOUTH CAROLINA	212.609	571.033	14.676	14.128	812.446
VIRGINIA	414.287	796.457	94.712	36.064	1341.520
WEST VIRGINIA	149.808	944.592	0.846	12.350	1107.596
EAST SOUTH CENTRAL:					
ALABAMA	282.551	1174.732	22.185	16.585	1496.052
KENTUCKY	293.697	1024.613	22.222	22.640	1363.172
MISSISSIPPI	194.642	593.283	4.976	14.520	807.421
TENNESSEE	348.659	1022.846	13.381	23.399	1408.285
WEST SOUTH CENTRAL:					
ARKANSAS	184.382	458.076	6.740	11.773	660.972
LOUISIANA	287.420	2344.730	34.987	50.531	2717.668
OKLAHOMA	252.455	783.032	9.935	22.462	1067.883
TEXAS	1045.831	5624.237	76.809	104.575	6851.452
ROCKY MOUNTAIN:					
ARIZONA	147.494	417.664	3.852	16.447	585.458
COLORADO	232.594	484.968	12.924	30.999	761.486
IDAHO	73.584	192.837	1.081	7.708	275.210
MONTANA	70.171	277.122	4.001	8.701	359.995
NEVADA	54.831	164.743	2.879	10.604	233.056
NEW MEXICO	104.638	488.212	8.838	23.891	625.579
UTAH	112.107	271.563	8.881	5.356	397.907
WYOMING	52.679	284.040	1.388	7.559	345.666
FAR WEST:					
ALASKA	34.676	145.222	23.715	10.209	213.822
CALIFORNIA	1782.578	3669.660	272.982	121.678	5846.898
HAWAII	32.918	190.676	6.154	1.574	231.322
OREGON	205.939	641.500	7.888	16.623	871.949
WASHINGTON	303.227	1255.442	21.933	24.003	1604.605

Table 20

Expenditures On Energy In Million Dollars, 1972, By State

Use By Sector

REGION AND STATE	HOUSEHOLD USE	BUSINESS USE	FEDERAL GOVERNMENT USE	STATE & LOCAL GOVERNMENT USE	ALL USE
NEW ENGLAND:					
CONNECTICUT	885.096	628.594	9.469	54.668	1577.827
MAINE	307.406	247.236	30.193	19.637	604.472
MASSACHUSETTS	1730.353	1063.691	40.697	126.516	2961.257
NEW HAMPSHIRE	247.393	133.815	1.962	12.097	395.266
RHODE ISLAND	261.962	146.504	13.885	18.025	440.377
VERMONT	162.978	71.399	1.476	7.979	243.833
MID ATLANTIC:					
NEW JERSEY	2155.406	1481.489	42.461	128.653	3808.009
NEW YORK	4492.715	3200.177	137.109	487.666	8317.667
PENNSYLVANIA	3009.848	2921.120	36.463	149.440	6116.870
EAST NORTH CENTRAL:					
ILLINOIS	2914.625	2564.489	54.750	221.815	5755.680
INDIANA	1381.613	1539.295	7.026	87.977	3015.910
MICHIGAN	2290.687	1964.154	42.400	176.706	4473.946
OHIO	2745.602	2585.917	26.661	178.097	5536.276
WISCONSIN	1136.109	905.456	12.198	73.083	2126.848
WEST NORTH CENTRAL:					
IOWA	744.134	627.200	4.588	55.994	1431.915
KANSAS	482.824	582.200	9.394	40.428	1114.846
MINNESOTA	994.044	806.370	15.090	74.435	1889.939
MISSOURI	1170.907	950.570	10.790	72.277	2204.544
NEBRASKA	379.656	339.096	5.607	31.512	755.872
NORTH DAKOTA	130.886	141.893	2.273	11.466	286.518
SOUTH DAKOTA	167.730	143.699	2.133	12.383	325.945
SOUTH ATLANTIC:					
DELAWARE	172.057	188.349	1.715	11.384	373.504
DISTRICT OF COLUMBIA	159.473	136.039	19.159	28.573	343.244
FLORIDA	1809.194	1404.703	34.991	161.823	3410.711
GEORGIA	1115.690	1031.520	16.268	89.769	2253.247
MARYLAND	962.405	877.775	36.616	73.632	1950.429
NORTH CAROLINA	1267.058	1139.253	21.357	96.347	2524.014
SOUTH CAROLINA	638.434	609.217	18.129	41.742	1307.523
VIRGINIA	1123.930	886.617	87.660	87.861	2186.069
WEST VIRGINIA	352.961	598.937	2.053	25.816	979.767
EAST SOUTH CENTRAL:					
ALABAMA	796.257	920.844	24.809	45.099	1787.010
KENTUCKY	715.589	792.601	28.641	46.951	1583.782
MISSISSIPPI	529.851	511.547	6.170	34.578	1082.146
TENNESSEE	901.354	933.683	13.999	53.904	1902.940
WEST SOUTH CENTRAL:					
ARKANSAS	468.136	474.295	8.976	28.880	980.288
LOUISIANA	737.470	1189.206	32.744	64.914	2024.335
OKLAHOMA	610.769	565.163	14.273	49.606	1239.811
TEXAS	2637.162	3218.546	88.840	189.072	6133.620
ROCKY MOUNTAIN:					
ARIZONA	434.499	474.244	9.622	41.131	959.496
COLORADO	534.459	469.843	17.678	48.506	1070.486
IDAHO	187.471	192.040	1.994	15.684	397.188
MONTANA	158.827	223.023	4.674	13.799	400.324
NEVADA	157.070	172.216	4.807	17.285	351.378
NEW MEXICO	243.182	296.753	12.841	24.766	577.542
UTAH	240.975	253.016	11.351	14.941	520.282
WYOMING	103.703	170.554	2.158	11.047	287.463
FAR WEST:					
ALASKA	88.335	144.952	32.028	12.481	277.796
CALIFORNIA	4237.465	3891.463	280.138	338.861	8747.927
HAWAII	137.452	254.627	9.014	9.265	410.358
OREGON	535.351	453.317	9.816	38.601	1037.083
WASHINGTON	744.053	737.247	26.838	53.647	1561.785

Table 21

Consumption Of Energy In Trillion BTU and Expenditures On Energy
    In Million Dollars, 1972, By Region

Use By Sector

REGION	HOUSEHOLD USE	BUSINESS USE	FEDERAL GOVERNMENT USE	STATE & LOCAL GOVERNMENT USE	ALL USE
Consumption In Trillion BTU					
NEW ENGLAND	1405.32	1672.68	92.99	98.40	3269.39
MID ATLANTIC	3883.03	6653.06	163.61	255.60	10955.29
EAST NORTH CENTRAL	4590.11	10099.44	91.54	293.53	15074.62
WEST NORTH CENTRAL	1734.43	3660.05	35.39	167.24	5597.10
SOUTH ATLANTIC	2630.39	6490.71	206.85	241.89	9569.84
EAST SOUTH CENTRAL	1119.55	3815.47	62.76	77.14	5074.93
WEST SOUTH CENTRAL	1770.09	9210.07	128.47	189.34	11297.98
ROCKY MOUNTAIN	848.10	2581.15	43.84	111.26	3584.36
FAR WEST	2359.34	5902.50	332.67	174.09	8768.60
TOTAL	20340.35	50085.13	1158.12	1608.50	73192.09
Expenditures In Million Dollars					
NEW ENGLAND	3595.19	2291.24	97.68	238.92	6223.03
MID ATLANTIC	9657.97	7602.79	216.03	765.76	18242.55
EAST NORTH CENTRAL	10468.64	9559.31	143.04	737.68	20908.66
WEST NORTH CENTRAL	4070.18	3591.03	49.88	298.49	8009.58
SOUTH ATLANTIC	7601.20	6872.41	237.95	616.95	15328.51
EAST SOUTH CENTRAL	2943.05	3158.68	73.62	180.53	6355.88
WEST SOUTH CENTRAL	4453.54	5447.21	144.83	332.47	10378.05
ROCKY MOUNTAIN	2060.19	2251.69	65.12	187.16	4564.16
FAR WEST	5742.66	5481.61	357.83	452.85	12034.95
TOTAL	50592.61	46255.95	1385.98	3810.82	102045.37

Table 22

Consumption Of Energy In Million BTU Per Capita, 1972, By State

Use By Sector

REGION AND STATE	HOUSEHOLD USE	BUSINESS USE	FEDERAL GOVERNMENT USE	STATE & LOCAL GOVERNMENT USE	ALL USE
NEW ENGLAND:					
CONNECTICUT	102.908	151.573	2.630	5.895	263.006
MAINE	118.895	188.500	26.479	7.804	341.678
MASSACHUSETTS	121.397	135.764	6.609	10.084	273.853
NEW HAMPSHIRE	124.759	133.324	2.183	5.966	266.230
RHODE ISLAND	108.660	87.719	17.871	7.223	221.474
VERMONT	132.402	81.206	0.894	4.735	219.238
MID ATLANTIC:					
NEW JERSEY	116.632	143.396	6.189	5.639	271.855
NEW YORK	96.768	136.950	4.703	8.542	246.962
PENNSYLVANIA	104.878	259.041	2.666	4.811	371.396
EAST NORTH CENTRAL:					
ILLINOIS	113.893	227.792	2.725	7.588	351.998
INDIANA	112.192	365.298	0.812	7.345	485.648
MICHIGAN	115.272	210.653	4.009	7.658	337.593
OHIO	112.292	267.913	1.058	6.778	388.042
WISCONSIN	104.618	184.711	2.015	6.116	297.461
WEST NORTH CENTRAL:					
IOWA	104.326	203.962	0.595	7.843	316.727
KANSAS	102.971	344.730	4.405	9.812	461.918
MINNESOTA	109.443	188.076	3.236	12.633	313.388
MISSOURI	102.024	188.825	1.024	8.752	300.626
NEBRASKA	109.544	209.896	2.628	13.459	335.526
NORTH DAKOTA	86.479	318.206	2.138	7.792	414.615
SOUTH DAKOTA	101.736	208.804	1.328	9.311	321.179
SOUTH ATLANTIC:					
DELAWARE	107.573	272.468	2.478	6.699	389.218
DISTRICT OF COLUMBIA	80.467	116.700	16.270	19.018	232.455
FLORIDA	72.848	172.879	2.786	8.661	257.174
GEORGIA	85.418	190.427	2.587	6.678	285.110
MARYLAND	87.019	176.666	8.309	7.040	279.034
NORTH CAROLINA	84.277	200.864	3.182	7.179	295.502
SOUTH CAROLINA	79.096	212.438	5.460	5.256	302.249
VIRGINIA	86.944	167.147	19.876	7.569	281.536
WEST VIRGINIA	83.459	526.235	0.471	6.880	617.045
EAST SOUTH CENTRAL:					
ALABAMA	80.247	333.636	6.301	4.710	424.894
KENTUCKY	88.838	309.925	6.722	6.848	412.333
MISSISSIPPI	86.277	262.980	2.206	6.436	357.899
TENNESSEE	85.623	251.190	3.286	5.746	345.846
WEST SOUTH CENTRAL:					
ARKANSAS	91.824	228.126	3.357	5.863	329.169
LOUISIANA	76.891	627.269	9.360	13.518	727.038
OKLAHOMA	95.881	297.391	3.773	8.531	405.577
TEXAS	90.127	484.681	6.619	9.012	590.439
ROCKY MOUNTAIN:					
ARIZONA	75.137	212.768	1.962	8.379	298.246
COLORADO	98.390	205.147	5.467	13.113	322.117
IDAHO	97.462	255.413	1.432	10.209	364.516
MONTANA	98.005	387.041	5.588	12.153	502.786
NEVADA	102.872	309.086	5.402	19.894	437.254
NEW MEXICO	97.247	453.729	8.214	22.203	581.393
UTAH	99.474	240.961	7.880	4.752	353.067
WYOMING	152.251	820.925	4.011	21.848	999.036
FAR WEST:					
ALASKA	106.696	446.838	72.970	31.411	657.915
CALIFORNIA	87.334	179.788	13.374	5.961	286.458
HAWAII	40.341	233.671	7.541	1.929	283.483
OREGON	94.251	293.593	3.610	7.608	399.061
WASHINGTON	88.715	367.303	6.417	7.023	469.457

Table 23

Expenditures On Energy In Dollars Per Capita, 1972, By State

Use By Sector

REGION AND STATE	HOUSEHOLD USE	BUSINESS USE	FEDERAL GOVERNMENT USE	STATE & LOCAL GOVERNMENT USE	ALL USE
NEW ENGLAND:					
CONNECTICUT	287.369	204.089	3.074	17.749	512.281
MAINE	299.616	240.971	29.428	19.140	589.154
MASSACHUSETTS	298.543	183.522	7.022	21.828	510.914
NEW HAMPSHIRE	319.629	172.888	2.535	15.629	510.680
RHODE ISLAND	270.343	151.191	14.330	18.602	454.466
VERMONT	354.300	155.216	3.210	17.345	530.071
MID ATLANTIC:					
NEW JERSEY	293.292	201.591	5.778	17.506	518.167
NEW YORK	244.608	174.235	7.465	26.551	452.859
PENNSYLVANIA	252.822	245.369	3.063	12.553	513.807
EAST NORTH CENTRAL:					
ILLINOIS	259.216	228.076	4.869	19.727	511.889
INDIANA	261.372	291.202	1.329	16.643	570.547
MICHIGAN	254.154	217.925	4.704	19.606	496.388
OHIO	256.072	241.179	2.487	16.610	516.347
WISCONSIN	251.018	200.057	2.695	16.147	469.918
WEST NORTH CENTRAL:					
IOWA	258.021	217.476	1.591	19.415	496.503
KANSAS	212.885	256.702	4.142	17.825	491.555
MINNESOTA	256.395	207.988	3.892	19.199	487.475
MISSOURI	246.663	200.246	2.273	15.226	464.408
NEBRASKA	248.466	221.922	3.669	20.623	494.680
NORTH DAKOTA	206.444	223.806	3.586	18.085	451.922
SOUTH DAKOTA	246.662	211.322	3.137	18.210	479.331
SOUTH ATLANTIC:					
DELAWARE	301.325	329.857	3.004	19.937	654.123
DISTRICT OF COLUMBIA	212.065	180.903	25.477	37.996	456.442
FLORIDA	246.249	191.194	4.763	22.026	464.232
GEORGIA	235.726	217.942	3.437	18.967	476.072
MARYLAND	237.748	216.842	9.046	18.190	481.825
NORTH CAROLINA	242.685	218.206	4.091	18.454	483.435
SOUTH CAROLINA	237.513	226.643	6.744	15.529	486.430
VIRGINIA	235.872	186.069	18.397	18.439	458.776
WEST VIRGINIA	196.636	333.670	1.144	14.382	545.831
EAST SOUTH CENTRAL:					
ALABAMA	226.145	261.529	7.046	12.809	507.529
KENTUCKY	216.452	239.746	8.663	14.202	479.063
MISSISSIPPI	234.863	226.749	2.735	15.327	479.674
TENNESSEE	221.354	229.293	3.438	13.238	467.323
WEST SOUTH CENTRAL:					
ARKANSAS	233.136	236.203	4.470	14.382	488.191
LOUISIANA	197.290	318.140	8.760	17.366	541.555
OKLAHOMA	231.967	214.646	5.421	18.840	470.874
TEXAS	227.263	277.365	7.656	16.294	528.578
ROCKY MOUNTAIN:					
ARIZONA	221.345	241.591	4.902	20.953	488.790
COLORADO	226.082	198.749	7.478	20.519	452.828
IDAHO	248.305	254.357	2.641	20.773	526.077
MONTANA	221.826	311.485	6.528	19.272	559.111
NEVADA	294.691	323.106	9.019	32.430	659.246
NEW MEXICO	226.006	275.793	11.934	23.017	536.749
UTAH	213.820	224.504	10.071	13.257	461.652
WYOMING	299.721	492.932	6.238	31.928	830.818
FAR WEST:					
ALASKA	271.800	446.007	98.547	38.403	854.757
CALIFORNIA	207.607	190.655	13.725	16.602	428.589
HAWAII	168.446	312.043	11.047	11.354	502.890
OREGON	245.012	207.468	4.492	17.666	474.638
WASHINGTON	217.687	215.695	7.852	15.695	456.929

Table 24

Consumption Of Energy In Million BTU Per Capita And Expenditures On Energy In Dollars Per Capita, 1972, By Region Use By Sector

REGION	HOUSEHOLD USE	BUSINESS USE	FEDERAL GOVERNMENT USE	STATE & LOCAL GOVERNMENT USE	TOTAL USE
Consumption In Million BTU Per Capita					
NEW ENGLAND	116.094	138.181	7.682	8.129	270.086
MID ATLANTIC	103.214	176.844	4.349	6.794	291.201
EAST NORTH CENTRAL	112.527	247.590	2.244	7.196	369.557
WEST NORTH CENTRAL	104.370	220.246	2.130	10.064	336.809
SOUTH ATLANTIC	82.406	203.343	6.480	7.578	299.807
EAST SOUTH CENTRAL	85.104	290.040	4.771	5.864	385.780
WEST SOUTH CENTRAL	88.580	460.896	6.429	9.475	565.379
ROCKY MOUNTAIN	95.507	290.670	4.937	12.530	403.644
FAR WEST	86.884	217.363	12.251	6.411	322.909
UNITED STATES	97.683	240.530	5.562	7.725	351.500
Expenditures In Dollars Per Capita					
NEW ENGLAND	297.000	189.280	8.070	19.738	514.088
MID ATLANTIC	256.718	202.089	5.742	20.355	484.903
EAST NORTH CENTRAL	256.641	234.349	3.507	18.084	512.580
WEST NORTH CENTRAL	244.926	216.093	3.001	17.962	481.982
SOUTH ATLANTIC	238.133	215.301	7.455	19.328	480.216
EAST SOUTH CENTRAL	223.721	240.112	5.596	13.723	483.153
WEST SOUTH CENTRAL	222.866	272.592	7.248	16.638	519.344
ROCKY MOUNTAIN	232.003	253.569	7.334	21.076	513.982
FAR WEST	211.477	201.864	13.177	16.677	443.195
UNITED STATES	242.967	222.141	6.656	18.301	490.066

Table 25

Consumption of Energy In Trillion BTU, 1972, By State

Use By Sectoral Class

REGION AND STATE	BUSINESS USE		USE BY FINAL DEMAND SECTORS	USE BY CUSTOMERS (Non-Energy Producers)	TOTAL USE
	Net Business Use	Use In Energy Production			
NEW ENGLAND:					
CONNECTICUT	200.693	266.151	343.214	543.907	810.058
MAINE	139.670	53.731	157.160	296.830	350.561
MASSACHUSETTS	443.802	343.084	800.366	1244.169	1587.253
NEW HAMPSHIRE	48.960	54.232	102.870	151.830	206.062
RHODE ISLAND	61.243	23.756	129.608	190.852	214.608
VERMONT	23.973	13.381	63.494	87.468	100.849
MID ATLANTIC:					
NEW JERSEY	570.754	483.061	944.049	1514.803	1997.864
NEW YORK	1384.689	1130.669	2020.599	3405.288	4535.957
PENNSYLVANIA	1902.597	1181.285	1337.587	3240.184	4421.469
EAST NORTH CENTRAL:					
ILLINOIS	1438.836	1122.456	1396.580	2835.415	3957.871
INDIANA	1241.324	689.638	636.171	1877.495	2567.134
MICHIGAN	1228.649	669.965	1144.107	2372.757	3042.722
OHIO	1831.246	1041.323	1288.017	3119.262	4160.585
WISCONSIN	501.662	334.338	510.306	1011.968	1346.307
WEST NORTH CENTRAL:					
IOWA	377.348	210.879	325.213	702.561	913.439
KANSAS	403.525	378.323	265.783	669.308	1047.631
MINNESOTA	458.319	270.851	485.835	944.155	1215.005
MISSOURI	504.505	391.849	530.718	1035.223	1427.072
NEBRASKA	208.583	112.138	191.964	400.547	512.684
NORTH DAKOTA	56.226	145.517	61.123	117.349	262.866
SOUTH DAKOTA	59.015	82.971	76.415	135.431	218.401
SOUTH ATLANTIC:					
DELAWARE	100.993	54.586	66.664	167.657	222.243
DISTRICT OF COLUMBIA	51.696	36.063	87.047	138.743	174.806
FLORIDA	532.790	737.349	619.316	1152.106	1889.455
GEORGIA	544.445	356.848	448.133	992.578	1349.426
MARYLAND	428.074	287.070	414.387	842.461	1129.531
NORTH CAROLINA	498.766	549.946	494.102	992.868	1542.814
SOUTH CAROLINA	318.674	252.359	241.413	560.087	812.446
VIRGINIA	463.796	332.662	545.063	1008.858	1341.520
WEST VIRGINIA	461.928	482.664	163.004	624.932	1107.596
EAST SOUTH CENTRAL:					
ALABAMA	664.604	510.127	321.320	985.925	1496.052
KENTUCKY	425.057	599.555	338.559	763.617	1363.172
MISSISSIPPI	357.441	235.841	214.138	571.580	807.421
TENNESSEE	521.134	501.712	385.439	906.572	1408.285
WEST SOUTH CENTRAL:					
ARKANSAS	314.231	143.845	202.895	517.127	660.972
LOUISIANA	1290.641	1054.089	372.938	1663.579	2717.668
OKLAHOMA	301.436	481.596	284.852	586.288	1067.883
TEXAS	2694.621	2929.616	1227.215	3921.836	6851.452
ROCKY MOUNTAIN:					
ARIZONA	225.744	191.920	167.793	393.538	585.458
COLORADO	311.973	172.995	276.518	588.491	761.486
IDAHO	113.533	79.304	82.373	195.906	275.210
MONTANA	132.303	144.818	82.873	215.177	359.995
NEVADA	70.649	94.094	68.313	138.962	233.056
NEW MEXICO	183.913	304.299	137.367	321.280	625.579
UTAH	207.393	64.170	126.344	333.737	397.907
WYOMING	123.151	160.889	61.626	184.777	345.666
FAR WEST:					
ALASKA	93.293	51.929	68.600	161.893	213.822
CALIFORNIA	2029.507	1640.153	2177.238	4206.745	5846.898
HAWAII	111.380	79.296	40.646	152.027	231.322
OREGON	268.559	372.941	230.449	499.009	871.949
WASHINGTON	412.363	843.079	349.164	761.526	1604.605

Table 26

Expenditures On Energy In Million Dollars, 1972, By State

Use By Sectoral Class

REGION AND STATE	BUSINESS USE		USE BY FINAL DEMAND SECTORS	USE BY CUSTOMERS (Non-Energy Producers)	TOTAL USE
	Net Business Use	Use In Energy Production			
NEW ENGLAND:					
CONNECTICUT	450.965	177.629	949.233	1400.198	1577.827
MAINE	215.835	31.401	357.236	573.072	604.472
MASSACHUSETTS	844.996	218.695	1897.566	2742.562	2961.257
NEW HAMPSHIRE	104.764	29.051	261.452	366.215	395.266
RHODE ISLAND	130.652	15.852	293.873	424.525	440.377
VERMONT	62.804	8.595	172.433	235.237	243.833
MID ATLANTIC:					
NEW JERSEY	1151.274	330.215	2326.520	3477.794	3808.009
NEW YORK	2524.929	675.248	5117.491	7642.420	8317.667
PENNSYLVANIA	2360.826	560.294	3195.751	5556.577	6116.870
EAST NORTH CENTRAL:					
ILLINOIS	2059.787	504.702	3191.190	5250.978	5755.680
INDIANA	1278.983	260.312	1476.615	2755.599	3015.910
MICHIGAN	1640.855	323.299	2509.793	4150.647	4473.946
OHIO	2159.138	426.779	2950.359	5109.497	5536.276
WISCONSIN	746.489	158.967	1221.391	1967.881	2126.848
WEST NORTH CENTRAL:					
IOWA	546.487	80.713	804.715	1351.202	1431.915
KANSAS	446.612	135.588	532.646	979.259	1114.846
MINNESOTA	686.748	119.621	1083.569	1770.318	1889.939
MISSOURI	819.882	130.688	1253.974	2073.856	2204.544
NEBRASKA	295.651	43.446	416.775	712.426	755.872
NORTH DAKOTA	103.544	38.349	144.625	248.169	286.518
SOUTH DAKOTA	107.325	36.374	182.246	289.572	325.945
SOUTH ATLANTIC:					
DELAWARE	153.930	34.419	185.156	339.085	373.504
DISTRICT OF COLUMBIA	111.502	24.537	207.205	318.707	343.244
FLORIDA	1042.558	362.145	2006.007	3048.566	3410.711
GEORGIA	872.220	159.300	1221.727	2093.947	2253.247
MARYLAND	708.438	169.338	1072.653	1781.091	1950.429
NORTH CAROLINA	887.373	251.880	1384.762	2272.134	2524.014
SOUTH CAROLINA	485.848	123.369	698.305	1184.154	1307.523
VIRGINIA	721.261	165.357	1299.452	2020.712	2186.069
WEST VIRGINIA	426.705	172.232	380.830	807.535	979.767
EAST SOUTH CENTRAL:					
ALABAMA	728.507	192.336	866.166	1594.674	1787.010
KENTUCKY	614.174	178.427	791.181	1405.355	1583.782
MISSISSIPPI	427.837	83.710	570.599	998.435	1082.146
TENNESSEE	760.628	173.055	969.257	1729.885	1902.940
WEST SOUTH CENTRAL:					
ARKANSAS	417.121	57.174	505.992	923.114	980.288
LOUISIANA	883.813	305.393	835.128	1718.941	2024.335
OKLAHOMA	446.123	119.040	674.648	1120.771	1239.811
TEXAS	2392.213	826.332	2915.074	5307.288	6133.620
ROCKY MOUNTAIN:					
ARIZONA	403.645	70.599	485.252	888.896	959.496
COLORADO	414.141	55.703	600.643	1014.784	1070.486
IDAHO	177.083	14.957	205.148	382.231	397.188
MONTANA	176.618	46.405	177.300	353.918	400.324
NEVADA	136.665	35.551	179.162	315.828	351.378
NEW MEXICO	234.735	62.018	280.790	515.524	577.542
UTAH	223.469	29.547	267.266	490.735	520.282
WYOMING	129.033	41.521	116.909	245.942	287.463
FAR WEST:					
ALASKA	122.554	22.398	132.844	255.398	277.796
CALIFORNIA	3130.115	761.348	4856.464	7986.579	8747.927
HAWAII	187.208	67.419	155.731	342.939	410.358
OREGON	379.067	74.249	583.767	962.834	1037.083
WASHINGTON	552.547	184.700	824.538	1377.085	1561.785

Table 27

Consumption of Energy In Trillion BTU and Expenditures On Energy
    In Million Dollars, 1972, By Region

Use By Sectoral Class

REGION	BUSINESS USE		USE BY FINAL DEMAND SECTORS	USE BY CUSTOMERS (Non-Energy Producers)	TOTAL USE
	Net Business Use	Use In Energy Production			
Consumption in Trillion BTU					
NEW ENGLAND	918.34	754.33	1596.71	2515.06	3269.39
MID ATLANTIC	3858.04	2795.02	4302.23	8160.27	10955.29
EAST NORTH CENTRAL	6241.72	3857.72	4975.18	11216.90	15074.62
WEST NORTH CENTRAL	2067.52	1592.53	1937.05	4004.57	5597.10
SOUTH ATLANTIC	3401.16	3089.55	3079.13	6480.29	9569.84
EAST SOUTH CENTRAL	1968.24	1847.24	1259.46	3227.69	5074.93
WEST SOUTH CENTRAL	4600.93	4609.15	2087.90	6688.83	11297.98
ROCKY MOUNTAIN	1368.66	1212.49	1003.21	2371.87	3584.36
FAR WEST	2915.10	2987.40	2866.10	5781.20	8768.60
TOTAL	27339.71	22745.41	23106.97	50446.68	73192.09
Expenditures In Million Dollars					
NEW ENGLAND	1810.02	481.22	3931.79	5741.81	6223.03
MID ATLANTIC	6037.03	1565.76	10639.76	16676.79	18242.55
EAST NORTH CENTRAL	7885.25	1674.06	11349.35	19234.60	20908.66
WEST NORTH CENTRAL	3006.25	584.78	4418.55	7424.80	8009.58
SOUTH ATLANTIC	5409.84	1462.58	8456.10	13865.93	15328.51
EAST SOUTH CENTRAL	2531.15	627.53	3197.20	5728.35	6355.88
WEST SOUTH CENTRAL	4139.27	1307.94	4930.84	9070.11	10378.05
ROCKY MOUNTAIN	1895.39	356.30	2312.47	4207.86	4564.16
FAR WEST	4371.49	1110.11	6553.34	10924.83	12034.95
TOTAL	37085.68	9170.28	55789.41	92875.09	102045.37

Table 28

Consumption of Energy In Million BTU Per Capita, 1972, By State

Use By Sectoral Class

REGION AND STATE	BUSINESS USE		USE BY FINAL DEMAND SECTORS	USE BY CUSTOMERS (Non-Energy Producers)	TOTAL USE
	Net Business Use	Use In Energy Production			
NEW ENGLAND:					
CONNECTICUT	65.160	86.413	111.433	176.593	263.006
MAINE	136.131	52.369	153.177	289.308	341.678
MASSACHUSETTS	76.570	59.193	138.089	214.660	273.853
NEW HAMPSHIRE	63.256	70.068	132.907	196.162	266.230
RHODE ISLAND	63.202	24.516	133.755	196.957	221.474
VERMONT	52.116	29.090	138.031	190.148	219.238
MID ATLANTIC:					
NEW JERSEY	77.664	65.731	128.460	206.124	271.855
NEW YORK	75.390	61.560	110.012	185.403	246.962
PENNSYLVANIA	159.815	99.226	112.355	272.170	371.396
EAST NORTH CENTRAL:					
ILLINOIS	127.965	99.827	124.207	252.171	351.998
INDIANA	234.832	130.465	120.350	355.183	485.648
MICHIGAN	136.320	74.333	126.940	263.259	337.593
OHIO	170.793	97.120	120.128	290.922	388.042
WISCONSIN	110.840	73.871	112.750	223.590	297.461
WEST NORTH CENTRAL:					
IOWA	130.842	73.120	112.764	243.606	316.727
KANSAS	177.921	166.809	117.188	295.109	461.918
MINNESOTA	118.215	69.861	125.312	243.527	313.388
MISSOURI	106.279	82.547	111.801	218.079	300.626
NEBRASKA	136.507	73.388	125.631	262.138	335.526
NORTH DAKOTA	88.685	229.522	96.409	185.093	414.615
SOUTH DAKOTA	86.787	122.016	112.375	199.163	321.179
SOUTH ATLANTIC:					
DELAWARE	176.871	95.597	116.749	293.620	389.218
DISTRICT OF COLUMBIA	68.744	47.956	115.755	184.499	232.455
FLORIDA	72.518	100.361	84.295	156.813	257.174
GEORGIA	115.032	75.396	94.683	209.714	285.110
MARYLAND	105.749	70.917	102.368	208.118	279.034
NORTH CAROLINA	95.531	105.333	94.638	190.168	295.502
SOUTH CAROLINA	118.554	93.883	89.811	208.366	302.249
VIRGINIA	97.334	69.814	114.389	211.723	281.536
WEST VIRGINIA	257.342	268.894	90.810	348.152	617.045
EAST SOUTH CENTRAL:					
ALABAMA	188.754	144.881	91.258	280.013	424.894
KENTUCKY	128.571	181.354	102.408	230.979	412.333
MISSISSIPPI	158.440	104.540	94.919	253.360	357.899
TENNESSEE	127.980	123.210	94.656	222.636	345.846
WEST SOUTH CENTRAL:					
ARKANSAS	156.490	71.636	101.043	257.533	329.169
LOUISIANA	345.276	281.993	99.769	445.045	727.038
OKLAHOMA	114.484	182.908	108.185	222.669	405.577
TEXAS	232.215	252.466	105.758	337.973	590.439
ROCKY MOUNTAIN:					
ARIZONA	115.000	97.769	85.478	200.478	298.246
COLORADO	131.968	73.179	116.970	248.939	322.117
IDAHO	150.374	105.038	109.103	259.478	364.516
MONTANA	184.781	202.260	115.745	300.526	502.786
NEVADA	132.550	176.536	128.167	260.718	437.254
NEW MEXICO	170.923	282.806	127.664	298.588	581.393
UTAH	184.022	56.939	112.106	296.128	353.067
WYOMING	355.927	464.998	178.110	534.037	999.036
FAR WEST:					
ALASKA	287.056	159.783	211.078	498.132	657.915
CALIFORNIA	99.432	80.356	106.670	206.102	286.458
HAWAII	136.495	97.176	49.812	186.307	283.483
OREGON	122.910	170.682	105.469	228.379	399.061
WASHINGTON	120.644	246.659	102.154	222.799	469.457

Table 29

Expenditures on Energy In Dollars Per Capita, 1972, By State

Use By Sectoral Class

REGION AND STATE	BUSINESS USE		USE BY FINAL DEMAND SECTORS	USE BY CUSTOMERS (Non-Energy Producers)	TOTAL USE
	Net Business Use	Use In Energy Production			
NEW ENGLAND:					
CONNECTICUT	146.417	57.672	308.193	454.610	512.281
MAINE	210.366	30.605	348.184	558.549	589.154
MASSACHUSETTS	145.790	37.732	327.392	473.182	510.914
NEW HAMPSHIRE	135.354	37.534	337.793	473.146	510.680
RHODE ISLAND	134.832	16.359	303.274	438.106	454.466
VERMONT	136.530	18.685	374.855	511.385	530.071
MID ATLANTIC:					
NEW JERSEY	156.657	44.933	316.576	473.234	518.167
NEW YORK	137.471	36.764	278.624	416.095	452.859
PENNSYLVANIA	198.305	47.064	268.438	466.743	513.807
EAST NORTH CENTRAL:					
ILLINOIS	183.190	44.886	283.813	467.003	511.889
INDIANA	241.957	49.246	279.345	521.301	570.547
MICHIGAN	182.054	35.870	278.464	460.518	496.388
OHIO	201.375	39.804	275.169	476.543	516.347
WISCONSIN	164.934	35.123	269.861	434.795	469.918
WEST NORTH CENTRAL:					
IOWA	189.489	27.986	279.027	468.517	496.503
KANSAS	196.919	59.783	234.853	431.772	491.555
MINNESOTA	177.134	30.854	279.486	456.620	487.475
MISSOURI	172.716	27.531	264.161	436.877	464.408
NEBRASKA	193.489	28.433	272.759	466.247	494.680
NORTH DAKOTA	163.319	60.487	228.115	391.434	451.922
SOUTH DAKOTA	157.831	53.491	268.009	425.840	479.331
SOUTH ATLANTIC:					
DELAWARE	269.579	60.278	324.266	593.845	654.123
DISTRICT OF COLUMBIA	148.274	32.629	275.539	423.813	456.442
FLORIDA	141.903	49.292	273.038	414.940	464.232
GEORGIA	184.285	33.657	258.130	442.414	476.072
MARYLAND	175.009	41.832	264.983	439.993	481.825
NORTH CAROLINA	169.962	48.244	265.229	435.191	483.435
SOUTH CAROLINA	180.747	45.896	259.786	440.533	486.430
VIRGINIA	151.366	34.702	272.708	424.074	458.776
WEST VIRGINIA	237.719	95.951	212.162	449.880	545.831
EAST SOUTH CENTRAL:					
ALABAMA	206.904	54.626	246.000	452.904	507.529
KENTUCKY	185.776	53.971	239.317	425.092	479.063
MISSISSIPPI	189.644	37.106	252.925	442.569	479.674
TENNESSEE	186.795	42.499	238.030	424.824	467.323
WEST SOUTH CENTRAL:					
ARKANSAS	207.730	28.473	251.988	459.718	488.191
LOUISIANA	236.440	81.700	223.416	459.856	541.555
OKLAHOMA	169.435	45.211	256.228	425.663	470.874
TEXAS	206.154	71.211	251.213	457.367	528.578
ROCKY MOUNTAIN:					
ARIZONA	205.626	35.965	247.199	452.826	488.790
COLORADO	175.186	23.563	254.079	429.266	452.828
IDAHO	234.546	19.811	271.720	506.266	526.077
MONTANA	246.673	64.812	247.626	494.299	559.111
NEVADA	256.407	66.699	336.140	592.547	659.246
NEW MEXICO	218.155	57.638	260.957	479.111	536.749
UTAH	198.287	26.217	237.148	435.435	461.652
WYOMING	372.929	120.003	337.887	710.815	830.818
FAR WEST:					
ALASKA	377.089	68.918	408.750	785.839	854.757
CALIFORNIA	153.354	37.301	237.934	391.288	428.589
HAWAII	229.421	82.621	190.847	420.269	502.890
OREGON	173.486	33.981	267.170	440.656	474.638
WASHINGTON	161.658	54.037	241.234	402.892	456.929

Table 30

Consumption Of Energy In Million BTU Per Capita and Expenditures On Energy
   In Dollars Per Capita, 1972, By Region

Use By Sectoral Class

REGION	BUSINESS USE		USE BY FINAL DEMAND SECTORS	USE BY CUSTOMERS (Non-Energy Producers)	TOTAL USE
	Net Business Use	Use In Energy Production			
Consumption In Million BTU Per Capita					
NEW ENGLAND	75.865	62.316	131.905	207.770	270.086
MID ATLANTIC	102.550	74.294	114.357	216.907	291.201
EAST NORTH CENTRAL	153.017	94.573	121.968	274.985	369.557
WEST NORTH CENTRAL	124.415	95.831	116.563	240.978	336.809
SOUTH ATLANTIC	106.553	96.790	96.464	203.017	299.807
EAST SOUTH CENTRAL	149.619	140.421	95.740	245.359	385.780
WEST SOUTH CENTRAL	230.242	230.653	104.484	334.726	565.379
ROCKY MOUNTAIN	154.128	136.542	112.974	267.102	403.644
FAR WEST	107.350	110.013	105.546	212.896	322.909
UNITED STATES	131.297	109.233	110.970	242.267	351.500
Expenditures In Dollars Per Capita					
NEW ENGLAND	149.526	39.754	324.807	474.334	514.088
MID ATLANTIC	160.470	41.619	282.814	443.284	484.903
EAST NORTH CENTRAL	193.309	41.040	278.232	471.540	512.580
WEST NORTH CENTRAL	180.903	35.189	265.889	446.793	481.982
SOUTH ATLANTIC	169.481	45.820	264.915	434.396	480.216
EAST SOUTH CENTRAL	192.409	47.703	243.041	435.450	483.153
WEST SOUTH CENTRAL	207.140	65.453	246.752	453.892	519.344
ROCKY MOUNTAIN	213.445	40.124	260.413	473.858	513.982
FAR WEST	160.983	40.881	241.331	402.314	443.195
UNITED STATES	178.101	44.040	267.925	446.026	490.066

Table 31

Consumption Of Energy As A Fraction Of Total Use, 1972, By State

Use By Sector

REGION AND STATE	USE AS FRACTION OF TOTAL USE				
	HOUSEHOLD USE	BUSINESS USE		FEDERAL GOVERNMENT USE	STATE & LOCAL GOVERNMENT USE
		Net Business Use	Energy Use		
NEW ENGLAND:					
CONNECTICUT	0.3913	0.2478	0.3286	0.0100	0.0224
MAINE	0.3480	0.3984	0.1533	0.0775	0.0228
MASSACHUSETTS	0.4433	0.2796	0.2161	0.0241	0.0368
NEW HAMPSHIRE	0.4686	0.2376	0.2632	0.0082	0.0224
RHODE ISLAND	0.4906	0.2854	0.1107	0.0807	0.0326
VERMONT	0.6039	0.2377	0.1327	0.0041	0.0216
MID ATLANTIC:					
NEW JERSEY	0.4290	0.2857	0.2418	0.0228	0.0207
NEW YORK	0.3918	0.3053	0.2493	0.0190	0.0346
PENNSYLVANIA	0.2824	0.4303	0.2672	0.0072	0.0130
EAST NORTH CENTRAL:					
ILLINOIS	0.3236	0.3635	0.2836	0.0077	0.0216
INDIANA	0.2310	0.4835	0.2686	0.0017	0.0151
MICHIGAN	0.3415	0.4038	0.2202	0.0119	0.0227
OHIO	0.2894	0.4401	0.2503	0.0027	0.0175
WISCONSIN	0.3517	0.3726	0.2483	0.0068	0.0206
WEST NORTH CENTRAL:					
IOWA	0.3294	0.4131	0.2309	0.0019	0.0248
KANSAS	0.2229	0.3852	0.3611	0.0095	0.0212
MINNESOTA	0.3492	0.3772	0.2229	0.0103	0.0403
MISSOURI	0.3394	0.3535	0.2746	0.0034	0.0291
NEBRASKA	0.3265	0.4068	0.2187	0.0078	0.0401
NORTH DAKOTA	0.2086	0.2139	0.5536	0.0052	0.0188
SOUTH DAKOTA	0.3168	0.2702	0.3799	0.0041	0.0290
SOUTH ATLANTIC:					
DELAWARE	0.2764	0.4544	0.2456	0.0064	0.0172
DISTRICT OF COLUMBIA	0.3462	0.2957	0.2063	0.0700	0.0818
FLORIDA	0.2833	0.2820	0.3902	0.0108	0.0337
GEORGIA	0.2996	0.4035	0.2644	0.0091	0.0234
MARYLAND	0.3119	0.3790	0.2541	0.0298	0.0252
NORTH CAROLINA	0.2852	0.3233	0.3565	0.0108	0.0243
SOUTH CAROLINA	0.2617	0.3922	0.3106	0.0181	0.0174
VIRGINIA	0.3088	0.3457	0.2480	0.0706	0.0269
WEST VIRGINIA	0.1353	0.4171	0.4358	0.0008	0.0112
EAST SOUTH CENTRAL:					
ALABAMA	0.1889	0.4442	0.3410	0.0148	0.0111
KENTUCKY	0.2155	0.3118	0.4398	0.0163	0.0166
MISSISSIPPI	0.2411	0.4427	0.2921	0.0062	0.0180
TENNESSEE	0.2476	0.3700	0.3563	0.0095	0.0166
WEST SOUTH CENTRAL:					
ARKANSAS	0.2790	0.4754	0.2176	0.0102	0.0178
LOUISIANA	0.1058	0.4749	0.3879	0.0129	0.0186
OKLAHOMA	0.2364	0.2823	0.4510	0.0093	0.0210
TEXAS	0.1526	0.3933	0.4276	0.0112	0.0153
ROCKY MOUNTAIN:					
ARIZONA	0.2519	0.3856	0.3278	0.0066	0.0281
COLORADO	0.3054	0.4097	0.2272	0.0170	0.0407
IDAHO	0.2674	0.4125	0.2882	0.0039	0.0280
MONTANA	0.1949	0.3675	0.4023	0.0111	0.0242
NEVADA	0.2353	0.3031	0.4037	0.0124	0.0455
NEW MEXICO	0.1673	0.2940	0.4864	0.0141	0.0382
UTAH	0.2817	0.5212	0.1613	0.0223	0.0135
WYOMING	0.1524	0.3563	0.4654	0.0040	0.0219
FAR WEST:					
ALASKA	0.1622	0.4363	0.2429	0.1109	0.0477
CALIFORNIA	0.3049	0.3471	0.2805	0.0467	0.0208
HAWAII	0.1423	0.4815	0.3428	0.0266	0.0068
OREGON	0.2362	0.3080	0.4277	0.0090	0.0191
WASHINGTON	0.1890	0.2570	0.5254	0.0137	0.0150

Table 32

Expenditures On Energy As A Fraction Of Total Expenditures, 1972, By State

Use By Sector

REGION AND STATE	HOUSEHOLD USE	USE AS FRACTION OF TOTAL USE		FEDERAL GOVERNMENT USE	STATE & LOCAL GOVERNMENT USE
		BUSINESS USE			
		Net Business Use	Energy Use		
NEW ENGLAND:					
CONNECTICUT	0.5610	0.2858	0.1126	0.0060	0.0346
MAINE	0.5086	0.3571	0.0519	0.0499	0.0325
MASSACHUSETTS	0.5843	0.2854	0.0739	0.0137	0.0427
NEW HAMPSHIRE	0.6259	0.2650	0.0735	0.0050	0.0306
RHODE ISLAND	0.5949	0.2967	0.0360	0.0315	0.0409
VERMONT	0.6684	0.2576	0.0353	0.0061	0.0327
MID ATLANTIC:					
NEW JERSEY	0.5660	0.3023	0.0867	0.0112	0.0338
NEW YORK	0.5401	0.3036	0.0812	0.0165	0.0586
PENNSYLVANIA	0.4921	0.3860	0.0916	0.0060	0.0244
EAST NORTH CENTRAL:					
ILLINOIS	0.5064	0.3579	0.0877	0.0095	0.0385
INDIANA	0.4581	0.4241	0.0863	0.0023	0.0292
MICHIGAN	0.5120	0.3668	0.0723	0.0095	0.0395
OHIO	0.4959	0.3900	0.0771	0.0048	0.0322
WISCONSIN	0.5342	0.3510	0.0747	0.0057	0.0344
WEST NORTH CENTRAL:					
IOWA	0.5197	0.3816	0.0564	0.0032	0.0391
KANSAS	0.4331	0.4006	0.1216	0.0084	0.0363
MINNESOTA	0.5260	0.3634	0.0633	0.0080	0.0394
MISSOURI	0.5311	0.3719	0.0593	0.0049	0.0328
NEBRASKA	0.5023	0.3911	0.0575	0.0074	0.0417
NORTH DAKOTA	0.4568	0.3614	0.1338	0.0079	0.0400
SOUTH DAKOTA	0.5146	0.3293	0.1116	0.0065	0.0380
SOUTH ATLANTIC:					
DELAWARE	0.4607	0.4121	0.0922	0.0046	0.0305
DISTRICT OF COLUMBIA	0.4646	0.3248	0.0715	0.0558	0.0832
FLORIDA	0.5304	0.3057	0.1062	0.0103	0.0474
GEORGIA	0.4951	0.3871	0.0707	0.0072	0.0398
MARYLAND	0.4934	0.3632	0.0868	0.0188	0.0378
NORTH CAROLINA	0.5020	0.3516	0.0998	0.0085	0.0382
SOUTH CAROLINA	0.4883	0.3716	0.0944	0.0139	0.0319
VIRGINIA	0.5141	0.3299	0.0756	0.0401	0.0402
WEST VIRGINIA	0.3602	0.4355	0.1758	0.0021	0.0263
EAST SOUTH CENTRAL:					
ALABAMA	0.4456	0.4077	0.1076	0.0139	0.0252
KENTUCKY	0.4518	0.3878	0.1127	0.0181	0.0296
MISSISSIPPI	0.4896	0.3954	0.0774	0.0057	0.0320
TENNESSEE	0.4737	0.3997	0.0909	0.0074	0.0283
WEST SOUTH CENTRAL:					
ARKANSAS	0.4775	0.4255	0.0583	0.0092	0.0295
LOUISIANA	0.3643	0.4366	0.1509	0.0162	0.0321
OKLAHOMA	0.4926	0.3598	0.0960	0.0115	0.0400
TEXAS	0.4300	0.3900	0.1347	0.0145	0.0308
ROCKY MOUNTAIN:					
ARIZONA	0.4528	0.4207	0.0736	0.0100	0.0429
COLORADO	0.4993	0.3869	0.0520	0.0165	0.0453
IDAHO	0.4720	0.4458	0.0377	0.0050	0.0395
MONTANA	0.3967	0.4412	0.1159	0.0117	0.0345
NEVADA	0.4470	0.3889	0.1012	0.0137	0.0492
NEW MEXICO	0.4211	0.4064	0.1074	0.0222	0.0429
UTAH	0.4632	0.4295	0.0568	0.0218	0.0287
WYOMING	0.3608	0.4489	0.1444	0.0075	0.0384
FAR WEST:					
ALASKA	0.3180	0.4412	0.0806	0.1153	0.0449
CALIFORNIA	0.4844	0.3578	0.0870	0.0320	0.0387
HAWAII	0.3350	0.4562	0.1643	0.0220	0.0226
OREGON	0.5162	0.3655	0.0716	0.0095	0.0372
WASHINGTON	0.4764	0.3538	0.1183	0.0172	0.0343

Table 33

Consumption and Expenditures On Energy As A Fraction Of Total Use, 1972, By Region

Use By Sector

REGION	USE AS FRACTION OF TOTAL USE				
	HOUSEHOLD USE	BUSINESS USE		FEDERAL GOVERNMENT USE	STATE & LOCAL GOVT. USE
		Net Business Use	Energy Use		
Consumption As Fraction of Total (BTU)					
NEW ENGLAND	0.4298	0.2809	0.2307	0.0284	0.0301
MID ATLANTIC	0.3544	0.3522	0.2551	0.0149	0.0233
EAST NORTH CENTRAL	0.3045	0.4141	0.2559	0.0061	0.0195
WEST NORTH CENTRAL	0.3099	0.3694	0.2845	0.0063	0.0299
SOUTH ATLANTIC	0.2749	0.3554	0.3228	0.0216	0.0253
EAST SOUTH CENTRAL	0.2206	0.3878	0.3640	0.0124	0.0152
WEST SOUTH CENTRAL	0.1567	0.4072	0.4080	0.0114	0.0168
ROCKY MOUNTAIN	0.2366	0.3818	0.3383	0.0122	0.0310
FAR WEST	0.2691	0.3324	0.3407	0.0379	0.0199
UNITED STATES	0.2779	0.3735	0.3108	0.0158	0.0220
Expenditures As Fraction of Total (Dollars)					
NEW ENGLAND	0.5777	0.2909	0.0773	0.0157	0.0384
MID ATLANTIC	0.5294	0.3309	0.0858	0.0118	0.0420
EAST NORTH CENTRAL	0.5007	0.3771	0.0801	0.0068	0.0353
WEST NORTH CENTRAL	0.5082	0.3753	0.0730	0.0062	0.0373
SOUTH ATLANTIC	0.4959	0.3529	0.0954	0.0155	0.0402
EAST SOUTH CENTRAL	0.4630	0.3982	0.0987	0.0116	0.0284
WEST SOUTH CENTRAL	0.4291	0.3988	0.1260	0.0140	0.0320
ROCKY MOUNTAIN	0.4514	0.4153	0.0781	0.0143	0.0410
FAR WEST	0.4772	0.3632	0.0922	0.0297	0.0376
UNITED STATES	0.4958	0.3634	0.0899	0.0136	0.0373

Table 34

Expenditures On Energy Per Capita As Fraction Of Income Per Capita, 1972, By State

Household Use Of Energy

REGION AND STATE	ENERGY AS FRACTION OF INCOME	REGION AND STATE	ENERGY AS FRACTION OF INCOME
NEW ENGLAND:		EAST SOUTH CENTRAL:	
CONNECTICUT	0.0534	ALABAMA	0.0651
MAINE	0.0811	KENTUCKY	0.0600
MASSACHUSETTS	0.0615	MISSISSIPPI	0.0737
NEW HAMPSHIRE	0.0764	TENNESSEE	0.0597
RHODE ISLAND	0.0600	WEST SOUTH CENTRAL:	
VERMONT	0.0912	ARKANSAS	0.0697
MID ATLANTIC:		LOUISIANA	0.0552
NEW JERSEY	0.0553	OKLAHOMA	0.0605
NEW YORK	0.0466	TEXAS	0.0554
PENNSYLVANIA	0.0558	ROCKY MOUNTAIN:	
EAST NORTH CENTRAL:		ARIZONA	0.0511
ILLINOIS	0.0505	COLORADO	0.0490
INDIANA	0.0598	IDAHO	0.0656
MICHIGAN	0.0513	MONTANA	0.0545
OHIO	0.0561	NEVADA	0.0573
WISCONSIN	0.0585	NEW MEXICO	0.0643
WEST NORTH CENTRAL:		UTAH	0.0572
IOWA	0.0600	WYOMING	0.0701
KANSAS	0.0469	FAR WEST:	
MINNESOTA	0.0592	ALASKA	0.0523
MISSOURI	0.0575	CALIFORNIA	0.0412
NEBRASKA	0.0559	HAWAII	0.0329
NORTH DAKOTA	0.0515	OREGON	0.0566
SOUTH DAKOTA	0.0650	WASHINGTON	0.0478
SOUTH ATLANTIC:			
DELAWARE	0.0577		
DISTRICT OF COLUMBIA	0.0358		
FLORIDA	0.0546		
GEORGIA	0.0594		
MARYLAND	0.0478		
NORTH CAROLINA	0.0630		
SOUTH CAROLINA	0.0677		
VIRGINIA	0.0536		
WEST VIRGINIA	0.0546		

Table 35

Consumption Of Energy In Trillion BTU, 1972, By State

Use By Function

REGION AND STATE	RESIDENTIAL USE	COMMERCIAL USE	INDUSTRIAL USE	TRANSPOR-TATION USE	ENERGY USE		MUNICIPAL-INSTITU-TIONAL USE	ALL USE
					Non Electric Utility Use	Electric Utility Use		
NEW ENGLAND:								
CONNECTICUT	184.782	49.464	105.501	199.113	2.475	263.676	5.048	810.058
MAINE	78.296	24.846	71.036	121.861	0.804	52.928	0.791	350.561
MASSACHUSETTS	474.612	200.844	166.890	395.088	11.357	331.727	6.735	1587.253
NEW HAMPSHIRE	61.504	14.500	24.698	50.825	1.331	52.902	0.302	206.062
RHODE ISLAND	69.437	22.662	29.641	67.800	6.496	17.260	1.313	214.608
VERMONT	39.597	6.060	8.683	32.517	0.521	12.860	0.611	100.849
MID ATLANTIC:								
NEW JERSEY	541.691	141.082	258.580	569.171	87.448	395.613	4.278	1997.664
NEW YORK	1204.652	404.107	594.046	1154.641	18.914	1111.755	47.843	4535.957
PENNSYLVANIA	792.984	184.551	1470.340	779.811	161.877	1019.408	12.498	4421.469
EAST NORTH CENTRAL:								
ILLINOIS	838.557	258.833	852.716	862.735	201.465	920.991	22.574	3957.871
INDIANA	370.549	110.036	980.955	410.493	128.317	561.321	5.462	2567.134
MICHIGAN	639.873	156.872	910.335	653.153	41.400	628.565	12.525	3042.722
OHIO	741.172	165.716	1452.136	729.998	105.462	935.860	30.242	4160.585
WISCONSIN	292.543	73.638	339.563	300.595	13.429	320.909	5.629	1346.307
WEST NORTH CENTRAL:								
IOWA	186.818	57.423	236.327	217.697	21.608	189.271	4.296	913.439
KANSAS	143.915	45.888	276.999	195.138	183.692	194.631	7.367	1047.630
MINNESOTA	266.566	72.987	276.034	301.883	34.499	236.351	26.685	1215.005
MISSOURI	278.639	81.548	241.292	414.051	33.544	358.305	19.694	1427.072
NEBRASKA	106.792	36.369	107.739	139.723	19.290	92.848	9.924	512.684
NORTH DAKOTA	36.057	14.874	14.848	50.986	29.153	116.363	0.584	262.866
SOUTH DAKOTA	42.659	14.272	20.150	56.131	1.104	81.867	2.218	218.401
SOUTH ATLANTIC:								
DELAWARE	35.203	15.904	72.214	44.206	5.114	49.472	0.130	222.243
DISTRICT OF COLUMBIA	36.572	58.081	6.968	34.721	0.871	35.191	2.402	174.806
FLORIDA	180.137	87.082	198.915	670.330	11.118	726.231	15.642	1889.455
GEORGIA	177.448	72.627	287.705	448.790	9.857	346.992	6.008	1349.426
MARYLAND	186.379	80.686	269.808	301.253	8.519	278.551	4.335	1129.531
NORTH CAROLINA	219.035	74.630	297.397	391.538	7.518	542.428	10.268	1542.814
SOUTH CAROLINA	93.781	30.793	219.934	212.209	4.629	247.730	3.369	812.446
VIRGINIA	207.104	72.652	225.466	483.459	32.488	300.174	20.157	1341.520
WEST VIRGINIA	92.359	24.542	395.915	108.915	21.034	461.630	3.201	1107.596
EAST SOUTH CENTRAL:								
ALABAMA	137.007	42.958	511.436	292.705	28.778	481.349	1.819	1496.052
KENTUCKY	164.431	37.903	286.680	262.632	65.418	534.138	11.971	1363.172
MISSISSIPPI	104.173	32.083	251.700	177.675	100.851	134.991	5.948	807.421
TENNESSEE	176.374	39.757	347.412	336.765	28.094	473.618	6.264	1408.285
WEST SOUTH CENTRAL:								
ARKANSAS	108.051	34.594	198.798	173.358	27.752	116.093	2.327	660.972
LOUISIANA	146.710	53.893	1072.925	352.573	652.562	401.527	37.478	2717.668
OKLAHOMA	142.696	41.821	165.212	227.920	198.668	282.928	8.639	1067.883
TEXAS	500.967	186.311	1927.628	1246.714	1553.424	1376.191	60.217	6851.452
ROCKY MOUNTAIN:								
ARIZONA	64.607	35.169	109.712	177.623	28.602	163.318	6.428	585.458
COLORADO	134.946	68.924	160.735	219.944	18.463	154.532	3.942	761.486
IDAHO	43.011	19.796	66.236	64.097	5.172	74.132	2.766	275.210
MONTANA	44.850	22.410	68.518	76.118	39.646	105.172	3.281	359.995
NEVADA	27.078	14.134	20.362	70.665	0.448	93.645	6.723	233.056
NEW MEXICO	58.965	23.587	104.292	116.546	98.418	205.881	17.890	625.579
UTAH	68.117	20.118	141.664	102.309	27.824	36.346	1.528	397.907
WYOMING	36.665	17.697	73.312	55.353	57.717	103.172	1.750	345.666
FAR WEST:								
ALASKA	26.024	10.178	35.307	83.086	26.724	25.205	7.298	213.822
CALIFORNIA	917.525	330.498	901.910	2022.562	407.335	1232.818	34.250	5846.898
HAWAII	8.168	6.156	14.935	122.543	27.106	52.190	0.225	231.322
OREGON	105.018	52.076	142.219	198.204	27.720	345.221	1.491	871.949
WASHINGTON	176.667	72.197	217.387	291.089	99.563	743.516	4.186	1604.605

Table 36

Expenditures On Energy In Million Dollars, 1972, By State

Use By Function

REGION AND STATE	RESIDENTIAL USE	COMMERCIAL USE	INDUSTRIAL USE	TRANSPOR- TATION USE	ENERGY USE		MUNICIPAL- INSTITU- TIONAL USE	ALL USE
					Non Electric Utility Use	Electric Utility Use		
NEW ENGLAND:								
CONNECTICUT	471.637	170.683	187.426	553.691	2.183	175.446	16.761	1577.827
MAINE	172.217	54.194	89.794	250.548	0.648	30.753	6.318	604.472
MASSACHUSETTS	1061.867	418.804	292.900	939.703	10.752	207.943	29.288	2961.257
NEW HAMPSHIRE	139.819	33.673	40.774	148.801	1.149	27.902	3.148	395.267
RHODE ISLAND	156.447	55.155	52.578	153.863	4.405	11.447	6.482	440.377
VERMONT	93.434	18.846	19.209	99.457	0.575	8.020	4.290	243.833
MID ATLANTIC:								
NEW JERSEY	1197.586	450.668	446.399	1354.953	57.444	272.771	28.188	3808.009
NEW YORK	2615.392	1198.039	757.826	2843.248	10.994	664.254	227.914	8317.667
PENNSYLVANIA	1649.296	517.206	1344.955	2002.207	96.534	463.760	42.912	6116.871
EAST NORTH CENTRAL:								
ILLINOIS	1565.737	691.311	835.243	2073.119	117.980	386.722	85.568	5755.680
INDIANA	732.638	257.124	683.754	1064.672	76.570	183.742	17.411	3015.910
MICHIGAN	1173.679	414.577	880.938	1633.696	21.431	301.868	47.758	4473.947
OHIO	1317.069	475.602	1226.243	2012.045	62.884	363.895	78.538	5536.276
WISCONSIN	634.668	210.385	349.452	753.746	7.235	151.732	19.630	2126.847
WEST NORTH CENTRAL:								
IOWA	406.608	149.852	200.997	580.751	5.452	75.261	12.994	1431.915
KANSAS	242.301	118.676	160.910	449.083	61.417	74.171	8.290	1114.847
MINNESOTA	536.297	168.126	295.694	741.399	18.668	100.953	28.802	1889.939
MISSOURI	591.365	219.419	265.499	974.902	16.246	114.442	22.671	2204.544
NEBRASKA	198.286	81.946	76.394	345.840	6.271	37.175	9.960	755.872
NORTH DAKOTA	82.287	34.483	16.561	112.275	11.890	26.459	2.564	286.518
SOUTH DAKOTA	98.420	35.715	17.592	134.565	1.009	35.365	3.280	325.945
SOUTH ATLANTIC:								
DELAWARE	90.371	41.447	88.421	117.231	3.486	30.933	1.616	373.504
DISTRICT OF COLUMBIA	85.090	121.091	8.181	97.916	0.487	24.049	6.430	343.244
FLORIDA	794.779	377.482	258.448	1560.589	5.875	356.270	57.268	3410.711
GEORGIA	457.843	238.899	301.967	1082.465	3.201	156.099	12.773	2253.247
MARYLAND	443.916	224.437	337.609	760.598	5.131	164.207	14.531	1950.429
NORTH CAROLINA	584.729	217.179	357.446	1091.724	4.022	247.857	21.056	2524.014
SOUTH CAROLINA	282.432	101.533	231.113	559.937	1.958	121.411	9.139	1307.523
VIRGINIA	515.959	214.388	229.755	1015.436	16.861	148.495	45.175	2186.069
WEST VIRGINIA	172.761	65.002	258.420	306.912	8.039	164.193	4.439	979.767
EAST SOUTH CENTRAL:								
ALABAMA	364.430	119.612	379.178	724.424	9.969	182.368	7.030	1787.010
KENTUCKY	331.828	94.535	292.424	660.817	26.083	152.344	25.751	1583.782
MISSISSIPPI	267.631	92.251	162.635	466.356	32.731	50.979	9.561	1082.146
TENNESSEE	404.092	85.350	390.253	832.992	7.148	165.907	17.198	1902.940
WEST SOUTH CENTRAL:								
ARKANSAS	248.047	88.385	141.881	437.932	9.041	48.133	6.869	980.288
LOUISIANA	352.056	154.706	489.956	693.716	195.121	110.272	28.507	2024.335
OKLAHOMA	298.957	117.431	116.656	570.079	50.391	68.649	17.648	1239.811
TEXAS	1187.347	566.992	893.059	2599.101	438.993	387.339	60.789	6133.620
ROCKY MOUNTAIN:								
ARIZONA	191.806	120.664	118.120	444.033	7.637	62.963	14.274	959.496
COLORADO	251.170	143.223	96.698	511.196	8.060	47.642	12.497	1070.486
IDAHO	100.835	50.551	65.527	162.404	1.462	13.496	2.915	397.188
MONTANA	86.849	41.055	52.386	170.063	19.117	27.288	3.566	400.324
NEVADA	68.884	46.345	26.075	168.943	0.382	35.169	5.581	351.378
NEW MEXICO	109.608	60.017	59.366	274.908	17.252	44.766	11.625	577.542
UTAH	113.173	46.874	87.050	237.960	14.544	15.003	5.678	520.282
WYOMING	58.652	30.824	44.747	110.159	20.446	21.075	1.560	287.463
FAR WEST:								
ALASKA	60.308	27.353	32.072	129.805	7.587	14.811	5.859	277.796
CALIFORNIA	1772.570	1055.597	878.985	4184.340	206.352	554.996	95.087	8747.927
HAWAII	54.052	33.432	45.548	208.160	22.032	45.387	1.747	410.358
OREGON	245.105	117.913	122.253	471.839	13.297	60.953	5.724	1037.084
WASHINGTON	374.464	149.743	164.306	676.183	53.610	131.090	12.390	1561.785

Table 37

Consumption Of Energy In Trillion BTU And Expenditures On Energy In Million Dollars, 1972, By Region

Use By Function

REGION	RESIDENTIAL USE	COMMERCIAL USE	INDUSTRIAL USE	TRANSPOR-TATION USE	ENERGY USE		MUNICIPAL-INSTITU-TIONAL USE	ALL USE
					Non Electric Utility Use	Electric Utility Use		
Consumption In Trillion BTU								
NEW ENGLAND	908.23	318.38	406.45	867.20	22.98	731.35	14.80	3269.39
MID ATLANTIC	2539.33	729.74	2322.97	2503.62	268.24	2526.78	64.62	10955.29
EAST NORTH CENTRAL	2882.69	765.10	4535.71	2956.97	490.07	3367.65	76.43	15074.62
WEST NORTH CENTRAL	1061.45	323.36	1173.39	1375.61	322.89	1269.64	70.77	5597.10
SOUTH ATLANTIC	1228.02	517.00	1974.34	2695.42	101.15	2988.40	65.51	9569.84
EAST SOUTH CENTRAL	581.99	152.70	1397.23	1069.78	223.14	2116.10	26.00	5074.93
WEST SOUTH CENTRAL	898.42	316.62	3364.56	2000.56	2432.41	2176.74	108.66	11297.98
ROCKY MOUNTAIN	478.24	221.84	744.83	882.66	276.29	936.20	44.31	3584.36
FAR WEST	1233.40	471.10	1311.76	2717.48	588.45	2398.95	47.45	8768.60
TOTAL	11811.76	3815.83	17231.23	17069.31	4725.62	18019.79	518.55	73192.09
Expenditures In Million Dollars								
NEW ENGLAND	2095.42	751.35	682.68	2146.06	19.71	461.51	66.29	6223.03
MID ATLANTIC	5462.27	2165.91	2549.18	6200.41	164.97	1400.78	299.01	18242.55
EAST NORTH CENTRAL	5423.79	2049.00	3975.63	7537.28	286.10	1387.96	248.91	20908.66
WEST NORTH CENTRAL	2155.56	808.22	1033.65	3338.82	120.95	463.83	88.56	8009.58
SOUTH ATLANTIC	3427.88	1601.46	2071.36	6592.81	49.06	1413.51	172.43	15328.51
EAST SOUTH CENTRAL	1367.98	391.75	1224.49	2684.59	75.93	551.60	59.54	6335.88
WEST SOUTH CENTRAL	2086.41	927.51	1641.55	4300.83	693.55	614.39	113.81	10378.05
ROCKY MOUNTAIN	980.98	539.55	549.97	2079.67	88.90	267.40	57.70	4564.16
FAR WEST	2506.50	1384.04	1243.16	5670.33	302.88	807.24	120.81	12034.95
TOTAL	25506.79	10618.80	14971.67	40550.78	1802.05	7368.22	1227.05	102045.37

Table 38

Consumption Of Energy In Million BTU Per Capita, 1972, By State

Use By Function

REGION AND STATE	RESI-DENTIAL USE	COMMER-CIAL USE	INDUSTRIAL USE	TRANSPOR-TATION USE	ENERGY USE		MUNICIPAL-INSTITU-TIONAL USE	ALL USE
					Non Electric Utility Use	Electric Utility Use		
NEW ENGLAND:								
CONNECTICUT	59.994	16.060	34.254	64.647	0.803	85.609	1.639	263.006
MAINE	76.312	24.217	69.236	118.773	0.783	51.586	0.771	341.678
MASSACHUSETTS	81.886	34.652	28.794	68.166	1.959	57.234	1.162	273.853
NEW HAMPSHIRE	79.462	18.734	31.910	65.666	1.719	68.348	0.390	266.230
RHODE ISLAND	71.658	23.386	30.589	69.969	6.704	17.812	1.355	221.474
VERMONT	86.080	13.175	18.876	70.689	1.133	27.957	1.328	219.238
MID ATLANTIC:								
NEW JERSEY	73.709	19.197	35.186	77.449	11.899	53.832	0.582	271.855
NEW YORK	65.588	22.002	32.343	62.865	1.030	60.530	2.605	246.962
PENNSYLVANIA	66.609	15.502	123.506	65.503	13.597	85.629	1.050	371.396
EAST NORTH CENTRAL:								
ILLINOIS	74.578	23.020	75.837	76.728	17.918	81.910	2.008	351.998
INDIANA	70.100	20.816	185.576	77.657	24.275	106.190	1.033	485.648
MICHIGAN	70.994	17.405	101.002	72.468	4.593	69.740	1.390	337.593
OHIO	69.126	15.456	135.435	68.084	9.836	87.284	2.821	388.042
WISCONSIN	64.636	16.270	75.025	66.415	2.967	70.903	1.244	297.461
WEST NORTH CENTRAL:								
IOWA	64.777	19.911	81.944	75.484	7.492	65.628	1.490	316.727
KANSAS	63.455	20.233	122.134	86.040	80.993	85.816	3.248	461.918
MINNESOTA	68.756	18.826	71.198	77.865	8.898	60.962	6.883	313.388
MISSOURI	58.698	17.179	50.830	87.224	7.066	75.480	4.149	300.626
NEBRASKA	69.890	23.802	70.510	91.442	12.624	60.764	6.495	335.526
NORTH DAKOTA	56.873	23.461	23.420	80.419	45.983	183.538	0.920	414.615
SOUTH DAKOTA	62.734	20.988	29.633	82.546	1.623	120.393	3.262	321.179
SOUTH ATLANTIC:								
DELAWARE	61.652	27.853	126.469	77.419	8.956	86.641	0.227	389.218
DISTRICT OF COLUMBIA	48.633	77.235	9.266	46.171	1.159	46.797	3.194	232.455
FLORIDA	24.518	11.853	27.074	91.239	1.513	98.847	2.129	257.174
GEORGIA	37.492	15.345	60.787	94.822	2.083	73.313	1.269	285.110
MARYLAND	46.042	19.932	66.652	74.420	2.105	68.812	1.071	279.034
NORTH CAROLINA	41.953	14.294	56.962	74.993	1.440	103.893	1.967	295.502
SOUTH CAROLINA	34.889	11.456	81.821	78.947	1.722	92.161	1.253	302.249
VIRGINIA	43.464	15.247	47.321	101.461	6.818	62.996	4.230	281.536
WEST VIRGINIA	51.454	13.672	220.566	60.677	11.718	257.175	1.783	617.045
EAST SOUTH CENTRAL:								
ALABAMA	38.911	12.201	145.253	83.131	8.173	136.708	0.517	424.894
KENTUCKY	49.737	11.465	86.715	79.441	19.788	161.566	3.621	412.333
MISSISSIPPI	46.176	14.221	111.569	78.757	44.703	59.836	2.637	357.899
TENNESSEE	43.314	9.764	85.317	82.703	6.899	116.311	1.538	345.846
WEST SOUTH CENTRAL:								
ARKANSAS	53.810	17.228	99.003	86.334	13.821	57.815	1.159	329.169
LOUISIANA	39.248	14.418	287.032	94.321	174.575	107.418	10.026	727.038
OKLAHOMA	54.195	15.883	62.747	86.563	75.453	107.455	3.281	405.577
TEXAS	43.172	16.056	166.110	107.438	133.870	118.596	5.189	590.439
ROCKY MOUNTAIN:								
ARIZONA	32.912	17.916	55.890	90.485	14.570	83.198	3.274	298.247
COLORADO	57.084	29.156	67.993	93.039	7.810	65.369	1.668	322.117
IDAHO	56.968	26.219	87.730	84.897	6.851	98.188	3.664	364.516
MONTANA	62.640	31.299	95.696	106.309	55.372	146.888	4.582	502.786
NEVADA	50.803	26.517	38.203	132.580	0.841	175.695	12.614	437.254
NEW MEXICO	54.800	21.921	96.926	108.314	91.466	191.339	16.627	581.393
UTAH	60.441	17.851	125.700	90.780	24.688	32.251	1.356	353.067
WYOMING	105.968	51.147	211.884	159.980	166.813	298.185	5.058	999.036
FAR WEST:								
ALASKA	80.075	31.317	108.638	255.648	82.228	77.555	22.455	657.915
CALIFORNIA	44.952	16.192	44.187	99.092	19.957	60.400	1.678	286.458
HAWAII	10.010	7.544	18.302	150.176	33.218	63.958	0.276	283.483
OREGON	48.063	23.834	65.089	90.711	12.686	157.996	0.682	399.061
WASHINGTON	51.687	21.123	63.601	85.163	29.129	217.529	1.225	469.457

Table 39

Expenditures On Energy In Dollars Per Capita, 1972, By State

Use By Function

REGION AND STATE	RESIDENTIAL USE	COMMER- CIAL USE	INDUSTRIAL USE	TRANSPOR- TATION USE	ENERGY USE		MUNICIPAL- INSTITU- TIONAL USE	ALL USE
					Non Electric Utility Use	Electric Utility Use		
NEW ENGLAND:								
CONNECTICUT	153.129	55.417	60.853	179.770	0.709	56.963	5.442	512.281
MAINE	167.853	52.821	87.518	244.199	0.631	29.974	6.158	589.154
MASSACHUSETTS	183.207	72.257	50.535	162.130	1.855	35.877	5.053	510.914
NEW HAMPSHIRE	180.645	43.505	52.680	192.250	1.485	36.049	4.067	510.680
RHODE ISLAND	161.452	56.920	54.260	158.785	4.546	11.813	6.689	454.466
VERMONT	203.118	40.970	41.759	216.212	1.250	17.435	9.326	530.071
MID ATLANTIC:								
NEW JERSEY	162.959	61.324	60.743	184.372	7.817	37.117	3.836	518.167
NEW YORK	142.396	65.228	41.260	154.802	0.599	36.166	12.409	452.859
PENNSYLVANIA	138.538	43.444	112.974	168.182	8.109	38.955	3.605	513.807
EAST NORTH CENTRAL:								
ILLINOIS	139.251	61.483	74.283	184.376	10.493	34.394	7.610	511.889
INDIANA	138.600	48.642	129.352	201.414	14.485	34.760	3.294	570.547
MICHIGAN	130.221	45.998	97.741	181.260	2.378	33.492	5.299	496.388
OHIO	122.838	44.358	114.367	187.656	5.865	33.939	7.325	516.347
WISCONSIN	140.227	46.484	77.210	166.537	1.599	33.524	4.337	469.918
WEST NORTH CENTRAL:								
IOWA	140.987	51.960	69.694	201.370	1.890	26.096	4.506	496.503
KANSAS	106.835	52.326	70.948	198.008	27.080	32.703	3.655	491.555
MINNESOTA	138.328	43.365	76.269	191.230	4.815	26.039	7.429	487.475
MISSOURI	124.577	46.223	55.930	205.372	3.422	24.108	4.776	464.408
NEBRASKA	129.768	53.630	49.996	226.335	4.104	24.329	6.518	494.680
NORTH DAKOTA	129.790	54.389	26.121	177.090	18.754	41.734	4.044	451.922
SOUTH DAKOTA	144.735	52.522	25.871	197.889	1.484	52.007	4.824	479.331
SOUTH ATLANTIC:								
DELAWARE	158.268	72.587	154.852	205.308	6.104	54.174	2.830	654.123
DISTRICT OF COLUMBIA	113.151	161.025	10.879	130.207	0.648	31.980	8.551	456.441
FLORIDA	108.177	51.379	35.177	212.412	0.800	48.492	7.795	464.232
GEORGIA	96.734	50.475	63.800	228.706	0.676	32.981	2.699	476.072
MARYLAND	109.663	55.444	83.401	187.895	1.268	40.565	3.590	481.825
NORTH CAROLINA	111.996	41.597	68.463	209.102	0.770	47.473	4.033	483.435
SOUTH CAROLINA	105.071	37.773	85.980	208.310	0.728	45.168	3.400	486.430
VIRGINIA	108.281	44.992	48.217	213.103	3.539	31.164	9.481	458.776
WEST VIRGINIA	96.246	36.213	143.967	170.982	4.479	91.472	2.473	545.831
EAST SOUTH CENTRAL:								
ALABAMA	103.502	33.971	107.690	205.744	2.831	51.794	1.997	507.529
KENTUCKY	100.372	28.595	88.453	199.884	7.890	46.081	7.789	479.063
MISSISSIPPI	118.631	40.892	72.090	206.718	14.508	22.597	4.238	479.674
TENNESSEE	99.237	20.960	95.838	204.566	1.755	40.743	4.223	467.323
WEST SOUTH CENTRAL:								
ARKANSAS	123.530	44.016	70.658	218.094	4.502	23.971	3.421	488.191
LOUISIANA	94.183	41.387	131.074	185.585	52.199	29.500	7.626	541.556
OKLAHOMA	113.542	44.600	44.305	216.513	19.138	26.073	6.703	470.874
TEXAS	102.322	48.862	76.961	223.983	37.831	33.380	5.239	528.578
ROCKY MOUNTAIN:								
ARIZONA	97.711	61.469	60.173	226.201	3.890	32.075	7.272	488.791
COLORADO	106.248	60.585	40.904	216.242	3.410	20.153	5.286	452.828
IDAHO	133.556	66.954	86.791	215.104	1.936	17.875	3.861	526.077
MONTANA	121.297	57.339	73.164	237.519	26.699	38.112	4.980	559.111
NEVADA	129.239	86.950	48.920	316.966	0.716	65.983	10.471	659.246
NEW MEXICO	101.866	55.778	55.173	255.491	16.033	41.604	10.804	536.749
UTAH	100.420	41.592	77.241	211.144	12.905	13.312	5.038	461.652
WYOMING	169.514	89.088	129.327	318.378	59.092	60.911	4.509	830.818
FAR WEST:								
ALASKA	185.564	84.164	98.684	399.399	23.345	45.574	18.028	854.758
CALIFORNIA	86.844	51.717	43.064	205.004	10.110	27.191	4.659	428.589
HAWAII	66.240	40.971	55.819	255.098	26.999	55.622	2.141	502.890
OREGON	112.176	53.965	55.951	215.945	6.085	27.896	2.620	474.638
WASHINGTON	109.556	43.810	48.071	197.830	15.685	38.353	3.625	456.929

Table 40

Consumption Of Energy In Million BTU Per Capita And Expenditures On Energy In Dollars Per Capita, 1972, By Region

Use By Function

REGION	RESI-DENTIAL USE	COMMER-CIAL USE	INDUSTRIAL USE	TRANSPOR-TATION USE	ENERGY USE		MUNICIPAL-INSTITU-TIONAL USE	ALL USE
					Non Electric Utility	Electric Utility		

Consumption In Million BTU Per Capita

REGION	RESI-DENTIAL USE	COMMER-CIAL USE	INDUSTRIAL USE	TRANSPOR-TATION USE	Non Electric Utility	Electric Utility	MUNICIPAL-INSTITU-TIONAL USE	ALL USE
NEW ENGLAND	75.029	26.301	33.577	71.640	1.899	60.417	1.222	270.086
MID ATLANTIC	67.498	19.397	61.747	66.549	7.130	67.164	1.718	291.201
EAST NORTH CENTRAL	70.670	18.756	111.194	72.491	12.014	82.559	1.874	369.557
WEST NORTH CENTRAL	63.873	19.458	70.610	82.778	19.430	76.401	4.258	336.809
SOUTH ATLANTIC	38.472	16.197	61.853	84.443	3.169	93.621	2.052	299.807
EAST SOUTH CENTRAL	44.241	11.608	106.213	81.321	16.962	123.458	1.977	385.780
WEST SOUTH CENTRAL	44.959	15.844	168.371	100.113	121.724	108.930	5.438	565.379
ROCKY MOUNTAIN	53.856	24.981	83.877	99.398	31.114	105.428	4.990	403.644
FAR WEST	45.421	17.349	48.306	100.073	21.670	88.343	1.747	322.909
UNITED STATES	56.725	18.325	82.752	81.974	22.694	86.539	2.490	351.500

Expenditures In Dollars Per Capita

REGION	RESI-DENTIAL USE	COMMER-CIAL USE	INDUSTRIAL USE	TRANSPOR-TATION USE	Non Electric Utility	Electric Utility	MUNICIPAL-INSTITU-TIONAL USE	ALL USE
NEW ENGLAND	173.104	62.070	56.397	177.287	1.628	38.126	5.476	514.088
MID ATLANTIC	145.192	57.572	67.760	164.812	4.385	37.234	7.948	484.903
EAST NORTH CENTRAL	132.965	50.232	97.463	184.778	7.014	34.026	6.102	512.580
WEST NORTH CENTRAL	129.713	48.635	62.200	200.916	7.278	27.911	5.329	481.982
SOUTH ATLANTIC	107.390	50.171	64.892	206.542	1.537	44.283	5.402	480.216
EAST SOUTH CENTRAL	103.990	29.779	93.082	204.074	5.772	41.931	4.526	483.153
WEST SOUTH CENTRAL	104.409	46.415	82.147	215.224	34.707	30.746	5.695	519.344
ROCKY MOUNTAIN	110.470	60.760	61.933	234.197	10.011	30.113	6.497	513.982
FAR WEST	92.303	50.968	45.780	208.813	11.154	29.727	4.449	443.195
UNITED STATES	122.495	50.996	71.900	194.742	8.654	35.385	5.893	490.066

Table 41

Per Capita Consumption Of Energy In Index Number Terms, U.S. = 100, 1972, By State (U.S. BTU Per Capita Set At 100.)

Use By Function

REGION AND STATE	RESIDENTIAL USE	COMMER- CIAL USE	INDUSTRIAL USE	TRANSPOR- TATION USE	ENERGY USE		MUNICIPAL- INSTITU- TIONAL USE	ALL USE
					Non Electric Utility Use	Electric Utility Use		
NEW ENGLAND:								
CONNECTICUT	105.763	87.640	41.394	78.863	3.538	98.925	65.823	74.824
MAINE	134.530	132.153	83.667	144.891	3.450	59.610	30.964	97.206
MASSACHUSETTS	144.356	189.097	34.796	83.156	8.632	66.137	46.667	77.910
NEW HAMPSHIRE	140.083	102.232	38.561	80.106	7.575	78.979	15.663	75.741
RHODE ISLAND	126.325	127.618	36.965	85.355	29.541	20.583	54.418	63.008
VERMONT	151.750	71.896	22.810	86.233	4.993	32.306	53.333	62.372
MID ATLANTIC:								
NEW JERSEY	129.941	104.759	42.520	94.480	52.432	62.205	23.373	77.341
NEW YORK	115.625	120.065	39.084	76.689	4.539	69.945	104.618	70.259
PENNSYLVANIA	117.424	84.595	149.248	79.907	59.915	98.948	42.169	105.660
EAST NORTH CENTRAL:								
ILLINOIS	131.473	125.621	91.644	93.600	78.955	94.651	80.643	100.142
INDIANA	123.579	113.593	224.256	94.734	106.967	122.708	41.486	138.164
MICHIGAN	125.155	94.980	122.054	88.404	20.239	80.588	55.823	96.044
OHIO	121.862	84.344	163.664	83.056	43.342	100.861	113.293	110.396
WISCONSIN	113.946	88.786	90.662	81.020	13.074	81.932	49.960	84.626
WEST NORTH CENTRAL:								
IOWA	114.195	108.655	99.024	92.083	33.013	75.836	59.839	90.107
KANSAS	111.864	110.412	147.590	104.960	356.892	99.165	130.442	131.413
MINNESOTA	121.209	102.734	86.038	94.987	39.209	70.445	276.426	89.157
MISSOURI	103.478	93.746	61.424	106.404	31.136	87.221	166.627	85.527
NEBRASKA	123.208	129.888	85.206	111.550	55.627	70.216	260.843	95.455
NORTH DAKOTA	100.261	128.027	28.301	98.103	202.622	212.087	36.948	117.956
SOUTH DAKOTA	110.593	114.532	35.809	100.698	7.152	139.120	131.004	91.374
SOUTH ATLANTIC:								
DELAWARE	108.686	151.995	152.829	94.443	39.464	100.118	9.116	110.731
DISTRICT OF COLUMBIA	85.735	421.473	11.197	56.324	5.107	54.076	128.273	66.132
FLORIDA	43.223	64.682	32.717	111.302	6.667	114.222	85.502	73.165
GEORGIA	66.094	83.738	73.457	115.673	9.179	84.717	50.964	81.112
MARYLAND	81.167	108.769	80.544	90.785	9.276	79.516	43.012	79.384
NORTH CAROLINA	73.959	78.003	68.835	91.484	6.345	120.053	78.996	84.069
SOUTH CAROLINA	61.506	62.516	98.875	96.307	7.588	106.496	50.321	85.988
VIRGINIA	76.622	83.203	57.184	123.772	30.043	72.795	169.880	80.096
WEST VIRGINIA	90.708	74.608	266.539	74.020	51.635	297.178	71.606	175.546
EAST SOUTH CENTRAL:								
ALABAMA	68.596	66.581	175.528	101.411	36.014	157.973	20.763	120.880
KENTUCKY	87.681	62.565	104.789	96.910	87.195	186.697	145.422	117.307
MISSISSIPPI	81.403	77.604	134.823	96.076	196.982	69.143	105.904	101.820
TENNESSEE	76.358	53.282	103.100	100.889	30.400	134.403	61.767	98.391
WEST SOUTH CENTRAL:								
ARKANSAS	94.861	94.014	119.638	105.319	60.902	66.808	46.546	93.647
LOUISIANA	69.190	78.679	346.858	115.062	769.256	124.127	402.651	206.839
OKLAHOMA	95.540	86.674	75.825	105.598	332.480	124.169	131.767	115.385
TEXAS	76.108	87.618	200.742	131.064	589.892	137.043	208.394	167.977
ROCKY MOUNTAIN:								
ARIZONA	58.020	97.768	67.539	110.383	64.202	96.139	131.486	84.850
COLORADO	100.633	159.105	82.165	113.498	34.414	75.537	66.988	91.641
IDAHO	100.428	143.078	106.016	103.566	30.189	113.461	147.149	103.703
MONTANA	110.428	170.799	115.642	129.686	243.994	169.736	184.016	143.040
NEVADA	89.560	144.704	46.166	161.734	3.706	203.024	506.586	124.397
NEW MEXICO	96.606	119.623	117.128	132.132	403.040	221.101	667.751	165.403
UTAH	106.551	97.413	151.900	110.742	108.786	37.268	54.458	100.446
WYOMING	186.810	279.110	256.047	195.159	735.053	344.567	203.133	284.221
FAR WEST:								
ALASKA	141.164	170.898	131.281	311.865	362.334	89.619	901.807	187.174
CALIFORNIA	79.245	88.360	53.397	120.882	87.940	69.795	67.390	81.496
HAWAII	17.647	41.168	22.117	183.200	146.373	73.907	11.084	80.650
OREGON	84.730	130.063	78.656	110.658	55.900	182.572	27.390	113.531
WASHINGTON	91.119	115.269	76.857	103.890	128.356	251.365	49.197	133.558

Table 42

Per Capita Expenditures On Energy In Index Number Terms, U.S. = 100, 1972, By State

Use By Function

REGION AND STATE	RESIDENTIAL USE	COMMER-CIAL USE	INDUSTRIAL USE	TRANSPOR-TATION USE	ENERGY USE		MUNICIPAL-INSTITU-TIONAL	ALL USE
					Non Electric Utility Use	Electric Utility Use		
NEW ENGLAND:								
CONNECTICUT	125.008	108.669	84.636	92.312	8.193	160.981	92.347	104.533
MAINE	137.028	103.579	121.722	125.396	7.291	84.708	104.497	120.219
MASSACHUSETTS	149.563	141.692	70.285	83.254	21.435	101.390	85.746	104.254
NEW HAMPSHIRE	147.471	85.311	73.268	98.720	17.160	101.877	69.014	104.206
RHODE ISLAND	131.803	111.617	75.466	81.536	52.531	33.384	113.508	92.736
VERMONT	165.817	80.340	58.079	111.025	14.444	49.272	158.256	108.163
MID ATLANTIC:								
NEW JERSEY	133.033	120.253	84.483	94.675	90.328	104.895	65.094	105.734
NEW YORK	116.246	127.908	57.385	79.491	6.922	102.207	210.572	92.408
PENNSYLVANIA	113.097	85.191	157.127	86.361	93.702	110.089	61.174	104.844
EAST NORTH CENTRAL:								
ILLINOIS	113.679	120.564	103.314	94.677	121.250	97.199	129.136	104.453
INDIANA	113.147	95.384	179.905	103.426	167.379	98.234	55.897	116.422
MICHIGAN	106.307	90.199	135.940	93.077	27.479	94.650	89.920	101.290
OHIO	100.280	86.983	159.064	96.361	67.772	95.914	124.300	105.363
WISCONSIN	114.476	91.152	107.385	85.517	18.477	94.741	73.596	95.889
WEST NORTH CENTRAL:								
IOWA	115.096	101.890	96.932	103.403	21.840	73.749	76.464	101.313
KANSAS	87.216	102.608	98.676	101.677	312.919	92.421	62.023	100.304
MINNESOTA	112.925	85.036	106.076	98.197	55.639	73.588	126.065	99.471
MISSOURI	101.700	90.640	77.789	105.459	39.542	68.131	81.045	94.764
NEBRASKA	105.937	105.165	69.535	116.223	47.423	68.755	110.606	100.942
NORTH DAKOTA	105.955	106.653	36.330	90.936	216.709	117.943	68.624	92.217
SOUTH DAKOTA	118.156	102.992	35.982	101.616	17.148	146.975	81.860	97.809
SOUTH ATLANTIC:								
DELAWARE	129.204	142.339	215.371	105.426	70.534	153.099	48.023	133.477
DISTRICT OF COLUMBIA	92.372	315.760	15.131	66.861	7.488	90.377	145.104	93.139
FLORIDA	88.311	100.751	48.925	109.074	9.244	137.041	132.276	94.728
GEORGIA	78.970	98.978	88.734	117.441	7.811	93.206	45.800	97.144
MARYLAND	89.524	108.722	115.996	96.484	14.652	114.639	60.920	98.318
NORTH CAROLINA	91.429	81.569	95.220	107.374	8.898	134.161	68.437	98.647
SOUTH CAROLINA	85.776	74.071	119.583	106.967	8.412	127.647	57.696	99.258
VIRGINIA	88.396	88.227	67.061	109.428	40.894	88.071	160.886	93.615
WEST VIRGINIA	78.571	71.011	200.232	87.799	51.756	258.505	41.965	111.379
EAST SOUTH CENTRAL:								
ALABAMA	84.495	66.615	149.777	105.650	32.713	146.373	33.888	103.563
KENTUCKY	81.940	56.073	123.022	102.640	91.172	130.227	132.174	97.755
MISSISSIPPI	96.846	80.187	100.264	106.150	167.645	63.860	71.916	97.879
TENNESSEE	81.013	41.101	133.293	105.045	20.280	115.142	71.661	95.359
WEST SOUTH CENTRAL:								
ARKANSAS	100.845	86.313	98.273	111.991	52.022	67.743	58.052	99.617
LOUISIANA	76.887	81.157	182.300	95.298	603.178	83.369	129.408	110.507
OKLAHOMA	92.691	87.458	61.620	111.179	221.146	73.684	113.745	96.084
TEXAS	83.532	95.815	107.039	115.015	437.150	94.334	88.902	107.859
ROCKY MOUNTAIN:								
ARIZONA	79.767	120.537	83.690	116.154	44.950	90.646	123.401	99.740
COLORADO	86.737	118.803	56.890	111.040	39.404	56.954	89.700	92.401
IDAHO	109.030	131.293	120.711	110.456	22.371	50.516	65.518	107.348
MONTANA	99.022	112.438	101.758	121.966	308.516	107.707	84.507	114.089
NEVADA	105.506	170.504	68.039	162.762	8.274	186.472	177.685	134.522
NEW MEXICO	83.159	109.377	76.736	131.195	185.267	117.575	183.336	109.526
UTAH	81.979	81.559	107.428	108.422	149.122	37.620	85.491	94.202
WYOMING	138.384	174.696	179.871	163.487	682.829	172.138	76.515	169.532
FAR WEST:								
ALASKA	151.487	165.040	137.252	205.091	269.760	128.795	305.922	174.417
CALIFORNIA	70.896	101.414	59.894	105.270	116.825	76.843	79.060	87.455
HAWAII	54.076	80.342	77.634	130.993	311.983	157.191	36.331	102.617
OREGON	91.576	105.822	77.818	110.888	70.314	78.836	44.460	96.852
WASHINGTON	89.437	85.909	66.858	101.586	181.246	108.388	61.514	93.238

Table 43

Per Capita Use Of Energy In Index Number Terms, U.S. = 100, 1972, Based On Consumption In Million BTU And Expenditures In Dollars, By Region

Use By Function

REGION	RESIDENTIAL USE	COMMERCIAL USE	INDUSTRIAL USE	TRANSPORTATION USE	ENERGY USE		MUNICIPAL-INSTITUTIONAL USE	ALL USE
					Non Electric Utility Use	Electric Utility Use		
Index Of Per Capita Consumption, U.S. = 100								
NEW ENGLAND	132.268	143.525	40.575	87.394	8.368	69.815	49.076	76.838
MID ATLANTIC	118.992	105.850	74.617	81.183	31.418	77.611	68.996	82.845
EAST NORTH CENTRAL	124.584	102.352	134.370	88.432	52.939	95.401	75.261	105.137
WEST NORTH CENTRAL	112.601	106.183	85.327	100.981	85.617	88.285	171.004	95.820
SOUTH ATLANTIC	67.822	88.387	74.745	103.012	13.964	108.184	82.410	85.294
EAST SOUTH CENTRAL	77.992	63.345	128.351	99.203	74.742	142.662	79.398	109.752
WEST SOUTH CENTRAL	79.258	86.461	203.465	122.128	536.371	125.874	218.394	160.848
ROCKY MOUNTAIN	94.942	136.322	101.359	121.256	137.102	121.827	200.402	114.835
FAR WEST	80.072	94.674	58.374	122.079	95.488	102.085	70.161	91.866
UNITED STATES	100.000	100.000	100.000	100.000	100.000	100.000	100.000	100.000
Index Of Per Capita Expenditures, U.S. = 100								
NEW ENGLAND	141.315	121.715	78.438	91.037	18.812	107.746	92.924	104.902
MID ATLANTIC	118.529	112.895	94.242	84.631	50.670	105.225	134.872	98.946
EAST NORTH CENTRAL	108.547	98.502	135.554	94.883	81.049	96.159	103.547	104.594
WEST NORTH CENTRAL	105.892	95.370	86.509	103.170	84.100	78.878	90.429	98.350
SOUTH ATLANTIC	87.669	98.382	90.253	106.059	17.761	125.146	91.668	97.990
EAST SOUTH CENTRAL	84.893	58.395	129.460	104.792	66.697	118.499	76.803	98.589
WEST SOUTH CENTRAL	85.235	91.017	114.252	110.518	401.052	86.890	96.640	105.974
ROCKY MOUNTAIN	90.183	119.147	86.138	120.260	115.681	85.101	110.249	104.880
FAR WEST	75.352	99.945	63.672	107.225	128.888	84.010	75.496	90.436
UNITED STATES	100.000	100.000	100.000	100.000	100.000	100.000	100.000	100.000

Table 44

Consumption Of Energy In Million BTU Per Capita, 1972, By State

Residential Use By Fuel Category

REGION AND STATE	PETROLEUM HEATING FUELS USE	OTHER PETROLEUM PRODUCTS USE	NATURAL GAS USE	ELECTRICITY USE	COAL USE	TOTAL RESIDENTIAL USE
NEW ENGLAND:						
CONNECTICUT	39.101	0.195	12.711	7.955	0.032	59.994
MAINE	68.120	0.091	0.963	7.040	0.097	76.312
MASSACHUSETTS	58.080	0.191	17.312	6.139	0.164	81.886
NEW HAMPSHIRE	63.830	0.198	6.750	8.296	0.388	79.462
RHODE ISLAND	50.475	0.111	15.464	5.556	0.052	71.658
VERMONT	71.757	0.265	3.038	10.585	0.435	86.080
MID ATLANTIC:						
NEW JERSEY	42.860	0.111	23.976	6.285	0.476	73.709
NEW YORK	35.701	0.122	23.932	5.106	0.727	65.588
PENNSYLVANIA	24.665	0.147	29.009	7.152	5.636	66.609
EAST NORTH CENTRAL:						
ILLINOIS	14.268	0.336	49.608	6.884	3.482	74.578
INDIANA	22.888	0.008	34.104	8.607	4.493	70.100
MICHIGAN	19.184	0.175	42.342	7.213	2.080	70.994
OHIO	9.534	0.336	48.316	7.616	3.325	69.126
WISCONSIN	26.153	0.038	25.606	8.088	4.750	64.636
WEST NORTH CENTRAL:						
IOWA	20.138	0.145	35.475	8.291	0.728	64.777
KANSAS	9.141	0.064	45.968	8.061	0.220	63.455
MINNESOTA	27.902	0.040	30.940	7.694	2.180	68.756
MISSOURI	13.534	0.097	36.634	7.885	0.548	58.698
NEBRASKA	18.653	0.028	41.989	8.566	0.654	69.890
NORTH DAKOTA	27.324	0.206	18.769	8.051	2.524	56.873
SOUTH DAKOTA	30.561	0.004	20.883	8.344	2.941	62.734
SOUTH ATLANTIC:						
DELAWARE	36.762	0.164	15.843	7.744	1.138	61.652
DISTRICT OF COLUMBIA	17.451	0.019	24.338	6.692	0.133	48.633
FLORIDA	7.569	0.314	3.174	13.365	0.095	24.518
GEORGIA	7.697	0.176	19.365	10.043	0.211	37.492
MARYLAND	18.650	0.057	20.377	6.477	0.482	46.042
NORTH CAROLINA	22.153	0.589	6.829	10.447	1.934	41.953
SOUTH CAROLINA	14.391	0.189	8.170	9.981	2.158	34.889
VIRGINIA	18.752	0.255	12.993	9.070	2.392	43.464
WEST VIRGINIA	5.407	0.060	34.485	7.379	4.123	51.454
EAST SOUTH CENTRAL:						
ALABAMA	10.179	0.237	16.016	11.969	0.511	38.911
KENTUCKY	10.439	0.332	26.997	9.337	2.632	49.737
MISSISSIPPI	15.326	2.272	18.138	9.731	0.709	46.176
TENNESSEE	8.431	0.515	14.110	17.238	3.021	43.314
WEST SOUTH CENTRAL:						
ARKANSAS	20.995	0.374	24.026	8.414	0.000	53.810
LOUISIANA	4.705	1.301	23.319	9.924	0.000	39.248
OKLAHOMA	13.802	0.280	31.014	9.100	0.000	54.195
TEXAS	9.840	0.801	22.200	10.322	0.009	43.172
ROCKY MOUNTAIN:						
ARIZONA	3.404	0.072	19.925	9.511	0.000	32.912
COLORADO	11.558	0.498	38.913	5.861	0.254	57.084
IDAHO	27.628	0.469	16.072	12.798	0.000	56.968
MONTANA	17.224	1.212	35.497	8.149	0.559	62.640
NEVADA	14.950	0.016	20.755	15.082	0.000	50.803
NEW MEXICO	13.386	0.833	35.686	4.896	0.000	54.800
UTAH	11.786	0.458	41.820	5.934	0.444	60.441
WYOMING	31.298	1.073	66.661	6.647	0.289	105.968
FAR WEST:						
ALASKA	45.088	0.070	28.710	5.900	0.308	80.075
CALIFORNIA	2.208	0.015	36.066	6.664	0.000	44.952
HAWAII	3.720	0.059	0.000	6.230	0.000	10.010
OREGON	17.963	0.103	12.911	17.041	0.046	48.063
WASHINGTON	18.850	0.027	14.151	18.630	0.029	51.687

Table 45

Expenditures On Energy In Dollars Per Capita, 1972, By State

Residential Use By Fuel Category

REGION AND STATE	PETROLEUM HEATING FUELS USE	OTHER PETROLEUM PRODUCTS USE	NATURAL GAS USE	ELECTRICITY USE	COAL USE	TOTAL RESIDENTIAL USE
NEW ENGLAND:						
CONNECTICUT	62.123	0.318	25.540	65.095	0.053	153.129
MAINE	108.402	0.148	2.873	56.279	0.151	167.853
MASSACHUSETTS	89.078	0.307	38.070	55.525	0.227	183.207
NEW HAMPSHIRE	101.902	0.313	13.006	64.913	0.511	180.645
RHODE ISLAND	79.578	0.182	30.853	50.765	0.073	161.452
VERMONT	120.882	0.438	5.192	75.930	0.676	203.118
MID ATLANTIC:						
NEW JERSEY	59.930	0.164	45.635	56.456	0.773	162.959
NEW YORK	55.528	0.204	36.877	48.742	1.045	142.396
PENNSYLVANIA	35.782	0.221	37.477	58.044	7.015	138.538
EAST NORTH CENTRAL:						
ILLINOIS	23.258	0.479	53.504	57.345	4.665	139.251
INDIANA	37.512	0.012	38.192	57.508	5.376	138.600
MICHIGAN	30.632	0.264	45.375	51.184	2.767	130.221
OHIO	15.709	0.502	49.340	53.065	4.223	122.838
WISCONSIN	43.817	0.057	33.010	56.681	6.662	140.227
WEST NORTH CENTRAL:						
IOWA	36.300	0.210	38.447	65.044	0.986	140.987
KANSAS	16.999	0.080	33.562	55.944	0.250	106.835
MINNESOTA	40.591	0.053	37.069	57.422	3.192	138.328
MISSOURI	24.341	0.136	39.186	60.273	0.641	124.577
NEBRASKA	32.173	0.038	40.396	56.284	0.878	129.768
NORTH DAKOTA	44.569	0.299	19.995	61.315	3.612	129.790
SOUTH DAKOTA	55.047	0.006	22.964	62.178	4.540	144.735
SOUTH ATLANTIC:						
DELAWARE	61.199	0.263	26.243	68.902	1.661	158.268
DISTRICT OF COLUMBIA	28.089	0.028	35.755	49.072	0.207	113.151
FLORIDA	18.121	0.530	6.426	82.973	0.128	108.177
GEORGIA	16.646	0.257	23.329	56.217	0.285	96.734
MARYLAND	26.159	0.081	32.641	50.080	0.703	109.663
NORTH CAROLINA	36.863	0.902	9.311	62.335	2.585	111.996
SOUTH CAROLINA	27.491	0.303	12.679	61.650	2.948	105.071
VIRGINIA	29.032	0.381	19.824	55.948	3.096	108.281
WEST VIRGINIA	8.897	0.088	32.230	50.077	4.953	96.246
EAST SOUTH CENTRAL:						
ALABAMA	24.579	0.322	19.472	58.491	0.638	103.502
KENTUCKY	24.160	0.505	24.469	48.227	3.010	100.372
MISSISSIPPI	39.405	3.279	19.047	56.045	0.854	118.631
TENNESSEE	16.880	0.758	14.055	63.807	3.737	99.237
WEST SOUTH CENTRAL:						
ARKANSAS	46.683	0.545	19.707	56.595	0.000	123.530
LOUISIANA	8.615	1.590	20.577	63.401	0.000	94.183
OKLAHOMA	22.372	0.312	26.798	64.059	0.000	113.542
TEXAS	16.975	0.999	21.580	62.757	0.012	102.322
ROCKY MOUNTAIN:						
ARIZONA	8.540	0.110	22.730	66.331	0.000	97.711
COLORADO	29.541	0.765	30.946	44.700	0.296	106.248
IDAHO	50.254	0.722	22.543	60.037	0.000	133.556
MONTANA	34.320	1.711	32.903	51.508	0.855	121.297
NEVADA	32.283	0.026	27.988	68.942	0.000	129.239
NEW MEXICO	29.819	1.094	31.840	39.112	0.000	101.866
UTAH	20.392	0.623	39.933	38.992	0.481	100.420
WYOMING	71.201	1.558	48.025	48.376	0.355	169.514
FAR WEST:						
ALASKA	84.140	0.131	43.080	57.615	0.598	185.564
CALIFORNIA	4.986	0.021	36.154	45.683	0.000	86.844
HAWAII	14.267	0.114	0.000	51.859	0.000	66.240
OREGON	27.807	0.147	20.357	63.822	0.043	112.176
WASHINGTON	33.010	0.045	19.042	57.433	0.028	109.556

Table 46

Consumption Of Energy In Million BTU Per Capita and Expenditures On Energy In Dollars Per Capita, 1972, By Region

Residential Use By Fuel Category

REGION	PETROLEUM HEATING FUELS USE	OTHER PETROLEUM PRODUCTS USE	NATURAL GAS USE	ELECTRICITY USE	COAL USE	TOTAL RESIDENTIAL USE
Consumption In Million BTU Per Capita						
NEW ENGLAND	54.380	0.181	13.390	6.938	0.140	75.029
MID ATLANTIC	33.607	0.128	25.547	5.984	2.231	67.498
EAST NORTH CENTRAL	16.546	0.225	42.991	7.506	3.403	70.670
WEST NORTH CENTRAL	19.126	0.082	35.545	8.023	1.098	63.873
SOUTH ATLANTIC	14.256	0.263	12.727	10.001	1.225	38.472
EAST SOUTH CENTRAL	10.586	0.696	18.550	12.555	1.855	44.241
WEST SOUTH CENTRAL	10.522	0.783	23.754	9.895	0.005	44.959
ROCKY MOUNTAIN	12.802	0.488	32.467	7.919	0.180	53.856
FAR WEST	6.129	0.025	30.272	8.983	0.011	45.421
UNITED STATES	19.210	0.268	27.387	8.380	1.480	56.725
Expenditures In Dollars Per Capita						
NEW ENGLAND	85.126	0.291	28.469	59.019	0.199	173.104
MID ATLANTIC	50.139	0.202	38.778	53.192	2.881	145.192
EAST NORTH CENTRAL	27.031	0.330	46.355	54.806	4.443	132.965
WEST NORTH CENTRAL	31.954	0.114	36.512	59.596	1.537	129.713
SOUTH ATLANTIC	24.892	0.410	17.752	62.728	1.607	107.390
EAST SOUTH CENTRAL	24.633	1.010	18.978	57.138	2.230	103.990
WEST SOUTH CENTRAL	19.107	0.973	21.892	62.430	0.007	104.409
ROCKY MOUNTAIN	27.705	0.701	30.310	51.531	0.222	110.470
FAR WEST	11.576	0.038	31.726	48.950	0.014	92.303
UNITED STATES	31.750	0.382	32.107	56.332	1.925	122.495

Table 47

Consumption Of Energy In Million BTU Per Capita, 1972, By State

Commercial Use By Fuel Category

REGION AND STATE	PETROLEUM HEATING FUELS USE	OTHER PETROLEUM PRODUCTS USE	NATURAL GAS USE	ELECTRICITY USE	COAL USE	TOTAL COMMERCIAL USE
NEW ENGLAND:						
CONNECTICUT	7.772	0.685	1.843	5.759	0.000	16.060
MAINE	19.020	0.974	0.232	3.991	0.000	24.217
MASSACHUSETTS	26.074	0.921	2.568	5.089	0.000	34.652
NEW HAMPSHIRE	13.416	0.740	1.303	3.275	0.000	18.734
RHODE ISLAND	16.168	0.625	1.826	4.768	0.000	23.386
VERMONT	7.522	0.876	0.548	4.228	0.000	13.175
MID ATLANTIC:						
NEW JERSEY	9.358	0.646	3.555	5.638	0.000	19.197
NEW YORK	13.238	0.480	3.224	5.060	0.000	22.002
PENNSYLVANIA	6.027	0.949	4.115	4.411	0.000	15.502
EAST NORTH CENTRAL:						
ILLINOIS	8.329	1.340	7.407	5.944	0.000	23.020
INDIANA	9.543	1.136	5.405	4.733	0.000	20.816
MICHIGAN	5.954	0.625	6.319	4.508	0.000	17.405
OHIO	3.038	0.697	6.454	5.267	0.000	15.456
WISCONSIN	8.131	0.560	3.318	4.261	0.000	16.270
WEST NORTH CENTRAL:						
IOWA	6.553	1.713	7.141	4.504	0.000	19.911
KANSAS	3.454	0.840	8.622	7.317	0.000	20.233
MINNESOTA	9.481	0.725	5.319	3.301	0.000	18.826
MISSOURI	5.640	0.571	6.192	4.776	0.000	17.179
NEBRASKA	6.740	0.955	8.773	7.333	0.000	23.802
NORTH DAKOTA	10.053	2.758	5.570	5.080	0.000	23.461
SOUTH DAKOTA	9.392	2.219	4.971	4.405	0.000	20.988
SOUTH ATLANTIC:						
DELAWARE	10.272	8.156	3.019	6.406	0.000	27.853
DISTRICT OF COLUMBIA	49.443	0.738	12.263	14.791	0.000	77.235
FLORIDA	2.706	0.911	1.280	6.955	0.000	11.853
GEORGIA	3.011	1.313	4.111	6.910	0.000	15.345
MARYLAND	10.451	0.827	3.321	5.334	0.000	19.932
NORTH CAROLINA	4.279	2.188	1.591	6.236	0.000	14.294
SOUTH CAROLINA	1.991	1.296	2.229	5.939	0.000	11.456
VIRGINIA	4.653	1.768	2.805	6.021	0.000	15.247
WEST VIRGINIA	2.316	0.415	6.330	4.611	0.000	13.672
EAST SOUTH CENTRAL:						
ALABAMA	0.811	1.394	4.898	5.097	0.000	12.201
KENTUCKY	1.035	0.815	4.938	4.678	0.000	11.465
MISSISSIPPI	0.780	3.936	4.189	5.316	0.000	14.221
TENNESSEE	1.166	0.781	4.824	2.992	0.000	9.764
WEST SOUTH CENTRAL:						
ARKANSAS	1.114	3.768	6.936	5.410	0.000	17.228
LOUISIANA	0.164	3.878	4.577	5.799	0.000	14.418
OKLAHOMA	0.734	0.956	7.549	6.644	0.000	15.883
TEXAS	0.917	2.960	4.083	8.095	0.000	16.056
ROCKY MOUNTAIN:						
ARIZONA	0.067	1.169	7.697	8.983	0.000	17.916
COLORADO	1.455	1.866	16.141	7.240	2.453	29.156
IDAHO	2.268	3.097	7.020	11.980	1.854	26.219
MONTANA	2.194	3.441	13.903	6.314	5.447	31.299
NEVADA	1.516	1.916	8.457	14.627	0.000	26.517
NEW MEXICO	0.349	3.547	10.814	7.211	0.000	21.921
UTAH	3.039	1.665	4.144	5.365	3.638	17.851
WYOMING	5.898	2.790	27.883	11.686	2.890	51.147
FAR WEST:						
ALASKA	2.765	3.990	17.614	5.102	1.846	31.317
CALIFORNIA	0.439	0.712	7.220	7.816	0.005	16.192
HAWAII	0.929	3.111	0.000	3.504	0.000	7.544
OREGON	8.664	0.978	3.902	9.969	0.320	23.834
WASHINGTON	6.225	1.669	4.301	8.665	0.263	21.123

Table 48

Expenditures On Energy In Dollars Per Capita, 1972, By State

Commercial Use By Fuel Category

REGION AND STATE	PETROLEUM HEATING FUELS USE	OTHER PETROLEUM PRODUCTS USE	NATURAL GAS USE	ELECTRICITY USE	COAL USE	TOTAL COMMERCIAL USE
NEW ENGLAND:						
CONNECTICUT	7.849	0.855	3.150	43.563	0.000	55.417
MAINE	19.758	1.190	0.416	31.457	0.000	52.821
MASSACHUSETTS	25.211	1.006	4.560	41.481	0.000	72.257
NEW HAMPSHIRE	13.035	0.966	2.184	27.320	0.000	43.505
RHODE ISLAND	17.049	0.732	3.368	35.771	0.000	56.920
VERMONT	8.086	1.193	0.728	30.963	0.000	40.970
MID ATLANTIC:						
NEW JERSEY	9.317	0.756	5.215	46.036	0.000	61.324
NEW YORK	12.116	0.605	4.238	48.268	0.000	65.228
PENNSYLVANIA	6.280	1.013	4.410	31.742	0.000	43.444
EAST NORTH CENTRAL:						
ILLINOIS	9.217	1.641	6.142	44.483	0.000	61.483
INDIANA	10.937	1.451	5.007	31.247	0.000	48.642
MICHIGAN	7.398	0.729	5.671	32.200	0.000	45.998
OHIO	3.715	0.877	5.589	34.176	0.000	44.358
WISCONSIN	10.098	0.730	3.363	32.292	0.000	46.484
WEST NORTH CENTRAL:						
IOWA	8.544	2.290	6.016	35.110	0.000	51.960
KANSAS	3.928	0.885	4.587	42.926	0.000	52.326
MINNESOTA	10.925	0.930	4.995	26.515	0.000	43.365
MISSOURI	6.392	0.641	5.073	34.118	0.000	46.223
NEBRASKA	8.433	1.193	5.422	38.581	0.000	53.630
NORTH DAKOTA	12.062	3.340	4.360	34.628	0.000	54.389
SOUTH DAKOTA	12.177	2.787	3.570	33.987	0.000	52.522
SOUTH ATLANTIC:						
DELAWARE	12.312	8.300	4.010	47.965	0.000	72.587
DISTRICT OF COLUMBIA	48.149	0.905	14.129	97.842	0.000	161.025
FLORIDA	2.532	1.120	1.682	46.044	0.000	51.379
GEORGIA	3.046	1.704	3.556	42.169	0.000	50.475
MARYLAND	10.756	0.899	4.263	39.526	0.000	55.444
NORTH CAROLINA	5.056	2.724	1.852	31.966	0.000	41.597
SOUTH CAROLINA	2.535	1.644	2.261	31.332	0.000	37.773
VIRGINIA	5.055	1.845	3.275	34.817	0.000	44.992
WEST VIRGINIA	2.483	0.519	4.607	28.603	0.000	36.213
EAST SOUTH CENTRAL:						
ALABAMA	0.841	1.513	3.506	28.111	0.000	33.971
KENTUCKY	1.225	1.052	3.753	22.565	0.000	28.595
MISSISSIPPI	0.852	4.815	2.869	32.356	0.000	40.892
TENNESSEE	1.306	0.975	4.192	14.487	0.000	20.960
WEST SOUTH CENTRAL:						
ARKANSAS	1.085	4.852	3.972	34.108	0.000	44.016
LOUISIANA	0.161	4.244	2.655	34.327	0.000	41.387
OKLAHOMA	0.640	1.012	4.177	38.770	0.000	44.600
TEXAS	0.862	3.539	2.493	41.968	0.000	48.862
ROCKY MOUNTAIN:						
ARIZONA	0.084	1.456	5.437	54.493	0.000	61.469
COLORADO	1.473	2.577	10.756	43.978	1.801	60.585
IDAHO	2.559	4.456	7.377	50.915	1.647	66.954
MONTANA	2.281	4.183	9.309	36.728	4.839	57.339
NEVADA	1.769	2.619	7.488	75.075	0.000	86.950
NEW MEXICO	0.357	4.047	6.870	44.504	0.000	55.778
UTAH	3.033	2.178	3.132	30.720	2.529	41.592
WYOMING	6.001	4.046	14.119	62.847	2.075	89.088
FAR WEST:						
ALASKA	4.089	5.593	18.998	53.037	2.447	84.164
CALIFORNIA	0.415	0.942	5.638	44.719	0.003	51.717
HAWAII	1.188	3.794	0.000	35.989	0.000	40.971
OREGON	8.817	1.246	5.433	38.288	0.180	53.965
WASHINGTON	6.585	1.833	4.754	30.491	0.148	43.810

Table 49

Consumption Of Energy In Million BTU Per Capita and Expenditures On Energy In Dollars Per Capita, 1972, By Region

Commercial Use By Fuel Category

REGION	PETROLEUM HEATING FUELS USE	OTHER PETROLEUM PRODUCTS USE	NATURAL GAS USE	ELECTRICITY USE	COAL USE	TOTAL COMMERCIAL USE
Consumption In Million BTU Per Capita						
NEW ENGLAND	18.512	0.829	1.969	4.992	0.000	26.301
MID ATLANTIC	10.198	0.661	3.571	4.967	0.000	19.397
EAST NORTH CENTRAL	6.549	0.900	6.203	5.105	0.000	18.756
WEST NORTH CENTRAL	6.819	1.028	6.648	4.963	0.000	19.458
SOUTH ATLANTIC	5.436	1.427	2.891	6.443	0.000	16.197
EAST SOUTH CENTRAL	0.972	1.495	4.763	4.378	0.000	11.608
WEST SOUTH CENTRAL	0.772	2.949	4.919	7.205	0.000	15.844
ROCKY MOUNTAIN	1.521	2.161	11.147	8.329	1.824	24.981
FAR WEST	1.872	0.965	6.493	7.934	0.085	17.349
UNITED STATES	6.024	1.240	5.043	5.929	0.089	18.325
Expenditures In Dollars Per Capita						
NEW ENGLAND	18.248	0.966	3.457	39.399	0.000	62.070
MID ATLANTIC	9.723	0.763	4.483	42.603	0.000	57.572
EAST NORTH CENTRAL	7.689	1.113	5.437	35.992	0.000	50.232
WEST NORTH CENTRAL	8.127	1.269	5.096	34.143	0.000	48.635
SOUTH ATLANTIC	5.688	1.683	3.101	39.699	0.000	50.171
EAST SOUTH CENTRAL	1.083	1.797	3.671	23.228	0.000	29.779
WEST SOUTH CENTRAL	0.724	3.470	2.894	39.328	0.000	46.415
ROCKY MOUNTAIN	1.580	2.806	7.672	47.290	1.411	60.760
FAR WEST	1.935	1.220	5.501	42.248	0.065	50.968
UNITED STATES	6.302	1.497	4.512	38.617	0.069	50.996

Table 50

Consumption Of Energy In Million BTU Per Capita, 1972, By State

Industrial Use By Fuel Category

REGION AND STATE	PETROLEUM HEATING FUELS USE	PETROLEUM PRODUCTS FOR INDUSTRIAL PROCESSING	NATURAL GAS USE	ELECTRICITY USE	COAL, HYDROPOWER & NUCLEAR POWER USE	TOTAL INDUSTRIAL USE
NEW ENGLAND:						
CONNECTICUT	3.107	17.510	6.989	6.125	0.523	34.254
MAINE	7.038	54.237	0.445	7.073	0.442	69.236
MASSACHUSETTS	8.459	9.522	5.435	4.818	0.560	28.794
NEW HAMPSHIRE	5.293	14.668	3.340	7.737	0.872	31.910
RHODE ISLAND	7.221	11.198	7.187	4.856	0.128	30.589
VERMONT	1.498	7.670	3.172	6.112	0.424	18.876
MID ATLANTIC:						
NEW JERSEY	3.132	10.711	13.461	7.518	0.364	35.186
NEW YORK	4.123	4.633	7.020	5.201	11.367	32.343
PENNSYLVANIA	2.395	8.112	33.414	11.944	67.640	123.506
EAST NORTH CENTRAL:						
ILLINOIS	1.634	4.727	40.428	8.854	20.195	75.838
INDIANA	1.683	8.418	60.632	13.265	101.579	185.576
MICHIGAN	0.232	5.433	45.082	10.814	39.441	101.002
OHIO	0.155	5.070	51.330	16.942	61.939	135.435
WISCONSIN	0.240	3.652	43.068	8.070	19.994	75.025
WEST NORTH CENTRAL:						
IOWA	0.053	4.811	56.237	7.107	13.737	81.944
KANSAS	0.026	7.056	106.014	7.450	1.588	122.134
MINNESOTA	0.238	10.856	39.728	8.648	11.728	71.198
MISSOURI	0.342	3.464	27.861	7.667	11.496	50.830
NEBRASKA	0.127	6.017	57.217	4.229	2.919	70.510
NORTH DAKOTA	0.091	4.975	2.724	2.282	13.348	23.420
SOUTH DAKOTA	0.003	4.186	17.887	1.872	5.685	29.633
SOUTH ATLANTIC:						
DELAWARE	1.278	41.002	19.321	16.504	48.364	126.469
DISTRICT OF COLUMBIA	1.893	1.381	1.569	0.699	3.723	9.266
FLORIDA	0.277	8.709	11.869	5.576	0.644	27.074
GEORGIA	0.964	12.324	36.733	9.374	1.392	60.787
MARYLAND	1.324	14.001	17.845	9.863	23.619	66.652
NORTH CAROLINA	0.924	15.613	20.969	11.880	7.576	56.962
SOUTH CAROLINA	0.189	13.056	39.110	16.933	12.532	81.821
VIRGINIA	0.508	12.059	13.197	5.964	15.594	47.321
WEST VIRGINIA	0.359	5.955	53.180	17.695	143.377	220.565
EAST SOUTH CENTRAL:						
ALABAMA	0.154	6.209	53.304	20.634	64.952	145.253
KENTUCKY	0.062	3.324	28.207	25.223	29.899	86.715
MISSISSIPPI	0.074	6.072	69.226	9.513	26.684	111.569
TENNESSEE	0.142	4.200	38.848	28.104	14.024	85.317
WEST SOUTH CENTRAL:						
ARKANSAS	0.229	7.060	79.792	11.179	0.743	99.003
LOUISIANA	0.002	12.543	259.442	13.921	1.124	287.032
OKLAHOMA	0.026	8.376	46.201	7.281	0.862	62.747
TEXAS	0.059	4.839	146.001	13.694	1.525	166.118
ROCKY MOUNTAIN:						
ARIZONA	0.000	8.126	37.209	9.183	1.372	55.890
COLORADO	0.192	5.258	39.981	3.718	18.843	67.993
IDAHO	0.221	11.658	47.164	24.689	3.999	87.730
MONTANA	0.156	13.386	43.332	28.059	10.763	95.696
NEVADA	0.048	7.790	18.973	11.049	0.344	38.203
NEW MEXICO	0.007	10.472	81.303	4.956	0.188	96.926
UTAH	0.346	19.368	45.341	5.949	54.697	125.700
WYOMING	0.289	22.825	156.329	15.571	16.871	211.884
FAR WEST:						
ALASKA	0.025	28.383	44.055	1.281	34.894	108.637
CALIFORNIA	0.080	6.453	27.730	7.371	2.554	44.187
HAWAII	0.070	9.210	0.000	9.019	0.003	18.303
OREGON	2.269	14.810	28.112	16.752	3.146	65.089
WASHINGTON	1.010	10.408	22.879	25.858	3.444	63.601

Table 51

Expenditures On Energy In Dollars Per Capita, 1972, By State

Industrial Use By Fuel Category

REGION AND STATE	PETROLEUM HEATING FUELS USE	PETROLEUM PRODUCTS FOR INDUSTRIAL PROCESSING	NATURAL GAS USE	ELECTRICITY USE	COAL, HYDROPOWER & NUCLEAR POWER USE	TOTAL INDUSTRIAL USE
NEW ENGLAND:						
CONNECTICUT	2.947	17.650	8.648	31.274	0.333	60.853
MAINE	6.810	53.553	0.748	26.182	0.224	87.518
MASSACHUSETTS	7.588	9.132	6.929	26.567	0.319	50.535
NEW HAMPSHIRE	4.678	13.598	2.900	31.075	0.429	52.680
RHODE ISLAND	6.960	11.511	9.044	26.669	0.076	54.260
VERMONT	1.452	8.208	1.967	29.865	0.267	41.759
MID ATLANTIC:						
NEW JERSEY	2.923	10.682	11.487	35.405	0.246	60.743
NEW YORK	3.588	4.652	6.430	20.437	6.153	41.260
PENNSYLVANIA	2.258	8.218	24.372	49.824	28.301	112.974
EAST NORTH CENTRAL:						
ILLINOIS	1.500	4.981	25.780	33.912	8.110	74.283
INDIANA	1.558	8.570	36.487	48.709	34.029	129.352
MICHIGAN	0.218	5.942	30.452	42.639	18.490	97.741
OHIO	0.143	5.766	33.667	50.208	24.583	114.367
WISCONSIN	0.221	4.167	27.742	35.204	9.876	77.210
WEST NORTH CENTRAL:						
IOWA	0.049	5.660	30.125	28.208	5.653	69.694
KANSAS	0.020	6.835	38.434	25.123	0.536	70.948
MINNESOTA	0.216	10.629	23.046	37.293	5.085	76.269
MISSOURI	0.275	3.664	16.638	31.678	3.675	55.930
NEBRASKA	0.117	6.691	26.857	15.019	1.312	49.996
NORTH DAKOTA	0.082	5.986	3.519	13.543	2.991	26.121
SOUTH DAKOTA	0.002	4.949	9.429	9.035	2.455	25.871
SOUTH ATLANTIC:						
DELAWARE	1.217	40.181	13.308	72.926	27.219	154.852
DISTRICT OF COLUMBIA	1.760	1.390	1.572	3.814	2.344	10.879
FLORIDA	0.215	8.158	5.523	20.995	0.286	35.177
GEORGIA	0.876	12.157	20.368	29.747	0.651	63.800
MARYLAND	1.220	13.573	14.328	40.963	13.317	83.401
NORTH CAROLINA	0.837	15.412	13.646	35.045	3.522	68.463
SOUTH CAROLINA	0.180	13.738	22.379	43.505	6.178	85.980
VIRGINIA	0.419	11.105	9.267	20.320	7.106	48.217
WEST VIRGINIA	0.334	6.580	29.574	54.559	52.920	143.967
EAST SOUTH CENTRAL:						
ALABAMA	0.135	6.374	23.557	52.050	25.574	107.690
KENTUCKY	0.058	4.037	16.337	59.201	8.819	88.453
MISSISSIPPI	0.062	6.745	24.737	30.391	10.156	72.090
TENNESSEE	0.121	4.794	20.755	65.031	5.137	95.838
WEST SOUTH CENTRAL:						
ARKANSAS	0.179	7.706	29.431	33.157	0.184	70.658
LOUISIANA	0.002	13.337	83.320	34.165	0.251	131.074
OKLAHOMA	0.019	7.436	15.108	21.564	0.179	44.305
TEXAS	0.045	4.745	38.156	33.675	0.341	76.961
ROCKY MOUNTAIN:						
ARIZONA	0.000	9.698	17.549	32.476	0.451	60.173
COLORADO	0.180	6.014	15.934	13.079	5.698	40.904
IDAHO	0.207	14.513	26.352	44.811	0.908	86.791
MONTANA	0.140	15.139	18.643	36.563	2.679	73.164
NEVADA	0.047	10.163	13.328	25.259	0.124	48.920
NEW MEXICO	0.006	11.235	27.147	16.755	0.030	55.173
UTAH	0.309	19.031	18.069	23.020	16.812	77.241
WYOMING	0.274	27.928	49.796	47.815	3.514	129.327
FAR WEST:						
ALASKA	0.024	33.934	33.084	6.914	24.729	98.684
CALIFORNIA	0.069	6.567	12.791	23.021	0.617	43.064
HAWAII	0.080	12.764	0.000	42.973	0.002	55.819
OREGON	2.066	15.102	15.626	22.595	0.562	55.951
WASHINGTON	0.928	11.558	10.629	24.344	0.612	48.071

Table 52

Consumption Of Energy In Million BTU Per Capita and Expenditures On Energy In Dollars Per Capita, 1972, By Region

Industrial Use By Fuel Category

REGION	PETROLEUM HEATING FUELS USE	PETROLEUM PRODUCTS FOR INDUSTRIAL PROCESSING	NATURAL GAS USE	ELECTRICITY USE	COAL, HYDRO-POWER & NUCLEAR POWER USE	TOTAL INDUSTRIAL USE
Consumption In Million BTU Per Capita						
NEW ENGLAND	6.410	15.737	5.328	5.581	0.521	33.577
MID ATLANTIC	3.382	6.921	16.631	7.788	27.025	61.747
EAST NORTH CENTRAL	0.787	5.332	47.233	11.898	45.944	111.194
WEST NORTH CENTRAL	0.181	6.235	47.552	7.010	9.631	70.610
SOUTH ATLANTIC	0.705	12.162	22.508	9.490	16.988	61.853
EAST SOUTH CENTRAL	0.114	4.838	45.253	22.192	33.816	106.213
WEST SOUTH CENTRAL	0.061	6.969	147.418	12.639	1.284	168.371
ROCKY MOUNTAIN	0.141	10.351	49.209	10.007	14.170	83.877
FAR WEST	0.372	7.968	26.512	10.430	3.024	48.306
UNITED STATES	1.328	8.027	42.375	10.478	20.544	82.752
Expenditures In Dollars Per Capita						
NEW ENGLAND	5.872	15.505	6.566	28.154	0.300	56.397
MID ATLANTIC	3.037	6.958	13.096	32.660	12.008	67.760
EAST NORTH CENTRAL	0.726	5.774	30.490	42.185	18.288	97.463
WEST NORTH CENTRAL	0.154	6.488	23.592	28.341	3.625	62.200
SOUTH ATLANTIC	0.631	11.859	13.547	31.329	7.526	64.892
EAST SOUTH CENTRAL	0.099	5.361	21.078	54.151	12.393	93.082
WEST SOUTH CENTRAL	0.047	7.004	42.690	32.119	0.287	82.147
ROCKY MOUNTAIN	0.130	11.674	20.188	25.750	4.191	61.933
FAR WEST	0.338	8.396	12.605	23.560	0.882	45.780
UNITED STATES	1.202	8.229	20.613	33.540	8.317	71.900

Table 53

Consumption Of Energy In Million BTU Per Capita, 1972, By State

Transportation Use By Fuel Category

REGION AND STATE	HOUSEHOLD PASSENGER CAR & MOTORCYCLE USE OF GASOLINE	ALL OTHER USE OF GASOLINE	ALL OTHER USE OF PETROLEUM PRODUCTS	ELECTRIC RAILROADS USE OF ELECTRICITY	TOTAL TRANSPOR- TATION USE
NEW ENGLAND:					
CONNECTICUT	42.533	10.841	11.273	0.000	64.647
MAINE	41.955	24.643	52.174	0.000	118.773
MASSACHUSETTS	39.164	10.907	18.082	0.013	68.166
NEW HAMPSHIRE	44.979	17.230	3.457	0.000	65.666
RHODE ISLAND	36.187	11.729	22.052	0.000	69.969
VERMONT	45.733	19.613	5.343	0.000	70.689
MID ATLANTIC:					
NEW JERSEY	42.311	11.650	23.485	0.003	77.449
NEW YORK	30.766	9.566	22.031	0.502	62.865
PENNSYLVANIA	38.019	12.897	14.336	0.250	65.503
EAST NORTH CENTRAL:					
ILLINOIS	38.881	13.562	24.166	0.119	76.728
INDIANA	41.532	21.172	14.940	0.013	77.657
MICHIGAN	43.622	17.777	11.069	0.000	72.468
OHIO	42.726	13.116	12.229	0.014	68.084
WISCONSIN	39.432	16.828	10.155	0.000	66.415
WEST NORTH CENTRAL:					
IOWA	38.985	24.074	12.425	0.000	75.484
KANSAS	38.983	28.424	18.634	0.000	86.040
MINNESOTA	40.053	21.170	16.643	0.000	77.865
MISSOURI	42.681	23.677	20.856	0.010	87.224
NEBRASKA	39.200	28.193	24.035	0.013	91.442
NORTH DAKOTA	29.052	31.660	19.708	0.000	80.419
SOUTH DAKOTA	38.486	32.969	11.091	0.000	82.546
SOUTH ATLANTIC:					
DELAWARE	45.632	16.755	15.032	0.000	77.419
DISTRICT OF COLUMBIA	31.684	8.038	6.308	0.141	46.171
FLORIDA	47.575	18.074	25.590	0.000	91.239
GEORGIA	47.327	23.211	24.284	0.000	94.822
MARYLAND	40.547	14.937	18.803	0.133	74.420
NORTH CAROLINA	41.784	22.528	10.681	0.000	74.993
SOUTH CAROLINA	43.610	21.883	13.454	0.000	78.947
VIRGINIA	43.012	19.110	39.339	0.000	101.461
WEST VIRGINIA	31.707	18.439	10.531	0.000	60.677
EAST SOUTH CENTRAL:					
ALABAMA	40.680	22.875	19.576	0.000	83.131
KENTUCKY	38.508	22.566	18.366	0.000	79.441
MISSISSIPPI	39.205	25.924	13.628	0.000	78.757
TENNESSEE	41.389	22.043	19.270	0.000	82.703
WEST SOUTH CENTRAL:					
ARKANSAS	37.357	31.217	17.739	0.020	86.334
LOUISIANA	35.823	20.909	37.589	0.001	94.321
OKLAHOMA	41.034	30.873	14.656	0.000	86.563
TEXAS	46.020	28.193	33.225	0.000	107.438
ROCKY MOUNTAIN:					
ARIZONA	41.411	27.429	21.645	0.000	90.485
COLORADO	40.911	25.420	26.708	0.000	93.039
IDAHO	39.645	31.702	13.550	0.000	84.897
MONTANA	34.699	35.680	35.545	0.386	106.309
NEVADA	50.838	34.013	47.729	0.000	132.580
NEW MEXICO	41.950	33.777	32.588	0.000	108.314
UTAH	38.560	27.015	25.205	0.000	90.780
WYOMING	45.369	45.914	68.697	0.000	159.980
FAR WEST:					
ALASKA	19.876	35.926	199.835	0.010	255.648
CALIFORNIA	41.865	20.662	36.554	0.011	99.092
HAWAII	29.522	11.750	108.904	0.000	150.176
OREGON	45.293	21.405	24.014	0.000	90.711
WASHINGTON	36.213	23.153	25.784	0.014	85.163

Table 54

Expenditures On Energy In Dollars Per Capita, 1972, By State

Transportation Use By Fuel Category

REGION AND STATE	HOUSEHOLD PASSENGER CAR & MOTORCYCLE USE OF GASOLINE	ALL OTHER USE OF GASOLINE	ALL OTHER USE OF PETROLEUM PRODUCTS	ELECTRIC RAILROADS USE OF ELECTRICITY	TOTAL TRANSPOR- TATION USE
NEW ENGLAND:					
CONNECTICUT	133.395	30.798	15.576	0.000	179.770
MAINE	130.351	65.811	48.038	0.000	244.199
MASSACHUSETTS	114.586	28.552	18.879	0.112	162.130
NEW HAMPSHIRE	138.232	48.234	5.783	0.000	192.250
RHODE ISLAND	107.139	30.896	20.750	0.000	158.785
VERMONT	149.745	58.727	7.740	0.000	216.212
MID ATLANTIC:					
NEW JERSEY	129.115	32.059	23.182	0.016	184.372
NEW YORK	101.275	28.189	22.177	3.161	154.802
PENNSYLVANIA	113.738	35.050	18.174	1.220	168.182
EAST NORTH CENTRAL:					
ILLINOIS	119.071	37.639	27.111	0.555	184.376
INDIANA	121.566	56.078	23.697	0.073	201.414
MICHIGAN	122.516	44.699	14.044	0.000	181.260
OHIO	132.195	37.077	18.321	0.063	187.656
WISCONSIN	109.626	42.008	14.903	0.000	166.537
WEST NORTH CENTRAL:					
IOWA	115.711	64.752	20.906	0.001	201.370
KANSAS	104.899	68.303	24.806	0.000	198.008
MINNESOTA	116.640	55.496	19.094	0.000	191.230
MISSOURI	120.684	60.515	24.140	0.033	205.372
NEBRASKA	117.581	76.649	32.055	0.050	226.335
NORTH DAKOTA	75.507	73.150	28.433	0.000	177.090
SOUTH DAKOTA	100.795	77.244	19.851	0.000	197.889
SOUTH ATLANTIC:					
DELAWARE	142.397	47.725	15.186	0.000	205.308
DISTRICT OF COLUMBIA	98.564	22.618	8.381	0.644	130.207
FLORIDA	136.412	46.509	29.491	0.000	212.412
GEORGIA	137.673	60.854	30.179	0.000	228.706
MARYLAND	127.160	41.973	18.143	0.619	187.895
NORTH CAROLINA	129.514	62.987	16.601	0.000	209.102
SOUTH CAROLINA	131.106	59.055	18.149	0.000	208.310
VIRGINIA	126.620	50.199	36.284	0.000	213.103
WEST VIRGINIA	99.797	52.991	18.194	0.000	170.982
EAST SOUTH CENTRAL:					
ALABAMA	121.283	60.758	23.703	0.000	205.744
KENTUCKY	114.963	60.489	24.432	0.000	199.884
MISSISSIPPI	114.525	68.247	23.946	0.000	206.718
TENNESSEE	120.326	57.694	26.546	0.000	204.566
WEST SOUTH CENTRAL:					
ARKANSAS	108.186	81.219	28.613	0.075	218.094
LOUISIANA	100.660	51.492	33.429	0.004	185.585
OKLAHOMA	116.917	79.286	20.311	0.000	216.513
TEXAS	123.173	67.036	33.775	0.000	223.983
ROCKY MOUNTAIN:					
ARIZONA	121.692	72.676	31.833	0.000	226.201
COLORADO	118.883	66.511	30.847	0.000	216.242
IDAHO	112.832	81.074	21.198	0.000	215.104
MONTANA	98.962	91.255	46.698	0.603	237.519
NEVADA	162.304	97.848	56.802	0.013	316.966
NEW MEXICO	122.918	88.329	44.244	0.000	255.491
UTAH	112.259	70.744	28.142	0.000	211.144
WYOMING	127.979	116.577	73.823	0.000	318.378
FAR WEST:					
ALASKA	69.626	104.830	224.818	0.126	399.399
CALIFORNIA	119.659	51.796	33.517	0.033	205.004
HAWAII	100.237	35.995	118.866	0.000	255.098
OREGON	130.946	55.508	29.491	0.000	215.945
WASHINGTON	106.508	60.663	30.627	0.032	197.830

Table 55

Consumption Of Energy In Million BTU Per Capita And Expenditures On Energy
       In Dollars Per Capita, 1972, By Region

Transportation Use By Fuel Category

REGION	HOUSEHOLD PASSENGER CAR & MOTORCYCLE USE OF GASOLINE	ALL OTHER USE OF GASOLINE	ALL OTHER USE OF PETROLEUM PRODUCTS	ELECTRIC RAILROADS USE OF ELECTRICITY	TOTAL ENERGY USE IN TRANSPOR-TATION
Consumption In Million BTU Per Capita					
NEW ENGLAND	40.641	12.855	18.138	0.006	71.640
MID ATLANTIC	35.317	11.028	19.880	0.325	66.549
EAST NORTH CENTRAL	41.344	15.725	15.384	0.038	72.491
WEST NORTH CENTRAL	39.910	24.909	17.955	0.004	82.778
SOUTH ATLANTIC	43.383	19.402	21.637	0.020	84.443
EAST SOUTH CENTRAL	40.101	23.063	18.157	0.000	81.321
WEST SOUTH CENTRAL	42.585	27.488	30.038	0.002	100.113
ROCKY MOUNTAIN	41.010	29.755	28.602	0.031	99.398
FAR WEST	40.795	20.950	38.318	0.010	100.073
UNITED STATES	40.367	18.878	22.656	0.073	81.974
Expenditures In Dollars Per Capita					
NEW ENGLAND	122.960	34.875	19.399	0.054	177.287
MID ATLANTIC	110.657	31.116	21.107	1.932	164.812
EAST NORTH CENTRAL	122.557	41.925	20.116	0.179	184.778
WEST NORTH CENTRAL	113.900	63.792	23.208	0.014	200.916
SOUTH ATLANTIC	129.545	52.187	24.716	0.094	206.542
EAST SOUTH CENTRAL	118.239	61.026	24.808	0.000	204.074
WEST SOUTH CENTRAL	116.631	67.167	31.417	0.008	215.224
ROCKY MOUNTAIN	119.992	78.120	36.035	0.049	234.197
FAR WEST	117.729	53.370	37.683	0.030	208.813
UNITED STATES	119.231	49.546	25.556	0.410	194.742

Table 56

Consumption Of Energy In Million BTU Per Capita And Expenditures On Energy
In Dollars Per Capita, 1972, By Region

Electric Utility Use By Fuel Category

REGION	PETROLEUM PRODUCTS USE	NATURAL GAS USE	COAL USE	HYDRO-POWER USE	NUCLEAR POWER USE	TOTAL ELECTRIC UTILITY USE
Consumption In Million BTU Per Capita						
NEW ENGLAND	45.602	0.750	2.677	3.971	7.416	60.417
MID ATLANTIC	27.539	2.882	26.649	7.303	2.791	67.164
EAST NORTH CENTRAL	4.221	4.859	68.204	0.991	4.283	82.559
WEST NORTH CENTRAL	1.927	24.424	39.880	8.146	2.023	76.401
SOUTH ATLANTIC	27.081	8.584	51.200	5.175	1.582	93.621
EAST SOUTH CENTRAL	1.937	10.097	93.350	18.074	0.000	123.458
WEST SOUTH CENTRAL	2.383	102.796	1.896	1.854	0.000	108.930
ROCKY MOUNTAIN	2.784	29.564	41.924	31.155	0.000	105.428
FAR WEST	11.773	24.013	0.221	50.236	2.100	88.343
UNITED STATES	14.764	19.677	37.259	12.388	2.452	86.539
Expenditures In Dollars Per Capita						
NEW ENGLAND	29.982	0.336	1.326	1.910	4.571	38.126
MID ATLANTIC	18.792	1.345	11.248	4.173	1.676	37.234
EAST NORTH CENTRAL	3.081	2.183	26.411	0.458	1.894	34.026
WEST NORTH CENTRAL	1.418	9.201	13.367	3.100	0.826	27.911
SOUTH ATLANTIC	15.875	3.401	21.818	2.421	0.768	44.283
EAST SOUTH CENTRAL	1.454	3.190	30.832	6.454	0.000	41.931
WEST SOUTH CENTRAL	1.623	28.140	0.404	0.578	0.000	30.746
ROCKY MOUNTAIN	2.003	10.850	9.037	8.222	0.000	30.113
FAR WEST	8.711	9.139	0.149	11.140	0.589	29.727
UNITED STATES	9.758	6.502	14.086	3.840	1.200	35.385

Table 57

Consumption Of Energy In Million BTU Per Capita And Expenditures On Energy
In Dollars Per Capita, 1972, By Region

Municipal-Institutional Use By Fuel Category

REGION	NATURAL GAS USE (State and Local Govt.)	ELECTRICITY STREET & HIGHWAY LIGHTING USE	ELECTRICITY USE BY OTHER PUBLIC AUTHORITIES	TOTAL MUNICIPAL- INSTITUTIONAL USE
Consumption In Million BTU Per Capita				
NEW ENGLAND	0.815	0.187	0.220	1.222
MID ATLANTIC	0.855	0.180	0.682	1.718
EAST NORTH CENTRAL	0.988	0.219	0.667	1.874
WEST NORTH CENTRAL	3.631	0.205	0.423	4.258
SOUTH ATLANTIC	1.023	0.153	0.875	2.052
EAST SOUTH CENTRAL	1.347	0.271	0.359	1.977
WEST SOUTH CENTRAL	4.351	0.187	0.900	5.438
ROCKY MOUNTAIN	3.857	0.183	0.950	4.990
FAR WEST	0.566	0.235	0.947	1.747
UNITED STATES	1.583	0.200	0.708	2.490
Expenditures In Dollars Per Capita				
NEW ENGLAND	0.977	3.266	1.233	5.476
MID ATLANTIC	0.821	2.685	4.443	7.948
EAST NORTH CENTRAL	0.711	2.270	3.121	6.102
WEST NORTH CENTRAL	1.733	1.871	1.726	5.329
SOUTH ATLANTIC	0.740	1.690	2.972	5.402
EAST SOUTH CENTRAL	0.792	2.242	1.492	4.526
WEST SOUTH CENTRAL	1.393	1.232	3.070	5.695
ROCKY MOUNTAIN	1.615	1.801	3.082	6.497
FAR WEST	0.267	2.267	1.915	4.449
UNITED STATES	0.883	2.160	2.849	5.893

Table 58

Consumption Of Energy By Source As Fraction Of Total Consumption (BTU), 1972, By State

Industrial Use By Fuel Category

REGION AND STATE	PETROLEUM HEATING FUELS USE	PETROLEUM PRODUCTS FOR INDUSTRIAL PROCESSING	NATURAL GAS USE	ELECTRICITY USE	COAL, HYDROPOWER & NUCLEAR POWER USE	TOTAL INDUSTRIAL USE
NEW ENGLAND:						
CONNECTICUT	0.0907	0.5112	0.2040	0.1788	0.0153	1.0000
MAINE	0.1017	0.7834	0.0064	0.1022	0.0064	1.0000
MASSACHUSETTS	0.2958	0.3307	0.1888	0.1673	0.0195	1.0000
NEW HAMPSHIRE	0.1659	0.4597	0.1047	0.2424	0.0273	1.0000
RHODE ISLAND	0.2361	0.3661	0.2349	0.1587	0.0042	1.0000
VERMONT	0.0793	0.4064	0.1681	0.3238	0.0225	1.0000
MID ATLANTIC:						
NEW JERSEY	0.0890	0.3044	0.3826	0.2137	0.0104	1.0000
NEW YORK	0.1275	0.1432	0.2171	0.1608	0.3514	1.0000
PENNSYLVANIA	0.0194	0.0657	0.2705	0.0967	0.5477	1.0000
EAST NORTH CENTRAL:						
ILLINOIS	0.0215	0.0623	0.5331	0.1168	0.2663	1.0000
INDIANA	0.0091	0.0454	0.3267	0.0715	0.5474	1.0000
MICHIGAN	0.0023	0.0538	0.4464	0.1071	0.3905	1.0000
OHIO	0.0011	0.0374	0.3790	0.1251	0.4573	1.0000
WISCONSIN	0.0032	0.0487	0.5741	0.1076	0.2665	1.0000
WEST NORTH CENTRAL:						
IOWA	0.0006	0.0587	0.6863	0.0867	0.1676	1.0000
KANSAS	0.0002	0.0578	0.8680	0.0610	0.0130	1.0000
MINNESOTA	0.0033	0.1525	0.5580	0.1215	0.1647	1.0000
MISSOURI	0.0067	0.0681	0.5481	0.1508	0.2262	1.0000
NEBRASKA	0.0018	0.0853	0.8115	0.0600	0.0414	1.0000
NORTH DAKOTA	0.0039	0.2124	0.1163	0.0974	0.5699	1.0000
SOUTH DAKOTA	0.0001	0.1413	0.6036	0.0632	0.1919	1.0000
SOUTH ATLANTIC:						
DELAWARE	0.0101	0.3242	0.1528	0.1305	0.3824	1.0000
DISTRICT OF COLUMBIA	0.2043	0.1491	0.1694	0.0754	0.4019	1.0000
FLORIDA	0.0102	0.3217	0.4384	0.2060	0.0238	1.0000
GEORGIA	0.0159	0.2027	0.6043	0.1542	0.0229	1.0000
MARYLAND	0.0199	0.2101	0.2677	0.1480	0.3544	1.0000
NORTH CAROLINA	0.0162	0.2741	0.3681	0.2086	0.1330	1.0000
SOUTH CAROLINA	0.0023	0.1596	0.4780	0.2070	0.1532	1.0000
VIRGINIA	0.0107	0.2548	0.2789	0.1260	0.3295	1.0000
WEST VIRGINIA	0.0016	0.0270	0.2411	0.0802	0.6500	1.0000
EAST SOUTH CENTRAL:						
ALABAMA	0.0011	0.0427	0.3670	0.1421	0.4472	1.0000
KENTUCKY	0.0007	0.0383	0.3253	0.2909	0.3448	1.0000
MISSISSIPPI	0.0007	0.0544	0.6205	0.0853	0.2392	1.0000
TENNESSEE	0.0017	0.0492	0.4553	0.3294	0.1644	1.0000
WEST SOUTH CENTRAL:						
ARKANSAS	0.0023	0.0713	0.8060	0.1129	0.0075	1.0000
LOUISIANA	0.0000	0.0437	0.9039	0.0485	0.0039	1.0000
OKLAHOMA	0.0004	0.1335	0.7363	0.1160	0.0137	1.0000
TEXAS	0.0004	0.0291	0.8789	0.0824	0.0092	1.0000
ROCKY MOUNTAIN:						
ARIZONA	0.0000	0.1454	0.6658	0.1643	0.0245	1.0000
COLORADO	0.0028	0.0773	0.5880	0.0547	0.2771	1.0000
IDAHO	0.0025	0.1329	0.5376	0.2814	0.0456	1.0000
MONTANA	0.0016	0.1399	0.4528	0.2932	0.1125	1.0000
NEVADA	0.0013	0.2039	0.4966	0.2892	0.0090	1.0000
NEW MEXICO	0.0001	0.1080	0.8388	0.0511	0.0019	1.0000
UTAH	0.0028	0.1541	0.3607	0.0473	0.4351	1.0000
WYOMING	0.0014	0.1077	0.7378	0.0735	0.0796	1.0000
FAR WEST:						
ALASKA	0.0002	0.2613	0.4055	0.0118	0.3212	1.0000
CALIFORNIA	0.0018	0.1460	0.6275	0.1668	0.0578	1.0000
HAWAII	0.0038	0.5032	0.0000	0.4928	0.0002	1.0000
OREGON	0.0349	0.2275	0.4319	0.2574	0.0483	1.0000
WASHINGTON	0.0159	0.1636	0.3597	0.4066	0.0542	1.0000

Table 59

Consumption Of Energy By Source As Fraction Of Total Consumption (BTU), 1972, By Region

Industrial Use By Fuel Category

REGION	PETROLEUM HEATING FUELS USE	PETROLEUM PRODUCTS FOR INDUSTRIAL PROCESSING	NATURAL GAS USE	ELECTRICITY USE	COAL, HYDROPOWER & NUCLEAR POWER USE	TOTAL INDUSTRIAL USE
NEW ENGLAND	0.1909	0.4687	0.1587	0.1662	0.0155	1.0000
MID ATLANTIC	0.0548	0.1121	0.2693	0.1261	0.4377	1.0000
EAST NORTH CENTRAL	0.0071	0.0480	0.4248	0.1070	0.4132	1.0000
WEST NORTH CENTRAL	0.0026	0.0883	0.6735	0.0993	0.1364	1.0000
SOUTH ATLANTIC	0.0114	0.1966	0.3639	0.1534	0.2746	1.0000
EAST SOUTH CENTRAL	0.0011	0.0456	0.4261	0.2089	0.3184	1.0000
WEST SOUTH CENTRAL	0.0004	0.0414	0.8756	0.0751	0.0076	1.0000
ROCKY MOUNTAIN	0.0017	0.1234	0.5867	0.1193	0.1689	1.0000
FAR WEST	0.0077	0.1650	0.5488	0.2159	0.0626	1.0000
UNITED STATES	0.0160	0.0970	0.5121	0.1266	0.2483	1.0000

Table 60

Consumption Of Energy By Source As Fraction Of Total Consumption (BTU), 1972, By State

Transportation Use By Fuel Category

REGION AND STATE	HOUSEHOLD PASSENGER CAR & MOTORCYCLE USE OF GASOLINE	ALL OTHER USE OF GASOLINE	ALL OTHER USE OF PETROLEUM PRODUCTS	ELECTRIC RAILROADS USE OF ELECTRICITY	TOTAL TRANSPOR- TATION USE
NEW ENGLAND:					
CONNECTICUT	0.6579	0.1677	0.1744	0.0000	1.0000
MAINE	0.3532	0.2075	0.4393	0.0000	1.0000
MASSACHUSETTS	0.5745	0.1600	0.2653	0.0002	1.0000
NEW HAMPSHIRE	0.6850	0.2624	0.0526	0.0000	1.0000
RHODE ISLAND	0.5172	0.1676	0.3152	0.0000	1.0000
VERMONT	0.6470	0.2775	0.0756	0.0000	1.0000
MID ATLANTIC:					
NEW JERSEY	0.5463	0.1504	0.3032	0.0000	1.0000
NEW YORK	0.4894	0.1522	0.3504	0.0080	1.0000
PENNSYLVANIA	0.5804	0.1969	0.2189	0.0038	1.0000
EAST NORTH CENTRAL:					
ILLINOIS	0.5067	0.1768	0.3150	0.0015	1.0000
INDIANA	0.5348	0.2726	0.1924	0.0002	1.0000
MICHIGAN	0.6019	0.2453	0.1527	0.0000	1.0000
OHIO	0.6275	0.1926	0.1796	0.0002	1.0000
WISCONSIN	0.5937	0.2534	0.1529	0.0000	1.0000
WEST NORTH CENTRAL:					
IOWA	0.5165	0.3189	0.1646	0.0000	1.0000
KANSAS	0.4531	0.3304	0.2166	0.0000	1.0000
MINNESOTA	0.5144	0.2719	0.2137	0.0000	1.0000
MISSOURI	0.4893	0.2714	0.2391	0.0001	1.0000
NEBRASKA	0.4287	0.3083	0.2628	0.0001	1.0000
NORTH DAKOTA	0.3613	0.3937	0.2451	0.0000	1.0000
SOUTH DAKOTA	0.4662	0.3994	0.1344	0.0000	1,0000
SOUTH ATLANTIC:					
DELAWARE	0.5894	0.2164	0.1942	0.0000	1.0000
DISTRICT OF COLUMBIA	0.6862	0.1741	0.1366	0.0030	1.0000
FLORIDA	0.5214	0.1981	0.2805	0.0000	1.0000
GEORGIA	0.4991	0.2448	0.2561	0.0000	1.0000
MARYLAND	0.5448	0.2007	0.2527	0.0018	1.0000
NORTH CAROLINA	0.5572	0.3004	0.1424	0.0000	1.0000
SOUTH CAROLINA	0.5524	0.2772	0.1704	0.0000	1.0000
VIRGINIA	0.4239	0.1883	0.3877	0.0000	1.0000
WEST VIRGINIA	0.5226	0.3039	0.1736	0.0000	1.0000
EAST SOUTH CENTRAL:					
ALABAMA	0.4893	0.2752	0.2355	0.0000	1.0000
KENTUCKY	0.4847	0.2841	0.2312	0.0000	1.0000
MISSISSIPPI	0.4978	0.3292	0.1730	0.0000	1.0000
TENNESSEE	0.5005	0.2665	0.2330	0.0000	1.0000
WEST SOUTH CENTRAL:					
ARKANSAS	0.4327	0.3616	0.2055	0.0002	1.0000
LOUISIANA	0.3798	0.2217	0.3985	0.0000	1.0000
OKLAHOMA	0.4740	0.3567	0.1693	0.0000	1.0000
TEXAS	0.4283	0.2624	0.3092	0.0000	1.0000
ROCKY MOUNTAIN:					
ARIZONA	0.4577	0.3031	0.2392	0.0000	1.0000
COLORADO	0.4397	0.2732	0.2871	0.0000	1.0000
IDAHO	0.4670	0.3734	0.1596	0.0000	1.0000
MONTANA	0.3264	0.3356	0.3343	0.0036	1.0000
NEVADA	0.3834	0.2565	0.3600	0.0000	1.0000
NEW MEXICO	0.3873	0.3118	0.3009	0.0000	1.0000
UTAH	0.4248	0.2976	0.2776	0.0000	1.0000
WYOMING	0.2836	0.2870	0.4294	0.0000	1.0000
FAR WEST:					
ALASKA	0.0777	0.1405	0.7817	0.0000	1.0000
CALIFORNIA	0.4225	0.2085	0.3689	0.0001	1.0000
HAWAII	0.1966	0.0782	0.7252	0.0000	1.0000
OREGON	0.4993	0.2360	0.2647	0.0000	1.0000
WASHINGTON	0.4252	0.2719	0.3028	0.0002	1.0000

Table 61

Consumption Of Energy By Source As Fraction Of Total Consumption (BTU), 1972, By Region

Transportation Use By Fuel Category

REGION	HOUSEHOLD PASSENGER CAR & MOTORCYCLE USE OF GASOLINE	ALL OTHER USE OF GASOLINE	ALL OTHER USE OF PETROLEUM PRODUCTS	ELECTRIC RAILROADS USE OF ELECTRICITY	TOTAL TRANSPOR- TATION USE
NEW ENGLAND	0.5673	0.1794	0.2532	0.0001	1.0000
MID ATLANTIC	0.5307	0.1657	0.2987	0.0049	1.0000
EAST NORTH CENTRAL	0.5703	0.2169	0.2122	0.0005	1.0000
WEST NORTH CENTRAL	0.4821	0.3009	0.2169	0.0000	1.0000
SOUTH ATLANTIC	0.5138	0.2298	0.2562	0.0002	1.0000
EAST SOUTH CENTRAL	0.4931	0.2836	0.2233	0.0000	1.0000
WEST SOUTH CENTRAL	0.4254	0.2746	0.3000	0.0000	1.0000
ROCKY MOUNTAIN	0.4126	0.2994	0.2878	0.0003	1.0000
FAR WEST	0.4077	0.2093	0.3829	0.0001	1.0000
UNITED STATES	0.4924	0.2303	0.2764	0.0009	1.0000

Table 62

Consumption Of Energy By Source As Fraction Of Total Consumption (BTU), 1972, By Region

Electric Utility Use By Fuel Category

REGION	PETROLEUM PRODUCTS USE	NATURAL GAS USE	COAL USE	HYDRO- POWER USE	NUCLEAR POWER USE	TOTAL ELECTRIC UTILITY USE
NEW ENGLAND	0.7548	0.0124	0.0443	0.0657	0.1228	1.0000
MID ATLANTIC	0.4100	0.0429	0.3968	0.1087	0.0416	1.0000
EAST NORTH CENTRAL	0.0511	0.0589	0.8261	0.0120	0.0519	1.0000
WEST NORTH CENTRAL	0.0252	0.3197	0.5220	0.1066	0.0265	1.0000
SOUTH ATLANTIC	0.2893	0.0917	0.5469	0.0553	0.0169	1.0000
EAST SOUTH CENTRAL	0.0157	0.0818	0.7561	0.1464	0.0000	1.0000
WEST SOUTH CENTRAL	0.0219	0.9437	0.0174	0.0170	0.0000	1.0000
ROCKY MOUNTAIN	0.0264	0.2804	0.3977	0.2955	0.0000	1.0000
FAR WEST	0.1333	0.2718	0.0025	0.5686	0.0238	1.0000
UNITED STATES	0.1706	0.2274	0.4305	0.1431	0.0283	1.0000

Table 63

Energy Prices In Dollars Per Million BTU, 1972, By State

Use By Sector

REGION AND STATE	HOUSEHOLD USE	FEDERAL GOVERNMENT USE	STATE & LOCAL GOVERNMENT USE	BUSINESS USE	ALL USE
NEW ENGLAND:					
CONNECTICUT	2.792	1.169	3.011	1.346	1.948
MAINE	2.520	1.111	2.453	1.278	1.724
MASSACHUSETTS	2.459	1.062	2.165	1.352	1.866
NEW HAMPSHIRE	2.562	1.161	2.620	1.297	1.918
RHODE ISLAND	2.488	0.802	2.575	1.724	2.052
VERMONT	2.676	3.591	3.663	1.911	2.418
MID ATLANTIC:					
NEW JERSEY	2.515	0.934	3.104	1.406	1.906
NEW YORK	2.528	1.587	3.108	1.272	1.834
PENNSYLVANIA	2.411	1.149	2.609	0.947	1.383
EAST NORTH CENTRAL:					
ILLINOIS	2.276	1.787	2.600	1.001	1.454
INDIANA	2.330	1.636	2.266	0.797	1.175
MICHIGAN	2.205	1.173	2.560	1.035	1.470
OHIO	2.280	2.350	2.451	0.900	1.331
WISCONSIN	2.399	1.337	2.640	1.083	1.580
WEST NORTH CENTRAL:					
IOWA	2.473	2.673	2.475	1.066	1.568
KANSAS	2.067	0.940	1.817	0.745	1.064
MINNESOTA	2.343	1.203	1.520	1.106	1.555
MISSOURI	2.418	2.219	1.740	1.060	1.545
NEBRASKA	2.268	1.396	1.532	1.057	1.474
NORTH DAKOTA	2.387	1.677	2.321	0.703	1.090
SOUTH DAKOTA	2.425	2.363	1.956	1.012	1.492
SOUTH ATLANTIC:					
DELAWARE	2.801	1.212	2.976	1.211	1.681
DISTRICT OF COLUMBIA	2.635	1.566	1.998	1.550	1.964
FLORIDA	3.380	1.709	2.543	1.106	1.805
GEORGIA	2.760	1.329	2.840	1.144	1.670
MARYLAND	2.732	1.089	2.584	1.227	1.727
NORTH CAROLINA	2.880	1.285	2.571	1.086	1.636
SOUTH CAROLINA	3.003	1.235	2.955	1.067	1.609
VIRGINIA	2.713	0.926	2.436	1.113	1.630
WEST VIRGINIA	2.356	2.427	2.090	0.634	0.885
EAST SOUTH CENTRAL:					
ALABAMA	2.818	1.118	2.719	0.784	1.194
KENTUCKY	2.436	1.289	2.074	0.774	1.162
MISSISSIPPI	2.722	1.240	2.381	0.862	1.340
TENNESSEE	2.585	1.046	2.304	0.913	1.351
WEST SOUTH CENTRAL:					
ARKANSAS	2.539	1.332	2.453	1.035	1.483
LOUISIANA	2.566	0.936	1.285	0.507	0.745
OKLAHOMA	2.419	1.437	2.208	0.722	1.161
TEXAS	2.522	1.157	1.808	0.572	0.895
ROCKY MOUNTAIN:					
ARIZONA	2.946	2.498	2.501	1.135	1.639
COLORADO	2.298	1.368	1.565	0.969	1.406
IDAHO	2.548	1.844	2.035	0.996	1.443
MONTANA	2.263	1.168	1.586	0.805	1.112
NEVADA	2.865	1.670	1.630	1.045	1.508
NEW MEXICO	2.324	1.453	1.037	0.608	0.923
UTAH	2.150	1.278	2.790	0.932	1.308
WYOMING	1.969	1.555	1.461	0.600	0.832
FAR WEST:					
ALASKA	2.547	1.351	1.223	0.998	1.299
CALIFORNIA	2.377	1.026	2.785	1.060	1.496
HAWAII	4.176	1.465	5.885	1.335	1.774
OREGON	2.600	1.244	2.322	0.707	1.189
WASHINGTON	2.454	1.224	2.235	0.587	0.973

Table 64

Energy Prices In Dollars Per Million BTU, 1972, By Region

Use By Sector

REGION	HOUSEHOLD USE	FEDERAL GOVERNMENT USE	STATE & LOCAL GOVERNMENT USE	BUSINESS USE	ALL USE
NEW ENGLAND	2.558	1.050	2.428	1.370	1.903
MID ATLANTIC	2.487	1.320	2.996	1.143	1.665
EAST NORTH CENTRAL	2.281	1.563	2.513	0.947	1.387
WEST NORTH CENTRAL	2.347	1.409	1.785	0.981	1.431
SOUTH ATLANTIC	2.890	1.150	2.551	1.059	1.602
EAST SOUTH CENTRAL	2.629	1.173	2.340	0.828	1.252
WEST SOUTH CENTRAL	2.516	1.127	1.756	0.591	0.919
ROCKY MOUNTAIN	2.429	1.485	1.682	0.872	1.273
FAR WEST	2.434	1.076	2.601	0.929	1.373
UNITED STATES	2.487	1.197	2.369	0.924	1.394

Table 65

Energy Prices In Dollars Per Million BTU, 1972, By State

Use By Function

REGION AND STATE	RESI-DENTIAL USE	COMMER-CIAL USE	INDUS-TRIAL USE	TRANSPOR-TATION USE	ENERGY USE		MUNICIPAL-INSTITU-TIONAL USE	ALL USE
					Non Electric Utility Use	Electric Utility Use		
NEW ENGLAND:								
CONNECTICUT	2.552	3.448	1.776	2.781	0.880	0.665	3.360	1.948
MAINE	2.199	2.185	1.265	2.055	0.750	0.582	7.875	1.724
MASSACHUSETTS	2.237	2.086	1.755	2.378	0.947	0.627	4.373	1.866
NEW HAMPSHIRE	2.273	2.324	1.652	2.929	0.846	0.527	10.333	1.918
RHODE ISLAND	2.254	2.432	1.777	2.270	0.677	0.659	5.000	2.052
VERMONT	2.359	3.082	2.207	3.062	1.200	0.620	7.167	2.419
MID ATLANTIC:								
NEW JERSEY	2.211	3.194	1.726	2.381	0.657	0.690	6.558	1.906
NEW YORK	2.171	2.965	1.276	2.462	0.582	0.597	4.768	1.834
PENNSYLVANIA	2.080	2.802	0.915	2.568	0.596	0.455	3.432	1.383
EAST NORTH CENTRAL:								
ILLINOIS	1.867	2.671	0.979	2.403	0.586	0.420	3.788	1.454
INDIANA	1.977	2.337	0.697	2.594	0.597	0.327	3.164	1.175
MICHIGAN	1.834	2.642	0.968	2.501	0.517	0.480	3.824	1.470
OHIO	1.777	2.870	0.844	2.756	0.596	0.389	2.599	1.331
WISCONSIN	2.170	2.859	1.029	2.507	0.537	0.473	3.500	1.580
WEST NORTH CENTRAL:								
IOWA	2.177	2.611	0.851	2.668	0.255	0.398	3.023	1.568
KANSAS	1.684	2.586	0.581	2.302	0.334	0.381	1.122	1.064
MINNESOTA	2.012	2.303	1.071	2.456	0.542	0.427	1.079	1.555
MISSOURI	2.123	2.692	1.100	2.354	0.484	0.319	1.152	1.545
NEBRASKA	1.857	2.250	0.709	2.475	0.326	0.401	1.010	1.474
NORTH DAKOTA	2.280	2.315	1.122	2.202	0.408	0.228	4.333	1.090
SOUTH DAKOTA	2.304	2.497	0.871	2.399	0.909	0.432	1.500	1.492
SOUTH ATLANTIC:								
DELAWARE	2.568	2.604	1.224	2.652	0.686	0.624	16.000	1.681
DISTRICT OF COLUMBIA	2.325	2.084	1.171	2.821	0.556	0.682	2.667	1.963
FLORIDA	4.413	4.334	1.299	2.328	0.532	0.491	3.673	1.805
GEORGIA	2.581	3.291	1.050	2.412	0.323	0.450	2.133	1.670
MARYLAND	2.381	2.781	1.251	2.524	0.600	0.589	3.372	1.727
NORTH CAROLINA	2.670	2.912	1.202	2.789	0.533	0.457	2.049	1.636
SOUTH CAROLINA	3.011	3.295	1.051	2.639	0.435	0.490	2.676	1.609
VIRGINIA	2.492	2.949	1.019	2.100	0.520	0.495	2.238	1.630
WEST VIRGINIA	1.870	2.653	0.653	2.818	0.381	0.356	1.375	0.885
EAST SOUTH CENTRAL:								
ALABAMA	2.660	2.781	0.741	2.475	0.347	0.379	3.889	1.194
KENTUCKY	2.018	2.493	1.020	2.516	0.399	0.285	2.150	1.162
MISSISSIPPI	2.568	2.875	0.646	2.625	0.324	0.378	1.627	1.340
TENNESSEE	2.291	2.146	1.123	2.473	0.253	0.350	2.730	1.351
WEST SOUTH CENTRAL:								
ARKANSAS	2.294	2.555	0.714	2.525	0.324	0.414	3.000	1.483
LOUISIANA	2.400	2.870	0.457	1.967	0.299	0.275	0.760	0.745
OKLAHOMA	2.095	2.809	0.706	2.502	0.254	0.242	2.047	1.161
TEXAS	2.370	3.043	0.463	2.085	0.283	0.281	1.010	0.895
ROCKY MOUNTAIN:								
ARIZONA	2.969	3.429	1.077	2.500	0.266	0.386	2.234	1.639
COLORADO	1.862	2.078	0.602	2.325	0.438	0.308	3.205	1.406
IDAHO	2.344	2.556	0.989	2.534	0.288	0.182	1.036	1.443
MONTANA	1.933	1.835	0.765	2.235	0.482	0.260	1.091	1.112
NEVADA	2.542	3.284	1.279	2.389	1.000	0.376	0.836	1.508
NEW MEXICO	1.858	2.542	0.570	2.360	0.176	0.218	0.648	0.923
UTAH	1.662	2.333	0.615	2.326	0.522	0.413	3.800	1.308
WYOMING	1.599	1.740	0.610	1.989	0.354	0.204	0.889	0.832
FAR WEST:								
ALASKA	2.319	2.686	0.909	1.562	0.285	0.587	0.808	1.299
CALIFORNIA	1.932	3.194	0.975	2.069	0.507	0.450	2.773	1.496
HAWAII	6.598	5.387	3.054	1.700	0.812	0.870	8.500	1.774
OREGON	2.334	2.263	0.860	2.380	0.480	0.177	3.800	1.189
WASHINGTON	2.119	2.073	0.756	2.323	0.538	0.176	2.952	0.973

Table 66

Energy Prices In Dollars Per Million BTU, 1972, By Region

Use By Function

REGION	RESI-DENTIAL USE	COMMER-CIAL USE	INDUS-TRIAL USE	TRANSPOR-TATION USE	ENERGY USE		MUNICIPAL INSTITU-TIONAL USE	ALL USE
					Non Electric Utility Use	Electric Utility Use		
NEW ENGLAND	2.307	2.360	1.680	2.475	0.857	0.631	4.510	1.903
MID ATLANTIC	2.151	2.968	1.097	2.477	0.615	0.554	4.628	1.665
EAST NORTH CENTRAL	1.881	2.678	0.877	2.549	0.584	0.412	3.258	1.387
WEST NORTH CENTRAL	2.031	2.499	0.881	2.427	0.375	0.365	1.253	1.431
SOUTH ATLANTIC	2.791	3.097	1.049	2.446	0.486	0.473	2.632	1.602
EAST SOUTH CENTRAL	2.350	2.564	0.876	2.509	0.340	0.340	2.292	1.252
WEST SOUTH CENTRAL	2.322	2.930	0.488	2.150	0.285	0.282	1.048	0.919
ROCKY MOUNTAIN	2.051	2.433	0.738	2.356	0.322	0.286	1.305	1.273
FAR WEST	2.032	2.937	0.948	2.087	0.515	0.337	2.543	1.373
UNITED STATES	2.159	2.783	0.869	2.376	0.381	0.409	2.367	1.394

Table 67

Energy Prices In Dollars Per Million BTU, 1972, By State

Prices For Natural Gas, Electricity and Coal, Hydropower and Nuclear Power, for
  Household Use And All Use (U.S. Weights)

REGION AND STATE	NATURAL GAS		ELECTRICITY		COAL, HYDROPOWER & NUCLEAR POWER	
	Household Use	All Use	Household Use	All Use	Household Use	All Use
NEW ENGLAND:						
CONNECTICUT	2.009	1.188	8.183	6.754	1.625	0.640
MAINE	2.983	1.631	7.994	6.203	1.553	0.587
MASSACHUSETTS	2.199	1.269	9.044	7.388	1.385	0.574
NEW HAMPSHIRE	1.927	1.052	7.824	6.475	1.318	0.497
RHODE ISLAND	1.995	1.235	9.136	7.212	1.424	0.593
VERMONT	1.709	0.881	7.174	6.308	1.554	0.642
MID ATLANTIC:						
NEW JERSEY	1.903	1.038	8.982	7.074	1.624	0.673
NEW YORK	1.541	0.950	9.546	7.191	1.437	0.554
PENNSYLVANIA	1.292	0.778	8.116	6.280	1.245	0.432
EAST NORTH CENTRAL:						
ILLINOIS	1.079	0.686	8.330	6.181	1.340	0.417
INDIANA	1.120	0.688	6.681	5.417	1.197	0.342
MICHIGAN	1.072	0.712	7.096	5.810	1.330	0.479
OHIO	1.021	0.693	6.968	5.190	1.270	0.404
WISCONSIN	1.289	0.748	7.008	5.989	1.402	0.496
WEST NORTH CENTRAL:						
IOWA	1.084	0.622	7.845	6.205	1.354	0.416
KANSAS	0.730	0.450	6.940	5.157	1.136	0.333
MINNESOTA	1.198	0.695	7.463	6.235	1.465	0.439
MISSOURI	1.070	0.651	7.644	6.003	1.170	0.325
NEBRASKA	0.962	0.554	6.571	4.940	1.341	0.447
NORTH DAKOTA	1.065	0.893	7.616	6.606	1.431	0.251
SOUTH DAKOTA	1.100	0.627	7.452	6.304	1.544	0.444
SOUTH ATLANTIC:						
DELAWARE	1.656	0.908	8.897	6.724	1.459	0.563
DISTRICT OF COLUMBIA	1.469	0.898	7.332	6.383	1.560	0.616
FLORIDA	2.024	0.866	6.208	5.275	1.342	0.453
GEORGIA	1.205	0.664	5.598	4.722	1.350	0.472
MARYLAND	1.602	0.886	7.732	6.153	1.460	0.564
NORTH CAROLINA	1.363	0.781	5.967	4.485	1.336	0.470
SOUTH CAROLINA	1.552	0.798	6.177	4.430	1.366	0.498
VIRGINIA	1.526	0.835	6.168	4.876	1.294	0.459
WEST VIRGINIA	0.935	0.601	6.786	5.117	1.202	0.375
EAST SOUTH CENTRAL:						
ALABAMA	1.216	0.589	4.887	4.037	1.247	0.400
KENTUCKY	0.906	0.577	5.165	3.941	1.144	0.303
MISSISSIPPI	1.050	0.522	5.760	4.751	1.205	0.387
TENNESSEE	0.996	0.580	3.702	3.400	1.237	0.374
WEST SOUTH CENTRAL:						
ARKANSAS	0.820	0.469	6.726	5.023	1.412	0.279
LOUISIANA	0.882	0.449	6.389	4.541	1.412	0.250
OKLAHOMA	0.864	0.440	7.040	4.978	0.914	0.223
TEXAS	0.972	0.448	6.080	4.327	1.412	0.247
ROCKY MOUNTAIN:						
ARIZONA	1.141	0.610	6.974	5.301	1.228	0.340
COLORADO	0.795	0.481	7.626	5.481	1.166	0.312
IDAHO	1.403	0.702	4.691	3.335	1.530	0.254
MONTANA	0.927	0.520	6.321	4.042	1.530	0.270
NEVADA	1.348	0.787	4.571	3.703	1.144	0.332
NEW MEXICO	0.892	0.454	7.989	5.572	1.068	0.182
UTAH	0.955	0.542	6.571	5.188	1.083	0.340
WYOMING	0.720	0.388	7.278	5.019	1.227	0.219
FAR WEST:						
ALASKA	1.501	0.814	9.765	8.052	1.942	0.710
CALIFORNIA	1.003	0.586	6.855	4.945	1.019	0.271
HAWAII	3.000	2.000	8.324	7.124	1.439	0.383
OREGON	1.577	0.789	3.745	2.775	0.943	0.193
WASHINGTON	1.346	0.698	3.083	2.280	0.943	0.193

Table 68

Energy Prices In Dollars Per Million BTU, By State

Weighted Prices For Petroleum Products In Household And Non-Household
    Use, And For All Use

REGION AND STATE	HOUSEHOLD USE	NON HOUSEHOLD USE	ALL USE
NEW ENGLAND:			
CONNECTICUT	2.628	1.474	1.968
MAINE	2.610	1.303	1.862
MASSACHUSETTS	2.470	1.296	1.798
NEW HAMPSHIRE	2.590	1.520	1.978
RHODE ISLAND	2.507	1.283	1.807
VERMONT	2.753	1.565	2.073
MID ATLANTIC:			
NEW JERSEY	2.509	1.307	1.821
NEW YORK	2.722	1.371	1.949
PENNSYLVANIA	2.487	1.382	1.855
EAST NORTH CENTRAL:			
ILLINOIS	2.589	1.342	1.876
INDIANA	2.504	1.465	1.910
MICHIGAN	2.412	1.394	1.830
OHIO	2.619	1.514	1.987
WISCONSIN	2.417	1.465	1.872
WEST NORTH CENTRAL:			
IOWA	2.586	1.619	2.033
KANSAS	2.416	1.282	1.767
MINNESOTA	2.436	1.360	1.821
MISSOURI	2.489	1.318	1.819
NEBRASKA	2.583	1.468	1.945
NORTH DAKOTA	2.282	1.368	1.759
SOUTH DAKOTA	2.351	1.537	1.885
SOUTH ATLANTIC:			
DELAWARE	2.643	1.376	1.918
DISTRICT OF COLUMBIA	2.620	1.460	1.956
FLORIDA	2.699	1.304	1.901
GEORGIA	2.656	1.369	1.920
MARYLAND	2.568	1.333	1.862
NORTH CAROLINA	2.627	1.516	1.991
SOUTH CAROLINA	2.644	1.471	1.973
VIRGINIA	2.485	1.242	1.774
WEST VIRGINIA	2.651	1.614	2.058
EAST SOUTH CENTRAL:			
ALABAMA	2.782	1.393	1.987
KENTUCKY	2.750	1.430	1.995
MISSISSIPPI	2.751	1.511	2.042
TENNESSEE	2.596	1.481	1.958
WEST SOUTH CENTRAL:			
ARKANSAS	2.668	1.482	1.990
LOUISIANA	2.438	1.174	1.715
OKLAHOMA	2.445	1.300	1.790
TEXAS	2.350	1.173	1.677
ROCKY MOUNTAIN:			
ARIZONA	2.788	1.542	2.075
COLORADO	2.775	1.356	1.963
IDAHO	2.508	1.557	1.964
MONTANA	2.558	1.330	1.856
NEVADA	2.854	1.522	2.092
NEW MEXICO	2.682	1.407	1.953
UTAH	2.521	1.298	1.821
WYOMING	2.633	1.300	1.870
FAR WEST:			
ALASKA	2.965	1.552	2.157
CALIFORNIA	2.656	1.217	1.833
HAWAII	3.518	1.486	2.356
OREGON	2.450	1.360	1.826
WASHINGTON	2.548	1.342	1.858

Table 69

Energy Prices In Dollars Per Million BTU, 1972, By State

Prices For Household Use Of Petroleum Products, By Product

REGION AND STATE	HOUSEHOLD PASSENGER CAR & MOTORCYCLE USE OF GASOLINE	ALL OTHER TRANSPOR- TATION	ALL OTHER PETROLEUM PRODUCTS
NEW ENGLAND:			
CONNECTICUT	3.136	2.216	1.589
MAINE	3.107	2.250	1.591
MASSACHUSETTS	2.926	2.159	1.534
NEW HAMPSHIRE	3.073	2.371	1.596
RHODE ISLAND	2.961	2.151	1.577
VERMONT	3.274	2.435	1.684
MID ATLANTIC:			
NEW JERSEY	3.052	1.995	1.398
NEW YORK	3.292	2.265	1.556
PENNSYLVANIA	2.992	2.185	1.451
EAST NORTH CENTRAL:			
ILLINOIS	3.062	2.061	1.625
INDIANA	2.927	2.153	1.639
MICHIGAN	2.809	2.160	1.596
OHIO	3.094	2.361	1.642
WISCONSIN	2.780	2.122	1.675
WEST NORTH CENTRAL:			
IOWA	2.968	2.348	1.800
KANSAS	2.691	2.157	1.855
MINNESOTA	2.912	2.251	1.455
MISSOURI	2.828	2.172	1.796
NEBRASKA	2.999	2.460	1.724
NORTH DAKOTA	2.599	2.069	1.630
SOUTH DAKOTA	2.619	2.191	1.801
SOUTH ATLANTIC:			
DELAWARE	3.121	2.291	1.664
DISTRICT OF COLUMBIA	3.111	2.353	1.609
FLORIDA	2.867	2.201	2.366
GEORGIA	2.909	2.200	2.147
MARYLAND	3.136	2.155	1.403
NORTH CAROLINA	3.100	2.178	1.661
SOUTH CAROLINA	3.006	2.238	1.906
VIRGINIA	2.944	2.072	1.547
WEST VIRGINIA	3.147	1.989	1.643
EAST SOUTH CENTRAL:			
ALABAMA	2.981	2.074	2.391
KENTUCKY	2.985	1.885	2.290
MISSISSIPPI	2.921	1.905	2.425
TENNESSEE	2.907	1.946	1.972
WEST SOUTH CENTRAL:			
ARKANSAS	2.896	2.162	2.210
LOUISIANA	2.810	1.344	1.699
OKLAHOMA	2.849	2.314	1.611
TEXAS	2.676	1.892	1.689
ROCKY MOUNTAIN:			
ARIZONA	2.939	2.386	2.488
COLORADO	2.906	2.403	2.514
IDAHO	2.846	2.257	1.814
MONTANA	2.852	2.352	1.954
NEVADA	3.193	2.557	2.159
NEW MEXICO	2.930	2.455	2.174
UTAH	2.911	2.417	1.716
WYOMING	2.821	2.436	2.248
FAR WEST:			
ALASKA	3.503	2.462	1.866
CALIFORNIA	2.858	2.136	2.252
HAWAII	3.395	2.430	3.805
OREGON	2.891	2.111	1.547
WASHINGTON	2.941	1.991	1.751

Table 70

Energy Prices In Dollars Per Million BTU, 1972, By State

Prices For Non-Household Use Of Petroleum Products, By Product

REGION AND STATE	GASOLINE	ALL OTHER TRANSPOR- TATION	HEATING FUELS	ALL OTHER PETROLEUM PRODUCTS (excluding electric utility use)	PETROLEUM PRODUCTS USED BY ELECTRIC UTILITIES
NEW ENGLAND:					
CONNECTICUT	2.862	1.382	0.992	1.010	0.683
MAINE	2.679	0.920	1.020	0.989	0.695
MASSACHUSETTS	2.629	1.044	0.950	0.929	0.636
NEW HAMPSHIRE	2.808	1.673	0.947	0.937	0.668
RHODE ISLAND	2.666	0.940	1.027	0.906	0.665
VERMONT	3.010	1.449	1.057	1.083	0.776
MID ATLANTIC:					
NEW JERSEY	2.766	0.985	0.980	0.828	0.718
NEW YORK	2.972	1.006	0.905	0.972	0.648
PENNSYLVANIA	2.725	1.268	1.014	0.824	0.735
EAST NORTH CENTRAL:					
ILLINOIS	2.788	1.122	1.076	0.775	0.690
INDIANA	2.660	1.587	1.113	0.777	0.792
MICHIGAN	2.527	1.269	1.231	0.982	0.749
OHIO	2.840	1.499	1.208	0.868	0.813
WISCONSIN	2.509	1.468	1.233	1.044	0.780
WEST NORTH CENTRAL:					
IOWA	2.698	1.683	1.301	1.204	0.833
KANSAS	2.408	1.331	1.135	0.657	0.627
MINNESOTA	2.632	1.147	1.146	0.900	0.762
MISSOURI	2.562	1.157	1.114	0.852	0.674
NEBRASKA	2.723	1.334	1.245	1.033	0.741
NORTH DAKOTA	2.315	1.443	1.197	0.826	0.808
SOUTH DAKOTA	2.345	1.790	1.296	1.148	0.733
SOUTH ATLANTIC:					
DELAWARE	2.856	1.010	1.171	0.946	0.711
DISTRICT OF COLUMBIA	2.823	1.329	0.972	1.053	0.695
FLORIDA	2.587	1.152	0.921	0.951	0.553
GEORGIA	2.632	1.243	0.987	1.011	0.611
MARYLAND	2.820	0.964	1.017	0.961	0.649
NORTH CAROLINA	2.810	1.555	1.133	1.017	0.634
SOUTH CAROLINA	2.711	1.349	1.245	1.062	0.714
VIRGINIA	2.635	0.922	1.061	0.859	0.547
WEST VIRGINIA	2.878	1.733	1.053	1.058	0.803
EAST SOUTH CENTRAL:					
ALABAMA	2.664	1.211	1.011	0.952	0.806
KENTUCKY	2.687	1.331	1.170	0.869	0.821
MISSISSIPPI	2.642	1.770	1.069	0.842	0.731
TENNESSEE	2.627	1.380	1.091	1.144	0.805
WEST SOUTH CENTRAL:					
ARKANSAS	2.608	1.615	0.941	1.031	0.685
LOUISIANA	2.472	0.886	0.978	0.685	0.682
OKLAHOMA	2.574	1.386	0.867	0.640	0.590
TEXAS	2.381	1.017	0.929	0.632	0.679
ROCKY MOUNTAIN:					
ARIZONA	2.658	1.471	1.246	1.196	0.825
COLORADO	2.620	1.155	1.003	1.041	0.644
IDAHO	2.566	1.564	1.111	1.281	0.845
MONTANA	2.561	1.314	1.030	0.803	0.605
NEVADA	2.889	1.190	1.160	1.302	0.772
NEW MEXICO	2.617	1.358	1.019	0.979	0.683
UTAH	2.622	1.117	0.987	0.841	0.630
WYOMING	2.541	1.075	1.014	0.841	0.790
FAR WEST:					
ALASKA	2.877	1.118	1.474	1.192	1.037
CALIFORNIA	2.512	0.917	0.933	0.795	0.711
HAWAII	3.064	1.090	1.269	0.956	0.871
OREGON	2.606	1.228	0.995	0.938	0.700
WASHINGTON	2.632	1.186	1.038	0.837	0.732

Table 71

Energy Prices In Dollars Per Million BTU And Energy Price Indexes,
U.S. = 100, 1972, By Region

Weighted Prices For Household Use Of Energy, By Energy Source

REGION	PETROLEUM PRODUCTS	NATURAL GAS	ELECTRICITY	COAL, HYDROPOWER & NUCLEAR POWER	ALL ENERGY USE
Prices In Dollars Per Million BTU					
NEW ENGLAND	2.543	2.165	8.594	1.466	2.940
MID ATLANTIC	2.606	1.533	8.983	1.413	2.834
EAST NORTH CENTRAL	2.528	1.091	7.339	1.308	2.519
WEST NORTH CENTRAL	2.479	1.047	7.433	1.307	2.485
SOUTH ATLANTIC	2.622	1.546	6.370	1.351	2.623
EAST SOUTH CENTRAL	2.711	1.042	4.740	1.211	2.394
WEST SOUTH CENTRAL	2.411	0.926	6.329	1.346	2.315
ROCKY MOUNTAIN	2.693	0.996	6.840	1.219	2.551
FAR WEST	2.655	1.158	6.209	1.027	2.516
UNITED STATES	2.577	1.285	7.138	1.300	2.587
Price Indexes, U.S. = 100					
NEW ENGLAND	98.68	168.44	120.40	112.76	113.65
MID ATLANTIC	101.11	119.27	125.85	108.70	109.56
EAST NORTH CENTRAL	98.07	84.87	102.81	100.62	97.38
WEST NORTH CENTRAL	96.17	81.47	104.13	100.57	96.04
SOUTH ATLANTIC	101.73	120.29	89.24	103.98	101.38
EAST SOUTH CENTRAL	105.18	81.04	66.40	93.16	92.55
WEST SOUTH CENTRAL	93.54	72.03	88.67	103.59	89.47
ROCKY MOUNTAIN	104.50	77.51	95.83	93.76	98.60
FAR WEST	103.03	90.13	86.98	79.02	97.25
UNITED STATES	100.00	100.00	100.00	100.00	100.00

Table 72

Energy Prices In Dollars Per Million BTU And Energy Price Indexes,
    U.S. = 100, 1972, By Region

Weighted Prices For All Use Of Energy, By Energy Source

REGION	PETROLEUM PRODUCTS	NATURAL GAS	ELECTRICITY	COAL, HYDROPOWER & NUCLEAR POWER	ALL ENERGY USE
Prices In Dollars Per Million BTU					
NEW ENGLAND	1.869	1.248	7.013	0.591	1.783
MID ATLANTIC	1.894	0.913	6.880	0.539	1.667
EAST NORTH CENTRAL	1.899	0.701	5.718	0.426	1.493
WEST NORTH CENTRAL	1.862	0.628	5.914	0.382	1.460
SOUTH ATLANTIC	1.911	0.801	5.088	0.479	1.494
EAST SOUTH CENTRAL	1.989	0.572	3.938	0.365	1.345
WEST SOUTH CENTRAL	1.731	0.449	4.523	0.248	1.221
ROCKY MOUNTAIN	1.964	0.551	4.992	0.295	1.391
FAR WEST	1.855	0.662	4.538	0.264	1.342
UNITED STATES	1.882	0.737	5.510	0.413	1.479
Price Indexes, U.S. = 100					
NEW ENGLAND	99.34	169.39	127.27	143.19	120.51
MID ATLANTIC	100.65	123.92	124.86	130.47	112.68
EAST NORTH CENTRAL	100.91	95.13	103.78	103.27	100.94
WEST NORTH CENTRAL	98.92	85.27	107.33	92.49	98.72
SOUTH ATLANTIC	101.55	108.73	92.33	115.99	101.00
EAST SOUTH CENTRAL	105.79	77.61	71.47	88.52	90.91
WEST SOUTH CENTRAL	91.95	60.98	82.08	59.98	82.55
ROCKY MOUNTAIN	104.37	74.76	90.59	71.54	94.03
FAR WEST	98.58	89.83	82.35	63.83	90.72
UNITED STATES	100.00	100.00	100.00	100.00	100.00

Table 73

Energy Prices In Dollars Per Million BTU And Energy Price Indexes, U.S. = 100, 1972, By State

Weighted Prices For Household Use And For All Use, For All Sources Of Energy

REGION AND STATE	PRICE IN DOLLARS PER MILLION BTU		PRICE INDEXES, U.S. = 100	
	Household Use	All Use	Household Use	All Use
NEW ENGLAND:				
CONNECTICUT	2.916	1.795	112.71	121.33
MAINE	3.160	1.839	122.14	124.31
MASSACHUSETTS	2.942	1.785	113.72	120.66
NEW HAMPSHIRE	2.834	1.706	109.54	115.32
RHODE ISLAND	2.916	1.769	112.71	119.58
VERMONT	2.821	1.708	109.04	115.45
MID ATLANTIC:				
NEW JERSEY	2.881	1.719	111.36	116.20
NEW YORK	2.957	1.727	114.30	116.74
PENNSYLVANIA	2.616	1.542	101.12	104.23
EAST NORTH CENTRAL:				
ILLINOIS	2.639	1.511	102.01	102.14
INDIANA	2.455	1.454	94.89	98.28
MICHIGAN	2.422	1.487	93.62	100.51
OHIO	2.524	1.483	97.56	100.24
WISCONSIN	2.479	1.532	95.82	103.56
WEST NORTH CENTRAL:				
IOWA	2.597	1.556	100.38	105.18
KANSAS	2.312	1.301	89.37	87.94
MINNESOTA	2.505	1.501	96.83	101.46
MISSOURI	2.513	1.445	97.14	97.67
NEBRASKA	2.452	1.413	94.78	95.51
NORTH DAKOTA	2.386	1.525	92.23	103.08
SOUTH DAKOTA	2.426	1.511	93.77	102.14
SOUTH ATLANTIC:				
DELAWARE	2.885	1.669	111.51	112.82
DISTRICT OF COLUMBIA	2.685	1.667	103.78	112.68
FLORIDA	2.790	1.519	107.84	102.68
GEORGIA	2.482	1.426	95.94	96.39
MARYLAND	2.723	1.597	105.25	107.95
NORTH CAROLINA	2.540	1.474	98.18	99.63
SOUTH CAROLINA	2.622	1.474	101.35	99.63
VIRGINIA	2.514	1.430	97.17	96.66
WEST VIRGINIA	2.503	1.471	96.75	99.43
EAST SOUTH CENTRAL:				
ALABAMA	2.500	1.364	96.63	92.20
KENTUCKY	2.416	1.336	93.39	90.31
MISSISSIPPI	2.509	1.415	96.98	95.65
TENNESSEE	2.222	1.297	85.89	87.67
WEST SOUTH CENTRAL:				
ARKANSAS	2.479	1.375	95.82	92.94
LOUISIANA	2.325	1.217	89.87	82.26
OKLAHOMA	2.373	1.270	91.72	85.85
TEXAS	2.269	1.185	87.70	80.10
ROCKY MOUNTAIN:				
ARIZONA	2.662	1.487	102.90	100.51
COLORADO	2.612	1.408	100.96	95.17
IDAHO	2.371	1.308	91.65	88.41
MONTANA	2.408	1.263	93.08	85.37
NEVADA	2.553	1.430	98.68	96.66
NEW MEXICO	2.611	1.375	100.92	92.94
UTAH	2.408	1.355	93.08	91.59
WYOMING	2.474	1.288	95.63	87.06
FAR WEST:				
ALASKA	3.122	1.864	120.68	126.00
CALIFORNIA	2.528	1.341	97.72	90.64
HAWAII	3.754	2.178	145.10	147.22
OREGON	2.294	1.226	88.67	82.87
WASHINGTON	2.233	1.174	86.31	79.36

Table 74

Energy Prices In Dollars Per Million BTU, And Energy Price Indexes,
U.S. = 100, 1972, By Region

Weighted Prices For Household Use And For All Use, For All Sources of Energy

REGION	PRICE IN DOLLARS PER MILLION BTU		PRICE INDEXES, U.S. = 100	
	Household Use	All Use	Household Use	All Use
NEW ENGLAND	2.940	1.783	113.65	120.51
MID ATLANTIC	2.834	1.667	109.55	112.68
EAST NORTH CENTRAL	2.519	1.493	97.38	100.94
WEST NORTH CENTRAL	2.484	1.460	96.03	98.72
SOUTH ATLANTIC	2.623	1.494	101.38	101.00
EAST SOUTH CENTRAL	2.394	1.345	92.55	90.91
WEST SOUTH CENTRAL	2.314	1.221	89.45	82.55
ROCKY MOUNTAIN	2.551	1.391	98.61	94.03
FAR WEST	2.516	1.342	97.25	90.72
UNITED STATES	2.587	1.479	100.00	100.00

Chapter 2

Petroleum Products

This chapter presents detailed information on the use of petroleum products, organized in four groups of tables. The first group consists of base data on total use, and includes Tables 75 through 86; the second group presents information on aggregate use of petroleum products by sector, and comprises Tables 87 through 95; the third group covers use of particular categories of petroleum products in terms of functions performed, and runs from Tables 96 through 109; finally, the last group deals with prices, and includes Tables 110 through 115. Each group will be discussed in terms of the organization and the content of its tables. The latter topic involves the presentation of some key findings, with focus on U.S. levels and relationships, seen as of intrinsic interest, as well as a basis of comparison for the corresponding state and regional data.

Base Information

Organization

The tables in the first group present base information on petroleum products under the major headings of gasoline, heating fuels, transportation and military use of non-gasoline products, and industrial, energy production and miscellaneous use. There are eight tables of state data, first on BTU consumption and then on expenditures, and these are followed by four regional aggregations of the state data. Explicitly, this cross-classification shows coverage by table numbers:

	Amounts of Use			
	Gasoline	Heat- ing Fuels	Transport& Military Non- Gasoline	Industrial Energy Prodn. & Misc.
States				
BTU consumed	75	76	77	78
Expenditures	79	80	81	82
Regions				
BTU and Expenditures	83	84	85	86

Some Key Findings

For the U.S. in 1972, the major categories of use of petroleum products were distributed in this fashion, for BTU consumption in trillions:

	Household	Business	Fed. Govt.	State & Local Govt.	Total
			Trillion BTU		
Gasoline	8,508.2	3,474.2	159.5	194.6	12,336.5
Heating Fuels	4,000.1	1,150.5	30.3	350.0	5,530.9
Transport-Military Non-Gasoline	20.4	3,853.4	843.9	——	4,717.7
Indl., Energy & Misc.	55.7	6,763.6	——	——	6,819.2
Total	12,584.4	15,241.7	1,033.7	544.6	29,404.3

Corresponding expenditures, in million dollars, were:

	Household	Business	Federal Govt.	State & Local Govt.	Total
	Million Dollars				
Gasoline	25,062.1	9,271.0	299.7	511.3	35,144.0
Heating Fuels	6,611.1	1,157.2	31.7	373.6	8,173.6
Transport-Military Non-Gasoline	23.7	4,633.4	664.3	——	5,321.5
Indl., Energy & Misc.	79.6	5,115.2	——	——	5,194.8
Total	31,776.5	20,176.8	995.7	884.8	53,833.9

The data indicate the considerable importance of gasoline, which accounts for 42 percent of total BTU and 65 percent of expenditures on petroleum products. Non-gasoline military use primarily involves transtation, which is why it was combined with that use.

The functional distributions of transportation and military use, in trillion BTU and million dollars, respectively, were:

	Highway	Aviation	Marine	Railroad	Total
	Trillion BTU				
Gasoline	12,163.0	87.7	85.8	——	12,336.5
Transport-Military Non-Gasoline	1,306.8	2,091.2	785.3	534.3	4,717.7
Total	13,469.8	2,178.9	871.1	534.3	17,054.2
	Million Dollars				
Gasoline	34,774.2	182.9	186.8	——	35,144.0
Transport-Military Non-Gasoline	2,606.8	1,782.0	510.0	422.6	5,321.5
Total	37,381.0	1,964.9	696.8	422.6	40,465.5

Gasoline used on highways accounts for 71 percent of BTU and 86 percent of expenditures for transportation employing petroleum products, which is essentially all of transportation (see Table 55, in Chapter 1).

The regional distributions of use for the four basic categories were as follows:

	Gasoline	Heating Fuels	Transport & Military Non-Gasoline	Industrial, Energy & Misc.	Total
			Trillion BTU		
New England	647.6	960.0	219.6	776.3	2,603.4
Mid Atlantic	1,743.5	1,775.3	747.9	1,549.5	5,816.1
East North Central	2,327.9	974.2	627.5	802.6	4,732.2
West North Central	1,077.2	434.2	298.4	248.9	2,058.6
South Atlantic	2,004.1	651.1	690.7	1,342.6	4,688.5
East South Central	830.9	153.5	238.9	175.3	1,398.6
West South Central	1,400.3	226.9	600.3	853.8	3,081.3
Rocky Mountain	628.4	128.4	254.0	213.6	1,224.4
Far West	1,676.7	227.4	1,040.5	856.6	3,801.1
Total	12,336.5	5,530.9	4,717.7	6,819.2	29,404.3
			Million Dollars		
New England	1,910.6	1,322.4	234.8	581.4	4,049.2
Mid Atlantic	5,333.7	2,366.3	794.1	1,150.5	9,644.5
East North Central	6,709.4	1,445.9	820.6	656.3	9,632.2
West North Central	2,952.9	668.6	385.7	210.2	4,217.4
South Atlantic	5,800.9	996.2	788.9	975.6	8,561.6
East South Central	2,358.2	339.6	326.3	161.8	3,186.0
West South Central	3,672.9	397.2	627.8	574.4	5,272.3
Rocky Mountain	1,759.2	261.2	320.0	199.4	2,539.9
Far West	4,646.2	376.0	1,023.3	685.2	6,730.8
Total	35,144.0	8,173.6	5,321.5	5,194.8	53,833.9

In aggregate terms, the East North Central region is the leading
consumer of gasoline; the Mid Atlantic region of heating fuels and of
industrial, energy production and miscellaneous use of petroleum
products; and the Far West of transportation and military use of non-
gasoline products.

Aggregate Use By Sector

Organization

Data on aggregate use of petroleum products by sector are presented
in terms of amounts of use, per capita use, and indexes of per capita
use (with U.S. use set at 100). The coverage by table number is:

	Amounts	Per Capita Use	Per Capita Indexes
States			
BTU Consumed	87	88	89
Expenditures	90	91	92
Regions			
BTU and Expenditures	93	94	95

Some Key Findings

The base data of the previous group of tables were combined to yield
various aggregates, including sectoral totals, which are presented in the
group of tables discussed in this section.

Amounts of U.S. use by sector were presented above; corresponding per
capita levels are:

	Household	Business	Federal Govt.	State & Local Govt.	Total
Consumption in Million BTU Per Capita	60.44	73.20	4.96	2.62	141.21
Expenditures in Dollars Per Capita	152.60	96.90	4.78	4.25	258.53

Per capita use over all sectors, by region, has the following values:

	Per Capita Use Of Petroleum Products			
			As Percent of U.S. Average (U.S. = 100)	
	Million BTU	Dollars	BTU	Dollars
New England	215.1	334.5	152.3	129.4
Mid Atlantic	154.6	256.4	109.5	99.2
East North Central	116.0	236.1	82.2	91.3
West North Central	123.9	253.8	87.7	98.2
South Atlantic	146.9	268.2	104.0	103.7
East South Central	106.3	242.2	75.3	93.7
West South Central	154.2	263.8	109.2	102.1
Rocky Mountain	137.9	286.0	97.6	110.6
Far West	140.0	247.9	99.1	95.9
United States	141.2	258.5	100.0	100.0

Aside from New England, with considerably higher per capita levels, all regions are within 25 percent of the U.S. average in terms of BTU, and within 10 percent in terms of expenditures (counting the Rocky Mountain differential of 10.6 percent as falling within the last category). The East South Central region has the lowest per capita use of petroleum products in terms of BTU (75% of the U.S. average) and the East North Central region has the lowest in terms of dollars spent (91% of the U.S. average).

Use of Particular Categories

Organization

The third group of tables contains information on use of particular categories of petroleum products, focusing on function performed. Topics covered include household passenger car use in the context of total

use, sectoral use by function, and the distribution of use by function.

The following cross-classification indicates coverage by table number:

	Household Passenger Car Use (amounts & fractions of total)	Sectoral Use By Function (per capita use & fractions of total)	Broad Categories (amounts & fractions of total)	Transportation, Energy Prodn. (amounts)
States				
BTU	} 96	——	} 104, 105	——
Expenditures		97, 98, 99, 100		107, 108
Regions				
BTU	} 101	——	} 106	——
Expenditures		102, 103		109

Data on both BTU and expenditures appear in Tables 96, 101, 104, 105 and 106.

Some Key Findings

Household passenger car and motorcycle use of gasoline accounts for

29 percent of total BTU and 46 percent of expenditures on petroleum products.

(It was noted earlier that all gasoline use, as a percentage of total petro-

leum products, was 42 percent of BTU and 65 percent of expenditures.) Since

the OPEC massive price increase, energy conservation policies have emphasized

the reduction of use of gasoline by passenger cars, no doubt on the basis of

the large percentages noted here. Regional values for those percentages are

presented in the following table on the next page.

Household Car and Motorcycle Gasoline Use As A
Percentage Of All Petroleum Product Use By All Sectors

	BTU	Expenditures
New England	18.9%	36.8%
Mid Atlantic	22.8	43.2
East North Central	35.6	51.9
West North Central	32.2	44.9
South Atlantic	29.5	48.3
East South Central	37.7	48.8
West South Central	27.6	44.2
Rocky Mountain	29.7	42.0
Far West	29.1	47.5
United States	28.6%	46.1%

Several tables present sectoral use by function, including the share of sector expenditures devoted to particular categories of use. For the household sector, the U.S. percentage distribution of expenditures by components was:

Passenger car and motorcycle gasoline	78.1%
Heating fuels	20.8
All other	1.1
Total	100.0

The gasoline share ranged from 59 percent in New England to 90 percent in the Far West, with heating fuels comprising almost all of the difference.

The U.S. distribution of business expenditures was:

Transportation	68.9%
Commercial	
Heating fuels	4.5
Miscellaneous	1.6
Industrial	
Heating fuels	1.2
Industrial processing	8.5
Energy Production	15.3
	100.0%

Finally, government expenditures were distributed in this fashion:

Federal	
Transport (and military)	51.3%
Heating fuels	1.7
State and local	
Transport	27.2
Heating fuels	19.8
	100.0%

Although the federal versus state and local shares were approximately equal for the nation, there was considerable regional variation, with the federal share ranging from 24 percent in the West North Central region to 78 percent in the Far West.

Classifying use of petroleum products by function, these U.S. distributions held for BTU use and expenditures, respectively:

	BTU Consumption	Expenditures
Transportation	58.0%	75.2%
Heating fuels	18.8	15.2
Industrial & Miscellaneous	6.8	3.9
Energy Production	16.4	5.7
	100.0%	100.0%

The U.S. distribution of expenditures for transportation, in dollars per capita, was:

Household passenger car & motorcycle gasoline	$119.23
All other highway use	60.29
Aviation use	9.44
Railroad use	2.03
Marine use	3.35
Total transportation	$194.33

The range of use for these categories, by region, was:

	Amount Per Capita		Region Of Occurrence	
	Minimum	Maximum	Minimum	Maximum
Household gasoline	$110.66	$129.55	MA	SA
All other highway	38.15	96.11	MA	RM
Aviation	5.22	21.19	ESC	FW
Railroad	0.58	5.67	NE	RM
Marine	1.02	6.07	RM	WSC
Total transportation	$162.88	$234.15	MA	RM

NE: New England, MA: Mid Atlantic, SA: South Atlantic, ESC: East South Central, WSC: West South Central, RM: Rocky Mountain, FW: Far West

Turning from regional to state patterns of use, the following list shows states with maximum and minimum per capita indexes of consumption and expenditures, first for household use and then for all sector use of petroleum products. Climate, specialization by fuel source and product mix can explain most of the variation in the list. High levels of household use occur for northern Atlantic seaboard states, with strong dependence on petroleum for residential heating, and relatively low levels occur for "sunbelt" states and for states relying on other fuels for residential heating. High use levels for all sectors also involves military expenditures (Alaska and Hawaii) and industrial use (Delaware); low use levels reflect reliance on cheaper, alternative fuels (West Virginia, Ohio, Tennessee).

Per Capita Use Levels, U.S.=100, Showing States with Extreme Levels of Use

Household Use of BTU	Per Capita BTU Index	Household Expenditures	Per Capita Expenditures Index
Vermont	195.8	Vermont	178.6
Maine	183.8	New Hampshire	158.1
New Hampshire	180.9	Maine	157.5
Massachusetts	161.8	Massachusetts	134.2
Rhode Island	144.9	Delaware	134.0
New Jersey	142.1	Wyoming	133.0
Arizona	75.6	Kansas	80.7
California	73.8	North Dakota	79.6
Louisiana	72.2	Hawaii	76.4
West Virginia	62.0	Louisiana	74.3
Hawaii	56.4	West Virginia	71.7

All Sector Use of BTU		All Sector Expenditures	
Alaska	246.5	Alaska	208.6
Maine	215.1	Wyoming	181.7
Wyoming	201.7	Maine	177.5
Hawaii	187.1	Hawaii	143.0
Delaware	161.3	Delaware	141.5
Massachusetts	159.3	Vermont	139.1
Wisconsin	76.3	California	90.1
Alabama	74.2	Michigan	90.1
Kentucky	72.9	Tennessee	88.9
Tennessee	69.7	Wisconsin	88.0
Ohio	68.0	Ohio	85.3
West Virginia	55.5	West Virginia	74.4

Prices

Organization

Price information on petroleum products appears in the form of (1) "base" prices, and (2) average consumer costs, weighted prices and price indexes. "Base" prices were best estimates of individual state prices for each of four major petroleum products: (1) gasoline purchased by household consumers at the service station, (2) number 2 fuel oil, in residential use, (3) number 6 fuel oil, in large commercial establishment use, and (4) petroleum products used by electric utilities. Those estimates were developed by drawing on a variety of sources, as described in some detail in the appendixes to this report. Regional "base" prices presented here are simple averages of state values. This is not as cavalier as it may seem, because the "base" state values, rather than those regional values, were employed in the subsequent development of average consumer costs, weighted prices and price indexes.

Average consumer costs equal expenditures divided by quantities to obtain costs actually paid per unit, while weighted prices are obtained by weighting state prices by U.S. quantity weights. Division of weighted state prices by corresponding U.S. average prices yields price indexes. These measures are discussed in detail in the last section of Chapter 1.

The tables in this group are organized as follows:

States	Base Prices	Average Costs & Weighted Prices
Money per unit	110	113
Indexes (U.S. = 100)	111	114
Regions		
Money per unit & indexes	112	115

Some Key Findings

The "base" price information in Tables 110 through 112 can be
summarized by these observations: (1) for gasoline, number 2 fuel oil
and number 6 fuel oil, price variation between states is quite limited,
with a few modest exceptions. Prices for the major producing states of
the West South Central region are well below the national average for fuel
oil and somewhat below the national average for gasoline. Prices for
Alaska and Hawaii are well above those for the continental United States.
Finally, prices for New England are a bit above the U.S. average. For
number 6 fuel oil, the geographic pattern seems most clear-cut, with prices
rising with distance from the major producing states of the West South
Central region, which has a price well below those of the other regions.
Middlemen margins account for a smaller portion of the number 6 fuel oil
price than they do of the number 2 fuel oil price, probably explaining the
more clear-cut pattern for the former. (2) Prices paid for petroleum products by electric utilities show a pattern with some marked divergences
from the other base prices. The central difference is that Atlantic Coast
states have considerably lower relative prices here than they do for the
other three "base" prices. Perhaps greater bulk purchases and relatively
low prices of imported oil at ports of entry account for much of the difference, but these explanations are admittedly speculative.

For the United States, the following averages for the base prices
were obtained:

Gasoline, household customers at
    service station   37.16 cents per gallon

No. 2 fuel oil, residential use   19.35 cents per gallon

No. 6 fuel oil, large commercial
   establishment use $ 4.68 per barrel

Petroleum products used by
   electric utilities $ 0.726 per million BTU

Tables 113 through 115 show average costs, weighted prices and price

indexes for petroleum products, comparing costs and weighted prices both

for states and for regions. Money measures are in dollars per million BTU.

In the comparison of costs per unit actually paid to weighted prices,

New England and the Mid Atlantic region had the lowest values for the

former measure (with respective indexes of 83.4 and 88.8 for all sector

consumption), but had values essentially equal to the U.S. average for the

latter (with all sector indexes of 99.3 and 100.7, respectively). These

patterns can be explained by product mix, given relatively greater reliance

on heating fuels than on higher priced gasoline in the Northeast than in

other regions. The West South Central region had the lowest weighted prices,

(with an index of 92.0 for all sectors), presumably reflecting its status

as the major petroleum producing region with consequent low transportation

costs for delivery from producer to refinery to consumer. The East South

Central region had the highest levels for all price measures, both in terms

of costs per unit actually paid (with an index of 121.41 for all sector

consumption) and in terms of weighted prices (with an index of 105.71 for

all sectors).

The Rocky Mountain region usually had price measures almost as high

as the East South Central values, and was the second highest region in all

cases except weighted prices for non-households, where the East North Central was a bit higher. High average costs to the East South Central region can probably be explained by product mix, with a consumption pattern reversing the emphasis in the Northeast. Perhaps the Rocky Mountain results also involve higher transportation costs, both because of distance from refineries and terrain.

U.S. average prices, in dollars per million BTU, were:

	Average Per Unit (Cost to Consumers)	Weighted Prices
Households	$2.57	$2.58
Non-households	1.38	1.36
All Sectors	1.88	1.88

As noted in Chapter 1, the difference between U.S. average cost per unit and corresponding weighted prices occurs because of weighting state values by population. In the case of petroleum products, weighted prices and average costs are quite close.

Table 75

Consumption Of Petroleum Products, 1972, In Billion BTU, By State

Gasoline Consumption By Sector and Function

REGION AND STATE	USE BY SECTOR					USE BY FUNCTION			TOTAL USE
	Household Passenger Car and Motorcycle	Household Total	Business	Federal Government	State and Local Government	Highway	Aviation	Marine	
NEW ENGLAND:									
CONNECTICUT	131000.9	132140.1	28775.7	1072.8	2401.9	162791.1	579.2	1020.1	164390.4
MAINE	43045.8	43643.1	19953.1	4051.0	682.8	66581.5	1239.4	509.1	68330.0
MASSACHUSETTS	226993.6	228826.5	54186.6	3999.3	3198.8	287059.8	1532.8	1618.7	290211.3
NEW HAMPSHIRE	34813.9	35059.3	12113.5	179.0	797.8	47773.4	176.1	200.1	48149.6
RHODE ISLAND	35065.5	35823.1	9389.4	587.4	631.4	45490.8	211.1	729.4	46431.3
VERMONT	21037.0	21300.7	8351.2	75.5	331.7	29723.5	101.4	234.3	30059.2
MID ATLANTIC:									
NEW JERSEY	310947.2	313979.7	73420.9	4141.4	5020.6	391833.8	2060.1	2668.5	396562.4
NEW YORK	565083.1	572144.4	141175.3	11290.2	16180.3	730536.4	3562.5	6691.2	740790.2
PENNSYLVANIA	452615.2	455314.8	141456.1	3240.8	6147.4	602180.5	1599.2	2379.4	606159.2
EAST NORTH CENTRAL:									
ILLINOIS	437180.5	441027.9	136350.6	3610.4	8684.1	583922.9	2438.1	3312.0	589673.0
INDIANA	219539.2	222333.9	104036.7	636.4	4446.8	327727.5	1300.1	2426.2	331453.8
MICHIGAN	393162.9	398979.3	135139.7	4881.3	14390.8	545218.9	2928.9	5243.3	553391.1
OHIO	458103.2	462552.6	128623.0	1407.6	6149.0	592977.7	1792.9	3961.6	598732.2
WISCONSIN	178471.4	180945.6	68499.5	1355.7	3833.6	251328.0	1089.2	2217.2	254634.4
WEST NORTH CENTRAL:									
IOWA	112433.6	114045.6	62907.6	320.9	4588.0	179588.5	939.1	1334.5	181862.1
KANSAS	88412.5	89620.9	59090.3	971.8	3194.2	150663.4	1360.9	853.1	152877.3
MINNESOTA	155285.0	157708.6	74345.5	1827.2	3478.4	233936.1	1288.3	2135.4	237359.7
MISSOURI	202606.8	205304.4	106381.8	745.3	2569.2	311302.0	1408.6	2290.0	315000.7
NEBRASKA	59898.3	60591.7	39922.8	504.4	1958.6	101748.7	736.0	492.8	102977.5
NORTH DAKOTA	18418.7	18770.2	18412.2	321.9	986.6	37874.8	369.4	246.7	38490.9
SOUTH DAKOTA	26170.5	26521.9	20936.3	281.4	849.7	47986.6	358.2	244.4	48589.2
SOUTH ATLANTIC:									
DELAWARE	26056.1	26205.7	8971.1	140.4	305.7	35395.8	102.9	124.3	35623.0
DISTRICT OF COLUMBIA	23826.7	23938.0	4790.1	667.8	475.2	29722.4	38.6	110.1	29871.1
FLORIDA	349534.1	354818.1	117238.9	2659.9	7605.5	473327.9	5138.9	3855.7	482322.4
GEORGIA	223998.1	226792.7	101041.1	1882.6	4137.4	329722.2	1771.6	2360.0	333853.8
MARYLAND	164134.2	165527.7	53060.7	4379.9	1631.6	221952.9	1391.6	1255.4	224599.9
NORTH CAROLINA	218155.8	220903.2	101766.9	2518.1	10587.0	331737.0	1627.2	2410.8	335775.1
SOUTH CAROLINA	117224.0	118785.0	51590.6	2210.1	3460.2	173664.1	977.3	1404.5	176045.9
VIRGINIA	204950.5	206845.5	78242.3	5056.8	5864.5	292511.1	1835.3	1662.6	296009.0
WEST VIRGINIA	56914.2	57248.6	30614.6	232.0	1917.3	89493.3	261.9	257.3	90012.4
EAST SOUTH CENTRAL:									
ALABAMA	143234.4	145055.5	70438.0	4861.8	3422.7	220164.0	2110.2	1503.8	223778.0
KENTUCKY	127308.0	128517.9	67947.3	2871.6	2575.9	199703.6	1168.0	1041.0	201912.7
MISSISSIPPI	88446.8	89808.3	54740.3	792.3	1590.1	144803.2	1048.0	1079.8	146931.1
TENNESSEE	168536.0	171082.8	79229.8	2112.0	5871.1	254492.7	1677.5	2125.4	258295.6
WEST SOUTH CENTRAL:									
ARKANSAS	75012.9	76177.4	58660.7	1244.8	1614.6	135639.3	1173.1	885.2	137697.6
LOUISIANA	133904.9	135979.5	67755.6	6060.7	2265.8	207712.2	2667.5	1681.9	212061.6
OKLAHOMA	108043.2	109759.1	74904.8	703.8	3964.4	186644.0	1361.4	1326.6	189332.0
TEXAS	534019.2	541852.5	297213.9	15385.7	6722.4	846813.9	7919.6	6441.0	861174.5
ROCKY MOUNTAIN:									
ARIZONA	81289.6	82887.6	48827.0	984.2	2434.2	132499.8	1453.5	1179.7	135133.0
COLORADO	96713.0	97648.5	54472.5	1573.7	3110.5	154900.0	1287.6	617.5	156805.2
IDAHO	29932.0	30573.3	21693.0	475.4	1125.3	52839.8	549.9	477.3	53867.0
MONTANA	24844.2	25321.1	23257.1	766.8	1046.2	49506.1	554.6	330.6	50391.3
NEVADA	27096.6	27752.8	16016.5	892.3	564.2	44105.6	632.8	487.4	45225.7
NEW MEXICO	45138.0	45673.4	32425.8	2210.0	1172.5	80129.2	1022.2	330.3	81481.7
UTAH	43457.4	43989.5	27865.8	1069.3	978.8	72918.7	577.7	407.0	73903.4
WYOMING	15697.7	16014.1	14635.8	271.0	663.1	30995.2	383.1	205.7	31584.0
FAR WEST:									
ALASKA	6459.7	7601.1	5883.3	3939.5	712.0	14999.0	2476.3	660.5	18135.8
CALIFORNIA	854501.7	863822.8	351643.0	41655.3	19114.0	1252892.1	16040.9	7302.1	1276235.1
HAWAII	24089.6	24466.8	7510.8	1086.3	613.6	32808.9	604.6	264.1	33677.6
OREGON	98965.3	100660.3	39892.5	1626.1	3555.4	143267.7	1014.6	1452.0	145734.3
WASHINGTON	123775.2	125870.9	68420.7	3632.8	4987.7	199407.5	1739.3	1765.3	202912.1

Table 76

Consumption Of Petroleum Products, 1972, In Billion BTU, By State

Consumption Of Petroleum Heating Fuels By Sector

REGION AND STATE	HOUSEHOLD USE	BUSINESS USE			FEDERAL GOVT.	STATE AND LOCAL GOVT.	TOTAL USE
		Commercial	Industrial	Total			
NEW ENGLAND:							
CONNECTICUT	120430.2	17350.0	9568.9	26918.9	297.3	6290.6	153937.0
MAINE	69891.0	13093.8	7220.9	20314.7	459.9	5960.8	96626.4
MASSACHUSETTS	336630.6	108617.6	49025.3	157642.9	2853.1	39654.7	536781.3
NEW HAMPSHIRE	49404.8	7405.9	4097.2	11503.2	133.8	2844.0	63885.8
RHODE ISLAND	48910.3	11200.2	6997.3	18197.5	412.4	4054.1	71574.3
VERMONT	33008.1	2417.2	688.9	3106.1	59.3	983.7	37157.2
MID ATLANTIC:							
NEW JERSEY	314981.5	49443.8	23015.3	72459.1	1098.6	18231.4	406770.6
NEW YORK	655716.6	173848.5	75720.5	249568.9	3909.1	65381.8	974576.4
PENNSYLVANIA	293637.4	52079.6	28516.6	80596.2	1393.5	18280.9	393908.0
EAST NORTH CENTRAL:							
ILLINOIS	160435.0	67676.6	18373.3	86049.9	1504.3	24467.2	272456.4
INDIANA	120984.4	34717.1	8896.0	43613.1	678.5	15049.0	180325.0
MICHIGAN	172905.4	36647.6	2089.9	38737.5	569.6	16446.1	228658.6
OHIO	102226.0	23105.0	1661.2	24766.2	476.8	8996.5	136465.5
WISCONSIN	118368.4	25969.1	1087.6	27056.7	466.3	10365.6	156257.0
WEST NORTH CENTRAL:							
IOWA	58077.0	13500.6	152.1	13652.7	251.4	5147.3	77128.4
KANSAS	20732.8	5622.6	59.9	5682.5	125.7	2084.4	28625.4
MINNESOTA	108174.2	25768.5	921.5	26689.9	521.2	10467.4	145852.7
MISSOURI	64243.7	19040.8	1624.5	20665.3	545.6	7185.2	92639.8
NEBRASKA	28501.7	7344.4	194.6	7539.0	164.5	2790.0	38995.2
NORTH DAKOTA	17323.3	4373.5	57.6	4431.1	136.5	1863.3	23754.2
SOUTH DAKOTA	20781.5	4392.9	1.7	4394.6	180.3	1813.3	27169.7
SOUTH ATLANTIC:							
DELAWARE	20991.1	3900.2	729.7	4629.9	92.6	1872.3	27585.9
DISTRICT OF COLUMBIA	13123.0	22314.4	1423.6	23737.9	7021.9	7845.1	51727.9
FLORIDA	55612.8	12917.4	2031.6	14949.0	418.9	6547.6	77528.3
GEORGIA	36429.1	8520.0	4564.7	13084.7	422.5	5309.5	55245.8
MARYLAND	75495.5	26904.3	5357.8	32262.1	2056.6	13343.7	123157.9
NORTH CAROLINA	115658.6	14354.8	4822.6	19177.4	356.1	7631.7	142823.8
SOUTH CAROLINA	38683.3	3299.8	509.1	3809.0	107.5	1945.6	44545.4
VIRGINIA	89354.8	13800.4	2418.2	16218.6	1120.4	7251.5	113945.3
WEST VIRGINIA	9706.4	2633.2	643.6	3276.9	83.0	1441.3	14507.6
EAST SOUTH CENTRAL:							
ALABAMA	35839.5	1757.5	543.2	2300.7	95.0	1003.6	39238.8
KENTUCKY	34511.9	2225.5	205.4	2430.8	79.9	1114.8	38137.4
MISSISSIPPI	34575.6	1072.1	167.3	1239.4	35.6	653.0	36503.6
TENNESSEE	34330.6	3022.3	579.1	3601.5	105.2	1621.4	39658.7
WEST SOUTH CENTRAL:							
ARKANSAS	42158.3	1395.3	459.5	1854.8	52.8	788.3	44854.2
LOUISIANA	17586.5	394.6	8.4	403.0	9.9	208.3	18207.7
OKLAHOMA	36339.8	1176.4	69.1	1245.5	77.1	680.4	38342.8
TEXAS	114182.4	6732.0	678.4	7410.4	269.7	3641.2	125503.7
ROCKY MOUNTAIN:							
ARIZONA	6681.7	88.8	0.0	88.8	3.4	39.7	6813.6
COLORADO	27322.4	2350.1	453.7	2803.9	99.9	990.4	31216.6
IDAHO	20859.3	1151.3	167.0	1318.3	30.8	530.4	22738.8
MONTANA	12332.5	1054.5	111.5	1166.0	36.7	480.0	14015.2
NEVADA	7968.3	530.2	25.6	555.8	20.3	257.7	8802.1
NEW MEXICO	14403.1	241.7	7.3	248.9	15.4	118.3	14785.7
UTAH	13283.2	2148.6	390.3	2538.9	226.3	1050.2	17098.6
WYOMING	10829.1	1257.5	99.9	1357.4	69.6	713.6	12969.7
FAR WEST:							
ALASKA	14653.5	567.8	8.3	576.1	59.9	271.0	15560.5
CALIFORNIA	45071.1	6179.5	1629.0	7808.6	214.9	2564.6	55659.2
HAWAII	3035.7	509.7	56.7	566.4	35.4	212.9	3850.4
OREGON	39249.3	13211.9	4958.4	18170.3	381.4	5336.9	63137.9
WASHINGTON	64430.8	14652.3	3453.7	18106.1	488.8	6135.3	89161.0

Table 77

Consumption Of Petroleum Products, 1972, In Billion BTU, By State

Transportation And Military Consumption Of Non-Gasoline Products By Sector And Function

REGION AND STATE	USE BY SECTOR			USE BY FUNCTION				TOTAL USE
	Household (Marine)	Business	Federal Government	Highway[a]	Aviation	Marine[b]	Railroad	
NEW ENGLAND:								
CONNECTICUT	34.4	28264.5	6423.4	12374.2	16490.6	3614.9	2242.6	34722.3
MAINE	46.6	31166.9	22317.3	7893.9	22351.1	22004.2	1281.5	53530.8
MASSACHUSETTS	178.8	74288.5	30334.5	19140.6	61538.1	20441.7	3681.4	104801.8
NEW HAMPSHIRE	0.0	1843.5	832.4	1661.8	663.6	251.5	99.0	2675.9
RHODE ISLAND	31.5	5360.6	15976.1	3941.8	3049.2	14179.0	198.2	21368.2
VERMONT	7.6	2365.1	85.2	1724.9	347.7	65.0	320.4	2457.9
MID ATLANTIC:								
NEW JERSEY	1454.5	131872.2	39261.7	36031.7	46507.9	83664.0	6384.7	172588.4
NEW YORK	537.1	341565.7	62532.4	44913.5	248706.9	98078.9	12936.0	404635.2
PENNSYLVANIA	274.4	145533.7	24861.5	63593.5	54001.9	33982.6	19091.6	170669.6
EAST NORTH CENTRAL:								
ILLINOIS	1031.0	252171.9	18525.1	64882.6	155910.7	7816.5	43118.3	271728.0
INDIANA	166.6	76702.7	2101.7	48552.9	14223.4	2272.9	13921.7	78971.0
MICHIGAN	94.4	70960.6	28706.4	37951.5	48165.6	1872.1	11772.2	99761.4
OHIO	269.7	126099.5	4749.7	70728.5	34018.9	3141.5	23230.1	131118.9
WISCONSIN	12.8	39404.5	6543.0	24352.0	15484.6	106.2	6017.5	45960.3
WEST NORTH CENTRAL:								
IOWA	13.4	35426.0	395.2	24591.0	3443.9	93.2	7706.5	35834.6
KANSAS	2.3	37063.8	5194.8	21548.2	7804.6	250.1	12658.1	42260.9
MINNESOTA	34.4	55267.3	9221.7	23142.4	31773.9	930.4	8676.7	64523.4
MISSOURI	365.8	97042.6	1593.8	33530.3	45630.3	2836.6	17005.0	99002.2
NEBRASKA	0.0	34836.7	1888.2	15491.7	5428.3	0.0	15804.8	36724.9
NORTH DAKOTA	0.0	11923.7	570.9	6661.9	1784.3	0.0	4048.4	12494.6
SOUTH DAKOTA	0.0	7498.1	43.9	5669.1	876.8	0.0	996.1	7542.0
SOUTH ATLANTIC:								
DELAWARE	15.1	7478.8	1089.5	1824.5	696.1	5744.3	318.6	8583.4
DISTRICT OF COLUMBIA	0.6	3032.8	1710.4	2166.8	685.8	917.4	973.7	4743.8
FLORIDA	257.5	177285.0	10465.3	33069.2	128144.7	13017.8	13776.1	188007.8
GEORGIA	42.5	106403.8	8490.4	39095.0	59491.6	1787.6	14562.5	114936.7
MARYLAND	344.8	49887.3	25882.1	16026.4	30894.2	23192.9	6000.7	76114.2
NORTH CAROLINA	69.9	43614.9	12078.3	28322.8	16917.2	1288.2	9234.9	55763.1
SOUTH CAROLINA	43.1	24952.6	11167.9	15112.9	11379.3	7206.5	2464.9	36163.6
VIRGINIA	337.3	108022.0	79091.1	32646.3	66702.1	72417.9	15684.1	187450.4
WEST VIRGINIA	200.4	18593.3	108.9	12790.8	566.3	1380.5	4164.9	18902.6
EAST SOUTH CENTRAL:								
ALABAMA	488.1	52278.2	16160.7	27363.1	15966.7	12671.6	12925.7	68927.0
KENTUCKY	748.5	42932.2	17038.1	23264.8	25033.3	5186.1	7234.6	60718.8
MISSISSIPPI	660.6	28424.5	1659.0	19702.3	2932.2	5523.3	2586.3	30744.1
TENNESSEE	1201.7	69582.6	7684.7	33322.6	23599.7	8289.0	13257.7	78469.0
WEST SOUTH CENTRAL:								
ARKANSAS	153.8	31792.4	3673.4	20707.9	4234.5	1060.1	9617.1	35619.6
LOUISIANA	4730.5	111557.5	24219.7	26660.1	33358.6	72328.2	8160.8	140507.7
OKLAHOMA	0.0	34920.7	3667.6	24464.9	10776.5	1867.2	1479.6	38588.3
TEXAS	3012.1	331741.3	50785.6	116211.2	126506.8	81838.5	60982.6	385539.0
ROCKY MOUNTAIN:								
ARIZONA	0.0	41199.9	1289.6	21205.8	15918.8	0.0	5364.8	42489.5
COLORADO	0.0	54540.3	8598.5	13956.4	40151.4	50.3	8980.7	63138.8
IDAHO	0.0	10112.9	117.1	5343.9	1117.3	0.0	3768.8	10230.0
MONTANA	0.0	22731.1	2718.8	9826.4	4689.5	201.2	10732.8	25449.9
NEVADA	0.0	23887.4	1552.3	5333.0	18456.3	25.1	1625.2	25439.7
NEW MEXICO	0.0	29921.4	5142.8	17118.9	8741.8	0.0	9203.5	35064.2
UTAH	0.0	22312.2	6093.5	9113.9	10540.5	62.9	8688.5	28405.7
WYOMING	0.0	23242.3	52.9	7647.6	1003.7	0.0	15117.9	23769.2
FAR WEST:								
ALASKA	1050.8	44815.1	19080.5	5102.7	50463.4	8742.6	637.7	64946.4
CALIFORNIA	1230.8	528934.4	215940.2	131966.9	421825.5	140659.6	51653.3	746105.4
HAWAII	283.7	83627.1	4954.9	2407.4	76347.0	10061.1	50.3	88865.7
OREGON	260.4	47084.5	5124.8	18979.1	13809.5	3334.4	16346.7	52469.7
WASHINGTON	689.1	71843.0	15596.8	17690.0	52075.2	10832.7	7531.0	88128.9

[a] Includes military use of distillate fuel oil, assumed to be primarily highway use

[b] Includes military use of residual fuel oil, assumed to be primarily marine use

Table 78

Consumption Of Petroleum Products, 1972, In Billion BTU, By State

Industrial, Energy Production And Miscellaneous Use, By Sector And Function

REGION AND STATE	HOUSEHOLD	BUSINESS USE						TOTAL USE
	Miscellaneous Use	Industrial Use	Oil Company Use	LPG for Utility Gas	Electrical Utility Use	All Energy Production	Miscellaneous Business Use	
NEW ENGLAND:								
CONNECTICUT	601.0	53930.1	838.2	1571.9	182935.9	185346.0	2109.2	241986.4
MAINE	93.6	55647.6	454.8	345.3	35673.4	36473.5	999.2	93213.9
MASSACHUSETTS	1108.5	55189.2	8261.9	1849.9	299903.3	310015.1	5340.9	371653.6
NEW HAMPSHIRE	153.1	11353.1	18.4	1312.4	15250.1	16580.9	572.9	28660.0
RHODE ISLAND	107.7	10850.6	6215.8	264.3	17038.8	23519.0	605.2	35082.5
VERMONT	121.9	3528.4	17.9	458.9	1213.4	1690.2	403.1	5743.6
MID ATLANTIC:								
NEW JERSEY	816.5	78712.1	82081.2	1279.5	301495.1	384855.8	4750.8	469135.2
NEW YORK	2245.3	85085.0	14415.8	292.0	567803.2	582511.0	8815.8	678657.1
PENNSYLVANIA	1752.0	96573.9	123417.6	1905.6	166742.2	292065.4	11294.5	401685.7
EAST NORTH CENTRAL:								
ILLINOIS	3776.2	53146.7	157600.1	871.6	83152.7	241624.4	15071.0	313618.3
INDIANA	42.5	44495.8	102607.0	47.3	5887.2	108541.6	6002.9	159082.8
MICHIGAN	1576.3	48965.7	19714.8	530.7	58847.6	79093.0	5630.4	135265.3
OHIO	3600.5	54357.6	77854.1	1629.3	18884.3	98367.6	7473.0	163798.6
WISCONSIN	172.9	16530.3	5780.4	388.3	5413.4	11582.1	2535.9	30821.2
WEST NORTH CENTRAL:								
IOWA	419.6	13876.1	122.3	871.6	4728.6	5722.5	4939.7	24957.9
KANSAS	144.6	16004.0	47064.7	0.0	4858.5	51923.2	1904.5	69976.2
MINNESOTA	155.9	42088.4	16368.0	587.2	12670.9	29626.1	2809.0	74679.4
MISSOURI	462.1	16443.7	13857.1	1506.1	4765.7	20129.0	2711.4	39746.1
NEBRASKA	42.5	9194.0	2415.5	1250.6	2809.5	6475.6	1459.1	17171.2
NORTH DAKOTA	130.4	3154.4	9594.5	312.5	226.9	10133.9	1748.6	15167.4
SOUTH DAKOTA	2.8	2846.6	235.5	681.9	1965.0	2882.4	1509.2	7240.9
SOUTH ATLANTIC:								
DELAWARE	93.6	23412.0	3928.8	69.4	26107.0	30105.2	4657.3	58268.1
DISTRICT OF COLUMBIA	14.2	1038.6	61.5	223.0	30917.5	31202.0	555.0	32809.7
FLORIDA	2307.7	63985.3	2852.4	1237.8	424906.8	428997.0	6695.1	501985.1
GEORGIA	830.7	58327.9	914.9	433.2	30530.5	31878.6	6215.4	97252.6
MARYLAND	229.6	56676.5	3010.5	1265.1	141562.3	145837.9	3347.4	206091.4
NORTH CAROLINA	3076.0	81513.7	490.5	97.5	30879.3	31467.5	11421.6	127478.8
SOUTH CAROLINA	507.5	35093.8	774.8	528.6	13988.6	15292.0	3484.5	54377.7
VIRGINIA	1216.2	57458.7	17797.1	931.8	161303.2	180032.0	8425.5	247132.5
WEST VIRGINIA	107.7	10688.6	1480.5	0.0	4225.5	5706.0	744.6	17247.0
EAST SOUTH CENTRAL:								
ALABAMA	833.5	21860.8	6565.7	29.7	2749.4	9344.8	4909.8	36948.9
KENTUCKY	1097.1	10987.7	21929.8	511.4	2431.8	24873.0	2693.0	39650.9
MISSISSIPPI	5125.7	13697.8	27004.2	489.7	19327.6	46821.6	8879.8	74524.9
TENNESSEE	2097.9	17102.6	483.5	284.0	978.6	1746.1	3178.7	24125.3
WEST SOUTH CENTRAL:								
ARKANSAS	751.3	14176.6	6101.3	0.0	27915.7	34017.0	7566.1	56510.9
LOUISIANA	4862.0	46887.3	153236.4	0.0	8069.0	161305.4	14494.6	227549.3
OKLAHOMA	737.1	22054.3	44519.4	0.0	926.1	45445.5	2516.3	70753.2
TEXAS	9290.3	56145.5	387997.9	540.7	10707.0	399245.6	34350.0	499031.4
ROCKY MOUNTAIN:								
ARIZONA	141.8	15952.1	169.8	0.0	9159.0	9328.8	2294.4	27717.1
COLORADO	1176.5	12430.7	7481.8	246.3	3315.0	11043.1	4410.2	29060.6
IDAHO	354.4	8801.8	104.8	0.0	5.8	110.6	2338.1	11604.9
MONTANA	867.5	9584.2	22921.4	0.0	110.2	23031.6	2463.4	35946.7
NEVADA	8.5	4152.0	163.1	0.0	808.9	972.0	1021.4	6153.9
NEW MEXICO	895.9	11267.4	4343.6	0.0	2721.5	7065.1	3816.6	23044.9
UTAH	516.0	21827.3	17804.5	0.0	7835.8	25640.3	1876.4	49860.0
WYOMING	371.4	7897.3	20218.4	0.0	767.8	20986.2	965.5	30220.4
FAR WEST:								
ALASKA	22.7	9224.4	1145.6	0.0	2785.3	3930.9	1296.8	14474.7
CALIFORNIA	300.5	131706.5	192959.9	3049.6	264350.0	460359.5	14530.4	606896.8
HAWAII	48.2	7515.8	26169.4	936.2	51982.1	79087.7	2538.3	89189.9
OREGON	224.0	32359.0	11300.7	0.0	162.2	11462.9	2137.8	46183.6
WASHINGTON	90.7	35575.0	57977.1	54.5	414.9	58446.5	5703.4	99815.7

Table 79

Expenditures On Petroleum Products, 1972, In Thousand Dollars, By State

Gasoline Expenditures By Sector And Function

REGION AND STATE	USE BY SECTOR					USE BY FUNCTION			TOTAL USE
	Household Passenger Car & Motorcycle	Household Total	Business	Federal Government	State and Local Government	Highway	Aviation	Marine	
NEW ENGLAND:									
CONNECTICUT	410858.11	413412.94	83479.74	2082.51	6741.82	502282.12	1215.20	2219.70	505717.02
MAINE	133740.13	135126.53	56772.59	7474.46	1888.08	197920.63	2207.57	1133.46	201261.66
MASSACHUSETTS	664142.15	668248.53	145677.73	7400.31	8305.01	823201.96	2924.15	3505.47	829631.57
NEW HAMPSHIRE	106991.90	107573.63	34196.25	363.13	2192.22	143440.48	446.06	438.69	144325.22
RHODE ISLAND	103818.13	105472.88	25529.39	1091.52	1662.96	131782.86	398.21	1575.68	133756.75
VERMONT	68882.81	69533.21	25203.28	185.55	975.12	95077.65	258.63	560.89	95897.17
MID ATLANTIC:									
NEW JERSEY	948869.79	956048.44	206581.60	8182.68	13662.16	1173967.14	4395.70	6112.05	1184474.89
NEW YORK	1860112.31	1876580.19	430916.99	22353.67	48009.73	2355559.60	6920.75	15380.20	2377860.51
PENNSYLVANIA	1354052.69	1360212.01	388338.19	6385.97	16383.96	1762620.90	3485.06	5214.17	1771320.09
EAST NORTH CENTRAL:									
ILLINOIS	1338835.02	1347677.69	383603.07	7037.38	23728.04	1749437.81	5291.29	7317.19	1762046.29
INDIANA	642598.96	648778.48	277422.97	1288.67	11537.39	930926.71	2940.94	5159.87	939027.53
MICHIGAN	1104239.72	1116890.64	345843.86	8611.02	35768.42	1489896.29	6268.00	10949.65	1507113.89
OHIO	1417390.69	1428200.79	366579.78	3159.10	16991.50	1801167.09	4417.16	9346.89	1814931.18
WISCONSIN	496165.20	501426.14	172999.87	2470.12	9396.77	679476.24	2249.74	4566.92	686292.92
WEST NORTH CENTRAL:									
IOWA	333709.31	337510.44	170090.25	740.11	12112.55	515184.28	2269.44	2999.65	520453.36
KANSAS	237911.76	240520.68	143113.56	1661.58	7526.45	388358.31	2782.89	1681.07	392822.27
MINNESOTA	452212.95	457709.82	197145.97	3537.15	8978.51	659902.97	2787.86	4680.61	667371.44
MISSOURI	572888.58	579121.43	272979.56	1653.30	6398.92	851751.65	3332.07	5069.50	860153.21
NEBRASKA	179663.48	181369.57	109165.49	1014.09	5234.62	293784.95	1934.76	1064.06	296783.76
NORTH DAKOTA	47871.74	48598.98	42805.87	609.25	2234.67	93041.12	744.23	463.42	94248.77
SOUTH DAKOTA	68540.39	69310.35	49232.78	575.72	1947.27	119744.17	857.89	464.06	121066.12
SOUTH ATLANTIC:									
DELAWARE	81308.60	81665.81	25742.31	299.32	852.26	108038.45	237.76	283.49	108559.70
DISTRICT OF COLUMBIA	74120.41	74382.95	13823.81	1596.94	1325.78	90801.24	69.48	258.75	91129.47
FLORIDA	1002219.06	1014055.75	305657.84	5047.68	19159.25	1324708.72	11242.19	7969.62	1343920.49
GEORGIA	651606.14	657795.24	267653.35	3533.87	10646.75	930835.09	3802.55	4991.53	939629.20
MARYLAND	514742.37	518085.79	153220.94	8770.31	4573.97	678980.96	2737.68	2932.36	684651.01
NORTH CAROLINA	676191.52	682240.31	288869.71	4576.57	29362.06	996595.58	3334.37	5118.70	1005046.67
SOUTH CAROLINA	352412.11	355944.75	141780.27	4156.39	9271.18	506112.75	1951.68	3088.15	511152.59
VIRGINIA	603345.12	607555.93	210449.39	9187.09	15352.18	835585.83	3394.86	3563.91	842544.59
WEST VIRGINIA	179135.75	179956.80	88327.08	561.38	5408.55	273012.43	647.79	593.58	274253.81
EAST SOUTH CENTRAL:									
ALABAMA	427037.90	431281.34	191667.79	8938.56	9077.38	633337.18	4347.97	3279.92	640965.08
KENTUCKY	380068.66	382820.38	185054.21	5329.76	6840.46	575503.57	2266.60	2274.66	580044.81
MISSISSIPPI	258367.31	261435.14	145250.77	1553.80	4093.89	407720.90	2322.52	2290.18	412333.60
TENNESSEE	489965.64	495805.03	209633.41	4323.24	15133.84	716499.33	3748.03	4648.15	724895.51
WEST SOUTH CENTRAL:									
ARKANSAS	217238.35	219904.48	154005.98	2296.69	4119.90	375917.19	2519.39	1890.47	380327.05
LOUISIANA	376268.47	380688.97	172476.42	9996.81	5582.84	560637.43	4727.64	3379.97	568745.03
OKLAHOMA	307841.58	311812.43	193318.41	1490.80	9979.10	510576.87	3146.46	2877.42	516600.75
TEXAS	1429298.00	1446741.80	717364.97	27364.32	15709.47	2178095.91	15474.16	13610.42	2207180.50
ROCKY MOUNTAIN:									
ARIZONA	238880.97	242693.59	130328.05	2203.26	6319.37	375488.64	3438.69	2616.95	381544.28
COLORADO	281040.40	283288.67	143819.21	3162.80	8001.70	434062.41	2860.29	1349.67	438272.38
IDAHO	85188.18	86635.84	55905.91	1029.84	2827.85	144072.61	1361.80	965.02	146399.43
MONTANA	70856.87	71978.75	59982.59	1601.65	2632.57	134224.32	1266.43	704.81	136195.56
NEVADA	86507.80	88185.65	46765.48	2114.38	1595.31	135924.34	1570.39	1166.09	138660.82
NEW MEXICO	132260.08	133574.44	86242.53	4452.02	3033.24	224406.76	2165.68	729.80	227302.24
UTAH	126515.42	127801.37	73772.18	2141.05	2529.24	203980.28	1371.90	891.66	206243.85
WYOMING	44280.63	45051.53	37332.81	579.88	1651.95	83203.55	980.60	432.02	84616.17
FAR WEST:									
ALASKA	22628.41	26386.37	18830.93	9250.50	2230.19	47765.05	6936.39	1996.56	56698.00
CALIFORNIA	2442357.91	2463474.50	914191.00	73648.98	48244.12	3454658.99	29369.89	15529.70	3499558.61
HAWAII	81793.68	82943.98	23619.21	2723.57	1878.73	108751.22	1665.78	748.49	111165.49
OREGON	286117.08	289937.82	105067.76	3283.43	9112.41	402015.94	2262.64	3122.85	407401.43
WASHINGTON	364043.71	368627.08	183146.46	6587.43	13029.86	564201.42	3551.37	3638.04	571390.83

Table 80

Expenditures On Petroleum Products, 1972, In Thousand Dollars, By State

Expenditures On Petroleum Heating Fuels, By Sector

REGION AND STATE	HOUSEHOLD USE	BUSINESS USE			FEDERAL GOVERNMENT	STATE AND LOCAL GOVT.	TOTAL EXPENDITURES
		Commercial	Industrial	Total			
NEW ENGLAND:							
CONNECTICUT	191339.90	17524.20	9077.10	26601.30	300.20	6352.10	224593.40
MAINE	111220.50	13257.60	6987.50	20245.10	502.40	6511.80	138479.80
MASSACHUSETTS	516296.70	102468.20	43981.50	146449.70	2930.10	40721.80	706398.40
NEW HAMPSHIRE	78871.90	7028.10	3620.60	10648.70	137.50	2923.90	92581.90
RHODE ISLAND	77111.10	11618.00	6744.30	18362.30	452.70	4449.80	100375.70
VERMONT	55605.70	2585.80	667.90	3253.70	64.50	1069.10	59993.00
MID ATLANTIC:							
NEW JERSEY	440422.90	48319.80	21481.50	69801.30	1145.50	19005.90	530375.50
NEW YORK	1019884.20	159130.00	65904.10	225034.10	3578.10	59835.60	1308331.90
PENNSYLVANIA	425980.80	53671.40	26886.60	80558.00	1493.90	19594.90	527627.60
EAST NORTH CENTRAL:							
ILLINOIS	261512.50	74511.20	16868.90	91380.10	1679.00	27446.40	382017.90
INDIANA	198288.70	39671.90	8234.90	47906.80	782.00	17357.90	264335.40
MICHIGAN	276082.40	45545.70	1962.70	47508.40	707.10	20421.20	344719.10
OHIO	168431.50	28251.70	1534.60	29786.30	582.00	11001.40	209801.20
WISCONSIN	198314.50	32299.70	1000.60	33300.30	576.50	12827.80	245019.30
WEST NORTH CENTRAL:							
IOWA	104689.40	17664.60	140.50	17805.10	324.30	6650.80	129469.70
KANSAS	38552.60	6400.80	45.70	6446.50	141.80	2365.80	47506.90
MINNESOTA	157372.10	29792.50	837.20	30629.70	592.50	11970.70	200565.00
MISSOURI	115545.80	21611.50	1305.30	22916.80	611.90	8117.10	147191.70
NEBRASKA	49160.10	9223.90	179.10	9403.00	202.40	3458.90	62224.60
NORTH DAKOTA	28256.80	5243.50	52.30	5295.80	164.10	2239.50	35956.10
SOUTH DAKOTA	37432.00	5709.30	1.70	5711.00	232.40	2338.70	45714.30
SOUTH ATLANTIC:							
DELAWARE	34944.90	4647.20	695.00	5342.20	112.30	2270.60	42670.00
DISTRICT OF COLUMBIA	21122.80	21540.70	1323.30	22864.00	6927.50	7739.60	58653.90
FLORIDA	133134.60	12074.90	1582.20	13657.10	392.80	6137.80	153322.30
GEORGIA	78787.10	8382.40	4147.10	12529.50	444.80	5588.90	97350.20
MARYLAND	105890.90	27041.50	4939.70	31981.20	2203.40	14295.90	154371.50
NORTH CAROLINA	192462.60	16949.40	4372.10	21321.50	421.10	9024.30	223229.50
SOUTH CAROLINA	73896.60	4201.00	483.10	4684.10	136.90	2476.90	81194.50
VIRGINIA	138335.60	14818.20	1998.50	16816.70	1240.40	8027.30	164420.10
WEST VIRGINIA	15970.20	2823.50	599.90	3423.40	89.00	1545.40	21027.90
EAST SOUTH CENTRAL:							
ALABAMA	86543.90	1813.30	475.90	2289.20	99.10	1048.30	89980.90
KENTUCKY	79873.00	2635.30	190.10	2825.40	94.70	1320.10	84113.20
MISSISSIPPI	88897.00	1170.10	138.90	1309.00	39.00	712.70	90957.80
TENNESSEE	68736.80	3378.70	491.90	3870.60	118.20	1821.80	74547.20
WEST SOUTH CENTRAL:							
ARKANSAS	93739.90	1351.90	359.60	1711.50	51.80	774.20	96277.50
LOUISIANA	32201.90	386.20	6.40	392.60	9.70	205.10	32809.30
OKLAHOMA	58906.30	1015.60	49.50	1065.10	68.30	602.50	60642.10
TEXAS	196973.40	6315.80	517.90	6833.70	254.20	3430.10	207491.50
ROCKY MOUNTAIN:							
ARIZONA	16763.50	110.60	0.00	110.60	4.30	49.40	16927.80
COLORADO	69834.50	2356.10	424.40	2780.50	103.20	1022.70	73740.80
IDAHO	37942.10	1282.40	156.20	1438.60	35.60	614.20	40030.40
MONTANA	24572.80	1090.20	100.20	1190.40	38.60	504.10	26306.00
NEVADA	17206.80	615.70	24.90	640.60	23.90	303.00	18174.40
NEW MEXICO	32085.30	247.10	6.30	253.40	15.80	120.90	32475.20
UTAH	22981.50	2115.90	347.90	2463.80	230.80	1071.20	26747.40
WYOMING	24635.60	1246.80	94.80	1341.60	73.70	755.70	26806.70
FAR WEST:							
ALASKA	27345.60	839.50	7.90	847.40	88.50	400.70	28682.30
CALIFORNIA	101760.40	5690.40	1408.40	7098.80	214.90	2565.40	111639.40
HAWAII	11642.10	651.40	65.00	716.40	45.20	272.50	12676.30
OREGON	60758.60	13332.40	4514.30	17846.70	395.70	5537.90	84538.90
WASHINGTON	112827.40	15319.20	3170.90	18490.10	530.30	6656.60	138504.50

156

Table 81

Expenditures On Petroleum Products, 1972, In Thousand Dollars, By State

Expenditures For Transportation And Military Use Of Non-Gasoline Products, By Sector And Function

REGION AND STATE	USE BY SECTOR			USE BY FUNCTION				TOTAL EXPENDITURES
	Household (Marine)	Business	Federal Government	Highway[a]	Aviation	Marine[b]	Railroad	
NEW ENGLAND:								
CONNECTICUT	46.23	42714.97	5212.57	28492.71	15117.67	2326.63	2036.77	47973.78
MAINE	62.39	28803.16	20421.13	13480.74	20300.47	14347.08	1158.39	49286.68
MASSACHUSETTS	237.15	85498.11	23686.23	38013.64	55631.38	12480.26	3296.20	109421.48
NEW HAMPSHIRE	0.00	3815.26	660.89	3660.46	589.40	138.90	87.39	4476.15
RHODE ISLAND	42.71	9541.98	10521.69	8448.11	2808.86	8693.46	155.96	20106.39
VERMONT	10.35	3474.18	75.71	2871.32	323.75	69.52	295.64	3560.23
MID ATLANTIC:								
NEW JERSEY	1771.95	140627.31	27962.59	70785.84	38711.04	55614.94	5250.03	170361.85
NEW YORK	742.88	350652.53	55934.20	102369.34	234234.47	58885.60	11840.20	407329.61
PENNSYLVANIA	339.46	198118.26	17908.33	133122.85	45678.21	21704.78	15860.21	216366.05
EAST NORTH CENTRAL:								
ILLINOIS	1210.26	288402.44	15218.57	137585.16	125595.86	7639.21	34011.03	304831.26
INDIANA	196.61	123346.06	1718.32	100788.87	11517.46	1861.48	11093.18	125261.00
MICHIGAN	117.36	101507.69	24957.36	74132.99	41241.88	1463.29	9744.24	126582.40
OHIO	331.98	192026.76	4077.93	145666.57	28699.18	2764.61	19306.31	196436.66
WISCONSIN	15.77	61799.80	5637.58	49321.66	13108.31	104.52	4918.65	67453.15
WEST NORTH CENTRAL:								
IOWA	15.90	59949.41	328.72	51221.33	2803.40	95.52	6173.78	60294.03
KANSAS	2.40	52546.03	3711.85	41812.13	5572.41	126.49	8749.25	56260.27
MINNESOTA	37.07	66986.18	7004.10	43421.40	23652.66	641.41	6311.89	74027.36
MISSOURI	420.12	112944.12	1227.38	62801.03	35947.02	2664.76	13178.79	114591.61
NEBRASKA	0.00	47505.52	1474.26	33172.18	4157.50	0.00	11650.09	48979.77
NORTH DAKOTA	0.00	17548.55	477.83	13295.51	1465.14	0.00	3265.74	18026.38
SOUTH DAKOTA	0.00	13460.47	38.03	11924.07	742.34	0.00	832.10	13498.51
SOUTH ATLANTIC:								
DELAWARE	20.08	7864.90	786.12	4147.30	627.91	3674.99	220.91	8671.10
DISTRICT OF COLUMBIA	0.72	5091.16	1210.51	4380.00	576.40	535.79	810.20	6302.40
FLORIDA	359.40	207085.28	9223.64	73863.09	121897.40	7924.21	12983.61	216668.32
GEORGIA	51.26	135981.14	6802.96	80693.99	49115.30	1172.83	11853.25	142835.37
MARYLAND	402.60	53131.73	19908.80	29044.99	24641.32	15029.42	4727.40	73443.13
NORTH CAROLINA	88.26	76182.81	10404.25	63260.20	14549.30	1001.91	7863.90	86675.31
SOUTH CAROLINA	57.16	38743.61	9983.38	31790.30	10243.25	4547.68	2202.93	48784.16
VIRGINIA	415.15	123428.16	49047.65	64547.06	56104.27	39218.58	13021.05	172890.96
WEST VIRGINIA	242.84	32324.57	91.01	27335.45	469.53	1445.54	3407.90	32658.42
EAST SOUTH CENTRAL:								
ALABAMA	545.43	70244.04	12669.43	52735.21	12293.42	8678.88	9751.40	83458.90
KENTUCKY	940.38	64866.67	14964.61	47347.04	21670.50	5617.40	6136.72	80771.66
MISSISSIPPI	784.60	51856.00	1382.31	44348.40	2389.83	5210.57	2074.10	54022.91
TENNESSEE	1456.35	100119.32	6520.28	68921.86	19646.95	8679.05	10848.10	108095.95
WEST SOUTH CENTRAL:								
ARKANSAS	184.41	54180.00	3089.84	45080.34	3488.71	1098.42	7786.78	57454.25
LOUISIANA	4724.39	103920.84	16311.52	48163.25	23044.76	48245.89	5502.85	124956.75
OKLAHOMA	0.00	51482.24	1996.22	44944.80	6791.96	835.31	906.40	53478.47
TEXAS	3073.23	352427.55	36419.96	211462.17	89105.94	49361.94	41990.70	391920.74
ROCKY MOUNTAIN:								
ARIZONA	0.00	61368.25	1120.64	44243.66	13696.88	0.00	4548.36	62488.90
COLORADO	0.00	65364.30	7559.07	30371.19	34865.89	29.40	7656.90	72923.38
IDAHO	0.00	15901.05	103.14	11805.69	969.39	0.00	3229.11	16004.19
MONTANA	0.00	31285.95	2149.74	21205.34	3748.04	113.04	8369.26	33435.69
NEVADA	0.00	28831.67	1443.61	11671.22	17100.94	15.30	1487.82	30275.28
NEW MEXICO	0.00	43699.63	3906.44	34423.31	6487.98	0.00	6694.78	47606.07
UTAH	0.00	26981.24	4734.67	17038.59	8116.13	35.03	6526.17	31715.91
WYOMING	0.00	25104.42	438.31	12846.21	824.86	0.00	11871.66	25542.73
FAR WEST:								
ALASKA	1640.23	51032.17	20393.35	8174.64	53515.15	10721.20	654.76	73065.76
CALIFORNIA	1420.57	513078.90	169606.54	225718.82	334052.17	84169.49	40165.53	684106.01
HAWAII	455.75	91084.64	5454.03	4706.58	83348.04	8903.86	35.94	96994.42
OREGON	307.63	60099.73	4030.64	37507.44	11192.41	2740.53	12997.61	64437.99
WASHINGTON	961.92	89392.94	14329.19	38653.96	49570.04	9387.87	7072.18	104684.05

[a] Includes military use of distillate fuel oil, assumed to be primarily highway use

[b] Includes military use of residual fuel oil, assumed to be primarily marine use

Table 82

Expenditures On Petroleum Products, 1972, In Thousand Dollars, By State

Expenditures On Industrial, Energy Production And Miscellaneous Use By Sector And Function

REGION AND STATE	HOUSEHOLD Miscellaneous Use (Kerosine)	BUSINESS USE						TOTAL USE
		Industrial Use	Oil Company Use	LPG for Utility Gas	Electrical Utility Use	All Energy Production	Miscellaneous Business Use	
NEW ENGLAND:								
CONNECTICUT	978.00	54362.47	598.68	1462.18	124945.20	127006.06	2632.30	184978.83
MAINE	151.48	54944.95	312.29	327.61	24793.00	25432.90	1220.63	81749.95
MASSACHUSETTS	1778.37	52926.41	5208.33	1627.57	190738.50	197574.41	5830.60	258109.77
NEW HAMPSHIRE	242.25	10524.75	12.34	1137.02	10187.10	11336.46	747.29	22850.76
RHODE ISLAND	176.79	11154.53	4144.52	249.83	11330.80	15725.15	708.98	27765.45
VERMONT	201.31	3775.65	13.97	436.21	941.60	1391.78	548.86	5917.60
MID ATLANTIC:								
NEW JERSEY	1207.56	78500.83	53073.61	1056.21	216473.50	270603.31	5552.62	355864.32
NEW YORK	3752.04	85446.17	8822.88	224.81	367936.50	376984.19	11115.83	477298.23
PENNSYLVANIA	2629.23	97832.55	80651.76	1590.16	122555.50	204797.42	12054.57	317313.78
EAST NORTH CENTRAL:								
ILLINOIS	5388.87	56009.12	100314.51	810.09	57375.40	158500.01	18449.26	238347.26
INDIANA	60.98	45299.01	66028.32	44.34	4662.70	70735.37	7671.74	123767.09
MICHIGAN	2376.33	53553.47	12904.96	504.46	44076.90	57486.32	6566.45	119982.58
OHIO	5378.29	61824.22	49937.74	1524.47	15352.90	66815.11	9398.36	143415.98
WISCONSIN	258.33	18859.53	3820.26	361.74·	4222.50	8404.50	3303.72	30826.08
WEST NORTH CENTRAL:								
IOWA	604.64	16322.78	88.96	840.95	3938.90	4868.81	6604.87	28401.09
KANSAS	181.58	15500.72	25197.62	0.00	3046.30	28243.92	2006.80	45933.01
MINNESOTA	205.12	41210.10	10283.61	557.49	9655.20	20496.30	3605.30	65516.82
MISSOURI	645.67	17392.51	7703.79	1263.92	3212.10	12179.82	3042.56	33260.55
NEBRASKA	57.51	10223.64	1546.91	1201.68	2081.80	4830.39	1823.56	16935.10
NORTH DAKOTA	189.28	3795.24	6027.24	296.64	183.30	6507.19	2117.37	12609.08
SOUTH DAKOTA	4.25	3365.19	162.17	632.06	1440.30	2234.52	1895.35	7499.32
SOUTH ATLANTIC:								
DELAWARE	150.09	22943.39	2587.73	66.92	18562.10	21216.75	4739.19	49049.42
DISTRICT OF COLUMBIA	21.27	1045.23	41.53	209.89	21487.70	21739.12	680.79	23486.41
FLORIDA	3890.43	59935.02	1996.09	976.41	234973.50	237946.00	8228.96	310000.42
GEORGIA	1216.05	57541.12	614.16	398.52	18654.10	19666.78	8064.86	86488.81
MARYLAND	325.89	54944.62	2058.79	1181.17	91873.90	95113.86	3637.43	154021.80
NORTH CAROLINA	4708.38	80467.43	341.90	89.47	19577.50	20008.87	14223.27	119407.95
SOUTH CAROLINA	814.14	36927.74	516.53	491.35	9987.90	10995.78	4419.76	53157.41
VIRGINIA	1816.76	52915.39	10212.20	780.06	88232.80	99225.06	8791.19	162748.41
WEST VIRGINIA	158.46	11810.39	926.51	0.00	3393.10	4319.61	932.33	17220.78
EAST SOUTH CENTRAL:								
ALABAMA	1133.99	22442.65	3978.69	25.23	2216.00	6219.92	5326.37	35122.93
KENTUCKY	1670.50	13347.73	14093.34	459.00	1996.50	16548.84	3476.96	35044.03
MISSISSIPPI	7397.79	15216.81	15706.41	394.26	14128.50	30229.17	10862.00	63705.78
TENNESSEE	3085.73	19519.91	359.14	234.06	787.80	1381.01	3971.90	27958.54
WEST SOUTH CENTRAL:								
ARKANSAS	1093.75	15474.60	3485.68	0.00	19122.30	22607.98	9742.16	48918.49
LOUISIANA	5943.38	49851.88	81192.97	0.00	5503.10	86696.07	15863.45	158354.78
OKLAHOMA	822.25	19577.83	21994.71	0.00	546.40	22541.11	2665.87	45607.05
TEXAS	11592.06	55064.50	206049.93	501.46	7270.10	213821.48	41063.59	321541.64
ROCKY MOUNTAIN:								
ARIZONA	215.83	19036.47	128.62	0.00	7556.20	7684.82	2858.25	29795.36
COLORADO	1809.02	14216.36	4966.60	294.60	2134.90	7396.10	6093.08	29514.56
IDAHO	544.88	10957.28	81.58	0.00	4.90	86.48	3364.58	14953.22
MONTANA	1225.14	10839.53	14238.81	0.00	66.70	14305.51	2995.09	29365.26
NEVADA	13.95	5416.70	135.60	0.00	624.50	760.10	1395.68	7586.43
NEW MEXICO	1177.60	12089.17	2575.87	0.00	1858.80	4434.67	4355.09	22056.53
UTAH	701.99	21448.15	11004.58	0.00	4936.60	15941.18	2454.45	40545.77
WYOMING	539.03	9663.15	13398.99	0.00	606.60	14005.59	1399.98	25607.74
FAR WEST:								
ALASKA	42.62	11028.51	1060.08	0.00	2888.40	3948.48	1817.75	16837.36
CALIFORNIA	421.96	134034.76	115573.61	3344.56	187952.90	306871.07	19232.29	460560.08
HAWAII	93.12	10415.53	20671.73	1359.79	45276.40	67307.92	3095.87	80912.43
OREGON	321.43	32998.26	7228.52	0.00	113.50	7342.02	2721.95	43383.66
WASHINGTON	152.94	39505.77	37244.63	63.50	303.70	37611.83	6263.95	83534.49

Table 83

Consumption In Billion BTU And Expenditures In Thousand Dollars, Petroleum Products, 1972, By Region

Gasoline Use, By Sector and Function

REGION	USE BY SECTOR					USE BY FUNCTION			TOTAL USE
	Household Passenger Car & Motorcycle	Household Total	Business	Federal Government	State And Local Govt.	Highway	Aviation	Marine	
Consumption In Billion BTU									
NEW ENGLAND	491956.70	496792.80	132769.50	9965.00	8044.40	639420.10	3840.00	4311.70	647571.79
MID ATLANTIC	1328645.50	1341438.91	356052.30	18672.40	27348.30	1724550.71	7221.80	11739.10	1743511.80
EAST NORTH CENTRAL	1686457.23	1705839.28	572649.50	11891.40	37504.30	2301175.00	9549.20	17160.30	2327884.49
WEST NORTH CENTRAL	663225.40	672553.31	381996.50	4972.90	17624.70	1063100.09	6460.50	7596.90	1077157.41
SOUTH ATLANTIC	1384792.71	1401064.51	547316.30	19637.60	3598.40	1977526.69	13145.30	13440.70	2004112.60
EAST SOUTH CENTRAL	527525.20	534464.50	272355.40	10637.70	13459.80	819163.51	6003.70	5750.00	830917.40
WEST SOUTH CENTRAL	850980.19	863768.50	498535.00	23395.00	14567.20	1376809.40	13121.60	10334.70	1400265.71
ROCKY MOUNTAIN	364168.49	369860.30	239193.50	8242.70	11094.80	617894.40	6461.40	4035.50	628391.30
FAR WEST	1107791.50	1122421.89	473350.30	51940.00	28982.70	1643375.20	21875.70	11444.00	1676694.88
TOTAL	8405543.86	8508214.13	3474218.36	159464.70	194610.60	12163015.30	87679.20	85812.90	12336507.30
Expenditures In Thousand Dollars									
NEW ENGLAND	1488433.24	1499367.71	370858.99	18597.48	21765.21	1893705.73	7449.82	9433.89	1910589.39
MID ATLANTIC	4163303.78	4192840.64	1025836.79	36922.32	78055.85	5292147.62	14801.51	26706.42	5333655.48
EAST NORTH CENTRAL	4999229.61	5042973.76	1546449.57	22566.29	97422.12	6650904.19	21167.13	37340.52	6709411.89
WEST NORTH CENTRAL	1892798.23	1914141.29	984533.48	9791.20	44432.99	2921767.42	14709.14	16422.37	2952898.93
SOUTH ATLANTIC	4135081.13	4171683.38	1495524.70	37729.55	95951.98	5744671.08	27418.36	28800.09	5800889.58
EAST SOUTH CENTRAL	1555439.51	1571341.88	731606.19	20145.36	35145.57	2333061.01	12685.12	12492.91	2358239.00
WEST SOUTH CENTRAL	2330640.44	2359147.69	1237165.78	41148.62	35391.31	3625227.40	25867.65	21758.28	3672853.34
ROCKY MOUNTAIN	1065530.34	1079209.85	634148.77	17284.88	28591.23	1735362.91	15015.78	8856.02	1759234.74
FAR WEST	3196940.79	3231369.74	1244855.37	95493.91	74495.31	4577392.64	43786.07	25035.64	4646214.36
TOTAL	24827134.40	25062075.60	9270979.76	299679.62	511251.56	34774239.40	182900.58	186846.14	35143986.30

Table 84

Consumption In Billion BTU And Expenditures in Thousand Dollars, Petroleum Products, 1972, By Region

Petroleum Heating Fuels Use, By Sector

REGION	HOUSEHOLD USE	BUSINESS USE			FEDERAL GOVT.	STATE AND LOCAL GOVT.	TOTAL USE
		Commercial	Industrial	Total			
Consumption In Billion BTU							
NEW ENGLAND	658274.99	160084.70	77598.50	237683.30	4215.80	59787.90	959962.00
MID ATLANTIC	1264335.49	275371.90	127252.40	402624.20	6401.20	101894.10	1775255.00
EAST NORTH CENTRAL	674919.20	188115.40	32108.00	220223.40	3695.50	75324.40	974162.50
WEST NORTH CENTRAL	317834.20	80043.30	3011.90	83055.10	1925.20	31350.90	434165.40
SOUTH ATLANTIC	455054.60	108644.50	22500.90	131145.50	11679.50	53188.30	651067.90
EAST SOUTH CENTRAL	139257.60	8077.40	1495.00	9572.40	315.70	4392.80	153538.50
WEST SOUTH CENTRAL	210267.00	9698.70	1215.40	10913.70	409.50	5318.20	226908.40
ROCKY MOUNTAIN	113679.60	8822.70	1255.30	10078.00	502.40	4180.30	128440.30
FAR WEST	166440.40	35121.20	10106.10	45227.50	1180.40	14520.70	227369.00
TOTAL	4000063.17	873979.39	276543.49	1150523.13	30325.20	349957.60	5530868.99
Expenditures in Thousand Dollars							
NEW ENGLAND	1030445.81	154481.90	71078.90	225560.80	4387.40	62028.50	1322422.20
MID ATLANTIC	1886287.89	261121.20	114272.20	375393.40	6217.50	98436.40	2366335.00
EAST NORTH CENTRAL	1102629.61	220280.20	29601.70	249601.70	4326.40	89041.50	1445892.88
WEST NORTH CENTRAL	531008.80	95646.10	2561.80	98207.90	2269.40	37141.50	668628.31
SOUTH ATLANTIC	794545.31	112478.80	20140.90	132619.70	11968.20	57106.70	996239.90
EAST SOUTH CENTRAL	324050.70	8997.40	1296.80	10294.20	351.00	4902.90	339599.10
WEST SOUTH CENTRAL	381821.50	9069.50	933.40	10002.90	384.00	5011.90	397220.40
ROCKY MOUNTAIN	246022.10	9064.80	1154.70	10219.50	525.90	4441.20	261208.70
FAR WEST	314334.00	35832.90	9166.50	44999.40	1274.60	15433.10	376041.40
TOTAL	6611145.96	906972.81	250206.90	1157179.69	31704.60	373556.90	8173587.84

Table 85

Consumption In Billion BTU And Expenditures In Thousand Dollars, Petroleum Products, By Region

Transportation And Military Use Of Non-Gasoline Products By Sector And Function

REGION	USE BY SECTOR			USE BY FUNCTION				TOTAL USE
	Household (Marine)	Business	Federal	Highway[a]	Aviation	Marine[b]	Railroad	
Consumption In Billion BTU								
NEW ENGLAND	298.90	143289.10	75968.90	46737.20	104440.30	60556.30	7823.10	219556.90
MID ATLANTIC	2266.00	618971.60	126655.60	144538.70	349216.70	215725.50	38412.30	747893.21
EAST NORTH CENTRAL	1574.50	565339.20	60625.90	246467.50	267803.20	15209.20	98059.80	627539.60
WEST NORTH CENTRAL	415.90	279058.20	18902.50	130634.60	96742.10	4410.30	66895.60	298382.60
SOUTH ATLANTIC	1311.20	539217.50	150083.90	181054.70	315477.30	126953.10	67180.40	690665.60
EAST SOUTH CENTRAL	3098.90	193217.50	42542.50	103652.80	67531.90	31670.00	36040.30	238058.90
WEST SOUTH CENTRAL	7896.40	510011.90	82346.30	188044.10	174876.40	157094.00	80240.10	600254.60
ROCKY MOUNTAIN	0.00	227947.50	26029.50	89545.90	100619.30	339.50	63482.20	253987.00
FAR WEST	3514.80	776304.10	260697.20	176146.10	614520.60	173630.40	76219.00	1040516.10
TOTAL	20376.60	3853409.59	843868.28	1306821.63	2091227.79	785288.31	534316.81	4717654.44
Expenditures In Thousand Dollars								
NEW ENGLAND	398.83	173847.66	60578.22	94966.98	94771.53	38055.85	7030.35	234824.71
MID ATLANTIC	2854.29	689398.10	101805.12	306278.03	318623.72	136205.32	32950.44	794057.52
EAST NORTH CENTRAL	1871.98	767082.75	51609.76	507495.25	220162.69	13833.11	79073.41	820564.48
WEST NORTH CENTRAL	475.49	370940.28	14262.17	257647.65	74340.47	3528.18	50161.64	385677.93
SOUTH ATLANTIC	1637.47	679833.37	107458.32	379906.38	278224.68	74550.95	57091.15	788929.18
EAST SOUTH CENTRAL	3726.76	287086.03	35536.63	213352.51	56000.70	28185.90	28810.32	326349.42
WEST SOUTH CENTRAL	7982.03	562010.63	57817.55	349650.56	122431.37	99541.56	56186.73	627810.21
ROCKY MOUNTAIN	0.00	298536.51	21455.62	183605.21	85810.11	192.77	50384.06	319992.15
FAR WEST	4786.10	804688.37	213813.75	314761.44	531677.81	115922.95	60926.02	1023288.23
TOTAL	23732.95	4633423.69	664337.14	2606820.02	1782043.09	510016.59	422614.13	5321493.89

[a] Includes military use of distillate fuel oil

[b] Includes military use of residual fuel oil

Table 86

Consumption In Billion BTU And Expenditures In Thousand Dollars, Petroleum Products, 1972, By Region

Industrial, Energy Production and Miscellaneous Use By Sector and Function

REGION	HOUSEHOLD USE	BUSINESS USE						TOTAL USE
	Miscellaneous Use (Kerosine)	Industrial Use	Oil Company Use	LPG for Utility Gas	Electrical Utility Use	All Energy Production	Miscellaneous Business Use	

Consumption In Billion BTU

REGION	Miscellaneous Use (Kerosine)	Industrial Use	Oil Company Use	LPG for Utility Gas	Electrical Utility Use	All Energy Production	Miscellaneous Business Use	TOTAL USE
NEW ENGLAND	2185.80	190499.00	15807.00	5802.70	552014.89	573624.70	10030.50	776340.00
MID ATLANTIC	4813.80	260371.00	219071.60	3477.10	1036040.50	1259432.21	24861.10	1549478.01
EAST NORTH CENTRAL	9168.40	217496.10	365556.40	3467.10	172185.20	539208.70	36713.20	802586.21
WEST NORTH CENTRAL	1357.90	103607.20	89657.60	5209.90	32025.10	126892.70	17081.50	24893.10
SOUTH ATLANTIC	8338.20	388195.10	31311.30	4786.40	864042.40	900518.20	45546.40	1342642.88
EAST SOUTH CENTRAL	9154.20	63648.90	55983.20	1314.80	25487.40	82785.50	19661.30	175250.00
WEST SOUTH CENTRAL	15640.70	139263.70	591855.00	540.70	47617.80	640013.50	58927.00	853844.80
ROCKY MOUNTAIN	4332.00	91912.80	73207.40	246.30	24724.00	98177.70	19186.00	213608.50
FAR WEST	686.10	216380.70	289552.70	4040.30	319694.50	613287.50	26206.70	856560.70
TOTAL	55722.10	1671374.48	1730845.18	28885.40	3074210.17	4833940.57	258213.71	6819249.99

Expenditures In Thousand Dollars

REGION	Miscellaneous Use (Kerosine)	Industrial Use	Oil Company Use	LPG for Utility Gas	Electrical Utility Use	All Energy Production	Miscellaneous Business Use	TOTAL USE
NEW ENGLAND	3528.20	187688.76	10290.13	5240.42	362936.20	378466.76	11688.66	581372.37
MID ATLANTIC	7588.83	261779.55	142548.25	2871.19	706965.50	852384.92	28723.02	1150476.35
EAST NORTH CENTRAL	13462.80	235545.35	233005.79	3245.10	125690.40	361941.31	45389.53	656338.99
WEST NORTH CENTRAL	1888.05	107810.18	51010.30	4792.75	23557.90	79360.95	21095.81	210154.97
SOUTH ATLANTIC	13101.47	378530.33	19295.44	4193.79	506742.60	530231.83	53717.78	975581.43
EAST SOUTH CENTRAL	13288.01	70527.10	34137.58	1112.55	19128.80	54378.94	23637.23	161831.28
WEST SOUTH CENTRAL	19451.44	139968.81	312723.29	501.46	32441.90	346566.64	69335.07	574421.96
ROCKY MOUNTAIN	6227.44	103666.81	46630.65	294.60	17789.20	64614.45	24916.20	199424.87
FAR WEST	1032.07	227982.83	181778.57	4767.85	236534.90	423081.32	33131.81	685228.03
TOTAL	79568.31	1713499.74	1031320.01	27019.70	2031787.43	3090127.04	311635.10	5194830.30

Table 87

Consumption Of Petroleum Products, 1972, In Billion BTU, By State

Aggregate Use By Sector

REGION AND STATE	HOUSEHOLD	BUSINESS	FEDERAL GOVERNMENT	STATE & LOCAL GOVERNMENT	ALL
NEW ENGLAND:					
CONNECTICUT	253205.7	325344.5	7793.5	8692.5	595036.1
MAINE	113674.3	164555.1	26828.2	6643.6	311701.1
MASSACHUSETTS	566744.4	656663.1	37186.9	42853.5	1303448.0
NEW HAMPSHIRE	84617.2	53967.1	1145.2	3641.8	143371.3
RHODE ISLAND	84872.6	67922.2	16975.9	4685.5	174456.3
VERMONT	54438.3	19444.1	220.0	1315.4	75417.9
MID ATLANTIC:					
NEW JERSEY	631232.2	746070.9	44501.7	23252.0	1445056.6
NEW YORK	1230643.4	1408721.7	77731.7	81562.1	2798658.9
PENNSYLVANIA	750978.6	767519.7	29495.8	24428.3	1572422.5
EAST NORTH CENTRAL:					
ILLINOIS	606270.1	784414.5	23639.8	33151.3	1447475.7
INDIANA	343527.4	383392.7	3416.6	19495.8	749832.6
MICHIGAN	573555.4	378526.9	34157.3	30836.9	1017076.4
OHIO	568648.8	439686.9	6634.1	15145.5	1030115.2
WISCONSIN	299499.7	165609.0	8365.0	14199.2	487672.9
WEST NORTH CENTRAL:					
IOWA	172555.6	136524.6	967.5	9735.3	319783.0
KANSAS	110500.6	171668.2	6292.3	5278.6	293739.8
MINNESOTA	266073.1	230826.2	11570.1	13945.8	522415.2
MISSOURI	270376.0	263373.7	2884.7	9754.4	546388.8
NEBRASKA	89135.9	99427.2	2557.1	4748.6	195868.8
NORTH DAKOTA	36223.9	49804.0	1029.3	2849.9	89907.1
SOUTH DAKOTA	47306.2	40067.1	505.6	2663.0	90541.8
SOUTH ATLANTIC:					
DELAWARE	47305.5	79254.3	1322.5	2178.0	130060.4
DISTRICT OF COLUMBIA	37075.8	64356.3	9400.1	8320.3	119152.5
FLORIDA	412996.1	809150.3	13544.1	14153.1	1249843.6
GEORGIA	264095.0	316951.5	10795.5	9446.9	601288.9
MARYLAND	241597.6	341071.9	32318.6	14975.3	629963.4
NORTH CAROLINA	339707.7	288962.0	14952.5	18218.7	661840.8
SOUTH CAROLINA	158018.9	134222.5	13485.5	5405.8	311132.6
VIRGINIA	297753.8	448399.2	85268.3	13116.0	844537.2
WEST VIRGINIA	67263.1	69624.1	423.9	3358.6	140669.6
EAST SOUTH CENTRAL:					
ALABAMA	182216.6	161132.3	21117.5	4426.3	368892.7
KENTUCKY	164875.4	151864.0	19989.6	3690.7	340419.8
MISSISSIPPI	130170.2	153803.4	2486.9	2243.1	288703.7
TENNESSEE	208713.0	174441.3	9901.9	7492.5	400548.6
WEST SOUTH CENTRAL:					
ARKANSAS	119240.8	148067.5	4971.0	2402.9	274682.3
LOUISIANA	163158.5	402403.4	30290.3	2474.1	598326.3
OKLAHOMA	146836.0	181087.1	4448.5	4644.8	337016.3
TEXAS	668337.3	1126106.7	66441.0	10363.6	1871248.6
ROCKY MOUNTAIN:					
ARIZONA	89711.1	117691.1	2277.2	2473.9	212153.2
COLORADO	126147.4	139700.8	10272.1	4100.9	280221.2
IDAHO	51787.0	44374.7	623.3	1655.7	98440.7
MONTANA	38521.1	82233.4	3522.3	1526.2	125803.1
NEVADA	35729.6	46605.0	2464.9	821.9	85621.4
NEW MEXICO	60972.4	84745.1	7368.2	1290.8	154376.5
UTAH	57788.7	102060.9	7389.1	2029.0	169267.7
WYOMING	27214.6	69084.5	867.5	1376.7	98543.3
FAR WEST:					
ALASKA	23328.1	65726.6	23079.9	983.0	113117.4
CALIFORNIA	910425.2	1494982.3	257810.4	21678.6	2684896.5
HAWAII	27834.4	180846.0	6076.6	826.5	215583.6
OREGON	140394.0	151106.9	7132.3	8892.3	307525.5
WASHINGTON	191081.5	258094.7	19718.4	11123.0	480017.7

Table 88

Consumption Of Petroleum Products, 1972, In Million BTU Per Capita, By State

Aggregate Use By Sector

REGION AND STATE	HOUSEHOLD	BUSINESS	FEDERAL GOVERNMENT	STATE & LOCAL GOVERNMENT	ALL
NEW ENGLAND:					
CONNECTICUT	82.210	105.631	2.530	2.822	193.194
MAINE	110.794	160.385	26.148	6.475	303.802
MASSACHUSETTS	97.782	113.296	6.416	7.394	224.888
NEW HAMPSHIRE	109.325	69.725	1.480	4.705	185.234
RHODE ISLAND	87.588	70.095	17.519	4.835	180.037
VERMONT	118.344	42.270	0.478	2.860	163.952
MID ATLANTIC:					
NEW JERSEY	85.894	101.520	6.055	3.164	196.633
NEW YORK	67.003	76.699	4.232	4.441	152.374
PENNSYLVANIA	63.081	64.470	2.478	2.052	132.081
EAST NORTH CENTRAL:					
ILLINOIS	53.919	69.763	2.102	2.948	128.733
INDIANA	64.988	72.530	0.646	3.688	141.853
MICHIGAN	63.636	41.998	3.790	3.421	112.845
OHIO	53.036	41.008	0.619	1.413	96.075
WISCONSIN	66.173	36.591	1.848	3.137	107.749
WEST NORTH CENTRAL:					
IOWA	59.832	47.339	0.335	3.376	110.882
KANSAS	48.722	75.691	2.774	2.327	129.515
MINNESOTA	68.629	59.537	2.984	3.597	134.747
MISSOURI	56.957	55.482	0.608	2.055	115.102
NEBRASKA	58.335	65.070	1.673	3.108	128.186
NORTH DAKOTA	57.135	78.555	1.624	4.495	141.809
SOUTH DAKOTA	69.568	58.922	0.744	3.916	133.150
SOUTH ATLANTIC:					
DELAWARE	82.847	138.799	2.316	3.814	227.777
DISTRICT OF COLUMBIA	49.303	85.580	12.500	11.064	158.447
FLORIDA	56.213	110.133	1.843	1.926	170.116
GEORGIA	55.799	66.966	2.281	1.996	127.042
MARYLAND	59.683	84.257	7.984	3.699	155.623
NORTH CAROLINA	65.066	55.346	2.864	3.490	126.765
SOUTH CAROLINA	58.787	49.934	5.017	2.011	115.749
VIRGINIA	62.488	94.103	17.895	2.753	177.238
WEST VIRGINIA	37.472	38.788	0.236	1.871	78.367
EAST SOUTH CENTRAL:					
ALABAMA	51.751	45.763	5.998	1.257	104.769
KENTUCKY	49.872	45.936	6.046	1.116	102.970
MISSISSIPPI	57.700	68.175	1.102	0.994	127.971
TENNESSEE	51.256	42.839	2.432	1.840	98.367
WEST SOUTH CENTRAL:					
ARKANSAS	59.383	73.739	2.476	1.197	136.794
LOUISIANA	43.649	107.652	8.103	0.662	160.066
OKLAHOMA	55.768	68.776	1.690	1.764	127.997
TEXAS	57.595	97.045	5.726	0.893	161.259
ROCKY MOUNTAIN:					
ARIZONA	45.701	59.955	1.160	1.260	108.076
COLORADO	53.362	59.095	4.345	1.735	118.537
IDAHO	68.592	58.774	0.826	2.193	130.385
MONTANA	53.800	114.851	4.919	2.132	175.703
NEVADA	67.035	87.439	4.625	1.542	160.641
NEW MEXICO	56.666	78.759	6.848	1.200	143.473
UTAH	51.277	90.560	6.556	1.800	150.193
WYOMING	78.655	199.666	2.507	3.979	284.807
FAR WEST:					
ALASKA	71.779	202.236	71.015	3.025	348.054
CALIFORNIA	44.605	73.244	12.631	1.062	131.542
HAWAII	34.111	221.625	7.447	1.013	264.196
OREGON	64.254	69.156	3.264	4.070	140.744
WASHINGTON	55.904	75.510	5.769	3.254	140.438

Table 89

Index Of Per Capita Consumption Of Petroleum Products, 1972 (U.S. BTU Per Capita Set at 100), By State

Aggregate Use By Sector

REGION & STATE	HOUSEHOLD	BUSINESS	FEDERAL GOVERNMENT	STATE & LOCAL GOVERNMENT	ALL
NEW ENGLAND:					
CONNECTICUT	136.0	144.3	51.0	107.9	136.8
MAINE	183.3	219.1	526.8	247.6	215.1
MASSACHUSETTS	161.8	154.8	129.2	282.7	159.3
NEW HAMPSHIRE	180.9	95.3	29.8	179.9	131.2
RHODE ISLAND	144.9	95.8	352.9	184.9	127.5
VERMONT	195.8	57.7	9.6	109.4	116.1
MID ATLANTIC:					
NEW JERSEY	142.1	138.7	122.0	121.0	139.2
NEW YORK	110.9	104.8	85.3	169.8	107.9
PENNSYLVANIA	104.4	88.1	49.9	78.5	93.5
EAST NORTH CENTRAL:					
ILLINOIS	89.2	95.3	42.4	112.7	91.2
INDIANA	107.5	99.1	13.0	141.0	100.5
MICHIGAN	105.3	57.4	76.3	130.8	79.9
OHIO	87.8	56.0	12.5	54.0	68.0
WISCONSIN	109.5	50.0	37.2	120.0	76.3
WEST NORTH CENTRAL:					
IOWA	99.0	64.7	6.8	129.1	78.5
KANSAS	80.6	103.4	55.9	89.0	91.7
MINNESOTA	113.6	81.3	60.1	137.6	95.4
MISSOURI	94.2	75.8	12.2	78.6	81.5
NEBRASKA	96.5	88.9	33.7	118.8	90.8
NORTH DAKOTA	94.5	107.3	32.7	171.9	100.4
SOUTH DAKOTA	115.1	80.5	15.0	149.8	94.3
SOUTH ATLANTIC:					
DELAWARE	137.1	189.6	46.7	145.9	161.3
DISTRICT OF COLUMBIA	81.6	116.9	251.8	423.1	112.2
FLORIDA	93.0	150.5	37.1	73.7	120.5
GEORGIA	92.3	91.5	45.9	76.3	90.0
MARYLAND	98.8	115.1	160.8	141.5	110.2
NORTH CAROLINA	107.7	75.6	57.7	133.4	89.8
SOUTH CAROLINA	97.3	68.2	101.1	76.9	82.0
VIRGINIA	103.4	128.6	360.5	105.3	125.5
WEST VIRGINIA	62.0	53.0	4.8	71.6	55.5
EAST SOUTH CENTRAL:					
ALABAMA	85.6	62.5	120.8	48.1	74.2
KENTUCKY	82.5	62.8	121.8	42.7	72.9
MISSISSIPPI	95.5	93.1	22.2	38.0	90.6
TENNESSEE	84.8	58.5	49.0	70.4	69.7
WEST SOUTH CENTRAL:					
ARKANSAS	98.3	100.7	49.9	45.8	96.9
LOUISIANA	72.2	147.1	163.2	25.3	113.4
OKLAHOMA	92.3	94.0	34.0	67.5	90.6
TEXAS	95.3	132.6	115.3	34.2	114.2
ROCKY MOUNTAIN:					
ARIZONA	75.6	81.9	23.4	48.2	76.5
COLORADO	88.3	80.7	87.5	66.3	83.9
IDAHO	113.5	80.3	16.6	83.9	92.3
MONTANA	89.0	156.9	99.1	81.5	124.4
NEVADA	110.9	119.5	93.2	59.0	113.8
NEW MEXICO	93.8	107.6	137.9	45.9	101.6
UTAH	84.8	123.7	132.1	68.8	106.4
WYOMING	130.1	272.8	50.5	152.2	201.7
FAR WEST:					
ALASKA	118.8	276.3	1430.6	115.7	246.5
CALIFORNIA	73.8	100.1	254.5	40.6	93.2
HAWAII	56.4	302.8	150.0	38.7	187.1
OREGON	106.3	94.5	65.8	155.6	99.7
WASHINGTON	92.5	103.2	116.2	124.4	99.5

Table 90

Expenditures On Petroleum Products, 1972, In Thousand Dollars, By State

Aggregate Use By Sector

REGION AND STATE	HOUSEHOLD	BUSINESS	FEDERAL GOVERNMENT	STATE & LOCAL GOVERNMENT	ALL
NEW ENGLAND:					
CONNECTICUT	605777.1	336796.8	7595.3	13093.9	963263.0
MAINE	246560.9	187419.3	28398.0	8399.9	470778.1
MASSACHUSETTS	1186560.8	633957.0	34016.6	49026.8	1903561.2
NEW HAMPSHIRE	186687.8	71268.7	1161.5	5116.1	264234.0
RHODE ISLAND	182803.5	81022.3	12065.9	6112.8	282004.3
VERMONT	125350.6	37647.5	325.8	2044.2	165368.0
MID ATLANTIC:					
NEW JERSEY	1399450.9	771667.0	37290.8	32668.1	2241076.6
NEW YORK	2900959.3	1480149.8	81866.0	107845.3	4570820.3
PENNSYLVANIA	1789161.5	981699.0	25788.2	35978.9	2832627.5
EAST NORTH CENTRAL:					
ILLINOIS	1615789.3	996344.0	23935.0	51174.4	2687242.7
INDIANA	847324.8	572381.9	3789.0	28895.3	1452391.0
MICHIGAN	1395466.7	612466.2	34275.5	56189.6	2098398.0
OHIO	1602342.6	726430.5	7819.0	27992.9	2364585.1
WISCONSIN	700014.7	298667.7	8684.2	22224.6	1029591.4
WEST NORTH CENTRAL:					
IOWA	442820.4	275641.2	1393.1	18763.4	738618.2
KANSAS	279257.3	247857.5	5515.2	9892.3	542522.4
MINNESOTA	615324.1	360073.6	11133.7	20949.2	1007480.6
MISSOURI	695733.0	441455.4	3492.6	14516.0	1155197.1
NEBRASKA	230587.2	182951.6	2690.7	8693.5	424923.2
NORTH DAKOTA	77045.1	78070.0	1251.2	4474.2	160840.3
SOUTH DAKOTA	106746.6	75899.3	846.2	4286.0	187778.2
SOUTH ATLANTIC:					
DELAWARE	116780.9	87848.7	1197.7	3122.9	208950.2
DISTRICT OF COLUMBIA	95527.7	65244.1	9735.0	9065.4	179572.2
FLORIDA	1151440.2	832510.2	14664.1	25297.1	2023911.6
GEORGIA	737849.6	501436.7	10781.6	16235.6	1266303.6
MARYLAND	624705.2	392029.8	30882.5	18869.9	1066487.4
NORTH CAROLINA	879499.6	501073.6	15401.9	38386.4	1434361.4
SOUTH CAROLINA	430712.7	237551.2	14276.7	11748.1	694288.7
VIRGINIA	748123.4	511625.9	59475.1	23379.5	1342604.1
WEST VIRGINIA	196328.3	141137.4	741.4	6954.0	345160.9
EAST SOUTH CENTRAL:					
ALABAMA	519504.7	298190.0	21707.1	10125.7	849527.8
KENTUCKY	465304.3	286119.8	20389.1	8160.6	779973.7
MISSISSIPPI	358514.5	254723.8	2975.1	4806.6	621020.1
TENNESSEE	569083.9	338496.1	10961.7	16955.6	935497.2
WEST SOUTH CENTRAL:					
ARKANSAS	314922.5	257722.2	5438.3	4894.1	582977.3
LOUISIANA	423558.6	429201.3	26318.0	5787.9	884865.9
OKLAHOMA	371541.0	290650.5	3555.3	10581.6	676328.4
TEXAS	1658380.5	1386575.8	64038.5	19139.6	3128134.4
ROCKY MOUNTAIN:					
ARIZONA	259672.9	221386.4	3328.2	6368.8	490756.3
COLORADO	354932.2	239669.6	10825.1	9024.4	614451.1
IDAHO	125122.8	87653.9	1168.6	3442.1	217387.2
MONTANA	97776.7	120599.1	3790.0	3136.7	225302.5
NEVADA	105406.4	83810.2	3581.9	1898.3	194696.9
NEW MEXICO	166837.3	151074.5	8374.3	3154.1	329440.0
UTAH	151484.9	143061.0	7106.5	3600.4	305252.9
WYOMING	70226.2	88847.5	1091.9	2407.6	162573.3
FAR WEST:					
ALASKA	55414.8	87505.2	29732.4	2630.9	175283.4
CALIFORNIA	2567077.4	1894506.8	243470.4	50809.5	4755864.1
HAWAII	95135.0	196239.6	8222.8	2151.2	301748.6
OREGON	351325.5	226076.4	7709.8	14650.3	599762.0
WASHINGTON	482569.3	374411.1	21446.9	19686.5	898113.9

Table 91

Expenditures On Petroleum Products, 1972, In Dollars Per Capita, By State

Aggregate Use By Sector

REGION AND STATE	HOUSEHOLD	BUSINESS	FEDERAL GOVT.	STATE & LOCAL GOVT.	ALL
NEW ENGLAND:					
CONNECTICUT	196.7	109.3	2.5	4.3	312.7
MAINE	240.3	182.7	27.7	8.2	458.8
MASSACHUSETTS	204.7	109.4	5.9	8.5	328.4
NEW HAMPSHIRE	241.2	92.1	1.5	6.6	341.4
RHODE ISLAND	188.7	83.6	12.5	6.3	291.0
VERMONT	272.5	81.8	0.7	4.4	359.5
MID ATLANTIC:					
NEW JERSEY	190.4	105.0	5.1	4.4	304.9
NEW YORK	157.9	80.6	4.5	5.9	248.9
PENNSYLVANIA	150.3	82.5	2.2	3.0	237.9
EAST NORTH CENTRAL:					
ILLINOIS	143.7	88.6	2.1	4.6	239.0
INDIANA	160.3	108.3	0.7	5.5	274.8
MICHIGAN	154.8	68.0	3.8	6.2	232.8
OHIO	149.4	67.8	0.7	2.6	220.5
WISCONSIN	154.7	66.0	1.9	4.9	227.5
WEST NORTH CENTRAL:					
IOWA	153.5	95.6	0.5	6.5	256.1
KANSAS	123.1	109.3	2.4	4.4	239.2
MINNESOTA	158.7	92.9	2.9	5.4	259.9
MISSOURI	146.6	93.0	0.7	3.1	243.4
NEBRASKA	150.9	119.7	1.8	5.7	278.1
NORTH DAKOTA	121.5	123.1	2.0	7.1	253.7
SOUTH DAKOTA	157.0	111.6	1.2	6.3	276.1
SOUTH ATLANTIC:					
DELAWARE	204.5	153.9	2.1	5.5	365.9
DISTRICT OF COLUMBIA	127.0	86.8	12.9	12.1	238.8
FLORIDA	156.7	113.3	2.0	3.4	275.5
GEORGIA	155.9	105.9	2.3	3.4	267.5
MARYLAND	154.3	96.8	7.6	4.7	263.5
NORTH CAROLINA	168.5	96.0	2.9	7.4	274.7
SOUTH CAROLINA	160.2	88.4	5.3	4.4	258.3
VIRGINIA	157.0	107.4	12.5	4.9	281.8
WEST VIRGINIA	109.4	78.6	0.4	3.9	192.3
EAST SOUTH CENTRAL:					
ALABAMA	147.5	84.7	6.2	2.9	241.3
KENTUCKY	140.7	86.5	6.2	2.5	235.9
MISSISSIPPI	158.9	112.9	1.3	2.1	275.3
TENNESSEE	139.8	83.1	2.7	4.2	229.7
WEST SOUTH CENTRAL:					
ARKANSAS	156.8	128.3	2.7	2.4	290.3
LOUISIANA	113.3	114.8	7.0	1.5	236.7
OKLAHOMA	141.1	110.4	1.4	4.0	256.9
TEXAS	142.9	119.5	5.5	1.6	269.6
ROCKY MOUNTAIN:					
ARIZONA	132.3	112.8	1.7	3.2	250.0
COLORADO	150.1	101.4	4.6	3.8	259.9
IDAHO	165.7	116.1	1.5	4.6	287.9
MONTANA	136.6	168.4	5.3	4.4	314.7
NEVADA	197.8	157.2	6.7	3.6	365.3
NEW MEXICO	155.1	140.4	7.8	2.9	306.2
UTAH	134.4	126.9	6.3	3.2	270.9
WYOMING	203.0	256.8	3.2	7.0	469.9
FAR WEST:					
ALASKA	170.5	269.2	91.5	8.1	539.3
CALIFORNIA	125.8	92.8	11.9	2.5	233.0
HAWAII	116.6	240.5	10.1	2.6	369.8
OREGON	160.8	103.5	3.5	6.7	274.5
WASHINGTON	141.2	109.5	6.3	5.8	262.8

Table 92

Index Of Per Capita Expenditures On Petroleum Products, 1972 (U.S. Spending Per Capita = 100), By State

Aggregate Use By Sector

REGION & STATE	HOUSEHOLD	BUSINESS	FEDERAL GOVERNMENT	STATE & LOCAL GOVERNMENT	TOTAL
NEW ENGLAND:					
CONNECTICUT	128.9	112.9	51.6	100.1	121.0
MAINE	157.5	188.5	578.8	192.7	177.5
MASSACHUSETTS	134.2	112.9	122.7	199.1	127.0
NEW HAMPSHIRE	158.1	95.0	31.4	155.6	132.0
RHODE ISLAND	123.6	86.3	260.4	148.5	112.6
VERMONT	178.6	84.5	14.8	104.6	139.1
MID ATLANTIC:					
NEW JERSEY	124.8	108.4	106.1	104.6	118.0
NEW YORK	103.5	83.2	93.2	138.2	96.3
PENNSYLVANIA	98.5	85.1	45.3	71.1	92.0
EAST NORTH CENTRAL:					
ILLINOIS	94.2	91.4	44.5	107.1	92.4
INDIANA	105.0	111.7	15.0	128.7	106.3
MICHIGAN	101.5	70.1	79.5	146.7	90.1
OHIO	97.9	69.9	15.2	61.4	85.3
WISCONSIN	101.4	68.1	40.1	115.6	88.0
WEST NORTH CENTRAL:					
IOWA	100.6	98.6	10.1	153.1	99.1
KANSAS	80.7	112.8	50.9	102.7	92.5
MINNESOTA	104.0	95.8	60.1	127.2	100.5
MISSOURI	96.0	96.0	15.4	72.0	94.1
NEBRASKA	98.9	123.6	36.8	133.9	107.6
NORTH DAKOTA	79.6	127.1	41.3	166.1	98.1
SOUTH DAKOTA	102.9	115.2	26.0	148.3	106.8
SOUTH ATLANTIC:					
DELAWARE	134.0	158.8	43.9	128.7	141.5
DISTRICT OF COLUMBIA	83.2	89.5	270.7	283.7	92.4
FLORIDA	102.7	116.9	41.7	81.0	106.6
GEORGIA	102.2	109.3	47.6	80.7	103.5
MARYLAND	101.1	99.9	159.5	109.7	101.9
NORTH CAROLINA	110.4	99.0	61.7	173.0	106.3
SOUTH CAROLINA	105.0	91.2	111.1	102.9	99.9
VIRGINIA	102.9	110.8	261.0	115.5	109.0
WEST VIRGINIA	71.7	81.1	8.6	91.2	74.4
EAST SOUTH CENTRAL:					
ALABAMA	96.7	87.4	128.9	67.7	93.3
KENTUCKY	92.2	89.3	129.0	58.1	91.3
MISSISSIPPI	104.1	116.5	27.6	50.1	106.5
TENNESSEE	91.6	85.8	56.3	98.0	88.9
WEST SOUTH CENTRAL:					
ARKANSAS	102.8	132.5	56.6	57.4	112.3
LOUISIANA	74.3	118.5	147.2	36.4	91.6
OKLAHOMA	92.5	113.9	28.2	94.6	99.4
TEXAS	93.7	123.3	115.4	38.8	104.3
ROCKY MOUNTAIN:					
ARIZONA	86.7	116.4	35.5	76.4	96.7
COLORADO	98.4	104.6	95.8	89.8	100.5
IDAHO	108.6	119.8	32.4	107.3	111.4
MONTANA	89.5	173.8	110.7	103.1	121.7
NEVADA	129.6	162.3	140.5	83.8	141.3
NEW MEXICO	101.6	144.9	162.8	69.0	118.4
UTAH	88.1	131.0	131.9	75.2	104.8
WYOMING	133.0	265.0	66.0	163.8	181.7
FAR WEST:					
ALASKA	111.7	277.9	1913.1	190.5	208.6
CALIFORNIA	82.4	95.8	249.4	58.6	90.1
HAWAII	76.4	248.2	210.7	62.0	143.0
OREGON	105.4	106.8	73.8	157.8	106.2
WASHINGTON	92.5	113.0	131.2	135.6	101.6

Table 93

Petroleum Product Consumption In Billion BTU And Expenditures In Thousand Dollars, 1972, By Region

Aggregate Use By Sector

REGION	HOUSEHOLD	BUSINESS	FEDERAL GOVERNMENT	STATE & LOCAL GOVERNMENT	ALL
Consumption In Billion BTU					
NEW ENGLAND	1157552.50	1287896.09	90149.70	67832.30	2603430.75
MID ATLANTIC	2612854.21	2922312.28	151729.20	129242.40	5816138.01
EAST NORTH CENTRAL	2391501.40	2151630.04	76212.80	112828.70	4732172.75
WEST NORTH CENTRAL	992171.29	991691.01	25806.60	48975.60	2058644.48
SOUTH ATLANTIC	1865813.51	2551992.09	181511.00	89172.70	4688489.06
EAST SOUTH CENTRAL	685975.20	641241.00	53495.90	17852.60	1398564.80
WEST SOUTH CENTRAL	1097572.59	1857664.70	106150.80	19885.40	3081273.51
ROCKY MOUNTAIN	487871.90	686495.50	34784.60	15275.10	1224427.09
FAR WEST	1293063.20	2150756.49	313817.60	43503.40	3801140.67
TOTAL	12584376.00	15241679.20	1033658.20	544568.20	29404281.10
Expenditures In Thousand Dollars					
NEW ENGLAND	2533740.70	1348111.59	83563.10	83793.70	4049208.61
MID ATLANTIC	6089571.71	3233515.81	144945.00	176492.30	9644524.53
EAST NORTH CENTRAL	6160938.07	3206290.27	78502.70	186476.80	9632208.12
WEST NORTH CENTRAL	2447513.70	1661948.60	26322.70	81574.60	4217359.98
SOUTH ATLANTIC	4980967.57	3270457.61	157156.00	153058.90	8561640.16
EAST SOUTH CENTRAL	1912407.41	1177529.70	56033.00	40048.50	3186018.76
WEST SOUTH CENTRAL	2768402.62	2364149.82	99350.10	40403.20	5272305.98
ROCKY MOUNTAIN	1331459.41	1136102.20	39266.50	33032.40	2539860.23
FAR WEST	3551522.01	2778739.11	310582.30	89928.40	6730771.96
TOTAL	31776523.60	20176844.50	995721.39	884808.80	53833898.20

Table   94

Per Capita Consumption Of Petroleum Products, 1972, In Million BTU
    And In Index Numbers, U.S. Average = 100, By Region

Aggregate Use By Sector

REGION	HOUSE-HOLD	BUSINESS	FEDERAL GOVT.	STATE & LOCAL GOVT.	TOTAL
Consumption In Million BTU Per Capita					
NEW ENGLAND	95.626	106.394	7.447	5.604	215.071
MID ATLANTIC	69.452	77.678	4.033	3.435	154.598
EAST NORTH CENTRAL	58.628	52.748	1.868	2.766	116.010
WEST NORTH CENTRAL	59.705	59.676	1.553	2.947	123.880
SOUTH ATLANTIC	58.453	79.950	5.686	2.794	146.882
EAST SOUTH CENTRAL	52.146	48.745	4.067	1.357	106.314
WEST SOUTH CENTRAL	54.925	92.962	5.312	0.995	154.195
ROCKY MOUNTAIN	54.941	77.308	3.917	1.720	137.886
FAR WEST	47.618	79.203	11.557	1.602	139.979
UNITED STATES	60.436	73.197	4.964	2.615	141.212
Index Of Per Capita Consumption, U.S. Average = 100 (BTU Use)					
NEW ENGLAND	158.2	145.4	150.0	214.3	152.3
MID ATLANTIC	114.9	106.1	81.2	131.4	109.5
EAST NORTH CENTRAL	97.0	72.1	37.6	105.8	82.2
WEST NORTH CENTRAL	98.8	81.5	31.3	112.7	87.7
SOUTH ATLANTIC	96.7	109.2	114.5	106.8	104.0
EAST SOUTH CENTRAL	86.3	66.6	81.9	51.9	75.3
WEST SOUTH CENTRAL	90.9	127.0	107.0	38.0	109.2
ROCKY MOUNTAIN	90.9	105.6	78.9	65.8	97.6
FAR WEST	78.8	108.2	232.8	61.3	99.1
UNITED STATES	100.0	100.0	100.0	100.0	100.0

Table 95

Per Capita Expenditures On Petroleum Products, 1972, In Dollars and
In Index Numbers, U.S. Average Equals 100, By Region

Aggregate Use By Sector

REGION	HOUSEHOLD	BUSINESS	FEDERAL GOVT.	STATE & LOCAL GOVT.	TOTAL
Expenditures In Dollars Per Capita					
NEW ENGLAND	209.314	111.368	6.903	6.922	334.507
MID ATLANTIC	161.866	85.950	3.853	4.691	256.360
EAST NORTH CENTRAL	151.037	78.603	1.925	4.572	236.136
WEST NORTH CENTRAL	147.281	100.009	1.584	4.909	253.783
SOUTH ATLANTIC	156.045	102.458	4.923	4.795	268.222
EAST SOUTH CENTRAL	145.375	89.512	4.259	3.044	242.191
WEST SOUTH CENTRAL	138.538	118.308	4.972	2.022	263.840
ROCKY MOUNTAIN	149.939	127.939	4.422	3.720	286.020
FAR WEST	130.787	102.329	11.437	3.312	247.865
UNITED STATES	152.604	96.898	4.782	4.249	258.533

Index Of Per Capita Expenditures, U.S. Average = 100

REGION	HOUSEHOLD	BUSINESS	FEDERAL GOVT.	STATE & LOCAL GOVT.	TOTAL
NEW ENGLAND	137.2	114.9	144.4	162.9	129.4
MID ATLANTIC	106.1	88.7	80.6	110.4	99.2
EAST NORTH CENTRAL	99.0	81.1	40.3	107.6	91.3
WEST NORTH CENTRAL	96.5	103.2	33.1	115.5	98.2
SOUTH ATLANTIC	102.3	105.7	102.9	112.9	103.7
EAST SOUTH CENTRAL	95.3	92.4	89.1	71.6	93.7
WEST SOUTH CENTRAL	90.8	122.1	104.0	47.6	102.1
ROCKY MOUNTAIN	98.3	132.0	92.5	87.6	110.6
FAR WEST	85.7	105.6	239.2	77.9	95.9
UNITED STATES	100.0	100.0	100.0	100.0	100.0

Table 96

Petroleum Product Consumption In Billion BTU And Expenditures In Thousand Dollars, 1972, By State

Household Passenger Car And Motorcycle Gasoline Use Relative To Use Of All Other Petroleum Products

REGION AND STATE	CONSUMPTION IN BILLION BTU			EXPENDITURES IN THOUSAND DOLLARS			RATIO OF HOUSEHOLD CAR & MOTORCYCLE GASOLINE TO TOTAL	
	Household Car And Motorcycle Gasoline	All Other Petroleum Products	Total Consumption	Household Car And Motorcycle Gasoline	All Other Petroleum Products	Total Expenditures	Consumption	Expenditures
NEW ENGLAND:								
CONNECTICUT	131000.9	464035.2	595036.1	410858.1	552404.9	963263.0	0.2202	0.4265
MAINE	43045.8	268655.3	311701.1	133740.1	337038.0	470778.1	0.1381	0.2841
MASSACHUSETTS	226993.6	1076454.4	1303448.0	664142.1	1239419.1	1903561.2	0.1741	0.3489
NEW HAMPSHIRE	34813.9	108557.4	143371.3	106991.9	157242.1	264234.0	0.2428	0.4049
RHODE ISLAND	35065.5	139390.8	174456.3	103818.1	178186.2	282004.3	0.2010	0.3681
VERMONT	21037.0	54380.9	75417.9	68882.8	96485.2	165368.0	0.2789	0.4165
MID ATLANTIC:								
NEW JERSEY	310947.2	1134109.4	1445056.6	948869.8	1292206.8	2241076.6	0.2152	0.4234
NEW YORK	565083.1	2233575.8	2798658.9	1860112.3	2710708.0	4570820.3	0.2019	0.4070
PENNSYLVANIA	452615.2	1119807.3	1572422.5	1354052.7	1478574.8	2832627.5	0.2878	0.4780
EAST NORTH CENTRAL:								
ILLINOIS	437180.5	1010295.2	1447475.7	1338835.0	1348407.7	2687242.7	0.3020	0.4982
INDIANA	219539.2	530293.4	749832.6	642599.0	809792.1	1452391.0	0.2928	0.4424
MICHIGAN	393162.9	623913.5	1017076.4	1104239.7	994158.3	2098398.0	0.3866	0.5262
OHIO	458103.2	572012.0	1030115.2	1417390.7	947194.4	2364585.1	0.4447	0.5994
WISCONSIN	178471.4	309201.5	487672.9	496165.2	533426.2	1029591.4	0.3660	0.4819
WEST NORTH CENTRAL:								
IOWA	112433.6	207349.4	319783.0	333709.3	404908.9	738618.2	0.3516	0.4518
KANSAS	88412.5	205327.3	293739.8	237911.8	304610.7	542522.4	0.3010	0.4385
MINNESOTA	155285.0	367130.2	522415.2	452212.9	555267.7	1007480.6	0.2972	0.4489
MISSOURI	202606.8	343782.0	546388.8	572888.6	582308.5	1195197.1	0.3708	0.4959
NEBRASKA	59898.3	135970.5	195868.8	179663.5	245259.8	424923.2	0.3058	0.4228
NORTH DAKOTA	18418.7	71488.4	89907.1	47871.7	112968.6	160840.3	0.2049	0.2976
SOUTH DAKOTA	26170.5	64371.3	90541.8	68540.4	119237.9	187778.2	0.2890	0.3650
SOUTH ATLANTIC:								
DELAWARE	26056.1	104004.3	130060.4	81308.6	127641.6	208950.2	0.2003	0.3891
DISTRICT OF COLUMBIA	23826.7	95325.8	119152.5	74120.4	105451.8	179572.2	0.2000	0.4128
FLORIDA	349534.1	900309.5	1249843.6	1002219.1	1021692.5	2023911.6	0.2797	0.4952
GEORGIA	223998.1	377290.8	601288.9	651606.1	614697.4	1266303.6	0.3725	0.5146
MARYLAND	164134.2	465829.2	629963.4	514742.4	551745.1	1066487.4	0.2605	0.4827
NORTH CAROLINA	218155.8	443685.0	661840.8	676191.5	758169.9	1434361.4	0.3296	0.4714
SOUTH CAROLINA	117224.0	193908.6	311132.6	352412.1	341876.6	694288.7	0.3768	0.5076
VIRGINIA	204950.5	639586.7	844537.2	603345.1	739259.0	1342604.1	0.2427	0.4494
WEST VIRGINIA	56914.2	83755.4	140669.6	179135.7	166025.2	345160.9	0.4046	0.5190
EAST SOUTH CENTRAL:								
ALABAMA	143234.4	225658.3	368892.7	427037.9	422489.9	849527.8	0.3883	0.5027
KENTUCKY	127308.0	213111.8	340419.8	380068.7	399905.1	779973.7	0.3740	0.4873
MISSISSIPPI	88446.8	200256.9	288703.7	258367.3	362652.8	621020.1	0.3064	0.4160
TENNESSEE	168536.0	232012.6	400548.6	489965.6	445531.6	935497.2	0.4208	0.5237
WEST SOUTH CENTRAL:								
ARKANSAS	75012.9	199669.4	274682.3	217238.3	365738.9	582977.3	0.2731	0.3726
LOUISIANA	133904.9	464421.4	598326.3	376268.5	508597.4	884865.9	0.2238	0.4252
OKLAHOMA	108043.2	228973.1	337016.3	307841.6	368486.8	676328.4	0.3206	0.4552
TEXAS	534019.2	1337229.4	1871248.6	1429298.0	1698836.4	3128134.4	0.2854	0.4569
ROCKY MOUNTAIN:								
ARIZONA	81289.6	130863.6	212153.2	238881.0	251875.4	490756.3	0.3832	0.4868
COLORADO	96713.0	183508.2	280221.2	281040.4	333410.7	614451.1	0.3451	0.4574
IDAHO	29932.0	68508.7	98440.7	85188.2	132199.1	217387.2	0.3041	0.3919
MONTANA	24844.2	100958.9	125803.1	70856.9	154445.6	225302.5	0.1975	0.3145
NEVADA	27096.6	58524.8	85621.4	86507.8	108189.1	194696.9	0.3165	0.4443
NEW MEXICO	45138.0	109238.5	154376.5	132260.1	197180.0	329440.0	0.2924	0.4015
UTAH	43457.4	125810.3	169267.7	126515.4	178737.5	305252.9	0.2567	0.4145
WYOMING	15697.7	82845.6	98543.3	44280.6	118292.7	162573.3	0.1593	0.2724
FAR WEST:								
ALASKA	6459.7	106657.7	113117.4	22628.4	152655.0	175283.4	0.0571	0.1291
CALIFORNIA	854501.7	1830394.8	2684896.5	2442357.9	2313506.2	4755864.1	0.3183	0.5135
HAWAII	24089.6	191494.0	215583.6	81793.7	219955.0	301748.6	0.1117	0.2711
OREGON	98965.3	208560.2	307525.5	286117.1	313644.9	599762.0	0.3218	0.4771
WASHINGTON	123775.2	356242.5	480017.7	364043.7	534070.2	898113.9	0.2579	0.4053

Table 97

Expenditures On Petroleum Products, 1972, In Dollars Per Capita, And As Fraction Of Total, By State

Household Sector Use By Category, And Category As Fraction Of Total

REGION AND STATE	DOLLARS PER CAPITA				FRACTION OF TOTAL		
	Passenger Car And Motorcycle Gasoline	Heating Fuels	All Other	Total Households	Passenger Car And Motorcycle Gasoline	Heating Fuels	All Other
NEW ENGLAND:							
CONNECTICUT	133.40	62.12	1.16	196.68	0.6782	0.3159	0.0059
MAINE	130.35	108.40	1.56	240.31	0.5424	0.4511	0.0065
MASSACHUSETTS	114.59	89.08	1.06	204.72	0.5597	0.4351	0.0052
NEW HAMPSHIRE	138.23	101.90	1.06	241.20	0.5731	0.4225	0.0044
RHODE ISLAND	107.14	79.58	1.93	188.65	0.5679	0.4218	0.0103
VERMONT	149.75	120.88	1.87	272.50	0.5495	0.4436	0.0069
MID ATLANTIC:							
NEW JERSEY	129.12	59.93	1.38	190.43	0.6780	0.3147	0.0073
NEW YORK	101.27	55.53	1.14	157.94	0.6412	0.3516	0.0072
PENNSYLVANIA	113.74	35.78	0.77	150.29	0.7568	0.2381	0.0051
EAST NORTH CENTRAL:							
ILLINOIS	119.07	23.26	1.37	143.70	0.8286	0.1618	0.0096
INDIANA	121.57	37.51	1.22	160.30	0.7584	0.2340	0.0076
MICHIGAN	122.52	30.63	1.68	154.83	0.7913	0.1978	0.0109
OHIO	132.19	15.71	1.54	149.44	0.8846	0.1051	0.0103
WISCONSIN	109.63	43.82	1.22	154.67	0.7088	0.2833	0.0079
WEST NORTH CENTRAL:							
IOWA	115.71	36.30	1.53	153.54	0.7536	0.2364	0.0100
KANSAS	104.90	17.00	1.23	123.13	0.8519	0.1381	0.0100
MINNESOTA	116.64	40.59	1.48	158.71	0.7349	0.2558	0.0093
MISSOURI	120.68	24.34	1.54	146.56	0.8234	0.1661	0.0105
NEBRASKA	117.58	32.17	1.15	150.91	0.7792	0.2132	0.0076
NORTH DAKOTA	75.51	44.57	1.45	121.52	0.6213	0.3668	0.0119
SOUTH DAKOTA	100.79	55.05	1.14	156.98	0.6421	0.3507	0.0073
SOUTH ATLANTIC:							
DELAWARE	142.40	61.20	0.92	204.52	0.6962	0.2992	0.0045
DISTRICT OF COLUMBIA	98.56	28.09	0.38	127.03	0.7759	0.2211	0.0030
FLORIDA	136.41	18.12	2.19	156.72	0.8704	0.1156	0.0140
GEORGIA	137.67	16.65	1.58	155.89	0.8831	0.1068	0.0101
MARYLAND	127.16	26.16	1.01	154.32	0.8240	0.1695	0.0065
NORTH CAROLINA	129.51	36.86	2.08	168.45	0.7688	0.2188	0.0123
SOUTH CAROLINA	131.11	27.49	1.64	160.24	0.8182	0.1716	0.0102
VIRGINIA	126.62	29.03	1.35	157.00	0.8065	0.1849	0.0086
WEST VIRGINIA	99.80	8.90	0.68	109.38	0.9124	0.0813	0.0062
EAST SOUTH CENTRAL:							
ALABAMA	121.28	24.58	1.68	147.54	0.8220	0.1666	0.0114
KENTUCKY	114.96	24.16	1.62	140.75	0.8168	0.1717	0.0115
MISSISSIPPI	114.52	39.40	4.99	158.92	0.7207	0.2480	0.0314
TENNESSEE	120.33	16.88	2.55	139.76	0.8610	0.1208	0.0182
WEST SOUTH CENTRAL:							
ARKANSAS	108.19	46.68	1.96	156.83	0.6898	0.2977	0.0125
LOUISIANA	100.66	8.61	4.04	113.31	0.8884	0.0760	0.0356
OKLAHOMA	116.92	22.37	1.82	141.11	0.8286	0.1585	0.0129
TEXAS	123.17	16.97	2.77	142.91	0.8619	0.1188	0.0194
ROCKY MOUNTAIN:							
ARIZONA	121.69	8.54	2.05	132.28	0.9199	0.0646	0.0155
COLORADO	118.88	29.54	1.72	150.14	0.7918	0.1968	0.0114
IDAHO	112.83	50.25	2.64	165.73	0.6808	0.3032	0.0159
MONTANA	98.96	34.32	3.28	136.56	0.7247	0.2513	0.0240
NEVADA	162.30	32.28	3.17	197.76	0.8207	0.1632	0.0161
NEW MEXICO	122.92	29.82	2.32	155.05	0.7927	0.1923	0.0149
UTAH	112.26	20.39	1.76	134.41	0.8352	0.1517	0.0131
WYOMING	127.98	71.20	3.79	202.97	0.6305	0.3508	0.0187
FAR WEST:							
ALASKA	69.63	84.14	16.74	170.51	0.4083	0.4935	0.0982
CALIFORNIA	119.66	4.99	1.12	125.77	0.9514	0.0396	0.0089
HAWAII	100.24	14.27	2.08	116.59	0.8598	0.1224	0.0179
OREGON	130.95	27.81	2.04	160.79	0.8144	0.1729	0.0127
WASHINGTON	106.51	33.01	1.67	141.18	0.7544	0.2338	0.0118

Table 98

Expenditures On Petroleum Products, 1972, In Dollars Per Capita, And As Fraction Of Total, By State

Business Sector Use By Functional Category, And Category as Fraction Of Total

REGION AND STATE	DOLLARS PER CAPITA					FRACTION OF TOTAL			
	Transpor-tation	Commercial	Industrial[a]	Energy Production	Total Business	Transpor-tation	Comml.	Indl.	Energy Production
NEW ENGLAND:									
CONNECTICUT	40.97	6.54	20.60	41.24	109.35	0.3747	0.0598	0.1884	0.3771
MAINE	83.41	14.11	60.36	24.79	182.67	0.4566	0.0773	0.3304	0.1357
MASSACHUSETTS	39.89	18.69	16.72	34.09	109.38	0.3647	0.1708	0.1529	0.3117
NEW HAMPSHIRE	49.11	10.05	18.28	14.65	92.08	0.5334	0.1091	0.1985	0.1591
RHODE ISLAND	36.19	12.72	18.47	16.23	83.61	0.4329	0.1521	0.2209	0.1941
VERMONT	62.34	6.81	9.66	3.03	81.84	0.7617	0.0833	0.1180	0.0370
MID ATLANTIC:									
NEW JERSEY	47.25	7.33	13.60	36.82	105.00	0.4499	0.0698	0.1296	0.3507
NEW YORK	42.55	9.27	8.24	20.53	80.59	0.5280	0.1150	0.1023	0.2547
PENNSYLVANIA	49.26	5.52	10.48	17.20	82.46	0.5974	0.0670	0.1270	0.2086
EAST NORTH CENTRAL:									
ILLINOIS	59.77	8.27	6.48	14.10	88.61	0.6745	0.0933	0.0731	0.1591
INDIANA	75.82	8.96	10.13	13.38	108.28	0.7002	0.0827	0.0935	0.1236
MICHIGAN	49.63	5.78	6.16	6.38	67.95	0.7304	0.0851	0.0906	0.0939
OHIO	52.10	3.51	5.91	6.23	67.75	0.7690	0.0518	0.0872	0.0920
WISCONSIN	51.88	7.87	4.39	1.86	65.99	0.7862	0.1192	0.0665	0.0281
WEST NORTH CENTRAL:									
IOWA	79.76	8.42	5.71	1.69	95.58	0.8346	0.0880	0.0597	0.0177
KANSAS	86.27	3.71	6.85	12.45	109.28	0.7894	0.0339	0.0627	0.1140
MINNESOTA	68.13	8.61	10.85	5.29	92.87	0.7336	0.0928	0.1168	0.0569
MISSOURI	81.30	5.19	3.94	2.57	93.00	0.8742	0.0558	0.0424	0.0276
NEBRASKA	102.53	7.23	6.81	3.16	119.73	0.8564	0.0604	0.0569	0.0264
NORTH DAKOTA	95.20	11.61	6.07	10.26	123.14	0.7731	0.0943	0.0493	0.0834
SOUTH DAKOTA	92.20	11.18	4.95	3.29	111.62	0.8260	0.1002	0.0444	0.0294
SOUTH ATLANTIC:									
DELAWARE	58.86	16.44	41.40	37.16	153.85	0.3826	0.1068	0.2691	0.2415
DISTRICT OF COLUMBIA	25.15	29.55	3.15	28.91	86.76	0.2899	0.3406	0.0363	0.3332
FLORIDA	69.79	2.76	8.37	32.39	113.31	0.6159	0.0244	0.0739	0.2858
GEORGIA	85.28	3.48	13.03	4.16	105.94	0.8050	0.0328	0.1230	0.0392
MARYLAND	50.98	7.58	14.79	23.50	96.85	0.5264	0.0783	0.1528	0.2426
NORTH CAROLINA	69.92	5.97	16.25	3.83	95.97	0.7285	0.0622	0.1693	0.0399
SOUTH CAROLINA	67.16	3.21	13.92	4.09	88.37	0.7599	0.0363	0.1575	0.0463
VIRGINIA	70.07	4.95	11.52	20.82	107.37	0.6526	0.0461	0.1073	0.1939
WEST VIRGINIA	67.22	2.09	6.91	2.41	78.63	0.8549	0.0266	0.0879	0.0306
EAST SOUTH CENTRAL:									
ALABAMA	74.39	2.03	6.51	1.77	84.69	0.8783	0.0239	0.0769	0.0209
KENTUCKY	75.60	1.85	4.09	5.01	86.55	0.8735	0.0214	0.0473	0.0578
MISSISSIPPI	87.37	5.33	6.81	13.40	112.91	0.7738	0.0472	0.0603	0.1187
TENNESSEE	76.07	1.81	4.91	0.34	83.13	0.9151	0.0217	0.0591	0.0041
WEST SOUTH CENTRAL:									
ARKANSAS	103.68	5.52	7.89	11.26	128.35	0.8078	0.0430	0.0614	0.0877
LOUISIANA	73.94	4.35	13.34	23.19	114.82	0.6440	0.0379	0.1162	0.2020
OKLAHOMA	92.97	1.40	7.45	8.56	110.39	0.8423	0.0127	0.0675	0.0776
TEXAS	92.19	4.08	4.79	18.43	119.49	0.7715	0.0342	0.0401	0.1542
ROCKY MOUNTAIN:									
ARIZONA	97.65	1.51	9.70	3.91	112.78	0.8659	0.0134	0.0860	0.0347
COLORADO	88.49	3.57	6.19	3.13	101.38	0.8728	0.0353	0.0611	0.0309
IDAHO	95.11	6.15	14.72	0.11	116.10	0.8192	0.0530	0.1268	0.0010
MONTANA	127.47	5.71	15.28	19.98	168.43	0.7568	0.0339	0.0907	0.1186
NEVADA	141.83	3.77	10.21	1.43	157.24	0.9020	0.0240	0.0649	0.0091
NEW MEXICO	120.76	4.28	11.24	4.12	140.40	0.8601	0.0305	0.0801	0.0294
UTAH	89.40	4.06	19.34	14.14	126.94	0.7043	0.0319	0.1524	0.1114
WYOMING	180.45	7.65	28.20	40.48	256.78	0.7027	0.0298	0.1098	0.1576
FAR WEST:									
ALASKA	214.96	8.18	33.96	12.15	269.25	0.7984	0.0304	0.1261	0.0451
CALIFORNIA	69.93	1.22	6.64	15.03	92.82	0.7534	0.0132	0.0715	0.1620
HAWAII	140.57	4.59	12.84	82.49	240.49	0.5845	0.0191	0.0534	0.3430
OREGON	75.59	7.35	17.17	3.36	103.47	0.7306	0.0710	0.1659	0.0325
WASHINGTON	79.74	6.31	12.49	11.00	109.54	0.7279	0.0576	0.1140	0.1005

[a] Includes estimated heating fuels used by industry.

Table 99

Expenditures On Petroleum Products, 1972, In Dollars Per Capita, By State

Detailed Use By Industrial And Commercial Categories Of Business Use

REGION AND STATE	INDUSTRIAL			COMMERCIAL		
	Heating Fuels	Industrial Processing	Total Industrial	Heating Fuels	Miscellaneous Business Use	Total Commercial
NEW ENGLAND:						
CONNECTICUT	2.95	17.65	20.60	5.69	0.85	6.54
MAINE	6.81	53.55	60.36	12.92	1.19	14.11
MASSACHUSETTS	7.59	9.13	16.72	17.68	1.01	18.69
NEW HAMPSHIRE	4.68	13.60	18.28	9.08	0.97	10.05
RHODE ISLAND	6.96	11.51	18.47	11.99	0.73	12.72
VERMONT	1.45	8.21	9.66	5.62	1.19	6.81
MID ATLANTIC:						
NEW JERSEY	2.92	10.68	13.60	6.58	0.76	7.33
NEW YORK	3.59	4.65	8.24	8.66	0.61	9.27
PENNSYLVANIA	2.26	8.22	10.48	4.51	1.01	5.52
EAST NORTH CENTRAL:						
ILLINOIS	1.50	4.98	6.48	6.63	1.64	8.27
INDIANA	1.56	8.57	10.13	7.51	1.45	8.96
MICHIGAN	0.22	5.94	6.16	5.05	0.73	5.78
OHIO	0.14	5.77	5.91	2.63	0.88	3.51
WISCONSIN	0.22	4.17	4.39	7.14	0.73	7.87
WEST NORTH CENTRAL:						
IOWA	0.05	5.66	5.71	6.13	2.29	8.42
KANSAS	0.02	6.83	6.85	2.82	0.88	3.71
MINNESOTA	0.22	10.63	10.85	7.68	0.93	8.61
MISSOURI	0.27	3.66	3.94	4.55	0.64	5.19
NEBRASKA	0.12	6.69	6.81	6.04	1.19	7.23
NORTH DAKOTA	0.08	5.99	6.07	8.27	3.34	11.61
SOUTH DAKOTA	0.00	4.95	4.95	8.40	2.79	11.18
SOUTH ATLANTIC:						
DELAWARE	1.22	40.18	41.40	8.14	8.30	16.44
DISTRICT OF COLUMBIA	1.76	1.39	3.15	28.64	0.91	29.55
FLORIDA	0.22	8.16	8.37	1.64	1.12	2.76
GEORGIA	0.88	12.16	13.03	1.77	1.70	3.48
MARYLAND	1.22	13.57	14.79	6.68	0.90	7.58
NORTH CAROLINA	0.84	15.41	16.25	3.25	2.72	5.97
SOUTH CAROLINA	0.18	13.74	13.92	1.56	1.64	3.21
VIRGINIA	0.42	11.11	11.52	3.11	1.84	4.95
WEST VIRGINIA	0.33	6.58	6.91	1.57	0.52	2.09
EAST SOUTH CENTRAL:						
ALABAMA	0.14	6.37	6.51	0.51	1.51	2.03
KENTUCKY	0.06	4.04	4.09	0.80	1.05	1.85
MISSISSIPPI	0.06	6.75	6.81	0.52	4.81	5.33
TENNESSEE	0.12	4.79	4.91	0.83	0.98	1.81
WEST SOUTH CENTRAL:						
ARKANSAS	0.18	7.71	7.89	0.67	4.85	5.52
LOUISIANA	0.00	13.34	13.34	0.10	4.24	4.35
OKLAHOMA	0.02	7.44	7.45	0.39	1.01	1.40
TEXAS	0.04	4.75	4.79	0.54	3.54	4.08
ROCKY MOUNTAIN:						
ARIZONA	0.00	9.70	9.70	0.06	1.46	1.51
COLORADO	0.18	6.01	6.19	1.00	2.58	3.57
IDAHO	0.21	14.51	14.72	1.70	4.46	6.15
MONTANA	0.14	15.14	15.28	1.52	4.18	5.71
NEVADA	0.05	10.16	10.21	1.16	2.62	3.77
NEW MEXICO	0.01	11.24	11.24	0.23	4.05	4.28
UTAH	0.31	19.03	19.34	1.88	2.18	4.06
WYOMING	0.27	27.93	28.20	3.60	4.05	7.65
FAR WEST:						
ALASKA	0.02	33.93	33.96	2.58	5.59	8.18
CALIFORNIA	0.07	6.57	6.64	0.28	0.94	1.22
HAWAII	0.08	12.76	12.84	0.80	3.79	4.59
OREGON	2.07	15.10	17.17	6.10	1.25	7.35
WASHINGTON	0.93	11.56	12.49	4.48	1.83	6.31

Table 100

Expenditures On Petroleum Products, 1972, In Dollars Per Capita, And As Fraction Of Total, By State Government Sector Use, and Fraction Of Use By Level Of Government And By Category Of Use

REGION AND STATE	DOLLARS PER CAPITA					FRACTION OF ALL GOVERNMENT USE			
	FEDERAL		STATE AND LOCAL		ALL GOVERNMENT	LEVEL		CATEGORY	
	Transport.[a]	Heating Fuels	Transport.	Heating Fuels		Federal	State & Local	Transport.	Heating Fuels
NEW ENGLAND:									
CONNECTICUT	2.37	0.10	2.19	2.06	6.72	0.3671	0.6329	0.6785	0.3215
MAINE	27.19	0.49	1.84	6.35	35.87	0.7717	0.2283	0.8094	0.1906
MASSACHUSETTS	5.36	0.51	1.43	7.03	14.33	0.4096	0.5904	0.4743	0.5257
NEW HAMPSHIRE	1.32	0.18	2.83	3.78	8.11	0.1850	0.8150	0.5123	0.4877
RHODE ISLAND	11.98	0.47	1.72	4.59	18.76	0.6637	0.3363	0.7303	0.2697
VERMONT	0.57	0.14	2.12	2.32	5.15	0.1375	0.8625	0.5217	0.4783
MID ATLANTIC:									
NEW JERSEY	4.92	0.16	1.86	2.59	9.52	0.5330	0.4670	0.7120	0.2880
NEW YORK	4.26	0.19	2.61	3.26	10.33	0.4315	0.5685	0.6657	0.3343
PENNSYLVANIA	2.04	0.13	1.38	1.65	5.19	0.4175	0.5825	0.6586	0.3414
EAST NORTH CENTRAL:									
ILLINOIS	1.98	0.15	2.11	2.44	6.68	0.3187	0.6813	0.6122	0.3878
INDIANA	0.57	0.15	2.18	3.28	6.18	0.1159	0.8841	0.4450	0.5550
MICHIGAN	3.72	0.08	3.97	2.27	10.04	0.3789	0.6211	0.7664	0.2336
OHIO	0.67	0.05	1.58	1.03	3.34	0.2183	0.7817	0.6765	0.3235
WISCONSIN	1.79	0.13	2.08	2.83	6.83	0.2810	0.7190	0.5663	0.4337
WEST NORTH CENTRAL:									
IOWA	0.37	0.11	4.20	2.31	6.99	0.0691	0.9309	0.6540	0.3460
KANSAS	2.37	0.06	3.32	1.04	6.79	0.3580	0.6420	0.8372	0.1628
MINNESOTA	2.72	0.15	2.32	3.09	8.28	0.3470	0.6530	0.6084	0.3916
MISSOURI	0.61	0.13	1.35	1.71	3.79	0.1939	0.8061	0.5153	0.4847
NEBRASKA	1.63	0.13	3.43	2.26	7.45	0.2364	0.7636	0.6784	0.3216
NORTH DAKOTA	1.71	0.26	3.52	3.53	9.03	0.2185	0.7815	0.5802	0.4198
SOUTH DAKOTA	0.90	0.34	2.86	3.44	7.55	0.1649	0.8351	0.4990	0.5010
SOUTH ATLANTIC:									
DELAWARE	1.90	0.20	1.49	3.98	7.57	0.2772	0.7228	0.4485	0.5515
DISTRICT OF COLUMBIA	3.73	9.21	1.76	10.29	25.00	0.5178	0.4822	0.2198	0.7802
FLORIDA	1.94	0.05	2.61	0.84	5.44	0.3670	0.6330	0.8366	0.1634
GEORGIA	2.18	0.09	2.25	1.18	5.71	0.3991	0.6009	0.7767	0.2233
MARYLAND	7.08	0.54	1.13	3.53	12.29	0.6207	0.3793	0.6684	0.3316
NORTH CAROLINA	2.87	0.08	5.62	1.73	10.30	0.2863	0.7137	0.8244	0.1756
SOUTH CAROLINA	5.26	0.05	3.45	0.92	9.68	0.5486	0.4514	0.8996	0.1004
VIRGINIA	12.22	0.26	3.22	1.68	17.39	0.7178	0.2822	0.8881	0.1119
WEST VIRGINIA	0.36	0.05	3.01	0.86	4.29	0.0963	0.9037	0.7876	0.2124
EAST SOUTH CENTRAL:									
ALABAMA	6.14	0.03	2.58	0.30	9.04	0.6819	0.3181	0.9640	0.0360
KENTUCKY	6.14	0.03	2.07	0.40	8.64	0.7142	0.2858	0.9504	0.0496
MISSISSIPPI	1.30	0.02	1.81	0.32	3.45	0.3823	0.6177	0.9034	0.0966
TENNESSEE	2.66	0.03	3.72	0.45	6.86	0.3926	0.6074	0.9305	0.0695
WEST SOUTH CENTRAL:									
ARKANSAS	2.68	0.03	2.05	0.39	5.15	0.5263	0.4737	0.9201	0.0799
LOUISIANA	7.04	0.00	1.49	0.05	8.59	0.8197	0.1803	0.9933	0.0067
OKLAHOMA	1.32	0.03	3.79	0.23	5.37	0.2515	0.7485	0.9525	0.0475
TEXAS	5.50	0.02	1.35	0.30	7.17	0.7699	0.2301	0.9557	0.0443
ROCKY MOUNTAIN:									
ARIZONA	1.69	0.00	3.22	0.03	4.94	0.3432	0.6568	0.9945	0.0055
COLORADO	4.54	0.04	3.38	0.43	8.40	0.5454	0.4546	0.9433	0.0567
IDAHO	1.50	0.05	3.75	0.81	6.11	0.2535	0.7465	0.8591	0.1409
MONTANA	5.24	0.05	3.68	0.70	9.67	0.5472	0.4528	0.9217	0.0783
NEVADA	6.68	0.04	2.99	0.57	10.28	0.6536	0.3464	0.9403	0.0597
NEW MEXICO	7.77	0.01	2.82	0.11	10.71	0.7264	0.2736	0.9881	0.0119
UTAH	6.10	0.20	2.24	0.95	9.50	0.6637	0.3363	0.8784	0.1216
WYOMING	2.94	0.21	4.77	2.18	10.11	0.3120	0.6880	0.7630	0.2370
FAR WEST:									
ALASKA	91.21	0.27	6.86	1.23	99.58	0.9187	0.0813	0.9849	0.0151
CALIFORNIA	11.92	0.01	2.36	0.13	14.42	0.8273	0.1727	0.9906	0.0094
HAWAII	10.02	0.06	2.30	0.33	12.71	0.7926	0.2074	0.9694	0.0306
OREGON	3.35	0.18	4.17	2.53	10.23	0.3448	0.6552	0.7346	0.2654
WASHINGTON	6.12	0.16	3.81	1.95	12.03	0.5214	0.4786	0.8253	0.1747

[a] Includes military use of distillate and residual fuel oils, assumed to be primarily transportation use.

Table 101

Petroleum Product Consumption In Billion BTU And Expenditures In Thousand Dollars, 1972, By Region

Household Passenger Car And Motorcycle Gasoline Use Relative To Use Of All Other Petroleum Products

REGION	CONSUMPTION IN BILLION BTU			EXPENDITURES IN THOUSAND DOLLARS			RATIO OF HOUSEHOLD CAR & MOTORCYCLE GASOLINE TO TOTAL	
	Household Car And Motorcycle Gasoline	All Other Petroleum Products	Total Consumption	Household Car And Motorcycle Gasoline	All Other Petroleum Products	Total Expenditures	Consumption	Expenditures
NEW ENGLAND	491956.7	2111474.0	2603430.8	1488433.1	2560775.5	4049208.6	0.1890	0.3676
MID ATLANTIC	1328645.5	4487492.5	5816138.0	4163034.8	5481489.6	9644524.5	0.2284	0.4316
EAST NORTH CENTRAL	1686457.2	3045715.6	4732172.8	4999229.6	4632978.7	9632208.1	0.3564	0.5190
WEST NORTH CENTRAL	663225.4	1395419.1	2058644.5	1892798.2	2324562.1	4217360.0	0.3222	0.4488
SOUTH ATLANTIC	1384793.7	3303695.3	4688489.1	4135081.0	4426559.1	8561640.2	0.2954	0.4830
EAST SOUTH CENTRAL	527525.2	871039.6	1398564.8	1555439.5	1630579.4	3186018.8	0.3772	0.4882
WEST SOUTH CENTRAL	850980.2	2230293.3	3081273.5	2330646.4	2941659.5	5272306.0	0.2762	0.4421
ROCKY MOUNTAIN	364168.5	860258.6	1224427.1	1065530.4	1474330.1	2539860.2	0.2974	0.4195
FAR WEST	1107791.5	2693349.2	3801140.7	3196940.8	3533831.3	6730772.0	0.2914	0.4750
UNITED STATES	8405543.9	20998737.0	29404281.1	24827134.1	29006765.0	53833898.2	0.2859	0.4612

Table 102

Expenditures On Petroleum Products, 1972, In Dollars Per Capita, And As Fraction Of Total, By Region

Household And Government Sector Use By Categories

Household Sector Use

REGION	DOLLARS PER CAPITA				FRACTION OF ALL HOUSEHOLD USE		
	Passenger Car & Motorcycle Gasoline	Heating Fuels	All Other	Total Household	Passenger Car & Motorcycle Gasoline	Heating Fuels	All Other
NEW ENGLAND	122.96	85.13	1.23	209.31	0.5874	0.4067	0.0059
MID ATLANTIC	110.66	50.14	1.07	161.87	0.6836	0.3098	0.0066
EAST NORTH CENTRAL	122.56	27.03	1.45	151.04	0.8114	0.1790	0.0096
WEST NORTH CENTRAL	113.90	31.95	1.43	147.28	0.7734	0.2170	0.0097
SOUTH ATLANTIC	129.55	24.89	1.61	156.05	0.8302	0.1595	0.0103
EAST SOUTH CENTRAL	118.24	24.63	2.50	145.37	0.8133	0.1694	0.0172
WEST SOUTH CENTRAL	116.63	19.11	2.80	138.54	0.8419	0.1379	0.0202
ROCKY MOUNTAIN	119.99	27.71	2.24	149.94	0.8003	0.1848	0.0150
FAR WEST	117.73	11.58	1.48	130.79	0.9002	0.0885	0.0113
UNITED STATES	119.23	31.75	1.62	152.60	0.7813	0.2081	0.0106

Government Sector Use

REGION	DOLLARS PER CAPITA					FRACTION OF ALL GOVERNMENT USE			
	Federal		State and Local		All Government	Level		Function	
	Transport	Heating Fuels	Transport	Heating Fuels		Federal	State & Local	Transport	Heating Fuels
NEW ENGLAND	6.54	0.36	1.80	5.12	13.83	0.4993	0.5007	0.6031	0.3969
MID ATLANTIC	3.69	0.17	2.07	2.62	8.54	0.4509	0.5491	0.6744	0.3256
EAST NORTH CENTRAL	1.82	0.11	2.39	2.18	6.50	0.2963	0.7037	0.6476	0.3524
WEST NORTH CENTRAL	1.45	0.14	2.67	2.24	6.49	0.2440	0.7560	0.6347	0.3653
SOUTH ATLANTIC	4.55	0.37	3.01	1.79	9.72	0.5066	0.4934	0.7773	0.2227
EAST SOUTH CENTRAL	4.23	0.03	2.67	0.37	7.30	0.5832	0.4168	0.9453	0.0547
WEST SOUTH CENTRAL	4.95	0.02	1.77	0.25	6.99	0.7109	0.2891	0.9614	0.0386
ROCKY MOUNTAIN	4.36	0.06	3.22	0.50	8.14	0.5431	0.4569	0.9313	0.0687
FAR WEST	11.39	0.05	2.74	0.57	14.75	0.7755	0.2245	0.9583	0.0417
UNITED STATES	4.63	0.15	2.46	1.79	9.03	0.5295	0.4705	0.7845	0.2155

Table 103

Expenditures On Petroleum Products, 1972, In Dollars Per Capita And As Fraction Of Total, By Region

Business Sector Use By Category, Category As Fraction Of Total, And Detailed Use By Industrial And Commercial Categories.

REGION	DOLLARS PER CAPITA					FRACTION OF TOTAL BUSINESS			
	Transportation	Commercial	Industrial	Energy Production	Total Business	Transportation	Commercial	Industrial	Energy Production
NEW ENGLAND	45.00	13.73	21.38	31.27	111.37	0.4041	0.1233	0.1919	0.2807
MID ATLANTIC	45.59	7.70	10.00	22.66	85.95	0.5305	0.0896	0.1163	0.2636
EAST NORTH CENTRAL	56.72	6.51	6.50	8.87	78.60	0.7216	0.0829	0.0827	0.1129
WEST NORTH CENTRAL	81.57	7.03	6.64	4.78	100.01	0.8156	0.0702	0.0664	0.0478
SOUTH ATLANTIC	68.15	5.21	12.49	16.61	102.46	0.6652	0.0508	0.1219	0.1621
EAST SOUTH CENTRAL	77.44	2.48	5.46	4.13	89.51	0.8651	0.0277	0.0610	0.0462
WEST SOUTH CENTRAL	90.04	3.92	7.05	17.30	118.31	0.7610	0.0332	0.0596	0.1462
ROCKY MOUNTAIN	105.03	3.83	11.80	7.28	127.94	0.8210	0.0299	0.0923	0.0569
FAR WEST	75.48	2.54	8.73	15.58	102.33	0.7376	0.0248	0.0853	0.1523
UNITED STATES	66.77	5.85	9.43	14.84	96.90	0.6891	0.0604	0.0973	0.1532

DOLLARS PER CAPITA

	INDUSTRIAL			COMMERCIAL		
	Heating Fuels	Industrial Processing	Total	Heating Fuels	Misc. Business Use	Total
NEW ENGLAND	5.87	15.51	21.38	12.76	0.97	13.73
MID ATLANTIC	3.04	6.96	10.00	6.94	0.76	7.70
EAST NORTH CENTRAL	0.73	5.77	6.50	5.40	1.11	6.51
WEST NORTH CENTRAL	0.15	6.49	6.64	5.76	1.27	7.03
SOUTH ATLANTIC	0.63	11.86	12.49	3.52	1.68	5.21
EAST SOUTH CENTRAL	0.10	5.36	5.46	0.68	1.80	2.48
WEST SOUTH CENTRAL	0.05	7.00	7.05	0.45	3.47	3.92
ROCKY MOUNTAIN	0.13	11.67	11.80	1.02	2.81	3.83
FAR WEST	0.34	8.40	8.73	1.32	1.22	2.54
UNITED STATES	1.20 *	8.23	9.43	4.36	1.50	5.85

Table 104

Petroleum Product Consumption In Billion BTU And Expenditures In Thousand Dollars, 1972, By State

Distribution Of Use By Category

REGION AND STATE	CONSUMPTION IN BILLION BTU				EXPENDITURES IN THOUSAND DOLLARS			
	Transpor- tation	Heating Fuels	Industrial[a] And Miscellaneous	Energy Production	Transpor- tation	Heating Fuels	Industrial[a] And Miscellaneous	Energy Production
NEW ENGLAND:								
CONNECTICUT	199112.7	153937.0	56640.4	185346.0	553690.8	224593.4	57972.8	127006.1
MAINE	121860.8	96626.4	56740.4	36473.5	250548.3	138479.8	56317.1	25432.9
MASSACHUSETTS	395013.1	536781.3	61638.5	310015.1	939053.1	706398.4	60535.4	197574.4
NEW HAMPSHIRE	50825.5	63885.8	12079.1	16580.9	148801.4	92581.9	11514.3	11336.5
RHODE ISLAND	67799.5	71574.3	11563.5	23519.0	153863.1	100375.7	12040.3	15725.1
VERMONT	32517.1	37157.2	4053.4	1690.2	99457.4	59993.0	4525.8	1391.8
MID ATLANTIC:								
NEW JERSEY	569150.8	406770.6	84279.4	384855.8	1354836.7	530375.5	85261.0	270603.3
NEW YORK	1145425.4	974576.4	96146.1	582511.0	2785190.1	1308331.9	100314.0	376984.2
PENNSYLVANIA	776828.8	393908.0	109620.3	292065.4	1987686.1	527627.6	112516.4	204797.4
EAST NORTH CENTRAL:								
ILLINOIS	861401.0	272456.4	71993.9	241624.4	2066877.6	382017.9	79847.2	158500.0
INDIANA	410424.8	180325.0	50541.2	108541.6	1064288.5	264335.4	53031.7	70735.4
MICHIGAN	653152.5	228658.6	56172.3	79093.0	1633696.3	344719.1	62496.3	57486.3
OHIO	729851.1	136465.5	65431.0	98367.6	2011367.8	209801.2	76600.9	66815.1
WISCONSIN	300594.7	156257.0	19239.1	11582.1	753746.1	245019.3	22421.6	8404.5
WEST NORTH CENTRAL:								
IOWA	217696.7	77128.4	19235.4	5722.5	580747.4	129469.7	23532.3	4868.8
KANSAS	195138.2	28625.4	18053.0	51923.2	449082.5	47506.9	17689.1	28243.9
MINNESOTA	301883.1	145852.7	45053.3	29626.1	741398.8	200565.0	45020.5	20496.3
MISSOURI	414002.9	92639.8	19617.1	20129.0	974744.8	147191.7	21080.7	12179.8
NEBRASKA	139702.4	38995.2	10695.6	6475.6	345763.5	62224.6	12104.7	4830.4
NORTH DAKOTA	50985.5	23754.2	5033.5	10133.9	112275.2	35956.1	6101.9	6507.2
SOUTH DAKOTA	56131.2	27169.7	4358.5	2882.4	134564.6	45714.3	5264.8	2234.5
SOUTH ATLANTIC:								
DELAWARE	44206.4	27585.9	28162.9	30105.2	117230.8	42670.0	27832.7	21216.7
DISTRICT OF COLUMBIA	34614.9	51727.9	1607.7	31202.0	97431.9	58653.9	1747.3	21739.1
FLORIDA	670330.2	77528.3	72988.1	428997.0	1560588.8	153322.3	72054.4	237946.0
GEORGIA	448790.5	55245.8	65374.0	31878.6	1082464.6	97350.2	66822.0	19666.8
MARYLAND	300714.1	123157.9	60253.5	145837.9	758094.1	154371.5	58907.9	95113.9
NORTH CAROLINA	391538.2	142823.8	96011.3	31467.5	1091724.0	223229.5	99399.1	20008.9
SOUTH CAROLINA	212209.5	44545.4	39085.7	15292.0	559936.7	81194.5	42161.6	10995.8
VIRGINIA	483459.4	113945.3	67100.5	100032.0	1015435.6	164420.1	63523.4	99225.1
WEST VIRGINIA	108915.0	14507.6	11541.0	5706.0	306912.2	21027.9	12901.2	4319.6
EAST SOUTH CENTRAL:								
ALABAMA	292705.0	39238.8	27604.1	9344.8	724424.0	89980.9	28903.0	6219.9
KENTUCKY	262631.5	38137.4	14777.9	24873.0	660816.5	84113.2	18495.2	16548.8
MISSISSIPPI	177675.2	36503.6	27703.3	46821.6	466356.5	90957.8	33476.6	30229.2
TENNESSEE	336764.6	39658.7	22379.2	1746.1	832991.5	74547.2	26577.5	1381.0
WEST SOUTH CENTRAL:								
ARKANSAS	173317.2	44854.2	22493.9	34017.0	437781.3	96277.5	26310.5	22608.0
LOUISIANA	352569.3	18207.7	66243.9	161305.4	693701.8	32809.3	71658.7	86696.1
OKLAHOMA	227920.3	38342.8	25307.7	45445.5	570079.2	60642.1	23065.9	22541.1
TEXAS	1246713.5	125503.7	99785.8	399245.6	2599101.3	207491.5	107720.2	213821.5
ROCKY MOUNTAIN:								
ARIZONA	177622.5	6813.6	18388.3	9328.8	444033.2	16927.8	22110.5	7684.8
COLORADO	219944.0	31216.6	18017.5	11043.1	511195.8	73740.8	22118.5	7396.1
IDAHO	64097.0	22738.8	11494.3	110.6	162403.6	40030.4	14866.7	86.5
MONTANA	75841.2	14015.2	12915.1	23031.6	169631.3	26306.0	15059.7	14305.5
NEVADA	70665.4	8802.1	5181.9	972.0	168936.1	18174.4	6826.3	760.1
NEW MEXICO	116545.9	14785.7	15979.8	7065.1	274908.3	32475.2	17621.9	4434.7
UTAH	102309.1	17098.6	24219.7	25640.3	237959.8	26747.4	24604.6	15941.4
WYOMING	55353.2	12969.7	9234.2	20986.2	110158.9	26806.7	11602.2	14005.6
FAR WEST:								
ALASKA	83082.2	15560.5	10543.8	3930.9	129763.8	28682.3	12888.9	3948.5
CALIFORNIA	2022340.5	55659.2	146537.3	460359.5	4183664.6	111639.4	153689.0	306871.1
HAWAII	122543.3	3850.4	10102.2	79087.7	208159.9	12676.3	13604.5	67307.9
OREGON	198204.0	63137.9	34720.7	11462.9	471839.4	84538.9	36041.6	7342.0
WASHINGTON	291041.0	89161.0	41369.2	58446.5	676074.9	138504.5	45922.7	37611.8

[a] Does not include industrial use of heating fuels, which appears as component of preceding column.

Table 105

Petroleum Product Consumption And Expenditures As Fraction Of Total, 1972, By State

Distribution Of Use By Category

REGION AND STATE	FRACTION OF CONSUMPTION				FRACTION OF EXPENDITURES			
	Transpor-tation	Heating Fuels	Industrial[a] And Miscellaneous	Energy Production	Transpor-tation	Heating Fuels	Industrial[a] And Miscellaneous	Energy Production
NEW ENGLAND:								
CONNECTICUT	0.3346	0.2587	0.0952	0.3115	0.5748	0.2332	0.0602	0.1318
MAINE	0.3910	0.3100	0.1820	0.1170	0.5322	0.2942	0.1196	0.0540
MASSACHUSETTS	0.3031	0.4118	0.0473	0.2378	0.4933	0.3711	0.0318	0.1038
NEW HAMPSHIRE	0.3545	0.4456	0.0843	0.1157	0.5631	0.3504	0.0436	0.0429
RHODE ISLAND	0.3886	0.4103	0.0663	0.1348	0.5456	0.3559	0.0427	0.0558
VERMONT	0.4312	0.4927	0.0537	0.0224	0.6014	0.3628	0.0274	0.0084
MID ATLANTIC:								
NEW JERSEY	0.3939	0.2815	0.0583	0.2663	0.6045	0.2367	0.0380	0.1207
NEW YORK	0.4093	0.3482	0.0344	0.2081	0.6093	0.2862	0.0219	0.0825
PENNSYLVANIA	0.4940	0.2505	0.0697	0.1857	0.7017	0.1863	0.0397	0.0723
EAST NORTH CENTRAL:								
ILLINOIS	0.5951	0.1882	0.0497	0.1669	0.7691	0.1422	0.0297	0.0590
INDIANA	0.5474	0.2405	0.0674	0.1448	0.7328	0.1820	0.0365	0.0487
MICHIGAN	0.6422	0.2248	0.0552	0.0778	0.7785	0.1643	0.0298	0.0274
OHIO	0.7085	0.1325	0.0635	0.0955	0.8506	0.0887	0.0324	0.0283
WISCONSIN	0.6164	0.3204	0.0395	0.0237	0.7321	0.2380	0.0218	0.0082
WEST NORTH CENTRAL:								
IOWA	0.6808	0.2412	0.0602	0.0179	0.7863	0.1753	0.0319	0.0066
KANSAS	0.6643	0.0975	0.0615	0.1768	0.8278	0.0876	0.0326	0.0521
MINNESOTA	0.5779	0.2792	0.0862	0.0567	0.7359	0.1991	0.0447	0.0203
MISSOURI	0.7577	0.1695	0.0359	0.0368	0.8438	0.1274	0.0182	0.0105
NEBRASKA	0.7132	0.1991	0.0546	0.0331	0.8137	0.1464	0.0285	0.0114
NORTH DAKOTA	0.5671	0.2642	0.0560	0.1127	0.6981	0.2236	0.0379	0.0405
SOUTH DAKOTA	0.6199	0.3001	0.0481	0.0318	0.7166	0.2434	0.0280	0.0119
SOUTH ATLANTIC:								
DELAWARE	0.3399	0.2121	0.2165	0.2315	0.5610	0.2042	0.1332	0.1015
DISTRICT OF COLUMBIA	0.2905	0.4341	0.0135	0.2619	0.5426	0.3266	0.0097	0.1211
FLORIDA	0.5363	0.0620	0.0584	0.3432	0.7711	0.0758	0.0356	0.1176
GEORGIA	0.7464	0.0919	0.1087	0.0530	0.8548	0.0769	0.0528	0.0155
MARYLAND	0.4774	0.1955	0.0956	0.2315	0.7108	0.1447	0.0552	0.0892
NORTH CAROLINA	0.5916	0.2158	0.1451	0.0475	0.7611	0.1556	0.0693	0.0139
SOUTH CAROLINA	0.6821	0.1432	0.1256	0.0491	0.8065	0.1169	0.0607	0.0158
VIRGINIA	0.5725	0.1349	0.0795	0.2132	0.7563	0.1225	0.0473	0.0739
WEST VIRGINIA	0.7743	0.1031	0.0820	0.0406	0.8892	0.0609	0.0374	0.0125
EAST SOUTH CENTRAL:								
ALABAMA	0.7935	0.1064	0.0748	0.0253	0.8527	0.1059	0.0340	0.0073
KENTUCKY	0.7715	0.1120	0.0434	0.0731	0.8472	0.1078	0.0237	0.0212
MISSISSIPPI	0.6154	0.1264	0.0960	0.1622	0.7510	0.1465	0.0539	0.0487
TENNESSEE	0.8408	0.0990	0.0559	0.0044	0.8904	0.0797	0.0284	0.0015
WEST SOUTH CENTRAL:								
ARKANSAS	0.6310	0.1633	0.0819	0.1238	0.7509	0.1651	0.0451	0.0388
LOUISIANA	0.5893	0.0304	0.1107	0.2696	0.7840	0.0371	0.0810	0.0980
OKLAHOMA	0.6763	0.1138	0.0751	0.1348	0.8429	0.0897	0.0341	0.0333
TEXAS	0.6662	0.0671	0.0533	0.2134	0.8309	0.0663	0.0344	0.0684
ROCKY MOUNTAIN:								
ARIZONA	0.8372	0.0321	0.0867	0.0440	0.9048	0.0345	0.0451	0.0157
COLORADO	0.7849	0.1114	0.0643	0.0394	0.8320	0.1200	0.0360	0.0120
IDAHO	0.6511	0.2310	0.1168	0.0011	0.7471	0.1841	0.0684	0.0004
MONTANA	0.6029	0.1114	0.1027	0.1831	0.7529	0.1168	0.0668	0.0635
NEVADA	0.8253	0.1028	0.0605	0.0114	0.8677	0.0933	0.0351	0.0039
NEW MEXICO	0.7549	0.0958	0.1035	0.0458	0.8345	0.0986	0.0535	0.0135
UTAH	0.6044	0.1010	0.1431	0.1515	0.7795	0.0876	0.0806	0.0522
WYOMING	0.5617	0.1316	0.0937	0.2130	0.6776	0.1649	0.0714	0.0861
FAR WEST:								
ALASKA	0.7345	0.1376	0.0932	0.0348	0.7403	0.1636	0.0735	0.0225
CALIFORNIA	0.7532	0.0207	0.0546	0.1715	0.8797	0.0235	0.0323	0.0645
HAWAII	0.5684	0.0179	0.0469	0.3669	0.6898	0.0420	0.0451	0.2231
OREGON	0.6445	0.2053	0.1129	0.0373	0.7867	0.1410	0.0601	0.0122
WASHINGTON	0.6063	0.1857	0.0862	0.1218	0.7528	0.1542	0.0511	0.0419

[a] Does not include industrial use of heating fuels, which appears as component of preceding column.

Table 106

Petroleum Product Consumption In Billion BTU, Expenditures In Thousand Dollars, And Fractions Of Totals, 1972, By Region

Distribution Of Use By Category

181

CONSUMPTION — Quantity Consumed In Billion BTU

Region	Transportation	Heating Fuels	Industrial [a] & Miscellaneous	Energy Production
NEW ENGLAND	867128.70	959962.00	202715.30	573624.70
MID ATLANTIC	2491404.99	1775255.00	290045.80	1259432.21
EAST NORTH CENTRAL	2955424.08	974162.50	263377.50	539208.70
WEST NORTH CENTRAL	1375540.01	434165.40	122046.40	126892.70
SOUTH ATLANTIC	2694778.22	651067.90	442124.70	900518.20
EAST SOUTH CENTRAL	1069776.29	153538.50	92464.50	82785.50
WEST SOUTH CENTRAL	2000520.30	226908.40	213831.10	640011.50
ROCKY MOUNTAIN	882378.30	128440.30	115430.80	98177.70
FAR WEST	2717210.99	227369.00	243273.20	613287.50
UNITED STATES	17054162.00	5530868.99	1985309.52	4833940.57

EXPENDITURES — Amount Spent In Thousand Dollars

Region	Transportation	Heating Fuels	Industrial [a] & Miscellaneous	Energy Production
NEW ENGLAND	2145414.09	1322422.20	202905.70	378466.80
MID ATLANTIC	6127712.88	2366335.00	298091.40	852384.90
EAST NORTH CENTRAL	752976.29	1445892.88	294397.70	361941.30
WEST NORTH CENTRAL	3338876.78	668628.31	130794.00	79360.90
SOUTH ATLANTIC	658818.67	996239.90	445349.60	530231.90
EAST SOUTH CENTRAL	2684588.51	339599.10	107452.30	54378.90
WEST SOUTH CENTRAL	4300663.55	397220.40	228775.30	345566.70
ROCKY MOUNTAIN	207226.99	261208.70	134810.40	64614.50
FAR WEST	5669502.47	376041.40	262146.70	423081.30
UNITED STATES	40465480.80	8173587.84	2104703.13	3090127.18

Fraction of Total BTU Consumed

Region	Transportation	Heating Fuels	Industrial & Miscellaneous	Energy Production
NEW ENGLAND	0.3331	0.3687	0.0779	0.2203
MID ATLANTIC	0.4284	0.3052	0.0499	0.2165
EAST NORTH CENTRAL	0.6245	0.2059	0.0557	0.1139
WEST NORTH CENTRAL	0.6682	0.2109	0.0593	0.0616
SOUTH ATLANTIC	0.5748	0.1389	0.0943	0.1921
EAST SOUTH CENTRAL	0.7649	0.1098	0.0661	0.0592
WEST SOUTH CENTRAL	0.6493	0.0736	0.0694	0.2077
ROCKY MOUNTAIN	0.7206	0.1049	0.0943	0.0802
FAR WEST	0.7148	0.0598	0.0640	0.1613
UNITED STATES	0.5800	0.1881	0.0675	0.1644

Fraction of Expenditures

Region	Transportation	Heating Fuels	Industrial & Miscellaneous	Energy Production
NEW ENGLAND	0.5298	0.3266	0.0501	0.0935
MID ATLANTIC	0.6354	0.2454	0.0309	0.0884
EAST NORTH CENTRAL	0.7817	0.1501	0.0306	0.0376
WEST NORTH CENTRAL	0.7916	0.1585	0.0310	0.0188
SOUTH ATLANTIC	0.7697	0.1164	0.0520	0.0619
EAST SOUTH CENTRAL	0.8426	0.1066	0.0337	0.0171
WEST SOUTH CENTRAL	0.8157	0.0753	0.0434	0.0656
ROCKY MOUNTAIN	0.8186	0.1028	0.0531	0.0254
FAR WEST	0.8423	0.0559	0.0389	0.0629
UNITED STATES	0.7517	0.1518	0.0391	0.0574

[a] Does not include industrial use of heating fuels, which appears as component of preceding column.

Table 107

Expenditures On Petroleum Products, 1972, In Dollars Per Capita, By State

Transportation Expenditures By Category Of Use

REGION AND STATE	HOUSEHOLD CAR & MOTORCYCLE GASOLINE	ALL OTHER HIGHWAY USE	AVIATION USE	RAILROAD USE	MARINE USE	TOTAL TRANSPORTATION
NEW ENGLAND:						
CONNECTICUT	133.395	38.934	5.303	0.661	1.476	179.770
MAINE	130.351	75.693	21.938	1.129	15.088	244.199
MASSACHUSETTS	114.586	34.002	10.103	0.569	2.758	162.017
NEW HAMPSHIRE	138.232	51.820	1.338	0.113	0.746	192.250
RHODE ISLAND	107.139	37.578	3.310	0.161	10.598	158.785
VERMONT	149.745	63.187	1.266	0.643	1.370	216.212
MID ATLANTIC:						
NEW JERSEY	129.115	40.262	5.866	0.714	8.399	184.357
NEW YORK	101.275	32.548	13.130	0.645	4.043	151.641
PENNSYLVANIA	113.738	45.501	4.130	1.332	2.261	166.962
EAST NORTH CENTRAL:						
ILLINOIS	119.071	48.754	11.641	3.025	1.330	183.820
INDIANA	121.566	73.613	2.735	2.099	1.328	201.341
MICHIGAN	122.516	51.014	5.271	1.081	1.377	181.260
OHIO	132.195	49.379	3.089	1.801	1.130	187.593
WISCONSIN	109.626	51.399	3.393	1.087	1.032	166.537
WEST NORTH CENTRAL:						
IOWA	115.711	80.685	1.759	2.141	1.073	201.369
KANSAS	104.899	84.770	3.684	3.858	0.797	198.008
MINNESOTA	116.640	64.770	6.820	1.628	1.373	191.230
MISSOURI	120.684	71.975	8.275	2.776	1.629	205.339
NEBRASKA	117.581	96.396	3.987	7.624	0.696	226.285
NORTH DAKOTA	75.507	92.216	3.485	5.151	0.731	177.090
SOUTH DAKOTA	100.795	92.835	2.353	1.224	0.682	197.889
SOUTH ATLANTIC:						
DELAWARE	142.397	54.076	1.516	0.387	6.933	205.308
DISTRICT OF COLUMBIA	98.564	28.006	0.859	1.077	1.057	129.564
FLORIDA	136.412	53.948	18.122	1.767	2.163	212.412
GEORGIA	137.673	76.045	11.181	2.504	1.302	228.706
MARYLAND	127.160	47.748	6.764	1.168	4.437	187.276
NORTH CAROLINA	129.514	73.485	3.425	1.506	1.172	209.102
SOUTH CAROLINA	131.106	69.007	4.537	0.820	2.841	208.310
VIRGINIA	126.620	62.285	12.487	2.733	8.978	213.103
WEST VIRGINIA	99.797	67.528	0.622	1.899	1.136	170.982
EAST SOUTH CENTRAL:						
ALABAMA	121.283	73.568	4.726	2.769	3.396	205.744
KENTUCKY	114.963	73.437	7.241	1.856	2.387	199.884
MISSISSIPPI	114.525	85.861	2.089	0.919	3.325	206.718
TENNESSEE	120.326	72.558	5.745	2.664	3.273	204.566
WEST SOUTH CENTRAL:						
ARKANSAS	108.186	101.474	2.992	3.878	1.488	218.019
LOUISIANA	100.660	62.208	7.430	1.472	13.811	185.581
OKLAHOMA	116.917	94.068	3.775	0.344	1.410	216.513
TEXAS	123.173	82.753	9.012	3.619	5.427	223.983
ROCKY MOUNTAIN:						
ARIZONA	121.692	92.130	8.729	2.317	1.333	226.201
COLORADO	118.883	77.577	15.959	3.239	0.583	216.242
IDAHO	112.832	93.629	3.088	4.277	1.278	215.104
MONTANA	98.962	118.118	7.003	11.689	1.142	236.915
NEVADA	162.304	114.611	35.031	2.791	2.216	316.953
NEW MEXICO	122.918	117.630	8.042	6.222	0.678	255.491
UTAH	112.259	83.854	8.419	5.791	0.822	211.144
WYOMING	127.979	149.622	5.218	34.311	1.249	318.378
FAR WEST:						
ALASKA	69.626	102.496	186.005	2.015	39.132	399.273
CALIFORNIA	119.659	60.655	17.805	1.968	4.885	204.971
HAWAII	100.237	38.804	104.184	0.044	11.829	255.098
OREGON	130.946	70.209	6.158	5.949	2.683	215.945
WASHINGTON	106.508	69.869	15.542	2.069	3.811	197.798

Table 108

Expenditures On Petroleum Products, 1972, In Dollars Per Capita, By State

Energy Production Expenditures By Category Of Use

REGION AND STATE	OIL COMPANY USE	LPG for UTILITY GAS	ELECTRIC UTILITY USE	TOTAL ENERGY PRODUCTION EXPENDITURES
NEW ENGLAND:				
CONNECTICUT	0.194	0.475	40.567	41.236
MAINE	0.304	0.319	24.165	24.788
MASSACHUSETTS	0.899	0.281	32.909	34.088
NEW HAMPSHIRE	0.016	1.469	13.162	14.647
RHODE ISLAND	4.277	0.258	11.693	16.228
VERMONT	0.030	0.948	2.047	3.026
MID ATLANTIC:				
NEW JERSEY	7.222	0.144	29.456	36.822
NEW YORK	0.480	0.012	20.032	20.525
PENNSYLVANIA	6.775	0.134	10.294	17.203
EAST NORTH CENTRAL:				
ILLINOIS	8.922	0.072	5.103	14.096
INDIANA	12.491	0.008	0.882	13.382
MICHIGAN	1.432	0.056	4.890	6.378
OHIO	4.658	0.142	1.432	6.232
WISCONSIN	0.844	0.080	0.933	1.857
WEST NORTH CENTRAL:				
IOWA	0.031	0.292	1.366	1.688
KANSAS	11.110	0.000	1.343	12.453
MINNESOTA	2.652	0.144	2.490	5.287
MISSOURI	1.623	0.266	0.677	2.566
NEBRASKA	1.012	0.786	1.362	3.161
NORTH DAKOTA	9.507	0.468	0.289	10.264
SOUTH DAKOTA	0.238	0.929	2.118	3.286
SOUTH ATLANTIC:				
DELAWARE	4.532	0.117	32.508	37.157
DISTRICT OF COLUMBIA	0.055	0.279	28.574	28.908
FLORIDA	0.272	0.133	31.982	32.387
GEORGIA	0.130	0.084	3.941	4.155
MARYLAND	0.509	0.292	22.696	23.497
NORTH CAROLINA	0.065	0.017	3.750	3.832
SOUTH CAROLINA	0.192	0.183	3.716	4.091
VIRGINIA	2.143	0.164	18.517	20.824
WEST VIRGINIA	0.516	0.000	1.890	2.406
EAST SOUTH CENTRAL:				
ALABAMA	1.130	0.007	0.629	1.767
KENTUCKY	4.263	0.139	0.604	5.006
MISSISSIPPI	6.962	0.175	6.263	13.399
TENNESSEE	0.088	0.057	0.193	0.339
WEST SOUTH CENTRAL:				
ARKANSAS	1.736	0.000	9.523	11.259
LOUISIANA	21.721	0.000	1.472	23.193
OKLAHOMA	8.353	0.000	0.208	8.561
TEXAS	17.757	0.043	0.627	18.427
ROCKY MOUNTAIN:				
ARIZONA	0.066	0.000	3.849	3.915
COLORADO	2.101	0.125	0.903	3.129
IDAHO	0.108	0.000	0.006	0.115
MONTANA	19.887	0.000	0.093	19.980
NEVADA	0.254	0.000	1.172	1.426
NEW MEXICO	2.394	0.000	1.728	4.121
UTAH	9.764	0.000	4.380	14.145
WYOMING	38.725	0.000	1.753	40.479
FAR WEST:				
ALASKA	3.262	0.000	8.887	12.149
CALIFORNIA	5.662	0.164	9.208	15.035
HAWAII	25.333	1.666	55.486	82.485
OREGON	3.308	0.000	0.052	3.360
WASHINGTON	10.897	0.019	0.089	11.004

Table 109

Expenditures On Petroleum Products, 1972, In Dollars Per Capita, By Region

Transportation And Energy Production Expenditures By Category Of Use

Transportation

REGION	HOUSEHOLD CAR AND MOTORCYCLE GASOLINE	ALL OTHER HIGHWAY USE	AVIATION USE	RAILROAD USE	MARINE USE	TOTAL TRANSPORTATION
NEW ENGLAND	122.960	41.325	8.445	0.581	3.923	177.234
MID ATLANTIC	110.657	38.154	8.863	0.876	4.330	162.880
EAST NORTH CENTRAL	122.557	52.933	5.916	1.939	1.255	184.599
WEST NORTH CENTRAL	113.900	77.423	5.359	3.019	1.201	200.901
SOUTH ATLANTIC	129.545	62.301	9.575	1.789	3.238	206.448
EAST SOUTH CENTRAL	118.239	75.331	5.221	2.190	3.092	204.074
WEST SOUTH CENTRAL	116.631	82.282	7.421	2.812	6.070	215.216
ROCKY MOUNTAIN	119.992	96.108	11.354	5.674	1.019	234.147
FAR WEST	117.729	62.427	21.192	2.244	5.191	208.783
UNITED STATES	119.231	60.289	9.437	2.030	3.347	194.333

Energy Production

REGION	OIL COMPANY USE	LPG FOR UTILITY GAS	ELECTRIC UTILITY USE	TOTAL ENERGY PRODUCTION
NEW ENGLAND	0.850	0.433	29.982	31.265
MID ATLANTIC	3.789	0.076	18.792	22.657
EAST NORTH CENTRAL	5.712	0.080	3.081	8.873
WEST NORTH CENTRAL	3.070	0.288	1.418	4.776
SOUTH ATLANTIC	0.604	0.131	15.875	16.611
EAST SOUTH CENTRAL	2.595	0.085	1.454	4.134
WEST SOUTH CENTRAL	15.649	0.025	1.623	17.298
ROCKY MOUNTAIN	5.240	0.033	2.003	7.276
FAR WEST	6.694	0.176	8.711	15.580
UNITED STATES	4.953	0.130	9.758	14.840

Table 110

Petroleum Product Prices Per Physical Unit, 1972, By State

Base Prices Employed

REGION AND STATE	GASOLINE, HOUSEHOLD CARS AND MOTORCYCLES (at service station) ¢ Per Gallon	NO. 2 FUEL OIL, RESIDENTIAL USE ¢ Per Gallon	NO. 6 FUEL OIL, LARGE COMMERCIAL USE $ Per BBL.	PETROLEUM PRODUCTS USED BY ELECTRIC UTILITIES $ Per Million BTU
NEW ENGLAND:				
CONNECTICUT	39.19	21.20	4.97	0.6830
MAINE	38.82	21.10	5.07	0.6950
MASSACHUSETTS	36.56	20.90	4.70	0.6360
NEW HAMPSHIRE	38.40	20.60	4.63	0.6680
RHODE ISLAND	37.00	21.40	5.05	0.6650
VERMONT	40.91	21.54	5.08	0.7760
MID ATLANTIC:				
NEW JERSEY	38.13	19.20	4.89	0.7180
NEW YORK	41.13	21.80	4.56	0.6480
PENNSYLVANIA	37.38	19.50	4.94	0.7350
EAST NORTH CENTRAL:				
ILLINOIS	38.27	18.50	4.81	0.6900
INDIANA	36.57	18.60	4.85	0.7920
MICHIGAN	35.09	19.60	4.92	0.7490
OHIO	38.66	19.40	4.84	0.8130
WISCONSIN	34.74	19.40	4.82	0.7800
WEST NORTH CENTRAL:				
IOWA	37.09	18.70	4.84	0.8330
KANSAS	33.62	16.20	4.00	0.6270
MINNESOTA	36.39	17.00	4.76	0.7620
MISSOURI	35.33	18.10	4.21	0.6740
NEBRASKA	37.48	17.50	4.82	0.7410
NORTH DAKOTA	32.48	18.83	4.76	0.8078
SOUTH DAKOTA	32.73	19.50	4.65	0.7330
SOUTH ATLANTIC:				
DELAWARE	38.99	20.90	4.99	0.7110
DISTRICT OF COLUMBIA	38.87	19.50	4.87	0.6950
FLORIDA	35.83	22.00	4.08	0.5530
GEORGIA	36.35	19.00	4.76	0.6110
MARYLAND	39.19	18.40	4.83	0.6490
NORTH CAROLINA	38.73	19.90	4.75	0.6340
SOUTH CAROLINA	37.56	20.90	4.81	0.7140
VIRGINIA	36.78	19.40	4.33	0.5470
WEST VIRGINIA	39.33	19.10	4.73	0.8030
EAST SOUTH CENTRAL:				
ALABAMA	37.25	17.61	4.59	0.8060
KENTUCKY	37.30	19.80	4.85	0.8210
MISSISSIPPI	36.50	18.72	4.35	0.7310
TENNESSEE	36.33	19.10	4.45	0.8050
WEST SOUTH CENTRAL:				
ARKANSAS	36.19	18.90	4.10	0.6850
LOUISIANA	35.11	15.74	4.00	0.6820
OKLAHOMA	35.60	14.30	3.75	0.5900
TEXAS	33.44	16.08	4.00	0.6790
ROCKY MOUNTAIN:				
ARIZONA	36.72	19.79	4.58	0.8250
COLORADO	36.31	20.00	4.90	0.6440
IDAHO	35.56	20.00	4.90	0.8448
MONTANA	35.64	18.30	4.71	0.6053
NEVADA	39.89	21.37	5.10	0.7720
NEW MEXICO	36.61	16.98	4.50	0.6830
UTAH	36.38	17.60	4.67	0.6300
WYOMING	35.25	18.84	4.97	0.7900
FAR WEST:				
ALASKA	43.77	24.60	5.00	1.0370
CALIFORNIA	35.71	18.19	4.53	0.7110
HAWAII	42.43	25.32	6.00	0.8710
OREGON	36.12	18.62	4.77	0.6998
WASHINGTON	36.75	22.00	4.81	0.7320

Table 111

Indexes Of Petroleum Prices Relative To U.S. Unweighted Average Price
  (U.S. Average = 100), 1972, By State

Base Prices Employed

REGION AND STATE	PETROLEUM PRODUCTS			
	Gasoline, Household Cars & Motorcycles (at service) station)	No. 2 Fuel Oil, Residential Use	No.6 Fuel Oil, Large Commercial Use	Petroleum Products Used By Electric Utilities
NEW ENGLAND:				
CONNECTICUT	105.60	109.28	105.74	94.69
MAINE	104.61	108.76	107.87	96.35
MASSACHUSETTS	98.52	107.73	100.00	88.17
NEW HAMPSHIRE	103.48	106.19	98.51	92.61
RHODE ISLAND	99.70	110.31	107.45	92.19
VERMONT	110.24	111.03	108.09	107.58
MID ATLANTIC:				
NEW JERSEY	102.75	98.97	104.04	99.54
NEW YORK	110.83	112.37	97.02	89.84
PENNSYLVANIA	100.73	100.52	105.11	101.90
EAST NORTH CENTRAL:				
ILLINOIS	103.13	95.36	102.34	95.66
INDIANA	98.54	95.88	103.19	109.80
MICHIGAN	94.56	101.03	104.68	103.84
OHIO	104.18	100.00	102.98	112.71
WISCONSIN	93.61	100.00	102.55	108.14
WEST NORTH CENTRAL:				
IOWA	99.95	96.39	102.98	115.49
KANSAS	90.60	83.51	85.11	86.93
MINNESOTA	98.06	87.63	101.28	105.64
MISSOURI	95.20	93.30	89.57	93.44
NEBRASKA	101.00	90.21	102.55	102.73
NORTH DAKOTA	87.52	97.06	101.28	111.99
SOUTH DAKOTA	88.20	100.52	98.94	101.62
SOUTH ATLANTIC:				
DELAWARE	105.07	107.73	106.17	98.57
DISTRICT OF COLUMBIA	104.74	100.52	103.62	96.35
FLORIDA	96.55	113.40	86.81	76.67
GEORGIA	97.95	97.94	101.28	84.71
MARYLAND	105.60	94.85	102.77	89.98
NORTH CAROLINA	104.37	102.58	101.06	87.90
SOUTH CAROLINA	101.21	107.73	102.34	98.99
VIRGINIA	99.11	100.00	92.13	75.84
WEST VIRGINIA	105.98	98.45	100.64	111.33
EAST SOUTH CENTRAL:				
ALABAMA	100.38	90.77	97.66	111.74
KENTUCKY	100.51	102.06	103.19	113.82
MISSISSIPPI	98.36	96.49	92.55	101.34
TENNESSEE	97.90	98.45	94.68	111.60
WEST SOUTH CENTRAL:				
ARKANSAS	97.52	97.42	87.23	94.97
LOUISIANA	94.61	81.13	85.11	94.55
OKLAHOMA	95.93	73.71	79.79	81.80
TEXAS	90.11	82.89	85.11	94.14
ROCKY MOUNTAIN:				
ARIZONA	98.95	102.01	97.45	114.38
COLORADO	97.84	103.09	104.26	89.28
IDAHO	95.82	103.09	104.26	117.12
MONTANA	96.04	94.33	100.21	83.92
NEVADA	107.49	110.15	108.51	107.03
NEW MEXICO	98.65	87.53	95.74	94.69
UTAH	98.03	90.72	99.36	87.34
WYOMING	94.99	97.11	105.74	109.52
FAR WEST:				
ALASKA	117.95	126.80	106.38	143.77
CALIFORNIA	96.23	93.76	96.38	98.57
HAWAII	114.34	130.52	127.66	120.75
OREGON	97.33	95.98	101.49	97.02
WASHINGTON	99.03	113.40	102.34	101.48

Table 112

Petroleum Product Prices Per Physical Unit, And Price Indexes Relative To U.S.
Unweighted Average Price (U.S. Average = 100), 1972, By Region

Base Prices Employed

	PETROLEUM PRODUCTS			
Prices Per Unit	Gasoline, Household Cars & Motorcycles (At Service Station)	No. 2 Fuel Oil, Residential Use	No. 6 Fuel Oil, Large Commercial Use	Petroleum Products Used By Electric Utilities
	¢ Per Gallon	¢ Per Gallon	$ Per BBL.	$ Per Million BTU
New England	38.48	21.12	4.91	0.687
Mid Atlantic	38.88	20.17	4.80	0.700
East North Central	36.66	19.10	4.84	0.765
West North Central	35.02	17.98	4.57	0.740
South Atlantic	37.95	19.89	4.68	0.657
East South Central	36.84	18.80	4.56	0.791
West South Central	35.09	16.25	3.96	0.659
Rocky Mountain	36.55	19.10	4.78	0.724
Far West	38.95	21.74	5.02	0.810
United States	37.16	19.35	4.68	0.726

Index Of Prices (U.S. = 100)

New England	103.69	108.88	104.61	95.27
Mid Atlantic	104.77	103.95	102.06	97.09
East North Central	98.80	98.45	103.15	106.03
West North Central	94.36	92.66	97.39	102.55
South Atlantic	102.29	102.58	99.64	91.15
East South Central	99.29	96.95	97.02	109.63
West South Central	94.54	83.79	84.31	91.36
Rocky Mountain	98.48	98.51	101.94	100.41
Far West	104.97	112.09	106.85	112.32
United States	100.00	100.00	100.00	100.00

Table 113

Prices Of Petroleum Products In Dollars Per Million BTU, 1972, By State

Use By Households, Non-Households And All Sectors Combined

REGION AND STATE	AVERAGE PRICE PAID FOR PETROLEUM PRODUCTS			AVERAGE PRICE PAID USING U.S. QUANTITY WEIGHTS		
	Households	Non-Households	All Sectors Combined	Households	Non-Households	All Sectors Combined
NEW ENGLAND:						
CONNECTICUT	2.393	1.046	1.619	2.628	1.474	1.968
MAINE	2.169	1.132	1.510	2.610	1.303	1.862
MASSACHUSETTS	2.094	0.973	1.460	2.470	1.296	1.798
NEW HAMPSHIRE	2.206	1.320	1.843	2.590	1.520	1.978
RHODE ISLAND	2.154	1.107	1.616	2.507	1.283	1.807
VERMONT	2.303	1.907	2.193	2.753	1.565	2.073
MID ATLANTIC:						
NEW JERSEY	2.219	1.034	1.551	2.509	1.307	1.821
NEW YORK	2.358	1.065	1.633	2.722	1.371	1.949
PENNSYLVANIA	2.383	1.270	1.801	2.487	1.382	1.855
EAST NORTH CENTRAL:						
ILLINOIS	2.668	1.274	1.857	2.589	1.342	1.876
INDIANA	2.467	1.489	1.937	2.504	1.465	1.910
MICHIGAN	2.433	1.585	2.063	2.412	1.394	1.830
OHIO	2.819	1.652	2.295	2.619	1.514	1.987
WISCONSIN	2.337	1.751	2.111	2.417	1.465	1.872
WEST NORTH CENTRAL:						
IOWA	2.566	2.009	2.310	2.586	1.619	2.033
KANSAS	2.527	1.437	1.847	2.416	1.282	1.767
MINNESOTA	2.313	1.530	1.929	2.436	1.360	1.821
MISSOURI	2.575	1.664	2.114	2.489	1.318	1.819
NEBRASKA	2.587	1.821	2.169	2.583	1.468	1.945
NORTH DAKOTA	2.127	1.561	1.789	2.282	1.368	1.759
SOUTH DAKOTA	2.257	1.874	2.074	2.351	1.537	1.885
SOUTH ATLANTIC:						
DELAWARE	2.469	1.114	1.607	2.643	1.376	1.918
DISTRICT OF COLUMBIA	2.577	1.024	1.507	2.620	1.460	1.956
FLORIDA	2.789	1.043	1.619	2.699	1.304	1.901
GEORGIA	2.794	1.567	2.106	2.656	1.369	1.920
MARYLAND	2.588	1.138	1.693	2.568	1.333	1.862
NORTH CAROLINA	2.589	1.722	2.167	2.627	1.516	1.991
SOUTH CAROLINA	2.726	1.721	2.231	2.644	1.471	1.973
VIRGINIA	2.514	1.087	1.590	2.485	1.242	1.774
WEST VIRGINIA	2.924	2.025	2.454	2.651	1.614	2.058
EAST SOUTH CENTRAL:						
ALABAMA	2.856	1.766	2.303	2.782	1.393	1.987
KENTUCKY	2.829	1.790	2.291	2.750	1.430	1.995
MISSISSIPPI	2.762	1.654	2.151	2.751	1.511	2.042
TENNESSEE	2.735	1.906	2.336	2.596	1.481	1.958
WEST SOUTH CENTRAL:						
ARKANSAS	2.643	1.724	2.122	2.668	1.482	1.990
LOUISIANA	2.644	1.059	1.479	2.438	1.174	1.715
OKLAHOMA	2.530	1.603	2.007	2.445	1.300	1.790
TEXAS	2.488	1.221	1.672	2.350	1.173	1.677
ROCKY MOUNTAIN:						
ARIZONA	2.895	1.887	2.313	2.788	1.542	2.075
COLORADO	2.814	1.684	2.193	2.775	1.356	1.963
IDAHO	2.416	1.978	2.208	2.508	1.557	1.964
MONTANA	2.538	1.461	1.791	2.558	1.330	1.856
NEVADA	2.950	1.790	2.274	2.854	1.522	2.092
NEW MEXICO	2.736	1.741	2.134	2.682	1.407	1.953
UTAH	2.621	1.379	1.803	2.521	1.298	1.821
WYOMING	2.580	1.295	1.650	2.633	1.300	1.870
FAR WEST:						
ALASKA	2.414	1.338	1.550	2.965	1.552	2.157
CALIFORNIA	2.822	1.233	1.771	2.656	1.217	1.833
HAWAII	3.437	1.101	1.400	3.518	1.486	2.356
OREGON	2.505	1.486	1.950	2.450	1.360	1.826
WASHINGTON	2.530	1.438	1.871	2.548	1.342	1.858

Table 114

Prices Of Petroleum Products In Index Number Terms, U.S. = 100, 1972, By State

Use By Households, Non-Households and All Sectors Combined

REGION AND STATE	AVERAGE PRICE PAID FOR PETROLEUM PRODUCTS			AVERAGE PRICE PAID USING U.S. QUANTITY WEIGHTS		
	Households	Non-Households	All Sectors Combined	Households	Non-Households	All Sectors Combined
NEW ENGLAND:						
CONNECTICUT	93.27	75.63	86.06	101.96	108.26	104.58
MAINE	84.54	81.85	80.26	101.26	95.70	98.94
MASSACHUSETTS	81.61	70.35	77.61	95.83	95.19	95.54
NEW HAMPSHIRE	85.98	95.44	97.96	100.49	111.64	105.11
RHODE ISLAND	83.95	80.04	85.90	97.27	94.23	96.02
VERMONT	89.76	137.88	116.57	106.81	114.95	110.15
MID ATLANTIC:						
NEW JERSEY	86.48	74.76	82.44	97.35	96.00	96.76
NEW YORK	91.90	77.00	86.80	105.61	100.70	103.57
PENNSYLVANIA	92.88	91.82	95.73	96.49	101.51	98.57
EAST NORTH CENTRAL:						
ILLINOIS	103.98	92.11	98.71	100.45	98.57	99.69
INDIANA	96.15	107.66	102.96	97.15	107.60	101.49
MICHIGAN	94.82	114.60	109.66	93.58	102.39	97.24
OHIO	109.87	119.44	121.99	101.61	111.20	105.58
WISCONSIN	91.08	126.60	112.21	93.78	107.60	99.47
WEST NORTH CENTRAL:						
IOWA	100.01	145.25	122.79	100.33	118.91	108.03
KANSAS	98.49	103.90	98.18	93.74	94.16	93.89
MINNESOTA	90.15	110.62	102.54	94.51	99.89	96.76
MISSOURI	100.36	120.31	112.37	96.57	96.80	96.66
NEBRASKA	100.83	131.66	115.29	100.22	107.82	103.35
NORTH DAKOTA	82.90	112.86	95.09	88.54	100.48	93.47
SOUTH DAKOTA	87.96	135.49	110.24	91.22	112.89	100.16
SOUTH ATLANTIC:						
DELAWARE	96.23	80.54	85.42	102.55	101.07	101.92
DISTRICT OF COLUMBIA	100.44	74.04	80.10	101.65	107.23	103.94
FLORIDA	108.70	75.41	86.06	104.72	95.78	101.01
GEORGIA	108.89	113.30	111.94	103.05	100.55	102.02
MARYLAND	100.87	82.28	89.99	99.64	97.91	98.94
NORTH CAROLINA	100.90	124.50	115.19	101.92	111.35	105.80
SOUTH CAROLINA	106.24	124.43	118.59	102.58	108.04	104.84
VIRGINIA	97.98	78.59	84.52	96.41	91.22	94.27
WEST VIRGINIA	113.96	146.41	130.44	102.86	118.55	109.36
EAST SOUTH CENTRAL:						
ALABAMA	111.31	127.68	122.42	107.94	102.31	105.58
KENTUCKY	110.26	129.42	121.78	106.70	105.03	106.01
MISSISSIPPI	107.65	119.59	114.34	106.74	110.98	108.51
TENNESSEE	106.59	137.81	124.17	100.72	108.78	104.04
WEST SOUTH CENTRAL:						
ARKANSAS	103.01	124.65	112.79	103.52	108.85	105.74
LOUISIANA	103.05	76.57	78.62	94.59	86.23	91.13
OKLAHOMA	98.60	115.90	106.68	94.86	95.48	95.12
TEXAS	96.97	88.28	88.87	91.18	86.15	89.11
ROCKY MOUNTAIN:						
ARIZONA	112.83	136.43	122.95	108.17	113.26	110.26
COLORADO	109.67	121.76	116.57	107.67	99.60	104.31
IDAHO	94.16	143.01	117.37	97.31	114.36	104.36
MONTANA	98.92	105.63	95.20	99.25	97.69	98.62
NEVADA	114.97	129.42	120.87	110.73	111.79	111.16
NEW MEXICO	106.63	125.88	113.43	104.06	103.34	103.78
UTAH	102.15	99.70	95.84	97.81	95.34	96.76
WYOMING	100.55	93.63	87.71	102.16	95.48	99.37
FAR WEST:						
ALASKA	94.08	96.74	82.39	115.04	113.99	114.62
CALIFORNIA	109.99	89.15	94.14	103.05	89.39	97.40
HAWAII	133.95	79.60	74.42	136.49	109.14	125.19
OREGON	97.63	107.44	103.65	95.06	99.89	97.03
WASHINGTON	98.60	103.97	99.45	98.86	98.57	98.73

Table 115

Prices Of Petroleum Products In Dollars Per Million BTU And Price Indexes, U.S. = 100, 1972, By Region

Use By Households, Non-Households And All Sectors Combined

REGION	AVERAGE PRICE PAID FOR PETROLEUM PRODUCTS			AVERAGE PRICE PAID USING U.S. QUANTITY WEIGHTS		
	Households	Non-Households	All Sectors	Households	Non-Households	All Sectors
Prices In Dollars Per Million BTU						
NEW ENGLAND	2.196	1.074	1.570	2.543	1.365	1.869
MID ATLANTIC	2.339	1.124	1.670	2.606	1.362	1.894
EAST NORTH CENTRAL	2.593	1.523	2.056	2.528	1.428	1.899
WEST NORTH CENTRAL	2.477	1.681	2.059	2.479	1.400	1.862
SOUTH ATLANTIC	2.682	1.364	1.882	2.622	1.379	1.911
EAST SOUTH CENTRAL	2.796	1.796	2.284	2.711	1.450	1.989
WEST SOUTH CENTRAL	2.538	1.292	1.725	2.411	1.221	1.731
ROCKY MOUNTAIN	2.741	1.695	2.115	2.693	1.419	1.964
FAR WEST	2.773	1.277	1.784	2.655	1.256	1.855
UNITED STATES	2.566	1.383	1.881	2.577	1.362	1.882
Price Indexes, U.S. = 100						
NEW ENGLAND	85.60	77.62	83.43	98.68	100.29	99.34
MID ATLANTIC	91.15	81.25	88.78	101.11	100.04	100.65
EAST NORTH CENTRAL	101.06	110.11	109.30	98.07	104.91	100.91
WEST NORTH CENTRAL	96.53	121.52	109.47	96.17	102.81	98.92
SOUTH ATLANTIC	104.53	98.58	100.02	101.73	101.30	101.55
EAST SOUTH CENTRAL	108.96	129.86	121.41	105.18	106.49	105.71
WEST SOUTH CENTRAL	98.93	93.38	91.70	93.54	89.68	91.95
ROCKY MOUNTAIN	106.82	122.57	112.44	104.50	104.20	104.37
FAR WEST	108.09	92.29	94.84	103.03	92.27	98.58
UNITED STATES	100.00	100.00	100.00	100.00	100.00	100.00

190

Chapter 3

Natural Gas

Detailed information on natural gas use is presented in this chapter in three groups of tables. The first group shows amounts of use for functions by sector and category of use, and includes Tables 116 through 124. The second group consolidates the tables of the preceding group to show aggregate amounts, per capita levels and indexes of use, first by function and then by sector; that group includes Tables 125 through 139. The last group, covering Tables 140 through 145, contains information on natural gas prices. Each group will be discussed in turn, first in terms of organization, and then in terms of key findings.

Use For Functions By Sector and Category

Organization

The cross-classification showing content by table number is:

	Amounts of Use		
	Residential, "Net" Commercial Use	Industrial	Municipal-Institutional, Energy Production
States			
BTU consumed	116	117	118
Expenditures	119	120	121
Regions			
BTU and expenditures	122	123	124

Tables 116, 119 and 122 show residential and commercial use as
distinct categories, the former being treated as entirely household
sector use, while the latter is distributed between business, federal
government and state and local government use. Commercial use is
identified here as "net" commercial use because an original measure of
commercial use was revised, with part transferred to residential use
(covering use in large multifamily residential buildings), and part
transferred to industrial use, the remainder then being termed "net" use
to distinguish it from the original measure. Industrial use is also
distributed between sectors, since a small portion of use under that
heading involved consumption by government agencies. Municipal-institutional use was allocated in its entirety to state and local government,
and energy production to the business sector. There was a further breakdown of energy production, by category, including use in electricity
generation; oil and gas production, and oil refining; pipeline fuel
(gas used in transmitting gas to consumers); and lease and plant fuel,
which consists of natural gas used in oil and gas field production.
The earlier category of use in oil and gas production consists of sales
by natural gas utilities, whereas lease and plant fuel use consists of
"direct" use by oil and gas producers without "middleman" involvement.

Key Findings

The amounts of natural gas use, cross-classified by function and
sector, were:

	Resi- dential	Commer- cial	Indus- trial	Muni- cipal- Instl.	Energy Prodn.	Total
			Trillion BTU			
Household	5,702.8	—	—	—	—	5,702.8
Business	—	708.5	8,769.5	—	7,045.6	16,523.6
Federal Govt.	—	24.7	20.4	—	—	45.1
State and Local Govt.	—	317.0	33.7	329.6	—	680.3
Total	5,702.8	1,050.2	8,823.6	329.6	7,045.6	22,951.8
			Million Dollars			
Household	6,685.5	—	—	—	—	6,685.5
Business	—	638.4	4,270.5	—	2,059.8	6,968.7
Federal Govt.	—	22.0	7.4	—	—	29.4
State and Local Govt.	—	279.2	14.3	184.0	—	477.5
Total	6,685.5	939.6	4,292.3	184.0	2,059.8	14,161.1

The cross-classification yields these fractions of total use, first by function, and then by sector:

	BTU	Expenditures
Residential	.248	.472
Commercial	.046	.066
Industrial	.384	.303
Municipal-Institutional	.014	.013
Energy Production	.307	.145
	1.000	1.000
Household	.248	.472
Business	.720	.492
Federal Government	.002	.002
State and Local Government	.030	.034
	1.000	1.000

The U.S. distributions of the use of natural gas for energy production were:

	Trillion BTU	Million Dollars
Electricity generation	4,097.2	1,354.0
Oil & gas production, oil refining	663.5	240.6
Pipeline fuel	786.0	178.2
Lease & plant fuel	1,498.8	287.0
Total	7,045.6	2,059.8

Thus, electricity generation accounts for about 60 percent of energy production BTU, and for two-thirds of expenditures on that use.

Consolidated Use Data

Organization

The organization of the second group of tables is shown by this cross-classification of table numbers:

	Amounts		Per Capita Use		Index Of Use
	Function	Sector	Function	Sector	Function
States					
BTU consumed	125	126	131	132	137
Expenditures	127	128	133	134	138
Regions					
BTU and expenditures	129	130	135	136	139

Some Key Findings

As a percentage of total U.S. use, regional consumption levels were:

	BTU	Expenditures
New England	1.18%	3.40%
Mid Atlantic	8.30	15.67
East North Central	18.71	24.86
West North Central	9.52	9.37
South Atlantic	6.92	8.83
East South Central	5.31	4.71
West South Central	32.66	16.33
Rocky Mountain	5.76	4.70
Far West	11.65	12.12
Total	100.00	100.00

The shift in percentage between BTU and expenditures is pronounced for the Mid Atlantic, East North Central and West South Central regions, and is explained by relative mix of functions, the last region having a much larger proportion of industrial and energy production use than the first two. This can be seen in the following indexes of per capita use by region:

Indexes of Per Capita Use Of BTU

	Residential Use	Industrial Use	Energy	Total Use
New England	48.9	12.6	2.4	20.2
Mid Atlantic	93.3	39.3	12.0	46.0
East North Central	157.0	111.5	23.2	95.5
West North Central	130.0	112.2	112.6	119.3
South Atlantic	46.5	53.1	31.3	45.1
East South Central	67.7	106.8	67.0	84.0
West South Central	86.7	347.9	575.3	340.3
Rocky Mountain	118.6	116.1	154.4	135.1
Far West	110.5	62.6	102.3	89.3
United States	100.0	100.0	100.0	100.0

In residential use, the North Central and Western regions exceed the U.S. average, while the West South Central region is about 15 percent below that average. However, its per capita industrial use is 3.5 times the national average, and its use in energy production is 5.75 times that average.

On a per capita basis, the following are the leading states in BTU consumption, with U.S. per capita use equal to 100.

Residential Use	Index
Wyoming	243.4
Illinois	181.1
Ohio	176.4

Industrial Use	
Louisiana	612.3
Wyoming	368.9
Texas	344.6
Kansas	250.2

Energy Production	
Louisiana	702.6
Texas	632.7
Oklahoma	474.1
New Mexico	434.0

Total Use	
Louisiana	484.5
Texas	354.3
Wyoming	337.5
Kansas	274.8

Proximity to areas of production, reducing transportation cost, seems a key factor in industrial use of natural gas.

In dollar terms, expenditures per capita for the United States were:

Residential use	$32.11
Net commercial use	4.51
Industrial use	20.61
Energy production	9.89
Municipal-Institutional	0.88
Total use	$68.01

Prices

Organization

The organization of the last group of tables is shown by this cross-classification of table numbers:

	Average Costs Paid		Weighted Prices & Indexes
	Function	Sector	
States			
Dollars per million BTU	140	141	} 144
Price indexes	—	—	
Regions			
Dollars per million BTU	142	143	} 145
Price indexes	—	—	

Some Key Findings

Tables 140 through 143 show average costs actually borne by consumers
for different classes of natural gas use. In dollars per million BTU,
these U.S. averages were obtained for use by function:

Residential use	$1.17
Net commercial use	0.90
Industrial use	0.49
Energy production	0.29
Municipal-Institutional	0.56
All use	$0.62

Corresponding values for use by sector were:

Household use	$1.17
Business use	0.42
Federal Govt. use	0.65
State and Local govt. use	0.70
All use	0.62

In constructing weighted prices, the usual procedures were carried out.
Prices for individual categories of use were weighted by U.S. quantity weights
to obtain state weighted prices. The state weighted prices were aggregated
to regional measures by weighting by the state share of the region's population. Similarly, weighting by the state's share of U.S. population yielded
U.S. averages, which consequently differed from the average costs actually
paid by consumers. Division by these U.S. averages and scaling by 100 gave
price indexes.

Quantity weights were based on the U.S. distribution of use by function, as follows:

Residential use	.24847
"Net" commercial use	.04575
Industrial use	.38445
Energy production	.30697
Municipal-Industrial	.01436
Total	1.00000

The estimated regional price indexes were:

	Residential Use	All Use
New England	168.4	169.4
Mid Atlantic	119.3	123.9
East North Central	84.9	95.1
West North Central	81.5	85.3
South Atlantic	120.3	108.7
East South Central	81.0	77.6
West South Central	72.0	61.0
Rocky Mountain	77.5	74.8
Far West	90.1	89.8
United States	100.0	100.0

New England's indexes are well above the U.S. average, while the Mid Atlantic and the South Atlantic regions indexes are 10 to 20 percent above the U.S. level. All other regions have indexes below the U.S. level, with the West South Central region's index the lowest, for both residential and all use.

Hawaii is shown with no consumption of natural gas in the tables through Table 143, following the raw data series drawn upon here. However, a price estimate was necessary if a weighted price for Hawaii were to be constructed. The estimate drew on American Gas Association data showing very low per capita use at very high prices in Hawaii. That use was inferred to be obtained from manufactured or imported liquified gas, presumably counted under petroleum products. (Appendix Table E.1.8 shows a substantial use of liquified petroleum gas for utility gas in Hawaii.) The price estimates derived from the American Gas Association data are shown in Table 144. They are well above the values for all other states save Maine, which probably relied on the same sort of supply. Those estimates are incorporated in the price indexes for the Far West shown in Table 145, but the effect is limited because of Hawaii's relatively small population.

Price indexes, by state, showed these extreme values for all use:

Hawaii	271.5
Maine	221.4
Massachusetts	172.3
Rhode Island	167.7
Louisiana	61.0
Texas	60.8
Oklahoma	59.7
Wyoming	52.8

The range of values for indexes of residential use are quite similar. Hence, in contrast to petroleum products, there is marked variation in natural gas price indexes between states and regions.

Table   116

Consumption Of Natural Gas, 1972, In Billion BTU, By State

Residential And "Net" Commercial Use, By Sector

REGION AND STATE	RESIDENTIAL USE	"NET" COMMERCIAL USE			
		BUSINESS SECTOR	FEDERAL GOVERNMENT	STATE & LOCAL GOVERNMENT	TOTAL "NET" COMMERCIAL
NEW ENGLAND:					
CONNECTICUT	39149.1	4133.6	70.9	1473.2	5677.7
MAINE	988.3	160.7	5.6	71.8	238.1
MASSACHUSETTS	100339.3	10740.2	282.5	3861.5	14884.2
NEW HAMPSHIRE	5224.6	722.7	13.0	272.9	1008.6
RHODE ISLAND	14984.9	1270.8	46.7	452.3	1769.8
VERMONT	1397.7	177.1	4.4	70.8	252.3
MID ATLANTIC:					
NEW JERSEY	176201.2	18865.1	419.0	6841.7	26125.8
NEW YORK	439557.6	42498.6	956.7	15759.9	59215.3
PENNSYLVANIA	345351.2	35706.2	954.8	12327.5	48988.4
EAST NORTH CENTRAL:					
ILLINOIS	557791.4	59598.7	1392.7	22288.2	83279.6
INDIANA	180273.1	19327.3	397.8	8843.3	28568.3
MICHIGAN	381628.8	38287.1	622.3	18042.0	56951.3
OHIO	518039.6	48343.3	1058.3	19794.1	69195.7
WISCONSIN	115894.3	10367.8	200.8	4448.1	15016.8
WEST NORTH CENTRAL:					
IOWA	102310.0	14071.3	308.1	6214.9	20594.3
KANSAS	104256.5	13239.1	411.9	5903.9	19554.8
MINNESOTA	119954.9	14100.2	315.7	6206.8	20622.8
MISSOURI	173903.1	20195.4	691.1	8505.8	29392.3
NEBRASKA	64159.2	9156.0	247.3	4002.4	13405.7
NORTH DAKOTA	11899.3	2364.3	79.0	1088.3	3531.6
SOUTH DAKOTA	14200.3	2215.8	106.1	1058.7	3380.6
SOUTH ATLANTIC:					
DELAWARE	9046.6	1146.9	27.7	549.1	1723.7
DISTRICT OF COLUMBIA	18302.4	5573.2	1710.1	1938.1	9221.4
FLORIDA	23322.6	6103.7	200.1	3101.2	9405.0
GEORGIA	91655.3	11597.0	576.9	7281.5	19455.3
MARYLAND	82486.0	8556.7	648.4	4237.8	13442.9
NORTH CAROLINA	35655.9	5337.7	134.2	2833.6	8305.5
SOUTH CAROLINA	21961.9	3688.4	121.1	2181.3	5990.8
VIRGINIA	61913.2	8326.2	672.7	4366.9	13365.8
WEST VIRGINIA	61899.9	7198.1	232.1	3931.9	11362.1
EAST SOUTH CENTRAL:					
ALABAMA	56392.4	10605.0	576.3	6063.6	17245.0
KENTUCKY	89253.7	10629.6	383.4	5310.5	16323.5
MISSISSIPPI	40918.8	5743.4	194.2	3511.7	9449.3
TENNESSEE	57454.0	12486.8	442.8	6715.7	19645.3
WEST SOUTH CENTRAL:					
ARKANSAS	48244.8	8685.1	337.0	4905.4	13927.5
LOUISIANA	87166.5	11006.8	279.8	5822.2	17108.9
OKLAHOMA	81660.0	12094.6	788.5	6994.6	19877.7
TEXAS	257612.2	29969.6	1205.8	16203.5	47378.9
ROCKY MOUNTAIN:					
ARIZONA	39112.6	9990.2	398.2	4720.9	15109.7
COLORADO	91990.6	25658.6	1122.6	11377.3	38158.5
IDAHO	12134.1	3499.4	96.6	1703.8	5299.8
MONTANA	25415.8	6563.6	236.6	3154.6	9954.8
NEVADA	11062.3	2908.7	114.8	1484.1	4507.7
NEW MEXICO	38397.8	7358.5	484.6	3793.0	11636.1
UTAH	47130.7	2872.8	314.5	1483.3	4670.7
WYOMING	23064.6	5851.8	325.6	3470.0	9647.4
FAR WEST:					
ALASKA	9330.7	3539.3	390.5	1794.6	5724.4
CALIFORNIA	736133.7	100140.1	3564.0	43666.4	147370.5
HAWAII	0.0	0.0	0.0	0.0	0.0
OREGON	28209.5	5857.8	172.2	2496.0	8526.0
WASHINGTON	48367.0	9967.2	339.4	4394.8	14701.4

Table 117

Consumption Of Natural Gas, 1972, In Billion BTU, By State

Industrial Use By Sector

REGION AND STATE	BUSINESS USE	FEDERAL GOVERNMENT USE	STATE & LOCAL GOVERNMENT USE	ALL INDUSTRIAL USE
NEW ENGLAND:				
CONNECTICUT	21525.0	0.0	0.0	21525.0
MAINE	456.8	0.0	0.0	456.8
MASSACHUSETTS	31501.0	0.0	0.0	31501.0
NEW HAMPSHIRE	2112.7	472.7	0.0	2585.4
RHODE ISLAND	6963.8	0.0	0.0	6963.8
VERMONT	1459.2	0.0	0.0	1459.2
MID ATLANTIC:				
NEW JERSEY	98924.8	0.0	0.0	98924.8
NEW YORK	128938.6	0.0	0.0	128938.6
PENNSYLVANIA	397797.9	0.0	0.0	397797.9
EAST NORTH CENTRAL:				
ILLINOIS	454508.8	0.0	61.5	454570.3
INDIANA	320499.9	0.0	0.0	320499.9
MICHIGAN	406328.6	0.0	0.0	406328.6
OHIO	550362.9	0.0	0.0	550362.9
WISCONSIN	194926.5	0.0	0.0	194926.5
WEST NORTH CENTRAL:				
IOWA	162186.8	0.0	0.0	162186.8
KANSAS	237139.2	2765.5	533.9	240438.6
MINNESOTA	154027.1	0.0	0.0	154027.1
MISSOURI	132256.4	0.0	0.0	132256.4
NEBRASKA	86773.1	600.8	53.4	87427.3
NORTH DAKOTA	1726.9	0.0	0.0	1726.9
SOUTH DAKOTA	12163.3	0.0	0.0	12163.3
SOUTH ATLANTIC:				
DELAWARE	10837.6	0.0	194.8	11032.4
DISTRICT OF COLUMBIA	1180.0	0.0	0.0	1180.0
FLORIDA	62397.4	2769.1	22035.9	87202.4
GEORGIA	173855.4	0.0	0.0	173855.4
MARYLAND	71943.6	0.0	294.3	72237.9
NORTH CAROLINA	109480.6	0.0	0.0	109480.6
SOUTH CAROLINA	105128.3	0.0	0.0	105128.3
VIRGINIA	62884.5	0.0	0.0	62884.5
WEST VIRGINIA	95458.0	0.0	0.0	95458.0
EAST SOUTH CENTRAL:				
ALABAMA	187684.1	0.0	0.0	187684.1
KENTUCKY	93253.7	0.0	0.0	93253.7
MISSISSIPPI	154392.2	1781.5	0.0	156173.7
TENNESSEE	155363.8	2759.4	64.4	158187.6
WEST SOUTH CENTRAL:				
ARKANSAS	159406.3	815.2	0.0	160221.5
LOUISIANA	966081.4	3153.9	557.7	969793.0
OKLAHOMA	119418.5	2161.0	67.1	121646.6
TEXAS	1690871.6	3149.8	178.7	1694200.1
ROCKY MOUNTAIN:				
ARIZONA	72843.9	0.0	197.0	73040.9
COLORADO	85078.6	0.0	9437.1	94515.7
IDAHO	35608.5	0.0	0.0	35608.5
MONTANA	31025.9	0.0	0.0	31025.9
NEVADA	10112.4	0.0	0.0	10112.4
NEW MEXICO	87482.4	0.0	0.0	87482.4
UTAH	51098.7	0.0	0.0	51098.7
WYOMING	54089.9	0.0	0.0	54089.9
FAR WEST:				
ALASKA	14317.7	0.0	0.0	14317.7
CALIFORNIA	565988.7	0.0	0.0	565988.7
HAWAII	0.0	0.0	0.0	0.0
OREGON	61424.5	0.0	0.0	61424.5
WASHINGTON	78201.4	0.0	0.0	78201.4

Table 118

Consumption Of Natural Gas, 1972, In Billion BTU, By State

Municipal-Institutional Use And Use In Energy Production, By Sector And Category

REGION AND STATE	MUNICIPAL INSTITUTIONAL	ENERGY PRODUCTION (BUSINESS USE)				
	State And Local Government	All Energy Production	Electricity Generation Use	Oil And Gas Production, Oil Refining	Pipeline Fuel	Lease And Plant Fuel
NEW ENGLAND:						
CONNECTICUT	4280.4	71.1	30.5	0.0	40.6	0.0
MAINE	16.2	0.0	0.0	0.0	0.0	0.0
MASSACHUSETTS	4799.9	8844.9	8180.0	0.0	664.9	0.0
NEW HAMPSHIRE	79.8	0.0	0.0	0.0	0.0	0.0
RHODE ISLAND	688.2	167.4	151.1	0.0	16.3	0.0
VERMONT	0.0	721.3	721.3	0.0	0.0	0.0
MID ATLANTIC:						
NEW JERSEY	2875.9	29685.0	25690.0	3247.0	748.0	0.0
NEW YORK	19581.8	81135.0	77092.6	570.0	3472.4	0.0
PENNSYLVANIA	9714.3	41941.9	5654.6	4882.0	28464.3	2941.0
EAST NORTH CENTRAL:						
ILLINOIS	6486.2	117561.5	74615.9	18814.0	23815.9	315.7
INDIANA	3906.3	43633.1	18079.8	12249.0	13304.3	0.0
MICHIGAN	7202.4	80726.2	59837.3	2353.0	16360.8	2175.1
OHIO	19794.0	42860.6	17072.8	9294.0	13018.7	3475.1
WISCONSIN	2892.9	35649.8	28607.4	690.0	6352.4	0.0
WEST NORTH CENTRAL:						
IOWA	2743.5	81847.4	61322.0	74.0	20451.4	0.0
KANSAS	6333.3	316252.1	179795.7	28399.0	79930.8	28126.6
MINNESOTA	24398.7	69389.8	52029.9	9877.0	7482.9	0.0
MISSOURI	16978.0	77355.6	59308.3	8361.0	9686.3	0.0
NEBRASKA	8289.8	65039.6	49532.1	1458.0	13229.0	820.5
NORTH DAKOTA	0.0	19567.4	338.2	5789.0	271.2	13169.0
SOUTH DAKOTA	1597.4	3709.2	3557.2	142.0	10.0	0.0
SOUTH ATLANTIC:						
DELAWARE	0.0	3570.6	2478.6	1092.0	0.0	0.0
DISTRICT OF COLUMBIA	2135.6	549.4	0.0	17.0	532.4	0.0
FLORIDA	4436.7	184032.0	177199.0	792.0	4185.9	1855.1
GEORGIA	4865.3	48082.1	39624.4	254.0	8203.7	0.0
MARYLAND	3581.1	11247.1	7197.9	836.0	3144.7	68.5
NORTH CAROLINA	6238.2	23569.2	17215.5	137.0	6216.7	0.0
SOUTH CAROLINA	1141.1	28500.5	25195.3	215.0	3090.2	0.0
VIRGINIA	7324.6	18224.5	4629.3	4945.0	8489.1	161.1
WEST VIRGINIA	2945.0	20020.7	470.3	411.0	15221.0	3918.4
EAST SOUTH CENTRAL:						
ALABAMA	1057.8	24720.4	2834.2	1126.0	19657.0	1103.2
KENTUCKY	7658.0	53058.1	10184.2	3761.0	37578.2	1534.7
MISSISSIPPI	4638.1	176256.0	102913.1	4631.0	59330.1	9381.8
TENNESSEE	4367.0	44100.7	16900.0	83.0	25942.4	1175.3
WEST SOUTH CENTRAL:						
ARKANSAS	971.9	94275.0	72641.4	3671.0	13203.6	4759.0
LOUISIANA	33254.2	888692.4	393457.7	92197.0	81840.5	321197.2
OKLAHOMA	4349.9	422375.4	268261.2	26786.0	25383.1	101945.1
TEXAS	48363.5	2484222.2	1319811.0	233446.0	107196.2	823769.0
ROCKY MOUNTAIN:						
ARIZONA	4250.8	109841.7	82300.2	70.0	27424.9	46.6
COLORADO	1239.9	75746.4	65188.8	3087.0	2916.2	4554.4
IDAHO	1988.3	5054.0	0.0	44.0	5010.0	0.0
MONTANA	2714.2	17910.2	1257.0	9456.0	1083.6	6113.6
NEVADA	6146.8	43393.5	43326.5	67.0	0.0	0.0
NEW MEXICO	16365.2	158014.7	64049.7	1792.0	39319.4	52853.6
UTAH	13.1	13486.1	3487.5	7345.0	798.2	1855.4
WYOMING	1528.4	40397.7	2922.7	8340.0	6217.8	22917.2
FAR WEST:						
ALASKA	6939.5	38718.6	13150.4	604.0	8827.9	16136.3
CALIFORNIA	7834.4	846235.0	638502.7	115561.0	19721.4	72449.9
HAWAII	0.0	0.0	0.0	0.0	0.0	0.0
OREGON	409.6	16757.0	426.4	5960.0	10370.6	0.0
WASHINGTON	177.2	38375.7	0.0	30575.0	7800.7	0.0

Table 119

Expenditures On Natural Gas, 1972, In Thousand Dollars, By State

Residential And "Net" Commercial Use, By Sector

REGION AND STATE	RESIDENTIAL USE	"NET" COMMERCIAL USE			
		Business Sector	Federal Government	State & Local Government	Total "Net" Commercial
NEW ENGLAND:					
CONNECTICUT	78663.6	7063.0	121.2	2517.2	9701.3
MAINE	2948.1	288.1	10.1	128.8	427.0
MASSACHUSETTS	220654.3	19071.3	501.6	6856.9	26429.7
NEW HAMPSHIRE	10066.3	1211.2	21.8	457.3	1690.3
RHODE ISLAND	29896.6	2343.6	86.1	834.2	3264.0
VERMONT	2388.5	235.2	5.8	94.0	335.0
MID ATLANTIC:					
NEW JERSEY	335374.4	27672.7	614.6	10035.9	38323.2
NEW YORK	677328.7	55860.2	1257.5	20714.8	77832.6
PENNSYLVANIA	446158.0	38263.8	1023.1	13210.5	52497.4
EAST NORTH CENTRAL:					
ILLINOIS	601594.6	49423.4	1154.9	18482.9	69061.3
INDIANA	201881.7	17905.8	368.5	8192.8	26467.1
MICHIGAN	408960.7	34364.2	558.5	16193.4	51116.1
OHIO	529023.6	41869.2	916.5	17143.3	59929.0
WISCONSIN	149404.2	10510.3	203.6	4509.3	15223.1
WEST NORTH CENTRAL:					
IOWA	110882.2	11853.8	259.5	5235.5	17348.8
KANSAS	76118.8	7044.0	219.1	3141.2	10404.3
MINNESOTA	143716.2	13241.7	296.5	5828.9	19367.1
MISSOURI	186015.1	16545.5	566.2	6968.5	24080.2
NEBRASKA	61725.7	5658.9	152.8	2473.7	8285.4
NORTH DAKOTA	12676.8	1850.5	61.8	851.8	2764.2
SOUTH DAKOTA	15615.4	1591.2	76.2	760.3	2427.7
SOUTH ATLANTIC:					
DELAWARE	14984.7	1523.7	36.8	729.4	2289.9
DISTRICT OF COLUMBIA	26887.4	6421.6	1970.3	2233.1	10625.0
FLORIDA	47208.7	8021.0	262.9	4075.4	12359.3
GEORGIA	110417.0	10033.6	499.1	6299.9	16832.5
MARYLAND	132129.9	10984.9	832.4	5440.4	17257.6
NORTH CAROLINA	48610.5	6213.5	156.3	3298.5	9668.3
SOUTH CAROLINA	34081.3	3742.2	122.9	2213.1	6078.1
VIRGINIA	94462.8	9721.9	785.5	5098.9	15606.3
WEST VIRGINIA	57853.6	5239.4	168.9	2862.0	8270.2
EAST SOUTH CENTRAL:					
ALABAMA	68560.3	7591.2	412.5	4340.4	12344.1
KENTUCKY	80893.8	8079.4	291.4	4036.4	12407.2
MISSISSIPPI	42970.9	3933.4	133.0	2405.0	6471.4
TENNESSEE	57232.4	10849.7	384.7	5835.2	17069.6
WEST SOUTH CENTRAL:					
ARKANSAS	39571.7	4974.0	193.0	2809.3	7976.3
LOUISIANA	76917.1	6385.7	162.3	3377.8	9925.9
OKLAHOMA	70559.9	6691.9	436.3	3870.1	10998.3
TEXAS	250412.3	18297.0	736.2	9892.6	28925.8
ROCKY MOUNTAIN:					
ARIZONA	44618.5	7056.2	281.3	3334.4	10672.1
COLORADO	73157.3	17097.1	748.0	7581.0	25426.2
IDAHO	17019.7	3677.4	101.5	1790.4	5569.3
MONTANA	23558.9	4394.8	158.4	2112.2	6665.4
NEVADA	14917.7	2575.4	101.7	1314.1	3991.2
NEW MEXICO	34259.8	4674.6	307.9	2409.5	7391.9
UTAH	45004.1	2171.3	237.7	1121.1	3530.1
WYOMING	16616.5	2963.2	164.9	1757.1	4885.2
FAR WEST:					
ALASKA	14001.0	3817.6	421.2	1935.7	6174.5
CALIFORNIA	737945.4	78193.4	2782.9	34096.5	115072.8
HAWAII	0.0	0.0	0.0	0.0	0.0
OREGON	44479.8	8156.2	239.7	3475.3	11871.3
WASHINGTON	65084.0	11015.7	375.1	4857.2	16248.0

Table 120

Expenditures On Natural Gas, 1972, In Thousand Dollars, By State

Industrial Use By Sector

REGION AND STATE	BUSINESS USE	FEDERAL GOVERNMENT USE	STATE & LOCAL GOVERNMENT USE	ALL INDUSTRIAL USE
NEW ENGLAND:				
CONNECTICUT	26637.2	0.0	0.0	26637.2
MAINE	767.9	0.0	0.0	767.9
MASSACHUSETTS	40159.8	0.0	0.0	40159.8
NEW HAMPSHIRE	1922.4	322.1	0.0	2244.5
RHODE ISLAND	8763.5	0.0	0.0	8763.5
VERMONT	904.6	0.0	0.0	904.6
MID ATLANTIC:				
NEW JERSEY	84415.7	0.0	0.0	84415.7
NEW YORK	118102.5	0.0	0.0	118102.5
PENNSYLVANIA	290153.7	0.0	0.0	290153.7
EAST NORTH CENTRAL:				
ILLINOIS	289829.2	0.0	36.6	289865.8
INDIANA	192868.4	0.0	0.0	192868.4
MICHIGAN	274459.8	0.0	0.0	274459.8
OHIO	360975.0	0.0	0.0	360975.0
WISCONSIN	125560.4	0.0	0.0	125560.4
WEST NORTH CENTRAL:				
IOWA	86880.1	0.0	0.0	86880.1
KANSAS	86057.1	931.8	179.9	87168.9
MINNESOTA	89348.9	0.0	0.0	89348.9
MISSOURI	78980.7	0.0	0.0	78980.7
NEBRASKA	40760.5	254.7	22.6	41037.8
NORTH DAKOTA	2231.1	0.0	0.0	2231.1
SOUTH DAKOTA	6412.0	0.0	0.0	6412.0
SOUTH ATLANTIC:				
DELAWARE	7477.5	0.0	121.4	7599.0
DISTRICT OF COLUMBIA	1182.1	0.0	0.0	1182.1
FLORIDA	29129.9	1277.8	10168.5	40576.2
GEORGIA	96402.7	0.0	0.0	96402.7
MARYLAND	57777.5	0.0	222.8	58000.4
NORTH CAROLINA	71248.2	0.0	0.0	71248.2
SOUTH CAROLINA	60154.8	0.0	0.0	60154.8
VIRGINIA	44158.6	0.0	0.0	44158.6
WEST VIRGINIA	53085.0	0.0	0.0	53085.0
EAST SOUTH CENTRAL:				
ALABAMA	82943.5	0.0	0.0	82943.5
KENTUCKY	54011.0	0.0	0.0	54011.0
MISSISSIPPI	55212.3	594.4	0.0	55806.7
TENNESSEE	83145.4	1339.2	31.3	84515.8
WEST SOUTH CENTRAL:				
ARKANSAS	58816.9	280.9	0.0	59097.8
LOUISIANA	310273.7	999.2	176.7	311449.6
OKLAHOMA	39146.4	613.5	19.1	39779.0
TEXAS	441914.0	797.4	45.2	442756.6
ROCKY MOUNTAIN:				
ARIZONA	34359.5	0.0	88.5	34448.0
COLORADO	34460.6	0.0	3207.1	37667.7
IDAHO	19896.0	0.0	0.0	19896.0
MONTANA	13348.7	0.0	0.0	13348.7
NEVADA	7103.9	0.0	0.0	7103.9
NEW MEXICO	29210.5	0.0	0.0	29210.5
UTAH	20363.6	0.0	0.0	20363.6
WYOMING	17229.5	0.0	0.0	17229.5
FAR WEST:				
ALASKA	10752.2	0.0	0.0	10752.2
CALIFORNIA	261073.0	0.0	0.0	261073.0
HAWAII	0.0	0.0	0.0	0.0
OREGON	34141.9	0.0	0.0	34141.9
WASHINGTON	36330.8	0.0	0.0	36330.8

Table 121

Expenditures On Natural Gas, 1972, In Thousand Dollars, By State

Municipal-Institutional Use And Use In Energy Production, By Sector And Category

REGION AND STATE	MUNICIPAL-INSTITUTIONAL (State & Local Government)	ENERGY PRODUCTION (BUSINESS USE)				
		All Energy Production	Electricity Generation Use	Oil And Gas Production / Oil Refining	Pipeline Fuel	Lease And Plant Fuel
NEW ENGLAND:						
CONNECTICUT	5338.0	27.0	13.0	0.0	14.0	0.0
MAINE	13.0	0.0	0.0	0.0	0.0	0.0
MASSACHUSETTS	5426.0	3896.0	3654.0	0.0	242.0	0.0
NEW HAMPSHIRE	69.0	0.0	0.0	0.0	0.0	0.0
RHODE ISLAND	982.0	82.0	76.0	0.0	6.0	0.0
VERMONT	0.0	322.0	322.0	0.0	0.0	0.0
MID ATLANTIC:						
NEW JERSEY	3215.0	14885.0	12244.0	2465.0	176.0	0.0
NEW YORK	19793.0	37054.0	35639.0	517.0	898.0	0.0
PENNSYLVANIA	7862.0	15910.0	2732.0	3384.0	8459.0	1335.0
EAST NORTH CENTRAL:						
ILLINOIS	3753.0	48350.0	31739.0	11197.0	5321.0	93.0
INDIANA	3149.0	17711.0	7656.0	6749.0	3306.0	0.0
MICHIGAN	5166.0	35376.0	28651.0	1467.0	4739.0	519.0
OHIO	15537.0	18993.0	8378.0	5687.0	3525.0	1403.0
WISCONSIN	1388.0	14670.0	12605.0	419.0	1646.0	0.0
WEST NORTH CENTRAL:						
IOWA	1248.0	27183.0	23095.0	34.0	4054.0	0.0
KANSAS	2069.0	103505.0	67919.0	9569.0	18661.0	7356.0
MINNESOTA	14391.0	27717.0	20615.0	5123.0	1979.0	0.0
MISSOURI	6946.0	28263.0	21674.0	4213.0	2376.0	0.0
NEBRASKA	3306.0	21317.0	18181.0	618.0	2336.0	182.0
NORTH DAKOTA	0.0	5634.0	132.0	3151.0	65.0	2286.0
SOUTH DAKOTA	832.0	1340.0	1283.0	54.0	3.0	0.0
SOUTH ATLANTIC:						
DELAWARE	0.0	1856.0	1176.0	680.0	0.0	0.0
DISTRICT OF COLUMBIA	2418.0	142.0	0.0	16.0	126.0	0.0
FLORIDA	2020.0	70390.0	68599.0	366.0	981.0	444.0
GEORGIA	3978.0	15689.0	13759.0	132.0	1798.0	0.0
MARYLAND	2885.0	3995.0	2592.0	633.0	738.0	32.0
NORTH CAROLINA	4295.0	9889.0	8440.0	83.0	1366.0	0.0
SOUTH CAROLINA	662.0	12771.0	11936.0	117.0	718.0	0.0
VIRGINIA	5297.0	7229.0	1882.0	3071.0	2217.0	59.0
WEST VIRGINIA	2058.0	7278.0	175.0	218.0	5636.0	1249.0
EAST SOUTH CENTRAL:						
ALABAMA	519.0	6222.0	968.0	463.0	4385.0	406.0
KENTUCKY	4895.0	14821.0	3655.0	2019.0	8794.0	353.0
MISSISSIPPI	2552.0	48777.0	32229.0	1545.0	13255.0	1748.0
TENNESSEE	2457.0	11386.0	5119.0	40.0	5838.0	389.0
WEST SOUTH CENTRAL:						
ARKANSAS	345.0	28212.0	22719.0	1265.0	3143.0	1085.0
LOUISIANA	10341.0	217821.0	104769.0	29209.0	18293.0	65550.0
OKLAHOMA	2129.0	92957.0	64726.0	7605.0	4722.0	15904.0
TEXAS	15022.0	597331.0	370113.0	59100.0	19727.0	148391.0
ROCKY MOUNTAIN:						
ARIZONA	2332.0	37393.0	32563.0	31.0	4791.0	8.0
COLORADO	528.0	23039.0	20614.0	1049.0	623.0	753.0
IDAHO	1179.0	1344.0	0.0	22.0	1322.0	0.0
MONTANA	1273.0	5046.0	418.0	3500.0	174.0	954.0
NEVADA	3431.0	18904.0	18860.0	44.0	0.0	0.0
NEW MEXICO	5153.0	36028.0	21823.0	558.0	6571.0	7076.0
UTAH	10.0	4649.0	1208.0	2850.0	237.0	354.0
WYOMING	433.0	7835.0	860.0	2454.0	1070.0	3451.0
FAR WEST:						
ALASKA	3218.0	12125.0	5666.0	411.0	2451.0	3597.0
CALIFORNIA	3702.0	322608.0	242316.0	51641.0	6586.0	22065.0
HAWAII	0.0	0.0	0.0	0.0	0.0	0.0
OREGON	243.0	6061.0	184.0	3108.0	2769.0	0.0
WASHINGTON	94.0	15757.0	0.0	13679.0	2078.0	0.0

Table 122

Consumption In Billion BTU And Expenditures In Thousand Dollars,
    Natural Gas, 1972, By Region

Residential And "Net" Commercial Use, By Sector

REGION	RESIDENTIAL USE	"NET" COMMERCIAL USE			
		Business Sector	Federal Government	State & Local Government	Total "Net" Commercial
Consumption In Billion BTU					
NEW ENGLAND	162083.90	17205.10	423.10	6202.50	23830.70
MID ATLANTIC	961110.00	97069.90	2330.50	34929.10	134329.50
EAST NORTH CENTRAL	1753627.19	175924.20	3671.90	73415.70	253011.70
WEST NORTH CENTRAL	590683.30	75342.10	2159.20	32980.80	110482.10
SOUTH ATLANTIC	406243.80	57527.90	4323.30	30421.40	92272.50
EAST SOUTH CENTRAL	244018.90	39464.80	1596.70	21601.50	62663.10
WEST SOUTH CENTRAL	474683.50	61756.10	2611.10	33925.70	98293.00
ROCKY MOUNTAIN	288308.50	64703.60	3093.50	31187.00	98984.70
FAR WEST	822040.90	119504.40	4466.10	52351.80	176322.30
TOTAL	5702800.15	708498.10	24675.40	317015.50	1050189.59
Expenditures In Thousand Dollars					
NEW ENGLAND	344617.40	30212.40	746.60	10888.40	41847.30
MID ATLANTIC	1458861.10	121796.70	2895.20	43961.20	168653.20
EAST NORTH CENTRAL	1890864.82	154072.90	3202.00	64521.70	221796.60
WEST NORTH CENTRAL	606750.20	57785.60	1632.10	25259.90	84677.70
SOUTH ATLANTIC	566635.91	61901.80	4835.10	32250.70	98987.20
EAST SOUTH CENTRAL	249657.40	30453.70	1221.60	16617.00	48292.30
WEST SOUTH CENTRAL	437461.00	36348.60	1527.80	19949.80	57826.30
ROCKY MOUNTAIN	269152.50	44610.00	2101.40	21419.80	68131.40
FAR WEST	861510.19	101182.90	3818.90	44364.70	149366.60
TOTAL	6685510.35	638364.59	21980.70	279233.20	939578.59

Table 123

Consumption In Billion BTU And Expenditures In Thousand Dollars,
    Natural Gas, 1972, By Region

Industrial Use By Sector

REGION	BUSINESS USE	FEDERAL GOVERNMENT USE	STATE & LOCAL GOVERNMENT USE	ALL INDUSTRIAL USE
Consumption In Billion BTU				
NEW ENGLAND	64018.50	472.70	0.00	64491.20
MID ATLANTIC	625661.30	0.00	0.00	625661.30
EAST NORTH CENTRAL	1926626.71	0.00	61.50	1926688.20
WEST NORTH CENTRAL	786272.79	3366.30	587.30	790226.39
SOUTH ATLANTIC	693165.40	2769.10	22525.00	718459.50
EAST SOUTH CENTRAL	590693.79	4540.90	64.40	595299.10
WEST SOUTH CENTRAL	2935777.83	9279.90	803.50	2945861.18
ROCKY MOUNTAIN	427340.30	0.00	9634.10	436974.40
FAR WEST	719932.30	0.00	0.00	719932.30
TOTAL	8769488.78	20428.90	33675.80	8823593.48
Expenditures In Thousand Dollars				
NEW ENGLAND	79155.40	322.10	0.00	79477.50
MID ATLANTIC	492671.90	0.00	0.00	492671.90
EAST NORTH CENTRAL	1243692.81	0.00	36.60	1243729.41
WEST NORTH CENTRAL	390670.40	1186.50	202.50	392059.50
SOUTH ATLANTIC	420616.30	1277.80	10512.70	432407.00
EAST SOUTH CENTRAL	275312.20	1933.60	31.30	277277.00
WEST SOUTH CENTRAL	850151.00	2691.00	241.00	853083.00
ROCKY MOUNTAIN	175972.30	0.00	3295.60	179267.90
FAR WEST	342297.90	0.00	0.00	342297.90
TOTAL	4270540.18	7411.00	14319.70	4292271.06

Table 124

Consumption In Billion BTU And Expenditures In Thousand Dollars, Natural Gas, 1972, By Region

Municipal-Institutional Use And Use In Energy Production By Sector And Category

REGION	MUNICIPAL-INSTITUTIONAL (State & Local Govt.)	ENERGY PRODUCTION (BUSINESS USE)				
		All Energy Production	Electricity Generation Use	Oil & Gas Production, Oil Refining	Pipeline Fuel	Lease & Plant Fuel
Consumption In Billion BTU						
NEW ENGLAND	9864.50	9804.70	9082.90	0.00	721.80	0.00
MID ATLANTIC	32172.00	152761.90	108437.20	8699.00	32684.70	2941.00
EAST NORTH CENTRAL	40281.80	320431.20	198213.20	43400.00	72852.10	5965.90
WEST NORTH CENTRAL	60340.70	633161.11	405883.40	54100.00	131061.60	42116.10
SOUTH ATLANTIC	32667.60	337796.10	274010.30	8699.00	49083.70	6003.10
EAST SOUTH CENTRAL	17720.90	298135.20	132831.50	9601.00	142507.70	13195.00
WEST SOUTH CENTRAL	86939.50	3889564.98	2054171.30	356100.00	227623.40	1251670.29
ROCKY MOUNTAIN	34246.70	463844.30	262532.40	30201.00	82770.10	88340.80
FAR WEST	15360.70	940086.31	652079.49	152700.00	46720.60	88586.20
TOTAL	329594.40	7045585.74	4097241.68	663500.00	786025.71	1498818.40
Expenditures In Thousand Dollars						
NEW ENGLAND	11828.00	4327.00	4065.00	0.00	262.00	0.00
MID ATLANTIC	30870.00	67849.00	50615.00	6366.00	9533.00	1335.00
EAST NORTH CENTRAL	28993.00	135100.00	89029.00	25519.00	18537.00	2015.00
WEST NORTH CENTRAL	28792.00	214959.00	152899.00	22762.00	29474.00	9824.00
SOUTH ATLANTIC	23613.00	129239.00	108559.00	5316.00	13580.00	1784.00
EAST SOUTH CENTRAL	10423.00	81206.00	41971.00	4067.00	32272.00	2896.00
WEST SOUTH CENTRAL	27837.00	936321.00	562327.00	97179.00	45885.00	230930.00
ROCKY MOUNTAIN	14339.00	134238.00	96346.00	10508.00	14788.00	12596.00
FAR WEST	7257.00	356551.00	248166.00	68839.00	13884.00	25662.00
TOTAL	183952.00	2059790.01	1353977.01	240556.00	178215.00	287042.00

Table 125

Consumption Of Natural Gas, 1972, In Billion BTU, By State

Use By Function

REGION & STATE	RESIDENTIAL USE	"NET" COMMERCIAL USE	INDUSTRIAL USE	ENERGY PRODUCTION USE	OTHER USE (Municipal-Institutional)	TOTAL USE
NEW ENGLAND:						
CONNECTICUT	39149.1	5677.7	21525.0	71.1	4280.4	70703.3
MAINE	988.3	238.1	456.8	0.0	16.2	1699.4
MASSACHUSETTS	100339.3	14884.2	31501.0	8844.9	4799.9	160369.3
NEW HAMPSHIRE	5224.6	1008.6	2585.4	0.0	79.8	8898.4
RHODE ISLAND	14984.9	1769.8	6963.8	167.4	688.2	24574.1
VERMONT	1397.7	252.3	1459.2	721.3	0.0	3830.5
MID ATLANTIC:						
NEW JERSEY	176201.2	26125.8	98924.8	29685.0	2875.9	333812.7
NEW YORK	439557.6	59215.3	128938.6	81135.0	19581.8	728428.3
PENNSYLVANIA	345351.2	48988.4	397797.9	41941.9	9714.3	843793.7
EAST NORTH CENTRAL:						
ILLINOIS	557791.4	83279.6	454570.3	117561.5	6486.2	1219689.0
INDIANA	180273.1	28568.3	320499.9	43633.1	3906.3	576880.7
MICHIGAN	381628.8	56951.3	406328.6	80726.2	7202.4	932837.3
OHIO	518039.6	69195.7	550362.9	42860.6	19794.0	1200252.8
WISCONSIN	115894.3	15016.8	194926.5	35649.8	2892.9	364380.3
WEST NORTH CENTRAL:						
IOWA	102310.0	20594.3	162186.8	81847.4	2743.5	369682.0
KANSAS	104256.5	19554.8	240438.6	316252.1	6333.3	686835.3
MINNESOTA	119954.9	20622.8	154027.1	69389.8	24398.7	388393.3
MISSOURI	173903.1	29392.3	132256.4	77355.6	16978.0	429885.4
NEBRASKA	64159.2	13405.7	87427.3	65039.6	8289.8	238321.6
NORTH DAKOTA	11899.3	3531.6	1726.9	19567.4	0.0	36725.2
SOUTH DAKOTA	14200.3	3380.6	12163.3	3709.2	1597.4	35050.8
SOUTH ATLANTIC:						
DELAWARE	9046.6	1723.7	11032.4	3570.6	0.0	25373.3
DISTRICT OF COLUMBIA	18302.4	9221.4	1180.0	549.4	2135.6	31388.8
FLORIDA	23322.6	9405.0	87202.4	184032.0	4436.7	308398.7
GEORGIA	91655.3	19455.3	173855.4	48082.1	4865.3	337913.4
MARYLAND	82486.0	13442.9	72237.9	11247.1	3581.1	182995.0
NORTH CAROLINA	35655.9	8305.5	109480.6	23569.2	6238.2	183249.4
SOUTH CAROLINA	21961.9	5990.8	105128.3	28500.5	1141.1	162722.6
VIRGINIA	61913.2	13365.8	62884.5	18224.5	7324.6	163712.6
WEST VIRGINIA	61899.9	11362.1	95458.0	20020.7	2945.0	191685.7
EAST SOUTH CENTRAL:						
ALABAMA	56392.4	17245.0	187684.1	24720.4	1057.8	287099.7
KENTUCKY	89253.7	16323.5	93253.7	53058.1	7658.0	259547.0
MISSISSIPPI	40918.8	9449.3	156173.7	176256.0	4638.1	387435.9
TENNESSEE	57454.0	19645.3	158187.6	44100.7	4367.0	283754.6
WEST SOUTH CENTRAL:						
ARKANSAS	48244.8	13927.5	160221.5	94275.0	971.9	317640.7
LOUISIANA	87166.5	17108.9	969793.0	888692.4	33254.2	1996015.0
OKLAHOMA	81660.0	19877.7	121646.6	422375.4	4349.9	649909.6
TEXAS	257612.2	47378.9	1694200.1	2484222.2	48363.5	4531776.9
ROCKY MOUNTAIN:						
ARIZONA	39112.6	15109.7	73040.9	109841.7	4250.8	241355.7
COLORADO	91990.6	38158.5	94515.7	75746.4	1239.9	301651.1
IDAHO	12134.1	5299.8	35608.5	5054.0	1988.3	60084.7
MONTANA	25415.8	9954.8	31025.9	17910.2	2714.2	87020.9
NEVADA	11062.3	4507.7	10112.4	43393.5	6146.8	75222.7
NEW MEXICO	38397.8	11636.1	87482.4	158014.7	16365.2	311896.2
UTAH	47130.7	4670.7	51098.7	13486.1	13.1	116399.3
WYOMING	23064.6	9647.4	54089.9	40397.7	1528.4	128728.0
FAR WEST:						
ALASKA	9330.7	5724.4	14317.7	38718.6	6939.5	75030.9
CALIFORNIA	736133.7	147370.5	565988.7	846235.0	7834.4	2303562.3
HAWAII	0.0	0.0	0.0	0.0	0.0	0.0
OREGON	28209.5	8526.0	61424.5	16757.0	409.6	115326.6
WASHINGTON	48367.0	14701.4	78201.4	38375.7	177.2	179822.7

Table 126

Consumption Of Natural Gas, 1972, In Billion BTU, By State

Use By Sector

REGION AND STATE	HOUSEHOLD USE	BUSINESS USE	FEDERAL GOVERNMENT	STATE & LOCAL GOVERNMENT USE	TOTAL USE
NEW ENGLAND:					
CONNECTICUT	39149.1	25729.7	70.9	5753.6	70703.3
MAINE	988.3	617.5	5.6	88.0	1699.4
MASSACHUSETTS	100339.3	51086.1	282.5	8661.4	160369.3
NEW HAMPSHIRE	5224.6	2835.4	485.7	352.7	8898.4
RHODE ISLAND	14984.9	8402.0	46.7	1140.5	24574.1
VERMONT	1397.7	2357.6	4.4	70.8	3830.5
MID ATLANTIC:					
NEW JERSEY	176201.2	147474.9	419.0	9717.6	333812.7
NEW YORK	439557.6	252572.2	956.7	35341.7	728428.3
PENNSYLVANIA	345351.2	475446.0	954.8	22041.8	843793.7
EAST NORTH CENTRAL:					
ILLINOIS	557791.4	631669.0	1392.7	28835.9	1219689.0
INDIANA	180273.1	383460.3	397.8	12749.6	576880.7
MICHIGAN	381628.8	525341.9	622.3	25244.4	932837.3
OHIO	518039.6	641566.8	1058.3	39588.1	1200252.8
WISCONSIN	115894.3	240944.1	200.8	7341.0	364380.3
WEST NORTH CENTRAL:					
IOWA	102310.0	258105.5	308.1	8958.4	369682.0
KANSAS	104256.5	566630.4	3177.4	12771.1	686835.3
MINNESOTA	119954.9	237517.1	315.7	30605.5	388393.3
MISSOURI	173903.1	229807.4	691.1	25483.8	429885.4
NEBRASKA	64159.2	160968.7	848.1	12345.6	238321.6
NORTH DAKOTA	11899.3	23658.6	79.0	1088.3	36725.2
SOUTH DAKOTA	14200.3	18088.3	106.1	2656.1	35050.8
SOUTH ATLANTIC:					
DELAWARE	9046.6	15555.1	27.7	743.9	25373.3
DISTRICT OF COLUMBIA	18302.4	7302.6	1710.1	4073.7	31388.8
FLORIDA	23322.6	252533.1	2969.2	29573.8	308398.7
GEORGIA	91655.3	233534.5	576.9	12146.8	337913.4
MARYLAND	82486.0	91747.4	648.4	8113.2	182995.0
NORTH CAROLINA	35655.9	138387.5	134.2	9071.8	183249.4
SOUTH CAROLINA	21961.9	137317.2	121.1	3322.4	162722.6
VIRGINIA	61913.2	89435.2	672.7	11691.5	163712.6
WEST VIRGINIA	61899.9	122676.8	232.1	6876.9	191685.7
EAST SOUTH CENTRAL:					
ALABAMA	56392.4	223009.5	576.3	7121.4	287099.7
KENTUCKY	89253.7	156941.4	383.4	12968.5	259547.0
MISSISSIPPI	40918.8	336391.6	1975.7	8149.8	387435.9
TENNESSEE	57454.0	211951.3	3202.2	11147.1	283754.6
WEST SOUTH CENTRAL:					
ARKANSAS	48244.8	262366.4	1152.2	5877.3	317640.7
LOUISIANA	87166.5	1865780.6	3433.7	39634.1	1996015.0
OKLAHOMA	81660.0	553888.5	2949.5	11411.6	649909.6
TEXAS	257612.2	4205063.4	4355.6	64745.7	4531776.9
ROCKY MOUNTAIN:					
ARIZONA	39112.6	192675.8	398.2	9168.7	241355.7
COLORADO	91990.6	186483.6	1122.6	22054.3	301651.1
IDAHO	12134.1	44161.9	96.6	3692.1	60084.7
MONTANA	25415.8	55499.7	236.6	5868.8	87020.9
NEVADA	11062.3	56414.6	114.8	7630.9	75222.7
NEW MEXICO	38397.8	252855.6	484.6	20158.2	311896.2
UTAH	47130.7	67457.6	314.5	1496.4	116399.3
WYOMING	23064.6	100339.4	325.6	4998.4	128728.0
FAR WEST:					
ALASKA	9330.7	56575.6	390.5	8734.1	75030.9
CALIFORNIA	736133.7	1512363.8	3564.0	51500.8	2303562.3
HAWAII	0.0	0.0	0.0	0.0	0.0
OREGON	28209.5	84039.3	172.2	2905.6	115326.6
WASHINGTON	48367.0	126544.3	339.4	4572.0	179822.7

Table 127

Expenditures On Natural Gas, 1972, In Thousand Dollars, By State

Use By Function

REGION AND STATE	RESIDENTIAL USE	"NET" COMMERCIAL USE	INDUSTRIAL USE	ENERGY PRODUCTION USE	OTHER USE (Municipal-Institutional)	TOTAL USE
NEW ENGLAND:						
CONNECTICUT	78663.6	9701.3	26637.2	27.0	5338.0	120367.1
MAINE	2948.1	427.0	767.9	0.0	13.0	4156.0
MASSACHUSETTS	220654.3	26429.7	40159.8	3896.0	5426.0	296565.8
NEW HAMPSHIRE	10066.3	1690.3	2244.5	0.0	69.0	14070.1
RHODE ISLAND	29896.6	3264.0	8763.5	82.0	982.0	42988.1
VERMONT	2388.5	335.0	904.6	322.0	0.0	3950.1
MID ATLANTIC:						
NEW JERSEY	335374.4	38323.2	84415.7	14885.0	3215.0	476213.3
NEW YORK	677328.7	77832.6	118102.5	37054.0	19793.0	930110.8
PENNSYLVANIA	446158.0	52497.4	290153.7	15910.0	7862.0	812581.1
EAST NORTH CENTRAL:						
ILLINOIS	601594.6	69061.3	289865.8	48350.0	3753.0	1012624.7
INDIANA	201881.7	26467.1	192868.4	17711.0	3149.0	442077.2
MICHIGAN	408960.7	51116.1	274459.8	35376.0	5166.0	775078.6
OHIO	529023.6	59929.0	360975.0	18993.0	15537.0	984457.6
WISCONSIN	149404.2	15223.1	125560.4	14670.0	1388.0	306245.7
WEST NORTH CENTRAL:						
IOWA	110882.2	17348.8	86880.1	27183.0	1248.0	243542.1
KANSAS	76118.8	10404.3	87168.9	103505.0	2069.0	279266.0
MINNESOTA	143716.2	19367.1	89348.9	27717.0	14391.0	294540.2
MISSOURI	186015.1	24080.2	78980.7	28263.0	6946.0	324285.0
NEBRASKA	61725.7	8285.4	41037.8	21317.0	3306.0	135671.9
NORTH DAKOTA	12676.8	2764.2	2231.1	5634.0	0.0	23306.1
SOUTH DAKOTA	15615.4	2427.7	6412.0	1340.0	832.0	26627.1
SOUTH ATLANTIC:						
DELAWARE	14984.7	2289.9	7599.0	1856.0	0.0	26729.6
DISTRICT OF COLUMBIA	26887.4	10625.0	1182.1	142.0	2418.0	41254.5
FLORIDA	47208.7	12359.3	40576.2	70390.0	2020.0	172554.2
GEORGIA	110417.0	16832.5	96402.7	15689.0	3978.0	243319.2
MARYLAND	132129.9	17257.6	58000.4	3995.0	2885.0	214267.9
NORTH CAROLINA	48610.5	9668.3	71248.2	9889.0	4295.0	143711.0
SOUTH CAROLINA	34081.3	6078.1	60154.8	12771.0	662.0	113747.2
VIRGINIA	94462.8	15606.3	44158.6	7229.0	5297.0	166753.7
WEST VIRGINIA	57853.6	8270.2	53085.0	7278.0	2058.0	128544.8
EAST SOUTH CENTRAL:						
ALABAMA	68560.3	12344.1	82943.5	6222.0	519.0	170588.9
KENTUCKY	80893.8	12407.2	54011.0	14821.0	4895.0	167028.0
MISSISSIPPI	42970.9	6471.4	55806.7	48777.0	2552.0	156578.0
TENNESSEE	57232.4	17069.6	84515.8	11386.0	2457.0	172660.8
WEST SOUTH CENTRAL:						
ARKANSAS	39571.7	7976.3	59097.8	28212.0	345.0	135202.8
LOUISIANA	76917.1	9925.9	311449.6	217821.0	10341.0	626454.6
OKLAHOMA	70559.9	10998.3	39779.0	92957.0	2129.0	216423.2
TEXAS	250412.3	28925.8	442756.6	597331.0	15022.0	1334447.7
ROCKY MOUNTAIN:						
ARIZONA	44618.5	10672.1	34448.0	37393.0	2332.0	129463.6
COLORADO	73157.3	25426.2	37667.7	23039.0	528.0	159818.2
IDAHO	17019.7	5569.3	19896.0	1344.0	1179.0	45008.0
MONTANA	23558.9	6665.4	13348.7	5046.0	1273.0	49892.0
NEVADA	14917.7	3991.2	7103.9	18904.0	3431.0	48347.8
NEW MEXICO	34259.8	7391.9	29210.5	36028.0	5153.0	112043.2
UTAH	45004.1	3530.1	20363.6	4649.0	10.0	73556.8
WYOMING	16616.5	4885.2	17229.5	7835.0	433.0	46999.2
FAR WEST:						
ALASKA	14001.0	6174.5	10752.2	12125.0	3218.0	46270.7
CALIFORNIA	737945.4	115072.8	261073.0	322608.0	3702.0	1440401.2
HAWAII	0.0	0.0	0.0	0.0	0.0	0.0
OREGON	44479.8	11871.3	34141.9	6061.0	243.0	96797.0
WASHINGTON	65084.0	16248.0	36330.8	15757.0	94.0	133513.8

Table 128

Expenditures On Natural Gas, 1972, In Thousand Dollars, By State

Use By Sector

REGION AND STATE	HOUSEHOLD USE	BUSINESS USE	FEDERAL GOVERNMENT USE	STATE & LOCAL GOVERNMENT USE	TOTAL USE
NEW ENGLAND:					
CONNECTICUT	78663.6	33727.2	121.2	7855.2	120367.1
MAINE	2948.1	1056.0	10.1	141.8	4156.0
MASSACHUSETTS	220654.3	63127.1	501.6	12282.9	296565.8
NEW HAMPSHIRE	10066.3	3133.6	343.9	526.3	14070.1
RHODE ISLAND	29896.6	11189.1	86.1	1816.2	42988.1
VERMONT	2388.5	1461.8	5.8	94.0	3950.1
MID ATLANTIC:					
NEW JERSEY	335374.4	126973.4	614.6	13250.9	476213.3
NEW YORK	677328.7	211016.7	1257.5	40507.8	930110.8
PENNSYLVANIA	446158.0	344327.5	1023.1	21072.5	812581.1
EAST NORTH CENTRAL:					
ILLINOIS	601594.6	387602.6	1154.9	22272.5	1012624.7
INDIANA	201881.7	228485.2	368.5	11341.8	442077.2
MICHIGAN	408960.7	344200.0	558.5	21359.4	775078.6
OHIO	529023.6	421837.2	916.5	32680.3	984457.6
WISCONSIN	149404.2	150740.7	203.6	5897.3	306245.7
WEST NORTH CENTRAL:					
IOWA	110882.2	125916.9	259.5	6483.5	243542.1
KANSAS	76118.8	196606.1	1150.9	5390.1	279266.0
MINNESOTA	143716.2	130307.6	296.5	20219.9	294540.2
MISSOURI	186015.1	123789.2	566.2	13914.5	324285.0
NEBRASKA	61725.7	67736.4	407.5	5802.3	135671.9
NORTH DAKOTA	12676.8	9715.6	61.8	851.8	23306.1
SOUTH DAKOTA	15615.4	9343.2	76.2	1592.3	26627.1
SOUTH ATLANTIC:					
DELAWARE	14984.7	10857.2	36.8	850.8	26729.6
DISTRICT OF COLUMBIA	26887.4	7745.7	1970.3	4651.1	41254.5
FLORIDA	47208.7	107540.9	1540.7	16263.9	172554.2
GEORGIA	110417.0	122125.3	499.1	10277.9	243319.2
MARYLAND	132129.9	72757.4	832.4	8548.2	214267.9
NORTH CAROLINA	48610.5	87350.7	156.3	7593.5	143711.0
SOUTH CAROLINA	34081.3	76668.0	122.9	2875.1	113747.2
VIRGINIA	94462.8	61109.5	785.5	10395.9	166753.7
WEST VIRGINIA	57853.6	65602.4	168.9	4920.0	128544.8
EAST SOUTH CENTRAL:					
ALABAMA	68560.3	96756.7	412.5	4859.4	170588.9
KENTUCKY	80893.8	76911.4	291.4	8931.4	167028.0
MISSISSIPPI	42970.9	107922.7	727.4	4957.0	156578.0
TENNESSEE	57232.4	105381.1	1723.9	8323.5	172660.8
WEST SOUTH CENTRAL:					
ARKANSAS	39571.7	92002.9	473.9	3154.3	135202.8
LOUISIANA	76917.1	534480.4	1161.5	13895.5	626454.6
OKLAHOMA	70559.9	138795.3	1049.8	6018.2	216423.2
TEXAS	250412.3	1057542.0	1533.6	24959.8	1334447.7
ROCKY MOUNTAIN:					
ARIZONA	44618.5	78808.7	281.3	5754.9	129463.6
COLORADO	73157.3	74596.7	748.0	11316.1	159818.2
IDAHO	17019.7	24917.4	101.5	2969.4	45008.0
MONTANA	23558.9	22789.5	158.4	3385.2	49892.0
NEVADA	14917.7	28583.3	101.7	4745.1	48347.8
NEW MEXICO	34259.8	69913.1	307.9	7562.5	112043.2
UTAH	45004.1	27183.9	237.7	1131.1	73556.8
WYOMING	16616.5	28027.7	164.9	2190.1	46999.2
FAR WEST:					
ALASKA	14001.0	26694.8	421.2	5153.7	46270.7
CALIFORNIA	737945.4	661874.4	2782.9	37798.5	1440401.2
HAWAII	0.0	0.0	0.0	0.0	0.0
OREGON	44479.8	48359.1	239.7	3718.3	96797.0
WASHINGTON	65084.0	63103.5	375.1	4951.2	133513.8

Table 129

Consumption In Billion BTU And Expenditures In Thousand Dollars, Natural Gas, 1972, By Region

Use By Function

REGION	RESIDENTIAL USE	"NET" COMMERCIAL USE	INDUSTRIAL USE	ENERGY PRODUCTION USE	OTHER USE (Municipal-Institutional)	TOTAL USE
Consumption In Billion BTU						
NEW ENGLAND	162083.90	23830.70	64491.20	9804.70	9864.50	270075.00
MID ATLANTIC	961110.00	134329.50	625661.30	152761.90	32172.00	1906034.70
EAST NORTH CENTRAL	1753627.19	253011.70	1926688.20	320431.20	40281.80	4294040.13
WEST NORTH CENTRAL	590683.30	110482.10	790226.39	633161.11	60340.70	2184893.60
SOUTH ATLANTIC	406243.80	92272.50	718459.50	337796.10	32667.60	1587439.50
EAST SOUTH CENTRAL	244018.90	62663.10	595299.10	298135.20	17720.90	1217837.20
WEST SOUTH CENTRAL	474683.50	98293.00	2945861.18	3889564.98	86939.50	7495342.20
ROCKY MOUNTAIN	288308.50	98984.70	436974.40	463844.30	34246.70	1322358.59
FAR WEST	822040.90	176322.30	719932.30	940086.31	15360.70	2673742.47
TOTAL	5702800.15	1050189.59	8823593.48	7045585.74	329594.40	22951763.70

Expenditures In Thousand Dollars						
NEW ENGLAND	344617.40	41847.30	79477.50	4327.00	11828.00	482097.21
MID ATLANTIC	1458861.10	168653.20	492671.90	67849.00	30870.00	2218905.18
EAST NORTH CENTRAL	1890864.82	221796.60	1243729.41	135100.00	28993.00	3520483.78
WEST NORTH CENTRAL	606750.20	84677.70	392059.50	214959.00	28792.00	1327238.40
SOUTH ATLANTIC	566635.91	98987.20	432407.00	129239.00	23613.00	1250882.09
EAST SOUTH CENTRAL	249657.40	48292.30	277277.00	81206.00	10423.00	666855.69
WEST SOUTH CENTRAL	437461.00	57826.30	853083.00	936321.00	27837.00	2312528.29
ROCKY MOUNTAIN	269152.50	68131.40	179267.90	134238.00	14339.00	665128.80
FAR WEST	861510.19	149366.60	342297.90	356551.00	7257.00	1716982.69
TOTAL	6685510.35	939578.59	4292271.06	2059790.01	183952.00	14161102.30

Table   130

Consumption In Billion BTU And Expenditures In Thousand Dollars, Natural Gas, 1972,
    By Region

Use By Sector

REGION	HOUSEHOLD USE	BUSINESS USE	FEDERAL GOVERNMENT USE	STATE & LOCAL GOVERNMENT USE	TOTAL USE
Consumption In Billion BTU					
NEW ENGLAND	162083.90	91028.30	895.80	16067.00	270075.00
MID ATLANTIC	961110.00	875493.10	2330.50	67101.10	1906034.70
EAST NORTH CENTRAL	1753627.19	2422982.10	3671.90	113759.00	4294040.13
WEST NORTH CENTRAL	590683.30	1494775.99	5525.50	93908.80	2184893.60
SOUTH ATLANTIC	406243.80	1088489.41	7092.40	85614.00	1587439.50
EAST SOUTH CENTRAL	244018.90	928293.79	6137.60	39386.80	1217837.20
WEST SOUTH CENTRAL	474683.50	6887098.85	11891.00	121668.70	7495342.20
ROCKY MOUNTAIN	288308.50	955888.20	3093.50	75067.80	1322358.59
FAR WEST	822040.90	1779522.99	4466.10	67712.50	2673742.47
TOTAL	5702800.15	16523572.80	45104.30	680285.70	22951763.70
Expenditures In Thousand Dollars					
NEW ENGLAND	344617.40	113694.80	1068.70	22716.40	482097.21
MID ATLANTIC	1458861.10	682317.60	2895.20	74831.20	2218905.18
EAST NORTH CENTRAL	1890864.82	1532865.71	3202.00	93551.30	3520483.78
WEST NORTH CENTRAL	606750.20	663415.01	2818.60	54254.40	1327238.40
SOUTH ATLANTIC	566635.91	611757.10	6112.90	66376.40	1250882.09
EAST SOUTH CENTRAL	249657.40	386971.90	3155.20	27071.30	666855.69
WEST SOUTH CENTRAL	437461.00	1822820.59	4218.80	48027.80	2312528.29
ROCKY MOUNTAIN	269152.50	354820.30	2101.40	39054.40	665128.80
FAR WEST	861510.19	800031.80	3818.90	51621.70	1716982.69
TOTAL	6685510.35	6968694.70	29391.70	477504.90	14161102.30

Table 131

Consumption Of Natural Gas, 1972, In Million BTU Per Capita, By State

Use By Function

REGION AND STATE	RESIDENTIAL USE	"NET" COMMERCIAL USE	INDUSTRIAL USE	ENERGY PRODUCTION USE	OTHER USE (Municipal Institutional)	TOTAL USE
NEW ENGLAND:						
CONNECTICUT	12.711	1.843	6.989	0.023	1.390	22.956
MAINE	0.963	0.232	0.445	0.000	0.016	1.656
MASSACHUSETTS	17.312	2.568	5.435	1.526	0.828	27.669
NEW HAMPSHIRE	6.750	1.303	3.340	0.000	0.103	11.497
RHODE ISLAND	15.464	1.826	7.187	0.173	0.710	25.360
VERMONT	3.038	0.548	3.172	1.568	0.000	8.327
MID ATLANTIC:						
NEW JERSEY	23.976	3.555	13.461	4.039	0.391	45.423
NEW YORK	23.932	3.224	7.020	4.417	1.066	39.660
PENNSYLVANIA	29.009	4.115	33.414	3.523	0.816	70.877
EAST NORTH CENTRAL:						
ILLINOIS	49.608	7.407	40.428	10.455	0.577	108.475
INDIANA	34.104	5.405	60.632	8.254	0.739	109.134
MICHIGAN	42.342	6.319	45.083	8.957	0.799	103.499
OHIO	48.316	6.454	51.330	3.997	1.846	111.943
WISCONSIN	25.606	3.318	43.068	7.877	0.639	80.508
WEST NORTH CENTRAL:						
IOWA	35.475	7.141	56.237	28.380	0.951	128.184
KANSAS	45.968	8.622	106.013	139.441	2.792	302.837
MINNESOTA	30.940	5.319	39.728	17.898	6.293	100.179
MISSOURI	36.634	6.192	27.861	16.296	3.577	90.559
NEBRASKA	41.989	8.773	57.217	42.565	5.425	155.970
NORTH DAKOTA	18.769	5.570	2.724	30.863	0.000	57.926
SOUTH DAKOTA	20.883	4.971	17.887	5.455	2.349	51.545
SOUTH ATLANTIC:						
DELAWARE	15.843	3.019	19.321	6.253	0.000	44.437
DISTRICT OF COLUMBIA	24.338	12.263	1.569	0.731	2.840	41.740
FLORIDA	3.174	1.280	11.869	25.049	0.604	41.976
GEORGIA	19.365	4.111	36.733	10.159	1.028	71.395
MARYLAND	20.377	3.321	17.845	2.778	0.885	45.206
NORTH CAROLINA	6.829	1.591	20.969	4.514	1.195	35.099
SOUTH CAROLINA	8.170	2.229	39.110	10.603	0.425	60.537
VIRGINIA	12.993	2.805	13.197	3.825	1.537	34.357
WEST VIRGINIA	34.485	6.330	53.180	11.154	1.641	106.789
EAST SOUTH CENTRAL:						
ALABAMA	16.016	4.898	53.304	7.021	0.300	81.539
KENTUCKY	26.997	4.938	28.207	16.049	2.316	78.508
MISSISSIPPI	18.138	4.189	69.226	78.128	2.056	171.736
TENNESSEE	14.110	4.824	38.848	10.830	1.072	69.684
WEST SOUTH CENTRAL:						
ARKANSAS	24.026	6.936	79.792	46.950	0.484	158.188
LOUISIANA	23.319	4.577	259.442	237.745	8.896	533.979
OKLAHOMA	31.014	7.549	46.201	160.416	1.652	246.832
TEXAS	22.200	4.083	146.001	214.083	4.168	390.536
ROCKY MOUNTAIN:						
ARIZONA	19.925	7.697	37.209	55.956	2.165	122.952
COLORADO	38.913	16.141	39.981	32.042	0.524	127.602
IDAHO	16.072	7.020	47.164	6.694	2.634	79.582
MONTANA	35.497	13.903	43.332	25.014	3.791	121.538
NEVADA	20.755	8.457	18.973	81.414	11.532	141.131
NEW MEXICO	35.686	10.814	81.303	146.854	15.209	289.866
UTAH	41.820	4.144	45.340	11.966	0.012	103.282
WYOMING	66.661	27.883	156.329	116.756	4.417	372.046
FAR WEST:						
ALASKA	28.710	17.614	44.054	119.134	21.352	230.864
CALIFORNIA	36.066	7.220	27.730	41.460	0.384	112.859
HAWAII	0.000	0.000	0.000	0.000	0.000	0.000
OREGON	12.911	3.902	28.112	7.669	0.187	52.781
WASHINGTON	14.151	4.301	22.879	11.228	0.052	52.611

Table   132

Consumption Of Natural Gas, 1972, In Million BTU Per Capita, By State

Use By Sector

REGION AND STATE	HOUSEHOLD USE	BUSINESS USE	FEDERAL GOVERNMENT USE	STATE & LOCAL GOVERNMENT USE	TOTAL USE
NEW ENGLAND:					
CONNECTICUT	12.711	8.354	0.023	1.868	22.956
MAINE	0.963	0.602	0.005	0.086	1.656
MASSACHUSETTS	17.312	8.814	0.049	1.494	27.669
NEW HAMPSHIRE	6.750	3.663	0.628	0.456	11.497
RHODE ISLAND	15.464	8.671	0.048	1.177	25.360
VERMONT	3.038	5.125	0.010	0.154	8.327
MID ATLANTIC:					
NEW JERSEY	23.976	20.067	0.057	1.322	45.423
NEW YORK	23.932	13.751	0.052	1.924	39.660
PENNSYLVANIA	29.009	39.937	0.080	1.851	70.877
EAST NORTH CENTRAL:					
ILLINOIS	49.608	56.178	0.124	2.565	108.475
INDIANA	34.104	72.543	0.075	2.412	109.134
MICHIGAN	42.342	58.287	0.069	2.801	103.499
OHIO	48.316	59.836	0.099	3.692	111.943
WISCONSIN	25.606	53.236	0.044	1.622	80.508
WEST NORTH CENTRAL:					
IOWA	35.475	89.496	0.107	3.106	128.184
KANSAS	45.968	249.837	1.401	5.631	302.837
MINNESOTA	30.940	61.263	0.081	7.894	100.179
MISSOURI	36.634	48.411	0.146	5.368	90.559
NEBRASKA	41.989	105.346	0.555	8.080	155.970
NORTH DAKOTA	18.769	37.316	0.125	1.717	57.926
SOUTH DAKOTA	20.883	26.600	0.156	3.906	51.545
SOUTH ATLANTIC:					
DELAWARE	15.843	27.242	0.049	1.303	44.437
DISTRICT OF COLUMBIA	24.338	9.711	2.274	5.417	41.740
FLORIDA	3.174	34.372	0.404	4.025	41.976
GEORGIA	19.365	49.342	0.122	2.566	71.395
MARYLAND	20.377	22.665	0.160	2.004	45.206
NORTH CAROLINA	6.829	26.506	0.026	1.738	35.099
SOUTH CAROLINA	8.170	51.085	0.045	1.236	60.537
VIRGINIA	12.993	18.769	0.141	2.454	34.357
WEST VIRGINIA	34.485	68.344	0.129	3.831	106.789
EAST SOUTH CENTRAL:					
ALABAMA	16.016	63.337	0.164	2.023	81.539
KENTUCKY	26.997	47.472	0.116	3.923	78.508
MISSISSIPPI	18.138	149.110	0.876	3.612	171.736
TENNESSEE	14.110	52.051	0.786	2.737	69.684
WEST SOUTH CENTRAL:					
ARKANSAS	24.026	130.661	0.574	2.927	158.188
LOUISIANA	23.319	499.139	0.919	10.603	533.979
OKLAHOMA	31.014	210.364	1.120	4.334	246.832
TEXAS	22.200	362.381	0.375	5.580	390.536
ROCKY MOUNTAIN:					
ARIZONA	19.925	98.154	0.203	4.671	122.952
COLORADO	38.913	78.885	0.475	9.329	127.602
IDAHO	16.072	58.493	0.128	4.890	79.582
MONTANA	35.497	77.514	0.330	8.197	121.538
NEVADA	20.755	105.844	0.215	14.317	141.131
NEW MEXICO	35.686	234.996	0.450	18.734	289.866
UTAH	41.820	59.856	0.279	1.328	103.282
WYOMING	66.661	289.998	0.941	14.446	372.046
FAR WEST:					
ALASKA	28.710	174.079	1.202	26.874	230.864
CALIFORNIA	36.066	74.096	0.175	2.523	112.859
HAWAII	0.000	0.000	0.000	0.000	0.000
OREGON	12.911	38.462	0.079	1.330	52.781
WASHINGTON	14.151	37.023	0.099	1.338	52.611

Table 133

Expenditures On Natural Gas, 1972, In Dollars Per Capita, By State

Use By Function

REGION AND STATE	RESIDENTIAL USE	"NET" COMMERCIAL USE	INDUSTRIAL USE	ENERGY PRODUCTION USE	OTHER USE (Municipal Institutional)	TOTAL USE
NEW ENGLAND:						
CONNECTICUT	25.540	3.150	8.648	0.009	1.733	39.080
MAINE	2.873	0.416	0.748	0.000	0.013	4.051
MASSACHUSETTS	38.070	4.560	6.929	0.672	0.936	51.167
NEW HAMPSHIRE	13.006	2.184	2.900	0.000	0.089	18.178
RHODE ISLAND	30.853	3.368	9.044	0.085	1.013	44.363
VERMONT	5.192	0.728	1.967	0.700	0.000	8.587
MID ATLANTIC:						
NEW JERSEY	45.635	5.215	11.487	2.025	0.437	64.800
NEW YORK	36.877	4.238	6.430	2.017	1.078	50.640
PENNSYLVANIA	37.477	4.410	24.372	1.336	0.660	68.255
EAST NORTH CENTRAL:						
ILLINOIS	53.504	6.142	25.780	4.300	0.334	90.059
INDIANA	38.192	5.007	36.487	3.351	0.596	83.632
MICHIGAN	45.375	5.671	30.452	3.925	0.573	85.996
OHIO	49.340	5.589	33.667	1.771	1.449	91.817
WISCONSIN	33.010	3.363	27.742	3.241	0.307	67.664
WEST NORTH CENTRAL:						
IOWA	38.447	6.016	30.125	9.425	0.433	84.446
KANSAS	33.562	4.587	38.434	45.637	0.912	123.133
MINNESOTA	37.069	4.995	23.046	7.149	3.712	75.971
MISSOURI	39.186	5.073	16.638	5.954	1.463	68.314
NEBRASKA	40.396	5.422	26.857	13.951	2.164	88.791
NORTH DAKOTA	19.995	4.360	3.519	8.886	0.000	36.760
SOUTH DAKOTA	22.964	3.570	9.429	1.971	1.224	39.157
SOUTH ATLANTIC:						
DELAWARE	26.243	4.010	13.308	3.250	0.000	46.812
DISTRICT OF COLUMBIA	35.755	14.129	1.572	0.189	3.215	54.860
FLORIDA	6.426	1.682	5.523	9.581	0.275	23.486
GEORGIA	23.329	3.556	20.368	3.315	0.840	51.409
MARYLAND	32.641	4.263	14.328	0.987	0.713	52.932
NORTH CAROLINA	9.311	1.852	13.646	1.894	0.823	27.526
SOUTH CAROLINA	12.679	2.261	22.379	4.751	0.246	42.317
VIRGINIA	19.824	3.275	9.267	1.517	1.112	34.996
WEST VIRGINIA	32.230	4.607	29.574	4.055	1.147	71.613
EAST SOUTH CENTRAL:						
ALABAMA	19.472	3.506	23.557	1.767	0.147	48.449
KENTUCKY	24.469	3.753	16.337	4.483	1.481	50.523
MISSISSIPPI	19.047	2.869	24.737	21.621	1.131	69.405
TENNESSEE	14.055	4.192	20.755	2.796	0.603	42.402
WEST SOUTH CENTRAL:						
ARKANSAS	19.707	3.972	29.431	14.050	0.172	67.332
LOUISIANA	20.577	2.655	83.320	58.272	2.766	167.591
OKLAHOMA	26.798	4.177	15.108	35.305	0.809	82.196
TEXAS	21.580	2.493	38.156	51.476	1.295	114.999
ROCKY MOUNTAIN:						
ARIZONA	22.730	5.437	17.549	19.049	1.188	65.952
COLORADO	30.946	10.756	15.934	9.746	0.223	67.605
IDAHO	22.543	7.377	26.352	1.780	1.562	59.613
MONTANA	32.903	9.309	18.643	7.047	1.778	69.682
NEVADA	27.988	7.488	13.328	35.467	6.437	90.709
NEW MEXICO	31.840	6.870	27.147	33.483	4.789	104.129
UTAH	39.933	3.132	18.069	4.125	0.009	65.268
WYOMING	48.025	14.119	49.796	22.645	1.251	135.836
FAR WEST:						
ALASKA	43.080	18.998	33.084	37.308	9.902	142.371
CALIFORNIA	36.154	5.638	12.791	15.806	0.181	70.570
HAWAII	0.000	0.000	0.000	0.000	0.000	0.000
OREGON	20.357	5.433	15.626	2.774	0.111	44.301
WASHINGTON	19.042	4.754	10.629	4.610	0.028	39.062

Table 134

Expenditures On Natural Gas, 1972, In Dollars Per Capita, By State

Use By Sector

REGION AND STATE	HOUSEHOLD USE	BUSINESS USS	FEDERAL GOVERNMENT USE	STATE & LOCAL GOVERNMENT USE	TOTAL USE
NEW ENGLAND:					
CONNECTICUT	25.540	10.950	0.039	2.550	39.080
MAINE	2.873	1.029	0.010	0.138	4.051
MASSACHUSETTS	38.070	10.891	0.087	2.119	51.167
NEW HAMPSHIRE	13.006	4.049	0.444	0.680	18.178
RHODE ISLAND	30.853	11.547	0.089	1.874	44.363
VERMONT	5.192	3.178	0.013	0.204	8.587
MID ATLANTIC:					
NEW JERSEY	45.635	17.278	0.084	1.803	64.800
NEW YORK	36.877	11.489	0.068	2.205	50.640
PENNSYLVANIA	37.477	28.923	0.086	1.770	68.255
EAST NORTH CENTRAL:					
ILLINOIS	53.504	34.472	0.103	1.981	90.059
INDIANA	38.192	43.225	0.070	2.146	83.632
MICHIGAN	45.375	38.189	0.062	2.370	85.996
OHIO	49.340	39.343	0.085	3.048	91.817
WISCONSIN	33.010	33.306	0.045	1.303	67.664
WEST NORTH CENTRAL:					
IOWA	38.447	43.661	0.090	2.248	84.446
KANSAS	33.562	86.687	0.507	2.377	123.133
MINNESOTA	37.069	33.610	0.076	5.215	75.971
MISSOURI	39.186	26.077	0.119	2.931	68.314
NEBRASKA	40.396	44.330	0.267	3.797	88.791
NORTH DAKOTA	19.995	15.324	0.097	1.344	36.760
SOUTH DAKOTA	22.964	13.740	0.112	2.342	39.157
SOUTH ATLANTIC:					
DELAWARE	26.243	19.014	0.064	1.490	46.812
DISTRICT OF COLUMBIA	35.755	10.300	2.620	6.185	54.860
FLORIDA	6.426	14.637	0.210	2.214	23.486
GEORGIA	23.329	25.803	0.105	2.172	51.409
MARYLAND	32.641	17.974	0.206	2.112	52.932
NORTH CAROLINA	9.311	16.731	0.030	1.454	27.526
SOUTH CAROLINA	12.679	28.522	0.046	1.070	42.317
VIRGINIA	19.824	12.825	0.165	2.182	34.996
WEST VIRGINIA	32.230	36.547	0.094	2.741	71.613
EAST SOUTH CENTRAL:					
ALABAMA	19.472	27.480	0.117	1.380	48.449
KENTUCKY	24.469	23.264	0.088	2.702	50.523
MISSISSIPPI	19.047	47.838	0.322	2.197	69.405
TENNESSEE	14.055	25.879	0.423	2.044	42.402
WEST SOUTH CENTRAL:					
ARKANSAS	19.707	45.818	0.236	1.571	67.332
LOUISIANA	20.577	142.986	0.311	3.717	167.591
OKLAHOMA	26.798	52.714	0.399	2.286	82.196
TEXAS	21.580	91.136	0.132	2.151	114.999
ROCKY MOUNTAIN:					
ARIZONA	22.730	40.147	0.143	2.932	65.952
COLORADO	30.946	31.555	0.316	4.787	67.605
IDAHO	22.543	33.003	0.134	3.933	59.613
MONTANA	32.903	31.829	0.221	4.728	69.682
NEVADA	27.988	53.627	0.191	8.903	90.709
NEW MEXICO	31.840	64.975	0.286	7.028	104.129
UTAH	39.933	24.121	0.211	1.004	65.268
WYOMING	48.025	81.005	0.477	6.330	135.836
FAR WEST:					
ALASKA	43.080	82.138	1.296	15.858	142.371
CALIFORNIA	36.154	32.427	0.136	1.852	70.570
HAWAII	0.000	0.000	0.000	0.000	0.000
OREGON	20.357	22.132	0.110	1.702	44.301
WASHINGTON	19.042	18.462	0.110	1.449	39.062

Table 135

Per Capita Use Of Natural Gas, 1972, In Million BTU Per Capita and In Dollars Per Capita By Region

Use By Function

REGION	RESIDENTIAL USE	"NET" COMMERCIAL USE	INDUSTRIAL USE	ENERGY PRODUCTION USE	OTHER USE (Municipal Institutional)	TOTAL USE
Consumption In Million BTU Per Capita						
NEW ENGLAND	13.390	1.969	5.328	0.810	0.815	22.311
MID ATLANTIC	25.547	3.571	16.631	4.061	0.855	50.664
EAST NORTH CENTRAL	42.991	6.203	47.233	7.855	0.988	105.269
WEST NORTH CENTRAL	35.545	6.648	47.552	38.101	3.631	131.478
SOUTH ATLANTIC	12.727	2.891	22.508	10.583	1.023	49.732
EAST SOUTH CENTRAL	18.550	4.763	45.253	22.663	1.347	92.576
WEST SOUTH CENTRAL	23.754	4.919	147.418	194.644	4.351	375.086
ROCKY MOUNTAIN	32.467	11.147	49.209	52.235	3.857	148.914
FAR WEST	30.272	6.493	26.512	34.619	0.566	98.462
TOTAL	27.387	5.043	42.375	33.836	1.583	110.224
Expenditures In Dollars Per Capita						
NEW ENGLAND	28.469	3.457	6.566	0.357	0.977	39.826
MID ATLANTIC	38.778	4.483	13.096	1.803	0.821	58.980
EAST NORTH CENTRAL	46.355	5.437	30.490	3.312	0.711	86.305
WEST NORTH CENTRAL	36.512	5.096	23.592	12.935	1.733	79.868
SOUTH ATLANTIC	17.752	3.101	13.547	4.049	0.740	39.188
EAST SOUTH CENTRAL	18.978	3.671	21.078	6.173	0.792	50.692
WEST SOUTH CENTRAL	21.892	2.894	42.690	46.856	1.393	115.725
ROCKY MOUNTAIN	30.310	7.672	20.188	15.117	1.615	74.902
FAR WEST	31.726	5.501	12.605	13.130	0.267	63.229
TOTAL	32.107	4.512	20.613	9.892	0.883	68.008

Table 136

Per Capita Use Of Natural Gas, 1972, In Million BTU Per Capita And
     In Dollars Per Capita, By Region

Use By Sector
_____

REGION	HOUSEHOLD USE	BUSINESS USE	FEDERAL GOVT. USE	STATE & LOCAL GOVT. USE	TOTAL USE
Consumption In Million BTU Per Capita					
NEW ENGLAND	13.390	7.520	0.074	1.327	22.311
MID ATLANTIC	25.547	23.271	0.062	1.784	50.664
EAST NORTH CENTRAL	42.991	59.400	0.090	2.789	105.269
WEST NORTH CENTRAL	35.545	89.949	0.333	5.651	131.478
SOUTH ATLANTIC	12.727	34.101	0.222	2.682	49.732
EAST SOUTH CENTRAL	18.550	70.566	0.467	2.994	92.576
WEST SOUTH CENTRAL	23.754	344.648	0.595	6.089	375.086
ROCKY MOUNTAIN	32.467	107.645	0.348	8.454	148.914
FAR WEST	30.272	65.532	0.164	2.494	98.462
TOTAL	27.387	79.353	0.217	3.267	110.224
Expenditures In Dollars Per Capita					
NEW ENGLAND	28.469	9.392	0.088	1.877	39.826
MID ATLANTIC	38.778	18.137	0.077	1.989	58.980
EAST NORTH CENTRAL	46.355	37.579	0.078	2.293	86.305
WEST NORTH CENTRAL	36.512	39.921	0.170	3.265	79.868
SOUTH ATLANTIC	17.752	19.165	0.192	2.079	39.188
EAST SOUTH CENTRAL	18.978	29.416	0.240	2.058	50.692
WEST SOUTH CENTRAL	21.892	91.219	0.211	2.403	115.725
ROCKY MOUNTAIN	30.310	39.957	0.237	4.398	74.902
FAR WEST	31.726	29.462	0.141	1.901	63.229
TOTAL	32.107	33.467	0.141	2.293	68.008

Table 137

Per Capita Consumption Of Natural Gas In Index Number Terms, U.S. = 100, 1972, By State

Use By Function

REGION AND STATE	RESIDENTIAL USE	"NET" COMMERCIAL USE	INDUSTRIAL USE	ENERGY PRODUCTION USE	OTHER USE (Municipal-Institu-tional)	TOTAL USE
NEW ENGLAND:						
CONNECTICUT	46.41	36.55	16.49	0.07	87.81	20.83
MAINE	3.52	4.60	1.05	0.00	1.01	1.50
MASSACHUSETTS	63.21	50.92	12.83	4.51	52.31	25.10
NEW HAMPSHIRE	24.65	25.84	7.88	0.00	6.51	10.43
RHODE ISLAND	56.46	36.21	16.96	0.51	44.85	23.01
VERMONT	11.09	10.87	7.49	4.63	0.00	7.55
MID ATLANTIC:						
NEW JERSEY	87.55	70.49	31.77	11.94	24.70	41.21
NEW YORK	87.38	63.93	16.57	13.05	67.34	35.98
PENNSYLVANIA	105.92	81.60	78.85	10.41	51.55	64.30
EAST NORTH CENTRAL:						
ILLINOIS	181.14	146.87	95.41	30.90	36.45	98.41
INDIANA	124.53	107.18	143.08	24.39	46.68	99.01
MICHIGAN	154.61	125.30	106.39	26.47	50.47	93.90
OHIO	176.42	127.98	121.13	11.81	116.61	101.56
WISCONSIN	93.50	65.80	101.64	23.28	40.37	73.04
WEST NORTH CENTRAL:						
IOWA	129.53	141.61	132.71	83.88	60.08	116.29
KANSAS	167.85	170.97	250.18	412.11	176.37	274.75
MINNESOTA	112.97	105.48	93.75	52.90	397.54	90.89
MISSOURI	133.76	122.78	65.75	48.16	225.96	82.16
NEBRASKA	153.32	173.97	135.03	125.80	342.70	141.50
NORTH DAKOTA	68.53	110.45	6.43	91.21	0.00	52.55
SOUTH DAKOTA	76.25	98.57	42.21	16.12	148.39	46.76
SOUTH ATLANTIC:						
DELAWARE	57.85	59.86	45.60	18.48	0.00	40.32
DISTRICT OF COLUMBIA	88.87	243.17	3.70	2.16	179.41	37.87
FLORIDA	11.59	25.38	28.01	74.03	38.16	38.08
GEORGIA	70.71	81.52	86.69	30.02	64.94	64.77
MARYLAND	74.40	65.85	42.11	8.21	55.91	41.01
NORTH CAROLINA	24.94	31.55	49.48	13.34	75.49	31.84
SOUTH CAROLINA	29.83	44.20	92.29	31.34	26.85	54.92
VIRGINIA	47.44	55.62	31.14	11.30	97.09	31.17
WEST VIRGINIA	125.92	125.52	125.50	32.96	103.66	96.88
EAST SOUTH CENTRAL:						
ALABAMA	58.48	97.12	125.79	20.75	18.95	73.98
KENTUCKY	98.58	97.92	66.57	47.43	146.30	71.23
MISSISSIPPI	66.23	83.06	163.37	230.90	129.88	155.81
TENNESSEE	51.52	95.65	91.68	32.01	67.72	63.22
WEST SOUTH CENTRAL:						
ARKANSAS	87.73	137.53	188.30	138.76	30.57	143.52
LOUISIANA	85.15	90.76	612.25	702.64	561.97	484.45
OKLAHOMA	113.24	149.69	109.03	474.10	104.36	223.94
TEXAS	81.06	80.96	344.55	632.71	263.30	354.31
ROCKY MOUNTAIN:						
ARIZONA	72.75	152.63	87.81	165.37	136.77	111.55
COLORADO	142.09	320.06	94.35	94.70	33.10	115.77
IDAHO	58.68	139.21	111.30	19.78	166.39	72.20
MONTANA	129.61	275.69	102.26	73.93	239.48	110.26
NEVADA	75.78	167.69	44.77	240.61	728.49	128.04
NEW MEXICO	130.30	214.43	191.87	434.02	960.77	262.98
UTAH	152.70	82.17	107.00	35.36	0.76	93.70
WYOMING	243.40	552.90	368.92	345.06	279.03	337.54
FAR WEST:						
ALASKA	104.83	349.28	103.96	352.09	1348.83	209.45
CALIFORNIA	131.69	143.17	65.44	122.53	24.26	102.39
HAWAII	0.00	0.00	0.00	0.00	0.00	0.00
OREGON	47.14	77.37	66.34	22.67	11.81	47.89
WASHINGTON	51.67	85.28	53.99	33.18	3.28	47.73

Table 138

Per Capita Expenditures On Natural Gas In Index Number Terms, U.S. = 100, 1972, By State

Use By Function

REGION AND STATE	RESIDENTIAL USE	"NET" COMMERCIAL USE	INDUSTRIAL USE	ENERGY PRODUCTION USE	OTHER USE (Municipal-Institu-tional)	TOTAL USE
NEW ENGLAND:						
CONNECTICUT	79.55	69.81	41.95	0.09	196.26	57.46
MAINE	8.95	9.22	3.63	0.00	1.47	5.96
MASSACHUSETTS	118.57	101.06	33.61	6.79	106.00	75.24
NEW HAMPSHIRE	40.51	48.40	14.07	0.00	10.08	26.73
RHODE ISLAND	96.09	74.65	43.88	0.86	114.72	65.23
VERMONT	16.17	16.13	9.54	7.08	0.00	12.63
MID ATLANTIC:						
NEW JERSEY	142.13	115.58	55.73	20.47	49.49	95.28
NEW YORK	114.86	93.93	31.19	20.39	122.08	74.46
PENNSYLVANIA	116.73	97.74	118.24	13.51	74.75	100.36
EAST NORTH CENTRAL:						
ILLINOIS	166.64	136.13	125.07	43.47	37.83	132.42
INDIANA	118.95	110.97	177.01	33.88	67.50	122.97
MICHIGAN	141.32	125.69	147.73	39.68	64.89	126.45
OHIO	153.67	123.87	163.33	17.90	164.10	135.01
WISCONSIN	102.81	74.53	134.58	32.76	34.77	99.49
WEST NORTH CENTRAL:						
IOWA	119.75	133.33	146.15	95.28	49.04	124.17
KANSAS	104.53	101.66	186.46	461.35	103.28	181.06
MINNESOTA	115.45	110.70	111.80	72.27	420.39	111.71
MISSOURI	122.05	112.43	80.72	60.19	165.69	100.45
NEBRASKA	125.82	120.17	130.29	141.03	245.07	130.56
NORTH DAKOTA	62.28	96.63	17.07	89.83	0.00	54.05
SOUTH DAKOTA	71.52	79.12	45.74	19.93	138.62	57.58
SOUTH ATLANTIC:						
DELAWARE	81.74	88.87	64.56	32.85	0.00	68.83
DISTRICT OF COLUMBIA	111.36	313.14	7.63	1.91	364.10	80.67
FLORIDA	20.01	37.28	26.79	96.86	31.14	34.53
GEORGIA	72.66	78.81	98.81	33.51	95.13	75.59
MARYLAND	101.66	94.48	69.51	9.98	80.75	77.83
NORTH CAROLINA	29.00	41.05	66.20	19.15	93.20	40.47
SOUTH CAROLINA	39.49	50.11	108.57	48.03	27.86	62.22
VIRGINIA	61.74	72.58	44.96	15.34	125.93	51.46
WEST VIRGINIA	100.38	102.11	143.47	40.99	129.90	105.30
EAST SOUTH CENTRAL:						
ALABAMA	60.65	77.70	114.28	17.86	16.65	71.24
KENTUCKY	76.21	83.18	79.26	45.32	167.72	74.29
MISSISSIPPI	59.32	63.59	120.01	218.57	128.09	102.05
TENNESSEE	43.78	92.91	100.69	28.27	68.29	62.35
WEST SOUTH CENTRAL:						
ARKANSAS	61.38	88.03	142.78	142.03	19.48	99.01
LOUISIANA	64.09	58.84	404.21	589.08	313.25	246.43
OKLAHOMA	83.46	92.58	73.29	356.90	91.62	120.86
TEXAS	67.21	55.25	185.11	520.38	146.66	169.10
ROCKY MOUNTAIN:						
ARIZONA	70.79	120.50	85.14	192.57	134.54	96.98
COLORADO	96.38	238.39	77.30	98.52	25.25	99.41
IDAHO	70.21	163.50	127.84	17.99	176.90	87.66
MONTANA	102.48	206.32	90.44	71.24	201.36	102.46
NEVADA	87.17	165.96	64.66	358.54	728.99	133.38
NEW MEXICO	99.17	152.26	131.70	338.49	542.36	153.11
UTAH	124.37	69.41	87.66	41.70	1.02	95.97
WYOMING	149.58	312.92	241.58	228.92	141.68	199.74
FAR WEST:						
ALASKA	134.18	421.05	160.50	377.15	1121.40	209.34
CALIFORNIA	112.60	124.96	62.05	159.79	20.50	103.77
HAWAII	0.00	0.00	0.00	0.00	0.00	0.00
OREGON	63.40	120.41	75.81	28.04	12.57	65.14
WASHINGTON	59.31	105.36	51.56	46.60	3.17	57.44

Table 139

Per Capita Use Of Natural Gas, In Index Number Terms, U.S. = 100, 1972, Based on Consumption
In BTU And Expenditures In Dollars, By Region

Use By Function

REGION	RESI-DENTIAL USE	"NET" COMMERCIAL USE	INDUSTRIAL USE	ENERGY PRODUCTION USE	OTHER USE (Municipal-Institu-tional)	TOTAL USE
Index Of Per Capita Consumption, U.S. = 100						
NEW ENGLAND	48.89	39.04	12.57	2.39	51.48	20.24
MID ATLANTIC	93.28	70.81	39.25	12.00	54.01	45.96
EAST NORTH CENTRAL	156.98	123.00	111.46	23.21	62.41	95.50
WEST NORTH CENTRAL	129.79	131.83	112.22	112.60	229.37	119.28
SOUTH ATLANTIC	46.47	57.33	53.12	31.28	64.62	45.12
EAST SOUTH CENTRAL	67.73	94.45	106.79	66.98	85.09	83.99
WEST SOUTH CENTRAL	86.73	97.54	347.89	575.26	274.86	340.29
ROCKY MOUNTAIN	118.55	221.04	116.13	154.38	243.65	135.10
FAR WEST	110.53	128.75	62.57	102.31	35.75	89.33
UNITED STATES	100.00	100.00	100.00	100.00	100.00	100.00

Index Of Per Capita Expenditures, U.S. = 100						
NEW ENGLAND	88.67	76.62	31.85	3.61	110.65	58.56
MID ATLANTIC	120.78	99.36	63.53	18.23	92.98	86.73
EAST NORTH CENTRAL	144.38	120.50	147.92	33.48	80.52	126.90
WEST NORTH CENTRAL	113.72	112.94	114.45	130.76	196.26	117.44
SOUTH ATLANTIC	55.29	68.73	65.72	40.93	83.81	57.62
EAST SOUTH CENTRAL	59.11	81.36	102.26	62.40	89.69	74.54
WEST SOUTH CENTRAL	68.18	64.14	207.10	473.68	157.76	170.16
ROCKY MOUNTAIN	94.40	170.04	97.94	152.82	182.90	110.14
FAR WEST	98.81	121.92	61.15	132.73	30.24	92.97
UNITED STATES	100.00	100.00	100.00	100.00	100.00	100.00

Table 140

Natural Gas Prices In Dollars Per Million BTU, 1972, By State

Use By Function

REGION AND STATE	RESIDENTIAL USE	"NET" COMMERCIAL USE	INDUSTRIAL USE	ENERGY PRODUCTION USE	OTHER USE (Municipal Institutional)	TOTAL USE
NEW ENGLAND:						
CONNECTICUT	2.009	1.709	1.238	0.380	1.247	1.702
MAINE	2.983	1.793	1.681	0.490	0.802	2.446
MASSACHUSETTS	2.199	1.776	1.275	0.440	1.130	1.849
NEW HAMPSHIRE	1.927	1.676	0.868	0.490	0.865	1.581
RHODE ISLAND	1.995	1.844	1.258	0.490	1.427	1.749
VERMONT	1.709	1.328	0.620	0.446	1.427	1.031
MID ATLANTIC:						
NEW JERSEY	1.903	1.467	0.853	0.501	1.118	1.427
NEW YORK	1.541	1.314	0.916	0.457	1.011	1.277
PENNSYLVANIA	1.292	1.072	0.729	0.379	0.809	0.963
EAST NORTH CENTRAL:						
ILLINOIS	1.079	0.829	0.638	0.411	0.579	0.830
INDIANA	1.120	0.926	0.602	0.406	0.806	0.766
MICHIGAN	1.072	0.898	0.675	0.438	0.717	0.831
OHIO	1.021	0.866	0.656	0.443	0.785	0.820
WISCONSIN	1.289	1.014	0.644	0.412	0.480	0.840
WEST NORTH CENTRAL:						
IOWA	1.084	0.842	0.536	0.332	0.455	0.659
KANSAS	0.730	0.532	0.363	0.327	0.327	0.407
MINNESOTA	1.198	0.939	0.580	0.399	0.590	0.758
MISSOURI	1.070	0.819	0.597	0.365	0.409	0.754
NEBRASKA	0.962	0.618	0.469	0.328	0.399	0.569
NORTH DAKOTA	1.065	0.783	1.292	0.288	0.521	0.635
SOUTH DAKOTA	1.100	0.718	0.527	0.361	0.521	0.760
SOUTH ATLANTIC:						
DELAWARE	1.656	1.328	0.689	0.520	0.806	1.053
DISTRICT OF COLUMBIA	1.469	1.152	1.002	0.258	1.132	1.314
FLORIDA	2.024	1.314	0.465	0.382	0.455	0.560
GEORGIA	1.205	0.865	0.554	0.326	0.818	0.720
MARYLAND	1.602	1.284	0.803	0.355	0.806	1.171
NORTH CAROLINA	1.363	1.164	0.651	0.420	0.688	0.784
SOUTH CAROLINA	1.552	1.015	0.572	0.448	0.580	0.699
VIRGINIA	1.526	1.168	0.702	0.397	0.723	1.019
WEST VIRGINIA	0.935	0.728	0.556	0.364	0.699	0.671
EAST SOUTH CENTRAL:						
ALABAMA	1.216	0.716	0.442	0.252	0.491	0.594
KENTUCKY	0.906	0.760	0.579	0.279	0.639	0.644
MISSISSIPPI	1.050	0.685	0.357	0.277	0.550	0.404
TENNESSEE	0.996	0.869	0.534	0.258	0.563	0.608
WEST SOUTH CENTRAL:						
ARKANSAS	0.820	0.573	0.369	0.299	0.355	0.426
LOUISIANA	0.882	0.580	0.321	0.245	0.311	0.314
OKLAHOMA	0.864	0.553	0.327	0.220	0.489	0.333
TEXAS	0.972	0.611	0.261	0.240	0.311	0.294
ROCKY MOUNTAIN:						
ARIZONA	1.141	0.706	0.472	0.340	0.549	0.536
COLORADO	0.795	0.666	0.399	0.304	0.426	0.530
IDAHO	1.403	1.051	0.559	0.266	0.593	0.749
MONTANA	0.927	0.670	0.430	0.282	0.469	0.573
NEVADA	1.349	0.885	0.702	0.436	0.558	0.643
NEW MEXICO	0.892	0.635	0.334	0.228	0.315	0.359
UTAH	0.955	0.756	0.399	0.345	0.763	0.632
WYOMING	0.720	0.506	0.319	0.194	0.283	0.365
FAR WEST:						
ALASKA	1.501	1.079	0.751	0.313	0.464	0.617
CALIFORNIA	1.002	0.781	0.461	0.381	0.473	0.625
HAWAII[a]	0.000	0.000	0.000	0.000	0.000	0.000
OREGON	1.577	1.392	0.556	0.362	0.593	0.839
WASHINGTON	1.346	1.105	0.465	0.411	0.530	0.742

[a] Zero use of natural gas.

Table 141

Natural Gas Prices In Dollars Per Million BTU, 1972, By State

Use By Sector

REGION AND STATE	HOUSEHOLD USE	BUSINESS USE	FEDERAL GOVERNMENT USE	STATE & LOCAL GOVERNMENT USE	TOTAL USE
NEW ENGLAND:					
CONNECTICUT	2.009	1.311	1.709	1.365	1.702
MAINE	2.983	1.710	1.804	1.611	2.446
MASSACHUSETTS	2.199	1.236	1.776	1.418	1.849
NEW HAMPSHIRE	1.927	1.105	0.708	1.492	1.581
RHODE ISLAND	1.995	1.332	1.844	1.593	1.749
VERMONT	1.709	0.620	1.318	1.328	1.031
MID ATLANTIC:					
NEW JERSEY	1.903	0.861	1.467	1.364	1.427
NEW YORK	1.541	0.836	1.314	1.146	1.277
PENNSYLVANIA	1.292	0.724	1.072	0.956	0.963
EAST NORTH CENTRAL:					
ILLINOIS	1.079	0.614	0.829	0.772	0.830
INDIANA	1.120	0.596	0.926	0.890	0.766
MICHIGAN	1.072	0.655	0.898	0.846	0.831
OHIO	1.021	0.657	0.866	0.826	0.820
WISCONSIN	1.289	0.626	1.014	0.803	0.841
WEST NORTH CENTRAL:					
IOWA	1.084	0.488	0.842	0.724	0.659
KANSAS	0.730	0.347	0.362	0.422	0.407
MINNESOTA	1.198	0.549	0.939	0.661	0.758
MISSOURI	1.070	0.539	0.819	0.546	0.754
NEBRASKA	0.962	0.421	0.481	0.470	0.569
NORTH DAKOTA	1.065	0.411	0.782	0.783	0.635
SOUTH DAKOTA	1.100	0.517	0.718	0.600	0.760
SOUTH ATLANTIC:					
DELAWARE	1.656	0.698	1.329	1.144	1.053
DISTRICT OF COLUMBIA	1.469	1.061	1.152	1.142	1.314
FLORIDA	2.024	0.426	0.519	0.550	0.560
GEORGIA	1.205	0.523	0.865	0.846	0.720
MARYLAND	1.602	0.793	1.284	1.054	1.171
NORTH CAROLINA	1.363	0.631	1.165	0.837	0.784
SOUTH CAROLINA	1.552	0.558	1.015	0.865	0.699
VIRGINIA	1.526	0.683	1.168	0.889	1.019
WEST VIRGINIA	0.935	0.535	0.728	0.715	0.671
EAST SOUTH CENTRAL:					
ALABAMA	1.216	0.434	0.716	0.682	0.594
KENTUCKY	0.906	0.490	0.760	0.689	0.644
MISSISSIPPI	1.050	0.321	0.368	0.608	0.404
TENNESSEE	0.996	0.497	0.538	0.747	0.609
WEST SOUTH CENTRAL:					
ARKANSAS	0.820	0.351	0.411	0.537	0.426
LOUISIANA	0.882	0.286	0.338	0.351	0.314
OKLAHOMA	0.864	0.251	0.356	0.527	0.333
TEXAS	0.972	0.251	0.352	0.385	0.295
ROCKY MOUNTAIN:					
ARIZONA	1.141	0.409	0.706	0.628	0.536
COLORADO	0.795	0.400	0.666	0.513	0.530
IDAHO	1.403	0.564	1.051	0.804	0.749
MONTANA	0.927	0.411	0.670	0.577	0.573
NEVADA	1.348	0.507	0.886	0.622	0.643
NEW MEXICO	0.892	0.277	0.635	0.375	0.359
UTAH	0.955	0.403	0.756	0.756	0.632
WYOMING	0.720	0.279	0.506	0.438	0.365
FAR WEST:					
ALASKA	1.501	0.472	1.079	0.590	0.617
CALIFORNIA	1.003	0.438	0.781	0.734	0.625
HAWAII [a]	0.000	0.000	0.000	0.000	0.000
OREGON	1.577	0.575	1.392	1.280	0.839
WASHINGTON	1.346	0.499	1.105	1.083	0.742

[a] Zero use of natural gas

Table 142

Natural Gas Prices In Dollars Per Million BTU, 1972, By Region

Use By Function

REGION	RESIDENTIAL USE	"NET" COMMERCIAL USE	INDUSTRIAL USE	ENERGY PRODUCTION USE	OTHER USE (Municipal Institutional)	TOTAL USE
NEW ENGLAND	2.126	1.756	1.232	0.441	1.199	1.785
MID ATLANTIC	1.518	1.256	0.787	0.444	0.960	1.164
EAST NORTH CENTRAL	1.078	0.877	0.646	0.422	0.720	0.820
WEST NORTH CENTRAL	1.027	0.766	0.496	0.340	0.477	0.607
SOUTH ATLANTIC	1.395	1.073	0.602	0.383	0.723	0.788
EAST SOUTH CENTRAL	1.023	0.771	0.466	0.272	0.588	0.548
WEST SOUTH CENTRAL	0.922	0.588	0.290	0.241	0.320	0.309
ROCKY MOUNTAIN	0.934	0.688	0.410	0.289	0.419	0.503
FAR WEST	1.048	0.847	0.475	0.379	0.472	0.642
UNITED STATES	1.172	0.895	0.486	0.292	0.558	0.617

Table 143

Natural Gas Prices In Dollars Per Million BTU, 1972, By Region

Use By Sector

REGION	HOUSEHOLD USE	BUSINESS USE	FEDERAL GOVERNMENT USE	STATE & LOCAL GOVERNMENT USE	TOTAL USE
NEW ENGLAND	2.126	1.249	1.193	1.414	1.785
MID ATLANTIC	1.518	0.779	1.242	1.115	1.164
EAST NORTH CENTRAL	1.078	0.633	0.872	0.822	0.820
WEST NORTH CENTRAL	1.027	0.444	0.510	0.578	0.607
SOUTH ATLANTIC	1.395	0.562	0.862	0.775	0.788
EAST SOUTH CENTRAL	1.023	0.417	0.514	0.687	0.548
WEST SOUTH CENTRAL	0.922	0.265	0.355	0.395	0.309
ROCKY MOUNTAIN	0.934	0.371	0.679	0.520	0.503
FAR WEST	1.048	0.450	0.855	0.762	0.642
UNITED STATES	1.172	0.422	0.652	0.702	0.617

Table 144

Natural Gas Prices In Dollars Per Million BTU And Price Indexes, U.S. = 100, 1972, By State

Use By Function

REGION AND STATE	PRICE IN DOLLARS FOR MILLION BTU			PRICE INDEXES, U.S. = 100		
	RESIDENTIAL USE	ALL USES	ALL USES GIVEN U.S. QUANTITY WEIGHTS	RESIDENTIAL USE	ALL USES	ALL USES (U.S. Quantity Weights)
NEW ENGLAND:						
CONNECTICUT	2.009	1.702	1.188	156.32	201.90	161.28
MAINE	2.983	2.446	1.631	232.10	290.15	221.42
MASSACHUSETTS	2.199	1.849	1.269	171.10	219.34	172.28
NEW HAMPSHIRE	1.927	1.581	1.052	149.94	187.54	142.82
RHODE ISLAND	1.995	1.749	1.235	155.23	207.47	167.66
VERMONT	1.709	1.031	0.881	132.98	122.30	119.60
MID ATLANTIC:						
NEW JERSEY	1.903	1.427	1.038	148.07	169.28	140.92
NEW YORK	1.541	1.277	0.950	119.90	151.48	128.97
PENNSYLVANIA	1.292	0.963	0.778	100.53	114.23	105.62
EAST NORTH CENTRAL:						
ILLINOIS	1.079	0.830	0.686	83.96	98.46	93.13
INDIANA	1.120	0.766	0.688	87.15	90.87	93.40
MICHIGAN	1.072	0.831	0.712	83.41	98.58	96.66
OHIO	1.021	0.820	0.693	79.44	97.27	94.08
WISCONSIN	1.289	0.840	0.748	100.30	99.64	101.55
WEST NORTH CENTRAL:						
IOWA	1.084	0.659	0.622	84.34	78.17	84.44
KANSAS	0.730	0.407	0.450	56.80	48.28	61.09
MINNESOTA	1.198	0.758	0.695	93.22	89.92	94.35
MISSOURI	1.070	0.754	0.651	83.26	89.44	88.38
NEBRASKA	0.962	0.569	0.554	74.85	67.50	75.21
NORTH DAKOTA	1.065	0.635	0.893	82.87	75.33	121.23
SOUTH DAKOTA	1.100	0.760	0.627	85.59	90.15	85.12
SOUTH ATLANTIC:						
DELAWARE	1.656	1.053	0.908	128.85	124.91	123.27
DISTRICT OF COLUMBIA	1.469	1.314	0.898	114.30	155.87	121.91
FLORIDA	2.024	0.560	0.866	157.49	66.43	117.57
GEORGIA	1.205	0.720	0.664	93.76	85.41	90.14
MARYLAND	1.602	1.171	0.886	124.65	138.91	120.28
NORTH CAROLINA	1.363	0.784	0.781	106.05	93.00	106.03
SOUTH CAROLINA	1.552	0.699	0.798	120.76	82.92	108.34
VIRGINIA	1.526	1.019	0.835	118.74	120.88	113.36
WEST VIRGINIA	0.935	0.671	0.601	72.75	79.60	81.59
EAST SOUTH CENTRAL:						
ALABAMA	1.216	0.594	0.589	94.62	70.46	79.96
KENTUCKY	0.906	0.644	0.577	70.49	76.39	78.33
MISSISSIPPI	1.050	0.404	0.522	81.70	47.92	70.87
TENNESSEE	0.996	0.608	0.580	77.50	72.12	78.74
WEST SOUTH CENTRAL:						
ARKANSAS	0.820	0.426	0.469	63.80	50.53	63.67
LOUISIANA	0.882	0.314	0.449	68.63	37.25	60.96
OKLAHOMA	0.864	0.333	0.440	67.23	39.50	59.73
TEXAS	0.972	0.294	0.448	75.63	34.88	60.82
ROCKY MOUNTAIN:						
ARIZONA	1.141	0.536	0.610	88.78	63.58	82.81
COLORADO	0.795	0.530	0.481	61.86	62.87	65.30
IDAHO	1.403	0.749	0.702	109.17	88.85	95.30
MONTANA	0.927	0.573	0.520	72.13	67.97	70.59
NEVADA	1.348	0.643	0.787	104.89	76.28	106.84
NEW MEXICO	0.892	0.359	0.454	69.41	42.59	61.63
UTAH	0.955	0.632	0.542	74.31	74.97	73.58
WYOMING	0.720	0.365	0.388	56.02	43.30	52.67
FAR WEST:						
ALASKA	1.501	0.617	0.814	116.79	73.19	110.51
CALIFORNIA	1.003	0.625	0.586	78.04	74.14	79.55
HAWAII[a]	3.000	2.000	2.000	233.43	0.00	271.52
OREGON	1.577	0.839	0.789	122.70	99.53	107.11
WASHINGTON	1.346	0.742	0.698	104.73	88.02	94.76

[a] Price data from American Gas Association Series

Table 145

Natural Gas Prices In Dollars Per Million BTU And
Price Indexes, U.S. = 100, 1972, By Region

Use By Function

REGION	PRICE IN DOLLARS PER MILLION BTU			PRICE INDEXES, U.S. = 100 (Regional Values Relative To U.S. Value)		
	RESIDENTIAL USE	ALL USES	ALL USES	RESIDENTIAL USE	ALL USES	ALL USES
	(State Population Weights)		(U.S. Quantity Weights)			(U.S. Quantity Weights)
NEW ENGLAND	2.165	1.806	1.248	168.44	214.30	169.39
MID ATLANTIC	1.533	1.207	0.913	119.27	143.22	123.92
EAST NORTH CENTRAL	1.091	0.820	0.701	84.88	97.35	95.13
WEST NORTH CENTRAL	1.047	0.670	0.628	81.47	79.48	85.27
SOUTH ATLANTIC	1.546	0.811	0.801	120.29	96.22	108.74
EAST SOUTH CENTRAL	1.042	0.578	0.572	81.04	68.62	77.61
WEST SOUTH CENTRAL	0.926	0.316	0.449	72.02	37.51	60.99
ROCKY MOUNTAIN	0.996	0.546	0.551	77.51	64.79	74.75
FAR WEST	1.158	0.698	0.662	90.13	82.85	89.82
UNITED STATES	1.285	0.843	0.737	100.00	100.00	100.00

Chapter 4

Electricity

Information on the use of electricity is presented in two groups of tables, the first covering consumption in BTU and expenditures by sector and function, and the second covering prices. The first group includes Tables 146 through 163, and the second includes Tables 164 through 167. The groups will be treated in the usual fashion, with a discussion of organization followed by the presentation of some key findings.

Consumption and Expenditures

Organization

Amounts of use, per capita use, and per capita indexes of use are covered in turn, with use by sector and then use by function shown for each category. The following cross-classification of table numbers shows content for each table:

	Amounts Of Use		Per Capita Use		Per Capita Index of Use	
States	Sector	Function	Sector	Function	Sector	Function
BTU consumed	146	147	152	153	158	159
Expenditures	148	149	154	155	160	161
Regions						
BTU & expenditures	150	151	156	157	162	163

Some Key Findings

For the United States, the distributions of use by sectors were:

	Trillion BTU	Million Dollars	Fraction of Total BTU	Fraction of Total Dollars
Household Use	1,745.0	11,729.8	.324	.420
Business Use	3,175.2	13,381.9	.590	.479
Federal Govt. Use	79.4	360.9	.015	.013
State & Local Govt. Use	383.6	2,448.5	.071	.088
Total	5,383.2	27,921.1	1.000	1.000

The corresponding distributions by function were:

	Trillion BTU	Million Dollars	Fraction of Total BTU	Fraction of Total Dollars
Residential	1,745.0	11,729.8	.324	.420
Commercial	1,234.7	8,041.1	.229	.288
Industrial	2,181.9	6,983.9	.405	.250
Street & Highway Lighting	41.6	449.8	.008	.016
Other Public Authorities	147.4	593.3	.027	.021
Railroads and Railways	15.1	85.3	.003	.003
Interdepartmental (use by electric utilities)	17.5	37.9	.003	.001
Total Use	5,383.2	27,921.1	1.000	1.000

At the regional level, the leading user was the East North Central region, followed by the South Atlantic region. The regional distributions of use were:

	Trillion BTU	Million Dollars	Percent of Total	
			BTU	Dollars
New England	217.6	1,591.2	4.0	5.7
Mid Atlantic	750.2	5,175.8	13.9	18.5
East North Central	1,038.3	5,655.5	19.3	20.3
West North Central	343.5	2,091.8	6.4	7.5
South Atlantic	862.6	4,426.2	16.0	15.9
East South Central	523.5	1,820.1	9.7	6.5
West South Central	620.6	2,767.7	11.5	9.9
Rocky Mountain	245.0	1,154.1	4.6	4.1
Far West	781.8	3,238.6	14.5	11.6
Total	5,383.2	27,921.1	100.0	100.0

Corresponding per capita use levels, and indexes of use, were:

	Million BTU Per Capita	Dollars Per Capita	Index Of Per Capita Use	
			BTU	Dollars
New England	17.98	$131.45	69.54	98.03
Mid Atlantic	19.94	137.58	77.13	102.60
East North Central	25.45	138.65	98.46	103.40
West North Central	20.67	125.88	79.96	93.88
South Atlantic	27.02	138.67	104.53	103.41
East South Central	39.80	138.36	153.93	103.19
West South Central	31.06	138.50	120.14	103.29
Rocky Mountain	27.59	129.98	106.72	96.93
Far West	28.79	119.26	111.37	88.94
United States	25.85	$134.09	100.00	100.00

Although the indexes of per capita use show considerable variation, the
indexes of expenditures are much more concentrated around the U.S. value of

100, suggesting an approximately unitary price elasticity. (That inference is supported by the evidence of the regression equations presented in Chapter 6.) Per capita use is higher in the South and West, at least in part reflecting climate influence, both in terms of greater use for cooling in summer, and in terms of greater use of electricity for heating in areas of mild climate. In the later case, there can be a net saving in paying a higher cost for "fuel" (electricity instead of fossil fuel), and a lower cost for the corresponding heating equipment needed in employing the fuel.

There is considerable variation in per capita electricity use between individual states. Washington leads in total use, with a per capita index of 213.8, followed by Idaho with 195.4 and Tennessee with 188.9, all three being states served by the Bonneville Power Authority or the TVA. At the lower end of the use range are Alaska, with an index of 51.9, South Dakota, with 60.3 and Rhode Island, with 61.2.

For the major functions and for street and highway lighting, the highest and lowest levels of use are as follows:

	Per Capita BTU Index	Per Capita Expenditures Index
Residential Use		
Washington	222.3	102.0
Tennessee	205.7	113.3
Oregon	203.3	113.3
Rhode Island	66.3	90.1
New York	60.9	86.5
New Mexico	58.4	69.4

	Per Capita BTU Index	Per Capita Expenditures Index
Commercial Use		
District of Columbia	249.5	253.4
Nevada	246.7	194.4
Idaho	202.1	131.9
Minnesota	55.7	68.7
New Hampshire	55.2	70.8
Tennessee	50.5	37.5
Industrial Use		
Tennessee	268.2	193.9
Montana	267.8	75.3
Washington	246.8	109.0
South Dakota	17.9	26.9
Alaska	12.2	20.6
District of Columbia	6.7	11.4
Street & Highway Lighting		
Tennessee	225.5	165.1
Wisconsin	163.5	132.0
Nevada	157.0	100.7
Virginia	59.5	53.3
South Carolina	51.0	47.1
West Virginia	48.5	51.4

Many of these entries seem easy to explain. Low prices per unit can
explain high residential and industrial use per capita in Washington,
Oregon, Tennessee and Montana, and similarly, high prices are probably a

major factor in low residential usage in New York and Rhode Island. The
mix of economic activity explains the District of Columbia's extreme
commercial and industrial values, and presumably explains the low levels
of industrial use for South Dakota and Alaska. Nevada's tourist trade can
be cited in explaining its indexes for commercial use and street and highway
use. Finally, poverty, relatively low levels of urbanization and generally
low levels of government service are likely factors explaining the low
extremes for the three Southern states in street and highway lighting.

Some of the entries, however, seem puzzling. Perhaps Tennessee's low
commercial use may be, in part, an artifact, with some commercial use mis-
classified as industrial use; or it may be that there has been a policy
emphasis on industrialization employing electricity, with a neglect of
commercial enterprise development. Minnesota's relatively low commercial
use level may, in part, reflect industry mix; yet, this is not likely to
be a full explanation. The investigation of such anomalies might make a
useful future extension of the present effort.

Prices

Organization

The organization of the tables on prices is shown by this cross-
classification of table numbers:

States	Average Costs Paid	Weighted Prices & Indexes
Dollars Per Million BTU	164	166
Price Indexes	—	
Regions		
Dollars Per Million BTU	165	167
Price Indexes	—	

Some Key Findings

Considering use by function, national average costs borne by users, in dollars per million BTU, were:

Residential	$ 6.72
Commercial	6.51
Industrial	3.20
Street & highway lighting	10.81
Other public authorities	4.03
Railroads and railways	5.63
Interdepartmental	2.16
All Use	$ 5.19

In residential use, state prices ranged from a low of $3.08 per million BTU in Washington to highs of $9.77 per million BTU in Alaska, and $9.55 per million BTU in New York. In all use, Washington and Alaska again had the extreme values, with $2.10 and $9.39 per million BTU, respectively. The next highest state cost per unit was that of Massachusetts, at $7.79, followed by New York, at $7.58.

In developing weighted prices, functional quantities were the basic components employed, using these U.S. fractions of total:

Residential use	.32416
Commercial use	.22936
Industrial use	.40530
Street & highway lighting	.00773
All other use	.03345
	1.00000

The last category was the aggregate of other public authorities, railroads and railways, and interdepartmental use. Hawaii had zero use for that last category, so in obtaining its weighted price, the price for that last category was set at 1.214 that of California's, which was the corresponding ratio of prices for residential use in the two states.

A U.S. average price was again obtained by weighting the state weighted prices by their share of population, and this was used to develop state and regional indexes, shown in Table 167, and summarized here, as follows:

	Residential Use	All Uses
New England	120.4	127.3
Mid Atlantic	125.9	124.9
East North Central	102.8	103.8
West North Central	104.1	107.3
South Atlantic	89.2	92.3
East South Central	66.4	71.5
West South Central	88.7	82.1
Rocky Mountain	95.8	90.6
Far West	87.0	82.3
United States	100.0	100.0

For both residential and all uses, there are pronounced regional differences, with the Northeast index well above average, the North Central roughly five percent above, and that for the South and West below the national average.

For the all uses index, the highest values were those for Alaska (146.1), Massachusetts (134.1), New Hampshire (130.9) and New York (130.5), while the lowest were those for Tennessee (61.7), Idaho (60.5) Oregon (50.4) and Washington (41.4).

Table 146

Consumption Of Electricity In Billion BTU, 1972, By State

Use By Sector

REGION AND STATE	HOUSEHOLD USE	BUSINESS USE	FEDERAL GOVERNMENT USE	STATE & LOCAL GOVERNMENT USE	TOTAL USE
NEW ENGLAND:					
CONNECTICUT	24501.6	33448.4	235.3	3711.9	61897.1
MAINE	7223.2	10521.0	333.5	1275.1	19352.9
MASSACHUSETTS	35583.8	52245.9	834.9	6929.5	95594.0
NEW HAMPSHIRE	6421.4	8063.8	58.4	622.9	15166.3
RHODE ISLAND	5384.1	8481.3	294.5	1173.5	15333.5
VERMONT	4868.9	4432.5	186.7	792.1	10280.4
MID ATLANTIC:					
NEW JERSEY	46191.7	89163.5	561.3	8472.5	144389.0
NEW YORK	93782.2	178432.8	7691.0	39982.7	319888.7
PENNSYLVANIA	85143.0	188651.5	1293.2	10800.4	285888.1
EAST NORTH CENTRAL:					
ILLINOIS	77404.6	154915.0	5606.9	23337.2	261263.7
INDIANA	45499.0	89808.5	480.4	6581.1	142369.1
MICHIGAN	65012.3	129386.0	1357.0	12943.1	208698.4
OHIO	81656.0	227305.7	3654.8	17941.6	330558.0
WISCONSIN	36607.4	52066.0	556.2	6142.6	95372.2
WEST NORTH CENTRAL:					
IOWA	23911.3	30760.2	440.5	3925.8	59037.8
KANSAS	18281.5	29971.7	521.9	4203.1	52978.1
MINNESOTA	29831.1	43705.9	661.0	4428.2	78626.1
MISSOURI	37429.6	54370.2	1285.8	6309.2	99395.0
NEBRASKA	13088.4	15357.3	610.4	3470.4	32526.6
NORTH DAKOTA	5104.4	4019.1	247.1	1001.9	10372.5
SOUTH DAKOTA	5674.2	3619.8	291.2	1012.4	10597.7
SOUTH ATLANTIC:					
DELAWARE	4422.0	12267.5	64.6	903.0	17657.1
DISTRICT OF COLUMBIA	5032.7	9025.7	1125.1	1907.3	17090.7
FLORIDA	98194.0	79602.7	3956.2	19906.6	201659.4
GEORGIA	47532.6	67380.2	871.2	10013.0	125797.0
MARYLAND	26217.8	56925.8	669.5	5410.7	89223.8
NORTH CAROLINA	54544.2	87476.2	1527.4	10190.0	153737.9
SOUTH CAROLINA	26828.6	57260.6	1069.5	5399.4	90557.9
VIRGINIA	43219.8	50075.6	8770.5	11256.8	113322.8
WEST VIRGINIA	13245.4	37995.0	189.7	2114.4	53544.5
EAST SOUTH CENTRAL:					
ALABAMA	42141.6	86128.3	491.1	5037.2	133798.2
KENTUCKY	30868.4	95437.8	1848.8	5981.0	134136.0
MISSISSIPPI	21952.8	30137.5	513.7	4127.3	56731.3
TENNESSEE	70191.7	123609.8	277.2	4759.0	198837.7
WEST SOUTH CENTRAL:					
ARKANSAS	16896.2	30613.9	616.8	3493.3	51620.2
LOUISIANA	37095.3	72345.8	1263.1	8422.4	119126.6
OKLAHOMA	23959.1	32046.1	2536.5	6405.8	64947.4
TEXAS	119781.7	229696.2	6012.1	29465.5	384955.5
ROCKY MOUNTAIN:					
ARIZONA	18670.5	32745.0	1176.3	4804.7	57396.7
COLORADO	13856.1	22410.0	1529.4	4844.2	42639.8
IDAHO	9662.8	25755.0	361.6	2359.9	38139.3
MONTANA	5834.5	23977.2	241.8	1306.2	31359.7
NEVADA	8038.7	12030.5	299.3	2150.8	22519.2
NEW MEXICO	5268.1	11299.3	985.0	2441.8	19994.3
UTAH	6687.5	11278.4	1177.3	1830.4	20973.6
WYOMING	2299.7	8297.4	194.7	1184.4	11976.1
FAR WEST:					
ALASKA	1917.5	1710.1	244.9	491.5	4363.9
CALIFORNIA	136019.4	280121.3	11607.4	48498.9	476247.0
HAWAII	5083.9	9619.4	77.1	747.7	15528.0
OREGON	37235.2	54148.3	583.0	4825.1	96791.6
WASHINGTON	63678.2	115029.6	1875.5	8308.5	188891.7

Table 147

Consumption Of Electricity In Billion BTU, 1972, By State

Use By Function

REGION AND STATE	RESIDENTIAL USE	COMMERCIAL USE	INDUSTRIAL USE	STREET & HIGHWAY LIGHTING	OTHER PUBLIC AUTHORITIES	RAILROADS AND RAILWAYS	INTER-DEPARTMENTAL	TOTAL USE
NEW ENGLAND:								
CONNECTICUT	24501.6	17739.0	18864.9	713.1	54.6	0.0	23.9	61897.1
MAINE	7223.2	4094.4	7257.3	184.3	590.3	0.0	3.4	19352.9
MASSACHUSETTS	35583.8	29493.3	27927.2	996.3	938.3	75.1	580.0	95594.0
NEW HAMPSHIRE	6421.4	2535.1	5988.1	119.4	102.4	0.0	0.0	15166.3
RHODE ISLAND	5384.1	4619.8	4705.2	194.5	429.9	0.0	0.0	15333.5
VERMONT	4868.9	1944.8	2811.5	61.4	549.3	0.0	44.4	10280.4
MID ATLANTIC:								
NEW JERSEY	46191.7	41431.9	55250.5	1313.6	88.7	20.5	92.1	144389.0
NEW YORK	93782.2	92936.1	95529.2	3783.9	24477.7	9215.8	163.8	319888.7
PENNSYLVANIA	85143.0	52514.1	142198.5	1685.5	1098.7	2982.1	266.1	285888.1
EAST NORTH CENTRAL:								
ILLINOIS	77404.6	68834.3	99555.3	2439.6	13648.0	1334.1	47.8	261263.7
INDIANA	45499.0	25020.2	70116.6	1050.9	505.0	68.2	109.2	142369.1
MICHIGAN	65012.3	40626.7	97470.6	1798.1	3524.6	0.0	266.1	208698.4
OHIO	81656.0	56468.6	181648.1	2176.9	8270.7	146.7	191.1	330558.0
WISCONSIN	36607.4	19284.6	36525.5	1480.8	1255.6	0.0	218.4	95372.2
WEST NORTH CENTRAL:								
IOWA	23911.3	12989.5	20495.9	665.3	887.1	0.0	88.7	59037.8
KANSAS	18281.5	16596.0	16896.2	494.7	539.1	0.0	170.6	52978.1
MINNESOTA	29831.1	12798.4	33526.3	726.8	1559.3	0.0	184.3	78626.1
MISSOURI	37429.6	22672.7	36395.8	890.5	1825.4	47.8	133.1	99395.0
NEBRASKA	13088.4	11205.0	6462.3	354.8	1279.5	20.5	116.0	32526.6
NORTH DAKOTA	5104.4	3220.9	1446.7	143.3	440.2	0.0	17.1	10372.5
SOUTH DAKOTA	5674.2	2995.7	1272.7	126.2	494.7	0.0	34.1	10597.7
SOUTH ATLANTIC:								
DELAWARE	4422.0	3657.7	9423.9	102.4	27.3	0.0	23.9	17657.1
DISTRICT OF COLUMBIA	5032.7	11123.1	525.4	235.4	30.7	105.8	37.5	17090.7
FLORIDA	98194.0	51098.1	40967.9	1436.4	9768.6	0.0	194.5	201659.4
GEORGIA	47532.6	32704.0	44366.2	750.6	392.4	0.0	51.2	125797.0
MARYLAND	26217.8	21591.1	39927.2	706.3	47.8	539.1	194.5	89223.8
NORTH CAROLINA	54544.2	32560.7	62026.8	655.1	3374.5	0.0	576.6	153737.9
SOUTH CAROLINA	26828.6	15964.8	45516.1	273.0	1955.1	0.0	20.5	90557.9
VIRGINIA	43219.8	28688.1	28418.5	566.4	12266.1	0.0	163.8	113322.8
WEST VIRGINIA	13245.4	8277.5	31762.3	174.0	81.9	0.0	3.4	53544.5
EAST SOUTH CENTRAL:								
ALABAMA	42141.6	17947.1	72651.7	692.6	68.2	0.0	296.8	133798.2
KENTUCKY	30868.4	15466.6	83385.9	566.4	3746.4	0.0	102.4	134136.0
MISSISSIPPI	21952.8	11993.2	21461.5	464.0	846.2	0.0	13.6	56731.3
TENNESSEE	70191.7	12184.2	114438.5	1835.7	61.4	0.0	126.2	198837.7
WEST SOUTH CENTRAL:								
ARKANSAS	16896.2	10863.8	22447.6	283.2	1071.4	40.9	17.1	51620.2
LOUISIANA	37095.3	21676.4	52036.4	757.5	3466.6	3.4	4091.0	119126.6
OKLAHOMA	23959.1	17493.3	19172.0	453.8	3835.1	0.0	34.1	64947.4
TEXAS	119781.7	93939.2	158907.1	2248.5	9604.8	0.0	474.3	384955.5
ROCKY MOUNTAIN:								
ARIZONA	18670.5	17633.2	18025.6	331.0	1845.9	0.0	890.5	57396.7
COLORADO	13856.1	17114.6	8789.3	412.9	2289.5	0.0	177.4	42639.8
IDAHO	9662.8	9045.2	18639.8	122.8	655.1	0.0	13.6	38139.3
MONTANA	5834.9	4520.9	20089.9	180.8	385.6	276.4	71.6	31359.7
NEVADA	8038.7	7796.4	5889.1	167.2	409.4	0.0	218.4	22519.2
NEW MEXICO	5268.1	7758.9	5333.0	160.4	1364.8	0.0	109.2	19994.3
UTAH	6687.5	6046.1	6704.6	191.1	1323.9	0.0	20.5	20973.6
WYOMING	2299.7	4043.2	5387.5	61.4	160.4	0.0	23.9	11976.1
FAR WEST:								
ALASKA	1917.5	1658.2	416.3	51.2	307.1	3.4	10.2	4363.9
CALIFORNIA	136019.4	159538.3	150459.0	4858.7	21557.0	221.8	3592.8	476247.0
HAWAII	5083.9	2859.3	7359.7	225.2	0.0	0.0	0.0	15528.0
OREGON	37235.2	21782.2	36603.9	508.4	573.2	0.0	88.7	96791.6
WASHINGTON	63678.2	29616.2	88384.5	730.2	3278.9	47.8	3156.1	188891.7

Table 148

Expenditures On Electricity In Thousand Dollars, 1972, By State

Use By Sector

REGION AND STATE	HOUSEHOLD USE	BUSINESS USE	FEDERAL GOVERNMENT USE	STATE & LOCAL GOVERNMENT USE	TOTAL USE
NEW ENGLAND:					
CONNECTICUT	200493.0	206555.5	1752.2	33719.3	442520.0
MAINE	57742.0	52570.7	1784.6	11095.7	123193.0
MASSACHUSETTS	321822.0	351206.3	6178.5	65206.2	744413.0
NEW HAMPSHIRE	50243.0	41365.8	456.5	6454.7	98520.0
RHODE ISLAND	49191.0	54179.4	1733.3	10096.3	115200.0
VERMONT	34928.0	25410.5	1144.8	5840.6	67324.0
MID ATLANTIC:					
NEW JERSEY	414898.0	536985.3	4555.4	82734.3	1039173.0
NEW YORK	895238.0	1135328.1	53985.7	339313.2	2423865.0
PENNSYLVANIA	691009.0	919696.6	9651.4	92389.0	1712746.0
EAST NORTH CENTRAL:					
ILLINOIS	644784.0	791742.3	29660.4	148368.3	1614555.0
INDIANA	303987.0	387128.0	2868.2	47739.9	741203.0
MICHIGAN	461322.0	611695.3	7565.7	99157.0	1179740.0
OHIO	568960.0	833901.7	17925.0	117423.3	1538210.0
WISCONSIN	256539.0	276445.8	3310.7	44961.5	581257.0
WEST NORTH CENTRAL:					
IOWA	187588.0	161111.4	2935.0	30746.7	382381.0
KANSAS	126880.0	133315.1	2728.3	25145.6	288069.0
MINNESOTA	222627.0	225592.2	3659.6	33266.2	485145.0
MISSOURI	286116.0	278324.4	6731.2	43846.4	615018.0
NEBRASKA	86002.0	69491.5	2508.7	17016.7	175019.0
NORTH DAKOTA	38874.0	26067.6	960.3	6140.1	72042.0
SOUTH DAKOTA	42281.0	24145.8	1210.8	6504.4	74142.0
SOUTH ATLANTIC:					
DELAWARE	39343.0	62905.3	480.5	7410.2	110139.0
DISTRICT OF COLUMBIA	36902.0	58725.0	7453.4	14856.7	117937.0
FLORIDA	609606.0	409849.4	18785.8	120261.8	1158503.0
GEORGIA	266073.0	281189.6	4987.7	63255.7	615506.0
MARYLAND	202722.0	289340.6	4901.3	46214.1	543178.0
NORTH CAROLINA	325452.0	312598.1	5798.6	50367.4	694216.0
SOUTH CAROLINA	165716.0	178904.2	3729.4	27119.3	375469.0
VIRGINIA	266591.0	221642.4	27399.8	54085.8	569719.0
WEST VIRGINIA	89888.0	136581.0	1142.6	13942.3	241554.0
EAST SOUTH CENTRAL:					
ALABAMA	205947.0	256666.1	2689.9	30114.0	495417.0
KENTUCKY	159439.0	253722.3	7960.7	29859.0	450981.0
MISSISSIPPI	126438.0	121366.3	2467.3	24814.4	275086.0
TENNESSEE	259821.0	308887.9	1313.8	28625.3	598648.0
WEST SOUTH CENTRAL:					
ARKANSAS	113642.0	117909.6	3064.0	20831.4	255447.0
LOUISIANA	236994.0	224585.6	5264.7	45230.7	512075.0
OKLAHOMA	168668.0	131870.1	9667.7	33006.2	343212.0
TEXAS	728228.0	760513.3	23267.9	144972.8	1656982.0
ROCKY MOUNTAIN:					
ARIZONA	130208.0	150320.9	6012.2	29006.9	315548.0
COLORADO	105670.0	112956.4	6104.7	28165.9	252897.0
IDAHO	45328.0	64048.7	724.1	9272.1	119373.0
MONTANA	36880.0	47448.3	725.8	7276.9	92331.0
NEVADA	36746.0	44071.6	1123.6	10641.8	92583.0
NEW MEXICO	42085.0	54648.4	4158.7	14049.9	114942.0
UTAH	43944.0	52114.3	4006.3	10209.4	110274.0
WYOMING	16738.0	32137.1	901.5	6449.4	56226.0
FAR WEST:					
ALASKA	18725.0	15663.3	1874.1	4696.5	40959.0
CALIFORNIA	932442.0	1197703.4	33884.6	250253.0	2414283.0
HAWAII	42317.0	58274.7	791.6	7113.7	108497.0
OREGON	139451.0	116604.7	1866.0	20232.2	278154.0
WASHINGTON	196305.0	166348.9	5016.4	29008.8	396679.0

Table 149

Expenditures On Electricity In Thousand Dollars, 1972, By State

Use By Function

REGION AND STATE	RESIDENTIAL	COMMERCIAL USE	INDUSTRIAL USE	STREET AND HIGHWAY LIGHTING	OTHER PUBLIC AUTHORITIES	RAILROADS AND RAILWAYS	INTER-DEPARTMENTAL	TOTAL USE
NEW ENGLAND:								
CONNECTICUT	200493.0	134173.0	96323.0	11117.0	306.0	0.0	108.0	442520.0
MAINE	57742.0	32275.0	26863.0	3649.0	2656.0	0.0	8.0	123193.0
MASSACHUSETTS	321822.0	240423.0	153982.0	18106.0	5756.0	650.0	3674.0	744413.0
NEW HAMPSHIRE	50243.0	21146.0	24052.0	2324.0	755.0	0.0	0.0	98520.0
RHODE ISLAND	49191.0	34662.0	25842.0	3280.0	2220.0	0.0	5.0	115200.0
VERMONT	34928.0	14243.0	13738.0	1062.0	3228.0	0.0	125.0	67324.0
MID ATLANTIC:								
NEW JERSEY	414898.0	338321.0	260192.0	24333.0	640.0	116.0	673.0	1039173.0
NEW YORK	895238.0	886547.0	375370.0	50417.0	157704.0	58058.0	531.0	2423865.0
PENNSYLVANIA	691009.0	377894.0	593158.0	26250.0	8800.0	14521.0	1114.0	1712746.0
EAST NORTH CENTRAL:								
ILLINOIS	644784.0	500164.0	381307.0	16748.0	65067.0	6241.0	244.0	1614555.0
INDIANA	303987.0	165173.0	257475.0	11779.0	2483.0	384.0	442.0	741723.0
MICHIGAN	461322.0	290220.0	384309.0	25292.0	17300.0	0.0	1297.0	1179740.0
OHIO	568960.0	366439.0	538326.0	25879.0	37122.0	677.0	807.0	1538210.0
WISCONSIN	256539.0	146154.0	159334.0	12909.0	5333.0	0.0	988.0	581257.0
WEST NORTH CENTRAL:								
IOWA	187588.0	101258.0	81351.0	6728.0	5018.0	4.0	434.0	382381.0
KANSAS	126880.0	97356.0	56979.0	4062.0	2159.0	0.0	633.0	288069.0
MINNESOTA	222627.0	102798.0	144584.0	7561.0	6850.0	0.0	725.0	485145.0
MISSOURI	286116.0	161956.0	150375.0	8036.0	7689.0	157.0	689.0	615018.0
NEBRASKA	86002.0	58952.0	22949.0	2154.0	4500.0	76.0	386.0	175019.0
NORTH DAKOTA	38874.0	21954.0	8586.0	1237.0	1327.0	0.0	64.0	72042.0
SOUTH DAKOTA	42281.0	23111.0	6144.0	1306.0	1142.0	0.0	158.0	74142.0
SOUTH ATLANTIC:								
DELAWARE	39343.0	27388.0	41641.0	1425.0	191.0	0.0	151.0	110139.0
DISTRICT OF COLUMBIA	36902.0	73577.0	2868.0	3796.0	216.0	484.0	94.0	117937.0
FLORIDA	609606.0	338288.0	154250.0	14168.0	41080.0	0.0	1111.0	1158503.0
GEORGIA	266073.0	199586.0	140794.0	7085.0	1710.0	0.0	258.0	615506.0
MARYLAND	202722.0	160001.0	165817.0	11388.0	258.0	2504.0	488.0	543178.0
NORTH CAROLINA	325452.0	166893.0	182968.0	5867.0	10894.0	0.0	2142.0	694216.0
SOUTH CAROLINA	165716.0	84220.0	116941.0	2736.0	5741.0	0.0	115.0	375469.0
VIRGINIA	266591.0	165904.0	96824.0	5489.0	34389.0	0.0	522.0	569719.0
WEST VIRGINIA	89888.0	51342.0	97933.0	1993.0	388.0	0.0	10.0	241554.0
EAST SOUTH CENTRAL:								
ALABAMA	205947.0	98980.0	183268.0	6172.0	339.0	0.0	711.0	495417.0
KENTUCKY	159439.0	74601.0	195720.0	5065.0	15791.0	0.0	365.0	450981.0
MISSISSIPPI	126438.0	72996.0	68561.0	3734.0	3275.0	0.0	82.0	275086.0
TENNESSEE	259821.0	58990.0	264808.0	14520.0	221.0	0.0	288.0	598648.0
WEST SOUTH CENTRAL:								
ARKANSAS	113642.0	68488.0	66580.0	2255.0	4269.0	151.0	62.0	255447.0
LOUISIANA	236994.0	128316.0	127709.0	5704.0	12462.0	14.0	876.0	512075.0
OKLAHOMA	168668.0	102081.0	56779.0	2562.0	12957.0	0.0	165.0	343212.0
TEXAS	728228.0	487002.0	390761.0	14106.0	31661.0	0.0	5224.0	1656982.0
ROCKY MOUNTAIN:								
ARIZONA	130208.0	106969.0	63751.0	3312.0	8630.0	0.0	2678.0	315548.0
COLORADO	105670.0	103965.0	30919.0	4403.0	7566.0	0.0	374.0	252897.0
IDAHO	45328.0	38441.0	33832.0	1162.0	574.0	0.0	36.0	119373.0
MONTANA	36880.0	26297.0	26179.0	1656.0	637.0	432.0	250.0	92331.0
NEVADA	36746.0	40015.0	13463.0	1159.0	991.0	7.0	202.0	92583.0
NEW MEXICO	42085.0	47886.0	18028.0	1535.0	4937.0	0.0	471.0	114942.0
UTAH	43944.0	34621.0	25943.0	2105.0	3563.0	0.0	98.0	110274.0
WYOMING	16738.0	21745.0	16544.0	658.0	469.0	0.0	72.0	56226.0
FAR WEST:								
ALASKA	18725.0	17237.0	2247.0	602.0	2039.0	41.0	68.0	40959.0
CALIFORNIA	932442.0	912759.0	469880.0	50142.0	41243.0	675.0	7142.0	2414283.0
HAWAII	42317.0	29367.0	35066.0	1747.0	0.0	0.0	0.0	108497.0
OREGON	139451.0	83660.0	49371.0	4328.0	1153.0	0.0	191.0	278154.0
WASHINGTON	196305.0	104218.0	83207.0	4728.0	7568.0	108.0	545.0	396679.0

Table 150

Consumption In Billion BTU And Expenditures In Thousand Dollars, Electricity, 1972, By Region
Use By Sector

REGION	HOUSEHOLD USE	BUSINESS USE	FEDERAL GOVERNMENT USE	STATE & LOCAL GOVERNMENT USE	TOTAL USE
Consumption In Billion BTU					
NEW ENGLAND	83983.00	117192.90	1943.30	14505.00	217624.20
MID ATLANTIC	225116.90	456247.80	9545.50	59255.60	750165.80
EAST NORTH CENTRAL	306179.30	653481.20	11655.30	66945.60	1038261.41
WEST NORTH CENTRAL	133320.50	181804.20	4057.90	24351.00	343533.80
SOUTH ATLANTIC	319237.10	458009.31	18243.70	67101.20	862591.10
EAST SOUTH CENTRAL	165154.50	335313.40	3130.80	19904.50	523503.20
WEST SOUTH CENTRAL	197732.30	364702.00	10428.50	47787.00	620649.70
ROCKY MOUNTAIN	70317.90	147792.80	5965.40	20922.40	244998.70
FAR WEST	243934.20	460628.70	14387.90	62871.70	781822.20
TOTAL	1744975.73	3175172.36	79358.30	383644.00	5383150.13
Expenditures In Thousand Dollars					
NEW ENGLAND	714419.00	731288.19	13049.90	132412.80	1591170.00
MID ATLANTIC	2001145.00	2592010.01	68192.50	514436.50	5175784.01
EAST NORTH CENTRAL	2235592.01	2900913.10	61330.00	457650.00	5655485.02
WEST NORTH CENTRAL	990368.00	918048.00	20733.90	162666.10	2091815.99
SOUTH ATLANTIC	2002293.00	1951735.60	74679.10	397513.30	4426220.99
EAST SOUTH CENTRAL	751645.00	940642.60	14431.70	113412.70	1820132.01
WEST SOUTH CENTRAL	1247532.00	1234878.59	41264.30	244041.10	2767716.01
ROCKY MOUNTAIN	457599.00	557745.70	23756.90	115072.30	1154174.00
FAR WEST	1329240.00	1554595.01	43432.70	311304.20	3238571.99
TOTAL	11729833.00	13381856.70	360871.01	2448509.04	27921070.20

Table 151

Consumption In Billion BTU And Expenditures In Thousand Dollars, Electricity, 1972, By Region

Use By Function

REGION	RESIDENTIAL USE	COMMERCIAL USE	INDUSTRIAL USE	STREET & HIGHWAY LIGHTING	OTHER PUBLIC AUTHORITIES	RAILROADS AND RAILWAYS	INTER-DEPARTMENTAL	TOTAL USE
Consumption In Billion BTU								
NEW ENGLAND	83983.00	60426.40	67554.20	2269.00	2664.80	75.10	651.70	217624.20
MID ATLANTIC	225116.90	186882.10	292978.20	6783.00	25665.10	12218.40	522.00	750165.80
EAST NORTH CENTRAL	306179.30	208234.40	485316.10	8946.30	27203.90	1549.60	832.60	1038261.41
WEST NORTH CENTRAL	133320.50	82478.20	116495.90	3401.60	7025.30	68.30	743.90	343533.80
SOUTH ATLANTIC	319237.10	205665.10	302934.30	4899.60	27944.40	644.90	126.90	862591.10
EAST SOUTH CENTRAL	165154.50	57591.10	291937.60	3558.70	4722.20	0.00	539.00	523503.20
WEST SOUTH CENTRAL	197732.30	143972.70	252563.10	3743.00	17977.90	44.30	4616.50	620649.70
ROCKY MOUNTAIN	70317.90	73958.40	88858.80	1627.60	8434.60	276.40	1525.10	244998.70
FAR WEST	243934.20	215454.20	283223.40	6373.70	25716.20	273.00	6847.80	781822.20
TOTAL	1744975.73	1234662.74	2181861.59	41602.50	147354.40	15149.40	17544.50	5383150.13
Expenditures In Thousand Dollars								
NEW ENGLAND	714419.00	476922.00	340800.00	39538.00	14921.00	650.00	3920.00	1591170.00
MID ATLANTIC	2001145.00	1602762.01	1228720.00	101000.00	167144.00	72695.00	2318.00	5175784.01
EAST NORTH CENTRAL	2235592.01	1468150.00	1720751.00	92607.00	127305.00	7302.00	3778.00	5655485.02
WEST NORTH CENTRAL	990368.00	567385.00	470968.00	31084.00	28685.00	237.00	3089.00	2091815.99
SOUTH ATLANTIC	2002293.00	1267198.99	1000036.00	53947.00	94867.00	2988.00	4891.00	4426220.99
EAST SOUTH CENTRAL	751645.00	305567.00	712357.00	29491.00	19626.00	0.00	1446.00	1820132.01
WEST SOUTH CENTRAL	1247532.00	785887.00	641829.00	24662.00	61349.00	165.00	6327.00	2767716.01
ROCKY MOUNTAIN	457599.00	419933.00	228655.00	15990.00	27367.00	439.00	4181.00	1154174.00
FAR WEST	1329240.00	1147241.00	639771.00	61547.00	52003.00	824.00	7946.00	3238571.99
TOTAL	11729833.00	8041052.00	6983890.98	449831.00	593267.00	85300.00	37896.00	27921070.20

Table 152

Consumption Of Electricity, 1972, In Million BTU Per Capita

Use By Sector

REGION AND STATE	HOUSEHOLD USE	BUSINESS USE	FEDERAL GOVERNMENT USE	STATE & LOCAL GOVERNMENT USE	TOTAL USE
NEW ENGLAND:					
CONNECTICUT	7.955	10.860	0.076	1.205	20.096
MAINE	7.040	10.254	0.325	1.243	18.862
MASSACHUSETTS	6.139	9.014	0.144	1.196	16.493
NEW HAMPSHIRE	8.296	10.418	0.075	0.805	19.595
RHODE ISLAND	5.556	8.753	0.304	1.211	15.824
VERMONT	10.585	9.636	0.406	1.722	22.349
MID ATLANTIC:					
NEW JERSEY	6.285	12.133	0.076	1.153	19.647
NEW YORK	5.106	9.715	0.419	2.177	17.416
PENNSYLVANIA	7.152	15.846	0.109	0.907	24.014
EAST NORTH CENTRAL:					
ILLINOIS	6.884	13.778	0.499	2.076	23.236
INDIANA	8.607	16.990	0.091	1.245	26.933
MICHIGAN	7.213	14.355	0.151	1.436	23.155
OHIO	7.616	21.200	0.341	1.673	30.830
WISCONSIN	8.088	11.504	0.123	1.357	21.072
WEST NORTH CENTRAL:					
IOWA	8.291	10.666	0.153	1.361	20.471
KANSAS	8.061	13.215	0.230	1.853	23.359
MINNESOTA	7.694	11.273	0.170	1.142	20.280
MISSOURI	7.885	11.454	0.271	1.329	20.938
NEBRASKA	8.566	10.051	0.399	2.271	21.287
NORTH DAKOTA	8.051	6.339	0.390	1.580	16.360
SOUTH DAKOTA	8.344	5.323	0.428	1.489	15.585
SOUTH ATLANTIC:					
DELAWARE	7.744	21.484	0.113	1.581	30.923
DISTRICT OF COLUMBIA	6.692	12.002	1.496	2.536	22.727
FLORIDA	13.365	10.835	0.538	2.709	27.448
GEORGIA	10.043	14.236	0.184	2.116	26.579
MARYLAND	6.477	14.063	0.165	1.337	22.041
NORTH CAROLINA	10.447	16.755	0.293	1.952	29.446
SOUTH CAROLINA	9.981	21.302	0.398	2.009	33.690
VIRGINIA	9.070	10.509	1.841	2.362	23.782
WEST VIRGINIA	7.379	21.167	0.106	1.178	29.830
EAST SOUTH CENTRAL:					
ALABAMA	11.969	24.461	0.139	1.431	38.000
KENTUCKY	9.337	28.868	0.559	1.809	40.574
MISSISSIPPI	9.731	13.359	0.228	1.829	25.147
TENNESSEE	17.238	30.356	0.068	1.169	48.830
WEST SOUTH CENTRAL:					
ARKANSAS	8.414	15.246	0.307	1.740	25.707
LOUISIANA	9.924	19.354	0.338	2.253	31.869
OKLAHOMA	9.100	12.171	0.963	2.433	24.667
TEXAS	10.322	19.795	0.518	2.539	33.174
ROCKY MOUNTAIN:					
ARIZONA	9.511	16.681	0.599	2.448	29.239
COLORADO	5.861	9.480	0.647	2.049	18.037
IDAHO	12.798	34.113	0.479	3.126	50.516
MONTANA	8.149	33.488	0.338	1.824	43.798
NEVADA	15.082	22.571	0.562	4.035	42.250
NEW MEXICO	4.896	10.501	0.915	2.269	18.582
UTAH	5.934	10.007	1.045	1.624	18.610
WYOMING	6.647	23.981	0.563	3.423	34.613
FAR WEST:					
ALASKA	5.900	5.262	0.754	1.512	13.427
CALIFORNIA	6.664	13.724	0.569	2.376	23.333
HAWAII	6.230	11.788	0.094	0.916	19.029
OREGON	17.041	24.782	0.267	2.208	44.298
WASHINGTON	18.630	33.654	0.549	2.431	55.264

Table 153

Consumption Of Electricity, 1972, In Million BTU Per Capita, By State

Use By Function

REGION AND STATE	RESIDENTIAL USE	COMMERCIAL USE	INDUSTRIAL USE	STREET & HIGHWAY LIGHTING	OTHER PUBLIC AUTHORITIES	RAILROADS AND RAILWAYS	INTER-DEPARTMENTAL	TOTAL USE
NEW ENGLAND:								
CONNECTICUT	7.955	5.759	6.125	0.232	0.018	0.000	0.008	20.096
MAINE	7.040	3.991	7.073	0.180	0.575	0.000	0.003	18.862
MASSACHUSETTS	6.139	5.089	4.818	0.172	0.162	0.013	0.100	16.493
NEW HAMPSHIRE	8.296	3.275	7.737	0.154	0.132	0.000	0.000	19.595
RHODE ISLAND	5.556	4.768	4.856	0.201	0.444	0.000	0.000	15.824
VERMONT	10.585	4.228	6.112	0.134	1.194	0.000	0.096	22.349
MID ATLANTIC:								
NEW JERSEY	6.285	5.638	7.518	0.179	0.012	0.003	0.013	19.647
NEW YORK	5.106	5.060	5.201	0.206	1.333	0.502	0.009	17.416
PENNSYLVANIA	7.152	4.411	11.944	0.142	0.092	0.250	0.022	24.014
EAST NORTH CENTRAL:								
ILLINOIS	6.884	5.944	8.854	0.217	1.214	0.119	0.004	23.236
INDIANA	8.607	4.733	13.265	0.199	0.096	0.013	0.021	26.933
MICHIGAN	7.213	4.508	10.814	0.200	0.391	0.000	0.030	23.155
OHIO	7.616	5.267	16.942	0.203	0.771	0.014	0.018	30.830
WISCONSIN	8.088	4.261	8.070	0.327	0.277	0.000	0.048	21.072
WEST NORTH CENTRAL:								
IOWA	8.291	4.504	7.107	0.231	0.308	0.000	0.031	20.471
KANSAS	8.061	7.317	7.450	0.218	0.238	0.000	0.075	23.359
MINNESOTA	7.694	3.301	8.647	0.187	0.402	0.000	0.048	20.280
MISSOURI	7.885	4.776	7.667	0.188	0.385	0.010	0.028	20.938
NEBRASKA	8.566	7.333	4.229	0.232	0.837	0.013	0.076	21.287
NORTH DAKOTA	8.051	5.080	2.282	0.226	0.694	0.000	0.027	16.360
SOUTH DAKOTA	8.344	4.405	1.872	0.186	0.728	0.000	0.050	15.585
SOUTH ATLANTIC:								
DELAWARE	7.744	6.406	16.504	0.179	0.048	0.000	0.042	30.923
DISTRICT OF COLUMBIA	6.692	14.791	0.699	0.313	0.041	0.141	0.050	22.727
FLORIDA	13.365	6.955	5.576	0.196	1.330	0.000	0.026	27.448
GEORGIA	10.043	6.910	9.374	0.159	0.083	0.000	0.011	26.579
MARYLAND	6.477	5.334	9.863	0.174	0.012	0.133	0.048	22.041
NORTH CAROLINA	10.447	6.236	11.880	0.125	0.646	0.000	0.110	29.446
SOUTH CAROLINA	9.981	5.939	16.933	0.102	0.727	0.000	0.008	33.690
VIRGINIA	9.070	6.021	5.964	0.119	2.574	0.000	0.034	23.782
WEST VIRGINIA	7.379	4.611	17.695	0.097	0.046	0.000	0.002	29.830
EAST SOUTH CENTRAL:								
ALABAMA	11.969	5.097	20.634	0.197	0.019	0.000	0.084	38.000
KENTUCKY	9.337	4.678	25.223	0.171	1.133	0.000	0.031	40.574
MISSISSIPPI	9.731	5.316	9.513	0.206	0.375	0.000	0.006	25.147
TENNESSEE	17.238	2.992	28.104	0.451	0.015	0.000	0.031	48.830
WEST SOUTH CENTRAL:								
ARKANSAS	8.414	5.410	11.179	0.141	0.534	0.020	0.008	25.707
LOUISIANA	9.924	5.799	13.921	0.203	0.927	0.001	1.094	31.869
OKLAHOMA	9.100	6.644	7.281	0.172	1.457	0.000	0.013	24.667
TEXAS	10.322	8.095	13.694	0.194	0.828	0.000	0.041	33.174
ROCKY MOUNTAIN:								
ARIZONA	9.511	8.983	9.183	0.169	0.940	0.000	0.454	29.239
COLORADO	5.861	7.240	3.718	0.175	0.968	0.000	0.075	18.037
IDAHO	12.798	11.980	24.688	0.163	0.868	0.000	0.018	50.516
MONTANA	8.149	6.314	28.058	0.253	0.538	0.386	0.100	43.798
NEVADA	15.082	14.627	11.049	0.314	0.768	0.000	0.410	42.250
NEW MEXICO	4.896	7.211	4.956	0.149	1.268	0.000	0.101	18.582
UTAH	5.934	5.365	5.949	0.170	1.175	0.000	0.018	18.610
WYOMING	6.647	11.686	15.571	0.178	0.463	0.000	0.069	34.613
FAR WEST:								
ALASKA	5.900	5.102	1.281	0.157	0.945	0.010	0.032	13.427
CALIFORNIA	6.664	7.816	7.371	0.238	1.056	0.011	0.176	23.333
HAWAII	6.230	3.504	9.019	0.276	0.000	0.000	0.000	19.029
OREGON	17.041	9.969	16.752	0.233	0.262	0.000	0.041	44.298
WASHINGTON	18.630	8.665	25.859	0.214	0.959	0.014	0.923	55.264

Table   154

Expenditures On Electricity, 1972, In Dollars Per Capita, By State

Use By Sector

REGION AND STATE	HOUSEHOLD USE	BUSINESS USE	FEDERAL GOVERNMENT USE	STATE & LOCAL GOVERNMENT USE	TOTAL USE
NEW ENGLAND:					
CONNECTICUT	65.095	67.063	0.569	10.948	143.675
MAINE	56.279	51.238	1.739	10.815	120.071
MASSACHUSETTS	55.525	60.595	1.066	11.250	128.436
NEW HAMPSHIRE	64.913	53.444	0.590	8.339	127.287
RHODE ISLAND	50.765	55.913	1.789	10.419	118.885
VERMONT	75.930	55.240	2.489	12.697	146.357
MID ATLANTIC:					
NEW JERSEY	56.456	73.069	0.620	11.258	141.403
NEW YORK	48.742	61.813	2.939	18.474	131.968
PENNSYLVANIA	58.044	77.253	0.811	7.761	143.868
EAST NORTH CENTRAL:					
ILLINOIS	57.345	70.415	2.638	13.195	143.593
INDIANA	57.508	73.236	0.543	9.031	140.318
MICHIGAN	51.184	67.868	0.839	11.002	130.893
OHIO	53.065	77.775	1.672	10.952	143.463
WISCONSIN	56.681	61.079	0.731	9.934	128.426
WEST NORTH CENTRAL:					
IOWA	65.044	55.864	1.018	10.661	132.587
KANSAS	55.944	58.781	1.203	11.087	127.015
MINNESOTA	57.422	58.187	0.944	8.580	125.134
MISSOURI	60.273	58.632	1.418	9.237	129.559
NEBRASKA	56.284	45.479	1.642	11.137	114.541
NORTH DAKOTA	61.315	41.116	1.515	9.685	113.631
SOUTH DAKOTA	62.178	35.509	1.781	9.565	109.032
SOUTH ATLANTIC:					
DELAWARE	68.902	110.167	0.842	12.978	192.888
DISTRICT OF COLUMBIA	49.072	78.092	9.911	19.756	156.831
FLORIDA	82.973	55.785	2.557	16.369	157.684
GEORGIA	56.217	59.410	1.054	13.365	130.046
MARYLAND	50.080	71.477	1.211	11.417	134.184
NORTH CAROLINA	62.335	59.873	1.111	9.647	132.966
SOUTH CAROLINA	61.650	66.557	1.387	10.089	139.683
VIRGINIA	55.948	46.515	5.750	11.351	119.563
WEST VIRGINIA	50.077	76.090	0.637	7.767	134.570
EAST SOUTH CENTRAL:					
ALABAMA	58.491	72.896	0.764	8.553	140.703
KENTUCKY	48.227	76.746	2.408	9.032	136.413
MISSISSIPPI	56.045	53.797	1.094	10.999	121.935
TENNESSEE	63.807	75.857	0.323	7.030	147.016
WEST SOUTH CENTRAL:					
ARKANSAS	56.595	58.720	1.526	10.374	127.215
LOUISIANA	63.401	60.082	1.408	12.100	136.992
OKLAHOMA	64.059	50.084	3.672	12.536	130.350
TEXAS	62.757	65.539	2.005	12.493	142.794
ROCKY MOUNTAIN:					
ARIZONA	66.331	76.577	3.063	14.777	160.748
COLORADO	44.700	47.782	2.582	11.915	106.978
IDAHO	60.037	84.833	0.959	12.281	158.110
MONTANA	51.508	66.269	1.014	10.163	128.954
NEVADA	68.942	82.686	2.108	19.966	173.702
NEW MEXICO	39.112	50.788	3.865	13.058	106.823
UTAH	38.992	46.242	3.555	9.059	97.847
WYOMING	48.376	92.882	2.605	18.640	162.503
FAR WEST:					
ALASKA	57.615	48.195	5.766	14.451	126.028
CALIFORNIA	45.683	58.679	1.660	12.261	118.283
HAWAII	51.859	71.415	0.970	8.718	132.962
OREGON	63.822	53.366	0.854	9.260	127.302
WASHINGTON	57.433	48.668	1.468	8.487	116.056

Table 155

Expenditures On Electricity, 1972, In Dollars Per Capita, By State

Use By Function

REGION AND STATE	RESIDENTIAL USE	COMMERCIAL USE	INDUSTRIAL USE	STREET & HIGHWAY LIGHTING	OTHER PUBLIC AUTHORITIES	RAILROADS AND RAILWAYS	INTER-DEPARTMENTAL	TOTAL USE
NEW ENGLAND:								
CONNECTICUT	65.095	43.563	31.274	3.609	0.099	0.000	0.035	143.675
MAINE	56.279	31.457	26.182	3.557	2.589	0.000	0.008	120.071
MASSACHUSETTS	55.525	41.481	26.567	3.124	0.993	0.112	0.634	128.436
NEW HAMPSHIRE	64.913	27.320	31.075	3.003	0.975	0.000	0.000	127.287
RHODE ISLAND	50.765	35.771	26.669	3.385	2.291	0.000	0.005	118.885
VERMONT	75.930	30.963	29.865	2.309	7.017	0.000	0.272	146.357
MID ATLANTIC:								
NEW JERSEY	56.456	46.036	35.405	3.311	0.087	0.016	0.092	141.403
NEW YORK	48.742	48.268	20.437	2.745	8.586	3.161	0.029	131.968
PENNSYLVANIA	58.044	31.742	49.824	2.205	0.739	1.220	0.094	143.868
EAST NORTH CENTRAL:								
ILLINOIS	57.345	44.483	33.912	1.490	5.787	0.555	0.022	143.593
INDIANA	57.508	31.247	48.709	2.228	0.470	0.073	0.084	140.318
MICHIGAN	51.184	32.200	42.639	2.806	1.919	0.000	0.144	130.893
OHIO	53.065	34.176	50.208	2.414	3.462	0.063	0.075	143.463
WISCONSIN	56.681	32.292	35.204	2.852	1.178	0.000	0.218	128.426
WEST NORTH CENTRAL:								
IOWA	65.044	35.110	28.208	2.333	1.740	0.001	0.150	132.587
KANSAS	55.944	42.926	25.123	1.791	0.952	0.000	0.279	127.015
MINNESOTA	57.422	26.515	37.293	1.950	1.767	0.000	0.187	125.134
MISSOURI	60.273	34.118	31.678	1.693	1.620	0.033	0.145	129.559
NEBRASKA	56.284	38.581	15.019	1.410	2.945	0.050	0.253	114.541
NORTH DAKOTA	61.315	34.628	13.543	1.951	2.093	0.000	0.101	113.631
SOUTH DAKOTA	62.178	33.987	9.035	1.921	1.679	0.000	0.232	109.032
SOUTH ATLANTIC:								
DELAWARE	68.902	47.965	72.926	2.496	0.335	0.000	0.264	192.888
DISTRICT OF COLUMBIA	49.072	97.842	3.814	5.048	0.287	0.644	0.125	156.831
FLORIDA	82.973	46.044	20.995	1.928	5.591	0.000	0.151	157.684
GEORGIA	56.217	42.169	29.747	1.497	0.361	0.000	0.055	130.046
MARYLAND	50.080	39.526	40.963	2.813	0.064	0.619	0.121	134.184
NORTH CAROLINA	62.335	31.966	35.045	1.124	2.087	0.000	0.410	132.966
SOUTH CAROLINA	61.650	31.332	43.505	1.018	2.136	0.000	0.043	139.683
VIRGINIA	55.948	34.817	20.320	1.152	7.217	0.000	0.110	119.563
WEST VIRGINIA	50.077	28.603	54.559	1.110	0.216	0.000	0.006	134.570
EAST SOUTH CENTRAL:								
ALABAMA	58.491	28.111	52.050	1.753	0.096	0.000	0.202	140.703
KENTUCKY	48.227	22.565	59.201	1.532	4.776	0.000	0.110	136.413
MISSISSIPPI	56.045	32.356	30.391	1.655	1.452	0.000	0.036	121.935
TENNESSEE	63.807	14.487	65.031	3.566	0.054	0.000	0.071	147.016
WEST SOUTH CENTRAL:								
ARKANSAS	56.595	34.108	33.157	1.123	2.126	0.075	0.031	127.215
LOUISIANA	63.401	34.327	34.165	1.526	3.334	0.004	0.234	136.992
OKLAHOMA	64.059	38.770	21.564	0.973	4.921	0.000	0.063	130.350
TEXAS	62.757	41.968	33.675	1.216	2.728	0.000	0.450	142.794
ROCKY MOUNTAIN:								
ARIZONA	66.331	54.493	32.476	1.687	4.396	0.000	1.364	160.748
COLORADO	44.700	43.978	13.079	1.863	3.201	0.000	0.158	106.978
IDAHO	60.037	50.915	44.811	1.539	0.760	0.000	0.048	158.110
MONTANA	51.508	36.728	36.563	2.313	0.890	0.603	0.349	128.954
NEVADA	68.942	75.075	25.259	2.174	1.859	0.013	0.379	173.702
NEW MEXICO	39.112	44.504	16.755	1.427	4.588	0.000	0.438	106.823
UTAH	38.992	30.720	23.020	1.868	3.161	0.000	0.087	97.847
WYOMING	48.376	62.847	47.815	1.902	1.355	0.000	0.208	162.503
FAR WEST:								
ALASKA	57.615	53.037	6.914	1.852	6.274	0.126	0.209	126.028
CALIFORNIA	45.683	44.719	23.021	2.457	2.021	0.033	0.350	118.283
HAWAII	51.859	35.989	42.973	2.141	0.000	0.000	0.000	132.962
OREGON	63.822	38.288	22.595	1.981	0.528	0.000	0.087	127.302
WASHINGTON	57.433	30.491	24.344	1.383	2.214	0.032	0.159	116.056

Table 156

Per Capita Use Of Electricity In Million BTU Per Capita And In Dollars Per Capita, 1972, By Region

Use By Sector

REGION	HOUSEHOLD USE	BUSINESS USE	FEDERAL GOVERNMENT USE	STATE & LOCAL GOVERNMENT USE	TOTAL USE
Consumption In Million BTU Per Capita					
NEW ENGLAND	6.938	9.681	0.161	1.198	17.978
MID ATLANTIC	5.984	12.127	0.254	1.575	19.940
EAST NORTH CENTRAL	7.506	16.020	0.286	1.641	25.453
WEST NORTH CENTRAL	8.023	10.940	0.244	1.465	20.672
SOUTH ATLANTIC	10.001	14.349	0.572	2.102	27.024
EAST SOUTH CENTRAL	12.555	25.489	0.238	1.513	39.795
WEST SOUTH CENTRAL	9.895	18.251	0.522	2.391	31.059
ROCKY MOUNTAIN	7.919	16.643	0.672	2.356	27.590
FAR WEST	8.983	16.963	0.530	2.315	28.791
TOTAL	8.380	15.249	0.381	1.842	25.852
Expenditures In Dollars Per Capita					
NEW ENGLAND	59.019	60.412	1.078	10.939	131.447
MID ATLANTIC	53.192	68.898	1.813	13.674	137.577
EAST NORTH CENTRAL	54.806	71.116	1.504	11.219	138.645
WEST NORTH CENTRAL	59.596	55.244	1.248	9.789	125.877
SOUTH ATLANTIC	62.728	61.145	2.340	12.453	138.666
EAST SOUTH CENTRAL	57.138	71.505	1.097	8.621	138.360
WEST SOUTH CENTRAL	62.430	61.796	2.065	12.212	138.504
ROCKY MOUNTAIN	51.531	62.809	2.675	12.959	129.975
FAR WEST	48.950	57.249	1.599	11.464	119.262
TOTAL	56.332	64.265	1.733	11.759	134.089

Table 157

Per Capita Use Of Electricity In Million BTU Per Capita And In Dollars Per Capita, 1972, By Region

Use By Function

REGION	RESIDENTIAL USE	COMMERCIAL USE	INDUSTRIAL USE	STREET & HIGHWAY LIGHTING	OTHER PUBLIC AUTHORITIES	RAILROADS AND RAILWAYS	INTER-DEPARTMENTAL	TOTAL USE
Consumption In Million BTU Per Capita								
NEW ENGLAND	6.938	4.992	5.581	0.187	0.220	0.006	0.054	17.978
MID ATLANTIC	5.984	4.967	7.788	0.180	0.682	0.325	0.014	19.940
EAST NORTH CENTRAL	7.506	5.105	11.898	0.219	0.667	0.038	0.020	25.453
WEST NORTH CENTRAL	8.023	4.963	7.010	0.205	0.423	0.004	0.045	20.672
SOUTH ATLANTIC	10.001	6.443	9.490	0.153	0.875	0.004	0.040	27.024
EAST SOUTH CENTRAL	12.555	4.378	22.192	0.271	0.359	0.000	0.041	39.795
WEST SOUTH CENTRAL	9.895	7.205	12.639	0.187	0.900	0.002	0.231	31.059
ROCKY MOUNTAIN	7.919	8.329	10.007	0.183	0.950	0.031	0.172	27.590
FAR WEST	8.983	7.934	10.430	0.235	0.947	0.010	0.252	28.791
TOTAL	8.380	5.929	10.478	0.200	0.708	0.073	0.084	25.852
Expenditures In Dollars Per Capita								
NEW ENGLAND	59.019	39.399	28.154	3.266	1.233	0.054	0.324	131.447
MID ATLANTIC	53.192	42.603	32.660	2.685	4.443	1.932	0.062	137.577
EAST NORTH CENTRAL	54.806	35.992	42.185	2.270	3.121	0.179	0.093	138.645
WEST NORTH CENTRAL	59.596	34.143	28.341	1.871	1.726	0.094	0.186	125.877
SOUTH ATLANTIC	62.728	39.699	31.329	1.690	2.972	0.001	0.153	138.666
EAST SOUTH CENTRAL	57.138	23.228	54.151	2.242	1.492	0.000	0.110	138.360
WEST SOUTH CENTRAL	62.430	39.328	32.119	1.232	3.070	0.008	0.317	138.504
ROCKY MOUNTAIN	51.531	47.290	25.750	1.801	3.082	0.049	0.471	129.975
FAR WEST	48.950	42.248	23.560	2.267	1.915	0.030	0.293	119.262
TOTAL	56.332	38.617	33.540	2.160	2.849	0.410	0.182	134.089

Table 158

Per Capita Consumption Of Electricity In Index Number Terms, U.S. = 100, 1972, By State

Use By Sector

REGION AND STATE	HOUSEHOLD USE	BUSINESS USE	FEDERAL GOVERNMENT	STATE & LOCAL GOVERNMENT USE	TOTAL USE
NEW ENGLAND:					
CONNECTICUT	94.93	71.22	19.95	65.42	77.73
MAINE	84.01	67.24	85.30	67.48	72.96
MASSACHUSETTS	73.26	59.11	37.80	64.93	63.80
NEW HAMPSHIRE	99.00	68.32	19.69	43.70	75.80
RHODE ISLAND	66.30	57.40	79.79	65.74	61.21
VERMONT	126.31	63.19	106.56	93.49	86.45
MID ATLANTIC:					
NEW JERSEY	75.00	79.57	19.95	62.60	76.00
NEW YORK	60.93	63.71	109.97	118.19	67.37
PENNSYLVANIA	85.35	103.92	28.61	49.24	92.89
EAST NORTH CENTRAL:					
ILLINOIS	82.15	90.35	130.97	112.70	89.88
INDIANA	102.71	111.42	23.88	67.59	104.18
MICHIGAN	86.07	94.14	39.63	77.96	89.57
OHIO	90.88	139.03	89.50	90.83	119.26
WISCONSIN	96.52	75.44	32.28	73.67	81.51
WEST NORTH CENTRAL:					
IOWA	98.94	69.95	40.16	73.89	79.19
KANSAS	96.19	86.66	60.37	100.60	90.36
MINNESOTA	91.81	73.93	44.62	62.00	78.45
MISSOURI	94.09	75.11	71.13	72.15	80.99
NEBRASKA	102.22	65.91	104.72	123.29	82.34
NORTH DAKOTA	96.07	41.57	102.36	85.78	63.28
SOUTH DAKOTA	99.57	34.91	112.34	80.84	60.29
SOUTH ATLANTIC:					
DELAWARE	92.41	140.89	29.66	85.83	119.62
DISTRICT OF COLUMBIA	79.86	78.71	392.65	137.68	87.91
FLORIDA	159.49	71.05	141.21	147.07	106.17
GEORGIA	119.84	93.36	48.29	114.88	102.81
MARYLAND	77.29	92.22	43.31	72.58	85.26
NORTH CAROLINA	124.67	109.88	76.90	105.97	113.90
SOUTH CAROLINA	119.11	139.69	104.46	109.07	130.32
VIRGINIA	108.23	68.92	483.20	128.23	91.99
WEST VIRGINIA	88.05	138.81	27.82	63.95	115.39
EAST SOUTH CENTRAL:					
ALABAMA	142.83	160.41	36.48	77.69	146.99
KENTUCKY	111.42	189.31	146.72	98.21	156.95
MISSISSIPPI	116.12	87.61	59.84	99.29	97.27
TENNESSEE	205.70	199.07	17.85	63.46	188.88
WEST SOUTH CENTRAL:					
ARKANSAS	100.41	99.98	80.58	94.46	99.44
LOUISIANA	118.42	126.92	88.71	122.31	123.27
OKLAHOMA	108.59	79.82	252.76	132.08	95.42
TEXAS	123.17	129.81	135.96	137.84	128.32
ROCKY MOUNTAIN:					
ARIZONA	113.50	109.39	157.22	132.90	113.10
COLORADO	69.94	62.17	169.82	111.24	69.77
IDAHO	152.72	223.71	125.72	169.71	195.40
MONTANA	97.24	219.61	88.71	99.02	169.42
NEVADA	179.98	148.02	147.51	219.06	163.43
NEW MEXICO	58.42	68.86	240.16	123.18	71.88
UTAH	70.81	65.62	274.28	88.17	71.99
WYOMING	79.32	157.26	147.77	185.83	133.89
FAR WEST:					
ALASKA	70.41	34.51	197.90	82.08	51.94
CALIFORNIA	79.52	90.00	149.34	128.99	90.26
HAWAII	74.34	77.30	24.67	49.73	73.61
OREGON	203.35	162.52	70.08	119.87	171.35
WASHINGTON	222.32	220.70	144.09	131.98	213.77

Table   159

Per Capita Consumption Of Electricity In Index Number Terms, U.S. = 100, 1972, By State

Use By Function

REGION AND STATE	RESIDENTIAL USE	COMMERCIAL USE	INDUSTRIAL USE	STREET & HIGHWAY LIGHTING	OTHER PUBLIC AUTHORITIES	RAILROADS AND RAILWAYS	INTER-DEPARTMENTAL	TOTAL USE
NEW ENGLAND:								
CONNECTICUT	94.93	97.13	58.46	116.00	2.54	0.00	9.52	77.73
MAINE	84.01	67.31	67.50	90.00	81.21	0.00	3.57	72.96
MASSACHUSETTS	73.26	85.83	45.98	86.00	22.88	17.81	119.05	63.80
NEW HAMPSHIRE	99.00	55.24	73.84	77.00	18.64	0.00	0.00	75.80
RHODE ISLAND	66.30	80.42	46.34	100.50	62.71	0.00	0.00	61.21
VERMONT	126.31	71.31	58.33	67.00	168.64	0.00	114.29	86.45
MID ATLANTIC:								
NEW JERSEY	75.00	95.09	71.75	89.50	1.69	4.11	15.48	76.00
NEW YORK	60.93	85.34	49.64	103.00	188.28	687.67	10.71	67.37
PENNSYLVANIA	85.35	74.40	113.99	71.00	12.99	342.47	26.19	92.89
EAST NORTH CENTRAL:								
ILLINOIS	82.15	100.25	84.50	108.50	171.47	163.01	4.76	89.88
INDIANA	102.71	79.83	126.60	99.50	13.56	17.81	25.00	104.18
MICHIGAN	86.07	76.03	103.21	100.00	55.23	0.00	35.71	89.57
OHIO	90.88	88.83	161.69	101.50	108.90	19.18	21.43	119.26
WISCONSIN	96.52	71.87	77.02	163.50	39.12	0.00	57.14	81.51
WEST NORTH CENTRAL:								
IOWA	98.94	75.97	67.83	115.50	43.50	0.00	36.90	79.19
KANSAS	96.19	123.41	71.10	109.00	33.62	0.00	89.29	90.36
MINNESOTA	91.81	55.68	82.53	93.50	56.78	0.00	57.14	78.45
MISSOURI	94.09	80.55	73.17	94.00	54.38	13.70	33.33	80.99
NEBRASKA	102.22	123.68	40.36	116.00	118.22	17.81	90.48	82.34
NORTH DAKOTA	96.07	85.68	21.78	113.00	98.02	0.00	32.14	63.28
SOUTH DAKOTA	99.57	74.30	17.87	93.00	102.82	0.00	59.52	60.29
SOUTH ATLANTIC:								
DELAWARE	92.41	108.05	157.51	89.50	6.78	0.00	50.00	119.62
DISTRICT OF COLUMBIA	79.86	249.47	6.67	156.50	5.79	193.15	59.52	87.91
FLORIDA	159.49	117.30	53.22	98.00	187.85	0.00	30.95	106.17
GEORGIA	119.84	116.55	89.46	79.50	11.72	0.00	13.10	102.81
MARYLAND	77.29	89.96	94.13	87.00	1.69	182.19	57.14	85.26
NORTH CAROLINA	124.67	105.18	113.38	62.50	91.24	0.00	130.95	113.90
SOUTH CAROLINA	119.11	100.17	161.61	51.00	102.68	0.00	9.52	130.32
VIRGINIA	108.23	101.55	56.92	59.50	363.56	0.00	40.48	91.99
WEST VIRGINIA	88.05	77.77	168.88	48.50	6.50	0.00	2.38	115.39
EAST SOUTH CENTRAL:								
ALABAMA	142.83	85.97	196.93	98.50	2.68	0.00	100.00	146.99
KENTUCKY	111.42	78.90	240.72	85.50	160.03	0.00	36.90	156.95
MISSISSIPPI	116.12	89.66	90.79	103.00	52.97	0.00	7.14	97.27
TENNESSEE	205.70	50.46	268.22	225.50	2.12	0.00	36.90	188.88
WEST SOUTH CENTRAL:								
ARKANSAS	100.41	91.25	106.69	70.50	75.42	27.40	9.52	99.44
LOUISIANA	118.42	97.81	132.86	101.50	130.93	1.37	1302.38	123.27
OKLAHOMA	108.59	112.06	69.49	86.00	205.79	0.00	15.48	95.42
TEXAS	123.17	136.53	130.69	97.00	116.95	0.00	48.81	128.32
ROCKY MOUNTAIN:								
ARIZONA	113.50	151.54	87.64	84.50	132.77	0.00	540.48	113.10
COLORADO	69.94	122.11	35.48	87.50	136.72	0.00	89.29	69.77
IDAHO	152.72	202.06	235.62	81.50	122.60	0.00	21.43	195.40
MONTANA	97.24	106.49	267.78	126.50	75.99	528.77	119.05	169.42
NEVADA	179.98	246.70	105.45	157.00	108.47	0.00	488.10	163.43
NEW MEXICO	58.42	121.62	47.30	74.50	179.10	0.00	120.24	71.88
UTAH	70.81	90.49	56.78	85.00	165.96	0.00	21.43	71.99
WYOMING	79.32	197.10	148.61	89.00	65.40	0.00	82.14	133.89
FAR WEST:								
ALASKA	70.41	86.05	12.23	78.50	133.47	13.70	38.10	51.94
CALIFORNIA	79.52	131.83	70.35	119.00	149.15	15.07	209.52	90.26
HAWAII	74.34	59.10	86.08	138.00	0.00	0.00	0.00	73.61
OREGON	203.35	168.14	159.88	116.50	37.01	0.00	48.81	171.35
WASHINGTON	222.32	146.15	246.79	107.00	135.45	19.18	1098.81	213.77

Table 160

Per Capita Expenditures On Electricity In Index Number Terms, U.S. = 100, 1972, By State

Use By Sector

REGION AND STATE	HOUSEHOLD USE	BUSINESS USE	FEDERAL GOVERNMENT USE	STATE & LOCAL GOVERNMENT USE	TOTAL USE
NEW ENGLAND:					
CONNECTICUT	115.56	104.35	32.83	93.10	107.15
MAINE	99.91	79.73	100.35	91.97	89.55
MASSACHUSETTS	98.57	94.29	61.51	95.67	95.78
NEW HAMPSHIRE	115.23	83.16	34.05	70.92	94.93
RHODE ISLAND	90.12	87.00	103.23	88.60	88.66
VERMONT	134.79	85.96	143.62	107.98	109.15
MID ATLANTIC:					
NEW JERSEY	100.22	113.70	35.78	95.74	105.45
NEW YORK	86.53	96.18	169.59	157.11	98.42
PENNSYLVANIA	103.04	120.21	46.80	66.00	107.29
EAST NORTH CENTRAL:					
ILLINOIS	101.80	109.57	152.22	112.21	107.09
INDIANA	102.09	113.96	31.33	76.80	104.65
MICHIGAN	90.86	105.61	48.41	93.56	97.62
OHIO	94.20	121.02	96.48	93.14	106.99
WISCONSIN	100.62	95.04	42.18	84.48	95.78
WEST NORTH CENTRAL:					
IOWA	115.47	86.93	58.74	90.66	98.88
KANSAS	99.31	91.47	69.42	94.29	94.72
MINNESOTA	101.93	90.54	54.47	72.97	93.32
MISSOURI	107.00	91.23	81.82	78.55	96.62
NEBRASKA	99.91	70.77	94.75	94.71	85.42
NORTH DAKOTA	108.85	63.98	87.42	82.36	84.74
SOUTH DAKOTA	110.38	55.25	102.77	81.34	81.31
SOUTH ATLANTIC:					
DELAWARE	122.31	171.43	48.59	110.37	143.85
DISTRICT OF COLUMBIA	87.11	121.52	571.90	168.01	116.96
FLORIDA	147.29	86.80	147.55	139.20	117.60
GEORGIA	99.80	92.45	60.82	113.66	96.98
MARYLAND	88.90	111.22	69.88	97.09	100.07
NORTH CAROLINA	110.66	93.17	64.11	82.04	99.16
SOUTH CAROLINA	109.44	103.57	80.03	85.80	104.17
VIRGINIA	99.32	72.38	331.79	96.53	89.17
WEST VIRGINIA	88.90	118.40	36.76	66.05	100.36
EAST SOUTH CENTRAL:					
ALABAMA	103.83	113.43	44.09	72.74	104.93
KENTUCKY	85.61	119.42	138.95	76.81	101.73
MISSISSIPPI	99.49	83.71	63.13	93.54	90.94
TENNESSEE	113.27	118.04	18.64	59.78	109.64
WEST SOUTH CENTRAL:					
ARKANSAS	100.47	91.37	88.06	88.22	94.87
LOUISIANA	112.55	93.49	81.25	102.90	102.16
OKLAHOMA	113.72	77.93	211.89	106.61	97.21
TEXAS	111.41	101.98	115.70	106.24	106.49
ROCKY MOUNTAIN:					
ARIZONA	117.75	119.16	176.75	125.67	119.88
COLORADO	79.35	74.35	148.99	101.33	79.78
IDAHO	106.58	132.00	55.34	104.44	117.91
MONTANA	91.44	103.12	58.51	86.43	96.17
NEVADA	122.39	128.66	121.64	169.79	129.54
NEW MEXICO	69.43	79.03	223.02	111.05	79.67
UTAH	69.22	71.96	205.14	77.04	72.97
WYOMING	85.88	144.53	150.32	158.52	121.19
FAR WEST:					
ALASKA	102.28	74.99	332.72	122.89	93.99
CALIFORNIA	81.10	91.31	95.79	104.27	88.21
HAWAII	92.06	111.13	55.97	74.14	99.16
OREGON	113.30	83.04	49.28	78.75	94.94
WASHINGTON	101.95	75.73	84.71	72.17	86.55

Table 161

Per Capita Expenditures On Electricity In Index Number Terms, U.S. = 100, 1972, By State

Use By Function

REGION AND STATE	RESIDENTIAL USE	COMMERCIAL USE	INDUSTRIAL USE	STREET & HIGHWAY LIGHTING	OTHER PUBLIC AUTHORITIES	RAILROADS AND RAILWAYS	INTER- DEPARTMENTAL	TOTAL USE
NEW ENGLAND:								
CONNECTICUT	115.56	112.81	93.24	167.08	3.47	0.00	19.23	107.15
MAINE	99.91	81.46	78.06	164.68	90.87	0.00	4.40	89.55
MASSACHUSETTS	98.57	107.42	79.21	144.63	34.85	27.32	348.35	95.78
NEW HAMPSHIRE	115.23	70.75	92.65	139.03	34.22	0.00	0.00	94.93
RHODE ISLAND	90.12	92.63	79.51	156.71	80.41	0.00	2.75	88.66
VERMONT	134.79	80.18	89.04	106.90	246.30	0.00	149.45	109.15
MID ATLANTIC:								
NEW JERSEY	100.22	119.21	105.56	153.29	3.05	3.90	50.55	105.45
NEW YORK	86.53	124.99	60.93	127.08	301.37	770.98	15.93	98.42
PENNSYLVANIA	103.04	82.20	148.55	102.08	25.94	297.56	51.65	107.29
EAST NORTH CENTRAL:								
ILLINOIS	101.80	115.19	101.11	68.98	203.12	135.37	12.09	107.09
INDIANA	102.09	80.92	145.23	103.15	16.50	17.80	46.15	104.65
MICHIGAN	90.86	83.38	127.13	129.91	67.36	0.00	79.12	97.62
OHIO	94.20	88.50	149.70	111.76	121.52	15.37	41.21	106.99
WISCONSIN	100.62	83.62	104.96	132.04	41.35	0.00	119.78	95.78
WEST NORTH CENTRAL:								
IOWA	115.47	90.92	84.10	108.01	61.07	0.24	82.42	98.88
KANSAS	99.31	111.16	74.90	82.92	33.42	0.00	153.30	94.72
MINNESOTA	101.93	68.66	111.19	90.28	62.02	0.00	102.75	93.32
MISSOURI	107.00	88.35	94.45	78.38	56.86	8.05	79.67	96.62
NEBRASKA	99.91	99.91	44.78	65.28	103.37	12.20	139.01	85.42
NORTH DAKOTA	108.85	89.67	40.38	90.32	73.46	0.00	55.49	84.74
SOUTH DAKOTA	110.38	88.01	26.94	88.94	58.93	0.00	127.47	81.31
SOUTH ATLANTIC:								
DELAWARE	122.31	124.21	217.43	115.56	11.76	0.00	145.05	143.85
DISTRICT OF COLUMBIA	87.11	253.37	11.37	233.70	10.07	157.07	68.68	116.96
FLORIDA	147.29	119.23	62.60	89.26	196.24	0.00	82.97	117.60
GEORGIA	99.80	109.20	88.69	69.31	12.67	0.00	30.22	96.98
MARYLAND	88.90	102.35	122.13	130.23	2.25	150.98	66.48	100.07
NORTH CAROLINA	110.66	82.78	104.49	52.04	73.25	0.00	225.27	99.16
SOUTH CAROLINA	109.44	81.14	129.71	47.13	74.97	0.00	23.63	104.17
VIRGINIA	99.32	90.16	60.58	53.33	253.32	0.00	60.44	89.17
WEST VIRGINIA	88.90	74.07	162.67	51.39	7.58	0.00	3.30	100.36
EAST SOUTH CENTRAL:								
ALABAMA	103.83	72.79	155.19	81.16	3.37	0.00	110.99	104.93
KENTUCKY	85.61	58.43	176.51	70.93	167.64	0.00	60.44	101.73
MISSISSIPPI	99.49	83.79	90.61	76.62	50.97	0.00	19.78	90.94
TENNESSEE	113.27	37.51	193.89	165.09	1.90	0.00	39.01	109.64
WEST SOUTH CENTRAL:								
ARKANSAS	100.47	88.32	98.86	51.99	74.62	18.29	17.03	94.87
LOUISIANA	112.55	88.89	101.86	70.65	117.02	0.98	128.57	102.16
OKLAHOMA	113.72	100.40	64.29	45.05	172.73	0.00	34.62	97.21
TEXAS	111.41	108.68	100.40	56.30	95.75	0.00	247.25	106.49
ROCKY MOUNTAIN:								
ARIZONA	117.75	141.11	96.83	78.10	154.30	0.00	749.45	119.88
COLORADO	79.35	113.88	39.00	86.25	112.36	0.00	86.81	79.78
IDAHO	106.58	131.85	133.60	71.25	26.68	0.00	26.37	117.91
MONTANA	91.44	95.11	109.01	107.08	31.24	147.07	191.76	96.17
NEVADA	122.39	194.41	75.31	100.65	65.25	3.17	208.24	129.54
NEW MEXICO	69.43	115.24	49.96	66.06	161.04	0.00	240.66	79.67
UTAH	69.22	79.55	68.63	86.48	110.95	0.00	47.80	72.97
WYOMING	85.88	162.74	142.56	88.06	47.56	0.00	114.29	121.19
FAR WEST:								
ALASKA	102.28	137.34	20.61	85.74	220.22	30.73	114.84	93.99
CALIFORNIA	81.10	115.80	68.64	113.75	70.94	8.05	192.31	88.21
HAWAII	92.06	93.19	128.12	99.12	0.00	0.00	0.00	99.16
OREGON	113.30	99.15	67.37	91.71	18.53	0.00	47.80	94.94
WASHINGTON	101.95	78.96	72.58	64.03	77.71	7.80	87.36	86.55

Table 162

Per Capita Use Of Electricity In Index Number Terms, U.S. = 100, 1972
    Based On Consumption In BTU And Expenditures In Dollars, By Region

Use By Sector

REGION	HOUSEHOLD USE	BUSINESS USE	FEDERAL GOVERNMENT USE	STATE & LOCAL GOVERNMENT USE	TOTAL USE
Index Of Per Capita Consumption, U.S. = 100					
NEW ENGLAND	82.79	63.49	42.26	65.04	69.54
MID ATLANTIC	71.41	79.53	66.67	85.50	77.13
EAST NORTH CENTRAL	89.57	105.06	75.07	89.09	98.46
WEST NORTH CENTRAL	95.74	71.74	64.04	79.53	79.96
SOUTH ATLANTIC	119.34	94.10	150.13	114.12	104.53
EAST SOUTH CENTRAL	149.82	167.15	62.47	82.14	153.93
WEST SOUTH CENTRAL	118.08	119.69	137.01	129.80	120.14
ROCKY MOUNTAIN	94.50	109.14	176.38	127.90	106.72
FAR WEST	107.20	111.24	139.11	125.68	111.37
TOTAL	100.00	100.00	100.00	100.00	100.00

Index Of Per Capita Expenditures, U.S. = 100					
NEW ENGLAND	104.77	94.00	62.20	93.03	98.03
MID ATLANTIC	94.43	107.21	104.62	116.29	102.60
EAST NORTH CENTRAL	97.29	110.66	86.79	95.41	103.40
WEST NORTH CENTRAL	105.79	85.96	72.01	83.25	93.88
SOUTH ATLANTIC	111.35	95.15	135.03	105.90	103.41
EAST SOUTH CENTRAL	101.43	111.27	63.30	73.31	103.19
WEST SOUTH CENTRAL	110.83	96.16	119.16	103.85	103.29
ROCKY MOUNTAIN	91.48	97.73	154.36	110.20	96.93
FAR WEST	86.90	89.08	92.27	97.49	88.94
TOTAL	100.00	100.00	100.00	100.00	100.00

Table 163

Per Capita Use Of Electricity In Index Number Terms, U.S. = 100, 1972, Based On Consumption In BTU And Expenditures In Dollars, By Region

Use By Function

REGION	RESIDENTIAL USE	COMMERCIAL USE	INDUSTRIAL USE	STREET & HIGHWAY LIGHTING	OTHER PUBLIC AUTHORITIES	RAILROADS AND RAILWAYS	INTER-DEPARTMENTAL	TOTAL USE
Index Of Per Capita Consumption, U.S. = 100								
NEW ENGLAND	82.79	84.20	53.26	93.50	31.07	8.22	64.29	69.54
MID ATLANTIC	71.41	83.77	74.33	90.00	96.33	445.21	16.67	77.13
EAST NORTH CENTRAL	89.57	86.10	113.55	109.50	94.21	52.05	23.81	98.46
WEST NORTH CENTRAL	95.74	83.71	66.90	102.50	59.75	5.48	53.57	79.96
SOUTH ATLANTIC	119.34	108.67	90.57	76.50	123.59	27.40	47.62	104.53
EAST SOUTH CENTRAL	149.82	73.84	211.80	135.50	50.71	0.00	48.81	153.93
WEST SOUTH CENTRAL	118.08	121.52	120.62	93.50	127.12	2.74	275.00	120.14
ROCKY MOUNTAIN	94.50	140.48	95.50	91.50	134.18	42.47	204.76	106.72
FAR WEST	107.20	133.82	99.54	117.50	133.76	13.70	300.00	111.37
TOTAL	100.00	100.00	100.00	100.00	100.00	100.00	100.00	100.00
Index Of Per Capita Expenditures, U.S. = 100								
NEW ENGLAND	104.77	102.03	83.94	151.20	43.28	13.17	178.02	98.03
MID ATLANTIC	94.43	110.32	97.38	124.31	155.95	471.22	34.07	102.60
EAST NORTH CENTRAL	97.29	93.20	125.78	105.09	109.55	43.66	51.10	103.40
WEST NORTH CENTRAL	105.79	88.41	84.50	86.62	60.58	3.41	102.20	93.88
SOUTH ATLANTIC	111.35	102.40	93.41	78.24	104.32	22.93	84.07	103.41
EAST SOUTH CENTRAL	101.43	60.15	161.45	103.80	52.37	0.00	60.44	103.19
WEST SOUTH CENTRAL	110.83	101.84	95.76	57.04	107.76	1.95	174.18	103.29
ROCKY MOUNTAIN	91.48	122.46	76.77	83.38	108.18	11.95	258.79	96.93
FAR WEST	86.90	109.40	70.24	104.95	67.22	7.32	160.99	88.94
TOTAL	100.00	100.00	100.00	100.00	100.00	100.00	100.00	100.00

Table 164

Electricity Prices In Dollars Per Million BTU, 1972, By State

Use By Function

REGION AND STATE	RESIDENTIAL USE	COMMERCIAL USE	INDUSTRIAL USE	STREET AND HIGHWAY LIGHTING	OTHER PUBLIC AUTHORITIES	RAILROADS AND RAILWAYS	INTER- DEPARTMENTAL	TOTAL USE
NEW ENGLAND:								
CONNECTICUT	8.183	7.564	5.106	15.590	5.605	0.000[a]	4.522	7.149
MAINE	7.994	7.883	3.702	19.805	4.500	0.000	2.345	6.366
MASSACHUSETTS	9.044	8.152	5.514	18.173	6.134	8.659	6.334	7.787
NEW HAMPSHIRE	7.824	8.341	4.017	19.461	7.376	0.000	0.000	6.496
RHODE ISLAND	9.136	7.503	5.492	16.865	5.164	0.000	6.015	7.513
VERMONT	7.174	7.323	4.886	17.292	5.876	0.000	2.818	6.549
MID ATLANTIC:								
NEW JERSEY	8.982	8.166	4.709	18.524	7.214	5.666	7.305	7.197
NEW YORK	9.546	9.539	3.929	13.324	6.443	6.300	3.242	7.577
PENNSYLVANIA	8.116	7.196	4.171	15.574	8.010	4.869	4.186	5.991
EAST NORTH CENTRAL:								
ILLINOIS	8.330	7.484	3.830	6.865	4.768	4.678	5.108	6.180
INDIANA	6.681	6.602	3.672	11.209	4.917	5.627	4.048	5.210
MICHIGAN	7.096	7.144	3.943	14.066	4.908	0.000	4.873	5.653
OHIO	6.968	6.489	2.964	11.888	4.488	4.614	4.224	4.653
WISCONSIN	7.008	7.579	4.362	8.718	4.247	0.000	4.524	6.095
WEST NORTH CENTRAL:								
IOWA	7.845	7.795	3.969	10.112	5.657	3.473	4.892	6.476
KANSAS	6.940	5.866	3.372	8.210	4.005	0.000	3.710	5.438
MINNESOTA	7.463	8.032	4.313	10.404	4.393	0.000	3.935	6.170
MISSOURI	7.644	7.143	4.132	9.024	4.212	3.287	5.178	6.188
NEBRASKA	6.571	5.261	3.551	6.070	3.517	3.712	3.327	5.381
NORTH DAKOTA	7.616	6.816	5.935	8.632	3.015	0.000	3.751	6.945
SOUTH DAKOTA	7.452	7.715	4.828	10.345	2.308	0.000	4.631	6.996
SOUTH ATLANTIC:								
DELAWARE	8.897	7.488	4.419	13.921	6.997	0.000	6.322	6.238
DISTRICT OF COLUMBIA	7.332	6.615	5.458	16.124	7.034	4.576	2.505	6.901
FLORIDA	6.208	6.620	3.765	9.863	4.205	0.000	5.713	5.745
GEORGIA	5.598	6.103	3.173	9.439	4.358	0.000	5.041	4.893
MARYLAND	7.732	7.410	4.153	16.124	5.401	4.645	2.509	6.088
NORTH CAROLINA	5.967	5.126	2.950	8.956	3.228	0.000	3.715	4.516
SOUTH CAROLINA	6.177	5.275	2.569	10.023	2.936	0.000	5.617	4.146
VIRGINIA	6.168	5.783	3.407	9.691	2.804	0.000	3.187	5.027
WEST VIRGINIA	6.786	6.203	3.083	11.453	4.738	0.000	2.931	4.511
EAST SOUTH CENTRAL:								
ALABAMA	4.887	5.515	2.523	8.911	4.968	0.000	2.395	3.703
KENTUCKY	5.165	4.823	2.347	8.943	4.215	0.000	3.566	3.362
MISSISSIPPI	5.760	6.086	3.195	8.047	3.870	0.000	6.008	4.849
TENNESSEE	3.702	4.841	2.314	7.910	3.598	0.000	2.281	3.011
WEST SOUTH CENTRAL:								
ARKANSAS	6.726	6.304	2.966	7.963	3.985	3.688	3.634	4.949
LOUISIANA	6.389	5.920	2.454	7.530	3.595	4.103	0.214	4.299
OKLAHOMA	7.040	5.835	2.962	5.646	3.379	0.000	4.836	5.284
TEXAS	6.080	5.184	2.459	6.273	3.296	0.000	11.015	4.304
ROCKY MOUNTAIN:								
ARIZONA	6.974	6.066	3.537	10.007	4.675	0.000	3.007	5.498
COLORADO	7.626	6.075	3.518	10.665	3.305	0.000	2.108	5.931
IDAHO	4.691	4.250	1.815	9.460	0.876	0.000	2.638	3.130
MONTANA	6.321	5.817	1.303	9.157	1.652	1.563	3.489	2.944
NEVADA	4.571	5.132	2.286	6.932	2.420	3.044	0.925	4.111
NEW MEXICO	7.989	6.172	3.380	9.572	3.617	0.000	4.314	5.749
UTAH	6.571	5.726	3.869	11.017	2.691	0.000	4.787	5.258
WYOMING	7.278	5.378	3.071	10.714	2.925	0.000	3.015	4.695
FAR WEST:								
ALASKA	9.765	10.395	5.398	11.762	6.640	12.016	6.643	9.386
CALIFORNIA	6.855	5.721	3.123	10.320	1.913	3.044	1.988	5.069
HAWAII	8.324	10.271	4.765	7.758	0.000	0.000	0.000	6.987
OREGON	3.745	3.841	1.349	8.513	2.011	0.000	2.153	2.874
WASHINGTON	3.083	3.519	0.941	6.475	2.308	2.261	0.173	2.100

[a] Zero indicates no use.

Table 165

Electricity Prices In Dollars Per Million BTU, 1972, By Region

Use By Function

REGION	RESI-DENTIAL USE	COMMER-CIAL USE	INDUS-TRIAL USE	STREET & HIGHWAY LIGHTING	OTHER PUBLIC AUTHOR-ITIES	RAILROADS AND RAILWAYS	INTER-DEPART-MENTAL	ALL USE
NEW ENGLAND	8.507	7.893	5.045	17.441	5.601	8.667	6.104	7.312
MID ATLANTIC	8.889	8.576	4.194	14.888	6.512	5.950	4.441	6.900
EAST NORTH CENTRAL	7.302	7.050	3.546	10.351	4.679	4.714	4.541	5.447
WEST NORTH CENTRAL	7.429	6.879	4.043	9.137	4.084	3.425	4.152	6.089
SOUTH ATLANTIC	6.272	6.161	3.301	11.014	3.395	4.633	3.866	5.131
EAST SOUTH CENTRAL	4.551	5.306	2.440	8.286	4.157	0.000[a]	2.683	3.477
WEST SOUTH CENTRAL	6.309	5.459	2.541	6.579	3.412	3.750	1.371	4.459
ROCKY MOUNTAIN	6.507	5.678	2.573	9.828	3.245	1.577	2.742	4.711
FAR WEST	5.449	5.325	2.259	9.657	2.022	3.018	1.160	4.142
UNITED STATES	6.722	6.513	3.201	10.813	4.026	5.630	2.160	5.187

[a] Zero indicates no use.

Table 166

Electricity Prices In Dollars Per Million BTU And Price Indexes, U.S. = 100, 1972, By State

Use By Function

REGION AND STATE	PRICE IN DOLLARS PER MILLION BTU			PRICE INDEXES, U.S. = 100		
	Residential Use	All Uses	All Uses Given U.S. Quantity Weights	Residential Use	All Uses	All Uses (U.S. Quantity Weights)
NEW ENGLAND:						
CONNECTICUT	8.183	7.149	6.754	114.64	129.09	122.57
MAINE	7.994	6.366	6.203	111.99	114.95	112.57
MASSACHUSETTS	9.044	7.787	7.388	126.70	140.61	134.09
NEW HAMPSHIRE	7.824	6.496	6.475	109.61	117.30	117.50
RHODE ISLAND	9.136	7.513	7.212	127.99	135.66	130.88
VERMONT	7.174	6.549	6.308	100.50	118.26	114.48
MID ATLANTIC:						
NEW JERSEY	8.982	7.197	7.074	125.83	129.96	128.38
NEW YORK	9.546	7.577	7.191	133.73	136.82	130.51
PENNSYLVANIA	8.116	5.991	6.280	113.70	108.18	113.98
EAST NORTH CENTRAL:						
ILLINOIS	8.330	6.180	6.181	116.70	111.59	112.18
INDIANA	6.681	5.210	5.417	93.60	94.08	98.31
MICHIGAN	7.096	5.653	5.810	99.41	102.08	105.44
OHIO	6.968	4.653	5.190	97.62	84.02	94.19
WISCONSIN	7.008	6.095	5.989	98.18	110.06	108.69
WEST NORTH CENTRAL:						
IOWA	7.845	6.476	6.205	109.90	116.94	112.60
KANSAS	6.940	5.438	5.157	97.22	98.19	93.59
MINNESOTA	7.463	6.170	6.235	104.55	111.41	113.16
MISSOURI	7.644	6.188	6.003	107.09	111.74	108.94
NEBRASKA	6.571	5.381	4.940	92.05	97.17	89.65
NORTH DAKOTA	7.616	6.945	6.606	106.69	125.41	119.89
SOUTH DAKOTA	7.452	6.996	6.304	104.40	126.33	114.41
SOUTH ATLANTIC:						
DELAWARE	8.897	6.238	6.724	124.64	112.64	122.02
DISTRICT OF COLUMBIA	7.332	6.901	6.383	102.71	124.61	115.85
FLORIDA	6.208	5.745	5.275	86.97	103.74	95.72
GEORGIA	5.598	4.893	4.722	78.42	88.35	85.69
MARYLAND	7.732	6.088	6.153	108.32	109.93	111.66
NORTH CAROLINA	5.967	4.516	4.485	83.59	81.55	81.40
SOUTH CAROLINA	6.177	4.146	4.430	86.53	74.86	80.40
VIRGINIA	6.168	5.027	4.876	86.41	90.77	88.48
WEST VIRGINIA	6.786	4.511	5.117	95.07	81.46	92.86
EAST SOUTH CENTRAL:						
ALABAMA	4.887	3.703	4.037	68.46	66.87	73.26
KENTUCKY	5.165	3.362	3.941	72.36	60.71	71.53
MISSISSIPPI	5.760	4.849	4.751	80.69	87.56	86.22
TENNESSEE	3.702	3.011	3.400	51.86	54.37	61.71
WEST SOUTH CENTRAL:						
ARKANSAS	6.726	4.949	5.023	94.23	89.36	91.15
LOUISIANA	6.389	4.299	4.541	89.50	77.63	82.41
OKLAHOMA	7.040	5.284	4.978	98.62	95.41	90.34
TEXAS	6.080	4.304	4.327	85.18	77.72	78.53
ROCKY MOUNTAIN:						
ARIZONA	6.974	5.498	5.301	97.70	99.28	96.21
COLORADO	7.626	5.931	5.481	106.83	107.10	99.48
IDAHO	4.691	3.130	3.335	65.72	56.52	60.52
MONTANA	6.321	2.944	4.042	88.55	53.16	73.36
NEVADA	4.571	4.111	3.703	64.04	74.23	67.20
NEW MEXICO	7.989	5.749	5.572	111.92	103.81	101.12
UTAH	6.571	5.258	5.188	92.05	94.94	94.15
WYOMING	7.278	4.695	5.019	101.96	84.78	91.08
FAR WEST:						
ALASKA	9.765	9.386	8.052	136.80	169.48	146.14
CALIFORNIA	6.855	5.069	4.945	96.03	91.53	89.73
HAWAII	8.324	6.987	7.124	116.61	126.16	129.28
OREGON	3.745	2.874	2.775	52.46	51.90	50.37
WASHINGTON	3.083	2.100	2.280	43.19	37.92	41.39

Table 167

Electricity Prices In Dollars Per Million BTU And Price Indexes, U.S. = 100, 1972, By Region

Use By Function

REGION	PRICE IN DOLLARS PER MILLION BTU			PRICE INDEXES, U.S. = 100		
	Residential Use	All Uses	All Uses Given U.S. Quantity Weights	Residential Use	All Uses	All Uses (U.S. Quantity Weights)
NEW ENGLAND	8.594	7.353	7.013	120.40	132.77	127.27
MID ATLANTIC	8.983	7.001	6.880	125.85	126.42	124.86
EAST NORTH CENTRAL	7.339	5.527	5.718	102.82	99.80	103.78
WEST NORTH CENTRAL	7.433	6.119	5.914	104.13	110.49	107.33
SOUTH ATLANTIC	6.370	5.186	5.088	89.24	93.65	92.33
EAST SOUTH CENTRAL	4.740	3.600	3.938	66.40	65.00	71.47
WEST SOUTH CENTRAL	6.329	4.497	4.523	88.67	81.20	82.08
ROCKY MOUNTAIN	6.840	5.091	4.992	95.82	91.94	90.60
FAR WEST	6.209	4.628	4.538	86.98	83.57	82.34
UNITED STATES	7.138	5.538	5.510	100.00	100.00	100.00

Chapter 5

Coal, Hydropower and Nuclear Power

This chapter presents detailed information on the use of coal, hydroelectric power and nuclear power, treated jointly because all of those energy sources are used primarily or exclusively in the production of electricity. There are three groups of tables. The first group shows amounts of use, first for each energy source individually, and then for the aggregate of those sources, by function; this group of tables runs from Table 168 through 176. The second group presents information on per capita use, both in original units and in indexes with the U.S. level set at 100; it covers Tables 177 through 188. The third and final group presents information on prices in Tables 189 through 192. The groups of tables will be discussed in the usual fashion, with organization covered first, followed by some key findings.

Amounts of Use

Organization

The coverage for the first group is shown by the following cross-classification of table numbers.

	Amounts of Use		
	Coal By Function	Hydropower & Nuclear Power By Function	Aggregate Use By Function & Sector
States			
BTU consumed	168	171	174
Expenditures	169	172	175
Regions			
BTU and expenditures	170	173	176

Some Key Findings

Hydropower and nuclear power use were estimated in fuel equivalent terms, that is, the amounts of BTU used and dollars expended that would be necessary to derive "equivalent" inputs from fossil fuels.[1] Details on procedures are presented in Appendix I, but a key point must be made here. In the initial development of estimates, transmission losses for electricity were built into the scale factors employed; at a later stage of the work, it seemed plausible that such was unnecessary and would lead to a 10 percent underestimate of hydroelectric and nuclear power, relative to Bureau of Mines BTU estimates. However, the lower figure was then justified by arguing that the use of hydropower or nuclear power instead of fossil fuel implied that the former were more efficient energy sources than their fossil fuel alternatives. In the absence of hard evidence, a 10 percent reduction in amount of input needed for given output could be defended as a rough way of accounting for the presumed efficiency differential. Admittedly, this argues that an improved estimate was obtained by inadvertance, but the case seemed strong enough to justify accepting the original estimates without further ado.

It should be added that if this rationale is not accepted, the amount of error introduced is relatively small, and is concentrated in energy used for energy production, so that "customer" estimates are unaffected. The difference between the Bureau of Mines estimate of hydropower plus nuclear

---

[1]A similar imputation procedure is used by the Bureau of Mines for hydropower and nuclear power (see chapter 1), and by Schurr and Netschert, et. al. in estimating BTU amount of fuel wood used for energy in the 19th century, in Sam H. Schurr and Bruce C. Netschert with V.F. Eliasberg, J. Lerner and Hans H. Landsberg, Energy in the American Economy, 1850-1975 (Baltimore: Johns Hopkins Press for Resources for the Future, 1960).

power and that used here amounts to 400 trillion BTU (chapter 1). This equals roughly one half of one percent of the total of 73,192 trillion BTU. Readers who do not accept the rationale can make adjustments in results in relatively straightforward fashion.

Under that rationale, the following U.S. levels were obtained for the individual energy sources, cross-classified by function:

	Coal	Hydro[a] Power	Nuclear[a] Power	Total
	Trillion BTU			
Residential use	308.2	—	—	308.2
Commercial use	18.5	—	—	18.5
Industrial use	4,245.9	32.0	—	4,277.9
Electric utility use	7,758.3	2,579.5	510.6	10,848.3
Total	12,330.9	2,611.5	510.6	15,452.9
	Million Dollars			
Residential use	400.7	—	—	400.7
Commercial use	14.3	—	—	14.3
Industrial use	1,721.9	9.9	—	1,731.8
Electric utility use	2,933.0	799.6	249.9	3,982.5
Total	5,070.0	809.5	249.9	6,129.3

[a] Fuel equivalent values

The distribution of use by region, in terms both of BTU consumed and percent of the U.S. total are presented in a table on the following page.

Clearly, there is considerable specialization of use between regions. This is most pronounced in the case of hydropower, with more than half of

1972 use located in the Far West region; roughly 80 percent of nuclear power is consumed in the Northeast and North Central regions; and coal use is concentrated near its major areas of production. Specialization and concentration seem even more pronounced at the state level; thus, Pennsylvania accounts for 13.8 percent of all coal BTU use, Washington for 27.7 percent of hydropower BTU equivalent, and Illinois for 24.2 percent of nuclear BTU equivalent. Hawaii had no coal use; New Jersey, Delaware, Mississippi and Louisiana had no hydropower use; and 35 states had no nuclear power use in 1972.

	Quantities Consumed					
	Coal	Hydro[a] Power	Nuclear[a] Power	Coal	Hydro Power	Nuclear Power
	Trillion BTU			Percent of U.S. Total		
New England	39.8	48.7	89.8	0.3%	1.9%	17.6%
Mid Atlantic	2,099.8	278.2	105.0	17.0	10.7	20.6
East North Central	4,794.5	40.9	174.7	38.9	1.6	34.2
West North Central	839.4	137.1	33.6	6.8	5.3	6.6
South Atlantic	2,213.6	167.2	50.5	18.0	6.4	9.9
East South Central	1,694.3	240.7	0.0	13.7	9.2	0.0
West South Central	63.2	37.5	0.0	0.5	1.4	0.0
Rocky Mountain	512.5	280.1	0.0	4.2	10.7	0.0
Far West	73.8	1,381.1	57.0	0.6	52.9	11.2
Total	12,330.9	2,611.4	510.6	100.0	100.0	100.0

[a]Fuel equivalent values.

Per Capita Use

Organization

The second group has the coverage shown in the following cross-classi-fication of table numbers:

	Use Per Capita		Indexes of Use Per Capita	
	By Energy Source	By Function	By Energy Source	By Function
States				
BTU consumed	177	180	183	186
Expenditures	178	181	184	187
Regions				
BTU and expenditures	179	182	185	188

Some Key Findings

National per capita use, by energy source and function, had the following distributions:

	Million BTU Per Capita	Dollars Per Capita
Coal	59.22	$24.35
Hydropower	12.54	3.89
Nuclear power	2.45	1.20
Total	74.21	29.44
Residential use	1.48	1.93
Commercial use	0.09	0.07
Industrial use	20.54	8.32
Electric utility use	52.10	19.13
Total	74.21	29.44

Regional distributions of per capita BTU consumption, relative to the U.S. level, by source and major function, were:

	Source			Major Function, All Sources	
	Coal Use	Hydro-Electric Power Use	Nuclear Power Use	Industrial Use	Electric Utility Use
Index Of Per Capita Consumption, U.S. = 100					
New England	5.6	32.1	302.5	2.5	27.0
Mid Atlantic	94.3	59.0	113.8	131.6	70.5
East North Central	198.5	8.0	174.7	223.6	141.0
West North Central	85.3	65.8	82.5	46.9	96.1
South Atlantic	117.1	41.8	64.5	82.7	111.2
East South Central	217.5	145.9	0.0	164.6	213.9
West South Central	5.3	15.0	0.0	6.3	7.2
Rocky Mountain	97.5	251.5	0.0	69.0	140.3
Far West	4.6	405.5	85.6	14.7	100.0
United States	100.0	100.0	100.0	100.0	100.0

Regional specialization is made even more explicit through the use of per capita measures. Per capita coal use is negligible in New England, the West South Central and Far West regions, while the East South Central use level is twice the national average. Per capita hydroelectric power use is only eight percent of the national level in the East North Central region, and 15 percent of that level in the West South Central region; in contrast, use in the Far West is four times the national average. Nuclear power is particularly important in New England with use three times the

national level. The West South Central region has next to no use of any
of these energy sources, concomitant with its heavy reliance on natural
gas for industrial and electric utility use (see Table 139 in Chapter 3).
Maximum per capita use by source occurred in the following states,
with the U.S. average set at an index value of 100:

Coal		Hydropower		Nuclear Power	
State	Index	State	Index	State	Index
W. Va.	674.1	Wash.	1689.9	Conn.	973.1
Wyo.	464.7	Ore.	1273.3	S. Car.	692.4
Ind.	349.7	Mont.	1006.2	Ill.	447.9
Ky.	302.7	S. Dak.	829.1	Minn.	353.7
N. Dak.	256.4	Idaho	792.6	Wash.	329.1
Ohio	251.9	N. Dak.	372.4	Wisc.	280.5
Pa.	241.4	Ariz.	263.1		

The major per capita coal consuming states are major coal producers-
or at least major producers per capita, as in the case of North Dakota.

The Pacific Northwest obviously is a dominant user of hydroelectric
power, with Idaho, Montana, Oregon and Washington having use levels eight
to 17 times the national average. Much of the high New England use of
nuclear power is attributable to use by Connecticut, which is roughly 10
times the national average.

Prices

Organization

Price information appears in Tables 189 through 192, organized
as follows. Table 189 shows estimated state coal prices in the sense of

costs per unit paid by consumers, and it also shows the estimated fuel equivalent price for hydropower and nuclear power, all prices being measured in dollars per million BTU. Table 190 shows the corresponding regional values for those measures. Tables 191 and 192 show prices for the aggregate use of coal, hydropower and nuclear power, first in terms of costs actually paid in residential and in all use, and then in terms of weighted prices and price indexes. Table 191 shows state values and Table 192 shows regional values.

Some Key Findings

Estimated U.S. average prices per million BTU were:

Coal Prices

Residential use	$1.30
Commercial use	0.77
Industrial use	0.41
Electric utility use	0.38

Hydro & Nuclear Power

(Fuel equivalent price)	0.34

Regional weighted price indexes for the aggregate of all three energy sources in all uses were:

New England	143.2
Mid Atlantic	130.5
East North Central	103.3
West North Central	92.5
South Atlantic	116.0
East South Central	88.5
West South Central	60.0
Rocky Mountain	71.5
Far West	63.8
United States	100.0

All of these values seem plausible given use rates for the three sources, and relative availability of energy from all sources. The latter factor should explain the very low value for the West South Central region, which seems anomalous at first glance. It is plausible that the very low prices of alternative sources (natural gas in particular) mean that only very low priced coal and hydropower can come into use, with relatively insignificant amounts of those sources that meet that condition. For all uses, minimum weighted prices occur for New Mexico, with a price index of 44.1; Oregon and Washington, each with a price index of 46.8; and Wyoming, with a price index of 53.1. The highest weighted price occurs for New Jersey, with an index of 163.0.

Table 168

Consumption Of Coal In Billion BTU, 1972, By State

Use By Function

REGION AND STATE	RESIDENTIAL USE	COMMERCIAL USE	INDUSTRIAL USE	ELECTRIC UTILITY USE	TOTAL USE
NEW ENGLAND:					
CONNECTICUT	100.0	0.0	1546.4	1934.7	3581.1
MAINE	100.0	0.0	246.4	26.8	373.2
MASSACHUSETTS	950.0	0.0	3155.2	2041.2	6146.4
NEW HAMPSHIRE	300.0	0.0	546.4	27313.3	28159.7
RHODE ISLAND	50.0	0.0	123.2	13.4	186.6
VERMONT	200.0	0.0	92.8	1078.6	1371.4
MID ATLANTIC:					
NEW JERSEY	3500.0	0.0	2677.6	27263.6	33441.2
NEW YORK	13350.0	0.0	205544.8	145493.1	364387.9
PENNSYLVANIA	67100.0	0.0	805073.6	829793.2	1701966.8
EAST NORTH CENTRAL:					
ILLINOIS	39150.0	0.0	227055.2	638481.8	904687.0
INDIANA	23750.0	0.0	536901.6	533716.1	1094367.7
MICHIGAN	18750.0	0.0	355287.2	474253.2	848290.4
OHIO	35650.0	0.0	664104.8	899818.1	1599572.9
WISCONSIN	21500.0	0.0	90246.4	235848.6	347595.0
WEST NORTH CENTRAL:					
IOWA	2100.0	0.0	39500.0	113836.3	155436.3
KANSAS	500.0	0.0	3600.0	9938.9	14038.9
MINNESOTA	8450.0	0.0	45369.6	129909.7	183729.3
MISSOURI	2600.0	0.0	54500.0	288447.7	345547.7
NEBRASKA	1000.0	0.0	4300.0	27541.0	32841.0
NORTH DAKOTA	1600.0	0.0	8100.0	86550.5	96250.5
SOUTH DAKOTA	2000.0	0.0	3000.0	6509.7	11509.7
SOUTH ATLANTIC:					
DELAWARE	650.0	0.0	27616.0	20886.4	49152.4
DISTRICT OF COLUMBIA	100.0	0.0	2800.0	4264.4	7164.4
FLORIDA	700.0	0.0	4700.0	121252.3	126652.3
GEORGIA	1000.0	0.0	6200.0	245349.2	252549.2
MARYLAND	1950.0	0.0	95340.8	108216.3	205507.1
NORTH CAROLINA	10100.0	0.0	38800.0	433578.6	482478.6
SOUTH CAROLINA	5800.0	0.0	33300.0	131717.2	170817.2
VIRGINIA	11400.0	0.0	74146.4	117136.7	202683.1
WEST VIRGINIA	7400.0	0.0	257300.0	451887.5	716587.5
EAST SOUTH CENTRAL:					
ALABAMA	1800.0	0.0	227500.0	379299.6	608599.6
KENTUCKY	8700.0	0.0	98400.0	485432.4	592532.4
MISSISSIPPI	1600.0	0.0	60200.0	12750.1	74550.1
TENNESSEE	12300.0	0.0	55800.0	350532.2	418632.2
WEST SOUTH CENTRAL:					
ARKANSAS	0.0	0.0	1300.0	0.0	1300.0
LOUISIANA	0.0	0.0	4200.0	0.0	4200.0
OKLAHOMA	0.0	0.0	2100.0	66.3	2166.3
TEXAS	100.0	0.0	17600.0	37830.0	55530.0
ROCKY MOUNTAIN:					
ARIZONA	0.0	0.0	1900.0	7873.0	9773.0
COLORADO	600.0	5800.0	44400.0	74291.1	125091.1
IDAHO	0.0	1400.0	2100.0	0.0	3500.0
MONTANA	400.0	3900.0	6600.0	14558.9	25458.9
NEVADA	0.0	0.0	0.0	34739.4	34739.4
NEW MEXICO	0.0	0.0	200.0	138920.9	139120.9
UTAH	500.0	4100.0	61500.0	13494.2	79594.2
WYOMING	100.0	1000.0	5700.0	88406.2	95206.2
FAR WEST:					
ALASKA	100.0	600.0	11300.0	6000.0	18000.0
CALIFORNIA	0.0	100.0	48400.0	0.0	48500.0
HAWAII	0.0	0.0	0.0	0.0	0.0
OREGON	100.0	700.0	2600.0	0.0	3400.0
WASHINGTON	100.0	900.0	2900.0	0.0	3900.0

Table 169

Expenditures On Coal In Thousand Dollars, 1972, By State

Use By Function

REGION AND STATE	RESIDENTIAL USE	COMMERCIAL USE	INDUSTRIAL USE	ELECTRIC UTILITY USE	TOTAL
NEW ENGLAND:					
CONNECTICUT	162.5	0.0	985.5	1174.3	2322.3
MAINE	155.3	0.0	158.6	16.4	330.3
MASSACHUSETTS	1315.9	0.0	1797.2	1107.4	4220.5
NEW HAMPSHIRE	395.5	0.0	274.8	13083.1	13753.4
RHODE ISLAND	71.2	0.0	73.3	7.6	152.1
VERMONT	310.9	0.0	59.7	661.2	1031.8
MID ATLANTIC:					
NEW JERSEY	5682.6	0.0	1809.3	17544.1	25036.0
NEW YORK	19189.3	0.0	111138.1	74928.9	205256.3
PENNSYLVANIA	83519.4	0.0	336842.8	330672.6	751034.8
EAST NORTH CENTRAL:					
ILLINOIS	52457.1	0.0	91185.4	244219.3	387861.8
INDIANA	28419.2	0.0	179862.0	170255.5	378536.7
MICHIGAN	24937.5	0.0	166558.6	211754.0	403250.1
OHIO	45275.5	0.0	263583.2	340131.2	648989.9
WISCONSIN	30151.6	0.0	44581.7	110966.7	185700.0
WEST NORTH CENTRAL:					
IOWA	2843.4	0.0	16258.2	44623.8	63725.4
KANSAS	567.9	0.0	1215.4	3195.4	4978.7
MINNESOTA	12376.7	0.0	19672.3	53652.7	85701.7
MISSOURI	3042.8	0.0	17423.6	87832.3	108298.7
NEBRASKA	1340.9	0.0	1941.5	11842.7	15125.1
NORTH DAKOTA	2289.9	0.0	1799.0	18305.4	22394.3
SOUTH DAKOTA	3087.4	0.0	1297.8	2682.0	7067.2
SOUTH ATLANTIC:					
DELAWARE	948.2	0.0	15542.3	11195.1	27685.6
DISTRICT OF COLUMBIA	156.0	0.0	1762.6	2556.5	4475.1
FLORIDA	939.1	0.0	2092.4	51411.0	54442.5
GEORGIA	1350.0	0.0	2906.6	109548.4	113805.0
MARYLAND	2847.6	0.0	53762.7	58112.2	114722.5
NORTH CAROLINA	13495.6	0.0	18045.9	192075.3	223616.8
SOUTH CAROLINA	7924.0	0.0	16416.9	61841.2	86182.1
VIRGINIA	14752.7	0.0	33788.5	50837.3	99378.5
WEST VIRGINIA	8891.1	0.0	94969.4	158838.5	262699.0
EAST SOUTH CENTRAL:					
ALABAMA	2245.3	0.0	89589.5	142237.3	234072.1
KENTUCKY	9951.9	0.0	29028.0	136406.5	175386.4
MISSISSIPPI	1927.4	0.0	22912.1	4621.9	29461.4
TENNESSEE	15216.3	0.0	20450.7	122335.7	158002.7
WEST SOUTH CENTRAL:					
ARKANSAS	0.0	0.0	290.7	0.0	290.7
LOUISIANA	0.0	0.0	939.1	0.0	939.1
OKLAHOMA	0.0	0.0	428.8	12.9	441.7
TEXAS	141.2	0.0	3935.4	8057.8	12134.4
ROCKY MOUNTAIN:					
ARIZONA	0.0	0.0	632.3	2495.8	3128.1
COLORADO	699.4	4257.2	13426.6	21395.8	39779.0
IDAHO	0.0	1243.6	518.1	0.0	1761.7
MONTANA	611.9	3464.4	1628.2	3421.3	9125.8
NEVADA	0.0	0.0	0.0	10352.3	10352.3
NEW MEXICO	0.0	0.0	31.8	21046.5	21078.3
UTAH	541.7	2850.7	18886.7	3947.1	26226.2
WYOMING	122.7	717.8	1190.7	17592.8	19624.0
FAR WEST:					
ALASKA	194.2	795.2	8009.4	4050.0	13048.8
CALIFORNIA	0.0	62.5	11180.4	0.0	11242.9
HAWAII	0.0	0.0	0.0	0.0	0.0
OREGON	94.3	394.0	475.0	0.0	963.3
WASHINGTON	94.3	506.5	529.8	0.0	1130.6

Table 170

Consumption In Billion BTU And Expenditures In Thousand Dollars For Coal, 1972, By Region

Use By Function

REGION	RESIDENTIAL USE	COMMER-CIAL USE	INDUSTRIAL USE	ELECTRIC UTILITY USE	TOTAL USE
Consumption In Billion BTU					
NEW ENGLAND	1700.00	0.00	5710.40	32408.00	39818.40
MID ATLANTIC	83950.00	0.00	1013296.00	1002549.90	2099795.90
EAST NORTH CENTRAL	138800.00	0.00	1873595.21	2782117.80	4794512.99
WEST NORTH CENTRAL	18250.00	0.00	158369.60	662733.81	839353.40
SOUTH ATLANTIC	39100.00	0.00	540203.21	1634288.62	2213591.82
EAST SOUTH CENTRAL	24400.00	0.00	441900.00	1228014.30	1694314.29
WEST SOUTH CENTRAL	100.00	0.00	25200.00	37896.30	63196.30
ROCKY MOUNTAIN	1600.00	16200.00	122400.00	372283.70	512483.70
FAR WEST	300.00	2300.00	65200.00	6000.00	73800.00
TOTAL	308200.00	18500.00	4245874.43	7758292.33	12330866.90

REGION	RESIDENTIAL USE	COMMER-CIAL USE	INDUSTRIAL USE	ELECTRIC UTILITY USE	TOTAL USE
Expenditures In Thousand Dollars					
NEW ENGLAND	2411.30	0.00	3349.10	16050.00	21810.40
MID ATLANTIC	108391.30	0.00	449790.19	423145.60	981327.09
EAST NORTH CENTRAL	181240.90	0.00	745770.91	1077326.70	2004338.50
WEST NORTH CENTRAL	25549.00	0.00	59607.80	222134.30	307291.10
SOUTH ATLANTIC	51304.30	0.00	239287.30	696415.50	987007.10
EAST SOUTH CENTRAL	29340.90	0.00	161980.30	405601.40	596922.60
WEST SOUTH CENTRAL	141.20	0.00	5594.00	8070.70	13805.90
ROCKY MOUNTAIN	1975.70	12533.70	36314.40	80251.60	131075.40
FAR WEST	382.80	1758.20	20194.60	4050.00	26385.60
TOTAL	400737.39	14291.90	1721888.61	2933045.92	5069963.71

Table 171

Fuel Equivalent Consumption Of Hydropower And Nuclear Power, In Billion BTU, 1972, By State

Use By Function And Energy Source

REGION AND STATE	HYDROELECTRIC POWER		NUCLEAR POWER	TOTAL HYDROELECTRIC & NUCLEAR POWER
	Industrial Use	Electric Utility Use		
NEW ENGLAND:				
CONNECTICUT	65.5	5282.6	73492.7	78840.7
MAINE	207.3	16717.1	510.3	17434.6
MASSACHUSETTS	92.1	7427.7	14175.0	21694.8
NEW HAMPSHIRE	128.2	10338.3	0.0	10466.5
RHODE ISLAND	0.7	56.7	0.0	57.4
VERMONT	102.3	8249.9	1597.0	9949.2
MID ATLANTIC:				
NEW JERSEY	0.0	0.0	41164.2	41164.2
NEW YORK	3227.4	260271.9	61094.3	324593.5
PENNSYLVANIA	179.6	14486.9	2731.1	17397.5
EAST NORTH CENTRAL:				
ILLINOIS	15.6	1256.9	123483.2	124755.6
INDIANA	45.1	3638.3	0.0	3683.4
MICHIGAN	192.8	15545.3	20081.2	35819.3
OHIO	1.1	85.1	0.0	86.1
WISCONSIN	246.9	19911.2	31128.3	51286.3
WEST NORTH CENTRAL:				
IOWA	116.4	9383.9	0.0	9500.2
KANSAS	0.5	37.8	0.0	38.3
MINNESOTA	100.7	8117.6	33623.1	41841.3
MISSOURI	71.7	5783.4	0.0	5855.1
NEBRASKA	160.8	12965.4	0.0	13126.2
NORTH DAKOTA	362.7	29247.8	0.0	29610.4
SOUTH DAKOTA	866.0	69835.5	0.0	70701.5
SOUTH ATLANTIC:				
DELAWARE	0.0	0.0	0.0	0.0
DISTRICT OF COLUMBIA	0.1	9.5	0.0	9.6
FLORIDA	27.9	2249.1	623.7	2900.7
GEORGIA	390.4	31487.4	0.0	31877.8
MARYLAND	267.5	21574.4	0.0	21841.9
NORTH CAROLINA	753.4	60754.1	0.0	61507.4
SOUTH CAROLINA	386.8	31194.5	45634.1	77215.3
VIRGINIA	159.6	12870.9	4233.6	17264.1
WEST VIRGINIA	62.6	5046.3	0.0	5108.9
EAST SOUTH CENTRAL:				
ALABAMA	1196.2	96465.6	0.0	97661.8
KENTUCKY	447.5	36089.6	0.0	36537.1
MISSISSIPPI	0.0	0.0	0.0	0.0
TENNESSEE	1304.6	105206.9	0.0	106511.4
WEST SOUTH CENTRAL:				
ARKANSAS	192.6	15535.8	0.0	15728.4
LOUISIANA	0.0	0.0	0.0	0.0
OKLAHOMA	169.6	13674.2	0.0	13843.7
TEXAS	97.3	7843.5	0.0	7940.8
ROCKY MOUNTAIN:				
ARIZONA	793.4	63986.0	0.0	64779.4
COLORADO	145.5	11736.9	0.0	11882.4
IDAHO	919.2	74125.8	0.0	75045.0
MONTANA	1106.6	89245.8	0.0	90352.4
NEVADA	183.2	14770.4	0.0	14953.5
NEW MEXICO	2.3	189.0	0.0	191.3
UTAH	143.0	11529.0	0.0	11672.0
WYOMING	137.3	11075.4	0.0	11212.7
FAR WEST:				
ALASKA	40.5	3269.7	0.0	3310.2
CALIFORNIA	3726.6	300528.9	29436.8	333692.2
HAWAII	2.6	207.9	0.0	210.5
OREGON	4273.4	344632.1	0.0	348905.5
WASHINGTON	8872.4	715516.2	27584.6	751973.2

Table 172

Fuel Equivalent Expenditures On Hydropower And Nuclear Power,
   In Thousand Dollars, 1972, By State

Use By Function And Energy Source

REGION AND STATE	HYDROELECTRIC POWER		NUCLEAR POWER	TOTAL HYDROELECTRIC AND NUCLEAR POWER
	Industrial Use	Electric Utility Use		
NEW ENGLAND:				
CONNECTICUT	41.0	3306.9	46006.4	49354.3
MAINE	71.5	5767.4	176.1	6015.0
MASSACHUSETTS	53.1	4278.4	8164.8	12496.2
NEW HAMPSHIRE	57.4	4631.6	0.0	4689.0
RHODE ISLAND	0.4	32.4	0.0	32.8
VERMONT	63.3	5106.7	988.6	6158.6
MID ATLANTIC:				
NEW JERSEY	0.0	0.0	26509.7	26509.7
NEW YORK	1865.4	150437.2	35312.5	187615.1
PENNSYLVANIA	81.4	6562.5	1237.2	7881.1
EAST NORTH CENTRAL:				
ILLINOIS	6.7	537.9	52850.8	53395.4
INDIANA	14.5	1167.9	0.0	1182.4
MICHIGAN	94.1	7586.1	9799.6	17479.8
OHIO	0.4	33.0	0.0	33.4
WISCONSIN	115.8	9338.3	14599.2	24053.3
WEST NORTH CENTRAL:				
IOWA	44.7	3603.4	0.0	3648.1
KANSAS	0.1	10.3	0.0	10.4
MINNESOTA	41.1	3312.0	13718.2	17071.3
MISSOURI	21.4	1723.5	0.0	1744.8
NEBRASKA	62.9	5069.5	0.0	5132.3
NORTH DAKOTA	97.2	7838.4	0.0	7935.6
SOUTH DAKOTA	371.5	29959.4	0.0	30330.9
SOUTH ATLANTIC:				
DELAWARE	0.0	0.0	0.0	0.0
DISTRICT OF COLUMBIA	0.1	5.1	0.0	5.2
FLORIDA	12.5	1007.6	279.4	1299.5
GEORGIA	175.3	14137.8	0.0	14313.2
MARYLAND	144.2	11628.6	0.0	11772.8
NORTH CAROLINA	344.3	27764.6	0.0	28108.9
SOUTH CAROLINA	189.5	15285.3	22360.7	37835.5
VIRGINIA	70.4	5676.1	1867.0	7613.5
WEST VIRGINIA	22.2	1786.4	0.0	1808.5
EAST SOUTH CENTRAL:				
ALABAMA	458.1	36946.3	0.0	37404.5
KENTUCKY	127.5	10285.5	0.0	10413.1
MISSISSIPPI	0.0	0.0	0.0	0.0
TENNESSEE	467.0	37664.1	0.0	38131.1
WEST SOUTH CENTRAL:				
ARKANSAS	78.0	6292.0	0.0	6370.0
LOUISIANA	0.0	0.0	0.0	0.0
OKLAHOMA	41.7	3363.8	0.0	3405.6
TEXAS	23.5	1898.1	0.0	1921.7
ROCKY MOUNTAIN:				
ARIZONA	252.3	20347.5	0.0	20599.8
COLORADO	43.4	3497.6	0.0	3541.0
IDAHO	167.3	13490.9	0.0	13658.2
MONTANA	289.9	23382.4	0.0	23672.3
NEVADA	66.1	5332.1	0.0	5398.2
NEW MEXICO	0.5	38.0	0.0	38.5
UTAH	60.9	4911.4	0.0	4972.3
WYOMING	25.0	2015.7	0.0	2040.7
FAR WEST:				
ALASKA	27.4	2207.0	0.0	2234.4
CALIFORNIA	1408.6	113599.9	11127.1	126135.7
HAWAII	1.4	111.0	0.0	112.4
OREGON	752.1	60655.2	0.0	61407.4
WASHINGTON	1561.5	125930.9	4854.9	132347.3

Table 173

Fuel Equivalent Consumption In Billion BTU And Expenditures
  In Thousand Dollars, Hydroelectric And Nuclear Power, 1972, By Region

Use By Function And Energy Source

REGION	HYDROELECTRIC POWER		NUCLEAR POWER	TOTAL HYDROELECTRIC AND NUCLEAR POWER
	Industrial Use	Electric Utility Use		
Consumption In Billion BTU				
NEW ENGLAND	596.10	48072.30	89775.00	138443.20
MID ATLANTIC	3407.00	274758.80	104989.60	383155.20
EAST NORTH CENTRAL	501.50	40436.80	174692.70	215630.70
WEST NORTH CENTRAL	1678.80	135371.40	33623.10	170673.00
SOUTH ATLANTIC	2048.30	165186.20	50491.40	217725.70
EAST SOUTH CENTRAL	2948.30	237762.10	0.00	240710.30
WEST SOUTH CENTRAL	459.50	37053.50	0.00	37512.90
ROCKY MOUNTAIN	3430.50	276658.30	0.00	280088.70
FAR WEST	16915.50	1364154.80	57021.40	1438091.60
TOTAL	31985.50	2579454.22	510593.21	3122031.32
Expenditures In Thousand Dollars				
NEW ENGLAND	286.70	23123.40	55335.90	78745.90
MID ATLANTIC	1946.80	156999.70	63059.40	222005.90
EAST NORTH CENTRAL	231.50	18663.20	77249.60	96144.30
WEST NORTH CENTRAL	638.90	51516.50	13718.20	65873.40
SOUTH ATLANTIC	958.50	77291.50	24507.10	102757.10
EAST SOUTH CENTRAL	1052.60	84895.90	0.00	85948.70
WEST SOUTH CENTRAL	143.20	11553.90	0.00	11697.30
ROCKY MOUNTAIN	905.40	73015.60	0.00	73921.00
FAR WEST	3751.00	302504.00	15982.00	322237.20
TOTAL	9914.60	799563.71	249852.20	1059330.81

Table 174

Consumption Of Coal And Fuel Equivalent Consumption Of Hydropower And
Nuclear Power, In Billion BTU, 1972, By State

Use By Function And Sector

REGION AND STATE	RESIDENTIAL USE (Household)	COMMERCIAL USE	INDUSTRIAL USE	ELECTRIC UTILITY USE	ALL BUSINESS USE	TOTAL
NEW ENGLAND:						
CONNECTICUT	100.0	0.0	1611.9	80710.0	82321.9	82421.9
MAINE	100.0	0.0	453.7	17254.2	17707.9	17807.9
MASSACHUSETTS	950.0	0.0	3247.3	23643.9	26891.2	27841.2
NEW HAMPSHIRE	300.0	0.0	674.6	37651.6	38326.2	38626.2
RHODE ISLAND	50.0	0.0	123.9	70.1	194.0	244.0
VERMONT	200.0	0.0	195.1	10925.5	11120.6	11320.6
MID ATLANTIC:						
NEW JERSEY	3500.0	0.0	2677.6	68427.8	71105.4	74605.4
NEW YORK	13350.0	0.0	208772.2	466859.3	675631.5	688981.5
PENNSYLVANIA	67100.0	0.0	805253.2	847011.2	1652264.4	1719364.4
EAST NORTH CENTRAL:						
ILLINOIS	39150.0	0.0	227070.8	763221.9	990292.7	1029442.7
INDIANA	23750.0	0.0	536946.7	537354.4	1074301.1	1098051.1
MICHIGAN	18750.0	0.0	355480.0	509879.7	865359.7	884109.7
OHIO	35650.0	0.0	664105.9	899903.2	1564009.1	1599659.1
WISCONSIN	21500.0	0.0	90493.3	286888.1	377381.4	398881.4
WEST NORTH CENTRAL:						
IOWA	2100.0	0.0	39616.4	123220.2	162836.6	164936.6
KANSAS	500.0	0.0	3600.5	9976.7	13577.2	14077.2
MINNESOTA	8450.0	0.0	45470.3	171650.4	217120.7	225570.7
MISSOURI	2600.0	0.0	54571.7	294231.1	348802.8	351402.8
NEBRASKA	1000.0	0.0	4460.8	40506.4	44967.2	45967.2
NORTH DAKOTA	1600.0	0.0	8462.7	115798.3	124261.0	125861.0
SOUTH DAKOTA	2000.0	0.0	3866.0	76345.2	80211.2	82211.2
SOUTH ATLANTIC:						
DELAWARE	650.0	0.0	27616.0	20886.4	48502.4	49152.4
DISTRICT OF COLUMBIA	100.0	0.0	2800.1	4273.9	7074.0	7174.0
FLORIDA	700.0	0.0	4727.9	124125.1	128853.0	129553.0
GEORGIA	1000.0	0.0	6590.4	276836.6	283427.0	284427.0
MARYLAND	1950.0	0.0	95608.3	129790.7	225399.0	227349.0
NORTH CAROLINA	10100.0	0.0	39553.4	494332.7	533886.1	543986.1
SOUTH CAROLINA	5800.0	0.0	33686.8	208545.8	242232.6	248032.6
VIRGINIA	11400.0	0.0	74306.0	134241.2	208547.2	219947.2
WEST VIRGINIA	7400.0	0.0	257362.6	456933.8	714296.4	721696.4
EAST SOUTH CENTRAL:						
ALABAMA	1800.0	0.0	228696.2	475765.2	704461.4	706261.4
KENTUCKY	8700.0	0.0	98847.5	521522.0	620369.5	629069.5
MISSISSIPPI	1600.0	0.0	60200.0	12750.1	72950.1	74550.1
TENNESSEE	12300.0	0.0	57104.6	455739.1	512843.7	525143.7
WEST SOUTH CENTRAL:						
ARKANSAS	0.0	0.0	1492.6	15535.8	17028.4	17028.4
LOUISIANA	0.0	0.0	4200.0	0.0	4200.0	4200.0
OKLAHOMA	0.0	0.0	2269.6	13740.5	16010.1	16010.1
TEXAS	100.0	0.0	17697.3	45673.5	63370.8	63470.8
ROCKY MOUNTAIN:						
ARIZONA	0.0	0.0	2693.4	71859.0	74552.4	74552.4
COLORADO	600.0	5800.0	44545.5	86028.0	136373.5	136973.5
IDAHO	0.0	1400.0	3019.2	74125.8	78545.0	78545.0
MONTANA	400.0	3900.0	7706.6	103804.7	115411.3	115811.3
NEVADA	0.0	0.0	183.2	49509.8	49693.0	49693.0
NEW MEXICO	0.0	0.0	202.3	139109.9	139312.2	139312.2
UTAH	500.0	4100.0	61643.0	25023.2	90766.2	91266.2
WYOMING	100.0	1000.0	5837.3	99481.6	106318.9	106418.9
FAR WEST:						
ALASKA	100.0	600.0	11340.5	9269.7	21210.2	21310.2
CALIFORNIA	0.0	100.0	52126.6	329965.7	382192.3	382192.3
HAWAII	0.0	0.0	2.6	207.9	210.5	210.5
OREGON	100.0	700.0	6873.4	344632.1	352205.5	352305.5
WASHINGTON	100.0	900.0	11772.4	743100.8	755773.2	755873.2

Table 175

Expenditures On Coal And Fuel Equivalent Expenditures On Hydropower And
Nuclear Power, In Thousand Dollars, 1972, By State

Use By Function And Sector

REGION AND STATE	RESIDENTIAL USE (Household)	COMMERCIAL USE	INDUSTRIAL USE	ELECTRIC UTILITY USE	ALL BUSINESS USE	TOTAL
NEW ENGLAND:						
CONNECTICUT	162.5	0.0	1026.5	50487.6	51514.1	51676.6
MAINE	155.3	0.0	230.1	5959.9	6190.0	6345.3
MASSACHUSETTS	1315.9	0.0	1850.3	13550.6	15400.9	16716.8
NEW HAMPSHIRE	395.5	0.0	332.2	17714.7	18046.9	18442.4
RHODE ISLAND	71.2	0.0	73.7	40.0	113.7	184.9
VERMONT	310.9	0.0	123.0	6756.5	6879.5	7190.4
MID ATLANTIC:						
NEW JERSEY	5682.6	0.0	1809.3	44053.8	45863.1	51545.7
NEW YORK	19189.3	0.0	113003.5	260678.6	373682.1	392871.4
PENNSYLVANIA	83519.4	0.0	336924.2	338472.3	675396.5	758915.9
EAST NORTH CENTRAL:						
ILLINOIS	52457.1	0.0	91192.1	297608.0	388800.1	441257.2
INDIANA	28419.2	0.0	179876.5	171423.4	351299.9	379719.1
MICHIGAN	24937.5	0.0	166652.7	229139.7	395792.4	420729.9
OHIO	45275.5	0.0	263583.6	340164.2	603747.8	649023.3
WISCONSIN	30151.6	0.0	44697.5	134904.2	179601.7	209753.3
WEST NORTH CENTRAL:						
IOWA	2843.4	0.0	16302.9	48227.2	64530.1	67373.5
KANSAS	567.9	0.0	1215.5	3205.7	4421.2	4989.1
MINNESOTA	12376.7	0.0	19713.4	70682.9	90396.3	102773.0
MISSOURI	3042.8	0.0	17445.0	89555.8	107000.8	110043.6
NEBRASKA	1340.9	0.0	2004.4	16912.2	18916.6	20257.5
NORTH DAKOTA	2289.9	0.0	1896.2	26143.8	28040.0	30329.9
SOUTH DAKOTA	3087.4	0.0	1669.3	32641.4	34310.7	37398.1
SOUTH ATLANTIC:						
DELAWARE	948.2	0.0	15542.3	11195.1	26737.4	27685.6
DISTRICT OF COLUMBIA	156.0	0.0	1762.7	2561.6	4324.3	4480.3
FLORIDA	939.1	0.0	2104.9	52698.0	54802.9	55742.0
GEORGIA	1350.0	0.0	3081.9	123686.2	126768.1	128118.1
MARYLAND	2847.6	0.0	53906.9	69740.8	123647.7	126495.3
NORTH CAROLINA	13495.6	0.0	18390.2	219839.9	238230.1	251725.7
SOUTH CAROLINA	7924.0	0.0	16606.4	99487.2	116093.6	124017.6
VIRGINIA	14752.7	0.0	33858.9	58380.4	92239.3	106992.0
WEST VIRGINIA	8891.1	0.0	94991.6	160624.9	255616.5	264507.6
EAST SOUTH CENTRAL:						
ALABAMA	2245.3	0.0	90047.6	179183.6	269231.2	271476.5
KENTUCKY	9951.9	0.0	29155.5	146692.0	175847.5	185799.4
MISSISSIPPI	1927.4	0.0	22912.1	4621.9	27534.0	29461.4
TENNESSEE	15216.3	0.0	20917.7	159999.8	180917.5	196133.8
WEST SOUTH CENTRAL:						
ARKANSAS	0.0	0.0	368.7	6292.0	6660.7	6660.7
LOUISIANA	0.0	0.0	939.1	0.0	939.1	939.1
OKLAHOMA	0.0	0.0	470.5	3376.7	3847.2	3847.2
TEXAS	141.2	0.0	3958.9	9955.9	13914.8	14056.0
ROCKY MOUNTAIN:						
ARIZONA	0.0	0.0	884.6	22843.3	23727.9	23727.9
COLORADO	699.4	4257.2	13470.0	24893.4	42620.6	43320.0
IDAHO	0.0	1243.6	685.4	13490.9	15419.9	15419.9
MONTANA	611.9	3464.4	1918.1	26803.7	32186.2	32798.1
NEVADA	0.0	0.0	66.1	15684.4	15750.5	15750.5
NEW MEXICO	0.0	0.0	32.3	21084.5	21116.8	21116.8
UTAH	541.7	2850.7	18947.6	8858.5	30656.8	31198.5
WYOMING	122.7	717.8	1215.7	19608.5	21542.0	21664.7
FAR WEST:						
ALASKA	194.2	795.2	8036.8	6257.0	15089.0	15283.2
CALIFORNIA	0.0	62.5	12589.0	124727.0	137378.5	137378.5
HAWAII	0.0	0.0	1.4	111.0	112.4	112.4
OREGON	94.3	394.0	1227.1	60655.2	62276.3	62370.6
WASHINGTON	94.3	506.5	2091.3	130785.8	133383.6	133477.9

Table 176

Consumption In Billion BTU And Expenditures In Thousand Dollars, Coal And Fuel Equivalent Values Of Hydropower and Nuclear Power, 1972, By Region

Use By Function And Sector

REGION	RESIDENTIAL USE (Household)	COMMERCIAL USE	INDUSTRIAL USE	ELECTRIC UTILITY USE	ALL BUSINESS USE	TOTAL
Consumption In Billion BTU						
NEW ENGLAND	1700.00	0.00	6306.50	170255.30	176561.80	178261.80
MID ATLANTIC	83950.00	0.00	1016703.00	1382298.30	2399001.29	2482951.28
EAST NORTH CENTRAL	138800.00	0.00	1874096.71	2997247.28	4871344.01	5010143.97
WEST NORTH CENTRAL	18250.00	0.00	160048.40	831728.29	991776.70	1010026.70
SOUTH ATLANTIC	39100.00	0.00	542251.50	1849966.20	2392217.72	2431317.72
EAST SOUTH CENTRAL	24000.00	0.00	444848.30	1465776.41	1910624.71	1935024.71
WEST SOUTH CENTRAL	100.00	0.00	25659.50	74949.80	100609.30	100709.30
ROCKY MOUNTAIN	1600.00	16200.00	125830.50	648942.01	790972.51	792572.51
FAR WEST	300.00	2300.00	82115.50	1427176.20	1511591.71	1511891.71
TOTAL	308200.00	18500.00	4277859.93	10848339.70	15144699.80	15452899.80
Expenditures In Thousand Dollars						
NEW ENGLAND	2411.30	0.00	3635.80	94509.30	98145.10	100556.40
MID ATLANTIC	108391.30	0.00	451737.00	643204.70	1094941.70	1203333.00
EAST NORTH CENTRAL	181240.90	0.00	746002.40	1173239.50	1919241.90	2100482.81
WEST NORTH CENTRAL	25549.00	0.00	60246.70	287369.00	347615.70	373164.70
SOUTH ATLANTIC	51304.30	0.00	240024.80	798214.10	1038459.90	1089764.20
EAST SOUTH CENTRAL	29340.90	0.00	163032.90	490497.30	653530.20	682871.10
WEST SOUTH CENTRAL	141.20	0.00	5737.20	19624.60	25361.80	25503.00
ROCKY MOUNTAIN	1975.70	12553.70	37219.80	153267.20	203020.70	204996.40
FAR WEST	382.80	1758.20	23945.60	322536.00	348239.80	348622.60
TOTAL	400737.39	14291.90	1731803.21	3982461.77	5728856.74	6129294.19

Table 177

Consumption Of Coal And Fuel Equivalent Consumption Of Hydropower And
Nuclear Power, In Million BTU Per Capita, 1972, By State

Use By Energy Source

REGION AND STATE	COAL USE	HYDRO-ELECTRIC POWER USE	NUCLEAR POWER USE	TOTAL USE
NEW ENGLAND:				
CONNECTICUT	1.163	1.736	23.861	26.760
MAINE	0.364	16.496	0.497	17.357
MASSACHUSETTS	1.060	1.297	2.446	4.804
NEW HAMPSHIRE	36.382	13.523	0.000	49.905
RHODE ISLAND	0.193	0.059	0.000	0.252
VERMONT	2.981	18.157	3.472	24.610
MID ATLANTIC:				
NEW JERSEY	4.550	0.000	5.601	10.152
NEW YORK	19.839	14.346	3.326	37.512
PENNSYLVANIA	142.962	1.232	0.229	144.424
EAST NORTH CENTRAL:				
ILLINOIS	80.460	0.113	10.982	91.555
INDIANA	207.031	0.697	0.000	207.728
MICHIGAN	94.119	1.746	2.228	98.093
OHIO	149.186	0.008	0.000	149.194
WISCONSIN	76.800	4.454	6.878	88.131
WEST NORTH CENTRAL:				
IOWA	53.896	3.294	0.000	57.190
KANSAS	6.190	0.017	0.000	6.207
MINNESOTA	47.390	2.120	8.672	58.182
MISSOURI	72.793	1.233	0.000	74.026
NEBRASKA	21.493	8.590	0.000	30.083
NORTH DAKOTA	151.815	46.704	0.000	198.519
SOUTH DAKOTA	16.926	103.973	0.000	120.899
SOUTH ATLANTIC:				
DELAWARE	86.081	0.000	0.000	86.081
DISTRICT OF COLUMBIA	9.527	0.013	0.000	9.540
FLORIDA	17.239	0.310	0.085	17.633
GEORGIA	53.359	6.735	0.000	60.094
MARYLAND	50.768	5.396	0.000	56.163
NORTH CAROLINA	92.411	11.781	0.000	104.192
SOUTH CAROLINA	63.548	11.749	16.977	92.274
VIRGINIA	42.536	2.735	0.888	46.159
WEST VIRGINIA	399.213	2.846	0.000	402.059
EAST SOUTH CENTRAL:				
ALABAMA	172.849	27.737	0.000	200.585
KENTUCKY	179.229	11.052	0.000	190.281
MISSISSIPPI	33.045	0.000	0.000	33.045
TENNESSEE	102.808	26.157	0.000	128.965
WEST SOUTH CENTRAL:				
ARKANSAS	0.647	7.833	0.000	8.480
LOUISIANA	1.124	0.000	0.000	1.124
OKLAHOMA	0.823	5.258	0.000	6.081
TEXAS	4.785	0.684	0.000	5.470
ROCKY MOUNTAIN:				
ARIZONA	4.979	33.000	0.000	37.979
COLORADO	52.915	5.026	0.000	57.941
IDAHO	4.636	99.397	0.000	104.033
MONTANA	35.557	126.191	0.000	161.748
NEVADA	65.177	28.056	0.000	93.233
NEW MEXICO	129.295	0.178	0.000	129.472
UTAH	70.625	10.357	0.000	80.982
WYOMING	275.162	32.407	0.000	307.569
FAR WEST:				
ALASKA	55.385	10.185	0.000	65.570
CALIFORNIA	2.376	14.906	1.442	18.725
HAWAII	0.000	0.258	0.000	0.258
OREGON	1.556	159.682	0.000	161.238
WASHINGTON	1.141	211.933	8.070	221.145

Table 178

Expenditures On Coal And Fuel Equivalent Expenditures On Hydropower And
Nuclear Power, In Dollars Per Capita, 1972, By State

Use By Energy Source

REGION AND STATE	COAL USE	HYDRO-ELECTRIC POWER USE	NUCLEAR POWER USE	TOTAL USE
NEW ENGLAND:				
CONNECTICUT	0.754	1.087	14.937	16.778
MAINE	0.322	5.691	0.172	6.185
MASSACHUSETTS	0.728	0.747	1.409	2.884
NEW HAMPSHIRE	17.769	6.058	0.000	23.827
RHODE ISLAND	0.157	0.034	0.000	0.191
VERMONT	2.243	11.239	2.149	15.631
MID ATLANTIC:				
NEW JERSEY	3.407	0.000	3.607	7.014
NEW YORK	11.175	8.292	1.923	21.390
PENNSYLVANIA	63.086	0.558	0.104	63.748
EAST NORTH CENTRAL:				
ILLINOIS	34.495	0.048	4.700	39.244
INDIANA	71.611	0.224	0.000	71.835
MICHIGAN	44.741	0.852	1.087	46.680
OHIO	60.529	0.003	0.000	60.532
WISCONSIN	41.030	2.089	3.226	46.344
WEST NORTH CENTRAL:				
IOWA	22.096	1.265	0.000	23.361
KANSAS	2.195	0.005	0.000	2.200
MINNESOTA	22.105	0.865	3.538	26.508
MISSOURI	22.814	0.368	0.000	23.182
NEBRASKA	9.899	3.359	0.000	13.258
NORTH DAKOTA	35.322	12.517	0.000	47.839
SOUTH DAKOTA	10.393	44.604	0.000	54.997
SOUTH ATLANTIC:				
DELAWARE	48.486	0.000	0.000	48.486
DISTRICT OF COLUMBIA	5.951	0.007	0.000	5.958
FLORIDA	7.410	0.139	0.038	7.587
GEORGIA	24.045	3.024	0.000	27.069
MARYLAND	28.341	2.908	0.000	31.249
NORTH CAROLINA	42.830	5.384	0.000	48.214
SOUTH CAROLINA	32.062	5.757	8.319	46.138
VIRGINIA	20.856	1.206	0.392	22.454
WEST VIRGINIA	146.350	1.008	0.000	147.358
EAST SOUTH CENTRAL:				
ALABAMA	66.479	10.623	0.000	77.102
KENTUCKY	53.051	3.150	0.000	56.201
MISSISSIPPI	13.059	0.000	0.000	13.059
TENNESSEE	38.802	9.364	0.000	48.166
WEST SOUTH CENTRAL:				
ARKANSAS	0.145	3.172	0.000	3.317
LOUISIANA	0.251	0.000	0.000	0.251
OKLAHOMA	0.168	1.293	0.000	1.461
TEXAS	1.046	0.166	0.000	1.211
ROCKY MOUNTAIN:				
ARIZONA	1.594	10.494	0.000	12.088
COLORADO	16.827	1.498	0.000	18.325
IDAHO	2.333	18.090	0.000	20.424
MONTANA	12.746	33.062	0.000	45.807
NEVADA	19.423	10.128	0.000	29.551
NEW MEXICO	19.589	0.036	0.000	19.625
UTAH	23.271	4.412	0.000	27.683
WYOMING	56.717	5.898	0.000	62.615
FAR WEST:				
ALASKA	40.150	6.875	0.000	47.025
CALIFORNIA	0.551	5.635	0.545	6.731
HAWAII	0.000	0.138	0.000	0.138
OREGON	0.441	28.104	0.000	28.545
WASHINGTON	0.331	37.300	1.420	39.051

Table 179

Per Capita Use Of Coal And Fuel Equivalent Use Of Hydropower And Nuclear Power In
  Million BTU Per Capita, And In Dollars Per Capita, 1972, By Region

Use By Energy Source

REGION	COAL USE	HYDRO-ELECTRIC POWER USE	NUCLEAR POWER USE	TOTAL USE
Consumption In Million BTU Per Capita				
NEW ENGLAND	3.289	4.021	7.416	14.726
MID ATLANTIC	55.814	7.394	2.791	65.999
EAST NORTH CENTRAL	117.539	1.004	4.283	122.825
WEST NORTH CENTRAL	50.509	8.247	2.023	60.779
SOUTH ATLANTIC	69.348	5.239	1.582	76.169
EAST SOUTH CENTRAL	128.796	18.298	0.000	147.094
WEST SOUTH CENTRAL	3.163	1.877	0.000	5.040
ROCKY MOUNTAIN	57.712	31.542	0.000	89.254
FAR WEST	2.718	50.859	2.100	55.676
UNITED STATES	59.218	12.541	2.452	74.211
Expenditures In Dollars Per Capita				
NEW ENGLAND	1.802	1.934	4.571	8.307
MID ATLANTIC	26.085	4.225	1.676	31.986
EAST NORTH CENTRAL	49.137	0.463	1.894	51.494
WEST NORTH CENTRAL	18.491	3.138	0.826	22.455
SOUTH ATLANTIC	30.921	2.451	0.768	34.140
EAST SOUTH CENTRAL	45.376	6.534	0.000	51.910
WEST SOUTH CENTRAL	0.691	0.585	0.000	1.276
ROCKY MOUNTAIN	14.761	8.324	0.000	23.085
FAR WEST	0.972	11.278	0.589	12.838
UNITED STATES	24.348	3.887	1.200	29.435

Table 180

Consumption Of Coal And Fuel Equivalent Consumption Of Hydropower And
    Nuclear Power, In Million BTU Per Capita, 1972, By State

Use By Function

REGION AND STATE	RESIDENTIAL USE	COMMERCIAL USE	INDUSTRIAL USE	ELECTRIC UTILITY USE	TOTAL USE
NEW ENGLAND:					
CONNECTICUT	0.032	0.000	0.523	26.205	26.760
MAINE	0.097	0.000	0.442	16.817	17.357
MASSACHUSETTS	0.164	0.000	0.560	4.079	4.804
NEW HAMPSHIRE	0.388	0.000	0.872	48.645	49.905
RHODE ISLAND	0.052	0.000	0.128	0.072	0.252
VERMONT	0.435	0.000	0.424	23.751	24.610
MID ATLANTIC:					
NEW JERSEY	0.476	0.000	0.364	9.311	10.152
NEW YORK	0.727	0.000	11.367	25.418	37.512
PENNSYLVANIA	5.636	0.000	67.640	71.148	144.424
EAST NORTH CENTRAL:					
ILLINOIS	3.482	0.000	20.195	67.878	91.555
INDIANA	4.493	0.000	101.579	101.656	207.728
MICHIGAN	2.080	0.000	39.441	56.572	98.093
OHIO	3.325	0.000	61.939	83.931	149.194
WISCONSIN	4.750	0.000	19.994	63.387	88.131
WEST NORTH CENTRAL:					
IOWA	0.728	0.000	13.737	42.725	57.190
KANSAS	0.220	0.000	1.588	4.399	6.207
MINNESOTA	2.180	0.000	11.728	44.274	58.182
MISSOURI	0.548	0.000	11.496	61.983	74.026
NEBRASKA	0.654	0.000	2.919	26.509	30.083
NORTH DAKOTA	2.524	0.000	13.348	182.647	198.519
SOUTH DAKOTA	2.941	0.000	5.685	112.272	120.899
SOUTH ATLANTIC:					
DELAWARE	1.138	0.000	48.364	36.579	86.081
DISTRICT OF COLUMBIA	0.133	0.000	3.724	5.683	9.540
FLORIDA	0.095	0.000	0.644	16.895	17.633
GEORGIA	0.211	0.000	1.392	58.491	60.094
MARYLAND	0.482	0.000	23.619	32.063	56.163
NORTH CAROLINA	1.934	0.000	7.576	94.682	104.192
SOUTH CAROLINA	2.158	0.000	12.532	77.584	92.274
VIRGINIA	2.392	0.000	15.594	28.172	46.159
WEST VIRGINIA	4.123	0.000	143.377	254.559	402.059
EAST SOUTH CENTRAL:					
ALABAMA	0.511	0.000	64.952	135.122	200.585
KENTUCKY	2.632	0.000	29.899	157.750	190.281
MISSISSIPPI	0.709	0.000	26.684	5.652	33.045
TENNESSEE	3.021	0.000	14.024	111.920	128.965
WEST SOUTH CENTRAL:					
ARKANSAS	0.000	0.000	0.743	7.737	8.480
LOUISIANA	0.000	0.000	1.124	0.000	1.124
OKLAHOMA	0.000	0.000	0.862	5.219	6.081
TEXAS	0.009	0.000	1.525	3.936	5.470
ROCKY MOUNTAIN:					
ARIZONA	0.000	0.000	1.372	36.607	37.979
COLORADO	0.254	2.453	18.843	36.391	57.941
IDAHO	0.000	1.854	3.999	98.180	104.033
MONTANA	0.559	5.447	10.763	144.979	161.748
NEVADA	0.000	0.000	0.344	92.889	93.233
NEW MEXICO	0.000	0.000	0.188	129.284	129.472
UTAH	0.444	3.638	54.697	22.203	80.982
WYOMING	0.289	2.890	16.871	287.519	307.569
FAR WEST:					
ALASKA	0.308	1.846	34.894	28.522	65.570
CALIFORNIA	0.000	0.005	2.554	16.166	18.725
HAWAII	0.000	0.000	0.003	0.255	0.258
OREGON	0.046	0.320	3.146	157.726	161.238
WASHINGTON	0.029	0.263	3.444	217.408	221.145

Table 181

Expenditures On Coal and Fuel Equivalent Expenditures On Hydropower And Nuclear Power,
  In Dollars Per Capita, 1972, By State

Use By Function

REGION AND STATE	RESIDENTIAL USE	COMMERCIAL USE	INDUSTRIAL USE	ELECTRIC UTILITY USE	TOTAL USE
NEW ENGLAND:					
CONNECTICUT	0.053	0.000	0.333	16.392	16.778
MAINE	0.151	0.000	0.224	5.809	6.185
MASSACHUSETTS	0.227	0.000	0.319	2.338	2.884
NEW HAMPSHIRE	0.511	0.000	0.429	22.887	23.827
RHODE ISLAND	0.073	0.000	0.076	0.041	0.191
VERMONT	0.676	0.000	0.267	14.688	15.631
MID ATLANTIC:					
NEW JERSEY	0.773	0.000	0.246	5.995	7.014
NEW YORK	1.045	0.000	6.153	14.193	21.390
PENNSYLVANIA	7.015	0.000	28.301	28.431	63.748
EAST NORTH CENTRAL:					
ILLINOIS	4.665	0.000	8.110	26.468	39.244
INDIANA	5.376	0.000	34.029	32.430	71.835
MICHIGAN	2.767	0.000	18.490	25.423	46.680
OHIO	4.223	0.000	24.583	31.726	60.532
WISCONSIN	6.662	0.000	9.876	29.806	46.344
WEST NORTH CENTRAL:					
IOWA	0.986	0.000	5.653	16.722	23.361
KANSAS	0.250	0.000	0.536	1.413	2.200
MINNESOTA	3.192	0.000	5.085	18.231	26.508
MISSOURI	0.641	0.000	3.675	18.866	23.182
NEBRASKA	0.878	0.000	1.312	11.068	13.258
NORTH DAKOTA	3.612	0.000	2.991	41.236	47.839
SOUTH DAKOTA	4.540	0.000	2.455	48.002	54.997
SOUTH ATLANTIC:					
DELAWARE	1.661	0.000	27.219	19.606	48.486
DISTRICT OF COLUMBIA	0.207	0.000	2.344	3.406	5.958
FLORIDA	0.128	0.000	0.286	7.173	7.587
GEORGIA	0.285	0.000	0.651	26.133	27.069
MARYLAND	0.703	0.000	13.317	17.228	31.249
NORTH CAROLINA	2.585	0.000	3.522	42.107	48.214
SOUTH CAROLINA	2.948	0.000	6.178	37.012	46.138
VIRGINIA	3.096	0.000	7.106	12.252	22.454
WEST VIRGINIA	4.953	0.000	52.920	89.485	147.358
EAST SOUTH CENTRAL:					
ALABAMA	0.638	0.000	25.574	50.890	77.102
KENTUCKY	3.010	0.000	8.819	44.371	56.201
MISSISSIPPI	0.854	0.000	10.156	2.049	13.059
TENNESSEE	3.737	0.000	5.137	39.293	48.166
WEST SOUTH CENTRAL:					
ARKANSAS	0.000	0.000	0.184	3.133	3.317
LOUISIANA	0.000	0.000	0.251	0.000	0.251
OKLAHOMA	0.000	0.000	0.179	1.282	1.461
TEXAS	0.012	0.000	0.341	0.858	1.211
ROCKY MOUNTAIN:					
ARIZONA	0.000	0.000	0.451	11.637	12.088
COLORADO	0.296	1.801	5.698	10.530	18.325
IDAHO	0.000	1.647	0.908	17.869	20.424
MONTANA	0.855	4.839	2.679	37.435	45.807
NEVADA	0.000	0.000	0.124	29.427	29.551
NEW MEXICO	0.000	0.000	0.030	19.595	19.625
UTAH	0.481	2.529	16.812	7.860	27.683
WYOMING	0.355	2.075	3.514	56.672	62.615
FAR WEST:					
ALASKA	0.598	2.447	24.729	19.252	47.025
CALIFORNIA	0.000	0.003	0.617	6.111	6.731
HAWAII	0.000	0.000	0.002	0.136	0.138
OREGON	0.043	0.180	0.562	27.760	28.545
WASHINGTON	0.028	0.148	0.612	38.264	39.051

Table 182

Per Capita Use Of Coal And Fuel Equivalent Use Of Hydropower And Nuclear Power In
Million BTU Per Capita, And In Dollars Per Capita, 1972, By Region

Use By Function

REGION	RESIDENTIAL USE	COMMERCIAL USE	INDUSTRIAL USE	ELECTRIC UTILITY USE	TOTAL USE
Consumption In Million BTU Per Capita					
NEW ENGLAND	0.140	0.000	0.521	14.065	14.726
MID ATLANTIC	2.231	0.000	27.025	36.743	65.999
EAST NORTH CENTRAL	3.403	0.000	45.944	73.478	122.825
WEST NORTH CENTRAL	1.098	0.000	9.631	50.050	60.779
SOUTH ATLANTIC	1.225	0.000	16.988	57.956	76.169
EAST SOUTH CENTRAL	1.855	0.000	33.816	111.424	147.094
WEST SOUTH CENTRAL	0.005	0.000	1.284	3.751	5.040
ROCKY MOUNTAIN	0.180	1.824	14.170	73.079	89.254
FAR WEST	0.011	0.085	3.024	52.557	55.676
UNITED STATES	1.480	0.089	20.544	52.098	74.211
Expenditures In Dollars Per Capita					
NEW ENGLAND	0.199	0.000	0.300	7.807	8.307
MID ATLANTIC	2.881	0.000	12.008	17.097	31.986
EAST NORTH CENTRAL	4.443	0.000	18.288	28.762	51.494
WEST NORTH CENTRAL	1.537	0.000	3.625	17.293	22.455
SOUTH ATLANTIC	1.607	0.000	7.526	25.007	34.140
EAST SOUTH CENTRAL	2.230	0.000	12.393	37.286	51.910
WEST SOUTH CENTRAL	0.007	0.000	0.287	0.982	1.276
ROCKY MOUNTAIN	0.222	1.411	4.191	17.260	23.085
FAR WEST	0.014	0.065	0.882	11.878	12.838
UNITED STATES	1.925	0.069	8.317	19.125	29.435

Table 183

Per Capita Consumption Of Coal and Fuel Equivalent Consumption Of Hydroelectric Power And
  Nuclear Power In Index Number Terms, U.S. BTU Per Capita = 100, 1972, By State

Use By Energy Source

REGION AND STATE	COAL USE	HYDRO-ELECTRIC POWER USE	NUCLEAR POWER USE	TOTAL USE
NEW ENGLAND:				
CONNECTICUT	1.96	13.84	973.12	36.06
MAINE	0.61	131.54	20.27	23.39
MASSACHUSETTS	1.79	10.34	99.76	6.47
NEW HAMPSHIRE	61.44	107.83	0.00	67.25
RHODE ISLAND	0.33	0.47	0.00	0.34
VERMONT	5.03	144.78	141.60	33.16
MID ATLANTIC:				
NEW JERSEY	7.68	0.00	228.43	13.68
NEW YORK	33.50	114.39	135.64	50.55
PENNSYLVANIA	241.42	9.82	9.34	194.61
EAST NORTH CENTRAL:				
ILLINOIS	135.87	0.90	447.88	123.37
INDIANA	349.61	5.56	0.00	279.92
MICHIGAN	158.94	13.92	90.86	132.18
OHIO	251.93	0.06	0.00	201.04
WISCONSIN	129.69	35.52	280.51	118.76
WEST NORTH CENTRAL:				
IOWA	91.01	26.27	0.00	77.06
KANSAS	10.45	0.14	0.00	8.36
MINNESOTA	80.03	16.90	353.67	78.40
MISSOURI	122.92	9.83	0.00	99.75
NEBRASKA	36.29	68.50	0.00	40.54
NORTH DAKOTA	256.37	372.41	0.00	267.51
SOUTH DAKOTA	28.58	829.06	0.00	162.91
SOUTH ATLANTIC:				
DELAWARE	145.36	0.00	0.00	115.99
DISTRICT OF COLUMBIA	16.09	0.10	0.00	12.86
FLORIDA	29.11	2.47	3.47	23.76
GEORGIA	90.11	53.70	0.00	80.98
MARYLAND	85.73	43.03	0.00	75.68
NORTH CAROLINA	156.05	93.94	0.00	140.40
SOUTH CAROLINA	107.31	93.68	692.37	124.34
VIRGINIA	71.83	21.81	36.22	62.20
WEST VIRGINIA	674.14	22.69	0.00	541.78
EAST SOUTH CENTRAL:				
ALABAMA	291.89	221.17	0.00	270.29
KENTUCKY	302.66	88.13	0.00	256.41
MISSISSIPPI	55.80	0.00	0.00	44.53
TENNESSEE	173.61	208.57	0.00	173.78
WEST SOUTH CENTRAL:				
ARKANSAS	1.09	62.46	0.00	11.43
LOUISIANA	1.90	0.00	0.00	1.51
OKLAHOMA	1.39	41.93	0.00	8.19
TEXAS	8.08	5.45	0.00	7.37
ROCKY MOUNTAIN:				
ARIZONA	8.41	263.14	0.00	51.18
COLORADO	89.36	40.08	0.00	78.08
IDAHO	7.83	792.58	0.00	140.19
MONTANA	60.04	1006.23	0.00	217.96
NEVADA	110.06	223.71	0.00	125.63
NEW MEXICO	218.34	1.42	0.00	174.46
UTAH	119.26	82.59	0.00	109.12
WYOMING	464.66	258.41	0.00	414.45
FAR WEST:				
ALASKA	93.53	81.21	0.00	88.36
CALIFORNIA	4.01	118.86	58.81	25.23
HAWAII	0.00	2.06	0.00	0.35
OREGON	2.63	1273.28	0.00	217.27
WASHINGTON	1.93	1689.92	329.12	297.99

Table 184

Per Capita Expenditures On Coal And Fuel Equivalent Expenditures On Hydroelectric Power And
    Nuclear Power In Index Number Terms, U.S. Spending Per Capita = 100, 1972, By State

Use By Energy Source

REGION AND STATE	COAL USE	HYDRO-ELECTRIC POWER USE	NUCLEAR POWER USE	TOTAL USE
NEW ENGLAND:				
CONNECTICUT	3.10	27.97	1244.75	57.00
MAINE	1.32	146.41	14.33	21.01
MASSACHUSETTS	2.99	19.22	117.42	9.80
NEW HAMPSHIRE	72.98	155.85	0.00	80.95
RHODE ISLAND	0.64	0.87	0.00	0.65
VERMONT	9.21	289.14	179.08	53.10
MID ATLANTIC:				
NEW JERSEY	13.99	0.00	300.58	23.83
NEW YORK	45.90	213.33	160.25	72.67
PENNSYLVANIA	259.10	14.36	8.67	216.57
EAST NORTH CENTRAL:				
ILLINOIS	141.67	1.23	391.67	133.32
INDIANA	294.11	5.76	0.00	244.05
MICHIGAN	183.76	21.92	90.58	158.59
OHIO	248.60	0.08	0.00	205.65
WISCONSIN	168.51	53.74	268.83	157.45
WEST NORTH CENTRAL:				
IOWA	90.75	32.54	0.00	79.36
KANSAS	9.02	0.13	0.00	7.47
MINNESOTA	90.79	22.25	294.83	90.06
MISSOURI	93.70	9.47	0.00	78.76
NEBRASKA	40.66	86.42	0.00	45.04
NORTH DAKOTA	145.07	322.02	0.00	162.52
SOUTH DAKOTA	42.69	1147.52	0.00	186.84
SOUTH ATLANTIC:				
DELAWARE	199.14	0.00	0.00	164.72
DISTRICT OF COLUMBIA	24.44	0.18	0.00	20.24
FLORIDA	30.43	3.58	3.17	25.78
GEORGIA	98.76	77.80	0.00	91.96
MARYLAND	116.40	74.81	0.00	106.16
NORTH CAROLINA	175.91	138.51	0.00	163.80
SOUTH CAROLINA	131.68	148.11	693.25	156.75
VIRGINIA	85.66	31.03	32.67	76.28
WEST VIRGINIA	601.08	25.93	0.00	500.62
EAST SOUTH CENTRAL:				
ALABAMA	273.04	273.30	0.00	261.94
KENTUCKY	217.89	81.04	0.00	190.93
MISSISSIPPI	53.63	0.00	0.00	44.37
TENNESSEE	159.36	240.91	0.00	163.64
WEST SOUTH CENTRAL:				
ARKANSAS	0.60	81.61	0.00	11.27
LOUISIANA	1.03	0.00	0.00	0.85
OKLAHOMA	0.69	33.26	0.00	4.96
TEXAS	4.30	4.27	0.00	4.11
ROCKY MOUNTAIN:				
ARIZONA	6.55	269.98	0.00	41.07
COLORADO	69.11	38.54	0.00	62.26
IDAHO	9.58	465.40	0.00	69.39
MONTANA	52.35	850.58	0.00	155.62
NEVADA	79.77	260.56	0.00	100.39
NEW MEXICO	80.45	0.93	0.00	66.67
UTAH	95.58	113.51	0.00	94.05
WYOMING	232.94	151.74	0.00	212.72
FAR WEST:				
ALASKA	164.90	176.87	0.00	159.76
CALIFORNIA	2.26	144.97	45.42	22.87
HAWAII	0.00	3.55	0.00	0.47
OREGON	1.81	723.03	0.00	96.98
WASHINGTON	1.36	959.61	118.33	132.67

Table 185

Per Capita Use Of Coal And Fuel Equivalent Use Of Hydropower And Nuclear Power
    In Index Number Terms, U.S. = 100, Based On Consumption In BTU And
    Expenditures In Dollars, 1972, By Region

Use By Energy Source

REGION	COAL USE	HYDRO-ELECTRIC POWER USE	NUCLEAR POWER USE	TOTAL USE

Index Of Per Capita Consumption, U.S. = 100

REGION	COAL USE	HYDRO-ELECTRIC POWER USE	NUCLEAR POWER USE	TOTAL USE
NEW ENGLAND	5.55	32.06	302.45	19.84
MID ATLANTIC	94.25	58.96	113.83	88.93
EAST NORTH CENTRAL	198.49	8.01	174.67	165.51
WEST NORTH CENTRAL	85.29	65.76	82.50	81.90
SOUTH ATLANTIC	117.11	41.77	64.52	102.64
EAST SOUTH CENTRAL	217.49	145.91	0.00	198.21
WEST SOUTH CENTRAL	5.34	14.97	0.00	6.79
ROCKY MOUNTAIN	97.46	251.51	0.00	120.27
FAR WEST	4.59	405.54	85.64	75.02
UNITED STATES	100.00	100.00	100.00	100.00

Index Of Per Capita Expenditures, U.S. = 100

REGION	COAL USE	HYDRO-ELECTRIC POWER USE	NUCLEAR POWER USE	TOTAL USE
NEW ENGLAND	7.40	49.76	380.92	28.22
MID ATLANTIC	107.13	108.70	139.67	108.67
EAST NORTH CENTRAL	201.81	11.91	157.83	174.94
WEST NORTH CENTRAL	75.94	80.73	68.83	76.29
SOUTH ATLANTIC	127.00	63.06	64.00	115.98
EAST SOUTH CENTRAL	186.36	168.10	0.00	176.35
WEST SOUTH CENTRAL	2.84	15.05	0.00	4.33
ROCKY MOUNTAIN	60.63	214.15	0.00	78.43
FAR WEST	3.99	290.15	49.08	43.61
UNITED STATES	100.00	100.00	100.00	100.00

Table 186

Per Capita Consumption Of Coal And Fuel Equivalent Consumption Of Hydroelectric Power And
   Nuclear Power In Index Number Terms, U.S. BTU Per Capita = 100, 1972, By State

Use By Function

REGION AND STATE	RESIDENTIAL USE	COMMERCIAL USE	INDUSTRIAL USE	ELECTRIC UTILITY USE	TOTAL USE
NEW ENGLAND:					
CONNECTICUT	2.16	0.00	2.55	50.30	36.06
MAINE	6.55	0.00	2.15	32.28	23.39
MASSACHUSETTS	11.08	0.00	2.73	7.83	6.47
NEW HAMPSHIRE	26.22	0.00	4.24	93.37	67.25
RHODE ISLAND	3.51	0.00	0.62	0.14	0.34
VERMONT	29.39	0.00	2.06	45.59	33.16
MID ATLANTIC:					
NEW JERSEY	32.16	0.00	1.77	17.87	13.68
NEW YORK	49.12	0.00	55.33	48.79	50.55
PENNSYLVANIA	380.81	0.00	329.24	136.57	194.61
EAST NORTH CENTRAL:					
ILLINOIS	235.27	0.00	98.30	130.29	123.37
INDIANA	303.58	0.00	494.45	195.12	279.92
MICHIGAN	140.54	0.00	191.98	108.59	132.18
OHIO	224.66	0.00	301.49	161.10	201.04
WISCONSIN	320.95	0.00	97.32	121.67	118.76
WEST NORTH CENTRAL:					
IOWA	49.19	0.00	66.87	82.01	77.06
KANSAS	14.86	0.00	7.73	8.44	8.36
MINNESOTA	147.30	0.00	57.09	84.98	78.40
MISSOURI	37.03	0.00	55.96	118.97	99.75
NEBRASKA	44.19	0.00	14.21	50.88	40.54
NORTH DAKOTA	170.54	0.00	64.97	350.58	267.51
SOUTH DAKOTA	198.72	0.00	27.67	215.50	162.91
SOUTH ATLANTIC:					
DELAWARE	76.89	0.00	235.42	70.21	115.99
DISTRICT OF COLUMBIA	8.99	0.00	18.13	10.91	12.86
FLORIDA	6.42	0.00	3.13	32.43	23.76
GEORGIA	14.26	0.00	6.78	112.27	80.98
MARYLAND	32.57	0.00	114.97	61.54	75.68
NORTH CAROLINA	130.68	0.00	36.88	181.74	140.40
SOUTH CAROLINA	145.81	0.00	61.00	148.92	124.34
VIRGINIA	161.62	0.00	75.91	54.08	62.20
WEST VIRGINIA	278.58	0.00	697.90	488.62	541.78
EAST SOUTH CENTRAL:					
ALABAMA	34.53	0.00	316.16	259.36	270.29
KENTUCKY	177.84	0.00	145.54	302.79	256.41
MISSISSIPPI	47.91	0.00	129.89	10.85	44.53
TENNESSEE	204.12	0.00	68.26	214.83	173.78
WEST SOUTH CENTRAL:					
ARKANSAS	0.00	0.00	3.62	14.85	11.43
LOUISIANA	0.00	0.00	5.47	0.00	1.51
OKLAHOMA	0.00	0.00	4.20	10.02	8.19
TEXAS	0.61	0.00	7.42	7.55	7.37
ROCKY MOUNTAIN:					
ARIZONA	0.00	0.00	6.68	70.27	51.18
COLORADO	17.16	2756.18	91.72	69.85	78.08
IDAHO	0.00	2083.15	19.47	188.45	140.19
MONTANA	37.77	6120.22	52.39	278.28	217.96
NEVADA	0.00	0.00	1.67	178.30	125.63
NEW MEXICO	0.00	0.00	0.92	248.16	174.46
UTAH	30.00	4087.64	266.24	42.62	109.12
WYOMING	19.53	3247.19	82.12	551.88	414.45
FAR WEST:					
ALASKA	20.81	2074.16	169.85	54.75	88.36
CALIFORNIA	0.00	5.62	12.43	31.03	25.23
HAWAII	0.00	0.00	0.01	0.49	0.35
OREGON	3.11	359.55	15.31	302.75	217.27
WASHINGTON	1.96	295.51	16.76	417.31	297.99

Table 187

Per Capita Expenditures On Coal and Fuel Equivalent Expenditures On Hydroelectric Power And
   Nuclear Power In Index Number Terms, U.S. Spending Per Capita = 100, 1972, By State

Use By Function

REGION AND STATE	RESIDENTIAL USE	COMMERCIAL USE	INDUSTRIAL USE	ELECTRIC UTILITY USE	TOTAL USE
NEW ENGLAND:					
CONNECTICUT	2.75	0.00	4.00	85.71	57.00
MAINE	7.84	0.00	2.69	30.37	21.01
MASSACHUSETTS	11.79	0.00	3.84	12.22	9.80
NEW HAMPSHIRE	26.55	0.00	5.16	119.67	80.95
RHODE ISLAND	3.79	0.00	0.91	0.21	0.65
VERMONT	35.12	0.00	3.21	76.80	53.10
MID ATLANTIC:					
NEW JERSEY	40.16	0.00	2.96	31.35	23.83
NEW YORK	54.29	0.00	73.98	74.21	72.67
PENNSYLVANIA	364.42	0.00	340.28	148.66	216.57
EAST NORTH CENTRAL:					
ILLINOIS	242.34	0.00	97.51	138.39	133.32
INDIANA	279.27	0.00	409.15	169.57	244.05
MICHIGAN	143.74	0.00	222.32	132.93	158.59
OHIO	219.38	0.00	295.58	165.89	205.65
WISCONSIN	346.08	0.00	118.74	155.85	157.45
WEST NORTH CENTRAL:					
IOWA	51.22	0.00	67.97	87.44	79.36
KANSAS	12.99	0.00	6.44	7.39	7.47
MINNESOTA	165.82	0.00	61.14	95.33	90.06
MISSOURI	33.30	0.00	44.19	98.65	78.76
NEBRASKA	45.61	0.00	15.77	57.87	45.04
NORTH DAKOTA	187.64	0.00	35.96	215.61	162.52
SOUTH DAKOTA	235.84	0.00	29.52	250.99	186.84
SOUTH ATLANTIC:					
DELAWARE	86.29	0.00	327.27	102.52	164.72
DISTRICT OF COLUMBIA	10.75	0.00	28.18	17.81	20.24
FLORIDA	6.65	0.00	3.44	37.51	25.78
GEORGIA	14.81	0.00	7.83	136.64	91.96
MARYLAND	36.52	0.00	160.12	90.08	106.16
NORTH CAROLINA	134.29	0.00	42.35	220.17	163.80
SOUTH CAROLINA	153.14	0.00	74.28	193.53	156.75
VIRGINIA	160.83	0.00	85.44	64.06	76.28
WEST VIRGINIA	257.30	0.00	636.29	467.90	500.62
EAST SOUTH CENTRAL:					
ALABAMA	33.14	0.00	307.49	266.09	261.94
KENTUCKY	156.36	0.00	106.04	232.01	190.93
MISSISSIPPI	44.36	0.00	122.11	10.71	44.37
TENNESSEE	194.13	0.00	61.77	205.45	163.64
WEST SOUTH CENTRAL:					
ARKANSAS	0.00	0.00	2.21	16.38	11.27
LOUISIANA	0.00	0.00	3.02	0.00	0.85
OKLAHOMA	0.00	0.00	2.15	6.70	4.96
TEXAS	0.62	0.00	4.10	4.49	4.11
ROCKY MOUNTAIN:					
ARIZONA	0.00	0.00	5.42	60.85	41.07
COLORADO	15.38	2610.14	68.51	55.06	62.26
IDAHO	0.00	2386.96	10.92	93.43	69.39
MONTANA	44.42	7013.04	32.21	195.74	155.62
NEVADA	0.00	0.00	1.49	153.87	100.39
NEW MEXICO	0.00	0.00	0.36	102.46	66.67
UTAH	24.99	3665.22	202.14	41.10	94.05
WYOMING	18.44	3007.25	42.25	296.32	212.72
FAR WEST:					
ALASKA	31.06	3546.38	297.33	100.66	159.76
CALIFORNIA	0.00	4.35	7.42	31.95	22.87
HAWAII	0.00	0.00	0.02	0.71	0.47
OREGON	2.23	260.87	6.76	145.15	96.98
WASHINGTON	1.45	214.49	7.36	200.07	132.67

Table 188

Per Capita Use Of Coal And Fuel Equivalent Use Of Hydropower And Nuclear Power
    In Index Number Terms, U.S. = 100, Based On Consumption In BTU And Expenditures
    In Dollars, 1972, By Region

Use By Function

REGION	RESIDENTIAL USE	COMMERCIAL USE	INDUSTRIAL USE	ELECTRIC UTILITY USE	TOTAL USE
Index Of Per Capita Consumption, U.S. = 100					
NEW ENGLAND	9.46	0.00	2.54	27.00	19.84
MID ATLANTIC	150.74	0.00	131.55	70.53	88.93
EAST NORTH CENTRAL	229.93	0.00	223.64	141.04	165.51
WEST NORTH CENTRAL	74.19	0.00	46.88	96.07	81.90
SOUTH ATLANTIC	82.77	0.00	82.69	111.24	102.64
EAST SOUTH CENTRAL	125.34	0.00	164.60	213.87	198.21
WEST SOUTH CENTRAL	0.34	0.00	6.25	7.20	6.79
ROCKY MOUNTAIN	12.16	2049.44	68.97	140.27	120.27
FAR WEST	0.74	95.51	14.72	100.88	75.02
UNITED STATES	100.00	100.00	100.00	100.00	100.00
Index Of Per Capita Expenditures, U.S. = 100					
NEW ENGLAND	10.3	0.0	3.6	40.8	28.22
MID ATLANTIC	149.7	0.0	144.4	89.4	108.67
EAST NORTH CENTRAL	230.8	0.0	219.9	150.4	174.94
WEST NORTH CENTRAL	79.8	0.0	43.6	90.4	76.29
SOUTH ATLANTIC	83.5	0.0	90.5	130.8	115.98
EAST SOUTH CENTRAL	115.8	0.0	149.0	195.0	176.35
WEST SOUTH CENTRAL	0.4	0.0	3.5	5.1	4.33
ROCKY MOUNTAIN	11.5	2044.9	50.4	90.2	78.43
FAR WEST	0.7	94.2	10.6	62.1	43.61
UNITED STATES	100.0	100.0	100.0	100.0	100.00

Table 189

Prices Of Coal And Fuel Equivalent Values Of Hydropower And Nuclear Power In
   Dollars Per Million BTU, 1972, By State

Use By Function And Energy Source

REGION AND STATE	COAL PRICES				FUEL EQUIVALENT VALUE HYDRO & NUCLEAR POWER
	Residential Use	Commercial Use	Industrial Use	Electric Utility Use	
NEW ENGLAND:					
CONNECTICUT	1.625	1.131	0.637	0.607	0.626
MAINE	1.553	1.098	0.644	0.613	0.345
MASSACHUSETTS	1.385	0.977	0.570	0.543	0.576
NEW HAMPSHIRE	1.318	0.911	0.503	0.479	0.448
RHODE ISLAND	1.424	1.010	0.595	0.567	0.572
VERMONT	1.554	1.099	0.644	0.613	0.619
MID ATLANTIC:					
NEW JERSEY	1.624	1.150	0.676	0.644	0.644
NEW YORK	1.437	0.989	0.541	0.515	0.578
PENNSYLVANIA	1.245	0.832	0.418	0.398	0.453
EAST NORTH CENTRAL:					
ILLINOIS	1.340	0.871	0.402	0.383	0.428
INDIANA	1.197	0.766	0.335	0.319	0.321
MICHIGAN	1.330	0.899	0.469	0.446	0.488
OHIO	1.270	0.833	0.397	0.378	0.388
WISCONSIN	1.402	0.948	0.494	0.471	0.469
WEST NORTH CENTRAL:					
IOWA	1.354	0.883	0.412	0.392	0.384
KANSAS	1.136	0.737	0.338	0.321	0.273
MINNESOTA	1.465	0.949	0.434	0.413	0.408
MISSOURI	1.170	0.745	0.320	0.305	0.298
NEBRASKA	1.341	0.896	0.452	0.430	0.391
NORTH DAKOTA	1.431	0.827	0.222	0.212	0.268
SOUTH DAKOTA	1.544	0.988	0.433	0.412	0.429
SOUTH ATLANTIC:					
DELAWARE	1.459	1.011	0.563	0.536	0.539
DISTRICT OF COLUMBIA	1.560	1.095	0.630	0.600	0.539
FLORIDA	1.342	0.893	0.445	0.424	0.448
GEORGIA	1.350	0.909	0.469	0.446	0.449
MARYLAND	1.460	1.012	0.564	0.537	0.539
NORTH CAROLINA	1.336	0.901	0.465	0.443	0.457
SOUTH CAROLINA	1.366	0.930	0.493	0.469	0.490
VIRGINIA	1.294	0.875	0.456	0.434	0.441
WEST VIRGINIA	1.202	0.785	0.369	0.352	0.354
EAST SOUTH CENTRAL:					
ALABAMA	1.247	0.821	0.394	0.375	0.383
KENTUCKY	1.144	0.719	0.295	0.281	0.285
MISSISSIPPI	1.205	0.793	0.381	0.363	0.370
TENNESSEE	1.237	0.802	0.367	0.349	0.358
WEST SOUTH CENTRAL:					
ARKANSAS	1.412	0.818	0.224	0.213	0.405
LOUISIANA	1.412	0.818	0.224	0.213	0.259
OKLAHOMA	0.914	0.559	0.204	0.195	0.246
TEXAS	1.412	0.818	0.224	0.213	0.242
ROCKY MOUNTAIN:					
ARIZONA	1.228	0.780	0.333	0.317	0.318
COLORADO	1.166	0.734	0.302	0.288	0.298
IDAHO	1.530	0.888	0.247	0.235	0.182
MONTANA	1.530	0.888	0.247	0.235	0.262
NEVADA	1.144	0.728	0.313	0.298	0.361
NEW MEXICO	1.068	0.613	0.159	0.151	0.201
UTAH	1.083	0.695	0.307	0.293	0.426
WYOMING	1.227	0.718	0.209	0.199	0.182
FAR WEST:					
ALASKA	1.942	1.325	0.709	0.675	0.675
CALIFORNIA	1.019	0.625	0.231	0.220	0.378
HAWAII	0.000	0.000	0.000	0.000	0.534
OREGON	0.943	0.563	0.183	0.174	0.176
WASHINGTON	0.943	0.563	0.183	0.174	0.176

Table 190

Prices Of Coal And Fuel Equivalent Values Of Hydropower and Nuclear Power
 In Dollars Per Million BTU, 1972, By Region

Use By Function and Energy Source

REGION	COAL PRICES				FUEL EQUIVALENT VALUE HYDRO & NUCLEAR POWER
	Residential Use	Commercial Use	Industrial Use	Electric Utility Use	
NEW ENGLAND	1.418	0.000[a]	0.586	0.495	0.569
MID ATLANTIC	1.291	0.000	0.444	0.422	0.579
EAST NORTH CENTRAL	1.306	0.000	0.398	0.387	0.446
WEST NORTH CENTRAL	1.400	0.000	0.376	0.335	0.386
SOUTH ATLANTIC	1.312	0.000	0.443	0.426	0.472
EAST SOUTH CENTRAL	1.202	0.000	0.367	0.330	0.357
WEST SOUTH CENTRAL	1.412	0.000	0.222	0.213	0.312
ROCKY MOUNTAIN	1.235	0.774	0.297	0.216	0.264
FAR WEST	1.276	0.764	0.310	0.675	0.224
UNITED STATES	1.300	0.773	0.406	0.378	0.339

[a] Zero indicates no consumption in commercial use

Table 191

Prices Of Coal And Fuel Equivalent Values Of Hydropower And Nuclear Power, Per Million BTU, And
Price Indexes, U.S. = 100, 1972, By State

Use By Function

REGION AND STATE	PRICE IN DOLLARS PER MILLION BTU			PRICE INDEXES, U.S. = 100		
	Residential Use (Household)	All Uses	All Uses Given U.S. Quantity Weights	Residential Use (Household)	All Uses	All Uses Given (U.S. Quantity Weights)
NEW ENGLAND:						
CONNECTICUT	1.625	0.627	0.640	125.03	148.23	155.04
MAINE	1.553	0.356	0.587	119.49	84.16	142.20
MASSACHUSETTS	1.385	0.600	0.574	106.56	141.84	139.05
NEW HAMPSHIRE	1.318	0.477	0.497	101.41	112.77	120.40
RHODE ISLAND	1.424	0.758	0.593	109.56	179.20	143.65
VERMONT	1.554	0.635	0.642	119.57	150.12	155.52
MID ATLANTIC:						
NEW JERSEY	1.624	0.691	0.673	124.95	163.36	163.03
NEW YORK	1.437	0.570	0.554	110.56	134.75	134.21
PENNSYLVANIA	1.245	0.441	0.432	95.79	104.26	104.65
EAST NORTH CENTRAL:						
ILLINOIS	1.340	0.429	0.417	103.10	101.42	101.02
INDIANA	1.197	0.346	0.342	92.10	81.80	82.85
MICHIGAN	1.330	0.476	0.479	102.33	112.53	116.04
OHIO	1.270	0.406	0.404	97.71	95.98	97.87
WISCONSIN	1.402	0.526	0.496	107.87	124.35	120.16
WEST NORTH CENTRAL:						
IOWA	1.354	0.408	0.416	104.18	96.45	100.78
KANSAS	1.136	0.354	0.333	87.40	83.69	80.67
MINNESOTA	1.465	0.456	0.439	112.72	107.80	106.35
MISSOURI	1.170	0.313	0.325	90.02	74.00	78.73
NEBRASKA	1.341	0.441	0.447	103.18	104.26	108.28
NORTH DAKOTA	1.431	0.241	0.251	110.10	56.97	60.80
SOUTH DAKOTA	1.544	0.455	0.444	118.80	107.57	107.56
SOUTH ATLANTIC:						
DELAWARE	1.459	0.563	0.563	112.26	133.10	136.39
DISTRICT OF COLUMBIA	1.560	0.625	0.616	120.03	147.75	149.22
FLORIDA	1.342	0.430	0.453	103.25	101.65	109.74
GEORGIA	1.350	0.450	0.472	103.87	106.38	114.34
MARYLAND	1.460	0.556	0.564	112.33	131.44	136.63
NORTH CAROLINA	1.336	0.463	0.470	102.79	109.46	113.86
SOUTH CAROLINA	1.366	0.500	0.498	105.10	118.20	120.64
VIRGINIA	1.294	0.486	0.459	99.56	114.89	111.19
WEST VIRGINIA	1.202	0.367	0.375	92.48	86.76	90.84
EAST SOUTH CENTRAL:						
ALABAMA	1.247	0.384	0.400	95.95	90.78	96.90
KENTUCKY	1.144	0.295	0.303	88.02	69.74	73.40
MISSISSIPPI	1.205	0.395	0.387	92.71	93.38	93.75
TENNESSEE	1.237	0.373	0.374	95.18	88.18	90.60
WEST SOUTH CENTRAL:						
ARKANSAS	1.412	0.391	0.279	108.64	92.43	67.59
LOUISIANA	1.412	0.224	0.250	108.64	52.96	60.56
OKLAHOMA	0.914	0.240	0.223	70.32	56.74	54.02
TEXAS	1.412	0.221	0.247	108.64	52.25	59.84
ROCKY MOUNTAIN:						
ARIZONA	1.228	0.318	0.340	94.48	75.18	82.36
COLORADO	1.166	0.316	0.312	89.71	74.70	75.58
IDAHO	1.530	0.196	0.254	117.72	46.34	61.53
MONTANA	1.530	0.283	0.270	117.72	66.90	65.41
NEVADA	1.144	0.317	0.332	88.02	74.94	80.43
NEW MEXICO	1.068	0.152	0.182	82.17	35.93	44.09
UTAH	1.083	0.342	0.340	83.33	80.85	82.36
WYOMING	1.227	0.204	0.219	94.41	48.23	53.05
FAR WEST:						
ALASKA	1.942	0.717	0.710	149.42	169.50	172.00
CALIFORNIA	1.019	0.359	0.271	78.40	84.87	65.65
HAWAII	1.439	0.534	0.383	110.72	126.24	92.78
OREGON	0.943	0.177	0.193	72.56	41.84	46.75
WASHINGTON	0.943	0.177	0.193	72.56	41.84	46.75

Table 192

Prices Of Coal And Fuel Equivalent Values Of Hydropower And Nuclear Power, Per Million BTU, And Price Indexes, U.S. = 100, 1972, By Region

Use By Function

REGION	PRICE IN DOLLARS PER MILLION BTU			PRICE INDEXES, U.S. = 100		
	Residential Use (Household)	All Uses	All Uses Given U.S. Quantity Weights	Residential Use (Household)	All Uses	All Uses Given U.S. Quantity Weights
NEW ENGLAND	1.466	0.592	0.591	112.76	139.94	143.17
MID ATLANTIC	1.413	0.553	0.539	108.70	130.61	130.47
EAST NORTH CENTRAL	1.308	0.433	0.426	100.62	102.38	103.27
WEST NORTH CENTRAL	1.307	0.383	0.382	100.57	90.55	92.46
SOUTH ATLANTIC	1.351	0.472	0.479	103.98	111.52	115.97
EAST SOUTH CENTRAL	1.211	0.360	0.365	93.16	85.08	88.49
WEST SOUTH CENTRAL	1.346	0.241	0.248	103.59	56.98	59.98
ROCKY MOUNTAIN	1.219	0.283	0.295	93.76	66.79	71.51
FAR WEST	1.027	0.331	0.264	79.02	78.20	63.83
UNITED STATES	1.300	0.423	0.413	100.00	100.00	100.00

Chapter 6

Estimation Procedures and Future Work

Overview

This final chapter reviews the estimation procedures and data sources
drawn on for this study, noting shortcomings in data and consequent difficulties in estimation, and applies that review to make some recommendations
for future development of data and their application in research. The
spirit of this review is implicit in two aphorisms of Frank Knight, who
said: "when you can't measure, measure anyway," and who also said "all
knowledge is provisional, subject to revision in the light of further inquiry."
To expand on the points at issue in less pithy fashion, it is freely acknowledged
that in this study there were some data gaps that were closed by expedient,
making most reasonable judgments and assumptions on the basis of what limited
information was available; and there were conflicts between sources that
were resolved either by choosing one as the most reliable, or simply by
combining the two series when choice between them was not obvious. The tenor
of this review, however, is not meant as carping criticism of the inadequacies
of data sources, nor as a defensive "mea culpa" of the estimates developed
here. The difficulties are common, even universal; what is not common is
their forthright acknowledgment. But such acknowledgment should be of help
in further inquiry, and it is in that spirit that this chapter is written.
The material is presented in summary fashion, drawing on the appendixes to this
report, which cover that material in considerable detail.

Categorizing data shortcomings under the headings of gaps and conflicts, the following were some major problems encountered. Major gaps included: (1) a general paucity of price information for petroleum products and (2) a general absence of information on use by sector, or on functional use cross-classified by sector; a subsidiary but related problem of some importance was poor or absent accounting for industrial use of petroleum fuels in space heating. There were a number of relatively minor gaps, including lack of publicly available series on state use of aviation fuel, although regional aggregates were available; lack of an individual state breakdown of use for certain industrial categories of coal and petroleum product use, though data for clusters of states were again available; and absence of a state breakdown for some categories of gasoline use.

Data conflicts include definitional problems and disagreements in numerical series. A common definitional problem is the use of the same term to embrace different components and this posed most difficulty in the work on natural gas; definitional problems also occurred for electricity use and industrial use of petroleum. Definitional differences can explain numerical disagreements between sources, but a number of such disagreements seemed wider based. In the case of data on quantities, the most important disagreement again occurred in natural gas, but there were also problems for electric utility use of petroleum and in highway use of "special fuels" (diesel fuel and liquified petroleum gas). Price series disagreements occurred in gasoline, in petroleum for electric utility use and in coal for electric utility use. There were also some marked differences in some of the natural gas series; though these did not affect the estimates of the present study, their notice may be useful in future work.

Some details on these gaps and conflicts, and on the estimating procedures employed to handle them, will now be presented as part of a more general discussion of the estimating procedures employed in this study. That discussion will begin with the petroleum price problem and then cover price estimates for other sources. The estimating of use by sector will follow, and will, in turn, serve as the introduction to a general discussion of the measurement of quantities. The chapter concludes with recommendations for future work, which draw on a comparative review of some related studies, and on the regression equation results which were summarized in chapter 1.

Prices

Information on petroleum prices is notable by its scarcity, a problem handled by tapping a large number of sources to develop a set of "patchwork" series for each of a number of products. Scarcity of information probably reflects the existence of a great number of petroleum products, sold at prices that vary by locale and by level of use, from producer level to retail, with middlemen markup a significant portion of the price. Hence, full and detailed information would involve a formidable effort. In the present study, gasoline at the service station, No. 2 fuel oil in residential heating and No. 6 fuel oil in large commercial (establishment) heating were treated as key fuels. Prices were estimated for each of those products, and then were used in conjunction with other information to generate price estimates for all other petroleum products.

The gasoline price series was based on data in Platt's Oil Price Handbook and The Oil and Gas Journal,[1] both of which present prices for regular gasoline for a number of major cities, the former covering at least one city in each

---

[1] Full citations for these and other references cited in this discussion are presented in the appendixes.

state, and the latter covering cities in 35 states. There was fairly good correspondence for the observations in common, with essentially equal averages for the 38 cities involved. However, the correlation between the two sets of prices for cities in common was only .58, and several cities showed marked disagreement. A 15 percent difference between respective readings occurred for Miami and for Chicago, and a 10 percent difference occurred for the respective New York City and Minneapolis figures. A final set of state estimates for regular gasoline was obtained by assuming the city data were applicable to the corresponding state, forming a weighted average based on population when more than one city appeared for a given state. Then, prices for the states common to both series were averaged, there being no basis for selecting one series rather than the other, and the Platt's values were employed for the remaining states. Prices actually paid by private sector passenger cars and motorcycles were estimated by accounting for the differential for premium relative to regular gasoline and applying the distribution of use for premium versus regular, by state.

Schedules of federal taxes, state and local taxes, estimated discounts for bulk purchases and premiums for aviation gasoline were applied to develop estimated prices for all modes of transport, distinguishing use by sector and function. A separate price series was developed for each of the modes in the following list:

Household	Business	Government
Passenger car	Passenger car	Federal Highway
Aviation	Truck & bus	State and Local highway
Marine	Aviation	Civilian aviation
		Military highway
		Military aviation

The tax schedules employed involved considerable complexity, but
even so, some extremely fine distinctions could not be incorporated in
the estimates; thus, some states exempt ambulances, the National Guard,
school buses and/or public transit, and there was no attempt to account
for such cases. Again, the estimated bulk discounts were based on informed
judgement. Errors introduced are probably minor, a conclusion supported
by several checks of the expenditure estimates obtained by multiplying
estimated prices by corresponding quantities. Total household expenditures
on gasoline nationally were estimated here as $25.06 billion, which compares
well to a corresponding Department of Commerce estimate of $24.6 billion. A
comparison of estimated gasoline tax collections to Federal Highway Administration (FHWA) data also shows good correspondence, as shown by these figures
in million dollars:

	This Study (1)	FHWA (2)	Ratio (1)/(2)
State taxes	7,732.1	7,828.0	.988
Federal taxes (paid by private sector)	4,132.4	3,995.2	1.034

Base prices for No. 2 fuel oil in residential use and No. 6 fuel oil in
"large" commercial establishment use were developed by drawing on data from
several sources, including two publications by Foster Associates. Price differentials by level of use are pronounced, reflecting additional transportation,
handling and accounting cost with movement from wholesale to retail level.
The following indexes were derived for prices at various levels of use relative
to each fuel's own base price:

	Index Relative To Own Base Price	
Level of Use	No. 2	No. 6
Residential	100.0	153.0
Small commercial	97.4	149.0
Large commercial	65.3	100.0
Large industrial	63.0	98.0
Wholesale	58.9	91.4

Over all states, the simple average of prices per gallon were 19.4 cents for No. 2 fuel oil in residential use and 11.2 cents for No. 6 fuel oil in large commercial use. Hence, if No. 6 oil were consumed in residential use, its price would be 17.15 cents, so that level of use accounts for most of the observed difference in price between the two fuels. Quality of product differences presumably account for the remaining price differential (from 17.15 to 19.4 cents).

Given the price estimate for No. 2 and No. 6 fuel oil, and the indexes for level of use, specific price estimates were developed for all other heating fuels (other distillates and residuals, kerosine, and LPG) by simple scaling of the base prices, that is, a given state base price was scaled by adding or multiplying by a constant (or both), to obtain the corresponding price for one of the other fuels. Scale factors were based on information in trade publications and on informed judgment (but there is obviously room for improvement).

Similar procedures were employed in estimating prices for non-gasoline fuels used in transportation, industrial uses, and miscellaneous uses of petroleum products. Data were available on the national average prices for civilian jet fuel, military aviation jet fuel and railroad fuel, so, in those cases, the respective national price was multiplied by a set of state weights to yield state price estimates. The state weights were those that held for fuels whose price had already been established and which were deemed most similar to the fuel in question--kerosine in the case of aviation jet fuel, and a weighted average of No. 2 and No. 6 fuel oil in the case of railroad fuel.

A National Coal Association (NCA) series was available on state prices of petroleum products used by electric utilities, and its data were compared to corresponding prices established using the heating oil base estimates. Correspondence seemed good except for Atlantic Coast states, whose prices in the NCA series were generally 15 to 20 percent below those derived from the heating oil data. It was speculated that such price differentials might reflect the relatively greater reliance on oil by utilities in those states than in other states, with subsequent greater discounts for bulk purchases, but it was not obvious that the NCA estimates were necessarily best, so a choice between the series was hedged by averaging them.

Considerably more price information was readily available for non-petroleum energy sources than for petroleum products, but there were some conflicts between different series covering the same source.

Alternative series were available from the Edison Electric Institute (EEI) and the National Coal Association (NCA) on the price of coal purchased by electric utilities. The two series showed generally good agreement; of the 41 states covered in both series, 36 differed by three percent or less between their respective entries. However, there were the following five cases of marked disagreement, with prices in cents per million BTU:

	EEI	NCA	EEI/NCA
Massachusetts	45.4¢	63.1¢	.719
Wyoming	17.1	22.7	.753
District of Columbia	53.9	66.0	.817
Montana	26.0	21.0	1.238
North Dakota	26.6	15.7	1.694

The practical decision, again, was to average the two series.

Prices for coal in other uses were obtained by scaling the prices established for electric utility use. The price per ton in residential use was estimated from a regression equation as $15 + 1.6 PEU, where PEU was the price per ton in electric utility use. It was assumed that the price in industrial use was five percent above that to electric utilities, because of presumed lower bulk discounts. It was also assumed that the price for commercial use was midway between the industrial and residential price.

Prices for electricity and natural gas were directly available, given source data on both quantities and expenditures. There were conflicts in alternative series covering natural gas use, but these caused no operational problems because the conflicts were resolved by splicing several quantity series together, and then applying the same splicing operations to the corresponding expenditures series. However, some comparisons of alternative series on natural gas prices may be useful in future work. The primary data series at issue are those of the Bureau of Mines (BOM) and the American Gas Association (AGA). Good correspondence between those series occurred for prices in residential and commercial use, but prices for industrial use showed much less agreement. Finally, prices in electric utility use showed considerably disagreement; here, data from the National

Coal Association (NCA) were also available, and tended to conform more closely to the AGA than BOM figures. The following list shows regional average prices for electric utility use of natural gas, in cents per million BTU, as presented by the respective sources:

	BOM	NCA	AGA
New England	44.8¢	46.2¢	51.7¢
Mid Atlantic	46.7	53.2	55.3
East North Central	44.9	51.7	49.2
West North Central	37.8	29.9	29.5
South Atlantic	39.6	39.9	42.2
East South Central	31.8	29.9	30.1
West South Central	27.4	24.1	24.7
Rocky Mountain	36.7	34.9	35.5
Far West	38.1	37.5	37.6
United States	33.1	30.3	33.1

Although the AGA and BOM values agree at the national level, there are marked disagreements at the regional level, and here the NCA and AGA estimates seem fairly close. Although many of the state values show good agreement between the series, some pronounced discrepancies occur, as shown by these examples, with prices again in cents per million BTU:

	BOM	NCA	AGA
New York	46.2¢	54.4¢	56.3¢
Pennsylvania	48.3	64.3	61.9
Illinois	42.5	51.4	48.5
Texas	28.0	23.4	23.7
Wyoming	29.4	48.1	33.3

The final set of price estimates developed were those for hydroelectric and nuclear power. The approach employed for those energy sources
was to estimate their input as the fuel equivalent of fossil fuels. In
most cases, the corresponding price estimate was the composite average
cost of all fossil fuels. However, where hydropower and nuclear power
furnished more than 20 percent of a state's electricity generation input,
the composite fuel price was checked against the composite price for
nearby states and against individual fossil fuel prices, and, in some
cases, this led to a reduction of the fuel equivalent price. The composite
price can be viewed as an overstatement because the alternative source
would not be employed unless there were cost advantages relative to fossil
fuels. Essentially that consideration led to the use of a quantity estimate 10 percent below the corresponding Bureau of Mines estimate, rationalized
as accounting for efficiency differences. Expressing the differences in
prices might have more intuitive appeal, but the approach used seems
defensible given the imprecision inherent in hydropower and nuclear power
estimation. The topic is examined further in the discussion of quantities.

Quantities

The most extensive problem involving quantities occurred in estimating
use by sector. To large extent, this involved the distribution of commercial use between sectors, because sectoral identification was usually obvious
for most other uses. A preliminary, related adjustment occurred in the case
of natural gas, as noted in Chapter 3. The original measure of commercial
use was revised, with part transferred to residential use, covering use in
large apartment buildings, and part transferred to industrial use, to cover
use by farms, fisheries and light industry, the remainder being retained as

"net" commercial use. (For the United States, 45 percent of the original
use was retained under the commercial heading, 19 percent transferred to
residential use, and 36 percent to industrial use.) That "net" commercial
use of natural gas, as well as commercial use for petroleum heating fuels
and for electricity, was distributed among five categories of commercial
use, including offices, retail, school, hospital, and all other commercial
use, on the basis of data appearing in a study by Arthur D. Little, Inc.
The Little data gave the distribution of specific energy use by commercial
category for the major U.S. census regions: Northeast, North Central, South
and West. State distributions were obtained from the regional distributions
by scale factors accounting for the relative concentration of commercial
activities within each state in the respective regions. Then, each of the
five categories of commercial use were distributed between sectors, applying
a set of fractions developed for each category by state. Office and hospital
use were respectively distributed between private business, federal government, and state and local government; school use was distributed between
business and state and local government, reflecting the distribution between
private and public schools; and retail trade and all other use were treated
as exclusively private business activities. Some sense of the process can
be had from these selected fractions for office and school use:

	Office Use			School Use	
	Business	Federal Govt.	State & Local Govt.	Business	State & Local Govt.
New York	.8545	.0372	.1083	.2115	.7885
District of Columbia	.3558	.5424	.1018	.3621	.6379
Nevada	.7742	.0859	.1419	.0263	.9737

Finally, the sectoral use figures by category were aggregated to sector totals within commercial use, and, as necessary, combined with sector values from other uses to yield aggregates.

In estimating sector use for petroleum heating fuels, a further complication arose because source statistics did not distinguish petroleum products used for space heating in industrial plants from other components of a "residential-commercial" use series, that is, industrial use could not be separately identified although it <u>was</u> included in the series. A detailed estimating process yielded a national figure of five percent of the total as the share attributable to industrial plant space heating; this, in turn, amounted to 23.5 percent of residual heating oil use, assuming that industrial space heating involved residual heating oils, only. That percentage was scaled up or down for individual states on the basis of state per capita employment in manufactures relative to the corresponding U.S. per capita figure. The estimated state percentages times the corresponding state residual oil totals gave an initial set of estimates, which, when scaled by .986, yielded a final set whose sum equalled the original national total (23.5 percent of all residual heating oil use).

A number of simplifying assumptions were necessary in estimating sectoral use, and future efforts might improve on those simplifications. For example, it was estimated that household use accounted for 91.5 percent, and business use for 8.5 percent of private passenger car mileage nationally; it was then assumed that these percentages were invariant between states. Of course, they well may not be. Again, following an interpretation applied to source data in the Arthur D. Little study, "large light and power" was identified as industrial use of electricity and "small light and power" as commercial use of electricity, a usage consistent with Edison Electric

Institute definitions, but nevertheless lending some imprecision to estimates.

There were several cases where quantities consumed were available for regions or groups of states but not for individual states. The group totals were distributed among the states in the group using what information was available. Oil refinery use of petroleum coke and refinery gas was distributed within a group on the basis of the individual state's share of residual oil consumption by refineries within the group. Industrial use of coal within a given group was distributed on the basis of the state's share both of electric utility use of coal and of industrial use of petroleum products within the group. Military use of gasoline and of aviation jet fuel within a region was distributed to states on the basis of military use of distillate fuels. Civilian aviation use of jet fuel was distributed among regions on the basis of scale factors derived from a confidential series, after accounting for under-reporting and adjusting the data to establish internal consistency.

Some apparent conflicts between alternative data series could be explained by differing definitions of the same terms. This was most obvious in the case of natural gas statistics; the American Gas Association included electric utility use under the industrial heading, while the Bureau of Mines treated that use as a separate category; both sources included oil refining and oil and gas producer purchases from gas utilities under industrial use, but those uses were reclassified here under the heading of use in energy production. Definitional differences also occurred in the Bureau of Mines handling of a series on "diesel type fuel oil use"; in one application, the series appeared under the heading of miscellaneous use, but in another it was included under industrial use, the definition applied here.

Some conflicts seemed more than definitional. Thus, National Coal Association (NCA) entries on electric utility use of petroleum products are generally considerably less than corresponding Bureau of Mines (BOM) entries, in part because consumption by certain institutional users is not included in the former series. There were some states where the NCA entry exceeded the BOM entry, but given the stated absence of complete coverage in the NCA series, the BOM series was employed here.

Again, there was disagreement between data from the Federal Highway Administration (FHWA) and the Bureau of Mines (BOM) on highway use of diesel fuel and liquified petroleum gas (LPG). Internal evidence and informed opinion implied that a large amount of LPG in the BOM series had been listed at its point of production rather than consumption, and when that estimated amount was transferred to non-highway use, the highway use estimates employed here fell between the FHWA and BOM values, viewed as a suitable compromise.

A final problem involved accounting for the quantity of hydroelectric and nuclear power. Data on power generated by those sources were scaled to fuel equivalent input by applying data on BTU of fossil fuel needed per BTU of electricity. It later appeared that a 10 percent underestimate had occurred, because transmission losses were built into the estimates, and should not have been. However, the lower figures were then justified as a way of accounting for presumed efficiency differences between energy sources. Future work might be directed to better resolution of the questions involved here, which include (1) how much more efficient hydroelectric and nuclear power really are, relative to fossil fuels, and (2) where the efficiency differences are best accounted for, in terms of less BTU of input for given output versus lower prices of input. Of course, lower expenditures emerge under either approach.

Some Comparisons With Other Studies

Energy studies have burgeoned in recent years, and one consequence is that a number of parallel studies have become available. Several of those studies[2] will now be compared to results appearing here. The comparisons generally show where further refinement and data reconcilations can be made in quantity data, and where some prospective future research can be facilitated. However, little information is to be found in those studies on expenditures, and on the distribution of use by sectors, the major contributions of the present report.

Hirst, Lin and Cope examine U.S. residential energy use and exhibit a U.S. expenditures estimate for 1972 of 25.5 billion dollars,[3] which squares exactly with the U.S. total developed here (Table 37). Their consumption figure is estimated as 11,950 trillion BTU,[4] which compares to this study's residential total of 11,812 trillion BTU (Table 37).

Considerably less agreement holds between results here and those in a study of residential use by Stephen Dole for 1970.[5] Dole presents regional levels of use, and their U.S. total is 88 percent of the corresponding total shown in the Arthur D. Little Project Independence report,[6] a major source employed in the present study. The difference reflects an adjustment made

---

[2] Jack Alterman of Resources for the Future cited most of the studies and made them available.

[3] Eric Hirst, William Lin, Jane Cope, An Engineering-Economic Model of Residential Energy Use, Oak Ridge National Laboratory, July, 1976, ORNL/TM-5470, table 2, p. 4.

[4] Derived from data in ibid. table 1.

[5] Stephen H. Dole, Energy Use and Conservation In The Residential Sector: A Regional Analysis, The Rand Corporation, June, 1975, R-1641-NSF.

[6] Arthur D. Little, Inc., Project Independence, Energy Conservation, Vol. I, Residential and Commercial Use Patterns, 1970-1990, Washington, D.C. 1974.

in the Little report to account for discerned understatement of residential energy use, because many series treat much of multifamily apartment use of energy as commercial, rather than residential use. That adjustment is built into corresponding estimates here.

By major Census regions, the totals for Dole, Little and the present study were:

Residential Use Estimates in Trillion BTU

Census Region	Dole, 1970	Little, 1970	This Study, 1972
Northeast	2,662	3,381	3,448
North Central	3,522	4,039	3,944
South	2,453	2,469	2,708
West	1,377	1,522	1,712
Total U.S.	10,014	11,411	11,811

Using the Little totals relative to those of this study as scale factors to convert 1972 to 1970 estimates, the Dole nine region data compare to those developed here, as shown in the table on the following page.

It seems plausible that much of the difference here can be explained by the treatment of multifamily apartment use, because the greatest discrepancies occur in regions with most multifamily housing. But the South Atlantic and East South Central ratios suggest that other factors are at work as well, including limitations of the Arthur D. Little data, which were presented only for the four major census regions, rather than the finer nine "division" breakdown.

Residential Use Estimates In Trillion BTU For Nine Regions

	Dole, 1970	This Study, 1972 Converted to 1970 Levels[a]	Ratio: (1)/(2)
	(1)	(2)	(3)
New England	659.8	890.7	.741
Mid Atlantic	2,002.6	2,490.3	.804
East North Central	2,544.2	2,952.2	.862
West North Central	977.6	1,087.0	.899
South Atlantic	1,172.0	1,119.5	1.047
East South Central	531.9	530.5	1,003
West South Central	749.1	819.0	.915
Mountain	386.5	425.3	.909
Pacific	990.5	1,096.7	.903
U.S. Total	10,014.1	11,411.2	.878

[a]From Table 37 times ratio for major Census regions of Arthur D. Little data to this study data.

It is worth noting that the Dole study seems an excellent source of data for some future analyses. It includes a detailed cross-classification of residential end use by energy source for each region. End uses include space heating, water heating, cooking, clothes drying, refrigeration, home food freezing, lighting, air conditioning and other. Sources include utility gas, electricity, fuel oil, bottled gas, and coal and other. Such data could be used with data from the present study to estimate demand elasticities for particular end uses.

The reliance on the Arthur D. Little study here implies not only that the residential BTU level will often be above those in alternate series, but concomitantly, that commercial BTU levels will often be below alternate series. This appears to be the case for a study of commercial use carried out by Jack Faucett Associates.[7]

Commercial use totals for the U.S. compare as follows, in trillion BTU:

> Faucett (1974)...................... 5,411
> Little (1970)....................... 3,375
> Present study (1972)................ 3,816

The Faucett study has a breakdown by Census divisions, so that regional totals can be compared to those in the present study; note that since there was no easy way to convert the present study's 1972 to 1974 BTU levels, some of the differences that appear reflect changes between 1972 and 1974. The comparisons are:

Commercial Use Estimates In Trillion BTU for Nine Regions

	Faucett, 1974	This Study, 1972	Ratio: (1)/(2)
	(1)	(2)	(3)
New England	329.5	318.4	1.035
Mid Atlantic	949.5	729.7	1.304
East North Central	1,006.6	765.1	1.316
West North Central	507.3	323.4	1.569
Aouth Atlantic	811.2	517.0	1.569
East South Central	255.6	152.7	1.674
West South Central	515.6	316.6	1.629
Rocky Mountain	316.5	221.8	1.427
Far West	719.4	471.1	1.527
U.S. Total	5,411.1	3,815.8	1.418
Source:	Table 1-2, p.15, Faucett Assoc. 1977	Table 37, this study	

[7] Jack Faucett Associates for the Federal Energy Administration, Energy Consumption in Commercial Industries by Census Division - 1974, March, 1977, FEA/B-77/167.

Besides the effects of different years, and of multifamily housing
use shifted to the residential category, some of the differences are
explained by this study's shift of some natural gas use from commercial
to industrial use, following an adjustment in the Little study.

The Faucett study contains a great deal of detailed information on
commercial use under the headings of communications; utilities (exclusive
of energy conversion); wholesale trade; retail trade; finance, insurance,
real estate and services; hospitals and nursing homes; schools; and public
administration. Data on all of these categories have a regional dimension.
Hence, the Faucett study could be quite useful in future analysis refining
the sort of estimates developed here. Some additional documentation on
commercial use appears in a study by Jackson and Johnson;[8] that document,
as cited, has not been released for public use, but when it does appear,
should be of help in further refinement of data.

Some limited additional refinement of transportation use statistics
could be based on some of the information in a report by Shonka, Loebl and
Patterson,[9] which consists of a miscellaneous collection of data on transportation. For example, their Table 1-16 shows the fleet inventory and
characteristics, including average miles per vehicle, of federal government
motor vehicles; Tables 1-79 and 1-80 have considerable detail on hours flown
in general aviation; and Table 2-9 compares Bureau of Mines data on U.S. transportation use of energy to other sources, noting differences in specific

[8] Jerry R. Jackson and W. Stan Johnson, "Commercial Energy Use: A
Disaggregation by Fuel, Building Type and End Use," Oak Ridge National
Laboratory, June, 1977.

[9] D. B. Shonka, A. S. Loebl and P. D. Patterson, Transportation Energy
Conservation Data Book: Edition 2, Oak Ridge National Laboratory, Oct. 1977,
ORNL-5320.

categories and in total. Some specific comparisons to the present study
may be noted. Table 2-16 contains a breakdown of marine transportation which
shows pleasure craft as consuming 8.2 percent of energy in marine use; this
compares to an estimated 12.2 percent of marine use allocated to the household
sector in the present study (based on total marine use of 871.1 trillion BTU,
and household marine use of 85.81 trillion BTU of gasoline and 20.37 trillion
BTU of distillates.) Tables 1-71 and 1-72 show for a sample of 21 metropolitan
areas that a small but non-negligible portion of the journey to work is by
truck, ranging from three percent in Chicago to 18 percent in San Bernardino.
Hence, treating truck use as entirely a business expenditure can understate
urban household use as well as rural farm household use of gasoline. Finally,
it was assumed here that rental car annual mileage per vehicle was roughly
50 percent above average vehicle mileage (Appendix A), an assumption that
turns out to be supported by data in tables 1-19 and 1-52, which show annual
mileages per vehicle of 13,900 for rental cars (1976) and 9,634 for all
passenger cars (1975), so the former is 1.44 times the latter.

A comparison across all functions is obtained by drawing on 1972 quantity
data presented by Hermelee.[10] Hermelee's major aggregates for the U.S. compare
to those presented here as shown on the following page.

The listing shows entries listed by Hermelee, followed by adjustments that
make them comparable in an accounting sense to the values presented here.
Hermelee follows Bureau of Mines conventions, noted in Chapter 1, of including
raw material use (feedstocks) as an energy use, and of excluding electricity

---

[10] Alan L. Hermelee, Regional Reference Energy Systems, Electric Power
Research Institute, June, 1977, EPRI EA-462.

BTU delivered to customers from his total. Electricity use appearing in the total is fuel inputs minus deliveries. Reversing those decisions, Hermelee's grand total becomes very close to that presented here. He also treats pipeline fuel as a component of transportation, in contrast to its treatment here under other energy production. Moving pipeline fuel from the former to the latter category makes the totals in each relatively close between the two studies.

Use By Function In Trillion BTU, U.S., 1972

Function	Hermelee, 1972	This Study, 1972
Residential	10,679.1	11,811.8
Commercial	6,390.4	3,815.8
Industrial	19,796.0	17,231.2
Feedstocks	− 4,189.9	0.0
"Net" industrial	15,606.1	17,231.2
Transportation	18,032.6	17,069.3
Pipelines	− 789.9	0.0
Rail use of coal	− 4.4	0.0
"net" transportation	17,238.3	17,069.3
Electric Utility (net)	13,168.9	
Electricity delivered	(5,394.9)	
Electricity total	(18,563.8)	18,019.8
Other Energy Production	4,099.9	
Pipelines	789.9	
Total other energy	4,889.8	4,725.6
Municipal-Institutional	0.0	518.6
Total (Hermelee listed)	72,166.9[a]	73,192.1
Minus feedstocks	− 4,189.9	
Plus electricity delivered	5,394.9	
	73,371.9	73,192.1
Source	Hermelee, Table A-1	Table 37

[a]Hermelee total equals sum of first entry in each category, i.e., 10,679.1 + 6,390.4 + 19,796.0 + 18,032.6 + 13,168.9 + 4,099.9 = 72,166.9

The deviations between respective residential, commercial and industrial use categories parallel those noted in the earlier comparisons, and reflect adjustments made here on the basis of corresponding adjustments in the Arthur D. Little study. When the three categories are summed (and feedstocks removed), these totals are obtained:

	U.S. Total, Trillion BTU
Hermelee	32,675.6
This study	32,858.8

The respective transportation categories compare in terms of components, as follows:

U.S. Transportation Use, 1972, In Trillion BTU

	Hermelee	This Study
Highway (automobile, truck & bus)	13,522.6	13,469.8
Rail & Transit	592.2	
Coal	4.4	
Use net of coal	587.8	549.5
Aviation	2,226.8	2,178.9
Marine	871.1	871.1
Pipelines	789.9	—
Total, excluding pipelines and coal	17,238.3	17,069.3

Again, the respective totals appear close.

Hermelee's "gross" electric utility use of 18,563.8 trillion BTU is the sum of electricity BTU delivered to users plus fuel inputs; it compares to a figure of 18,019.8 trillion BTU presented in the present study. As noted in Chapter 5, hydropower plus nuclear power BTU here is below the corresponding

Bureau of Mines figure by about 10 percent, equalling 400 trillion BTU,

and accounting for most of the difference between the electric utility

figures. Excluding that 400 trillion BTU, the Hermelee U.S. total is 1.002

times that presented here. Adding the 400 trillion BTU to the total here,

the Hermelee total becomes 0.997 of the "amended" total here. In both cases,

the differences could be viewed as equivalent to round-off error.

The consistency in totals between the two studies also holds at the

regional level, as indicated in the set of comparisons shown on the following

page.

Hermelee's data include cross-classifications that can be useful in

future research. Both residential and commercial use have the following

subcategories: space heating, water heating, air conditioning and cooking.

In addition, appliances and lighting appears under residential, and miscel-

laneous electricity under commercial use. Industrial use has the following

subcategories: aluminum, iron, steel, process heat, electric drive and

feedstocks. All items are cross-classified by energy source.

A final comparison can be made by considering a report by Vogt, Rice

and Pai for 1972.[11] Their study used the Bureau of Mines study by Crump

and Readling[12] as the major source of state and regional data. Then, consump-

tion was classified into the following major categories: (1) final end use,

which they label "final demand" but which corresponds best to use by customers,

in the terminology of the present study; (2) energy conversion losses, which

---

[11]D. P. Vogt, P. L. Rice and V. P. Pai, Energy Availabilities For State
and Local Development: 1972 Data Volume, Oak Ridge National Laboratory,
September, 1977.

[12]Lulie H. Crump and Charles L. Readling, Fuel and Energy Data,
United States by States and Regions, 1972, Bureau of Mines Information
Circular 8647, Washington, 1974, cited in Vogt, Rice and Pai, op. cit.,
13-15.

All Energy Use In Trillion BTU For Nine Regions, 1972

	Hermelee Data				This Study Total	Ratio (4)/(5)
	Total Listed	Electricity End Use	Feed-Stocks	Revised Total (1)+(2)-(3) =(4)		
	(1)	(2)	(3)		(5)	(6)
New England	3,184.0	216.5	117.4	3,283.1	3,269.4	1.004
Mid Atlantic	10,709.4	723.9	530.2	10,903.1	10,955.3	0.995
East North Central	15,165.7	1,020.5	1,122.9	15,063.3	15,074.6	0.999
West North Central	5,557.4	362.1	359.4	5,660.1	5,597.1	1.011
South Atlantic	9,251.3	864.8	447.5	9,668.6	9,569.8	1.010
East South Central	4,789.9	497.7	232.5	5,055.1	5,074.9	0.996
West South Central	11,504.8	643.0	878.4	11,269.4	11,298.0	0.997
Rocky Mountain	3,469.9	258.3	151.8	3,576.4	3,584.4	0.998
Far West	8,533.9	808.3	449.8	8,892.4	8,768.6	1.014
United States	72,166.9	5,394.9	4,189.9	73,374.9	73,192.1	1.002

Sources: Hermelee - tables A-2 through A-10; table 37 this study

they label "transformation use," and which consists of inputs into energy
production minus energy provided to final end use; (3) the sum of the first
two categories; (4) losses and omissions; and (5) net usage, which more-or-
less corresponds to total use in the present study. A close comparison of
results between studies is not possible because of the following differences
in measurement and definition. Vogt, Rice and Pai follow the Bureau of Mines
convention of including "raw material" use of energy in their consumption
figures, as opposed to the present study; and they diverge from both the
Bureau of Mines and the present study by not measuring hydroelectric and
nuclear power input as fossil fuel equivalents, but rather at end use levels.
Thus, they multiply kilowatt-hours from those fuels by 3,412.8 BTU per kilowatt-hour to obtain a BTU total, rather than by a figure of around 10,500 BTU
per kilowatt-hour, which is used by the Bureau of Mines.[13] This reduces
their total from 72,000 trillion BTU to 69,600 trillion BTU. Finally,
their "losses and omissions" category includes U.S. energy consumption not
specifically allocated to individual states, distribution losses of electricity, and errors found between Bureau of Mines data on computer tape and
in published sources; these items did not appear or were handled in different
fashion in the present study.

Though a close comparison is not possible, the following listing of
more-or-less corresponding results seems of some use.

Their use by customers (column (1) in the table) has four components:
(1) residential-commercial, (2) industrial, (3) transportation and (4) miscellaneous uses. Column (1) exceeds use by customers in this study (column (6))
because it includes raw materials and also because it appears to include some
use classified under the heading of energy production in the present study.

_____

[13]Vogt, Rice and Pai, op. cit., 12 and Crump and Readling, op. cit., 82.

Energy Use By "Customers" And In Energy Production In Trillion BTU For Nine Regions, 1972

| | Vogt, Rice and Pai, 1972 | | | | | This Study, 1972 | | |
	Use by Customers (Their "Final Demand") (1)	Energy Conversion Loss (Their "Transformation" Use) (2)	Gross Flows (1) + (2) (3)	Losses & Omissions (4)	Net Usage (5)	Use By Customers (6)	Energy Production Use (7)	Total Use (8)
New England	2,696.3	412.3	3,108.5	− 39.4	3,069.1	2,515.1	754.3	3,269.4
Mid Atlantic	9,083.9	1,504.8	10,588.8	154.9	10,743.7	8,160.3	2,795.0	10,955.3
East North Central	12,196.2	2,128.5	14,324.6	449.0	14,773.6	11,216.9	3,857.7	15,074.6
West North Central	4,573.2	813.2	5,386.4	10.4	5,396.9	4,004.6	1,592.5	5,597.1
South Atlantic	7,271.0	1,894.4	9,165.4	234.8	9,400.2	6,480.3	3,089.6	9,569.8
East South Central	3,710.1	962.8	4,672.9	204.9	4,877.8	3,227.7	1,847.2	5,074.9
West South Central	9,867.1	1,632.0	11,499.1	− 279.4	11,219.6	6,688.8	4,609.2	11,298.0
Rocky Mountain	2,780.6	449.9	3,230.6	11.3	3,241.9	2,371.9	1,212.5	3,584.4
Far West	6,277.0	724.0	7,001.0	− 90.0	6,911.0	5,781.2	2,987.4	8,768.6
United States	58,455.3	10,522.0	68,977.4	656.5	69,633.9	50,446.7	22,745.4	73,192.1

Sources: Vogt, Rice, and Pai, U.S. totals – page 5, regional totals – pages 251-259; this study – Table 27.

The U.S. raw materials total is 3,428 trillion BTU (chapter 1), while
the second item may well correspond to U.S. non-electric utility energy
production of 4,726 trillion BTU (Table 37). These two items yield a total
of 8,154 trillion BTU, roughly corresponding to the differences between
columns (1) and (6) of 8,009 trillion BTU. It follows that column (2)
is considerably less than column (7) because of exclusion of electricity
in end use, a considerably lower estimate of hydropower and nuclear power,
and omission of most or all of the non-electric utility energy production
use. The first two factors seem to explain the difference in totals
between columns (5) and (8).

The state data presented by Vogt, Rice and Pai could also be compared
to the state figures in the present study, though the utility of that comparison would be limited because of the general measurement and definition problems
noted above. However, their work seems most important for future research
because of two extensions. First, results have been published for 1973 and
1974,[14] as well as for 1972. Second, their state data were disaggregated to
data covering BEA areas. There are 173 BEA areas, referring to areas defined
by the Bureau of Economic Analysis of the U.S. Department of Commerce, with
those areas encompassing all of the area of the United States, and with
metropolitan areas (SMSA's) usually encompassed within specific BEA areas.
Vogt, Rice and Pai do not give details of their estimating procedure, beyond
noting that a voluminous listing of sources is available at Oak Ridge National
Laboratory.[15]

---

[14] D. P. Vogt, P. L. Rice and V. P. Pai, Energy Availabilities for State
and Local Development: 1973 Data Volume, and Energy Availabilities for State
and Local Development: 1974 Data Volume, Regional and Urban Studies Section,
Energy Division, Oak Ridge National Laboratory, Oak Ridge, Tenn. Nov. 1977.

[15] Vogt, Rice and Pai, 1972 report, op cit., 21

A further difficulty is that BEA areas include both urban and rural territory, so that behavioral differences attributable to urbanization tend to become obscured. Nevertheless, the availability of such data could be of great help in future work, with the possibility of some blending of the approaches of the present study with those of the Oak Ridge reports. In particular, the development of price series and the detailed estimation of sectoral relationships, as carried out here, might be joined with the finer geographic breakdown of the Oak Ridge Study to forge some powerful tools of analysis.

Regression Equation Results

As noted at several points, a major future application of the data of the present study, and of similar data for future years, will be in statistical inference, particularly in the fitting of demand curves by regression analysis. By way of example, this section reports on regression equations that were estimated for residential consumption of energy per capita, and industrial consumption of energy per worker in manufactures. The dependent variable in those equations is consumption of a particular energy source, but it would be a relatively straightforward procedure to combine all sources and treat consumption of all energy as the dependent variable.

For the sample of 51 jurisdictions (50 states and the District of Columbia), average residential consumption in million BTU per capita was:

Petroleum products	22.656
Natural gas	24.580
Electricity	8.823

Similarly, average industrial consumption per worker in manufactures, in million BTU per worker, was:

Petroleum Products	265.932
Natural gas	1,123.336
Electricity	237.474

Tables 193 through 195 present the results obtained by relating each dependent variable to a number of explanatory variables, with all equations in logarithmic form.

The first two tables show the residential consumption relationship, with Table 193 presenting estimates for a "full set" of explanatory variables, while Table 194 limits the explanatory variables to those that are statistically significant. (A nonsignificant variable is retained if it causes another variable to become statistically significant.)

Table 195 presents the industrial use results, again in logarithmic form, and including coal and hydropower consumption as a fourth category of use.

The logarithmic form of the equation implies that coefficients are direct measures of elasticities. Thus, a coefficient of 1.0 involves unitary elasticity; a one percent increase in the corresponding variable leads to a one percent increase in energy consumption. Similarly, a coefficient of 2.0 implies that a one percent increase in the explanatory variable yields a two percent increase in consumption.

In all of the equations, each energy source has a negative value for its own price elasticity, while the cross-elasticity for competitive sources is usually positive, i.e., a price increase for a given energy source reduces its use, while a price increase for a competitive source usually increases

its use. The residential use equations employed "real" disposable
income per capita as an explanatory variable; this consisted of
disposable income deflated by accounting for price level differences
between North and South, and between urban areas of different size.
The variable performed somewhat better than disposable income, but
the improvement was marginal. Its elasticity was always positive,
but statistically significant only in the case of electricity, although
its elasticity was higher for petroleum and natural gas (1.3 and 1.0,
respectively) than it was for electricity (0.7). In Table 193, climate
effects are measured by degree days for petroleum products and natural gas,
but by summer temperature and winter temperature (degrees fahrenheit) for
electricity, to account for presumed air conditioning demand for the latter
source. Degree days performed as the best climate measure for petroleum
products use, and so it was retained in Table 194, but summer temperature
had higher explanatory power for natural gas use then did degree days, and
so it replaced degree days in Table 194.

Climate affected consumption in reasonable fashion, even though
different measures of climate worked "best" (had most statistical explanatory
power) in different equations. Warmer climate(measured by lower degree days
or higher summer temperatures) yields lower energy use for petroleum products
and natural gas, while increased summer temperature has a positive effect
on electricity use (presumably reflecting increased use of air conditioning)
and increased winter temperature has a negative effect on that use (presumably
reflecting decreased heating, and perhaps lighting). The combined effect
of the two climate variables suggests increased use as temperature increases,

perhaps reflecting a tendency to use electricity as the heating source in areas of warmer climate.

Urbanization was statistically significant in a number of equations, being measured best by fraction of population in metropolitan areas. (The fraction, rather than the log of the fraction, was used because it performed much better than did the alternative measure.) In residential consumption, urbanization had a positive impact on consumption of natural gas and a negative impact on consumption of electricity and petroleum products. The explanation for these differences may be merely the occurence of pipelines to serve metropolitan areas, or it may reflect lower use of energy as urban size increases. In industrial use, urbanization typically had a negative effect on energy consumption per worker. Perhaps there is less floor area per worker with increased size of metropolitan area, and perhaps industrial processes using energy are correlated with floor area, but this is purely speculative. In the residential equations, population growth was statistically significant only in the case of electricity, perhaps indirectly measuring increased income and suburbanization; its negative coefficient for petroleum products and natural gas may be a muted regional effect, since growth has been strongest in the South and West, with lower heating consumption than occurs in the Northeast and North Central regions.

Regional effects are explicitly estimated in the equations through the use of dummy variables for regions; a dummy variable corresponding to a specific region takes on a value of one when the region appears and a value of zero when it does not appear. The coefficient of the dummy variable can be

interpreted as an effect attributable to regional location that has <u>not</u>
been accounted for by other variables, which often vary considerably
between regions.   It turned out that such regional effects were only of
limited importance.   This is most apparent in Table 194 where only a
few coefficients were statistically significant.   Petroleum product
consumption is above the amount predicted by the other explanatory
variables for the Northeast, and below the predicted amount for Pennsylvania
and West Virginia (presumably accounting for some substitution of coal
for petroleum); and Rocky Mountain consumption falls below prediction for
natural gas and above prediction for electricity, effects that may roughly
balance out.

Explained variance is high in most of the equations, with the residential equation values ranging from .75 to .90.   In conjunction with the
generally "reasonable" nature of the estimated coefficients, the regression
results thus seem quite encouraging, and that seems a pleasant note on which
to conclude this report.

Table 193

Regression Results For Residential Consumption of Energy Per Capita

	LOG RESIDENTIAL CONSUMPTION PER CAPITA		
	Petroleum Products	Natural Gas	Electricity
		Coefficients	
constant term	-2.948	-2.120*	-3.747*
log petroleum products price	-0.661	-0.989	-0.008
log natural gas price	1.707*	-1.886*	0.185*
log electricity price	0.469	1.111*	-1.244*
fraction SMSA population	-0.481	0.360*	-0.182*
log pop. growth 1960-1970	-0.809	-0.552	0.883*
log "real" disposable income	1.289	1.029	0.690*
log degree day	0.300*	1.193	—
log summer temperature	—	—	0.824*
log winter temperature	—	—	-0.025
Regions			
New England	.031	-0.442*	0.037
Middle Atlantic	.119	-0.289*	0.046
East North Central	.111	-0.187	0.056
West North Central	.064	-0.230*	0.062
South Atlantic	-.096	-0.295*	0.013
East South Central	.164	-0.020	0.017
West South Central	.219	-0.313*	0.076
Mountain	.163	-0.060	-0.029
Pacific[a/]	.000	0.000	0.000
		t ratios	
Constant term	0.905	2.784	2.938
log petroleum product price	0.918	1.608	0.060
log natural gas price	4.268	5.516	2.656
log electricity price	1.479	4.101	16.400
fraction SMSA population	3.385	2.966	4.909
log pop. growth 1960-1970	0.855	0.682	4.253
log "real" disposable income	1.418	1.324	3.238
log degree day	2.621	1.217	—
log summer temperature	—	—	1.885
log winter temperature	—	—	0.280
Regions			
New England	0.195	3.292	0.854
Middle Atlantic	0.706	2.009	0.911
East North Central	0.843	1.622	1.244
West North Central	0.501	2.102	1.081
South Atlantic	0.889	3.189	0.310
East South Central	1.126	0.164	0.262
West South Central	1.514	2.524	1.477
Mountain	1.378	0.596	0.695
Pacific[a/]	—	—	—
$\bar{R}^2$	0.747	0.851	0.913

[a/] Omitted from equation. One dummy variable from a set must be omitted (have coefficient set equal to zero) to avoid exact collinearity.

* significant at 10% level
__ indicates variable does not enter equation

Table 194

Regression Results for Residential Consumption of Energy Per Capita ,
Significant Variables Only

	LOG RESIDENTIAL CONSUMPTION PER CAPITA		
	Petroleum Products	Natural Gas	Electricity
	Coefficients		
Constant term	0.373	4.769*	-3.780*
log petroleum products price	-0.854*	-0.721*	——
log natural gas price	0.962*	-2.572*	0.234*
log electricity price	0.415*	0.725*	-1.227*
fraction SMSA population	-0.467*	0.479*	-0.154*
log pop. growth 1960-1970	—	—	0.595*
log "real" disposable income	—	—	0.814*
log degree day	0.245*	—	—
log summer temperature	—	-2.069*	1.002*
log winter temperature	—	—	-0.124*
Regions			
Coal producing region (Pa. and W.Va.)	-0.344*	—	—
New England	0.167[a]	—	—
Middle Atlantic	0.301*	—	—
West South Central	—	-0.204*	0.076*
	t ratios		
constant term	0.765	3.632	3.899
log petroleum products price	1.869	2.743	—
log natural gas price	3.675	16.545	4.947
log electricity price	1.691	3.528	18.912
fraction SMSA population	4.819	5.673	4.779
log pop. growth 1960-1970	—	—	3.063
log "real" disposable income	—	—	4.073
log degree day	3.125	—	—
log summer temperature	—	2.903	4.215
log winter temperature	—	—	2.474
Regions			
Coal producing region (Pa. and W.Va.)	2.623	—	—
New England	1.588[a]	—	—
Middle Atlantic	2.489	—	—
West South Central	—	2.449	3.081
$\bar{R}^2$	.772	0.851	0.898

[a]Retained in equation because it causes another variable to become significant.

*Significant at 10% level.

——Indicates variable does not enter equation.

Table 195

Regression Results for Industrial Consumption of Energy Relative to Manufacturing
   Employment

VARIABLE	LOG INDUSTRIAL CONSUMPTION PER WORKER IN MANUFACTURES			
	Petroleum Products	Natural Gas	Electricity	Coal & Hydropower
	Coefficients			
constant term	3.290*	2.048*	2.222*	2.274*
log petroleum products price	-2.924*	1.684	2.991*	-6.295
log natural gas price	0.963*	-1.977*	0.016	0.824
log electricity price	0.340	0.409	-0.800*	0.430
log coal and hydropower price	0.322	0.009	-0.511	-0.434
fraction SMSA population	-0.619*	-0.052	0.049	-0.998*
Regions:				
New England	-0.892*	-0.583*	0.061	-1.478*
Middle Atlantic	-0.819*	-0.115	0.131	0.185
East North Central	-0.845*	0.060	0.012	1.075*
West North Central	-0.585*	0.102	0.062	0.371
South Atlantic	-0.551*	-0.095	0.217	0.350
East South Central	-0.767*	-0.141	0.131	0.931*
West South Central	-0.191	0.198	0.159	-0.449
Mountain	0.232	0.288	0.232*	0.664
Pacific [a]	0.000	0.000	0.000	0.000
	t ratios			
Constant	8.606	4.430	6.848	1.880
log petroleum product price	2.248	1.071	2.709	1.530
log natural gas price	2.677	4.547	0.052	0.725
log electricity price	1.090	1.084	3.024	0.436
log coal and hydropower price	0.838	0.019	1.566	0.357
fraction SMSA population	4.033	0.281	0.375	2.055
Regions				
New England	3.936	2.125	0.317	2.061
Middle Atlantic	3.911	0.455	0.737	0.279
East North Central	5.406	0.316	0.088	2.173
West North Central	3.753	0.542	0.468	0.752
South Atlantic	3.194	0.455	1.484	0.641
East South Central	4.703	0.714	0.943	1.805
West South Central	1.021	0.875	1.001	0.761
Mountain	1.571	1.610	1.849	1.421
Pacific [a]	---	---	---	---
$\bar{R}^2$: measure of explained variance	0.615	0.779	0.618	0.338

a/ Omitted from equation. One dummy variable from a set must be omitted (have
   coefficient set equal to zero) to avoid exact collinearity.

* significant at 10% level

PART II

Appendixes and Supporting Materials

Introduction to Part II

This part of the report contains the present introduction; a set of
appendixes, comprising the bulk of Part II; a detailed set of source notes
on the construction of the tables in the report; and a list of references
covering the citations appearing in the appendixes.

In contrast to the goals of Part I, which primarily involved subject
matter, the specific goals of this Part primarily involve method. Those
goals are (1) to present a finer breakdown of categories of use than appeared
in text, the tables here being the components used to construct the aggregate
tables of the main body of the report; (2) to document sources and procedures
in considerable detail, not only for the record, but to serve as a basis
for possible future efforts to revise and extend the present estimates; and
(3) to point out problems in the form of gaps and conflicts in source data.

The fine breakdown of categories of use aims at bringing detailed
use statistics together in one place, so that analysts interested in
specific categories of use or in alternative forms of aggregation will be
able to draw on the data in economic fashion.

Some of the present estimates were obtained only through the use
of involved estimating techniques and assumptions, occasionally entailing
a fair amount of expedience. Making those procedures quite explicit
may facilitate possible refinements and extensions, particularly in
extensions to subsequent years.

Most of the complications, the assumptions and the expedients employed in developing estimates occurred because of gaps and conflicts in source data. Making those problems manifest can be useful both to data consumers, who may better avoid pitfalls in using the data, and to data producers, who may be helped in clarifying the problems and in receiving support for their future solution.

There are nine appendixes, labeled A through I. The first five deal with petroleum products, in this order: Appendix A deals with gasoline use, Appendix B with heating fuels, Appendix C with use by electric utilities, Appendix D with transportation and military use of petroleum products other than gasoline, and Appendix E with industrial, refinery and miscellaneous use. The remaining appendixes are Appendix F, on natural gas; Appendix G, on electricity; Appendix H on coal; and Appendix I on hydroelectric and nuclear power.

The length of an appendix was more a consequence of the reporting of difficulties in estimation, and of data conflicts that had to be resolved, than of the relative importance of the subject matter. Appendix B is the longest, in part reflecting the occurrence there of the most formidable set of estimation problems, and in part reflecting the development at that point of some use distributions and prices that were applied in much of the subsequent work.

Each appendix consists of a narrative describing procedures used followed by a set of tables showing state and regional energy use. (The District of Columbia is treated as a state.) The regions are the standard "divisions" defined by the Census Bureau, with states entering each region indicated in the tables of state data and illustrated in a map presented in Part I.

In both text and tables the coverage begins with information on quantities, moves to prices and concludes with expenditures. There are some unnumbered tables in the narrative sections of the appendixes, documenting estimation procedures, but they are to be distinguished from the tables following the narrative, which present results, and are numbered. The table numbers (or codes) assigned consist of three symbols; the first is the letter denoting the appendix; the second denotes the subtopic, with 1 indicating quantities, 2 indicating prices, and 3 indicating expenditures; and the third simply shows place in sequence. Thus, Table B.3.11 would be the eleventh table on prices in Appendix B, and Table D.3.7 would be the seventh table on expenditures in Appendix D.

Several sets of scale factors were applied throughout the report, including data on population and on energy units. Base population data, showing state populations as of July 1, 1972, appear in the first column of Table 196; those data were used in deriving per capita levels of energy use. Columns 2 and 3 of Table 196 respectively show each state population's share of its regional population and of the U.S. total. The former is measured in fractions and the latter in percentages to facilitate the joint presentation of significant digits for the two series. The shares of population were employed as weights in constructing regional and U.S. price indexes. The state population figures were also aggregated to form regional totals, employed in deriving per capita energy use by regions, and those regional totals were as follows:

Regional Population, July 1, 1972 (in 000)

New England	12,105
Mid Atlantic	37,621
East North Central	40,791
West North Central	16,618
South Atlantic	31,920
East South Central	13,155
West South Central	19,983
Rocky Mountain	8,880
Far West	27,155
United States	208,228

All consumption quantities are eventually converted to BTU units, e.g., billion BTU or trillion BTU. Appendix A reports gasoline consumption in barrels, with the corresponding BTU measures presented in chapters 1 and 2 of this report; some of the other appendixes present initial estimates of consumption in units specific to a particular energy source or use, but thereafter, quantities consumed are measured in BTU units.

The Bureau of Mines report by Crump and Readling ([7], page 2, table 6, 82) was a primary source for scale factors converting original measures to BTU. The following scale factors for petroleum products and electricity were obtained from that source.

Petroleum products, BTU per barrel (in millions):

Natural gasoline	4.620
Liquefied gases	4.011
Jet fuel, naphtha-type	5.355
Jet fuel, kerosine-type	5.670
Gasoline (including aviation)	5.248
Special naphtha	5.248
Kerosine	5.670
Distillate (including diesel)	5.825
Residual fuel oil	6.287
Still gas	6.000
Petroleum coke	6.024

Electricity, BTU per kilowatt-hour (in thousands)   3.412

Natural gas data in cubic feet were converted to BTU applying individual state values from data in an American Gas Association report ([1], table 65, 79). Coal data employed appeared in BTU form in Crump and Readling [7], and a National Coal Association report [23], the sources drawn on for the base series on coal use. Kilowatt-hours of electricity generated by hydro-power and nuclear power were converted to estimated fuel equivalent inputs starting with an estimate of 10,520 BTU per kilowatt-hour for the fuel equivalent input and then accounting for conversion and other losses, primarily in transmission. As noted in chapter 5, a better estimate might have been obtained by disregarding the transmission losses, though the ten percent reduction in use has been rationalized as accounting for efficiency differences.

A number of other scale factors were employed in distributing the use of energy to underlying sectors. Data on manufacturing employment were employed in estimating industrial use of petroleum heating fuels, and are presented in Table B.1.6. The distribution of commercial use between sectors for office, school and hospital use of energy was based on data appearing in Table B.1.13, and applied to the use of petroleum heating fuels, natural gas and electricity.

Supporting materials in Part II include a detailed list of source notes which shows how each table in both parts of the report was constructed, often on a column by column basis. The material is presented with the aim of improving the accessibility of the data in the report, thus making them more susceptible to refinement and further application.

In the citation of references in Part II, including citations in the source notes for the tables, source documents and personal communications are referenced in abbreviated fashion followed by a reference number in square brackets, or are cited only by that reference number in brackets. A corresponding list of references at the conclusion of this report lists the full citations and their reference numbers in alphabetic order. Where such seemed helpful, table numbers and page numbers of source documents were also included in the references at the point of citation.

There is a trivial but noticeable flaw involving round-off error in the regional tables presenting totals of large values, consisting of entries with seven or more digits. The computer program generating those totals can introduce small errors in the last digit of such large numbers, typically involving plus or minus .01. For example, in Table D.1.13, the total for the Mid Atlantic region should be 747,893.20, but appears as 747,893.21.

Since the problem is essentially a matter of appearance rather than of

substance, and was embedded in the standard round-off routine of the

package of computer programs drawn upon, it was decided to live with it,

rather than attempt a cosmetic repair job. Hence, the last digit in

totals involving large numbers should generally be disregarded.

The concluding chapter of Part I contains a brief review of the work

covered in the appendixes, as part of a critical analysis of the adequacy

of available data. Hence, there is some focus on data gaps and shortfalls,

and on estimation problems encountered here, in an effort to generalize

from this experience, and to draw on it in making recommendations for

future development of data and for prospective applications of that data

in research.

Table 196

Population By State, And State Population As Share Of Region And U.S. Population, 1972

REGION AND STATE	POPULATION IN THOUSANDS	FRACTION OF REGION POPULATION	PERCENT OF U.S. POPULATION
NEW ENGLAND:			
CONNECTICUT	3080.0	0.2544	1.4792
MAINE	1026.0	0.0848	0.4927
MASSACHUSETTS	5796.0	0.4788	2.7835
NEW HAMPSHIRE	774.0	0.0639	0.3717
RHODE ISLAND	969.0	0.0800	0.4654
VERMONT	460.0	0.0380	0.2209
MID ATLANTIC:			
NEW JERSEY	7349.0	0.1953	3.5293
NEW YORK	18367.0	0.4882	8.8206
PENNSYLVANIA	11905.0	0.3164	5.7173
EAST NORTH CENTRAL:			
ILLINOIS	11244.0	0.2757	5.3999
INDIANA	5286.0	0.1296	2.5386
MICHIGAN	9013.0	0.2210	4.3284
OHIO	10722.0	0.2629	5.1492
WISCONSIN	4526.0	0.1110	2.1736
WEST NORTH CENTRAL:			
IOWA	2884.0	0.1736	1.3850
KANSAS	2268.0	0.1365	1.0892
MINNESOTA	3877.0	0.2333	1.8619
MISSOURI	4747.0	0.2856	2.2797
NEBRASKA	1528.0	0.0920	0.7338
NORTH DAKOTA	634.0	0.0381	0.3045
SOUTH DAKOTA	680.0	0.0409	0.3266
SOUTH ATLANTIC:			
DELAWARE	571.0	0.0179	0.2742
DISTRICT OF COLUMBIA	752.0	0.0236	0.3611
FLORIDA	7347.0	0.2302	3.5283
GEORGIA	4733.0	0.1483	2.2730
MARYLAND	4048.0	0.1268	1.9440
NORTH CAROLINA	5221.0	0.1636	2.5073
SOUTH CAROLINA	2688.0	0.0842	1.2909
VIRGINIA	4765.0	0.1493	2.2884
WEST VIRGINIA	1795.0	0.0562	0.8620
EAST SOUTH CENTRAL:			
ALABAMA	3521.0	0.2677	1.6909
KENTUCKY	3306.0	0.2513	1.5877
MISSISSIPPI	2256.0	0.1715	1.0834
TENNESSEE	4072.0	0.3095	1.9555
WEST SOUTH CENTRAL:			
ARKANSAS	2008.0	0.1005	0.9643
LOUISIANA	3738.0	0.1871	1.7952
OKLAHOMA	2633.0	0.1318	1.2645
TEXAS	11604.0	0.5807	5.5727
ROCKY MOUNTAIN:			
ARIZONA	1963.0	0.2211	0.9427
COLORADO	2364.0	0.2662	1.1353
IDAHO	755.0	0.0850	0.3626
MONTANA	716.0	0.0806	0.3439
NEVADA	533.0	0.0600	0.2560
NEW MEXICO	1076.0	0.1212	0.5167
UTAH	1127.0	0.1269	0.5412
WYOMING	346.0	0.0390	0.1662
FAR WEST:			
ALASKA	325.0	0.0120	0.1561
CALIFORNIA	20411.0	0.7516	9.8022
HAWAII	816.0	0.0301	0.3919
OREGON	2185.0	0.0805	1.0493
WASHINGTON	3418.0	0.1259	1.6415

Appendix A

Gasoline Use

Gasoline Quantities - Overview

Civilian highway use accounts for the bulk of gasoline consumption, and that use for individual states was estimated by subtracting a series on diesel fuel and LPG (liquified petroleum gas) from a series on civilian highway fuel use. Individual state data could be drawn on to distribute nonmilitary highway gasoline use between four categories of use: (1) private sector passenger car and motorcycle use; (2) private sector truck and bus use; (3) federal government civilian highway use and (4) state and local government highway use. Three additional series rounded out an initial accounting for all gasoline consumption; (5) civilian aviation use; (6) marine use; and (7) military use. Total military use was obtained as a residual by subtracting the sum of the U.S. totals of the previous six categories from total U.S. gasoline consumption of 2350.7 million barrels, to yield 25 million barrels in military use. The 25 million barrels were distributed between states in the same proportions as military use of distillate fuel. Table A.1.1 shows the gasoline use by individual states for these initial seven categories, while Table A.1.2 shows the corresponding regional consumption figures.

A finer breakdown of private sector car and motorcycle use, civilian aviation use and military use was then carried out by applying proportions that held at the national level, assuming that those proportions were

invariant between states. On the basis of the U.S. data, it was estimated that for private sector automobile consumption, .915 was in household use and .085 in business use; for civilian aviation, the proportions
were estimated as .30, .63, and .07 in household, business and government
use, respectively; and for military use, the proportions were set at .24
in aviation use and .76 in highway use, given an estimate of six million
barrels of gasoline used in military aviation.

On the basis of available evidence, it was assumed that all of
marine use of gasoline was by the household sector, and all private truck
and bus use was by the business sector. The latter assumption may understate household consumption in states where the farm population comprises
a large proportion of the total, because of the likely use of trucks for
household travel as well as in the farm enterprise; however, the evidence
suggested this problem was generally minor.

The culmination of these operations and inferences was the development
of a cross classification of gasoline consumption by sector and function.
The cross classification for the United States as a whole, both in million
barrels and in percentage terms, is as follows:

U.S. Gasoline Consumption, 1972, By Sector and Function

USE OF GASOLINE BY FUNCTION	USE BY SECTOR, IN MILLION BARRELS				PERCENTAGE DISTRIBUTION OF USE BY SECTOR			
	House-hold	Busi-ness	Govt.	Total	House-hold	Busi-ness	Govt.	Total
Highway Use								
Civilian	1601.67	655.26	41.72	2298.65	68.14	27.88	1.77	97.79
Military	—	—	18.25	18.25	—	—	0.80	0.80
Aviation Use								
Civilian	3.21	6.75	0.75	10.71	0.14	0.29	0.03	0.46
Military	—	—	6.75	6.75	—	—	0.26	0.26
Marine Use	16.35	—	—	16.35	0.69	—	—	0.69
Total Use	1621.23	662.01	67.47	2350.71	68.97	28.17	2.86	100.00

This cross classification of use is disaggregated to the corresponding state values in Tables A.1.3 through A.1.5, and to regional values in Tables A.1.6 through A.1.8. The first table in each set shows the breakdown into sectoral or functional components of private sector car and motorcycle use, civilian aviation use and military use. The second table in each set shows use by sectors (households, business and government) subclassified by function. Finally, the last table in each set shows the aggregate use by sectors and by major functions (highway, aviation and marine), as well as the total use of gasoline by state or region. The remainder of this section presents detailed documentation on sources and estimating procedures employed in developing Tables A.1.1 through A.1.8. In those tables the unit of measure is millions of barrels; in later applications, those units were converted to BTU by using the conversion factor of 5.248 million BTU per barrel.

Highway Use of Gasoline

The Federal Highway Administration report Highway Statistics, 1972 [48], contains data by state on civilian highway fuel use and highway use of "special fuels" (diesel fuel and liquified petroleum gas). Hence, subtraction of the latter from the former gave gasoline use by state. Highway use of gasoline was distributed between sectors as follows. In the source document, Table MF-21, page 5, listed highway use of fuel (1) by households and business (labeled private and commercial use in the source document) and (2) by government broken down into (a) federal (civilian only) and (b), state, county, and municipal government, including school buses. Table MF-25, page 9, listed highway use of special fuels. It was assumed that civilian government use of special fuels was negligible, so that subtraction of

special fuels from household and business fuel use gave household
and business gasoline use. Then the latter result was allocated between
private sector automobiles versus private sector trucks and buses on the
basis of data on registrations and fuel consumption per vehicle. Finally,
outside data were employed to distribute private sector automobile use
between the household and business sectors.

As a preliminary step, the ratio of special fuel use to special fuel
vehicles was calculated and found to vary considerably between states.
This suggested that similar variations in gasoline use per vehicle could
be of some importance. In particular, the source document, Table MV-9,
page 35, listed the registrations of "diesel, butane and other" trucks,
under the heading of "private and commercial truck registrations," and
Table MV-10, page 36, listed "private and commercial diesel, butane and
other" buses (with a U.S. total of 903,053 for the trucks, and 68,984 for
the buses). The ratio of gallons of special fuel to number of buses and
trucks using special fuel was calculated for each state, (Table A.1.9) and
region (Table A.1.10). Source document Table VM-1, page 52, listed annual
gallons of fuel consumption per vehicle in terms of U.S. averages, as
follows:

Motorcycles	90
Passenger cars	755
Single unit trucks	1090
Combination trucks	8687
Commercial buses	6318

It was assumed that combination trucks corresponded to "diesel, butane, etc.," trucks, the registration totals for the two categories being approximately equal. It then followed that single unit trucks corresponded to gasoline-using trucks. It was further assumed that the ratio of fuel use for gasoline-using trucks relative to automobiles was 1092 to 755 or 1.44, for _every_ state; similarly it was assumed that the ratio of fuel use for gasoline-using buses to automobiles was 6318 to 755 or 8.66. (The number of gasoline using buses relative to gasoline using trucks was quite small.) Finally, it was assumed that fuel use for motorcycles was everywhere equal to .12 that for passenger cars (from 90/755). Registrations for private sector passenger cars and motorcycles appeared in source document Table MV-1, page 33; registrations for private sector gasoline-using buses appeared in Table MV-10, page 36. The registrations were multiplied by the previously derived gasoline consumption scale factors for motorcycles, automobiles, trucks, and buses, respectively: 0.12, 1.00, 1.44, and 8.66. The resultant products were summed to give an "auto-equivalent" number of vehicles using gasoline. The partial sum of the automobile and motorcycle products, when divided by the "auto-equivalent" total, gave the share of fuel consumed by automobiles plus motorcycles. That fraction could then be used to break gasoline consumption into two components: (1) gallons consumed by private sector automobiles and motorcycles, and (2) gallons consumed by trucks and buses. (These estimates are presented in Table A.1.1 in terms of barrels consumed by virtue of division of the gallon figures by 42.)

As a derivative statistic, gallons of gasoline consumed per automobile were obtained by dividing total gasoline consumed by the "auto-equivalent"

total, and results by state are presented in Table A.1.9, which also
shows the fraction of private sector highway gasoline consumed by
automobiles and motorcycles, and, for comparison, "special fuel" (diesel,
butane, and other) consumed per special fuel vehicle. Table A.1.10 presents
this information at the regional level.

In Table A.1.10, the calculated U.S. annual average of 759 gallons
per passenger car squares very well with the source estimate of 755 gallons.
That latter estimate was employed only in developing use ratios by vehicle
type, and did not otherwise enter the estimation process. The U.S. annual
average of 8,765 gallons per special fuel vehicle in Table A.1.10 squares
rather well with the initial special truck figure of 8,687. The difference
might be rationalized as reflecting greater fuel consumption by special
fuel buses than by trucks. On the whole, then, the correspondence between
calculated averages and listed averages seems close.

It should be noted that the ratio of fuel use to vehicle registrations
is not exactly the same as the actual average use of fuel by vehicles
registered in a state because some of the fuel use is by vehicles driven
in the state but registered outside of the state, including trucks
moving interstate freight, automobiles on business or recreation trips
between states, and vehicles belonging to people who have moved from
one state to another during the year.

Inspection of the estimates of gallons of fuel use per registered
vehicle showed much greater variation between states for the special
fuel vehicles than for the gasoline using vehicles. This may reflect
(1) variations in travel patterns, e.g., states with high fuel use per
vehicle may tend to be on major routes between origin and destination
states, and (2) possible incentives to register trucks in some states

rather than others, e.g., because of lower vehicle taxes. These variations are not a problem here, since gallons of fuel use is the primary variable of interest, and information on that variable was one of the givens.

Variation in gallons of fuel use per automobile can reflect variations in factors such as (1) miles of use per vehicle, in turn reflecting (a) number of vehicles per consumer unit and (b) settlement pattern, affecting use of car in journey to work, length of work trip, recreation activities, etc., and (2) miles per gallon, probably reflecting congestion associated with density of settlement. The variation may also reflect errors stemming from simplifying assumptions; for example, it is possible that farm trucks in highway use used relatively less gasoline than other trucks, which would lead to overstatement of truck use, and understatement of automobile use in rural states. The resolution of such question awaits better data; for the present, however, the problem seems relatively minor.

Estimates developed to this point cover civilian highway use of gasoline. It was assumed that all non-aviation use of gasoline by the military could be treated as a highway use. (Details on estimation of military use are presented below). Total highway use of gasoline then was obtained as the sum of use by (1) private sector automobiles and motorcycles, (2) trucks and buses, (3) civilian federal government, (4) state and local government and (5) the military.

These estimates of total highway use of gasoline were compared to another series on highway use, and generally good agreement was found between the two series. (The alternative series is from a set of confidential data whose reproduction and citation were not permitted.) However, the comparison did suggest that the FHWA highway use data might involve overstatement of use in New England by about 10 percent, and of use in the Mid Atlantic region by about 5 percent; contrariwise, use in the Rocky Mountain and East North Central region may be under-stated by a few percent, and that in the West North Central region by 5 to 10 percent.

A final step in developing estimates of highway use by sector involved distributing passenger car and motorcycle use between households and business use. The latter category includes business fleet use, travel by salesmen, intercity and intracity business trips by automobile, rental car use, taxicabs and driver training school use. Little data seems available on such use; however, Automobile Facts and Figures, 1975 Edition [21] lists some 1969 U.S. data based on an FHWA study [47] which led to an estimate of 8.5 percent of gasoline use by passenger cars and motor-cycles as attributable to business use.

Business travel is shown as accounting for 4.3 percent of all auto-mobile trips and 7.9 percent of all automobile travel, or mileage ([21], p. 41).

Rental cars comprise 0.35 percent of private sector automobiles, and assuming that their trip mileage is about 1.5 times the average implies that rental car travel accounts for 0.5 percent of mileage (and gasoline use). Taxi trips were estimated to be 0.1 percent of all trips, and

this percentage was assumed to hold for mileage, also ([21], pp. 40, 52).
Hence, mileage attributed to business sector use amounts to 8.5 percent
of the total (7.9 + 0.5 + 0.1). The journey to and from work by automobile is treated as personal consumption and hence, a component of
household use; such was estimated as accounting for 34 percent of all
automobile travel ([21], p. 40).

It was assumed that the 1969 percentages of use held for 1972, and
of more importance, that the U.S. distribution between household and
business use (.915 versus .085) held for every state. The application of
those fractions gave the distribution of passenger car use between the
household and business sectors that is presented in Table A.1.3.

Marine Use of Gasoline

The Boating Industry Association, Chicago, Illinois, listed a figure
of 880 million gallons of fuel used for recreational boating for 1973 [5].
A Department of Transportation report ([46], p. 77) lists the following
fuel consumption for vessels:

	Million Gallons, 1972	Million Gallons, 1973
Residual fuel	3273	3859
Distillate fuel	929	1125
Gasoline	687	717

Data from the two sources were reconciled by assuming that all 717 million gallons of gasoline in 1973 were used in recreational boating, leaving 163 million gallons (880-717) as obtained from distillate fuel. Similarly, it was inferred that all 687 million gallons of gasoline were used in recreational boating (by the household sector) in 1972. The figure of 687 million gallons exactly equals the U.S. total for marine use in Highway Statistics, 1972 [48] and it seems likely this was the source for that datum in [46]. Hence, [48], Table MF-24, p. 8 was used in obtaining marine use of gasoline by individual state, with all of that use allocated to the household sector.

It may be noted that if some marine use of gasoline is commercial, household use of gasoline will be overstated while household use of distillate fuel will be understated, with the reverse errors for business use of fuels. But such errors seem minor.

Aviation Use of Gasoline

The Bureau of Mines, Mineral Industry Surveys ([42], p. 13) lists these data for aviation use of gasoline in 1972:

Commercial	Million Barrels
Airlines	0.925
Factory	0.152
General Aviation	9.630
Total	10.707
Military Use	5.926

The figure of 10.707 million barrels was accepted as a control total for civilian aviation use of gasoline. Then, individual state estimates were derived from Highway Statistics [48] and the confidential series noted earlier, with greater reliance placed on the latter source, based on internal comparisons and some checks against outside information. The initial set of state estimates was then revised by scaling to yield the control total of 10.707 million barrels.

A check of the final set of state estimates was carried out by aggregating the individual state figures into P.A.D. regional totals and then comparing those totals to data listed for P.A.D. districts in ([42], p. 13). The Bureau of Mines does not list aviation fuel consumption by state, but does present regional totals in terms of consumption in "Petroleum Administration for Defense" districts, usually and hereafter referred to as P.A.D. districts. There are five P.A.D. districts, with each a grouping of states. States entering each district are shown in the figure on the following page, and are also enumerated in later tables on aviation fuel consumption. The comparison of aggregated state figures to the Bureau of Mines totals revealed good correspondence, as shown in these comparisons:

P.A.D. Regions	Millions of Barrels		Fraction of U.S. Total	
	State Aggregation To P.A.D. Totals	Bureau of Mines P.A.D. Totals	State Aggregation To P.A.D. Totals	Bureau of Mines P.A.D. Totals
P.A.D. 1	2.800	2.843	.262	.266
P.A.D. 2	3.139	3.103	.293	.290
P.A.D. 3	1.822	1.762	.170	.165
P.A.D. 4	0.373	0.486	.051	.045
P.A.D. 5	2.573	2.513	.224	.235
Total	10.707	10.707	1.000	1.000

PETROLEUM ADMINISTRATION FOR DEFENSE (PAD) DISTRICTS

Source: Bureau of Mines Mineral Industry Surveys, <u>Crude Petroleum</u>,
<u>Petroleum Products and Natural-Gas Liquids: 1972</u>, 1974, p. 44

The civilian aviation use of gasoline by state was distributed

between sectors by applying these proportions for all states: .30 to

households, .63 to business, and .07 to government.   (In later stages

of the work, it was assumed that all of this civilian government use was

by state and local government.)   The proportions employed here were based

on limited information, so the estimates may be subject to considerable

revision.   That information included the following items.   The <u>Statistical</u>

<u>Abstract, 1974</u> [45] p. 577, citing the <u>FAA Statistical Handbook</u>, presents

data on miles flown in general aviation by category.   Fuel consumption

in general aviation was distributed as .69 from gasoline and .31 from jet

fuel. It was assumed that all of the jet fuel use was in business
use, with a corresponding proportion in miles flown. Given that
assumption, the data was used to infer that nongovernmental general
aviation miles flown using gasoline could be distributed as .36 to
households (personal use) and .64 to business (including corporation
not-for-hire aviation, instruction, for-hire aviation, cropdusting and
spraying).

Then, applying data in [42], [48] and the confidential series, total
civilian aviation consumption was distributed as follows:

	Million Barrels		
	Household	Business	Government
Airlines and factories	—	1.077	—
All other civilian aviation	3.189	5.668	0.773
Sector totals	3.189	6.745	0.773

As fractions of the grand total of 10.7 million barrels, the sector totals
yielded .30, .63, and .07 for household, business and government shares,
respectively, and these national proportions were then assumed to hold for
all states.

In considering the adequacy of available data, it may be noted that
there are some conflicts regarding total civilian aviation use of gasoline.
Thus, the DOT report [46] lists a total of 14.215 million barrels distributed
as 13.905 million barrels in general aviation and 0.310 million barrels

used by certified carriers. In contrast, [48] shows civilian aviation use as 8.457 million barrels, perhaps corresponding to general aviation use, only. The decision to use the Bureau of Mines total of 10.7 million barrels was reinforced because that figure fell between these extreme alternative estimates.

Military Use of Gasoline

The U.S. total of gasoline consumption to this point included civilian highway, marine and aviation use, and equaled 2325.7 million barrels, which was 25.0 million barrels less than the U.S. total for gasoline use appearing in the Minerals Yearbook [43]. This residual was inferred to be the military use of gasoline, with six million barrels attributable to military aviation [42], leaving 19 million barrels attributable to ground use, interpreted as military highway use, as noted above. The two categories comprise .24 and .76 of the total, respectively. (The exact figures available were 5.296 and 19.074 million barrels, respectively, rounded here to 6 and 19 million barrels.)

The 25.0 million barrel total was distributed among individual states using the distribution of distillate fuel for military use by state ([39] p. 10). It was assumed that the state fraction of total military distillate fuel use was equal to the state fraction of total military gasoline use.

Gasoline Prices - Overview

Gasoline prices for regular gasoline at the service station, exclusive of taxes, were available for a major city or cities in every state except Alaska and Hawaii, which were estimated from other evidence. The city data were assumed applicable to the corresponding state. Premium gasoline price was set at two cents above the regular price, and the distribution of regular versus premium sales, by state, was used to obtain a weighted average base price. The addition of federal, state, and local highway and sales taxes gave a price taken as applicable to purchases by household passenger cars and motorcycles. Estimates for other sectors and functions were obtained by adding or subtracting appropriate amounts to the base price, reflecting (1) a three cent "premium" for aviation gasoline, (2) varying tax schedules between subsectors and functions, and (3) varying discounts reflecting the advantages of bulk purchases, shifting prices from the retail toward the wholesale level. Price estimates by state are presented in Table A.2.1, covering the household and business sectors, and Table A.2.2, covering the government sector. The price estimates were used at a later stage to develop expenditures by category by state, using prices times corresponding quantities. Expenditures totaled by region, when divided by corresponding quantities, yield weighted average prices by region, and those averages are presented as Table A.2.3. The components entering the price estimates, including taxes and the ratio of premium to regular gasoline use, are presented as Table A.2.4. A detailed discussion of procedures follows.

Gasoline Base Price and Price For Household - Passenger Cars and Motorcycles

Data on 1972 gasoline prices at service stations, for regular gasoline, exclusive of taxes, were available for a set of cities in both Platt's Oil Price Handbook [25] and the Oil and Gas Journal [24]. These were taken as applicable to passenger cars and motorcycles. The Platt's data were annual averages, while an annual average for the second series was derived by averaging 12 monthly prices, employing the data appearing in the first Journal issue of each month. (There was generally little or no variation in price within a given month, so no appreciable difference would emerge for averages based on the 52 weekly observations. Some cities, in fact, showed no listed variation over the entire year.) Platt's covered at least one major city in the 48 conterminous states and the District of Columbia, while the Journal's coverage excluded 16 states and the District of Columbia. Observations on the 38 cities common to both series are shown in the following table, in turn followed by a table of prices for cities covered in only one of the series. There was fairly good correspondence between the two series for the observations in common. Thus, the average of the ratio of Platt to Journal price was essentially one (.9979), with the average price equal to 24.3 cents for the Platt data, and to 24.4 cents for the Journal data. The correlation between the two was only .584, however, there being several cases with considerable differences in value. (Nine of the cases had percentage differences of more than five percent, with the most pronounced differences occurring for Chicago, Miami and New York.) The regression of one series on the other yielded statistically significant results (t = 4.318; the fitted equation was Platt's = 13.368 + .448 Journal). Hence, it was decided there would be no appreciable problem in combining the two series, which would reduce the risk attached to relying on only one of them.

Gasoline Prices At Service Stations Exclusive of Tax, 1972,
 Regular Gasoline In Cents Per Gallon

Comparison Of Platts and Oil & Gas Journal Data For Cities Common To Both
Series

| City | Sources | | Difference: Platt's - Oil & Gas Journal | Ratio: Platt Oil & Gas Journal |
	Platt's	Oil & Gas Journal		
	Cents Per Gallon			
Albuquerque, N.M.	25.48	24.65	0.83	1.0337
Atlanta, Ga.	24.23	22.73	1.50	1.0660
Baltimore, Md.	25.65	26.90	-1.25	0.9535
Birmingham, Ala.	24.79	23.82	0.97	1.0407
Boston, Mass.	24.48	23.98	0.50	1.0209
Buffalo, N.Y.	23.33	24.32	-0.99	0.9593
Charlotte, N.C.	23.11	24.23	-1.12	0.9538
Cheyenne, Wyo.	23.99	23.65	0.34	1.0144
Chicago, Ill.	23.70	27.40	-3.70	0.8650
Cleveland, Ohio	26.90	26.90	0.00	1.0000
Dallas, Tex.	24.15	24.07	0.08	1.0033
Denver, Colo.	24.15	25.40	-1.25	0.9508
Des Moines, Iowa	26.23	25.07	1.16	1.0463
Detroit, Mich.	23.23	23.98	-0.75	0.9687
Houston, Tex.	23.34	23.40	-0.06	0.9974
Indianapolis, Ind.	23.56	24.40	-0.84	0.9656
Little Rock, Ark.	23.56	24.23	-0.67	0.9723
Los Angeles, Calif.	23.32	23.07	0.25	1.0108
Louisville, Ky.	25.28	23.65	1.63	1.0689
Memphis, Tenn.	24.48	24.23	0.25	1.0103
Miami, Fla.	23.98	20.98	3.00	1.1430
Milwaukee, Wisc.	22.73	23.90	-1.17	0.9510
Minneapolis, Minn.	26.06	23.98	2.08	1.0867
Newark, N.J.	24.81	26.48	-1.67	0.9369
New Orleans, La.	22.06	22.23	-0.17	0.9924
New York, N.Y.	26.57	28.90	-2.33	0.9194
Norfolk, Va.	24.90	22.90	2.00	1.0873
Omaha, Nebr.	24.98	24.23	0.75	1.0310
Philadelphia, Pa.	24.74	24.40	0.34	1.0139
Phoenix, Ariz.	24.40	25.48	-1.08	0.9576
Portland, Ore.	24.23	24.07	0.16	1.0066
St. Louis, Mo.	25.98	26.82	-0.84	0.9687
Salt Lake, Utah	24.56	25.15	-0.59	0.9765
San Francisco, Calif.	24.16	23.65	0.51	1.0216
Seattle, Wash.	23.35	22.73	0.62	1.0273
Spokane, Wash.	22.95	22.90	0.05	1.0022
Tulsa, O.K.	24.40	25.30	-0.90	0.9644
Wichita, Kans.	21.40	22.98	-1.58	0.9312
Average	24.30	24.40	-0.10	0.9979

Gasoline Prices At Service Stations Exclusive Of Tax, 1972,
Regular Gasoline In Cents Per Gallon

Prices For Cities Covered In Only One Series

City	Platt's	City	Oil & Gas Journal
	Cents Per Gallon		Cents Per Gallon
Boise, Ida.	22.81	Albany, N.Y.	25.48
Burlington, Vt.	27.23	Amarillo, Tex.	24.48
Charleston, S.C.	24.56	Corpus Christi, Tex.	23.40
Charleston, W. Va.	25.90	Fort Worth, Tex.	22.73
Cincinnati, Ohio	26.48	Jacksonville, Fla.	23.32
El Paso, Tex.	26.90	Kansas City, Mo.	22.82
Fargo, N.D.	21.23	Oklahoma City, O.K.	23.97
Great Falls, Mont.	24.23	Pittsburgh, Pa.	24.65
Hartford, Conn.	24.31	San Antonio, Tex.	22.73
Huron, S.D.	21.48	San Diego, Calif.	23.48
Jackson, Miss.	23.66	Springfield, Ill.	25.23
Manchester, N.H.	24.65	Tampa, Fla.	21.57
Portland, Me.	25.23	Texarkana, Tex.	21.57
Providence, R.I.	24.15	Wichita Falls, Tex.	20.57
Reno, Nev.	27.02		
Washington, D.C.	26.15		
Wilmington, Del.	25.56		

This was done by averaging the observations common to both series; for the other states, the Platt's observation was employed. When only one city was covered for a state, that city's price was assumed to hold for the entire state. In the few cases where more than one city appeared for a state, a weighted average over those cities was employed, based on a rough estimate of the state population corresponding to the observed city coverage. (For example, for the state of Washington, the weights employed were Seattle: .70, Spokane: 30.) Hawaii and Alaska were not covered in either price series, so their values were estimated from outside sources, relying primarily on the transportation cost index for Honolulu and Anchorage in a BLS cost-of-living report for 1972 [38]. (Some additional, confirming data were obtained from the office of one of the U.S. Senators from Alaska.)

Available evidence (from The Oil and Gas Journal [24], Independent Petroleum Association data, and Platt's Oilgram [26], October 3, 1972, 5A) indicated that premium gasoline was almost always two cents per gallon higher than regular gasoline. The ratio of regular and of premium to all gasoline consumed was available in a confidential series; hence, the ratio of the regular to the total quantity times the regular price plus the ratio of the premium to total quantity times the premium price gave the average price at the retail level, and this was treated as a base price. Algebraically, for each state, let

PR = regular price per gallon

QR = regular quantity in gallons

QP = premium quantity in gallons

Q = QR + QP = total quantity

then

$$(PR) \; \frac{QR}{Q} + (PR+2) \; \frac{QP}{Q} \quad = \text{weighted average price.}$$

Data on gasoline taxes were available in Platt's Oil Price Handbook
[25], and were modified for six states on the basis of data in Highway Statistics
([48], Table MFL, p. 10), accounting for state tax changes during the
year apparently not included in the Platt's data. Taxes included federal
tax at four cents per gallon, state taxes and local taxes, where such
occurred. Adding the taxes to the base price gave the average price
for passenger cars and motorcycles in the household sector. The components for this calculation appear in Table A.2.4, which shows regular
price exclusive of taxes; taxes; the ratio of premium quantity to all
gasoline use; and the weighted average emerging at the end of the process.
Table A.2.4 also shows the data sources employed for each state in estimating the regular gasoline price.

Parenthetically, the prices for Hawaii and Alaska were calculated
initially at the retail level, using an estimated price ratio relative
to Los Angeles of 1.1.9 for Honolulu and 1.25 for Anchorage. (In Table A.2.4,
the retail price ratios are respectively 1.24 and 1.18 because the California
figure is an average of Los Angeles, San Francisco and San Diego data.)
Subtracting respective state taxes yielded the Alaska and Hawaii price net
of taxes.

Gasoline Prices for Other Uses

Prices for other uses were obtained by adding to the base price or subtracting from it, amounts to account for (1) a higher price for aviation
gasoline, reflecting both higher octane rating and higher prices for given
octane; (2) tax differences; and (3) bulk use discounts. In all cases

it was assumed that the same distribution between premium and regular

gasoline held for all uses (as indicated by the ratio of premium to all

use in Table A.2.4), there being no evidence available to support a more

refined assumption.

The increments per gallon assigned to the base price by subsector are

indicated in the following chart, where the state and local tax schedule

that held for highway use of gasoline is indicated by A, the corresponding

schedule for aviation use by B, and that for marine use by C. (Available

evidence indicated that category C consisted only of a four cent per gallon

tax by the State of Alaska.) Details on these estimates follow.

Components of Gasoline Prices Per Gallon (Increments to Base Price)

	Aviation Premium	Federal Tax	State and Local Tax	Bulk Discount
Household				
Passenger Car	0	4¢	A	0
Aviation	3¢	7¢	B	0
Marine	0	2¢	C	0
Business				
Passenger Car	0	4¢	A	-2¢
Truck & Bus	0	4¢	A	-3.5¢
Aviation	3¢	3.5¢	B	-1.5¢
Government				
Federal Highway	0	4¢	0	0
State & Local Highway	0	0	A	0
Civilian Aviation	3¢	0	B	-3
Military Highway	0	4¢	0	-6
Military Aviation	3¢	0	0	-6

A,B,C: schedule of state and local taxes on highway, aviation and marine
use of gasoline, respectively.

Aviation gasoline was estimated to cost three cents more per gallon than gasoline for passenger cars, on the basis of data appearing in Platt's Oilgram ([26]; five issues spread over 1972: 1/4, 4/17, 7/17, 10/17 and 12/29). Aviation gasoline for similar octane levels was priced above that for automotive use, and higher octane levels occur for aviation gasoline. The distribution of octane levels is not known, but the range of price data available led to the estimated differential of three cents.

Information on federal tax rates in Highway Statistics, 1972 ([48], p. 59) was extended on the basis of additional information obtained from federal government agencies. Federal taxes include a four cent per gallon tax on highway use, a net two cent gallon tax on marine use (three cent tax and one cent rebate), and a "basic" seven cent per gallon tax on aviation use, taken as applicable to all household sector use and to half of all business sector use. All aircraft under 6,000 pounds pay the tax, which should include most executive and business planes but will normally exclude "for hire" planes [12].

State and federal government exempt one another in gasoline taxes, but make their own agencies liable to their own taxes. (There are some state exemptions to the state taxes; some states exempt ambulances, the National Guard, school buses and public transit [30].)

Federal taxation of federal agency gasoline use applies to the military, but there is an exemption for war vessels and military aircraft [6].

State and local tax rates per gallon for highway use can be derived from Table A.2.4 by subtracting the four cent federal tax. State taxation per gallon of gasoline for aviation use in 1972 was as follows:

New Hampshire	4 ¢	Montana	1
Pennsylvania	1.5	Utah	4
Michigan	3	Wyoming	4
Nebraska	5	Alaska	4
South Dakota	4	Hawaii	1
Alabama	2.7	Oregon	1
Idaho	3.5	California	2

Alaska had a four cent per gallon tax on marine use.   Aviation and marine

use tax information were obtained from Highway Statistics, 1972 ([48]

Table MF101, p. 13, footnote 2, and Table MF102, p. 16, footnote 5).

Assumed discounts for bulk purchases were based on spotty information

and inferences that seemed "most reasonable."

Gasoline prices for business sector truck use were estimated as 3.5

cents per gallon less than those for passenger cars, to account for bulk

purchase discounts for trucking fleets.   The price differential between

retail and wholesale levels (service station versus tank wagon) as

listed in Platt's [25] averaged 7 cents per gallon.   There was some

information to the effect that large trucking operations saved most of

this differential by buying in bulk [27].   Data in Foster Associates

[15], [16] showed that a similar differential held for the price of dis-

tillates as between large industrial versus residential use; however the

differential between all industrial use (including small plants) and

residential use was about half that.   It was assumed that a similar situation

held in trucking, so half the 7 cent retail and wholesale differential was

employed in estimating average price paid by trucks.

Remaining bulk discount estimates were assigned on the basis of
the likelihood of large purchases at one time. Thus, in the case of
business passenger cars, it seemed plausible that fleet use of gasoline
would entail bulk purchases, but that a substantial amount of business
car use would involve single car trips. The scale of operations in
aviation was hypothesized to merit a three cent discount in government
aviation and half that in business aviation. Finally, it was hypothesized that military purchases would be so large that their average price
would be close to the wholesale level.

Gasoline Expenditures and Taxes - Overview

The quantity and price data developed in the previous sections were combined to yield expenditure estimates. Tax rates multiplied by quantities gave estimated taxes collected by all levels of government. Taxes on special fuels were included here for comparison with estimates appearing in Highway Statistics [48].

Total expenditures checked well with Department of Commerce data for the U.S. as a whole, as did state taxes with the Highway Statistics data. However, federal tax estimates exceeded those in the latter source by about 3.5 percent. Total U.S. expenditures on gasoline were estimated as $35 billion, with $25 billion spent by the household sector. Total federal taxes on gasoline and special fuel were estimated as $4.2 billion, state taxes were estimated as $7.8 billion and local taxes as $0.3 billion.

Details on procedures and results follow.

Expenditures on Gasoline

Data on gasoline price in cents per gallon, as shown in Tables A.2.1 and A.2.2, were converted to price in dollars per barrel by multiplication by .42. Then, multiplication by data on corresponding gasoline quantities used, as shown in Table A.1.4, yielded expenditures on gasoline for the 11 sector and function categories, by state. Results, in millions of dollars, are presented in Table A.3.1 for the household and business subsectors, and in Table A.3.2 for the government subsectors.   Table A.3.3

presents aggregate expenditures by sector, function and total, for

each state.   Table A.3.4 presents the regional aggregates of the state

data of Tables A.3.1 and A.3.2, and Table A.3.5 presents regional

aggregates for the state data of Table A.3.3.   The grand total of

$25.06 billion for household expenditures shows good agreement with

the U.S. Department of Commerce, Bureau of Economic Analysis (BEA)

estimate of $25.5 billion in personal consumption expenditures for

gasoline and oil in 1972 (Survey of Current Business [44]; January 1974,

P.9).   Lubricating oil is not included in the $25.06 billion total here.

Data in Highway Statistics([48] p.59 and Table FE-7, p.62) indicate

that U.S. lubricating oil sales, in terms of gallons sold, equal a

bit less than one percent of the total of gasoline and oil (0.95%).

Assuming a lubricating oil price of about four times that for gasoline

implies a refined BEA estimate of $24.6 billion for gasoline only,

which is 98 percent of the estimate developed here.

Taxes on Gasoline and Special Fuel

Amounts collected in gasoline taxes were obtained by multiplying

estimated quantities consumed by corresponding tax rates, using the

series developed above.   Data on taxes collected on gasoline sales

were seen as both a useful by-product of the estimation process, and

as a check on that process, since similar estimates appear in Highway

Statistics, 1972 [48].   That source includes taxes on highway special

fuel use (diesel, etc.) in the totals it presents, so taxes from special

fuel sales were also estimated and employed here, insuring that consis-

tently defined series would be compared.

Table A.3.6 presents estimates of taxes collected by the federal government by detailed category, for each state. Table A.3.7 aggregates the categories of Table A.3.6 to obtain highway and non-highway totals, by state. Tables A.3.8 through A.3.10 present corresponding taxes collected by state and local governments. Taxes here are primarily the excise taxes imposed by state governments, but in some cases, local sales taxes on gasoline are included in the estimates. Table A.3.8 presents detailed subsector data on highway taxes, Table A.3.9 presents corresponding data on non-highway taxes, and Table A.3.10 presents the totals for each of those major categories, and their grand total.

Tables A.3.11 and A.3.12 present the corresponding tax data by regions, with the former covering federal taxes and the latter covering state and local taxes.

Table A.3.13 combines the federal with the state and local taxes, to show taxes collected by all levels of government, by function (highway versus non-highway), sector (household, business, and government), and the grand total, for each state. Table A.3.14 shows corresponding regional values. Total U.S. taxes collected are estimated as $12.2 billion, with roughly one-third collected by the federal government, and two-thirds by state and local governments. Taxes account for roughly one-third of spending on gasoline and special fuel by ultimate consumers, a result suggested by the list of tax rates and gasoline prices of Table A.2.4. For gasoline use only, taxes paid by household passenger cars account for .317 of gasoline purchased by that subsector, while .327 of all other gasoline purchased is accounted for by taxes.

Table A.3.15 carries out the comparison of the tax estimates developed here to those appearing in Highway Statistics, by state. Table A.3.16 makes the comparison by region.

The series being compared seem generally close, although the alternative state tax estimates are closer in percentage terms than are the federal tax estimates. For the U.S. as a whole, state tax collections estimated here are about one percent below the corresponding total in Highway Statistics, while estimated federal taxes here are 3.5 percent above the corresponding figure in that document.

In making the comparisons of state tax collections, local taxes were first estimated and then subtracted from the series developed here. Most states did not have local taxes on gasoline, but such taxes were of some importance in several states. They were estimated employing the difference between the state tax rates shown in Highway Statistics, 1972 ([48] Table MF-1, p. 10) and the state plus local tax rates used here.

For the U.S. as a whole, local taxes amounted to four percent of state and local tax collections. After the local taxes were removed, the remaining state taxes were compared to the listed gross tax collections made by states shown in Highway Statistics, 1972 (in Table MF-1). Since the taxes listed as collected are stated to be "compiled from the reports of state authorities and other sources" the comparison can be interpreted as essentially involving independently derived series. Good correspondence occurred at both regional and state levels, with most of the figures compared differing by only a few percentage points.

The federal tax comparisons utilized estimated private sector motor fuel taxes, as listed in Highway Statistics, 1972 ([48] Table FE-7, p. 62).

Those data were "estimated by the Federal Highway Administration, based on U.S. Internal Revenue Service collections." Hence, independence--or at least, quasi-independence--of the series being compared seems assured.

There was a small "overstatement" of taxes for the estimates here relative to those in Highway Statistics for every region and almost every state. At the national level, the difference amounted to 137 million dollars. It seemed possible that private special fuel taxes had been overstated here, since all special fuel use had been treated as non-governmental; however, federal taxes from that source were estimated as $341 million here, and $321 million in Highway Statistics. Hence, no ready explanation emerges for the small, but persistent and regular differential that occurs between the alternative federal tax series.

Table A.1.1

Gasoline Quantities, 1972, In Thousand Barrels, By State

Categories Of Use For Which State Data Were Available

REGION AND STATE	CIVILIAN HIGHWAY USE				ALL OTHER USE		
	Passenger Car and Motorcycle	Truck And Bus	Federal Govt. Highway	State and Local Govt. Highway	Civilian Aviation	Marine	Military
NEW ENGLAND:							
CONNECTICUT	27280.95	3116.67	59.52	452.38	75.59	194.38	144.90
MAINE	8964.29	3004.76	21.43	126.19	56.04	97.00	750.48
MASSACHUSETTS	47271.43	6221.43	111.90	600.00	136.03	308.45	650.17
NEW HAMPSHIRE	7250.00	1673.81	14.29	150.00	28.81	38.12	19.81
RHODE ISLAND	7302.38	1157.14	19.05	119.05	17.94	138.98	92.88
VERMONT	4380.95	1207.14	11.90	61.90	18.73	44.64	2.48
MID ATLANTIC:							
NEW JERSEY	64754.76	8340.48	116.67	940.48	231.16	508.48	672.46
NEW YORK	117678.57	16750.00	302.38	3066.67	235.08	1275.00	1848.96
PENNSYLVANIA	94257.14	18814.29	195.24	1157.14	203.38	453.40	422.30
EAST NORTH CENTRAL:							
ILLINOIS	91042.86	18028.57	169.05	1630.95	340.04	631.10	518.90
INDIANA	45719.05	15790.48	64.29	830.95	234.06	462.31	56.97
MICHIGAN	81876.19	18561.91	121.43	2716.67	364.00	999.10	808.69
OHIO	95400.00	16204.76	135.71	1150.00	309.83	754.88	132.51
WISCONSIN	37166.67	9790.48	73.81	719.05	163.26	422.48	184.52
WEST NORTH CENTRAL:							
IOWA	23414.29	9885.71	50.00	861.90	176.27	254.29	11.15
KANSAS	18411.90	9552.38	45.24	592.86	225.72	162.55	139.94
MINNESOTA	32338.10	11302.38	88.10	650.00	183.06	406.90	260.07
MISSOURI	42192.86	16521.43	102.38	471.43	258.90	436.36	39.63
NEBRASKA	12473.81	6466.67	42.86	364.29	127.46	93.90	53.25
NORTH DAKOTA	3835.71	3140.48	45.24	183.33	66.53	47.00	16.10
SOUTH DAKOTA	5450.00	3483.33	52.38	157.14	67.96	46.57	1.24
SOUTH ATLANTIC:							
DELAWARE	5426.19	1238.10	11.90	57.14	16.03	23.69	14.86
DISTRICT OF COLUMBIA	4961.90	490.48	100.00	90.48	0.81	20.98	27.25
FLORIDA	72790.48	15580.95	207.14	1385.71	907.28	734.69	299.70
GEORGIA	46647.62	15114.29	102.38	769.05	276.06	449.69	256.35
MARYLAND	34180.95	7150.00	95.24	304.76	87.73	239.21	739.34
NORTH CAROLINA	45430.95	15395.24	78.57	2002.38	213.77	459.38	401.25
SOUTH CAROLINA	24411.90	7692.86	59.52	652.38	99.44	267.62	361.62
VIRGINIA	42680.95	11188.10	121.43	1107.14	147.60	316.81	842.13
WEST VIRGINIA	11852.38	4795.24	40.48	361.90	49.02	49.02	3.72
EAST SOUTH CENTRAL:							
ALABAMA	29828.57	10759.52	90.48	638.10	201.48	286.55	835.93
KENTUCKY	26511.90	10626.19	66.67	483.33	107.25	198.36	480.51
MISSISSIPPI	18419.05	8752.38	64.29	290.48	178.89	205.76	86.69
TENNESSEE	35097.62	11945.24	185.71	1100.00	267.63	405.00	216.72
WEST SOUTH CENTRAL:							
ARKANSAS	15621.43	9738.10	45.24	295.24	177.47	168.67	191.96
LOUISIANA	27885.71	10383.33	76.19	414.29	249.41	320.48	1078.66
OKLAHOMA	22500.00	12204.76	83.33	738.10	247.23	252.79	50.78
TEXAS	111209.52	46623.81	328.57	1219.05	884.31	1227.33	2603.16
ROCKY MOUNTAIN:							
ARIZONA	16928.57	7697.62	140.48	445.24	265.67	224.79	47.06
COLORADO	20140.48	8540.48	119.05	578.57	201.97	117.67	180.81
IDAHO	6233.33	3538.10	88.10	207.14	104.19	90.95	2.48
MONTANA	5173.81	3933.33	92.86	192.86	92.89	63.00	53.25
NEVADA	5642.86	2504.76	114.29	100.00	107.19	92.88	55.73
NEW MEXICO	9400.00	5297.62	152.38	214.29	130.27	62.93	268.74
UTAH	9050.00	4490.48	76.19	180.95	79.47	77.55	127.56
WYOMING	3269.05	2466.67	40.48	121.43	70.32	39.19	11.15
FAR WEST:							
ALASKA	1345.24	814.29	57.14	114.29	305.42	125.86	693.52
CALIFORNIA	177950.00	51071.43	545.24	3552.38	1282.47	1391.40	7392.13
HAWAII	5016.67	959.52	26.19	111.90	71.81	50.33	180.81
OREGON	20609.52	5752.38	147.62	666.67	154.40	276.67	162.23
WASHINGTON	25776.19	10714.29	185.71	935.71	209.86	336.38	506.51

Table A.1.2

Gasoline Quantities, 1972, In Thousand Barrels, By Region

Categories Of Use For Which State Data Were Available

REGION	CIVILIAN HIGHWAY USE				ALL OTHER USE		
	Passenger Car and Motorcycle	Truck And Bus	Federal Govt. Highway	State and Local Govt. Highway	Civilian Aviation	Marine	Military
NEW ENGLAND	102450.001	16380.950	238.090	1509.520	333.140	821.570	1660.720
MID ATLANTIC	276690.468	43904.770	614.290	5164.290	669.620	2236.880	2943.720
EAST NORTH CENTRAL	351204.775	78376.202	564.290	7047.620	1411.190	3269.870	1701.590
WEST NORTH CENTRAL	138116.673	60352.381	426.200	3280.950	1105.900	1447.570	521.380
SOUTH ATLANTIC	288383.320	78645.261	816.660	6730.940	1797.740	2561.090	2946.220
EAST SOUTH CENTRAL	109857.141	42083.330	407.150	2511.910	755.250	1095.670	1619.850
WEST SOUTH CENTRAL	177216.662	78950.000	533.330	2666.680	1558.420	1969.270	3924.560
ROCKY MOUNTAIN	75838.101	38469.060	823.830	2040.480	1051.970	768.960	746.780
FAR WEST	230697.619	69311.910	961.900	5380.950	2023.960	2180.640	8935.200
TOTAL:	1750454.740	506473.862	5385.740	36333.340	10707.190	16351.520	25000.020

Table A.1.3

Gasoline Quantities, 1972, In Thousand Barrels, By State

Distribution Of Three Major Categories Of Use By Sector Or Function Using U.S. Proportions

REGION AND STATE	PASSENGER CAR AND MOTORCYCLE		CIVILIAN AVIATION			MILITARY	
	Household	Business	Household	Business	Government	Highway	Aviation
NEW ENGLAND:							
CONNECTICUT	24962.07	2318.88	22.68	47.62	5.29	110.12	34.78
MAINE	8202.33	761.96	16.81	35.31	3.92	570.36	180.12
MASSACHUSETTS	43253.36	4018.07	40.81	85.70	9.52	494.13	156.04
NEW HAMPSHIRE	6633.75	616.25	8.64	18.15	2.02	15.06	4.75
RHODE ISLAND	6681.68	620.70	5.38	11.30	1.26	70.59	22.29
VERMONT	4008.57	372.38	5.62	11.80	1.31	1.88	0.60
MID ATLANTIC:							
NEW JERSEY	59250.61	5504.15	69.35	145.63	16.18	511.07	161.39
NEW YORK	107675.89	10002.68	70.52	148.10	16.46	1405.21	443.75
PENNSYLVANIA	86245.28	8011.86	61.01	128.13	14.24	320.95	101.35
EAST NORTH CENTRAL:							
ILLINOIS	83304.22	7738.64	102.01	214.23	23.80	394.36	124.54
INDIANA	41832.93	3886.12	70.22	147.46	16.38	43.30	13.67
MICHIGAN	74916.71	6959.48	109.20	229.32	25.48	614.60	194.09
OHIO	87291.00	8109.00	92.95	195.19	21.69	100.71	31.80
WISCONSIN	34007.50	3159.17	48.98	102.85	11.43	140.24	44.28
WEST NORTH CENTRAL:							
IOWA	21424.08	1990.21	52.88	111.05	12.34	8.47	2.68
KANSAS	16846.89	1565.01	67.72	142.20	15.80	106.35	33.59
MINNESOTA	29589.36	2748.74	54.92	115.33	12.81	197.65	62.42
MISSOURI	38606.47	3586.39	77.67	163.11	18.12	30.12	9.51
NEBRASKA	11413.54	1060.27	38.24	80.30	8.92	40.47	12.78
NORTH DAKOTA	3509.67	326.04	19.96	41.91	4.66	12.24	3.86
SOUTH DAKOTA	4986.75	463.25	20.39	42.81	4.76	0.94	0.30
SOUTH ATLANTIC:							
DELAWARE	4964.96	461.23	4.81	10.10	1.12	11.29	3.57
DISTRICT OF COLUMBIA	4540.14	421.76	0.24	0.51	0.06	20.71	6.54
FLORIDA	66603.29	6187.19	272.18	571.59	63.51	227.77	71.93
GEORGIA	42682.57	3965.05	82.82	173.92	19.32	194.83	61.52
MARYLAND	31275.57	2905.38	26.32	55.27	6.14	561.90	177.44
NORTH CAROLINA	41569.32	3861.63	64.13	134.68	14.96	304.95	96.30
SOUTH CAROLINA	22336.89	2075.01	29.83	62.65	6.96	274.83	86.79
VIRGINIA	39053.07	3627.88	44.28	92.99	10.33	640.02	202.11
WEST VIRGINIA	10844.93	1007.45	14.71	30.88	3.43	2.83	0.89
EAST SOUTH CENTRAL:							
ALABAMA	27293.14	2535.43	60.45	126.93	14.10	635.31	200.62
KENTUCKY	24258.39	2253.51	32.17	67.57	7.51	365.19	115.32
MISSISSIPPI	16853.43	1565.62	53.67	112.70	12.52	65.88	20.81
TENNESSEE	32114.32	2983.30	80.29	168.61	18.73	164.71	52.01
WEST SOUTH CENTRAL:							
ARKANSAS	14293.61	1327.82	53.24	111.81	12.42	145.89	46.07
LOUISIANA	25515.42	2370.29	74.82	157.13	17.46	819.78	258.88
OKLAHOMA	20587.50	1912.50	74.17	155.75	17.31	38.59	12.19
TEXAS	101756.71	9452.81	265.29	557.12	61.90	1978.40	624.76
ROCKY MOUNTAIN:							
ARIZONA	15489.64	1438.93	79.70	167.37	18.60	35.77	11.29
COLORADO	18428.54	1711.94	60.59	127.24	14.14	137.42	43.39
IDAHO	5703.50	529.83	31.26	65.64	7.29	1.88	0.60
MONTANA	4734.04	439.77	27.87	58.52	6.50	40.47	12.78
NEVADA	5163.22	479.64	32.16	67.53	7.50	42.35	13.38
NEW MEXICO	8601.00	799.00	39.08	82.07	9.12	204.24	64.50
UTAH	8280.75	769.25	23.84	50.07	5.56	96.95	30.61
WYOMING	2991.18	277.87	21.10	44.30	4.92	8.47	2.68
FAR WEST:							
ALASKA	1230.89	114.35	91.63	192.41	21.38	527.08	166.44
CALIFORNIA	162824.25	15125.75	384.74	807.96	89.77	5618.02	1774.11
HAWAII	4590.25	426.24	21.54	45.24	5.03	137.42	43.39
OREGON	18857.71	1751.81	46.32	97.27	10.81	123.29	38.94
WASHINGTON	23585.21	2190.98	62.96	132.21	14.69	384.95	121.56

Table A.1.4

Gasoline Quantities, 1972, In Thousand Barrels, By State

Sector Use Subclassified By Function

REGION AND STATE	HOUSEHOLD			BUSINESS			GOVERNMENT				
	Passenger Car and Motorcycle	Aviation	Marine	Passenger Car and Motorcycle	Truck and Bus	Aviation	Federal Govt. Highway	State and Local Highway	Civilian Aviation	Military Highway	Military Aviation
NEW ENGLAND:											
CONNECTICUT	24962.07	22.68	194.38	2318.88	3116.67	47.62	59.52	452.38	5.29	110.12	34.78
MAINE	8202.33	16.81	97.00	761.96	3004.76	35.31	21.43	126.19	3.92	570.36	180.12
MASSACHUSETTS	43253.36	40.81	308.45	4018.07	6221.43	85.70	111.90	600.00	9.52	494.13	156.04
NEW HAMPSHIRE	6633.75	8.64	38.12	616.25	1673.81	18.15	14.29	150.00	2.02	15.06	4.75
RHODE ISLAND	6681.68	5.38	138.98	620.70	1157.14	11.30	19.05	119.05	1.26	70.59	22.29
VERMONT	4008.57	5.62	44.64	372.38	1207.14	11.80	11.90	61.90	1.31	1.88	0.60
MID ATLANTIC:											
NEW JERSEY	59250.61	69.35	508.48	5504.15	8340.48	145.63	116.67	940.48	16.18	511.07	161.39
NEW YORK	107675.89	70.52	1275.00	10002.68	16750.00	148.10	302.38	3066.67	16.46	1405.21	443.75
PENNSYLVANIA	86245.28	61.01	453.40	8011.86	18814.29	128.13	195.24	1157.14	14.24	320.95	101.35
EAST NORTH CENTRAL:											
ILLINOIS	83304.22	102.01	631.10	7738.64	18028.57	214.23	169.05	1630.95	23.80	394.36	124.54
INDIANA	41832.93	70.22	462.31	3886.12	15790.48	147.46	64.29	830.95	16.38	43.30	13.67
MICHIGAN	74916.71	109.20	999.10	6959.48	18561.91	229.32	121.43	2716.67	25.48	614.60	194.09
OHIO	87291.00	92.95	754.88	8109.00	16204.76	195.19	135.71	1150.00	21.69	100.71	31.80
WISCONSIN	34007.50	48.98	422.48	3159.17	9790.48	102.85	73.81	719.05	11.43	140.24	44.28
WEST NORTH CENTRAL:											
IOWA	21424.08	52.88	254.29	1990.21	9885.71	111.05	50.00	861.90	12.34	8.47	2.68
KANSAS	16846.89	67.72	162.55	1565.01	9552.38	142.20	45.24	592.86	15.80	106.35	33.59
MINNESOTA	29589.36	54.92	406.90	2748.74	11302.38	115.33	88.10	650.00	12.81	197.65	62.42
MISSOURI	38606.47	77.67	436.36	3586.39	16521.43	163.11	102.38	471.43	18.12	30.12	9.51
NEBRASKA	11413.54	38.24	93.90	1060.27	6446.67	80.30	42.86	364.29	8.92	40.47	12.78
NORTH DAKOTA	3509.67	19.96	47.00	326.04	3140.48	41.91	45.24	183.33	4.66	12.24	3.86
SOUTH DAKOTA	4986.75	20.39	46.57	463.25	3483.33	42.81	52.38	157.14	4.76	0.94	0.30
SOUTH ATLANTIC:											
DELAWARE	4964.96	4.81	23.69	461.23	1238.10	10.10	11.90	57.14	1.12	11.29	3.57
DISTRICT OF COLUMBIA	4540.14	0.24	20.98	421.76	490.48	0.51	100.00	90.48	0.06	20.71	6.54
FLORIDA	66603.29	272.18	734.69	6187.19	15580.95	571.59	207.14	1385.71	63.51	227.77	71.93
GEORGIA	42682.57	82.82	449.69	3965.05	15114.29	173.92	102.38	769.05	19.32	194.83	61.52
MARYLAND	31275.57	26.32	239.21	2905.38	7150.00	55.27	95.24	304.76	6.14	561.90	177.44
NORTH CAROLINA	41569.32	64.13	459.38	3861.63	15395.24	134.68	78.57	2002.38	14.96	304.95	96.30
SOUTH CAROLINA	22336.89	29.83	267.62	2075.01	7692.86	62.65	59.52	652.38	6.96	274.83	86.79
VIRGINIA	39053.07	44.28	316.81	3627.88	11188.10	92.99	121.43	1107.14	10.33	640.02	202.11
WEST VIRGINIA	10844.93	14.71	49.02	1007.45	4795.24	30.88	40.48	361.90	3.43	2.83	0.89
EAST SOUTH CENTRAL:											
ALABAMA	27293.14	60.45	286.55	2535.43	10759.52	126.93	90.48	638.10	14.10	635.31	200.62
KENTUCKY	24258.39	32.17	198.36	2253.51	10626.19	67.57	66.67	483.33	7.51	365.19	115.32
MISSISSIPPI	16853.43	53.67	205.76	1565.62	8752.38	112.70	64.29	290.48	12.52	65.88	20.81
TENNESSEE	32114.32	80.29	405.00	2983.30	11945.24	168.61	185.71	1100.00	18.73	164.71	52.01
WEST SOUTH CENTRAL:											
ARKANSAS	14293.61	53.24	168.67	1327.82	9738.10	111.81	45.24	295.24	12.42	145.89	46.07
LOUISIANA	25515.42	74.82	320.48	2370.29	10383.33	157.13	76.19	414.29	17.46	819.78	258.88
OKLAHOMA	20587.50	74.17	252.79	1912.50	12204.76	155.75	83.33	738.10	17.31	38.59	12.19
TEXAS	101756.71	265.29	1227.33	9452.81	46623.81	557.12	328.57	1219.05	61.90	1978.40	624.76
ROCKY MOUNTAIN:											
ARIZONA	15489.64	79.70	224.79	1438.93	7697.62	167.37	140.48	445.24	18.60	35.77	11.29
COLORADO	18428.54	60.59	117.67	1711.94	8540.48	127.24	119.05	578.57	14.14	137.42	43.39
IDAHO	5703.50	31.26	90.95	529.83	3538.10	65.64	88.10	207.14	7.29	1.88	0.60
MONTANA	4734.04	27.87	63.00	439.77	3933.33	58.52	92.86	192.86	6.50	40.47	12.78
NEVADA	5163.22	32.16	92.88	479.64	2504.76	67.53	114.29	100.00	7.50	42.35	13.38
NEW MEXICO	8601.00	39.08	62.93	799.00	5297.62	82.07	152.38	214.29	9.12	204.24	64.50
UTAH	8280.75	23.84	77.55	769.25	4490.48	50.07	76.19	180.95	5.56	96.95	30.61
WYOMING	2991.18	21.10	39.19	277.87	2466.67	44.30	40.48	121.43	4.92	8.47	2.68
FAR WEST:											
ALASKA	1230.89	91.63	125.86	114.35	814.29	192.41	57.14	114.29	21.38	527.08	166.44
CALIFORNIA	162824.25	384.74	1391.40	15125.75	51071.43	807.76	545.24	3552.38	89.77	5618.02	1774.11
HAWAII	4590.25	21.54	50.33	426.42	959.52	45.24	26.19	111.90	5.03	137.42	43.39
OREGON	18857.71	46.32	276.67	1751.81	5752.38	97.27	147.62	666.67	10.81	123.29	38.94
WASHINGTON	23585.21	62.96	336.38	2190.98	10744.29	132.21	185.71	935.71	14.69	384.95	121.56

Table A.1.5

Gasoline Quantities, 1972, In Thousand Barrels, By State

Aggregate Use By Sectors, Functions and Total

REGION AND STATE	SECTORS			FUNCTIONS			TOTAL (Sector sum = Function sum)
	Household	Business	Government	Highway	Aviation	Marine	
NEW ENGLAND:							
CONNECTICUT	25179.13	5483.17	662.09	31019.64	110.37	194.38	31324.39
MAINE	8316.14	3802.03	902.02	12687.03	236.16	97.00	13020.19
MASSACHUSETTS	43602.62	10325.20	1371.59	54698.89	292.07	308.45	55299.41
NEW HAMPSHIRE	6680.51	2308.21	186.12	9103.16	33.56	38.12	9174.84
RHODE ISLAND	6826.04	1789.14	232.24	8668.21	40.23	138.98	8847.42
VERMONT	4058.83	1591.32	77.59	5663.77	19.33	44.64	5727.74
MID ATLANTIC:							
NEW JERSEY	59828.44	13990.26	1745.79	74663.46	392.55	508.48	75564.49
NEW YORK	109021.41	26900.78	5234.47	139202.83	678.83	1275.00	141156.66
PENNSYLVANIA	86759.69	26954.28	1788.92	114744.76	304.73	453.40	115502.89
EAST NORTH CENTRAL:							
ILLINOIS	84037.33	25981.44	2342.70	111265.80	464.58	631.10	112361.47
INDIANA	42365.46	19824.06	968.59	62448.07	247.73	462.31	63158.11
MICHIGAN	76025.01	25750.71	3672.27	103890.80	558.09	999.10	105447.99
OHIO	88138.83	24508.95	1439.91	112991.18	341.63	754.88	114087.69
WISCONSIN	34478.96	13052.50	988.81	47890.25	207.54	422.48	48520.27
WEST NORTH CENTRAL:							
IOWA	21731.25	11986.97	935.39	34220.37	178.95	254.29	34653.61
KANSAS	17077.16	11259.59	793.84	28708.73	259.31	162.55	29130.59
MINNESOTA	30051.18	14166.45	1010.98	44576.23	245.48	406.90	45228.61
MISSOURI	39120.50	20270.93	631.56	59318.22	268.41	436.36	60022.99
NEBRASKA	11545.68	7607.24	469.32	19388.10	140.24	93.90	19622.24
NORTH DAKOTA	3576.63	3508.43	249.33	7217.00	70.39	47.00	7334.39
SOUTH DAKOTA	5053.71	3989.39	215.52	9143.79	68.26	46.57	9258.62
SOUTH ATLANTIC:							
DELAWARE	4993.46	1709.43	85.02	6744.62	19.60	23.69	6787.91
DISTRICT OF COLUMBIA	4561.36	912.75	217.79	5663.57	7.35	20.98	5691.90
FLORIDA	67610.16	22339.73	1956.06	90192.05	979.21	734.69	91905.95
GEORGIA	43215.08	19253.26	1147.10	62828.17	337.58	449.69	63615.44
MARYLAND	31541.10	10110.65	1145.48	42292.85	265.17	239.21	42797.23
NORTH CAROLINA	42092.83	19391.55	2497.16	63212.09	310.07	459.38	63981.54
SOUTH CAROLINA	22634.34	9830.52	1080.48	33091.49	186.23	267.62	33545.34
VIRGINIA	39414.16	14908.97	2081.03	55737.64	349.71	316.81	56404.16
WEST VIRGINIA	10908.66	5833.57	409.53	17052.83	49.91	49.02	17151.76
EAST SOUTH CENTRAL:							
ALABAMA	27640.14	13421.88	1578.61	41951.98	402.10	286.55	42640.63
KENTUCKY	24488.92	12947.27	1038.02	38053.28	222.57	198.36	38474.21
MISSISSIPPI	17112.86	10430.70	453.98	27592.08	199.70	205.76	27997.54
TENNESSEE	32599.61	15097.15	1521.16	48493.28	319.64	405.00	49217.92
WEST SOUTH CENTRAL:							
ARKANSAS	14515.52	11177.73	544.86	25845.90	223.54	168.67	26238.11
LOUISIANA	25910.72	12910.75	1586.60	39579.30	508.29	320.48	40408.07
OKLAHOMA	20914.46	14273.01	889.52	35564.78	259.42	252.79	36076.99
TEXAS	103249.33	56633.74	4212.68	161359.35	1509.07	1227.33	164095.75
ROCKY MOUNTAIN:							
ARIZONA	15794.13	9303.92	651.38	25247.68	276.96	224.79	25749.43
COLORADO	18606.80	10379.66	892.57	29516.00	245.36	117.67	29879.03
IDAHO	5825.71	4133.57	305.01	10068.55	104.79	90.95	10264.29
MONTANA	4824.91	4431.62	345.47	9433.33	105.67	63.00	9602.00
NEVADA	5288.26	3051.93	277.52	8404.26	120.57	92.88	8617.71
NEW MEXICO	8703.01	6178.69	644.53	15268.53	194.77	62.93	15526.23
UTAH	8382.14	5309.80	390.26	13894.57	110.08	77.55	14082.20
WYOMING	3051.47	2788.84	177.98	5906.10	73.00	39.19	6018.29
FAR WEST:							
ALASKA	1448.38	1121.05	886.33	2858.04	471.86	125.86	3455.76
CALIFORNIA	164600.39	67005.14	11579.52	238737.07	3056.58	1391.40	243185.05
HAWAII	4662.12	1431.18	323.93	6251.70	115.20	50.33	6417.23
OREGON	19180.70	7601.46	987.33	27299.48	193.34	276.67	27769.49
WASHINGTON	23984.55	13037.48	1642.62	37996.85	331.42	336.38	38664.65

Table A.1.6

Gasoline Quantities, 1972, In Thousand Barrels, By Region

Distribution Of Three Major Categories Of Use

REGION	PASSENGER CAR AND MOTORCYCLE		CIVILIAN AVIATION			MILITARY	
	Households	Business	Households	Business	Government	Highway	Aviation
NEW ENGLAND	93741.760	8708.240	99.940	209.880	23.320	1262.140	398.580
MID ATLANTIC	253171.783	23518.690	200.880	421.860	46.880	2237.230	706.490
EAST NORTH CENTRAL	321352.363	29852.410	423.360	889.050	98.780	1293.210	408.380
WEST NORTH CENTRAL	126376.761	11739.910	331.780	696.710	77.410	396.240	125.140
SOUTH ATLANTIC	263870.742	24512.580	539.320	1132.590	125.830	2239.130	707.090
EAST SOUTH CENTRAL	100519.280	9337.860	226.580	475.810	52.860	1231.090	388.760
WEST SOUTH CENTRAL	162153.240	15063.420	467.520	981.810	109.090	2982.660	941.900
ROCKY MOUNTAIN	69391.870	6446.230	315.600	662.740	73.630	567.550	179.230
FAR WEST	211088.313	19609.310	607.190	1275.090	141.680	6790.760	2144.440
TOTAL:	1601666.100	148788.650	3212.170	6745.540	749.480	19000.010	6000.010

Table A.1.7

Gasoline Quantities, 1972, In Thousand Barrels, By Region

Sector Use Subclassified By Function

REGION	HOUSEHOLD			BUSINESS		
	Passenger Car and Motorcycle	Aviation	Marine	Passenger Car and Motorcycle	Truck and Bus	Aviation
NEW ENGLAND	93741.760	99.940	821.570	8708.240	16380.950	209.880
MID ATLANTIC	253171.783	200.880	2236.880	23518.690	43904.770	421.860
EAST NORTH CENTRAL	321352.363	423.360	3269.870	29852.410	78376.202	889.050
WEST NORTH CENTRAL	126376.761	331.780	1447.570	11739.910	60352.381	696.710
SOUTH ATLANTIC	263870.742	539.320	2561.090	24512.580	78645.261	1132.590
EAST SOUTH CENTRAL	100519.280	226.580	1095.670	9337.860	42083.330	475.810
WEST SOUTH CENTRAL	162153.240	467.520	1969.270	15063.420	78950.000	981.810
ROCKY MOUNTAIN	69391.870	315.600	768.960	6446.230	38469.060	662.740
FAR WEST	211088.313	607.190	2180.640	19609.310	69311.910	1275.090
TOTAL	1601666.100	3212.170	16351.520	148788.650	506473.862	6745.540

GOVERNMENT					
	Federal Govt. Highway	State and Local Govt. Highway	Civilian Aviation	Military Highway	Military Aviation
NEW ENGLAND	238.090	1509.520	23.320	1262.140	398.580
MID ATLANTIC	614.290	5164.290	46.880	2237.230	706.490
EAST NORTH CENTRAL	564.290	7047.620	98.780	1293.210	408.380
WEST NORTH CENTRAL	426.200	3280.950	77.410	396.240	125.140
SOUTH ATLANTIC	816.660	6730.940	125.830	2239.130	707.090
EAST SOUTH CENTRAL	407.150	2511.910	52.860	1231.090	388.760
WEST SOUTH CENTRAL	533.330	2666.680	109.090	2982.660	941.900
ROCKY MOUNTAIN	823.830	2040.480	73.630	567.550	179.230
FAR WEST	961.900	5380.950	141.680	6790.760	2144.440
TOTAL	5385.740	36333.340	749.480	19000.010	6000.010

Table A.1.8

Gasoline Quantities, 1972, In Thousand Barrels, By Region

Aggregate Use By Sectors, Functions and Total

REGION	SECTORS			FUNCTIONS			TOTAL
	Households	Business	Government	Highway	Aviation	Marine	
NEW ENGLAND	94663.271	25299.070	3431.650	121840.701	731.720	821.570	1233393.990
MID ATLANTIC	255609.542	67845.320	8769.180	328611.050	1376.110	2236.880	332224.037
EAST NORTH CENTRAL	325045.593	109117.660	9412.280	438486.099	1819.570	3269.870	443575.531
WEST NORTH CENTRAL	128156.109	72789.000	4305.940	202572.441	1231.040	1447.570	205251.051
SOUTH ATLANTIC	266971.149	104290.430	10619.650	376815.315	2504.830	2561.090	381881.233
EAST SOUTH CENTRAL	101841.530	51897.000	4591.770	156090.621	1144.010	1095.670	158330.301
WEST SOUTH CENTRAL	164590.031	94995.230	7233.660	262349.334	2500.320	1969.270	266818.922
ROCKY MOUNTAIN	70476.431	45578.030	3684.720	117739.021	1231.200	768.960	119739.180
FAR WEST	213876.141	90196.309	15419.730	313143.142	4168.400	2180.640	319492.180
TOTAL:	1621229.780	662008.040	67468.579	2317647.650	16707.200	16351.520	2350706.480

Table A.1.9

Annual Gasoline and "Special Fuel" Use Per Vehicle, 1972, By State

Passenger Car and Motorcycle Share of Total Gasoline Use, and Fuel Use Per Vehicle

REGION	SHARE OF TOTAL Passenger Car and Motorcycle Use As Fraction of Private Sector Highway Gasoline	FUEL USE PER VEHICLE IN GALLONS PER YEAR	
		Gasoline Use Per Passenger Car	"Special Fuel" Use Per Special Fuel Vehicle
NEW ENGLAND:			
CONNECTICUT	0.898	676.770	6847.390
MAINE	0.749	835.400	8474.580
MASSACHUSETTS	0.884	781.980	4936.720
NEW HAMPSHIRE	0.812	827.230	4220.930
RHODE ISLAND	0.863	646.230	4347.830
VERMONT	0.784	856.090	7247.850
MID ATLANTIC:			
NEW JERSEY	0.886	788.880	7220.620
NEW YORK	0.875	791.440	5375.820
PENNSYLVANIA	0.834	725.650	8057.570
EAST NORTH CENTRAL:			
ILLINOIS	0.835	780.680	12642.420
INDIANA	0.743	830.790	11443.130
MICHIGAN	0.815	805.680	8601.140
OHIO	0.855	728.900	9897.270
WISCONSIN	0.792	792.070	8516.000
WEST NORTH CENTRAL:			
IOWA	0.703	676.420	11472.300
KANSAS	0.658	631.510	11084.070
MINNESOTA	0.741	724.200	8923.410
MISSOURI	0.719	872.670	12214.130
NEBRASKA	0.659	673.170	7941.000
NORTH DAKOTA	0.550	556.720	14336.590
SOUTH DAKOTA	0.610	733.730	11101.330
SOUTH ATLANTIC:			
DELAWARE	0.814	851.690	2049.560
DISTRICT OF COLUMBIA	0.910	896.940	7248.370
FLORIDA	0.824	740.730	5923.930
GEORGIA	0.755	825.370	12068.330
MARYLAND	0.827	784.660	6397.280
NORTH CAROLINA	0.747	757.410	7039.980
SOUTH CAROLINA	0.760	854.160	9887.060
VIRGINIA	0.792	832.280	11641.170
WEST VIRGINIA	0.712	742.670	11547.980
EAST SOUTH CENTRAL:			
ALABAMA	0.735	717.170	7751.600
KENTUCKY	0.714	735.280	11840.970
MISSISSIPPI	0.678	840.150	12517.630
TENNESSEE	0.746	810.030	10937.540
WEST SOUTH CENTRAL:			
ARKANSAS	0.616	897.340	11581.700
LOUISIANA	0.729	774.330	9752.040
OKLAHOMA	0.648	709.780	4160.700
TEXAS	0.705	842.230	10435.080
ROCKY MOUNTAIN:			
ARIZONA	0.687	733.170	12161.930
COLORADO	0.702	664.880	6163.610
IDAHO	0.638	684.050	6011.480
MONTANA	0.568	576.690	19006.320
NEVADA	0.693	801.560	19055.340
NEW MEXICO	0.639	793.270	15833.860
UTAH	0.668	705.540	8071.340
WYOMING	0.570	789.430	10770.020
FAR WEST:			
ALASKA	0.623	560.980	7202.390
CALIFORNIA	0.777	707.610	8458.190
HAWAII	0.840	540.380	5051.700
OREGON	0.782	705.550	11249.920
WASHINGTON	0.706	637.400	7132.960

Table A.1.10

Annual Gasoline and "Special Fuel" Use Per Vehicle, 1972, By Region

Passenger Car and Motorcycle Share of Total Gasoline Use, and Fuel
Use Per Vehicle

REGION	SHARE OF TOTAL	FUEL USE PER VEHICLE IN GALLONS PER YEAR	
	Car and Motorcycle Use As Fraction Of Private Sector Highway Use	Gasoline Use Per Passenger Car	Special Fuel Use Per Vehicle (Trucks & Buses)
New England	.8621	751.83	5,669.55
Mid Atlantic	.8631	766.37	6,988.85
East North Central	.8176	779.90	10,350.27
West North Central	.6959	724.62	10,606.60
South Atlantic	.7857	788.05	8,174.51
East South Central	.7230	769.24	10,286.38
West South Central	.6918	815.88	8,527.12
Rocky Mountain	.6635	705.81	10,396.41
Far West	.7690	692.58	8,479.48
United States	.7756	759.02	8,764.52

Table A.2.1

Gasoline Prices, 1972, In Cents Per Gallon By State

Weighted Averages, Premium and Regular Gasoline, Estimates For Private Sector Use

Region and State	Household			Business		
	Passenger Car and Motorcycle	Aviation	Marine	Passenger Car and Motorcycle	Truck and Bus	Aviation
NEW ENGLAND:						
CONNECTICUT	39.19	35.18	27.19	37.19	35.69	30.18
MAINE	38.82	35.83	27.82	36.82	35.32	30.83
MASSACHUSETTS	36.56	35.06	27.06	34.56	33.06	30.06
NEW HAMPSHIRE	38.40	39.42	27.40	36.40	34.90	34.42
RHODE ISLAND	36.99	34.99	26.99	34.99	33.49	29.99
VERMONT	40.91	37.92	29.92	38.91	37.41	32.92
MID ATLANTIC:						
NEW JERSEY	38.13	36.62	28.62	36.13	34.63	31.62
NEW YORK	41.13	36.72	28.72	39.13	37.63	31.72
PENNSYLVANIA	37.38	36.88	27.38	35.38	33.88	31.88
EAST NORTH CENTRAL:						
ILLINOIS	38.27	35.61	27.61	36.27	34.77	30.61
INDIANA	36.57	34.57	26.57	34.57	33.07	29.57
MICHIGAN	35.09	37.09	26.09	33.09	31.59	32.09
OHIO	38.66	37.48	29.48	36.66	35.16	32.48
WISCONSIN	34.74	33.74	25.74	32.74	31.24	28.74
WEST NORTH CENTRAL:						
IOWA	37.09	36.09	28.09	35.09	33.59	31.09
KANSAS	33.62	32.62	24.62	31.62	30.12	27.62
MINNESOTA	36.39	35.39	27.39	34.39	32.89	30.39
MISSOURI	35.33	35.66	27.66	33.33	31.83	30.66
NEBRASKA	37.48	39.98	26.98	35.48	33.98	34.98
NORTH DAKOTA	32.48	31.47	23.48	30.48	28.98	26.47
SOUTH DAKOTA	32.73	35.72	23.73	30.73	29.22	30.72
SOUTH ATLANTIC:						
DELAWARE	38.99	36.49	28.49	36.99	35.49	31.49
DISTRICT OF COLUMBIA	38.87	37.62	29.36	36.87	35.37	32.62
FLORIDA	35.83	33.83	25.83	33.83	32.33	28.83
GEORGIA	36.35	34.43	26.43	34.35	32.85	29.43
MARYLAND	39.19	37.19	29.19	37.19	35.69	32.19
NORTH CAROLINA	38.73	34.53	26.53	36.73	35.23	29.53
SOUTH CAROLINA	37.56	35.48	27.47	35.56	34.06	30.48
VIRGINIA	36.78	34.78	26.78	34.78	33.28	29.78
WEST VIRGINIA	39.33	36.82	28.83	37.33	35.83	31.82
EAST SOUTH CENTRAL:						
ALABAMA	37.25	37.95	27.25	35.25	33.75	32.95
KENTUCKY	37.30	35.31	27.30	35.30	33.80	30.31
MISSISSIPPI	36.50	34.50	26.50	34.50	33.00	29.50
TENNESSEE	36.33	35.33	27.33	34.33	32.83	30.33
WEST SOUTH CENTRAL:						
ARKANSAS	36.19	34.69	26.69	34.19	32.69	29.69
LOUISIANA	35.11	33.11	25.11	33.11	31.61	28.11
OKLAHOMA	35.60	35.10	27.10	33.60	32.10	30.10
TEXAS	33.44	34.40	26.40	31.44	29.94	29.40
ROCKY MOUNTAIN:						
ARIZONA	36.72	35.72	27.72	34.72	33.22	30.72
COLORADO	36.31	35.31	27.31	34.31	32.81	30.31
IDAHO	35.56	36.76	25.26	33.56	32.06	31.76
MONTANA	35.64	35.63	26.64	33.64	32.14	30.63
NEVADA	39.89	37.89	29.89	37.89	36.39	32.89
NEW MEXICO	36.61	35.61	27.61	34.61	33.11	30.61
UTAH	36.38	39.38	27.38	34.38	32.88	34.38
WYOMING	35.25	38.24	26.25	33.25	31.75	33.24
FAR WEST:						
ALASKA	43.77	45.77	37.77	41.77	40.27	40.77
CALIFORNIA	35.71	34.57	26.57	33.71	32.21	29.57
HAWAII	42.43	44.41	35.41	40.43	38.93	39.41
OREGON	36.12	35.87	26.87	34.12	32.62	30.87
WASHINGTON	36.75	35.75	25.75	34.75	33.25	30.75

Table A.2.2

Gasoline Prices, 1972, in Cents Per Gallon, By State

Weighted Averages, Premium and Regular Gasoline, Estimates For Public Sector

Region and State	Government				
	Federal Highway	State and Local Govt.	Civilian Aviation	Military Highway	Military Aviation
NEW ENGLAND:					
CONNECTICUT	29.19	35.19	25.18	23.19	19.19
MAINE	29.82	34.82	25.83	23.82	19.82
MASSACHUSETTS	29.06	32.56	25.06	23.06	19.06
NEW HAMPSHIRE	29.40	34.40	29.42	23.40	19.40
RHODE ISLAND	28.99	32.99	24.99	22.99	18.99
VERMONT	31.91	36.91	27.92	25.91	21.91
MID ATLANTIC:					
NEW JERSEY	30.62	34.13	26.62	24.62	20.62
NEW YORK	30.72	37.13	26.72	24.72	20.72
PENNSYLVANIA	29.38	33.38	26.88	23.38	19.38
EAST NORTH CENTRAL:					
ILLINOIS	29.61	34.27	25.61	23.61	19.61
INDIANA	28.57	32.57	24.57	22.57	18.57
MICHIGAN	28.09	31.09	27.09	22.09	18.09
OHIO	31.48	34.66	27.48	25.48	21.48
WISCONSIN	27.74	30.74	23.74	21.74	17.74
WEST NORTH CENTRAL:					
IOWA	30.09	33.09	26.09	24.09	20.09
KANSAS	26.62	29.62	22.62	20.62	16.62
MINNESOTA	29.39	32.39	25.39	23.39	19.39
MISSOURI	29.66	31.33	25.66	23.66	19.66
NEBRASKA	28.98	33.48	29.98	22.98	18.98
NORTH DAKOTA	25.48	28.48	21.47	19.48	15.48
SOUTH DAKOTA	25.72	28.73	25.72	19.72	15.73
SOUTH ATLANTIC:					
DELAWARE	30.49	34.99	26.49	24.49	20.49
DISTRICT OF COLUMBIA	31.37	34.87	27.62	25.37	21.37
FLORIDA	27.83	31.83	23.83	21.83	17.83
GEORGIA	28.43	32.35	24.43	22.43	18.43
MARYLAND	31.19	35.19	27.19	25.19	21.19
NORTH CAROLINA	28.53	34.73	24.53	22.53	18.53
SOUTH CAROLINA	29.47	33.56	25.48	23.47	19.47
VIRGINIA	28.78	32.78	24.78	22.78	18.78
WEST VIRGINIA	30.83	35.33	26.82	24.83	20.83
EAST SOUTH CENTRAL:					
ALABAMA	29.25	33.25	27.95	23.25	19.25
KENTUCKY	29.30	33.30	25.31	23.30	19.30
MISSISSIPPI	28.50	32.50	24.50	22.50	18.50
TENNESSEE	29.33	32.33	25.33	23.33	19.33
WEST SOUTH CENTRAL:					
ARKANSAS	28.69	32.19	24.69	22.69	18.69
LOUISIANA	27.11	31.11	23.11	21.11	17.11
OKLAHOMA	29.10	31.60	25.10	23.10	19.10
TEXAS	28.40	29.44	24.40	22.40	18.40
ROCKY MOUNTAIN:					
ARIZONA	29.72	32.72	25.72	23.72	19.72
COLORADO	29.31	32.31	25.31	23.31	19.31
IDAHO	27.26	31.56	26.76	21.26	17.26
MONTANA	28.64	31.64	25.63	22.64	18.64
NEVADA	31.89	35.89	27.89	25.89	21.89
NEW MEXICO	29.61	32.61	25.61	23.61	19.61
UTAH	29.38	32.38	29.38	23.38	19.38
WYOMING	28.25	31.25	28.24	22.25	18.25
FAR WEST:					
ALASKA	35.77	39.77	35.77	29.77	25.77
CALIFORNIA	28.57	31.71	24.57	22.57	18.57
HAWAII	37.41	38.43	34.41	31.41	27.41
OREGON	28.87	32.12	25.87	22.87	18.87
WASHINGTON	27.75	32.75	25.75	21.75	17.75

Table A.2.3

Gasoline Prices, 1972, In Cents Per Gallon, By Region

Weighted Averages (Obtained By Dividing Region Expenditures By Region Quantities)
For Sectors and Functions

Region	Household			Business		
	Passenger and Motorcycle	Aviation	Marine	Passenger and Motorcycle	Truck and Bus	Aviation
NEW ENGLAND	37.8047	35.7357	27.3286	35.8035	34.5145	27.7937
MID ATLANTIC	39.1512	36.7431	28.4303	37.1508	35.4539	28.7277
EAST NORTH CENTRAL	37.0401	35.9932	27.1891	35.0398	33.3149	28.0128
WEST NORTH CENTRAL	35.6606	35.3074	27.0075	33.6601	31.9777	27.3052
SOUTH ATLANTIC	37.3116	34.4349	26.7743	35.3113	33.8894	26.4459
EAST SOUTH CENTRAL	36.8430	35.8330	27.1415	34.8428	33.3460	27.8222
WEST SOUTH CENTRAL	34.2217	34.3250	26.3090	32.2209	30.8348	26.3362
ROCKY MOUNTAIN	36.5601	36.3631	27.4335	34.5606	32.9690	28.3815
FAR WEST	36.0596	36.8207	27.3402	34.0594	32.5959	28.8308
TOTAL	36.9067	35.6531	27.2073	34.9067	32.9603	27.6479

Region	Government					All Uses Combined
	Federal Highway	State and Local Govt. Highway	Civilian Aviation	Military Highway	Military Aviation	
NEW ENGLAND	29.3006	33.9275	25.5248	23.4107	19.4142	36.8658
MID ATLANTIC	30.2711	35.7446	26.9178	24.5095	20.4903	38.2248
EAST NORTH CENTRAL	29.3669	32.5473	26.0319	22.7930	18.7734	36.0137
WEST NORTH CENTRAL	28.3234	31.6473	25.2213	22.5332	18.4555	34.2542
SOUTH ATLANTIC	29.2422	33.4843	24.4094	23.3403	19.3280	36.1674
EAST SOUTH CENTRAL	29.1808	32.7677	25.6743	23.2469	19.2309	35.4629
WEST SOUTH CENTRAL	28.3484	30.6070	24.4446	22.0720	18.0739	32.7746
ROCKY MOUNTAIN	29.4501	32.4153	26.5161	23.5767	19.5280	34.9814
FAR WEST	29.1338	32.2567	26.8882	23.2704	19.2747	34.6250
TOTAL	29.2262	32.9738	25.6368	23.2055	19.2063	35.5962

Table A.2.4

Gasoline Prices, 1972, In Cents Per Gallon, By State

Components of Gasoline Price At Service Station, Passenger Car and Motorcycle Use

Region and State	Source Of Data Code a/	Regular Gasoline Price, Net of Taxes At The Service Station	Ratio Of Premium Gasoline Quantity To All Gasoline Use	Gasoline Taxes, All Levels of Govt.	Gasoline Weighted Average Prices, Including Taxes, At The Service Station
NEW ENGLAND:					
CONNECTICUT	2	24.31	0.4394	14.00	39.1888
MAINE	2	25.23	0.2959	13.00	38.8218
MASSACHUSETTS	1	24.23	0.4144	11.50	36.5588
NEW HAMPSHIRE	2	24.65	0.3755	13.00	38.4010
RHODE ISLAND	2	24.15	0.4223	12.00	36.9946
VERMONT	2	27.23	0.3420	13.00	40.9140
MID ATLANTIC:					
NEW JERSEY	1	25.65	0.4874	11.51	38.1298
NEW YORK	1	25.93	0.3981	14.41	41.1312
PENNSYLVANIA	1	24.63	0.3730	12.00	37.3810
EAST NORTH CENTRAL:					
ILLINOIS	1	25.01	0.2979	12.66	38.2658
INDIANA	1	23.98	0.2970	12.00	36.5740
MICHIGAN	1	23.61	0.2446	11.00	35.0942
OHIO	1	26.81	0.3354	11.18	38.6608
WISCONSIN	1	23.31	0.2114	11.00	34.7378
WEST NORTH CENTRAL:					
IOWA	1	25.65	0.2183	11.00	37.0866
KANSAS	2	22.19	0.2169	11.00	33.6238
MINNESOTA	1	25.02	0.1840	11.00	36.3880
MISSOURI	1	25.10	0.2782	9.67	35.3314
NEBRASKA	1	24.61	0.1871	12.50	37.4792
NORTH DAKOTA	1	21.23	0.1230	11.00	32.4761
SOUTH DAKOTA	2	21.48	0.1225	11.00	32.7250
SOUTH ATLANTIC:					
DELAWARE	2	25.56	0.4658	12.50	38.9916
DISTRICT OF COLUMBIA	1	26.15	0.6102	11.50	38.8704
FLORIDA	1	22.97	0.4288	12.00	35.8276
GEORGIA	1	23.48	0.4742	11.92	36.3484
MARYLAND	1	26.27	0.4557	12.00	39.1864
NORTH CAROLINA	1	23.67	0.4300	14.20	38.7300
SOUTH CAROLINA	1	24.56	0.4573	12.09	37.5646
VIRGINIA	1	23.90	0.4421	12.00	36.7842
WEST VIRGINIA	1	25.90	0.4642	12.50	39.3284
EAST SOUTH CENTRAL:					
ALABAMA	1	24.31	0.4741	12.00	37.2532
KENTUCKY	1	24.46	0.4193	12.00	37.3036
MISSISSIPPI	2	23.66	0.4203	12.00	36.5006
TENNESSEE	1	24.36	0.4855	11.00	36.3260
WEST SOUTH CENTRAL:					
ARKANSAS	2	23.89	0.3957	11.50	36.1864
LOUISIANA	1	22.14	0.4831	12.00	35.1112
OKLAHOMA	1	24.52	0.2910	10.50	35.6020
TEXAS	1	23.61	0.3992	9.04	33.4434
ROCKY MOUNTAIN:					
ARIZONA	1	24.94	0.3895	11.00	36.7190
COLORADO	1	24.78	0.2676	11.00	36.3102
IDAHO	2	22.81	0.2261	12.30	35.5622
MONTANA	1	24.23	0.2035	11.00	35.6370
NEVADA	2	27.02	0.4360	12.00	39.8920
NEW MEXICO	2	25.06	0.2738	11.00	36.6126
UTAH	1	24.85	0.2609	11.00	36.3768
WYOMING	2	23.82	0.2135	11.00	35.2470
FAR WEST:					
ALASKA	3	31.09	0.3404	12.00	43.7709
CALIFORNIA	1	23.49	0.5421	11.14	35.7142
HAWAII	3	32.00	0.7031	9.02	42.4262
OREGON	1	24.15	0.3624	11.25	36.1248
WASHINGTON	1	23.03	0.3628	13.00	36.7506

a/ Regular gasoline price data obtained as follows:

1. Average of data in Platt's Oil Price Handbook [25] and Oil and Gas Journal [24].
2. From Platt's Oil Price Handbook [25].
3. From Other Sources (see text).

Table A.3.1

Gasoline Expenditures, 1972, In Million Dollars, By State

Estimated Expenditures By Private Sectors

Region and State	Household			Business		
	Passenger Car and Motorcycle	Aviation	Marine	Passenger Car and Motorcycle	Truck and Bus	Aviation
NEW ENGLAND:						
CONNECTICUT	410.858	0.335	2.220	36.219	46.717	0.544
MAINE	133.740	0.253	1.133	11.784	44.576	0.413
MASSACHUSETTS	664.142	0.601	3.506	58.321	86.383	0.974
NEW HAMPSHIRE	106.992	0.143	0.439	9.421	24.535	0.239
RHODE ISLAND	103.818	0.079	1.576	9.123	16.278	0.128
VERMONT	68.883	0.089	0.561	6.086	18.969	0.148
MID ATLANTIC:						
NEW JERSEY	948.870	1.067	6.112	83.523	121.308	1.751
NEW YORK	1860.112	1.088	15.380	164.395	264.736	1.786
PENNSYLVANIA	1354.053	0.945	5.214	119.056	267.728	1.554
EAST NORTH CENTRAL:						
ILLINOIS	1338.835	1.526	7.317	117.872	263.247	2.484
INDIANA	642.599	1.020	5.160	56.431	219.347	1.646
MICHIGAN	1104.240	1.701	10.950	96.734	246.308	2.802
OHIO	1417.391	1.463	9.347	124.859	239.304	2.417
WISCONSIN	496.165	0.694	4.567	43.438	128.450	1.112
WEST NORTH CENTRAL:						
IOWA	333.709	0.802	3.000	29.329	139.452	1.310
KANSAS	237.912	0.928	1.681	20.786	120.857	1.470
MINNESOTA	452.213	0.816	4.681	39.700	156.119	1.327
MISSOURI	572.889	1.163	5.070	50.207	220.878	1.895
NEBRASKA	179.663	0.642	1.064	15.799	92.288	1.079
NORTH DAKOTA	47.872	0.264	0.463	4.173	38.219	0.413
SOUTH DAKOTA	68.540	0.306	0.464	5.978	42.756	0.499
SOUTH ATLANTIC:						
DELAWARE	81.309	0.074	0.284	7.166	18.456	0.121
DISTRICT OF COLUMBIA	74.120	0.004	0.259	6.531	7.286	0.006
FLORIDA	1002.219	3.867	7.970	87.905	211.552	6.201
GEORGIA	651.606	1.198	4.992	57.201	208.522	1.931
MARYLAND	514.742	0.411	2.932	45.377	107.166	0.678
NORTH CAROLINA	676.192	0.930	5.119	59.572	227.797	1.501
SOUTH CAROLINA	352.412	0.444	3.088	30.995	110.063	0.723
VIRGINIA	603.345	0.647	3.564	53.001	156.402	1.046
WEST VIRGINIA	179.136	0.228	0.594	15.795	72.158	0.374
EAST SOUTH CENTRAL:						
ALABAMA	427.038	0.964	3.280	37.540	152.531	1.597
KENTUCKY	380.069	0.477	2.275	33.414	150.865	0.775
MISSISSIPPI	258.367	0.778	2.290	22.686	121.310	1.254
TENNESSEE	489.966	1.191	4.648	43.010	164.688	1.935
WEST SOUTH CENTRAL:						
ARKANSAS	217.238	0.776	1.891	19.065	133.687	1.253
LOUISIANA	376.269	1.041	3.380	32.963	137.856	1.657
OKLAHOMA	307.842	1.093	2.877	26.991	164.555	1.773
TEXAS	1429.298	3.833	13.610	124.836	586.352	6.177
ROCKY MOUNTAIN:						
ARIZONA	238.881	1.196	2.617	20.982	107.397	1.949
COLORADO	281.040	0.899	1.350	24.670	117.690	1.460
IDAHO	85.188	0.483	0.965	7.469	47.644	0.793
MONTANA	70.857	0.417	0.705	6.213	53.090	0.679
NEVADA	86.508	0.512	1.166	7.633	38.284	0.848
NEW MEXICO	132.260	0.585	0.730	11.615	73.675	0.952
UTAH	126.515	0.394	0.892	11.107	62.006	0.660
WYOMING	44.281	0.339	0.432	3.880	32.890	0.563
FAR WEST:						
ALASKA	22.628	1.761	1.997	2.006	13.773	3.052
CALIFORNIA	2442.358	5.587	15.530	214.180	690.995	9.016
HAWAII	81.794	0.402	0.749	7.240	15.687	0.692
OREGON	286.117	0.698	3.123	25.108	78.821	1.139
WASHINGTON	364.044	0.945	3.638	31.978	149.628	1.541

Table A.3.2

Gasoline Expenditures, 1972, In Million Dollars, By State

Estimated Expenditures By Public Sector

Region and State	Federal Highway	State and Local Government	Civilian Aviation	Military Highway	Military Aviation
NEW ENGLAND:					
CONNECTICUT	0.730	6.686	0.056	1.073	0.280
MAINE	0.268	1.846	0.043	5.706	1.500
MASSACHUSETTS	1.366	8.205	0.100	4.785	1.249
NEW HAMPSHIRE	0.176	2.167	0.025	0.148	0.039
RHODE ISLAND	0.232	1.650	0.013	0.682	0.178
VERMONT	0.160	0.960	0.015	0.021	0.006
MID ATLANTIC:					
NEW JERSEY	1.500	13.481	0.181	5.285	1.398
NEW YORK	3.902	47.825	0.185	14.590	3.862
PENNSYLVANIA	2.409	16.223	0.161	3.152	0.825
EAST NORTH CENTRAL:					
ILLINOIS	2.102	23.472	0.256	3.910	1.025
INDIANA	0.771	11.368	0.169	0.411	0.107
MICHIGAN	1.433	35.478	0.290	5.703	1.475
OHIO	1.794	16.741	0.250	1.078	0.287
WISCONSIN	0.860	9.283	0.114	1.280	0.330
WEST NORTH CENTRAL:					
IOWA	0.632	11.977	0.135	0.086	0.023
KANSAS	0.506	7.376	0.150	0.921	0.235
MINNESOTA	1.087	8.842	0.137	1.942	0.508
MISSOURI	1.275	6.204	0.195	0.299	0.078
NEBRASKA	0.522	5.122	0.112	0.391	0.102
NORTH DAKOTA	0.484	2.193	0.042	0.100	0.025
SOUTH DAKOTA	0.566	1.896	0.051	0.008	0.002
SOUTH ATLANTIC:					
DELAWARE	0.152	0.840	0.013	0.116	0.031
DISTRICT OF COLUMBIA	1.318	1.325	0.001	0.221	0.059
FLORIDA	2.421	18.524	0.636	2.088	0.539
GEORGIA	1.222	10.449	0.198	1.835	0.476
MARYLAND	1.248	4.504	0.070	5.944	1.579
NORTH CAROLINA	0.942	29.208	0.154	2.886	0.749
SOUTH CAROLINA	0.737	9.197	0.075	2.710	0.710
VIRGINIA	1.468	15.245	0.107	6.125	1.595
WEST VIRGINIA	0.524	5.370	0.039	0.029	0.008
EAST SOUTH CENTRAL:					
ALABAMA	1.112	8.912	0.166	6.205	1.622
KENTUCKY	0.821	6.761	0.080	3.574	0.935
MISSISSIPPI	0.770	3.965	0.129	0.623	0.162
TENNESSEE	2.287	14.935	0.199	1.614	0.422
WEST SOUTH CENTRAL:					
ARKANSAS	0.545	3.991	0.129	1.390	0.362
LOUISIANA	0.868	5.413	0.170	7.269	1.861
OKLAHOMA	1.019	9.797	0.183	0.374	0.098
TEXAS	3.920	15.075	0.634	18.616	4.829
ROCKY MOUNTAIN:					
ARIZONA	1.753	6.119	0.201	0.356	0.094
COLORADO	1.465	7.851	0.150	1.345	0.352
IDAHO	1.009	2.746	0.082	0.017	0.004
MONTANA	1.117	2.563	0.070	0.385	0.100
NEVADA	1.531	1.508	0.088	0.461	0.123
NEW MEXICO	1.895	2.935	0.098	2.025	0.531
UTAH	0.940	2.461	0.069	0.952	0.249
WYOMING	0.480	1.594	0.058	0.079	0.021
FAR WEST:					
ALASKA	0.859	1.909	0.321	6.591	1.802
CALIFORNIA	6.543	47.318	0.927	53.265	13.840
HAWAII	0.411	1.806	0.073	1.813	0.499
OREGON	1.790	8.995	0.118	1.185	0.309
WASHINGTON	2.165	12.871	0.159	3.517	0.906

Table A.3.3

Gasoline Expenditures, 1972, In Million Dollars, By State

Aggregate Expenditures By Sector, Function and Total

Region and State	Sector			Function			Total
	Household	Business	Government	Highway	Aviation	Marine	
NEW ENGLAND:							
CONNECTICUT	413.413	83.480	8.824	502.282	1.215	2.220	505.717
MAINE	135.127	56.773	9.363	197.921	2.208	1.133	201.262
MASSACHUSETTS	668.249	145.678	15.705	823.202	2.924	3.506	829.632
NEW HAMPSHIRE	107.574	34.196	2.555	143.440	0.446	0.439	144.325
RHODE ISLAND	105.473	25.529	2.754	131.783	0.398	1.576	133.757
VERMONT	69.533	25.203	1.161	95.078	0.259	0.561	95.897
MID ATLANTIC:							
NEW JERSEY	956.048	206.582	21.845	1173.967	4.396	6.112	1184.475
NEW YORK	1876.580	430.917	70.363	2355.560	6.921	15.380	2377.861
PENNSYLVANIA	1360.212	388.338	22.770	1762.621	3.485	5.214	1771.320
EAST NORTH CENTRAL:							
ILLINOIS	1347.678	383.603	30.765	1749.438	5.291	7.317	1762.046
INDIANA	648.779	277.423	12.826	930.927	2.941	5.160	939.028
MICHIGAN	1116.891	345.844	44.379	1489.896	6.268	10.950	1507.114
OHIO	1428.201	366.580	20.151	1801.167	4.417	9.347	1814.931
WISCONSIN	501.426	173.000	11.867	679.476	2.250	4.567	686.293
WEST NORTH CENTRAL:							
IOWA	337.510	170.090	12.853	515.184	2.269	3.000	520.453
KANSAS	240.521	143.114	9.188	388.358	2.783	1.681	392.822
MINNESOTA	457.710	197.146	12.516	659.903	2.788	4.681	667.371
MISSOURI	579.121	272.980	8.052	851.752	3.332	5.070	860.153
NEBRASKA	181.370	109.166	6.249	293.785	1.935	1.064	296.784
NORTH DAKOTA	48.599	42.806	2.844	93.041	0.744	0.463	94.249
SOUTH DAKOTA	69.310	49.233	2.523	119.744	0.858	0.464	121.066
SOUTH ATLANTIC:							
DELAWARE	81.666	25.742	1.152	108.038	0.238	0.284	108.560
DISTRICT OF COLUMBIA	74.383	13.824	2.923	90.801	0.070	0.259	91.130
FLORIDA	1014.056	305.658	24.207	1324.709	11.242	7.970	1343.921
GEORGIA	657.795	267.653	14.181	930.835	3.803	4.992	939.629
MARYLAND	518.086	153.221	13.344	678.981	2.738	2.932	684.651
NORTH CAROLINA	682.240	288.870	33.939	996.596	3.334	5.119	1005.049
SOUTH CAROLINA	355.945	141.780	13.428	506.113	1.952	3.088	511.153
VIRGINIA	607.556	210.449	24.539	835.586	3.395	3.564	842.545
WEST VIRGINIA	179.957	88.327	5.970	273.012	0.648	0.594	274.254
EAST SOUTH CENTRAL:							
ALABAMA	431.281	191.668	18.016	633.337	4.348	3.280	640.965
KENTUCKY	382.820	185.054	12.170	575.504	2.267	2.275	580.045
MISSISSIPPI	261.435	145.251	5.648	407.721	2.322	2.290	412.334
TENNESSEE	495.805	209.633	19.457	716.499	3.748	4.648	724.895
WEST SOUTH CENTRAL:							
ARKANSAS	219.905	154.006	6.417	375.917	2.519	1.891	380.327
LOUISIANA	380.689	172.476	15.580	560.637	4.728	3.380	568.745
OKLAHOMA	311.812	193.318	11.470	510.577	3.147	2.877	516.601
TEXAS	1446.742	717.365	43.074	2178.096	15.474	13.610	2207.181
ROCKY MOUNTAIN:							
ARIZONA	242.694	130.328	8.523	375.489	3.439	2.617	381.544
COLORADO	283.289	143.819	11.165	434.062	2.860	1.350	438.272
IDAHO	86.636	55.906	3.858	144.073	1.362	0.965	146.399
MONTANA	71.979	59.983	4.234	134.224	1.266	0.705	136.196
NEVADA	88.186	46.765	3.710	135.924	1.570	1.166	138.661
NEW MEXICO	133.574	86.242	7.485	224.407	2.166	0.730	227.302
UTAH	127.801	73.772	4.670	203.980	1.372	0.892	206.244
WYOMING	45.052	37.333	2.232	83.204	0.981	0.432	84.616
FAR WEST:							
ALASKA	26.386	18.831	11.481	47.765	6.936	1.997	56.698
CALIFORNIA	2463.475	914.191	121.893	3454.659	29.370	15.530	3499.559
HAWAII	82.944	23.619	4.602	108.751	1.666	0.749	111.166
OREGON	289.938	105.068	12.396	402.016	2.263	3.123	407.401
WASHINGTON	368.627	183.146	19.617	564.201	3.551	3.638	571.391

Table A.3.4

Gasoline Expenditures, 1972, in Million Dollars, By Region

Expenditures By Sector Cross-Classified By Function

Region	Household			Business		
	Passenger Car and Motorcycle	Aviation	Marine	Passenger Car and Motorcycle	Truck and Bus	Aviation
NEW ENGLAND	1488.43	1.50	9.43	130.95	237.46	2.45
MID ATLANTIC	4163.03	3.10	26.71	366.97	653.77	5.09
EAST NORTH CENTRAL	4999.23	6.40	37.34	439.33	1096.66	10.46
WEST NORTH CENTRAL	1892.80	4.92	16.42	165.97	810.57	7.99
SOUTH ATLANTIC	4135.08	7.80	28.80	363.54	1119.40	12.58
EAST SOUTH CENTRAL	1555.44	3.41	12.49	136.65	589.39	5.56
WEST SOUTH CENTRAL	2330.65	6.74	21.76	203.85	1022.45	10.86
ROCKY MOUNTAIN	1065.53	4.82	8.86	93.57	532.68	7.90
FAR WEST	3196.94	9.39	25.04	280.51	948.90	15.44
TOTAL	24827.13	48.10	186.85	2181.36	7011.28	78.33

Region	Government				
	Federal Highway	State and Local Govt. Highway	Civilian Aviation	Military Highway	Military Aviation
NEW ENGLAND	2.93	21.51	0.25	12.41	3.25
MID ATLANTIC	7.81	77.53	0.53	23.03	6.08
EAST NORTH CENTRAL	6.96	96.34	1.08	12.38	3.22
WEST NORTH CENTRAL	5.07	43.61	0.82	3.75	0.97
SOUTH ATLANTIC	10.03	94.66	1.29	21.95	5.74
EAST SOUTH CENTRAL	4.99	34.57	0.57	12.02	3.14
WEST SOUTH CENTRAL	6.35	34.28	1.12	27.65	7.15
ROCKY MOUNTAIN	10.19	27.78	0.82	5.62	1.47
FAR WEST	11.77	72.90	1.60	66.37	17.36
TOTAL	66.11	503.18	8.07	185.18	48.40

Table A.3.5

Gasoline Expenditures, 1972, in Million Dollars, By Region

Aggregate Use By Sector, Function and Total

Region	Sector			Function			Total
	Households	Business	Government	Highway	Aviation	Marine	
NEW ENGLAND	1499.37	370.86	40.36	1893.71	7.45	9.43	1910.59
MID ATLANTIC	4192.84	1025.84	114.98	5292.15	14.80	26.71	5333.66
EAST NORTH CENTRAL	5042.97	1546.45	119.99	6650.90	21.17	37.34	6709.41
WEST NORTH CENTRAL	1914.14	984.53	54.22	2921.77	14.71	16.42	2952.90
SOUTH ATLANTIC	4171.68	1495.52	133.68	5744.67	27.42	28.80	5800.89
EAST SOUTH CENTRAL	1571.34	731.61	55.29	2333.06	12.69	12.49	2358.24
WEST SOUTH CENTRAL	2359.15	1237.17	76.54	3625.23	25.87	21.76	3672.85
ROCKY MOUNTAIN	1079.21	634.15	45.88	1735.36	15.02	8.86	1759.23
FAR WEST	3231.37	1244.86	169.99	4577.39	43.79	25.04	4646.21
TOTAL	25062.08	9270.98	810.93	34774.24	182.90	186.85	35143.99

Table A.3.6

Gasoline and Special Fuel Taxes, 1972, In Thousand Dollars, By State

Taxes Collected By Federal Government By Sector And Functional Source

Region and State	Highway					Non-Highway		
	Household Passenger Car and Motorcycle	Business Passenger Car and Motorcycle	Truck And Bus Gasoline	Truck And Bus Special Fuel	Federal Highway And Military Highway	Household Aviation	Business Aviation	Marine (Household)
NEW ENGLAND:								
CONNECTICUT	41936.28	3895.72	5236.01	3396.00	285.00	66.68	70.00	163.28
MAINE	13779.91	1280.09	5048.00	1452.00	994.21	49.42	51.91	81.48
MASSACHUSETTS	72665.64	6750.36	10452.00	4604.00	1018.13	119.98	125.98	259.10
NEW HAMPSHIRE	11144.70	1035.30	2812.00	656.00	49.31	25.40	26.68	32.02
RHODE ISLAND	11225.22	1042.78	1944.00	952.00	150.60	15.82	16.61	116.74
VERMONT	6734.40	625.60	2028.00	608.00	23.15	16.52	17.35	37.50
MID ATLANTIC:								
NEW JERSEY	99541.03	9246.97	14012.01	10544.00	1054.60	203.89	214.08	427.12
NEW YORK	180895.50	16804.50	28140.00	10692.00	2868.75	207.33	217.71	1071.00
PENNSYLVANIA	144892.07	13459.92	31608.01	21632.00	867.20	179.37	188.35	380.86
EAST NORTH CENTRAL:								
ILLINOIS	139951.09	13000.92	30288.00	16744.00	946.53	299.91	314.92	530.12
INDIANA	70279.32	6528.68	26528.01	13636.00	180.75	206.45	216.77	388.34
MICHIGAN	125860.07	11691.93	31184.01	9964.00	1236.53	321.05	337.10	839.24
OHIO	146648.88	13623.12	27224.00	19796.00	397.19	273.27	286.93	634.10
WISCONSIN	57132.60	5307.41	16448.01	6524.00	359.60	144.00	151.19	354.88
WEST NORTH CENTRAL:								
IOWA	35992.46	3343.55	16607.99	7140.00	98.23	155.47	163.24	213.60
KANSAS	28302.78	2629.22	16048.00	5104.00	254.67	199.10	209.03	136.54
MINNESOTA	49710.13	4617.88	18988.00	6112.00	480.06	161.46	169.54	341.80
MISSOURI	64858.87	6025.14	27756.00	9488.00	222.60	228.35	239.77	366.54
NEBRASKA	19174.75	1781.25	10864.01	3952.00	139.99	112.43	118.04	78.88
NORTH DAKOTA	5896.25	547.75	5276.01	1528.00	96.57	58.68	61.61	39.48
SOUTH DAKOTA	8377.74	778.26	5851.99	1508.00	89.58	59.95	62.93	39.12
SOUTH ATLANTIC:								
DELAWARE	8341.13	774.87	2080.01	620.00	38.96	14.14	14.85	19.90
DISTRICT OF COLUMBIA	7627.44	708.56	824.01	668.00	202.79	0.71	0.75	17.62
FLORIDA	111893.53	10394.48	26176.00	10672.00	730.65	800.21	840.24	617.14
GEORGIA	71706.72	6661.28	25392.01	11952.00	499.31	243.49	255.66	377.74
MARYLAND	52542.96	4881.04	12012.00	4188.00	1104.00	77.38	81.25	200.94
NORTH CAROLINA	69836.46	6487.54	25864.00	9228.00	644.31	188.54	197.98	385.88
SOUTH CAROLINA	37525.98	3486.02	12924.00	4992.00	561.71	87.70	92.10	224.80
VIRGINIA	65609.16	6094.84	18796.01	9520.00	1279.24	130.18	136.70	266.12
WEST VIRGINIA	18219.48	1692.52	8056.00	3708.00	72.76	43.25	45.39	41.18
EAST SOUTH CENTRAL:								
ALABAMA	45852.48	4259.52	18075.99	6608.00	1219.33	177.72	186.59	240.70
KENTUCKY	40754.10	3785.90	17852.00	5916.00	725.52	94.58	99.33	166.62
MISSISSIPPI	28313.76	2630.24	14704.00	4728.00	218.69	157.79	165.67	172.84
TENNESSEE	53952.06	5011.94	20068.00	9100.00	588.71	236.05	247.86	340.20
WEST SOUTH CENTRAL:								
ARKANSAS	24013.27	2230.74	16360.01	5276.00	321.10	156.53	164.36	141.68
LOUISIANA	42865.91	3982.09	17443.99	5312.00	1505.23	219.97	230.98	269.20
OKLAHOMA	34587.00	3213.00	20504.00	6116.00	204.83	218.06	228.95	212.34
TEXAS	170951.27	15880.72	78328.00	23856.00	3875.71	779.95	818.97	1030.96
ROCKY MOUNTAIN:								
ARIZONA	26022.59	2417.40	12932.00	5072.00	296.10	234.32	246.03	188.82
COLORADO	30959.95	2876.06	14348.01	3608.00	430.87	178.13	187.04	98.84
IDAHO	9581.88	890.11	5944.01	1360.00	151.17	91.90	96.49	76.40
MONTANA	7953.19	738.81	6607.99	2764.00	223.99	81.94	86.02	52.92
NEVADA	8674.21	805.80	4208.00	1776.00	263.16	94.55	99.27	78.02
NEW MEXICO	14449.68	1342.32	8900.00	3820.00	599.12	114.90	120.64	52.86
UTAH	13911.66	1292.34	7544.01	2440.00	290.88	70.09	73.60	65.14
WYOMING	5025.18	466.82	4144.01	1884.00	82.24	62.03	65.12	32.92
FAR WEST:								
ALASKA	2067.90	192.11	1368.01	460.00	981.49	269.39	282.84	105.72
CALIFORNIA	273544.74	25411.26	85800.00	28376.00	10354.28	1131.14	1187.70	1168.78
HAWAII	7711.62	716.39	1611.99	424.00	274.86	63.33	66.50	42.28
OREGON	31680.95	2943.04	9664.00	5480.00	455.13	136.18	142.99	232.40
WASHINGTON	39623.15	3680.85	18000.01	4824.00	958.71	185.10	194.35	282.56

Table A.3.7

Gasoline and Special Fuel Taxes, 1972, In Thousand Dollars, By State

Aggregate Taxes Collected By Federal Government

Region and State	Highway Taxes	Non-Highway Taxes	Total Taxes
NEW ENGLAND:			
CONNECTICUT	54749.00	299.96	55048.96
MAINE	22554.21	182.81	22737.02
MASSACHUSETTS	95490.14	505.06	95995.20
NEW HAMPSHIRE	15697.31	84.10	15781.41
RHODE ISLAND	15314.59	149.17	15463.76
VERMONT	10019.14	71.37	10090.51
MID ATLANTIC:			
NEW JERSEY	134398.61	845.09	135243.70
NEW YORK	239400.75	1496.04	240896.79
PENNSYLVANIA	212459.21	748.58	213207.78
EAST NORTH CENTRAL:			
ILLINOIS	200930.53	1144.95	202075.49
INDIANA	117152.76	811.55	117964.32
MICHIGAN	179936.54	1497.39	181433.93
OHIO	207689.18	1194.30	208883.49
WISCONSIN	85771.62	650.07	86421.69
WEST NORTH CENTRAL:			
IOWA	63182.23	532.31	63714.55
KANSAS	52338.66	544.67	52883.34
MINNESOTA	79908.07	672.80	80580.86
MISSOURI	108350.61	834.66	109185.27
NEBRASKA	35912.00	309.34	36221.34
NORTH DAKOTA	13344.57	159.77	13504.34
SOUTH DAKOTA	16605.57	162.00	16767.57
SOUTH ATLANTIC:			
DELAWARE	11854.97	48.89	11903.85
DISTRICT OF COLUMBIA	10030.79	19.08	10049.87
FLORIDA	159866.65	2257.59	162124.24
GEORGIA	116211.32	876.89	117088.21
MARYLAND	74727.99	359.56	75087.56
NORTH CAROLINA	112060.31	772.40	112832.71
SOUTH CAROLINA	59489.71	404.60	59894.30
VIRGINIA	101299.24	533.00	101832.24
WEST VIRGINIA	31748.76	129.82	31878.58
EAST SOUTH CENTRAL:			
ALABAMA	76015.32	605.01	76620.33
KENTUCKY	69033.52	360.53	69394.05
MISSISSIPPI	50594.69	496.30	51090.99
TENNESSEE	88720.71	824.11	89544.82
WEST SOUTH CENTRAL:			
ARKANSAS	48201.11	462.57	48663.68
LOUISIANA	71109.22	720.16	71829.37
OKLAHOMA	64624.82	659.36	65284.18
TEXAS	292891.71	2629.88	295521.58
ROCKY MOUNTAIN:			
ARIZONA	46740.10	669.18	47409.27
COLORADO	52222.88	464.02	52686.90
IDAHO	17927.17	264.79	18191.96
MONTANA	18287.99	220.88	18508.87
NEVADA	15727.16	271.84	15999.00
NEW MEXICO	29111.12	288.40	29399.52
UTAH	25478.88	208.83	25687.72
WYOMING	11602.25	160.07	11762.32
FAR WEST:			
ALASKA	5069.50	657.96	5727.46
CALIFORNIA	423486.29	3487.61	426973.90
HAWAII	10738.86	172.11	10910.97
OREGON	50223.12	511.57	50734.69
WASHINGTON	67086.72	662.01	67748.73

Table A.3.8

Gasoline and Special Fuel Taxes, 1972, In Thousand Dollars, By State

Highway Taxes Collected By State and Local Governments By Sector and Functional Source

Region and State	Household Passenger Car and Motorcycle	Business Passenger Car and Motorcycle	Truck and Bus Gasoline	Truck and Bus Special Fuel	State and Local Govt. Highway	Total Highway Taxes
NEW ENGLAND:						
CONNECTICUT	104840.69	9739.30	13090.01	8490.00	1900.00	138060.00
MAINE	31004.81	2880.21	11357.99	3267.00	477.00	48987.01
MASSACHUSETTS	136248.08	12656.92	19597.51	8632.50	1890.00	179025.01
NEW HAMPSHIRE	25075.57	2329.42	6327.00	1476.00	567.00	35775.00
RHODE ISLAND	22450.45	2085.55	3887.99	1904.00	400.01	30728.00
VERMONT	15152.39	1407.60	4562.99	0.00	233.98	21356.96
MID ATLANTIC:						
NEW JERSEY	186888.28	17361.19	26307.54	19796.36	2966.46	253319.83
NEW YORK	470780.53	43733.72	73234.35	33171.93	13408.09	634328.62
PENNSYLVANIA	289784.15	26919.85	63216.01	43264.00	3887.99	427072.00
EAST NORTH CENTRAL:						
ILLINOIS	302994.11	28146.98	65573.51	36250.76	5932.09	438897.46
INDIANA	140558.65	13057.36	53056.01	27272.00	2791.99	236736.02
MICHIGAN	220255.13	20460.87	54572.02	17437.00	7987.01	320712.03
OHIO	263234.75	24453.50	48867.08	35533.82	3467.94	375557.08
WISCONSIN	99982.05	9287.96	28784.01	11417.00	2114.01	151585.03
WEST NORTH CENTRAL:						
IOWA	62986.80	5851.22	29063.99	14280.00	2533.99	114715.99
KANSAS	49529.86	4601.13	28084.00	10208.00	1743.01	94165.99
MINNESOTA	86992.72	8081.30	33229.00	10696.00	1911.00	140910.02
MISSOURI	91937.45	8540.63	39344.13	13449.24	1122.66	154394.11
NEBRASKA	40746.34	3785.16	23086.01	8398.00	1300.52	77316.03
NORTH DAKOTA	10318.43	958.56	9233.01	2674.00	538.99	23722.99
SOUTH DAKOTA	14661.04	1361.95	10240.99	2639.00	461.99	29364.98
SOUTH ATLANTIC:						
DELAWARE	17724.91	1646.59	4420.02	1317.50	203.99	25313.01
DISTRICT OF COLUMBIA	14301.44	1328.54	1545.01	1252.50	285.01	18712.51
FLORIDA	223787.05	20788.96	52351.99	21344.00	4655.99	322927.99
GEORGIA	141979.30	13189.34	50276.17	23664.96	2558.17	231667.94
MARYLAND	105085.91	9762.08	24024.00	8376.00	1023.99	148271.99
NORTH CAROLINA	178082.97	16543.22	65953.21	23531.40	8578.20	292688.99
SOUTH CAROLINA	75896.29	7050.47	26138.80	10096.32	2216.66	121398.53
VIRGINIA	131218.31	12189.68	37592.02	19040.00	3719.99	203760.00
WEST VIRGINIA	38716.40	3596.60	17119.01	7879.50	1291.98	68603.49
EAST SOUTH CENTRAL:						
ALABAMA	91704.95	8519.04	36151.99	14868.00	2144.02	153388.00
KENTUCKY	81508.19	7571.79	35704.00	11832.00	1623.99	138239.97
MISSISSIPPI	56627.52	5260.48	29408.00	11820.00	976.01	104092.02
TENNESSEE	94416.10	8770.90	35119.01	18200.00	3234.00	159740.01
WEST SOUTH CENTRAL:						
ARKANSAS	45024.87	4182.63	30675.02	11211.50	930.01	92024.03
LOUISIANA	85731.81	7964.17	34887.99	10624.00	1392.01	140599.99
OKLAHOMA	56203.88	5221.13	33318.99	9938.50	2015.01	106697.51
TEXAS	215398.60	20009.71	98693.28	39004.56	2580.49	375686.63
ROCKY MOUNTAIN:						
ARIZONA	45539.54	4230.45	22631.00	8876.00	1309.01	82586.00
COLORADO	54179.91	5033.10	25109.01	6314.00	1701.00	92337.02
IDAHO	19882.40	1846.99	12333.82	2822.00	722.09	37607.30
MONTANA	13918.08	1292.92	11563.99	6219.00	567.01	33561.00
NEVADA	17348.42	1611.59	8415.99	3552.00	336.00	31264.00
NEW MEXICO	25286.94	2349.06	15575.00	6685.00	630.01	50526.02
UTAH	24345.41	2261.59	13202.01	4270.00	531.99	44611.00
WYOMING	8794.07	816.94	7252.01	0.00	357.00	17220.02
FAR WEST:						
ALASKA	4135.79	384.22	2736.01	920.00	384.01	8560.04
CALIFORNIA	488277.37	45359.10	153153.01	50651.16	10652.88	748093.50
HAWAII	9678.08	899.06	2023.05	532.12	235.93	13368.25
OREGON	57421.73	5334.26	17516.00	9932.50	2030.01	92234.50
WASHINGTON	89152.09	8281.90	40500.02	10854.00	3536.98	152325.00

Table A.3.9

Gasoline and Special Fuel Taxes, 1972, In Thousand Dollars, By State

Non-Highway Taxes Collected By State Governments By Sector and Functional Source

Region and State	Household Aviation	Business Aviation	Govt. Civilian Aviation	Marine (Household)	Total Taxes Collected
NEW ENGLAND:					
CONNECTICUT	0.00	0.00	0.00	0.00	0.00
MAINE	0.00	0.00	0.00	0.00	0.00
MASSACHUSETTS	0.00	0.00	0.00	0.00	0.00
NEW HAMPSHIRE	14.52	30.49	3.39	0.00	48.40
RHODE ISLAND	0.00	0.00	0.00	0.00	0.00
VERMONT	0.00	0.00	0.00	0.00	0.00
MID ATLANTIC:					
NEW JERSEY	0.00	0.00	0.00	0.00	0.00
NEW YORK	0.00	0.00	0.00	0.00	0.00
PENNSYLVANIA	38.44	80.72	8.97	0.00	128.13
EAST NORTH CENTRAL:					
ILLINOIS	0.00	0.00	0.00	0.00	0.00
INDIANA	0.00	0.00	0.00	0.00	0.00
MICHIGAN	137.59	288.94	32.10	0.00	458.64
OHIO	0.00	0.00	0.00	0.00	0.00
WISCONSIN	0.00	0.00	0.00	0.00	0.00
WEST NORTH CENTRAL:					
IOWA	0.00	0.00	0.00	0.00	0.00
KANSAS	0.00	0.00	0.00	0.00	0.00
MINNESOTA	0.00	0.00	0.00	0.00	0.00
MISSOURI	0.00	0.00	0.00	0.00	0.00
NEBRASKA	80.30	168.63	18.73	0.00	267.67
NORTH DAKOTA	0.00	0.00	0.00	0.00	0.00
SOUTH DAKOTA	34.26	71.92	8.00	0.00	114.17
SOUTH ATLANTIC:					
DELAWARE	0.00	0.00	0.00	0.00	0.00
DISTRICT OF COLUMBIA	0.00	0.00	0.00	0.00	0.00
FLORIDA	0.00	0.00	0.00	0.00	0.00
GEORGIA	0.00	0.00	0.00	0.00	0.00
MARYLAND	0.00	0.00	0.00	0.00	0.00
NORTH CAROLINA	0.00	0.00	0.00	0.00	0.00
SOUTH CAROLINA	0.00	0.00	0.00	0.00	0.00
VIRGINIA	0.00	0.00	0.00	0.00	0.00
WEST VIRGINIA	0.00	0.00	0.00	0.00	0.00
EAST SOUTH CENTRAL:					
ALABAMA	68.31	143.43	15.93	0.00	227.67
KENTUCKY	0.00	0.00	0.00	0.00	0.00
MISSISSIPPI	0.00	0.00	0.00	0.00	0.00
TENNESSEE	0.00	0.00	0.00	0.00	0.00
WEST SOUTH CENTRAL:					
ARKANSAS	0.00	0.00	0.00	0.00	0.00
LOUISIANA	0.00	0.00	0.00	0.00	0.00
OKLAHOMA	0.00	0.00	0.00	0.00	0.00
TEXAS	0.00	0.00	0.00	0.00	0.00
ROCKY MOUNTAIN:					
ARIZONA	0.00	0.00	0.00	0.00	0.00
COLORADO	0.00	0.00	0.00	0.00	0.00
IDAHO	45.95	96.49	10.72	0.00	153.16
MONTANA	11.71	24.58	2.73	0.00	39.01
NEVADA	0.00	0.00	0.00	0.00	0.00
NEW MEXICO	0.00	0.00	0.00	0.00	0.00
UTAH	40.05	84.12	9.34	0.00	133.51
WYOMING	35.45	74.42	8.27	0.00	118.14
FAR WEST:					
ALASKA	153.94	323.25	35.92	211.44	724.55
CALIFORNIA	0.00	0.00	0.00	0.00	0.00
HAWAII	9.05	19.00	2.11	0.00	30.16
OREGON	19.45	40.85	4.54	0.00	64.85
WASHINGTON	52.89	111.06	12.34	0.00	176.28

Table A.3.10

Gasoline and Special Fuel Taxes, 1972, In Thousand Dollars, By State

Aggregate Taxes Collected By State and Local Governments

Region and State	Highway Taxes	Non-Highway Taxes	Total Taxes
NEW ENGLAND:			
CONNECTICUT	138060.00	0.00	138060.00
MAINE	48987.01	0.00	48987.01
MASSACHUSETTS	179025.01	0.00	179025.01
NEW HAMPSHIRE	35775.00	48.40	35823.40
RHODE ISLAND	30728.00	0.00	30728.00
VERMONT	21356.96	0.00	21356.96
MID ATLANTIC:			
NEW JERSEY	253319.83	0.00	253319.83
NEW YORK	634328.62	0.00	634328.62
PENNSYLVANIA	427072.00	128.13	427200.13
EAST NORTH CENTRAL:			
ILLINOIS	438897.46	0.00	438897.46
INDIANA	236736.02	0.00	236736.02
MICHIGAN	320712.03	458.64	321170.67
OHIO	375557.08	0.00	375557.08
WISCONSIN	151585.03	0.00	151585.03
WEST NORTH CENTRAL:			
IOWA	114715.99	0.00	114715.99
KANSAS	94165.99	0.00	94165.99
MINNESOTA	140910.02	0.00	140910.02
MISSOURI	154394.11	0.00	154394.11
NEBRASKA	77316.03	267.67	77583.70
NORTH DAKOTA	23722.99	0.00	23722.99
SOUTH DAKOTA	29364.98	114.17	29479.15
SOUTH ATLANTIC:			
DELAWARE	25313.01	0.00	25313.01
DISTRICT OF COLUMBIA	18712.51	0.00	18712.51
FLORIDA	322927.99	0.00	322927.99
GEORGIA	231667.94	0.00	231667.94
MARYLAND	148271.99	0.00	148271.99
NORTH CAROLINA	292688.99	0.00	292688.99
SOUTH CAROLINA	121398.53	0.00	121398.53
VIRGINIA	203760.00	0.00	203760.00
WEST VIRGINIA	68603.49	0.00	68603.49
EAST SOUTH CENTRAL:			
ALABAMA	153388.00	227.67	153615.67
KENTUCKY	138239.97	0.00	138239.97
MISSISSIPPI	104092.02	0.00	104092.02
TENNESSEE	159740.01	0.00	159740.01
WEST SOUTH CENTRAL:			
ARKANSAS	92024.03	0.00	92024.03
LOUISIANA	140599.99	0.00	140599.99
OKLAHOMA	106697.51	0.00	106697.51
TEXAS	375686.63	0.00	375686.63
ROCKY MOUNTAIN:			
ARIZONA	82586.00	0.00	82586.00
COLORADO	92337.02	0.00	92337.02
IDAHO	37607.30	153.16	37760.45
MONTANA	33561.00	39.01	33600.01
NEVADA	31264.00	0.00	31264.00
NEW MEXICO	50526.02	0.00	50526.02
UTAH	44611.00	133.51	44744.52
WYOMING	17220.02	118.14	17338.16
FAR WEST:			
ALASKA	8560.04	724.55	9284.59
CALIFORNIA	748093.50	0.00	748093.50
HAWAII	13368.25	30.16	13398.41
OREGON	92234.50	64.85	92299.34
WASHINGTON	152325.00	176.28	152501.28

Table A.3.11

Gasoline And Special Fuel Taxes, 1972, In Thousand Dollars, By Region

Taxes Collected By Federal Government

| REGION | HIGHWAY | | | | |
	Household Passenger Car And Motorcycle	Business Passenger Car And Motorcycle	Truck & Bus Gasoline	Truck & Bus Special Fuel	Federal Govt. And Military Highway
NEW ENGLAND	157486.16	14629.84	27520.00	11668.00	2520.39
MID ATLANTIC	425328.60	39511.40	73760.01	42868.60	4790.55
EAST NORTH CENTRAL	539871.97	50152.05	131672.02	66664.00	3120.60
WEST NORTH CENTRAL	212312.96	19723.05	101392.00	34832.00	1381.70
SOUTH ATLANTIC	443302.84	41181.13	132124.04	55548.00	5133.73
EAST SOUTH CENTRAL	168872.39	15687.60	70699.99	26352.00	2752.24
WEST SOUTH CENTRAL	272417.44	25306.55	132636.00	40560.00	5906.86
ROCKY MOUNTAIN	116578.34	10829.67	64628.02	22724.00	2337.52
FAR WEST	354628.36	32943.64	116444.01	39564.00.	13024.47
TOTAL	2690799.09	249964.93	850876.09	340780.00	40968.06

| REGION | NON-HIGHWAY | | | ALL TAXES | | |
	Household Aviation	Business Aviation	Marine (Household)	All Highway	All Non-Highway	All Taxes Collected
NEW ENGLAND	293.82	308.52	690.12	213824.39	1292.47	215116.85
MID ATLANTIC	590.59	620.13	1878.98	586258.57	3089.70	589348.27
EAST NORTH CENTRAL	1244.68	1306.90	2746.69	791480.63	5298.27	796778.92
WEST NORTH CENTRAL	975.43	1024.16	1215.96	369641.70	3215.56	372857.26
SOUTH ATLANTIC	1585.60	1664.91	2151.32	677289.75	5401.82	682691.58
EAST SOUTH CENTRAL	666.15	699.44	920.36	284364.24	2285.95	286650.19
WEST SOUTH CENTRAL	1374.51	1443.26	1654.19	476826.86	4471.96	481298.81
ROCKY MOUNTAIN	927.86	974.23	645.93	217097.55	2548.02	219645.57
FAR WEST	1785.14	1874.38	1831.74	556604.49	5491.26	562095.75
TOTAL	9443.78	9915.94	13735.28	4173388.22	33095.00	4206483.36

Table A.3.12

Gasoline and Special Fuel Taxes, 1972, In Thousand Dollars, By Region
Taxes Collected By State and Local Governments

Region	Household Passenger Car and Motorcycle	Business Passenger Car and Motorcycle	Highway Truck and Bus Gasoline	Truck and Bus Special Fuel	State and Local Govt. Highway
NEW ENGLAND	334771.99	31099.00	58823.49	23769.50	5467.98
MID ATLANTIC	947452.96	88014.76	162757.91	96232.29	20262.55
EAST NORTH CENTRAL	1027024.70	95406.68	250852.63	127910.58	22293.04
WEST NORTH CENTRAL	357172.64	33179.95	172281.13	62344.24	9612.15
SOUTH ATLANTIC	926792.58	86095.48	279420.23	116502.18	24533.98
EAST SOUTH CENTRAL	324256.77	30122.22	136382.99	56720.00	7978.02
WEST SOUTH CENTRAL	402359.16	37377.64	197575.28	70778.56	6917.52
ROCKY MOUNTAIN	209294.76	19442.65	116082.84	38738.00	6154.11
FAR WEST	648665.06	60258.54	215928.09	72889.78	16839.82
TOTAL	5177790.67	480996.92	1590104.59	665885.14	120059.16

Region	Household Aviation	Business Aviation	Non-Highway Civilian Aviation	Marine (Household)	All Highway	All Taxes All Non-Highway	Total Taxes Collected
NEW ENGLAND	14.52	30.49	3.39	0.00	453931.98	48.40	453980.38
MID ATLANTIC	38.44	80.72	8.97	0.00	1314720.46	128.13	1314848.59
EAST NORTH CENTRAL	137.59	288.94	32.10	0.00	1523487.62	458.64	1523946.26
WEST NORTH CENTRAL	114.56	240.55	26.73	0.00	634590.12	381.84	634971.95
SOUTH ATLANTIC	0.00	0.00	0.00	0.00	1433344.45	0.00	1433344.45
EAST SOUTH CENTRAL	68.31	143.43	15.93	0.00	555460.00	227.67	555687.67
WEST SOUTH CENTRAL	0.00	0.00	0.00	0.00	715008.15	0.00	715008.15
ROCKY MOUNTAIN	133.16	279.61	31.05	0.00	389712.36	443.82	390156.19
FAR WEST	235.33	494.16	54.91	211.44	1014581.29	995.84	1015577.12
TOTAL	741.89	1557.91	173.09	211.44	8034836.50	2684.34	8037520.80

Table A.3.13

Gasoline and Special Fuel Taxes, 1972, In Million Dollars, By State

Aggregate Taxes Collected By State and Local and Federal Governments Combined, By Function and Sector

Region and State	Function		Sector			Total Taxes Collected
	Highway	Non-Highway	Household	Business	Government	
NEW ENGLAND:						
CONNECTICUT	192.809	0.300	147.007	43.917	2.185	193.109
MAINE	71.541	0.183	44.916	25.337	1.471	71.724
MASSACHUSETTS	274.515	0.505	209.293	62.819	2.908	275.020
NEW HAMPSHIRE	51.472	0.133	36.292	14.693	0.620	51.605
RHODE ISLAND	46.043	0.149	33.808	11.833	0.551	46.192
VERMONT	31.376	0.071	21.941	9.250	0.257	31.447
MID ATLANTIC:						
NEW JERSEY	387.718	0.845	287.060	97.482	4.021	388.563
NEW YORK	873.729	1.496	652.954	205.994	16.277	875.225
PENNSYLVANIA	639.531	0.877	435.275	200.369	4.764	640.408
EAST NORTH CENTRAL:						
ILLINOIS	639.828	1.145	443.775	190.319	6.879	640.973
INDIANA	353.889	0.812	211.433	140.295	2.973	354.700
MICHIGAN	500.649	1.956	347.413	145.936	9.256	502.605
OHIO	583.246	1.194	410.791	169.784	3.865	584.441
WISCONSIN	237.357	0.650	157.614	77.920	2.474	238.007
WEST NORTH CENTRAL:						
IOWA	177.898	0.532	99.348	76.450	2.632	178.430
KANSAS	146.505	0.545	78.168	66.883	1.998	147.049
MINNESOTA	220.818	0.673	137.206	81.894	2.391	221.491
MISSOURI	262.745	0.835	157.391	104.843	1.345	263.579
NEBRASKA	113.228	0.577	60.193	52.153	1.459	113.805
NORTH DAKOTA	37.068	0.160	16.313	20.279	0.636	37.227
SOUTH DAKOTA	45.971	0.276	23.172	22.515	0.560	46.247
SOUTH ATLANTIC:						
DELAWARE	37.168	0.049	26.100	10.874	0.243	37.217
DISTRICT OF COLUMBIA	28.743	0.019	21.947	6.327	0.488	28.762
FLORIDA	482.795	2.258	337.098	142.568	5.387	485.052
GEORGIA	347.879	0.877	214.307	131.391	3.058	348.756
MARYLAND	223.000	0.360	157.907	63.324	2.128	223.360
NORTH CAROLINA	404.749	0.772	248.494	147.805	9.222	405.522
SOUTH CAROLINA	180.888	0.405	113.735	64.780	2.778	181.293
VIRGINIA	305.059	0.533	197.224	103.369	4.999	305.592
WEST VIRGINIA	100.352	0.130	57.020	42.097	1.365	100.482
EAST SOUTH CENTRAL:						
ALABAMA	229.403	0.833	138.044	88.813	3.379	230.236
KENTUCKY	207.274	0.361	122.524	82.761	2.350	207.634
MISSISSIPPI	154.687	0.496	85.272	68.716	1.195	155.183
TENNESSEE	248.461	0.824	148.944	96.518	3.823	249.285
WEST SOUTH CENTRAL:						
ARKANSAS	140.225	0.463	69.336	70.100	1.251	140.688
LOUISIANA	211.709	0.720	129.087	80.445	2.897	212.429
OKLAHOMA	171.322	0.659	91.221	78.541	2.220	171.982
TEXAS	668.578	2.630	388.161	276.591	6.456	671.208
ROCKY MOUNTAIN:						
ARIZONA	129.326	0.669	71.985	56.405	1.605	129.995
COLORADO	144.560	0.464	85.417	57.475	2.132	145.024
IDAHO	55.534	0.418	29.679	25.390	0.884	55.952
MONTANA	51.849	0.260	22.018	29.297	0.794	52.109
NEVADA	46.991	0.272	26.195	20.469	0.599	47.263
NEW MEXICO	79.637	0.288	39.904	38.792	1.229	79.925
UTAH	70.090	0.342	38.432	31.168	0.832	70.432
WYOMING	28.822	0.278	13.950	14.703	0.448	29.101
FAR WEST:						
ALASKA	13.630	1.383	6.944	6.666	1.401	15.012
CALIFORNIA	1171.580	3.488	764.122	389.938	21.007	1175.067
HAWAII	24.107	0.202	17.504	6.292	0.513	24.309
OREGON	142.458	0.576	89.491	51.054	2.490	143.034
WASHINGTON	219.412	0.838	129.296	86.446	4.508	220.250

Table A.3.14

Gasoline and Special Fuel Taxes, 1972, in Million Dollars, By Region

Aggregate Taxes Collected By State and Local and Federal Governments Combined, By Function and Sector

Region	Function		Sector			Total Taxes Collected
	Highway	Non-Highway	Household	Business	Government	
NEW ENGLAND	667.76	1.34	493.26	167.85	7.99	669.10
MID ATLANTIC	1900.98	3.22	1375.29	503.85	25.06	1904.20
EAST NORTH CENTRAL	2314.97	5.76	1571.03	724.25	25.45	2320.73
WEST NORTH CENTRAL	1004.23	3.60	571.79	425.02	11.02	1007.83
SOUTH ATLANTIC	2110.63	5.40	1373.83	712.54	29.67	2116.04
EAST SOUTH CENTRAL	839.82	2.51	494.78	336.81	10.75	842.34
WEST SOUTH CENTRAL	1191.83	4.47	677.81	505.68	12.82	1196.31
ROCKY MOUNTAIN	606.81	2.99	327.58	273.70	8.52	609.80
FAR WEST	1571.19	6.49	1007.36	540.40	29.92	1577.67
TOTAL	12208.22	35.78	7892.72	4190.08	161.20	12244.00

Table A.3.15

Gasoline and Special Fuel Taxes, 1972, In Thousand Dollars, By State

Comparison Of Estimates, This Study versus Highway Statistics

	This Study Estimates			Highway Statistics	This Study Estimated	Highway Statistics	Ratio Of This Study To Highway Statistics	
Region and State	State and Local Taxes	Local Taxes	Net State Taxes	State Taxes	Federal Taxes, Private Sector		State Taxes	Federal Taxes
NEW ENGLAND:								
CONNECTICUT	138060.00	0.00	138060.00	140426.00	54464.00	53112.00	0.9832	1.0255
MAINE	48987.01	0.00	48987.01	49957.00	21560.01	20903.00	0.9806	1.0314
MASSACHUSETTS	179025.01	0.00	179025.01	177656.00	94472.01	91802.00	1.0077	1.0291
NEW HAMPSHIRE	35823.40	0.00	35823.40	36289.00	15648.00	15290.00	0.9872	1.0234
RHODE ISLAND	30728.00	0.00	30728.00	31477.00	15163.99	14950.00	0.9762	1.0143
VERMONT	21356.96	0.00	21356.96	21759.00	9995.99	9792.00	0.9815	1.0208
MID ATLANTIC:								
NEW JERSEY	253319.83	0.00	253319.83	253913.00	133344.01	124327.00	0.9977	1.0725
NEW YORK	634328.62	152316.00	482012.62	500310.00	236532.00	234882.00	0.9634	1.0070
PENNSYLVANIA	427200.13	0.00	427200.13	415032.00	211592.01	199884.00	1.0293	1.0586
EAST NORTH CENTRAL:								
ILLINOIS	438897.46	58900.00	379997.46	390970.00	199984.00	190747.00	0.9719	1.0484
INDIANA	236736.02	0.00	236736.02	243541.00	116972.01	111486.00	0.9721	1.0492
MICHIGAN	321170.67	0.00	321170.67	315463.00	178700.01	175757.00	1.0181	1.0167
OHIO	375557.08	9517.00	366040.08	366015.00	207291.99	201798.00	1.0001	1.0272
WISCONSIN	151585.03	0.00	151585.03	158533.00	85412.01	82445.00	0.9562	1.0360
WEST NORTH CENTRAL:								
IOWA	114715.99	0.00	114715.99	125499.00	63084.00	61326.00	0.9141	1.0287
KANSAS	94165.99	0.00	94165.99	96993.00	52083.99	49616.00	0.9709	1.0497
MINNESOTA	140910.02	0.00	140910.02	150473.00	79428.01	77894.00	0.9364	1.0197
MISSOURI	154394.11	0.00	154394.11	153252.00	108128.01	105038.00	1.0075	1.0294
NEBRASKA	77583.70	0.00	77583.70	81189.00	35772.01	33891.00	0.9556	1.0555
NORTH DAKOTA	23722.99	0.00	23722.99	30133.00	13248.00	12765.00	0.7873	1.0378
SOUTH DAKOTA	29479.15	0.00	29479.15	35224.00	16515.99	15673.00	0.8369	1.0538
SOUTH ATLANTIC:								
DELAWARE	25313.01	1500.00	23813.01	24069.00	11816.01	11202.00	0.9894	1.0548
DISTRICT OF COLUMBIA	18712.51	0.00	18712.51	18282.00	9828.00	10032.00	1.0235	0.9797
FLORIDA	322927.99	0.00	322927.99	330555.00	159136.00	149556.00	0.9769	1.0641
GEORGIA	231667.94	12286.00	219381.94	222566.00	115712.01	112185.00	0.9857	1.0314
MARYLAND	148271.99	0.00	148271.99	150535.00	73624.00	71870.00	0.9850	1.0244
NORTH CAROLINA	292688.99	34358.00	258330.99	262619.00	111416.00	109157.00	0.9837	1.0207
SOUTH CAROLINA	121398.53	6329.00	115069.53	111812.00	58928.00	56956.00	1.0291	1.0346
VIRGINIA	203760.00	0.00	203760.00	196942.00	100020.00	97874.00	1.0346	1.0219
WEST VIRGINIA	68603.49	0.00	68603.49	71145.00	31676.00	31326.00	0.9643	1.0112
EAST SOUTH CENTRAL:								
ALABAMA	153615.67	19219.00	134396.67	138591.00	74795.99	73456.00	0.9697	1.0182
KENTUCKY	138239.97	0.00	138239.97	140707.00	68307.99	66692.00	0.9825	1.0242
MISSISSIPPI	104092.02	0.00	104092.02	105775.00	50376.00	47938.00	0.9841	1.0509
TENNESSEE	159740.01	0.00	159740.01	163442.00	88132.01	82984.00	0.9773	1.0620
WEST SOUTH CENTRAL:								
ARKANSAS	92024.03	0.00	92024.03	91373.00	47880.01	45425.00	1.0071	1.0540
LOUISIANA	140599.99	0.00	140599.99	144203.00	69603.99	66328.00	0.9750	1.0494
OKLAHOMA	106697.51	0.00	106697.51	107676.00	64420.00	63028.00	0.9909	1.0221
TEXAS	375686.63	0.00	375686.63	378841.00	289016.00	274786.00	0.9917	1.0518
ROCKY MOUNTAIN:								
ARIZONA	82586.00	0.00	82586.00	85620.00	46444.00	44131.00	0.9646	1.0524
COLORADO	92337.02	0.00	92337.02	91009.00	51792.01	50344.00	1.0146	1.0288
IDAHO	37760.45	0.00	37760.45	39165.00	17776.00	17215.00	0.9641	1.0326
MONTANA	33600.01	0.00	33600.01	35354.00	18064.00	17962.00	0.9504	1.0057
NEVADA	31264.00	7815.00	23449.00	24582.00	15464.00	14950.00	0.9539	1.0344
NEW MEXICO	50526.02	0.00	50526.02	51021.00	28512.00	27811.00	0.9903	1.0252
UTAH	44744.52	0.00	44744.52	44702.00	25188.01	24175.00	1.0010	1.0419
WYOMING	17338.16	0.00	17338.16	23111.00	11520.01	11067.00	0.7502	1.0409
FAR WEST:								
ALASKA	9284.59	0.00	9284.59	10133.00	4088.01	4363.00	0.9163	0.9370
CALIFORNIA	748093.50	0.00	748093.50	735000.00	413132.01	403020.00	1.0178	1.0251
HAWAII	13398.41	0.00	13398.41	13622.00	10464.00	10388.00	0.9836	1.0073
OREGON	92299.34	3181.00	89118.34	82215.00	49767.99	49125.00	1.0840	1.0131
WASHINGTON	152501.28	0.00	152501.28	159203.00	66128.01	66476.00	0.9579	0.9948

Table A.3.16

Gasoline and Special Fuel Taxes, 1972, In Million Dollars, By Region

Comparison of Estimates, This Study Versus Highway Statistics

| | This Study Estimates | | | Highway Statistics | Ratio | This Study Estimates | Highway Statistics | Ratio |
| | State and Local Taxes | Local Taxes | Net State Taxes | State Taxes | (3)/(4) | Federal Taxes | Federal Taxes | (6)/(7) |
	(1)	(2)	(3)	(4)	(5)	(6)	(7)	(8)
	All Taxes Collected					Private Sector Highway Taxes		
New England	453.980	0	453.980	457.564	0.992	211.304	205.849	1.027
Mid Atlantic	1314.849	152.316	1162.533	1169.255	0.994	581.468	559.093	1.040
East North Central	1523.946	68.417	1455.529	1474.522	0.987	788.360	762.233	1.034
West North Central	634.972	0	634.763	672.763	0.944	368.260	356.203	1.034
South Atlantic	1433.344	54.473	1378.871	1388.525	0.993	672.156	650.158	1.034
East South Central	555.688	19.219	536.469	548.515	0.978	281.612	271.070	1.039
West South Central	715.008	0	715.008	722.093	0.990	470.920	449.567	1.047
Rocky Mountain	390.156	7.815	382.341	394.564	0.969	214.760	207.655	1.034
Far West	1015.577	3.181	1012.396	1000.173	1.012	543.580	533.372	1.019
Total	8037.521	305.421	7732.100	7827.974	0.988	4132.420	3995.200	1.034

Appendix B.

Petroleum Heating Fuels

Quantities of Petroleum Heating Fuels - Overview

Petroleum heating fuels are used almost exclusively in space heating. Good data are available on total consumption of heating fuels by fuel type: residual oils, distillate oils, kerosine and LPG. That data is presented here by state, first in terms of barrels, and then in terms of BTU. Some data are available on consumption by broad category of use, consisting of residential versus commercial use, the latter classified into office, retail, school, hospital and all other subcategories. But next to nothing is available on sectoral use, and much of the work of this section is devoted to developing estimates of such use.

Residential use is equivalent to household use, but commercial use includes both business and government sector use. Previous studies sometimes identify industrial use as a component of space heating use of petroleum heating fuels, but estimates of that use are inadequate, insofar as they are made at all.

In this section, industrial use is estimated as five percent of all U.S. use of petroleum heating fuels, and then industrial use by state is estimated on the basis of the importance of manufactures in the state economy, under the constraint that national use by industry equals five percent of total use, and assuming that "manufactures" and "industry" are roughly equivalent.

The distribution of residential and commercial use by state is developed next. A small portion of residential use is estimated to be obtained from residual fuels (estimated as about 1.5 percent of total

use of fuels, accounted for by high rise apartment buildings, with most of
that use concentrated in New York City). The bulk of residential use,
however, is obtained from distillates, with a small portion from kerosine
and LPG. Regional data on commercial use as a share of total was modified to account for relative intensity of given commercial activities
between states. Then, quantities consumed by commercial categories were
distributed to their sectoral sources, and sectoral components were summed
to obtain consumption by sector. In summary form the cross-classification
of use by region and sector had this distribution (in fractions of total)
for all petroleum fuels combined:

	Household	Business	Government	All Sectors
Northeast	.348	.116	.031	.495
North Central	.180	.055	.020	.255
South	.145	.027	.014	.186
West	.050	.010	.004	.064
U.S.	.723	.208	.069	1.000

Basic Data

The Bureau of Mines publishes detailed information on petroleum fuels
used for heating, by state. Data on 1972 sales in thousand barrels of
distillate-type heating oils (No. 1, No. 2 and No. 4), residual-type heating
oils (No. 5 and No. 6) and kerosine appear in Mineral Industry Surveys,
Fuel Oil Sales Annual ([39] Tables 5, 6, and 7, pages 3, 4 and 5). Data on

1972 sales in thousand gallons of LPG for residential and commercial use appear in Mineral Industry Surveys, Liquified Petroleum Gas Sales, Annual ([40] Table 3 , page 5). That state data has been assembled and reproduced here as Table B.1.1, covering the specific distillate and residual heating oils, and Table B.1.2 covering aggregate distillate heating oil, residual heating oil, kerosine used for heating and LPG used for heating, all in units of thousand barrels. The corresponding regional totals appear as Table B.1.3. Much of the available information on quantities of petroleum heating fuels is presented in terms of BTUs rather than barrels; hence, conversion of quantities in barrels to quantities in BTU is a useful step in the analysis. Conversion factors showing million BTU per barrel are listed in Crump and Readling ([7], 82) as follows:

Distillates:	5.825
Residual fuel oil:	6.287
Kerosine:	5.670
LPG (Liquified Petroleum Gas)	4.011

Thus, one barrel of distillates contains 5.825 million BTU.

These conversion factors were applied to the Table B.1.2 entries to yield quantities consumed by state in terms of billion BTU, with results appearing as Table B.1.4. The regional and U.S. totals, obtained by summing the state entries, appear as Table B.1.5. The U.S. totals here check with those presented in the Minerals Yearbook for 1972 [43].

Functional and Sectoral Coverage: Problems and Proposed Solutions

Heating fuels are used primarily in space heating, although small amounts are used for water heating, cooking and clothes drying. The sectoral distribution into household, government and business use poses great difficulty because of serious gaps in information. Major problems turn on questions of (1) industrial use of fuels for space heating, (2) residential use of residual heating oil, and (3) the distribution of fuel use within the commercial sector.

The following section reviews the available information, presenting data on the functional distribution of use and then noting the sources of difficulty for the sectoral distribution in some detail. Then, the procedures employed to handle each difficulty and the estimates derived using those procedures are presented. This is done first for industrial use and then for residential and commercial use.

Functional Classification: Space Heating Versus Other Uses

In Stanford Research Institute (SRI) Patterns of Energy Consumption in the United States [29], the following information is given on petroleum for heating in 1968, with consumption measured in trillion BTU ([29], pages 7, 35 , 65 and 85):

Residential use of direct heat:	3192
space heating:	2988
water heating:	146
cooking	49
clothes drying	9
Commercial use of direct heat:	2405
(all commercial use was for space heating)	

A Project Independence study by Arthur D. Little, Inc., Residential and Commercial Energy Use Patterns, 1970-1990 [20] contains the following U.S. breakdown by sector and function (from [20] Appendix Table A.b, pages A.54 and A.56):

	LPG	Heating Oils & Kerosine	All
Residential Total	580	3475	4055
Space Heating	427	3228	3655
Water Heating	102	245	347
Cooking	51	2	53
Commercial Total	96	1164	1260
Space Heating	96	1096	1192
Water Heating	0	68	68
Grand Total	675	4639	5314

Space heating predominates, accounting for 91 percent of total use.

Sectoral Use: The Question of Industrial Use of Heating Fuels For

  Space Heating.

The use of fuel for industrial space heating is not separately
identified in the SRI study, but is included in "process steam" and
"direct heat" and is seen as a relatively small share of these uses.
Viewing all sources of heating (all other fuels, as well as petroleum), it
is argued that "residential space heating is much larger than commercial
space heating, which in turn is probably much larger than industrial space
heating." It is further suggested that industrial space heating is probably about 1% to 2% of total U.S. energy consumption ([29] page 7). For 1968,
this yields a "guesstimate" of total industrial space heating of 600 to 1200
trillion BTU (from ([29] p. 6). Petroleum accounts for 23 percent of all fuel

consumption by industry ([29] p. 86), and assuming this percentage holds for industrial space heating yields a further "guesstimate" of about 140 to 280 trillion BTU from petroleum fuels. This in turn implies an industrial share of total BTU falling between 2.4% to 4.8%; that is, we have these values for BTU from petroleum:

Residential Use:	3192	trillion BTU
Commercial Use:	2405	" "
Industrial Use:	140 to 280	" "
Total	5737 to 5877	" "

In the Minerals Yearbook [43], the Bureau of Mines classifies the U.S. aggregate use of petroleum fuels (corresponding to the totals in Table B.1.5) under the heading of residential-commercial use. However, those data include petroleum used in space heating in industrial plants, without differentiating that particular use. As a corollary, there is no direct source of information on industrial use, no doubt the source of the gap in the SRI coverage. (To make matters worse, it is possible that industrial use for space heating is understated, as well as obscured, because sellers of fuel who submit data on transactions sometimes neglect to separate sales for industrial space heating from other industrial uses [9].) The SRI study recognizes the industrial use problem but its estimated U.S. heating use of petroleum of around 5800 trillion BTU shows some disagreement with the Minerals Yearbook estimate of 5,145 trillion BTU (1969 edition, page 29, use for 1968).

In contrast, the Arthur D. Little Study shows almost exact agreement with the Bureau of Mines total, but treats "residential-commercial" consumption as exclusively by residential and commercial units, excluding industrial plant use ([20] page 63, and footnote on that page). There is some recognition of the problem of industrial use, but it seems incomplete, at best.

The listed values for the U.S. use of petroleum for space heating in 1970, in trillion BTU, compare as follows, drawing on ([20], appendix A, pages A.54 and A.56) and ([43], 1971 edition, page 27):

	Bureau of Mines	Little
LPG	722.8	675
Heating Oils & Kerosine	4648.0	4639
Total	5370.8	5314

The Little study notes ([20] page 5) that it relied on the Bureau of Mines data, which were felt to be reliable, in aggregate. However, it argues that the Bureau of Mines counts as commercial consumption such sectors of the economy as farms, fisheries, laundries and light industrial customers "which logically belong in the industrial sector, or in a miscellaneous category. The Bureau of Mines figures were adjusted [downward] to "reflect the inconsistency," presumably accounting for the reduction in LPG and the modest reduction in heating oils and kerosine in the Little data relative to the Bureau of Mines data.

The total reduction from this source for all residential and commercial energy use was 3.3 percent. The Little study states that in 1970 'the Continental United States consumed 15.3 quadrillion BTUs (quads) of energy in the residential and commercial building sector .... The total for the commercial sector includes 0.5 quads which we believe are misallocated to the commercial sector in the Bureau of Mines data; this amount is not analyzed in our work but is carried as an 'unallocated amount'" ([20], page 6). The ratio of 0.5 to 15.3 is .033.

Since a percentage of 3.3% corresponds nicely to the SRI "guesstimate' of 2.4% to 4.8% for industrial use, the course of least resistance would be to assume that the Little study has properly accounted for the industrial use problem. There are several difficulties with this assumption, however: (1) The sectors of the economy listed by Little as "illegitimately" appearing in the commercial sector do not include medium and heavy industrial users. (2) There is essentially no downward adjustment in heating oils and kerosine, which seems defensible only if industry obtains next to no BTU for space heating from those fuels. (3) The Little study recognizes (footnote, page 7) that "despite our adjustments, our derived demand for the commercial sector may be somewhat overestimated." All of these reasons suggest that much or most of the industrial use implicit in the Bureau of Mines data has not been removed by the Little adjustments.

In the present study, available evidence yielded an estimate of five percent for industrial use as a percentage of all petroleum fuels used in space heating. The estimate was based on population and employment data scaled by estimated space heating use factors. The initial step was to treat population as an indicator of residential use, and persons at work,

in schools and in hospitals as indicators of non-residential use of space
heating. The employed labor force was distributed between "commercial,"
"industrial," and "other" places, where the first category includes all
non-residential indoor work places except industrial, and the last category
includes all places of outdoor work (agriculture, construction, places
employing outdoor labor), transportation, household service and home enterprises. The employed labor force in 1972 was 81.702 million, and it was
estimated that 64% worked in commercial places, 20% in industrial places
and 16% in other places. This percentage distribution was developed from
detailed occupational data in the 1970 census of population, allocated to
one of the three classifications on the basis of job category, and adjusted
to account for employment trends from 1970 to 1972. A summary of the data
employed is as follows:

1970 U.S. Employment Distribution: Commercial, Industrial and Other Categories

Occupation	Estimated Workers In 000		
	Commercial Places	Industrial Places	Other Places
Professional, Tech. & Kindred	11561	0	0
Managers & Administrators	5963	361	139
Sales Workers	5625	0	0
Clerical Workers	13500	709	0
Craftsmen	2485	4359	3686
Operatives (non-transport)	1077	10006	161
Transp. Equipt. Operatives	0	0	3091
Laborers (non-farm)	935	1155	1661
Farmers & Farm Managers	0	0	1429
Farm Laborers	0	0	1021
Service Workers	9047	0	0
Household Service	0	0	1204
Total	50193	16590	12392
Percent of Total	63.4%	21.0%	15.6%

Source: Developed from data in U.S. Statistical Abstract, 1974,
[45], 352-356.

Number of patients plus employment in hospitals was taken as an initial

indicator of hospital use of fuels, and school enrollment plus school

employment was taken as an initial indicator of school use of fuel . Then

commercial employment (using the 64% times 81.702 million figures shown

above) minus hospital and school employment yielded an "All Other Commercial"

category of employment. The categories employed here corresponded to

categories in Little [20] for which fuel consumption data were available,

and for which some marked variations in consumption per capita occurred.

The following table shows the initial set of indicators and a set of scale

factors, derived from data in Little ([20], Table A.b, pp. A.54 and A.56).

Source of Estimated Industrial Share of Petroleum Heating Fuel Use, 1970 Data

Category	Measure of Use	Initial Indicator	Scale Factor	Adjusted Figure (in 000)
		(base figure in 000)		(base times scale factor)
Residential	Population	208,837	1.15	240,163
Hospitals	Patients & Employment	3,871	2.00	7,742
Schools	Students & Employment	63,053	0.33	20,807
All Other Commercial	Employment Net of Hospitals & Schools	46,708	1.00	46,708
Industrial	Employment	16,340	1.00	16,340
Total		338,809		331,760

Sources: Census Bureau, Statistical Abstract of the United States, 1974,
[45], Hospital Patients and Personnel (in 000) = 1200 and 2671, respectively,
from pp. 77 and 78; School Enrollment and Employment (in 000) = 60142 and
2911, respectively, from pp. 113, 126 and 133; Employed Labor Force, p. 350.
The Employed Labor Force was distributed between Commercial and Industrial
and Other Categories using the respective fractions .64, .20 and .16, based on
previous table results updated to 1972. Subtraction of Hospital and School
Employment from Commercial Employment (in 000) of 52,270 yielded 46,709 of
All Other Commercial Employment.

The scale factors account for intensity of per capita use of fuel for space heating; much of the difference in intensity reflects different hours of operation for the categories of use. In particular, Little ([20], p. 116) shows the following estimated hours of operation per year:

hospitals	8800
schools	2500
offices	3500
retail stores	4000

Remaining differences presumably reflect differences in persons per square foot of floor space.

The product of the initial indicator (or base figure) times the scale factor yielded an adjusted figure for each category. The sum over categories when divided into the industrial component yielded .0492; hence, it seemed appropriate to set industrial use at five percent of the total. In this process, it was assumed that the scale factor for industrial use was equal to that for All Other Commercial use. It is also worth noting that the scale factors from Little have implicit in them the assumption that industrial use does not occur; but the small share of industrial use in the total makes this a trivial problem in the present context.

It was now assumed that all industrial use consisted of residual heating oils; given the estimate that industrial use was five percent of total use, it followed that it comprised 23.5 percent of residual heating oil use, in BTU terms. (From Table B.1.5 it can be seen that residual heating oil is .213 of the total; hence .05/.213 = .235.) This percentage is the estimate for aggregate U.S. use, and it seemed plausible to assume that the percentage would vary between states with variation in the relative importance of industry in the state economy. Relative importance was measured by man-hours worked in manufactures relative to population, employing data in [31].

The process is exhibited in Table B.1.6, with initial columns presenting data on employment in manufactures by state, both in terms of number of production workers and man-hours of employment, drawing on [31]. It turned out that these were essentially equivalent measures, with a correlation of .9992, but man-hours seemed a shade more precise a measure, so it was employed. Table B.1.6 next presents the ratio of millions of man-hours in manufactures to population in thousands. This, in turn, is divided by the U.S. average for that ratio, which was .12822, to yield per capita employment in manufactures relative to the U.S. level. High levels for the fraction occur in the east and low levels in the west; somewhat surprisingly, the highest levels occur for North Carolina and South Carolina. The regional values were as follows:

Region	Thousand man-hours in mfg. per capita	Per capita employment in mfg. relative to U.S. level
New England	.1531	1.1938
Mid Atlantic	.1354	1.0558
East North Central	.1719	1.3408
West North Central	.0991	0.7731
South Atlantic	.1320	1.0292
East South Central	.1497	1.1676
West South Central	.0896	0.6984
Rocky Mountain	.0594	0.4634
Far West	.0955	0.7451

Each state fraction was then multiplied by .235, the fraction of residual oil used in industry for the U.S. as a whole (established earlier). This gave an initial estimate of the fraction of residual oil employed in industry for each state, which in turn was multiplied by total residual oil in billions of BTU. The initial estimates were summed, and totaled an

amount slightly larger than the control total, which was 276.5 trillion

BTU (obtained by multiplying the residual oil total by .235). The initial

estimates, when scaled by a factor of .986, yielded the control total.

The final, scaled estimates, and the final estimates of BTU in manufactures

as a fraction of residual oil BTU, appear as the last two columns, respec-

tively, of Table B.1.6. (Use in manufactures is here treated as equivalent to

industrial use.)

As a final step in the analysis of industrial use, estimated fuel

use by industry was distributed between No. 5 and No. 6 fuel oil by the

following simple rule: if No. 6 BTU exceeded industrial use, all of the

industrial use was assumed to come from that source; if the reverse oc-

curred, and industrial use exceeded the No. 6 level, all of No. 6 was

assumed to be used by industry, with the difference accounted for by No. 5

oil. Table B.1.7 shows the allocation of No. 5 and No. 6 oil between in-

dustrial and non-industrial use that is obtained at the state level under

this procedure, while Table B.1.8 shows the corresponding allocation at

the regional level.

The further allocation of residual oil between residential and com-

mercial uses, and a corresponding allocation for other fuels, is considered

next.

Sectoral Use: Residential and Commercial Use

The correspondence between industrial use and residual oil is part

of a broader correspondence to be found in the literature in which there

tends to be an identification of No. 2 fuel oil with residential use, and

of No. 5 and No. 6 fuel oils with commercial and industrial use. This

occurs in Foster Associates [15] and [16], and it also seems to occur
in the Little study [20], as can be seen in this comparison of the Little
sectoral distribution to the Bureau of Mines fuel type distribution, for
the U.S. as a whole:

Heating Oils & Kerosine Use As presented in Little [20]		Residential & Commercial Use as presented in Bur. of Mines [43]	
Sector	Trillion BTU	Fuel Type	Trillion BTU
Residential	3475	Distillates & Kerosine	3474.9
Commercial	1164	Residuals	1173.1
Total	4639		4648.0

It would appear a simple correspondence has been established between residential use and distillates plus kerosine, and between commercial use and
the residuals. (The Little report treats LPG as a separate category.)

In reality, of course, the correspondence is likely to be approximate,
with distillates and kerosine used predominantly, but not exclusively,
in the residential sector, and residuals used predominantly, but not
exclusively, in the commercial (and industrial) sector. Further, in the
case of the Little data [20], the almost exact correspondence at the
national level is not fully paralleled at the regional level, as shown in the
following table. Total use is generally close between the two sources for
all four major census regions, with North Central and Western totals in
almost exact agreement. However, the Northeast and North Central regions
show some divergence in the residential-distillate plus kerosine comparison,
and those regions and the South show even greater divergence in the commercial-
residual oil comparison.

Consumption of Heating Oils Plus Kerosine, 1970, in Trillion BTU, By Region

Comparison of Data From Study By Little and From Bureau of Mines

Region a/	Little Study, Residential Use	Bureau of Mines, Distillates & Kerosine	Little Study, Commercial Use	Bureau of Mines, Residual Oil	Little Study, Total	Bureau of Mines, Total
Northeast	1942	1773	567	815	2509	2588
North Central	749	895	286	141	1035	1036
South	590	591	246	140	836	732
West	195	191	65	72	260	263
U.S.	3475	3451	1164	1168	4639	4638

Sources: [20] and [39], 1971 issue.

Notes: a/ Northeast = New England and Mid-Atlantic

North Central = East North Central + West North Central

South = South Atlantic + East South Central + West South Central

West = Rocky Mountain + Far West

In noting its reliance on the Bureau of Mines data, the Little study

states: "The difficulty with these data arises in dividing [the] total

energy consumption between the residential and commercial markets, and

to a lesser extent, in dividing this demand among the four [major]

census regions " ([20] page 5). It can be surmised that the Little

analysis took as its starting point the identification of fuel type

with specific sectoral use, and then refined that first approximation on

the basis of other evidence. The process was not made too explicit,

however. The Little study notes that apartment buildings are sometimes

classified as commercial users, although it (the Little study) treats

apartment building use as residential. This is seen as explaining the

divergence between the SRI and Little studies in the residential versus

commercial shares of total use. For all energy sources, the SRI distri-

bution was 62% residential, 38% commercial; in contrast, the Little

distribution was 75%-25% ([20], pages 6 and 7). For petroleum heating

fuels, the SRI distribution was 57%-43% (excluding industrial use),

drawing on data presented earlier. The Little distribution for all

petroleum heating fuels (including LPG) was 76%-24%. Following up on

this clue, it can be hypothesized that apartment building use of residual

fuel oil helps explain why the northeast residential BTU total

is somewhat above the distillate plus kerosine BTU total, and why the

commercial total, correspondingly, is below the residual total. Two

points are worth noting in this connection: (1) Some older, larger

apartment buildings in the northeast (particularly in New York City)

do use residual fuel oil for heating [8], and (2) the payment for heating

that is a component of the rent paid by apartment dwellers is properly

treated as consumption by the household sector, rather than as furnished
by the business sector, following the standard convention in national
income accounting [28]. (In practice, utility payments are imputed, removed
from gross rent and treated as a separate household consumption item when
rent includes utility service furnished by the landlord.)

It is also plausible that some commercial uses, including schools and
hospitals, utilize distillate oil for heating, helping to explain why the
commercial BTU total differs from the residual BTU total for the north central
and southern regions. A final discrepancy occurs in total BTU use, with the
Little study figure below that of the Bureau of Mines for the northeast, and
above it for the south by roughly the same amount. Perhaps some offsetting
errors were identified, but they are not made explicit in the discussion.

These general observations helped shape the estimating procedures for
the distribution of residential and commercial use, which, in summary form,
involved the following steps: (1) The Little study contained useful information on petroleum product use exclusive of LPG, i.e., on the aggregate
of distillates, kerosine and residuals; it also contained separate information on LPG use. The smallest geographic units reported were the major
census regions (as shown in the preceding table in text). For those
regions, the Bureau of Mines distribution between distillates plus kerosine
use versus residual use was taken as the initial given. (2) Industrial use,
as estimated in the previous section, yielded a fraction of residual oil use
and of total use (exclusive of LPG) for each census region. This was used to
modify the Little study data, with residential and commercial use reduced
given the recognition of industrial use. Most of this reduction occurred in
residential use; for the northeast region all of the reduction was in that

use, on the basis of internal evidence; for the other regions, the reduction was made proportionate to initial estimated use, so about three-fourths of the reduction was in the residential category. (3) For all of the regions except the northeast, residential use was treated as consisting exclusively of distillates plus kerosine. For the northeast, the roughly .7 of total use that was residential had approximately 10% occurring in high rise apartment buildings; roughly half of this amount was treated as consumption of residual oils. Internal evidence led to a final estimate for high rise apartments as a fraction of total as about .03 in residuals and .04 in distillates plus kerosine. (4) Given the Bureau of Mines distribution between types of fuel, the allocation of all industrial use to residual fuels and of residential use primarily to distillates and kerosine, the remaining amounts of both types of fuel were then allocated to commercial use. In gross terms, this was the distribution that emerged for each region:

	Residential	Commercial	Industrial
Northeast			
Distillates & Kerosine	.67	.02	—
Residuals	.03	.21	.07
North Central			
Distillates & Kerosine	.70	.19	—
Residuals	—	.08	.03
South			
Distillates & Kerosine	.68	.11	—
Residuals	—	.17	.04
West			
Distillates & Kerosine	.72	.04	—
Residuals	—	.20	.04

Residential use as a fraction of total is quite similar for all regions. Commercial use primarily involves residual oil except in the north central region, which surprisingly emerged with about 70 percent in distillates and kerosine. The Little study allots commercial use between the five categories of office, retail, school, hospital and other use. For each region, the share of each category as a fraction of commercial use was taken as a basic datum and in turn, distributed between fuel types, in the same proportions that were established for total commercial use. Results are shown in the table on the next page. (5) Individual state consumption estimates were then derived by adjusting the regional data to account for relative concentration of particular activities within states in each region. In the case of high rise use of residual fuel in the northeast region, the adjustment was based on data showing the distribution of high rise apartment buildings by state. As might be expected, New York State accounted for the bulk of that consumption. Office, school and hospital uses of fuel were also adjusted by scale factors estimating relative concentration of those activities by state. Retail trade and other use were assumed proportionate to population, equivalent to accepting the regional fraction as applicable to the state. After those adjustments were carried out, a final adjustment consisted in forcing the sum of the commercial categories to equal their initial total (as obtained from the following table.) This was done by multiplying by a scale factor derived for each state. The consequence was that the sum across categories for each state equalled the initial state total, and the sum over states yielded the regional total for each major category of use.

Use By Function: Fraction of Total Use of Petroleum Heating Fuels in Residential, Commercial and Industrial Consumption, 1972

	Northeast		North Central		South		West	
	Distillates & Kerosine	Residuals	Distillates & Kerosine	Residuals	Distillates & Kerosine	Residuals	Distillates & Kerosine	Residuals
Residential								
High Rise	.0386	.0289						
All Other	.6300							
Total	.6686	.0289	.7000	——	.6810	——	.7180	——
Commercial								
Office	.0039	.0471	.0357	.0153	.0268	.0402	.0091	.0469
Retail	.0027	.0316	.0294	.0126	.0152	.0228	.0058	.0302
School	.0045	.0538	.0525	.0225	.0344	.0516	.0100	.0520
Hospital	.0020	.0249	.0189	.0081	.0100	.0150	.0032	.0168
Other	.0043	.0513	.0505	.0215	.0266	.0402	.0109	.0551
Total	.0174	.2086	.1870	.0800	.1130	.1700	.0390	.2010
Industrial		.0760		.0330		.0360		.0420
Total a/	.6860	.3140	.8870	.1130	.7940	.2060	.7570	.2430

Source: based on data appearing in Little [20], Table A.b., modified to account for industrial use, and for totals to exactly equal the distribution of use between Distillates + Kerosine versus Residuals to be found in Bureau of Mines [39], 1972 data.

a/ For each region the total for Distillates + Kerosine plus the total for Residuals sum to 1.000, accounting for total use of heating fuels exclusive of LPG. —— indicates zero.

(6) Quantities consumed by sector were then derived using information on
the distribution of each category of use between household, business and
government use, in terms of fraction of total use. Residential use was treated
as identical to household use. Office and hospital use were respectively
distributed between private business, federal government, and state and local
government components. School use was distributed between business and state
and local government, reflecting the distribution between private and public
schools. Retail trade and all other use were treated as exclusively private
business activities. The sectoral distributions in terms of fractions were
obtained for each state; then, multiplying the quantity of each category by
the estimated fractions yielded the distribution of each category between
sectors, and the sum of components for a given sector in turn gave the
sector total. (7) Finally, a simplified version of the procedure outlined
above was applied in the case of LPG. For all regions except the North Central,
LPG use was exclusively residential. In the North Central regions, the
regional distribution of use by categories (from Little [20]) was assumed to
hold for each state. Application of this distribution yielded quantity
consumed by category for each state, which was then distributed between sectors
using the procedures described above.

The remainder of this section presents some additional detail on estimating
procedures and problems, and exhibits the estimates of consumption that were
obtained.

Estimates were obtained and are described in this sequence: residential
use of residual fuel; commercial scale factors; and category and sector use
of residual fuel, distillates and kerosine, and LPG, respectively. The
section concludes by presenting the aggregates of category and sector use
for all fuels combined.

Residential Use of Residual Fuel

It was assumed that residential use of residual fuels occurred only in the northeast region, accounted for by older high rise apartment building use. The 1960 Census of Housing contained data on the number of dwelling units in high rise structures (four floors or more, with elevator) by city ([32], Table 21 , pp. 1-208, 1-209).

The time period covered seemed appropriate, because buildings constructed since 1960 would obviously not appear, and estimated use by "older" buildings was what was wanted. From this data, the state distribution of high rise buildings in the Northeast was estimated as follows, ordered by the size of fraction:

New York State	.879
(New York City = .841)	
New Jersey	.042
Pennsylvania	.036
Massachusetts	.030
Connecticut	.010
Maine	.002
Rhode Island	.001
Total	1.000

These fractions were multiplied by the estimated regional use of residual fuel in residential heating and the results were allocated to the individual state. (In an initial trial, that regional use was estimated as .05 of total petroleum use, net of LPG, but this was scaled down to .0289 to establish a consistent pattern for the New York estimates.)

Commercial Scale Factors

Because of likely variation in intensity of office employment, school enrollment and hospital facilities by state, scale factors were developed to account for such variation. Office employment relative to total employment, enrollment relative to population, and hospital employment relative to population were found for each state. Those measures, in turn, were divided by corresponding regional averages to yield the scale factors measuring intensity.

Data on office employment are not directly available in statistical series; however, Census data on employment by occupation (1970 Census of Population [34], Table 165, 1-506 and 1-507) were used to estimate office employment. Specifically, this was the estimation formula used:

Office employment =

Professional, technical, kindred employment

- Health workers

- Teachers, elementary and secondary schools

- Teachers, colleges and universities

+ Managers in industries other than manufactures and retail trade

+ Clerical and kindred workers

Data on teachers in colleges and universities were obtained from The Statistical Abstract [45], 1972 edition.

The census data list workers by place of residence, but fuel oil usage occurs at place of work. This posed a problem in the case of the District of Columbia, with a considerable inflow of workers from Virginia and Maryland. Data in [34], [36], and [37] were used to derive

the following estimates of workers commuting into the District of
Columbia in terms of total workers, **workers in offices, and**
office workers in public administration (primarily in federal government employment):

	Thousands of Commuting Workers	
	from Maryland	from Virginia
Total	140.6	110.5
Office workers	112.5	88.4
Public administration	78.7	61.9

The number of in-commuting office workers was added to the District
of Columbia total and subtracted from the respective Maryland and Virginia
totals. The public administration data were employed at a later point in
distributing office employment between sectors. (Considerable federal
government employment occurs in the Washington, D.C., metropolitan area
but outside the central city; there were 95,000 workers in such employment,
and that number is not included in the estimates of commuters into the
District of Columbia.)

For each state, the estimate of office workers was then divided by
total employment, as listed in the basic source document [34] .

Elementary and secondary school enrollment for 1972, distributed between public and non-public schools, was obtained from The Statistical
Abstract ([45], 1973 edition, p . 109); and higher education enrollment,
in terms of public versus private enrollment was also obtained from that
source ([45], 1974 edition, p. 111). The enrollment figures were aggregated and then the totals were divided by state population to yield the
measure of school intensity.

Hospital employment was used to measure hospital activity with data on total employment drawn from The Statistical Abstract ([45], 1974 edition, p.79). Employment was divided by population to yield the measure of hospital intensity. For each measure of intensity of activity, the weighted average by region was obtained, with these results:

	Office Employment Relative to All Employment	School Enrollment Relative to Population	Hospital Employment Relative to Population
Northeast	.3417	.2816	.01500
North Central	.2926	.2959	.01289
South	.2891	.2773	.01205
West	.3453	.3061	.01118
U.S.	.3128	.2884	.01284

The division of the state ratios by these regional ratios then yielded the scale factors employed in estimating state commercial fuel use. The state ratios and scale factors appear in Table B.1.9.

Residual Oil Consumption

Commercial use as a fraction of residual oil use can be obtained from the preceding table of use by function to yield these results, by region:

	Office	Retail	School	Hospital	All Other	Total Commercial
Northeast	.1345	.0916	.1546	.0687	.1488	.5988
North Central	.1356	.1117	.1994	.0718	.1914	.7099
South	.1959	.1112	.2515	.0731	.1959	.8276
West	.1926	.1240	.2136	.0691	.2272	.8265

These regional proportions were multiplied by total residual fuel use and then adjusted by the scale factors (of Table B.1.9) to yield estimates of commercial fuel use by state. The commercial uses for each state were then forced to sum to the initial commercial total, by appropriate scaling, so that given total fuel use by states, and regional use by category, were unaffected. Table B.1.10 presents the state estimates of residual fuel consumption by the commercial categories, and Table B.1.11 presents the distribution of state residual fuel use between the residential, commercial and industrial categories.

The corresponding regional consumption for these categories appears as Table B.1.12.

Office, school and hospital use were now distributed between the business and government sectors, with the fraction of use by sector assumed equal to the estimated fraction of activity in the sector, derived as follows.

In the case of the office category, public administration employment is listed in the basic source document [34]; this is employment in non-educational government agencies, and was taken as a good estimate of government office employment. Hence, the ratio of public administration to office employment was taken as the fraction of government use, and one

minus that ratio as the fraction of business use. The distribution
between federal and state and local employment was based on data in
Public Employment in 1972, excluding estimated school and hospital
employment ([36], Tables 5 and 8, pp.11, 19-20). As noted above,
the District of Columbia, Maryland and Virginia data were adjusted to
account for in-commuting office workers.

School enrollment had been obtained in terms of public versus non-
public enrollment (sources listed above), so the ratio of non-public
to total enrollment was taken as the fraction of business use (including
non-profit and parochial schools), and that of public to total enrollment as the fraction of state and local government use. Data on full-
time equivalent employment in hospitals for state and local government
were obtained from Public Employment In 1972 ([36], p. 21); data on employment in Veterans Administration hospitals were used to measure
federal hospital employment, and obtained from The Statistical Abstract,
([45], 1973 edition, p. 407); and non-government employment in hospitals
was obtained by subtracting the government employment total from all
hospital employment (source noted above).

The ratios established for the three categories appear in Table
B.1.13. In addition, it was assumed that the retail and all other categories represented business use, exclusively.

Table B.1.14 exhibits the state sectoral distribution of residual fuel
use obtained after the categories of use are allocated between sectors,
and the sectoral components are combined. The corresponding regional
distribution appears as Table B.1.15.

The residual fuel oil totals obtained to this point were then distributed between No. 5 and No. 6 fuel oil employing the hypothesis that industrial fuel use would predominantly involve No. 6 fuel oil, while residential and government use would predominantly use No. 5 fuel oil. The hypothesis led to the following allocation rules, which complete the process initiated in the industrial-nonindustrial allocation of Table B.1.7:

(1) Allocate No. 6 fuel in steps, by sector and function. In the first step, distribute No. 6 fuel oil to industrial use to the extent possible. If industrial use exceeds No. 6 fuel use, account for the remainder by No. 5 fuel oil. If No. 6 fuel oil use exceeds industrial use, apply the net amount to business commercial use as the next step. If business commercial use exceeds the net amount, account for the remainder by No. 5 fuel oil. If net No. 6 fuel oil use exceeds business commercial use, apply the net amount of this step to government use. Finally, any remaining net amount is applied to household use.

(2) Contrariwise, No. 5 fuel oil is distributed in the reverse direction, being applied to household use first, to the extent possible, then to government use, next to business commercial use, and finally to industrial use.

The results of this allocation process are shown for states in Tables B.1.16 and B.1.17, which exhibit No. 5 and No. 6 use, respectively. Table B.1.18 shows No. 5 and No. 6 use by region. In these tables, government use was not distributed between federal versus state and local government. Such could be carried out by applying the proportions implicit in Table B.1.14, which shows a breakdown of total residual use between the two levels of government.

Distillates and Kerosine Use

The table of use by function yields the following ratios of use by categories relative to total use of distillates and kerosine:

	Residential	Office	Retail	School	Hospital	All Other	Total Commercial
Northeast	.9746	.0057	.0039	.0066	.0029	.0063	.0254
North Central	.7892	.0403	.0331	.0593	.0213	.0568	.2108
South	.8577	.0337	.0191	.0432	.0126	.0337	.1423
West	.9485	.0121	.0077	.0133	.0042	.0142	.0515

Residential use accounts for the bulk of use here; this is particularly the case for the Northeast and West regions, since most of the commercial use of fuel oil, net of LPG, was estimated to be furnished by residual oil in those regions.

The procedures used in the residual oil estimating process were now applied here. The regional ratios of use multiplied by total use were then multiplied by the scale factors of Table B.1.9 . Further scaling made totals equal to initial totals, and then the sectoral fractions of Table B.1.13 were applied to distribute use by sectors. Table B.1.19 lists use by category, and Table B.1.20 lists use by sector, for states. Available evidence led to the assumption that all kerosine use occurred in the household sector, as exhibited in Table B.1.20 . Table B.1.21 exhibits regional use by category and sector.

Liquified Petroleum Gas (LPG)

LPG use is exclusively residential in all regions except the North Central, where commercial use occurs as well. In the North Central region, this distribution of LPG use appears in Little ([20], Table A.b) and was applied here:

Residential	.720
Office	.041
Retail	.058
School	.066
Hospital	.020
All Other	.095
Total Commercial	.280

For simplicity, it was assumed that those proportions held for all of the states in the North Central region, so total use times the appropriate ratio gave the corresponding use by category, as shown in Table B.1.22.

Use by categories was then distributed into use by sectors by again applying the fractions of Table B.1.13. Results for states appear as Table B.1.23 . Regional use by category and sector is shown in Table B.1.24

All Fuels Combined

Results for residual oil, distillates plus kerosine and LPG were now combined to obtain tables showing use of all petroleum heating fuels.

Table B.1.25 presents all fuel consumption by state by broad categories of use (household, commercial and industrial) and Table B.1.26 presents state data on the commercial categories of use (office, retail, school, hospital and all other). Table B.1.27 exhibits regional consumption for those categories of use.

Table B.1.28 presents the sectoral distribution of all fuel use, by state, and Table B.1.29 presents that distribution by region.

Aggregating to major census regions, the following sectoral totals are obtained in trillions of BTU:

	Household	Business	Federal Govt.	State and Local Govt.	All Sectors
Northeast	1922.61	640.31	10.62	161.68	2735.22
North Central	992.75	303.28	5.62	106.68	1408.33
South	804.58	151.63	12.40	62.90	1031.51
West	280.12	55.31	1.68	18.70	355.81
United States	4000.06	1150.52	30.33	349.96	5530.87

Presented in terms of fraction of total, this data yields:

	Household	Business	Federal Govt.	State and Local Govt.	All Sectors
Northeast	.3476	.1158	.0019	.0292	.4945
North Central	.1795	.0548	.0010	.0193	.2546
South	.1455	.0274	.0022	.0114	.1865
West	.0506	.0100	.0004	.0034	.0644
United States	.7232	.2080	.0055	.0633	1.0000

Heating Fuel Prices - Overview

A number of sources were drawn on to estimate the price of No. 2
fuel oil in residential use, and of No. 6 fuel oil in "large commercial"
use, by state. Those series were then treated as base prices and all
other fuel price estimates were derived from them by scaling. The scale
factors reflected differences in price both by level of use, ranging
from the wholesale to the retail level, and by fuel type, presumably
reflecting refining and distribution cost differences. Several internal
checks for consistency gave good results.

Prices for specific fuels and specific levels of use were then
converted from prices per gallon or per barrel to prices per million BTU,
and applied to the quantity estimates developed in the previous section
to yield expenditure estimates.

Price of No. 2 Fuel Oil in Residential Heating

A major source of data on No. 2 fuel oil prices for residential
heating was a series published by the Independent National Gas Association of America, Comparison of Seasonal Heating Costs For Gas, Fuel Oil,
Coal and Electricity, 1971 and 1972 [18]. In that series, price data
appeared for one or more major cities in each of thirty-three states and
the District of Columbia, with fifty-six cities covered in all. Where
only one city appeared, its price was assumed to hold for the state; when
more than one city appeared, the cities' average price was employed as the
state price estimate. (Within states, individual city prices were usually
close in magnitude.)

Prices for the remaining seventeen states were estimated by drawing on several sources. Seven cases were estimated from data in Foster Associates [16], which consisted of No. 2 oil prices for 1973 for major cities in a number of states, assumed to hold generally for their respective states. Those values were multiplied by .86 to yield corresponding price estimates for 1972. The .86 figure was derived from a comparison of 1972 to 1973 values for nine cases appearing in both Foster Associates [15], covering 1972 prices, and Foster Associates [16], covering 1973 prices. (The 1972 to 1973 ratio was obtained for each case, and ranged from .785 to 1.024, with four of the cases falling between .842 and .884. The average of the nine cases was .86, and this was then applied as a general scale factor.)

Prices for three additional states were estimated on the basis of 1969 prices for those states appearing in American Petroleum Institute [3]; prices for a number of other states appeared in that reference and their pattern of price change between 1969 and 1972 was used to estimate the 1972 price for the three states of interest. For example, the price increase for Arkansas, Louisiana and Oklahoma averaged 70 percent between the two dates, and this percentage increase was applied to the 1969 price listed for New Nexico to obtain the 1972 estimate.

Prices for the seven remaining states were estimated on the basis of the ratio of the No. 2 fuel oil price relative to the price of gasoline at the service station, which averaged .79 for the initial set of thirty-four states. It was assumed that the .79 figure also applied to the final set of seven states, and that fraction times the previously estimated gasoline price for each state yielded the No. 2 fuel oil price estimate.

Estimated prices for No. 2 fuel oil in cents per gallon, and the source of the estimates, by state, are presented in Table B.2.1.

Price of Number 6 Fuel Oil in "Large Commercial" Heating

The prices by state of No. 6 fuel oil used by large commercial establishments were estimated primarily from data appearing in Foster Associates [15] and [16]. Five groups of estimates were involved, with procedures and data specific to each group.

In the first group, covering eight states and the District of Columbia, 1972 data for major cities appeared in Foster Associates [15], and were taken as applicable to the respective states in which the cities were located. The second group contained four states; 1969 prices for those states appeared in American Petroleum Institute [3], and these were sealed to 1972 levels using price data for other states in the same region which appeared both in [3] and in the first group. The third group contained twenty-two states; for this group, 1973 data in Foster Associates [16] were scaled to 1972 levels on the basis of the ratio of the 1972 to 1973 price that held in the respective region, applying regional ratios derived for the first group. (For a few states in this group, 1969 data from [3] yielded divergent results, and the final estimate employed was a compromise value falling between the alternative estimates.)

For thirteen states, comprising the fourth group, the No. 2 oil price estimated previously was converted to dollars per barrel and multiplied by .568 to yield the No. 6 price estimate. The .568 figure was obtained as the average ratio of the No. 2 to the No. 6 price per barrel that held for the first group. Some additional support for this ratio seemed apparent in a similar figure of .552 obtained from data on 1969 refinery prices for

eighteen states appearing in American Petroleum Institute [2]. The
ratio of No. 6 to No. 2 price per barrel at the refinery was calculated
for each of eighteen states, and ranged from .42 to .79, with an average
value of .552.

A fifth group of three states consisted of special cases where initial
estimates were modified. A price listing for Illinois (the 1972 Chicago
price) appeared in Foster Associates [15], but ultimately was not used
because a good deal of evidence indicated it was overstated. (The evidence
consisted of the prices for the other states in the region, the relative
price for No. 2 fuel oil in Illinois, and the data for Illinois in Foster
Associates [16].) Hence, the Illinois price employed was that derived from
the procedure employed for the third group. Data in [2] showed a well-
head price for oil produced in Alaska as approximately equal to that for
the "lower 48" states; this bit of evidence suggested that the initial,
very high price estimated for Alaska might be overstated, and it was therefore reduced somewhat. (A high price at the point of consumption seemed
reasonable given a generally higher price level in Alaska.) Finally, the
price for Oklahoma was initially obtained in the same fashion as that used
for the fourth group, but data in the Minerals Year Book [43], 1972 edition,
indicated the Oklahoma price for residual fuel oil was less than the price
that held for Texas and Louisiana, rather than equal to that price, as
initially estimated. The Oklahoma price was then reduced on the basis of
that evidence in [43].

The estimated prices for No. 6 fuel oil, in dollars per barrel, and
the source of the estimates, by state, are presented in Table B.2.1.

Price Differentials By Level Of Use

Data in Foster Associates ([15], pp. 185, 193, 195, 203, 205, 238-249)

were used to establish estimated price differentials by level of use, moving
from the wholesale level through the large, bulk buyer and finally to
the small purchaser at the retail level. Prices increase considerably
in this process, reflecting the growing importance of distribution
charges (middleman and delivery costs) with movement from wholesale to
retail level. Employing these data, the following estimated index numbers
were derived for prices at various levels of use relative to the price
of No. 2 oil in residential heating, and of No. 6 oil in large commercial
heating, treated as base prices for those fuels, respectively:

Use	No. 2	No. 6
Residential	100.0	153.0 [a]
Small Commercial	97.4	149.0 [a]
Large Commercial	65.3	100.0
Large Industrial	63.0	98.0
Wholesale	58.9	91.4

[a] Inferred from other entries in list.

It is not at all obvious how Foster Associates defines "large" versus
"small" enterprises, for an explicit definition of those terms was not found
in either [15] or [16]. However, for No. 2 fuel oil, "all industrial use" is
shown with an average price equal to 84.2, given a residential index of 100
(from data in [16], Schedule V-56). This figure, in turn, implies a distribution of industrial enterprises using No. 2 fuel oil that is one-third large
and two-thirds small. (This result follows from estimating the small industrial price as .96 of the small commercial price, or 94 in index number terms,
paralleling the corresponding price ratio for the large categories. Then,

for an index number price of 94 for the small industrial category, and
a price of 63 for the large, the 2/3 - 1/3 distribution yields an average
index number price of 84.) It seems plausible that smaller industrial
enterprises would be more likely to use No. 2 than No. 6 heating oil;
hence, for No. 6 use, an estimate of half "small" and half "large" enterprises seems reasonable. This yields an average price index of 120 for
all industrial use, given the base index of 100 for large commercial use
of No. 6 oil. The same assumption applied to commercial use yields an
average price index of 122 for all commercial use.

Price Differences Between Fuels

In 1972, No. 1 fuel oil typically cost 0.75 cents more per gallon than
No. 2 fuel oil, on the basis of data in The Oil and Gas Journal ([24], first
issue of each month in 1972). Kerosine is shown as equivalent to No. 1
fuel oil in the Minerals Yearbook ([43], 1973, Vol. 1, 966), but the price
of kerosine is shown as about one cent higher per gallon than the price
of No. 1 fuel oil in Foster Associates ([16], Schedule V-54) and in The
Oil and Gas Journal. It seemed likely that these differences reflect different grade varieties involving different uses of kerosine, so a price equal
to No. 1 fuel oil was assumed for kerosine used in heating.

In 1972, the price of No. 5 fuel oil typically was around 50 cents
per barrel more than the price of No. 6 fuel oil, on the basis of data in
Platt's Oil Handbook and Oilmanac [25], and The Oil and Gas Journal. The
first source also yields data indicating that the No. 4 fuel oil price is
roughly equal to the No. 6 price plus 70 cents per barrel. (Although
pegged to the No. 6 price, it seems worth recalling that the Bureau of Mines
treats No. 4 heating oil as a distillate-type oil, in Sales of Fuel Oil and
Kerosine In 1972, [39], Table 6, p. 4.)

The question of price differentials between heating oils is compli-
cated because of regulations forcing the use of low sulfur residual fuels
in many states as of 1972. Foster Associates ([15], p. 83) note "Residual
fuel oil has been the lowest cost fuel for industrial use in the coastal
parts of the nation, although the cost difference between fuel oil and
other fuels has recently narrowed or disappeared, primarily because of
sulfur regulations." Data in that source (p. 82) and in The Oil and Gas
Journal yield some suggestion that regulation of sulfur content may have
narrowed the price differential between No. 6 and other heating fuels,
and, more generally, between residuals and distillates. A review of
the available evidence led to the following simple adjustments: (1) the
No. 5 price per barrel was set at the No. 6 price plus 30 cents for
Atlantic Coast states from Maine to Maryland, and for Illinois; (2) the
price of No. 4 fuel oil per gallon was set at 0.25 cents less than No. 2
fuel oil, which was the rough equivalent of setting No. 4 price per barrel
equal to the No. 6 price plus 70 cents. (This equivalency was confirmed
through the use of the data of Table B.2.1, applying the index number
converting commercial to residential level, and weighting by relative
use of No. 4 oil, employing as weight the ratio of state use to total use.)

The LPG price pattern involved complications because of regional
variations The Minerals Year Book [43] shows refinery and wholesale
prices of LPG below that for No. 2 fuel oil (for the cases listed, the
differential is about three cents per gallon). However, Foster Associates
([16], Schedule V-56) shows the price for LPG in industrial use typically
was below the price for No. 6 fuel oil (consistent with the Minerals
Yearbook data), but it also shows the price for LPG in small commercial

use to be well _above_ that of the price for No. 2 fuel oil in small commercial use. It seems likely, then, that distribution costs for LPG increase faster than for fuel oil with movement from wholesale to retail level.

On the basis of thirty-five observations on prices for small commercial use and thirty-three observations on prices for industrial use, the following regional price ratios were estimated.

Region	Price of LPG Relative to Price of Fuel Oil	
	Relative to No. 2 Fuel Oil In Small Commercial Use	Relative to No. 2 Fuel Oil In Industrial Use
1. New England	1.50	0.92
2. Mid Atlantic	1.25	0.83
3. East North Central	1.40	0.95
4. West North Central	1.20	0.98
5. South Atlantic	1.40	0.95
6. East South Central	1.50	0.91
7. West South Central	1.20	1.14
8. Rocky Mountain	1.50	1.20
9. Far West	1.70	1.19

It was now assumed that the factors for industrial use also held for all commercial use (the average of large and small commercial), and that the factors for small commercial use applied to household use of LPG, given the relationships established earlier.

A Note On The Relation of No. 2 to No. 6 Prices

In the development of price estimates here, the initial sets of estimates for No. 2 and No. 6 fuel oil prices were the key starting points. Hence, it is of some interest to compare those data in a check for internal consistency. Results of the comparison seem good.

Table B.2.2 presents the following prices for each state: No. 6 fuel oil in commercial use, converted to cents per gallon; No. 2 fuel oil in residential use, in cents per gallon; and the price of No. 6 if it were consumed at the residential level, obtained by dividing the initial No. 6 figure by .653, the estimate presented earlier for price at the commercial level relative to the residential level. (The .653 figure accounts for lower prices to the bulk buyer relative to the retail purchaser.) The last column of the table then presents the ratio of the No. 2 price to the No. 6 price "as if at the residential level.' The simple average values for these estimates are:

No. 6, commercial use:	11.197¢
No. 2, residential use:	19.403¢
No. 6, residential use:	17.148¢
No. 2/No. 6 residential	1.132

Thus, level of use accounts for most of the observed difference between No. 2 and No. 6 price, i.e., the movement from 11.197 to 17.148. Quality of product differences presumably account for the remaining price difference (between 17.148 and 19.403). In quantitative terms, 72.5 percent and 27.5 percent are the respective percentages accounted for by the level of use and by quality differences, when the two sets of prices are compared.

The ratio of No. 2 price to No. 6 price, residential level, is fairly stable between states, with a standard error of .090. The simple average for the ratio, by region, was:

New England	1.177
Mid Atlantic	1.157
East North Central	1.080
West North Central	1.080
South Atlantic	1.171
East South Central	1.133
West South Central	1.122
Rocky Mountain	1.094
Far West	1.186

These results seem reasonably consistent, with differences presumably reflecting both differences in raw product prices, and in middlemen and distribution mark-up. When the No. 2 price was related to the No. 6 price, residential level, by regression analysis, the fitted equation was: No. 2 = 2.208 + 1.003 No. 6R, with a t ratio of 6.356 and $\bar{r}^2$ of .4407, where No. 2 is No. 2 price and No. 6R is No. 6 price, residential level. The regression equation states that the No. 2 price equals the No. 6 price, residential level, plus 2.2 cents. (The regression of No. 2 price on No. 6 price, commercial level yielded a slope of 1.536.) The coefficient essentially equal to one appears to show good internal consistency with the factor (.653) translating the commercial to the residential level. Admittedly, a subset of No. 6 prices, covering thirteen states, were initially estimated as a fraction of No. 2 prices, so some of this relationship was "built-in." Yet most of the price estimates were obtained independently, and the consistency here therefore seems reassuring. Put another way, the consistency lends support to the simple scaling of prices which was used to develop price estimates for most of the fuels, given the No. 2 and No. 6 prices as base series.

Specific Price Estimates

Specific price estimates were now developed to correspond to the quantity measures appearing in the tables of heating fuel consumption, in terms of fuel type, sector of use, level of use and units (BTU measures rather than gallons or barrels).

In the tables covering distillate use, the usage of No. 1, No. 2, and No. 4 fuel oil were aggregated, with no attempt to allocate specific distillates to specific uses. It seemed plausible that little could be gained by such refinement. In particular, it seemed likely that No. 4 use occurred in apartment buildings (residential use) as well as in commercial structures. More than half of all No. 4 use occurred in New York and New Jersey, consistent with this hypothesis. (See Tables B.1.1 and B.1.3 .) Further, No. 2 use accounted for the bulk of distillate use (80 percent for the simple average over states), and the prices of No. 1, No. 2 and No. 4 were close enough that disaggregation seemed a needless refinement.

Hence, an average distillate fuel price was calculated by first estimating the price for No. 1, No. 2 and No. 4 fuel oil at the residential level, and then weighting those prices by the fraction of total distillate use accounted for by each fuel in each state. Table B.2.3 presents the average price computed, and the underlying components used in estimating this price, for each state.

Government expenditures on residual fuel oils (No. 5 and No. 6)
were broken down into federal versus state and local expenditures for
the combined consumption of No. 5 and No. 6 fuel oil. It was assumed
that the fraction consumed at each level of government held for the
individual fuels as well as for their total, and the fractions were
then applied in estimating the distribution of expenditures for each
of the two fuels. Table B.2.4 presents these fractions by state; the
preponderance of consumption occurs for state and local government,
reflecting the relatively large consumption by schools. The federal
share is almost half of the total in the District of Columbia, and is
relatively large in Maryland and Virginia (reflecting the "spill-over"
of federal offices from the District of Columbia) and in the western
states.

In all applications, it was assumed that the prices paid by government equaled those that had been estimated for the "all commercial" category.

Estimated prices for LPG were obtained by multiplying the previously
established regional scale factors for LPG relative to No. 2 and No. 6
fuel oil by the state prices for the latter fuels. The resulting estimates
for LPG prices at the residential and "all commercial" levels appear in
Table B.2.4 .

As a final step, all of the fuel price estimates established in terms
of cents per gallon were converted to dollars per barrel by multiplying
by .42. Then all prices in dollars per barrel were converted to dollars
per million BTU using the following scale factors, based on data in Crump
and Readling [7] showing million BTU per barrel:

Distillates	5.825
Residual fuel oil	6.287
Kerosine	5.670
LPG	4.011

Table B.2.5 compares prices for major specific fuels estimated to hold at the "all commercial" level (the estimated average of prices at the large and small commercial level). The prices for LPG are considerably above those for No. 6 fuel oil; this reflects the considerably lower amounts of BTU per barrel for LPG than for the other fuels. Price differences are even more pronounced between LPG and distillates at the residential level, reflecting the scale factors for prices per gallon established earlier, as well as the BTU conversion difference noted at this point. No doubt LPG requires special handling and extra distribution charges because of its physical characteristics and primary locale of use -- by farms, mobile homes, etc.

Given the array of prices for fuels and levels corresponding to the quantity estimates of the previous section, expenditure estimates were obtained by multiplying prices by quantities. Results are presented in the next section.

Expenditures on Petroleum Heating Fuels

Multiplication of prices by quantities was carried out by state for each of the major fuel categories, with results presented in Tables B.3.1 through B.3.4. The first two of these tables cover No. 5 and No. 6 fuel oils, respectively, and the last two cover Kerosine - Distillates and LPG, respectively. Regional summaries using these groupings appear as Tables B.3.5 and B.3.6. Table B.3.7 lists total expenditures by state on each of the individual fuel types, and Table B.3.8 presents total expenditures by state for individual sectors: households; business, sub-classified into commercial versus industrial; federal government and state and local government. Table B.3.9 presents the regional totals corresponding to the state data of Tables B.3.7 and B.3.8.

Estimated total U.S. expenditures is $8.17 billion, with roughly 80 percent of the total attributable to household spending. Fractions of total spending, by sector are:

Household	.809
Business	
Commercial	.111
Industrial	.031
Government	
Federal	.004
State and Local	.045
	————
	1.000

Fractions of total spending by fuel type are:

No. 5 fuel oil	.032
No. 6 fuel oil	.104
Residual fuel oil total (No. 5 & No. 6)	(.136)
Kerosine	.069
Distillates	.556
LPG	.239
Total	1.000

It is somewhat surprising that the federal government fraction is so low and that the LPG fraction is so high. Perhaps part of the explanation for the first result is that military expenditures for residuals and distillates are treated separately, and it seems likely that military use of fuels for heating is included in that separate accounting. More generally, the low fraction for federal expenditures seems a concomitant of the large fraction attributed to households (.8 of total).

To considerable extent, the LPG result reflects high consumption of physical quantities. In terms of BTU consumption, LPG accounts for .142 of the total (Table B.1.5). but in terms of barrels consumed, LPG accounts for .197 of the total (Table B.1.3). The higher fraction for expenditures reflects the higher than average costs for LPG.

Nevertheless, future work aimed at improving these estimates might take as points of departure more detailed investigations of LPG, federal government consumption, and the over-all share of residential (household) use in total consumption.

Table B.1.1

Consumption Of Petroleum Heating Fuels, 1972, In Thousand Barrels, By State
Distillate and Residual Heating Oils

Region and State	Distillate Oils			Residual Oils	
	No. 1	No. 2	No. 4	No. 5	No. 6
NEW ENGLAND:					
CONNECTICUT	230.0	17258.0	2203.0	61.0	4916.0
MAINE	817.0	9046.0	315.0	867.0	3151.0
MASSACHUSETTS	1017.0	52100.0	3322.0	8086.0	22694.0
NEW HAMPSHIRE	412.0	7088.0	50.0	510.0	1613.0
RHODE ISLAND	207.0	7705.0	210.0	1203.0	2221.0
VERMONT	177.0	4623.0	175.0	30.0	504.0
MID ATLANTIC:					
NEW JERSEY	412.0	40721.0	11314.0	2592.0	11301.0
NEW YORK	1972.0	80036.0	12100.0	1384.0	57768.0
PENNSYLVANIA	1260.0	38907.0	4581.0	7216.0	8068.0
EAST NORTH CENTRAL:					
ILLINOIS	3191.0	20473.0	1349.0	4163.0	6045.0
INDIANA	3138.0	15129.0	414.0	592.0	3379.0
MICHIGAN	6951.0	23234.0	1167.0	356.0	691.0
OHIO	1819.0	12968.0	318.0	117.0	713.0
WISCONSIN	3522.0	15249.0	833.0	313.0	288.0
WEST NORTH CENTRAL:					
IOWA	1815.0	4803.0	10.0	82.0	42.0
KANSAS	139.0	698.0	0.0	23.0	36.0
MINNESOTA	3790.0	12127.0	1194.0	410.0	411.0
MISSOURI	980.0	5644.0	17.0	740.0	422.0
NEBRASKA	460.0	2045.0	0.0	99.0	106.0
NORTH DAKOTA	595.0	2037.0	2.0	93.0	130.0
SOUTH DAKOTA	1038.0	1801.0	0.0	4.0	0.0
SOUTH ATLANTIC:					
DELAWARE	222.0	3252.0	18.0	244.0	252.0
DISTRICT OF COLUMBIA	13.0	2257.0	105.0	518.0	5190.0
FLORIDA	656.0	3310.0	29.0	31.0	2696.0
GEORGIA	196.0	2866.0	5.0	890.0	1687.0
MARYLAND	341.0	12436.0	136.0	1742.0	3777.0
NORTH CAROLINA	997.0	10778.0	35.0	1020.0	809.0
SOUTH CAROLINA	378.0	3390.0	90.0	152.0	55.0
VIRGINIA	727.0	11203.0	280.0	457.0	1282.0
WEST VIRGINIA	50.0	1208.0	3.0	488.0	71.0
EAST SOUTH CENTRAL:					
ALABAMA	58.0	1267.0	0.0	201.0	123.0
KENTUCKY	345.0	1201.0	4.0	0.0	152.0
MISSISSIPPI	133.0	1126.0	0.0	0.0	100.0
TENNESSEE	302.0	1561.0	0.0	16.0	270.0
WEST SOUTH CENTRAL:					
ARKANSAS	70.0	947.0	0.0	18.0	254.0
LOUISIANA	73.0	218.0	6.0	2.0	8.0
OKLAHOMA	232.0	1103.0	0.0	32.0	54.0
TEXAS	1036.0	3318.0	129.0	25.0	647.0
ROCKY MOUNTAIN:					
ARIZONA	35.0	349.0	0.0	0.0	0.0
COLORADO	889.0	650.0	0.0	54.0	480.0
IDAHO	1341.0	1441.0	21.0	58.0	110.0
MONTANA	773.0	446.0	0.0	163.0	46.0
NEVADA	193.0	755.0	1.0	72.0	17.0
NEW MEXICO	328.0	162.0	3.0	0.0	21.0
UTAH	403.0	912.0	183.0	339.0	186.0
WYOMING	80.0	499.0	43.0	87.0	214.0
FAR WEST:					
ALASKA	785.0	1371.0	405.0	0.0	20.0
CALIFORNIA	348.0	2851.0	3.0	417.0	1064.0
HAWAII	0.0	105.0	0.0	113.0	10.0
OREGON	1764.0	4571.0	21.0	2105.0	1408.0
WASHINGTON	3133.0	7578.0	77.0	1923.0	1501.0

Table B.1.2

Consumption of Petroleum Heating Fuels, 1972, In Thousand Barrels, By State

Major Fuels

Region and State	Distillate Heating Oil	Residual Heating Oil	Kerosine	LPG
NEW ENGLAND:				
CONNECTICUT	19691.0	4977.0	690.0	1005.8
MAINE	10178.0	4018.0	1763.0	519.1
MASSACHUSETTS	56439.0	30780.0	1687.0	1232.9
NEW HAMPSHIRE	7550.0	2123.0	652.0	713.8
RHODE ISLAND	8122.0	3424.0	345.0	194.7
VERMONT	4975.0	534.0	460.0	551.5
MID ATLANTIC:				
NEW JERSEY	52447.0	13893.0	1687.0	1086.1
NEW YORK	94108.0	59152.0	6938.0	3782.2
PENNSYLVANIA	44748.0	15284.0	4868.0	2383.1
EAST NORTH CENTRAL:				
ILLINOIS	25013.0	10208.0	2985.0	11382.0
INDIANA	18681.0	3971.0	2169.0	8537.6
MICHIGAN	31352.0	1047.0	2089.0	6882.6
OHIO	15105.0	830.0	3721.0	5525.5
WISCONSIN	19604.0	601.0	1472.0	7464.2
WEST NORTH CENTRAL:				
IOWA	6628.0	124.0	358.0	8903.2
KANSAS	837.0	59.0	99.0	5688.8
MINNESOTA	17111.0	821.0	915.0	8933.3
MISSOURI	6641.0	1162.0	318.0	11181.1
NEBRASKA	2505.0	205.0	756.0	4694.1
NORTH DAKOTA	2634.0	223.0	139.0	1551.0
SOUTH DAKOTA	2839.0	4.0	6.0	2636.1
SOUTH ATLANTIC:				
DELAWARE	3492.0	496.0	383.0	487.5
DISTRICT OF COLUMBIA	2375.0	5708.0	31.0	456.7
FLORIDA	3995.0	2727.0	1840.0	6651.7
GEORGIA	3067.0	2577.0	153.0	5063.9
MARYLAND	12913.0	5519.0	1723.0	865.7
NORTH CAROLINA	11810.0	1829.0	8443.0	3654.9
SOUTH CAROLINA	3858.0	207.0	2032.0	2306.1
VIRGINIA	12210.0	1739.0	4293.0	1881.7
WEST VIRGINIA	1261.0	559.0	345.0	421.8
EAST SOUTH CENTRAL:				
ALABAMA	1325.0	324.0	388.0	6802.2
KENTUCKY	1550.0	152.0	1870.0	4375.5
MISSISSIPPI	1259.0	100.0	377.0	6582.8
TENNESSEE	1863.0	286.0	2587.0	3076.6
WEST SOUTH CENTRAL:				
ARKANSAS	1017.0	272.0	269.0	8899.3
LOUISIANA	297.0	10.0	375.0	3562.3
OKLAHOMA	1335.0	86.0	418.0	6894.9
TEXAS	4483.0	672.0	4008.0	18060.4
ROCKY MOUNTAIN:				
ARIZONA	384.0	0.0	53.0	1066.1
COLORADO	1539.0	534.0	213.0	4409.6
IDAHO	2803.0	168.0	180.0	1080.6
MONTANA	1219.0	209.0	77.0	1287.5
NEVADA	949.0	89.0	6.0	668.3
NEW MEXICO	493.0	21.0	344.0	2451.1
UTAH	1498.0	525.0	196.0	987.5
WYOMING	622.0	301.0	237.0	1523.4
FAR WEST:				
ALASKA	2561.0	20.0	13.0	110.5
CALIFORNIA	3202.0	1481.0	1039.0	5436.4
HAWAII	105.0	123.0	35.0	565.2
OREGON·	6356.0	3513.0	38.0	950.5
WASHINGTON	10788.0	3424.0	116.0	1031.3

Table B.1.3

Consumption Of Petroleum Heating Fuels, 1972, In Thousand Barrels, By Region
Distillate and Residual Heating Oils, and Major Fuels

Region	Distillate Heating Oils			Residual Heating Oils	
	No. 1	No. 2	No. 4	No. 5	No. 6
NEW ENGLAND	2860.00	97820.00	6275.00	10757.00	35099.00
MID ATLANTIC	3644.00	159664.00	27995.00	11192.00	77137.00
EAST NORTH CENTRAL	18621.00	87053.00	4081.00	5541.00	11116.00
WEST NORTH CENTRAL	8817.00	29155.00	1223.00	1451.00	1147.00
SOUTH ATLANTIC	3580.00	50700.00	701.00	5542.00	15819.00
EAST SOUTH CENTRAL	838.00	5155.00	4.00	217.00	645.00
WEST SOUTH CENTRAL	1411.00	5586.00	135.00	77.00	963.00
ROCKY MOUNTAIN	4042.00	5214.00	251.00	773.00	1074.00
FAR WEST	6030.00	16476.00	506.00	4558.00	4003.00
TOTAL	49843.00	456823.00	41171.00	40108.00	147003.00

Region	Distillate Heating Oil	Residual Heating Oil	Kerosine	LPG
NEW ENGLAND	106955.00	45856.00	5597.00	4217.69
MID ATLANTIC	191303.00	88329.00	13493.00	7251.43
EAST NORTH CENTRAL	109755.00	16657.00	12436.00	39791.76
WEST NORTH CENTRAL	39195.00	2598.00	2591.00	43587.64
SOUTH ATLANTIC	54981.00	21361.00	19243.00	21789.91
EAST SOUTH CENTRAL	5997.00	862.00	5222.00	20837.17
WEST SOUTH CENTRAL	7132.00	1040.00	5070.00	37416.88
ROCKY MOUNTAIN	9507.00	1847.00	1306.00	13474.17
FAR WEST	23012.00	8561.00	1241.00	8093.83
TOTAL	547837.00	187111.00	66199.00	196460.48

Table **B.1.4**

Consumption of Petroleum Heating Fuels, 1972, In Billion BTU, By State

Major Fuels and Aggregates of Fuels

State and Region	Distillate Heating Oil	Residual Heating Oil	Kerosine	LPG	Non-Residual Heating Fuels	All Heating Fuels
NEW ENGLAND:						
CONNECTICUT	114700.08	31290.40	3912.30	4034.11	122646.49	153936.89
MAINE	59286.85	25261.17	9996.21	2082.09	71365.15	96626.32
MASSACHUSETTS	328757.17	193513.86	9565.29	4944.99	343267.45	536781.31
NEW HAMPSHIRE	43978.75	13347.30	3696.84	2862.90	50538.49	63885.79
RHODE ISLAND	47310.65	21526.69	1956.15	780.81	50047.61	71574.30
VERMONT	28979.37	3357.26	2608.20	2212.26	33799.83	37157.09
MID ATLANTIC:						
NEW JERSEY	305503.77	87345.29	9565.29	4356.33	319425.39	406770.68
NEW YORK	548179.11	371888.63	39338.46	15170.37	602687.93	974576.56
PENNSYLVANIA	260657.10	96090.51	27601.56	9558.79	297817.45	393907.95
EAST NORTH CENTRAL:						
ILLINOIS	145700.73	64177.70	16924.95	45653.01	208278.69	272456.38
INDIANA	108816.82	24965.68	12298.23	34244.20	155359.25	180324.93
MICHIGAN	182625.40	6582.49	11844.63	27605.99	222076.03	228658.51
OHIO	87986.62	5218.21	21098.07	22162.59	131247.29	136465.50
WISCONSIN	114193.30	3778.49	8346.24	29938.96	152478.50	156256.99
WEST NORTH CENTRAL:						
IOWA	38608.10	779.59	2029.86	35710.79	76348.75	77128.34
KANSAS	4875.53	370.93	561.33	22817.62	28254.48	28625.41
MINNESOTA	99671.58	5161.63	5188.05	35831.50	140691.13	145852.76
MISSOURI	38683.83	7305.49	1803.06	44847.47	85334.35	92639.85
NEBRASKA	14591.62	1288.84	4286.52	18828.21	37706.35	38995.19
NORTH DAKOTA	15343.05	1402.00	788.13	6221.06	22352.24	23754.24
SOUTH DAKOTA	16537.18	25.15	34.02	10573.38	27144.57	27169.72
SOUTH ATLANTIC:						
DELAWARE	20340.90	3118.35	2171.61	1955.17	24467.68	27586.03
DISTRICT OF COLUMBIA	13834.37	35886.20	175.77	1831.69	15841.83	51728.03
FLORIDA	23270.88	17144.65	10432.80	26680.03	60383.70	77528.35
GEORGIA	17865.27	16201.60	867.51	20311.42	39044.20	55245.80
MARYLAND	75218.22	34697.95	9769.41	3472.28	88459.92	123157.87
NORTH CAROLINA	68793.25	11498.92	47871.81	14659.73	131324.79	142823.71
SOUTH CAROLINA	22472.85	1301.41	11521.44	9249.65	43243.94	44545.35
VIRGINIA	71123.25	10933.09	24341.31	7547.65	103012.21	113945.30
WEST VIRGINIA	7345.32	3514.43	1956.15	1691.69	10993.16	14507.59
EAST SOUTH CENTRAL:						
ALABAMA	7718.12	2036.99	2199.96	27283.78	37201.86	39238.85
KENTUCKY	9028.75	955.62	10602.90	17550.13	37181.78	38137.40
MISSISSIPPI	7333.67	628.70	2137.59	26403.65	35874.91	36503.61
TENNESSEE	10851.97	1798.08	14668.29	12340.32	37860.59	39658.67
WEST SOUTH CENTRAL:						
ARKANSAS	5924.03	1710.06	1525.23	35694.94	43144.19	44854.26
LOUISIANA	1730.03	62.87	2126.25	14288.52	18144.79	18207.66
OKLAHOMA	7776.37	540.68	2370.06	27655.56	37801.99	38342.68
TEXAS	26113.48	4224.86	22725.36	72440.09	121278.92	125503.79
ROCKY MOUNTAIN:						
ARIZONA	2236.80	0.00	300.51	4276.30	6813.61	6813.61
COLORADO	8964.67	3357.26	1207.71	17686.89	27859.27	31216.53
IDAHO	16327.48	1056.22	1020.60	4334.46	21682.53	22738.75
MONTANA	7100.67	1313.98	436.59	5164.07	12701.33	14015.32
NEVADA	5527.92	559.54	34.02	2680.59	8242.53	8802.08
NEW MEXICO	2871.73	132.03	1950.48	9831.44	14653.64	14785.67
UTAH	8725.85	3300.68	1111.32	3960.77	13797.94	17098.61
WYOMING	3623.15	1892.39	1343.79	6110.38	11077.32	12969.70
FAR WEST:						
ALASKA	14917.83	125.74	73.71	443.22	15434.75	15560.49
CALIFORNIA	18651.65	9311.05	5891.13	21805.32	46348.10	55659.15
HAWAII	611.63	773.30	198.45	2267.07	3077.15	3850.45
OREGON	37023.70	22086.23	215.46	3812.36	41051.52	63137.75
WASHINGTON	62840.10	21526.69	657.72	4136.39	67634.21	89160.90

Table B.1.5

Consumption of Petroleum Heating Fuels, 1972, In Billion BTU, By Region

Major Fuels and Aggregates of Fuels

Region	Distillate Heating Oil	Residual Heating Oil	Kerosine	LPG	Nonresidual Heating Fuels	All Heating Fuels
NEW ENGLAND	623012.88	288296.67	31734.99	16917.16	671665.02	959961.70
MID ATLANTIC	1114339.99	555324.43	76505.31	29085.48	1219930.77	1775255.20
EAST NORTH CENTRAL	639322.88	104722.56	70512.12	159604.76	869439.76	974162.31
WEST NORTH CENTRAL	228310.88	16333.63	14690.97	174830.03	417831.88	434165.51
SOUTH ATLANTIC	320264.32	134296.61	109107.81	87399.31	516771.44	651068.05
EAST SOUTH CENTRAL	34932.53	5419.39	29608.74	83577.88	148119.14	153538.53
WEST SOUTH CENTRAL	41543.90	6538.48	28746.90	150079.11	220369.91	226908.39
ROCKY MOUNTAIN	55378.27	11612.09	7405.02	54044.88	116828.18	128440.27
FAR WEST	134044.90	53823.01	7036.47	32464.37	173545.73	227368.74
TOTAL	3191150.58	1176366.87	375348.33	788002.96	4354501.74	5530868.77

Table .B.1.6

Consumption Of Petroleum Heating Fuels, 1972, Scale Factors, By State
Data Employed To Develop Estimates, And Estimates, For Fuel Oil Use In Manufactures

Region and State	Number Of Production Workers In 000	Man-Hours In Millions	Thousand Man-Hours In Manufactures Per Capita	Per Capita Employment In Manufactures Relative To U.S. Level	Estimated Fuel Oil Use In Manufactures In Billion BTU	Estimated BTU in Manufactures As Fraction Of Residual Fuel Oil BTU
NEW ENGLAND:						
CONNECTICUT	258.20	520.90	0.1691	1.3190	9568.92	0.3058
MAINE	82.60	162.20	0.1581	1.2329	7220.85	0.2858
MASSACHUSETTS	416.00	812.10	0.1401	1.0927	49025.26	0.2533
NEW HAMPSHIRE	67.70	131.40	0.1698	1.3240	4097.21	0.3070
RHODE ISLAND	91.40	174.20	0.1798	1.4020	6997.33	0.3251
VERMONT	26.10	52.20	0.1135	0.8850	688.87	0.2052
MID ATLANTIC:						
NEW JERSEY	546.60	1070.90	0.1457	1.1365	23015.26	0.2635
NEW YORK	1076.20	2068.20	0.1126	0.8782	75720.46	0.2036
PENNSYLVANIA	1015.00	1953.90	0.1641	1.2800	28516.58	0.2968
EAST NORTH CENTRAL:						
ILLINOIS	901.00	1780.30	0.1583	1.2348	18373.32	0.2863
INDIANA	526.10	1041.70	0.1971	1.5369	8896.02	0.3563
MICHIGAN	768.10	1582.60	0.1756	1.3694	2089.91	0.3175
OHIO	940.00	1887.80	0.1761	1.3731	1661.23	0.3184
WISCONSIN	360.50	720.50	0.1592	1.2415	1087.61	0.2878
WEST NORTH CENTRAL:						
IOWA	157.00	311.20	0.1079	0.8415	152.10	0.1951
KANSAS	101.30	202.50	0.0893	0.6963	59.88	0.1614
MINNESOTA	196.10	382.80	0.0987	0.7700	921.48	0.1785
MISSOURI	299.80	583.80	0.1230	0.9591	1624.50	0.2224
NEBRASKA	63.20	127.60	0.0835	0.6513	194.62	0.1510
NORTH DAKOTA	7.10	14.40	0.0227	0.1771	57.57	0.0411
SOUTH DAKOTA	12.90	25.10	0.0369	0.2879	1.68	0.0667
SOUTH ATLANTIC:						
DELAWARE	37.70	73.90	0.1294	1.0093	729.71	0.2340
DISTRICT OF COLUMBIA	9.40	16.50	0.0219	0.1711	1423.59	0.0397
FLORIDA	242.00	481.50	0.0655	0.5111	2031.62	0.1185
GEORGIA	368.60	737.50	0.1558	1.2152	4564.70	0.2817
MARYLAND	175.70	345.70	0.0854	0.6660	5357.78	0.1544
NORTH CAROLINA	604.00	1211.00	0.2319	1.8089	4822.57	0.4194
SOUTH CAROLINA	282.70	581.60	0.2164	1.6874	509.14	0.3912
VIRGINIA	293.20	582.90	0.1223	0.9540	2418.23	0.2212
WEST VIRGINIA	92.70	181.80	0.1013	0.7899	643.63	0.1831
EAST SOUTH CENTRAL:						
ALABAMA	262.20	519.30	0.1475	1.1502	543.21	0.2667
KENTUCKY	200.40	392.90	0.1188	0.9269	205.37	0.2149
MISSISSIPPI	166.90	332.00	0.1472	1.1477	167.29	0.2661
TENNESSEE	367.00	725.30	0.1781	1.3891	579.10	0.3221
WEST SOUTH CENTRAL:						
ARKANSAS	150.10	298.40	0.1486	1.1590	459.52	0.2687
LOUISIANA	134.30	274.60	0.0735	0.5729	8.35	0.1328
OKLAHOMA	95.70	186.10	0.0707	0.5512	69.10	0.1278
TEXAS	516.60	1030.50	0.0888	0.6926	678.43	0.1606
ROCKY MOUNTAIN:						
ARIZONA	62.30	121.10	0.0617	0.4811	0.00	0.0000
COLORADO	89.00	176.70	0.0747	0.5829	453.72	0.1351
IDAHO	34.30	66.00	0.0874	0.6818	166.96	0.1581
MONTANA	17.10	33.60	0.0469	0.3660	111.50	0.0849
NEVADA	6.90	13.50	0.0253	0.1975	25.62	0.0458
NEW MEXICO	17.20	32.90	0.0306	0.2385	7.30	0.0553
UTAH	38.80	73.70	0.0654	0.5100	390.28	0.1182
WYOMING	5.10	10.10	0.0292	0.2277	99.90	0.0528
FAR WEST:						
ALASKA	6.20	11.90	0.0366	0.2856	8.33	0.0662
CALIFORNIA	1020.00	1974.90	0.0968	0.7546	1629.00	0.1750
HAWAII	17.70	33.10	0.0406	0.3164	56.73	0.0734
OREGON	141.50	271.30	0.1242	0.9683	4958.36	0.2245
WASHINGTON	159.80	303.30	0.0887	0.6920	3453.74	0.1604

Table B.1.7

Consumption Of Petroleum Heating Fuels, 1972, In Billion BTU, By State

Estimated Residual Oil Consumption For Space Heating In Industrial and Non-Industrial Use

REGION and STATE	NO. 5 HEATING OIL TOTAL	NO. 6 HEATING OIL TOTAL	NO. 5 HEATING OIL		NO. 6 HEATING OIL	
			Industrial Use	Non-Industrial Use	Industrial Use	Non-Industrial Use
NEW ENGLAND:						
CONNECTICUT	383.51	30906.89	0.00	383.51	9568.92	21337.97
MAINE	5450.83	19810.34	0.00	5450.83	7220.85	12589.49
MASSACHUSETTS	50836.68	142677.18	0.00	50836.68	49025.26	93651.92
NEW HAMPSHIRE	3206.37	10140.93	0.00	3206.37	4097.21	6043.72
RHODE ISLAND	7563.26	13963.43	0.00	7563.26	6997.33	6966.10
VERMONT	188.61	3168.65	0.00	188.61	688.87	2479.78
MID ATLANTIC:						
NEW JERSEY	16295.90	71049.39	0.00	16295.90	23015.26	48034.13
NEW YORK	8701.21	363187.42	0.00	8701.21	75720.46	287466.96
PENNSYLVANIA	45366.99	50723.52	0.00	45366.99	28516.58	22206.94
EAST NORTH CENTRAL:						
ILLINOIS	26172.78	38004.92	0.00	26172.78	18373.32	19631.59
INDIANA	3721.90	21243.77	0.00	3721.90	8896.02	12347.75
MICHIGAN	2238.17	4344.32	0.00	2238.17	2089.91	2254.41
OHIO	735.58	4482.63	0.00	735.58	1661.23	2821.40
WISCONSIN	1967.83	1810.66	0.00	1967.83	1087.61	723.05
WEST NORTH CENTRAL:						
IOWA	515.53	264.05	0.00	515.53	152.10	111.96
KANSAS	144.60	226.33	0.00	144.60	59.88	166.45
MINNESOTA	2577.67	2583.96	0.00	2577.67	921.48	1662.48
MISSOURI	4652.38	2653.11	0.00	4652.38	1624.50	1028.61
NEBRASKA	622.41	666.42	0.00	622.41	194.62	471.80
NORTH DAKOTA	584.69	817.31	0.00	584.69	57.57	759.74
SOUTH DAKOTA	25.15	0.00	1.68	23.47	0.00	0.00
SOUTH ATLANTIC:						
DELAWARE	1534.03	1584.32	0.00	1534.03	729.71	854.61
DISTRICT OF COLUMBIA	3256.67	32629.53	0.00	3256.67	1423.59	31205.94
FLORIDA	194.90	16949.75	0.00	194.90	2031.62	14918.14
GEORGIA	5595.43	10606.17	0.00	5595.43	4564.70	6041.47
MARYLAND	10951.95	23746.00	0.00	10951.95	5357.78	18388.22
NORTH CAROLINA	6412.74	5086.18	0.00	6412.74	4822.57	263.61
SOUTH CAROLINA	955.62	345.78	163.36	792.27	345.78	0.00
VIRGINIA	2873.16	8059.93	0.00	2873.16	2418.23	5641.70
WEST VIRGINIA	3068.06	446.38	197.25	2870.81	446.38	0.00
EAST SOUTH CENTRAL:						
ALABAMA	1263.69	773.30	0.00	1263.69	543.21	230.09
KENTUCKY	0.00	955.62	0.00	0.00	205.37	750.26
MISSISSIPPI	0.00	628.70	0.00	0.00	167.29	461.41
TENNESSEE	100.59	1697.49	0.00	100.59	579.10	1118.39
WEST SOUTH CENTRAL:						
ARKANSAS	113.17	1596.90	0.00	113.17	459.52	1137.38
LOUISIANA	12.57	50.30	0.00	12.57	8.35	41.95
OKLAHOMA	201.18	339.50	0.00	201.18	69.10	270.40
TEXAS	157.17	4067.69	0.00	157.17	678.43	3389.26
ROCKY MOUNTAIN:						
ARIZONA	0.00	0.00	0.00	0.00	0.00	0.00
COLORADO	339.50	3017.76	0.00	339.50	453.72	2564.04
IDAHO	364.65	691.57	0.00	364.65	166.96	524.61
MONTANA	1024.78	289.20	0.00	1024.78	111.50	177.70
NEVADA	452.66	106.88	0.00	452.66	25.62	81.26
NEW MEXICO	0.00	132.03	0.00	0.00	7.30	124.73
UTAH	2131.29	1169.38	0.00	2131.29	390.28	779.10
WYOMING	546.97	1345.42	0.00	546.97	99.90	1245.51
FAR WEST:						
ALASKA	0.00	125.74	0.00	0.00	8.33	117.41
CALIFORNIA	2621.68	6689.37	0.00	2621.68	1629.00	5060.36
HAWAII	710.43	62.87	0.00	710.43	56.73	6.14
OREGON	13234.13	8852.10	0.00	13234.13	4958.36	3893.73
WASHINGTON	12089.90	9436.79	0.00	12089.90	3453.74	5983.04

Table B.1.8

Consumption Of Petroleum Heating Fuels, 1972, In Billion BTU, By Region

Estimated Residual Oil Consumption For Space Heating In Industrial And Non-Industrial Use

REGION	NO. 5 HEATING OIL TOTAL	NO. 6 HEATING OIL TOTAL	NO. 5 OIL Industrial Use	NO. 5 OIL Non-Ind. Use	NO. 6 OIL Industrial Use	NO. 6 OIL Non-Ind. Use
NEW ENGLAND	67629.26	220667.42	0.00	67629.26	77598.43	143068.98
MID ATLANTIC	70364.10	484960.33	0.00	70364.10	127252.30	357708.03
EAST NORTH CENTRAL	34836.27	69886.29	0.00	34836.27	32108.09	37778.20
WEST NORTH CENTRAL	9122.44	7211.19	1.68	9120.76	3010.15	4201.04
SOUTH ATLANTIC	34842.55	99454.05	360.61	34481.95	22140.37	77313.69
EAST SOUTH CENTRAL	1364.28	4055.12	0.00	1364.28	1494.97	2560.15
WEST SOUTH CENTRAL	484.10	6054.38	0.00	484.10	1215.39	4838.99
ROCKY MOUNTAIN	4859.85	6752.24	0.00	4859.85	1255.29	5496.95
FAR WEST	28656.15	25166.86	0.00	28656.15	10106.17	15060.69
TOTAL	252159.00	924207.88	362.29	251796.71	276181.14	648026.74

Table B.1.9

Consumption Of Petroleum Heating Fuels, 1972, Scale Factors, By State

Scale Factors For Office Employment, School Enrollment and Hospital Employment,
    Relative To Regional Average , And Base Data

REGION AND STATE	STATE SCALE FACTORS RELATIVE TO REGIONAL AVERAGE			DATA BASE FOR SCALE FACTORS		
	Offices	Schools	Hospitals	Off. Emp. Relative To Total Employment	School Enrollment Relative To Pop.	Hospital Employment Relative To Pop.
NEW ENGLAND:						
CONNECTICUT	1.0100	1.0423	0.8658	0.3451	0.2935	0.0130
MAINE	0.7073	1.0522	0.8447	0.2417	0.2963	0.0127
MASSACHUSETTS	1.0258	1.0563	1.2422	0.3505	0.2974	0.0186
NEW HAMPSHIRE	0.8054	1.0369	0.7752	0.2752	0.2920	0.0116
RHODE ISLAND	0.8548	1.0151	1.0320	0.2921	0.2859	0.0155
VERMONT	0.8153	1.1194	1.0145	0.2786	0.3152	0.0152
MID ATLANTIC:						
NEW JERSEY	1.0301	0.9732	0.7167	0.3520	0.2741	0.0107
NEW YORK	1.1048	0.9893	1.1071	0.3775	0.2786	0.0166
PENNSYLVANIA	0.8557	0.9814	0.9520	0.2924	0.2764	0.0143
EAST NORTH CENTRAL:						
ILLINOIS	1.1227	0.9849	1.0970	0.3285	0.2914	0.0141
INDIANA	0.9111	0.9782	0.8659	0.2666	0.2894	0.0112
MICHIGAN	0.9850	1.0754	0.9554	0.2882	0.3182	0.0123
OHIO	0.9990	0.9869	0.9406	0.2923	0.2920	0.0121
WISCONSIN	0.8982	1.0469	1.0113	0.2628	0.3098	0.0130
WEST NORTH CENTRAL:						
IOWA	0.8657	0.9691	0.9146	0.2533	0.2868	0.0118
KANSAS	1.0075	0.9209	1.0604	0.2948	0.2725	0.0137
MINNESOTA	1.0458	1.0321	1.0405	0.3060	0.3054	0.0134
MISSOURI	1.0345	0.9419	1.0950	0.3027	0.2787	0.0141
NEBRASKA	0.9265	0.9732	1.0662	0.2711	0.2880	0.0137
NORTH DAKOTA	0.8281	0.9755	0.9789	0.2423	0.2886	0.0126
SOUTH DAKOTA	0.8021	1.0089	1.0268	0.2347	0.2985	0.0132
SOUTH ATLANTIC:						
DELAWARE	1.1892	1.1368	1.1627	0.3438	0.3152	0.0140
DISTRICT OF COLUMBIA	2.1190	1.1653	2.5382	0.6126	0.3231	0.0306
FLORIDA	1.0716	0.9257	0.9940	0.3098	0.2567	0.0120
GEORGIA	0.9557	0.9623	0.9994	0.2763	0.2668	0.0120
MARYLAND	1.2324	1.0735	1.0865	0.3563	0.2977	0.0131
NORTH CAROLINA	0.8122	0.9594	0.9060	0.2348	0.2660	0.0109
SOUTH CAROLINA	0.7769	1.0049	0.8336	0.2246	0.2786	0.0100
VIRGINIA	1.0457	0.9922	0.9753	0.3023	0.2751	0.0118
WEST VIRGINIA	0.8530	0.9764	1.1096	0.2466	0.2708	0.0134
EAST SOUTH CENTRAL:						
ALABAMA	0.8592	0.9802	0.9899	0.2484	0.2718	0.0119
KENTUCKY	0.8558	0.9643	0.9288	0.2474	0.2674	0.0112
MISSISSIPPI	0.7707	1.0758	0.8828	0.2228	0.2983	0.0106
TENNESSEE	0.8893	0.9503	1.1005	0.2571	0.2635	0.0133
WEST SOUTH CENTRAL:						
ARKANSAS	0.7755	0.9482	0.8679	0.2242	0.2629	0.0105
LOUISIANA	0.9727	1.0824	1.0212	0.2812	0.3002	0.0123
OKLAHOMA	1.0505	1.0163	0.9771	0.3037	0.2818	0.0118
TEXAS	1.0630	1.0402	0.9726	0.3073	0.2884	0.0117
ROCKY MOUNTAIN:						
ARIZONA	0.9406	1.0635	1.0936	0.3248	0.3255	0.0122
COLORADO	1.0139	1.0226	1.2108	0.3501	0.3130	0.0135
IDAHO	0.7324	0.9779	0.8293	0.2529	0.2993	0.0093
MONTANA	0.7828	0.9947	0.9994	0.2703	0.3045	0.0112
NEVADA	0.9403	0.9317	0.8391	0.3247	0.2852	0.0094
NEW MEXICO	0.9823	1.0535	0.9975	0.3392	0.3225	0.0112
UTAH	0.9942	1.1363	0.7937	0.3433	0.3478	0.0089
WYOMING	0.8436	1.0103	1.0341	0.2913	0.3092	0.0116
FAR WEST:						
ALASKA	1.1086	1.0052	0.8257	0.3828	0.3077	0.0092
CALIFORNIA	1.0455	0.9943	1.0211	0.3610	0.3043	0.0114
HAWAII	0.9959	0.9849	0.9865	0.3439	0.3015	0.0110
OREGON	0.8593	0.9270	0.8597	0.2967	0.2838	0.0096
WASHINGTON	0.9548	0.9845	0.9159	0.3297	0.3013	0.0102

Table B.1.10

Consumption of Petroleum Heating Fuels, 1972, in Billion BTU, By State

Commercial Consumption of Residual Oil By Category of Use

			Commercial Use of Residual Fuel Oil			
Region and State	Office	Retail	School	Hospital	All Other	Total Commercial
NEW ENGLAND:						
CONNECTICUT	4766.27	3213.39	5652.39	2087.98	5223.66	20943.70
MAINE	3058.47	2944.47	5228.54	1866.61	4786.79	17884.88
MASSACHUSETTS	31276.30	20761.52	37010.24	19355.14	33751.46	142154.67
NEW HAMPSHIRE	1781.81	1506.45	2636.13	876.42	2449.27	9250.09
RHODE ISLAND	2848.61	2269.21	3887.40	1757.52	3688.90	14451.64
VERMONT	493.54	412.21	778.71	313.84	670.08	2668.39
MID ATLANTIC:						
NEW JERSEY	14618.73	9663.55	15871.37	5197.80	15710.85	61062.31
NEW YORK	54759.45	33750.64	56348.90	28042.35	54881.34	227782.69
PENNSYLVANIA	13016.62	10358.17	17155.55	7400.58	16842.19	64773.11
EAST NORTH CENTRAL:						
ILLINOIS	9545.58	7003.77	12313.91	4938.67	12002.45	45804.38
INDIANA	2903.03	2624.69	4583.30	1460.89	4497.75	16069.65
MICHIGAN	833.74	697.25	1338.54	428.20	1194.85	4492.58
OHIO	685.53	565.27	995.87	341.77	968.53	3556.98
WISCONSIN	464.07	425.60	795.39	276.67	729.15	2690.88
WEST NORTH CENTRAL:						
IOWA	108.42	103.16	178.47	60.65	176.79	627.49
KANSAS	60.75	49.67	81.65	33.86	85.12	311.05
MINNESOTA	828.89	652.89	1202.91	436.67	1118.79	4240.15
MISSOURI	1122.67	893.95	1503.11	629.22	1532.04	5680.99
NEBRASKA	196.57	174.77	303.63	119.78	299.47	1094.22
NORTH DAKOTA	221.95	220.78	384.47	138.92	378.32	1344.43
SOUTH DAKOTA	3.72	3.82	6.87	2.52	6.54	23.47
SOUTH ATLANTIC:						
DELAWARE	610.88	291.59	749.71	222.87	513.58	2388.64
DISTRICT OF COLUMBIA	11912.97	3191.24	8410.66	5324.73	5623.01	34462.61
FLORIDA	3857.17	2043.18	4277.70	1335.07	3599.91	15113.03
GEORGIA	2691.74	1598.76	3479.57	1050.35	2816.48	11636.90
MARYLAND	7888.65	3633.47	8821.79	2595.16	6401.12	29340.17
NORTH CAROLINA	1372.93	959.52	2082.03	571.47	1690.40	6676.35
SOUTH CAROLINA	156.00	113.98	259.05	62.46	200.78	792.27
VIRGINIA	2094.54	1136.98	2551.44	728.96	2002.94	8514.86
WEST VIRGINIA	599.02	398.62	880.28	290.76	702.12	2870.81
EAST SOUTH CENTRAL:						
ALABAMA	316.53	209.12	463.59	136.08	368.46	1493.78
KENTUCKY	160.20	106.25	231.74	64.88	187.20	750.26
MISSISSIPPI	87.83	64.69	157.40	37.54	113.95	461.41
TENNESSEE	265.20	169.27	363.82	122.46	298.23	1218.99
WEST SOUTH CENTRAL:						
ARKANSAS	249.66	182.74	391.90	104.26	321.98	1250.55
LOUISIANA	12.30	7.18	17.57	4.82	12.65	54.52
OKLAHOMA	115.54	62.43	143.50	40.10	110.00	471.59
TEXAS	870.82	465.01	1093.99	297.31	819.30	3546.44
ROCKY MOUNTAIN:						
ARIZONA	0.00	0.00	0.00	0.00	0.00	0.00
COLORADO	668.18	424.29	747.40	286.28	777.39	2903.54
IDAHO	165.39	145.39	244.91	67.19	266.37	889.25
MONTANA	231.39	190.31	326.08	105.99	348.72	1202.48
NEVADA	122.50	83.88	134.62	39.22	153.70	533.92
NEW MEXICO	28.28	18.54	33.64	10.30	33.96	124.73
UTAH	663.24	429.50	840.69	189.97	786.98	2910.39
WYOMING	363.61	277.50	482.95	159.91	508.50	1792.48
FAR WEST:						
ALASKA	29.97	17.41	30.14	8.01	31.89	117.41
CALIFORNIA	1851.47	1140.14	1952.78	648.76	2088.90	7682.04
HAWAII	167.30	108.15	183.49	59.46	198.18	716.57
OREGON	3661.88	2743.62	4381.10	1314.40	5026.86	17127.87
WASHINGTON	4109.86	2771.28	4699.75	1414.44	5077.61	18072.94

Table B.1.11

Consumption of Petroleum Heating Fuels, 1972, In Billion BTU, By State

Consumption of Residual Oil By Major Category Of Use

Region and State	Residual Fuel Oil Uee In Billion BTU			
	Residential	Commercial	Industrial	Total
NEW ENGLAND:				
CONNECTICUT	777.78	20943.70	9568.92	31290.40
MAINE	155.44	17884.88	7220.85	25261.17
MASSACHUSETTS	2333.92	142154.67	49025.26	193513.86
NEW HAMPSHIRE	0.00	9250.09	4097.21	13347.30
RHODE ISLAND	77.72	14451.64	6997.33	21526.69
VERMONT	0.00	2668.39	688.87	3357.26
MID ATLANTIC:				
NEW JERSEY	3267.72	61062.31	23015.26	87345.29
NEW YORK	68385.48	227782.69	75720.46	371888.63
PENNSYLVANIA	2800.82	64773.11	28516.58	96090.51
EAST NORTH CENTRAL:				
ILLINOIS	0.00	45804.38	18373.32	64177.70
INDIANA	0.00	16069.65	8896.02	24965.68
MICHIGAN	0.00	4492.58	2089.91	6582.49
OHIO	0.00	3556.98	1661.23	5218.21
WISCONSIN	0.00	2690.88	1087.61	3778.49
WEST NORTH CENTRAL:				
IOWA	0.00	627.49	152.10	779.59
KANSAS	0.00	311.05	59.88	370.93
MINNESOTA	0.00	4240.15	921.48	5161.63
MISSOURI	0.00	5680.99	1624.50	7305.49
NEBRASKA	0.00	1094.22	194.62	1288.84
NORTH DAKOTA	0.00	1344.43	57.57	1402.00
SOUTH DAKOTA	0.00	23.47	1.68	25.15
SOUTH ATLANTIC:				
DELAWARE	0.00	2388.64	729.71	3118.35
DISTRICT OF COLUMBIA	0.00	34462.61	1423.59	35886.20
FLORIDA	0.00	15113.03	2031.62	17144.65
GEORGIA	0.00	11636.90	4564.70	16201.60
MARYLAND	0.00	29340.17	5357.78	34697.95
NORTH CAROLINA	0.00	6676.35	4822.57	11498.92
SOUTH CAROLINA	0.00	792.27	509.14	1301.41
VIRGINIA	0.00	8514.86	2418.23	10933.09
WEST VIRGINIA	0.00	2870.81	643.63	3514.43
EAST SOUTH CENTRAL:				
ALABAMA	0.00	1493.78	543.21	2036.99
KENTUCKY	0.00	750.26	205.37	955.62
MISSISSIPPI	0.00	461.41	167.29	628.70
TENNESSEE	0.00	1218.99	579.10	1798.08
WEST SOUTH CENTRAL:				
ARKANSAS	0.00	1250.55	459.52	1710.06
LOUISIANA	0.00	54.52	8.35	62.87
OKLAHOMA	0.00	471.59	69.10	540.68
TEXAS	0.00	3546.44	678.43	4224.86
ROCKY MOUNTAIN:				
ARIZONA	0.00	0.00	0.00	0.00
COLORADO	0.00	2903.54	453.72	3357.26
IDAHO	0.00	889.25	166.96	1056.22
MONTANA	0.00	1202.48	111.50	1313.98
NEVADA	0.00	533.92	25.62	559.54
NEW MEXICO	0.00	124.73	7.30	132.03
UTAH	0.00	2910.39	390.28	3300.68
WYOMING	0.00	1792.48	99.90	1892.39
FAR WEST:				
ALASKA	0.00	117.41	8.33	125.74
CALIFORNIA	0.00	7682.04	1629.00	9311.05
HAWAII	0.00	716.57	56.73	773.30
OREGON	0.00	17127.87	4958.36	22086.23
WASHINGTON	0.00	18072.94	3453.74	21526.69

Table B.1.12

Consumption of Petroleum Heating Fuels, 1972, In Billion BTU, By Region

Estimated Residual Fuel Oil Consumption In Residential, Commercial and Industrial Use, And In Commercial Categories Of Use

REGION	RESIDENTIAL	COMMERCIAL	INDUSTRIAL	TOTAL
NEW ENGLAND	3344.86	207353.37	77598.43	288296.67
MID ATLANTIC	74454.02	353618.11	127252.30	555324.43
EAST NORTH CENTRAL	0.00	72614.47	32108.09	104722.56
WEST NORTH CENTRAL	0.00	13321.80	3011.82	16333.63
SOUTH ATLANTIC	0.00	111795.63	22500.98	134296.61
EAST SOUTH CENTRAL	0.00	3924.43	1494.97	5419.39
WEST SOUTH CENTRAL	0.00	5323.09	1215.39	6538.48
ROCKY MOUNTAIN	0.00	10356.80	1255.29	11612.09
FAR WEST	0.00	43716.84	10106.17	53823.01
TOTAL	77798.88	822024.54	276543.43	1176366.87

REGION	OFFICE	RETAIL	SCHOOL	HOSPITAL	ALL OTHER	TOTAL COMMERCIAL
NEW ENGLAND	44225.00	31107.26	55193.42	26257.53	50570.17	207353.37
MID ATLANTIC	82394.80	53772.37	89375.82	40640.74	87434.38	353618.11
EAST NORTH CENTRAL	14431.95	11316.59	20027.01	7446.19	19392.73	72614.47
WEST NORTH CENTRAL	2542.96	2099.04	3661.12	1421.61	3597.06	13321.80
SOUTH ATLANTIC	31183.90	13367.33	31512.22	12181.84	23550.34	111795.63
EAST SOUTH CENTRAL	829.75	549.34	1646.55	360.96	967.84	3924.43
WEST SOUTH CENTRAL	1248.32	717.32	1646.97	446.49	1263.93	5323.09
ROCKY MOUNTAIN	2242.61	1569.41	2810.29	858.87	2875.62	10356.80
FAR WEST	9820.47	6780.60	11247.27	3445.06	12423.44	43716.84
TOTAL	188919.77	121279.30	216690.67	93059.28	202075.53	822024.54

Table B.1.13

Consumption Of Petroleum Heating Fuels, 1972, Scale Factors, By State

Fraction Of Commercial Category Allocated To Business, Federal Government And State and Local Government

REGION AND STATE	OFFICE USE			SCHOOL USE		HOSPITAL USE		
	BUSINESS	FEDERAL GOVT.	STATE and LOCAL GOVT.	BUSINESS (Private Schools)	STATE and LOCAL GOVT.	BUSINESS	FEDERAL GOVT.	STATE and LOCAL GOVT.
NEW ENGLAND:								
CONNECTICUT	0.8878	0.0283	0.0839	0.1759	0.8241	0.7250	0.0600	0.2150
MAINE	0.7964	0.0861	0.1175	0.0921	0.9079	0.7231	0.0846	0.1923
MASSACHUSETTS	0.8534	0.0486	0.0980	0.2239	0.7761	0.6546	0.0602	0.2852
NEW HAMPSHIRE	0.8517	0.0450	0.1033	0.1858	0.8142	0.7223	0.0444	0.2333
RHODE ISLAND	0.7876	0.1006	0.1118	0.2130	0.7870	0.7400	0.0533	0.2067
VERMONT	0.8308	0.0473	0.1219	0.1655	0.8345	0.7715	0.0714	0.1571
MID ATLANTIC:								
NEW JERSEY	0.8543	0.0483	0.0974	0.1634	0.8366	0.6608	0.0519	0.2873
NEW YORK	0.8545	0.0372	0.1083	0.2115	0.7885	0.5531	0.0580	0.3889
PENNSYLVANIA	0.8385	0.0625	0.0990	0.2064	0.7936	0.7229	0.0600	0.2171
EAST NORTH CENTRAL:								
ILLINOIS	0.8662	0.0444	0.0894	0.1758	0.8242	0.6830	0.0698	0.2472
INDIANA	0.8597	0.0501	0.0902	0.1046	0.8954	0.5390	0.0542	0.4068
MICHIGAN	0.8667	0.0360	0.0973	0.1102	0.8898	0.6118	0.0450	0.3432
OHIO	0.8557	0.0505	0.0938	0.1329	0.8671	0.6877	0.0585	0.2538
WISCONSIN	0.8552	0.0313	0.1135	0.1569	0.8431	0.6627	0.0780	0.2593
WEST NORTH CENTRAL:								
IOWA	0.8574	0.0375	0.1051	0.1306	0.8694	0.5442	0.0882	0.3676
KANSAS	0.8308	0.0561	0.1131	0.0777	0.9223	0.5678	0.0935	0.3387
MINNESOTA	0.8762	0.0360	0.0878	0.1242	0.8758	0.5846	0.0808	0.3346
MISSOURI	0.8271	0.0793	0.0936	0.1179	0.8821	0.5971	0.0716	0.3313
NEBRASKA	0.8386	0.0508	0.1106	0.1318	0.8682	0.5762	0.0857	0.3381
NORTH DAKOTA	0.7761	0.0969	0.1270	0.0710	0.9290	0.7375	0.0625	0.2000
SOUTH DAKOTA	0.7782	0.0859	0.1359	0.0887	0.9113	0.6111	0.1667	0.2222
SOUTH ATLANTIC:								
DELAWARE	0.8717	0.0343	0.0940	0.1222	0.8778	0.7125	0.0750	0.2125
DISTRICT OF COLUMBIA	0.3558	0.5424	0.1018	0.3621	0.6379	0.8609	0.0087	0.1304
FLORIDA	0.8197	0.0566	0.1237	0.0832	0.9168	0.4920	0.0750	0.4330
GEORGIA	0.7889	0.1014	0.1097	0.0459	0.9541	0.2456	0.0684	0.6860
MARYLAND	0.7398	0.1634	0.0968	0.1228	0.8772	0.6566	0.0528	0.2906
NORTH CAROLINA	0.8502	0.0475	0.1023	0.0569	0.9431	0.6176	0.0719	0.3105
SOUTH CAROLINA	0.8274	0.0722	0.1004	0.0734	0.9266	0.4074	0.0741	0.5185
VIRGINIA	0.7259	0.1749	0.0992	0.0717	0.9283	0.6250	0.0875	0.2875
WEST VIRGINIA	0.8347	0.0471	0.1182	0.0473	0.9527	0.6042	0.1000	0.2958
EAST SOUTH CENTRAL:								
ALABAMA	0.7666	0.1138	0.1196	0.0742	0.9258	0.4738	0.1000	0.4262
KENTUCKY	0.8099	0.0798	0.1103	0.0916	0.9084	0.6729	0.0730	0.2541
MISSISSIPPI	0.8140	0.0654	0.1206	0.1129	0.8871	0.3459	0.0958	0.5583
TENNESSEE	0.8488	0.0564	0.0948	0.0662	0.9338	0.4815	0.0981	0.4204
WEST SOUTH CENTRAL:								
ARKANSAS	0.8297	0.0565	0.1138	0.0398	0.9602	0.5048	0.1476	0.3476
LOUISIANA	0.8357	0.0451	0.1192	0.1435	0.8565	0.5130	0.0674	0.4196
OKLAHOMA	0.7427	0.1402	0.1171	0.0431	0.9569	0.5581	0.0645	0.3774
TEXAS	0.8226	0.0773	0.1001	0.0607	0.9393	0.5912	0.0757	0.3331
ROCKY MOUNTAIN:								
ARIZONA	0.8040	0.0857	0.1102	0.0516	0.9484	0.7042	0.0833	0.2125
COLORADO	0.8101	0.0954	0.0945	0.0676	0.9324	0.6625	0.0719	0.2656
IDAHO	0.8004	0.0734	0.1262	0.0575	0.9425	0.5858	0.0571	0.3571
MONTANA	0.7807	0.0930	0.1263	0.0642	0.9358	0.6250	0.0625	0.3125
NEVADA	0.7742	0.0839	0.1419	0.0263	0.9737	0.3600	0.0800	0.5600
NEW MEXICO	0.7379	0.1444	0.1177	0.0490	0.9510	0.5083	0.1000	0.3917
UTAH	0.6330	0.2498	0.1172	0.0918	0.9082	0.5900	0.1400	0.2700
WYOMING	0.7830	0.0803	0.1367	0.0280	0.9720	0.1250	0.2000	0.6750
FAR WEST:								
ALASKA	0.5695	0.2507	0.1798	0.0300	0.9700	0.8667	0.0333	0.1000
CALIFORNIA	0.8203	0.0712	0.1085	0.0766	0.9234	0.6176	0.0807	0.3017
HAWAII	0.6691	0.1957	0.1352	0.1016	0.8984	0.7556	0.0111	0.2333
OREGON	0.8360	0.0584	0.1056	0.0645	0.9355	0.6381	0.1000	0.2619
WASHINGTON	0.8305	0.0676	0.1019	0.0650	0.9350	0.6200	0.0971	0.2829

Table B.1.14

Consumption Of Petroleum Heating Fuels, 1972, In Billion BTU, By State

Estimated Residual Fuel Oil Consumption By Sector

REGION AND STATE	HOUSEHOLD USE	BUSINESS USE			GOVERNMENT USE			TOTAL USE
		Commercial	Industrial	Total	Federal Govt.	State and Local Govt.	Total	
NEW ENGLAND:								
CONNECTICUT	777.78	15176.60	9568.92	24745.51	260.16	5506.94	5767.11	31290.40
MAINE	155.44	11998.32	7220.85	19219.17	421.25	5465.31	5886.56	25261.17
MASSACHUSETTS	2333.92	102160.65	49025.26	151185.92	2685.21	37308.81	39994.02	193513.86
NEW HAMPSHIRE	0.00	6596.12	4097.21	10693.34	119.09	2534.87	2653.97	13347.30
RHODE ISLAND	77.72	10330.26	6997.33	17327.58	380.25	3741.14	4121.38	21526.69
VERMONT	0.00	1863.34	688.87	2552.20	45.75	759.30	805.06	3357.26
MID ATLANTIC:								
NEW JERSEY	3267.72	43891.28	23015.26	66906.54	975.85	16195.18	17171.03	87345.29
NEW YORK	68385.48	162851.95	75720.46	238572.42	3663.51	61267.23	64930.73	371888.63
PENNSYLVANIA	2800.82	47005.58	28516.58	75522.16	1257.57	16509.96	17767.53	96090.51
EAST NORTH CENTRAL:								
ILLINOIS	0.00	32812.50	18373.32	51185.82	768.54	12223.34	12991.88	64177.70
INDIANA	0.00	10885.00	8896.02	19781.03	224.62	4960.03	5184.65	24965.68
MICHIGAN	0.00	3024.18	2089.91	5114.09	49.28	1419.11	1468.40	6582.49
OHIO	0.00	2487.80	1661.23	4149.04	54.61	1014.56	1069.17	5218.21
WISCONSIN	0.00	1859.77	1087.61	2947.38	36.11	795.01	831.11	3778.49
WEST NORTH CENTRAL:								
IOWA	0.00	429.22	152.10	581.32	9.41	188.85	198.27	779.59
KANSAS	0.00	210.83	59.88	270.71	6.57	93.65	100.22	370.93
MINNESOTA	0.00	2902.63	921.48	3824.11	65.12	1272.40	1337.52	5161.63
MISSOURI	0.00	3907.47	1624.50	5531.98	134.08	1639.44	1773.52	7305.49
NEBRASKA	0.00	748.12	194.62	942.74	20.25	325.85	346.10	1288.84
NORTH DAKOTA	0.00	901.10	57.57	958.67	30.19	413.14	443.33	1402.00
SOUTH DAKOTA	0.00	15.40	1.68	17.08	0.74	7.33	8.07	25.15
SOUTH ATLANTIC:								
DELAWARE	0.00	1588.09	729.71	2317.81	37.67	762.88	800.54	3118.35
DISTRICT OF COLUMBIA	0.00	20682.44	1423.59	22106.03	6507.92	7272.25	13780.17	35886.20
FLORIDA	0.00	9817.57	2031.62	11849.19	318.45	4977.01	5295.46	17144.65
GEORGIA	0.00	6956.43	4564.70	11521.13	344.79	4335.68	4680.47	16201.60
MARYLAND	0.00	18657.90	5357.78	24015.68	1426.03	9256.24	10682.27	34697.95
NORTH CAROLINA	0.00	4288.59	4822.57	9111.16	106.30	2281.46	2387.76	11498.92
SOUTH CAROLINA	0.00	488.29	509.14	997.44	15.89	288.08	303.97	1301.41
VIRGINIA	0.00	5298.89	2418.23	7717.12	430.12	2785.85	3215.97	10933.09
WEST VIRGINIA	0.00	1818.06	643.63	2461.69	57.29	995.45	1052.74	3514.43
EAST SOUTH CENTRAL:								
ALABAMA	0.00	919.10	543.21	1462.31	49.63	525.05	574.68	2036.99
KENTUCKY	0.00	488.08	205.37	693.44	17.52	244.66	262.18	955.62
MISSISSIPPI	0.00	280.89	167.29	448.18	9.34	171.18	180.52	628.70
TENNESSEE	0.00	775.66	579.10	1354.75	26.97	416.36	443.33	1798.08
WEST SOUTH CENTRAL:								
ARKANSAS	0.00	780.10	459.52	1239.62	29.49	440.95	470.45	1710.06
LOUISIANA	0.00	35.10	8.35	43.45	0.88	18.54	19.42	62.87
OKLAHOMA	0.00	286.82	69.10	355.91	18.79	165.98	184.77	540.68
TEXAS	0.00	2242.83	678.43	2921.25	89.82	1213.79	1303.61	4224.86
ROCKY MOUNTAIN:								
ARIZONA	0.00	0.00	0.00	0.00	0.00	0.00	0.00	0.00
COLORADO	0.00	1983.16	453.72	2436.88	84.33	836.05	920.38	3357.26
IDAHO	0.00	597.58	166.96	764.54	15.98	275.70	291.67	1056.22
MONTANA	0.00	806.85	111.50	918.35	28.14	367.49	395.64	1313.98
NEVADA	0.00	350.08	25.62	375.70	13.42	170.42	183.84	559.54
NEW MEXICO	0.00	80.25	7.30	87.56	5.11	39.36	44.47	132.03
UTAH	0.00	1825.58	390.28	2215.86	192.27	892.54	1084.82	3300.68
WYOMING	0.00	1104.23	99.90	1204.13	61.18	627.07	688.25	1892.39
FAR WEST:								
ALASKA	0.00	74.21	8.33	82.54	7.78	35.42	43.20	125.74
CALIFORNIA	0.00	5298.05	1629.00	6927.05	184.18	2199.82	2383.99	9311.05
HAWAII	0.00	481.84	56.73	538.56	33.40	201.34	234.74	773.30
OREGON	0.00	11953.11	4958.36	16911.48	345.29	4829.46	5174.75	22086.23
WASHINGTON	0.00	12444.56	3453.74	15898.31	415.17	5213.21	5628.38	21526.69

Table B.1.15

Consumption Of Petroleum Heating Fuels, 1972, In Billion BTU, By Region

Estimated Residual Fuel Oil Consumption By Sector

REGION	HOUSEHOLD USE	BUSINESS USE			GOVERNMENT USE			TOTAL USE
		Commercial	Industrial	Total Business	Federal Government	State and Local Govt.	Total Government	
NEW ENGLAND	3344.86	148125.28	77598.43	225723.72	3911.72	55316.38	59228.09	288296.67
MID ATLANTIC	74454.02	253748.81	127252.30	381001.11	5896.93	93972.36	99869.30	555324.43
EAST NORTH CENTRAL	0.00	51069.25	32108.09	83177.35	1133.17	20412.05	21545.21	104722.56
WEST NORTH CENTRAL	0.00	9114.78	3011.82	12126.60	266.37	3940.65	4207.02	16333.63
SOUTH ATLANTIC	0.00	69596.27	22500.98	92097.24	9244.45	32954.91	42199.36	134296.61
EAST SOUTH CENTRAL	0.00	2463.72	1494.97	3958.69	103.46	1357.25	1460.71	5419.39
WEST SOUTH CENTRAL	0.00	3344.84	1215.39	4560.23	138.98	1839.27	1978.25	6538.48
ROCKY MOUNTAIN	0.00	6747.73	1255.29	8003.02	400.43	3208.64	3609.07	11612.09
FAR WEST	0.00	30251.77	10106.17	40357.94	985.82	12479.24	13465.07	53823.01
TOTAL	77798.88	574462.45	276543.43	851005.90	22081.33	225480.75	247562.08	1176366.87

Table B.1.16

Consumption Of Petroleum Heating Fuels, 1972, In Billion BTU, By State

Distribution Of No. 5 Heating Oil Consumption By Sector

REGION AND STATE	HOUSEHOLD CONSUMPTION	BUSINESS CONSUMPTION		GOVERNMENT CONSUMPTION	TOTAL CONSUMPTION NO.5 FUEL OIL
		Commercial	Industrial		
NEW ENGLAND:					
CONNECTICUT	383.51	0.00	0.00	0.00	383.51
MAINE	155.44	0.00	0.00	5295.39	5450.83
MASSACHUSETTS	2333.92	8508.74	0.00	39994.02	50836.68
NEW HAMPSHIRE	0.00	552.40	0.00	2653.97	3206.37
RHODE ISLAND	77.72	3364.16	0.00	4121.38	7563.26
VERMONT	0.00	0.00	0.00	188.61	188.61
MID ATLANTIC:					
NEW JERSEY	3267.72	0.00	0.00	13028.18	16295.90
NEW YORK	8701.21	0.00	0.00	0.00	8701.21
PENNSYLVANIA	2800.82	24798.64	0.00	17767.53	45366.99
EAST NORTH CENTRAL:					
ILLINOIS	0.00	13180.90	0.00	12991.88	26172.78
INDIANA	0.00	0.00	0.00	3721.90	3721.90
MICHIGAN	0.00	769.78	0.00	1468.40	2238.17
OHIO	0.00	0.00	0.00	735.58	735.58
WISCONSIN	0.00	1136.72	0.00	831.11	1967.83
WEST NORTH CENTRAL:					
IOWA	0.00	317.27	0.00	198.27	515.53
KANSAS	0.00	44.38	0.00	100.22	144.60
MINNESOTA	0.00	1240.15	0.00	1337.52	2577.67
MISSOURI	0.00	2878.86	0.00	1773.52	4652.38
NEBRASKA	0.00	276.31	0.00	346.10	622.41
NORTH DAKOTA	0.00	141.36	0.00	443.33	584.69
SOUTH DAKOTA	0.00	15.40	1.68	8.07	25.15
SOUTH ATLANTIC:					
DELAWARE	0.00	733.48	0.00	800.54	1534.03
DISTRICT OF COLUMBIA	0.00	0.00	0.00	3256.67	3256.67
FLORIDA	0.00	0.00	0.00	194.90	194.90
GEORGIA	0.00	914.96	0.00	4680.47	5595.43
MARYLAND	0.00	269.68	0.00	10682.27	10951.95
NORTH CAROLINA	0.00	4024.98	0.00	2387.76	6412.74
SOUTH CAROLINA	0.00	488.29	163.36	303.97	955.62
VIRGINIA	0.00	0.00	0.00	2873.16	2873.16
WEST VIRGINIA	0.00	1818.06	197.25	1052.74	3068.06
EAST SOUTH CENTRAL:					
ALABAMA	0.00	689.01	0.00	574.68	1263.69
KENTUCKY	0.00	0.00	0.00	0.00	0.00
MISSISSIPPI	0.00	0.00	0.00	0.00	0.00
TENNESSEE	0.00	0.00	0.00	100.59	100.59
WEST SOUTH CENTRAL:					
ARKANSAS	0.00	0.00	0.00	113.17	113.17
LOUISIANA	0.00	0.00	0.00	12.57	12.57
OKLAHOMA	0.00	16.41	0.00	184.77	201.18
TEXAS	0.00	0.00	0.00	157.17	157.17
ROCKY MOUNTAIN:					
ARIZONA	0.00	0.00	0.00	0.00	0.00
COLORADO	0.00	0.00	0.00	339.50	339.50
IDAHO	0.00	72.97	0.00	291.67	364.65
MONTANA	0.00	629.15	0.00	395.64	1024.78
NEVADA	0.00	268.82	0.00	183.84	452.66
NEW MEXICO	0.00	0.00	0.00	0.00	0.00
UTAH	0.00	1046.48	0.00	1084.82	2131.29
WYOMING	0.00	0.00	0.00	546.97	546.97
FAR WEST:					
ALASKA	0.00	0.00	0.00	0.00	0.00
CALIFORNIA	0.00	237.68	0.00	2383.99	2621.68
HAWAII	0.00	475.69	0.00	234.74	710.43
OREGON	0.00	8059.38	0.00	5174.75	13234.13
WASHINGTON	0.00	6461.52	0.00	5628.38	12089.90

Table B.1.17

Consumption Of Petroleum Heating Fuels, 1972, In Billion BTU, By State

Distribution Of No. 6 Heating Oil Consumption By Sector

REGION AND STATE	HOUSEHOLD CONSUMP-TION	BUSINESS CONSUMPTION		GOVERNMENT CONSUMP-TION	TOTAL CONSUMPTION NO. 6 FUEL OIL
		Commercial	Industrial		
NEW ENGLAND:					
CONNECTICUT	394.27	15176.60	9568.92	5767.11	30906.89
MAINE	0.00	11998.32	7220.85	591.17	19810.34
MASSACHUSETTS	0.00	93651.92	49025.26	0.00	142677.18
NEW HAMPSHIRE	0.00	6043.72	4097.21	0.00	10140.93
RHODE ISLAND	0.00	6966.10	6997.33	0.00	13963.43
VERMONT	0.00	1863.34	688.87	616.45	3168.65
MID ATLANTIC:					
NEW JERSEY	0.00	43891.28	23015.26	4142.85	71049.39
NEW YORK	59684.27	162851.96	75720.46	64930.73	363187.42
PENNSYLVANIA	0.00	22206.94	28516.58	0.00	50723.52
EAST NORTH CENTRAL:					
ILLINOIS	0.00	19631.59	18373.32	0.00	38004.92
INDIANA	0.00	10885.00	8896.02	1462.75	21243.77
MICHIGAN	0.00	2254.41	2089.91	0.00	4344.32
OHIO	0.00	2487.80	1661.23	333.60	4482.63
WISCONSIN	0.00	723.05	1087.61	0.00	1810.66
WEST NORTH CENTRAL:					
IOWA	0.00	111.96	152.10	0.00	264.05
KANSAS	0.00	166.45	59.88	0.00	226.33
MINNESOTA	0.00	1662.48	921.48	0.00	2583.96
MISSOURI	0.00	1028.61	1624.50	0.00	2653.11
NEBRASKA	0.00	471.80	194.62	0.00	666.42
NORTH DAKOTA	0.00	759.74	57.57	0.00	817.31
SOUTH DAKOTA	0.00	0.00	0.00	0.00	0.00
SOUTH ATLANTIC:					
DELAWARE	0.00	854.61	729.71	0.00	1584.32
DISTRICT OF COLUMBIA	0.00	20682.44	1423.59	10523.50	32629.53
FLORIDA	0.00	9817.57	2031.62	5100.56	16949.75
GEORGIA	0.00	6041.47	4564.70	0.00	10606.17
MARYLAND	0.00	18388.22	5357.78	0.00	23746.00
NORTH CAROLINA	0.00	263.61	4822.57	0.00	5086.18
SOUTH CAROLINA	0.00	0.00	345.78	0.00	345.78
VIRGINIA	0.00	5298.89	2418.23	342.81	8059.93
WEST VIRGINIA	0.00	0.00	446.38	0.00	446.38
EAST SOUTH CENTRAL:					
ALABAMA	0.00	230.09	543.21	0.00	773.30
KENTUCKY	0.00	488.08	205.37	262.18	955.62
MISSISSIPPI	0.00	280.89	167.29	180.52	628.70
TENNESSEE	0.00	775.66	579.10	342.74	1697.49
WEST SOUTH CENTRAL:					
ARKANSAS	0.00	780.10	459.52	357.28	1596.90
LOUISIANA	0.00	35.10	8.35	6.85	50.30
OKLAHOMA	0.00	270.40	69.10	0.00	339.50
TEXAS	0.00	2242.83	678.43	1146.44	4067.69
ROCKY MOUNTAIN:					
ARIZONA	0.00	0.00	0.00	0.00	0.00
COLORADO	0.00	1983.16	453.72	580.88	3017.76
IDAHO	0.00	524.61	166.96	0.00	691.57
MONTANA	0.00	177.70	111.50	0.00	289.20
NEVADA	0.00	81.26	25.62	0.00	106.88
NEW MEXICO	0.00	80.25	7.30	44.47	132.03
UTAH	0.00	779.10	390.28	0.00	1169.38
WYOMING	0.00	1104.23	99.90	141.29	1345.42
FAR WEST:					
ALASKA	0.00	74.21	8.33	43.20	125.74
CALIFORNIA	0.00	5060.36	1629.00	0.00	6689.37
HAWAII	0.00	6.14	56.73	0.00	62.87
OREGON	0.00	3893.73	4958.36	0.00	8852.10
WASHINGTON	0.00	5983.04	3453.74	0.00	9436.79

Table B.1.18

Consumption Of Petroleum Heating Fuels, 1972, In Billion BTU, By Region

Distribution Of No. 5 and No. 6 Heating Oil Consumption By Sector

REGION	HSHLD. CONS. OF NO. 5	BUSINESS CONSUMPTION OF NO. 5		GOVT. CONS. OF NO.5	TOTAL CONS. OF NO. 5
		Commercial	Industrial		
NEW ENGLAND	2950.59	12425.30	0.00	52253.37	67629.26
MID ATLANTIC	14769.75	24798.64	0.00	30795.71	70364.10
EAST NORTH CENTRAL	0.00	15087.40	0.00	19748.87	34836.27
WEST NORTH CENTRAL	0.00	4913.74	1.68	4207.02	9122.44
SOUTH ATLANTIC	0.00	8249.46	360.61	26232.49	34842.55
EAST SOUTH CENTRAL	0.00	689.01	0.00	675.27	1364.28
WEST SOUTH CENTRAL	0.00	16.41	0.00	467.68	484.10
ROCKY MOUNTAIN	0.00	2017.42	0.00	2842.43	4859.85
FAR WEST	0.00	15234.28	0.00	13421.86	28656.15
TOTAL	17720.33	83431.66	362.29	150644.71	252159.00

REGION	HSHD. CONS. OF NO. 6	BUSINESS CONSUMPTION OF NO. 6		GOVT. CONS. OF NO. 6	TOTAL CONS. OF NO. 6
		Commercial	Industrial		
NEW ENGLAND	394.27	135699.99	77598.43	6974.72	220667.42
MID ATLANTIC	59684.27	228950.18	127252.30	69073.58	484960.33
EAST NORTH CENTRAL	0.00	35981.86	32108.09	1796.34	69886.29
WEST NORTH CENTRAL	0.00	4201.04	3010.15	0.00	7211.19
SOUTH ATLANTIC	0.00	61346.81	22140.37	15966.87	99454.05
EAST SOUTH CENTRAL	0.00	1774.71	1494.97	785.44	4055.12
WEST SOUTH CENTRAL	0.00	3328.42	1215.39	1510.57	6054.38
ROCKY MOUNTAIN	0.00	4730.31	1255.29	766.64	6752.24
FAR WEST	0.00	15017.49	10106.17	43.20	25166.86
TOTAL	60078.54	491030.82	276181.14	96917.37	924207.88

Table B.1.19

Consumption Of Petroleum Heating Fuels, 1972, In Billion BTU, By State

Consumption Of Distillates And Kerosine By Category Of Use

REGION AND STATE	RESIDENTIAL CONSUMPTION	COMMERCIAL CONSUMPTION					TOTAL DISTILLATES & KEROSINE
		Office	Retail	School	Hospital	All Other	
NEW ENGLAND:							
CONNECTICUT	115618.27	682.85	462.59	803.59	297.81	747.26	118612.38
MAINE	67653.49	279.32	270.20	473.85	169.72	436.48	69283.06
MASSACHUSETTS	329351.71	1978.19	1319.46	2322.91	1218.77	2131.43	338322.46
NEW HAMPSHIRE	46541.93	218.87	185.93	321.33	107.18	300.36	47675.59
RHODE ISLAND	48051.72	240.05	192.14	325.07	147.45	310.38	49266.80
VERMONT	30795.82	146.79	123.19	229.83	92.93	199.00	31587.58
MID ATLANTIC:							
NEW JERSEY	307357.50	1849.95	1228.77	1993.06	654.85	1984.94	315069.06
NEW YORK	572160.80	3699.81	2291.32	3778.00	1886.28	3701.36	587517.57
PENNSYLVANIA	281277.79	1405.98	1124.21	1838.83	795.82	1816.03	288258.66
EAST NORTH CENTRAL:							
ILLINOIS	127564.83	7313.08	5350.07	9440.14	3776.75	9180.79	162625.68
INDIANA	96328.59	4481.71	4040.18	7080.35	2251.23	6932.99	121115.05
MICHIGAN	153029.06	7697.20	6418.29	12365.63	3945.99	11013.86	194470.03
OHIO	86268.98	4400.94	3618.29	6397.39	2190.08	6209.02	109084.70
WISCONSIN	96812.36	4440.50	4060.52	7615.77	2642.49	6967.90	122539.54
WEST NORTH CENTRAL:							
IOWA	32365.20	1430.67	1357.36	2356.62	798.87	2329.24	40637.96
KANSAS	4304.13	221.43	180.52	297.82	123.18	309.77	5436.85
MINNESOTA	82375.52	4399.06	3454.89	6388.26	2313.28	5928.63	104859.62
MISSOURI	31953.52	1687.91	1340.12	2261.38	944.30	2299.66	40486.89
NEBRASKA	14945.39	707.13	626.87	1092.96	430.10	1075.71	18878.14
NORTH DAKOTA	12844.17	543.13	538.69	941.45	339.34	924.41	16131.18
SOUTH DAKOTA	13168.63	539.35	552.29	998.26	364.93	947.74	16571.20
SOUTH ATLANTIC:							
DELAWARE	19035.97	889.49	423.93	1090.00	325.16	747.97	22512.51
DISTRICT OF COLUMBIA	11291.36	940.04	251.43	662.68	421.00	443.62	14010.14
FLORIDA	28932.76	1218.23	644.32	1349.03	422.50	1136.84	33703.67
GEORGIA	16117.65	605.20	358.91	781.16	236.62	633.25	18732.78
MARYLAND	72023.26	3487.34	1603.78	3894.02	1149.51	2829.71	84987.63
NORTH CAROLINA	100998.89	3223.27	2249.25	4880.76	1344.32	3968.57	116665.06
SOUTH CAROLINA	29433.65	898.48	655.46	1489.77	360.45	1156.49	33994.29
VIRGINIA	81807.11	3361.15	1821.73	4088.22	1172.09	3214.26	95464.56
WEST VIRGINIA	8014.70	268.61	178.48	394.15	130.64	314.90	9301.47
EAST SOUTH CENTRAL:							
ALABAMA	8555.69	288.84	190.53	422.41	124.42	336.18	9918.08
KENTUCKY	16961.74	570.38	377.74	823.86	231.45	666.48	19631.65
MISSISSIPPI	8171.91	247.47	181.99	442.81	105.98	321.10	9471.27
TENNESSEE	21990.25	768.35	489.68	1052.50	355.50	863.99	25520.27
WEST SOUTH CENTRAL:							
ARKANSAS	6463.35	196.94	143.93	308.68	82.41	253.95	7449.25
LOUISIANA	3297.94	126.04	73.44	179.80	49.48	129.58	3856.28
OKLAHOMA	8684.19	358.45	193.39	444.54	124.66	341.22	10146.44
TEXAS	41742.35	1743.44	929.56	2186.97	596.41	1640.11	48838.84
ROCKY MOUNTAIN:							
ARIZONA	2405.39	28.86	19.53	35.87	11.65	36.01	2537.31
COLORADO	9635.48	124.62	78.22	138.16	51.66	144.25	10172.38
IDAHO	16524.83	154.40	134.15	226.60	60.68	247.40	17348.07
MONTANA	7168.46	71.58	58.19	99.98	31.72	107.32	7537.27
NEVADA	5287.70	63.43	42.93	69.08	19.65	79.16	5561.94
NEW MEXICO	4571.64	57.29	37.11	67.53	20.19	68.44	4822.21
UTAH	9322.40	118.23	75.68	148.53	32.76	139.56	9837.17
WYOMING	4718.75	50.78	38.31	66.85	21.61	70.64	4966.94
FAR WEST:							
ALASKA	14210.26	200.96	115.35	200.28	51.95	212.73	14991.54
CALIFORNIA	23265.77	310.29	188.87	324.36	105.19	348.30	24542.78
HAWAII	768.59	9.76	6.24	10.61	3.36	11.51	810.07
OREGON	35436.91	388.47	287.69	460.64	134.90	530.54	37239.16
WASHINGTON	60294.41	734.40	489.47	832.35	244.53	902.66	63497.82

Table B.1.20

Consumption of Petroleum Heating Fuels, 1972, In Billion BTU, By State

Consumption Of Distillates And Kerosine By Sector

REGION AND STATE	HOUSEHOLD USE		BUSINESS USE	GOVERNMENT USE			TOTAL DISTILLATES	TOTAL DISTILLATES + KEROSINE
	Kerosine	Distillates		Federal	State and Local	Total Govt.		
NEW ENGLAND:								
CONNECTICUT	3912.30	111705.97	2173.35	37.19	783.56	820.76	114700.08	118612.38
MAINE	9996.21	57657.27	1095.50	38.41	495.66	534.07	59286.85	69283.06
MASSACHUSETTS	9565.29	319786.42	6456.98	169.51	2344.26	2513.77	328757.17	338322.46
NEW HAMPSHIRE	3696.84	42845.09	809.82	14.61	309.24	323.85	43978.75	47675.59
RHODE ISLAND	1956.15	46095.57	869.93	32.01	313.14	345.15	47310.65	49266.80
VERMONT	2608.20	28187.62	553.88	13.58	224.29	237.87	28979.37	31587.58
MID ATLANTIC:								
NEW JERSEY	9565.29	297792.21	5552.51	123.34	2035.72	2159.06	305503.77	315069.06
NEW YORK	39338.46	532822.33	10996.51	247.04	4113.22	4360.25	548179.11	587517.57
PENNSYLVANIA	27601.56	253676.23	5073.99	135.62	1771.26	1906.88	260657.10	288258.66
EAST NORTH CENTRAL:								
ILLINOIS	16924.95	110639.88	25104.56	588.32	9367.97	9956.29	145700.73	162625.68
INDIANA	12298.23	84030.37	16780.11	346.55	7659.80	8006.35	108816.82	121115.05
MICHIGAN	11844.63	141184.43	27880.17	454.67	13106.14	13560.81	182625.40	194470.03
OHIO	21098.07	65170.91	15949.52	350.37	6515.83	6866.19	87986.62	109084.70
WISCONSIN	8346.24	88466.12	17772.03	345.10	7610.05	7955.15	114193.30	122539.54
WEST NORTH CENTRAL:								
IOWA	2029.86	30335.34	5655.77	124.11	2492.87	2616.98	38608.10	40637.96
KANSAS	561.33	3742.80	767.34	23.94	341.45	365.39	4875.53	5436.85
MINNESOTA	5188.05	77187.47	15383.73	345.28	6755.10	7100.37	99671.58	104859.62
MISSOURI	1803.06	30150.46	5866.30	201.46	2465.60	2667.06	38683.83	40486.89
NEBRASKA	4286.52	10658.87	2687.45	72.78	1172.53	1245.31	14591.62	18878.14
NORTH DAKOTA	788.13	12056.04	2201.73	73.84	1011.45	1085.29	15343.05	16131.18
SOUTH DAKOTA	34.02	13134.61	2231.31	107.16	1064.1u	1171.26	16537.18	16571.20
SOUTH ATLANTIC:								
DELAWARE	2171.61	16864.35	2312.14	54.90	1109.51	1164.40	20340.90	22512.51
DISTRICT OF COLUMBIA	175.77	11115.59	1631.92	513.54	573.32	1086.86	13834.37	14010.14
FLORIDA	10432.80	18499.96	3099.85	100.64	1570.43	1671.07	23270.88	33703.67
GEORGIA	867.51	15250.14	1563.57	77.55	974.02	1051.57	17865.27	18732.78
MARYLAND	9769.41	62253.85	8246.39	630.53	4087.46	4717.98	75218.22	84987.63
NORTH CAROLINA	47871.81	53127.08	10066.21	249.76	5350.20	5599.96	68793.25	116665.06
SOUTH CAROLINA	11521.44	17912.21	2811.55	91.58	1657.52	1749.10	22472.85	33994.29
VIRGINIA	24341.31	57465.80	8501.53	690.42	4465.49	5155.92	71123.25	95464.56
WEST VIRGINIA	1956.15	6058.55	815.16	25.72	445.90	471.61	7345.32	9301.47
EAST SOUTH CENTRAL:								
ALABAMA	2199.96	6355.73	838.43	45.31	478.65	523.96	7718.12	9918.08
KENTUCKY	10602.90	6358.84	1737.38	62.41	870.12	932.53	9028.75	19631.65
MISSISSIPPI	2137.59	6034.32	791.18	26.34	481.84	508.17	7333.67	9471.27
TENNESSEE	14668.29	7321.96	2246.69	78.21	1205.12	1283.33	10851.97	25520.27
WEST SOUTH CENTRAL:								
ARKANSAS	1525.23	4938.12	615.17	23.29	347.45	370.74	5924.03	7449.25
LOUISIANA	2126.25	1171.69	359.54	9.02	189.78	198.80	1730.03	3856.28
OKLAHOMA	2370.06	6314.13	889.56	58.29	514.39	572.69	7776.37	10146.44
TEXAS	22725.36	19016.99	4489.16	179.92	2427.41	2607.32	26113.48	48838.84
ROCKY MOUNTAIN:								
ARIZONA	300.51	2104.88	88.80	3.44	39.68	43.12	2236.80	2537.31
COLORADO	1207.71	8427.77	366.98	15.60	154.31	169.92	8964.67	10172.38
IDAHO	1020.60	15504.23	553.72	14.80	254.73	269.52	16327.48	17348.07
MONTANA	436.59	6731.87	247.64	8.64	112.52	121.16	7100.67	7537.27
NEVADA	34.02	5253.68	180.08	6.89	87.27	94.16	5527.92	5561.94
NEW MEXICO	1950.48	2621.16	161.40	10.29	78.88	89.17	2871.73	4822.21
UTAH	1111.32	8211.08	323.05	34.12	157.60	191.72	8725.85	9837.17
WYOMING	1343.79	3374.96	153.28	8.40	86.50	94.90	3623.15	4966.94
FAR WEST:								
ALASKA	73.71	14136.55	493.57	52.11	235.60	287.71	14917.83	14991.54
CALIFORNIA	5891.13	17374.64	881.51	30.58	364.92	395.50	18651.65	24542.78
HAWAII	198.45	570.14	27.89	1.95	11.64	13.59	611.63	810.07
OREGON	215.46	35221.45	1258.79	36.18	507.28	543.46	37023.70	37239.16
WASHINGTON	657.72	59636.69	2207.76	73.39	922.26	995.65	62840.10	63497.82

Table B.1.21

Consumption Of Petroleum Heating Fuels, 1972, In Billion BTU, By Region

Consumption Of Distillates And Kerosine, By Category And Sector

REGION	RESIDENTIAL USE	COMMERCIAL CONSUMPTION					TOTAL DISTILLATES & KEROSINE
		Office	Retail	School	Hospital	All Other	
NEW ENGLAND	638012.94	3546.07	2553.52	4476.58	2033.85	4124.91	654747.87
MID ATLANTIC	1160796.09	6955.74	4644.30	7609.90	3336.95	7502.33	1190845.30
EAST NORTH CENTRAL	560003.84	28333.43	23487.35	42899.28	14806.54	4030.58	709835.00
WEST NORTH CENTRAL	191956.56	9528.68	8050.73	14336.75	5313.98	13815.15	243001.84
SOUTH ATLANTIC	367655.34	14891.82	8187.28	18629.79	5562.29	14445.62	429372.14
EAST SOUTH CENTRAL	55679.60	1875.03	1239.94	2741.59	817.35	2187.75	64541.27
WEST SOUTH CENTRAL	60187.83	2424.87	1340.32	3119.98	852.95	2336.86	70290.80
ROCKY MOUNTAIN	59634.67	669.20	484.12	852.61	249.92	892.79	62783.29
FAR WEST	133975.94	1643.89	1087.62	1828.25	539.94	2005.74	141081.37
TOTAL	3227902.80	69868.73	51075.17	96494.71	33513.78	87643.71	3566498.79

REGION	HOUSEHOLD USE		BUSINESS USE	GOVERNMENT USE			TOTAL DISTILLATES	TOTAL DISTILLATES & KEROSINE
	Kerosine	Distillates		Federal	State & Local	Total Govt.		
NEW ENGLAND	31734.99	606277.94	11959.47	305.31	4470.16	4775.46	623012.88	654747.87
MID ATLANTIC	76505.31	1084290.76	21623.01	506.00	7920.20	8426.20	1114339.99	1190845.30
EAST NORTH CENTRAL	70512.12	489491.72	103486.39	2085.01	44259.78	46344.78	639322.88	709835.00
WEST NORTH CENTRAL	14690.97	177265.58	34793.62	948.57	15303.09	16251.67	228310.88	243001.84
SOUTH ATLANTIC	109107.81	258547.53	39048.32	2434.63	20233.84	22668.48	320264.32	429372.14
EAST SOUTH CENTRAL	29608.74	26070.86	5613.68	212.27	3035.72	3247.99	34932.53	64541.27
WEST SOUTH CENTRAL	28746.90	31440.93	6353.42	270.52	3479.03	3749.55	41543.90	70290.80
ROCKY MOUNTAIN	7405.02	52229.65	2074.95	102.19	971.48	1073.67	55378.27	62783.29
FAR WEST	7036.47	126939.47	4869.52	194.21	2041.70	2235.91	134044.90	141081.37
TOTAL	375348.33	2852554.43	229822.39	7058.71	101715.00	108773.71	3191150.58	3566498.79

Table B.1.22

Consumption Of Petroleum Heating Fuels, 1972, In Billion BTU, By State

Consumption Of LPG By Category Of Use

REGION AND STATE	RESIDENTIAL USE	COMMERCIAL CONSUMPTION					TOTAL LPG
		Office	Retail	School	Hospital	Other	
NEW ENGLAND:							
CONNECTICUT	4034.11	0.00	0.00	0.00	0.00	0.00	4034.11
MAINE	2082.09	0.00	0.00	0.00	0.00	0.00	2082.09
MASSACHUSETTS	4944.99	0.00	0.00	0.00	0.00	0.00	4944.99
NEW HAMPSHIRE	2862.90	0.00	0.00	0.00	0.00	0.00	2862.90
RHODE ISLAND	780.81	0.00	0.00	0.00	0.00	0.00	780.81
VERMONT	2212.26	0.00	0.00	0.00	0.00	0.00	2212.26
MID ATLANTIC:							
NEW JERSEY	4356.33	0.00	0.00	0.00	0.00	0.00	4356.33
NEW YORK	15170.37	0.00	0.00	0.00	0.00	0.00	15170.37
PENNSYLVANIA	9558.79	0.00	0.00	0.00	0.00	0.00	9558.79
EAST NORTH CENTRAL:							
ILLINOIS	32870.17	1871.77	2647.87	3013.10	913.06	4337.04	45653.01
INDIANA	24655.82	1404.01	1986.16	2260.12	684.88	3253.20	34244.20
MICHIGAN	19876.32	1131.85	1601.15	1822.00	552.12	2622.57	27605.99
OHIO	15957.06	908.67	1285.43	1462.73	443.25	2105.45	22162.59
WISCONSIN	21556.05	1227.50	1736.46	1975.97	598.78	2844.20	29938.96
WEST NORTH CENTRAL:							
IOWA	25711.77	1464.14	2071.23	2356.91	714.22	3392.53	35710.79
KANSAS	16428.69	935.52	1323.42	1505.96	456.35	2167.67	22817.62
MINNESOTA	25798.68	1469.09	2078.23	2364.88	716.63	3403.99	35831.50
MISSOURI	32290.18	1838.75	2601.15	2959.93	896.95	4260.51	44847.47
NEBRASKA	13556.31	771.96	1092.04	1242.66	376.56	1788.68	18828.21
NORTH DAKOTA	4479.16	255.06	360.82	410.59	124.42	591.00	6221.06
SOUTH DAKOTA	7612.83	433.51	613.26	697.84	211.47	1004.47	10573.38
SOUTH ATLANTIC:							
DELAWARE	1955.17	0.00	0.00	0.00	0.00	0.00	1955.17
DISTRICT OF COLUMBIA	1831.69	0.00	0.00	0.00	0.00	0.00	1831.69
FLORIDA	26680.03	0.00	0.00	0.00	0.00	0.00	26680.03
GEORGIA	20311.42	0.00	0.00	0.00	0.00	0.00	20311.42
MARYLAND	3472.28	0.00	0.00	0.00	0.00	0.00	3472.28
NORTH CAROLINA	14659.73	0.00	0.00	0.00	0.00	0.00	14659.73
SOUTH CAROLINA	9249.65	0.00	0.00	0.00	0.00	0.00	9249.65
VIRGINIA	7547.65	0.00	0.00	0.00	0.00	0.00	7547.65
WEST VIRGINIA	1691.69	0.00	0.00	0.00	0.00	0.00	1691.69
EAST SOUTH CENTRAL:							
ALABAMA	27283.78	0.00	0.00	0.00	0.00	0.00	27283.78
KENTUCKY	17550.13	0.00	0.00	0.00	0.00	0.00	17550.13
MISSISSIPPI	26403.65	0.00	0.00	0.00	0.00	0.00	26403.65
TENNESSEE	12340.32	0.00	0.00	0.00	0.00	0.00	12340.32
WEST SOUTH CENTRAL:							
ARKANSAS	35694.94	0.00	0.00	0.00	0.00	0.00	35694.94
LOUISIANA	14288.52	0.00	0.00	0.00	0.00	0.00	14288.52
OKLAHOMA	27655.56	0.00	0.00	0.00	0.00	0.00	27655.56
TEXAS	72440.09	0.00	0.00	0.00	0.00	0.00	72440.09
ROCKY MOUNTAIN:							
ARIZONA	4276.30	0.00	0.00	0.00	0.00	0.00	4276.30
COLORADO	17686.89	0.00	0.00	0.00	0.00	0.00	17686.89
IDAHO	4334.46	0.00	0.00	0.00	0.00	0.00	4334.46
MONTANA	5164.07	0.00	0.00	0.00	0.00	0.00	5164.07
NEVADA	2680.59	0.00	0.00	0.00	0.00	0.00	2680.59
NEW MEXICO	9831.44	0.00	0.00	0.00	0.00	0.00	9831.44
UTAH	3960.77	0.00	0.00	0.00	0.00	0.00	3960.77
WYOMING	6110.38	0.00	0.00	0.00	0.00	0.00	6110.38
FAR WEST:							
ALASKA	443.22	0.00	0.00	0.00	0.00	0.00	443.22
CALIFORNIA	21805.32	0.00	0.00	0.00	0.00	0.00	21805.32
HAWAII	2267.07	0.00	0.00	0.00	0.00	0.00	2267.07
OREGON	3812.36	0.00	0.00	0.00	0.00	0.00	3812.36
WASHINGTON	4136.39	0.00	0.00	0.00	0.00	0.00	4136.39

Table B.1.23

Consumption Of Petroleum Heating Fuels, 1972, In Billion BTU, By State

Consumption Of LPG By Sector

REGION AND STATE	HOUSEHOLD USE	BUSINESS USE	GOVERNMENT USE			TOTAL LPG
			Federal	State and Local	Total	
NEW ENGLAND:						
CONNECTICUT	4034.11	0.00	0.00	0.00	0.00	4034.11
MAINE	2082.09	0.00	0.00	0.00	0.00	2082.09
MASSACHUSETTS	4944.99	0.00	0.00	0.00	0.00	4944.99
NEW HAMPSHIRE	2862.90	0.00	0.00	0.00	0.00	2862.90
RHODE ISLAND	780.81	0.00	0.00	0.00	0.00	780.81
VERMONT	2212.26	0.00	0.00	0.00	0.00	2212.26
MID ATLANTIC:						
NEW JERSEY	4356.33	0.00	0.00	0.00	0.00	4356.33
NEW YORK	15170.37	0.00	0.00	0.00	0.00	15170.37
PENNSYLVANIA	9558.79	0.00	0.00	0.00	0.00	9558.79
EAST NORTH CENTRAL:						
ILLINOIS	32870.17	9759.56	146.84	2876.44	3023.28	45653.01
INDIANA	24655.82	7051.95	107.46	2428.96	2536.42	34244.20
MICHIGAN	19876.32	5743.26	65.59	1920.83	1986.42	27605.99
OHIO	15957.06	4667.64	71.82	1466.06	1537.88	22162.59
WISCONSIN	21556.05	6337.26	85.13	1960.53	2045.65	29938.96
WEST NORTH CENTRAL:						
IOWA	25711.77	7415.60	117.90	2465.53	2583.43	35710.79
KANSAS	16428.69	4644.46	95.15	1649.32	1744.48	22817.62
MINNESOTA	25798.68	7482.10	110.79	2439.93	2550.72	35831.50
MISSOURI	32290.18	9267.03	210.03	3080.22	3290.26	44847.47
NEBRASKA	13556.31	3908.84	71.49	1291.57	1363.06	18828.21
NORTH DAKOTA	4479.16	1270.69	32.49	438.72	471.21	6221.06
SOUTH DAKOTA	7612.83	2146.21	72.49	741.85	814.34	10573.38
SOUTH ATLANTIC:						
DELAWARE	1955.17	0.00	0.00	0.00	0.00	1955.17
DISTRICT OF COLUMBIA	1831.69	0.00	0.00	0.00	0.00	1831.69
FLORIDA	26680.03	0.00	0.00	0.00	0.00	26680.03
GEORGIA	20311.42	0.00	0.00	0.00	0.00	20311.42
MARYLAND	3472.28	0.00	0.00	0.00	0.00	3472.28
NORTH CAROLINA	14659.73	0.00	0.00	0.00	0.00	14659.73
SOUTH CAROLINA	9249.65	0.00	0.00	0.00	0.00	9249.65
VIRGINIA	7547.65	0.00	0.00	0.00	0.00	7547.65
WEST VIRGINIA	1691.69	0.00	0.00	0.00	0.00	1691.69
EAST SOUTH CENTRAL:						
ALABAMA	27283.78	0.00	0.00	0.00	0.00	27283.78
KENTUCKY	17550.13	0.00	0.00	0.00	0.00	17550.13
MISSISSIPPI	26403.65	0.00	0.00	0.00	0.00	26403.65
TENNESSEE	12340.32	0.00	0.00	0.00	0.00	12340.32
WEST SOUTH CENTRAL:						
ARKANSAS	35694.94	0.00	0.00	0.00	0.00	35694.94
LOUISIANA	14288.52	0.00	0.00	0.00	0.00	14288.52
OKLAHOMA	27655.56	0.00	0.00	0.00	0.00	27655.56
TEXAS	72440.09	0.00	0.00	0.00	0.00	72440.09
ROCKY MOUNTAIN:						
ARIZONA	4276.30	0.00	0.00	0.00	0.00	4276.30
COLORADO	17686.89	0.00	0.00	0.00	0.00	17686.89
IDAHO	4334.46	0.00	0.00	0.00	0.00	4334.46
MONTANA	5164.07	0.00	0.00	0.00	0.00	5164.07
NEVADA	2680.59	0.00	0.00	0.00	0.00	2680.59
NEW MEXICO	9831.44	0.00	0.00	0.00	0.00	9831.44
UTAH	3960.77	0.00	0.00	0.00	0.00	3960.77
WYOMING	6110.38	0.00	0.00	0.00	0.00	6110.38
FAR WEST:						
ALASKA	443.22	0.00	0.00	0.00	0.00	443.22
CALIFORNIA	21805.32	0.00	0.00	0.00	0.00	21805.32
HAWAII	2267.07	0.00	0.00	0.00	0.00	2267.07
OREGON	3812.36	0.00	0.00	0.00	0.00	3812.36
WASHINGTON	4136.39	0.00	0.00	0.00	0.00	4136.39

Table B.1.24

Consumption Of Petroleum Heating Fuels, 1972, In Billion BTU, By Region

Consumption Of LPG By Category And Sector

REGION	RESIDENTIAL USE	COMMERCIAL USE					TOTAL LPG
		Office	Retail	School	Hospital	Other	
NEW ENGLAND	16917.16	0.00	0.00	0.00	0.00	0.00	16917.16
MID ATLANTIC	29085.48	0.00	0.00	0.00	0.00	0.00	29085.48
EAST NORTH CENTRAL	114915.42	6543.79	9257.08	10553.91	3192.10	15162.45	159604.76
WEST NORTH CENTRAL	125877.62	7168.03	10140.14	11538.78	3496.60	16608.85	174830.03
SOUTH ATLANTIC	87399.31	0.00	0.00	0.00	0.00	0.00	87399.31
EAST SOUTH CENTRAL	83577.88	0.00	0.00	0.00	0.00	0.00	83577.88
WEST SOUTH CENTRAL	150079.11	0.00	0.00	0.00	0.00	0.00	150079.11
ROCKY MOUNTAIN	54044.88	0.00	0.00	0.00	0.00	0.00	54044.88
FAR WEST	32464.37	0.00	0.00	0.00	0.00	0.00	32464.37
TOTAL	694361.22	13711.83	19397.22	22072.70	6688.70	31771.31	788002.96

REGION	HOUSEHOLD USE	BUSINESS USE	GOVERNMENT USE			TOTAL LPG
			Federal	State and Local	Total	
NEW ENGLAND	16917.16	0.00	0.00	0.00	0.00	16917.16
MID ATLANTIC	29085.48	0.00	0.00	0.00	0.00	29085.48
EAST NORTH CENTRAL	114915.42	33559.68	476.84	10652.82	11129.66	159604.76
WEST NORTH CENTRAL	125877.62	36134.92	710.34	12107.14	12817.49	174830.03
SOUTH ATLANTIC	87399.31	0.00	0.00	0.00	0.00	87399.31
EAST SOUTH CENTRAL	83577.88	0.00	0.00	0.00	0.00	83577.88
WEST SOUTH CENTRAL	150079.11	0.00	0.00	0.00	0.00	150079.11
ROCKY MOUNTAIN	54044.88	0.00	0.00	0.00	0.00	54044.88
FAR WEST	32464.37	0.00	0.00	0.00	0.00	32464.37
TOTAL	694361.22	69694.60	1187.18	22759.96	23947.14	788002.96

Table B.1.25

Consumption of Petroleum Heating Fuels, 1972, In Billion BTU, By State

Consumption Of All Fuels By Major Category Of Use

REGION AND STATE	RESIDENTIAL	COMMERCIAL	INDUSTRIAL	TOTAL
NEW ENGLAND:				
CONNECTICUT	120430.16	23937.81	9568.92	153936.89
MAINE	69891.02	19514.45	7220.85	96626.32
MASSACHUSETTS	336630.62	151125.43	49025.26	536781.31
NEW HAMPSHIRE	49404.83	10383.75	4097.21	63885.79
RHODE ISLAND	48910.25	15666.72	6997.33	71574.30
VERMONT	33008.08	3460.15	688.87	37157.09
MID ATLANTIC:				
NEW JERSEY	314981.55	68773.88	23015.26	406770.68
NEW YORK	655716.65	243139.46	75720.46	974576.56
PENNSYLVANIA	293637.40	71753.99	28516.58	393907.95
EAST NORTH CENTRAL:				
ILLINOIS	160435.00	93648.06	18373.32	272456.38
INDIANA	120984.42	50444.49	8896.02	180324.93
MICHIGAN	172905.38	53663.23	2089.91	228658.51
OHIO	102226.04	32578.22	1661.23	136465.50
WISCONSIN	118368.41	36800.97	1087.61	156256.99
WEST NORTH CENTRAL:				
IOWA	58076.97	18899.27	152.10	77128.34
KANSAS	20732.82	7832.71	59.88	28625.41
MINNESOTA	108174.20	36757.08	921.48	145852.76
MISSOURI	64243.70	26771.64	1624.50	92639.85
NEBRASKA	28501.70	10298.87	194.62	38995.19
NORTH DAKOTA	17323.33	6373.34	57.57	23754.24
SOUTH DAKOTA	20781.46	6386.58	1.68	27169.72
SOUTH ATLANTIC:				
DELAWARE	20991.14	5865.18	729.71	27586.03
DISTRICT OF COLUMBIA	13123.05	37181.39	1423.59	51728.03
FLORIDA	55612.78	19883.95	2031.62	77528.35
GEORGIA	36429.06	14252.04	4564.70	55245.80
MARYLAND	75495.55	42304.54	5357.78	123157.87
NORTH CAROLINA	115658.61	22342.52	4822.57	142823.71
SOUTH CAROLINA	38683.30	5352.91	509.14	44545.35
VIRGINIA	89354.76	22172.31	2418.23	113945.30
WEST VIRGINIA	9706.39	4157.58	643.63	14507.59
EAST SOUTH CENTRAL:				
ALABAMA	35839.47	2856.17	543.21	39238.85
KENTUCKY	34511.87	3420.17	205.37	38137.40
MISSISSIPPI	34575.56	1760.76	167.29	36503.61
TENNESSEE	34330.57	4749.00	579.10	39658.67
WEST SOUTH CENTRAL:				
ARKANSAS	42158.29	2236.45	459.52	44854.26
LOUISIANA	17586.46	612.85	8.35	18207.66
OKLAHOMA	36339.75	1933.83	69.10	38342.68
TEXAS	114182.44	10642.92	678.43	125503.79
ROCKY MOUNTAIN:				
ARIZONA	6681.69	131.92	0.00	6813.61
COLORADO	27322.37	3440.44	453.72	31216.53
IDAHO	20859.29	1712.50	166.96	22738.75
MONTANA	12332.53	1571.29	111.50	14015.32
NEVADA	7968.29	808.16	25.62	8802.08
NEW MEXICO	14403.08	375.29	7.30	14785.67
UTAH	13283.17	3425.16	390.28	17098.61
WYOMING	10829.13	2040.67	99.90	12969.70
FAR WEST:				
ALASKA	14653.47	898.69	8.33	15560.49
CALIFORNIA	45071.09	8959.06	1629.00	55659.15
HAWAII	3035.67	758.06	56.73	3850.45
OREGON	39249.27	18930.11	4958.36	63137.75
WASHINGTON	64430.80	21276.35	3453.74	89160.90

Table B.1.26

Consumption of Petroleum Heating Fuels, 1972, In Billion BTU, By State

Commercial Consumption of Fuels By Category Of Use

REGION AND STATE	OFFICE	RETAIL	SCHOOL	HOSPITAL	ALL OTHER
NEW ENGLAND					
CONNECTICUT	5449.12	3675.98	6455.98	2385.80	5970.92
MAINE	3337.79	3214.67	5702.39	2036.33	5223.27
MASSACHUSETTS	33254.49	22080.98	39333.15	20573.91	35882.90
NEW HAMPSHIRE	2000.67	1692.39	2957.46	983.60	2749.63
RHODE ISLAND	3088.66	2461.35	4212.47	1904.97	3999.28
VERMONT	640.34	535.40	1008.55	406.78	869.09
MID ATLANTIC:					
NEW JERSEY	16468.68	10892.32	17864.43	5852.65	17695.78
NEW YORK	58459.26	36041.96	60126.90	29928.63	58582.70
PENNSYLVANIA	14422.60	11482.38	18994.38	8196.40	18658.22
EAST NORTH CENTRAL:					
ILLINOIS	18730.43	15001.72	24767.15	9628.48	25520.28
INDIANA	8788.75	8651.03	13923.77	4397.00	14683.94
MICHIGAN	9662.79	8716.69	15526.16	4926.31	14831.28
OHIO	5995.14	5468.99	8855.99	2975.10	9283.00
WISCONSIN	6132.07	6222.58	10387.13	3517.93	10541.25
WEST NORTH CENTRAL:					
IOWA	3003.23	3531.75	4892.00	1573.74	5898.55
KANSAS	1217.71	1553.61	1885.44	613.39	2562.56
MINNESOTA	6697.04	6186.00	9956.05	3466.58	10451.42
MISSOURI	4649.33	4835.22	6724.43	2470.46	8092.20
NEBRASKA	1675.46	1893.67	2639.25	926.44	3163.86
NORTH DAKOTA	1020.14	1120.30	1736.50	602.68	1893.73
SOUTH DAKOTA	976.58	1169.36	1702.98	578.91	1958.75
SOUTH ATLANTIC:					
DELAWARE	1500.38	715.52	1839.70	548.03	1261.56
DISTRICT OF COLUMBIA	12853.01	3442.67	9073.35	5745.73	6066.63
FLORIDA	5075.41	2687.50	5626.73	1757.57	4736.75
GEORGIA	3296.94	1957.66	4260.73	1286.97	3449.73
MARYLAND	11375.99	5237.25	12715.81	3744.67	9230.83
NORTH CAROLINA	4596.20	3208.77	6962.79	1915.79	5658.97
SOUTH CAROLINA	1054.48	769.44	1748.82	422.91	1357.27
VIRGINIA	5455.69	2958.71	6639.66	1901.05	5217.20
WEST VIRGINIA	867.63	577.10	1274.43	421.40	1017.03
EAST SOUTH CENTRAL:					
ALABAMA	605.37	399.65	886.01	260.50	704.64
KENTUCKY	730.57	483.99	1055.60	296.32	853.68
MISSISSIPPI	335.30	246.68	600.21	143.52	435.05
TENNESSEE	1033.54	658.95	1416.32	477.96	1162.22
WEST SOUTH CENTRAL:					
ARKANSAS	446.60	326.67	700.58	186.67	575.93
LOUISIANA	138.34	80.62	197.37	54.29	142.23
OKLAHOMA	473.99	255.82	588.04	164.76	451.22
TEXAS	2614.25	1394.57	3280.97	893.73	2459.41
ROCKY MOUNTAIN:					
ARIZONA	28.86	19.53	35.87	11.65	36.01
COLORADO	792.81	502.51	885.55	337.94	921.63
IDAHO	319.79	279.55	471.51	127.87	513.77
MONTANA	302.97	248.50	426.06	137.71	456.04
NEVADA	185.93	126.80	203.70	58.87	232.86
NEW MEXICO	85.57	55.65	101.17	30.50	102.40
UTAH	781.48	505.18	989.23	222.73	926.55
WYOMING	414.40	315.81	549.79	181.52	579.15
FAR WEST:					
ALASKA	230.93	132.76	230.42	59.96	244.62
CALIFORNIA	2161.76	1329.00	2277.15	753.95	2437.20
HAWAII	177.06	114.39	194.10	62.81	209.68
OREGON	4050.35	3031.31	4841.75	1449.30	5557.40
WASHINGTON	4844.26	3260.75	5532.10	1658.97	5980.27

Table B.1.27

Consumption of Petroleum Heating Fuels, 1972, In Billion BTU, By Region

Consumption of All Fuels and of Commercial Consumption By Category of Use

REGION	RESIDENTIAL	COMMERCIAL	INDUSTRIAL	TOTAL
NEW ENGLAND	658274.95	224088.31	77598.43	959961.70
MID ATLANTIC	1264335.61	383667.32	127252.30	1775255.20
EAST NORTH CENTRAL	674919.26	267134.97	32108.09	974162.31
WEST NORTH CENTRAL	317834.18	113319.50	3011.82	434165.51
SOUTH ATLANTIC	455054.65	173512.43	22500.98	651068.05
EAST SOUTH CENTRAL	139257.47	12786.09	1494.97	153538.53
WEST SOUTH CENTRAL	210266.94	15426.06	1215.39	226908.39
ROCKY MOUNTAIN	113679.55	13505.43	1255.29	128440.27
FAR WEST	166440.30	50822.27	10106.17	227368.74
TOTAL	4000062.83	1254262.40	276543.43	5530868.77

COMMERCIAL USE

REGION	Office	Retail	School	Hospital	All Other
NEW ENGLAND	47771.07	33660.77	59669.99	28291.38	54695.08
MID ATLANTIC	89350.54	58416.67	96985.71	43977.69	94936.70
EAST NORTH CENTRAL	49309.17	44061.01	73460.20	25444.82	74859.76
WEST NORTH CENTRAL	19239.67	20289.92	29536.65	10232.20	34021.07
SOUTH ATLANTIC	46075.71	21554.62	50142.01	17744.12	37995.97
EAST SOUTH CENTRAL	2704.79	1789.27	3958.14	1178.31	3155.58
WEST SOUTH CENTRAL	3673.19	2057.69	4766.95	1299.44	3628.79
ROCKY MOUNTAIN	2911.81	2053.53	3662.89	1108.79	3768.41
FAR WEST	11464.36	7868.21	13075.52	3985.00	14429.18
TOTAL	272500.31	191751.68	335258.08	133261.76	321490.55

Table B.1.28

Consumption Of Petroleum Heating Fuels, 1972, In Billion BTU, By State

Consumption Of All Fuels By Sector

REGION AND STATE	HOUSEHOLD	BUSINESS	GOVERNMENT			ALL SECTORS
			Federal	State and Local	Total Govt.	
NEW ENGLAND:						
CONNECTICUT	120430.16	26918.86	297.36	6290.50	6587.86	153936.89
MAINE	69891.01	20314.67	459.66	5960.97	6420.63	96626.32
MASSACHUSETTS	336630.62	157642.90	2854.72	39653.08	42507.79	536781.31
NEW HAMPSHIRE	49404.82	11503.15	133.70	2844.11	2977.81	63885.79
RHODE ISLAND	48910.25	18197.51	412.25	4054.28	4466.54	71574.29
VERMONT	33008.08	3106.09	59.33	983.59	1042.93	37157.09
MID ATLANTIC:						
NEW JERSEY	314981.55	72459.05	1099.19	18230.90	19330.09	406770.68
NEW YORK	655716.64	249568.94	3910.55	65380.44	69290.99	974576.57
PENNSYLVANIA	293637.40	80596.15	1393.20	18281.22	19674.41	393907.95
EAST NORTH CENTRAL:						
ILLINOIS	160435.00	86049.94	1503.70	24467.75	25971.45	272456.39
INDIANA	120984.42	43613.09	678.63	15048.79	15727.42	180324.93
MICHIGAN	172905.38	38737.52	569.54	16446.08	17015.62	228658.51
OHIO	102226.05	24766.20	476.80	8996.45	9473.25	136465.49
WISCONSIN	118368.41	27056.66	466.33	10365.58	10831.91	156256.99
WEST NORTH CENTRAL:						
IOWA	58076.97	13652.69	251.42	5147.25	5398.68	77128.34
KANSAS	20732.82	5682.51	125.67	2084.42	2210.08	28625.41
MINNESOTA	108174.20	26689.94	521.19	10467.42	10988.62	145852.76
MISSOURI	64243.70	20665.31	545.58	7185.26	7730.84	92639.85
NEBRASKA	28501.70	7539.02	164.52	2789.95	2954.47	38995.19
NORTH DAKOTA	17323.33	4431.09	136.52	1863.31	1999.82	23754.24
SOUTH DAKOTA	20781.46	4394.60	180.39	1813.27	1993.67	27169.72
SOUTH ATLANTIC:						
DELAWARE	20991.14	4629.95	92.57	1872.38	1964.95	27586.03
DISTRICT OF COLUMBIA	13123.05	23737.95	7021.46	7845.57	14867.03	51728.03
FLORIDA	55612.78	14949.04	419.09	6547.44	6966.53	77528.35
GEORGIA	36429.06	13084.70	422.34	5309.70	5732.04	55245.80
MARYLAND	75495.55	32262.07	2056.55	13343.70	15400.26	123157.87
NORTH CAROLINA	115658.61	19177.37	356.06	7631.66	7987.72	142823.71
SOUTH CAROLINA	38683.30	3808.98	107.47	1945.60	2053.07	44545.35
VIRGINIA	89354.76	16218.65	1120.54	7251.35	8371.89	113945.30
WEST VIRGINIA	9706.39	3276.85	83.01	1441.35	1524.36	14507.59
EAST SOUTH CENTRAL:						
ALABAMA	35839.47	2300.75	94.94	1003.69	1098.64	39238.85
KENTUCKY	34511.87	2430.82	79.93	1114.78	1194.71	38137.40
MISSISSIPPI	34575.56	1239.36	35.68	653.01	688.69	36503.61
TENNESSEE	34330.57	3601.44	105.18	1621.48	1726.65	39658.67
WEST SOUTH CENTRAL:						
ARKANSAS	42158.29	1854.78	52.79	788.40	841.19	44854.26
LOUISIANA	17586.46	402.99	9.90	208.32	218.22	18207.66
OKLAHOMA	36339.75	1245.47	77.08	680.38	757.46	38342.67
TEXAS	114182.44	7410.41	269.74	3641.20	3910.93	125503.79
ROCKY MOUNTAIN:						
ARIZONA	6681.69	88.80	3.44	39.68	43.12	6813.61
COLORADO	27322.37	2803.86	99.93	990.37	1090.30	31216.53
IDAHO	20859.29	1318.26	30.77	530.42	561.20	22738.75
MONTANA	12332.53	1165.99	36.78	480.01	516.79	14015.32
NEVADA	7968.29	555.79	20.31	257.69	278.00	8802.08
NEW MEXICO	14403.08	248.95	15.41	118.23	133.64	14785.67
UTAH	13283.17	2538.91	226.40	1050.14	1276.54	17098.61
WYOMING	10829.13	1357.42	69.58	713.58	783.16	12969.70
FAR WEST:						
ALASKA	14653.47	576.10	59.89	271.03	330.92	15560.49
CALIFORNIA	45071.09	7808.56	214.76	2564.74	2779.50	55659.15
HAWAII	3035.67	566.46	35.35	212.98	248.33	3850.45
OREGON	39249.27	18170.27	381.47	5336.74	5718.21	63137.75
WASHINGTON	64430.80	18106.07	488.56	6135.47	6624.02	89160.90

Table B.1.29

Consumption of Petroleum Heating Fuels, 1972, In Billion BTU, By Region

Consumption of All Fuels By Sector

REGION	HOUSEHOLD	BUSINESS	GOVERNMENT			ALL SECTORS
			Federal	State and Local	Total Govt.	
NEW ENGLAND	658274.94	237683.19	4217.02	59786.54	64003.56	959961.70
MID ATLANTIC	1264335.59	402624.13	6402.93	101892.56	108295.50	1775255.20
EAST NORTH CENTRAL	674919.26	220223.41	3695.01	75324.64	79019.65	974162.31
WEST NORTH CENTRAL	317834.18	83055.15	1925.29	31350.89	33276.18	434165.52
SOUTH ATLANTIC	455054.65	131145.57	11679.09	53188.75	64867.84	651068.05
EAST SOUTH CENTRAL	139257.47	9572.36	315.73	4392.97	4708.70	153538.53
WEST SOUTH CENTRAL	210266.94	10913.65	409.50	5318.30	5727.80	226908.39
ROCKY MOUNTAIN	113679.55	10077.97	502.62	4180.12	4682.74	128440.27
FAR WEST	166440.30	45227.46	1180.03	14520.95	15700.98	227368.75
TOTAL	4000062.83	1150522.90	30327.22	349955.73	380282.95	5530868.84

Table B.2.1
Heating Fuel Prices, 1972, By State

Prices Of No. 2 Fuel Oil, Residential Use, And No. 6 Fuel Oil,
    Large Commercial Establishment Use

REGION AND STATE	NO. 2 FUEL OIL		NO. 6 FUEL OIL	
	Price, Cents Per Gallon Residential	Code For Source Of Estimate [a/]	Price, Dollars Per bbl., Large Comm.	Code For Source Of Estimate [b/]
NEW ENGLAND:				
CONNECTICUT	21.20	3	4.97	2
MAINE	21.10	3	5.07	2
MASSACHUSETTS	20.90	1	4.70	1
NEW HAMPSHIRE	20.60	1	4.63	4
RHODE ISLAND	21.40	1	5.05	2
VERMONT	21.54	4	5.08	4
MID ATLANTIC:				
NEW JERSEY	19.20	1	4.89	3
NEW YORK	21.80	1	4.56	1
PENNSYLVANIA	19.50	1	4.94	3
EAST NORTH CENTRAL:				
ILLINOIS	18.50	1	4.81	5
INDIANA	18.60	1	4.85	3
MICHIGAN	19.60	1	4.92	1
OHIO	19.40	1	4.84	3
WISCONSIN	19.40	1	4.82	3
WEST NORTH CENTRAL:				
IOWA	18.70	1	4.84	3
KANSAS	16.20	1	4.00	4
MINNESOTA	17.00	1	4.76	1
MISSOURI	18.10	1	4.21	1
NEBRASKA	17.50	1	4.82	3
NORTH DAKOTA	18.83	2	4.76	3
SOUTH DAKOTA	19.50	1	4.65	4
SOUTH ATLANTIC:				
DELAWARE	20.90	1	4.99	4
DISTRICT OF COLUMBIA	19.50	1	4.87	1
FLORIDA	22.00	1	4.08	1
GEORGIA	19.00	1	4.76	3
MARYLAND	18.40	1	4.83	3
NORTH CAROLINA	19.90	1	4.75	4
SOUTH CAROLINA	20.90	1	4.81	3
VIRGINIA	19.40	1	4.33	3
WEST VIRGINIA	19.10	1	4.73	3
EAST SOUTH CENTRAL:				
ALABAMA	17.61	2	4.59	3
KENTUCKY	19.80	1	4.85	3
MISSISSIPPI	18.72	4	4.35	4
TENNESSEE	19.10	1	4.45	4
WEST SOUTH CENTRAL:				
ARKANSAS	18.90	4	4.10	3
LOUISIANA	15.74	2	4.00	3
OKLAHOMA	14.30	1	3.75	5
TEXAS	16.08	2	4.00	3
ROCKY MOUNTAIN:				
ARIZONA	19.79	2	4.58	3
COLORADO	20.00	1	4.90	4
IDAHO	20.00	1	4.90	4
MONTANA	18.30	1	4.71	3
NEVADA	21.37	4	5.10	4
NEW MEXICO	16.98	3	4.50	2
UTAH	17.60	1	4.67	1
WYOMING	18.84	4	4.97	4
FAR WEST:				
ALASKA	24.60	4	5.00	5
CALIFORNIA	18.19	2	4.53	3
HAWAII	25.32	4	6.00	4
OREGON	18.62	2	4.77	3
WASHINGTON	22.00	1	4.81	1

a/ Sources for No. 2 fuel oil price:
   1. Independent National Gas Association of America [18]
   2. Foster Associates [16]
   3. American Petroleum Institute [3]
   4. From .79 (ratio of No. 2 fuel oil to gasoline price for other states) times state gasoline price (Table A.2.4).

b/ Sources for No. 6 fuel oil price:
   1. Foster Associates [15]
   2. American Petroleum Institute [3]
   3. Foster Associates [16]
   4. From No. 2 fuel
   5. Special cases - see text

Table B.2.2

Heating Fuel Prices, 1972, By State

Relation Of No. 2 And No. 6 Price

REGION AND STATE	FUEL OIL PRICES IN CENTS PER GALLON			PRICE RATIO NO.6/NO.2,
	No.6 Large Commercial Level	No. 2, Residential Level	No. 6, Residential Level	Residential Level
NEW ENGLAND:				
CONNECTICUT	11.83	21.20	18.121	1.170
MAINE	12.07	21.10	18.486	1.141
MASSACHUSETTS	11.19	20.90	17.137	1.220
NEW HAMPSHIRE	11.02	20.60	16.882	1.220
RHODE ISLAND	12.02	21.40	18.413	1.162
VERMONT	12.10	21.54	18.523	1.163
MID ATLANTIC:				
NEW JERSEY	11.64	19.20	17.830	1.077
NEW YORK	10.86	21.80	16.627	1.311
PENNSYLVANIA	11.76	19.50	18.012	1.083
EAST NORTH CENTRAL:				
ILLINOIS	11.45	18.50	17.538	1.055
INDIANA	11.55	18.60	17.684	1.052
MICHIGAN	11.71	19.60	17.939	1.093
OHIO	11.52	19.40	17.647	1.099
WISCONSIN	11.48	19.40	17.575	1.104
WEST NORTH CENTRAL:				
IOWA	11.52	18.70	17.647	1.060
KANSAS	9.52	16.20	14.585	1.111
MINNESOTA	11.33	17.00	17.356	0.980
MISSOURI	10.02	18.10	15.350	1.179
NEBRASKA	11.48	17.50	17.575	0.996
NORTH DAKOTA	11.33	18.83	17.356	1.085
SOUTH DAKOTA	11.07	19.50	16.955	1.150
SOUTH ATLANTIC:				
DELAWARE	11.88	20.90	18.194	1.149
DISTRICT OF COLUMBIA	11.60	19.50	17.757	1.098
FLORIDA	9.71	22.00	14.876	1.479
GEORGIA	11.33	19.00	17.356	1.095
MARYLAND	11.50	18.40	17.611	1.045
NORTH CAROLINA	11.31	19.90	17.319	1.149
SOUTH CAROLINA	11.45	20.90	17.538	1.192
VIRGINIA	10.31	19.40	15.788	1.229
WEST VIRGINIA	11.26	19.10	17.246	1.107
EAST SOUTH CENTRAL:				
ALABAMA	10.93	17.61	16.736	1.052
KENTUCKY	11.55	19.80	17.684	1.120
MISSISSIPPI	10.36	18.72	15.861	1.180
TENNESSEE	10.60	19.10	16.225	1.177
WEST SOUTH CENTRAL:				
ARKANSAS	9.76	18.90	14.949	1.264
LOUISIANA	9.52	15.74	14.585	1.079
OKLAHOMA	8.93	14.30	13.673	1.046
TEXAS	9.52	16.08	14.585	1.103
ROCKY MOUNTAIN:				
ARIZONA	10.90	19.79	16.699	1.185
COLORADO	11.67	20.00	17.866	1.119
IDAHO	11.67	20.00	17.866	1.119
MONTANA	11.21	18.30	17.173	1.066
NEVADA	12.14	21.37	18.595	1.149
NEW MEXICO	10.71	16.98	16.408	1.035
UTAH	11.12	17.60	17.028	1.034
WYOMING	11.83	18.84	18.121	1.040
FAR WEST:				
ALASKA	11.90	24.60	18.231	1.349
CALIFORNIA	10.79	18.19	16.517	1.101
HAWAII	14.29	25.32	21.877	1.157
OREGON	11.36	18.62	17.392	1.071
WASHINGTON	11.45	22.00	17.538	1.254

Table B.2.3

Heating Fuel Prices, 1972, By State

Average Price of Distillate Oil, Residential Level, and Data Used In Estimate of Price

REGION AND STATE	AVG. PRICE DISTILLATE, IN ¢/GAL. RESIDENTIAL	USE OF SPECIFIC DISTILLATES RELATIVE TO ALL DISTILLATES (Fraction of Total)			ESTIMATED PRICE OF DISTILLATE OIL AT RESIDENTIAL LEVEL IN CENTS PER GAL.		
		No. 1	No. 2	No. 4	No. 1	No. 2	No. 4
NEW ENGLAND:							
CONNECTICUT	21.181	0.0117	0.8764	0.1119	21.95	21.20	20.95
MAINE	21.152	0.0803	0.8888	0.0309	21.85	21.10	20.85
MASSACHUSETTS	20.899	0.0180	0.9231	0.0589	21.65	20.90	20.65
NEW HAMPSHIRE	20.639	0.0546	0.9388	0.0066	21.35	20.60	20.35
RHODE ISLAND	21.415	0.0255	0.9487	0.0259	22.15	21.40	21.15
VERMONT	21.558	0.0356	0.9292	0.0352	22.29	21.54	21.29
MID ATLANTIC:							
NEW JERSEY	19.152	0.0079	0.7764	0.2157	19.95	19.20	18.95
NEW YORK	21.786	0.0210	0.8505	0.1286	22.55	21.80	21.55
PENNSYLVANIA	19.497	0.0282	0.8695	0.1024	20.25	19.50	19.25
EAST NORTH CENTRAL:							
ILLINOIS	18.582	0.1276	0.8185	0.0539	19.25	18.50	18.25
INDIANA	18.722	0.1680	0.8099	0.0222	19.35	18.60	18.35
MICHIGAN	19.757	0.2217	0.7411	0.0372	20.35	19.60	19.35
OHIO	19.485	0.1204	0.8585	0.0211	20.15	19.40	19.15
WISCONSIN	19.526	0.1797	0.7779	0.0425	20.15	19.40	19.15
WEST NORTH CENTRAL:							
IOWA	18.905	0.2738	0.7247	0.0015	19.45	18.70	18.45
KANSAS	16.325	0.1661	0.8339	0.0000	16.95	16.20	15.95
MINNESOTA	17.149	0.2215	0.7087	0.0698	17.75	17.00	16.75
MISSOURI	18.212	0.1476	0.8499	0.0026	18.85	18.10	17.85
NEBRASKA	17.638	0.1836	0.8164	0.0000	18.25	17.50	17.25
NORTH DAKOTA	18.999	0.2259	0.7733	0.0008	19.58	18.83	18.58
SOUTH DAKOTA	19.774	0.3656	0.6344	0.0000	20.25	19.50	19.25
SOUTH ATLANTIC:							
DELAWARE	20.948	0.0636	0.9313	0.0052	21.65	20.90	20.65
DISTRICT OF COLUMBIA	19.493	0.0055	0.9503	0.0442	20.25	19.50	19.25
FLORIDA	22.121	0.1642	0.8285	0.0073	22.75	22.00	21.75
GEORGIA	19.048	0.0639	0.9345	0.0016	19.75	19.00	18.75
MARYLAND	18.417	0.0264	0.9631	0.0105	19.15	18.40	18.15
NORTH CAROLINA	19.963	0.0844	0.9126	0.0030	20.65	19.90	19.65
SOUTH CAROLINA	20.968	0.0980	0.8787	0.0233	21.65	20.90	20.65
VIRGINIA	19.437	0.0595	0.9175	0.0229	20.15	19.40	19.15
WEST VIRGINIA	19.131	0.0397	0.9580	0.0024	19.85	19.10	18.85
EAST SOUTH CENTRAL:							
ALABAMA	17.643	0.0438	0.9562	0.0000	18.36	17.61	17.36
KENTUCKY	19.966	0.2226	0.7748	0.0026	20.55	19.80	19.55
MISSISSIPPI	18.799	0.1056	0.8944	0.0000	19.47	18.72	18.47
TENNESSEE	19.222	0.1621	0.8379	0.0000	19.85	19.10	18.85
WEST SOUTH CENTRAL:							
ARKANSAS	18.952	0.0688	0.9312	0.0000	19.65	18.90	18.65
LOUISIANA	15.919	0.2458	0.7340	0.0202	16.49	15.74	15.49
OKLAHOMA	14.430	0.1738	0.8262	0.0000	15.05	14.30	14.05
TEXAS	16.246	0.2311	0.7401	0.0288	16.83	16.08	15.83
ROCKY MOUNTAIN:							
ARIZONA	19.858	0.0911	0.9089	0.0000	20.54	19.79	19.54
COLORADO	20.433	0.5776	0.4224	0.0000	20.75	20.00	19.75
IDAHO	20.357	0.4784	0.5141	0.0075	20.75	20.00	19.75
MONTANA	18.776	0.6341	0.3659	0.0000	19.05	18.30	18.05
NEVADA	21.524	0.2034	0.7956	0.0011	22.12	21.37	21.12
NEW MEXICO	17.477	0.6653	0.3286	0.0061	17.73	16.98	16.73
UTAH	17.771	0.2690	0.6088	0.1222	18.35	17.60	17.35
WYOMING	18.919	0.1286	0.8023	0.0691	19.59	18.84	18.59
FAR WEST:							
ALASKA	24.788	0.3065	0.5353	0.1581	25.35	24.60	24.35
CALIFORNIA	18.271	0.1087	0.8904	0.0009	18.94	18.19	17.94
HAWAII	25.320	0.0000	1.0000	0.0000	26.07	25.32	25.07
OREGON	18.827	0.2775	0.7192	0.0033	19.37	18.62	18.37
WASHINGTON	22.214	0.2904	0.7024	0.0071	22.75	22.00	21.75

Table B.2.4

Heating Fuel Prices, 1972, By State

Factors Used In Allocating Government Purchases Of Residual Fuel Oils,
And Estimated Prices For LPG

REGION AND STATE	FRACTION OF GOVT. PURCHASE		LPG PRICE ESTIMATE	
	Federal	State and Local	Residential ¢ Per Gal.	Commercial $ Per BBL
NEW ENGLAND:				
CONNECTICUT	0.0451	0.9549	31.80	5.49
MAINE	0.0716	0.9284	31.65	5.60
MASSACHUSETTS	0.0671	0.9329	31.35	5.19
NEW HAMPSHIRE	0.0449	0.9551	30.90	5.11
RHODE ISLAND	0.0923	0.9077	32.10	5.58
VERMONT	0.0568	0.9432	32.31	5.61
MID ATLANTIC:				
NEW JERSEY	0.0568	0.9432	24.00	4.87
NEW YORK	0.0564	0.9436	27.25	4.54
PENNSYLVANIA	0.0708	0.9292	24.38	4.92
EAST NORTH CENTRAL:				
ILLINOIS	0.0592	0.9408	25.90	5.48
INDIANA	0.0433	0.9567	26.04	5.53
MICHIGAN	0.0336	0.9664	27.44	5.61
OHIO	0.0511	0.9489	27.16	5.52
WISCONSIN	0.0434	0.9566	27.16	5.49
WEST NORTH CENTRAL:				
IOWA	0.0475	0.9525	22.44	5.69
KANSAS	0.0656	0.9344	19.44	4.70
MINNESOTA	0.0487	0.9513	20.40	5.60
MISSOURI	0.0756	0.9244	21.72	4.95
NEBRASKA	0.0585	0.9415	21.00	5.67
NORTH DAKOTA	0.0681	0.9319	22.60	5.60
SOUTH DAKOTA	0.0916	0.9084	23.40	5.47
SOUTH ATLANTIC:				
DELAWARE	0.0471	0.9529	29.26	5.69
DISTRICT OF COLUMBIA	0.4723	0.5277	27.30	5.55
FLORIDA	0.0601	0.9399	30.80	4.65
GEORGIA	0.0737	0.9263	26.60	5.43
MARYLAND	0.1335	0.8665	25.76	5.51
NORTH CAROLINA	0.0445	0.9555	27.86	5.42
SOUTH CAROLINA	0.0523	0.9477	29.26	5.48
VIRGINIA	0.1337	0.8663	27.16	4.94
WEST VIRGINIA	0.0544	0.9456	26.74	5.39
EAST SOUTH CENTRAL:				
ALABAMA	0.0864	0.9136	26.42	5.01
KENTUCKY	0.0668	0.9332	29.70	5.30
MISSISSIPPI	0.0517	0.9483	28.08	4.75
TENNESSEE	0.0608	0.9392	28.65	4.86
WEST SOUTH CENTRAL:				
ARKANSAS	0.0627	0.9373	22.68	5.61
LOUISIANA	0.0453	0.9547	18.89	5.47
OKLAHOMA	0.1017	0.8983	17.16	5.13
TEXAS	0.0689	0.9311	19.30	5.47
ROCKY MOUNTAIN:				
ARIZONA	0.0000	0.0000	29.68	6.60
COLORADO	0.0916	0.9084	30.00	7.06
IDAHO	0.0548	0.9452	30.00	7.06
MONTANA	0.0711	0.9289	27.45	6.78
NEVADA	0.0730	0.9270	32.06	7.34
NEW MEXICO	0.1150	0.8850	25.47	6.48
UTAH	0.1772	0.8228	26.40	6.72
WYOMING	0.0889	0.9111	28.26	7.16
FAR WEST:				
ALASKA	0.1801	0.8199	41.82	7.14
CALIFORNIA	0.0773	0.9227	30.92	6.47
HAWAII	0.1423	0.8577	43.04	8.57
OREGON	0.0667	0.9333	31.65	6.81
WASHINGTON	0.0738	0.9262	37.40	6.87

Table B.2.5

Heating Fuel Prices, 1972, By State

Comparison Of Prices In Dollars Per Million BTU At "All Commercial" Level

REGION AND STATE	DISTILLATES	NO. 2 FUEL OIL	KEROSINE	NO. 5 FUEL OIL	NO. 6 FUEL OIL	LPG
NEW ENGLAND:						
CONNECTICUT	1.329	1.330	1.415	1.061	0.964	1.368
MAINE	1.327	1.324	1.408	1.081	0.984	1.395
MASSACHUSETTS	1.311	1.311	1.395	1.009	0.912	1.294
NEW HAMPSHIRE	1.295	1.292	1.376	0.995	0.898	1.274
RHODE ISLAND	1.343	1.342	1.427	1.077	0.980	1.390
VERMONT	1.352	1.351	1.436	1.083	0.986	1.398
MID ATLANTIC:						
NEW JERSEY	1.201	1.204	1.286	1.046	0.949	1.214
NEW YORK	1.367	1.368	1.453	0.982	0.885	1.132
PENNSYLVANIA	1.223	1.223	1.305	1.056	0.959	1.227
EAST NORTH CENTRAL:						
ILLINOIS	1.166	1.160	1.241	1.030	0.933	1.367
INDIANA	1.174	1.167	1.247	1.038	0.941	1.378
MICHIGAN	1.239	1.230	1.311	1.052	0.955	1.398
OHIO	1.222	1.217	1.299	1.036	0.939	1.376
WISCONSIN	1.225	1.217	1.299	1.032	0.935	1.370
WEST NORTH CENTRAL:						
IOWA	1.186	1.173	1.253	1.036	0.939	1.419
KANSAS	1.024	1.016	1.092	0.873	0.776	1.173
MINNESOTA	1.076	1.066	1.144	1.021	0.924	1.396
MISSOURI	1.142	1.135	1.215	0.914	0.817	1.234
NEBRASKA	1.106	1.098	1.176	1.032	0.935	1.413
NORTH DAKOTA	1.192	1.181	1.262	1.021	0.924	1.396
SOUTH DAKOTA	1.240	1.223	1.305	0.999	0.902	1.363
SOUTH ATLANTIC:						
DELAWARE	1.314	1.311	1.395	1.065	0.968	1.418
DISTRICT OF COLUMBIA	1.223	1.223	1.305	1.042	0.945	1.384
FLORIDA	1.388	1.380	1.466	0.889	0.792	1.160
GEORGIA	1.195	1.192	1.273	1.021	0.924	1.353
MARYLAND	1.155	1.154	1.234	1.034	0.937	1.373
NORTH CAROLINA	1.252	1.248	1.331	1.019	0.922	1.350
SOUTH CAROLINA	1.315	1.311	1.395	1.030	0.933	1.367
VIRGINIA	1.219	1.217	1.299	0.937	0.840	1.231
WEST VIRGINIA	1.200	1.198	1.279	1.015	0.918	1.344
EAST SOUTH CENTRAL:						
ALABAMA	1.107	1.105	1.183	0.988	0.891	1.250
KENTUCKY	1.252	1.242	1.324	1.038	0.941	1.320
MISSISSIPPI	1.179	1.174	1.255	0.941	0.844	1.184
TENNESSEE	1.206	1.198	1.279	0.961	0.864	1.212
WEST SOUTH CENTRAL:						
ARKANSAS	1.189	1.186	1.266	0.893	0.796	1.398
LOUISIANA	0.999	0.987	1.063	0.873	0.776	1.364
OKLAHOMA	0.905	0.897	0.970	0.825	0.728	1.279
TEXAS	1.019	1.009	1.085	0.873	0.776	1.364
ROCKY MOUNTAIN:						
ARIZONA	1.246	1.241	1.324	0.986	0.889	1.644
COLORADO	1.282	1.255	1.337	1.048	0.951	1.759
IDAHO	1.277	1.255	1.337	1.048	0.951	1.759
MONTANA	1.178	1.148	1.228	1.011	0.914	1.691
NEVADA	1.350	1.341	1.426	1.087	0.990	1.831
NEW MEXICO	1.096	1.065	1.143	0.970	0.873	1.616
UTAH	1.115	1.104	1.183	1.003	0.906	1.677
WYOMING	1.187	1.182	1.262	1.061	0.964	1.784
FAR WEST:						
ALASKA	1.555	1.543	1.634	1.067	0.970	1.780
CALIFORNIA	1.146	1.141	1.221	0.976	0.879	1.613
HAWAII	1.588	1.588	1.680	1.261	1.164	2.136
OREGON	1.181	1.168	1.248	1.023	0.926	1.698
WASHINGTON	1.393	1.380	1.466	1.030	0.933	1.712

Table B.3.1

Expenditures On Petroleum Heating Fuels, 1972, In Thousand Dollars, By State

Expenditures On No. 5 Fuel Oil By Sector

REGION AND STATE	HOUSEHOLD	BUSINESS		GOVERNMENT		TOTAL
		Commercial	Industrial	Federal	State and Local	
NEW ENGLAND:						
CONNECTICUT	490.5	0.0	0.0	0.0	0.0	490.5
MAINE	202.4	0.0	0.0	409.8	5314.1	5926.3
MASSACHUSETTS	2837.7	8585.8	0.0	2707.9	37648.5	51780.0
NEW HAMPSHIRE	0.0	549.9	0.0	118.6	2523.5	3192.0
RHODE ISLAND	100.9	3623.3	0.0	409.7	4029.1	8162.9
VERMONT	0.0	0.0	0.0	11.6	192.6	204.2
MID ATLANTIC:						
NEW JERSEY	4118.1	0.0	0.0	774.0	12852.3	17744.3
NEW YORK	10294.0	0.0	0.0	0.0	0.0	10294.0
PENNSYLVANIA	3562.6	26179.1	0.0	1328.0	17428.6	48498.3
EAST NORTH CENTRAL:						
ILLINOIS	0.0	13581.8	0.0	792.5	12594.5	26968.7
INDIANA	0.0	0.0	0.0	167.3	3696.8	3864.2
MICHIGAN	0.0	809.6	0.0	51.9	1492.5	2354.0
OHIO	0.0	0.0	0.0	39.0	723.3	762.3
WISCONSIN	0.0	1173.5	0.0	37.2	820.8	2031.5
WEST NORTH CENTRAL:						
IOWA	0.0	328.8	0.0	9.8	195.7	534.2
KANSAS	0.0	38.8	0.0	5.7	81.8	126.3
MINNESOTA	0.0	1265.8	0.0	66.5	1298.7	2630.9
MISSOURI	0.0	2631.3	0.0	122.6	1498.5	4252.4
NEBRASKA	0.0	285.3	0.0	20.9	336.4	642.6
NORTH DAKOTA	0.0	144.3	0.0	30.8	421.7	596.8
SOUTH DAKOTA	0.0	15.4	1.7	0.7	7.3	25.1
SOUTH ATLANTIC:						
DELAWARE	0.0	781.4	0.0	40.2	812.7	1634.2
DISTRICT OF COLUMBIA	0.0	0.0	0.0	1602.7	1790.7	3393.5
FLORIDA	0.0	0.0	0.0	10.4	162.8	173.2
GEORGIA	0.0	933.9	0.0	352.1	4425.1	5711.0
MARYLAND	0.0	278.9	0.0	1475.0	9573.8	11327.8
NORTH CAROLINA	0.0	4100.7	0.0	108.3	2324.4	6533.4
SOUTH CAROLINA	0.0	503.1	165.6	16.4	296.8	981.9
VIRGINIA	0.0	0.0	0.0	360.1	2333.0	2693.1
WEST VIRGINIA	0.0	1845.2	196.9	58.1	1010.3	3110.5
EAST SOUTH CENTRAL:						
ALABAMA	0.0	680.5	0.0	49.0	518.6	1248.2
KENTUCKY	0.0	0.0	0.0	0.0	0.0	0.0
MISSISSIPPI	0.0	0.0	0.0	0.0	0.0	0.0
TENNESSEE	0.0	0.0	0.0	5.9	90.7	96.6
WEST SOUTH CENTRAL:						
ARKANSAS	0.0	0.0	0.0	6.3	94.7	101.0
LOUISIANA	0.0	0.0	0.0	0.5	10.5	11.0
OKLAHOMA	0.0	13.5	0.0	15.5	136.9	165.9
TEXAS	0.0	0.0	0.0	9.5	127.8	137.3
ROCKY MOUNTAIN:						
ARIZONA	0.0	0.0	0.0	0.0	0.0	0.0
COLORADO	0.0	0.0	0.0	32.6	323.2	355.7
IDAHO	0.0	76.5	0.0	16.7	288.9	382.1
MONTANA	0.0	636.1	0.0	28.4	371.6	1036.1
NEVADA	0.0	292.1	0.0	14.6	185.2	491.9
NEW MEXICO	0.0	0.0	0.0	0.0	0.0	0.0
UTAH	0.0	1049.8	0.0	192.8	895.5	2138.1
WYOMING	0.0	0.0	0.0	51.6	528.9	580.6
FAR WEST:						
ALASKA	0.0	0.0	0.0	0.0	0.0	0.0
CALIFORNIA	0.0	232.0	0.0	179.9	2147.2	2559.1
HAWAII	0.0	600.0	0.0	42.1	254.0	896.1
OREGON	0.0	8241.6	0.0	353.0	4938.8	13533.3
WASHINGTON	0.0	6658.0	0.0	428.0	5371.5	12457.6

Table B.3.2

Expenditures On Petroleum Heating Fuels, 1972, In Thousand Dollars, By State

Expenditures On No. 6 Fuel Oil By Sector

REGION AND STATE	HOUSEHOLD	BUSINESS		GOVERNMENT		TOTAL
		Commercial	Industrial	Federal	State and Local	
NEW ENGLAND:						
CONNECTICUT	458.2	14636.5	9077.1	250.8	5311.0	29733.6
MAINE	0.0	11804.0	6987.5	41.6	540.0	19373.1
MASSACHUSETTS	0.0	85417.3	43981.5	0.0	0.0	129398.8
NEW HAMPSHIRE	0.0	5429.7	3620.6	0.0	0.0	9050.3
RHODE ISLAND	0.0	6826.1	6744.3	0.0	0.0	13570.4
VERMONT	0.0	1836.8	667.9	34.5	573.2	3112.4
MID ATLANTIC:						
NEW JERSEY	0.0	41649.1	21481.5	223.3	3707.9	67061.9
NEW YORK	63634.8	144102.2	65904.1	3240.5	54214.5	331096.0
PENNSYLVANIA	0.0	21286.6	26886.6	0.0	0.0	48173.1
EAST NORTH CENTRAL:						
ILLINOIS	0.0	18324.6	16868.9	0.0	0.0	35193.5
INDIANA	0.0	10244.0	8234.9	59.6	1317.0	19855.4
MICHIGAN	0.0	2152.4	1962.7	0.0	0.0	4115.1
OHIO	0.0	2336.4	1534.6	16.0	297.3	4184.3
WISCONSIN	0.0	676.3	1000.6	0.0	0.0	1677.0
WEST NORTH CENTRAL:						
IOWA	0.0	105.1	140.5	0.0	0.0	245.7
KANSAS	0.0	129.2	45.7	0.0	0.0	174.9
MINNESOTA	0.0	1535.6	837.2	0.0	0.0	2372.8
MISSOURI	0.0	840.3	1305.3	0.0	0.0	2145.6
NEBRASKA	0.0	441.3	179.1	0.0	0.0	620.4
NORTH DAKOTA	0.0	701.7	52.3	0.0	0.0	754.0
SOUTH DAKOTA	0.0	0.0	0.0	0.0	0.0	0.0
SOUTH ATLANTIC:						
DELAWARE	0.0	827.5	695.0	0.0	0.0	1522.5
DISTRICT OF COLUMBIA	0.0	19545.2	1323.3	4696.9	5247.9	30813.2
FLORIDA	0.0	7773.4	1582.2	242.7	3795.8	13394.1
GEORGIA	0.0	5580.3	4147.1	0.0	0.0	9727.4
MARYLAND	0.0	17235.8	4939.7	0.0	0.0	22175.4
NORTH CAROLINA	0.0	243.0	4372.1	0.0	0.0	4615.1
SOUTH CAROLINA	0.0	0.0	317.5	0.0	0.0	317.5
VIRGINIA	0.0	4452.2	1998.5	38.5	249.5	6738.8
WEST VIRGINIA	0.0	0.0	403.0	0.0	0.0	403.0
EAST SOUTH CENTRAL:						
ALABAMA	0.0	204.9	475.9	0.0	0.0	680.9
KENTUCKY	0.0	459.3	190.1	16.5	230.3	896.2
MISSISSIPPI	0.0	237.1	138.9	7.9	144.5	528.4
TENNESSEE	0.0	669.8	491.9	18.0	278.0	1457.6
WEST SOUTH CENTRAL:						
ARKANSAS	0.0	620.6	359.6	17.8	266.4	1264.4
LOUISIANA	0.0	27.2	6.4	0.2	5.1	38.9
OKLAHOMA	0.0	196.8	49.5	0.0	0.0	246.2
TEXAS	0.0	1740.8	517.9	61.3	828.5	3148.6
ROCKY MOUNTAIN:						
ARIZONA	0.0	0.0	0.0	0.0	0.0	0.0
COLORADO	0.0	1885.7	424.4	50.6	501.7	2862.4
IDAHO	0.0	498.8	156.2	0.0	0.0	655.0
MONTANA	0.0	162.4	100.2	0.0	0.0	262.7
NEVADA	0.0	80.4	24.9	0.0	0.0	105.4
NEW MEXICO	0.0	70.1	6.3	4.5	34.4	115.2
UTAH	0.0	706.0	347.9	0.0	0.0	1053.9
WYOMING	0.0	1064.9	94.8	12.1	124.1	1296.0
FAR WEST:						
ALASKA	0.0	72.0	7.9	7.5	34.4	121.9
CALIFORNIA	0.0	4448.1	1408.4	0.0	0.0	5856.5
HAWAII	0.0	7.1	65.0	0.0	0.0	72.1
OREGON	0.0	3604.1	4514.3	0.0	0.0	8118.4
WASHINGTON	0.0	5584.7	3170.9	0.0	0.0	8755.6

Table B.3.3

Expenditures On Petroleum Heating Fuels, 1972, In Thousand Dollars, By State

Expenditures On Distillates And Kerosine, By Sector

REGION AND STATE	KEROSINE (Household)	DISTILLATES					DISTILLATES & KEROSINE TOTAL
		Household	Business	Fed. Govt.	State & Local Govt.	Total	
NEW ENGLAND:							
CONNECTICUT	6361.0	170597.4	2887.7	49.4	1041.1	174575.5	180936.5
MAINE	16178.9	87938.9	1453.6	51.0	657.7	90101.2	106280.1
MASSACHUSETTS	15339.9	481886.2	8465.1	222.2	3073.3	493646.8	508986.7
NEW HAMPSHIRE	5846.6	63762.1	1048.5	18.9	400.4	65229.9	71076.4
RHODE ISLAND	3209.5	71176.2	1168.6	43.0	420.7	72808.5	76017.9
VERMONT	4306.4	43814.8	749.0	18.4	303.3	44885.5	49191.9
MID ATLANTIC:							
NEW JERSEY	14135.6	411221.3	6670.7	148.2	2445.7	420485.8	434621.4
NEW YORK	65711.0	836957.3	15027.8	337.6	5621.1	857943.8	923654.8
PENNSYLVANIA	41402.3	356618.0	6205.7	165.9	2166.3	365156.0	406558.3
EAST NORTH CENTRAL:							
ILLINOIS	24133.3	148235.3	29262.5	685.8	10919.5	189103.1	213236.4
INDIANA	17627.1	113432.6	19706.8	407.0	8995.8	142542.1	160169.2
MICHIGAN	17854.6	201117.2	34552.3	563.5	16242.6	252475.6	270330.2
OHIO	31491.0	91558.6	19494.5	428.2	7964.1	119445.4	150936.4
WISCONSIN	12457.6	124551.5	21768.5	422.7	9321.3	156064.0	168521.6
WEST NORTH CENTRAL:							
IOWA	2924.4	41350.1	6707.2	147.2	2956.3	51160.7	54085.2
KANSAS	704.8	4405.6	785.8	24.5	349.7	5565.7	6270.5
MINNESOTA	6821.2	95442.3	16549.1	371.4	7266.8	119629.7	126450.9
MISSOURI	2517.6	39590.6	6701.6	230.1	2816.7	49339.1	51856.7
NEBRASKA	5794.9	13554.9	2973.3	80.5	1297.3	17906.0	23701.0
NORTH DAKOTA	1143.1	16515.6	2624.1	88.0	1205.5	20433.1	21576.2
SOUTH DAKOTA	51.0	18727.3	2767.8	132.9	1320.0	22948.0	22999.1
SOUTH ATLANTIC:							
DELAWARE	3482.6	25471.9	3038.3	72.1	1457.9	30040.3	33522.9
DISTRICT OF COLUMBIA	263.7	15623.0	1995.5	627.9	701.0	18947.4	19211.1
FLORIDA	17581.4	29507.4	4301.5	139.7	2179.2	36127.8	53709.2
GEORGIA	1269.2	20944.5	1868.2	92.7	1163.8	24069.3	25338.4
MARYLAND	13857.9	82666.9	9526.8	728.4	4722.1	97644.3	111502.2
NORTH CAROLINA	73224.7	76471.1	12605.7	312.8	6699.9	96089.5	169314.2
SOUTH CAROLINA	18476.9	27079.7	3697.9	120.5	2180.1	33078.1	51555.1
VIRGINIA	36331.8	80538.3	10366.0	841.8	5444.8	97190.9	133522.7
WEST VIRGINIA	2876.3	8357.2	978.3	30.9	535.1	9901.4	12777.7
EAST SOUTH CENTRAL:							
ALABAMA	2991.9	8085.1	927.9	50.1	529.7	9592.9	12584.9
KENTUCKY	16139.7	9154.2	2176.0	78.2	1089.8	12498.1	28637.9
MISSISSIPPI	3082.8	8179.5	933.0	31.1	568.2	9711.8	12794.7
TENNESSEE	21568.3	10147.5	2708.9	94.3	1453.1	14403.8	35972.0
WEST SOUTH CENTRAL:							
ARKANSAS	2220.1	6747.9	731.3	27.7	413.1	7920.0	10140.2
LOUISIANA	2597.2	1344.9	359.0	9.0	189.5	1902.4	4499.6
OKLAHOMA	2642.1	6569.9	805.3	52.8	465.6	7893.5	10535.7
TEXAS	28331.7	22276.5	4575.0	183.4	2473.8	29508.7	57840.4
ROCKY MOUNTAIN:							
ARIZONA	457.2	3013.8	110.6	4.3	49.4	3178.1	3635.3
COLORADO	1856.3	12416.6	470.4	20.0	197.8	13104.8	14961.1
IDAHO	1568.7	22757.1	707.1	18.9	325.3	23808.4	25377.0
MONTANA	616.1	9113.6	291.7	10.2	132.5	9548.0	10164.1
NEVADA	55.7	8153.7	243.2	9.3	117.8	8524.0	8579.7
NEW MEXICO	2561.6	3303.2	177.0	11.3	86.5	3577.9	6139.5
UTAH	1510.6	10521.7	360.1	38.0	175.7	11095.6	12606.2
WYOMING	1950.0	4603.8	181.9	10.0	102.7	4898.3	6848.3
FAR WEST:							
ALASKA	138.4	25266.3	767.5	81.0	366.3	26481.1	26619.5
CALIFORNIA	8265.3	22889.4	1010.3	35.0	418.2	24353.0	32618.2
HAWAII	383.2	1040.8	44.3	3.1	18.5	1106.7	1490.0
OREGON	309.1	47813.1	1486.7	42.7	599.1	49941.6	50250.8
WASHINGTON	1108.4	95520.1	3076.5	102.3	1285.1	99984.0	101092.4

Table   B.3.4

Expenditures On Petroleum Heating Fuels, 1972, In Thousand Dollars, By State

Expenditures On LPG, By Sector

REGION AND STATE	HOUSEHOLD	BUSINESS	FEDERAL GOVT.	STATE AND LOCAL GOVT.	TOTAL
NEW ENGLAND:					
CONNECTICUT	13432.8	0.0	0.0	0.0	13432.8
MAINE	6900.3	0.0	0.0	0.0	6900.3
MASSACHUSETTS	16232.9	0.0	0.0	0.0	16232.9
NEW HAMPSHIRE	9263.2	0.0	0.0	0.0	9263.2
RHODE ISLAND	2624.5	0.0	0.0	0.0	2624.5
VERMONT	7484.5	0.0	0.0	0.0	7484.5
MID ATLANTIC:					
NEW JERSEY	10947.9	0.0	0.0	0.0	10947.9
NEW YORK	43287.1	0.0	0.0	0.0	43287.1
PENNSYLVANIA	24397.9	0.0	0.0	0.0	24397.9
EAST NORTH CENTRAL:					
ILLINOIS	89143.9	13342.3	200.7	3932.4	106619.3
INDIANA	67229.0	9721.1	148.1	3348.3	80446.6
MICHIGAN	57110.6	8031.4	91.7	2686.1	67919.8
OHIO	45381.9	6420.8	98.8	2016.7	53918.2
WISCONSIN	61305.4	8681.4	116.6	2685.7	72789.2
WEST NORTH CENTRAL:					
IOWA	60414.9	10523.5	167.3	3498.8	74604.6
KANSAS	33442.2	5447.0	111.6	1934.3	40935.2
MINNESOTA	55108.6	10442.0	154.6	3405.2	69110.4
MISSOURI	73437.6	11438.3	259.2	3801.9	88937.0
NEBRASKA	29810.3	5524.0	101.0	1825.2	37260.6
NORTH DAKOTA	10598.1	1773.4	45.3	612.3	13029.1
SOUTH DAKOTA	18653.7	2926.1	98.8	1011.4	22690.1
SOUTH ATLANTIC:					
DELAWARE	5990.4	0.0	0.0	0.0	5990.4
DISTRICT OF COLUMBIA	5236.1	0.0	0.0	0.0	5236.1
FLORIDA	86045.8	0.0	0.0	0.0	86045.8
GEORGIA	56573.4	0.0	0.0	0.0	56573.4
MARYLAND	9366.1	0.0	0.0	0.0	9366.1
NORTH CAROLINA	42766.8	0.0	0.0	0.0	42766.8
SOUTH CAROLINA	28340.0	0.0	0.0	0.0	28340.0
VIRGINIA	21465.5	0.0	0.0	0.0	21465.5
WEST VIRGINIA	4736.7	0.0	0.0	0.0	4736.7
EAST SOUTH CENTRAL:					
ALABAMA	75466.9	0.0	0.0	0.0	75466.9
KENTUCKY	54579.1	0.0	0.0	0.0	54579.1
MISSISSIPPI	77634.7	0.0	0.0	0.0	77634.7
TENNESSEE	37021.0	0.0	0.0	0.0	37021.0
WEST SOUTH CENTRAL:					
ARKANSAS	84771.9	0.0	0.0	0.0	84771.9
LOUISIANA	28259.8	0.0	0.0	0.0	28259.8
OKLAHOMA	49694.3	0.0	0.0	0.0	49694.3
TEXAS	146365.2	0.0	0.0	0.0	146365.2
ROCKY MOUNTAIN:					
ARIZONA	13292.5	0.0	0.0	0.0	13292.5
COLORADO	55561.6	0.0	0.0	0.0	55561.6
IDAHO	13616.3	0.0	0.0	0.0	13616.3
MONTANA	14843.1	0.0	0.0	0.0	14843.1
NEVADA	8997.4	0.0	0.0	0.0	8997.4
NEW MEXICO	26220.5	0.0	0.0	0.0	26220.5
UTAH	10949.2	0.0	0.0	0.0	10949.2
WYOMING	18081.8	0.0	0.0	0.0	18081.8
FAR WEST:					
ALASKA	1940.9	0.0	0.0	0.0	1940.9
CALIFORNIA	70605.6	0.0	0.0	0.0	70605.6
HAWAII	10218.1	0.0	0.0	0.0	10218.1
OREGON	12636.4	0.0	0.0	0.0	12636.4
WASHINGTON	16198.9	0.0	0.0	0.0	16198.9

Table B.3.5

Expenditures On Petroleum Heating Fuels, 1972, In Thousand Dollars, By Region

Expenditures On No. 5 and No. 6 Fuel Oil, By Sector

EXPENDITURES ON NO. 5 FUEL OIL

REGION	HOUSEHOLD	BUSINESS		GOVERNMENT		TOTAL
		Commercial	Industrial	Federal	State & Local	
NEW ENGLAND	3631.50	12759.00	0.00	3657.60	49707.80	69755.90
MID ATLANTIC	17974.70	26179.10	0.00	2102.00	30280.90	76536.60
EAST NORTH CENTRAL	0.00	15564.90	1.70	1087.90	19327.90	35980.70
WEST NORTH CENTRAL	0.00	4709.70	362.50	257.00	3840.10	8808.30
SOUTH ATLANTIC	0.00	8443.20	0.00	4023.30	22729.60	35558.60
EAST SOUTH CENTRAL	0.00	680.50	0.00	54.90	609.30	1344.80
WEST SOUTH CENTRAL	0.00	13.50	0.00	31.80	369.90	415.20
ROCKY MOUNTAIN	0.00	2054.50	0.00	336.70	2593.30	4984.50
FAR WEST	0.00	15731.60	0.00	1003.00	12711.50	29446.10
TOTAL	21606.20	86136.00	364.20	12554.20	142170.30	262830.70

EXPENDITURES ON NO. 6 FUEL OIL

REGION	HOUSEHOLD	BUSINESS		GOVERNMENT		TOTAL
		Commercial	Industrial	Federal	State & Local	
NEW ENGLAND	458.20	125950.40	71078.90	326.90	6424.20	204238.60
MID ATLANTIC	63634.80	207037.90	114272.20	3463.80	57922.40	446331.00
EAST NORTH CENTRAL	0.00	33733.70	29601.70	75.60	1614.30	65025.30
WEST NORTH CENTRAL	0.00	3753.20	2560.10	0.00	0.00	6313.40
SOUTH ATLANTIC	0.00	55657.40	19778.40	4978.10	9293.20	89707.00
EAST SOUTH CENTRAL	0.00	1571.10	1296.80	42.40	652.80	3563.10
WEST SOUTH CENTRAL	0.00	2585.40	933.40	79.30	1100.00	4698.10
ROCKY MOUNTAIN	0.00	4468.30	1154.70	67.20	660.20	6350.60
FAR WEST	0.00	13716.00	9166.50	7.50	34.40	22924.50
TOTAL	64093.00	448473.41	249842.70	9040.80	77701.50	849151.60

Table B.3.6

Expenditures On Petroleum Heating Fuels, 1972, In Thousand Dollars, By Region

Expenditures On Kerosine, Distillates And LPG, By Sector

REGION	KEROSINE (Household)	DISTILLATES					DISTILLATES AND KEROSINE TOTAL
		Household	Business	Federal Govt.	State & Local Govt.	Total	
NEW ENGLAND	51242.30	919175.60	15772.50	402.90	5896.50	941247.40	992489.50
MID ATLANTIC	121248.90	1604796.59	27904.20	651.70	10233.10	1643585.60	1764834.50
EAST NORTH CENTRAL	103563.60	678895.20	124784.60	2507.20	53443.30	859630.20	963193.80
WEST NORTH CENTRAL	19957.00	229586.40	39108.90	1074.60	17212.30	286982.30	306939.60
SOUTH ATLANTIC	167364.50	366660.00	48378.20	2966.80	25083.90	443089.00	610453.51
EAST SOUTH CENTRAL	43782.70	35566.30	6745.80	253.70	3640.80	46206.60	89989.50
WEST SOUTH CENTRAL	35791.10	36939.20	6470.60	272.90	3542.00	47224.60	83015.90
ROCKY MOUNTAIN	10576.20	73883.50	2542.00	122.00	1187.70	77735.10	88311.20
FAR WEST	10204.40	192529.70	6385.30	264.10	2687.20	201866.40	212070.90
TOTAL	563730.71	4138032.50	278092.10	8515.90	122926.80	4547567.26	5111298.34

LPG

REGION	Household	Business	Federal Govt.	State & Local Govt.	Total
NEW ENGLAND	55938.20	0.00	0.00	0.00	55938.20
MID ATLANTIC	78632.90	0.00	0.00	0.00	78632.90
EAST NORTH CENTRAL	320170.80	46197.00	655.90	14669.20	381693.10
WEST NORTH CENTRAL	281465.40	48074.30	937.80	16089.10	346567.00
SOUTH ATLANTIC	260520.80	0.00	0.00	0.00	260520.80
EAST SOUTH CENTRAL	244701.70	0.00	0.00	0.00	244701.70
WEST SOUTH CENTRAL	309091.20	0.00	0.00	0.00	309091.20
ROCKY MOUNTAIN	161562.40	0.00	0.00	0.00	161562.40
FAR WEST	111599.90	0.00	0.00	0.00	111599.90
TOTAL	1823683.29	94271.30	1593.70	30758.30	1950307.21

Table B.3.7

Expenditures On Petroleum Heating Fuels, 1972, In Thousand Dollars, By State

Expenditures By Fuel

REGION AND STATE	NO. 5 FUEL OIL	NO. 6 FUEL OIL	RESIDUAL FUEL OIL (No.5 & No.6)	KEROSINE	DISTILLATES	LPG	TOTAL
NEW ENGLAND:							
CONNECTICUT	490.5	29733.6	30224.1	6361.0	174575.5	13432.8	224593.5
MAINE	5926.3	19373.1	25299.4	16178.9	90101.2	6900.3	138479.8
MASSACHUSETTS	51780.0	129398.8	181178.8	15339.9	493646.8	16232.9	706398.3
NEW HAMPSHIRE	3192.0	9050.3	12242.3	5846.6	65229.9	9263.2	92582.0
RHODE ISLAND	8162.9	13570.4	21733.3	3209.5	72808.5	2624.5	100375.9
VERMONT	204.2	3112.4	3316.6	4306.4	44885.5	7484.5	59993.0
MID ATLANTIC:							
NEW JERSEY	17744.3	67061.9	84806.2	14135.6	420485.8	10947.9	530375.6
NEW YORK	10294.0	331096.0	341390.0	65711.0	857943.8	43287.1	1308332.0
PENNSYLVANIA	48498.3	48173.1	96671.4	41402.3	365156.0	24397.9	527627.6
EAST NORTH CENTRAL:							
ILLINOIS	26968.7	35193.5	62162.2	24133.3	189103.1	106619.3	382018.0
INDIANA	3864.2	19855.4	23719.6	17627.1	142542.1	80446.6	264335.4
MICHIGAN	2354.0	4115.1	6469.1	17854.6	252475.6	67919.8	344719.1
OHIO	762.3	4184.3	4946.6	31491.0	119445.4	53918.2	209801.2
WISCONSIN	2031.5	1677.0	3708.5	12457.6	156064.0	72789.2	245019.1
WEST NORTH CENTRAL:							
IOWA	534.2	245.7	779.9	2924.4	51160.7	74604.6	129469.6
KANSAS	126.3	174.9	301.2	704.8	5565.7	40935.2	47506.7
MINNESOTA	2630.9	2372.8	5003.7	6821.2	119629.7	69110.4	200565.0
MISSOURI	4252.4	2145.6	6398.0	2517.6	49339.1	88937.0	147191.6
NEBRASKA	642.6	620.4	1263.0	5794.9	17906.0	37260.6	62224.4
NORTH DAKOTA	596.8	754.0	1350.8	1143.1	20433.1	13029.1	35956.2
SOUTH DAKOTA	25.1	0.0	25.1	51.0	22948.0	22690.1	45714.1
SOUTH ATLANTIC:							
DELAWARE	1634.2	1522.5	3156.7	3482.6	30040.3	5990.4	42670.0
DISTRICT OF COLUMBIA	3393.5	30813.2	34206.7	263.7	18947.4	5236.1	58653.9
FLORIDA	173.2	13394.1	13567.3	17581.4	36127.8	86045.8	153322.3
GEORGIA	5711.0	9727.4	15438.4	1269.2	24069.3	56573.4	97350.3
MARYLAND	11327.8	22175.4	33503.2	13857.9	97644.3	9366.1	154371.4
NORTH CAROLINA	6533.4	4615.1	11148.5	73224.7	96089.5	42766.8	223229.5
SOUTH CAROLINA	981.9	317.5	1299.4	18476.9	33078.1	28340.0	81194.5
VIRGINIA	2693.1	6738.8	9431.9	36331.8	97190.9	21465.5	164420.0
WEST VIRGINIA	3110.5	403.0	3513.5	2876.3	9901.4	4736.7	21028.0
EAST SOUTH CENTRAL:							
ALABAMA	1248.2	680.9	1929.1	2991.9	9592.9	75466.9	89980.5
KENTUCKY	0.0	896.2	896.2	16139.7	12498.1	54579.1	84113.2
MISSISSIPPI	0.0	528.4	528.4	3082.8	9711.8	77634.7	90957.7
TENNESSEE	96.6	1457.6	1554.2	21568.3	14403.8	37021.0	74547.4
WEST SOUTH CENTRAL:							
ARKANSAS	101.0	1264.4	1365.4	2220.1	7920.0	84771.9	96277.4
LOUISIANA	11.0	38.9	49.9	2597.2	1902.4	28259.8	32809.3
OKLAHOMA	165.9	246.2	412.1	2642.1	7893.5	49694.3	60642.2
TEXAS	137.3	3148.6	3285.9	28331.7	29508.7	146365.2	207491.4
ROCKY MOUNTAIN:							
ARIZONA	0.0	0.0	0.0	457.2	3178.1	13292.5	16927.8
COLORADO	355.7	2862.4	3218.1	1856.3	13104.8	55561.6	73740.9
IDAHO	382.1	655.0	1037.1	1568.7	23800.4	13610.3	40030.5
MONTANA	1036.1	262.7	1298.8	616.1	9548.0	14843.1	26305.9
NEVADA	491.9	105.4	597.3	55.7	8524.0	8997.4	18174.3
NEW MEXICO	0.0	115.2	115.2	2561.6	3577.9	26220.5	32475.4
UTAH	2138.1	1053.9	3192.0	1510.6	11095.6	10949.2	26747.3
WYOMING	580.6	1296.0	1876.6	1950.0	4898.3	18081.8	26806.6
FAR WEST:							
ALASKA	0.0	121.9	121.9	138.4	26481.1	1940.9	28682.2
CALIFORNIA	2559.1	5856.5	8415.6	8265.3	24353.0	70605.6	111639.4
HAWAII	896.1	72.1	968.2	383.2	1106.7	10218.1	12676.2
OREGON	13533.3	8118.4	21651.7	309.1	49941.6	12636.4	84538.9
WASHINGTON	12457.6	8755.6	21213.2	1108.4	99984.0	16198.9	138504.4

Table B.3.8

Expenditures On Petroleum Heating Fuels, 1972, In Thousand Dollars, By State

Expenditures By Sector

REGION AND STATE	HOUSEHOLD	BUSINESS		GOVERNMENT		TOTAL
		Commercial	Industrial	Federal	State and Local	
NEW ENGLAND:						
CONNECTICUT	191339.9	17524.2	9077.1	300.2	6352.1	224593.5
MAINE	111220.5	13257.6	6987.5	502.4	6511.8	138479.8
MASSACHUSETTS	516296.7	102468.2	43981.5	2930.1	40721.8	706398.3
NEW HAMPSHIRE	78871.9	7028.1	3620.6	137.5	2923.9	92582.0
RHODE ISLAND	77111.1	11618.0	6744.3	452.7	4449.8	100375.9
VERMONT	55605.7	2585.8	667.9	64.5	1069.1	59993.0
MID ATLANTIC:						
NEW JERSEY	440422.9	48319.8	21481.5	1145.5	19005.9	530375.6
NEW YORK	1019884.2	159130.0	65904.1	3578.1	59835.6	1308332.0
PENNSYLVANIA	425980.8	53671.4	26886.6	1493.9	19594.9	527627.6
EAST NORTH CENTRAL:						
ILLINOIS	261512.5	74511.2	16868.9	1679.0	27446.4	382018.0
INDIANA	198288.7	39671.9	8234.9	782.0	17357.9	264335.4
MICHIGAN	276082.4	45545.7	1962.7	707.1	20421.2	344719.1
OHIO	168431.5	28251.7	1534.6	582.0	11001.4	209801.2
WISCONSIN	198314.5	32299.7	1000.6	576.5	12827.8	245019.1
WEST NORTH CENTRAL:						
IOWA	104689.4	17664.6	140.5	324.3	6650.8	129469.6
KANSAS	38552.6	6400.8	45.7	141.8	2365.8	47506.7
MINNESOTA	157372.1	29792.5	837.2	592.5	11970.7	200565.0
MISSOURI	115545.8	21611.5	1305.3	611.9	8117.1	147191.6
NEBRASKA	49160.1	9223.9	179.1	202.4	3458.9	62224.4
NORTH DAKOTA	28256.8	5243.5	52.3	164.1	2239.5	35956.2
SOUTH DAKOTA	37432.0	5709.3	1.7	232.4	2338.7	45714.1
SOUTH ATLANTIC:						
DELAWARE	34944.9	4647.2	695.0	112.3	2270.6	42670.0
DISTRICT OF COLUMBIA	21122.8	21540.7	1323.3	6927.5	7739.6	58653.9
FLORIDA	133134.6	12074.9	1582.2	392.8	6137.8	153322.3
GEORGIA	78787.1	8382.4	4147.1	444.8	5588.9	97350.3
MARYLAND	105890.9	27041.5	4939.7	2203.4	14295.9	154371.4
NORTH CAROLINA	192462.6	16949.4	4372.1	421.1	9024.3	223229.5
SOUTH CAROLINA	73896.6	4201.0	483.1	136.9	2476.9	81194.5
VIRGINIA	138335.6	14818.2	1998.5	1240.4	8027.3	164420.0
WEST VIRGINIA	15970.2	2823.5	599.9	89.0	1545.4	21028.0
EAST SOUTH CENTRAL:						
ALABAMA	86543.9	1813.3	475.9	99.1	1048.3	89980.5
KENTUCKY	79873.0	2635.3	190.1	94.7	1320.1	84113.2
MISSISSIPPI	88897.0	1170.1	138.9	39.0	712.7	90957.7
TENNESSEE	68736.8	3378.7	491.9	118.2	1821.8	74547.4
WEST SOUTH CENTRAL:						
ARKANSAS	93739.9	1351.9	359.6	51.8	774.2	96277.4
LOUISIANA	32201.9	386.2	6.4	9.7	205.1	32809.3
OKLAHOMA	58906.3	1015.6	49.5	68.3	602.5	60642.2
TEXAS	196973.4	6315.8	517.9	254.2	3430.1	207491.4
ROCKY MOUNTAIN:						
ARIZONA	16763.5	110.6	0.0	4.3	49.4	16927.8
COLORADO	69834.5	2356.1	424.4	103.2	1022.7	73740.9
IDAHO	37942.1	1282.4	156.2	35.6	614.2	40030.5
MONTANA	24572.8	1090.2	100.2	38.6	504.1	26305.9
NEVADA	17206.8	615.7	24.9	23.9	303.0	18174.3
NEW MEXICO	32085.3	247.1	6.3	15.8	120.9	32475.4
UTAH	22981.5	2115.9	347.9	230.8	1071.2	26747.3
WYOMING	24635.6	1246.8	94.8	73.7	755.7	26806.6
FAR WEST:						
ALASKA	27345.6	839.5	7.9	88.5	400.7	28682.2
CALIFORNIA	101760.3	5690.4	1408.4	214.9	2565.4	111639.4
HAWAII	11642.1	651.4	65.0	45.2	272.5	12676.2
OREGON	60758.6	13332.4	4514.3	395.7	5537.9	84538.9
WASHINGTON	112827.4	15319.2	3170.9	530.3	6656.6	138504.4

Table B.3.9

Expenditures On Petroleum Heating Fuels, 1972, In Thousand Dollars, By State

Expenditures By Fuel

EXPENDITURES BY FUEL

REGION	NO. 5 FUEL OIL	NO. 6 FUEL OIL	RESIDUAL FUEL OIL (No.5 & No.6)	KEROSINE	DISTILLATES	LPG	TOTAL
NEW ENGLAND	69755.90	204238.60	273994.50	51242.30	941247.40	55938.20	1322422.49
MID ATLANTIC	76536.60	446331.00	522867.60	121248.90	1643585.60	78632.90	2366335.22
EAST NORTH CENTRAL	35980.70	65025.30	101006.00	103563.60	859630.20	381693.10	1445892.79
WEST NORTH CENTRAL	8808.30	6313.40	15121.70	19957.00	286982.30	346567.00	668627.60
SOUTH ATLANTIC	35558.60	89707.00	125265.60	167364.50	443089.00	260520.80	996239.91
EAST SOUTH CENTRAL	1344.80	3563.10	4907.90	43782.70	46206.60	244701.70	339598.80
WEST SOUTH CENTRAL	415.20	4698.10	5113.30	35791.10	47224.60	309091.20	397220.30
ROCKY MOUNTAIN	4984.50	6350.60	11335.10	10576.20	77735.10	161562.40	261208.70
FAR WEST	29446.10	22924.50	52370.60	10204.40	201866.40	111599.90	376041.10
TOTAL	262830.70	849151.60	1111982.32	563730.71	4547567.26	1950307.21	8173586.73

EXPENDITURES BY SECTOR

REGION	HOUSEHOLD	BUSINESS		GOVERNMENT		TOTAL
		Commercial	Industrial	Federal	State & Local	
NEW ENGLAND	1030445.81	154481.90	71078.90	4387.40	62028.50	1322422.49
MID ATLANTIC	1886287.89	261121.20	114272.20	6217.50	98436.40	2366335.22
EAST NORTH CENTRAL	1102629.61	220280.20	29601.70	4326.60	89054.70	1445892.79
WEST NORTH CENTRAL	531008.80	95646.10	2561.80	2269.40	37141.50	668627.60
SOUTH ATLANTIC	794545.31	112478.80	20140.90	11968.20	57106.70	996239.91
EAST SOUTH CENTRAL	324050.70	8997.40	1296.80	351.00	4902.90	339598.80
WEST SOUTH CENTRAL	381821.50	9069.50	933.40	384.00	5011.90	397220.30
ROCKY MOUNTAIN	246022.10	9064.80	1154.70	525.90	4441.20	261208.70
FAR WEST	314334.00	35832.90	9166.50	1274.60	15433.10	376041.10
TOTAL	6611145.96	906972.81	250206.90	31704.60	373556.90	8173586.73

Appendix C

Electric Utility Use of Fuel Oils

Overview

Data on electric utility company use of fuel oil, by state, appears in both Bureau of Mines and National Coal Association (NCA) series. Because the latter involves some understatement, the former series was employed for estimates of quantity consumed. The latter series also contains information on prices paid, by state, and these data were combined with earlier estimates.of fuel oil prices to construct a price series specific to electric utility use of fuel oil. Estimated prices times quantities then yielded expenditures by state.

Quantities

The Bureau of Mines, Mineral Industry Surveys ([39], Tables 13 and 13a) presents data on sales of distillate-type and of residual-type oils for electric utility company use, and on total oil burned in generating electricity. Table C.1.1 lists these data by state, in thousand barrels, and compares amounts purchased to amounts burned, with differences accounted for by changes in inventories. Table C.1.2 presents corresponding regional totals. For the U.S. as a whole, residual oils account for .86 of total oil use, while the amount bought is quite close in magnitude to the amount burned, equalling 1.02 times the latter figure.

For individual regions, Table C.1.2 yields these fractions:

	Residuals Bought / Total Bought	Total Bought / Total Burned
New England	.9621	0.9997
Mid Atlantic	.8344	1.0137
East North Central	.5146	1.0152
West North Central	.3523	1.0094
South Atlantic	.9216	1.0101
East South Central	.3487	1.0642
West South Central	.5287	0.8610
Rocky Mountain	.6960	1.1785
Far West	.9826	1.1124
United States	.8643	1.0197

For the first five regions, purchases and use were quite close, with a one percent addition to inventories the typical pattern; greater variability occurred in the other regions, but some addition to inventory usually took place.

An alternative data series on electric utility use of oil, by state, appears in National Coal Association (NCA), Steam - Electric Plant Factors [23]. That source shows billions of BTU of oil burned in 1972. A corresponding estimate was obtained from the data of Table C.1.1 using the plausible assumption that residuals and distillates as a fraction of total were the same for both fuel bought and fuel burned. Then, amount burned (in thousand barrels) times fraction allotted to distillates times 5.8250 yielded billions of BTU of distillates; similarly, amount burned times fraction allotted to residuals times 6.2870 yielded billions of BTU of residuals; summing these results yielded the estimate of total BTU burned. The

conversion factors, 5.8250 and 6.2870, show millions of BTU per barrel of
distillate and residual oil respectively [7]. Table C.1.3 converts
the data of Table C.1.1 from thousands of barrels to billion BTU,
using these procedures. Then Table C.1.4 compares the Bureau of Mines
data (from Table C.1.3) to the NCA data, by state, listing the corresponding state figures for each series, the differences between them,
and their ratios. Table C.1.5 carries out the comparison at the regional
level.

The National Coal Association data generally are considerably below
the corresponding Bureau of Mines figures; for the U.S. as a whole, the
total for the former was .86 of the latter. By region, the following
ratios were obtained for Coal Association regional totals relative to
Bureau of Mines regional totals:

New England	.9396
Mid Atlantic	.8173
East North Central	.6619
West North Central	.5437
South Atlantic	.9088
East South Central	.7940
West South Central	.9062
Rocky Mountain	.9475
Far West	.8478
United States	.8588

The National Coal Association ([23] P.V) notes that its report
covers all publicly and privately owned steam-electric plants in the
U.S., excluding Alaska and Hawaii. The exclusion of those two states

accounts for roughly 12 percent of the total difference between the
sources. The National Coal Association suggests the following additional
sources of differences between its data and government series: (1) its
statistics are obtained from utilities' annual reports, which may differ
from totals based on aggregates of monthly reports; (2) its series do
not include data from some military installations, schools, universities
and cooperatives, which do not file annual reports with the Federal Power
Commission, and (3) some company annual reports are filed too late for
inclusion in their report. The internal evidence of Table C.1.4 , and
explanations (2) and (3), suggest that the National Coal Association
series may involve considerable understatement, so the Bureau of Mines
data were taken to be the best estimates of quantities and were used in
subsequent steps.

(Parenthetically, it seems worth noting that for individual states,
three of the NAC estimates exceeded those of the Bureau of Mines (Table C.1.4),
so differences involve more than under-reporting by the NAC.)

Prices

Given the distribution between distillates and residuals in Table C.1.1,
an average price could be estimated by applying the price data developed in
the work on heating oils (Appendix B). The prices of No. 2 and No. 6 oil
in dollars per million BTU were respectively multiplied by the fraction of
distillates and of residuals relative to all oil used, for each state.
This process was used to yield prices at both the large industrial level
and the wholesale level. These estimates are presented in Table C.2.1,

which also presents their average, since it seemed a good guess that the price to an electric utility would fall roughly halfway between the large industrial and the wholesale level.

Table C.2.1 also presents average prices by state listed by the National Coal Association ([23], Table 2), and a comparison is then carried out by dividing the NCA estimates by the prices established using the heating fuel data, here labeled the "wholesale-industrial average" (Avg. W+I) estimates.

There were five states for which the NCA listed neither quantities nor prices, and these appear with zero entries in Table C.2.1. When those states are excluded, the ratio of NCA to (Avg. W+I) is generally below 1.0, and the simple average for the ratio is .874.

Inspection of the last two columns of Table C.2.1 shows a very low NCA price and ratio for Maine, New Hampshire, Vermont and Utah.[1] If the ratios for those four states were arbitrarily increased by .5 (moving the New Hampshire figure from .343 to .843, for example), the over-all average for the ratio would move from .874 to around .92. The standard deviation for the ratio, excluding the zero cases, was .211 prior to the increase of .5 in the ratio for the four states, and .149 after that increase. Hence, the average value for the ratio lies within one standard deviation of 1.0, which would represent equality, both before and after the adjustment. This furnishes support for the argument that the two series are "reasonably" close.

Now, it is possible that the price facing the upper New England states and Utah is indeed as low as shown in the NAC data; for example, perhaps

---

[1]The NCA lists a small amount of oil burned in Vermont (107 Billion BTU) but shows the price as "not available." The value used here was based on the listed Maine and New Hampshire price.

the first group of states obtained oil from Canada at very favorable terms. However, prices that low suggest a quantity limitation must have been in force; otherwise, it would have been quite profitable to buy large amounts for resale. It therefore seems reasonable to assume the NCA price estimate for the four states involves considerable understatement relative to the market price that prevailed in those states. If the utilities did indeed have a low price, someone was subsidizing them, and the "proper" accounting price is taken here to be the market price. Alternatively, and perhaps more plausibly, the listed price is likely to be an underestimate of the price actually paid.

Aside from the very low ratio for the upper New England states and Utah, a relatively low ratio seems to prevail for Atlantic Coast states, suggesting either that utilities in those states had price advantages, relative to other uses, or that one series of estimates contains a bias, with either some overstatement in the Avg. W+I price estimates or some understatement in the NCA estimates. Price advantages to Atlantic Coast utilities might arise because of location differences from other users in those states, or because low sulfur regulations may not have been as pressing for utilities, or because of relatively greater purchases of oil than by utilities in other states, yielding larger bulk purchase discounts. The situation is illustrated in Table C.2.2 which shows regional prices, consisting of the simple average of state prices for each region. Because the NCA data excluded some states, comparisons were carried out by excluding the same states when computing the large industrial and wholesale level prices. In Table C.2.2 the regional ratio is close for a number of regions but seems well below 1.0 for the Mid-Atlantic and South Atlantic regions, as well as for New England. This relationship was examined further by relating the two price series by regression analysis, including a dummy variable for Atlantic Coast states, which was defined to cover New England, the Mid-Atlantic and the South Atlantic regions, excluding three states: Vermont, Pennsylvania and West Virginia. (In the regression analysis, the five states without NCA data were omitted, and the NCA price for Maine and New Hampshire was augmented by .30 dollars per million BTU, putting those states at roughly the same level as the other New England states, on the basis of the earlier discussion of the upper New England states.) The results were:

$$(\text{Avg. W + I}) = .568 + .237 \text{ NCA} + .430 \text{ ATL}$$
$$(9.940) \ (3.041) \qquad (2.197)$$
$$\bar{R}^2 = .144$$

where (Avg. W + I) and NCA are the respective price estimates, ATL is the Atlantic Coast dummy variable and t ratios are listed in parentheses. The explained variance was relatively low (.144), but both t ratios are statistically significant at the .05 level. The results tend to confirm the impression of a reasonably good association between the two price series, but suggest that future effort might be devoted to refining the estimates for the Atlantic Coast states.

Given the uncertainty attached to price estimation, it was decided to use a simple average of Avg. W + I and NAC prices as the price to multiply by quantity in estimating expenditures.

Expenditures

Table C.3.1 lists estimated expenditures on oil used by electric utility companies, by state, and the underlying quantity and price data used to obtain the expenditure estimates. Table C.32 lists corresponding data by region. Here the state quantity and expenditure figures were summed within regions to obtain the regional totals, and then the regional expenditures were divided by the regional quantities to obtained weighted average prices, which appear last in the table to reflect this procedure. Total U.S. expenditures were a bit above two billion dollars, with the Mid Atlantic region accounting for about a third of the total. That region plus the New England and South Atlantic region account for more than three-fourths (77%) of total expenditures in this use.

Relative to the classification by sectors, all use here has been classi- fied as business use, although some electric utilities are publicly owned and operated. Given their sale of electricity to ultimate consumers, however, it seems reasonable to treat their purchase of fuel as a business sector transaction.

Table C.1.1

Quantities Of Oil Used By Electric Utility Companies, 1972, In Thousand Barrels, By State

Distribution Of Quantities Bought And Relation To Total Burned

REGION & STATE	DISTILLATES BOUGHT	RESIDUALS BOUGHT	TOTAL BOUGHT	TOTAL BURNED	BURNED MINUS BOUGHT	BOUGHT DIVIDED BY BURNED
NEW ENGLAND:						
CONNECTICUT	1105.0	27963.0	29068.0	29179.0	111.0	0.9962
MAINE	276.0	5542.0	5818.0	5694.0	-124.0	1.0218
MASSACHUSETTS	1494.0	46284.0	47778.0	47812.0	34.0	0.9993
NEW HAMPSHIRE	222.0	2215.0	2437.0	2442.0	5.0	0.9980
RHODE ISLAND	52.0	2655.0	2707.0	2714.0	7.0	0.9974
VERMONT	195.0	17.0	212.0	207.0	-5.0	1.0242
MID ATLANTIC:						
NEW JERSEY	7816.0	41193.0	49009.0	48524.0	-485.0	1.0100
NEW YORK	13037.0	79855.0	92892.0	91255.0	-1637.0	1.0179
PENNSYLVANIA	7149.0	20055.0	27204.0	27044.0	-160.0	1.0059
EAST NORTH CENTRAL:						
ILLINOIS	6597.0	7139.0	13736.0	13710.0	-26.0	1.0019
INDIANA	644.0	397.0	1041.0	981.0	-60.0	1.0612
MICHIGAN	3783.0	5862.0	9645.0	9638.0	-7.0	1.0007
OHIO	2591.0	825.0	3416.0	3181.0	-235.0	1.0739
WISCONSIN	379.0	610.0	989.0	886.0	-103.0	1.1163
WEST NORTH CENTRAL:						
IOWA	785.0	78.0	863.0	806.0	-57.0	1.0707
KANSAS	507.0	304.0	811.0	810.0	-1.0	1.0012
MINNESOTA	1452.0	751.0	2203.0	2118.0	-85.0	1.0401
MISSOURI	366.0	341.0	707.0	788.0	81.0	0.8972
NEBRASKA	314.0	155.0	469.0	470.0	1.0	0.9979
NORTH DAKOTA	13.0	26.0	39.0	37.0	-2.0	1.0541
SOUTH DAKOTA	58.0	246.0	304.0	317.0	13.0	0.9590
SOUTH ATLANTIC:						
DELAWARE	90.0	4162.0	4252.0	4159.0	-93.0	1.0224
DISTRICT OF COLUMBIA	277.0	4673.0	4950.0	4938.0	-12.0	1.0024
FLORIDA	3983.0	64050.0	68033.0	67877.0	-156.0	1.0023
GEORGIA	1225.0	3572.0	4797.0	4949.0	152.0	0.9693
MARYLAND	1857.0	22038.0	23895.0	22646.0	-1249.0	1.0552
NORTH CAROLINA	1172.0	4048.0	5220.0	4994.0	-226.0	1.0453
SOUTH CAROLINA	893.0	1385.0	2278.0	2291.0	13.0	0.9943
VIRGINIA	1439.0	24171.0	25610.0	25763.0	153.0	0.9941
WEST VIRGINIA	12.0	643.0	655.0	673.0	18.0	0.9733
EAST SOUTH CENTRAL:						
ALABAMA	667.0	0.0	667.0	472.0	-195.0	1.4131
KENTUCKY	57.0	333.0	390.0	391.0	1.0	0.9974
MISSISSIPPI	1963.0	1244.0	3207.0	3219.0	12.0	0.9963
TENNESSEE	259.0	0.0	259.0	168.0	-91.0	1.5417
WEST SOUTH CENTRAL:						
ARKANSAS	1605.0	2081.0	3686.0	4587.0	901.0	0.8036
LOUISIANA	278.0	959.0	1237.0	1305.0	68.0	0.9479
OKLAHOMA	52.0	25.0	77.0	155.0	78.0	0.4968
TEXAS	1248.0	506.0	1754.0	1797.0	43.0	0.9761
ROCKY MOUNTAIN:						
ARIZONA	1219.0	936.0	2155.0	1520.0	-635.0	1.4178
COLORADO	51.0	484.0	535.0	531.0	-4.0	1.0075
IDAHO	1.0	0.0	1.0	1.0	0.0	1.0000
MONTANA	9.0	16.0	25.0	18.0	-7.0	1.3889
NEVADA	24.0	75.0	99.0	131.0	32.0	0.7557
NEW MEXICO	112.0	396.0	508.0	440.0	-68.0	1.1545
UTAH	9.0	1272.0	1281.0	1247.0	-34.0	1.0273
WYOMING	12.0	111.0	123.0	123.0	0.0	1.0000
FAR WEST:						
ALASKA	479.0	2.0	481.0	478.0	-3.0	1.0063
CALIFORNIA	369.0	47340.0	47709.0	42071.0	-5638.0	1.1340
HAWAII	135.0	8236.0	8371.0	8278.0	-93.0	1.0112
OREGON	2.0	17.0	19.0	26.0	7.0	0.7308
WASHINGTON	0.0	60.0	60.0	66.0	6.0	0.9091

Table C.1.2

Quantities of Oil Used By Electric Utility Companies, 1972, In Thousand Barrels, By Region

Distribution of Quantities Bought and Relation to Total Burned

REGION	DISTILLATES BOUGHT	RESIDUALS BOUGHT	TOTAL BOUGHT	TOTAL BURNED	BURNED MINUS BOUGHT
NEW ENGLAND	3344.00	84676.00	88020.00	88048.00	28.00
MID ATLANTIC	28002.00	141103.00	169105.00	166823.00	-2282.00
EAST NORTH CENTRAL	13994.00	14833.00	28827.00	28396.00	-431.00
WEST NORTH CENTRAL	3495.00	1901.00	5396.00	5346.00	-50.00
SOUTH ATLANTIC	10948.00	128742.00	139690.00	138290.00	-1400.00
EAST SOUTH CENTRAL	2946.00	1577.00	4523.00	4250.00	-273.00
WEST SOUTH CENTRAL	3183.00	3571.00	6754.00	7844.00	1090.00
ROCKY MOUNTAIN	1437.00	3290.00	4727.00	4011.00	-716.00
FAR WEST	985.00	55655.00	56640.00	50919.00	-5721.00
TOTAL	68334.00	435348.00	503682.00	493927.00	-9755.00

Table C.1.3

Quantities Of Oil Used By Electric Utility Companies, 1972, In Billion BTU, By State

Comparison Of Quantities Bought And Burned

REGION & STATE	TOTAL BOUGHT	TOTAL BURNED	BURNED MINUS BOUGHT	BOUGHT DIVIDED BY BURNED
NEW ENGLAND:				
CONNECTICUT	182240.0	182935.9	695.9	0.9962
MAINE	36450.3	35673.4	-776.9	1.0218
MASSACHUSETTS	299690.1	299903.3	213.3	0.9993
NEW HAMPSHIRE	15218.9	15250.1	31.2	0.9980
RHODE ISLAND	16994.9	17038.8	43.9	0.9974
VERMONT	1242.8	1213.4	-29.3	1.0242
MID ATLANTIC:				
NEW JERSEY	304508.6	301495.1	-3013.5	1.0100
NEW YORK	577988.9	567803.2	-10185.7	1.0179
PENNSYLVANIA	167728.7	166742.2	-986.5	1.0059
EAST NORTH CENTRAL:				
ILLINOIS	83310.4	83152.7	-157.7	1.0019
INDIANA	6247.2	5887.2	-360.1	1.0612
MICHIGAN	58890.4	58847.6	-42.7	1.0007
OHIO	20279.4	18884.3	-1395.1	1.0739
WISCONSIN	6042.7	5413.4	-629.3	1.1163
WEST NORTH CENTRAL:				
IOWA	5063.0	4728.6	-334.4	1.0707
KANSAS	4864.5	4858.5	-6.0	1.0012
MINNESOTA	13179.4	12670.9	-508.5	1.0401
MISSOURI	4275.8	4765.7	489.9	0.8972
NEBRASKA	2803.5	2809.5	6.0	0.9979
NORTH DAKOTA	239.2	226.9	-12.3	1.0541
SOUTH DAKOTA	1884.5	1965.0	80.6	0.9590
SOUTH ATLANTIC:				
DELAWARE	26690.7	26107.0	-583.8	1.0224
DISTRICT OF COLUMBIA	30992.7	30917.5	-75.1	1.0024
FLORIDA	425883.3	424906.8	-976.6	1.0023
GEORGIA	29592.8	30530.5	937.7	0.9693
MARYLAND	149369.9	141562.3	-7807.6	1.0552
NORTH CAROLINA	32276.7	30879.3	-1397.4	1.0453
SOUTH CAROLINA	13909.2	13988.6	79.4	0.9943
VIRGINIA	160345.3	161303.2	957.9	0.9941
WEST VIRGINIA	4112.4	4225.5	113.0	0.9733
EAST SOUTH CENTRAL:				
ALABAMA	3885.3	2749.4	-1135.9	1.4131
KENTUCKY	2425.6	2431.8	6.2	0.9974
MISSISSIPPI	19255.5	19327.6	72.1	0.9963
TENNESSEE	1508.7	978.6	-530.1	1.5417
WEST SOUTH CENTRAL:				
ARKANSAS	22432.4	27915.7	5483.3	0.8036
LOUISIANA	7648.6	8069.0	420.5	0.9479
OKLAHOMA	460.1	926.1	466.1	0.4968
TEXAS	10450.8	10707.0	256.2	0.9761
ROCKY MOUNTAIN:				
ARIZONA	12985.3	9159.0	-3826.3	1.4178
COLORADO	3340.0	3315.0	-25.0	1.0075
IDAHO	5.8	5.8	0.0	1.0000
MONTANA	153.0	110.2	-42.8	1.3889
NEVADA	611.3	808.9	197.6	0.7557
NEW MEXICO	3142.1	2721.5	-420.6	1.1545
UTAH	8049.5	7835.8	-213.6	1.0273
WYOMING	767.8	767.8	0.0	1.0000
FAR WEST:				
ALASKA	2802.7	2785.3	-17.5	1.0063
CALIFORNIA	299776.0	264350.0	-35426.0	1.1340
HAWAII	52566.1	51982.1	-584.0	1.0112
OREGON	118.5	162.2	43.7	0.7308
WASHINGTON	377.2	414.9	37.7	0.9091

Table C.1.4

Quantities of Oil Used By Electric Utility Companies, 1972, In Billion BTU, By State

Comparison of Bureau Of Mines (BOM) And National Coal Association (NCA) Series

REGION & STATE	BOM	NCA	BOM - NCA	NCA/BOM
NEW ENGLAND:				
CONNECTICUT	182935.9	168076.7	14859.2	0.9188
MAINE	35673.4	33853.2	1820.2	0.9490
MASSACHUSETTS	299903.3	286373.2	13530.1	0.9549
NEW HAMPSHIRE	15250.1	13875.3	1374.8	0.9099
RHODE ISLAND	17038.8	16413.0	625.8	0.9633
VERMONT	1213.4	107.1	1106.3	0.0883
MID ATLANTIC:				
NEW JERSEY	301495.1	234121.4	67373.7	0.7765
NEW YORK	567803.2	471509.5	96293.7	0.8304
PENNSYLVANIA	166742.2	141077.4	25664.8	0.8461
EAST NORTH CENTRAL:				
ILLINOIS	83152.7	47772.6	35380.1	0.5745
INDIANA	5887.2	4169.2	1718.0	0.7082
MICHIGAN	58847.6	52514.0	6333.6	0.8924
OHIO	18884.3	5041.7	13842.6	0.2670
WISCONSIN	5413.4	4476.7	936.7	0.8270
WEST NORTH CENTRAL:				
IOWA	4728.6	1475.3	3253.3	0.3120
KANSAS	4858.5	3732.7	1125.8	0.7683
MINNESOTA	12670.9	5803.4	6867.5	0.4580
MISSOURI	4765.7	3693.3	1072.4	0.7750
NEBRASKA	2809.5	909.6	1899.9	0.3238
NORTH DAKOTA	226.9	187.2	39.7	0.8250
SOUTH DAKOTA	1965.0	1610.6	354.4	0.8196
SOUTH ATLANTIC:				
DELAWARE	26107.0	25471.6	635.4	0.9757
DISTRICT OF COLUMBIA	30917.5	28439.9	2477.6	0.9199
FLORIDA	424906.8	393718.2	31188.6	0.9266
GEORGIA	30530.5	24280.7	6249.8	0.7953
MARYLAND	141562.3	128829.8	12732.5	0.9101
NORTH CAROLINA	30879.3	19847.2	11032.1	0.6427
SOUTH CAROLINA	13988.6	8698.6	5290.0	0.6218
VIRGINIA	161303.2	152605.3	8697.9	0.9461
WEST VIRGINIA	4225.5	3719.6	505.9	0.8803
EAST SOUTH CENTRAL:				
ALABAMA	2749.4	5.5	2743.9	0.0020
KENTUCKY	2431.8	2068.2	363.6	0.8505
MISSISSIPPI	19327.6	18162.5	1165.1	0.9397
TENNESSEE	978.6	0.0	978.6	0.0000
WEST SOUTH CENTRAL:				
ARKANSAS	27915.7	28643.4	-727.7	1.0261
LOUISIANA	8069.0	4989.4	3079.6	0.6183
OKLAHOMA	926.1	576.2	349.9	0.6222
TEXAS	10707.0	8944.1	1762.9	0.8353
ROCKY MOUNTAIN:				
ARIZONA	9159.0	8421.1	737.9	0.9194
COLORADO	3315.0	3006.3	308.7	0.9069
IDAHO	5.8	0.0	5.8	0.0000
MONTANA	110.2	86.6	23.6	0.7860
NEVADA	808.9	763.6	45.3	0.9440
NEW MEXICO	2721.5	2615.3	106.2	0.9610
UTAH	7835.8	7894.3	-58.5	1.0075
WYOMING	767.8	640.0	127.8	0.8336
FAR WEST:				
ALASKA	2785.3	0.0	2785.3	0.0000
CALIFORNIA	264350.0	270634.3	-6284.3	1.0238
HAWAII	51982.1	0.0	51982.1	0.0000
OREGON	162.2	0.0	162.2	0.0000
WASHINGTON	414.9	411.2	3.7	0.9910

Table C.1.5

Quantities of Oil Used By Electric Utility Companies, 1972,
    In Billion BTU, By Region

Comparison of Bureau of Mines (BOM) and
    National Coal Association (NCA) Series

REGION	BOM	NCA	BOM - NCA
NEW ENGLAND	552014.89	518698.50	33316.40
MID ATLANTIC	1036040.50	846708.30	189332.20
EAST NORTH CENTRAL	172185.20	113974.20	58211.00
WEST NORTH CENTRAL	32025.10	17412.10	14613.00
SOUTH ATLANTIC	864420.70	785610.90	78809.80
EAST SOUTH CENTRAL	25487.40	20236.20	5251.20
WEST SOUTH CENTRAL	47617.80	43153.10	4464.70
ROCKY MOUNTAIN	24724.00	23427.20	1296.80
FAR WEST	319694.50	271045.50	48649.00
TOTAL	3074210.17	2640266.01	433944.10

Table C.2.1

Prices In Dollars Per Million BTU, 1972, By State

Comparison Of Alternative Price Estimates

REGION & STATE	ESTIMATES BASED ON HEATING OIL RELATIONSHIPS			NCA ESTIMATES	NCA AVG. W+I
	Large Industrial Level (I)	Wholesale Level (W)	Avg. W+I: (W+I)/2		
NEW ENGLAND:					
CONNECTICUT	0.782	0.729	0.756	0.611	0.809
MAINE	0.798	0.745	0.771	0.319	0.414
MASSACHUSETTS	0.739	0.690	0.715	0.557	0.779
NEW HAMPSHIRE	0.741	0.691	0.716	0.320	0.447
RHODE ISLAND	0.791	0.737	0.764	0.566	0.741
VERMONT	0.963	0.901	0.932	0.320	0.343
MID ATLANTIC:					
NEW JERSEY	0.780	0.728	0.754	0.682	0.905
NEW YORK	0.750	0.700	0.725	0.570	0.786
PENNSYLVANIA	0.800	0.747	0.774	0.696	0.900
EAST NORTH CENTRAL:					
ILLINOIS	0.793	0.741	0.767	0.613	0.799
INDIANA	0.811	0.758	0.784	0.800	1.020
MICHIGAN	0.815	0.761	0.788	0.710	0.901
OHIO	0.851	0.795	0.823	0.803	0.976
WISCONSIN	0.801	0.748	0.775	0.784	1.012
WEST NORTH CENTRAL:					
IOWA	0.841	0.786	0.813	0.854	1.050
KANSAS	0.694	0.648	0.671	0.582	0.867
MINNESOTA	0.762	0.712	0.737	0.788	1.069
MISSOURI	0.742	0.693	0.718	0.629	0.876
NEBRASKA	0.781	0.729	0.755	0.726	0.962
NORTH DAKOTA	0.780	0.728	0.754	0.862	1.144
SOUTH DAKOTA	0.756	0.705	0.730	0.736	1.008
SOUTH ATLANTIC:					
DELAWARE	0.781	0.729	0.755	0.666	0.882
DISTRICT OF COLUMBIA	0.766	0.715	0.740	0.650	0.878
FLORIDA	0.657	0.613	0.635	0.470	0.740
GEORGIA	0.773	0.721	0.747	0.475	0.636
MARYLAND	0.759	0.708	0.734	0.564	0.769
NORTH CAROLINA	0.777	0.725	0.751	0.517	0.688
SOUTH CAROLINA	0.828	0.773	0.801	0.627	0.783
VIRGINIA	0.687	0.640	0.663	0.432	0.651
WEST VIRGINIA	0.740	0.690	0.715	0.890	1.245
EAST SOUTH CENTRAL:					
ALABAMA	0.800	0.748	0.774	0.837	1.082
KENTUCKY	0.777	0.725	0.751	0.890	1.185
MISSISSIPPI	0.784	0.732	0.758	0.704	0.929
TENNESSEE	0.868	0.811	0.839	0.000 [a]	0.000 [a]
WEST SOUTH CENTRAL:					
ARKANSAS	0.735	0.686	0.710	0.659	0.928
LOUISIANA	0.644	0.601	0.623	0.742	1.192
OKLAHOMA	0.628	0.587	0.608	0.571	0.939
TEXAS	0.700	0.654	0.677	0.681	1.006
ROCKY MOUNTAIN:					
ARIZONA	0.819	0.765	0.792	0.857	1.083
COLORADO	0.778	0.725	0.752	0.536	0.713
IDAHO	0.909	0.849	0.879	0.000 [a]	0.000 [a]
MONTANA	0.769	0.718	0.744	0.466	0.627
NEVADA	0.838	0.782	0.810	0.734	0.907
NEW MEXICO	0.717	0.669	0.693	0.674	0.973
UTAH	0.728	0.679	0.704	0.255	0.362
WYOMING	0.783	0.730	0.756	0.824	1.089
FAR WEST:					
ALASKA	1.116	1.043	1.080	0.000 [a]	0.000 [a]
CALIFORNIA	0.707	0.659	0.683	0.739	1.082
HAWAII	0.939	0.876	0.907	0.000 [a]	0.000 [a]
OREGON	0.754	0.704	0.729	0.000 [a]	0.000 [a]
WASHINGTON	0.750	0.699	0.725	0.739	1.020

[a] A zero indicates not listed because NCA quantity not listed.

Table C.2.2

Prices in Dollars Per Million BTU, By Region

Comparison of Alternative Price Estimates for States Covered In Both Series

| | PRICES IN DOLLARS PER MILLION BTU | | NCA | NUMBER OF CASES |
	(AVG. W+I)[a]	NCA[b]	(AVG. W+I)	
New England	.775	.448	.588	6
Mid-Atlantic	.750	.650	.863	3
East North Central	.788	.742	.942	5
West North Central	.740	.740	.997	7
South Atlantic	.727	.588	.808	9
East South Central	.761	.777	1.065	3[c]
West South Central	.655	.663	1.018	4
Rocky Mountain	.750	.621	0.822	7[c]
Far West	.704	.739	1.051	2[c]
United States	.767	—	—	51

—— not applicable because of missing data.

[a] Price estimates derived from heating oil relationships, average of wholesale and large industrial levels.

[b] National Coal Association data [23].

[c] Some states in region omitted; listed prices apply to included states.

Table C.3.1

Expenditures On Oil Used By Electric Utility Companies, 1972,
   In Thousand Dollars, By State

Quantities And Prices Used In Estimating Expenditures,
   and The Resultant Expenditures Estimates

REGION & STATE	CONSUMPTION IN BILLION BTU	PRICE IN $ PER MILLION BTU	EXPENDITURES IN THOUSAND $
NEW ENGLAND:			
CONNECTICUT	182935.9	0.683	124945.2
MAINE	35673.4	0.695	24793.0
MASSACHUSETTS	299903.3	0.636	190738.5
NEW HAMPSHIRE	15250.1	0.668	10187.1
RHODE ISLAND	17038.8	0.665	11330.8
VERMONT	1213.4	0.776	941.6
MID ATLANTIC:			
NEW JERSEY	301495.1	0.718	216473.5
NEW YORK	567803.2	0.648	367936.5
PENNSYLVANIA	166742.2	0.735	122555.5
EAST NORTH CENTRAL:			
ILLINOIS	83152.7	0.690	57375.4
INDIANA	5887.2	0.792	4662.7
MICHIGAN	58847.6	0.749	44076.9
OHIO	18884.3	0.813	15352.9
WISCONSIN	5413.4	0.780	4222.5
WEST NORTH CENTRAL:			
IOWA	4728.6	0.833	3938.9
KANSAS	4858.5	0.627	3046.3
MINNESOTA	12670.9	0.762	9655.2
MISSOURI	4765.7	0.674	3212.1
NEBRASKA	2809.5	0.741	2081.8
NORTH DAKOTA	226.9	0.808	183.3
SOUTH DAKOTA	1965.0	0.733	1440.3
SOUTH ATLANTIC:			
DELAWARE	26107.0	0.711	18562.1
DISTRICT OF COLUMBIA	30917.5	0.695	21487.7
FLORIDA	424906.8	0.553	234973.5
GEORGIA	30530.5	0.611	18654.1
MARYLAND	141562.3	0.649	91873.9
NORTH CAROLINA	30879.3	0.634	19577.5
SOUTH CAROLINA	13988.6	0.714	9987.9
VIRGINIA	161303.2	0.547	88232.8
WEST VIRGINIA	4225.5	0.803	3393.1
EAST SOUTH CENTRAL:			
ALABAMA	2749.4	0.806	2216.0
KENTUCKY	2431.8	0.821	1996.5
MISSISSIPPI	19327.6	0.731	14128.5
TENNESSEE	978.6	0.805	787.8
WEST SOUTH CENTRAL:			
ARKANSAS	27915.7	0.685	19122.3
LOUISIANA	8069.0	0.682	5503.1
OKLAHOMA	926.1	0.590	546.4
TEXAS	10707.0	0.679	7270.1
ROCKY MOUNTAIN:			
ARIZONA	9159.0	0.825	7556.2
COLORADO	3315.0	0.644	2134.9
IDAHO	5.8	0.844	4.9
MONTANA	110.2	0.605	66.7
NEVADA	808.9	0.772	624.5
NEW MEXICO	2721.5	0.683	1858.8
UTAH	7835.8	0.630	4936.6
WYOMING	767.8	0.790	606.6
FAR WEST:			
ALASKA	2785.3	1.037	2888.4
CALIFORNIA	264350.0	0.711	187952.9
HAWAII	51982.1	0.871	45276.4
OREGON	162.2	0.700	113.5
WASHINGTON	414.9	0.732	303.7

Table C.3.2

Expenditures on Oil Used By Electric Utility Companies, 1972,
    In Thousand Dollars, By Region

Quantities, Expenditures and Prices

REGION	CONSUMPTION IN BILLION BTU	EXPENDITURES IN THOUSAND $	PRICES IN $ PER MILLION BTU [a]
NEW ENGLAND	552014.9	362936.2	0.657
MID ATLANTIC	1036040.5	706965.5	0.682
EAST NORTH CENTRAL	172185.2	125690.4	0.730
WEST NORTH CENTRAL	32025.1	23557.9	0.736
SOUTH ATLANTIC	864420.7	506742.6	0.586
EAST SOUTH CENTRAL	25487.4	19128.8	0.751
WEST SOUTH CENTRAL	47617.8	32441.9	0.681
ROCKY MOUNTAIN	24724.0	17789.2	0.720
FAR WEST	319694.5	236534.9	0.740
TOTAL	3074210.2	2031787.4	0.661

[a] Prices obtained by dividing regional expenditures by regional
    consumption.

Appendix D

Transportation and Military Use of
Non-Gasoline Petroleum Products

Quantities-Overview

This section presents data on distillate and residual fuel consumption by the military; highway use of diesel and LPG fuels; civilian and military aviation consumption of jet fuel; and railroad use and marine use (vessel bunkering) of distillate and residual fuel. The Bureau of Mines presents state consumption data on all categories except aviation use of jet fuel. In that latter case, regional data are available, and the regional data were used in conjunction with data from a confidential series to develop a state series on civilian aviation. Military aviation estimates were made by employing the simplifying assumption that the distribution of use within regions paralleled the use pattern for non-aviation military use. There were some conflicts between the Bureau of Mines highway fuel use data and a corresponding series published by the Federal Highway Administration, and some reconciliation of the two was carried out here.

Military Use of Distillates and Residual Fuel Oils

In Sales of Fuel Oil and Kerosine in 1972 ([39] Table 12, P. 10), distillate and residual fuel oil use by the military are listed by state. The data for those categories, and their sum, appear as Table D.1.1, and the corresponding regional totals appear as Table D.1.2. The largest regional total occurs for the South Atlantic region, probably accounted for by the naval bases in the region. Given the heavy military reliance on vehicles, it seemed proper to subsume military use in the transportation functional category, following the classification practice used by the Bureau of Mines.

Highway Use of Diesel and LPG

The Bureau of Mines lists 1972 consumption, by state, of diesel type fuel on highways in Sales of Fuel Oil and Kerosine in 1972 ([39], Table 14, P. 13) and of liquified petroleum gases for internal-combustion engine fuel in Sales of Liquified Petroleum Gases and Ethane in 1973 ([40] Table 4, P. 6, which includes data for 1972 as well as 1973). Presumably the bulk of LPG use as internal combustion engine fuel occurs as highway use.

In its 1972 Highway Statistics, the Federal Highway Administration (FHWA) lists highway use of "special fuels" by state, where special fuels is the aggregate of diesel fuel and liquified petroleum gases ([48], Table MF-25, P. 9). Table D.1.3 compares these state data, listing the Bureau of Mines (BOM) series on diesel fuel and LPG,[1] and their total; the FHWA series on special fuels; the difference between the two totals, in terms of FHWA minus BOM values; and the ratio of BOM to FHWA values. Some pronounced differences appear, with the major source of difference occurring in estimated LPG use in Texas (and hence, in the West South Central region). Specifically, the Texas LPG figure in the BOM series is an order of magnitude above that of the next highest state, and its listed consumption is 47 percent of the U.S. total. The Texas consumption is also 77 percent of its region's

---

[1] The BOM series on LPG consumption lists a combined figure for Maryland and the District of Columbia, which was distributed as two-thirds to the former and one-third to the latter on the basis of total oil consumption in the respective jurisdictions.

consumption of 21.5 million barrels of LPG - a figure that corresponds

almost exactly to the difference of 21.4 million barrels between the FHWA

and BOM totals (see Table D.1.5).

A plausible hypothesis, based on informed opinion, [13] is that a large

Texas producer listed its output as being used at the point of production,

rather than at the actual point of consumption. One response would be to

distribute "excess" Texas production among the other states--say on the

basis of their listed consumption. However, this procedure would not attach

any weight to the lower levels of consumption listed in the FHWA data.

Hence, the following modified procedure was adopted. The use of LPG relative

to diesel fuel was calculated for each state, and appears as the first column

of Table D.1.4. It was hypothesized that a high ratio occurred near major

producing centers, presumably reflecting low prices for LPG relative to

diesel fuel, in turn probably reflecting transportation cost differentials.

It was then assumed that the "proper" LPG to diesel ratio for Mississippi,

Arkansas, Lousiana and Oklahoma was .34 (equal to the Lousiana figure), and

that for Texas was .40. The difference between these ratios and those in

Table D.1.4 were assumed to reflect shipments by producers or trans-shipments

by distributors, which had been counted at their place of origin rather than

at their place of consumption. It was further assumed that the amounts

involved were not used on the highways, but rather were a miscellaneous use;

for example, perhaps some farm machinery uses LPG as a fuel. The reductions

in quantities (to be transferred to a miscellaneous classification), the

revised LPG figures, and the revised totals for diesel plus LPG, by state,

are presented in Table D.1.4. Regional quantity estimates corresponding
to that table and the preceding table appear in Table D.1.5. U.S. totals
for LPG and for diesel plus LPG compare as follows:

	Millions of Gallons	
	LPG	Diesel + LPG
Bureau of Mines	35.219	224.274
Final Estimate Here	21.936	210.991
FHWA	13.790[a]	202.845

[a] Inferred by subtracting diesel total (from BOM) from diesel +
LPG total (special fuels, from FHWA).

Hence, the final totals are somewhat closer to the HWFA than to the
BOM totals. Of course, the individual state figures, outside of the reduced
LPG cases, are those listed by the Bureau of Mines.

Aviation Jet Fuel

The Bureau of Mines does not list jet fuel consumption by state, but
does present regional totals in terms of consumption in "Petroleum Administration for Defense" or P.A.D. districts, as defined in Appendix A. States
entering each district are indicated in Tables D.1.6 and D.1.7. In Bureau
of Mines Crude Petroleum, Petroleum Products and Natural Gas Liquids: 1972
([42], table 11, p. 13), the following data are presented on 1972 shipments
to P.A.D. districts, assumed here as equivalent to consumption in those
districts:

Jet Fuel in Thousand Barrels:

P.A.D. DISTRICT	I	II	III	IV	V	U.S.
A. For Commercial Use, Total	103,016	58,667	20,923	7,324	78,467	268,397
1. Kerosine-type, total[1]	100,354	58,379	20,881	7,322	74,882	261,818
a. Airlines	92,851	55,057	18,916	6,934	73,185	246,943
b. Factory	626	554	290	——	645	2,115
c. General aviation	6,877	2,768	1,675	388	1,052	12,760
2. Naphtha-type, total	2,662	288	42	2	3,585	6,579
a. Airlines	1,154	7	——	——	3,308	4,469
b. Factory	1,015	166	20	——	20	1,221
c. General aviation	493	115	22	2	257	889
B. For Military Use, Total[2]	27,020	17,047	13,516	2,965	35,537	96,085
1. JP-4	16,935[2]	16,786	11,183	2,650	25,153[2]	72,707
2. JP-5	9,197	249	1,485	——	9,816	20,747
3. Other	888	12	848	315	568	2,631

[1] Excludes shipments for non-aviation use, by P.A.D. District: I, 6,891,000 barrels; II, 1,464,000 barrels; III, 2,000 barrels; IV, 55,000 barrels; V, 409,000 barrels.

[2] Excludes direct imports by the military into: P.A.D. District I, 6,939,000 barrels; P.A.D. District V, 2,129,000 barrels.

A confidential alternative series listed 1972 aviation turbine fuel consumed by state in Thousands of gallons, excluding sales to the military. When converted to thousands of barrels, aggregated by P.A.D. district and compared to the Bureau of Mines civilian totals listed above, these comparisons emerged:

P.A.D. District	Bureau Of Mines (BOM)	Alternative Series (AS)	BOM / AS
I	103,016	92,369	1.115
II	58,667	51,506	1.139
III	20,923	20,421	1.025
IV	7,324	8,040	0.911
V	78,467	71,141	1.103
U.S. Total	268,397	243,476	1.102

The alternative series understate the Bureau of Mines estimates in four of the five P.A.D. districts, but in all cases the P.A.D. totals are fairly close, differing by less than 15 percent.

Some of the values in the alternative series for 1972 were adjusted on the basis of revisions in the series for later years. Then the regional ratios (BOM/AS) were taken as scale factors and multiplied by the adjusted individual state figures in the alternative series. Table D.1.6 presents the final state estimates, first in terms of individual P.A.D. districts, and then, by combining those district data, in terms of a single series.

The military aviation use of jet fuel by P.A.D. district was distributed among the states in each district according to the share of military
distillate use in the state relative to military distillate use in the
given P.A.D. district, applying the data of Table D.1.1. It was assumed
that distillate use would parallel that of aviation fuel. Military
aviation use consisted of shipments plus direct imports into P.A.D.
districts 1 and 5. Results appear as Table D.1.7.

Table D.1.8 lists regional totals for both civilian and military
aviation fuel use, with each use distributed by P.A.D. district and
then listed in combined form. Civilian use totaled 268.4 million
barrels, and military use totaled 105.1 million barrels, (almost 40%
of the civilian level), for an aggregate use of 363.5 million barrels of
jet fuel.

Railroad Use and Vessel Bunkering

Sales of Fuel Oil and Kerosine in 1972 ([39], Tables 10 & 11, pp. 8,9)
lists railroad use and vessel bunkering use of distillate and residual-
type oils. In the Appendix A discussion of marine use of gasoline, it was
inferred that household use accounted for all marine use of gasoline, in
the form of recreational boating, and that there was some distillate fuel
used in recreational boating, as well. That earlier discussion yields
an estimate of .145 of total distillate use as accounted for by recreational boating, and that fraction was applied to distillate consumption
at this point, to distribute distillate use between households and business.

Table D.1.9 lists distillate, residual and total use by railroads and
for vessel bunkering, in thousands of barrels, by state. Table D.1.10
lists the corresponding regional totals.

Consumption in Billion BTU

Consumption in thousands of barrels was converted to consumption in billion BTU by using the standard scale factors (from [7]):

Fuel	Million BTU Per Barrel
Distillate fuel oil	5.825
Residual fuel oil	6.287
LPG	4.011
Jet fuel, naphtha type	5.355
Jet fuel, kerosine type	5.670

In the case of aviation consumption, a weighted scale factor was determined for each P.A.D. district for both civilian and military aviation. The former's use was primarily of kerosine-type fuel, while the latter's was naphtha-type (JP-4 being a naphtha fuel and JP-5 a kerosine fuel). The factors employed were:

P.A.D. District	Civilian Aviation	Military Aviation
I	5.662	5.473
II	5.668	5.359
III	5.669	5.409
IV	5.670	5.388
V	5.656	5.447

Tables D.1.11 and D.1.12 exhibit the distribution of use in terms of billion BTU by function and sector, respectively. Table D.1.13 presents the corresponding regional totals. For the U.S. as a whole, the following fractional shares of total held for the individual categories:

Functional Distribution	
Military Use	.062
Highway Use	.195
Aviation Use	.447
Railroad Use	.122
Vessel Bunkering	.144
Total	1.000

Sectoral Distribution	
Households	.005
Business	.803
Federal Government	.192
Total	1.000

The aviation share amounts to almost half of the total. Even with the exclusion of military aviation, the civilian aviation component amounts to around 35 percent of the total, considerably more than the other non-gasoline using transportation modes.

Prices-Overview

The development of estimated price series was carried out in several steps, with the sequence imposed by characteristics of the fuel prices and by the information available. Substantial taxes appear in the prices of highway fuels, making them the highest priced fuels at the point of consumption, so diesel fuel and LPG for highway use were estimated as the first step. Data were available on the national average price for each of three fuels: civilian aviation jet fuel, military aviation jet fuel and railroad fuel. In each case, the national average price was multiplied by a set of state weights to yield state price estimates. The state weights were the ratios of state to national prices for a fuel seen as corresponding closely to the specific transportation fuel. Thus, aviation and railroad fuel prices were estimated as a second step. In the final step, vessel bunkering fuel and military fuel prices were estimated on the basis of the relation (or the inferred relation) of the specific fuel price to the No. 2 fuel oil or the No. 6 fuel oil price.

Prices of Highway Fuels

Data in the 1972 issues of The Oil and Gas Journal ([24] statistical section on refined products prices) showed diesel fuel with a price ranging from about one-half cent to one and a half cents per gallon more than the price of No. 2 fuel oil, at the refinery. Hence, it was assumed that the typical differential was one cent a gallon. The price of No. 2 fuel oil at the residential level (Table B.2.1, above) was then taken as the starting point and scaled by a factor of .84, to convert the level of use to the "all industrial" level, with .84 the scale factor established in Appendix B for that purpose, it being assumed here that diesel use by trucks and buses would correspond to the "all industrial" level. The one cent differential for diesel was then added, and so were federal, state and local taxes.

In the case of LPG, the initial starting point was LPG price in all commercial use (from Table B.2.5), assumed to correspond to the level of use that held for highway users. The initial set of prices were converted to cents per gallon and all highway taxes were added to yield a final price series.

Table D.2.1 presents comparative tax and price information for highway fuels. The first three columns present highway gasoline taxes (from Table A.2.5), diesel and LPG taxes respectively. Data for the latter two series were obtained from <u>Highway Statistics</u> ([48], Table MF-1, P. 10, and

Table FE-101, P. 64). All three sets of taxes contain a federal tax of

four cents per gallon.

The last three columns of Table D.2.1 present the prices per gallon

for the three highway fuels. The gasoline price is that estimated earlier

for trucks and buses (in Table A.2.1). The diesel price is somewhat less

than the gasoline price, which squares with general information on those

fuels, and the LPG price is below the diesel price, perhaps reflecting the

lower BTU content of LPG. The simple averages of the respective prices, in

cents per gallon, are: gasoline, 33.61; diesel fuel, 29.06; and LPG, 26.09.

Aviation and Railroad Fuel Prices

Data were available on the U.S. national average price for civilian

aviation jet fuel, for military aviation jet fuel, and for railroad fuel,

but no finer geographic breakdown was available for any of those cases. A

similar estimation procedure was adopted for all three.

In the case of civilian aviation, data from the Civil Aeronautics Board

yielded an average price of 11.597 cents per gallon of jet fuel consumed in

1972 domestic operations.[3] That price estimate was obtained from the cost of

7.823 billion gallons of jet fuel listed as consumed, which amounts to

about 70 percent of the total obtained from the Bureau of Mines data. (From

Table D.1.8, the Bureau of Mines total is 11.273 billion gallons. However,

---

[3] The data applied to trunk and local service of eleven major carriers
and ninety-five local service carriers, viewed as covering almost all domestic
operations. A total of 7,822,980,000 gallons was listed as consumed at a
cost of $907,238,000. The data were obtained from CAB Schedule T2B, fuel
consumption, and CAB Schedule P5.2, fuel cost [19].

restricting use to that consumed by airlines, the Bureau of Mines total
is 10.559 billion gallons, from [42], which increases the CAB estimate
to 74 percent of the Bureau of Mines figure.)

Data covering a large part of 1972 military jet fuel consumption was
listed in a Defense Fuel Supply release in Platt's Oilgram ([26], July 18, 1972,
P. 3-A). The data covered awards for grade JP-4 jet fuel totaling 1.978
billion gallons, which comprises a large portion of the total use of 4.416
billion gallons (from Table D.1.8). Average price was 10.75 cents per
gallon.[4]

To develop series of individual state prices for both civilian and
military jet fuel, it seemed reasonable to begin by assuming that those fuels
were physically quite close to kerosine used in space heating, since a form
of kerosine was a major jet fuel. Hence, relative prices for kerosine
could be applied here. A relative fuel price in the form of a ratio was
developed for each state by dividing the previously estimated price of
kerosine for that state by the simple average price, using the data in
Table B.2.5, above. Then the respective national average prices for jet
fuel were multiplied by the state ratios to generate price series for each
fuel. These price estimates were used as a first approximation, and the
weighted price was obtained, using quantities consumed as weights. The
ratio of given national price to weighted average was then used as a
scale factor to yield the final price series. The respective scale factors
were 0.9934 for civilian jet fuel and 1.0132 for military jet fuel. (The
closeness to 1.0 of the scale factors indicate the simple average was a

---

[4] There was a total of 64 awards, ranging in size from 1.3 million
to 175.0 million gallons, and in price per gallon from 6.70 cents to
13.12 cents, but the bulk of the cases ranged between 10 and 11.5 cents
in price per gallon.

good first approximation.)

Average fuel cost for railroads in 1972 was 10.97 cents per gallon [4]. Railroad fuel is preponderantly distillates, that fuel type accounting for .988 of the total (from Table D.1.10). Given the general pattern of distillate versus residual prices in [26], it was assumed that the railroad national average distillate price was 11 cents per gallon, and the national average residual price was 8 cents per gallon, yielding a weighted average of 10.97 cents. Then, relative prices for No. 2 fuel oil and No. 6 fuel oil were developed by finding the ratio of the state price to the respective simple average for each fuel, again applying the data of Table B.2.5, under the assumption that those fuels corresponded "well enough" to be employed in estimating railroad fuel prices.

The product of the distillate price by the No. 2 ratio, and of the residual price by the No. 6 ratio yielded initial series. These were scaled by 1.048, the ratio of the national price to the weighted average that emerged using the initial price series, to obtain the final series.

Results, in the form of the aviation and railroad fuel price estimates, appear as Table D.2.2.

Prices For Military and Marine Fuel Use

Data in a number of 1972 issues of Platt's Oilgram [26] led to the estimates that marine diesel fuel had a price that was .88 of No. 2 fuel oil, and that bunker C fuel oil, treated as corresponding to residual fuel in vessel bunkering, had a price that was .82 of No. 6 fuel oil. Level of use then accounted for further price differentials. Household use of marine distillate fuel in recreation boating was treated as a purchase at retail, with price then estimated as .88 of No. 2 fuel oil at the residential level. Business use of distillates was treated as occurring at the "all commercial" level, with a price .85 of the residential level, or .75 of No. 2 fuel oil at the residential level. Marine users of residual fuel were assumed to have a price corresponding to the large industrial level, which implied a final price of .80 times No. 6 fuel oil at the large commercial level (.98 times .82 equals .80).

Military use was assumed to be preponderantly diesel fuel and bunker C fuel oil, under the distillate and residual categories, respectively, and it was further assumed that purchases occurred at the wholesale level. These assumptions implied that the military distillate price was .6 times the No. 2 price, residential level, plus one cent a gallon, while the military residual price was .75 times the No. 6 price, large commercial level.

These estimated scale factors were applied to the No. 2 and No. 6 fuel oil prices, and the resultant price series, in cents per gallon, appear as Table D.2.3.

Expenditures

The prices estimated in the previous section were converted to dollars per barrel and multiplied by the quantities developed earlier to yield expenditures in thousands of dollars. Tables D.3.1 and D.3.2 show expenditures by particular function and fuel type, by state; Table D.3.3 presents the aggregates of those tables, by function, showing the respective expenditures for military, highway, aviation, railroad and vessel bunkering uses; and Table D.3.4 presents expenditures by sector: household, federal government

and business. Tables D.3.5 and D.3.6 are the regional analogues of the
preceding state tables, with the detailed breakdown by function and fuel
type presented in Table D.3.5, and the functional and sectoral aggregates
in Table D.3.6.

Table D.3.6 shows total expenditures of $5.3 billion in 1972; in
conjunction with Table D.1.13, this implies an average cost of $1.21 per
million BTU. The business sector accounted for 87 percent, the federal
government for 12.5 percent, and the household sector for only 0.5 percent
of total expenditures. In terms of the functional classification, highway
use accounted for almost half the total, with 47 percent, followed by
aviation with 33 percent, and then, at some remove, by vessel bunkering
and railroad use, each with only eight percent, and finally, by military
use, which made up the remaining four percent.

Table D.1.1

Transportation And Military Consumption Of Petroleum Products (Non-Gasoline), 1972, In Thousands of Barrels, By State

Military Use Of Distillate And Residual Fuels

REGION AND STATE	DISTILLATES	RESIDUALS	TOTAL
NEW ENGLAND:			
CONNECTICUT	117.0	346.0	463.0
MAINE	606.0	50.0	656.0
MASSACHUSETTS	525.0	1793.0	2318.0
NEW HAMPSHIRE	16.0	40.0	56.0
RHODE ISLAND	75.0	2108.0	2183.0
VERMONT	2.0	2.0	4.0
MID ATLANTIC:			
NEW JERSEY	543.0	3109.0	3652.0
NEW YORK	1493.0	1324.0	2817.0
PENNSYLVANIA	341.0	1985.0	2326.0
EAST NORTH CENTRAL:			
ILLINOIS	419.0	20.0	439.0
INDIANA	46.0	13.0	59.0
MICHIGAN	653.0	5.0	658.0
OHIO	107.0	8.0	115.0
WISCONSIN	149.0	0.0	149.0
WEST NORTH CENTRAL:			
IOWA	9.0	0.0	9.0
KANSAS	113.0	37.0	150.0
MINNESOTA	210.0	0.0	210.0
MISSOURI	32.0	30.0	62.0
NEBRASKA	43.0	0.0	43.0
NORTH DAKOTA	13.0	0.0	13.0
SOUTH DAKOTA	1.0	0.0	1.0
SOUTH ATLANTIC:			
DELAWARE	12.0	104.0	116.0
DISTRICT OF COLUMBIA	22.0	145.0	167.0
FLORIDA	242.0	267.0	509.0
GEORGIA	207.0	155.0	362.0
MARYLAND	597.0	669.0	1266.0
NORTH CAROLINA	324.0	50.0	374.0
SOUTH CAROLINA	292.0	90.0	382.0
VIRGINIA	680.0	8653.0	9333.0
WEST VIRGINIA	3.0	0.0	3.0
EAST SOUTH CENTRAL:			
ALABAMA	675.0	26.0	701.0
KENTUCKY	388.0	0.0	388.0
MISSISSIPPI	70.0	0.0	70.0
TENNESSEE	175.0	0.0	175.0
WEST SOUTH CENTRAL:			
ARKANSAS	155.0	0.0	155.0
LOUISIANA	871.0	569.0	1440.0
OKLAHOMA	41.0	297.0	338.0
TEXAS	2102.0	154.0	2256.0
ROCKY MOUNTAIN:			
ARIZONA	38.0	0.0	38.0
COLORADO	146.0	8.0	154.0
IDAHO	2.0	0.0	2.0
MONTANA	43.0	32.0	75.0
NEVADA	45.0	4.0	49.0
NEW MEXICO	217.0	0.0	217.0
UTAH	103.0	10.0	113.0
WYOMING	9.0	0.0	9.0
FAR WEST:			
ALASKA	560.0	12.0	572.0
CALIFORNIA	5969.0	2126.0	8095.0
HAWAII	146.0	0.0	146.0
OREGON	131.0	108.0	239.0
WASHINGTON	409.0	273.0	682.0

Table D.1.2

Transportation And Military Consumption Of Petroleum Products
(Non-Gasoline), 1972, In Thousands of Barrels, By Region

Military Use Of Distillate And Residual Fuels

REGION	DISTILLATES	RESIDUALS	TOTAL
NEW ENGLAND	1341.00	4339.00	5680.00
MID ATLANTIC	2377.00	6418.00	8795.00
EAST NORTH CENTRAL	1374.00	46.00	1420.00
WEST NORTH CENTRAL	421.00	67.00	488.00
SOUTH ATLANTIC	2379.00	10133.00	12512.00
EAST SOUTH CENTRAL	1308.00	26.00	1334.00
WEST SOUTH CENTRAL	3169.00	1020.00	4189.00
ROCKY MOUNTAIN	603.00	54.00	657.00
FAR WEST	7215.00	2519.00	9734.00
TOTAL	20187.00	24622.00	44809.00

Table D.1.3

Transportation and Military Consumption Of Petroleum Products (Non-Gasoline), 1972,
In Thousand Barrels, By State

Comparison Of Bureau Of Mines (BOM) And Federal Highway Administration (FHWA)
Estimates Of Diesel Fuel And LPG Consumed In Highway Use

REGION and STATE	BUREAU OF MINES (BOM)			FHWA "SPECIAL FUELS" TOTAL	FHWA MINUS BOM	FHWA/BOM
	Diesel Fuel	LPG	Total			
NEW ENGLAND:						
CONNECTICUT	1962.00	65.83	2027.83	2021.43	-6.40	0.997
MAINE	743.00	8.98	751.98	864.29	112.31	1.149
MASSACHUSETTS	2695.00	95.76	2790.76	2740.48	-50.29	0.982
NEW HAMPSHIRE	259.00	14.95	273.95	390.48	116.52	1.425
RHODE ISLAND	544.00	83.79	627.79	566.67	-61.12	0.903
VERMONT	290.00	5.98	295.98	361.90	65.93	1.223
MID ATLANTIC:						
NEW JERSEY	5449.00	281.31	5730.31	6276.19	545.88	1.095
NEW YORK	5964.00	368.10	6332.10	6364.29	32.19	1.005
PENNSYLVANIA	10294.00	410.02	10704.02	12876.19	2172.17	1.203
EAST NORTH CENTRAL:						
ILLINOIS	9768.00	1382.02	11150.02	9966.67	-1183.36	0.894
INDIANA	8070.00	318.43	8388.43	8116.67	-271.76	0.968
MICHIGAN	5713.00	216.79	5929.79	5930.95	1.17	1.000
OHIO	11718.00	460.69	12178.69	11783.33	-395.36	0.968
WISCONSIN	3859.00	250.67	4109.67	3883.33	-226.33	0.945
WEST NORTH CENTRAL:						
IOWA	4110.00	149.05	4259.05	4250.00	-9.05	0.998
KANSAS	2909.00	983.55	3892.55	3038.10	-854.45	0.780
MINNESOTA	3567.00	284.55	3851.55	3638.10	-213.45	0.945
MISSOURI	5575.00	216.79	5791.79	5647.62	-144.17	0.975
NEBRASKA	2206.00	596.19	2802.19	2352.38	-449.81	0.839
NORTH DAKOTA	1126.00	6.79	1132.79	909.52	-223.26	0.803
SOUTH DAKOTA	858.00	165.90	1023.90	897.62	-126.29	0.877
SOUTH ATLANTIC:						
DELAWARE	260.00	59.86	319.86	369.05	49.19	1.154
DISTRICT OF COLUMBIA	339.00	15.95	354.95	397.62	42.67	1.120
FLORIDA	5065.00	537.50	5602.50	6352.38	749.88	1.134
GEORGIA	6315.00	275.33	6590.33	7114.29	523.95	1.080
MARYLAND	2087.00	97.76	2184.76	2492.86	308.10	1.141
NORTH CAROLINA	4367.00	248.74	4615.74	5492.86	877.12	1.190
SOUTH CAROLINA	2150.00	221.45	2371.45	2971.43	599.98	1.253
VIRGINIA	4805.00	173.57	4978.57	5666.67	688.10	1.138
WEST VIRGINIA	2164.00	41.90	2205.90	2207.14	1.24	1.001
EAST SOUTH CENTRAL:						
ALABAMA	3810.00	308.64	4118.64	3933.33	-185.31	0.955
KENTUCKY	3494.00	162.60	3656.60	3521.43	-135.17	0.963
MISSISSIPPI	2684.00	1426.02	4110.02	2814.29	-1295.74	0.685
TENNESSEE	5387.00	230.36	5617.36	5416.67	-200.69	0.964
WEST SOUTH CENTRAL:						
ARKANSAS	2755.00	2367.24	5122.24	3140.48	-1981.76	0.613
LOUISIANA	3003.00	1020.71	4023.71	3161.90	-861.81	0.786
OKLAHOMA	3370.00	1411.67	4781.67	3640.48	-1141.19	0.761
TEXAS	13994.00	16670.14	30664.14	14200.00	-16464.14	0.463
ROCKY MOUNTAIN:						
ARIZONA	3462.00	204.02	3666.02	3019.05	-646.98	0.824
COLORADO	1847.00	585.19	2432.19	2147.62	-284.57	0.883
IDAHO	879.00	52.88	931.88	809.52	-122.36	0.869
MONTANA	1507.00	198.86	1705.86	1645.24	-60.62	0.964
NEVADA	855.00	22.57	877.57	1057.14	179.57	1.205
NEW MEXICO	2159.00	817.43	2976.43	2273.81	-702.62	0.764
UTAH	1446.00	22.67	1468.67	1452.38	-16.29	0.989
WYOMING	1030.00	397.76	1427.76	1121.43	-306.33	0.785
FAR WEST:						
ALASKA	316.00	0.00	316.00	273.81	-42.19	0.866
CALIFORNIA	15945.00	1076.50	17021.50	16890.48	-131.02	0.992
HAWAII	230.00	54.14	284.14	252.38	-31.76	0.888
OREGON	3093.00	49.69	3142.69	3261.90	119.21	1.038
WASHINGTON	2558.00	101.52	2659.52	2871.43	211.90	1.080

Table D.1.4

Transportation And Military Consumption Of Petroleum Products (Non-Gasoline), 1972,
In Thousands Of Barrels, By State

Revision Of Estimated Highway Use Of LPG And Special Fuels Total

REGION AND STATE	LPG DIESEL (BOM data)	LPG TRANSFER OUT (other uses)	REVISED LPG	REVISED TOTAL, SPECIAL FUELS
NEW ENGLAND:				
CONNECTICUT	0.034	0.000	65.830	2027.830
MAINE	0.012	0.000	8.980	751.980
MASSACHUSETTS	0.036	0.000	95.760	2790.760
NEW HAMPSHIRE	0.058	0.000	14.950	273.950
RHODE ISLAND	0.154	0.000	83.790	627.790
VERMONT	0.021	0.000	5.980	295.980
MID ATLANTIC:				
NEW JERSEY	0.052	0.000	281.310	5730.310
NEW YORK	0.062	0.000	368.100	6332.100
PENNSYLVANIA	0.040	0.000	410.020	10704.020
EAST NORTH CENTRAL:				
ILLINOIS	0.141	0.000	1382.020	11150.020
INDIANA	0.039	0.000	318.430	8388.430
MICHIGAN	0.038	0.000	216.790	5929.790
OHIO	0.039	0.000	460.690	12178.690
WISCONSIN	0.065	0.000	250.670	4109.670
WEST NORTH CENTRAL:				
IOWA	0.036	0.000	149.050	4259.050
KANSAS	0.338	0.000	983.550	3892.550
MINNESOTA	0.080	0.000	284.550	3851.550
MISSOURI	0.039	0.000	216.790	5791.790
NEBRASKA	0.270	0.000	596.190	2802.190
NORTH DAKOTA	0.006	0.000	6.790	1132.790
SOUTH DAKOTA	0.193	0.000	165.900	1023.900
SOUTH ATLANTIC:				
DELAWARE	0.230	0.000	59.860	319.860
DISTRICT OF COLUMBIA	0.047	0.000	15.950	354.950
FLORIDA	0.106	0.000	537.500	5602.500
GEORGIA	0.044	0.000	275.330	6590.330
MARYLAND	0.047	0.000	97.760	2184.760
NORTH CAROLINA	0.057	0.000	248.740	4615.740
SOUTH CAROLINA	0.103	0.000	221.450	2371.450
VIRGINIA	0.036	0.000	173.570	4978.570
WEST VIRGINIA	0.019	0.000	41.900	2205.900
EAST SOUTH CENTRAL:				
ALABAMA	0.081	0.000	308.640	4118.640
KENTUCKY	0.047	0.000	162.600	3656.600
MISSISSIPPI	0.531	513.460	912.560	3596.560
TENNESSEE	0.043	0.000	230.360	5617.360
WEST SOUTH CENTRAL:				
ARKANSAS	0.859	1430.540	936.700	3691.700
LOUISIANA	0.340	0.000	1020.710	4023.710
OKLAHOMA	0.419	265.870	1145.800	4515.800
TEXAS	1.191	11072.540	5597.600	19591.600
ROCKY MOUNTAIN:				
ARIZONA	0.059	0.000	204.020	3666.020
COLORADO	0.317	0.000	585.190	2432.190
IDAHO	0.060	0.000	52.880	931.880
MONTANA	0.132	0.000	198.860	1705.860
NEVADA	0.026	0.000	22.570	877.570
NEW MEXICO	0.379	0.000	817.430	2976.430
UTAH	0.016	0.000	22.670	1468.670
WYOMING	0.386	0.000	397.760	1427.760
FAR WEST:				
ALASKA	0.000	0.000	0.000	316.000
CALIFORNIA	0.068	0.000	1076.500	17021.500
HAWAII	0.235	0.000	54.140	284.140
OREGON	0.016	0.000	49.690	3142.690
WASHINGTON	0.040	0.000	101.520	2659.520

Table D.1.5

Transportation And Military Consumption Of Petroleum Products (Non-Gasoline), 1972, In Thousands Of Barrels, By Region

Comparison Of Bureau Of Mines (BOM) And Federal Highway Administration (FHWA) Estimates Of Diesel Fuel And LPG Consumed In Highway Use, And Revised Estimates Of Use Of LPG And Special Fuels Total

REGION	BUREAU OF MINES			FHWA "SPECIAL FUELS" TOTAL	FHWA MINUS BOM	FHWA/BOM
	Diesel	LPG	Total			
NEW ENGLAND	6493.00	275.29	6768.29	6945.25	176.95	1.026
MID ATLANTIC	21707.00	1059.43	22766.43	25516.67	2750.24	1.121
EAST NORTH CENTRAL	39128.00	2628.60	41756.60	39680.95	-2075.64	0.950
WEST NORTH CENTRAL	20351.00	2402.82	22753.82	20733.34	-2020.48	0.911
SOUTH ATLANTIC	27552.00	1672.06	29224.06	33064.30	3840.23	1.131
EAST SOUTH CENTRAL	15375.00	2127.62	17502.62	15685.72	-1816.91	0.896
WEST SOUTH CENTRAL	23122.00	21469.76	44591.76	24142.86	-20448.90	0.541
ROCKY MOUNTAIN	13185.00	2301.38	15486.38	13526.19	-1960.20	0.873
FAR WEST	22142.00	1281.85	23423.85	23550.00	126.14	1.005
TOTAL	189055.00	35218.81	224273.81	202845.28	-21428.57	0.904

REGION	LPG TRANSFER OUT	REVISED LPG	REVISED TOTAL
NEW ENGLAND	0.00	275.29	6768.29
MID ATLANTIC	0.00	1059.43	22766.43
EAST NORTH CENTRAL	0.00	2628.60	41756.60
WEST NORTH CENTRAL	0.00	2402.82	22753.82
SOUTH ATLANTIC	0.00	1672.06	29224.06
EAST SOUTH CENTRAL	513.46	1614.16	16989.16
WEST SOUTH CENTRAL	12768.95	8700.81	31822.81
ROCKY MOUNTAIN	0.00	2301.38	15486.38
FAR WEST	0.00	1281.85	23423.85
TOTAL	13282.41	21936.40	210991.40

Table D.1.6

Transportation And Military Consumption Of Petroleum Products (Non-Gasoline), 1972, In Thousands Of Barrels, By State

Civilian Aviation Use Of Jet Fuel

REGION AND STATE	SCALED ESTIMATES TO YIELD BOM TOTALS BY P.A.D. DISTRICT					FINAL ESTIMATES (Districts Combined)
	P.A.D. I	P.A.D. II	P.A.D. III	P.A.D. IV	P.A.D. V	
NEW ENGLAND:						
CONNECTICUT	2282.59	0.00	0.00	0.00	0.00	2282.59
MAINE	684.94	0.00	0.00	0.00	0.00	684.94
MASSACHUSETTS	8042.06	0.00	0.00	0.00	0.00	8042.06
NEW HAMPSHIRE	31.07	0.00	0.00	0.00	0.00	31.07
RHODE ISLAND	134.76	0.00	0.00	0.00	0.00	134.76
VERMONT	50.64	0.00	0.00	0.00	0.00	50.64
MID ATLANTIC:						
NEW JERSEY	5290.60	0.00	0.00	0.00	0.00	5290.60
NEW YORK	35887.53	0.00	0.00	0.00	0.00	35887.53
PENNSYLVANIA	7701.71	0.00	0.00	0.00	0.00	7701.71
EAST NORTH CENTRAL:						
ILLINOIS	0.00	24687.25	0.00	0.00	0.00	24687.25
INDIANA	0.00	2199.92	0.00	0.00	0.00	2199.92
MICHIGAN	0.00	4109.09	0.00	0.00	0.00	4109.09
OHIO	0.00	5281.97	0.00	0.00	0.00	5281.97
WISCONSIN	0.00	1730.39	0.00	0.00	0.00	1730.39
WEST NORTH CENTRAL:						
IOWA	0.00	547.04	0.00	0.00	0.00	547.04
KANSAS	0.00	617.52	0.00	0.00	0.00	617.52
MINNESOTA	0.00	4193.95	0.00	0.00	0.00	4193.95
MISSOURI	0.00	7834.10	0.00	0.00	0.00	7834.10
NEBRASKA	0.00	668.64	0.00	0.00	0.00	668.64
NORTH DAKOTA	0.00	227.40	0.00	0.00	0.00	227.40
SOUTH DAKOTA	0.00	147.94	0.00	0.00	0.00	147.94
SOUTH ATLANTIC:						
DELAWARE	58.34	0.00	0.00	0.00	0.00	58.34
DISTRICT OF COLUMBIA	2.68	0.00	0.00	0.00	0.00	2.68
FLORIDA	21329.51	0.00	0.00	0.00	0.00	21329.51
GEORGIA	9392.70	0.00	0.00	0.00	0.00	9392.70
MARYLAND	2242.25	0.00	0.00	0.00	0.00	2242.25
NORTH CAROLINA	1243.47	0.00	0.00	0.00	0.00	1243.47
SOUTH CAROLINA	437.69	0.00	0.00	0.00	0.00	437.69
VIRGINIA	8119.64	0.00	0.00	0.00	0.00	8119.64
WEST VIRGINIA	83.86	0.00	0.00	0.00	0.00	83.86
EAST SOUTH CENTRAL:						
ALABAMA	0.00	0.00	688.06	0.00	0.00	688.06
KENTUCKY	0.00	1809.01	0.00	0.00	0.00	1809.01
MISSISSIPPI	0.00	0.00	296.47	0.00	0.00	296.47
TENNESSEE	0.00	2987.19	0.00	0.00	0.00	2987.19
WEST SOUTH CENTRAL:						
ARKANSAS	0.00	0.00	258.20	0.00	0.00	258.20
LOUISIANA	0.00	0.00	3137.54	0.00	0.00	3137.54
OKLAHOMA	0.00	1625.49	0.00	0.00	0.00	1625.49
TEXAS	0.00	0.00	15685.08	0.00	0.00	15685.08
ROCKY MOUNTAIN:						
ARIZONA	0.00	0.00	0.00	0.00	2626.09	2626.09
COLORADO	0.00	0.00	0.00	5723.75	0.00	5723.75
IDAHO	0.00	0.00	0.00	178.46	0.00	178.46
MONTANA	0.00	0.00	0.00	427.22	0.00	427.22
NEVADA	0.00	0.00	0.00	0.00	3040.00	3040.00
NEW MEXICO	0.00	0.00	857.68	0.00	0.00	857.68
UTAH	0.00	0.00	0.00	901.21	0.00	901.21
WYOMING	0.00	0.00	0.00	93.33	0.00	93.33
FAR WEST:						
ALASKA	0.00	0.00	0.00	0.00	6139.76	6139.76
CALIFORNIA	0.00	0.00	0.00	0.00	44919.88	44919.88
HAWAII	0.00	0.00	0.00	0.00	12775.00	12775.00
OREGON	0.00	0.00	0.00	0.00	1790.77	1790.77
WASHINGTON	0.00	0.00	0.00	0.00	7175.46	7175.46

Table D.1.7

Transportation and Military Consumption Of Petroleum Products (Non-Gasoline), 1972,
    In Thousands Of Barrels, By State

Military Aviation Use Of Jet Fuel

REGION AND STATE	ESTIMATED USE BY P.A.D. DISTRICT					FINAL ESTIMATES
	P.A.D. I	P.A.D. II	P.A.D. III	P.A.D. IV	P.A.D. V	(Districts) Combined)
NEW ENGLAND:						
CONNECTICUT	651.66	0.00	0.00	0.00	0.00	651.66
MAINE	3375.29	0.00	0.00	0.00	0.00	3375.29
MASSACHUSETTS	2924.14	0.00	0.00	0.00	0.00	2924.14
NEW HAMPSHIRE	89.11	0.00	0.00	0.00	0.00	89.11
RHODE ISLAND	417.73	0.00	0.00	0.00	0.00	417.73
VERMONT	11.14	0.00	0.00	0.00	0.00	11.14
MID ATLANTIC:						
NEW JERSEY	3024.39	0.00	0.00	0.00	0.00	3024.39
NEW YORK	8315.68	0.00	0.00	0.00	0.00	8315.68
PENNSYLVANIA	1899.29	0.00	0.00	0.00	0.00	1899.29
EAST NORTH CENTRAL:						
ILLINOIS	0.00	2977.37	0.00	0.00	0.00	2977.37
INDIANA	0.00	326.87	0.00	0.00	0.00	326.87
MICHIGAN	0.00	4640.15	0.00	0.00	0.00	4640.15
OHIO	0.00	760.33	0.00	0.00	0.00	760.33
WISCONSIN	0.00	1058.78	0.00	0.00	0.00	1058.78
WEST NORTH CENTRAL:						
IOWA	0.00	63.95	0.00	0.00	0.00	63.95
KANSAS	0.00	802.97	0.00	0.00	0.00	802.97
MINNESOTA	0.00	1492.24	0.00	0.00	0.00	1492.24
MISSOURI	0.00	227.39	0.00	0.00	0.00	227.39
NEBRASKA	0.00	305.55	0.00	0.00	0.00	305.55
NORTH DAKOTA	0.00	92.38	0.00	0.00	0.00	92.38
SOUTH DAKOTA	0.00	7.11	0.00	0.00	0.00	7.11
SOUTH ATLANTIC:						
DELAWARE	66.83	0.00	0.00	0.00	0.00	66.83
DISTRICT OF COLUMBIA	122.54	0.00	0.00	0.00	0.00	122.54
FLORIDA	1347.89	0.00	0.00	0.00	0.00	1347.89
GEORGIA	1152.95	0.00	0.00	0.00	0.00	1152.95
MARYLAND	3325.16	0.00	0.00	0.00	0.00	3325.16
NORTH CAROLINA	1804.61	0.00	0.00	0.00	0.00	1804.61
SOUTH CAROLINA	1626.37	0.00	0.00	0.00	0.00	1626.37
VIRGINIA	3787.45	0.00	0.00	0.00	0.00	3787.45
WEST VIRGINIA	16.71	0.00	0.00	0.00	0.00	16.71
EAST SOUTH CENTRAL:						
ALABAMA	0.00	0.00	2230.61	0.00	0.00	2230.61
KENTUCKY	0.00	2757.09	0.00	0.00	0.00	2757.09
MISSISSIPPI	0.00	0.00	231.32	0.00	0.00	231.32
TENNESSEE	0.00	1243.53	0.00	0.00	0.00	1243.53
WEST SOUTH CENTRAL:						
ARKANSAS	0.00	0.00	512.21	0.00	0.00	512.21
LOUISIANA	0.00	0.00	2878.31	0.00	0.00	2878.31
OKLAHOMA	0.00	291.34	0.00	0.00	0.00	291.34
TEXAS	0.00	0.00	6946.27	0.00	0.00	6946.27
ROCKY MOUNTAIN:						
ARIZONA	0.00	0.00	0.00	0.00	196.12	196.12
COLORADO	0.00	0.00	0.00	1428.68	0.00	1428.68
IDAHO	0.00	0.00	0.00	19.57	0.00	19.57
MONTANA	0.00	0.00	0.00	420.78	0.00	420.78
NEVADA	0.00	0.00	0.00	0.00	232.25	232.25
NEW MEXICO	0.00	0.00	717.10	0.00	0.00	717.10
UTAH	0.00	0.00	0.00	1007.91	0.00	1007.91
WYOMING	0.00	0.00	0.00	88.07	0.00	88.07
FAR WEST:						
ALASKA	0.00	0.00	0.00	0.00	2890.22	2890.22
CALIFORNIA	0.00	0.00	0.00	0.00	30806.61	30806.61
HAWAII	0.00	0.00	0.00	0.00	753.52	753.52
OREGON	0.00	0.00	0.00	0.00	676.10	676.10
WASHINGTON	0.00	0.00	0.00	0.00	2110.89	2110.89

Table D.1.8

Transportation And Military Consumption Of Petroleum Products (Non-Gasoline), 1972,
   In Thousands Of Barrels, By Region

Civilian And Military Aviation Use Of Jet Fuel

CIVILIAN AVIATION

REGION	SCALED ESTIMATES TO YIELD BOM TOTALS BY P.A.D. DISTRICT					FINAL ESTIMATED CIVILIAN USE
	P.A.D. I	P.A.D. II	P.A.D. III	P.A.D. IV	P.A.D. V	
NEW ENGLAND	11226.08	0.00	0.00	0.00	0.00	11226.08
MID ATLANTIC	48879.84	0.00	0.00	0.00	0.00	48879.84
EAST NORTH CENTRAL	0.00	38008.62	0.00	0.00	0.00	38008.62
WEST NORTH CENTRAL	0.00	14236.59	0.00	0.00	0.00	14236.59
SOUTH ATLANTIC	42910.14	0.00	0.00	0.00	0.00	42910.14
EAST SOUTH CENTRAL	0.00	4796.20	984.53	0.00	0.00	5780.73
WEST SOUTH CENTRAL	0.00	1625.49	19080.82	0.00	0.00	20706.31
ROCKY MOUNTAIN	0.00	0.00	857.68	7323.97	5666.09	13847.74
FAR WEST	0.00	0.00	0.00	0.00	72800.87	72800.87
TOTAL	103016.06	58666.90	20923.03	7323.97	78466.96	268396.92

MILITARY AVIATION

REGION	ESTIMATED USE BY P.A.D. DISTRICTS					FINAL ESTIMATED MILITARY USE
	P.A.D. I	P.A.D. II	P.A.D. III	P.A.D. IV	P.A.D. V	
NEW ENGLAND	7469.07	0.00	0.00	0.00	0.00	7469.07
MID ATLANTIC	13239.36	0.00	0.00	0.00	0.00	13239.36
EAST NORTH CENTRAL	0.00	9763.50	0.00	0.00	0.00	9763.50
WEST NORTH CENTRAL	0.00	2991.59	0.00	0.00	0.00	2991.59
SOUTH ATLANTIC	13250.51	0.00	0.00	0.00	0.00	13250.51
EAST SOUTH CENTRAL	0.00	4000.62	2461.93	0.00	0.00	6462.55
WEST SOUTH CENTRAL	0.00	291.34	10336.79	0.00	0.00	10628.13
ROCKY MOUNTAIN	0.00	0.00	717.10	2965.01	428.37	4110.48
FAR WEST	0.00	0.00	0.00	0.00	37237.34	37237.34
TOTAL	33958.94	17047.05	13515.82	2965.01	37665.71	105152.53

Table D.1.9

Transportation And Military Consumption Of Petroleum Products (Non-Gasoline), 1972,
   In Thousands Of Barrels, By State

Railroad And Vessel Bunkering Use Of Fuel Oil

REGION AND STATE	RAILROAD USE			VESSEL BUNKERING USE			
	Distillates	Residuals	Total	Distillates		Residuals (Business)	Total
				Household	Business		
NEW ENGLAND:							
CONNECTICUT	385.0	0.0	385.0	5.9	35.1	191.0	232.0
MAINE	220.0	0.0	220.0	8.0	47.0	3399.0	3454.0
MASSACHUSETTS	632.0	0.0	632.0	30.7	181.3	1262.0	1474.0
NEW HAMPSHIRE	17.0	0.0	17.0	0.0	0.0	0.0	0.0
RHODE ISLAND	20.0	13.0	33.0	5.4	31.6	113.0	150.0
VERMONT	55.0	0.0	55.0	1.3	7.7	0.0	9.0
MID ATLANTIC:							
NEW JERSEY	1095.0	1.0	1096.0	249.7	1472.3	8603.0	10325.0
NEW YORK	2115.0	98.0	2213.0	92.2	543.8	13687.0	14323.0
PENNSYLVANIA	3216.0	57.0	3273.0	47.1	277.9	3119.0	3444.0
EAST NORTH CENTRAL:							
ILLINOIS	7276.0	117.0	7393.0	177.0	1044.0	92.0	1313.0
INDIANA	2390.0	0.0	2390.0	28.6	168.4	166.0	363.0
MICHIGAN	1926.0	88.0	2014.0	16.2	95.8	189.0	301.0
OHIO	3988.0	0.0	3988.0	46.3	272.7	196.0	515.0
WISCONSIN	978.0	51.0	1029.0	2.2	12.8	3.0	18.0
WEST NORTH CENTRAL:							
IOWA	1323.0	0.0	1323.0	2.3	13.7	0.0	16.0
KANSAS	2145.0	26.0	2171.0	0.4	2.6	0.0	3.0
MINNESOTA	1482.0	7.0	1489.0	5.9	35.1	110.0	151.0
MISSOURI	2915.0	4.0	2919.0	62.8	370.2	20.0	453.0
NEBRASKA	2519.0	180.0	2699.0	0.0	0.0	0.0	0.0
NORTH DAKOTA	695.0	0.0	695.0	0.0	0.0	0.0	0.0
SOUTH DAKOTA	171.0	0.0	171.0	0.0	0.0	0.0	0.0
SOUTH ATLANTIC:							
DELAWARE	18.0	34.0	52.0	2.6	15.4	793.0	811.0
DISTRICT OF COLUMBIA	165.0	2.0	167.0	0.1	0.9	0.0	1.0
FLORIDA	2365.0	0.0	2365.0	44.2	260.8	1521.0	1826.0
GEORGIA	2500.0	0.0	2500.0	7.3	42.7	83.0	133.0
MARYLAND	1028.0	2.0	1030.0	59.2	348.8	2642.0	3050.0
NORTH CAROLINA	1580.0	5.0	1585.0	12.0	71.0	78.0	161.0
SOUTH CAROLINA	421.0	2.0	423.0	7.4	43.6	1009.0	1060.0
VIRGINIA	2685.0	7.0	2692.0	57.9	341.1	2496.0	2895.0
WEST VIRGINIA	715.0	0.0	715.0	34.4	202.6	0.0	237.0
EAST SOUTH CENTRAL:							
ALABAMA	2219.0	0.0	2219.0	83.8	494.2	1454.0	2032.0
KENTUCKY	1242.0	0.0	1242.0	128.5	757.5	4.0	890.0
MISSISSIPPI	444.0	0.0	444.0	113.4	668.6	154.0	936.0
TENNESSEE	2276.0	0.0	2276.0	206.3	1216.7	0.0	1423.0
WEST SOUTH CENTRAL:							
ARKANSAS	1651.0	0.0	1651.0	26.4	155.6	0.0	182.0
LOUISIANA	1401.0	0.0	1401.0	812.1	4788.9	5746.0	11347.0
OKLAHOMA	254.0	0.0	254.0	0.0	0.0	0.0	0.0
TEXAS	10454.0	14.0	10468.0	517.1	3048.9	9559.0	13125.0
ROCKY MOUNTAIN:							
ARIZONA	921.0	0.0	921.0	0.0	0.0	0.0	0.0
COLORADO	1518.0	22.0	1540.0	0.0	0.0	0.0	0.0
IDAHO	647.0	0.0	647.0	0.0	0.0	0.0	0.0
MONTANA	1808.0	32.0	1840.0	0.0	0.0	0.0	0.0
NEVADA	279.0	0.0	279.0	0.0	0.0	0.0	0.0
NEW MEXICO	1580.0	0.0	1580.0	0.0	0.0	0.0	0.0
UTAH	1470.0	20.0	1490.0	0.0	0.0	0.0	0.0
WYOMING	2332.0	244.0	2576.0	0.0	0.0	0.0	0.0
FAR WEST:							
ALASKA	103.0	6.0	109.0	180.4	1063.6	226.0	1470.0
CALIFORNIA	8806.0	57.0	8863.0	211.3	1245.7	18897.0	20354.0
HAWAII	0.0	8.0	8.0	48.7	287.3	1289.0	1625.0
OREGON	2775.0	29.0	2804.0	44.7	263.3	137.0	445.0
WASHINGTON	1281.0	11.0	1292.0	118.3	697.7	694.0	1510.0

Table D.1.10

Transportation And Military Consumption Of Petroleum Products (Non-Gasoline), 1972,
In Thousands Of Barrels, By Region

Railroad And Vessel Bunkering Use Of Fuel Oil

| REGION | RAILROAD USE | | | VESSEL BUNKERING USE | | | |
| | Distillates | Residuals | Total | Distillates | | Residuals (Business) | Total |
				Household	Business		
NEW ENGLAND	1329.00	13.00	1342.00	51.30	302.70	4965.00	5319.00
MID ATLANTIC	6426.00	156.00	6582.00	389.00	2294.00	25409.00	28092.00
EAST NORTH CENTRAL	16558.00	256.00	16814.00	270.30	1593.70	646.00	2510.00
WEST NORTH CENTRAL	11250.00	217.00	11467.00	71.40	421.60	130.00	623.00
SOUTH ATLANTIC	11477.00	52.00	11529.00	225.10	1326.90	8622.00	10174.00
EAST SOUTH CENTRAL	6181.00	0.00	6181.00	532.00	3137.00	1612.00	5281.00
WEST SOUTH CENTRAL	13760.00	14.00	13774.00	1355.60	7993.40	15305.00	24654.00
ROCKY MOUNTAIN	10555.00	318.00	10873.00	0.00	0.00	0.00	0.00
FAR WEST	12965.00	111.00	13076.00	603.40	3557.60	21243.00	25404.00
TOTAL	90501.00	1137.00	91638.00	3498.10	20626.90	77932.00	102057.00

Table D.1.11

Transportation and Military Consumption Of Petroleum Products (Non-Gasoline), 1972, In Billion BTU, By State

Distribution Of Use By Function

REGION AND STATE	MILITARY USE	HIGHWAY USE	AVIATION USE	RAILROAD USE	VESSEL BUNKERING	TOTAL
NEW ENGLAND:						
CONNECTICUT	2856.8	11692.7	16490.6	2242.6	1439.6	34722.3
MAINE	3844.3	4364.0	22351.1	1281.5	21689.9	53530.8
MASSACHUSETTS	14330.7	16082.5	61538.1	3681.4	9169.1	104801.8
NEW HAMPSHIRE	344.7	1568.6	663.6	99.0	0.0	2675.9
RHODE ISLAND	13689.9	3504.9	3049.2	198.2	926.0	21368.2
VERMONT	24.2	1713.2	347.7	320.4	52.4	2457.9
MID ATLANTIC:						
NEW JERSEY	22709.3	32868.8	46507.9	6384.7	64117.7	172588.4
NEW YORK	17020.7	36216.7	248706.9	12936.0	89754.9	404635.2
PENNSYLVANIA	14466.7	61607.1	54001.9	19091.6	21502.3	170669.6
EAST NORTH CENTRAL:						
ILLINOIS	2566.4	62441.9	155910.7	43118.3	7690.7	271728.0
INDIANA	349.7	48285.0	14223.4	13921.7	2191.2	78971.0
MICHIGAN	3835.2	34147.8	48165.6	11772.2	1840.6	99761.4
OHIO	674.3	70105.2	34018.9	23230.1	3090.4	131118.9
WISCONSIN	867.9	23484.1	15484.6	6017.5	106.2	45960.3
WEST NORTH CENTRAL:						
IOWA	52.4	24538.6	3443.9	7706.5	93.2	35834.6
KANSAS	890.8	20889.9	7804.6	12658.1	17.5	42260.9
MINNESOTA	1223.3	21919.1	31773.9	8676.7	930.4	64523.4
MISSOURI	375.0	33343.9	45630.3	17005.0	2648.0	99002.2
NEBRASKA	250.5	15241.3	5428.3	15804.8	0.0	36724.9
NORTH DAKOTA	75.7	6586.2	1784.3	4048.4	0.0	12494.6
SOUTH DAKOTA	5.8	5663.3	876.8	996.1	0.0	7542.0
SOUTH ATLANTIC:						
DELAWARE	723.7	1754.6	696.1	318.6	5090.4	8583.4
DISTRICT OF COLUMBIA	1039.8	2038.7	685.8	973.7	5.8	4743.8
FLORIDA	3088.3	31659.5	128144.7	13776.1	11339.2	188007.8
GEORGIA	2180.3	37889.2	59491.6	14562.5	813.1	114936.7
MARYLAND	7683.5	12548.9	30894.2	6000.7	18986.9	76114.2
NORTH CAROLINA	2201.6	26435.5	16917.2	9234.9	973.9	55763.1
SOUTH CAROLINA	2266.7	13412.0	11379.3	2464.9	6640.7	36163.6
VIRGINIA	58362.4	28685.3	66702.1	15684.1	18016.5	187450.4
WEST VIRGINIA	17.5	12773.4	566.3	4164.9	1380.5	18902.6
EAST SOUTH CENTRAL:						
ALABAMA	4095.3	23431.2	15966.7	12925.7	12508.1	68927.0
KENTUCKY	2260.1	21004.7	25033.3	7234.6	5186.1	60718.8
MISSISSIPPI	407.7	19294.6	2932.2	2586.3	5523.3	30744.1
TENNESSEE	1019.4	32303.2	23599.7	13257.7	8289.0	78469.0
WEST SOUTH CENTRAL:						
ARKANSAS	902.9	19805.0	4234.5	9617.1	1060.1	35619.6
LOUISIANA	8650.9	21586.5	33358.6	8160.8	68750.9	140507.7
OKLAHOMA	2106.1	24226.1	10776.5	1479.6	0.0	38588.3
TEXAS	13213.2	103967.0	126506.8	60982.6	80869.4	385539.0
ROCKY MOUNTAIN:						
ARIZONA	221.4	20984.5	15918.8	5364.8	0.0	42489.5
COLORADO	900.7	13106.0	40151.4	8980.7	0.0	63138.8
IDAHO	11.6	5332.3	1117.3	3768.8	0.0	10230.0
MONTANA	451.7	9575.9	4689.5	10732.8	0.0	25449.9
NEVADA	287.3	5070.9	18456.3	1625.2	0.0	25439.7
NEW MEXICO	1264.0	15854.9	8741.8	9203.5	0.0	35064.2
UTAH	662.8	8513.9	10540.5	8688.5	0.0	28405.7
WYOMING	52.4	7595.2	1003.7	15117.9	0.0	23769.2
FAR WEST:						
ALASKA	3337.4	1840.7	50463.4	637.7	8667.2	64946.4
CALIFORNIA	48136.6	97197.5	421825.5	51653.3	127292.5	746105.4
HAWAII	850.4	1556.9	76347.0	50.3	10061.1	88865.7
OREGON	1442.1	18216.0	13809.5	16346.7	2655.4	52469.7
WASHINGTON	4098.8	15307.5	52075.2	7531.0	9116.4	88128.9

Table D.1.12

Transportation And Military Consumption Of Petroleum Products (Non-Gasoline), 1972,
    In Billion BTU, By State

Distribution Of Use By Sector

REGION AND STATE	HOUSEHOLD	BUSINESS	FEDERAL GOVT.	TOTAL
NEW ENGLAND:				
CONNECTICUT	34.4	28264.5	6423.4	34722.3
MAINE	46.6	31166.9	22317.3	53530.8
MASSACHUSETTS	178.8	74288.5	30334.5	104801.8
NEW HAMPSHIRE	0.0	1843.5	832.4	2675.9
RHODE ISLAND	31.5	5360.6	15976.1	21368.2
VERMONT	7.6	2365.1	85.2	2457.9
MID ATLANTIC:				
NEW JERSEY	1454.5	131872.2	39261.7	172588.4
NEW YORK	537.1	341565.7	62532.4	404635.2
PENNSYLVANIA	274.4	145533.7	24861.5	170669.6
EAST NORTH CENTRAL:				
ILLINOIS	1031.0	252171.9	18525.1	271728.0
INDIANA	166.6	76702.7	2101.7	78971.0
MICHIGAN	94.4	70960.6	28706.4	99761.4
OHIO	269.7	126099.5	4749.7	131118.9
WISCONSIN	12.8	39404.5	6543.0	45960.3
WEST NORTH CENTRAL:				
IOWA	13.4	35426.0	395.2	35834.6
KANSAS	2.3	37063.8	5194.8	42260.9
MINNESOTA	34.4	55267.3	9221.7	64523.4
MISSOURI	365.8	97042.6	1593.8	99002.2
NEBRASKA	0.0	34836.7	1888.2	36724.9
NORTH DAKOTA	0.0	11923.7	570.9	12494.6
SOUTH DAKOTA	0.0	7498.1	43.9	7542.0
SOUTH ATLANTIC:				
DELAWARE	15.1	7478.8	1089.5	8583.4
DISTRICT OF COLUMBIA	0.6	3032.8	1710.4	4743.8
FLORIDA	257.5	177285.0	10465.3	188007.8
GEORGIA	42.5	106403.8	8490.4	114936.7
MARYLAND	344.8	49887.3	25882.1	76114.2
NORTH CAROLINA	69.9	43614.9	12078.3	55763.1
SOUTH CAROLINA	43.1	24952.6	11167.9	36163.6
VIRGINIA	337.3	108022.0	79091.1	187450.4
WEST VIRGINIA	200.4	18593.3	108.9	18902.6
EAST SOUTH CENTRAL:				
ALABAMA	488.1	52278.2	16160.7	68927.0
KENTUCKY	748.5	42932.2	17038.1	60718.8
MISSISSIPPI	660.6	28424.5	1659.0	30744.1
TENNESSEE	1201.7	69582.6	7684.7	78469.0
WEST SOUTH CENTRAL:				
ARKANSAS	153.8	31792.4	3673.4	35619.6
LOUISIANA	4730.5	111557.5	24219.7	140507.7
OKLAHOMA	0.0	34920.7	3667.6	38588.3
TEXAS	3012.1	331741.3	50785.6	385539.0
ROCKY MOUNTAIN:				
ARIZONA	0.0	41199.9	1289.6	42489.5
COLORADO	0.0	54540.3	8598.5	63138.8
IDAHO	0.0	10112.9	117.1	10230.0
MONTANA	0.0	22731.1	2718.8	25449.9
NEVADA	0.0	23887.4	1552.3	25439.7
NEW MEXICO	0.0	29921.4	5142.8	35064.2
UTAH	0.0	22312.2	6093.5	28405.7
WYOMING	0.0	23242.3	526.9	23769.2
FAR WEST:				
ALASKA	1050.8	44815.1	19080.5	64946.4
CALIFORNIA	1230.8	528934.4	215940.2	746105.4
HAWAII	283.7	83627.1	4954.9	88865.7
OREGON	260.4	47084.5	5124.8	52469.7
WASHINGTON	689.1	71843.0	15596.8	88128.9

Table D.1.13

Transportation and Military Consumption of Petroleum Products (Non-Gasoline), 1972, In Billion BTU, By Region

Distribution Of Use By Function And Sector

FUNCTIONAL DISTRIBUTION

REGION	MILITARY USE	HIGHWAY USE	AVIATION USE	RAILROAD USE	VESSEL BUNKERING	TOTAL
NEW ENGLAND	35090.60	38925.90	104440.30	7823.10	33277.00	219556.90
MID ATLANTIC	54196.70	130692.60	349216.70	38412.30	175374.90	747893.21
EAST NORTH CENTRAL	8293.50	238464.00	267803.20	98059.80	14919.10	627539.60
WEST NORTH CENTRAL	2873.50	128182.30	96742.10	66895.60	3689.10	298382.60
SOUTH ATLANTIC	77563.80	167197.10	315477.90	67180.40	63247.00	690665.60
EAST SOUTH CENTRAL	7782.50	96033.70	67531.90	36004.30	31506.50	238858.90
WEST SOUTH CENTRAL	24873.10	169584.60	174876.40	80240.10	150680.40	600254.60
ROCKY MOUNTAIN	3851.90	86033.60	100619.30	63482.20	0.00	253987.00
FAR WEST	57865.30	134118.60	614520.60	76219.00	157792.60	1040516.10
TOTAL	272390.90	1189232.42	2091227.79	534316.81	630486.59	4717654.44

SECTORAL DISTRIBUTION

REGION	HOUSEHOLD	BUSINESS	FEDERAL GOVT.	TOTAL
NEW ENGLAND	298.90	143289.10	75968.90	219556.90
MID ATLANTIC	2266.00	618971.60	126655.60	747893.21
EAST NORTH CENTRAL	1574.50	565339.20	60625.90	627539.60
WEST NORTH CENTRAL	415.90	279058.20	18908.50	298382.60
SOUTH ATLANTIC	1311.20	539270.50	150083.90	690665.60
EAST SOUTH CENTRAL	3098.90	193217.50	42542.50	238858.90
WEST SOUTH CENTRAL	7896.40	510011.90	82346.30	600254.60
ROCKY MOUNTAIN	0.00	227947.50	26033.50	253987.00
FAR WEST	3514.80	776304.10	260697.20	1040516.10
TOTAL	20376.60	3853409.59	843868.28	4717654.44

Table D.2.1

Prices For Transportation And Military Consumption Of Petroleum Products, (Non-Gasoline), 1972,
    In Cents Per Gallon, By State

Taxes and Prices Of Diesel Fuel And LPG For Highway Use Compared To Gasoline Taxes And Prices

REGION AND STATE	TAXES, ALL LEVELS OF GOVERNMENT			PRICES TO TRUCKS AND BUSES		
	Gasoline	Diesel	LPG	Gasoline	Diesel	LPG
NEW ENGLAND:						
CONNECTICUT	14.0	14.0	14.0	35.69	32.81	28.33
MAINE	13.0	13.0	13.0	35.32	31.72	27.62
MASSACHUSETTS	11.5	11.5	11.5	33.06	30.06	25.06
NEW HAMPSHIRE	13.0	13.0	13.0	34.90	31.30	26.35
RHODE ISLAND	12.0	12.0	12.0	33.50	30.98	26.56
VERMONT	13.0	4.0	4.0	37.41	23.09	18.65
MID ATLANTIC:						
NEW JERSEY	11.5	11.5	7.5	34.63	28.64	20.23
NEW YORK	14.4	16.4	14.4	37.63	35.72	26.27
PENNSYLVANIA	12.0	12.0	12.0	33.88	29.38	24.85
EAST NORTH CENTRAL:						
ILLINOIS	12.7	12.7	12.7	34.77	29.20	26.98
INDIANA	12.0	12.0	12.0	33.07	28.62	26.44
MICHIGAN	11.0	11.0	11.0	31.59	28.46	25.65
OHIO	11.2	11.2	11.2	35.16	28.48	25.60
WISCONSIN	11.0	11.0	11.0	31.24	28.30	25.35
WEST NORTH CENTRAL:						
IOWA	11.0	12.0	11.0	33.59	28.71	25.87
KANSAS	11.0	12.0	9.0	30.12	26.61	21.29
MINNESOTA	11.0	11.0	11.0	32.89	26.28	25.62
MISSOURI	9.7	9.7	9.7	31.83	25.87	22.60
NEBRASKA	12.5	12.5	12.5	33.98	28.20	27.30
NORTH DAKOTA	11.0	11.0	11.0	28.98	27.82	25.62
SOUTH DAKOTA	11.0	11.0	10.0	29.23	28.38	24.28
SOUTH ATLANTIC:						
DELAWARE	12.5	12.5	12.5	35.49	31.06	27.36
DISTRICT OF COLUMBIA	11.5	11.5	8.0	35.37	28.88	22.50
FLORIDA	12.0	12.0	12.0	32.33	31.48	24.15
GEORGIA	11.9	11.9	11.9	32.85	28.88	26.09
MARYLAND	12.0	12.0	12.0	35.69	28.46	26.38
NORTH CAROLINA	14.2	14.2	14.2	35.23	31.92	28.34
SOUTH CAROLINA	12.1	12.1	12.1	34.06	30.65	26.41
VIRGINIA	12.0	12.0	12.0	33.28	29.30	24.90
WEST VIRGINIA	12.5	12.5	12.5	35.83	29.54	26.58
EAST SOUTH CENTRAL:						
ALABAMA	12.0	13.0	13.0	33.75	28.79	26.10
KENTUCKY	12.0	12.0	12.0	33.80	29.63	25.83
MISSISSIPPI	12.0	14.0	12.0	33.00	30.72	24.40
TENNESSEE	11.0	12.0	11.0	32.83	29.04	23.70
WEST SOUTH CENTRAL:						
ARKANSAS	11.5	12.5	11.5	32.69	29.38	26.15
LOUISIANA	12.0	12.0	12.0	31.61	26.22	26.29
OKLAHOMA	10.5	10.5	10.5	32.10	23.51	23.90
TEXAS	9.0	10.5	9.0	29.94	25.05	23.33
ROCKY MOUNTAIN:						
ARIZONA	11.0	11.0	11.0	33.22	28.62	28.22
COLORADO	11.0	11.0	11.0	32.81	28.80	29.43
IDAHO	12.3	12.3	12.3	32.06	30.10	30.73
MONTANA	11.0	13.0	11.0	32.14	29.37	28.72
NEVADA	12.0	12.0	12.0	36.39	30.95	31.18
NEW MEXICO	11.0	11.0	11.0	33.11	26.26	27.93
UTAH	11.0	11.0	11.0	32.88	26.78	28.57
WYOMING	11.0	4.0	4.0	31.75	20.83	22.69
FAR WEST:						
ALASKA	12.0	12.0	8.0	40.27	33.66	26.65
CALIFORNIA	11.1	11.1	10.1	32.21	27.42	27.04
HAWAII	9.0	9.0	8.0	38.93	31.29	30.40
OREGON	11.2	11.2	11.2	32.62	27.89	29.04
WASHINGTON	13.0	13.0	13.0	33.25	32.48	30.95

Table D.2.2

Prices For Transportation And Military Consumption Of Petroleum Products (Non-Gasoline), 1972,
In Cents Per Gallon, By State

Prices of Aviation and Railroad Fuel

REGION and STATE	AVIATION JET FUEL		RAILROAD FUEL	
	Civilian	Military	Distillate	Residual
NEW ENGLAND:				
CONNECTICUT	12.38	11.87	12.60	8.86
MAINE	12.32	11.81	12.53	9.04
MASSACHUSETTS	12.21	11.70	12.42	8.38
NEW HAMPSHIRE	12.05	11.55	12.24	8.25
RHODE ISLAND	12.49	11.98	12.72	9.00
VERMONT	12.57	12.05	12.80	9.05
MID ATLANTIC:				
NEW JERSEY	11.25	10.79	11.41	8.72
NEW YORK	12.72	12.19	12.96	8.13
PENNSYLVANIA	11.42	10.95	11.59	8.80
EAST NORTH CENTRAL:				
ILLINOIS	10.86	10.41	10.99	8.58
INDIANA	10.91	10.46	11.06	8.64
MICHIGAN	11.47	11.00	11.65	8.77
OHIO	11.37	10.90	11.53	8.63
WISCONSIN	11.37	10.90	11.53	8.59
WEST NORTH CENTRAL:				
IOWA	10.97	10.52	11.11	8.63
KANSAS	9.56	9.17	9.63	7.13
MINNESOTA	10.01	9.60	10.10	8.48
MISSOURI	10.63	10.19	10.76	7.50
NEBRASKA	10.30	9.87	10.40	8.59
NORTH DAKOTA	11.04	10.58	11.18	8.48
SOUTH DAKOTA	11.42	10.95	11.59	8.29
SOUTH ATLANTIC:				
DELAWARE	12.21	11.70	12.42	8.90
DISTRICT OF COLUMBIA	11.42	10.95	11.59	8.69
FLORIDA	12.83	12.30	13.08	7.28
GEORGIA	11.14	10.68	11.29	8.48
MARYLAND	10.80	10.35	10.93	8.61
NORTH CAROLINA	11.65	11.17	11.83	8.47
SOUTH CAROLINA	12.21	11.70	12.42	8.58
VIRGINIA	11.37	10.90	11.53	7.72
WEST VIRGINIA	11.20	10.73	11.35	8.43
EAST SOUTH CENTRAL:				
ALABAMA	10.36	9.93	10.47	8.18
KENTUCKY	11.58	11.11	11.76	8.64
MISSISSIPPI	10.98	10.53	11.13	7.76
TENNESSEE	11.20	10.73	11.35	7.93
WEST SOUTH CENTRAL:				
ARKANSAS	11.08	10.63	11.23	7.31
LOUISIANA	9.31	8.93	9.35	7.13
OKLAHOMA	8.49	8.14	8.50	6.68
TEXAS	9.49	9.10	9.56	7.13
ROCKY MOUNTAIN:				
ARIZONA	11.58	11.11	11.76	8.17
COLORADO	11.71	11.22	11.89	8.74
IDAHO	11.71	11.22	11.89	8.74
MONTANA	10.74	10.30	10.87	8.40
NEVADA	12.48	11.97	12.69	9.09
NEW MEXICO	9.99	9.58	10.09	8.02
UTAH	10.34	9.92	10.46	8.33
WYOMING	11.05	10.59	11.20	8.86
FAR WEST:				
ALASKA	14.30	13.71	14.62	8.91
CALIFORNIA	10.68	10.24	10.82	8.07
HAWAII	14.70	14.09	15.05	10.70
OREGON	10.92	10.47	11.07	8.50
WASHINGTON	12.83	12.30	13.08	8.58

Table D.2.3

Prices For Transportation And Military Consumption Of Petroleum Products (Non-Gasoline), 1972,
In Cents Per Gallon, By State

Prices For Military And Marine Fuel Use

REGION AND STATE	MILITARY USE		VESSEL BUNKERING		
			Distillates		Residuals
	Distillates	Residuals	Household	Business	(Business)
NEW ENGLAND:					
CONNECTICUT	13.72	8.88	18.66	15.69	9.47
MAINE	13.66	9.05	18.57	15.61	9.66
MASSACHUSETTS	13.54	8.39	18.39	15.47	8.95
NEW HAMPSHIRE	13.36	8.27	18.13	15.24	8.82
RHODE ISLAND	13.84	9.02	18.83	15.84	9.62
VERMONT	13.92	9.07	18.96	15.94	9.68
MID ATLANTIC:					
NEW JERSEY	12.52	8.73	16.90	14.21	9.31
NEW YORK	14.08	8.14	19.18	16.13	8.69
PENNSYLVANIA	12.70	8.82	17.16	14.43	9.41
EAST NORTH CENTRAL:					
ILLINOIS	12.10	8.59	16.28	13.69	9.16
INDIANA	12.16	8.66	16.37	13.76	9.24
MICHIGAN	12.76	8.79	17.25	14.50	9.37
OHIO	12.64	8.64	17.07	14.36	9.22
WISCONSIN	12.64	8.61	17.07	14.36	9.18
WEST NORTH CENTRAL:					
IOWA	12.22	8.64	16.46	13.84	9.22
KANSAS	10.72	7.14	14.26	11.99	7.62
MINNESOTA	11.20	8.50	14.96	12.58	9.07
MISSOURI	11.86	7.52	15.93	13.39	8.02
NEBRASKA	11.50	8.61	15.40	12.95	9.18
NORTH DAKOTA	12.30	8.50	16.57	13.93	9.07
SOUTH DAKOTA	12.70	8.30	17.16	14.43	8.86
SOUTH ATLANTIC:					
DELAWARE	13.54	8.91	18.39	15.47	9.50
DISTRICT OF COLUMBIA	12.70	8.70	17.16	14.43	9.28
FLORIDA	14.20	7.29	19.36	16.28	7.77
GEORGIA	12.40	8.50	16.72	14.06	9.07
MARYLAND	12.04	8.62	16.19	13.62	9.20
NORTH CAROLINA	12.94	8.48	17.51	14.73	9.05
SOUTH CAROLINA	13.54	8.59	18.39	15.47	9.16
VIRGINIA	12.64	7.73	17.07	14.36	8.25
WEST VIRGINIA	12.46	8.45	16.81	14.13	9.01
EAST SOUTH CENTRAL:					
ALABAMA	11.57	8.20	15.50	13.03	8.74
KENTUCKY	12.88	8.66	17.42	14.65	9.24
MISSISSIPPI	12.23	7.77	16.47	13.85	8.29
TENNESSEE	12.46	7.95	16.81	14.13	8.48
WEST SOUTH CENTRAL:					
ARKANSAS	12.34	7.32	16.63	13.99	7.81
LOUISIANA	10.44	7.14	13.85	11.65	7.62
OKLAHOMA	9.58	6.70	12.58	10.58	7.14
TEXAS	10.65	7.14	14.15	11.90	7.62
ROCKY MOUNTAIN:					
ARIZONA	12.87	8.18	17.42	14.64	8.72
COLORADO	13.00	8.75	17.60	14.80	9.33
IDAHO	13.00	8.75	17.60	14.80	9.33
MONTANA	11.98	8.41	16.10	13.54	8.97
NEVADA	13.82	9.11	18.81	15.81	9.71
NEW MEXICO	11.19	8.04	14.94	12.57	8.57
UTAH	11.56	8.34	15.49	13.02	8.90
WYOMING	12.30	8.88	16.58	13.94	9.47
FAR WEST:					
ALASKA	15.76	8.93	21.65	18.20	9.52
CALIFORNIA	11.91	8.09	16.01	13.46	8.63
HAWAII	16.19	10.71	22.28	18.74	11.43
OREGON	12.17	8.52	16.39	13.78	9.09
WASHINGTON	14.20	8.59	19.36	16.28	9.16

Table D.3.1

Expenditures For Transportation And Military Use Of Petroleum Products (Non-Gasoline), 1972,
    In Thousand Dollars, By State

Military, Highway And Aviation Expenditures

REGION AND STATE	MILITARY USE		HIGHWAY USE		AVIATION USE OF JET FUEL	
	Distillates	Residuals	Diesel	LPG	Civilian	Military
NEW ENGLAND:						
CONNECTICUT	674.2	1289.7	27035.2	783.3	11869.0	3248.7
MAINE	3476.7	190.1	9899.8	104.2	3546.2	16754.3
MASSACHUSETTS	2985.6	6320.3	34020.3	1007.7	41251.0	14380.3
NEW HAMPSHIRE	89.8	138.9	3405.3	165.4	157.2	432.2
RHODE ISLAND	436.0	7984.0	7077.4	934.8	707.2	2101.7
VERMONT	11.7	7.6	2812.8	46.8	267.4	56.4
MID ATLANTIC:						
NEW JERSEY	2855.3	11402.3	65540.6	2390.0	25006.0	13705.0
NEW YORK	8829.0	4528.1	89479.1	4061.2	191657.4	42577.1
PENNSYLVANIA	1818.9	7354.8	127023.8	4280.1	36943.6	8734.6
EAST NORTH CENTRAL:						
ILLINOIS	2129.4	72.2	119794.8	15661.1	112578.8	13017.1
INDIANA	234.9	47.3	97018.3	3535.6	10081.4	1436.1
MICHIGAN	3499.6	18.5	68298.3	2335.1	19802.5	21439.3
OHIO	568.0	29.5	140146.1	4952.4	25218.8	3480.4
WISCONSIN	791.0	0.0	45861.5	2669.1	8261.7	4846.6
WEST NORTH CENTRAL:						
IOWA	46.2	0.0	49555.9	1619.2	2520.9	282.5
KANSAS	508.8	111.0	32509.2	8794.1	2480.5	3092.1
MINNESOTA	987.8	0.0	39371.1	3062.4	17636.4	6016.3
MISSOURI	159.4	94.7	60584.1	2057.6	34973.8	973.3
NEBRASKA	207.7	0.0	26127.9	6836.6	2890.9	1266.6
NORTH DAKOTA	67.1	0.0	13155.3	73.1	1054.5	410.7
SOUTH DAKOTA	5.3	0.0	10227.0	1691.7	709.6	32.7
SOUTH ATLANTIC:						
DELAWARE	68.2	389.2	3391.3	687.7	299.2	328.7
DISTRICT OF COLUMBIA	117.3	529.6	4111.9	150.7	12.9	563.5
FLORIDA	1443.3	817.0	66967.4	5452.4	114934.1	6963.3
GEORGIA	1078.1	553.4	76598.4	3017.5	43943.7	5171.6
MARYLAND	3018.9	2423.5	24942.8	1083.3	10174.9	14466.4
NORTH CAROLINA	1760.9	178.1	58538.3	2961.0	6084.1	8465.2
SOUTH CAROLINA	1660.5	324.7	27673.3	2456.5	2245.1	7998.2
VIRGINIA	3610.0	28100.6	59122.2	1814.9	38767.2	17337.1
WEST VIRGINIA	15.7	0.0	26852.0	467.8	394.2	75.3
EAST SOUTH CENTRAL:						
ALABAMA	3278.9	89.5	46073.6	3382.7	2992.4	9301.0
KENTUCKY	2098.9	0.0	43484.2	1763.9	8804.8	12865.7
MISSISSIPPI	359.6	0.0	34635.4	9353.4	1367.1	1022.7
TENNESSEE	915.8	0.0	65713.3	2292.7	14042.5	5604.5
WEST SOUTH CENTRAL:						
ARKANSAS	803.3	0.0	33990.9	10286.1	1202.2	2286.5
LOUISIANA	3820.6	1707.0	33072.3	11270.3	12260.9	10783.9
OKLAHOMA	165.0	835.3	33278.7	11501.1	5796.0	995.9
TEXAS	9400.6	462.4	147214.1	54847.5	62549.0	26557.0
ROCKY MOUNTAIN:						
ARIZONA	205.5	0.0	41619.8	2418.4	12781.7	915.2
COLORADO	797.2	29.4	22341.3	7232.7	28133.4	6732.5
IDAHO	10.9	0.0	11112.3	682.4	877.2	92.2
MONTANA	216.4	113.0	18590.7	2398.3	1927.7	1820.3
NEVADA	261.2	15.3	11114.4	295.6	15933.9	1167.1
NEW MEXICO	1019.7	0.0	23814.8	9588.8	3601.2	2886.8
UTAH	500.1	35.0	16266.5	272.0	3916.6	4199.6
WYOMING	46.5	0.0	9009.2	3790.5	433.1	391.8
FAR WEST:						
ALASKA	3706.8	45.0	4467.9	0.0	36873.6	16641.6
CALIFORNIA	29868.3	7223.6	183625.8	12224.7	201537.5	132514.6
HAWAII	992.9	0.0	3022.5	691.2	78886.9	4461.1
OREGON	669.7	386.4	36231.7	606.0	8217.8	2974.6
WASHINGTON	2439.3	984.8	34895.2	1319.5	38665.0	10905.1

Table D.3.2

Expenditures For Transportation And Military Use Of Petroleum Products (Non-Gasoline), 1972,
    In Thousand Dollars, By State

Railroad And Vessel Bunkering Expenditures

REGION AND STATE	RAILROAD USE		VESSEL BUNKERING		
	Distillates	Residuals	Distillates		Residuals
			Household	Business	(Business)
NEW ENGLAND:					
CONNECTICUT	2036.8	0.0	46.2	231.3	759.4
MAINE	1158.4	0.0	62.4	308.2	13786.3
MASSACHUSETTS	3296.2	0.0	237.1	1177.7	4745.1
NEW HAMPSHIRE	87.4	0.0	0.0	0.0	0.0
RHODE ISLAND	106.8	49.2	42.7	210.2	456.5
VERMONT	295.6	0.0	10.3	51.5	0.0
MID ATLANTIC:					
NEW JERSEY	5246.4	3.7	1771.9	8785.8	33654.9
NEW YORK	11505.6	334.6	742.9	3684.5	49930.2
PENNSYLVANIA	15649.4	210.8	339.5	1684.2	12326.3
EAST NORTH CENTRAL:					
ILLINOIS	33589.7	421.4	1210.3	6002.8	354.0
INDIANA	11093.2	0.0	196.6	973.5	644.1
MICHIGAN	9420.1	324.2	117.4	583.6	743.9
OHIO	19306.3	0.0	332.0	1644.2	758.9
WISCONSIN	4734.6	184.1	15.8	77.2	11.6
WEST NORTH CENTRAL:					
IOWA	6173.8	0.0	15.9	79.6	0.0
KANSAS	8671.4	77.9	2.4	13.1	0.0
MINNESOTA	6286.9	24.9	37.1	185.5	418.9
MISSOURI	13166.2	12.6	420.1	2082.6	67.4
NEBRASKA	11000.5	649.6	0.0	0.0	0.0
NORTH DAKOTA	3265.7	0.0	0.0	0.0	0.0
SOUTH DAKOTA	832.1	0.0	0.0	0.0	0.0
SOUTH ATLANTIC:					
DELAWARE	93.9	127.0	20.1	100.0	3165.7
DISTRICT OF COLUMBIA	802.9	7.3	0.7	5.5	0.0
FLORIDA	12983.6	0.0	359.4	1783.2	4964.5
GEORGIA	11853.3	0.0	51.3	252.2	316.1
MARYLAND	4720.2	7.2	402.6	1994.7	10208.7
NORTH CAROLINA	7846.1	17.8	88.3	439.1	296.4
SOUTH CAROLINA	2195.7	7.2	57.2	283.2	3882.6
VIRGINIA	12998.4	22.7	415.2	2056.7	8646.1
WEST VIRGINIA	3407.9	0.0	242.8	1202.7	0.0
EAST SOUTH CENTRAL:					
ALABAMA	9751.4	0.0	545.4	2704.9	5339.1
KENTUCKY	6136.7	0.0	940.4	4661.5	15.5
MISSISSIPPI	2074.1	0.0	784.6	3890.0	535.9
TENNESSEE	10848.1	0.0	1456.4	7222.7	0.0
WEST SOUTH CENTRAL:					
ARKANSAS	7786.8	0.0	184.4	914.0	0.0
LOUISIANA	5502.8	0.0	4724.4	23427.3	18387.2
OKLAHOMA	906.4	0.0	0.0	0.0	0.0
TEXAS	41948.8	41.9	3073.2	15237.5	30588.8
ROCKY MOUNTAIN:					
ARIZONA	4548.4	0.0	0.0	0.0	0.0
COLORADO	7576.2	80.7	0.0	0.0	0.0
IDAHO	3229.1	0.0	0.0	0.0	0.0
MONTANA	8256.4	112.9	0.0	0.0	0.0
NEVADA	1487.8	0.0	0.0	0.0	0.0
NEW MEXICO	6694.8	0.0	0.0	0.0	0.0
UTAH	6456.2	69.9	0.0	0.0	0.0
WYOMING	10963.7	908.0	0.0	0.0	0.0
FAR WEST:					
ALASKA	632.3	22.5	1640.2	8132.0	904.0
CALIFORNIA	39972.2	193.3	1420.6	7042.6	68482.7
HAWAII	0.0	35.9	455.7	2260.9	6187.2
OREGON	12894.0	103.6	307.6	1523.7	522.8
WASHINGTON	7032.6	39.6	961.9	4770.6	2670.5

Table D.3.3

Expenditures For Transportation And Military Use Of Petroleum Products (Non-Gasoline), 1972,
In Thousand Dollars, By State

Expenditures By Function

REGION AND STATE	MILITARY	HIGHWAY	AVIATION	RAILROAD	VESSEL BUNKERING	TOTAL
NEW ENGLAND:						
CONNECTICUT	1963.9	27818.5	15117.7	2036.8	1036.9	47973.8
MAINE	3666.9	10004.0	20300.5	1158.4	14157.0	49286.7
MASSACHUSETTS	9305.9	35028.1	55631.4	3296.2	6159.9	109421.5
NEW HAMPSHIRE	228.7	3570.7	589.4	87.4	0.0	4476.2
RHODE ISLAND	8420.0	8012.1	2808.9	156.0	709.4	20106.4
VERMONT	19.3	2859.6	323.8	295.6	61.9	3560.2
MID ATLANTIC:						
NEW JERSEY	14257.6	67930.5	38711.0	5250.0	44212.7	170361.8
NEW YORK	13357.1	93540.3	234234.5	11840.2	54357.5	407329.6
PENNSYLVANIA	9173.7	131304.0	45678.2	15860.2	14350.0	216366.1
EAST NORTH CENTRAL:						
ILLINOIS	2201.5	135455.8	125595.9	34011.0	7567.1	304831.3
INDIANA	·282.2	100553.9	11517.5	11093.2	1814.2	125261.0
MICHIGAN	3518.0	70633.4	41241.9	9744.2	1444.8	126582.4
OHIO	597.5	145098.5	28699.2	19306.3	2735.1	196436.7
WISCONSIN	791.0	48530.6	13108.3	4918.7	104.5	67453.1
WEST NORTH CENTRAL:						
IOWA	46.2	51175.1	2803.4	6173.8	95.5	60294.0
KANSAS	619.8	41303.4	5572.4	8749.2	15.5	56260.3
MINNESOTA	987.8	42433.6	23652.7	6311.9	641.4	74027.4
MISSOURI	254.1	62641.6	35947.0	13178.8	2570.0	114591.6
NEBRASKA	207.7	32964.5	4157.5	11650.1	0.0	48979.8
NORTH DAKOTA	67.1	13228.4	1465.1	3265.7	0.0	18026.4
SOUTH DAKOTA	5.3	11918.7	742.3	832.1	0.0	13498.5
SOUTH ATLANTIC:						
DELAWARE	457.5	4079.1	627.9	220.9	3285.8	8671.1
DISTRICT OF COLUMBIA	647.0	4262.7	576.4	810.2	6.2	6302.4
FLORIDA	2260.3	72419.8	121897.4	12983.6	7107.2	216668.3
GEORGIA	1631.4	79615.9	49115.3	11853.3	619.5	142835.4
MARYLAND	5442.4	26026.1	24641.3	4727.4	12606.0	73443.1
NORTH CAROLINA	1939.0	61499.3	14549.3	7863.9	823.8	86675.3
SOUTH CAROLINA	1985.2	30129.8	10243.2	2202.9	4223.0	48784.2
VIRGINIA	31710.6	60937.1	56104.3	13021.0	11118.0	172891.0
WEST VIRGINIA	15.7	27319.7	469.5	3407.9	1445.5	32658.4
EAST SOUTH CENTRAL:						
ALABAMA	3368.5	49456.3	12293.4	9751.4	8589.4	83458.9
KENTUCKY	2098.9	45248.1	21670.5	6136.7	5617.4	80771.7
MISSISSIPPI	359.6	43988.8	2389.8	2074.1	5210.6	54022.9
TENNESSEE	915.8	68006.0	19646.9	10848.1	8679.1	108096.0
WEST SOUTH CENTRAL:						
ARKANSAS	803.3	44277.0	3488.7	7786.8	1098.4	57454.2
LOUISIANA	5527.6	44342.6	23044.8	5502.8	46538.9	124956.7
OKLAHOMA	1000.3	44779.8	6792.0	906.4	0.0	53478.5
TEXAS	9863.0	202061.6	89105.9	41990.7	48899.5	391920.7
ROCKY MOUNTAIN:						
ARIZONA	205.5	44038.2	13696.9	4548.4	0.0	62488.9
COLORADO	826.6	29574.0	34865.9	7656.9	0.0	72923.4
IDAHO	10.9	11794.8	969.4	3229.1	0.0	16004.2
MONTANA	329.4	20989.0	3748.0	8369.3	0.0	33435.7
NEVADA	276.5	11410.0	17100.9	1487.8	0.0	30275.3
NEW MEXICO	1019.7	33403.6	6488.0	6694.8	0.0	47606.1
UTAH	535.1	16538.5	8116.1	6526.2	0.0	31715.9
WYOMING	46.5	12799.7	824.9	11871.7	0.0	25542.7
FAR WEST:						
ALASKA	3751.8	4467.9	53515.2	654.8	10676.2	73065.8
CALIFORNIA	37091.9	195850.5	334052.2	40165.5	76945.9	684106.0
HAWAII	992.9	3713.7	83348.0	35.9	8903.9	96994.4
OREGON	1056.1	36837.7	11192.4	12997.6	2354.2	64438.0
WASHINGTON	3424.1	36214.7	49570.0	7072.2	8403.0	104684.1

Table D.3.4

Expenditures For Transportation And Military Use Of Petroleum Products (Non-Gasoline), 1972,
In Thousand Dollars, By State

Expenditures By Sector

REGION AND STATE	HOUSEHOLD	FEDERAL GOVT.	BUSINESS	TOTAL
NEW ENGLAND:				
CONNECTICUT	46.2	5212.6	42715.0	47973.8
MAINE	62.4	20421.1	28803.2	49286.7
MASSACHUSETTS	237.1	23686.2	85498.1	109421.5
NEW HAMPSHIRE	0.0	660.9	3815.3	4476.2
RHODE ISLAND	42.7	10521.7	9542.0	20106.4
VERMONT	10.3	75.7	3474.2	3560.2
MID ATLANTIC:				
NEW JERSEY	1771.9	27962.6	140627.3	170361.8
NEW YORK	742.9	55934.2	350652.5	407329.6
PENNSYLVANIA	339.5	17908.3	198118.3	216366.1
EAST NORTH CENTRAL:				
ILLINOIS	1210.3	15218.6	288402.4	304831.3
INDIANA	196.6	1718.3	123346.1	125261.0
MICHIGAN	117.4	24957.4	101507.7	126582.4
OHIO	332.0	4077.9	192026.8	196436.7
WISCONSIN	15.8	5637.6	61799.8	67453.1
WEST NORTH CENTRAL:				
IOWA	15.9	328.7	59949.4	60294.0
KANSAS	2.4	3711.8	52546.0	56260.3
MINNESOTA	37.1	7004.1	66986.2	74027.4
MISSOURI	420.1	1227.4	112944.1	114591.6
NEBRASKA	0.0	1474.3	47505.5	48979.8
NORTH DAKOTA	0.0	477.8	17548.5	18026.4
SOUTH DAKOTA	0.0	38.0	13460.5	13498.5
SOUTH ATLANTIC:				
DELAWARE	20.1	786.1	7864.9	8671.1
DISTRICT OF COLUMBIA	0.7	1210.5	5091.2	6302.4
FLORIDA	359.4	9223.6	207085.3	216668.3
GEORGIA	51.3	6803.0	135981.1	142835.4
MARYLAND	402.6	19908.8	53131.7	73443.1
NORTH CAROLINA	88.3	10404.2	76182.8	86675.3
SOUTH CAROLINA	57.2	9983.4	38743.6	48784.2
VIRGINIA	415.2	49047.7	123428.2	172891.0
WEST VIRGINIA	242.8	91.0	32324.6	32658.4
EAST SOUTH CENTRAL:				
ALABAMA	545.4	12669.4	70244.0	83458.9
KENTUCKY	940.4	14964.6	64866.7	80771.7
MISSISSIPPI	784.6	1382.3	51856.0	54022.9
TENNESSEE	1456.4	6520.3	100119.3	108096.0
WEST SOUTH CENTRAL:				
ARKANSAS	184.4	3089.8	54180.0	57454.2
LOUISIANA	4724.4	16311.5	103920.8	124956.7
OKLAHOMA	0.0	1996.2	51482.2	53478.5
TEXAS	3073.2	36420.0	352427.5	391920.7
ROCKY MOUNTAIN:				
ARIZONA	0.0	1120.6	61368.3	62488.9
COLORADO	0.0	7559.1	65364.3	72923.4
IDAHO	0.0	103.1	15901.0	16004.2
MONTANA	0.0	2149.7	31286.0	33435.7
NEVADA	0.0	1443.6	28831.7	30275.3
NEW MEXICO	0.0	3906.4	43699.6	47606.1
UTAH	0.0	4734.7	26981.2	31715.9
WYOMING	0.0	438.3	25104.4	25542.7
FAR WEST:				
ALASKA	1640.2	20393.3	51032.2	73065.8
CALIFORNIA	1420.6	169606.5	513078.9	684106.0
HAWAII	455.7	5454.0	91084.6	96994.4
OREGON	307.6	4030.6	60099.7	64438.0
WASHINGTON	961.9	14329.2	89392.9	104684.1

Table D.3.5

Expenditures For Transportation And Military Use Of Petroleum Products (Non-Gasoline), 1972
In Thousand Dollars, By Region

Expenditures By Function And Fuel Type

Military, Highway And Aviation Use

REGION	MILITARY USE		HIGHWAY USE		AVIATION USE OF JET FUEL	
	Distillates	Residuals	Diesel	LPG	Civilian	Military
NEW ENGLAND	7674.00	15930.60	84250.80	3042.20	57798.00	36973.60
MID ATLANTIC	13503.20	23285.20	28043.50	10731.30	253607.00	65016.70
EAST NORTH CENTRAL	7222.90	167.50	471119.00	29153.30	175943.20	44219.50
WEST NORTH CENTRAL	1982.30	205.70	231530.50	24134.70	6226.40	12074.20
SOUTH ATLANTIC	12772.90	33316.10	348197.60	18091.80	216855.40	61369.30
EAST SOUTH CENTRAL	6653.20	89.50	189906.50	16792.70	27206.80	28793.90
WEST SOUTH CENTRAL	14189.50	3004.70	247556.00	87905.00	81808.10	40623.30
ROCKY MOUNTAIN	3057.50	192.70	153869.00	26678.70	67604.80	1805.50
FAR WEST	37677.00	8639.80	262243.10	14841.40	364180.80	167497.00
TOTAL	104732.50	84831.80	2270716.00	231371.10	1307270.53	474773.01

Railroad And Vessel Bunkering Expenditures

REGION	RAILROAD USE		VESSEL BUNKERING		
	Distillates	Residuals	Distillates		Residuals (Business)
			Household	Business	
NEW ENGLAND	6981.20	49.20	398.70	1978.90	19747.30
MID ATLANTIC	3201.40	549.10	2854.30	14154.50	95911.40
EAST NORTH CENTRAL	78143.90	929.70	1872.10	9281.30	2512.50
WEST NORTH CENTRAL	49336.60	765.00	475.50	2360.80	486.30
SOUTH ATLANTIC	56902.00	189.20	1637.60	8117.30	31480.10
EAST SOUTH CENTRAL	28810.30	0.00	3726.80	18479.10	5890.50
WEST SOUTH CENTRAL	56144.80	41.90	7982.00	39578.80	48976.00
ROCKY MOUNTAIN	49212.60	1171.50	0.00	0.00	0.00
FAR WEST	60531.10	394.90	4786.00	23729.80	78767.20
TOTAL	418523.89	4090.50	23733.00	117680.50	283771.30

Table D.3.6

Expenditures For Transportation And Military Use Of Petroleum Products (Non-Gasoline), 1972,
In Thousand Dollars, By Region

Expenditures By Function And Sector

Function

REGION	MILITARY	HIGHWAY	AVIATION	RAILROAD	VESSEL BUNKERING	TOTAL
NEW ENGLAND	23604.70	87293.00	94771.70	7030.40	22125.10	234824.71
MID ATLANTIC	36788.40	292774.80	31623.70	32950.40	112920.20	794057.52
EAST NORTH CENTRAL	7390.20	500272.20	20162.80	79073.40	13665.70	820564.48
WEST NORTH CENTRAL	2188.00	255665.30	74340.40	50161.60	3322.40	385677.93
SOUTH ATLANTIC	46089.10	366289.50	278224.60	57091.10	41235.00	788929.18
EAST SOUTH CENTRAL	6742.80	206699.20	56000.60	28810.30	28096.50	326349.42
WEST SOUTH CENTRAL	17194.20	335461.00	122431.40	56186.70	96536.80	627810.21
ROCKY MOUNTAIN	3250.20	180547.80	85810.10	50384.20	0.00	319992.15
FAR WEST	46316.80	277084.50	531677.80	60926.00	107283.20	1023288.23
TOTAL	189564.40	2502087.24	1782043.13	422614.10	425184.89	5321493.89

Sector

REGION	HOUSEHOLD	FEDERAL GOVT.	BUSINESS	TOTAL
NEW ENGLAND	398.70	60578.20	173847.80	234824.71
MID ATLANTIC	2854.30	101805.10	689398.10	794057.52
EAST NORTH CENTRAL	1872.10	51609.80	767082.80	820564.48
WEST NORTH CENTRAL	475.50	14262.10	370940.20	385677.93
SOUTH ATLANTIC	1637.60	107458.30	679833.40	788929.18
EAST SOUTH CENTRAL	3726.80	35536.60	287086.00	326349.42
WEST SOUTH CENTRAL	7982.00	57817.50	562010.50	627810.21
ROCKY MOUNTAIN	0.00	21455.50	298536.49	319992.15
FAR WEST	4786.00	213813.60	804688.30	1023288.23
TOTAL	23733.00	664336.71	4633423.57	5321493.89

Appendix E

Industrial, Refinery and Miscellaneous Uses
of Petroleum Products

<u>Quantities-Overview</u>

Remaining uses of petroleum products were categorized under the
heading of industrial, refinery and miscellaneous uses, with good data
on quantities available in Bureau of Mines publications [39], [40] and
[42]. Specific uses, and the source of quantity data for each, were as
follows:

<u>Industrial Use</u>

Industrial distillates	[39] Table 8, P. 6
Industrial residuals	[39] Table 8, P. 6
Industrial diesel fuel	[39] Table 14, P. 13
Industrial LPG	[40] Table 5, P. 7

<u>Refinery & Other Energy Use</u>

Oil company use of distillates	[39] Table 9, P. 7
Oil company use of residuals	[39] Table 9, P. 7
Refinery use of petroleum coke	[42] Table 18, P. 20
Refinery use of refinery gas (still gas)	[40] Table 18, P. 20
LPG for use as utility gas	[40] Table 6, P. 8

<u>Miscellaneous Use</u>

Miscellaneous use of kerosine	[39] Table 5, P. 3
Miscellaneous use of distillates	[39] Table 14, P. 13
Miscellaneous use of residuals	[39] Table 14, P. 13
Miscellaneous use of LPG	[40] Table 7, P. 9
Transfer LPG	Appendix D, Table D.1.4

In most of these data series, an entry occurred for each state, so
that use of the series could be made immediately and directly. In the
case of petroleum coke and refinery gas, a number of states had been
grouped, and aggregate entries were presented. Disaggregation was

carried out on the basis of refinery use of residual oil. The "transfer LPG" series initially consisted of that part of LPG listed as used in highway transportation that was inferred to be consumed in other uses. The original entries were reassigned on the basis of "reasonable" assumptions on use. All of the data on LPG use were initially listed in thousand of gallons, and were divided by 42 to convert to thousands of barrels, the units employed in the final set of data presented for each use. The specific data series, and procedures employed to obtain them, are considered next.

Industrial Use

In [39], Table 14, diesel type fuel oil use is a subheading under distillate-type oils for miscellaneous uses." However, in the Minerals Year Book ([43], 1973, Vol. I, Table 22, P. 43), this category is included under "industrial use" as a subcomponent of distillates, and it was decided to follow that precedent, and further, to treat the series as a distinct use. The latter decision is justified by price differences (albeit small differences) between diesel fuel and other distillates. Quantities consumed in industrial use, by state, are presented in Table E.1.1. Corresponding regional totals are shown in Table E.1.2.

Refinery and Other Energy Use

Energy production and distribution is itself an important use of energy; hence it was decided to recognize such use explicitly, and to include LPG for utility gas in the subclassification set up for refinery use of petroleum products.

Data on that use and on distillates and residuals used by oil companies (assumed for simplicity to be identical to refinery use) could be utilized directly. Data on petroleum coke and refinery gas posed some difficulty; use information was available for nineteen individual states and for twenty-one states aggregated into groupings of from two to five states. It seemed apparent that there was no refinery activity in the remaining eleven jurisdictions (including the District of Columbia). For each of the aggregate groupings, use was distributed within the grouping on the basis of the individual state's share of residual oil consumption by refineries in the grouping. A zero entry appears for some states other than the eleven cases not listed; this occurs because use of petroleum coke or refinery gas is listed as zero for a grouping in the source document, or because residual oil consumption by refineries is zero (which occurred for Tennessee).

In the source document, petroleum coke was measured in units of thousand short tons, and refinery gas in units of million cubic feet. These measures were converted to barrels as follows: for petroleum coke, 1,000 short tons times 5 equals 1,000 barrels; for refinery gas, one million cubic feet times .165 equals 1,000 barrels. The scale factors were derived from [42], Table 19, P. 21, and from [7].

Quantities consumed in refinery and other energy use are presented in Table E.1.3 for states, and in Table E.1.4 for regions.

Miscellaneous Use

"Transfer" LPG was the only category of miscellaneous use for which quantities by state were not directly available. The category consisted of the estimated "excess" amounts of LPG used for internal combustion

engine fuel inferred as not consumed in highway use. The amounts
transferred, in thousands of barrels, by state, were:

Mississippi	513.5
Arkansas	1,430.5
Oklahoma	265.9
Texas	11,072.5

These amounts were distributed among the fifty states and the
District of Columbia by assigning one-third to the state of origin, one-
third on the basis of industrial use of LPG, and one-third on the basis
of miscellaneous use of LPG, for that category in [40]. For the
last two categories, each jurisdiction's fraction of total consumption
was obtained, and multiplied by one-third of the transferred amount.

The reassigned transfer LPG and the quantities for the other categories of miscellaneous use are shown in Table E.1.5 for states, and in
Table E.1.6, for regions.

In the subsequent distribution of use between sectors, it was
assumed that all fuels except kerosine were consumed entirely in the
business sector. Kerosine for miscellaneous uses includes use in
"lamps, tractors, cooking stoves, etc." ([39], P. 3, footnote 2); it
was therefore assumed that half of the total use was by households, and
half by business.

Conversion to BTU units

Consumption in thousand gallons was converted to consumption in
billion BTU by applying these scale factors from [7]:

Fuel	Millions of BTU per barrel
Distillate	5.825
Residual	6.287
LPG	4.011
Petroleum Coke	6.024
Petroleum Gas	6.000

The individual category consumption in billions of BTU, by state, appear as Tables E.1.7 through E.1.9; corresponding regional consumption appears in Table E.1.10.

Table E.1.11 presents totals for the individual categories, in billions of BTU by state, and the grand total. The regional analogue appears as Table E.1.12.

Prices

Price relationships established earlier were drawn upon here. Table B.2.5, in particular, lists estimated prices for No. 2 fuel oil, kerosine, No. 6 fuel oil and LPG in commercial use, with these prices pegged to use at the "all commercial" level. Scale factors developed earlier also established that industrial prices equalled .98 commercial prices for residual fuel oil, and .96 commercial prices for distillate fuel oil; household prices were 1.15 the all commercial price level; and wholesale prices were .68 the all commercial level for No. 2 fuel oil, and .75 that level for No. 6 fuel oil.

It was assumed here that industrial prices could be derived directly from Table B.2.5 by applying the scale factors. This involved the further assumption that the distribution of use was 50 percent large industrial and 50 percent small industrial; if the percentage of large industrial

use were in fact greater, the price employed here would be an overstatement. If use were 100 percent large industrial, the price used
here would involve a 20 percent overstatement.

The price of diesel fuel oil was estimated to be one-half cent per
gallon (and hence 21 cents per barrel) above that of No. 2 fuel oil, on
the basis of data on diesel for plant use in Platt's Oilgram for 1972
([26], various issues).

Energy use prices were assumed to be somewhat _below_ the wholesale
level, corresponding, in effect, to the "factory" or producer level.
The wholesale markup was assumed to be 10 percent, so that the scale
factors to apply to Table B.2.5 become .62 for distillates (with No. 2
fuel oil price employed) and .68 for residuals (with No. 6 fuel oil
price employed). Prices for petroleum coke and refinery gas were set at
.96 and .95 the residual fuel oil price, respectively, on the basis of
relative heat content of those fuels. The same procedure has been
employed by oil industry technical experts in imputing such prices
([17], 80). The price for LPG was also scaled by .68, assuming the
same price level relationships held for that product.

Finally, fuels in miscellaneous business uses were assumed to be
used at the all commercial level, while kerosine in household use was
obtained by scaling the kerosine price in business use by 1.15. Prices
established employing these procedures are shown for individual categories
of use in Table E.2.1.

Expenditures

The multiplication of prices and quantities yielded expenditures in
thousands of dollars, shown for states in Table E.3.1, and for regions

in Table E.3.2. Total expenditures for the U.S. are shown as a bit

above three billion dollars, with industrial use accounting for about

half the total, energy use for about one-third, and miscellaneous use

for the roughly 15 percent remainder. Texas and California are the

leading states, with each accounting for almost 10 percent of the total.

A large portion of those states' expenditures is accounted for by

refinery spending.

Table E.1.1

Industrial, Refinery and Miscellaneous Use Of Petroleum Products, 1972,
    In Thousand Barrels, By State

Industrial Consumption Of Fuel Oils And LPG

REGION AND STATE	DISTILLATE FUEL OIL	RESIDUAL FUEL OIL	DIESEL FUEL OIL	LPG
NEW ENGLAND:				
CONNECTICUT	980.0	7036.0	349.0	487.0
MAINE	347.0	8237.0	232.0	121.9
MASSACHUSETTS	1059.0	7249.0	395.0	285.5
NEW HAMPSHIRE	105.0	1580.0	93.0	66.4
RHODE ISLAND	136.0	1398.0	163.0	79.7
VERMONT	78.0	397.0	81.0	26.5
MID ATLANTIC:				
NEW JERSEY	2205.0	9015.0	738.0	1219.6
NEW YORK	2454.0	9212.0	1543.0	969.0
PENNSYLVANIA	2912.0	10818.0	1051.0	1365.4
EAST NORTH CENTRAL:				
ILLINOIS	2380.0	4007.0	1210.0	1755.9
INDIANA	1724.0	4184.0	1075.0	470.4
MICHIGAN	2504.0	3232.0	2184.0	333.7
OHIO	4784.0	1758.0	2047.0	876.2
WISCONSIN	493.0	765.0	972.0	794.6
WEST NORTH CENTRAL:				
IOWA	706.0	123.0	1143.0	581.5
KANSAS	243.0	533.0	1672.0	373.5
MINNESOTA	962.0	4365.0	970.0	845.6
MISSOURI	1131.0	505.0	836.0	451.5
NEBRASKA	406.0	79.0	870.0	315.3
NORTH DAKOTA	100.0	10.0	307.0	179.7
SOUTH DAKOTA	50.0	67.0	273.0	135.6
SOUTH ATLANTIC:				
DELAWARE	219.0	3371.0	139.0	33.2
DISTRICT OF COLUMBIA	11.0	119.0	35.0	5.6
FLORIDA	1070.0	7248.0	1882.0	304.6
GEORGIA	1522.0	6449.0	1348.0	265.6
MARYLAND	973.0	6981.0	1034.0	273.3
NORTH CAROLINA	2563.0	9534.0	720.0	610.8
SOUTH CAROLINA	1259.0	3486.0	639.0	528.9
VIRGINIA	1559.0	6659.0	862.0	371.8
WEST VIRGINIA	749.0	495.0	314.0	345.2
EAST SOUTH CENTRAL:				
ALABAMA	1285.0	1033.0	1102.0	364.5
KENTUCKY	775.0	50.0	768.0	420.2
MISSISSIPPI	658.0	270.0	1004.0	578.2
TENNESSEE	1281.0	233.0	1318.0	124.3
WEST SOUTH CENTRAL:				
ARKANSAS	514.0	576.0	982.0	459.0
LOUISIANA	1644.0	1005.0	2652.0	3875.5
OKLAHOMA	1199.0	703.0	1416.0	598.9
TEXAS	2683.0	1785.0	4015.0	1472.8
ROCKY MOUNTAIN:				
ARIZONA	2197.0	69.0	435.0	46.6
COLORADO	290.0	730.0	960.0	139.6
IDAHO	650.0	70.0	676.0	159.0
MONTANA	774.0	227.0	481.0	211.1
NEVADA	294.0	74.0	285.0	78.3
NEW MEXICO	449.0	163.0	1157.0	221.3
UTAH	923.0	1953.0	630.0	125.3
WYOMING	410.0	130.0	601.0	296.9
FAR WEST:				
ALASKA	202.0	842.0	416.0	82.5
CALIFORNIA	5211.0	11028.0	3649.0	2683.6
HAWAII	267.0	551.0	365.0	92.3
OREGON	1473.0	2793.0	984.0	121.5
WASHINGTON	1525.0	3123.0	1113.0	143.2

Table E.1.2

Industrial, Refinery and Miscellaneous Use Of Petroleum Products, 1972,
      In Thousand Barrels, By Region

Industrial Consumption Of Fuel Oils And LPG

REGION	DISTILLATE FUEL OIL	RESIDUAL FUEL OIL	DIESEL FUEL OIL	LPG
NEW ENGLAND	2705.00	25897.00	1313.00	1067.00
MID ATLANTIC	7571.00	29045.00	3332.00	3554.00
EAST NORTH CENTRAL	11885.00	13946.00	7488.00	4230.80
WEST NORTH CENTRAL	3598.00	5682.00	6071.00	2882.70
SOUTH ATLANTIC	9925.00	44342.00	6973.00	2739.00
EAST SOUTH CENTRAL	3999.00	1586.00	4192.00	1487.20
WEST SOUTH CENTRAL	6040.00	4069.00	9065.00	6406.20
ROCKY MOUNTAIN	5987.00	3416.00	5225.00	1278.10
FAR WEST	8678.00	18337.00	6527.00	3123.10
TOTAL	60388.00	146320.00	50186.00	26768.10

Table E.1.3

Industrial, Refinery And Miscellaneous Use Of Petroleum Products, 1972,
    In Thousand Barrels, By State

Oil Company Use Of Petroleum Products And LPG Use As Utility Gas

REGION AND STATE	OIL COMPANY USE OF PETROLEUM PRODUCTS				LPG FOR UTILITY GAS
	Distillate Fuel Oils	Residual Fuel Oils	Petroleum Coke	Refinery Gas	
NEW ENGLAND:					
CONNECTICUT	50.0	87.0	0.0	0.0	391.9
MAINE	9.0	64.0	0.0	0.0	86.1
MASSACHUSETTS	83.0	62.0	510.0	719.4	461.2
NEW HAMPSHIRE	1.0	2.0	0.0	0.0	327.2
RHODE ISLAND	10.0	49.0	405.0	568.3	65.9
VERMONT	2.0	1.0	0.0	0.0	114.4
MID ATLANTIC:					
NEW JERSEY	297.0	4795.0	3150.0	5204.9	319.0
NEW YORK	119.0	526.0	235.0	1500.0	72.8
PENNSYLVANIA	555.0	6023.0	2670.0	11039.0	475.1
EAST NORTH CENTRAL:					
ILLINOIS	1022.0	7547.0	5100.0	12246.1	217.3
INDIANA	1025.0	5549.0	2010.0	8273.6	11.8
MICHIGAN	199.0	628.0	540.0	1892.4	132.3
OHIO	515.0	2083.0	2240.0	8044.1	406.2
WISCONSIN	216.0	246.0	185.0	310.2	96.8
WEST NORTH CENTRAL:					
IOWA	21.0	0.0	0.0	0.0	217.3
KANSAS	706.0	940.0	1410.0	4758.1	0.0
MINNESOTA	71.0	869.0	650.0	1095.9	146.4
MISSOURI	25.0	410.0	560.0	1293.4	375.5
NEBRASKA	54.0	63.0	85.0	198.8	311.8
NORTH DAKOTA	12.0	518.0	390.0	653.1	77.9
SOUTH DAKOTA	21.0	18.0	0.0	0.0	170.0
SOUTH ATLANTIC:					
DELAWARE	7.0	31.0	255.0	359.5	17.3
DISTRICT OF COLUMBIA	3.0	7.0	0.0	0.0	55.6
FLORIDA	249.0	223.0	0.0	0.0	308.6
GEORGIA	61.0	89.0	0.0	0.0	108.0
MARYLAND	308.0	191.0	0.0	2.6	315.4
NORTH CAROLINA	40.0	41.0	0.0	0.0	24.3
SOUTH CAROLINA	24.0	101.0	0.0	0.0	131.8
VIRGINIA	60.0	139.0	1145.0	1612.7	232.3
WEST VIRGINIA	8.0	50.0	0.0	186.6	0.0
EAST SOUTH CENTRAL:					
ALABAMA	24.0	151.0	190.0	722.0	7.4
KENTUCKY	129.0	620.0	520.0	2358.0	127.5
MISSISSIPPI	276.0	597.0	750.0	2854.2	122.1
TENNESSEE	83.0	0.0	0.0	0.0	70.8
WEST SOUTH CENTRAL:					
ARKANSAS	170.0	184.0	35.0	623.9	0.0
LOUISIANA	1153.0	159.0	5305.0	18927.2	0.0
OKLAHOMA	54.0	219.0	1625.0	5506.5	0.0
TEXAS	3212.0	620.0	16510.0	44322.3	134.8
ROCKY MOUNTAIN:					
ARIZONA	27.0	2.0	0.0	0.0	0.0
COLORADO	184.0	120.0	175.0	766.9	61.4
IDAHO	18.0	0.0	0.0	0.0	0.0
MONTANA	40.0	967.0	810.0	1954.9	0.0
NEVADA	28.0	0.0	0.0	0.0	0.0
NEW MEXICO	10.0	13.0	200.0	499.8	0.0
UTAH	129.0	738.0	795.0	1270.7	0.0
WYOMING	381.0	573.0	685.0	1711.7	0.0
FAR WEST:					
ALASKA	176.0	3.0	5.0	11.9	0.0
CALIFORNIA	852.0	5364.0	4715.0	20978.4	760.3
HAWAII	15.0	744.0	655.0	2909.8	233.4
OREGON	236.0	283.0	250.0	1106.8	0.0
WASHINGTON	435.0	1582.0	1390.0	6187.3	13.6

Table E.1.4

Industrial, Refinery and Miscellaneous Use Of Petroleum Products, 1972,
    In Thousand Barrels, By Region

Oil Company Use Of Petroleum Products And LPG Use As A Utility Gas

| | OIL COMPANY USE OF PETROLEUM PRODUCTS | | | | LPG FOR |
	Distillate Fuel Oils	Residual Fuel Oils	Petroleum Coke	Refinery Gas	UTILITY GAS
NEW ENGLAND	155.00	265.00	915.00	1287.70	1446.70
MID ATLANTIC	971.00	11344.00	6055.00	17743.90	866.90
EAST NORTH CENTRAL	2977.00	16053.00	10075.00	30766.40	864.40
WEST NORTH CENTRAL	910.00	2818.00	3095.00	7999.30	1298.90
SOUTH ATLANTIC	760.00	872.00	1400.00	2161.40	1193.30
EAST SOUTH CENTRAL	512.00	1368.00	1460.00	5934.20	327.80
WEST SOUTH CENTRAL	4589.00	1182.00	23475.00	69379.90	134.80
ROCKY MOUNTAIN	817.00	2413.00	2665.00	6204.00	61.40
FAR WEST	1714.00	7976.00	7015.00	31194.20	1007.30
TOTAL	13405.00	44291.00	56155.00	172671.00	7201.50

Table E.1.5

Industrial, Refinery And Miscellaneous Use Of Petroleum Products, 1972,
   In Thousand Barreļs, By State

Miscellaneous Use Of Petroleum Products

REGION & STATE	KEROSINE	DISTILLATE FUEL OIL	RESIDUAL FUEL OIL	LPG[a]	TRANSFER LPG [b]
NEW ENGLAND:					
CONNECTICUT	212.0	55.0	106.0	31.2	98.8
MAINE	33.0	78.0	55.0	3.9	22.4
MASSACHUSETTS	391.0	82.0	500.0	66.2	86.2
NEW HAMPSHIRE	54.0	40.0	1.0	21.4	23.6
RHODE ISLAND	38.0	17.0	51.0	3.9	15.5
VERMONT	43.0	42.0	3.0	0.0	4.4
MID ATLANTIC:					
NEW JERSEY	288.0	347.0	152.0	23.4	215.3
NEW YORK	792.0	606.0	269.0	111.0	225.4
PENNSYLVANIA	618.0	166.0	1149.0	70.1	266.9
EAST NORTH CENTRAL:					
ILLINOIS	1332.0	370.0	451.0	806.7	765.0
INDIANA	15.0	381.0	46.0	492.8	367.8
MICHIGAN	556.0	234.0	337.0	55.1	87.6
OHIO	1270.0	240.0	140.0	159.1	238.4
WISCONSIN	61.0	116.0	20.0	162.4	226.9
WEST NORTH CENTRAL:					
IOWA	148.0	234.0	0.0	435.0	352.1
KANSAS	51.0	31.0	75.0	135.0	141.2
MINNESOTA	55.0	113.0	20.0	205.4	260.6
MISSOURI	163.0	147.0	80.0	92.7	129.2
NEBRASKA	15.0	85.0	24.0	88.1	104.0
NORTH DAKOTA	46.0	235.0	4.0	16.5	39.4
SOUTH DAKOTA	1.0	198.0	0.0	41.3	46.7
SOUTH ATLANTIC:					
DELAWARE	33.0	43.0	649.0	33.1	25.0
DISTRICT OF COLUMBIA	5.0	86.0	2.0	3.7	3.1
FLORIDA	814.0	332.0	289.0	68.2	90.5
GEORGIA	293.0	196.0	35.0	603.7	399.3
MARYLAND	81.0	230.0	231.0	22.7	58.5
NORTH CAROLINA	1085.0	371.0	341.0	570.6	436.8
SOUTH CAROLINA	179.0	135.0	115.0	175.3	190.6
VIRGINIA	429.0	321.0	666.0	142.2	145.1
WEST VIRGINIA	38.0	69.0	1.0	0.0	57.0
EAST SOUTH CENTRAL:					
ALABAMA	294.0	408.0	182.0	49.3	89.2
KENTUCKY	387.0	181.0	0.0	41.3	93.7
MISSISSIPPI	1808.0	273.0	0.0	171.5	368.0
TENNESSEE	740.0	153.0	4.0	12.9	28.1
WEST SOUTH CENTRAL:					
ARKANSAS	265.0	381.0	70.0	303.6	732.4
LOUISIANA	1715.0	744.0	219.0	212.4	765.4
OKLAHOMA	260.0	107.0	25.0	38.5	210.5
TEXAS	3277.0	758.0	441.0	323.6	4132.1
ROCKY MOUNTAIN:					
ARIZONA	50.0	103.0	132.0	108.6	71.6
COLORADO	415.0	249.0	86.0	180.5	129.3
IDAHO	125.0	190.0	8.0	113.2	92.9
MONTANA	306.0	240.0	2.0	7.1	39.1
NEVADA	3.0	165.0	0.0	0.0	12.9
NEW MEXICO	316.0	392.0	28.0	49.4	65.6
UTAH	182.0	102.0	20.0	87.5	72.2
WYOMING	131.0	22.0	10.0	32.4	68.1
FAR WEST:					
ALASKA	8.0	150.0	55.0	0.0	13.6
CALIFORNIA	106.0	337.0	685.0	970.1	1014.5
HAWAII	17.0	23.0	365.0	0.0	15.3
OREGON	79.0	109.0	97.0	92.4	74.4
WASHINGTON	32.0	165.0	645.0	78.7	70.0

[a] As listed in [25] under heading of miscellaneous use.

[b] Reallocated amounts of portion of LPG listed as internal combustion engine fuel but inferred
as not used on highways.

Table E.1.6

Industrial, Refinery and Miscellaneous Use Of Petroleum Products, 1972,
     In Thousand Barrels, By State

Miscellaneous Use Of Petroleum Products

REGION	KEROSINE	DISTILLATE FUEL OIL	RESIDUAL FUEL OIL	LPG [a]	TRANSFER LPG [b]
NEW ENGLAND	771.00	314.00	716.00	126.60	250.90
MID ATLANTIC	1698.00	1119.00	1570.00	204.50	707.60
EAST NORTH CENTRAL	3234.00	1341.00	994.00	1676.10	1685.70
WEST NORTH CENTRAL	479.00	1043.00	203.00	1014.00	1073.20
SOUTH ATLANTIC	2957.00	1783.00	2329.00	1619.50	1405.90
EAST SOUTH CENTRAL	3229.00	1015.00	186.00	275.00	579.00
WEST SOUTH CENTRAL	5517.00	1990.00	755.00	878.10	5840.40
ROCKY MOUNTAIN	1528.00	1463.00	286.00	578.70	551.70
FAR WEST	242.00	784.00	1847.00	1141.20	1187.80
TOTAL	19655.00	10852.00	8886.00	7513.70	13282.20

[a] As listed in [25] under heading of Miscellaneous Use.

[b] Reallocated amounts of portion of LPG listed as internal combustion engine fuel,
   but inferred as not used on highways.

Table E.1.7

Industrial, Refinery And Miscellaneous Use Of Petroleum Products, 1972,
    In Billion BTU, By State

Industrial Consumption Of Fuel Oils And LPG

REGION AND STATE	DISTILLATE FUEL OIL	RESIDUAL FUEL OIL	DIESEL FUEL OIL	LPG	TOTAL INDUSTRIAL
NEW ENGLAND:					
CONNECTICUT	5708.5	44235.3	2032.9	1953.4	53930.1
MAINE	2021.3	51786.0	1351.4	488.9	55647.6
MASSACHUSETTS	6168.7	45574.5	2300.9	1145.1	55189.2
NEW HAMPSHIRE	611.6	9933.5	541.7	266.3	11353.1
RHODE ISLAND	792.2	8789.2	949.5	319.7	10850.6
VERMONT	454.3	2495.9	471.8	106.3	3528.4
MID ATLANTIC:					
NEW JERSEY	12844.1	56677.3	4298.8	4891.8	78712.1
NEW YORK	14294.6	57915.8	8988.0	3886.7	85085.0
PENNSYLVANIA	16962.4	68012.8	6122.1	5476.6	96573.9
EAST NORTH CENTRAL:					
ILLINOIS	13863.5	25192.0	7048.2	7042.9	53146.7
INDIANA	10042.3	26304.8	6261.9	1886.8	44495.8
MICHIGAN	14585.8	20319.6	12721.8	1338.5	48965.7
OHIO	27866.8	11052.5	11923.8	3514.4	54357.6
WISCONSIN	2871.7	4809.6	5661.9	3187.1	16530.3
WEST NORTH CENTRAL:					
IOWA	4112.4	773.3	6658.0	2332.4	13876.1
KANSAS	1415.5	3351.0	9739.4	1498.1	16004.0
MINNESOTA	5603.6	27442.8	5650.3	3391.7	42088.4
MISSOURI	6588.1	3174.9	4869.7	1811.0	16443.7
NEBRASKA	2364.9	496.7	5067.7	1264.7	9194.0
NORTH DAKOTA	582.5	62.9	1788.3	720.8	3154.4
SOUTH DAKOTA	291.3	421.2	1590.2	543.9	2846.6
SOUTH ATLANTIC:					
DELAWARE	1275.7	21193.5	809.7	133.2	23412.0
DISTRICT OF COLUMBIA	64.1	748.2	203.9	22.5	1038.6
FLORIDA	6232.7	45568.2	10962.6	1221.8	63985.3
GEORGIA	8865.6	40544.9	7852.1	1065.3	58327.9
MARYLAND	5667.7	43889.5	6023.0	1096.2	56676.5
NORTH CAROLINA	14929.5	59940.3	4194.0	2449.9	81513.7
SOUTH CAROLINA	7333.7	21916.5	3722.2	2121.4	35093.8
VIRGINIA	9081.2	41865.1	5021.1	1491.3	57458.7
WEST VIRGINIA	4362.9	3112.1	1829.0	1384.6	10688.6
EAST SOUTH CENTRAL:					
ALABAMA	7485.1	6494.5	6419.1	1462.0	21860.8
KENTUCKY	4514.4	314.3	4473.6	1685.4	10987.7
MISSISSIPPI	3832.9	1697.5	5848.3	2319.2	13697.8
TENNESSEE	7461.8	1464.9	7677.3	498.6	17102.6
WEST SOUTH CENTRAL:					
ARKANSAS	2994.0	3621.3	5720.1	1841.0	14176.6
LOUISIANA	9576.3	6318.4	15447.9	15544.6	46887.3
OKLAHOMA	6984.2	4419.8	8248.2	2402.2	22054.3
TEXAS	15628.5	11222.3	23387.4	5907.4	56145.5
ROCKY MOUNTAIN:					
ARIZONA	12797.5	433.8	2533.9	186.9	15952.1
COLORADO	1689.3	4589.5	5592.0	559.9	12430.7
IDAHO	3786.3	440.1	3937.7	637.7	8801.8
MONTANA	4508.5	1427.1	2801.8	846.7	9584.2
NEVADA	1712.5	465.2	1660.1	314.1	4152.0
NEW MEXICO	2615.4	1024.8	6739.5	887.6	11267.4
UTAH	5376.5	12278.5	3669.7	502.6	21827.3
WYOMING	2388.3	817.3	3500.8	1190.9	7897.3
FAR WEST:					
ALASKA	1176.6	5293.7	2423.2	330.9	9224.4
CALIFORNIA	30354.1	69333.0	21255.4	10763.9	131706.5
HAWAII	1555.3	3464.1	2126.1	370.2	7515.8
OREGON	8580.2	17559.6	5731.8	487.3	32359.0
WASHINGTON	8883.1	19634.3	6483.2	574.4	35575.0

Table E.1.8

Industrial, Refinery And Miscellaneous Use Of Petroleum Products, 1972, In Billion BTU, By State

Oil Company Use Of Petroleum Products And LPG Use As Utility Gas

REGION AND STATE	OIL COMPANY USE OF PETROLEUM PRODUCTS					LPG FOR UTILITY GAS	TOTAL ENERGY USE
	Distillate Fuel Oils	Residual Fuel Oils	Petroleum Gas	Refinery Gas	Total Oil Co. Use		
NEW ENGLAND:							
CONNECTICUT	291.3	547.0	0.0	0.0	838.2	1571.9	2410.1
MAINE	52.4	402.4	0.0	0.0	454.8	345.3	800.1
MASSACHUSETTS	483.5	389.8	3072.2	4316.4	8261.9	1849.9	10111.8
NEW HAMPSHIRE	5.8	12.6	0.0	0.0	18.4	1312.4	1330.8
RHODE ISLAND	58.3	308.1	2439.7	3409.8	6215.8	264.3	6480.2
VERMONT	11.6	6.3	0.0	0.0	17.9	458.9	476.8
MID ATLANTIC:							
NEW JERSEY	1730.0	30146.2	18975.6	31229.4	82081.2	1279.5	83360.7
NEW YORK	693.2	3307.0	1415.6	9000.0	14415.8	292.0	14707.8
PENNSYLVANIA	3232.9	37866.6	16084.1	66234.0	123417.6	1905.6	125323.2
EAST NORTH CENTRAL:							
ILLINOIS	5953.1	47448.0	30722.4	73476.6	157600.1	871.6	158471.7
INDIANA	5970.6	34886.6	12108.2	49641.6	102607.0	47.3	102654.4
MICHIGAN	1159.2	3948.2	3253.0	11354.4	19714.8	530.7	20245.4
OHIO	2999.9	13095.8	13493.8	48264.6	77854.1	1629.3	79483.3
WISCONSIN	1258.2	1546.6	1114.4	1861.2	5780.4	388.3	6168.7
WEST NORTH CENTRAL:							
IOWA	122.3	0.0	0.0	0.0	122.3	871.6	993.9
KANSAS	4112.4	5909.8	8493.8	28548.6	47064.7	0.0	47064.7
MINNESOTA	413.6	5463.4	3915.6	6575.4	16368.0	587.2	16955.2
MISSOURI	145.6	2577.7	3373.4	7760.4	13857.1	1506.1	15363.3
NEBRASKA	314.5	396.1	512.0	1192.8	2415.5	1250.6	3666.1
NORTH DAKOTA	69.9	3256.7	2349.4	3918.6	9594.5	312.5	9907.0
SOUTH DAKOTA	122.3	113.2	0.0	0.0	235.5	681.9	917.4
SOUTH ATLANTIC:							
DELAWARE	40.8	194.9	1536.1	2157.0	3928.8	69.4	3998.2
DISTRICT OF COLUMBIA	17.5	44.0	0.0	0.0	61.5	223.0	284.5
FLORIDA	1450.4	1402.0	0.0	0.0	2852.4	1237.8	4090.2
GEORGIA	355.3	559.5	0.0	0.0	914.9	433.2	1348.1
MARYLAND	1794.1	1200.8	0.0	15.6	3010.5	1265.1	4275.6
NORTH CAROLINA	233.0	257.8	0.0	0.0	490.8	97.5	588.2
SOUTH CAROLINA	139.8	635.0	0.0	0.0	774.8	528.6	1303.4
VIRGINIA	349.5	873.9	6897.5	9676.2	17797.1	931.8	18728.8
WEST VIRGINIA	46.6	314.3	0.0	1119.6	1480.5	0.0	1480.5
EAST SOUTH CENTRAL:							
ALABAMA	139.8	949.3	1144.6	4332.0	6565.7	29.7	6595.4
KENTUCKY	751.4	3897.9	3132.5	14148.0	21929.8	511.4	22441.2
MISSISSIPPI	1607.7	3753.3	4518.0	17125.2	27004.2	489.7	27494.0
TENNESSEE	483.5	0.0	0.0	0.0	483.5	284.0	767.5
WEST SOUTH CENTRAL:							
ARKANSAS	990.2	1156.8	210.8	3743.4	6101.3	0.0	6101.3
LOUISIANA	6716.2	999.6	31957.3	113563.2	153236.4	0.0	153236.4
OKLAHOMA	314.5	1376.9	9789.0	33039.0	44519.4	0.0	44519.4
TEXAS	18709.9	3897.9	99456.2	265933.8	387997.9	540.7	388538.6
ROCKY MOUNTAIN:							
ARIZONA	157.3	12.6	0.0	0.0	169.8	0.0	169.8
COLORADO	1071.8	754.4	1054.2	4601.4	7481.8	246.3	7728.1
IDAHO	104.8	0.0	0.0	0.0	104.8	0.0	104.8
MONTANA	233.0	6079.5	4879.4	11729.4	22921.4	0.0	22921.4
NEVADA	163.1	0.0	0.0	0.0	163.1	0.0	163.1
NEW MEXICO	58.3	81.7	1204.8	2998.8	4343.6	0.0	4343.6
UTAH	751.4	4639.8	4789.1	7624.2	17804.5	0.0	17804.5
WYOMING	2219.3	3602.5	4126.4	10270.2	20218.4	0.0	20218.4
FAR WEST:							
ALASKA	1025.2	18.9	30.1	71.4	1145.6	0.0	1145.6
CALIFORNIA	4962.9	33723.5	28403.2	125870.4	192959.9	3049.6	196009.5
HAWAII	87.4	4677.5	3945.7	17458.8	26169.4	936.2	27105.6
OREGON	1374.7	1779.2	1506.0	6640.8	11300.7	0.0	11300.7
WASHINGTON	2533.9	9946.0	8373.4	37123.8	57977.1	54.5	58031.6

Table E.1.9

Industrial, Refinery And Miscellaneous Use Of Petroleum Products, 1972, In Billion BTU By State

Miscellaneous Use Of Petroleum Products

REGION AND STATE	KEROSINE	DISTILLATE FUEL OIL	RESIDUAL FUEL OIL	LPG	TRANSFER LPG	TOTAL MISC. USE
NEW ENGLAND:						
CONNECTICUT	1202.0	320.4	666.4	125.1	396.3	2710.3
MAINE	187.1	454.3	345.8	15.6	89.8	1092.7
MASSACHUSETTS	2217.0	477.6	3143.5	265.5	345.7	6449.4
NEW HAMPSHIRE	306.2	233.0	6.3	85.8	94.7	726.0
RHODE ISLAND	215.5	99.0	320.6	15.6	62.2	712.9
VERMONT	243.8	244.6	18.9	0.0	17.6	525.0
MID ATLANTIC:						
NEW JERSEY	1633.0	2021.3	955.6	93.9	863.6	5567.3
NEW YORK	4490.6	3529.9	1691.2	445.2	904.1	11061.1
PENNSYLVANIA	3504.1	966.9	7223.8	281.2	1070.5	13046.5
EAST NORTH CENTRAL:						
ILLINOIS	7552.4	2155.2	2835.4	3235.7	3068.4	18847.2
INDIANA	85.1	2219.3	289.2	1976.6	1475.2	6045.4
MICHIGAN	3152.5	1363.1	2118.7	221.0	351.4	7206.7
OHIO	7200.9	1398.0	880.2	638.2	956.2	11073.5
WISCONSIN	345.9	675.7	125.7	651.4	910.1	2708.8
WEST NORTH CENTRAL:						
IOWA	839.2	1363.1	0.0	1744.8	1412.3	5359.3
KANSAS	289.2	180.6	471.5	541.5	566.4	2049.1
MINNESOTA	311.9	658.2	125.7	823.9	1045.3	2964.9
MISSOURI	924.2	856.3	503.0	371.8	518.2	3173.5
NEBRASKA	85.1	495.1	150.9	353.4	417.1	1501.6
NORTH DAKOTA	260.8	1368.9	25.1	66.2	158.0	1879.1
SOUTH DAKOTA	5.7	1153.3	0.0	165.7	187.3	1512.0
SOUTH ATLANTIC:						
DELAWARE	187.1	250.5	4080.3	132.8	100.3	4750.9
DISTRICT OF COLUMBIA	28.4	501.0	12.6	14.8	12.4	569.1
FLORIDA	4615.4	1933.9	1816.9	273.6	363.0	9002.8
GEORGIA	1661.3	1141.7	220.0	2421.4	1601.6	7046.1
MARYLAND	459.3	1339.7	1452.3	91.0	234.6	3577.0
NORTH CAROLINA	6151.9	2161.1	2143.9	2288.7	1752.0	14497.6
SOUTH CAROLINA	1014.9	786.4	723.0	703.1	764.5	3991.9
VIRGINIA	2432.4	1869.8	4187.1	570.4	582.0	9641.8
WEST VIRGINIA	215.5	401.9	6.3	0.0	228.6	852.3
EAST SOUTH CENTRAL:						
ALABAMA	1667.0	2376.6	1144.2	197.7	357.8	5743.3
KENTUCKY	2194.3	1054.3	0.0	165.7	375.8	3790.1
MISSISSIPPI	10251.4	1590.2	0.0	687.9	1476.0	14005.5
TENNESSEE	4195.8	891.2	25.1	51.7	112.7	5276.6
WEST SOUTH CENTRAL:						
ARKANSAS	1502.6	2219.3	440.1	1217.7	2937.7	8317.4
LOUISIANA	9724.1	4333.8	1376.9	851.9	3070.0	19356.7
OKLAHOMA	1474.2	623.3	157.2	154.4	844.3	3253.4
TEXAS	18580.6	4415.3	2772.6	1298.0	16573.9	43640.3
ROCKY MOUNTAIN:						
ARIZONA	283.5	600.0	829.9	435.6	287.2	2436.1
COLORADO	2353.1	1450.4	540.7	724.0	518.6	5586.8
IDAHO	708.8	1106.7	50.3	454.0	372.6	2692.5
MONTANA	1735.0	1398.0	12.6	28.5	156.8	3330.9
NEVADA	17.0	961.1	0.0	0.0	51.7	1029.9
NEW MEXICO	1791.7	2283.4	176.0	198.1	263.1	4712.4
UTAH	1031.9	594.1	125.7	351.0	289.6	2392.4
WYOMING	742.8	128.1	62.9	130.0	273.1	1336.9
FAR WEST:						
ALASKA	45.4	873.8	345.8	0.0	54.5	1319.4
CALIFORNIA	601.0	1963.0	4306.6	3891.1	4069.2	14830.9
HAWAII	96.4	134.0	2294.8	0.0	61.4	2586.5
OREGON	447.9	634.9	609.8	370.6	298.4	2361.7
WASHINGTON	181.4	961.1	4055.1	315.7	280.8	5794.1

Table E.1.10

Industrial, Reginery and Miscellaneous Use Of Petroleum Products, 1972,
In Billion BTU, By Region

Category Components And Total Consumption By Category

Industrial Use

	DISTILLATES	RESIDUALS	DIESEL	LPG	INDUSTRIAL TOTAL
NEW ENGLAND	15756.60	162814.40	7648.20	4279.70	190499.00
MID ATLANTIC	44101.10	182605.90	19408.90	14255.10	260371.00
EAST NORTH CENTRAL	69230.10	87678.50	43617.60	16969.70	217496.10
WEST NORTH CENTRAL	20958.30	35722.80	35363.60	11562.60	103607.20
SOUTH ATLANTIC	57813.10	278778.30	40617.60	10986.20	388195.10
EAST SOUTH CENTRAL	23294.20	9971.20	24418.30	5965.20	63648.90
WEST SOUTH CENTRAL	35183.00	25581.80	52803.60	25695.20	139263.70
ROCKY MOUNTAIN	34874.30	21476.30	30435.50	5126.40	91912.80
FAR WEST	50549.30	115284.70	38019.70	12526.70	216380.70
TOTAL	351760.00	919913.88	292333.00	107366.80	1671374.48

Energy Use

	OIL COMPANY USE					LPG-UT. GAS	ENERGY TOTAL
	Distillates	Residuals	Pet. Coke	Ref. Gas	Oil Co. Total		
NEW ENGLAND	902.90	1666.20	5511.90	7726.20	15807.00	5802.70	21609.80
MID ATLANTIC	5656.10	71319.80	36475.30	106463.40	219914.60	3477.10	223391.70
EAST NORTH CENTRAL	17341.00	100925.20	60691.80	184598.40	363556.40	3467.20	367023.50
WEST NORTH CENTRAL	5300.60	17716.90	18644.20	47995.80	89657.60	5209.90	94867.60
SOUTH ATLANTIC	4427.00	5482.20	8433.60	12968.40	31311.30	4786.40	36097.50
EAST SOUTH CENTRAL	2982.40	8600.50	8795.10	35605.20	55983.20	1314.80	57298.10
WEST SOUTH CENTRAL	26730.80	7431.20	141413.30	416279.40	591855.00	540.70	592395.70
ROCKY MOUNTAIN	4759.00	15170.50	16053.90	37224.00	73207.40	246.30	73453.70
FAR WEST	9984.10	50145.10	42258.40	187165.20	289552.70	4040.30	293593.00
TOTAL	78083.90	278457.60	338277.50	1036025.99	1730845.18	28885.40	1759730.58

Miscellaneous Use

	KEROSINE	DISTILLATES	RESIDUALS	LPG	TRANSFER LPG	MISCELLANEOUS TOTAL
NEW ENGLAND	4371.60	1828.90	4501.50	507.60	1006.30	12216.30
MID ATLANTIC	9627.70	6518.10	9870.60	820.30	2838.20	29674.90
EAST NORTH CENTRAL	18336.80	7811.30	6249.20	6722.90	6761.30	45881.60
WEST NORTH CENTRAL	2716.10	6075.50	1276.20	4067.30	4304.60	18439.50
SOUTH ATLANTIC	16766.20	10386.00	14642.40	6495.80	5639.00	53929.50
EAST SOUTH CENTRAL	18308.50	5912.30	1169.30	1103.00	2322.30	28815.50
WEST SOUTH CENTRAL	31281.50	11591.70	4746.80	3522.00	23425.90	74567.80
ROCKY MOUNTAIN	8663.80	8521.80	1798.10	2321.20	2212.70	23517.90
FAR WEST	1372.10	4566.80	11612.10	4577.40	4764.30	26892.60
TOTAL	111444.30	63212.40	55866.20	30137.50	53274.60	313935.59

Table E.1.11

Industrial, Refinery And Miscellaneous Use Of Petroleum Products, 1972, In Billion BTU, By State

Aggregate Use By Categories Of Use

REGION AND STATE	INDUSTRIAL USE TOTAL	ENERGY USE			MISCELLANEOUS USE			TOTAL ALL USES
		Oil Co. Total	LPG For Utility Gas	Energy Use Total	Household Kerosine Use	Business Use	Misc. Total	
NEW ENGLAND:								
CONNECTICUT	53930.1	838.2	1571.9	2410.1	601.0	2109.2	2710.3	59050.5
MAINE	55647.6	454.8	345.3	800.1	93.6	999.2	1092.7	57540.5
MASSACHUSETTS	55189.2	8261.9	1849.9	10111.8	1108.5	5340.9	6449.4	71750.3
NEW HAMPSHIRE	11353.1	18.4	1312.4	1330.8	153.1	572.9	726.0	13409.9
RHODE ISLAND	10850.6	6215.8	264.3	6480.2	107.7	605.2	712.9	18043.7
VERMONT	3528.4	17.9	458.9	476.8	121.9	403.1	525.0	4530.2
MID ATLANTIC:								
NEW JERSEY	78712.1	82081.2	1279.5	83360.7	816.5	4750.8	5567.3	167640.1
NEW YORK	85085.0	14415.8	292.0	14707.8	2245.3	8815.8	11061.1	110853.9
PENNSYLVANIA	96573.9	123417.6	1905.6	125323.2	1752.0	11294.5	13046.5	234943.5
EAST NORTH CENTRAL:								
ILLINOIS	53146.7	157600.1	871.6	158471.7	3776.2	15071.0	18847.2	230465.6
INDIANA	44495.8	102607.0	47.3	102654.4	42.5	6002.9	6045.4	153195.6
MICHIGAN	48965.7	19714.8	530.7	20245.4	1576.3	5630.4	7206.7	76417.7
OHIO	54357.6	77854.1	1629.3	79483.3	3600.5	7473.0	11073.5	144914.3
WISCONSIN	16530.3	5780.4	388.3	6168.7	172.9	2535.9	2708.8	25407.8
WEST NORTH CENTRAL:								
IOWA	13876.1	122.3	871.6	993.9	419.6	4939.7	5359.3	20229.3
KANSAS	16004.0	47064.7	0.0	47064.7	144.6	1904.5	2049.1	65117.7
MINNESOTA	42088.4	16368.0	587.2	16955.2	155.9	2809.0	2964.9	62008.5
MISSOURI	16443.7	13857.1	1506.1	15363.3	462.1	2711.4	3173.5	34980.4
NEBRASKA	9194.0	2415.5	1250.6	3666.1	42.5	1459.1	1501.6	14361.7
NORTH DAKOTA	3154.4	9594.5	312.5	9907.0	130.4	1748.6	1879.1	14940.5
SOUTH DAKOTA	2846.6	235.5	681.9	917.4	2.8	1509.2	1512.0	5275.9
SOUTH ATLANTIC:								
DELAWARE	23412.0	3928.8	69.4	3998.2	93.6	4657.3	4750.9	32161.1
DISTRICT OF COLUMBIA	1038.6	61.5	223.0	284.5	14.2	555.0	569.1	1892.2
FLORIDA	63985.3	2852.4	1237.8	4090.2	2307.7	6695.1	9002.8	77078.3
GEORGIA	58327.9	914.9	433.2	1348.1	830.7	6215.4	7046.1	66722.1
MARYLAND	56676.5	3010.5	1265.1	4275.6	229.6	3347.4	3577.0	64529.1
NORTH CAROLINA	81513.7	490.8	97.5	588.2	3076.0	11421.6	14497.6	96599.5
SOUTH CAROLINA	35093.8	774.8	528.6	1303.4	507.5	3484.5	3991.9	40389.1
VIRGINIA	57458.7	17797.1	931.8	18728.8	1216.2	8425.5	9641.8	85829.3
WEST VIRGINIA	10688.6	1480.5	0.0	1480.5	107.7	744.6	852.3	13021.5
EAST SOUTH CENTRAL:								
ALABAMA	21860.8	6565.7	29.7	6595.4	833.5	4909.8	5743.3	34199.5
KENTUCKY	10987.2	21929.8	511.4	22441.2	1097.1	2693.0	3790.1	37219.1
MISSISSIPPI	13697.8	27004.2	489.7	27494.0	5125.7	8879.8	14005.5	55197.3
TENNESSEE	17102.6	483.5	284.0	767.5	2097.9	3178.7	5276.6	23146.7
WEST SOUTH CENTRAL:								
ARKANSAS	14176.6	6101.3	0.0	6101.3	751.3	7566.1	8317.4	28595.2
LOUISIANA	46887.3	153236.4	0.0	153236.4	4862.0	14494.6	19356.7	219480.3
OKLAHOMA	22054.4	44519.4	0.0	44519.4	737.1	2516.3	3253.4	69827.1
TEXAS	56145.5	387997.9	540.7	388538.6	9290.3	34350.0	43640.3	488324.4
ROCKY MOUNTAIN:								
ARIZONA	15952.1	169.8	0.0	169.8	141.8	2294.4	2436.1	18558.1
COLORADO	12430.7	7481.8	246.3	7728.1	1176.5	4410.2	5586.8	25745.6
IDAHO	8801.8	104.8	0.0	104.8	354.4	2338.1	2692.5	11599.1
MONTANA	9584.2	22921.4	0.0	22921.4	867.5	2463.4	3330.9	35836.5
NEVADA	4152.0	163.1	0.0	163.1	8.5	1021.4	1029.9	5345.0
NEW MEXICO	11267.4	4343.6	0.0	4343.6	895.9	3816.6	4712.4	20323.4
UTAH	21827.3	17804.5	0.0	17804.5	516.0	1876.4	2392.4	42024.2
WYOMING	7897.3	20218.4	0.0	20218.4	371.4	965.5	1336.9	29452.6
FAR WEST:								
ALASKA	9224.4	1145.6	0.0	1145.6	22.7	1296.8	1319.4	11689.4
CALIFORNIA	131706.5	192959.9	3049.6	196009.5	300.5	14530.4	14830.9	342546.8
HAWAII	7515.8	26169.4	936.2	27105.6	48.2	2538.3	2586.5	37207.8
OREGON	32359.0	11300.7	0.0	11300.7	224.0	2137.8	2361.7	46021.4
WASHINGTON	35575.0	57977.1	54.5	58031.6	90.7	5703.4	5794.1	99400.8

Table E.1.12

Industrial, Refinery And Miscellaneous Use Of Petroleum Products, 1972, In Billion BTU, By Region

Aggregate Use By Categories Of Use

REGION	INDUSTRIAL USE TOTAL	ENERGY USE			MISCELLANEOUS USE			TOTAL, ALL USE
		Oil Co. Use	LPG for Utility Gas	Energy Use Total	Household Kerosine Use	Business Use	Misc. Total	
NEW ENGLAND	190499.00	15807.00	5802.70	21609.80	2185.80	10030.50	12216.30	224325.10
MID ATLANTIC	260371.00	219914.60	3477.10	223391.70	4813.80	24861.10	29674.90	513437.50
EAST NORTH CENTRAL	217496.10	363556.40	3467.20	367023.50	9168.40	36713.20	45881.60	630400.99
WEST NORTH CENTRAL	103607.20	89657.60	5209.90	94867.60	1357.90	17081.50	18439.50	216914.00
SOUTH ATLANTIC	388195.10	31311.30	4786.40	36097.50	8383.20	45546.40	53929.50	478222.20
EAST SOUTH CENTRAL	63648.90	55983.20	1314.80	57298.10	9154.20	19661.30	28815.50	149762.60
WEST SOUTH CENTRAL	139263.70	591855.00	540.70	592395.70	15640.70	58927.00	74567.80	806227.00
ROCKY MOUNTAIN	91912.80	73207.40	246.30	73453.70	4332.00	19186.00	23517.90	188884.50
FAR WEST	216380.70	289552.70	4040.30	293593.00	686.10	26206.70	26892.60	536866.20
TOTAL	1671374.48	1730845.18	28885.40	1759730.58	55722.10	258213.71	313935.59	3745040.11

Table E.2.1

Prices For Industrial, Refinery And Miscellaneous Use Of Petroleum Products, 1972, In Dollars Per Barrel

Prices For Individual Categories Of Use [a]

REGION AND STATE	INDUSTRIAL USE				ENERGY USE					MISCELLANEOUS USE			
	Dis.	Res.	Dsl.	LPG	Dis.	Oil Co. Use			LPG-Ut. Gas	Kero.	Dis.	Res.	LPG
						Res.	Coke	R Gas					
NEW ENGLAND:													
CONNECTICUT	7.44	5.94	7.65	5.38	4.80	4.12	3.96	3.91	3.73	8.02	7.75	6.06	5.49
MAINE	7.40	6.06	7.61	5.48	4.78	4.21	4.04	4.00	3.80	7.98	7.71	6.19	5.60
MASSACHUSETTS	7.33	5.62	7.54	5.09	4.74	3.90	3.74	3.70	3.53	7.91	7.64	5.73	5.19
NEW HAMPSHIRE	7.23	5.53	7.44	5.01	4.67	3.84	3.69	3.65	3.48	7.80	7.53	5.65	5.11
RHODE ISLAND	7.50	6.04	7.71	5.46	4.85	4.19	4.02	3.98	3.79	8.09	7.82	6.16	5.57
VERMONT	7.56	6.08	7.77	5.50	4.88	4.22	4.05	4.00	3.81	8.14	7.87	6.20	5.61
MID ATLANTIC:													
NEW JERSEY	6.73	5.85	6.94	4.77	4.35	4.06	3.89	3.85	3.31	7.29	7.01	5.97	4.87
NEW YORK	7.65	5.45	7.86	4.45	4.94	3.78	3.63	3.59	3.09	8.24	7.97	5.56	4.54
PENNSYLVANIA	6.84	5.91	7.05	4.82	4.42	4.10	3.94	3.89	3.35	7.40	7.12	6.03	4.92
EAST NORTH CENTRAL:													
ILLINOIS	6.49	5.75	6.70	5.37	4.19	3.99	3.83	3.79	3.73	7.04	6.76	5.87	5.48
INDIANA	6.53	5.80	6.74	5.42	4.22	4.02	3.86	3.82	3.76	7.07	6.80	5.92	5.53
MICHIGAN	6.88	5.88	7.09	5.50	4.44	4.08	3.92	3.88	3.81	7.43	7.16	6.00	5.61
OHIO	6.81	5.79	7.01	5.41	4.39	4.01	3.85	3.81	3.75	7.37	7.09	5.90	5.52
WISCONSIN	6.81	5.76	7.01	5.38	4.39	4.00	3.84	3.80	3.74	7.37	7.09	5.88	5.50
WEST NORTH CENTRAL:													
IOWA	6.56	5.79	6.77	5.58	4.24	4.01	3.85	3.81	3.87	7.11	6.83	5.90	5.69
KANSAS	5.68	4.78	5.89	4.61	3.67	3.32	3.19	3.15	3.20	6.19	5.92	4.88	4.70
MINNESOTA	5.96	5.69	6.17	5.49	3.85	3.95	3.79	3.75	3.81	6.49	6.21	5.81	5.60
MISSOURI	6.35	5.03	6.56	4.85	4.10	3.49	3.35	3.32	3.37	6.89	6.61	5.14	4.95
NEBRASKA	6.14	5.76	6.35	5.55	3.96	4.00	3.84	3.80	3.85	6.67	6.40	5.88	5.67
NORTH DAKOTA	6.60	5.69	6.81	5.49	4.27	3.95	3.79	3.75	3.81	7.16	6.88	5.81	5.60
SOUTH DAKOTA	6.84	5.56	7.05	5.36	4.42	3.86	3.70	3.66	3.72	7.40	7.12	5.67	5.47
SOUTH ATLANTIC:													
DELAWARE	7.33	5.96	7.54	5.57	4.74	4.14	3.97	3.93	3.87	7.91	7.64	6.09	5.69
DISTRICT OF COLUMBIA	6.84	5.82	7.05	5.44	4.42	4.04	3.88	3.84	3.78	7.40	7.12	5.94	5.55
FLORIDA	7.72	4.88	7.93	4.56	4.98	3.39	3.25	3.22	3.16	8.31	8.04	4.98	4.65
GEORGIA	6.67	5.69	6.88	5.32	4.31	3.95	3.79	3.75	3.69	7.22	6.94	5.81	5.43
MARYLAND	6.45	5.77	6.66	5.40	4.17	4.01	3.85	3.81	3.74	7.00	6.72	5.89	5.51
NORTH CAROLINA	6.98	5.68	7.19	5.31	4.51	3.94	3.78	3.74	3.68	7.55	7.27	5.80	5.42
SOUTH CAROLINA	7.33	5.75	7.54	5.37	4.74	3.99	3.83	3.79	3.73	7.91	7.64	5.87	5.48
VIRGINIA	6.81	5.17	7.01	4.84	4.39	3.59	3.45	3.41	3.36	7.37	7.09	5.28	4.94
WEST VIRGINIA	6.70	5.66	6.91	5.28	4.33	3.93	3.77	3.73	3.67	7.25	6.98	5.77	5.39
EAST SOUTH CENTRAL:													
ALABAMA	6.18	5.49	6.39	4.91	3.99	3.81	3.66	3.62	3.41	6.71	6.44	5.60	5.01
KENTUCKY	6.94	5.80	7.16	5.19	4.48	4.02	3.86	3.82	3.60	7.51	7.23	5.92	5.30
MISSISSIPPI	6.56	5.20	6.78	4.65	4.24	3.61	3.46	3.43	3.23	7.12	6.84	5.31	4.75
TENNESSEE	6.70	5.32	6.91	4.76	4.33	3.69	3.55	3.51	3.31	7.25	6.98	5.43	4.86
WEST SOUTH CENTRAL:													
ARKANSAS	6.63	4.90	6.84	5.50	4.28	3.40	3.27	3.23	3.81	7.18	6.91	5.00	5.61
LOUISIANA	5.52	4.78	5.73	5.36	3.56	3.32	3.19	3.15	3.72	6.03	5.75	4.88	5.47
OKLAHOMA	5.02	4.48	5.23	5.03	3.24	3.11	2.99	2.96	3.49	5.50	5.23	4.58	5.13
TEXAS	5.64	4.78	5.85	5.36	3.64	3.32	3.19	3.15	3.72	6.15	5.88	4.88	5.47
ROCKY MOUNTAIN:													
ARIZONA	6.94	5.48	7.15	6.46	4.48	3.80	3.65	3.61	4.48	7.51	7.23	5.59	6.59
COLORADO	7.02	5.86	7.23	6.91	4.53	4.07	3.90	3.86	4.80	7.58	7.31	5.98	7.05
IDAHO	7.02	5.86	7.23	6.91	4.53	4.07	3.90	3.86	4.80	7.58	7.31	5.98	7.05
MONTANA	6.42	5.63	6.63	6.65	4.15	3.91	3.75	3.71	4.61	6.96	6.69	5.75	6.78
NEVADA	7.50	6.10	7.71	7.20	4.84	4.23	4.06	4.02	4.99	8.09	7.81	6.22	7.34
NEW MEXICO	5.95	5.38	6.17	6.35	3.85	3.73	3.58	3.55	4.41	6.48	6.20	5.49	6.48
UTAH	6.17	5.58	6.38	6.59	3.99	3.87	3.72	3.68	4.57	6.71	6.43	5.70	6.73
WYOMING	6.61	5.94	6.82	7.01	4.27	4.12	3.96	3.91	4.87	7.16	6.89	6.06	7.16
FAR WEST:													
ALASKA	8.63	5.98	8.84	7.00	5.57	4.15	3.98	3.94	4.86	9.27	8.99	6.10	7.14
CALIFORNIA	6.38	5.42	6.59	6.34	4.12	3.76	3.61	3.57	4.40	6.92	6.65	5.53	6.47
HAWAII	8.88	7.17	9.09	8.40	5.73	4.98	4.78	4.73	5.83	9.53	9.25	7.32	8.57
OREGON	6.53	5.71	6.74	6.67	4.22	3.96	3.80	3.76	4.63	7.08	6.80	5.82	6.81
WASHINGTON	7.72	5.75	7.93	6.73	4.98	3.99	3.83	3.79	4.67	8.31	8.04	5.87	6.87

[a] Meaning of abbreviations: Dis. = Distillate Fuel Oil; Res. = Residual Fuel Oil; Dsl. = Diesel Fuel Oil; Coke = Petroleum Coke; R Gas = Refinery Gas; Ut. Gas = Utility Gas; Kero. = Kerosine Business Use

Table E.3.1

Expenditures For Industrial, Refinery And Miscellaneous Use Of Petroleum Products, 1972, In Thousand Dollars, By State

Aggregate Expenditures By Category Of Use

REGION AND STATE	INDUSTRIAL USE	ENERGY USE			MISCELLANEOUS USE			TOTAL ALL USE
		Oil Co. Use	LPG For Ut. Gas	Energy Total	Household Kerosine Use	Business Use	Misc. Use Total	
NEW ENGLAND:								
CONNECTICUT	54362.5	598.7	1462.2	2060.9	978.0	2632.3	3610.3	60033.6
MAINE	54944.9	312.3	327.6	639.9	151.5	1220.6	1372.1	56957.0
MASSACHUSETTS	52926.4	5208.3	1627.6	6835.9	1778.4	5830.6	7609.0	67371.3
NEW HAMPSHIRE	10524.8	12.3	1137.0	1149.4	242.3	747.3	989.5	12663.7
RHODE ISLAND	11154.5	4144.5	249.8	4394.4	176.8	709.0	885.8	16434.7
VERMONT	3775.6	14.0	436.2	450.2	201.3	548.9	750.2	4976.0
MID ATLANTIC:								
NEW JERSEY	78500.8	53073.6	1056.2	54129.8	1207.6	5552.6	6760.2	139390.8
NEW YORK	85446.2	8822.9	224.8	9047.7	3752.0	11115.8	14867.9	109361.7
PENNSYLVANIA	97832.6	80651.8	1590.2	82241.9	2629.2	12054.6	14683.8	194758.3
EAST NORTH CENTRAL:								
ILLINOIS	56009.1	100314.5	810.1	101124.6	5388.9	18449.3	23838.1	180971.9
INDIANA	45299.0	66028.3	44.3	66072.7	61.0	7671.7	7732.7	119104.4
MICHIGAN	53553.5	12905.0	504.5	13409.4	2376.3	6566.5	8942.8	75905.7
OHIO	61824.2	49937.7	1524.5	51462.2	5378.3	9398.4	14776.6	128063.1
WISCONSIN	18859.5	3820.3	361.7	4182.0	258.3	3303.7	3562.0	26603.6
WEST NORTH CENTRAL:								
IOWA	16322.8	89.0	841.0	929.9	604.6	6604.9	7209.5	24462.2
KANSAS	15500.7	25197.6	0.0	25197.6	181.6	2006.8	2188.4	42886.7
MINNESOTA	41210.1	10283.6	557.5	10841.1	205.1	3605.3	3810.4	55861.6
MISSOURI	17392.5	7703.8	1263.9	8967.7	645.7	3042.6	3688.2	30048.5
NEBRASKA	10223.6	1546.9	1201.7	2748.6	57.5	1823.6	1881.1	14853.3
NORTH DAKOTA	3795.2	6027.2	296.6	6323.9	189.3	2117.4	2306.6	12425.8
SOUTH DAKOTA	3365.2	162.2	632.1	794.2	4.3	1895.3	1899.6	6059.0
SOUTH ATLANTIC:								
DELAWARE	22943.4	2587.7	66.9	2654.6	150.1	4739.2	4889.3	30487.3
DISTRICT OF COLUMBIA	1045.2	41.5	209.9	251.4	21.3	680.8	702.1	1998.7
FLORIDA	59935.0	1996.1	976.4	2972.5	3890.4	8229.0	12119.4	75026.9
GEORGIA	57541.1	614.2	398.5	1012.7	1216.1	8064.9	9280.9	67834.7
MARYLAND	54944.6	2058.8	1181.2	3240.0	325.9	3637.4	3963.3	62147.9
NORTH CAROLINA	80467.4	341.9	89.5	431.4	4708.4	14223.3	18931.7	99830.5
SOUTH CAROLINA	36927.7	516.5	491.4	1007.9	814.1	4419.8	5233.9	43169.5
VIRGINIA	52915.4	10212.2	780.1	10992.3	1816.8	8791.2	10608.0	74515.6
WEST VIRGINIA	11810.4	926.5	0.0	926.5	158.5	932.3	1090.8	13827.7
EAST SOUTH CENTRAL:								
ALABAMA	22442.7	3978.7	25.2	4003.9	1134.0	5326.4	6460.4	32906.9
KENTUCKY	13347.7	14093.3	459.0	14552.3	1670.5	3477.0	5147.5	33047.5
MISSISSIPPI	15216.8	15706.4	394.3	16100.7	7397.8	10862.0	18259.8	49577.3
TENNESSEE	19519.9	359.1	234.1	593.2	3085.7	3971.9	7057.6	27170.7
WEST SOUTH CENTRAL:								
ARKANSAS	15474.6	3485.7	0.0	3485.7	1093.7	9742.2	10835.9	29796.2
LOUISIANA	49851.9	81193.0	0.0	81193.0	5943.4	15863.5	21806.8	152851.7
OKLAHOMA	19577.8	21994.7	0.0	21994.7	822.3	2665.9	3488.1	45060.7
TEXAS	55064.5	206049.9	501.5	206551.4	11592.1	41063.6	52655.7	314271.5
ROCKY MOUNTAIN:								
ARIZONA	19036.5	128.6	0.0	128.6	215.8	2858.2	3074.1	22239.2
COLORADO	14216.4	4966.6	294.6	5261.2	1809.0	6093.1	7902.1	27379.7
IDAHO	10957.3	81.6	0.0	81.6	544.9	3364.6	3909.5	14948.3
MONTANA	10839.5	14238.8	0.0	14238.8	1225.1	2995.1	4220.2	29298.6
NEVADA	5416.7	135.6	0.0	135.6	13.9	1395.7	1409.6	6961.9
NEW MEXICO	12089.2	2575.9	0.0	2575.9	1177.6	4355.1	5532.7	20197.7
UTAH	21448.1	11004.6	0.0	11004.6	702.0	2454.5	3156.4	35609.2
WYOMING	9663.1	13399.0	0.0	13399.0	539.0	1400.0	1939.0	25001.1
FAR WEST:								
ALASKA	11028.5	1060.1	0.0	1060.1	42.6	1817.8	1860.4	13949.0
CALIFORNIA	134034.8	115573.6	3344.6	118918.2	422.0	19232.3	19654.2	272607.2
HAWAII	10415.5	20671.7	1359.8	22031.5	93.1	3095.9	3189.0	35636.0
OREGON	32998.3	7228.5	0.0	7228.5	321.4	2721.9	3043.4	43270.2
WASHINGTON	39505.8	37244.6	63.5	37308.1	152.9	6264.0	6416.9	83230.8

Table E.3.2

Expenditures For Industrial, Refinery And Miscellaneous Use Of Petroleum Products, 1972,
In Thousand Dollars, By Region

Aggregate Expenditures By Category Of Use

| REGION | INDUSTRIAL USE TOTAL | ENERGY USE | | | MISCELLANEOUS USE | | | TOTAL ALL USE |
		Oil Co. Use	LPG for Ut. Gas	Energy Use Total	Household Kerosine Use	Business Use	Misc. Total	
NEW ENGLAND	187688.70	10290.10	5240.40	15530.70	3528.30	11688.70	15216.90	218436.30
MID ATLANTIC	261779.60	142548.30	2871.20	145419.40	7588.80	28723.00	36311.90	443510.80
EAST NORTH CENTRAL	235545.30	233005.80	3245.10	236250.90	13462.80	45389.60	58852.20	530648.69
WEST NORTH CENTRAL	107810.10	51010.30	4792.80	55803.00	1888.10	21095.90	22983.80	186597.10
SOUTH ATLANTIC	378530.20	19295.40	4193.90	23489.30	13101.60	53717.90	66819.40	468838.80
EAST SOUTH CENTRAL	70527.10	34137.50	1112.60	35250.10	13288.00	23637.30	36925.30	142702.40
WEST SOUTH CENTRAL	139968.80	312723.30	501.50	313224.80	19451.50	69335.20	88786.50	541980.10
ROCKY MOUNTAIN	103666.80	46530.70	294.60	46825.30	6227.30	24916.30	31143.60	181635.70
FAR WEST	227982.90	181778.50	4767.90	186546.40	1032.00	33131.90	34163.90	448693.20
TOTAL	1713499.54	1031319.92	27020.00	1058339.90	79568.40	311635.80	391203.50	3163043.04

Appendix F

Natural Gas

Overview

The work on natural gas consumption had two phases which can be categorized as analysis and synthesis. In the analysis phase, statistical series were compared and conflicts noted. In the synthesis phase, the conflicts were resolved by a series of decisions aimed at integrating the various series into a coherent whole. The major data sources employed were the Natural Gas tables in the Minerals Yearbook, 1972 edition [43] and the American Gas Association 1972 Gas Facts [1]. Data in Crump and Readling [7] and in Steam Electric Plant Factors [23], were employed in the analysis phase; the Little report [20] furnished data which were of major importance in the synthesis phase. Other documents drawn on were Main Line Gas Sales To Industrial Users [41] and The Census of Housing [33].

In comparing the various series on natural gas consumption, a major semantic problem became manifest, because different series employed the same terms to cover different classes of use. The Bureau of Mines (BOM) and Crump and Readling distinguished gas for electric generation as a separate category from industrial use and "other" use, while the American Gas Association (AGA) had electric generation appearing as a subcategory of both industrial and other use. When there is an accounting for these definitional differences, the AGA and BOM data show generally good correspondence. However, some divergence occurred in sales for industrial use (net of electric generation) and available information led to the decision to splice the series together, using the AGA data for the first five regions (New England through South Atlantic), and the BOM data for the remaining four.

In addition to quantities sold to consumers, the BOM series included categories of (1) lease and plant fuel, and (2) pipeline fuel, listing both quantities and dollar values for these categories. The first consists of natural gas used in oil and gas field production, presumably involving direct use (and "expense") by producers ([43], 1972 edition, 813). The second category refers to natural gas used in the transmission of gas in pipelines. These categories were included under the general heading of natural gas used in energy production. (Any concern about "double-counting" should be avoided by noting that the double-counting occurs and is made explicit by this categorization; on the one hand, all gas consumed "productively" is accounted for; on the other, the cost of that production is passed on to the ultimate consumer, and thus is counted twice, but a net cost is obtainable by subtracting the energy cost figures from the total.)

In addition to plant and lease fuel, oil and gas producers and oil refiners purchase substantial amounts of natural gas from gas utilities. The AGA source document [1] contained information on these purchases by region. The regional totals were distributed among the states in each region by applying the corresponding fractions for oil company use of petroleum products, as developed in Appendix E. This use, the use for electric generation, and the natural gas employed as pipeline fuel in the transmission of gas, were all combined into the category of energy use.

In the Little study, the level of commercial use, covering office, retail, school, hospital and other use (such as warehouses), was considerably less than the BOM and AGA commercial totals. The Little study argued that the difference consisted of multifamily residential use and some industrial use classified as commercial use by the BOM (and AGA), which would be better allocated to the non-commercial categories. This argument was accepted here, and the allocation carried out on the basis of available information. The Little study gave a distribution of the "net" commercial categories (office, retail, school, hospital and other) by region; this was extended to a state distribution by applying relative concentration factors developed earlier (in the petroleum analysis).

Finally, the distribution of use between sectors was carried out by drawing on several sources. Residential use, of course, was identified with the household sector. The state distributions of net commercial use were, in turn, allocated among the business, federal government, and state and local government sectors by applying scale factors developed earlier.

A small portion of industrial use was allocated to the government sectors on the basis of data in [41], with the remainder treated as business sector use.

All of electrical generation use was treated as private sector use, following the convention adopted in the work with petroleum products. The AGA data exhibit a substantial amount of sales for electric generation under the "other" category; these were inferred to be sales to public enterprises, and/or sales for street and highway lighting, and were treated here as a component of electric utility use, subsumed under the business sector. (Since 1976 the American Gas Association has treated all electrical generation as industrial use, supporting the approach adopted here.) Subsequent "purchase" and use of electricity for street and highway lighting would be treated as a government purchase of electricity.

The "other" category in the BOM series, and "other" net of electric generation in the AGA series consisted primarily of sales to municipalities and public authorities for institutional heating, street lighting and related uses; hence, it seemed reasonable to treat this use as consumption by state and local government.

A schematic outline of the categorization of uses between sources may help to clarify this discussion. The following symbols and corresponding definitions will be employed, first covering functional and then sectoral categories:

Symbols For Categories Of Use

R1: residential use by mobile homes, single-family housing, and multifamily housing of 1 to 4 units.

R2: residential use by multifamily housing of more than 4 units.

C1: "net" commercial use, including office, retail, school, hospital and other net commercial use (by warehouses, religious, social-recreational, non-housekeeping residential, and miscellaneous buildings).

I1: industrial use classified as "commercial" in the BOM and AGA series.

I2: industrial use net of energy production in the BOM and AGA series.

E1: oil and gas producer and oil refinery purchases from gas utilities.

E2: electric utility use, classified under the industrial heading in the AGA series.

E3: electric utility use, classified under the "other" heading in the AGA series.

E4: pipeline fuel.

E5: lease and plant fuel.

O1: other use (municipal, public authorities).

H: household sector use.

B: business sector use.

F: federal government use.

SL: state and local government use.

These categories are distributed as follows:

BOM	AGA	This Study	This Study
Functional Distribution	Functional Distribution	Functional Distribution	Sectoral Distribution
<u>Sales</u>	<u>Sales</u>	<u>All Use</u>	<u>All Use</u>
Residential	Residential	Residential	
R1	R1	R1 R2	H
<u>Commercial</u>	<u>Commercial</u>	<u>Commercial</u>	
R2 C1 I1	R2 C1 I1	-- C1 --	B, FG, SL
<u>Industrial</u>	<u>Industrial</u>	<u>Industrial</u>	
-- I2 E1 --	-- I2 E1 E2	I1 I2 -- --	B, FG, SL
Electric Utilities	___*	Energy Production	
E2 E3		E1 E2 E3 E4 E5	B
<u>Other</u>	<u>Other</u>	<u>Other</u>	
O1	O1 E3	O1	SL
<u>Non-Sales</u>			
E4 E5	-- --		

*The AGA does show electric utility use, in terms of the E2 and E3
categories, in a separate table ([1] Table 69, 83).

The basic series employed here (the BOM and AGA data) list expenditures as well as quantities consumed. Hence, the major estimation problem faced in the petroleum products work was not repeated here. When a subcategory of use was shifted between major consumption categories, such as the shift of part of "commercial" use (BOM definition) to residential and industrial use, the prices that held for the original category were retained for the subcategory. Those prices were obtained directly by dividing expenditures by physical quantities.

The remainder of this section presents more details on estimation procedures, a fuller citation of sources employed, and the data in its various stages of processing, moving from the analysis to the synthesis phase. The tables presenting the data are organized in the usual sequence, with tables on physical quantities presented first, followed by tables containing prices, in turn followed by tables of expenditures. In each case, the order is roughly the same, so that triplets of quantity, price and expenditure data can usually be identified.

Quantities: Analysis

The BOM data appeared in units of million cubic feet. The AGA source document presents average BTU value per cubic foot, by state ([1], Table 65, 79) and those conversion factors were applied to the BOM data to yield consumption in billion BTU. Table F.1.1 compares the respective BOM and AGA state series on residential and commercial use, while Table F.1.2 shows the corresponding regional comparisons. Both the residential and the commercial series seem reasonably consistent between sources, with U.S. totals only about two percent apart in each case. California and Illinois are the leading consuming states, and the East North Central is the leading region, for both categories of use.

Crump and Readling present combined residential-commercial figures which are the same as the BOM data in cubic feet terms, but differ somewhat from the BTU data presented in Table F.1.1 because they apply a scale factor of 1,021 BTU per cubic foot, rather than scale factors which vary by state. (Those employed here ranged from 938 to 1,083.)

Tables F.1.3 and F.1.4 present data on industrial use by state, the former comparing data from BOM, Crump and Readling and AGA, while the latter makes the BOM-AGA comparisons in terms of differences and ratios. Table F.1.3 involves an attempt to reconcile the BOM series with the greater values to be found in Crump and Readling, first by adding lease and plant fuel to sales, and then by adding "other" sales to the previous total. (This was done because Crump and Readling omit "other sales.") These additions establish greater correspondence between the BOM and Crump and Readling series, but a considerable gap often remains, and for five states the augmented BOM total is somewhat above that of Crump and Readling.

Since use for electric generation is carried as a separate category in the BOM series, the AGA figure for the industrial component of such use was subtracted from the AGA industrial total so that proper comparisons could be made. It turns out that the AGA net figures are generally above the corresponding BOM entries in the New England through the South Atlantic regions. In the other regions, the two series are close, except for the three producing states of Louisiana, Texas and New Mexico, and

the relatively low use case of Hawaii. It seems plausible that in
Louisiana, Texas and New Mexico, much of the sales were made by non-
utilities, e.g., a plant producing its own fuel might sell some of its
"excess" production. The BOM listed zero sales for Hawaii, while
the AGA listed a small amount--presumably consisting of manufactured or
imported liquified gas. (In data on total gas sales, an "all gas" figure is
slightly above the "natural gas" figure.)

Table F.1.5 carries out the industrial use comparisons at the
regional level. For the first five regions, the net sales listed by
the AGA exceed the corresponding BOM sales figure, and in turn are
equalled or exceeded by the Crump and Readling figure. (It does seem
noteworthy that essentially equal values hold for BOM and Crump and
Readling in the two North Central regions.) The difference in U.S.
totals between BOM and AGA primarily reflects the West South Central
region differences between the two.

Tables F.1.6 and F.1.7 present pipeline fuel and "other" consumption
for states and regions, respectively. The proper comparison again involves
removing electric generation from the AGA figures. The U.S. totals for
the two cases are almost exactly the same, but there are some marked
regional differences, with the West South Central figure much higher in
the AGA than in the BOM series, and the readings for the North Central
and Far West regions appreciably lower. Perhaps some exported fuel is
counted in the region of origin by the AGA, and in the region of destination (and use) by the BOM.

Tables F.1.8 and F.1.9 respectively show state and regional data
on electric utility use, and bring national Coal Association (NCA)

data [23] into the comparisons. The AGA data here consist not only
of the sales by gas utilities (corresponding to the "included" electric
generation values in Tables F.1.3 and F.1.6) but also include "transfers"
from the gas department to the electric department of companies sell-
ing both gas and electricity. Such transfers are not carried in the
general set of statistics presented by the AGA, but are noted in a
special table ([1], table 69, p. 83). Direct sales to electric companies
by producers which are not handled by gas companies, and gas used for
electric generation by industrial plants producing their own power are
not included in the AGA statistics, but presumably appear (at least in
part) in both the NCA and BOM series, thus accounting for most or all
of the deviation from the AGA values. The BOM and NCA values are quite
close; perhaps the coverage of the former is somewhat more extensive,
accounting for its somewhat higher values. The BOM values (in cubic
feet) are identical to Federal Power Commission data appearing in both
the AGA Gas Facts ([1], table 68, p. 82) and Crump and Readling.

For the sake of completeness, Tables F.1.10 through F.1.13 present
data on firm versus interruptible usage as reported in Gas Facts ([1],
table 72, p. 86 and table 83, p. 102). (Interruptible gas deliveries
can be stopped or "interrupted" if there are temporary shortages in
the general supply of gas.) Tables F.1.10 and F.1.11 respectively
show state and regional figures for commercial and industrial use,
while Tables F.1.12 and F.1.13 show similar data for electric utilities,
as well as the "transfers" from gas to electric departments of combined
companies. Given the AGA definitions, the industrial supplies of Tables F.1.12
and F.1.13 are a subcategory of those shown in Tables F.1.10 and F.1.11.

Quantities - Synthesis

For the residential and commercial use categories it was decided to rely on the BOM series as base data; since the BOM values were generally close to the AGA values, alternative procedures (such as averaging the two series) would not much affect estimates. Then, part of the commercial use was shifted to the residential category, and part to the industrial category, on the basis of information in the Arthur D. Little study [20].

The Little study lists 1970 energy use for individual fuels by major census region; in that study, it is argued that the commercial category in the BOM series (and by implication, in the AGA series) includes residential use by multifamily housing units, and some industrial use by farms, fisheries, and light industrial customers ([20], p. 5). Comparing the Little "net" commercial sales (for offices, retail, school, hospital, and other categories) to the BOM commercial sales in 1970 ([20], Appendix Table A.b, and 12, 1970 edition) this distribution emerged:

Census Region	Little Categories Relative To BOM Commercial			
	"Net" Commercial	Multifamily Residential	Industrial	Total
Northeast	.438	.393	.169	1.000
North Central	.362	.166	.472	1.000
South	.479	.101	.420	1.000
West	.617	.202	.181	1.000
U.S.	.448	.191	.361	1.000

It was assumed that these regional fractions held for 1972 as
well as 1970, so that multiplication by the 1972 BOM commercial total
yielded the corresponding subtotals, by region. The multifamily residential totals for major census regions were then distributed to the states
within each region on the basis of data in the Census of Housing [33],
Table 21. That data is summarized in Table F.1.14 which lists number
of housing units by state, and the percentage of housing units in
structures with five or more units ("large multifamily"), which corresponds exactly to the Little definition of the multifamily residential
grouping falling within the commercial category of BOM. The multiplication of the large multifamily percentage by number of housing units
(and scaling by .01) gave the number of large multifamily units by state.
The sum over states within a major census region gave the regional total,
and the division of the state figure by the regional total gave the
state fraction of the regional total. The corresponding percentages are
shown for each state within its region in Table F.1.14.

The fractions established by this procedure were then multiplied by
the regional large multifamily gas usage estimated earlier to yield an
initial set of state consumption estimates.

After the "net" commercial estimates by state were estimated (to be
described below), the initial large multifamily use estimates were added
to the net commercial estimates, and subtracted from the state BOM
commercial figure. The residual was identified as the amount to transfer
to industrial use. In the initial subtraction, negative residuals
occurred for Maine, Vermont, New York and Hawaii. The last result
occurred because Hawaiian use was zero in the BOM series; the other

three cases reflected lower than proportionate total gas sales in the states in question. The Maine and Vermont multifamily residential use were reduced accordingly, and the amounts involved were allotted to Massachusetts; similarly, the Hawaiian figure was set at zero, and the increment allotted to California, and the New York use was reduced and its increment distributed between New Jersey and Pennsylvania on the basis of the respective amounts of total commercial use (BOM data) in those states.

The "net" commercial regional totals were obtained by multiplying the "net" commercial fraction (from Little) by the BOM commercial total. Then individual state estimates were obtained as follows. The information in Little yielded these regional distributions of the five subcategories of use:

	Office Use	Retail Use	School Use	Hospital Use	Other Use	Total
Northeast	.225	.159	.254	.116	.246	1.000
North Central	.190	.156	.282	.101	.271	1.000
South	.233	.135	.302	.094	.236	1.000
West	.241	.149	.270	.079	.261	1.000

An initial set of state estimates were obtained by assuming the state fraction was the same as the regional fraction for both "net" commercial relative to BOM commercial, and for the individual subcategories relative to the "net" commercial total. Then scale factors on the relative concentration of activity for offices, schools and hospitals were multiplied by the initial amounts of those respective activities. The scale factors exhibit the per capita level of each activity relative to the regional level, as developed in the work on petroleum products

(Table B.1.9). It was assumed that the retail and other commercial subcategories had the same concentration of activity as held at the regional level, i.e., their scale factors equalled 1.0 after the multiplications were carried out. The revised regional sums were obtained and compared to the initial sums for each subcategory. The before and after sums were essentially the same in all cases, so no further adjustments were necessary. The first three columns of Table F.1.15 exhibit the scale factors employed in the process. Table F.1.16 shows the estimated state use levels for each of the five subcategories and for their total, 'net" commercial use. Table F.1.17 exhibits the corresponding regional levels of use.

Table F.1.18 shows the components and resultants of the shifts in the commercial use data for each state, including the original BOM commercial use level; the component estimated as residential use in large multifamily structures; the "net" commercial use; the residual, identified as industrial use; the original residential level of use; and the revised residential use, obtained by adding the multifamily component to the original residential figure.

The data of Table F.1.16 were distributed by use of the sectoral fractions appearing on the right side of Table F.1.15, with all retail use and other commercial use allocated to the business sector. The data in Table F.1.15 were developed in the work on petroleum products (and first appear in Table B.1.13). The resulting distribution of use by sector is presented for the states in Table F.1.19. Table F.1.20 is the regional analogue of Tables F.1.18 and F.1.19.

In developing the final estimates of industrial use, the evidence

of Tables F.1.3 through F.1.5 led to the decision to splice the AGA and

BOM series together, employing the AGA data for the first five regions,

and the BOM data for the remaining four. The closeness of the Crump

and Readling figures to the AGA figures in the North Central region was

a major source of this decision. The decision itself was based on the

inferences that the AGA data for the first five regions were somewhat

more accurate, perhaps because of fuller coverage, while the BOM data

for the last four regions certainly had fuller coverage, since there

was an accounting for natural gas obtained from sources other than gas

utilities, including direct sales from producers.

The AGA data were net of gas used in electrical generation, of

course. More generally, following the convention employed earlier, a

separate functional category for the use of energy in energy production

was set up here; as a consequence, it was decided to estimate and sub-

tract gas used in oil and gas production and refining from the industrial

series. The AGA report ([1], table 70, p. 84) lists gas sales for

petroleum and natural gas production, with a U.S. total of 185.5 trillion

BTU, and for petroleum refining, with a U.S. total of 478.1 trillion

BTU. Regional subtotals are also given. For each of the nine regions, the

regional total was distributed among the states in the region on the basis

of the state share of oil company use of petroleum products in the region,

drawing on the earlier petroleum work. It seemed plausible that petroleum

and gas use would be highly correlated. Lease and plant fuel accounts for

producer use of natural gas employed in gas and oil fields. It is possible

that there were some additional direct sales to oil and gas producers or oil refineries that were made by other producers without intermediate sale to gas utilities, but this was assumed to be minor.

In accounting for sales by sector, it turned out that a small portion of industrial sales were to government agencies. The publication Main Line Gas Sales to Industrial Users: 1974 [41], Table 2, contained a breakdown by Standard Industrial Classification (SIC) of industrial users, by state, and over the years 1970 through 1974. The SIC codes included the code 90 series, covering governmental functions. In addition, Table 4 of that source identified specific customer by SIC code, company making sale and delivery point, so it was possible to identify the state of purchase by this information, and to classify the public agency for each purchase under the heading of federal or state and local government. Individual sales data were then aggregated by state.

Table F.1.21 lists the components of the various industrial use series, including the initial sales estimates, obtained by splicing together the AGA and BOM data; the transfer-in from the commercial sector (as estimated in Table F.1.18); the federal and the state and local government industrial purchases; the oil and gas production and refinery use to be transferred to the energy production category; and the lease and plant fuel series, defined here as a component of energy production, but possibly appearing in some industrial series (e.g., Crump and Readling).

The net results for industrial use of natural gas are presented in tables in the text. (See Tables 117 and 123 of the main body of this report.)

In developing the functional category for the use of energy in energy production, the Bureau of Mines series on electrical utility use was taken to be the best estimate of electrical generation use, because of fuller coverage than the AGA series. In the 1972 report, the AGA distinguished industrial from other use for electrical generation, the latter referring (apparently) to publicly owned electric utilities [14]. Following previous convention, publicly owned utilities are treated here as part of the business sector. (The AGA now follows this convention, classifying all electric utility use as industrial, as of 1976 [14].)

As a check, the AGA "other" electric utility series was subtracted from the BOM (total) electric utility series; all differences were positive, except for a small negative value for Tennessee. In that case, the AGA figure was substituted for the BOM entry.

Pipeline fuel is treated by Crump and Readling as a form of transportation consumption; but it seemed more reasonable to treat the item as a component of energy production (here viewing distribution as a component of production).

The remaining category of use is the BOM "other" category identified as primarily use by municipalities and public authorities for institutional heating, street lighting and miscellaneous uses ([43], 1972 edition, table 13, footnote 2, p. 837). It seemed simplest to treat the category as exclusively use by state and local government.

This other use series and the components of the energy producing series are presented for states in Table F.1.23 and for regions in Table F.1.24. The energy producing components are the AGA other electric

utility use; electric utility use net of that AGA series (so the sum
of the two equals total electric utility use); the oil and gas production
and oil refinery use transferred from industrial use; pipeline fuel;
lease and plant fuel; and the energy use total.

Prices

Given the synthesis phase of the work on natural gas quantities,
corresponding estimates of natural gas expenditures were obtained directly
by carrying out the same operations on the expenditures series. Thus, if
two quantity series were averaged to obtain a final series, the same operation
was performed on the corresponding expenditures series, which were directly
available in the same sources as the quantity series. Then, in contrast
to the work on petroleum products, where prices were estimated separately
by drawing on a variety of sources, natural gas prices were obtained directly
by dividing expenditures by quantities. Those prices, corresponding to the
synthesis stage of the work on quantities and expenditures, are presented
in the main body of this report. This appendix presents natural gas prices
corresponding to the consumption data presented in the analysis phase of
the work on quantities, which involved a series of comparisons. Similar
price comparisons are made in Tables F.2.1 through F.2.12. These date
may be useful in future work aimed at further refinement and reconciliation
of source data.

Table F.2.1 compares the respective BOM and AGA prices for residential
and commercial use by state, while Table F.2.2 carries out that comparison
by region. The two series have essentially the same average value for the
U.S. as a whole, and regional averages are quite close. However, considerable

differences between the series occur for some states; Florida and Utah

show marked differences in prices for residential use, while four of

the New England states, Alabama, Utah and Alaska show similar disagree-

ments in prices for commercial use. The deviation for Hawaii is an

artifact of the non-use of natural gas in that state in the BOM series.

(In the main body of this report the AGA data on prices for Hawaii were

utilized in constructing price indexes. It was assumed that the very

small quantities involved were either manufactured gas or imported liqui-

fied gas.) Tables F.2.3 and F.2.4 present price comparisons for industrial

use at the state and regional level, respectively. The Bureau of Mines

data exclude electricity generation by virtue of the definition of indus-

trial use, and a corresponding AGA series is obtained by removing that

use from the industrial series. When that is done, the AGA values are

considerably above the BOM values for the U.S. as a whole, and for the

six regions from the West North Central through the Far West region. Some

marked differences occur at the state level, e.g., Maine, Missouri, Delaware

and Nevada.

Tables F.2.5 and F.2.6 present price data for pipeline fuel and "other"

consumption, comparing BOM and AGA values for the latter category, with

state values shown in Table F.2.5, and regional values shown in Table F.2.6.

Pipeline fuel prices average about 20 percent of residential natural gas

prices and about half of the price in industrial use; presumably that cost

is a component of the price paid by consumers. Prices for "other use"

show considerable variability between the BOM and AGA series, perhaps

reflecting definitional differences.

Prices paid by electric utilities are tabulated for states in Table F.2.7, and for regions in Table F.2.8. Those tables make a three-way comparison, showing prices appearing in the National Coal Association series, as well as those of the Bureau of Mines and American Gas Association series. For the U.S. as a whole, the BOM and AGA averages are quite close, while the NCA value is about 10 percent lower. At the regional level, however, the NCA and AGA figures usually show good agreement (New England and the South Atlantic regions are the exceptions), while the BOM figure usually shows considerable divergence from those of the other series. This is most pronounced for the North Central regions, with BOM prices generally lower in the East North Central region and higher in the West North Central region than the corresponding prices in the other series. These differences hold for most of the states in those regions, and similar deviations also occur for some other states (Pennsylvania, Delaware, West Virginia and New Mexico), with BOM prices differing substantially from those of the other series.

Again for the sake of completeness, as in the case of quantity data, Tables F.2.9 through F.2.12 present price data on firm versus interruptible use, based on AGA data, with commercial and industrial use covered in the first two tables and electric utility use in the last two. The first table in each set covers states and the second covers regions. As expected, prices for interruptible use are below those for firm use, for commercial and industrial sales (Tables F.2.9 and F.2.10). Somewhat surprisingly, however, interruptible prices are sometimes above firm prices in electric utility use (Table F.2.11 and F.2.12). Perhaps this can be explained as an aggregation effect; some jurisdictions with high prices in interruptible use may also have little or no firm use; similarly, some jurisdictions with low prices for firm use may have little or no interruptible use. This hypothesis receive some support at the state level from the data of Table F.2.11; note the values for Georgia, North Carolina and South Carolina, where only interruptible usage occurs.

Expenditures

As noted in the discussion of prices, operations on expenditure series were the direct analogues of operation on corresponding quantity series. The analysis phase of the work on expenditures in effect is reported in Tables F.3.1 through F.3.12, while the synthesis phase is covered in Tables F.3.13 through F.3.19. Comparisons of expenditures series by data source are carried out for residential and commercial use in Tables F.3.1 and F.3.2; for industrial use in Tables F.3.3 and F.3.4; for pipeline fuel and "other" consumption in Tables F.3.5 and F.3.6, and for electric utility use in Tables F.3.7 and F.3.8. Expenditures on firm versus interruptible use are presented for commercial and interruptible sales in Tables F.3.9 and F.3.10, and for electric utility sales in Tables F.3.11 and F.3.12, drawing on AGA data. In all of these sets of tables, the first table presents state data and the second presents regional data.

The variations between sources that is manifest in Tables F.3.1 through F.3.8 of course parallels and is explained by the corresponding variations in quantities and prices to be found in the earlier tables of this section.

In the synthesis phase of the work, Table F.3.13 displays the revisions carried out in the commercial use series and the resulting revised residential and commercial use series, while Table F.3.14 shows the sectoral components of the revised commercial use series. Both of those tables cover states, and their regional analogue appears as Table F.3.15. Tables F.3.16 and F.3.17 show the components that were employed to estimate the series on expenditures for industrial use, by states and regions, respectively. Finally, Tables F.3.18 and F.3.19 display expenditures on "other" use for municipal-industrial purposes, and expenditures for energy production, classified into electricity generation and components of other energy production (non-electric utility use). In the usual fashion, the first table in the set shows state values, and the second shows regional values. The industrial use totals (from Tables F.1.21 and F.3.16), the electric utility use totals and the other energy use totals (from Tables F.1.23 and F.3.18) are presented in the main body of this report.

Table F.1.1

Natural Gas Consumption in Billion BTU, 1972, by State

Residential and Commercial Use: Comparison of Data From Bureau of Mines (BOM) And American Gas Association (AGA).

REGION AND STATE	RESIDENTIAL USE				COMMERCIAL USE			
	BOM	AGA	BOM MINUS AGA	BOM/AGA	BOM	AGA	BOM MINUS AGA	BOM/AGA
NEW ENGLAND:								
CONNECTICUT	33405.1	33400.0	5.1	1.000	12996.7	12200.0	796.7	1.065
MAINE	698.3	800.0	-101.7	0.873	584.9	500.0	84.9	1.170
MASSACHUSETTS	87205.1	92200.0	-4994.9	0.946	32419.4	34800.0	-2380.6	0.932
NEW HAMPSHIRE	4267.3	4900.0	-632.7	0.871	2451.3	2100.0	351.3	1.167
RHODE ISLAND	13573.2	13700.0	-126.8	0.991	4145.3	4500.0	-354.7	0.921
VERMONT	1127.7	1300.0	-172.3	0.867	581.5	500.0	81.5	1.163
MID ATLANTIC:								
NEW JERSEY	153822.0	152400.0	1422.0	1.009	61677.0	64100.0	-2423.0	0.962
NEW YORK	371043.7	375300.0	-4256.3	0.989	130838.1	114400.0	16438.1	1.144
PENNSYLVANIA	315573.2	325600.0	-10026.8	0.969	116846.8	116300.0	546.8	1.005
EAST NORTH CENTRAL:								
ILLINOIS	500041.1	486300.0	13741.1	1.028	223614.0	222900.0	714.0	1.003
INDIANA	170282.6	165600.0	4682.6	1.028	81907.5	78300.0	3607.5	1.046
MICHIGAN	360595.0	375600.0	-15005.0	0.960	155167.1	179200.0	-24032.9	0.866
OHIO	489332.6	495000.0	-5667.4	0.989	193059.5	202100.0	-9040.5	0.955
WISCONSIN	106636.3	126100.0	-19463.7	0.846	41691.4	53000.0	-11308.6	0.787
WEST NORTH CENTRAL:								
IOWA	97331.2	100800.0	-3468.8	0.966	59434.1	60300.0	-865.9	0.986
KANSAS	100518.6	97300.0	3218.6	1.033	54830.1	37000.0	17830.1	1.482
MINNESOTA	107333.2	113200.0	-5866.8	0.948	55748.3	51300.0	4448.3	1.087
MISSOURI	161202.6	154400.0	6802.6	1.044	81210.5	76700.0	4510.5	1.059
NEBRASKA	60457.8	56400.0	4057.8	1.072	37592.4	30700.0	6892.4	1.225
NORTH DAKOTA	10666.7	9700.0	966.7	1.100	10180.1	9300.0	880.1	1.095
SOUTH DAKOTA	13234.7	12100.0	1134.7	1.094	9651.5	9500.0	151.5	1.016
SOUTH ATLANTIC:								
DELAWARE	8525.2	8600.0	-74.8	0.991	3269.1	3500.0	-230.9	0.934
DISTRICT OF COLUMBIA	14591.8	14500.0	91.8	1.006	13229.3	10900.0	2329.3	1.214
FLORIDA	13363.3	16400.0	-3036.7	0.815	19759.2	21100.0	-1340.8	0.936
GEORGIA	87898.9	80900.0	6998.9	1.087	41521.5	39200.0	2321.5	1.059
MARYLAND	76323.0	75400.0	923.0	1.012	25880.1	21200.0	4680.1	1.221
NORTH CAROLINA	33836.0	29400.0	4436.0	1.151	18542.6	17900.0	642.6	1.036
SOUTH CAROLINA	21204.6	19600.0	1604.6	1.082	13391.8	13400.0	-8.2	0.999
VIRGINIA	56868.1	54500.0	2368.1	1.043	27740.0	28800.0	-1060.0	0.963
WEST VIRGINIA	61249.2	58200.0	3049.2	1.052	24482.0	25000.0	-518.0	0.979
EAST SOUTH CENTRAL:								
ALABAMA	55052.3	52300.0	2752.3	1.053	37490.3	28000.0	9490.3	1.339
KENTUCKY	87341.0	85300.0	2041.0	1.024	35913.3	37900.0	-1986.7	0.948
MISSISSIPPI	40317.4	30500.0	9817.4	1.322	20581.0	15100.0	5481.0	1.363
TENNESSEE	54945.8	45500.0	9445.8	1.208	42342.5	38300.0	4042.5	1.106
WEST SOUTH CENTRAL:								
ARKANSAS	47576.5	47600.0	-23.5	1.000	31615.0	29100.0	2515.0	1.086
LOUISIANA	85249.6	68500.0	16749.6	1.245	35000.4	26900.0	8100.4	1.301
OKLAHOMA	80091.5	74700.0	5391.5	1.072	40905.4	37600.0	3305.4	1.088
TEXAS	247159.9	240500.0	6659.9	1.028	96575.0	105700.0	-9125.0	0.914
ROCKY MOUNTAIN:								
ARIZONA	36280.3	35500.0	780.3	1.022	24241.6	22400.0	1841.6	1.082
COLORADO	86868.1	87100.0	-231.9	0.997	60272.1	58500.0	1772.1	1.030
IDAHO	11551.1	9300.0	2251.1	1.242	9377.1	7600.0	1777.1	1.234
MONTANA	24548.2	25900.0	-1351.8	0.948	17049.7	16900.0	149.7	1.009
NEVADA	9794.3	8300.0	1494.3	1.180	7654.1	6900.0	754.1	1.109
NEW MEXICO	37494.5	27500.0	9994.5	1.363	18674.2	12500.0	6174.2	1.494
UTAH	45826.0	42300.0	3526.0	1.083	7428.0	14300.0	-6872.0	0.519
WYOMING	22753.6	13100.0	9653.6	1.737	16156.2	8500.0	7656.2	1.901
FAR WEST:								
ALASKA	8436.0	6000.0	2436.0	1.406	9151.5	7100.0	2051.5	1.289
CALIFORNIA	671702.6	636200.0	35502.6	1.056	236204.6	229000.0	7204.6	1.031
HAWAII	0.0	1000.0	-1000.0	0.000	0.0	700.0	-700.0	0.000
OREGON	24380.9	23200.0	1180.9	1.051	14774.2	13500.0	1274.2	1.094
WASHINGTON	40755.7	38600.0	2155.7	1.056	24355.7	23400.0	955.7	1.041

Table F.1.2

Natural Gas Consumption In Billion BTU, 1972, By Region

Residential And Commercial Use: Comparisons Of Data From Bureau of Mines (BOM)
    and American Gas Association (AGA)

Residential Use

	BOM	AGA	BOM MINUS AGA	BOM/AGA
NEW ENGLAND	140276.7	146300.0	-6023.3	0.959
MID ATLANTIC	840438.9	853300.0	-12861.1	0.985
EAST NORTH CENTRAL	1626887.6	1648600.0	-21712.4	0.987
WEST NORTH CENTRAL	550744.8	543900.0	6844.8	1.013
SOUTH ATLANTIC	373860.1	357500.0	16360.1	1.046
EAST SOUTH CENTRAL	237656.5	213600.0	24056.5	1.113
WEST SOUTH CENTRAL	460077.5	431300.0	28777.5	1.067
ROCKY MOUNTAIN	275116.1	249000.0	26116.1	1.105
FAR WEST	745275.2	705000.0	40275.2	1.057
TOTAL	5250333.5	5148500.0	101833.4	1.020

Commercial Use

	BOM	AGA	BOM MINUS AGA	BOM/AGA
NEW ENGLAND	53179.1	54600.0	-1420.9	0.974
MID ATLANTIC	309361.9	294800.0	14561.9	1.049
EAST NORTH CENTRAL	695439.5	735500.0	-40060.5	0.946
WEST NORTH CENTRAL	308647.0	274800.0	33847.0	1.123
SOUTH ATLANTIC	187815.6	181000.0	6815.6	1.038
EAST SOUTH CENTRAL	136327.1	119300.0	17027.1	1.143
WEST SOUTH CENTRAL	204095.8	199300.0	4795.8	1.024
ROCKY MOUNTAIN	160853.0	147600.0	13253.0	1.090
FAR WEST	284486.0	273700.0	10786.0	1.039
TOTAL	2340204.9	2280600.0	59605.0	1.026

Table F.1.3

Natural Gas Consumption in Billion BTU, 1972, By State

Industrial Use: Comparison of Alternative Series and Definitions, Data From Bureau of Mines (BOM), Crump and Readling,
    and American Gas Association (AGA)

REGION AND STATE	BOM Sales = (1)	BOM (1) Plus Lease and Plant Fuel = (2)	BOM (2) Plus Other	Crump and Readling	AGA Net Of Electric Gener.	AGA Including Electric Gener.
NEW ENGLAND:						
CONNECTICUT	14278.9	14278.9	18559.3	21482.8	19950.0	20000.0
MAINE	327.9	327.9	344.1	392.6	400.0	400.0
MASSACHUSETTS	28934.1	28934.1	33734.0	39164.7	27100.0	32900.0
NEW HAMPSHIRE	1719.0	1719.0	1798.8	1959.3	2100.0	2100.0
RHODE ISLAND	4392.3	4392.3	5080.5	1386.4	6000.0	6100.0
VERMONT	814.9	814.9	814.9	1366.1	1400.0	1400.0
MID ATLANTIC:						
NEW JERSEY	84828.7	84828.7	87704.5	99614.6	89000.0	94900.0
NEW YORK	105248.8	105248.8	124830.5	129927.4	126400.0	126400.0
PENNSYLVANIA	377122.5	380063.4	389777.8	408991.9	364600.0	366800.0
EAST NORTH CENTRAL:						
ILLINOIS	408582.4	408898.1	415384.3	425509.2	390800.0	456100.0
INDIANA	292929.1	292929.1	296835.4	309410.9	289400.0	295100.0
MICHIGAN	276403.8	278578.9	285781.4	292489.3	331500.0	373900.0
OHIO	438450.6	441925.8	461719.8	473298.7	464500.0	466100.0
WISCONSIN	140741.2	140741.2	143634.2	153887.8	178200.0	189800.0
WEST NORTH CENTRAL:						
IOWA	106334.5	106334.5	109077.9	107261.3	128400.0	140500.0
KANSAS	177317.7	205444.3	211777.6	216927.1	237300.0	359500.0
MINNESOTA	105117.8	105117.8	129516.5	134507.1	141400.0	171600.0
MISSOURI	99805.8	99805.8	116783.8	124922.7	101500.0	153600.0
NEBRASKA	56436.9	57257.4	65547.2	76259.9	68400.0	105600.0
NORTH DAKOTA	2978.1	16147.5	16147.5	17300.0	2100.0	2100.0
SOUTH DAKOTA	6162.6	6162.6	7759.9	8472.2	7000.0	9400.0
SOUTH ATLANTIC:						
DELAWARE	10296.9	10296.9	10296.9	10190.1	11100.0	11100.0
DISTRICT OF COLUMBIA	827.0	827.0	2962.7	985.5	900.0	900.0
FLORIDA	90435.8	92290.9	96727.6	98445.7	87600.0	116600.0
GEORGIA	159294.7	159294.7	164159.9	169600.0	155800.0	203400.0
MARYLAND	61733.9	61802.4	65383.5	75237.4	66800.0	66800.0
NORTH CAROLINA	85781.5	85781.5	92019.7	96540.1	101200.0	111500.0
SOUTH CAROLINA	84132.5	84132.5	85273.6	92430.3	98700.0	102000.0
VIRGINIA	54492.9	54654.0	61978.6	66575.6	58500.0	58500.0
WEST VIRGINIA	96630.3	100548.7	103493.7	133939.7	83400.0	84000.0
EAST SOUTH CENTRAL:						
ALABAMA	169904.7	171007.8	172065.7	178400.0	168900.0	169800.0
KENTUCKY	79337.2	80871.8	88529.9	99135.3	76900.0	76900.0
MISSISSIPPI	150274.2	159656.1	164294.2	174180.4	82100.0	174600.0
TENNESSEE	138081.4	139256.7	143623.7	149880.1	160800.0	160800.0
WEST SOUTH CENTRAL:						
ARKANSAS	146873.2	151632.1	152604.0	176844.2	140100.0	209400.0
LOUISIANA	1046015.5	1367212.8	1400466.9	1413452.8	375500.0	560300.0
OKLAHOMA	128973.2	230918.3	235268.1	255247.3	121800.0	145500.0
TEXAS	1888902.5	2712671.6	2761035.0	2753874.1	1037900.0	1487700.0
ROCKY MOUNTAIN:						
ARIZONA	66811.3	66857.8	71108.7	76112.4	69800.0	118900.0
COLORADO	80611.2	85165.6	86405.5	94188.0	80700.0	139700.0
IDAHO	32157.8	32157.8	34146.2	38179.5	32400.0	32400.0
MONTANA	34254.1	40367.7	43081.9	44142.8	36700.0	36700.0
NEVADA	8301.1	8301.1	14447.9	16266.7	14800.0	58500.0
NEW MEXICO	83139.7	135993.4	152358.6	161031.9	35800.0	82400.0
UTAH	56991.0	58846.4	58859.5	71146.1	56500.0	60000.0
WYOMING	56232.3	79149.5	80677.9	76005.6	49000.0	49000.0
FAR WEST:						
ALASKA	12389.6	28525.9	35465.4	37821.5	11400.0	11400.0
CALIFORNIA	657146.9	729596.7	737431.1	748432.0	609700.0	903400.0
HAWAII	0.0	0.0	0.0	0.0	1700.0	1700.0
OREGON	64964.5	64964.5	65374.2	70342.4	63600.0	63600.0
WASHINGTON	106733.3	106733.3	106910.5	116142.1	126000.0	126000.0

Table F.1.4

Natural Gas Consumption in Billion BTU, 1972, by State

Industrial Sales Net of Use for Electricity Generation: Comparison of Data From
   Bureau of Mines (BOM) and American Gas Association (AGA)

REGION AND STATE	BOM	AGA	BOM Minus AGA	BOM/AGA
NEW ENGLAND:				
CONNECTICUT	14278.9	19950.0	-5671.1	0.716
MAINE	327.9	400.0	-72.1	0.820
MASSACHUSETTS	28934.1	27100.0	1834.1	1.068
NEW HAMPSHIRE	1719.0	2100.0	-381.0	0.819
RHODE ISLAND	4392.3	6000.0	-1607.7	0.732
VERMONT	814.9	1400.0	-585.1	0.582
MID ATLANTIC:				
NEW JERSEY	84828.7	89000.0	-4171.3	0.953
NEW YORK	105248.8	126400.0	-21151.2	0.833
PENNSYLVANIA	377122.5	364600.0	12522.5	1.034
EAST NORTH CENTRAL:				
ILLINOIS	408582.4	390800.0	17782.4	1.046
INDIANA	292929.1	289400.0	3529.1	1.012
MICHIGAN	276403.8	331500.0	-55096.2	0.834
OHIO	438450.6	464500.0	-26049.4	0.944
WISCONSIN	140741.2	178200.0	-37458.8	0.790
WEST NORTH CENTRAL:				
IOWA	106334.5	128400.0	-22065.5	0.828
KANSAS	177317.7	237300.0	-59982.3	0.747
MINNESOTA	105117.8	141400.0	-36282.2	0.743
MISSOURI	99805.8	101500.0	-1694.2	0.983
NEBRASKA	56436.9	68400.0	-11963.1	0.825
NORTH DAKOTA	2978.6	2100.0	878.6	1.418
SOUTH DAKOTA	6162.6	7000.0	-837.4	0.880
SOUTH ATLANTIC:				
DELAWARE	10296.9	11100.0	-803.1	0.928
DISTRICT OF COLUMBIA	827.0	900.0	-73.0	0.919
FLORIDA	90435.8	87600.0	2835.8	1.032
GEORGIA	159294.7	155800.0	3494.7	1.022
MARYLAND	61733.9	66800.0	-5066.1	0.924
NORTH CAROLINA	85781.5	101200.0	-15418.5	0.848
SOUTH CAROLINA	84132.5	98700.0	-14567.5	0.852
VIRGINIA	54492.9	58500.0	-4007.1	0.932
WEST VIRGINIA	96630.3	83400.0	13230.3	1.159
EAST SOUTH CENTRAL:				
ALABAMA	169904.7	168900.0	1004.7	1.006
KENTUCKY	79337.2	76900.0	2437.2	1.032
MISSISSIPPI	150274.2	82100.0	68174.2	1.830
TENNESSEE	138081.4	160800.0	-22718.6	0.859
WEST SOUTH CENTRAL:				
ARKANSAS	146873.2	140100.0	6773.2	1.048
LOUISIANA	1046015.5	375500.0	670515.6	2.786
OKLAHOMA	128973.2	121800.0	7173.2	1.059
TEXAS	1888902.5	1037900.0	851002.6	1.820
ROCKY MOUNTAIN:				
ARIZONA	66811.3	69800.0	-2988.7	0.957
COLORADO	80611.2	80700.0	-88.8	0.999
IDAHO	32157.8	32400.0	-242.2	0.993
MONTANA	34254.1	36700.0	-2445.9	0.933
NEVADA	8301.1	14800.0	-6498.9	0.561
NEW MEXICO	83139.7	35800.0	47339.7	2.322
UTAH	56991.0	56500.0	491.0	1.009
WYOMING	56232.3	49000.0	7232.3	1.148
FAR WEST:				
ALASKA	12389.6	11400.0	989.6	1.087
CALIFORNIA	657146.9	609700.0	47446.9	1.078
HAWAII	0.0	1700.0	-1700.0	0.000
OREGON	64964.5	63600.0	1364.5	1.021
WASHINGTON	106733.3	126000.0	-19266.7	0.847

Table F.1.5

Natural Gas Consumption In Billion BTU, 1972, By Region

Industrial Use: Comparison Of Alternative Series And Definitions, Data From Bureau of Mines (BOM), Crump And Readling, And American Gas Association (AGA)

REGION	BOM SALES = (1)	BOM(1) PLUS LEASE & PLANT FUEL = (2)	BOM (2) PLUS OTHER	CRUMP & READLING	AGA NET OF ELECTRIC GENER.	AGA INCLUDING ELECTRIC GENER.
NEW ENGLAND	50467.10	50467.10	60331.60	65751.90	56950.00	62900.00
MID ATLANTIC	567200.10	570140.90	602312.80	638533.90	580000.00	588100.00
EAST NORTH CENTRAL	1557107.10	1563073.10	1603355.09	1654595.90	1654400.01	1780999.99
WEST NORTH CENTRAL	554153.90	596269.91	656610.40	685650.30	686100.00	942300.00
SOUTH ATLANTIC	643625.50	649628.60	682296.20	743944.41	664000.00	754800.00
EAST SOUTH CENTRAL	537597.50	550792.40	568513.50	601595.80	488700.00	582100.00
WEST SOUTH CENTRAL	3210764.42	4462434.80	4549373.98	4599418.38	1675300.00	2402899.99
ROCKY MOUNTAIN	418498.50	506839.30	541086.20	577073.00	375700.00	577600.00
FAR WEST	841234.30	929820.39	945181.20	972738.00	812400.00	1106100.00
TOTAL	8380648.34	9879466.52	10209061.10	10539301.70	6993549.99	8797800.02

Industrial Sales Net Of Use For Electricity Generation

	BOM	AGA	BOM MINUS AGA	BOM/AGA
NEW ENGLAND	50467.1	56950.0	-6482.9	0.886
MID ATLANTIC	567200.0	580000.0	-12800.0	0.978
EAST NORTH CENTRAL	1557107.1	1654400.0	-97292.9	0.941
WEST NORTH CENTRAL	554153.9	686100.0	-131946.1	0.808
SOUTH ATLANTIC	643625.5	664000.0	-20374.5	0.969
EAST SOUTH CENTRAL	537597.5	488700.0	48897.5	1.100
WEST SOUTH CENTRAL	3210764.4	1675300.0	1535464.6	1.917
ROCKY MOUNTAIN	418498.5	375700.0	42798.5	1.114
FAR WEST	841234.3	812400.0	28834.3	1.035
TOTAL	8380648.3	6993550.0	1387098.5	1.198

Table F.1.6

Natural Gas Consumption In Billion BTU, 1972, By State

Consumption Of Pipeline Fuel And "Other" Consumption, Comparing Bureau of Mines (BOM) and
American Gas Association (AGA) Data

REGION AND STATE	Pipeline Fuel (BOM Data)	BOM Other (Excludes Electric Generation)	AGA Other Net Of Electric Generation	AGA Other Including Electric Generation
NEW ENGLAND:				
CONNECTICUT	40.6	4280.4	100.0	100.0
MAINE	0.0	16.2	100.0	100.0
MASSACHUSETTS	664.9	4799.9	3900.0	4600.0
NEW HAMPSHIRE	0.0	79.8	1100.0	1100.0
RHODE ISLAND	16.3	688.2	300.0	300.0
VERMONT	0.0	0.0	0.0	0.0
MID ATLANTIC:				
NEW JERSEY	748.0	2875.9	2200.0	2400.0
NEW YORK	3472.4	19581.8	26600.0	27000.0
PENNSYLVANIA	28464.3	9714.3	11200.0	11200.0
EAST NORTH CENTRAL:				
ILLINOIS	23815.9	6486.2	4400.0	8100.0
INDIANA	13304.3	3906.3	3500.0	3600.0
MICHIGAN	16360.8	7202.4	100.0	11500.0
OHIO	13018.7	19794.0	8900.0	15500.0
WISCONSIN	6352.4	2892.9	1100.0	14300.0
WEST NORTH CENTRAL:				
IOWA	20451.4	2743.5	1900.0	19500.0
KANSAS	79930.8	6333.3	10200.0	11100.0
MINNESOTA	7482.9	24398.7	7700.0	7700.0
MISSOURI	9686.3	16978.0	1400.0	12600.0
NEBRASKA	13229.0	8289.8	2200.0	11100.0
NORTH DAKOTA	271.2	0.0	100.0	400.0
SOUTH DAKOTA	10.0	1597.4	400.0	400.0
SOUTH ATLANTIC:				
DELAWARE	0.0	0.0	1400.0	1400.0
DISTRICT OF COLUMBIA	532.4	2135.6	2100.0	2100.0
FLORIDA	4185.9	4436.7	5900.0	23500.0
GEORGIA	8203.7	4865.3	2300.0	2300.0
MARYLAND	3144.7	3581.1	3500.0	3500.0
NORTH CAROLINA	6216.7	6238.2	1700.0	7100.0
SOUTH CAROLINA	3090.2	1141.1	7000.0	7000.0
VIRGINIA	8489.1	7324.6	6400.0	8300.0
WEST VIRGINIA	15221.0	2945.0	1800.0	1800.0
EAST SOUTH CENTRAL:				
ALABAMA	19657.0	1057.8	400.0	400.0
KENTUCKY	37578.2	7658.0	7700.0	7700.0
MISSISSIPPI	59330.1	4638.1	5600.0	11300.0
TENNESSEE	25942.4	4367.0	4100.0	21000.0
WEST SOUTH CENTRAL:				
ARKANSAS	13203.6	971.9	1200.0	2100.0
LOUISIANA	81840.5	33254.2	12100.0	12200.0
OKLAHOMA	25383.1	4349.9	5200.0	114200.0
TEXAS	107196.2	48363.5	138500.0	142500.0
ROCKY MOUNTAIN:				
ARIZONA	27424.9	4250.8	10000.0	10000.0
COLORADO	2916.2	1239.9	1800.0	1800.0
IDAHO	5010.0	1988.3	1300.0	1300.0
MONTANA	1083.6	2714.2	2700.0	3300.0
NEVADA	0.0	6146.8	1500.0	1500.0
NEW MEXICO	39319.4	16365.2	12500.0	13100.0
UTAH	798.2	13.1	0.0	0.0
WYOMING	6217.8	1528.4	1700.0	1700.0
FAR WEST:				
ALASKA	8827.9	6939.5	0.0	0.0
CALIFORNIA	19721.4	7834.4	4000.0	319400.0
HAWAII	0.0	0.0	0.0	0.0
OREGON	10370.6	409.6	0.0	0.0
WASHINGTON	7800.7	177.2		

Table F.1.7

Natural Gas Consumption In Billion BTU, 1972, By Region

Consumption Of Pipeline Fuel And "Other" Consumption, Comparing Bureau of Mines (BOM) and American Gas Association (AGA) Data

REGION	Pipeline Fuel (BOM Data)	BOM Other (Excludes Electric Generation)	AGA Other Net Of Electric Generation	AGA Other Including Electric Generation
NEW ENGLAND	721.80	9864.50	5500.00	6200.00
MID ATLANTIC	32684.70	32172.00	40000.00	40600.00
EAST NORTH CENTRAL	72852.10	40281.80	18000.00	53000.00
WEST NORTH CENTRAL	131061.60	60340.70	23900.00	62800.00
SOUTH ATLANTIC	49083.70	32667.60	32100.00	57000.00
EAST SOUTH CENTRAL	142507.70	17720.90	17800.00	40400.00
WEST SOUTH CENTRAL	227623.40	86939.50	157000.00	271000.00
ROCKY MOUNTAIN	82770.10	34246.70	31500.00	32700.00
FAR WEST	46720.60	15360.70	4000.00	319400.00
TOTAL	786025.71	329594.40	329800.00	883100.00

Table F.1.8

Natural Gas Consumption In Billion BTU, 1972, By State

Use By Electric Utilities: Comparison of Data From Bureau Of Mines (BOM)
    National Coal Association (NCA), And American Gas Association (AGA)

REGION AND STATE	BOM	NCA	AGA	BOM MINUS NCA	BOM MINUS AGA
NEW ENGLAND:					
CONNECTICUT	30.5 [a]	0.0 [a]	100.0	30.5	-69.5
MAINE	0.0 [a]	0.0	0.0	0.0	0.0
MASSACHUSETTS	8180.0	6797.1	7300.0	1382.9	880.0
NEW HAMPSHIRE	0.0	0.0	0.0	0.0	0.0
RHODE ISLAND	151.1	150.9	100.0	0.2	51.1
VERMONT	721.3	373.8	0.0	347.5	721.3
MID ATLANTIC:					
NEW JERSEY	25690.0	18798.1	21500.0	6891.9	4190.0
NEW YORK	77092.6	53146.7	78600.0	23945.9	-1507.4
PENNSYLVANIA	5654.6	3344.5	5000.0	2310.1	654.6
EAST NORTH CENTRAL:					
ILLINOIS	74615.9	58349.0	80200.0	16266.9	-5584.1
INDIANA	18079.8	14476.7	18400.0	3603.1	-320.2
MICHIGAN	59837.3	40048.7	57100.0	19788.6	2737.3
OHIO	17072.8	9368.3	9500.0	7704.5	7572.8
WISCONSIN	28607.4	22085.1	28100.0	6522.3	507.4
WEST NORTH CENTRAL:					
IOWA	61322.0	53888.3	55600.0	7433.7	5722.0
KANSAS	179795.7	165646.3	181000.0	14149.4	-1204.3
MINNESOTA	52029.9	47848.5	48600.0	4181.4	3429.9
MISSOURI	59308.3	51733.8	78700.0	7574.5	-19391.7
NEBRASKA	49532.1	43507.4	46100.0	6024.7	3432.1
NORTH DAKOTA	338.2	13.0	300.0	325.2	38.2
SOUTH DAKOTA	3557.2	3068.4	3600.0	488.8	-42.8
SOUTH ATLANTIC:					
DELAWARE	2478.6	2218.2	1600.0	260.4	878.6
DISTRICT OF COLUMBIA	0.0	0.0	0.0	0.0	0.0
FLORIDA	177199.0	157562.9	46600.0	19636.1	130599.0
GEORGIA	39624.4	37767.0	47600.0	1857.4	-7975.6
MARYLAND	7197.9	0.0	6700.0	7197.9	497.9
NORTH CAROLINA	17215.5	5486.0	15700.0	11729.5	1515.5
SOUTH CAROLINA	25195.3	17098.6	17800.0	8096.7	7395.3
VIRGINIA	4629.3	1904.2	4200.0	2725.1	429.3
WEST VIRGINIA	470.3	45.1	600.0	425.2	-129.7
EAST SOUTH CENTRAL:					
ALABAMA	2834.2	2835.6	900.0	-1.4	1934.2
KENTUCKY	10184.2	10348.7	10200.0	-164.5	-15.8
MISSISSIPPI	102913.1	93206.5	98600.0	9706.6	4313.1
TENNESSEE	16520.6	19572.8	17200.0	-3052.2	-679.4
WEST SOUTH CENTRAL:					
ARKANSAS	72641.4	73219.9	70300.0	-578.5	2341.4
LOUISIANA	393457.7	381517.7	280700.0	11940.0	112757.7
OKLAHOMA	268261.2	267797.4	132700.0	463.8	135561.2
TEXAS	1319811.1	1300189.0	514900.0	19622.1	804911.1
ROCKY MOUNTAIN:					
ARIZONA	82300.2	79549.8	98100.0	2750.4	-15799.8
COLORADO	65188.8	57677.0	101500.0	7511.8	-36311.2
IDAHO	0.0	0.0	0.0	0.0	0.0
MONTANA	1257.0	869.9	1200.0	387.1	57.0
NEVADA	43326.5	40480.4	60100.0	2846.1	-16773.5
NEW MEXICO	64049.7	62118.6	47300.0	1931.1	16749.7
UTAH	3487.5	3408.6	3500.0	78.9	-12.5
WYOMING	2922.7	2658.8	3.0	263.9	2919.7
FAR WEST:					
ALASKA	13150.4	0.0	0.0	13150.4	13150.4
CALIFORNIA	638502.7	623615.0	609200.0	14887.7	29302.7
HAWAII	0.0	0.0	0.0	0.0	0.0
OREGON	426.4	437.8	0.0	-11.4	426.4
WASHINGTON	0.0	0.0	0.0	0.0	0.0

a Zero indicates no use of natural gas

Table   F.1.9

Natural Gas Consumption In Billion BTU, 1972, By Region

Use By Electric Utilities: Comparison Of Data From Bureau of Mines (BOM),
   National Coal Association (NCA), And American Gas Association (AGA)

REGION	BOM	NCA	AGA	BOM MINUS NCA	BOM MINUS AGA
NEW ENGLAND	9082.90	7321.80	7500.00	1761.10	1582.90
MID ATLANTIC	108437.20	75289.30	105100.00	33147.90	3337.20
EAST NORTH CENTRAL	198213.20	144327.80	193300.00	53885.40	4913.20
WEST NORTH CENTRAL	405883.40	365705.70	413900.00	40177.70	-8016.60
SOUTH ATLANTIC	274010.30	222082.00	140800.00	51928.30	133210.30
EAST SOUTH CENTRAL	132452.10	125963.60	126900.00	6488.50	5552.10
WEST SOUTH CENTRAL	2054171.39	2022724.00	998600.00	31447.40	1055571.39
ROCKY MOUNTAIN	262532.40	246763.10	311703.00	15769.30	-49170.60
FAR WEST	652079.49	624052.80	609200.00	28026.70	42879.50
TOTAL	4096862.38	3834230.15	2907003.02	262632.30	1189859.43

Table   F.1.10

Natural Gas Consumption in Billion BTU, 1972, by State

Commercial and Industrial Firm and Interruptible Sales, American Gas Association Data

REGION AND STATE	COMMERCIAL			INDUSTRIAL		
	Firm	Interruptible	Total	Firm	Interruptible	Total
NEW ENGLAND:						
CONNECTICUT	12000.0	200.0	12200.0	13700.0	6400.0	20000.0
MAINE	500.0	0.0	500.0	300.0	0.0	400.0
MASSACHUSETTS	33700.0	1200.0	34800.0	18300.0	14600.0	32900.0
NEW HAMPSHIRE	2100.0	0.0	2100.0	1200.0	900.0	2100.0
RHODE ISLAND	4300.0	100.0	4500.0	3700.0	2400.0	6100.0
VERMONT	500.0	0.0	500.0	100.0	1300.0	1400.0
MID ATLANTIC:						
NEW JERSEY	58300.0	5800.0	64100.0	39100.0	55800.0	94900.0
NEW YORK	113000.0	1500.0	114400.0	88400.0	38000.0	126400.0
PENNSYLVANIA	116300.0	0.0	116300.0	322700.0	44100.0	366800.0
EAST NORTH CENTRAL:						
ILLINOIS	216600.0	6300.0	222900.0	373900.0	82200.0	456100.0
INDIANA	74500.0	3700.0	78300.0	243400.0	51800.0	295100.0
MICHIGAN	174700.0	4500.0	179200.0	227600.0	146300.0	373900.0
OHIO	199800.0	2300.0	202100.0	423900.0	42100.0	466100.0
WISCONSIN	48100.0	4900.0	53000.0	51600.0	138300.0	189800.0
WEST NORTH CENTRAL:						
IOWA	46200.0	14100.0	60300.0	72000.0	68500.0	140500.0
KANSAS	35000.0	2100.0	37000.0	87300.0	272200.0	359500.0
MINNESOTA	44200.0	7100.0	51300.0	70400.0	101200.0	171600.0
MISSOURI	66200.0	10500.0	76700.0	63100.0	90400.0	153600.0
NEBRASKA	26900.0	3700.0	30700.0	38800.0	66900.0	105600.0
NORTH DAKOTA	9300.0	0.0	9300.0	1400.0	700.0	2100.0
SOUTH DAKOTA	8200.0	1300.0	9500.0	200.0	9200.0	9400.0
SOUTH ATLANTIC:						
DELAWARE	3500.0	0.0	3500.0	9100.0	2000.0	11100.0
DISTRICT OF COLUMBIA	9000.0	1800.0	10900.0	800.0	200.0	900.0
FLORIDA	19900.0	1100.0	21100.0	33800.0	82800.0	116600.0
GEORGIA	39200.0	0.0	39200.0	29100.0	174300.0	203400.0
MARYLAND	17200.0	3900.0	21200.0	38700.0	28000.0	66800.0
NORTH CAROLINA	17800.0	100.0	17900.0	40200.0	71300.0	111500.0
SOUTH CAROLINA	10800.0	2600.0	13400.0	20500.0	81500.0	102000.0
VIRGINIA	25300.0	3500.0	28800.0	35700.0	22800.0	58500.0
WEST VIRGINIA	25000.0	0.0	25000.0	79500.0	4600.0	84000.0
EAST SOUTH CENTRAL:						
ALABAMA	27700.0	300.0	28000.0	127900.0	41900.0	169800.0
KENTUCKY	34300.0	3600.0	37900.0	37800.0	39100.0	76900.0
MISSISSIPPI	15100.0	0.0	15100.0	157400.0	17200.0	174600.0
TENNESSEE	34900.0	3400.0	38300.0	84700.0	76100.0	160800.0
WEST SOUTH CENTRAL:						
ARKANSAS	29000.0	100.0	29100.0	190200.0	19200.0	209400.0
LOUISIANA	26600.0	300.0	26900.0	545100.0	15200.0	560300.0
OKLAHOMA	36500.0	1200.0	37600.0	68800.0	76700.0	145500.0
TEXAS	103700.0	2000.0	105700.0	1067500.0	420200.0	1487700.0
ROCKY MOUNTAIN:						
ARIZONA	22400.0	0.0	22400.0	118200.0	600.0	118900.0
COLORADO	58200.0	400.0	58500.0	51300.0	88400.0	139700.0
IDAHO	7600.0	0.0	7600.0	24100.0	8300.0	32400.0
MONTANA	16900.0	0.0	16900.0	2200.0	34500.0	36700.0
NEVADA	6900.0	0.0	6900.0	19100.0	39400.0	58500.0
NEW MEXICO	12100.0	400.0	12500.0	42300.0	40100.0	82400.0
UTAH	14300.0	0.0	14300.0	4700.0	55300.0	60000.0
WYOMING	8500.0	0.0	8500.0	6600.0	42300.0	49000.0
FAR WEST:						
ALASKA	7100.0	0.0	7100.0	11400.0	0.0	11400.0
CALIFORNIA	196400.0	32800.0	229000.0	68200.0	835200.0	903400.0
HAWAII	700.0	0.0	700.0	1700.0	0.0	1700.0
OREGON	13100.0	400.0	13500.0	22600.0	41000.0	63600.0
WASHINGTON	22400.0	1100.0	23400.0	37000.0	89000.0	126000.0

Table F.1.11

Natural Gas Consumption in Billion BTU, 1972, by Region

Commercial and Industrial Firm and Interruptible Sales, American Gas Association Data

REGION	COMMERCIAL			INDUSTRIAL		
	Firm	Interruptible	Total	Firm	Interruptible	Total
NEW ENGLAND	53100.00	1500.00	54600.00	37300.00	25600.00	62900.00
MID ATLANTIC	287600.00	7300.00	294800.00	450200.00	137900.00	588100.00
EAST NORTH CENTRAL	713700.00	21700.00	735500.00	1320400.00	460700.00	1780999.99
WEST NORTH CENTRAL	236000.00	38800.00	274800.00	333200.00	609100.00	942300.00
SOUTH ATLANTIC	167700.00	13000.00	181000.00	287400.00	467500.00	754800.00
EAST SOUTH CENTRAL	112000.00	7300.00	119300.00	407800.00	174300.00	582100.00
WEST SOUTH CENTRAL	195800.00	3600.00	199300.00	1871600.00	531300.00	2402899.99
ROCKY MOUNTAIN	146900.00	800.00	147600.00	268500.00	308900.00	577600.00
FAR WEST	239500.00	34300.00	273700.00	140900.00	965200.00	1106100.00
TOTAL	2152299.99	128300.00	2280600.00	5117300.00	3680500.02	8797800.02

Table   F.1.12

Natural Gas Consumption In Billion BTU, 1972, By State

Quantities Employed By Electric Utilities For Different Classes Of Use, American Gas Association Data

REGION AND STATE	SALES				TRANSFERS WITHIN COMBINED GAS-ELECTRIC UTILITIES	TOTAL SALES AND TRANSFERS
	INDUSTRIAL		OTHER SALES	TOTAL SALES		
	Firm	Interruptible				
NEW ENGLAND:						
CONNECTICUT	50.0	0.0	0.0	50.0	50.0	100.0
MAINE	0.0	0.0	0.0	0.0	0.0	0.0
MASSACHUSETTS	2500.0	3300.0	700.0	6500.0	900.0	7300.0
NEW HAMPSHIRE	0.0	0.0	0.0	0.0	0.0	0.0
RHODE ISLAND	0.0	100.0	0.0	100.0	0.0	100.0
VERMONT	0.0	0.0	0.0	0.0	0.0	0.0
MID ATLANTIC:						
NEW JERSEY	0.0	5900.0	200.0	6100.0	15400.0	21500.0
NEW YORK	0.0	0.0	400.0	400.0	78200.0	78600.0
PENNSYLVANIA	2200.0	0.0	0.0	2200.0	2800.0	5000.0
EAST NORTH CENTRAL:						
ILLINOIS	56500.0	8800.0	3700.0	69000.0	11200.0	80200.0
INDIANA	100.0	5600.0	100.0	5900.0	12500.0	18400.0
MICHIGAN	23100.0	19300.0	11400.0	53700.0	3400.0	57100.0
OHIO	700.0	900.0	6600.0	8300.0	1300.0	9500.0
WISCONSIN	0.0	11600.0	13200.0	24700.0	3400.0	28100.0
WEST NORTH CENTRAL:						
IOWA	0.0	12100.0	17600.0	29700.0	25900.0	55600.0
KANSAS	100.0	122100.0	900.0	123200.0	57800.0	181000.0
MINNESOTA	40.0	30160.0	0.0	30200.0	18500.0	48600.0
MISSOURI	16600.0	35500.0	11200.0	63300.0	15500.0	78700.0
NEBRASKA	400.0	36800.0	8900.0	46100.0	0.0	46100.0
NORTH DAKOTA	0.0	0.0	300.0	300.0	0.0	300.0
SOUTH DAKOTA	0.0	2400.0	0.0	2400.0	1200.0	3600.0
SOUTH ATLANTIC:						
DELAWARE	0.0	0.0	0.0	0.0	1600.0	1600.0
DISTRICT OF COLUMBIA	0.0	0.0	0.0	0.0	0.0	0.0
FLORIDA	5200.0	23800.0	17600.0	46600.0	0.0	46600.0
GEORGIA	0.0	47600.0	0.0	47600.0	0.0	47600.0
MARYLAND	0.0	0.0	0.0	0.0	6700.0	6700.0
NORTH CAROLINA	0.0	10300.0	5400.0	15700.0	15.0	15700.0
SOUTH CAROLINA	0.0	3300.0	0.0	3300.0	14600.0	17800.0
VIRGINIA	0.0	0.0	1900.0	1900.0	2300.0	4200.0
WEST VIRGINIA	560.0	40.0	0.0	600.0	0.0	600.0
EAST SOUTH CENTRAL:						
ALABAMA	100.0	800.0	0.0	900.0	0.0	900.0
KENTUCKY	0.0	0.0	0.0	0.0	10200.0	10200.0
MISSISSIPPI	80600.0	11900.0	5700.0	98300.0	300.0	98600.0
TENNESSEE	0.0	0.0	16900.0	16900.0	300.0	17200.0
WEST SOUTH CENTRAL:						
ARKANSAS	68800.0	500.0	900.0	70300.0	0.0	70300.0
LOUISIANA	171600.0	13200.0	100.0	184900.0	95800.0	280700.0
OKLAHOMA	6800.0	16900.0	109000.0	132700.0	15.0	132700.0
TEXAS	405900.0	43900.0	4000.0	453800.0	61100.0	514900.0
ROCKY MOUNTAIN:						
ARIZONA	48600.0	500.0	0.0	49000.0	49100.0	98100.0
COLORADO	29400.0	29600.0	0.0	58900.0	42600.0	101500.0
IDAHO	0.0	0.0	0.0	0.0	0.0	0.0
MONTANA	0.0	0.0	600.0	600.0	600.0	1200.0
NEVADA	15500.0	28200.0	0.0	43700.0	16400.0	60100.0
NEW MEXICO	10600.0	36000.0	600.0	47300.0	0.0	47300.0
UTAH	0.0	3500.0	0.0	3500.0	0.0	3500.0
WYOMING	0.0	0.0	0.0	0.0	3.0	3.0
FAR WEST:						
ALASKA	0.0	0.0	0.0	0.0	0.0	0.0
CALIFORNIA	0.0	293700.0	315400.0	609200.0	0.0	609200.0
HAWAII	0.0	0.0	0.0	0.0	0.0	0.0
OREGON	0.0	0.0	0.0	0.0	0.0	0.0
WASHINGTON	0.0	0.0	0.0	0.0	0.0	0.0

Table F.1.13

Natural Gas Consumption In Billion BTU, 1972, By Region

Quantities Employed By Electric Utilities For Different Classes Of Use, American Gas Association Data

REGION	SALES				TRANSFERS WITHIN COMBINED GAS-ELECTRIC UTILITIES	TOTAL SALES AND TRANSFERS
	INDUSTRIAL		OTHER SALES	TOTAL SALES		
	Firm	Interruptible				
NEW ENGLAND	2550.00	3400.00	700.00	6650.00	950.00	7500.00
MID ATLANTIC	2200.00	5900.00	600.00	8700.00	96400.00	105100.00
EAST NORTH CENTRAL	80400.00	46200.00	35000.00	161600.00	31800.00	193300.00
WEST NORTH CENTRAL	17140.00	239060.00	38900.00	295200.00	118900.00	413900.00
SOUTH ATLANTIC	5760.00	85040.00	24900.00	115700.00	25215.00	140800.00
EAST SOUTH CENTRAL	80700.00	12700.00	22600.00	116100.00	10800.00	126900.00
WEST SOUTH CENTRAL	653100.00	74500.00	114000.00	841700.00	156915.00	998600.00
ROCKY MOUNTAIN	104100.00	97800.00	1200.00	203000.00	108703.00	311703.00
FAR WEST	0.00	293700.00	315400.00	609200.00	0.00	609200.00
TOTAL	945950.00	858300.00	553300.00	2357850.00	549683.00	2907003.02

Table F.1.14

Natural Gas Consumption, Scale Factors, 1972, By State

Housing Units, Percent In Large Multi-family Structures, and State Large Multi-family Units As
A Percent Of Regional Total

REGION AND STATE	NUMBER OF HOUSING UNITS IN THOUSANDS	PERCENTAGE IN STRUCTURES WITH 5 + UNITS (Large Multi-family)	STATE LARGE MULTI-FAMILY UNITS AS PERCENTAGE OF REGIONAL TOTAL			
			Northeast	North Central	South	West
NEW ENGLAND:						
CONNECTICUT	968.8	15.1	4.0315	0.0000	0.0000	0.0000
MAINE	339.4	8.1	0.7576	0.0000	0.0000	0.0000
MASSACHUSETTS	1839.0	16.9	8.5648	0.0000	0.0000	0.0000
NEW HAMPSHIRE	248.8	9.8	0.6719	0.0000	0.0000	0.0000
RHODE ISLAND	307.3	11.7	0.9908	0.0000	0.0000	0.0000
VERMONT	149.8	7.0	0.2890	0.0000	0.0000	0.0000
MID ATLANTIC:						
NEW JERSEY	2305.3	19.2	12.1978	0.0000	0.0000	0.0000
NEW YORK	6159.3	36.6	62.1246	0.0000	0.0000	0.0000
PENNSYLVANIA	3880.1	9.7	10.3721	0.0000	0.0000	0.0000
EAST NORTH CENTRAL:						
ILLINOIS	3692.4	20.1	0.0000	34.6478	0.0000	0.0000
INDIANA	1711.9	7.5	0.0000	5.9939	0.0000	0.0000
MICHIGAN	2845.4	9.5	0.0000	12.6194	0.0000	0.0000
OHIO	3447.9	10.7	0.0000	17.2230	0.0000	0.0000
WISCONSIN	1416.4	8.4	0.0000	5.5544	0.0000	0.0000
WEST NORTH CENTRAL:						
IOWA	955.0	6.7	0.0000	2.9871	0.0000	0.0000
KANSAS	787.5	6.1	0.0000	2.2426	0.0000	0.0000
MINNESOTA	1219.6	13.3	0.0000	7.5725	0.0000	0.0000
MISSOURI	1665.5	9.8	0.0000	7.6198	0.0000	0.0000
NEBRASKA	511.5	9.3	0.0000	2.2207	0.0000	0.0000
NORTH DAKOTA	200.5	7.9	0.0000	0.7395	0.0000	0.0000
SOUTH DAKOTA	221.6	5.6	0.0000	0.5793	0.0000	0.0000
SOUTH ATLANTIC:						
DELAWARE	175.0	11.4	0.0000	0.0000	0.9772	0.0000
DISTRICT OF COLUMBIA	278.4	51.0	0.0000	0.0000	6.9549	0.0000
FLORIDA	2490.8	15.3	0.0000	0.0000	18.6672	0.0000
GEORGIA	1466.7	9.8	0.0000	0.0000	7.0407	0.0000
MARYLAND	1234.7	19.1	0.0000	0.0000	11.5516	0.0000
NORTH CAROLINA	1619.5	4.3	0.0000	0.0000	3.4111	0.0000
SOUTH CAROLINA	804.9	3.6	0.0000	0.0000	1.4194	0.0000
VIRGINIA	1485.0	13.0	0.0000	0.0000	9.4562	0.0000
WEST VIRGINIA	592.8	4.2	0.0000	0.0000	1.2196	0.0000
EAST SOUTH CENTRAL:						
ALABAMA	1114.8	4.6	0.0000	0.0000	2.5119	0.0000
KENTUCKY	1060.7	6.9	0.0000	0.0000	3.5850	0.0000
MISSISSIPPI	697.3	3.3	0.0000	0.0000	1.1272	0.0000
TENNESSEE	1297.0	7.4	0.0000	0.0000	4.7013	0.0000
WEST SOUTH CENTRAL:						
ARKANSAS	673.0	3.8	0.0000	0.0000	1.2527	0.0000
LOUISIANA	1146.1	6.4	0.0000	0.0000	3.5929	0.0000
OKLAHOMA	937.8	6.4	0.0000	0.0000	2.9399	0.0000
TEXAS	3809.1	10.5	0.0000	0.0000	19.5912	0.0000
ROCKY MOUNTAIN:						
ARIZONA	578.8	11.0	0.0000	0.0000	0.0000	3.1485
COLORADO	742.9	15.5	0.0000	0.0000	0.0000	5.6943
IDAHO	238.3	5.5	0.0000	0.0000	0.0000	0.6481
MONTANA	240.8	8.1	0.0000	0.0000	0.0000	0.9645
NEVADA	171.7	16.6	0.0000	0.0000	0.0000	1.4095
NEW MEXICO	322.3	6.3	0.0000	0.0000	0.0000	1.0041
UTAH	312.0	9.4	0.0000	0.0000	0.0000	1.4503
WYOMING	114.6	6.1	0.0000	0.0000	0.0000	0.3457
FAR WEST:						
ALASKA	88.6	22.7	0.0000	0.0000	0.0000	0.9946
CALIFORNIA	6976.3	20.0	0.0000	0.0000	0.0000	68.9971
HAWAII	215.9	24.6	0.0000	0.0000	0.0000	2.6264
OREGON	735.6	11.7	0.0000	0.0000	0.0000	4.2560
WASHINGTON	1204.9	14.2	0.0000	0.0000	0.0000	8.4609

Table F.1.15

Natural Gas Consumption, Scale Factors, 1972, By State

Relative Concentration of Activity and Fraction of Category Allocated to Business (Bus.) Federal Government (FG) and State and Local Government (SL)

REGION AND STATE	RELATIVE CONCENTRATION OF ACTIVITY			FRACTION OF CATEGORY ALLOCATED TO SECTOR							
				Office Use			School Use		Hospital Use		
	Office	School	Hospital	B	FG	SL	B	SL	B	FG	SL
NEW ENGLAND:											
CONNECTICUT	1.0100	1.0423	0.8658	0.8878	0.0283	0.0839	0.1759	0.8241	0.7250	0.0600	0.2150
MAINE	0.7073	1.0522	0.8447	0.7964	0.0861	0.1175	0.0921	0.9079	0.7231	0.0846	0.1923
MASSACHUSETTS	1.0258	1.0563	1.2422	0.8534	0.0486	0.0980	0.2239	0.7761	0.6546	0.0602	0.2852
NEW HAMPSHIRE	0.8054	1.0369	0.7752	0.8517	0.0450	0.1033	0.1858	0.8142	0.7223	0.0444	0.2333
RHODE ISLAND	0.8548	1.0151	1.0320	0.7876	0.1006	0.1118	0.2130	0.7870	0.7400	0.0533	0.2067
VERMONT	0.8153	1.1194	1.0145	0.8308	0.0473	0.1219	0.1655	0.8345	0.7715	0.0714	0.1571
MID ATLANTIC:											
NEW JERSEY	1.0301	0.9732	0.7167	0.8543	0.0483	0.0974	0.1634	0.8366	0.6608	0.0519	0.2873
NEW YORK	1.1048	0.9893	1.1071	0.8545	0.0372	0.1083	0.2115	0.7885	0.5531	0.0580	0.3889
PENNSYLVANIA	0.8557	0.9814	0.9520	0.8385	0.0625	0.0990	0.2064	0.7936	0.7229	0.0600	0.2171
EAST NORTH CENTRAL:											
ILLINOIS	1.1227	0.9849	1.0970	0.8662	0.0444	0.0894	0.1758	0.8242	0.6830	0.0698	0.2472
INDIANA	0.9111	0.9782	0.8659	0.8597	0.0501	0.0902	0.1046	0.8954	0.6118	0.0450	0.3432
MICHIGAN	0.9850	1.0754	0.9554	0.8667	0.0360	0.0973	0.1102	0.8898	0.6877	0.0585	0.2538
OHIO	0.9990	0.9869	0.9406	0.8557	0.0505	0.0938	0.1329	0.8671	0.6877	0.0585	0.2538
WISCONSIN	0.8982	1.0469	1.0113	0.8552	0.0313	0.1135	0.1569	0.8431	0.6627	0.0780	0.2593
WEST NORTH CENTRAL:											
IOWA	0.8657	0.9691	0.9146	0.8574	0.0375	0.1051	0.1306	0.8694	0.5442	0.0882	0.3676
KANSAS	1.0075	0.9209	1.0604	0.8308	0.0561	0.1131	0.0777	0.9223	0.5678	0.0935	0.3387
MINNESOTA	1.0458	1.0321	1.0405	0.8762	0.0360	0.0878	0.1242	0.8758	0.5846	0.0808	0.3346
MISSOURI	1.0345	0.9419	1.0950	0.8271	0.0793	0.0936	0.1179	0.8821	0.5971	0.0716	0.3313
NEBRASKA	0.9265	0.9732	1.0662	0.8386	0.0508	0.1106	0.1318	0.8682	0.5762	0.0857	0.3381
NORTH DAKOTA	0.8281	0.9755	0.9789	0.7761	0.0969	0.1270	0.0710	0.9290	0.7375	0.0625	0.2000
SOUTH DAKOTA	0.8021	1.0089	1.0268	0.7782	0.0859	0.1359	0.0887	0.9113	0.6111	0.1667	0.2222
SOUTH ATLANTIC:											
DELAWARE	1.1892	1.1368	1.1627	0.8717	0.0343	0.0940	0.1222	0.8778	0.7125	0.0750	0.2125
DISTRICT OF COLUMBIA	2.1190	1.1653	2.5382	0.3558	0.5424	0.1018	0.3621	0.6379	0.8609	0.0087	0.1304
FLORIDA	1.0716	0.9257	0.9940	0.8197	0.0566	0.1237	0.0832	0.9168	0.4920	0.0750	0.4330
GEORGIA	0.9557	0.9623	0.9994	0.7889	0.1014	0.1097	0.0459	0.9541	0.2456	0.0684	0.6860
MARYLAND	1.2324	1.0735	1.0865	0.7398	0.1634	0.0968	0.1228	0.8772	0.6566	0.0528	0.2906
NORTH CAROLINA	0.8122	0.9594	0.9060	0.8502	0.0475	0.1023	0.0569	0.9431	0.6176	0.0719	0.3105
SOUTH CAROLINA	0.7769	1.0049	0.8336	0.8274	0.0722	0.1004	0.0734	0.9266	0.6250	0.0875	0.2875
VIRGINIA	1.0457	0.9922	0.9753	0.7259	0.1749	0.0992	0.0717	0.9283	0.6042	0.1000	0.2958
WEST VIRGINIA	0.8530	0.9764	1.1096	0.8347	0.0471	0.1182	0.0473	0.9527	0.6042	0.1000	0.2958
EAST SOUTH CENTRAL:											
ALABAMA	0.8592	0.9802	0.9899	0.7666	0.1138	0.1196	0.0742	0.9258	0.4738	0.1000	0.4262
KENTUCKY	0.8558	0.9643	0.9288	0.8099	0.0798	0.1103	0.0916	0.9084	0.6729	0.0730	0.2541
MISSISSIPPI	0.7707	1.0758	0.8828	0.8140	0.0654	0.1206	0.1129	0.8871	0.3459	0.0958	0.5583
TENNESSEE	0.8893	0.9503	1.1005	0.8488	0.0564	0.0948	0.0662	0.9338	0.4815	0.0981	0.4204
WEST SOUTH CENTRAL:											
ARKANSAS	0.7755	0.9482	0.8679	0.8297	0.0565	0.1138	0.0398	0.9602	0.5048	0.1476	0.3476
LOUISIANA	0.9727	1.0824	1.0212	0.8357	0.0451	0.1192	0.1435	0.8565	0.5130	0.0674	0.4196
OKLAHOMA	1.0505	1.0163	0.9771	0.7427	0.1402	0.1171	0.0431	0.9569	0.5581	0.0645	0.3774
TEXAS	1.0630	1.0402	0.9726	0.8226	0.0773	0.1001	0.0607	0.9393	0.5912	0.0757	0.3331
ROCKY MOUNTAIN:											
ARIZONA	0.9406	1.0635	1.0936	0.8040	0.0857	0.1102	0.0516	0.9484	0.7042	0.0833	0.2125
COLORADO	1.0139	1.0226	1.2108	0.8101	0.0954	0.0945	0.0676	0.9324	0.6625	0.0719	0.2656
IDAHO	0.7324	0.9779	0.8293	0.8004	0.0734	0.1262	0.0575	0.9425	0.5858	0.0571	0.3571
MONTANA	0.7828	0.9947	0.9994	0.7807	0.0930	0.1263	0.0642	0.9358	0.6250	0.0625	0.3125
NEVADA	0.9403	0.9317	0.8391	0.7742	0.0839	0.1419	0.0263	0.9737	0.3600	0.0800	0.5600
NEW MEXICO	0.9823	1.0535	0.9975	0.7379	0.1444	0.1177	0.0490	0.9510	0.5083	0.1000	0.3917
UTAH	0.9942	1.1363	0.7937	0.6330	0.2498	0.1172	0.0918	0.9082	0.5900	0.1400	0.2700
WYOMING	0.8436	1.0103	1.0341	0.7830	0.0803	0.1367	0.0280	0.9720	0.1250	0.2000	0.6750
FAR WEST:											
ALASKA	1.1086	1.0052	0.8257	0.5695	0.2507	0.1798	0.0300	0.9700	0.8667	0.0333	0.1000
CALIFORNIA	1.0455	0.9943	1.0211	0.8203	0.0712	0.1085	0.0766	0.9234	0.6176	0.0807	0.3017
HAWAII	0.9959	0.9849	0.9865	0.6691	0.1957	0.1352	0.1016	0.8984	0.7556	0.0111	0.2333
OREGON	0.8593	0.9270	0.8597	0.8360	0.0584	0.1056	0.0645	0.9355	0.6381	0.1000	0.2619
WASHINGTON	0.9548	0.9845	0.9159	0.8305	0.0676	0.1019	0.0650	0.9350	0.6200	0.0971	0.2829

Table   F.1.16

Natural Gas Consumption In Billion BTU, 1972, By State

Estimated Use By "Net" Commercial Subcategories, And Total "Net" Commercial Use

REGION AND STATE	OFFICE USE	RETAIL USE	SCHOOL USE	HOSPITAL USE	OTHER COMMERCIAL USE	TOTAL "NET" COMMERCIAL USE
NEW ENGLAND:						
CONNECTICUT	1293.9	905.1	1506.8	571.5	1400.4	5677.7
MAINE	40.8	40.7	68.5	25.1	63.0	238.1
MASSACHUSETTS	3277.3	2257.8	3809.8	2046.2	3493.1	14884.2
NEW HAMPSHIRE	194.5	170.7	282.8	96.5	264.1	1008.6
RHODE ISLAND	349.1	288.7	468.1	217.3	446.6	1769.8
VERMONT	46.7	40.5	72.4	30.0	62.7	252.3
MID ATLANTIC:						
NEW JERSEY	6262.0	4295.3	6678.0	2244.9	6645.6	26125.8
NEW YORK	14246.5	9111.8	14401.3	7358.2	14097.5	59215.3
PENNSYLVANIA	9851.9	8137.4	12758.9	5650.2	12590.0	48988.4
EAST NORTH CENTRAL:						
ILLINOIS	17266.3	12627.9	22479.3	8969.1	21937.0	83279.6
INDIANA	5132.5	4625.5	8180.6	2594.4	8035.3	28568.3
MICHIGAN	10509.5	8762.6	17036.5	5420.5	15222.2	56951.3
OHIO	13264.7	10902.5	19449.7	6639.3	18939.5	69195.7
WISCONSIN	2576.3	2354.4	4455.2	1540.9	4090.0	15016.8
WEST NORTH CENTRAL:						
IOWA	3539.2	3356.4	5880.1	1988.0	5830.6	20594.3
KANSAS	3799.0	3096.4	5154.7	2125.8	5378.9	19554.8
MINNESOTA	4009.9	3148.2	5874.7	2121.0	5469.0	20622.8
MISSOURI	5779.7	4586.1	7808.2	3251.4	7966.9	29392.3
NEBRASKA	2395.1	2122.9	3734.2	1465.6	3687.9	13405.7
NORTH DAKOTA	579.7	574.9	1013.8	364.5	998.7	3531.6
SOUTH DAKOTA	532.5	545.0	994.0	362.3	946.8	3380.6
SOUTH ATLANTIC:						
DELAWARE	433.9	211.4	537.6	171.2	369.6	1723.7
DISTRICT OF COLUMBIA	3128.5	855.5	2229.9	1512.0	1495.5	9221.4
FLORIDA	2363.3	1277.7	2646.3	884.0	2233.7	9405.0
GEORGIA	4429.2	2685.0	5779.7	1867.6	4693.8	19455.3
MARYLAND	3559.1	1673.5	4019.0	1265.7	2925.6	13442.9
NORTH CAROLINA	1680.5	1199.1	2573.1	756.7	2096.1	8305.5
SOUTH CAROLINA	1161.1	866.0	1946.9	502.9	1513.9	5990.8
VIRGINIA	3236.8	1793.8	3980.9	1218.5	3135.8	13365.8
WEST VIRGINIA	2330.1	1583.1	3458.3	1223.1	2767.5	11362.1
EAST SOUTH CENTRAL:						
ALABAMA	3595.2	2424.3	5315.5	1671.9	4238.1	17245.0
KENTUCKY	3430.2	2322.3	5009.4	1501.8	4059.8	16323.5
MISSISSIPPI	1770.6	1330.9	3203.0	818.2	2326.6	9449.3
TENNESSEE	4202.4	2738.1	5821.0	2097.2	4786.6	19645.3
WEST SOUTH CENTRAL:						
ARKANSAS	2736.4	2044.4	4337.1	1235.7	3573.9	13927.6
LOUISIANA	3799.0	2263.3	5480.5	1609.5	3956.6	17108.9
OKLAHOMA	4796.5	2645.1	6013.3	1798.7	4624.1	19877.7
TEXAS	11458.5	6245.0	14530.1	4228.1	10917.2	47378.9
ROCKY MOUNTAIN:						
ARIZONA	3390.8	2228.6	4294.2	1292.3	3903.8	15109.7
COLORADO	9085.0	5541.0	10267.6	3558.9	9706.0	38158.5
IDAHO	1021.2	862.1	1527.4	379.0	1510.1	5299.8
MONTANA	1985.1	1567.4	2825.6	831.1	2745.6	9954.8
NEVADA	1070.1	703.7	1188.2	313.1	1232.6	4507.7
NEW MEXICO	2727.3	1716.8	3276.9	907.9	3007.2	11636.1
UTAH	1098.1	682.9	1406.1	287.4	1196.2	4670.7
WYOMING	2026.6	1485.3	2719.4	814.4	2601.7	9647.4
FAR WEST:						
ALASKA	1508.7	841.3	1532.5	368.2	1473.7	5724.4
CALIFORNIA	36726.0	21715.0	39130.7	11761.1	38037.7	147370.5
HAWAII	0.0	0.0	0.0	0.0	0.0	0.0
OREGON	1887.9	1358.2	2281.7	619.0	2379.2	8526.0
WASHINGTON	3457.8	2239.1	3994.3	1088.0	3922.2	14701.4

Table F.1.17

Natural Gas Consumption In Billion BTU, 1972, By Region

Estimated Use By "Net" Commercial Subcategories And Total "Net" Commercial Use

REGION	OFFICE USE	RETAIL USE	SCHOOL USE	HOSPITAL USE	OTHER COMMERCIAL USE	TOTAL "NET" COMMERCIAL USE
NEW ENGLAND	5202.30	3703.50	6208.40	2986.60	5729.90	23830.70
MID ATLANTIC	30360.40	21544.50	33838.20	15253.30	33333.10	134329.50
EAST NORTH CENTRAL	48749.30	39272.90	71601.30	25164.20	68224.00	253011.70
WEST NORTH CENTRAL	20635.10	17429.90	30459.70	11678.60	30278.80	110482.10
SOUTH ATLANTIC	22322.50	12145.10	27171.70	9401.70	21231.50	92272.50
EAST SOUTH CENTRAL	12998.40	8815.60	19348.90	6089.10	15411.10	62663.10
WEST SOUTH CENTRAL	22790.40	13197.80	30361.00	8872.00	23071.80	98293.00
ROCKY MOUNTAIN	22404.20	14787.80	27505.40	8384.10	25903.20	98984.70
FAR WEST	43580.40	26153.60	46939.20	13836.30	45812.80	176322.30
TOTAL	229043.00	157050.70	293433.80	101665.90	268996.19	1050189.59

Table F.1.18

Natural Gas Consumption In Billion BTU, 1972, By State

Revision Of Commercial Use: Components And Resultants Of Shifts

REGION AND STATE	COMMERCIAL USE (BOM) "INITIAL" DATA	RESIDENTIAL USE IN LARGE MULTI-FAMILY STRUCTURES	"NET" COMMERCIAL USE	RESIDUAL TO INDUSTRIAL USE	INITIAL RESIDENTIAL USE	REVISED RESIDENTIAL USE
NEW ENGLAND:						
CONNECTICUT	12996.7	5744.0	5677.7	1575.0	33405.1	39149.1
MAINE	584.9	290.0	238.1	56.8	698.3	988.3
MASSACHUSETTS	32419.4	13134.2	14884.2	4401.0	87205.1	100339.3
NEW HAMPSHIRE	2451.3	957.3	1008.6	485.4	4267.3	5224.6
RHODE ISLAND	4145.3	1411.7	1769.8	963.8	13573.2	14984.9
VERMONT	581.5	270.0	252.3	59.2	1127.7	1397.7
MID ATLANTIC:						
NEW JERSEY	61677.0	22379.2	26125.8	13172.0	153822.0	176201.2
NEW YORK	130838.1	68513.9	59215.3	3108.9	371043.7	439557.6
PENNSYLVANIA	116846.8	29778.0	48988.4	38080.4	315573.2	345351.2
EAST NORTH CENTRAL:						
ILLINOIS	223614.0	57750.3	83279.6	82584.1	500041.1	557791.4
INDIANA	81907.5	9990.5	28568.3	43348.7	170282.6	180273.1
MICHIGAN	155167.1	21033.8	56951.3	77182.0	360595.0	381628.8
OHIO	193059.5	28707.0	69195.7	95156.8	489332.6	518039.6
WISCONSIN	41691.4	9258.0	15016.8	17416.6	106636.3	115894.3
WEST NORTH CENTRAL:						
IOWA	59434.1	4978.8	20594.3	33861.0	97331.2	102310.0
KANSAS	54830.1	3737.9	19554.8	31537.4	100518.6	104256.5
MINNESOTA	55748.3	12621.7	20622.8	22503.8	107333.2	119954.9
MISSOURI	81210.5	12700.5	29392.3	39117.7	161202.6	173903.1
NEBRASKA	37592.4	3701.4	13405.7	20485.3	60457.8	64159.2
NORTH DAKOTA	10180.1	1232.6	3531.6	5415.9	10666.7	11899.3
SOUTH DAKOTA	9651.5	965.6	3380.6	5305.3	13234.7	14200.3
SOUTH ATLANTIC:						
DELAWARE	3269.1	521.4	1723.7	1024.0	8525.2	9046.6
DISTRICT OF COLUMBIA	13229.3	3710.6	9221.4	297.3	14591.8	18302.4
FLORIDA	19759.2	9959.3	9405.0	394.9	13363.3	23322.6
GEORGIA	41521.5	3756.4	19455.3	18309.8	87898.9	91655.3
MARYLAND	25880.1	6163.0	13442.9	6274.2	76323.0	82486.0
NORTH CAROLINA	18542.6	1819.9	8305.5	8417.2	33836.0	35655.9
SOUTH CAROLINA	13391.8	757.3	5990.8	6643.7	21204.6	21961.9
VIRGINIA	27740.0	5045.1	13365.8	9329.1	56868.1	61913.2
WEST VIRGINIA	24482.0	650.7	11362.1	12469.2	61249.2	61899.9
EAST SOUTH CENTRAL:						
ALABAMA	37490.3	1340.1	17245.0	18905.2	55052.3	56392.4
KENTUCKY	35913.3	1912.7	16323.5	17677.1	87341.0	89253.7
MISSISSIPPI	20581.0	601.4	9449.3	10530.3	40317.4	40918.8
TENNESSEE	42342.5	2508.2	19645.3	20189.0	54945.8	57454.0
WEST SOUTH CENTRAL:						
ARKANSAS	31615.0	668.3	13927.5	17019.2	47576.5	48244.8
LOUISIANA	35000.4	1916.9	17108.9	15974.6	85249.6	87166.5
OKLAHOMA	40905.4	1568.5	19877.7	19459.2	80091.5	81660.0
TEXAS	96575.0	10452.3	47378.9	38743.8	247159.9	257612.2
ROCKY MOUNTAIN:						
ARIZONA	24241.6	2832.3	15109.7	6299.6	36280.3	39112.6
COLORADO	60272.1	5122.5	38158.5	16991.1	86868.1	91990.6
IDAHO	9377.1	583.0	5299.8	3494.3	11551.1	12134.1
MONTANA	17049.7	867.6	9954.8	6227.3	24548.2	25415.8
NEVADA	7654.1	1268.0	4507.7	1878.4	9794.3	11062.3
NEW MEXICO	18674.2	903.3	11636.1	6134.8	37494.5	38397.8
UTAH	7428.0	1304.7	4670.7	1452.6	45826.0	47130.7
WYOMING	16156.2	311.0	9647.4	6197.8	22753.6	23064.6
FAR WEST:						
ALASKA	9151.5	894.7	5724.4	2532.4	8436.0	9330.7
CALIFORNIA	236204.6	64431.1	147370.5	24403.0	671702.6	736133.7
HAWAII	0.0	0.0	0.0	0.0	0.0	0.0
OREGON	14774.2	3828.6	8526.0	2419.6	24380.9	28209.5
WASHINGTON	24355.7	7611.3	14701.4	2043.0	40755.7	48367.0

Table F.1.19

Natural Gas Consumption In Billion BTU, 1972, By State

Distribution Of "Net" Commercial Use By Sector

REGION AND STATE	BUSINESS USE	FEDERAL GOVERNMENT USE	STATE AND LOCAL GOVERNMENT USE	TOTAL "NET" COMMERCIAL USE
NEW ENGLAND:				
CONNECTICUT	4133.6	70.9	1473.2	5677.7
MAINE	160.7	5.6	71.8	238.1
MASSACHUSETTS	10740.2	282.5	3861.5	14884.2
NEW HAMPSHIRE	722.7	13.0	272.9	1008.6
RHODE ISLAND	1270.8	46.7	452.3	1769.8
VERMONT	177.1	4.4	70.8	252.3
MID ATLANTIC:				
NEW JERSEY	18865.1	419.0	6841.7	26125.8
NEW YORK	42498.6	956.7	15759.9	59215.3
PENNSYLVANIA	35706.2	954.8	12327.5	48988.4
EAST NORTH CENTRAL:				
ILLINOIS	59598.7	1392.7	22288.2	83279.6
INDIANA	19327.3	397.8	8843.3	28568.3
MICHIGAN	38287.1	622.3	18042.0	56951.3
OHIO	48343.3	1058.3	19794.1	69195.7
WISCONSIN	10367.8	200.8	4448.1	15016.8
WEST NORTH CENTRAL:				
IOWA	14071.3	308.1	6214.9	20594.3
KANSAS	13239.1	411.9	5903.9	19554.8
MINNESOTA	14100.2	315.7	6206.8	20622.8
MISSOURI	20195.4	691.1	8505.8	29392.3
NEBRASKA	9156.0	247.3	4002.4	13405.7
NORTH DAKOTA	2364.3	79.0	1088.3	3531.6
SOUTH DAKOTA	2215.8	106.1	1058.7	3380.6
SOUTH ATLANTIC:				
DELAWARE	1146.9	27.7	549.1	1723.7
DISTRICT OF COLUMBIA	5573.2	1710.1	1938.1	9221.4
FLORIDA	6103.7	200.1	3101.2	9405.0
GEORGIA	11597.0	576.9	7281.5	19455.3
MARYLAND	8556.7	648.4	4237.8	13442.9
NORTH CAROLINA	5337.7	134.2	2833.6	8305.5
SOUTH CAROLINA	3688.4	121.1	2181.3	5990.8
VIRGINIA	8326.2	672.7	4366.9	13365.8
WEST VIRGINIA	7198.1	232.1	3931.9	11362.1
EAST SOUTH CENTRAL:				
ALABAMA	10605.0	576.3	6063.6	17245.0
KENTUCKY	10629.6	383.4	5310.5	16323.5
MISSISSIPPI	5743.4	194.2	3511.7	9449.3
TENNESSEE	12486.8	442.8	6715.7	19645.3
WEST SOUTH CENTRAL:				
ARKANSAS	8685.1	337.0	4905.4	13927.5
LOUISIANA	11006.8	279.8	5822.2	17108.9
OKLAHOMA	12094.6	788.5	6994.6	19877.7
TEXAS	29969.6	1205.8	16203.5	47378.9
ROCKY MOUNTAIN:				
ARIZONA	9990.2	398.2	4720.9	15109.4
COLORADO	25658.6	1122.6	11377.3	38158.5
IDAHO	3499.4	96.6	1703.8	5299.8
MONTANA	6563.6	236.6	3154.6	9954.8
NEVADA	2908.7	114.8	1484.1	4507.7
NEW MEXICO	7358.5	484.6	3793.0	11636.1
UTAH	2872.8	314.5	1483.3	4670.7
WYOMING	5851.8	325.6	3470.0	9647.4
FAR WEST:				
ALASKA	3539.3	390.5	1794.6	5724.4
CALIFORNIA	100140.1	3564.0	43666.4	147370.5
HAWAII	0.0	0.0	0.0	0.0
OREGON	5857.8	172.2	2496.0	8526.0
WASHINGTON	9967.2	339.4	4394.8	14701.4

Table F.1.20

Natural Gas Consumption In Billion BTU, 1972, By Region

Revision Of Commercial Use: Components And Resultants Of Shifts, And
    Distribution Of "Net" Commercial Use By Sector

Revision Of Commercial Use

REGION	COMMERCIAL USE (BOM) INITIAL DATA	RESIDENTIAL USE IN LARGE MULTI-FAMILY STRUCTURES	"NET" COMMERCIAL USE	RESIDUAL TO INDUSTRIAL USE	INITIAL RESIDENTIAL USE	REVISED RESIDENTIAL USE
NEW ENGLAND	53179.10	21807.20	23830.70	7541.20	140276.70	162083.90
MID ATLANTIC	309361.90	120671.10	134329.50	54361.30	840438.91	961110.00
EAST NORTH CENTRAL	695439.50	126739.60	253011.70	315688.20	1626887.60	1753627.19
WEST NORTH CENTRAL	308647.00	39938.50	110482.10	158226.40	550744.80	590683.30
SOUTH ATLANTIC	187815.60	32383.70	92272.50	63159.40	373860.10	406243.80
EAST SOUTH CENTRAL	136327.10	6362.40	62663.10	67301.60	237656.50	244018.90
WEST SOUTH CENTRAL	204095.80	14606.00	98293.00	91196.80	460077.50	474683.50
ROCKY MOUNTAIN	160853.00	13192.40	98984.70	48675.90	275116.10	288308.50
FAR WEST	284486.00	76765.70	176322.30	31398.00	745275.19	822040.90
TOTAL	2340204.94	452466.61	1050189.59	837548.80	5250333.47	5702800.15

Distribution Of "Net" Commercial Use By Sector

REGION	BUSINESS USE	FEDERAL GOVERNMENT USE	STATE & LOCAL GOVERNMENT USE	TOTAL "NET" COMMERCIAL USE
NEW ENGLAND	17205.10	423.10	6202.50	23830.70
MID ATLANTIC	97069.90	2330.50	34929.10	134329.50
EAST NORTH CENTRAL	175924.20	3671.90	73415.70	253011.70
WEST NORTH CENTRAL	75342.10	2159.20	32980.80	110482.10
SOUTH ATLANTIC	57527.90	4323.30	30421.40	92272.50
EAST SOUTH CENTRAL	39464.80	1596.70	21601.50	62663.10
WEST SOUTH CENTRAL	61756.10	2611.10	33925.70	98293.00
ROCKY MOUNTAIN	64703.60	3093.50	31187.00	98984.40
FAR WEST	119504.40	4466.10	52351.80	176322.30
TOTAL	708498.10	24675.40	317015.50	1050189.28

Table F.1.21

Natural Gas Consumption In Billion BTU, 1972, By State

Components Of Industrial Use Series

REGION AND STATE	INDUSTRIAL SALES (Combining AGA and BOM data)	TRANSFER IN FROM COMMERCIAL SALES	USE IN OIL & GAS PRODUCTION & OIL REFINING	FEDERAL GOVERNMENT INDUSTRIAL USE	STATE & LOCAL GOVERNMENT INDUSTRIAL USE	LEASE AND PLANT FUEL
NEW ENGLAND:						
CONNECTICUT	19950.0	1575.0	0.0	0.0	0.0	0.0
MAINE	400.0	56.8	0.0	0.0	0.0	0.0
MASSACHUSETTS	27100.0	4401.0	0.0	0.0	0.0	0.0
NEW HAMPSHIRE	2100.0	485.4	0.0	472.7	0.0	0.0
RHODE ISLAND	6000.0	963.8	0.0	0.0	0.0	0.0
VERMONT	1400.0	59.2	0.0	0.0	0.0	0.0
MID ATLANTIC:						
NEW JERSEY	89000.0	13172.0	3247.2	0.0	0.0	0.0
NEW YORK	126400.0	3108.9	570.3	0.0	0.0	0.0
PENNSYLVANIA	364600.0	38080.4	4882.5	0.0	0.0	2941.0
EAST NORTH CENTRAL:						
ILLINOIS	390800.0	82584.1	18813.8	0.0	61.5	315.7
INDIANA	289400.0	43348.7	12248.8	0.0	0.0	0.0
MICHIGAN	331500.0	77182.0	2353.4	0.0	0.0	2175.1
OHIO	464500.0	95156.8	9293.9	0.0	0.0	3475.1
WISCONSIN	178200.0	17416.6	690.1	0.0	0.0	0.0
WEST NORTH CENTRAL:						
IOWA	128400.0	33861.0	74.2	0.0	0.0	0.0
KANSAS	237300.0	31537.4	28398.8	2765.5	533.9	28126.6
MINNESOTA	141400.0	22503.8	9876.7	0.0	0.0	0.0
MISSOURI	101500.0	39117.7	8361.3	0.0	0.0	0.0
NEBRASKA	68400.0	20485.3	1458.0	600.8	53.4	820.5
NORTH DAKOTA	2100.0	5415.9	5789.0	0.0	0.0	13169.0
SOUTH DAKOTA	7000.0	5305.3	142.0	0.0	0.0	0.0
SOUTH ATLANTIC:						
DELAWARE	11100.0	1024.0	1091.6	0.0	194.8	0.0
DISTRICT OF COLUMBIA	900.0	297.3	17.3	0.0	0.0	0.0
FLORIDA	87600.0	394.9	792.5	2769.1	22035.9	1855.1
GEORGIA	155800.0	18309.8	254.4	0.0	0.0	0.0
MARYLAND	66800.0	6274.2	836.3	0.0	294.3	68.5
NORTH CAROLINA	101200.0	8417.2	136.6	0.0	0.0	0.0
SOUTH CAROLINA	98700.0	6643.7	215.4	0.0	0.0	0.0
VIRGINIA	58500.0	9329.1	4944.6	0.0	0.0	161.1
WEST VIRGINIA	83400.0	12469.2	411.2	0.0	0.0	3918.4
EAST SOUTH CENTRAL:						
ALABAMA	169904.7	18905.2	1125.8	0.0	0.0	1103.2
KENTUCKY	79337.2	17677.1	3760.6	0.0	0.0	1534.7
MISSISSIPPI	150274.2	10530.3	4630.8	1781.5	0.0	9381.8
TENNESSEE	138081.4	20189.0	82.8	2759.4	64.4	1175.3
WEST SOUTH CENTRAL:						
ARKANSAS	146873.2	17019.2	3670.9	815.2	0.0	4759.0
LOUISIANA	1046015.5	15974.6	92197.1	3153.9	557.7	321197.2
OKLAHOMA	128973.2	19459.2	26785.8	2161.0	67.1	101945.1
TEXAS	1888902.5	38743.8	233446.2	3149.8	178.7	823769.0
ROCKY MOUNTAIN:						
ARIZONA	66811.3	6299.6	70.0	0.0	197.0	46.6
COLORADO	80611.2	16991.1	3086.6	0.0	9437.1	4554.4
IDAHO	32157.8	3494.3	43.6	0.0	0.0	0.0
MONTANA	34254.1	6227.3	9455.5	0.0	0.0	6113.6
NEVADA	8301.1	1878.4	67.1	0.0	0.0	0.0
NEW MEXICO	83139.7	6134.8	1792.1	0.0	0.0	52853.6
UTAH	56991.0	1452.6	7344.9	0.0	0.0	1855.4
WYOMING	56232.3	6197.8	8340.2	0.0	0.0	22917.2
FAR WEST:						
ALASKA	12389.6	2532.4	604.3	0.0	0.0	16136.3
CALIFORNIA	657146.9	24403.0	115561.2	0.0	0.0	72449.9
HAWAII	0.0	0.0	0.0	0.0	0.0	0.0
OREGON	64964.5	2419.6	5959.6	0.0	0.0	0.0
WASHINGTON	106733.3	2043.0	30574.9	0.0	0.0	0.0

Table F.1.22

Natural Gas Consumption in Billion Btu, 1972, by Region

Components of Industrial Use Series

REGION	INDUSTRIAL SALES (Combining AGA and BOM data)	TRANSFER IN FROM COMMERCIAL SALES	USE IN OIL & GAS PRODUCTION & OIL REFINING	FEDERAL GOVERNMENT INDUSTRIAL USE	STATE & LOCAL GOVERNMENT INDUSTRIAL USE	LEASE AND PLANT FUEL
NEW ENGLAND	56950.00	7541.20	0.00	472.70	0.00	0.00
MID ATLANTIC	580000.00	54361.30	8700.00	0.00	0.00	2941.00
EAST NORTH CENTRAL	1654400.01	315688.20	43400.00	0.00	61.50	5965.90
WEST NORTH CENTRAL	686100.00	158226.40	54100.00	3366.30	587.30	42116.10
SOUTH ATLANTIC	664000.00	63159.40	8699.90	2769.10	22525.00	6003.10
EAST SOUTH CENTRAL	537597.50	67301.60	9600.00	4540.90	64.40	13195.00
WEST SOUTH CENTRAL	3210764.42	91196.80	356100.00	9279.90	803.50	1251670.29
ROCKY MOUNTAIN	418498.50	48675.90	30200.00	0.00	9634.10	88340.80
FAR WEST	841234.30	31398.00	152700.00	0.00	0.00	88586.20
TOTAL	8649544.72	837548.80	663499.91	20428.90	33675.80	1498818.40

Table F.1.23

Natural Gas Consumption In Billion BTU, 1972, By State

Other (Municipal-Institutional) And Energy Production Use Of Natural Gas

REGION AND STATE	OTHER: MUNICIPAL-INSTITUTIONAL (State & Local Govt.)	ENERGY PRODUCTION					
		ELECTRIC GENERATION		OIL & GAS PRODUCTION, OIL REFINING	PIPELINE FUEL	LEASE AND PLANT FUEL	TOTAL
		BOM Minus AGA Other	AGA Other				
NEW ENGLAND:							
CONNECTICUT	4280.4	30.5	0.0	0.0	40.6	0.0	71.1
MAINE	16.2	0.0	0.0	0.0	0.0	0.0	0.0
MASSACHUSETTS	4799.9	7480.0	700.0	0.0	664.9	0.0	8844.9
NEW HAMPSHIRE	79.8	0.0	0.0	0.0	0.0	0.0	0.0
RHODE ISLAND	688.2	151.1	0.0	0.0	16.3	0.0	167.4
VERMONT	0.0	721.3	0.0	0.0	0.0	0.0	721.3
MID ATLANTIC:							
NEW JERSEY	2875.9	25490.0	200.0	3247.0	748.0	0.0	29685.0
NEW YORK	19581.8	76692.6	400.0	570.0	3472.4	0.0	81135.0
PENNSYLVANIA	9714.3	5654.6	0.0	4882.0	28464.3	2941.0	41941.9
EAST NORTH CENTRAL:							
ILLINOIS	6486.2	70915.9	3700.0	18814.0	23815.9	315.7	117561.5
INDIANA	3906.3	17979.8	100.0	12249.0	13304.3	0.0	43633.1
MICHIGAN	7202.4	48437.3	11400.0	2353.0	16360.8	2175.1	80726.2
OHIO	19794.0	10472.8	6600.0	9294.0	13018.7	3475.1	42860.6
WISCONSIN	2892.9	15407.4	13200.0	690.0	6352.4	0.0	35649.8
WEST NORTH CENTRAL:							
IOWA	2743.5	43722.0	17600.0	74.0	20451.4	0.0	81847.4
KANSAS	6333.3	178895.7	900.0	28399.0	79930.8	28126.6	316252.1
MINNESOTA	24398.7	52029.9	0.0	9877.0	7482.9	0.0	69389.8
MISSOURI	16978.0	48108.3	11200.0	8361.0	9686.3	0.0	77355.6
NEBRASKA	8289.8	40632.1	8900.0	1458.0	13229.0	820.5	65039.6
NORTH DAKOTA	0.0	38.2	300.0	5789.0	271.2	13169.0	19567.4
SOUTH DAKOTA	1597.4	3557.2	0.0	142.0	10.0	0.0	3709.2
SOUTH ATLANTIC:							
DELAWARE	0.0	2478.6	0.0	1092.0	0.0	0.0	3570.6
DISTRICT OF COLUMBIA	2135.6	0.0	0.0	17.0	532.4	0.0	549.4
FLORIDA	4436.7	159599.0	17600.0	792.0	4185.9	1855.1	184032.0
GEORGIA	4865.3	39624.4	0.0	254.0	8203.7	0.0	48082.1
MARYLAND	3581.1	7197.9	0.0	836.0	3144.7	68.5	11247.1
NORTH CAROLINA	6238.2	11815.5	5400.0	137.0	6216.7	0.0	23569.2
SOUTH CAROLINA	1141.1	25195.3	0.0	215.0	3090.2	0.0	28500.5
VIRGINIA	7324.6	2729.3	1900.0	4945.0	8489.1	161.1	18224.5
WEST VIRGINIA	2945.0	470.3	0.0	411.0	15221.0	3918.4	20020.7
EAST SOUTH CENTRAL:							
ALABAMA	1057.8	2834.2	0.0	1126.0	19657.0	1103.2	24720.4
KENTUCKY	7658.0	10184.2	0.0	3761.0	37578.2	1534.7	53058.1
MISSISSIPPI	4638.1	97213.1	5700.0	4631.0	59330.1	9381.8	176256.0
TENNESSEE	4367.0	0.0	16900.0	83.0	25942.4	1175.3	44100.7
WEST SOUTH CENTRAL:							
ARKANSAS	971.9	71741.4	900.0	3671.0	13203.6	4759.0	94275.0
LOUISIANA	33254.2	393357.7	100.0	92197.0	81840.5	321197.2	888692.4
OKLAHOMA	4349.9	159261.2	109000.0	26786.0	25383.1	101945.1	422375.4
TEXAS	48363.5	1315811.0	4000.0	233446.0	107196.2	823769.0	2484222.2
ROCKY MOUNTAIN:							
ARIZONA	4250.8	82300.2	0.0	70.0	27424.9	46.6	109841.7
COLORADO	1239.9	65188.8	0.0	3087.0	2916.2	4554.4	75746.4
IDAHO	1988.3	0.0	0.0	44.0	5010.0	0.0	5054.0
MONTANA	2714.2	657.0	600.0	9456.0	1083.6	6113.6	17910.2
NEVADA	6146.8	43326.5	0.0	67.0	0.0	0.0	43393.5
NEW MEXICO	16365.2	63449.7	600.0	1792.0	39319.4	52853.6	158014.7
UTAH	13.1	3487.5	0.0	7345.0	798.2	1855.4	13486.1
WYOMING	1528.4	2922.7	0.0	8340.0	6217.8	22917.2	40397.7
FAR WEST:							
ALASKA	6939.5	13150.4	0.0	604.0	8827.9	16136.3	38718.6
CALIFORNIA	7834.4	323102.7	315400.0	115561.0	19721.4	72449.9	846235.0
HAWAII	0.0	0.0	0.0	0.0	0.0	0.0	0.0
OREGON	409.6	426.4	0.0	5960.0	10370.6	0.0	16757.0
WASHINGTON	177.2	0.0	0.0	30575.0	7800.7	0.0	38375.7

Table F.1.24

Natural Gas Consumption In Billion BTU, 1972, By Region

Other (Municipal-Institutional) And Energy Production Use Of Natural Gas

REGION	OTHER: MUNICIPAL-INSTITUTIONAL (State & Local Govt.)	ELECTRIC GENERATION		ENERGY PRODUCTION			
		BOM Minus AGA Other	AGA Other	OIL & GAS PRO-DUCTION, OIL REFINING	PIPELINE FUEL	LEASE AND PLANT FUEL	TOTAL
NEW ENGLAND	9864.50	8382.90	700.00	0.00	721.80	0.00	9804.70
MID ATLANTIC	32172.00	107837.20	600.00	8699.00	3684.70	2941.00	152761.90
EAST NORTH CENTRAL	40281.80	163213.20	35000.00	43400.00	72852.10	5965.90	320431.20
WEST NORTH CENTRAL	60340.70	366983.40	38900.00	54100.00	131061.60	42116.10	633161.11
SOUTH ATLANTIC	32667.60	249110.30	24900.00	8699.00	49083.70	6003.10	337796.10
EAST SOUTH CENTRAL	17720.90	110231.50	22600.00	9601.00	142507.70	13195.00	298135.20
WEST SOUTH CENTRAL	86939.50	1940171.29	114000.00	356100.00	227623.40	1251670.29	3889564.98
ROCKY MOUNTAIN	34246.70	261332.40	1200.00	30201.00	82770.10	88340.80	463844.30
FAR WEST	15360.70	336679.50	315400.00	152700.00	46720.60	88586.20	940086.31
TOTAL	329594.40	3543941.68	553300.00	663500.00	786025.71	1498818.40	7045585.74

Table F.2.1

Natural Gas Prices In Dollars Per Million BTU, 1972, By State

Residential and Commercial Use: Comparison of Data From Bureau of Mines (BOM) and American Gas Association (AGA)

REGION AND STATE	RESIDENTIAL USE			COMMERCIAL USE		
	BOM	AGA	BOM Minus AGA	BOM	AGA	BOM Minus AGA
NEW ENGLAND:						
CONNECTICUT	2.061	2.245	-0.184	1.709	1.966	-0.258
MAINE	3.477	3.495	-0.018	1.793	2.288	-0.495
MASSACHUSETTS	2.263	2.183	0.080	1.776	1.731	0.045
NEW HAMPSHIRE	1.983	1.990	-0.007	1.676	2.133	-0.457
RHODE ISLAND	2.011	2.142	-0.132	1.844	1.776	0.068
VERMONT	1.800	1.799	0.001	1.328	1.682	-0.354
MID ATLANTIC:						
NEW JERSEY	1.967	1.782	0.185	1.467	1.454	0.013
NEW YORK	1.583	1.596	-0.013	1.314	1.422	-0.108
PENNSYLVANIA	1.313	1.328	-0.016	1.072	1.084	-0.012
EAST NORTH CENTRAL:						
ILLINOIS	1.107	1.108	0.000	0.829	0.824	0.006
INDIANA	1.131	1.135	-0.004	0.926	0.930	-0.003
MICHIGAN	1.082	1.074	0.007	0.898	0.881	0.017
OHIO	1.030	1.023	0.007	0.866	0.860	0.006
WISCONSIN	1.313	1.304	0.009	1.014	1.078	-0.065
WEST NORTH CENTRAL:						
IOWA	1.096	1.062	0.034	0.842	0.791	0.052
KANSAS	0.737	0.739	-0.002	0.532	0.567	-0.035
MINNESOTA	1.229	1.201	0.027	0.939	0.963	-0.024
MISSOURI	1.089	1.074	0.015	0.819	0.750	0.069
NEBRASKA	0.983	0.972	0.011	0.618	0.745	-0.127
NORTH DAKOTA	1.098	1.110	-0.012	0.783	0.760	0.023
SOUTH DAKOTA	1.127	1.119	0.009	0.718	0.773	-0.055
SOUTH ATLANTIC:						
DELAWARE	1.676	1.652	0.025	1.329	1.261	0.068
DISTRICT OF COLUMBIA	1.550	1.550	0.000	1.152	1.195	-0.043
FLORIDA	2.553	1.806	0.747	1.314	1.218	0.096
GEORGIA	1.219	1.250	-0.031	0.865	0.878	-0.013
MARYLAND	1.628	1.637	-0.010	1.284	1.339	-0.055
NORTH CAROLINA	1.374	1.421	-0.047	1.164	1.193	-0.029
SOUTH CAROLINA	1.571	1.569	0.002	1.015	1.020	-0.006
VIRGINIA	1.557	1.619	-0.062	1.168	1.164	0.004
WEST VIRGINIA	0.937	0.887	0.050	0.728	0.691	0.037
EAST SOUTH CENTRAL:						
ALABAMA	1.228	1.332	-0.104	0.716	0.838	-0.122
KENTUCKY	0.910	0.936	-0.026	0.760	0.777	-0.017
MISSISSIPPI	1.056	1.073	-0.018	0.685	0.715	-0.030
TENNESSEE	1.002	1.053	-0.051	0.869	0.852	0.017
WEST SOUTH CENTRAL:						
ARKANSAS	0.824	0.826	-0.002	0.573	0.586	-0.013
LOUISIANA	0.889	0.902	-0.013	0.580	0.565	0.015
OKLAHOMA	0.870	0.860	0.010	0.553	0.560	-0.006
TEXAS	0.987	0.973	0.014	0.611	0.608	0.002
ROCKY MOUNTAIN:						
ARIZONA	1.175	1.227	-0.052	0.706	0.717	-0.011
COLORADO	0.803	0.779	0.024	0.666	0.637	0.029
IDAHO	1.420	1.497	-0.077	1.051	1.077	-0.027
MONTANA	0.936	0.871	0.065	0.670	0.645	0.024
NEVADA	1.408	1.431	-0.023	0.885	0.925	-0.040
NEW MEXICO	0.898	0.913	-0.014	0.635	0.664	-0.029
UTAH	0.961	0.773	0.188	0.756	0.541	0.215
WYOMING	0.723	0.701	0.023	0.506	0.521	-0.015
FAR WEST:						
ALASKA	1.545	1.396	0.150	1.079	0.537	0.542
CALIFORNIA	1.024	1.031	-0.008	0.781	0.743	0.038
HAWAII	0.000 [a]	3.397	-3.397	0.000	2.457	-2.457
OREGON	1.606	1.607	-0.001	1.392	1.356	0.036
WASHINGTON	1.391	1.441	-0.051	1.105	1.193	-0.087

[a] Zero indicates no quantities in category.

Table F.2.2

Natural Gas Prices In Dollars Per Million BTU, 1972, by Region

Residential And Commerical Use: Comparison Of Data From Bureau of Mines (BOM) and American Gas Association (AGA)

REGION	RESIDENTIAL			COMMERCIAL		
	BOM	AGA	BOM Minus AGA	BOM	AGA	BOM Minus AGA
NEW ENGLAND	2.184	2.191	-0.006	1.755	1.807	-0.052
MID ATLANTIC	1.552	1.527	0.024	1.253	1.296	-0.042
EAST NORTH CENTRAL	1.094	1.093	0.002	0.877	0.877	-0.000
WEST NORTH CENTRAL	1.043	1.029	0.013	0.765	0.775	-0.009
SOUTH ATLANTIC	1.413	1.408	0.005	1.065	1.059	0.006
EAST SOUTH CENTRAL	1.029	1.077	-0.048	0.770	0.807	-0.037
WEST SOUTH CENTRAL	0.932	0.926	0.006	0.588	0.590	-0.002
ROCKY MOUNTAIN	0.944	0.911	0.033	0.690	0.673	0.017
FAR WEST	1.069	1.079	-0.010	0.850	0.811	0.039
UNITED STATES	1.185	1.186	-0.000	0.900	0.906	-0.006

Table F.2.3

Natural Gas Prices in Dollars Per Million BTU, 1972, by State

Industrial Use: Comparison of Data From Bureau of Mines and American Gas Association

REGION AND STATE	BUREAU OF MINES			AMERICAN GAS ASSOCIATION	
	Sales	Lease and Plant Fuel	All (Net of Elect. Gen.)	Net of Electric Generation	Including Electric Generation
NEW ENGLAND:					
CONNECTICUT	1.1545	0.0000[a]	1.1545	1.2003	1.1979
MAINE	2.1684	0.0000	2.1684	1.6650	1.6650
MASSACHUSETTS	1.2194	0.0000	1.2194	1.1935	1.0771
NEW HAMPSHIRE	0.8877	0.0000	0.8877	0.6814	0.6814
RHODE ISLAND	1.1245	0.0000	1.1245	1.1643	1.1536
VERMONT	0.7731	0.0000	0.7731	0.5900	0.5900
MID ATLANTIC:					
NEW JERSEY	0.7905	0.0000	0.7905	0.7591	0.7403
NEW YORK	0.8384	0.0000	0.8384	0.9061	0.9061
PENNSYLVANIA	0.6980	0.4539	0.6961	0.6932	0.6925
EAST NORTH CENTRAL:					
ILLINOIS	0.6215	0.2946	0.6212	0.5951	0.5826
INDIANA	0.5537	0.0000	0.5537	0.5510	0.5499
MICHIGAN	0.6227	0.2386	0.6197	0.6234	0.6186
OHIO	0.6158	0.4037	0.6142	0.6119	0.6120
WISCONSIN	0.6241	0.0000	0.6241	0.6079	0.5970
WEST NORTH CENTRAL:					
IOWA	0.4599	0.0000	0.4599	0.4547	0.4471
KANSAS	0.3337	0.2615	0.3238	0.3369	0.3136
MINNESOTA	0.4840	0.0000	0.4840	0.5187	0.4865
MISSOURI	0.4409	0.0000	0.4409	0.5039	0.4365
NEBRASKA	0.4841	0.2218	0.4804	0.4239	0.4012
NORTH DAKOTA	0.4801	0.1736	0.2301	0.5443	0.5443
SOUTH DAKOTA	0.3805	0.0000	0.3805	0.3794	0.3747
SOUTH ATLANTIC:					
DELAWARE	0.7412	0.0000	0.7412	0.6233	0.6233
DISTRICT OF COLUMBIA	0.9214	0.0000	0.9214	0.9511	0.9511
FLORIDA	0.4793	0.2393	0.4745	0.4614	0.4405
GEORGIA	0.5189	0.0000	0.5189	0.5179	0.4806
MARYLAND	0.7314	0.4673	0.7311	0.7572	0.7572
NORTH CAROLINA	0.5830	0.0000	0.5830	0.6080	0.6026
SOUTH CAROLINA	0.5331	0.0000	0.5331	0.5424	0.5421
VIRGINIA	0.5799	0.3663	0.5793	0.6211	0.6211
WEST VIRGINIA	0.5423	0.3187	0.5336	0.5303	0.5303
EAST SOUTH CENTRAL:					
ALABAMA	0.4113	0.3680	0.4110	0.4467	0.4463
KENTUCKY	0.5369	0.2300	0.5311	0.5322	0.5322
MISSISSIPPI	0.3337	0.1863	0.3250	0.3980	0.3431
TENNESSEE	0.4853	0.3310	0.4840	0.4677	0.4677
WEST SOUTH CENTRAL:					
ARKANSAS	0.3446	0.2280	0.3410	0.3455	0.3351
LOUISIANA	0.3168	0.2041	0.2903	0.2725	0.2576
OKLAHOMA	0.2839	0.1560	0.2274	0.2992	0.2972
TEXAS	0.2532	0.1801	0.2310	0.2757	0.2636
ROCKY MOUNTAIN:					
ARIZONA	0.4495	0.1717	0.4493	0.4604	0.4298
COLORADO	0.3398	0.1653	0.3305	0.3294	0.3172
IDAHO	0.5052	0.0000	0.5052	0.4868	0.4868
MONTANA	0.3701	0.1560	0.3377	0.3443	0.3443
NEVADA	0.6608	0.0000	0.6608	0.4907	0.4605
NEW MEXICO	0.3112	0.1339	0.2423	0.3706	0.3149
UTAH	0.3881	0.1908	0.3818	0.3087	0.3086
WYOMING	0.2942	0.1506	0.2526	0.2876	0.2876
FAR WEST:					
ALASKA	0.6806	0.2229	0.4217	0.3536	0.3536
CALIFORNIA	0.4469	0.3046	0.4327	0.4684	0.4342
HAWAII	0.0000	0.0000	0.0000	2.2124	2.2124
OREGON	0.5215	0.0000	0.5215	0.5253	0.5253
WASHINGTON	0.4474	0.0000	0.4474	0.4766	0.4766

[a] Zero indicates no quantities in category.

Table F.2.4

Natural Gas Prices in Dollars Per Million BTU, 1972, by Region

Industrial Use: Comparison of Data From Bureau of Mines and American Gas Association

| REGION | BUREAU OF MINES | | | AMERICAN GAS ASSOCIATION | |
	Sales	Lease and Plant Fuel	All (Net of Elect. Gen)	Net of Electric Generation	Including Electric Generation
NEW ENGLAND	1.1804	0.0000 a	1.1804	1.1624	1.1026
MID ATLANTIC	0.7379	0.4539	0.7364	0.7497	0.7461
EAST NORTH CENTRAL	0.6076	0.3378	0.6066	0.5992	0.5940
WEST NORTH CENTRAL	0.4224	0.2333	0.4090	0.4309	0.3960
SOUTH ATLANTIC	0.5569	0.2972	0.5545	0.5649	0.5443
EAST SOUTH CENTRAL	0.4271	0.2195	0.4222	0.4589	0.4326
WEST SOUTH CENTRAL	0.2793	0.1845	0.2527	0.2825	0.2705
ROCKY MOUNTAIN	0.3736	0.1426	0.3334	0.3705	0.3624
FAR WEST	0.4561	0.2897	0.4403	0.4761	0.4462
UNITED STATES	0.4395	0.1915	0.4019	0.4842	0.4495

a Zero indicates no quantities in category.

Table F.2.5

Natural Gas Prices in Dollars Per Million BTU, 1972, By State

Pipeline Fuel and "Other" Consumption: Comparison of Data From Bureau of Mines (BOM)
And American Gas Association (AGA)

REGION AND STATE	Pipeline Fuel (BOM Data)	BOM Other (Excludes Electric Generation)	AGA Other Net Of Electric Generation	AGA Other Including Electric Generation
NEW ENGLAND:				
CONNECTICUT	0.3448	1.2471	0.6200	0.6200
MAINE	0.0000[a]	0.8025	1.7400	1.7400
MASSACHUSETTS	0.3640	1.1304	1.3526	1.2252
NEW HAMPSHIRE	0.0000	0.8647	0.8055	0.8055
RHODE ISLAND	0.3681	1.4269	1.6933	1.6933
VERMONT	0.0000	0.0000	0.0000	0.0000
MID ATLANTIC:				
NEW JERSEY	0.2353	1.1179	0.4723	0.5458
NEW YORK	0.2586	1.0108	1.0234	1.0194
PENNSYLVANIA	0.2972	0.8093	0.7834	0.7834
EAST NORTH CENTRAL:				
ILLINOIS	0.2234	0.5786	0.0641	0.1765
INDIANA	0.2485	0.8061	0.7763	0.7753
MICHIGAN	0.2897	0.7173	0.0000	0.5579
OHIO	0.2708	0.7849	0.7410	0.6788
WISCONSIN	0.2591	0.4798	0.5400	0.4494
WEST NORTH CENTRAL:				
IOWA	0.1982	0.4549	0.4716	0.3756
KANSAS	0.2335	0.3267	0.3342	0.3360
MINNESOTA	0.2645	0.5898	0.3100	0.3100
MISSOURI	0.2453	0.4091	0.4836	0.3448
NEBRASKA	0.1766	0.3988	0.3977	0.3511
NORTH DAKOTA	0.2397	0.0000	0.7400	0.4600
SOUTH DAKOTA	0.3000	0.5208	0.4750	0.4750
SOUTH ATLANTIC:				
DELAWARE	0.0000	0.0000	0.4764	0.4764
DISTRICT OF COLUMBIA	0.2367	1.1322	0.9543	0.9543
FLORIDA	0.2344	0.4553	0.5098	0.4883
GEORGIA	0.2192	0.8176	0.9430	0.9430
MARYLAND	0.2347	0.8056	0.6834	0.6834
NORTH CAROLINA	0.2197	0.6885	0.9953	0.6141
SOUTH CAROLINA	0.2323	0.5801	0.6709	0.6709
VIRGINIA	0.2612	0.7232	0.7359	0.6533
WEST VIRGINIA	0.3703	0.6988	0.5139	0.5139
EAST SOUTH CENTRAL:				
ALABAMA	0.2231	0.4906	0.8775	0.8775
KENTUCKY	0.2340	0.6392	0.6439	0.6439
MISSISSIPPI	0.2234	0.5502	0.5279	0.4497
TENNESSEE	0.2250	0.5626	0.8868	0.4169
WEST SOUTH CENTRAL:				
ARKANSAS	0.2380	0.3550	0.3475	0.3533
LOUISIANA	0.2235	0.3110	0.3587	0.3612
OKLAHOMA	0.1860	0.4894	0.7508	0.2912
TEXAS	0.1840	0.3106	0.2603	0.2597
ROCKY MOUNTAIN:				
ARIZONA	0.1747	0.5486	0.6391	0.6391
COLORADO	0.2136	0.4258	0.3772	0.3772
IDAHO	0.2639	0.5930	0.5915	0.5915
MONTANA	0.1606	0.4690	0.4004	0.3933
NEVADA	0.0000	0.5582	0.3533	0.3533
NEW MEXICO	0.1671	0.3149	0.3295	0.3276
UTAH	0.2969	0.7634	0.0000	0.0000
WYOMING	0.1721	0.2833	0.2559	0.2559
FAR WEST:				
ALASKA	0.2776	0.4637	0.0000	0.0000
CALIFORNIA	0.3340	0.4725	0.5460	0.3907
HAWAII	0.0000	0.0000	0.0000	0.0000
OREGON	0.2670	0.5933	0.0000	0.0000
WASHINGTON	0.2664	0.5305	0.0000	0.0000

[a] Zero indicates no quantities in category.

Table   F.2.6

Natural Gas Prices In Dollars Per Million BTU, 1972, By Region

Pipeline Fuel Use And "Other" Consumption: Comparison of Data From
Bureau of Mines (BOM) And American Gas Association (AGA)

REGION	PIPELINE FUEL (BOM Data)	BOM OTHER (Excludes Electric Generation)	AGA OTHER Net of Electric Generation	AGA OTHER Including Electric Generation
NEW ENGLAND	0.3630	1.1990	1.2555	1.1719
MID ATLANTIC	0.2917	0.9595	0.9259	0.9263
EAST NORTH CENTRAL	0.2544	0.7198	0.5660	0.5205
WEST NORTH CENTRAL	0.2249	0.4772	0.3560	0.3512
SOUTH ATLANTIC	0.2767	0.7228	0.6936	0.5984
EAST SOUTH CENTRAL	0.2265	0.5882	0.6686	0.4739
WEST SOUTH CENTRAL	0.2016	0.3202	0.2848	0.2783
ROCKY MOUNTAIN	0.1787	0.4187	0.4446	0.4402
FAR WEST	0.2972	0.4724	0.5460	0.3907
UNITED STATES	0.2267	0.5581	0.4782	0.4103

Table F.2.7

Natural Gas Prices In Dollars Per Million BTU, 1972, By State

Prices Paid By Electric Utilities: Comparison of Data From Bureau of Mines (BOM),
    National Coal Association (NCA), and American Gas Association (AGA)

REGION AND STATE	BOM	NCA	AGA
NEW ENGLAND:			
CONNECTICUT	0.4265 [a]	0.0000 [a]	0.2200
MAINE	0.0000 [a]	0.0000	0.0000
MASSACHUSETTS	0.4467	0.4620	0.5211
NEW HAMPSHIRE	0.0000	0.0000	0.0000
RHODE ISLAND	0.5030	0.5360	0.5100
VERMONT	0.4464	0.4340	0.0000
MID ATLANTIC:			
NEW JERSEY	0.4766	0.4800	0.5013
NEW YORK	0.4623	0.5440	0.5628
PENNSYLVANIA	0.4831	0.6430	0.6192
EAST NORTH CENTRAL:			
ILLINOIS	0.4254	0.5140	0.4851
INDIANA	0.4235	0.4630	0.4634
MICHIGAN	0.4788	0.5850	0.5234
OHIO	0.4907	0.5450	0.5601
WISCONSIN	0.4406	0.4280	0.4436
WEST NORTH CENTRAL:			
IOWA	0.3766	0.3460	0.3483
KANSAS	0.3778	0.2610	0.2623
MINNESOTA	0.3962	0.3190	0.3287
MISSOURI	0.3654	0.3050	0.2748
NEBRASKA	0.3671	0.3530	0.3555
NORTH DAKOTA	0.3903	0.3720	0.3667
SOUTH DAKOTA	0.3607	0.3720	0.3453
SOUTH ATLANTIC:			
DELAWARE	0.4745	0.5500	0.5162
DISTRICT OF COLUMBIA	0.0000	0.0000	0.0000
FLORIDA	0.3871	0.3910	0.4165
GEORGIA	0.3472	0.3800	0.3583
MARYLAND	0.3601	0.0000	0.4694
NORTH CAROLINA	0.4903	0.4530	0.5308
SOUTH CAROLINA	0.4737	0.4710	0.4842
VIRGINIA	0.4065	0.4750	0.4057
WEST VIRGINIA	0.3721	0.4850	0.5367
EAST SOUTH CENTRAL:			
ALABAMA	0.3415	0.3400	0.3644
KENTUCKY	0.3589	0.3220	0.3144
MISSISSIPPI	0.3132	0.2990	0.2983
TENNESSEE	0.3209	0.2780	0.3016
WEST SOUTH CENTRAL:			
ARKANSAS	0.3128	0.3070	0.3142
LOUISIANA	0.2663	0.2510	0.2365
OKLAHOMA	0.2413	0.2450	0.2724
TEXAS	0.2804	0.2340	0.2371
ROCKY MOUNTAIN:			
ARIZONA	0.3957	0.3890	0.3932
COLORADO	0.3162	0.2830	0.2962
IDAHO	0.0000	0.0000	0.0000
MONTANA	0.3325	0.2470	0.3092
NEVADA	0.4353	0.4580	0.4604
NEW MEXICO	0.3407	0.2850	0.2717
UTAH	0.3464	0.3110	0.3069
WYOMING	0.2942	0.4810	0.3333
FAR WEST:			
ALASKA	0.4309	0.0000	0.0000
CALIFORNIA	0.3795	0.3750	0.3764
HAWAII	0.0000	0.0000	0.0000
OREGON	0.4316	0.4370	0.0000
WASHINGTON	0.0000	0.0000	0.0000

[a] Zero indicates no use of natural gas

Table F.2.8

Natural Gas Prices In Dollars Per Million BTU, 1972, By Region

Prices Paid By Electric Utilities: Comparison Of Data From Bureau of
    Mines (BOM) , National Coal Association (NCA), And American Gas
    Association (AGA)

REGION	BOM	NCA	AGA
NEW ENGLAND	0.4475	0.4621	0.5169
MID ATLANTIC	0.4668	0.5324	0.5529
EAST NORTH CENTRAL	0.4492	0.5174	0.4920
WEST NORTH CENTRAL	0.3767	0.2992	0.2952
SOUTH ATLANTIC	0.3962	0.3991	0.4219
EAST SOUTH CENTRAL	0.3183	0.2985	0.3005
WEST SOUTH CENTRAL	0.2737	0.2413	0.2471
ROCKY MOUNTAIN	0.3670	0.3488	0.3548
FAR WEST	0.3806	0.3750	0.3764
UNITED STATES	0.3305	0.3031	0.3314

Table   F.2.9

Natural Gas Prices In Dollars Per Million BTU, 1972, by State

Commercial and Industrial Firm and Interruptible Sales, American Gas Association Data

REGION AND STATE	COMMERCIAL			INDUSTRIAL		
	Firm	Interruptible	Total	Firm	Interruptible	Total
NEW ENGLAND:						
CONNECTICUT	1.9843	0.8850 a	1.9663	1.3899	0.7681	1.1979
MAINE	2.2880	0.0000	2.2880	2.1233	0.0000	1.6650
MASSACHUSETTS	1.7669	0.5792	1.7311	1.4802	0.5718	1.0771
NEW HAMPSHIRE	2.1329	0.0000	2.1329	0.7525	0.5867	0.6814
RHODE ISLAND	1.8440	0.6400	1.7762	1.5081	0.6071	1.1536
VERMONT	1.6820	0.0000	1.6820	1.2600	0.5385	0.5900
MID ATLANTIC:						
NEW JERSEY	1.5437	0.5529	1.4540	1.0961	0.4910	0.7403
NEW YORK	1.4296	0.7660	1.4222	0.8624	1.0078	0.9061
PENNSYLVANIA	1.0837	0.0000	1.0837	0.7073	0.5846	0.6925
EAST NORTH CENTRAL:						
ILLINOIS	0.8347	0.4389	0.8235	0.6126	0.4463	0.5826
INDIANA	0.9431	0.6824	0.9296	0.5655	0.4759	0.5499
MICHIGAN	0.8908	0.4989	0.8809	0.6653	0.5459	0.6186
OHIO	0.8637	0.5796	0.8605	0.6254	0.4788	0.6120
WISCONSIN	1.0691	1.1702	1.0784	0.7722	0.5311	0.5970
WEST NORTH CENTRAL:						
IOWA	0.8742	0.5172	0.7907	0.4929	0.3990	0.4471
KANSAS	0.5808	0.3114	0.5671	0.3751	0.2939	0.3136
MINNESOTA	1.0271	0.5662	0.9633	0.5262	0.4589	0.4865
MISSOURI	0.7893	0.5011	0.7498	0.5559	0.3537	0.4365
NEBRASKA	0.7759	0.5376	0.7447	0.4499	0.3723	0.4012
NORTH DAKOTA	0.7601	0.0000	0.7601	0.6071	0.4186	0.5443
SOUTH DAKOTA	0.8118	0.5300	0.7733	0.4650	0.3727	0.3747
SOUTH ATLANTIC:						
DELAWARE	1.2609	0.0000	1.2609	0.6440	0.5295	0.6233
DISTRICT OF COLUMBIA	1.3147	0.6617	1.1948	0.9275	0.5700	0.9511
FLORIDA	1.2572	0.6273	1.2184	0.3401	0.4815	0.4405
GEORGIA	0.8780	0.0000	0.8781	0.7163	0.4412	0.4806
MARYLAND	1.4952	0.6841	1.3389	0.9395	0.5079	0.7572
NORTH CAROLINA	1.1960	0.6400	1.1929	0.6406	0.5812	0.6026
SOUTH CAROLINA	1.1428	0.5108	1.0201	0.6625	0.5118	0.5421
VIRGINIA	1.2168	0.7797	1.1637	0.6852	0.5209	0.6211
WEST VIRGINIA	0.6906	0.0000	0.6913	0.5301	0.5233	0.5303
EAST SOUTH CENTRAL:						
ALABAMA	0.8410	0.5400	0.8378	0.4563	0.4158	0.4463
KENTUCKY	0.7980	0.5747	0.7768	0.4594	0.6026	0.5322
MISSISSIPPI	0.7144	0.0000	0.7146	0.3434	0.3406	0.3431
TENNESSEE	0.8944	0.4109	0.8515	0.5202	0.4093	0.4677
WEST SOUTH CENTRAL:						
ARKANSAS	0.5864	0.3300	0.5855	0.3322	0.3640	0.3351
LOUISIANA	0.5673	0.3533	0.5649	0.2575	0.2591	0.2576
OKLAHOMA	0.5675	0.2708	0.5595	0.3230	0.2741	0.2972
TEXAS	0.6139	0.3065	0.6081	0.3531	0.0362	0.2636
ROCKY MOUNTAIN:						
ARIZONA	0.7175	0.0000	0.7175	0.4300	0.4700	0.4298
COLORADO	0.6378	0.4075	0.6373	0.3333	0.3079	0.3172
IDAHO	1.0774	0.0000	1.0774	0.5107	0.4173	0.4868
MONTANA	0.6453	0.0000	0.6453	0.4700	0.3363	0.3443
NEVADA	0.9246	0.0000	0.9251	0.4236	0.4783	0.4605
NEW MEXICO	0.6712	0.4475	0.6641	0.3577	0.2697	0.3149
UTAH	0.5410	0.0000	0.5410	0.4545	0.2961	0.3086
WYOMING	0.5211	0.0000	0.5211	0.3736	0.2749	0.2876
FAR WEST:						
ALASKA	0.5370	0.0000	0.5370	0.3536	0.0000	0.3536
CALIFORNIA	0.7865	0.4817	0.7428	0.6712	0.4149	0.4342
HAWAII	2.4571	0.0000	2.4571	2.2124	0.0000	2.2124
OREGON	1.3799	0.5850	1.3564	0.6596	0.4513	0.5253
WASHINGTON	1.2200	0.5282	1.1927	0.5564	0.4435	0.4766

a Zero indicates no quantities in category.

Table F.2.10

Natural Gas Prices in Dollars Per Million BTU, 1972, by Region

Commercial and Industrial Firm and Interruptible Sales, American Gas Association Data

REGION	COMMERCIAL			INDUSTRIAL		
	Firm	Interruptible	Total	Firm	Interruptible	Total
NEW ENGLAND	1.8409	0.6240	1.8075	1.4310	0.6241	1.1026
MID ATLANTIC	1.3129	0.5967	1.2956	0.7715	0.6633	0.7461
EAST NORTH CENTRAL	0.8836	0.6729	0.8773	0.6233	0.5097	0.5940
WEST NORTH CENTRAL	0.8176	0.5131	0.7746	0.4765	0.3520	0.3960
SOUTH ATLANTIC	1.0917	0.6685	1.0595	0.6306	0.4911	0.5443
EAST SOUTH CENTRAL	0.8274	0.4975	0.8072	0.4263	0.4474	0.4326
WEST SOUTH CENTRAL	0.5949	0.2992	0.5898	0.3221	0.0888	0.2705
ROCKY MOUNTAIN	0.6736	0.4312	0.6727	0.4063	0.3245	0.3624
FAR WEST	0.8570	0.4844	0.8106	0.6321	0.4191	0.4462
TOTAL	0.9271	0.5469	0.9057	0.4961	0.3848	0.4495

Table F.2.11

Natural Gas Prices in Dollars Per Million BTU, By State

Prices Paid By Electric Utilities For Different Classes Of Use, American Gas Association Data

REGION AND STATE	INDUSTRIAL SALES		OTHER SALES	TOTAL SALES	TRANSFERS	ALL USES
	Firm	Interruptible				
NEW ENGLAND:						
CONNECTICUT	0.2200	0.0000	0.0000	0.2200	0.2200	0.2200
MAINE	0.0000	0.0000a	0.0000	0.0000	0.0000	0.0000
MASSACHUSETTS	0.5568	0.5148	0.5157	0.5311	0.3911	0.5211
NEW HAMPSHIRE	0.0000	0.0000	0.0000	0.0000	0.0000	0.0000
RHODE ISLAND	0.0000	0.5100	0.0000	0.5100	0.0000	0.5100
VERMONT	0.0000	0.0000	0.0000	0.0000	0.0000	0.0000
MID ATLANTIC:						
NEW JERSEY	0.0000	0.4571	1.3550	0.4866	0.5072	0.5013
NEW YORK	0.0000	0.0000	0.7550	0.7550	0.5619	0.5628
PENNSYLVANIA	0.5832	0.0000	0.0000	0.5832	0.6475	0.6192
EAST NORTH CENTRAL:						
ILLINOIS	0.5241	0.4031	0.3103	0.4972	0.4110	0.4851
INDIANA	1.0000	0.4871	0.7400	0.4919	0.4500	0.4634
MICHIGAN	0.6324	0.5190	0.3166	0.5258	0.4859	0.5234
OHIO	0.8200	0.4889	0.5948	0.5952	0.2931	0.5601
WISCONSIN	0.0000	0.4294	0.4419	0.4378	0.4859	0.4436
WEST NORTH CENTRAL:						
IOWA	0.0000	0.3664	0.3652	0.3657	0.3284	0.3483
KANSAS	0.3100	0.2684	0.3567	0.2688	0.2485	0.2623
MINNESOTA	0.3250	0.3359	0.0000	0.3359	0.3150	0.3287
MISSOURI	0.3225	0.2972	0.3275	0.3092	0.1327	0.2748
NEBRASKA	0.5200	0.3576	0.3396	0.3555	0.0000	0.3555
NORTH DAKOTA	0.0000	0.0000	0.3667	0.3667	0.0000	0.3667
SOUTH DAKOTA	0.0000	0.3608	0.0000	0.3608	0.3142	0.3453
SOUTH ATLANTIC:						
DELAWARE	0.0000	0.0000	0.0000	0.0000	0.5162	0.5162
DISTRICT OF COLUMBIA	0.0000	0.0000	0.0000	0.0000	0.0000	0.0000
FLORIDA	0.2510	0.4049	0.4811	0.4165	0.0000	0.4165
GEORGIA	0.0000	0.3583	0.0000	0.3583	0.0000	0.3583
MARYLAND	0.0000	0.0000	0.0000	0.0000	0.4694	0.4694
NORTH CAROLINA	0.0000	0.5492	0.4941	0.5303	0.5333	0.5308
SOUTH CAROLINA	0.0000	0.5330	0.0000	0.5330	0.4698	0.4842
VIRGINIA	0.0000	0.0000	0.3747	0.3747	0.4313	0.4057
WEST VIRGINIA	0.5357	0.5500	0.0000	0.5367	0.0000	0.5367
EAST SOUTH CENTRAL:						
ALABAMA	0.5200	0.3450	0.0000	0.3644	0.0000	0.3644
KENTUCKY	0.0000	0.0000	0.0000	0.0000	0.3144	0.3144
MISSISSIPPI	0.2925	0.3071	0.3730	0.2986	0.1900	0.2983
TENNESSEE	0.0000	0.0000	0.3029	0.3029	0.2267	0.3016
WEST SOUTH CENTRAL:						
ARKANSAS	0.3138	0.3420	0.3611	0.3142	0.0000	0.3142
LOUISIANA	0.2249	0.2585	0.6700	0.2276	0.2538	0.2365
OKLAHOMA	0.3313	0.2689	0.2692	0.2724	0.2667	0.2724
TEXAS	0.2326	0.2641	0.2395	0.2357	0.2476	0.2371
ROCKY MOUNTAIN:						
ARIZONA	0.3864	0.3960	0.0000	0.3872	0.3991	0.3932
COLORADO	0.3105	0.2908	0.0000	0.3012	0.2894	0.2962
IDAHO	0.0000	0.0000	0.0000	0.0000	0.0000	0.0000
MONTANA	0.0000	0.0000	0.3617	0.3617	0.2567	0.3092
NEVADA	0.3939	0.4812	0.0000	0.4502	0.4875	0.4604
NEW MEXICO	0.3594	0.2463	0.2883	0.2717	0.0000	0.2717
UTAH	0.0000	0.3069	0.0000	0.3069	0.0000	0.3069
WYOMING	0.0000	0.0000	0.0000	0.0000	0.3333	0.3333
FAR WEST:						
ALASKA	0.0000	0.0000	0.0000	0.0000	0.0000	0.0000
CALIFORNIA	0.0000	0.3634	0.3888	0.3764	0.0000	0.3764
HAWAII	0.0000	0.0000	0.0000	0.0000	0.0000	0.0000
OREGON	0.0000	0.0000	0.0000	0.0000	0.0000	0.0000
WASHINGTON	0.0000	0.0000	0.0000	0.0000	0.0000	0.0000

a Zero indicates no quantities in category

Table F.2.12

Natural Gas Prices In Dollars Per Million BTU, 1972, By Region

Prices Paid By Electric Utilities For Different Classes Of Use, American Gas Association Data

REGION	SALES				TRANSFERS WITHIN COMBINED GAS-ELECTRIC UTILITIES	TOTAL SALES AND TRANSFERS
	INDUSTRIAL		OTHER SALES	TOTAL SALES		
	Firm	Interrupt- ible				
NEW ENGLAND	0.5502	0.5147	0.5157	0.5284	0.3821	0.5169
MID ATLANTIC	0.5832	0.4571	0.9550	0.5233	0.5556	0.5529
EAST NORTH CENTRAL	0.5584	0.4700	0.4169	0.5024	0.4375	0.4920
WEST NORTH CENTRAL	0.3271	0.3008	0.3483	0.3085	0.2618	0.2952
SOUTH ATLANTIC	0.2786	0.4013	0.4758	0.4112	0.4692	0.4219
EAST SOUTH CENTRAL	0.2927	0.3094	0.3206	0.2997	0.3085	0.3005
WEST SOUTH CENTRAL	0.2402	0.2647	0.2693	0.2463	0.2514	0.2471
ROCKY MOUNTAIN	0.3633	0.3304	0.3250	0.3474	0.3687	0.3548
FAR WEST	0.0000 a	0.3634	0.3888	0.3764	0.0000	0.3764
UNITED STATES	0.2887	0.3436	0.3648	0.3265	0.3523	0.3314

a Zero indicates no quantities in category.

Table F. 3.1

Expenditures On Natural Gas In Thousand Dollars, 1972, By State

Residential And Commercial Use: Comparison Of Data From Bureau Of Mines (BOM) and American Gas Association (AGA)

REGION AND STATE	RESIDENTIAL				COMMERCIAL			
	BOM	AGA	BOM Minus AGA	BOM/AGA	BOM	AGA	BOM Minus AGA	BOM/AGA
NEW ENGLAND:								
CONNECTICUT	68849.0	74992.0	-6143.0	0.918	22207.0	23989.0	-1782.0	0.926
MAINE	2428.0	2796.0	-368.0	0.868	1049.0	1144.0	-95.0	0.917
MASSACHUSETTS	197332.0	201249.0	-3917.0	0.981	57567.0	60241.0	-2674.0	0.956
NEW HAMPSHIRE	8462.0	9749.0	-1287.0	0.868	4108.0	4479.0	-371.0	0.917
RHODE ISLAND	27293.0	29351.0	-2058.0	0.930	7645.0	7993.0	-348.0	0.956
VERMONT	2030.0	2339.0	-309.0	0.868	772.0	841.0	-69.0	0.918
MID ATLANTIC:								
NEW JERSEY	302547.0	271613.0	30934.0	1.114	90472.0	93203.0	-2731.0	0.971
NEW YORK	587274.0	599074.0	-11800.0	0.980	171973.0	162694.0	9279.0	1.057
PENNSYLVANIA	414247.0	432517.0	-18270.0	0.958	125217.0	126035.0	-818.0	0.994
EAST NORTH CENTRAL:								
ILLINOIS	553704.0	538683.0	15021.0	1.028	185436.0	183559.0	1877.0	1.010
INDIANA	192626.0	188025.0	4601.0	1.024	75883.0	72786.0	3097.0	1.043
MICHIGAN	390082.0	403569.0	-13487.0	0.967	139268.0	157862.0	-18594.0	0.882
OHIO	504161.0	506471.0	-2310.0	0.995	167205.0	173899.0	-6694.0	0.962
WISCONSIN	140019.0	164416.0	-24397.0	0.852	42264.0	57156.0	-14892.0	0.739
WEST NORTH CENTRAL:								
IOWA	106688.0	107045.0	-357.0	0.997	50068.0	47682.0	2386.0	1.050
KANSAS	74130.0	71951.0	2179.0	1.030	29173.0	20983.0	8190.0	1.390
MINNESOTA	131863.0	135989.0	-4126.0	0.970	52354.0	49417.0	2937.0	1.059
MISSOURI	175610.0	165813.0	9797.0	1.059	66533.0	57512.0	9021.0	1.157
NEBRASKA	59438.0	54803.0	4635.0	1.085	23234.0	22861.0	373.0	1.016
NORTH DAKOTA	11712.0	10767.0	945.0	1.088	7968.0	7069.0	899.0	1.127
SOUTH DAKOTA	14922.0	13538.0	1384.0	1.102	6931.0	7346.0	-415.0	0.944
SOUTH ATLANTIC:								
DELAWARE	14292.0	14206.0	86.0	1.006	4343.0	4413.0	-70.0	0.984
DISTRICT OF COLUMBIA	22612.0	22476.0	136.0	1.006	15243.0	13023.0	2220.0	1.170
FLORIDA	34121.0	29623.0	4498.0	1.152	25966.0	25709.0	257.0	1.010
GEORGIA	107167.0	101123.0	6044.0	1.060	35924.0	34420.0	1504.0	1.044
MARYLAND	124218.0	123446.0	772.0	1.006	33224.0	28385.0	4839.0	1.170
NORTH CAROLINA	46492.0	41783.0	4709.0	1.113	21585.0	21353.0	232.0	1.011
SOUTH CAROLINA	33313.0	30751.0	2562.0	1.083	13587.0	13670.0	-83.0	0.994
VIRGINIA	88572.0	88257.0	315.0	1.004	32390.0	33514.0	-1124.0	0.966
WEST VIRGINIA	57380.0	51638.0	5742.0	1.111	17820.0	17282.0	538.0	1.031
EAST SOUTH CENTRAL:								
ALABAMA	67601.0	69667.0	-2066.0	0.970	26836.0	23458.0	3378.0	1.144
KENTUCKY	79440.0	79835.0	-395.0	0.995	27297.0	29440.0	-2143.0	0.927
MISSISSIPPI	42559.0	32734.0	9825.0	1.300	14095.0	10791.0	3304.0	1.306
TENNESSEE	55053.0	47897.0	7156.0	1.149	36791.0	32613.0	4178.0	1.128
WEST SOUTH CENTRAL:								
ARKANSAS	39189.0	39306.0	-117.0	0.997	18106.0	17039.0	1067.0	1.063
LOUISIANA	75805.0	61785.0	14020.0	1.227	20306.0	15195.0	5111.0	1.336
OKLAHOMA	69692.0	64258.0	5434.0	1.085	22633.0	21039.0	1594.0	1.076
TEXAS	244031.0	233969.0	10062.0	1.043	58961.0	64276.0	-5315.0	0.917
ROCKY MOUNTAIN:								
ARIZONA	42618.0	43552.0	-934.0	0.979	17122.0	16071.0	1051.0	1.065
COLORADO	69744.0	67872.0	1872.0	1.028	40161.0	37281.0	2880.0	1.077
IDAHO	16407.0	13923.0	2484.0	1.178	9854.0	8188.0	1666.0	1.203
MONTANA	22978.0	22560.0	418.0	1.019	11416.0	10906.0	510.0	1.047
NEVADA	13795.0	11879.0	1916.0	1.161	6777.0	6383.0	394.0	1.062
NEW MEXICO	33686.0	25095.0	8591.0	1.342	11863.0	8301.0	3562.0	1.429
UTAH	44018.0	32697.0	11321.0	1.346	5614.0	7737.0	-2123.0	0.726
WYOMING	16459.0	9177.0	7282.0	1.794	8181.0	4429.0	3752.0	1.847
FAR WEST:								
ALASKA	13036.0	8373.0	4663.0	1.557	9871.0	3813.0	6058.0	2.589
CALIFORNIA	687635.0	656074.0	31561.0	1.048	184437.0	170103.0	14334.0	1.084
HAWAII	0.0	3397.0	-3397.0	0.000	0.0	1720.0	-1720.0	0.000
OREGON	39149.0	37280.0	1869.0	1.050	20571.0	18311.0	2260.0	1.123
WASHINGTON	56672.0	55626.0	1046.0	1.019	26918.0	27909.0	-991.0	0.964

Table F.3.2

Expenditures On Natural Gas In Thousand Dollars, 1972, By Region

Residential And Commercial Use: Comparison Of Data From Bureau of Mines (BOM)
     And American Gas Association (AGA)

Residential

	BOM	AGA	BOM MINUS AGA	BOM/AGA
NEW ENGLAND	306394.0	320476.0	-14082.0 •	0.956
MID ATLANTIC	1304068.0	1303204.0	864.0	1.001
EAST NORTH CENTRAL	1780592.0	1801164.0	-20572.0	0.989
WEST NORTH CENTRAL	574363.0	559906.0	14457.0	1.026
SOUTH ATLANTIC	528167.0	503303.0	24864.0	1.049
EAST SOUTH CENTRAL	244653.0	230133.0	14520.0	1.063
WEST SOUTH CENTRAL	428717.0	399318.0	29399.0	1.074
ROCKY MOUNTAIN	259705.0	226755.0	32950.0	1.145
FAR WEST	796492.0	760750.0	35742.0	1.047
TOTAL	6223151.0	6105009.0	118142.0	1.019

Commercial

	BOM	AGA	BOM - MINUS AGA	BOM/AGA
NEW ENGLAND	93348.0	98687.0	-5339.0	0.946
MID ATLANTIC	387662.0	381932.0	5730.0	1.015
EAST NORTH CENTRAL	610056.0	645262.0	-35206.0	0.945
WEST NORTH CENTRAL	236261.0	212870.0	23391.0	1.110
SOUTH ATLANTIC	200082.0	191769.0	8313.0	1.043
EAST SOUTH CENTRAL	105019.0	96302.0	8717.0	1.091
WEST SOUTH CENTRAL	120006.0	117549.0	2457.0	1.021
ROCKY MOUNTAIN	110988.0	99296.0	11692.0	1.118
FAR WEST	241797.0	221856.0	19941.0	1.090
TOTAL	2105219.0	2065523.0	39696.0	1.019

Table F.3.3

Expenditures On Natural Gas in Thousand Dollars, 1972, By State

Industrial Use Net of Use For Electricity Generation: Comparison of Data From Bureau of Mines (BOM) and
American Gas Association (AGA)

REGION AND STATE	BOM Sales (1)	BOM Lease And Plant Fuel (2)	BOM Total (3)	AGA Sales (4)	BOM Sales Minus AGA Sales: (1) - (4)	BOM Sales ÷ By AGA Sales (1) / (4)
NEW ENGLAND:						
CONNECTICUT	16485.0	0.0	16485.0	23946.0	-7461.0	0.688
MAINE	711.0	0.0	711.0	666.0	45.0	1.068
MASSACHUSETTS	35281.0	0.0	35281.0	32345.0	2936.0	1.091
NEW HAMPSHIRE	1526.0	0.0	1526.0	1431.0	95.0	1.066
RHODE ISLAND	4939.0	0.0	4939.0	6986.0	-2047.0	0.707
VERMONT	630.0	0.0	630.0	826.0	-196.0	0.763
MID ATLANTIC:						
NEW JERSEY	67053.0	0.0	67053.0	67559.0	-506.0	0.993
NEW YORK	88240.0	0.0	88240.0	114533.0	-26293.0	0.770
PENNSYLVANIA	263219.0	1335.0	264554.0	252730.0	10489.0	1.042
EAST NORTH CENTRAL:						
ILLINOIS	253919.0	93.0	254012.0	232578.0	21341.0	1.092
INDIANA	162188.0	0.0	162188.0	159457.0	2731.0	1.017
MICHIGAN	172106.0	519.0	172625.0	206653.0	-34547.0	0.833
OHIO	270014.0	1403.0	271417.0	284249.0	-14235.0	0.950
WISCONSIN	87842.0	0.0	87842.0	108324.0	-20482.0	0.811
WEST NORTH CENTRAL:						
IOWA	48899.0	0.0	48899.0	58389.0	-9490.0	0.837
KANSAS	59165.0	7356.0	66521.0	79958.0	-20793.0	0.740
MINNESOTA	50880.0	0.0	50880.0	73338.0	-22458.0	0.694
MISSOURI	44006.0	0.0	44006.0	51146.0	-7140.0	0.860
NEBRASKA	27323.0	182.0	27505.0	28995.0	-1672.0	0.942
NORTH DAKOTA	1430.0	2286.0	3716.0	1143.0	287.0	1.251
SOUTH DAKOTA	2345.0	0.0	2345.0	2656.0	-311.0	0.883
SOUTH ATLANTIC:						
DELAWARE	7632.0	0.0	7632.0	6919.0	713.0	1.103
DISTRICT OF COLUMBIA	762.0	0.0	762.0	856.0	-94.0	0.890
FLORIDA	43350.0	444.0	43794.0	40423.0	2927.0	1.072
GEORGIA	82660.0	0.0	82660.0	80693.0	1967.0	1.024
MARYLAND	45152.0	32.0	45184.0	50579.0	-5427.0	0.893
NORTH CAROLINA	50011.0	0.0	50011.0	61533.0	-11522.0	0.813
SOUTH CAROLINA	44849.0	0.0	44849.0	53531.0	-8682.0	0.838
VIRGINIA	31602.0	59.0	31661.0	36337.0	-4735.0	0.870
WEST VIRGINIA	52401.0	1249.0	53650.0	44227.0	8174.0	1.185
EAST SOUTH CENTRAL:						
ALABAMA	69874.0	406.0	70280.0	75452.0	-5578.0	0.926
KENTUCKY	42594.0	353.0	42947.0	40928.0	1666.0	1.041
MISSISSIPPI	50140.0	1748.0	51888.0	32679.0	17461.0	1.534
TENNESSEE	67014.0	389.0	67403.0	75209.0	-8195.0	0.891
WEST SOUTH CENTRAL:						
ARKANSAS	50616.0	1085.0	51701.0	48401.0	2215.0	1.046
LOUISIANA	331391.0	65550.0	396941.0	102317.0	229074.0	3.239
OKLAHOMA	36617.0	15904.0	52521.0	36446.0	171.0	1.005
TEXAS	478203.0	148391.0	626594.0	286161.0	192042.0	1.671
ROCKY MOUNTAIN:						
ARIZONA	30030.0	8.0	30038.0	32133.0	-2103.0	0.935
COLORADO	27395.0	753.0	28148.0	26579.0	816.0	1.031
IDAHO	16246.0	0.0	16246.0	15771.0	475.0	1.030
MONTANA	12679.0	954.0	13633.0	12635.0	44.0	1.003
NEVADA	5485.0	0.0	5485.0	7262.0	-1777.0	0.755
NEW MEXICO	25871.0	7076.0	32947.0	13268.0	12603.0	1.950
UTAH	22116.0	354.0	22470.0	17439.0	4677.0	1.268
WYOMING	16545.0	3451.0	19996.0	14094.0	2451.0	1.174
FAR WEST:						
ALASKA	8432.0	3597.0	12029.0	4031.0	4401.0	2.092
CALIFORNIA	293659.0	22065.0	315724.0	285561.0	8098.0	1.028
HAWAII	0.0	0.0	0.0	3761.0	-3761.0	0.000
OREGON	33881.0	0.0	33881.0	33411.0	470.0	1.014
WASHINGTON	47752.0	0.0	47752.0	60054.0	-12302.0	0.795

Table F.3.4

Expenditures On Natural Gas In Thousand Dollars, 1972, By Region

Industrial Use Net of Use For Electricity Generation: Comparison Of Data From Bureau Of Mines (BOM) and American Gas Association (AGA)

REGION	BOM Sales (1)	Lease And Plant Fuel (2)	BOM Total (3)	AGA Sales (4)	BOM Sales Minus AGA Sales (1)-(4)	BOM Sales ÷By AGA Sales (1)/(4)
NEW ENGLAND	59572.0	0.0	59572.0	66200.0	-6628.0	0.900
MID ATLANTIC	418512.0	1335.0	419847.0	434822.0	-16310.0	0.962
EAST NORTH CENTRAL	946069.0	2015.0	948084.0	991261.0	-45192.0	0.954
WEST NORTH CENTRAL	234048.0	9824.0	243872.0	295625.0	-61577.0	0.792
SOUTH ATLANTIC	358419.0	1784.0	360203.0	375098.0	16679.0	0.956
EAST SOUTH CENTRAL	229622.0	2896.0	232518.0	224268.0	5354.0	1.024
WEST SOUTH CENTRAL	896827.0	230930.0	1127757.0	473325.0	423502.0	1.895
ROCKY MOUNTAIN	156367.0	12596.0	168963.0	139181.0	17186.0	1.123
FAR WEST	383724.0	25662.0	409386.0	386818.0	-3094.0	0.992
TOTAL	3683160.0	287042.0	3970202.0	3386598.0	296562.0	1.088

Table F.3.5

Expenditures On Natural Gas In Thousand Dollars, 1972, By State

Pipeline Fuel And "Other" Consumption: Comparison Of Bureau of Mines (BOM)
and American Gas Association (AGA) Data

REGION AND STATE	Pipeline Fuel (BOM Data)	BOM Other (Excludes Electric Generation)	AGA Other Net Of Electric Generation	AGA Other Including Electric Generation
NEW ENGLAND:				
CONNECTICUT	14.0	5338.0	62.0	62.0
MAINE	0.0	13.0	174.0	174.0
MASSACHUSETTS	242.0	5426.0	5275.0	5636.0
NEW HAMPSHIRE	0.0	69.0	886.0	886.0
RHODE ISLAND	6.0	982.0	508.0	508.0
VERMONT	0.0	0.0	0.0	0.0
MID ATLANTIC:				
NEW JERSEY	176.0	3215.0	1039.0	1310.0
NEW YORK	898.0	19793.0	27223.0	27525.0
PENNSYLVANIA	8459.0	7862.0	8774.0	8774.0
EAST NORTH CENTRAL:				
ILLINOIS	5321.0	3753.0	282.0	1430.0
INDIANA	3306.0	3149.0	2717.0	2791.0
MICHIGAN	4739.0	5166.0	2807.0	6416.0
OHIO	3525.0	15537.0	6595.0	10521.0
WISCONSIN	1646.0	1388.0	594.0	6427.0
WEST NORTH CENTRAL:				
IOWA	4054.0	1248.0	896.0	7324.0
KANSAS	18661.0	2069.0	3409.0	3730.0
MINNESOTA	1979.0	14391.0	2387.0	2387.0
MISSOURI	2376.0	6946.0	677.0	4345.0
NEBRASKA	2336.0	3306.0	875.0	3897.0
NORTH DAKOTA	65.0	0.0	74.0	184.0
SOUTH DAKOTA	3.0	832.0	190.0	190.0
SOUTH ATLANTIC:				
DELAWARE	0.0	0.0	667.0	667.0
DISTRICT OF COLUMBIA	126.0	2418.0	2004.0	2004.0
FLORIDA	981.0	2020.0	3008.0	11476.0
GEORGIA	1798.0	3978.0	2169.0	2169.0
MARYLAND	738.0	2885.0	2392.0	2392.0
NORTH CAROLINA	1366.0	4295.0	1692.0	4360.0
SOUTH CAROLINA	718.0	662.0	4696.0	4696.0
VIRGINIA	2217.0	5297.0	4710.0	5422.0
WEST VIRGINIA	5636.0	2058.0	925.0	925.0
EAST SOUTH CENTRAL:				
ALABAMA	4385.0	519.0	351.0	351.0
KENTUCKY	8794.0	4895.0	4958.0	4958.0
MISSISSIPPI	13255.0	2552.0	2956.0	5082.0
TENNESSEE	5838.0	2457.0	3636.0	8755.0
WEST SOUTH CENTRAL:				
ARKANSAS	3143.0	345.0	417.0	742.0
LOUISIANA	18293.0	10341.0	4340.0	4407.0
OKLAHOMA	4722.0	2129.0	3904.0	33251.0
TEXAS	19727.0	15022.0	36052.0	37010.0
ROCKY MOUNTAIN:				
ARIZONA	4791.0	2332.0	6391.0	6391.0
COLORADO	623.0	528.0	679.0	679.0
IDAHO	1322.0	1179.0	769.0	769.0
MONTANA	174.0	1273.0	1081.0	1298.0
NEVADA	0.0	3431.0	530.0	530.0
NEW MEXICO	6571.0	5153.0	4119.0	4292.0
UTAH	237.0	10.0	11.0	11.0
WYOMING	1070.0	433.0	435.0	435.0
FAR WEST:				
ALASKA	2451.0	3218.0	0.0	0.0
CALIFORNIA	6586.0	3702.0	2184.0	124796.0
HAWAII	0.0	0.0	0.0	0.0
OREGON	2769.0	243.0	0.0	0.0
WASHINGTON	2078.0	94.0	24.0	24.0

Table F.3.6

Expenditures on Natural Gas in Thousand Dollars 1972, By Region

Pipeline Fuel And "Other" Consumption: Comparison Of
Bureau of Mines (BOM) And American Gas Association (AGA) Data

REGION	Pipeline Fuel (BOM Data)	BOM Other (Excludes Electric Generation)	AGA Other Net Of Electric Generation	AGA Other Including Electric Generation
NEW ENGLAND	262.00	11828.00	6905.00	7266.00
MID ATLANTIC	9533.00	30870.00	37036.00	37609.00
EAST NORTH CENTRAL	18537.00	28993.00	12995.00	27585.00
WEST NORTH CENTRAL	29474.00	28792.00	8508.00	22057.00
SOUTH ATLANTIC	13580.00	23613.00	22263.00	34111.00
EAST SOUTH CENTRAL	32272.00	10423.00	11901.00	19146.00
WEST SOUTH CENTRAL	45885.00	27837.00	44713.00	75410.00
ROCKY MOUNTAIN	14788.00	14339.00	14015.00	14405.00
FAR WEST	13884.00	7257.00	2208.00	124820.00
TOTAL	178215.00	183952.00	160544.00	362409.00

Table F.3.7

Expenditures on Natural Gas In Thousand Dollars, 1972, By State

Expenditures By Electric Utilities: Comparison of Data From Bureau Of Mines (BOM),
  National Coal Association (NCA) and American Gas Association (AGA)

REGION AND STATE	BOM	NCA	AGA	BOM MINUS NCA	BOM MINUS AGA
NEW ENGLAND:					
CONNECTICUT	13.00	0.00[a]	22.00	13.00	-9.00
MAINE	0.00 [a]	0.00	0.00	0.00	0.00
MASSACHUSETTS	3654.00	3140.26	3804.00	513.74	-150.00
NEW HAMPSHIRE	0.00	0.00	0.00	0.00	0.00
RHODE ISLAND	76.00	80.88	51.00	-4.88	25.00
VERMONT	322.00	162.23	0.00	159.77	322.00
MID ATLANTIC:					
NEW JERSEY	12244.00	9023.09	10779.00	3220.91	1465.00
NEW YORK	35639.00	28911.80	44240.00	6727.20	-8601.00
PENNSYLVANIA	2732.00	2150.51	3096.00	581.49	-364.00
EAST NORTH CENTRAL:					
ILLINOIS	31739.00	29991.39	38908.00	1747.61	-7169.00
INDIANA	7656.00	6702.71	8527.00	953.29	-871.00
MICHIGAN	28651.00	23428.49	29886.00	5222.51	-1235.00
OHIO	8378.00	5105.72	5321.00	3272.28	3057.00
WISCONSIN	12605.00	9452.42	12466.00	3152.58	139.00
WEST NORTH CENTRAL:					
IOWA	23095.00	18645.35	19366.00	4449.65	3729.00
KANSAS	67919.00	43233.68	47484.00	24685.32	20435.00
MINNESOTA	20615.00	15263.67	15973.00	5351.33	4642.00
MISSOURI	21674.00	15778.81	21630.00	5895.19	44.00
NEBRASKA	18181.00	15358.11	16390.00	2822.89	1791.00
NORTH DAKOTA	132.00	4.84	110.00	127.16	22.00
SOUTH DAKOTA	1283.00	1141.44	1243.00	141.56	40.00
SOUTH ATLANTIC:					
DELAWARE	1176.00	1220.01	826.00	-44.01	350.00
DISTRICT OF COLUMBIA	0.00	0.00	0.00	0.00	0.00
FLORIDA	68599.00	61607.09	19409.00	6991.91	49190.00
GEORGIA	13759.00	14351.46	17053.00	-592.46	-3294.00
MARYLAND	2592.00	0.00	3145.00	2592.00	-553.00
NORTH CAROLINA	8440.00	2485.16	8333.00	5954.84	107.00
SOUTH CAROLINA	11936.00	8053.44	8618.00	3882.56	3318.00
VIRGINIA	1882.00	904.50	1704.00	977.50	178.00
WEST VIRGINIA	175.00	21.87	322.00	153.13	-147.00
EAST SOUTH CENTRAL:					
ALABAMA	968.00	964.10	328.00	3.90	640.00
KENTUCKY	3655.00	3332.28	3207.00	322.72	448.00
MISSISSIPPI	32229.00	27868.74	29409.00	4360.26	2820.00
TENNESSEE	5302.00	5441.24	5187.00	-139.24	115.00
WEST SOUTH CENTRAL:					
ARKANSAS	22719.00	22478.51	22088.00	240.49	631.00
LOUISIANA	104769.00	95760.94	66394.00	9008.06	38375.00
OKLAHOMA	64726.00	65610.36	36149.00	-884.36	28577.00
TEXAS	370113.00	304244.23	122105.00	65868.77	248008.00
ROCKY MOUNTAIN:					
ARIZONA	32563.00	30944.87	38572.00	1618.13	-6009.00
COLORADO	20614.00	16322.59	30065.00	4291.41	-9451.00
IDAHO	0.00	0.00	0.00	0.00	0.00
MONTANA	418.00	214.87	371.00	203.13	47.00
NEVADA	18860.00	18540.02	27670.00	319.98	-8810.00
NEW MEXICO	21823.00	17703.80	12851.00	4119.20	8972.00
UTAH	1208.00	1060.07	1074.00	147.93	134.00
WYOMING	860.00	1278.88	1.00	-418.88	859.00
FAR WEST:					
ALASKA	5666.00	0.00	0.00	5666.00	5666.00
CALIFORNIA	242316.00	233855.63	229330.00	8460.37	12986.00
HAWAII	0.00	0.00	0.00	0.00	0.00
OREGON	184.00	191.32	0.00	-7.32	184.00
WASHINGTON	0.00	0.00	0.00	0.00	0.00

[a] Zero indicates no use of natural gas

Table F.3.8

Expenditures On Natural Gas In Thousand Dollars, 1972, By Region

Expenditures By Electric Utilities: Comparison Of Data From Bureau of Mines (BOM),
   National Coal Association (NCA), and American Gas Association (AGA)

REGION	BOM	NCA	AGA	BOM MINUS NCA	BOM MINUS AGA
NEW ENGLAND	4065.00	3383.37	3877.00	681.63	188.00
MID ATLANTIC	50615.00	40085.40	58115.00	10529.60	-7500.00
EAST NORTH CENTRAL	89029.00	74680.73	95108.00	14348.27	-6079.00
WEST NORTH CENTRAL	152899.00	109425.90	122196.00	43473.10	30703.00
SOUTH ATLANTIC	108559.00	88643.53	59410.00	19915.47	49149.00
EAST SOUTH CENTRAL	42154.00	37606.36	38131.00	4547.64	4023.00
WEST SOUTH CENTRAL	562327.00	488094.04	246736.00	74232.96	315591.00
ROCKY MOUNTAIN	96346.00	86065.10	110604.00	10280.90	-14258.00
FAR WEST	248166.00	234046.95	229330.00	14119.05	18836.00
TOTAL	1354159.99	1162031.39	963507.00	192128.62	390653.00

Table F.3.9

Expenditures On Natural Gas in Thousand Dollars, 1972, By State

Commercial and Industrial Firm and Interruptible Sales, American Gas Association Data

REGION AND STATE	COMMERCIAL			INDUSTRIAL		
	Firm	Interruptible	Total	Firm	Interruptible	Total
NEW ENGLAND:						
CONNECTICUT	23812.0	177.0	23989.0	19041.0	4916.0	23957.0
MAINE	1144.0	0.0	1144.0	637.0	29.0	666.0
MASSACHUSETTS	59546.0	695.0	60241.0	27088.0	8348.0	35436.0
NEW HAMPSHIRE	4479.0	0.0	4479.0	903.0	528.0	1431.0
RHODE ISLAND	7929.0	64.0	7993.0	5580.0	1457.0	7037.0
VERMONT	841.0	0.0	841.0	126.0	700.0	826.0
MID ATLANTIC:						
NEW JERSEY	89996.0	3207.0	93203.0	42858.0	27398.0	70256.0
NEW YORK	161545.0	1149.0	162694.0	76236.0	38297.0	114533.0
PENNSYLVANIA	126035.0	0.0	126035.0	228233.0	25780.0	254013.0
EAST NORTH CENTRAL:						
ILLINOIS	180794.0	2765.0	183559.0	229051.0	36684.0	265735.0
INDIANA	70261.0	2525.0	72786.0	137631.0	24654.0	162285.0
MICHIGAN	155617.0	2245.0	157862.0	151411.0	79867.0	231278.0
OHIO	172566.0	1333.0	173899.0	265107.0	20156.0	285263.0
WISCONSIN	51422.0	5734.0	57156.0	39847.0	73458.0	113305.0
WEST NORTH CENTRAL:						
IOWA	40389.0	7293.0	47682.0	35489.0	27333.0	62822.0
KANSAS	20329.0	654.0	20983.0	32748.0	80009.0	112757.0
MINNESOTA	45397.0	4020.0	49417.0	37044.0	46439.0	83483.0
MISSOURI	52250.0	5262.0	57512.0	35075.0	31976.0	67051.0
NEBRASKA	20872.0	1989.0	22861.0	17456.0	24907.0	42363.0
NORTH DAKOTA	7069.0	0.0	7069.0	850.0	293.0	1143.0
SOUTH DAKOTA	6657.0	689.0	7346.0	93.0	3429.0	3522.0
SOUTH ATLANTIC:						
DELAWARE	4413.0	0.0	4413.0	5860.0	1059.0	6919.0
DISTRICT OF COLUMBIA	11832.0	1191.0	13023.0	742.0	114.0	856.0
FLORIDA	25019.0	690.0	25709.0	11495.0	39869.0	51364.0
GEORGIA	34417.0	3.0	34420.0	20843.0	76903.0	97746.0
MARYLAND	25717.0	2668.0	28385.0	36359.0	14220.0	50579.0
NORTH CAROLINA	21289.0	64.0	21353.0	25752.0	41438.0	67190.0
SOUTH CAROLINA	12342.0	1328.0	13670.0	13581.0	41709.0	55290.0
VIRGINIA	30785.0	2729.0	33514.0	24461.0	11876.0	36337.0
WEST VIRGINIA	17265.0	17.0	17282.0	42142.0	2407.0	44549.0
EAST SOUTH CENTRAL:						
ALABAMA	23296.0	162.0	23458.0	58358.0	17422.0	75780.0
KENTUCKY	27371.0	2069.0	29440.0	17365.0	23563.0	40928.0
MISSISSIPPI	10787.0	4.0	10791.0	54047.0	5858.0	59905.0
TENNESSEE	31216.0	1397.0	32613.0	44063.0	31146.0	75209.0
WEST SOUTH CENTRAL:						
ARKANSAS	17006.0	33.0	17039.0	63175.0	6989.0	70164.0
LOUISIANA	15089.0	106.0	15195.0	140388.0	3939.0	144327.0
OKLAHOMA	20714.0	325.0	21039.0	22222.0	21022.0	43244.0
TEXAS	63663.0	613.0	64276.0	376972.0	15207.0	392179.0
ROCKY MOUNTAIN:						
ARIZONA	16071.0	0.0	16071.0	50826.0	282.0	51108.0
COLORADO	37118.0	163.0	37281.0	17100.0	27217.0	44317.0
IDAHO	8188.0	0.0	8188.0	12307.0	3464.0	15771.0
MONTANA	10906.0	0.0	10906.0	1034.0	11601.0	12635.0
NEVADA	6380.0	3.0	6383.0	8091.0	18846.0	26937.0
NEW MEXICO	8122.0	179.0	8301.0	15130.0	10816.0	25946.0
UTAH	7737.0	0.0	7737.0	2136.0	16377.0	18513.0
WYOMING	4429.0	0.0	4429.0	2466.0	11628.0	14094.0
FAR WEST:						
ALASKA	3813.0	0.0	3813.0	4031.0	0.0	4031.0
CALIFORNIA	154302.0	15801.0	170103.0	45778.0	346501.0	392279.0
HAWAII	1720.0	0.0	1720.0	3761.0	0.0	3761.0
OREGON	18077.0	234.0	18311.0	14907.0	18504.0	33411.0
WASHINGTON	27328.0	581.0	27909.0	20586.0	39468.0	60054.0

Table F.3.10

Expenditures on Natural Gas, In Thousand Dollars, 1972, By Region

Commercial and Industrial Firm and Interruptible Sales, American Gas Association Data

REGION	COMMERCIAL			INDUSTRIAL		
	Firm	Interruptible	Total	Firm	Interruptible	Total
NEW ENGLAND	97751.00	936.00	98687.00	53375.00	15978.00	69353.00
MID ATLANTIC	377576.00	4356.00	381932.00	347327.00	91475.00	438802.00
EAST NORTH CENTRAL	630660.00	14602.00	645262.00	823047.00	234819.00	1057866.00
WEST NORTH CENTRAL	192963.00	19907.00	212870.00	158755.00	214386.00	373141.00
SOUTH ATLANTIC	183079.00	8690.00	191769.00	181235.00	229595.00	410830.00
EAST SOUTH CENTRAL	92670.00	3632.00	96302.00	173833.00	77989.00	251822.00
WEST SOUTH CENTRAL	116472.00	1077.00	117549.00	602757.00	47157.00	649914.00
ROCKY MOUNTAIN	98951.00	345.00	99296.00	109090.00	100231.00	209321.00
FAR WEST	205240.00	16616.00	221856.00	89063.00	404473.00	493536.00
TOTAL	1995362.01	70161.00	2065523.01	2538481.99	1416103.00	3954585.01

Table F.3.11

Expenditures On Natural Gas In Thousand Dollars, 1972, By State

Expenditures By Electric Utilities For Different Classes Of Use, American Gas Association Data

REGION AND STATE	SALES				TRANSFERS WITHIN COMBINED GAS-ELECTRIC UTILITIES	TOTAL SALES AND TRANSFERS
	INDUSTRIAL		OTHER SALES	TOTAL SALES		
	Firm	Interruptible				
NEW ENGLAND:						
CONNECTICUT	11.0	0.0	0.0	11.0	11.0	22.0
MAINE	0.0	0.0	0.0	0.0	0.0	0.0
MASSACHUSETTS	1392.0	1699.0	361.0	3452.0	352.0	3804.0
NEW HAMPSHIRE	0.0	0.0	0.0	0.0	0.0	0.0
RHODE ISLAND	0.0	51.0	0.0	51.0	0.0	51.0
VERMONT	0.0	0.0	0.0	0.0	0.0	0.0
MID ATLANTIC:						
NEW JERSEY	0.0	2697.0	271.0	2968.0	7811.0	10779.0
NEW YORK	0.0	0.0	302.0	302.0	43938.0	44240.0
PENNSYLVANIA	1283.0	0.0	0.0	1283.0	1813.0	3096.0
EAST NORTH CENTRAL:						
ILLINOIS	29610.0	3547.0	1148.0	34305.0	4603.0	38908.0
INDIANA	100.0	2728.0	74.0	2902.0	5625.0	8527.0
MICHIGAN	14608.0	10017.0	3609.0	28234.0	1652.0	29886.0
OHIO	574.0	440.0	3926.0	4940.0	381.0	5321.0
WISCONSIN	0.0	4981.0	5833.0	10814.0	1652.0	12466.0
WEST NORTH CENTRAL:						
IOWA	0.0	4433.0	6428.0	10861.0	8505.0	19366.0
KANSAS	31.0	32768.0	321.0	33120.0	14364.0	47484.0
MINNESOTA	13.0	10132.0	0.0	10145.0	5828.0	15973.0
MISSOURI	5354.0	10551.0	3668.0	19573.0	2057.0	21630.0
NEBRASKA	208.0	13160.0	3022.0	16390.0	0.0	16390.0
NORTH DAKOTA	0.0	0.0	110.0	110.0	0.0	110.0
SOUTH DAKOTA	0.0	866.0	0.0	866.0	377.0	1243.0
SOUTH ATLANTIC:						
DELAWARE	0.0	0.0	0.0	0.0	826.0	826.0
DISTRICT OF COLUMBIA	0.0	0.0	0.0	0.0	0.0	0.0
FLORIDA	1305.0	9636.0	8468.0	19409.0	0.0	19409.0
GEORGIA	0.0	17053.0	0.0	17053.0	0.0	17053.0
MARYLAND	0.0	0.0	0.0	0.0	3145.0	3145.0
NORTH CAROLINA	0.0	5657.0	2668.0	8325.0	8.0	8333.0
SOUTH CAROLINA	0.0	1759.0	0.0	1759.0	6859.0	8618.0
VIRGINIA	0.0	0.0	712.0	712.0	992.0	1704.0
WEST VIRGINIA	300.0	22.0	0.0	322.0	0.0	322.0
EAST SOUTH CENTRAL:						
ALABAMA	52.0	276.0	0.0	328.0	0.0	328.0
KENTUCKY	0.0	0.0	0.0	0.0	3207.0	3207.0
MISSISSIPPI	23572.0	3654.0	2126.0	29352.0	57.0	29409.0
TENNESSEE	0.0	0.0	5119.0	5119.0	68.0	5187.0
WEST SOUTH CENTRAL:						
ARKANSAS	21592.0	171.0	325.0	22088.0	0.0	22088.0
LOUISIANA	38598.0	3412.0	67.0	42077.0	24317.0	66394.0
OKLAHOMA	2253.0	4545.0	29347.0	36145.0	4.0	36149.0
TEXAS	94423.0	11595.0	958.0	106976.0	15129.0	122105.0
ROCKY MOUNTAIN:						
ARIZONA	18777.0	198.0	0.0	18975.0	19597.0	38572.0
COLORADO	9130.0	8608.0	0.0	17738.0	12327.0	30065.0
IDAHO	0.0	0.0	0.0	0.0	0.0	0.0
MONTANA	0.0	0.0	217.0	217.0	154.0	371.0
NEVADA	6106.0	13569.0	0.0	19675.0	7995.0	27670.0
NEW MEXICO	3810.0	8868.0	173.0	12851.0	0.0	12851.0
UTAH	0.0	1074.0	0.0	1074.0	0.0	1074.0
WYOMING	0.0	0.0	0.0	0.0	1.0	1.0
FAR WEST:						
ALASKA	0.0	0.0	0.0	0.0	0.0	0.0
CALIFORNIA	0.0	106718.0	122612.0	229330.0	0.0	229330.0
HAWAII	0.0	0.0	0.0	0.0	0.0	0.0
OREGON	0.0	0.0	0.0	0.0	0.0	0.0
WASHINGTON	0.0	0.0	0.0	0.0	0.0	0.0

Table F.3.12

Expenditures On Natural Gas In Thousand Dollars, 1972, By Region

Expenditures By Electric Utilities For Different Classes Of Use, American Gas Association Data

REGION	SALES				TRANSFERS WITHIN COMBINED GAS - ELECTRIC UTILITIES	TOTAL SALES AND TRANSFERS
	INDUSTRIAL		OTHER SALES	TOTAL SALES		
	Firm	Interruptible				
NEW ENGLAND	1403.00	1750.00	361.00	3514.00	363.00	3877.00
MID ATLANTIC	1283.00	2697.00	573.00	4553.00	53562.00	58115.00
EAST NORTH CENTRAL	44892.00	21713.00	14590.00	81195.00	13913.00	95108.00
WEST NORTH CENTRAL	5606.00	71910.00	13549.00	91065.00	31131.00	122196.00
SOUTH ATLANTIC	1605.00	34127.00	11848.00	47580.00	11830.00	59410.00
EAST SOUTH CENTRAL	23624.00	3930.00	7245.00	34799.00	3332.00	38131.00
WEST SOUTH CENTRAL	156866.00	19723.00	30697.00	207286.00	39450.00	246736.00
ROCKY MOUNTAIN	37823.00	32317.00	390.00	70530.00	40074.00	110604.00
FAR WEST	0.00	106718.00	122612.00	229330.00	0.00	229330.00
TOTAL	273102.00	294885.00	201865.00	769852.00	193655.00	963507.00

Table F.3.13

Expenditures On Natural Gas In Thousand Dollars, 1972, By State

Revision Of Commercial Use: Components and Resultants Of Shifts

REGION AND STATE	COMMERCIAL USE (BOM) "INITIAL" DATA	RESIDENTIAL USE IN LARGE MULTI-FAMILY STRUCTURES	"NET" COMMERCIAL USE	RESIDUAL TO INDUSTRIAL USE	INITIAL RESIDENTIAL USE	REVISED RESIDENTIAL USE
NEW ENGLAND:						
CONNECTICUT	22207.1	9814.6	9701.3	2691.2	68849.0	78663.6
MAINE	1048.9	520.1	427.0	101.9	2428.0	2948.1
MASSACHUSETTS	57566.8	23322.3	26429.7	7814.8	197332.0	220654.3
NEW HAMPSHIRE	4108.1	1604.3	1690.3	813.5	8462.0	10066.3
RHODE ISLAND	7645.1	2603.6	3264.0	1777.5	27293.0	29896.6
VERMONT	772.0	358.5	335.0	78.6	2030.0	2388.5
MID ATLANTIC:						
NEW JERSEY	90472.1	32827.4	38323.2	19321.6	302547.0	335374.4
NEW YORK	171973.6	90054.7	77832.6	4086.3	587274.0	677328.7
PENNSYLVANIA	125216.5	31911.0	52497.4	40808.1	414247.0	446158.0
EAST NORTH CENTRAL:						
ILLINOIS	185436.4	47890.6	69061.3	68484.5	553704.0	601594.6
INDIANA	75883.2	9255.7	26467.1	40160.4	192626.0	201881.7
MICHIGAN	139268.7	18878.7	51116.1	69273.9	390082.0	408960.7
OHIO	167205.0	24862.6	59929.0	82413.4	504161.0	529023.6
WISCONSIN	42264.2	9385.2	15223.1	17655.9	140019.0	149404.2
WEST NORTH CENTRAL:						
IOWA	50067.9	4194.2	17348.8	28524.8	106688.0	110882.2
KANSAS	29172.9	1988.8	10404.3	16779.8	74130.0	76118.8
MINNESOTA	52353.8	11853.2	19367.1	21133.5	131863.0	143716.2
MISSOURI	66533.3	10405.1	24080.2	32048.0	175610.0	186015.1
NEBRASKA	23234.0	2287.7	8285.4	12660.9	59438.0	61725.7
NORTH DAKOTA	7968.0	964.8	2764.2	4239.0	11712.0	12676.8
SOUTH DAKOTA	6931.0	693.4	2427.7	3809.9	14922.0	15615.4
SOUTH ATLANTIC:						
DELAWARE	4343.0	692.7	2289.9	1360.4	14292.0	14984.7
DISTRICT OF COLUMBIA	15242.9	4275.4	10625.0	342.6	22612.0	26887.4
FLORIDA	25966.0	13087.6	12359.3	518.9	34121.0	47208.7
GEORGIA	35924.0	3250.0	16832.5	15841.5	107167.0	110417.0
MARYLAND	33224.1	7911.9	17257.6	8054.6	124218.0	132129.9
NORTH CAROLINA	21585.1	2118.5	9668.3	9798.3	46492.0	48610.5
SOUTH CAROLINA	13587.1	768.3	6078.1	6740.6	33313.0	34081.3
VIRGINIA	32390.1	5890.8	15606.3	10892.9	88572.0	94462.8
WEST VIRGINIA	17820.0	473.6	8270.2	9076.1	57380.0	57853.6
EAST SOUTH CENTRAL:						
ALABAMA	26835.9	959.3	12344.1	13532.5	67601.0	68560.3
KENTUCKY	27297.0	1453.8	12407.2	13436.0	79440.0	80893.8
MISSISSIPPI	14095.1	411.9	6471.4	7211.8	42559.0	42970.9
TENNESSEE	36791.0	2179.3	17069.6	17542.0	55053.0	57232.4
WEST SOUTH CENTRAL:						
ARKANSAS	18105.9	382.7	7976.3	9746.9	39189.0	39571.7
LOUISIANA	20305.8	1112.1	9925.9	9267.8	75805.0	76917.1
OKLAHOMA	22633.0	867.9	10998.3	10766.8	69692.0	70559.9
TEXAS	58961.0	6381.3	28925.8	23653.9	244031.0	250412.3
ROCKY MOUNTAIN:						
ARIZONA	17122.1	2000.5	10672.1	4449.5	42618.0	44618.5
COLORADO	40161.1	3413.3	25426.2	11321.7	69744.0	73157.3
IDAHO	9854.0	612.7	5569.3	3672.0	16407.0	17019.7
MONTANA	11416.0	580.9	6665.4	4169.6	22978.0	23558.9
NEVADA	6777.0	1122.7	3991.2	1663.2	13795.0	14917.7
NEW MEXICO	11863.0	573.8	7391.9	3897.2	33686.0	34259.8
UTAH	5614.0	986.1	3530.1	1097.9	44018.0	45004.1
WYOMING	8181.0	157.5	4885.2	3138.4	16459.0	16616.5
FAR WEST:						
ALASKA	9871.0	965.0	6174.5	2731.5	13036.0	14001.0
CALIFORNIA	184438.0	50310.4	115072.8	19054.8	687635.0	737945.4
HAWAII	0.0	0.0	0.0	0.0	0.0	0.0
OREGON	20571.0	5330.8	11871.3	3369.0	39149.0	44479.8
WASHINGTON	26917.9	8412.0	16248.0	2257.9	56672.0	65084.0

Table F.3.14

Expenditures On Natural Gas In Thousand Dollars, 1972, By State

Distribution Of Net Commercial Use By Sector

REGION AND STATE	BUSINESS USE	FEDERAL GOVERNMENT USE	STATE AND LOCAL GOVERNMENT USE	TOTAL "NET" COMMERCIAL USE
NEW ENGLAND:				
CONNECTICUT	7063.0	121.2	2517.2	9701.3
MAINE	288.1	10.1	128.8	427.0
MASSACHUSETTS	19071.3	501.6	6856.9	26429.7
NEW HAMPSHIRE	1211.2	21.8	457.3	1690.3
RHODE ISLAND	2343.6	86.1	834.2	3264.0
VERMONT	235.2	5.8	94.0	335.0
MID ATLANTIC:				
NEW JERSEY	27672.7	614.6	10035.9	38323.2
NEW YORK	55860.2	1257.5	20714.8	77832.6
PENNSYLVANIA	38263.8	1023.1	13210.5	52497.4
EAST NORTH CENTRAL:				
ILLINOIS	49423.4	1154.9	18482.9	69061.3
INDIANA	17905.8	368.5	8192.8	26467.1
MICHIGAN	34364.2	558.5	16193.4	51116.1
OHIO	41869.2	916.5	17143.3	59929.0
WISCONSIN	10510.3	203.6	4509.3	15223.1
WEST NORTH CENTRAL:				
IOWA	11853.8	259.5	5235.5	17348.8
KANSAS	7044.0	219.1	3141.2	10404.3
MINNESOTA	13241.7	296.5	5828.9	19367.1
MISSOURI	16545.5	566.2	6968.5	24080.2
NEBRASKA	5658.9	152.8	2473.7	8285.4
NORTH DAKOTA	1850.5	61.8	851.8	2764.2
SOUTH DAKOTA	1591.2	76.2	760.3	2427.7
SOUTH ATLANTIC:				
DELAWARE	1523.7	36.8	729.4	2289.9
DISTRICT OF COLUMBIA	6421.6	1970.3	2233.1	10625.0
FLORIDA	8021.0	262.9	4075.4	12359.3
GEORGIA	10033.6	499.1	6299.9	16832.5
MARYLAND	10984.9	832.4	5440.4	17257.6
NORTH CAROLINA	6213.5	156.3	3298.5	9668.3
SOUTH CAROLINA	3742.2	122.9	2213.1	6078.1
VIRGINIA	9721.9	785.5	5098.9	15606.3
WEST VIRGINIA	5239.4	168.9	2862.0	8270.2
EAST SOUTH CENTRAL:				
ALABAMA	7591.2	412.5	4340.4	12344.1
KENTUCKY	8079.4	291.4	4036.4	12407.2
MISSISSIPPI	3933.4	133.0	2405.0	6471.4
TENNESSEE	10849.7	384.7	5835.2	17069.6
WEST SOUTH CENTRAL:				
ARKANSAS	4974.0	193.0	2809.3	7976.3
LOUISIANA	6385.7	162.3	3377.8	9925.9
OKLAHOMA	6691.9	436.3	3870.1	10998.3
TEXAS	18297.0	736.2	9892.6	28925.8
ROCKY MOUNTAIN:				
ARIZONA	7056.2	281.3	3334.4	10671.9
COLORADO	17097.1	748.0	7581.0	25426.2
IDAHO	3677.4	101.5	1790.4	5569.3
MONTANA	4394.8	158.4	2112.2	6665.4
NEVADA	2575.4	101.7	1314.1	3991.2
NEW MEXICO	4674.6	307.9	2409.5	7391.9
UTAH	2171.3	237.7	1121.1	3530.1
WYOMING	2963.2	164.9	1757.1	4885.2
FAR WEST:				
ALASKA	3817.6	421.2	1935.7	6174.5
CALIFORNIA	78193.4	2782.9	34096.5	115072.8
HAWAII	0.0	0.0	0.0	0.0
OREGON	8156.2	239.7	3475.3	11871.3
WASHINGTON	11015.7	375.1	4857.2	16248.0

Table F.3.15

Expenditures On Natural Gas In Thousand Dollars, 1972, By Region

Revision Of Commercial Use: Components And Resultants Of Shifts, And Distribution Of
    "Net" Commercial Use By Sector

Revision Of Commercial Use

REGION	COMMERCIAL USE (BOM) INITIAL DATA	RESIDENTIAL USE IN MULTI-FAMILY STRUCTURES	"NET" COMMERCIAL USE	RESIDUAL TO INDUSTRIAL USE	INITIAL RESIDENTIAL USE	REVISED RESIDENTIAL USE
NEW ENGLAND	93348.00	38223.40	41847.30	13277.50	306394.00	344617.40
MID ATLANTIC	387662.20	154793.10	168653.20	64216.00	1304068.01	1458861.10
EAST NORTH CENTRAL	610057.51	110272.80	221796.60	277988.10	1780592.00	1890864.82
WEST NORTH CENTRAL	236260.90	32387.20	84677.70	119195.90	574363.00	606750.20
SOUTH ATLANTIC	200082.30	38468.90	98987.20	62625.90	528167.00	566635.91
EAST SOUTH CENTRAL	105019.00	5004.30	48292.30	51722.30	244653.00	249657.40
WEST SOUTH CENTRAL	120005.70	8744.00	57826.30	53435.40	428717.00	437461.00
ROCKY MOUNTAIN	110988.20	9447.50	68131.40	33409.50	259705.00	269152.50
FAR WEST	241797.90	65018.20	149366.60	27413.20	796492.00	861510.19
TOTAL	2105221.69	462359.40	939578.59	703283.79	6223151.01	6685510.35

Distribution Of "Net" Commercial Use By Sector

	BUSINESS USE	FEDERAL GOVERNMENT USE	STATE & LOCAL GOVERNMENT USE	TOTAL "NET" COMMERCIAL USE
NEW ENGLAND	30212.40	746.60	10888.40	41847.30
MID ATLANTIC	121796.70	2895.20	43961.20	168653.20
EAST NORTH CENTRAL	154072.90	3202.00	64521.70	221796.60
WEST NORTH CENTRAL	57785.60	1632.10	25259.90	84677.70
SOUTH ATLANTIC	61901.80	4835.10	32250.70	98987.20
EAST SOUTH CENTRAL	30453.70	1221.60	16617.00	48292.30
WEST SOUTH CENTRAL	36348.60	1527.80	19949.80	57826.30
ROCKY MOUNTAIN	44610.00	2101.40	21419.80	68131.20
FAR WEST	101182.90	3818.90	44364.70	149366.60
TOTAL	638364.59	21980.70	279233.20	939578.39

Table F.3.16

Expenditures On Natural Gas In Thousand Dollars, 1972, By State

Components Of Industrial Use Series

REGION AND STATE	INDUSTRIAL SALES (Combining AGA and BOM data)	TRANSFER IN FROM COMMERCIAL SALES	USE IN OIL & GAS PRODUCTION & OIL REFINING	FEDERAL GOVERNMENT INDUSTRIAL USE	STATE & LOCAL GOVERNMENT INDUSTRIAL USE	LEASE AND PLANT FUEL
NEW ENGLAND:						
CONNECTICUT	23946.0	2691.2	0.0	0.0	0.0	0.0
MAINE	666.0	101.9	0.0	0.0	0.0	0.0
MASSACHUSETTS	32345.0	7814.8	0.0	0.0	0.0	0.0
NEW HAMPSHIRE	1431.0	813.5	0.0	322.1	0.0	0.0
RHODE ISLAND	6986.0	1777.5	0.0	0.0	0.0	0.0
VERMONT	826.0	78.6	0.0	0.0	0.0	0.0
MID ATLANTIC:						
NEW JERSEY	67559.0	19321.6	2464.9	0.0	0.0	0.0
NEW YORK	114533.0	4086.3	516.8	0.0	0.0	0.0
PENNSYLVANIA	252730.0	40808.1	3384.4	0.0	0.0	1335.0
EAST NORTH CENTRAL:						
ILLINOIS	232578.0	68484.5	11196.7	0.0	36.6	93.0
INDIANA	159457.0	40160.4	6749.0	0.0	0.0	0.0
MICHIGAN	206653.0	69273.9	1467.1	0.0	0.0	519.0
OHIO	284249.0	82413.4	5687.4	0.0	0.0	1403.0
WISCONSIN	108324.0	17655.9	419.5	0.0	0.0	0.0
WEST NORTH CENTRAL:						
IOWA	58389.0	28524.8	33.7	0.0	0.0	0.0
KANSAS	79958.0	16779.8	9568.9	931.8	179.9	7356.0
MINNESOTA	73338.0	21133.5	5122.6	0.0	0.0	0.0
MISSOURI	51146.0	32048.0	4213.3	0.0	0.0	0.0
NEBRASKA	28995.0	12660.9	618.1	254.7	22.6	182.0
NORTH DAKOTA	1143.0	4239.0	3150.9	0.0	0.0	2286.0
SOUTH DAKOTA	2656.0	3809.9	53.9	0.0	0.0	0.0
SOUTH ATLANTIC:						
DELAWARE	6919.0	1360.4	680.4	0.0	121.4	0.0
DISTRICT OF COLUMBIA	856.0	342.6	16.5	0.0	0.0	0.0
FLORIDA	40423.0	518.9	365.7	1277.8	10168.5	444.0
GEORGIA	80693.0	15841.5	131.8	0.0	0.0	0.0
MARYLAND	50579.0	8054.6	633.2	0.0	222.8	32.0
NORTH CAROLINA	61533.0	9798.3	83.1	0.0	0.0	0.0
SOUTH CAROLINA	53531.0	6740.6	116.8	0.0	0.0	0.0
VIRGINIA	36337.0	10892.9	3071.3	0.0	0.0	59.0
WEST VIRGINIA	44227.0	9076.1	218.1	0.0	0.0	1249.0
EAST SOUTH CENTRAL:						
ALABAMA	69874.0	13532.5	463.0	0.0	0.0	406.0
KENTUCKY	42594.0	13436.0	2019.0	0.0	0.0	353.0
MISSISSIPPI	50140.0	7211.8	1545.1	594.4	0.0	1748.0
TENNESSEE	67014.0	17542.0	40.2	1339.2	31.3	389.0
WEST SOUTH CENTRAL:						
ARKANSAS	50616.0	9746.9	1265.1	280.9	0.0	1085.0
LOUISIANA	331391.0	9267.8	29209.2	999.2	176.7	65550.0
OKLAHOMA	36617.0	10766.8	7604.8	613.5	19.1	15904.0
TEXAS	478203.0	23653.9	59100.3	797.4	45.2	148391.0
ROCKY MOUNTAIN:						
ARIZONA	30030.0	4449.5	31.5	0.0	88.5	8.0
COLORADO	27395.0	11321.7	1049.0	0.0	3207.1	753.0
IDAHO	16246.0	3672.0	22.0	0.0	0.0	0.0
MONTANA	12679.0	4169.6	3499.9	0.0	0.0	954.0
NEVADA	5485.0	1663.2	44.3	0.0	0.0	0.0
NEW MEXICO	25871.0	3897.2	557.7	0.0	0.0	7076.0
UTAH	22116.0	1097.9	2850.3	0.0	0.0	354.0
WYOMING	16545.0	3138.4	2453.9	0.0	0.0	3451.0
FAR WEST:						
ALASKA	8432.0	2731.5	411.3	0.0	0.0	3597.0
CALIFORNIA	293659.0	19054.8	51640.8	0.0	0.0	22065.0
HAWAII	0.0	0.0	0.0	0.0	0.0	0.0
OREGON	33881.0	3369.0	3108.1	0.0	0.0	0.0
WASHINGTON	47752.0	2257.9	13679.1	0.0	0.0	0.0

Table F.3.17

Expenditures on Natural Gas in Thousand Dollars, 1972, by State

Components of Industrial Use Series

REGION	INDUSTRIAL SALES (Combining AGA and BOM data)	TRANSFER IN FROM COMMERCIAL SALES	USE IN OIL & GAS PRODUCTION & OIL REFINING	FEDERAL GOVERNMENT INDUSTRIAL USE	STATE & LOCAL GOVERNMENT INDUSTRIAL USE	LEASE AND PLANT FUEL
NEW ENGLAND	66200.00	13277.50	0.00	322.10	0.00	0.00
MID ATLANTIC	434822.00	64216.00	6366.10	0.00	0.00	1335.00
EAST NORTH CENTRAL	991261.00	277988.10	25519.70	0.00	36.60	2015.00
WEST NORTH CENTRAL	295625.00	119195.90	22761.40	1186.50	202.50	9824.00
SOUTH ATLANTIC	375098.00	62625.90	5316.90	1277.80	10512.70	1784.00
EAST SOUTH CENTRAL	229622.00	51722.30	4067.30	1933.60	31.30	2896.00
WEST SOUTH CENTRAL	896827.00	53435.40	97179.40	2691.00	241.00	230930.00
ROCKY MOUNTAIN	156367.00	33409.50	10508.60	0.00	3295.60	12596.00
FAR WEST	383724.00	27413.20	68839.30	0.00	0.00	25662.00
TOTAL	3829546.01	703283.79	240558.70	7411.00	14319.70	287042.00

Table   F.3.18

Expenditures On Natural Gas In Thousand Dollars, 1972, By State

Other (Municipal-Institutional) And Energy Production Use Of Natural Gas

REGION AND STATE	OTHER: MUNICIPAL-INSTITUTIONAL (State & Local Govt.)	ENERGY PRODUCTION					
		ELECTRIC GENERATION		OIL & GAS PRO-DUCTION, OIL REFINING	PIPELINE FUEL	LEASE AND PLANT FUEL	TOTAL
		BOM Minus AGA Other	AGA Other				
NEW ENGLAND:							
CONNECTICUT	5338.0	13.0	0.0	0.0	14.0	0.0	27.0
MAINE	13.0	0.0	0.0	0.0	0.0	0.0	0.0
MASSACHUSETTS	5426.0	3293.0	361.0	0.0	242.0	0.0	3896.0
NEW HAMPSHIRE	69.0	0.0	0.0	0.0	0.0	0.0	0.0
RHODE ISLAND	982.0	76.0	0.0	0.0	6.0	0.0	82.0
VERMONT	0.0	322.0	0.0	0.0	0.0	0.0	322.0
MID ATLANTIC:							
NEW JERSEY	3215.0	11973.0	271.0	2465.0	176.0	0.0	14885.0
NEW YORK	19793.0	35337.0	302.0	517.0	898.0	0.0	37054.0
PENNSYLVANIA	7862.0	2732.0	0.0	3384.0	8459.0	1335.0	15910.0
EAST NORTH CENTRAL:							
ILLINOIS	3753.0	30591.0	1148.0	11197.0	5321.0	93.0	48350.0
INDIANA	3149.0	7582.0	74.0	6749.0	3306.0	0.0	17711.0
MICHIGAN	5166.0	25042.0	3609.0	1467.0	4739.0	519.0	35376.0
OHIO	15537.0	4452.0	3926.0	5687.0	3525.0	1403.0	18993.0
WISCONSIN	1388.0	6772.0	5833.0	419.0	1646.0	0.0	14670.0
WEST NORTH CENTRAL:							
IOWA	1248.0	16667.0	6428.0	34.0	4054.0	0.0	27183.0
KANSAS	2069.0	67598.0	321.0	9569.0	18661.0	7356.0	103505.0
MINNESOTA	14391.0	20615.0	0.0	5123.0	1979.0	0.0	27717.0
MISSOURI	6946.0	18006.0	3668.0	4213.0	2376.0	0.0	28263.0
NEBRASKA	3306.0	15159.0	3022.0	618.0	2336.0	182.0	21317.0
NORTH DAKOTA	0.0	22.0	110.0	3151.0	65.0	2286.0	5634.0
SOUTH DAKOTA	832.0	1283.0	0.0	54.0	3.0	0.0	1340.0
SOUTH ATLANTIC:							
DELAWARE	0.0	1176.0	0.0	680.0	0.0	0.0	1856.0
DISTRICT OF COLUMBIA	2418.0	0.0	0.0	16.0	126.0	0.0	142.0
FLORIDA	2020.0	60131.0	8468.0	366.0	981.0	444.0	70390.0
GEORGIA	3978.0	13759.0	0.0	132.0	1798.0	0.0	15689.0
MARYLAND	2885.0	2592.0	0.0	633.0	738.0	32.0	3995.0
NORTH CAROLINA	4295.0	5772.0	2668.0	83.0	1366.0	0.0	9889.0
SOUTH CAROLINA	662.0	11936.0	0.0	117.0	718.0	0.0	12771.0
VIRGINIA	5297.0	1170.0	712.0	3071.0	2217.0	59.0	7229.0
WEST VIRGINIA	2058.0	175.0	0.0	218.0	5636.0	1249.0	7278.0
EAST SOUTH CENTRAL:							
ALABAMA	519.0	968.0	0.0	463.0	4385.0	406.0	6222.0
KENTUCKY	4895.0	3655.0	0.0	2019.0	8794.0	353.0	14821.0
MISSISSIPPI	2552.0	30103.0	2126.0	1545.0	13255.0	1748.0	48777.0
TENNESSEE	2457.0	0.0	5119.0	40.0	5838.0	389.0	11386.0
WEST SOUTH CENTRAL:							
ARKANSAS	345.0	22394.0	325.0	1265.0	3143.0	1085.0	28212.0
LOUISIANA	10341.0	104702.0	67.0	29209.0	18293.0	65550.0	217821.0
OKLAHOMA	2129.0	35379.0	29347.0	7605.0	4722.0	15904.0	92957.0
TEXAS	15022.0	369155.0	958.0	59100.0	19727.0	148391.0	597331.0
ROCKY MOUNTAIN:							
ARIZONA	2332.0	32563.0	0.0	31.0	4791.0	8.0	37393.0
COLORADO	528.0	20614.0	0.0	1049.0	623.0	753.0	23039.0
IDAHO	1179.0	0.0	0.0	22.0	1322.0	0.0	1344.0
MONTANA	1273.0	201.0	217.0	3500.0	174.0	954.0	5046.0
NEVADA	3431.0	18860.0	0.0	44.0	0.0	0.0	18904.0
NEW MEXICO	5153.0	21650.0	173.0	558.0	6571.0	7076.0	36028.0
UTAH	10.0	1208.0	0.0	2850.0	237.0	354.0	4649.0
WYOMING	433.0	860.0	0.0	2454.0	1070.0	3451.0	7835.0
FAR WEST:							
ALASKA	3218.0	5666.0	0.0	411.0	2451.0	3597.0	12125.0
CALIFORNIA	3702.0	119704.0	122612.0	51641.0	6586.0	22065.0	322608.0
HAWAII	0.0	0.0	0.0	0.0	0.0	0.0	0.0
OREGON	243.0	184.0	0.0	3108.0	2769.0	0.0	6061.0
WASHINGTON	94.0	0.0	0.0	13679.0	2078.0	0.0	15757.0

Table F.3.19

Expenditures On Natural Gas In Thousand Dollars, 1972, By Region

Other (Muncipal-Institutional) And Energy Production Use Of Natural Gas

REGION	OTHER: MUNICIPAL-INSTITUTIONAL (State & Local Govt.)	ELECTRIC GENERATION		ENERGY PRODUCTION			TOTAL
		BOM Minus AGA Other	AGA Other	OIL & GAS PRODUCTION, OIL REFINING	PIPELINE FUEL	LEASE AND PLANT FUEL	
NEW ENGLAND	11828.00	3704.00	361.00	0.00	262.00	0.00	4327.00
MID ATLANTIC	30870.00	50042.00	573.00	6366.00	9533.00	1335.00	67849.00
EAST NORTH CENTRAL	28993.00	74439.00	14590.00	25519.00	18537.00	2015.00	135100.00
WEST NORTH CENTRAL	28792.00	139350.00	13549.00	22762.00	29474.00	9824.00	214959.00
SOUTH ATLANTIC	23613.00	96711.00	11848.00	5316.00	13580.00	1784.00	129239.00
EAST SOUTH CENTRAL	10423.00	34726.00	7245.00	4067.00	32272.00	2896.00	81206.00
WEST SOUTH CENTRAL	27837.00	531630.00	30697.00	97179.00	45885.00	230930.00	936321.00
ROCKY MOUNTAIN	14339.00	95956.00	390.00	10508.00	14788.00	12596.00	134238.00
FAR WEST	7257.00	125554.00	122612.00	68839.00	13884.00	25662.00	356551.00
TOTAL	183952.00	1152112.00	201865.00	240556.00	178215.00	287042.00	2059790.01

Appendix G

Electricity

Quantities

The primary source of data on electricity use was the Edison Electric Institute, <u>Statistical Yearbook</u> [10]. Usage in kilowatt-hours was converted to BTU by multiplying by 3,412, the BTU per kilowatt-hour (from [7], 2).

Residential and commercial use for 1970 were compared to the corresponding values in the Arthur D. Little report [20] and generally good correspondence was found. There seemed to be some shifting between residential and commercial categories within regions as between the two sets of data, but the magnitude of the shifts was both small (about 10 percent of a given category) and without consistent pattern. Hence, the primary source data were accepted without further question.

In trillion BTU, the 1970 U.S. comparative values were:

	Little	Edison Electric
Residential	1523	1528
Commercial	1061	1067
Total	2584	2595

By major region, these values were listed, again in trillion BTU:

	North-east	North Central	South	West	U.S.
Little					
Residential	255	379	583	306	1523
Commercial	232	276	347	206	1061
Total	487	655	930	512	2584
Edison Electric					
Residential	275	393	591	269	1528
Commercial	215	257	343	252	1067
Total	490	650	934	521	2595

Comparing the two series, it can be seen that corresponding regional
totals are approximately equal; corresponding residential and commercial
values show good agreement for the south; the Little residential figure
is below the Edison Electric figure in the northeast and north central
regions and above it in the west, the difference ranging from about 5 to
10 percent of the residential amount; and the differences in the commercial
figures for those regions are about the same magnitude, in the reverse
direction.

Besides residential and commercial use, The Statistical Yearbook [10]
lists industrial use, street and highway lighting, use by other public
authorities, railroads and railway use, and interdepartmental use. A
combined category of "Commercial and Industrial" use is disaggregated into
"Small light and power" and "Large light and power," which basically corresponds
to commercial and industrial use, respectively, on the basis of definitions in
([11], 16) and usage in the Little study. Table G.1.1 shows the 1972 state

consumption by these categories of use, and Table G.1.2 shows the corresponding regional values. In those tables, use in kilowatt-hours has been converted to BTU by employing the scale factor of 3,412 BTU per kilowatt-hour.

Commercial use was now distributed among office, retail, school, hospital and other categories on the basis of data on commercial use in Little ([20], Appendix A.b). The following distribution of 1970 commercial use of electricity by region was derived, and assumed applicable to 1972:

	Northeast	North Central	South	West
Office	.1164	.0978	.1153	.1311
Retail	.2974	.3044	.2594	.2864
School	.1422	.1594	.1816	.1553
Hospital	.1724	.1522	.1383	.1165
Other	.2716	.2862	.3054	.3107
Total	1.0000	1.0000	1.0000	1.0000

Then, the factors accounting for relative concentration of office, school and hospital activity by state (which were developed earlier and described in the work on petroleum heating fuels) were used to scale the corresponding regional distribution components to yield state estimates. These scaled fractions were added to the fractions for the retail and the all other categories, assumed invariant within each region, and the sum was divided into the individual components, so the revised fractions would sum to 1.0. Table G.1.3 shows the resulting fraction of commercial use estimated to hold for each category within each state. Table G.1.4 shows the product of each fraction and total commercial use, yielding consumption by each

category of use. A check was carried out by obtaining regional totals

and comparing the distribution by category to the initial distribution,

with excellent results - next to no change occurred in the distribution.

The fractions allocating each category of use between sectors were then

applied, and the sectoral components derived were added to yield commer-

cial use by sector, as shown in Table G.1.5. The state data of tables

G.1.4 and G.1.5 are aggregated to regional totals in Table G.1.6.

The functional category of use by "other public authorities" was

distributed between levels of government by the expedient of assuming that

the respective share for each level of government equalled its share of

total government office employment, so that the factors used in distributing

government office employment were applied again here. Obviously, the

assumption is open to question, but perhaps it is fairly reasonable to

expect some correlation between government office employment and other

use by public authorities. Table G.1.7 exhibits the estimated fraction of

use and corresponding consumption by level of government for the category

of other use by public authorities.

The remaining set of tables showing quantities consumed develop

sectoral totals. Table G.1.8 shows the components classified under the

heading of business use; here, interdepartmental use is treated as an

energy production use. Table G.1.9 brings all of the government categories

together; besides commercial use and use by public authorities, the category

of street and highway lighting appears and, for simplicity, is classified

as solely a state and local government use. Table G.1.10 exhibits the

totals obtained by sector by state. Table G.1.11 shows the regional totals

for the preceding three tables, exhibiting the business and government
components, and then, the sectoral totals by region.

Prices

Prices were obtained directly by dividing given data on expenditures
by the corresponding data listed for consumption. Table G.2.1 lists prices
in dollars per million BTU by state, and Table G.2.2 shows the corresponding
weighted average prices by region, which were obtained by dividing regional
expenditures by regional quantities.

Considerable variation in price occurs between states, with lowest
prices occurring in regions with major federal power projects; thus the
Pacific Northwest and the TVA area states have electricity prices that are
roughly half the country average.

Expenditures

The work with expenditures was carried out in parallel with the work
on consumption, given the direct availability of both series. Tables G.3.1
and G.3.2 show the given expenditures by function for states and regions,
respectively. Given the estimated distribution of commercial use in BTU
by sector in Table G.1.5, the corresponding expenditure data were obtained
by multiplying quantities consumed by the corresponding commercial prices
shown in Table G.2.1, assuming that price did not vary between categories
of commercial use. The estimated state commercial expenditures appear in
Table G.3.3, and the corresponding regional totals in Table G.3.4. State
expenditures by categories of business and government use respectively
appear in Tables G.3.5 and G.3.6, while the state distribution of use by
sector appears in Table G.3.7. Finally, the regional totals for this set
of three tables are presented in Table G.3.8, exhibiting the development of
sectoral totals from the functional categories.

Table G.1.1

Consumption Of Electricity In Billion BTU, 1972, By State

Use By Function

REGION AND STATE	RESIDENTIAL USE	COMMERCIAL USE	INDUSTRIAL USE	STREET & HIGHWAY LIGHTING	OTHER PUBLIC AUTHOR-ITIES	RAILROADS AND RAILWAYS	INTER-DEPART-MENTAL	ALL USE
NEW ENGLAND:								
CONNECTICUT	24501.6	17739.0	18864.9	713.1	54.6	0.0	23.9	61897.1
MAINE	7223.2	4094.4	7257.3	184.3	590.3	0.0	3.4	19352.9
MASSACHUSETTS	35583.8	29493.3	27927.2	996.3	938.3	75.1	580.0	95594.0
NEW HAMPSHIRE	6421.4	2535.1	5988.1	119.4	102.4	0.0	0.0	15166.3
RHODE ISLAND	5384.1	4619.8	4705.2	194.5	429.9	0.0	0.0	15333.5
VERMONT	4868.9	1944.8	2811.5	61.4	549.3	0.0	44.4	10280.4
MID ATLANTIC:								
NEW JERSEY	46191.7	41431.9	55250.5	1313.6	88.7	20.5	92.1	144389.0
NEW YORK	93782.2	92936.1	95529.2	3783.9	24477.7	9215.8	163.8	319888.7
PENNSYLVANIA	85143.0	52514.1	142198.5	1685.5	1098.7	2982.1	266.1	285888.1
EAST NORTH CENTRAL:								
ILLINOIS	77404.6	66834.3	99555.3	2439.6	13648.0	1334.1	47.8	261263.7
INDIANA	45499.0	25020.2	70116.6	1050.9	505.0	68.2	109.2	142369.1
MICHIGAN	65012.3	40626.7	97470.6	1798.1	3524.6	0.0	266.1	208698.4
OHIO	81656.0	56468.6	181648.1	2176.9	8270.7	146.7	191.1	330558.0
WISCONSIN	36607.4	19284.6	36525.5	1480.8	1255.6	0.0	218.4	95372.2
WEST NORTH CENTRAL:								
IOWA	23911.3	12989.5	20495.9	665.3	887.1	0.0	88.7	59037.8
KANSAS	18281.5	16596.0	16896.2	494.7	539.1	0.0	170.6	52978.1
MINNESOTA	29831.1	12798.4	33526.3	726.8	1559.3	0.0	184.3	78626.1
MISSOURI	37429.6	22672.7	36395.8	890.5	1825.4	47.8	133.1	99395.0
NEBRASKA	13088.4	11205.0	6462.3	354.8	1279.5	20.5	116.0	32526.6
NORTH DAKOTA	5104.4	3220.9	1446.7	143.3	440.2	0.0	17.1	10372.5
SOUTH DAKOTA	5674.2	2995.7	1272.7	126.2	494.7	0.0	34.1	10597.7
SOUTH ATLANTIC:								
DELAWARE	4422.0	3657.7	9423.9	102.4	27.3	0.0	23.9	17657.1
DISTRICT OF COLUMBIA	5032.7	11123.1	525.4	235.4	30.7	105.8	37.5	17090.7
FLORIDA	98194.0	51098.1	40967.9	1436.4	9768.6	0.0	194.5	201659.4
GEORGIA	47532.6	32704.0	44366.2	750.6	392.4	0.0	51.2	125797.0
MARYLAND	26217.8	21591.1	39927.2	706.3	47.8	539.1	194.5	89223.8
NORTH CAROLINA	54544.2	32560.7	62026.8	655.1	3374.5	0.0	576.6	153737.9
SOUTH CAROLINA	26828.6	15964.8	45516.1	273.0	1955.1	0.0	20.5	90557.9
VIRGINIA	43219.8	28688.1	28418.5	566.4	12266.1	0.0	163.8	113322.8
WEST VIRGINIA	13245.4	8277.5	31762.3	174.0	81.9	0.0	3.4	53544.5
EAST SOUTH CENTRAL:								
ALABAMA	42141.6	17947.1	72651.7	692.6	68.2	0.0	296.8	133798.2
KENTUCKY	30868.4	15466.6	83385.9	566.4	3746.4	0.0	102.4	134136.0
MISSISSIPPI	21952.8	11993.2	21461.5	464.0	846.2	0.0	13.6	56731.3
TENNESSEE	70191.7	12184.2	114438.5	1835.7	61.4	0.0	126.2	198837.7
WEST SOUTH CENTRAL:								
ARKANSAS	16896.2	10863.8	22447.6	283.2	1071.4	40.9	17.1	51620.2
LOUISIANA	37095.3	21676.4	52036.4	757.5	3466.6	3.4	4091.0	119126.6
OKLAHOMA	23959.1	17493.3	19172.0	453.8	3835.1	0.0	34.1	64947.4
TEXAS	119781.7	93939.2	158907.1	2248.5	9604.8	0.0	474.3	384955.5
ROCKY MOUNTAIN:								
ARIZONA	18670.5	17633.2	18025.6	331.0	1845.9	0.0	890.5	57396.7
COLORADO	13856.1	17114.6	8789.3	412.9	2289.5	0.0	177.4	42639.8
IDAHO	9662.8	9045.2	18639.8	122.8	655.1	0.0	13.6	38139.3
MONTANA	5834.9	4520.9	20089.9	180.8	385.6	276.4	71.6	31359.7
NEVADA	8038.7	7796.4	5889.1	167.2	409.4	0.0	218.4	22519.2
NEW MEXICO	5268.1	7758.9	5333.0	160.4	1364.8	0.0	109.2	19994.3
UTAH	6687.5	6046.1	6704.6	191.1	1323.9	0.0	20.5	20973.6
WYOMING	2299.7	4043.2	5387.5	61.4	160.4	0.0	23.9	11976.1
FAR WEST:								
ALASKA	1917.5	1658.2	416.3	51.2	307.1	3.4	10.2	4363.9
CALIFORNIA	136019.4	159538.3	150459.0	4858.7	21557.0	221.8	3592.8	476247.0
HAWAII	5083.9	2859.3	7359.7	225.2	0.0	0.0	0.0	15528.0
OREGON	37235.2	21782.2	36603.9	508.4	573.2	0.0	88.7	96791.6
WASHINGTON	63678.2	29616.2	88384.5	730.2	3278.9	47.8	3156.1	188891.7

Table G.1.2

Consumption Of Electricity In Billion BTU, 1972, By Region

Use By Function

REGION	RESIDENTIAL USE	COMMERCIAL USE	INDUSTRIAL USE	STREET & HIGHWAY LIGHTING	OTHER PUBLIC AUTHOR- ITIES	RAILROADS AND RAILWAYS	INTER- DEPART- MENTAL	ALL USE
NEW ENGLAND	83983.00	60426.40	67554.20	2269.00	2664.80	75.10	651.70	217624.20
MID ATLANTIC	225116.90	186882.10	292978.20	6783.00	25665.10	12218.40	522.00	750165.80
EAST NORTH CENTRAL	306179.30	208234.40	485316.10	8946.30	27203.90	1549.00	832.60	1038261.41
WEST NORTH CENTRAL	133320.50	82478.20	116495.90	3401.60	7025.30	68.30	743.90	343533.80
SOUTH ATLANTIC	319237.10	205665.10	302934.30	4899.60	27944.40	644.90	1265.90	862591.10
EAST SOUTH CENTRAL	165154.50	57591.10	291937.60	3558.70	4722.20	0.00	539.00	523503.20
WEST SOUTH CENTRAL	197732.30	143972.70	252563.10	3743.00	17977.90	44.30	4616.50	620649.70
ROCKY MOUNTAIN	70317.90	73958.50	88858.80	1627.60	8434.60	276.40	1525.10	244998.70
FAR WEST	243934.20	215454.20	283223.40	6373.70	25716.20	273.00	6847.80	781822.20
TOTAL	1744975.73	1234662.74	2181861.59	41602.50	147354.40	15149.40	17544.50	5383150.13

Table G.1.3

Consumption Of Electricity, Scale Factors, 1972, By State

Fraction Of Total Commercial Use Consumed In Office, Retail, School, Hospital and Other Use

REGION AND STATE	FRACTION OF COMMERCIAL USE				
	OFFICE USE	RETAIL USE	SCHOOL USE	HOSPITAL USE	OTHER USE
NEW ENGLAND:					
CONNECTICUT	0.1195	0.3022	0.1506	0.1517	0.2760
MAINE	0.0869	0.3142	0.1580	0.1538	0.2871
MASSACHUSETTS	0.1134	0.2825	0.1427	0.2035	0.2579
NEW HAMPSHIRE	0.0993	0.3151	0.1562	0.1416	0.2878
RHODE ISLAND	0.1004	0.3002	0.1456	0.1796	0.2742
VERMONT	0.0951	0.2980	0.1595	0.1753	0.2721
MID ATLANTIC:					
NEW JERSEY	0.1261	0.3128	0.1455	0.1300	0.2856
NEW YORK	0.1250	0.2890	0.1367	0.1855	0.2638
PENNSYLVANIA	0.1024	0.3059	0.1436	0.1688`	0.2793
EAST NORTH CENTRAL:					
ILLINOIS	0.1072	0.2971	0.1533	0.1630	0.2794
INDIANA	0.0921	0.3147	0.1612	0.1362	0.2958
MICHIGAN	0.0959	0.3032	0.1708	0.1448	0.2853
OHIO	0.0988	0.3078	0.1591	0.1448	0.2895
WISCONSIN	0.0879	0.3046	0.1670	0.1540	0.2865
WEST NORTH CENTRAL:					
IOWA	0.0874	0.3142	0.1595	0.1437	0.2952
KANSAS	0.0988	0.3052	0.1472	0.1618	0.2870
MINNESOTA	0.1007	0.2997	0.1619	0.1559	0.2818
MISSOURI	0.1003	0.3018	0.1488	0.1653	0.2838
NEBRASKA	0.0907	0.3048	0.1553	0.1625	0.2867
NORTH DAKOTA	0.0830	0.3119	0.1593	0.1526	0.2932
SOUTH DAKOTA	0.0795	0.3087	0.1631	0.1585	0.2902
SOUTH ATLANTIC:					
DELAWARE	0.1282	0.2426	0.1930	0.1504	0.2858
DISTRICT OF COLUMBIA	0.1781	0.1891	0.1542	0.2559	0.2227
FLORIDA	0.1244	0.2610	0.1691	0.1383	0.3072
GEORGIA	0.1115	0.2626	0.1769	0.1399	0.3091
MARYLAND	0.1351	0.2466	0.1852	0.1429	0.2902
NORTH CAROLINA	0.0977	0.2708	0.1818	0.1308	0.3189
SOUTH CAROLINA	0.0941	0.2724	0.1917	0.1211	0.3207
VIRGINIA	0.1206	0.2593	0.1801	0.1348	0.3052
WEST VIRGINIA	0.0990	0.2610	0.1784	0.1544	0.3072
EAST SOUTH CENTRAL:					
ALABAMA	0.1012	0.2650	0.1819	0.1399	0.3120
KENTUCKY	0.1021	0.2683	0.1811	0.1329	0.3156
MISSISSIPPI	0.0915	0.2671	0.2012	0.1257	0.3145
TENNESSEE	0.1033	0.2615	0.1740	0.1534	0.3078
WEST SOUTH CENTRAL:					
ARKANSAS	0.0945	0.2741	0.1820	0.1268	0.3226
LOUISIANA	0.1106	0.2556	0.1938	0.1392	0.3008
OKLAHOMA	0.1204	0.2580	0.1836	0.1343	0.3037
TEXAS	0.1213	0.2566	0.1869	0.1331	0.3021
ROCKY MOUNTAIN:					
ARIZONA	0.1217	0.2827	0.1631	0.1258	0.3067
COLORADO	0.1290	0.2781	0.1542	0.1370	0.3017
IDAHO	0.1020	0.3042	0.1613	0.1026	0.3299
MONTANA	0.1057	0.2951	0.1592	0.1199	0.3201
NEVADA	0.1281	0.2975	0.1503	0.1016	0.3225
NEW MEXICO	0.1281	0.2848	0.1627	0.1155	0.3089
UTAH	0.1308	0.2874	0.1771	0.0928	0.3119
WYOMING	0.1123	0.2907	0.1593	0.1223	0.3154
FAR WEST:					
ALASKA	0.1461	0.2879	0.1569	0.0967	0.3124
CALIFORNIA	0.1361	0.2843	0.1533	0.1181	0.3082
HAWAII	0.1312	0.2877	0.1537	0.1154	0.3120
OREGON	0.1181	0.3002	0.1510	0.1050	0.3257
WASHINGTON	0.1275	0.2917	0.1557	0.1087	0.3164

Table G.1.4

Consumption Of Electricity In Billion BTU, 1972, By State

Commercial Use By Consumption Categories

REGION AND STATE	OFFICE USE	RETAIL USE	SCHOOL USE	HOSPITAL USE	OTHER USE	TOTAL COMMERCIAL USE
NEW ENGLAND:						
CONNECTICUT	2119.8	5360.7	2671.5	2691.0	4896.0	17739.0
MAINE	355.8	1286.5	646.9	629.7	1175.5	4094.4
MASSACHUSETTS	3344.5	8331.9	4208.7	6001.9	7606.3	29493.3
NEW HAMPSHIRE	251.7	798.8	396.0	359.0	729.6	2535.1
RHODE ISLAND	463.8	1386.9	672.6	829.7	1266.7	4619.8
VERMONT	185.0	579.6	310.2	340.9	529.2	1944.8
MID ATLANTIC:						
NEW JERSEY	5224.6	12959.9	6028.3	5386.1	11833.0	41431.9
NEW YORK	11617.0	26858.5	12704.4	17239.6	24516.5	92936.1
PENNSYLVANIA	5377.4	16064.1	7541.0	8864.4	14667.2	52514.1
EAST NORTH CENTRAL:						
ILLINOIS	7164.6	19856.5	10245.7	10894.0	18673.5	66834.3
INDIANA	2304.4	7873.9	4033.3	3407.8	7401.0	25020.2
MICHIGAN	3896.1	12318.0	6939.0	5882.7	11590.8	40626.7
OHIO	5579.1	17381.0	8984.2	8176.7	16347.7	56468.6
WISCONSIN	1695.1	5874.1	3220.5	2969.8	5525.0	19284.6
WEST NORTH CENTRAL:						
IOWA	1135.3	4081.3	2071.8	1866.6	3834.5	12989.5
KANSAS	1639.7	5065.1	2442.9	2685.2	4763.1	16596.0
MINNESOTA	1288.8	3835.7	2072.1	1995.3	3606.6	12798.4
MISSOURI	2274.1	6842.6	3373.7	3747.8	6434.5	22672.7
NEBRASKA	1016.3	3415.3	1740.1	1820.8	3212.5	11205.0
NORTH DAKOTA	267.3	1004.6	513.1	491.5	944.4	3220.9
SOUTH DAKOTA	238.2	924.8	488.6	474.8	869.4	2995.7
SOUTH ATLANTIC:						
DELAWARE	468.9	887.4	705.9	550.1	1045.4	3657.7
DISTRICT OF COLUMBIA	1981.0	2103.4	1715.2	2846.4	2477.1	11123.1
FLORIDA	6356.6	13336.6	8640.7	7066.9	15697.3	51098.1
GEORGIA	3646.5	8588.1	5785.3	4575.3	10108.8	32704.0
MARYLAND	2917.0	5324.4	3998.7	3085.4	6265.7	21591.1
NORTH CAROLINA	3181.2	8817.4	5919.5	4258.9	10383.6	32560.7
SOUTH CAROLINA	1502.3	4348.8	3060.5	1933.3	5119.9	15964.8
VIRGINIA	3459.8	7438.8	5166.7	3867.2	8755.6	28688.1
WEST VIRGINIA	819.5	2160.4	1476.7	1278.0	2542.8	8277.5
EAST SOUTH CENTRAL:						
ALABAMA	1816.2	4756.0	3264.6	2510.8	5599.5	17947.1
KENTUCKY	1579.1	4149.7	2801.0	2055.5	4881.3	15466.6
MISSISSIPPI	1097.4	3203.4	2413.0	1507.5	3771.9	11993.2
TENNESSEE	1258.6	3186.2	2120.1	1869.1	3750.3	12184.2
WEST SOUTH CENTRAL:						
ARKANSAS	1026.6	2977.8	1977.2	1377.5	3504.7	10863.8
LOUISIANA	2397.4	5540.5	4200.9	3017.4	6520.3	21676.4
OKLAHOMA	2106.2	4513.3	3211.8	2349.4	5312.7	17493.3
TEXAS	11394.8	24104.8	17557.2	12503.3	28379.0	93939.2
ROCKY MOUNTAIN:						
ARIZONA	2146.0	4984.9	2876.0	2218.3	5408.1	17633.2
COLORADO	2207.8	4759.6	2639.1	2344.7	5163.5	17114.6
IDAHO	922.6	2751.5	1459.0	928.0	2984.0	9045.2
MONTANA	477.9	1334.1	719.7	542.1	1447.1	4520.9
NEVADA	998.7	2319.4	1171.8	792.1	2514.3	7796.4
NEW MEXICO	993.9	2209.7	1262.4	896.2	2396.7	7758.9
UTAH	790.8	1737.6	1070.8	561.1	1885.8	6046.1
WYOMING	454.1	1175.4	644.1	494.5	1275.2	4043.2
FAR WEST:						
ALASKA	242.3	477.4	260.2	160.3	518.0	1658.2
CALIFORNIA	21713.2	45356.7	24457.2	18841.5	49169.7	159538.3
HAWAII	375.1	822.6	439.5	330.0	892.1	2859.3
OREGON	2572.5	6539.0	3289.1	2287.1	7094.5	21782.2
WASHINGTON	3776.1	8639.0	4611.2	3219.3	9370.6	29616.2

Table G.1.5

Consumption Of Electricity In Billion BTU, 1972, By State

Commercial Use By Sector

REGION AND STATE	BUSINESS USE	FEDERAL GOVERNMENT USE	STATE & LOCAL GOVERNMENT USE	TOTAL COMMERCIAL USE
NEW ENGLAND:				
CONNECTICUT	14559.6	221.5	2958.0	17739.0
MAINE	3260.3	83.9	750.2	4094.4
MASSACHUSETTS	23663.6	523.9	5305.9	29493.3
NEW HAMPSHIRE	2075.7	27.3	432.2	2535.1
RHODE ISLAND	3776.2	90.9	752.7	4619.8
VERMONT	1576.7	33.1	335.0	1944.8
MID ATLANTIC:				
NEW JERSEY	33800.4	531.9	7099.6	41431.9
NEW YORK	73524.0	1432.1	17980.0	92936.1
PENNSYLVANIA	43204.8	868.0	8441.4	52514.1
EAST NORTH CENTRAL:				
ILLINOIS	53977.8	1078.5	11778.0	66834.3
INDIANA	19514.5	300.1	5205.5	25020.2
MICHIGAN	31649.3	405.0	8572.4	40626.7
OHIO	45319.8	760.1	10388.7	56468.6
WISCONSIN	15322.2	284.7	3677.7	19284.6
WEST NORTH CENTRAL:				
IOWA	10175.6	207.2	2606.7	12989.5
KANSAS	12904.9	343.1	3348.1	16596.0
MINNESOTA	9995.3	207.6	2595.5	12798.4
MISSOURI	17793.6	448.7	4430.4	22672.7
NEBRASKA	8758.5	207.7	2238.8	11205.0
NORTH DAKOTA	2555.4	56.6	608.9	3220.9
SOUTH DAKOTA	2313.0	99.6	583.1	2995.7
SOUTH ATLANTIC:				
DELAWARE	2819.7	57.3	780.6	3657.7
DISTRICT OF COLUMBIA	8356.9	1099.3	1667.0	11123.1
FLORIDA	38440.3	889.8	11768.0	51098.1
GEORGIA	22962.8	682.7	9058.5	32704.0
MARYLAND	16265.0	639.5	4686.6	21591.1
NORTH CAROLINA	24872.8	457.3	7230.5	32560.7
SOUTH CAROLINA	11724.0	251.7	3989.1	15964.8
VIRGINIA	21493.3	943.5	6251.3	28688.1
WEST VIRGINIA	6229.3	166.4	1881.8	8277.5
EAST SOUTH CENTRAL:				
ALABAMA	13179.7	457.8	4309.7	17947.1
KENTUCKY	11949.6	276.1	3240.9	15466.6
MISSISSIPPI	8662.4	216.2	3114.6	11993.2
TENNESSEE	9045.1	254.3	2884.8	12184.2
WEST SOUTH CENTRAL:				
ARKANSAS	8108.3	261.3	2494.2	10863.8
LOUISIANA	16215.0	311.5	5149.9	21676.4
OKLAHOMA	12839.9	446.8	4206.6	17493.3
TEXAS	70314.9	1827.3	21797.0	93939.2
ROCKY MOUNTAIN:				
ARIZONA	13828.9	368.7	3435.4	17633.0
COLORADO	13443.3	379.2	3292.1	17114.6
IDAHO	7101.6	120.7	1822.9	9045.2
MONTANA	3539.3	78.3	903.3	4520.9
NEVADA	5923.0	147.2	1726.3	7796.4
NEW MEXICO	5857.2	233.1	1668.5	7758.9
UTAH	4553.4	276.1	1216.6	6046.1
WYOMING	2886.0	135.4	1021.9	4043.2
FAR WEST:				
ALASKA	1280.2	66.1	312.0	1658.2
CALIFORNIA	125847.7	3066.5	30624.1	159538.3
HAWAII	2259.7	77.1	522.5	2859.3
OREGON	17455.6	378.9	3947.6	21782.2
WASHINGTON	23441.3	567.9	5607.0	29616.2

Table G.1.6

Consumption Of Electricity In Billion BTU, 1972, By Region

Commercial Use By Consumption Categories And By Sector

Use By Consumption Categories

REGION	OFFICE	RETAIL USE	SCHOOL USE	HOSPITAL USE	OTHER USE	COMMERCIAL USE
NEW ENGLAND	6720.60	17744.40	8905.90	10852.20	16203.30	60426.40
MID ATLANTIC	22219.00	55882.50	26273.70	31490.10	51016.70	186882.10
EAST NORTH CENTRAL	20639.30	63303.50	33422.70	31331.00	59538.00	208234.40
WEST NORTH CENTRAL	7859.70	25169.40	12702.30	13082.00	23665.00	82478.20
SOUTH ATLANTIC	24332.80	53005.30	36469.20	29461.50	62396.20	205665.10
EAST SOUTH CENTRAL	5751.30	15295.30	10598.70	7942.90	18003.00	57591.10
WEST SOUTH CENTRAL	16925.00	37136.40	26947.10	19247.60	43716.70	143972.70
ROCKY MOUNTAIN	8991.80	21272.20	11842.90	8777.00	23074.70	73958.50
FAR WEST	28679.20	61834.70	33057.20	24838.20	67044.90	215454.20
TOTAL	142118.70	350643.70	200219.70	177022.50	364658.51	1234662.74

Use By Sector

REGION	BUSINESS USE	FEDERAL GOVERNMENT USE	STATE & LOCAL GOVERNMENT USE	TOTAL COMMERCIAL USE
NEW ENGLAND	48912.10	980.60	10534.00	60426.40
MID ATLANTIC	150529.20	2832.00	33521.00	186882.10
EAST NORTH CENTRAL	165783.60	2828.40	39622.30	208234.40
WEST NORTH CENTRAL	64496.30	1570.50	16411.50	82478.20
SOUTH ATLANTIC	153164.10	5187.50	47313.40	205665.10
EAST SOUTH CENTRAL	42836.80	1204.40	13550.00	57591.10
WEST SOUTH CENTRAL	107478.10	2846.90	33647.70	143972.70
ROCKY MOUNTAIN	57132.70	1738.70	15087.00	73958.30
FAR WEST	170284.50	4156.50	41013.20	215454.20
TOTAL	960617.40	23345.50	250700.10	1234662.53

Table G.1.7

Consumption Of Electricity In Billion BTU, 1972, By State

Distribution Of Other Public Authorities Use By Levels Of Government

REGION AND STATE	OTHER PUBLIC AUTHORITIES USE			
	FRACTION OF TOTAL		ESTIMATED CONSUMPTION	
	Federal Govt.	State & Local Govt.	Federal Govt.	State & Local Govt.
NEW ENGLAND:				
CONNECTICUT	0.2522	0.7478	13.8	40.8
MAINE	0.4229	0.5771	249.6	340.7
MASSACHUSETTS	0.3315	0.6685	311.0	627.3
NEW HAMPSHIRE	0.3034	0.6966	31.1	71.3
RHODE ISLAND	0.4736	0.5264	203.6	226.3
VERMONT	0.2796	0.7204	153.6	395.7
MID ATLANTIC:				
NEW JERSEY	0.3315	0.6685	29.4	59.3
NEW YORK	0.2557	0.7443	6258.9	18218.8
PENNSYLVANIA	0.3870	0.6130	425.2	673.5
EAST NORTH CENTRAL:				
ILLINOIS	0.3318	0.6682	4528.4	9119.6
INDIANA	0.3571	0.6429	180.3	324.7
MICHIGAN	0.2701	0.7299	952.0	2572.6
OHIO	0.3500	0.6500	2894.7	5376.0
WISCONSIN	0.2162	0.7838	271.5	984.1
WEST NORTH CENTRAL:				
IOWA	0.2630	0.7370	233.3	653.8
KANSAS	0.3316	0.6684	178.8	360.3
MINNESOTA	0.2908	0.7092	453.4	1105.9
MISSOURI	0.4586	0.5414	837.1	988.3
NEBRASKA	0.3147	0.6853	402.7	876.8
NORTH DAKOTA	0.4328	0.5672	190.5	249.7
SOUTH DAKOTA	0.3873	0.6127	191.6	303.1
SOUTH ATLANTIC:				
DELAWARE	0.2673	0.7327	7.3	20.0
DISTRICT OF COLUMBIA	0.8420	0.1580	25.8	4.9
FLORIDA	0.3139	0.6861	3066.4	6702.2
GEORGIA	0.4803	0.5197	188.5	203.9
MARYLAND	0.6280	0.3720	30.0	17.8
NORTH CAROLINA	0.3171	0.6829	1070.1	2304.4
SOUTH CAROLINA	0.4183	0.5817	817.8	1137.3
VIRGINIA	0.6381	0.3619	7827.0	4439.1
WEST VIRGINIA	0.2849	0.7151	23.3	58.6
EAST SOUTH CENTRAL:				
ALABAMA	0.4876	0.5124	33.3	34.9
KENTUCKY	0.4198	0.5802	1572.7	2173.7
MISSISSIPPI	0.3516	0.6484	297.5	548.7
TENNESSEE	0.3730	0.6270	22.9	38.5
WEST SOUTH CENTRAL:				
ARKANSAS	0.3318	0.6682	355.5	715.9
LOUISIANA	0.2745	0.7255	951.6	2515.0
OKLAHOMA	0.5449	0.4551	2089.7	1745.4
TEXAS	0.4357	0.5643	4184.8	5420.0
ROCKY MOUNTAIN:				
ARIZONA	0.4375	0.5625	807.6	1038.3
COLORADO	0.5024	0.4976	1150.2	1139.3
IDAHO	0.3677	0.6323	240.9	414.2
MONTANA	0.4241	0.5759	163.5	222.1
NEVADA	0.3716	0.6284	152.1	257.3
NEW MEXICO	0.5509	0.4491	751.9	612.9
UTAH	0.6807	0.3193	901.2	422.7
WYOMING	0.3700	0.6300	59.3	101.1
FAR WEST:				
ALASKA	0.5823	0.4177	178.8	128.3
CALIFORNIA	0.3962	0.6038	8540.9	13016.1
HAWAII	0.5914	0.4086	0.0	0.0
OREGON	0.3561	0.6439	204.1	369.1
WASHINGTON	0.3988	0.6012	1307.6	1971.3

Table G.1.8

Consumption Of Electricity In Billion BTU, 1972, By State

Distribution Of Business Use, By Function

REGION & STATE	COMMERCIAL USE	INDUSTRIAL USE	RAILROADS AND RAILWAYS	INTER- DEPARTMENTAL	TOTAL BUSINESS USE
NEW ENGLAND:					
CONNECTICUT	14559.6	18864.9	0.0	23.9	33448.4
MAINE	3260.3	7257.3	0.0	3.4	10521.0
MASSACHUSETTS	23663.6	27927.2	75.1	580.0	52245.9
NEW HAMPSHIRE	2075.7	5988.1	0.0	0.0	8063.8
RHODE ISLAND	3776.2	4705.2	0.0	0.0	8481.3
VERMONT	1576.7	2811.5	0.0	44.4	4432.5
MID ATLANTIC:					
NEW JERSEY	33800.4	55250.5	20.5	92.1	89163.5
NEW YORK	73524.0	95529.2	9215.8	163.8	178432.8
PENNSYLVANIA	43204.8	142198.5	2982.1	266.1	188651.5
EAST NORTH CENTRAL:					
ILLINOIS	53977.8	99555.3	1334.1	47.8	154915.0
INDIANA	19514.5	70116.6	68.2	109.2	89808.5
MICHIGAN	31649.3	97470.6	0.0	266.1	129386.0
OHIO	45319.8	181648.1	146.7	191.1	227305.7
WISCONSIN	15322.2	36525.5	0.0	218.4	52066.0
WEST NORTH CENTRAL:					
IOWA	10175.6	20495.9	0.0	88.7	30760.2
KANSAS	12904.9	16896.2	0.0	170.6	29971.7
MINNESOTA	9995.3	33526.3	0.0	184.3	43705.9
MISSOURI	17793.6	36395.8	47.8	133.1	54370.2
NEBRASKA	8758.5	6462.3	20.5	116.0	15357.3
NORTH DAKOTA	2555.4	1446.7	0.0	17.1	4019.1
SOUTH DAKOTA	2313.0	1272.7	0.0	34.1	3619.8
SOUTH ATLANTIC:					
DELAWARE	2819.7	9423.9	0.0	23.9	12267.5
DISTRICT OF COLUMBIA	8356.9	525.4	105.8	37.5	9025.7
FLORIDA	38440.3	40967.9	0.0	194.5	79602.7
GEORGIA	22962.8	44366.2	0.0	51.2	67380.2
MARYLAND	16265.0	39927.2	539.1	194.5	56925.8
NORTH CAROLINA	24872.8	62026.8	0.0	576.6	87476.2
SOUTH CAROLINA	11724.0	45516.1	0.0	20.5	57260.6
VIRGINIA	21493.3	28418.5	0.0	·163.8	50075.6
WEST VIRGINIA	6229.3	31762.3	0.0	3.4	37995.0
EAST SOUTH CENTRAL:					
ALABAMA	13179.7	72651.7	0.0	296.8	86128.3
KENTUCKY	11949.6	83385.9	0.0	102.4	95437.8
MISSISSIPPI	8662.4	21461.5	0.0	13.6	30137.5
TENNESSEE	9045.1	114438.5	0.0	126.2	123609.8
WEST SOUTH CENTRAL:					
ARKANSAS	8108.3	22447.6	40.9	17.1	30613.9
LOUISIANA	16215.0	52036.4	3.4	4091.0	72345.8
OKLAHOMA	12839.9	19172.0	0.0	34.1	32046.1
TEXAS	70314.9	158907.1	0.0	474.3	229696.2
ROCKY MOUNTAIN:					
ARIZONA	13828.9	18025.6	0.0	890.5	32745.0
COLORADO	13443.3	8789.3	0.0	177.4	22410.0
IDAHO	7101.6	18639.8	0.0	13.6	25755.0
MONTANA	3539.3	20089.9	276.4	71.6	23977.2
NEVADA	5923.0	5889.1	0.0	218.4	12030.5
NEW MEXICO	5857.2	5333.0	0.0	109.2	11299.3
UTAH	4553.4	6704.6	0.0	20.5	11278.4
WYOMING	2886.0	5387.5	0.0	23.9	8297.4
FAR WEST:					
ALASKA	1280.2	416.3	3.4	10.2	1710.1
CALIFORNIA	125847.7	150459.0	221.8	3592.8	280121.3
HAWAII	2259.7	7359.7	0.0	0.0	9619.4
OREGON	17455.6	36603.9	0.0	88.7	54148.3
WASHINGTON	23441.3	88384.5	47.8	3156.1	115029.6

Table G.1.9

Consumption Of Electricity In Billion BTU, 1972, By State

Distribution Of Government Use, By Function

REGION AND STATE	FEDERAL GOVERNMENT			STATE AND LOCAL GOVERNMENT				ALL GOVERNMENT
	Commercial Use	Other Public Authorities	Total Federal Government	Commercial Use	Other Public Authorities	Street And Highway Lighting	Total State & Local Govt.	Total Use
NEW ENGLAND:								
CONNECTICUT	221.5	13.8	235.3	2958.0	40.8	713.1	3711.9	3947.2
MAINE	83.9	249.6	333.5	750.2	340.7	184.3	1275.1	1608.6
MASSACHUSETTS	523.9	311.0	834.9	5305.9	627.3	996.3	6929.5	7764.4
NEW HAMPSHIRE	27.3	31.1	58.4	432.2	71.3	119.4	622.9	681.3
RHODE ISLAND	90.9	203.6	294.5	752.7	226.3	194.5	1173.5	1468.0
VERMONT	33.1	153.6	186.7	335.0	395.7	61.4	792.1	978.8
MID ATLANTIC:								
NEW JERSEY	531.9	29.4	561.3	7099.6	59.3	1313.6	8472.5	9033.8
NEW YORK	1432.1	6258.9	7691.0	17980.0	18218.8	3783.9	39982.7	47673.7
PENNSYLVANIA	868.0	425.2	1293.2	8441.4	673.5	1685.5	10800.4	12093.6
EAST NORTH CENTRAL:								
ILLINOIS	1078.5	4528.4	5606.9	11778.0	9119.6	2439.6	23337.2	28944.1
INDIANA	300.1	180.3	480.4	5205.5	324.7	1050.9	6581.1	7061.5
MICHIGAN	405.0	952.0	1357.0	8572.4	2572.6	1798.1	12943.1	14300.1
OHIO	760.1	2894.7	3654.8	10388.7	5376.0	2176.9	17941.6	21596.4
WISCONSIN	284.7	271.5	556.2	3677.7	984.1	1480.8	6142.6	6698.8
WEST NORTH CENTRAL:								
IOWA	207.2	233.3	440.5	2606.7	653.8	665.3	3925.8	4366.3
KANSAS	343.1	178.8	521.9	3348.1	360.3	494.7	4203.1	4725.0
MINNESOTA	207.6	453.4	661.0	2595.5	1105.9	726.8	4428.2	5089.2
MISSOURI	448.7	837.1	1285.8	4430.4	988.3	890.5	6309.2	7595.0
NEBRASKA	207.7	402.7	610.4	2238.8	876.8	354.8	3470.4	4080.8
NORTH DAKOTA	56.6	190.5	247.1	608.9	249.7	143.3	1001.9	1249.0
SOUTH DAKOTA	99.6	191.6	291.2	583.1	303.1	126.2	1012.4	1303.6
SOUTH ATLANTIC:								
DELAWARE	57.3	7.3	64.6	780.6	20.0	102.4	903.0	967.6
DISTRICT OF COLUMBIA	1099.3	25.8	1125.1	1667.0	4.9	235.4	1907.3	3032.4
FLORIDA	889.8	3066.4	3956.2	11768.0	6702.2	1436.4	19906.6	23862.8
GEORGIA	682.7	188.5	871.2	9058.5	203.9	750.6	10013.0	10884.2
MARYLAND	639.5	30.0	669.5	4686.6	17.8	706.3	5410.7	6080.2
NORTH CAROLINA	457.3	1070.1	1527.4	7230.5	2304.4	655.1	10190.0	11717.4
SOUTH CAROLINA	251.7	817.8	1069.5	3989.1	1137.3	273.0	5399.4	6468.9
VIRGINIA	943.5	7827.0	8770.5	6251.3	4439.1	566.4	11256.8	20027.3
WEST VIRGINIA	166.4	23.3	189.7	1881.8	58.6	174.0	2114.4	2304.1
EAST SOUTH CENTRAL:								
ALABAMA	457.8	33.3	491.1	4309.7	34.9	692.6	5037.2	5528.3
KENTUCKY	276.1	1572.7	1848.8	3240.9	2173.7	566.4	5981.0	7829.8
MISSISSIPPI	216.2	297.5	513.7	3114.6	548.7	464.0	4127.3	4641.0
TENNESSEE	254.3	22.9	277.2	2884.8	38.5	1835.7	4759.0	5036.2
WEST SOUTH CENTRAL:								
ARKANSAS	261.3	355.5	616.8	2494.2	715.9	283.2	3493.3	4110.1
LOUISIANA	311.5	951.6	1263.1	5149.9	2515.0	757.5	8422.4	9685.5
OKLAHOMA	446.8	2089.7	2536.5	4206.6	1745.4	453.8	6405.8	8942.3
TEXAS	1827.3	4184.8	6012.1	21797.0	5420.0	2248.5	29465.5	35477.6
ROCKY MOUNTAIN:								
ARIZONA	368.7	807.6	1176.3	3435.4	1038.3	331.0	4804.7	5981.0
COLORADO	379.2	1150.2	1529.4	3292.1	1139.3	412.9	4844.2	6373.6
IDAHO	120.7	240.9	361.6	1822.9	414.2	122.8	2359.9	2721.5
MONTANA	78.3	163.5	241.8	903.3	222.1	180.8	1306.2	1548.0
NEVADA	147.2	152.1	299.3	1726.3	257.3	167.2	2150.8	2450.1
NEW MEXICO	233.1	751.9	985.0	1668.5	612.9	160.4	2441.8	3426.8
UTAH	276.1	901.2	1177.3	1216.6	422.7	191.1	1830.4	3007.7
WYOMING	135.4	59.3	194.7	1021.9	101.1	61.4	1184.4	1379.1
FAR WEST:								
ALASKA	66.1	178.8	244.9	312.0	128.3	51.2	491.5	736.4
CALIFORNIA	3066.5	8540.9	11607.4	30624.1	13016.1	4858.7	48498.9	60106.3
HAWAII	77.1	0.0	77.1	522.5	0.0	225.2	747.7	824.8
OREGON	378.9	204.1	583.0	3947.6	369.1	508.4	4825.1	5408.1
WASHINGTON	567.9	1307.6	1875.5	5607.0	1971.3	730.2	8308.5	10184.0

Table G.1.10

Consumption Of Electricity In Billion BTU, 1972, By State

Use By Sector

REGION & STATE	HOUSEHOLD USE	BUSINESS USE	FEDERAL GOVERNMENT USE	STATE & LOCAL GOVERNMENT USE	TOTAL USE
NEW ENGLAND:					
CONNECTICUT	24501.6	33448.4	235.3	3711.9	61897.1
MAINE	7223.2	10521.0	333.5	1275.1	19352.9
MASSACHUSETTS	35583.8	52245.9	834.9	6929.5	95594.0
NEW HAMPSHIRE	6421.4	8063.8	58.4	622.9	15166.3
RHODE ISLAND	5384.1	8481.3	294.5	1173.5	15333.5
VERMONT	4868.9	4432.5	186.7	792.1	10280.4
MID ATLANTIC:					
NEW JERSEY	46191.7	89163.5	561.3	8472.5	144389.0
NEW YORK	93782.2	178432.8	7691.0	39982.7	319888.7
PENNSYLVANIA	85143.0	188651.5	1293.2	10800.4	285888.1
EAST NORTH CENTRAL:					
ILLINOIS	77404.6	154915.0	5606.9	23337.2	261263.7
INDIANA	45499.0	89808.5	480.4	6581.1	142369.1
MICHIGAN	65012.3	129386.0	1357.0	12943.1	208698.4
OHIO	81656.0	227305.7	3654.8	17941.6	330558.0
WISCONSIN	36607.4	52066.0	556.2	6142.6	95372.2
WEST NORTH CENTRAL:					
IOWA	23911.3	30760.2	440.5	3925.8	59037.8
KANSAS	18281.5	29971.7	521.9	4203.1	52978.1
MINNESOTA	29831.1	43705.9	661.0	4428.2	78626.1
MISSOURI	37429.6	54370.2	1285.8	6309.2	99395.0
NEBRASKA	13088.4	15357.3	610.4	3470.4	32526.6
NORTH DAKOTA	5104.4	4019.1	247.1	1001.9	10372.5
SOUTH DAKOTA	5674.2	3619.8	291.2	1012.4	10597.7
SOUTH ATLANTIC:					
DELAWARE	4422.0	12267.5	64.6	903.0	17657.1
DISTRICT OF COLUMBIA	5032.7	9025.7	1125.1	1907.3	17090.7
FLORIDA	98194.0	79602.7	3956.2	19906.6	201659.4
GEORGIA	47532.6	67380.2	871.2	10013.0	125797.0
MARYLAND	26217.8	56925.8	669.5	5410.7	89223.8
NORTH CAROLINA	54544.2	87476.2	1527.4	10190.0	153737.9
SOUTH CAROLINA	26828.6	57260.6	1069.5	5399.4	90557.9
VIRGINIA	43219.8	50075.6	8770.5	11256.8	113322.8
WEST VIRGINIA	13245.4	37995.0	189.7	2114.4	53544.5
EAST SOUTH CENTRAL:					
ALABAMA	42141.6	86128.3	491.1	5037.2	133798.2
KENTUCKY	30868.4	95437.8	1848.8	5981.0	134136.0
MISSISSIPPI	21952.8	30137.5	513.7	4127.3	56731.3
TENNESSEE	70191.7	123609.8	277.2	4759.0	198837.7
WEST SOUTH CENTRAL:					
ARKANSAS	16896.2	30613.9	616.8	3493.3	51620.2
LOUISIANA	37095.3	72345.8	1263.1	8422.4	119126.6
OKLAHOMA	23959.1	32046.1	2536.5	6405.8	64947.4
TEXAS	119781.7	229696.2	6012.1	29465.5	384955.5
ROCKY MOUNTAIN:					
ARIZONA	18670.5	32745.0	1176.3	4804.7	57396.7
COLORADO	13856.1	22410.0	1529.4	4844.2	42639.8
IDAHO	9662.8	25755.0	361.6	2359.9	38139.3
MONTANA	5834.5	23977.2	241.8	1306.2	31359.7
NEVADA	8038.7	12030.5	299.3	2150.8	22519.2
NEW MEXICO	5268.1	11299.3	985.0	2441.8	19994.3
UTAH	6687.5	11278.4	1177.3	1830.4	20973.6
WYOMING	2299.7	8297.4	194.7	1184.4	11976.1
FAR WEST:					
ALASKA	1917.5	1710.1	244.9	491.5	4363.9
CALIFORNIA	136019.4	280121.3	11607.4	48498.9	476247.0
HAWAII	5083.9	9619.4	77.1	747.7	15528.0
OREGON	37235.2	54148.3	583.0	4825.1	96791.6
WASHINGTON	63678.2	115029.6	1875.5	8308.5	188891.7

Table G.1.11

Consumption Of Electricity In Billion BTU, 1972, By Region

Distribution Of Use, By Sector And Function

DISTRIBUTION OF BUSINESS USE, BY FUNCTION

REGION	COMMERCIAL USE	INDUSTRIAL USE	RAILWAYS AND RAILROADS	INTER-DEPARTMENTAL	TOTAL BUSINESS USE
NEW ENGLAND	48912.10	67554.20	75.10	651.70	117192.90
MID ATLANTIC	150529.20	292978.20	12218.40	522.00	456247.80
EAST NORTH CENTRAL	165783.60	485316.10	1549.00	832.60	653481.20
WEST NORTH CENTRAL	64496.30	116495.90	68.30	743.90	181804.20
SOUTH ATLANTIC	153164.10	302934.30	644.90	1265.90	458009.31
EAST SOUTH CENTRAL	42836.80	291937.60	0.00	539.00	335313.40
WEST SOUTH CENTRAL	107478.10	252563.10	44.30	4616.50	364702.00
ROCKY MOUNTAIN	57132.70	88858.80	276.40	1525.10	147792.80
FAR WEST	170284.50	283223.40	273.00	6847.80	460628.70
TOTAL	960617.40	2181861.59	15149.40	17544.50	3175172.36

DISTRIBUTION OF GOVERNMENT USE, BY FUNCTION

REGION	FEDERAL GOVERNMENT			STATE AND LOCAL GOVERNMENT				ALL GOVERNMENT
	Commercial Use	Other Public Authorities	Total Federal Government	Commercial Use	Other Public Authorities	Street & Highway Lighting	State & Local Government	Total Use
NEW ENGLAND	980.60	962.70	1943.30	10534.00	1702.10	2269.00	14505.00	16448.30
MID ATLANTIC	2832.00	6713.50	9545.50	33521.00	18951.60	6783.00	59255.60	68801.10
EAST NORTH CENTRAL	2828.40	8826.90	11655.30	39622.30	18377.00	8946.30	66945.60	78600.90
WEST NORTH CENTRAL	1570.50	2487.40	4057.90	16411.50	4537.90	3401.60	24351.00	28408.90
SOUTH ATLANTIC	5187.50	13056.20	18243.70	47313.40	14888.20	4899.60	67101.20	85344.90
EAST SOUTH CENTRAL	1204.40	1926.40	3130.80	13550.00	2795.80	3558.70	19904.50	23035.30
WEST SOUTH CENTRAL	2846.90	7581.60	10428.50	33647.70	10396.30	3743.00	47787.00	58215.50
ROCKY MOUNTAIN	1738.70	4226.70	5965.40	15087.00	4207.90	1627.60	20922.40	26887.80
FAR WEST	4156.50	10231.40	14387.90	41013.20	15484.80	6373.70	62871.70	77259.60
TOTAL	23345.50	56012.80	79358.30	250700.10	91341.60	41602.50	383644.00	463002.31

USE BY SECTOR

REGION	HOUSEHOLD USE	BUSINESS USE	FEDERAL GOVERNMENT USE	STATE & LOCAL GOVERNMENT USE	TOTAL USE
NEW ENGLAND	83983.00	117192.90	1943.30	14505.00	217624.20
MID ATLANTIC	225116.90	456247.80	9545.50	59255.60	750165.80
EAST NORTH CENTRAL	306179.30	653481.20	11655.30	66945.60	1038261.41
WEST NORTH CENTRAL	133320.50	181804.20	4057.90	24351.00	343533.80
SOUTH ATLANTIC	319237.10	458009.31	18243.70	67101.20	862591.10
EAST SOUTH CENTRAL	165154.50	335313.40	3130.80	19904.50	523503.20
WEST SOUTH CENTRAL	197732.30	364702.00	10428.50	47787.00	620649.70
ROCKY MOUNTAIN	70317.90	147792.80	5965.40	20922.40	244998.70
FAR WEST	243934.20	460628.70	14387.90	62871.70	781822.20
TOTAL	1744975.73	3175172.36	79358.30	383644.00	5383150.13

Table G.2.1

Electricity Prices In Dollars Per Million BTU, 1972, By State

Use By Function

REGION AND STATE	RESI- DENTIAL USE	COMMER- CIAL USE	INDUS- TRIAL USE	STREET & HIGHWAY LIGHTING	OTHER PUBLIC AUTHOR- ITIES	RAILROADS AND RAILWAYS	INTER- DEPART- MENTAL	ALL USE
NEW ENGLAND:								
CONNECTICUT	8.183	7.564	5.106	15.590	5.605	0.000[a]	4.522	7.149
MAINE	7.994	7.883	3.702	19.805	4.500	0.000	2.345	6.366
MASSACHUSETTS	9.044	8.152	5.514	18.173	6.134	8.659	6.334	7.787
NEW HAMPSHIRE	7.824	8.341	4.017	19.461	7.376	0.000	0.000	6.496
RHODE ISLAND	9.136	7.503	5.492	16.865	5.164	0.000	6.015	7.513
VERMONT	7.174	7.323	4.886	17.292	5.876	0.000	2.818	6.549
MID ATLANTIC:								
NEW JERSEY	8.982	8.166	4.709	18.524	7.214	5.666	7.305	7.197
NEW YORK	9.546	9.539	3.929	13.324	6.443	6.300	3.242	7.577
PENNSYLVANIA	8.116	7.196	4.171	15.574	8.010	4.869	4.186	5.991
EAST NORTH CENTRAL:								
ILLINOIS	8.330	7.484	3.830	6.865	4.768	4.678	5.108	6.180
INDIANA	6.681	6.602	3.672	11.209	4.917	5.627	4.048	5.210
MICHIGAN	7.096	7.144	3.943	14.066	4.908	0.000	4.873	5.653
OHIO	6.968	6.489	2.964	11.888	4.488	4.614	4.224	4.653
WISCONSIN	7.008	7.579	4.362	8.718	4.247	0.000	4.524	6.095
WEST NORTH CENTRAL:								
IOWA	7.845	7.795	3.969	10.112	5.657	3.473	4.892	6.476
KANSAS	6.940	5.866	3.372	8.210	4.005	0.000	3.710	5.438
MINNESOTA	7.463	8.032	4.313	10.404	4.393	0.000	3.935	6.170
MISSOURI	7.644	7.143	4.132	9.024	4.212	3.287	5.178	6.188
NEBRASKA	6.571	5.261	3.551	6.070	3.517	3.712	3.327	5.381
NORTH DAKOTA	7.616	6.816	5.935	8.632	3.015	0.000	3.751	6.945
SOUTH DAKOTA	7.452	7.715	4.828	10.345	2.308	0.000	4.631	6.996
SOUTH ATLANTIC:								
DELAWARE	8.897	7.488	4.419	13.921	6.997	0.000	6.322	6.238
DISTRICT OF COLUMBIA	7.332	6.615	5.458	16.124	7.034	4.576	2.505	6.901
FLORIDA	6.208	6.620	3.765	9.863	4.205	0.000	5.713	5.745
GEORGIA	5.598	6.103	3.173	9.439	4.358	0.000	5.041	4.893
MARYLAND	7.732	7.410	4.153	16.124	5.401	4.645	2.509	6.088
NORTH CAROLINA	5.967	5.126	2.950	8.956	3.228	0.000	3.715	4.516
SOUTH CAROLINA	6.177	5.275	2.569	10.023	2.936	0.000	5.617	4.146
VIRGINIA	6.168	5.783	3.407	9.691	2.804	0.000	3.187	5.027
WEST VIRGINIA	6.786	6.203	3.083	11.453	4.738	0.000	2.931	4.511
EAST SOUTH CENTRAL:								
ALABAMA	4.887	5.515	2.523	8.911	4.968	0.000	2.395	3.703
KENTUCKY	5.165	4.823	2.347	8.943	4.215	0.000	3.566	3.362
MISSISSIPPI	5.760	6.086	3.195	8.047	3.870	0.000	6.008	4.849
TENNESSEE	3.702	4.841	2.314	7.910	3.598	0.000	2.281	3.011
WEST SOUTH CENTRAL:								
ARKANSAS	6.726	6.304	2.966	7.963	3.985	3.688	3.634	4.949
LOUISIANA	6.389	5.920	2.454	7.530	3.595	4.103	0.214	4.299
OKLAHOMA	7.040	5.835	2.962	5.646	3.379	0.000	4.836	5.284
TEXAS	6.080	5.184	2.459	6.273	3.296	0.000	11.015	4.304
ROCKY MOUNTAIN:								
ARIZONA	6.974	6.066	3.537	10.007	4.675	0.000	3.007	5.498
COLORADO	7.626	6.075	3.518	10.665	3.305	0.000	2.108	5.931
IDAHO	4.691	4.250	1.815	9.460	0.876	0.000	2.638	3.130
MONTANA	6.321	5.817	1.303	9.157	1.652	1.563	3.489	2.944
NEVADA	4.571	5.132	2.286	6.932	2.420	3.044	0.925	4.111
NEW MEXICO	7.989	6.172	3.380	9.572	3.617	0.000	4.314	5.749
UTAH	6.571	5.726	3.869	11.017	2.691	0.000	4.787	5.258
WYOMING	7.278	5.378	3.071	10.714	2.925	0.000	3.015	4.695
FAR WEST:								
ALASKA	9.765	10.395	5.398	11.762	6.640	12.016	6.643	9.386
CALIFORNIA	6.855	5.721	3.123	10.320	1.913	3.044	1.988	5.069
HAWAII	8.324	10.271	4.765	7.758	0.000	0.000	0.000	6.987
OREGON	3.745	3.841	1.349	8.513	2.011	0.000	2.153	2.874
WASHINGTON	3.083	3.519	0.941	6.475	2.308	2.261	0.173	2.100

[a] Zero indicates no use.

Table G.2.2

Electricity Prices In Dollars Per Million BTU, 1972, By Region

Use By Function

REGION	RESIDENTIAL USE	COMMERCIAL USE	INDUSTRIAL USE	STREET & HIGHWAY LIGHTING	OTHER PUBLIC AUTHORITIES	RAILROADS AND RAILWAYS	INTERDEPARTMENTAL	ALL USE
NEW ENGLAND	8.507	7.893	5.045	17.441	5.601	8.667	6.014	7.312
MID ATLANTIC	8.889	8.576	4.194	14.888	6.512	5.950	4.441	6.900
EAST NORTH CENTRAL	7.302	7.050	3.546	10.351	4.679	4.714	4.541	5.447
WEST NORTH CENTRAL	7.429	6.879	4.043	9.137	4.084	3.425	4.152	6.089
SOUTH ATLANTIC	6.272	6.161	3.301	11.014	3.395	4.633	3.866	5.131
EAST SOUTH CENTRAL	4.551	5.306	2.440	8.286	4.157	0.000[a]	2.683	3.477
WEST SOUTH CENTRAL	6.309	5.459	2.541	6.579	3.412	3.750	1.371	4.459
ROCKY MOUNTAIN	6.507	5.678	2.573	9.828	3.245	1.577	2.742	4.711
FAR WEST	5.449	5.325	2.259	9.657	2.022	3.018	1.160	4.142
UNITED STATES	6.722	6.513	3.201	10.813	4.026	5.630	2.160	5.187

[a] Zero indicates no use.

Table G.3.1

Expenditures On Electricity In Thousand Dollars, 1972, By State

Use By Function

REGION & STATE	RESIDENTIAL USE	COMMERCIAL USE	INDUSTRIAL USE	STREET & HIGHWAY LIGHTING	OTHER PUBLIC AUTHOR- ITIES	RAILROADS AND RAILWAYS	INTER- DEPART- MENTAL	ALL USE
NEW ENGLAND:								
CONNECTICUT	200493.0	134173.0	96323.0	11117.0	306.0	0.0	108.0	442520.0
MAINE	57742.0	32275.0	26863.0	3649.0	2656.0	0.0	8.0	123193.0
MASSACHUSETTS	321822.0	240423.0	153982.0	18106.0	5756.0	650.0	3674.0	744413.0
NEW HAMPSHIRE	50243.0	21146.0	24052.0	2324.0	755.0	0.0	0.0	98520.0
RHODE ISLAND	49191.0	34662.0	25842.0	3280.0	2220.0	0.0	5.0	115200.0
VERMONT	34928.0	14243.0	13738.0	1062.0	3228.0	0.0	125.0	67324.0
MID ATLANTIC:								
NEW JERSEY	414898.0	338321.0	260192.0	24333.0	640.0	116.0	673.0	1039173.0
NEW YORK	895238.0	886547.0	375370.0	50417.0	157704.0	58058.0	531.0	2423865.0
PENNSYLVANIA	691009.0	377894.0	593158.0	26250.0	8800.0	14521.0	1114.0	1712746.0
EAST NORTH CENTRAL:								
ILLINOIS	644784.0	500164.0	381307.0	16748.0	65067.0	6241.0	244.0	1614555.0
INDIANA	303987.0	165173.0	257475.0	11779.0	2483.0	384.0	442.0	741723.0
MICHIGAN	461322.0	290220.0	384309.0	25292.0	17300.0	0.0	1297.0	1179740.0
OHIO	568960.0	366439.0	538326.0	25879.0	37122.0	677.0	807.0	1538210.0
WISCONSIN	256539.0	146154.0	159334.0	12909.0	5333.0	0.0	988.0	581257.0
WEST NORTH CENTRAL:								
IOWA	187588.0	101258.0	81351.0	6728.0	5018.0	4.0	434.0	382381.0
KANSAS	126880.0	97356.0	56979.0	4062.0	2159.0	0.0	633.0	288069.0
MINNESOTA	222627.0	102798.0	144584.0	7561.0	6850.0	0.0	725.0	485145.0
MISSOURI	286116.0	161956.0	150375.0	8036.0	7689.0	157.0	689.0	615018.0
NEBRASKA	86002.0	58952.0	22949.0	2154.0	4500.0	76.0	386.0	175019.0
NORTH DAKOTA	38874.0	21954.0	8586.0	1237.0	1327.0	0.0	64.0	72042.0
SOUTH DAKOTA	42281.0	23111.0	6144.0	1306.0	1142.0	0.0	158.0	74142.0
SOUTH ATLANTIC:								
DELAWARE	39343.0	27388.0	41641.0	1425.0	191.0	0.0	151.0	110139.0
DISTRICT OF COLUMBIA	36902.0	73577.0	2868.0	3796.0	216.0	484.0	94.0	117937.0
FLORIDA	609606.0	338288.0	154250.0	14168.0	41080.0	0.0	1111.0	1158503.0
GEORGIA	266073.0	199586.0	140794.0	7085.0	1710.0	0.0	258.0	615506.0
MARYLAND	202722.0	160001.0	165817.0	11388.0	258.0	2504.0	488.0	543178.0
NORTH CAROLINA	325452.0	166893.0	182968.0	5867.0	10894.0	0.0	2142.0	694216.0
SOUTH CAROLINA	165716.0	84220.0	116941.0	2736.0	5741.0	0.0	115.0	375469.0
VIRGINIA	266591.0	165904.0	96824.0	5489.0	34389.0	0.0	522.0	569719.0
WEST VIRGINIA	89888.0	51342.0	97933.0	1993.0	388.0	0.0	10.0	241554.0
EAST SOUTH CENTRAL:								
ALABAMA	205947.0	98980.0	183268.0	6172.0	339.0	0.0	711.0	495417.0
KENTUCKY	159439.0	74601.0	195720.0	5065.0	15791.0	0.0	365.0	450981.0
MISSISSIPPI	126438.0	72996.0	68561.0	3734.0	3275.0	0.0	82.0	275086.0
TENNESSEE	259821.0	58990.0	264808.0	14520.0	221.0	0.0	288.0	598648.0
WEST SOUTH CENTRAL:								
ARKANSAS	113642.0	68488.0	66580.0	2255.0	4269.0	151.0	62.0	255447.0
LOUISIANA	236994.0	128316.0	127709.0	5704.0	12462.0	14.0	876.0	512075.0
OKLAHOMA	168668.0	102081.0	56779.0	2562.0	12957.0	0.0	165.0	343212.0
TEXAS	728228.0	487002.0	390761.0	14106.0	31661.0	0.0	5224.0	1656982.0
ROCKY MOUNTAIN:								
ARIZONA	130208.0	106969.0	63751.0	3312.0	8630.0	0.0	2678.0	315548.0
COLORADO	105670.0	103965.0	30919.0	4403.0	7566.0	0.0	374.0	252897.0
IDAHO	45328.0	38441.0	33832.0	1162.0	574.0	0.0	36.0	119373.0
MONTANA	36880.0	26297.0	26179.0	1656.0	637.0	432.0	250.0	92331.0
NEVADA	36746.0	40015.0	13463.0	1159.0	991.0	7.0	202.0	92583.0
NEW MEXICO	42085.0	47886.0	18028.0	1535.0	4937.0	0.0	471.0	114942.0
UTAH	43944.0	34621.0	25943.0	2105.0	3563.0	0.0	98.0	110274.0
WYOMING	16738.0	21745.0	16544.0	658.0	469.0	0.0	72.0	56226.0
FAR WEST:								
ALASKA	18725.0	17237.0	2247.0	602.0	2039.0	41.0	68.0	40959.0
CALIFORNIA	932442.0	912759.0	469880.0	50142.0	41243.0	675.0	7142.0	2414283.0
HAWAII	42317.0	29367.0	35066.0	1747.0	0.0	0.0	0.0	108497.0
OREGON	139451.0	83660.0	49371.0	4328.0	1153.0	0.0	191.0	278154.0
WASHINGTON	196305.0	104218.0	83207.0	4728.0	7568.0	108.0	545.0	396679.0

Table G.3.2

Expenditures On Electricity In Thousand Dollars, 1972, By State

Use By Function

REGION	RESIDENTIAL USE	COMMERCIAL USE	INDUSTRIAL USE	STREET & HIGHWAY LIGHTING	OTHER PUBLIC AUTHORITIES	RAILROADS AND RAILWAYS	INTERDEPARTMENTAL	ALL USE
NEW ENGLAND	714419.00	476922.00	340800.00	39538.00	14921.00	650.00	3920.00	1591170.00
MID ATLANTIC	2001145.00	1602762.01	1228720.00	101000.00	167144.00	72695.00	2318.00	5175784.01
EAST NORTH CENTRAL	2235592.01	1468150.00	1720751.00	92607.00	127305.00	7302.00	3778.00	5655485.02
WEST NORTH CENTRAL	990368.00	567385.00	470968.00	31084.00	28685.00	237.00	3089.00	2091815.99
SOUTH ATLANTIC	2002293.00	1267198.99	1000036.00	53947.00	94867.00	2988.00	4891.00	4426220.99
EAST SOUTH CENTRAL	751645.00	305567.00	712357.00	29491.00	19626.00	0.00	1446.00	1820132.01
WEST SOUTH CENTRAL	1247532.00	785887.00	641829.00	24627.00	61349.00	165.00	6327.00	2767716.01
ROCKY MOUNTAIN	457599.00	419939.00	228659.00	15990.00	27367.00	439.00	4181.00	1154174.00
FAR WEST	1329240.00	1147241.00	639771.00	61547.00	52003.00	824.00	7946.00	3238571.99
TOTAL	11729833.00	8041052.00	6983890.98	449831.00	593267.00	85300.00	37896.00	27921070.20

Table G.3.3

Expenditures On Electricity In Thousand Dollars, 1972, By State

Commercial Use By Sector

REGION AND STATE	BUSINESS USE	FEDERAL GOVERNMENT USE	STATE & LOCAL GOVERNMENT USE	TOTAL USE
NEW ENGLAND:				
CONNECTICUT	110124.5	1675.0	22373.5	134173.0
MAINE	25699.7	661.4	5913.9	32275.0
MASSACHUSETTS	192900.3	4270.4	43252.3	240423.0
NEW HAMPSHIRE	17313.8	227.4	3604.8	21146.0
RHODE ISLAND	28332.4	681.9	5647.7	34662.0
VERMONT	11547.5	242.3	2453.1	14243.0
MID ATLANTIC:				
NEW JERSEY	276004.3	4343.2	57973.5	338321.0
NEW YORK	701369.1	13660.8	171517.1	886547.0
PENNSYLVANIA	310903.6	6245.8	60744.6	377894.0
EAST NORTH CENTRAL:				
ILLINOIS	403950.3	8071.2	88142.5	500164.0
INDIANA	128827.0	1981.5	34364.6	165173.0
MICHIGAN	226089.3	2893.0	61237.7	290220.0
OHIO	294091.7	4932.3	67415.0	366439.0
WISCONSIN	116123.8	2157.7	27872.5	146154.0
WEST NORTH CENTRAL:				
IOWA	79322.4	1615.3	20320.4	101258.0
KANSAS	75703.1	2012.4	19640.5	97356.0
MINNESOTA	80283.2	1667.6	20847.2	102798.0
MISSOURI	127103.4	3205.0	31647.6	161956.0
NEBRASKA	46080.5	1092.6	11778.9	58952.0
NORTH DAKOTA	17417.6	386.0	4150.4	21954.0
SOUTH DAKOTA	17843.8	768.5	4498.7	23111.0
SOUTH ATLANTIC:				
DELAWARE	21113.3	429.4	5845.3	27388.0
DISTRICT OF COLUMBIA	55279.0	7271.5	11026.6	73577.0
FLORIDA	254488.4	5890.8	77908.8	338288.0
GEORGIA	140137.6	4166.4	55282.0	199586.0
MARYLAND	120531.6	4739.3	34730.1	160001.0
NORTH CAROLINA	127488.1	2344.1	37060.9	166893.0
SOUTH CAROLINA	61848.2	1327.9	21043.8	84220.0
VIRGINIA	124296.4	5456.2	36151.4	165904.0
WEST VIRGINIA	38638.0	1032.1	11671.8	51342.0
EAST SOUTH CENTRAL:				
ALABAMA	72687.1	2524.6	23768.3	98980.0
KENTUCKY	57637.3	1331.6	15632.1	74601.0
MISSISSIPPI	52723.3	1315.8	18956.9	72996.0
TENNESSEE	43791.9	1231.4	13966.7	58990.0
WEST SOUTH CENTRAL:				
ARKANSAS	51116.6	1647.5	15723.9	68488.0
LOUISIANA	95986.6	1843.9	30485.5	128316.0
OKLAHOMA	74926.1	2607.4	24547.5	102081.0
TEXAS	364528.3	9473.2	113000.5	487002.0
ROCKY MOUNTAIN:				
ARIZONA	83890.6	2236.6	20840.5	106967.7
COLORADO	81663.4	2303.5	19998.1	103965.0
IDAHO	30180.7	513.0	7747.2	38441.0
MONTANA	20587.3	455.6	5254.1	26297.0
NEVADA	30399.6	755.3	8860.1	40015.0
NEW MEXICO	36149.4	1438.9	10297.7	47886.0
UTAH	26073.3	1581.0	6966.7	34621.0
WYOMING	15521.1	728.0	5495.9	21745.0
FAR WEST:				
ALASKA	13307.3	686.8	3242.8	17237.0
CALIFORNIA	720006.4	17544.1	175208.5	912759.0
HAWAII	23208.7	791.6	5366.7	29367.0
OREGON	67042.7	1455.4	15161.8	83660.0
WASHINGTON	82488.9	1998.3	19730.9	104218.0

Table G.3.4

Expenditures On Electricity In Thousand Dollars, 1972, By Region

Commercial Use By Sector

REGION	BUSINESS USE	FEDERAL GOVERNMENT USE	STATE & LOCAL GOVERNMENT USE	TOTAL USE
NEW ENGLAND	385918.20	7758.40	83245.30	476922.00
MID ATLANTIC	1288277.00	24249.80	290235.20	1602762.01
EAST NORTH CENTRAL	1169082.09	20035.70	279032.30	1468150.00
WEST NORTH CENTRAL	443754.00	10747.40	112883.70	567385.00
SOUTH ATLANTIC	943820.60	32657.70	290720.70	1267198.99
EAST SOUTH CENTRAL	226839.60	6403.40	72324.00	305567.00
WEST SOUTH CENTRAL	586557.60	15572.00	183757.40	785887.00
ROCKY MOUNTAIN	324465.40	10011.90	85460.30	419937.70
FAR WEST	906054.00	22476.20	218710.70	1147241.00
TOTAL	6274768.64	149912.50	1616369.62	8041050.66

Table G.3.5

Expenditures On Electricity In Thousand Dollars, 1972, By State

Distribution Of Business Use

REGION AND STATE	COMMERCIAL USE	INDUSTRIAL USE	RAILROADS AND RAILWAYS	INTER-DEPARTMENTAL	TOTAL BUSINESS USE
NEW ENGLAND:					
CONNECTICUT	110124.5	96323.0	0.0	108.0	206555.5
MAINE	25699.7	26863.0	0.0	8.0	52570.7
MASSACHUSETTS	192900.3	153982.0	650.0	3674.0	351206.3
NEW HAMPSHIRE	17313.8	24052.0	0.0	0.0	41365.8
RHODE ISLAND	28332.4	25842.0	0.0	5.0	54179.4
VERMONT	11547.5	13738.0	0.0	125.0	25410.5
MID ATLANTIC:					
NEW JERSEY	276004.3	260192.0	116.0	673.0	536985.3
NEW YORK	701369.1	375370.0	58058.0	531.0	1135328.1
PENNSYLVANIA	310903.6	593158.0	14521.0	1114.0	919696.6
EAST NORTH CENTRAL:					
ILLINOIS	403950.3	381307.0	6241.0	244.0	791742.3
INDIANA	128827.0	257475.0	384.0	442.0	387128.0
MICHIGAN	226089.3	384309.0	0.0	1297.0	611695.3
OHIO	294091.7	538326.0	677.0	807.0	833901.7
WISCONSIN	116123.8	159334.0	0.0	988.0	276445.8
WEST NORTH CENTRAL:					
IOWA	79322.4	81351.0	4.0	434.0	161111.4
KANSAS	75703.1	56979.0	0.0	633.0	133315.1
MINNESOTA	80283.2	144584.0	0.0	725.0	225592.2
MISSOURI	127103.4	150375.0	157.0	689.0	278324.4
NEBRASKA	46080.5	22949.0	76.0	386.0	69491.5
NORTH DAKOTA	17417.6	8586.0	0.0	64.0	26067.6
SOUTH DAKOTA	17843.8	6144.0	0.0	158.0	24145.8
SOUTH ATLANTIC:					
DELAWARE	21113.3	41641.0	0.0	151.0	62905.3
DISTRICT OF COLUMBIA	55279.0	2868.0	484.0	94.0	58725.0
FLORIDA	254488.4	154250.0	0.0	1111.0	409849.4
GEORGIA	140137.6	140794.0	0.0	258.0	281189.6
MARYLAND	120531.6	165817.0	2504.0	488.0	289340.6
NORTH CAROLINA	127488.1	182968.0	0.0	2142.0	312598.1
SOUTH CAROLINA	61848.2	116941.0	0.0	115.0	178904.2
VIRGINIA	124296.4	96824.0	0.0	522.0	221642.4
WEST VIRGINIA	38638.0	97933.0	0.0	10.0	136581.0
EAST SOUTH CENTRAL:					
ALABAMA	72687.1	183268.0	0.0	711.0	256666.1
KENTUCKY	57637.3	195720.0	0.0	365.0	253722.3
MISSISSIPPI	52723.3	68561.0	0.0	82.0	121366.3
TENNESSEE	43791.9	264808.0	0.0	288.0	308887.9
WEST SOUTH CENTRAL:					
ARKANSAS	51116.6	66580.0	151.0	62.0	117909.6
LOUISIANA	95986.6	127709.0	14.0	876.0	224585.6
OKLAHOMA	74926.1	56779.0	0.0	165.0	131870.1
TEXAS	364528.3	390761.0	0.0	5224.0	760513.3
ROCKY MOUNTAIN:					
ARIZONA	83891.9	63751.0	0.0	2678.0	150320.9
COLORADO	81663.4	30919.0	0.0	374.0	112956.4
IDAHO	30180.7	33832.0	0.0	36.0	64048.7
MONTANA	20587.3	26179.0	432.0	250.0	47448.3
NEVADA	30399.6	13463.0	7.0	202.0	44071.6
NEW MEXICO	36149.4	18028.0	0.0	471.0	54648.4
UTAH	26073.3	25943.0	0.0	98.0	52114.3
WYOMING	15521.1	16544.0	0.0	72.0	32137.1
FAR WEST:					
ALASKA	13307.3	2247.0	41.0	68.0	15663.3
CALIFORNIA	720006.4	469880.0	675.0	7142.0	1197703.4
HAWAII	23208.7	35066.0	0.0	0.0	58274.7
OREGON	67042.7	49371.0	0.0	191.0	116604.7
WASHINGTON	82488.9	83207.0	108.0	545.0	166348.9

Table G.3.6

Expenditures On Electricity In Thousand Dollars, 1972, By State

Distribution Of Government Use, By Function

REGION AND STATE	FEDERAL GOVERNMENT			STATE AND LOCAL GOVERNMENT				TOTAL GOVERNMENT
	Commercial Use	Other Public Authorities	Total Federal Government	Commercial Use	Other Public Authorities	Street And Highway Lighting	Total State & Local Government	
NEW ENGLAND:								
CONNECTICUT	1675.0	77.2	1752.2	22373.5	228.8	11117.0	33719.3	35471.5
MAINE	661.4	1123.2	1784.6	5913.9	1532.8	3649.0	11095.7	12880.3
MASSACHUSETTS	4270.4	1908.1	6178.5	43252.3	3847.9	18106.0	65206.2	71384.7
NEW HAMPSHIRE	227.4	229.1	456.5	3604.8	525.9	2324.0	6454.7	6911.2
RHODE ISLAND	681.9	1051.4	1733.3	5647.7	1168.6	3280.0	10096.3	11829.6
VERMONT	242.3	902.5	1144.8	2453.1	2325.5	1062.0	5840.6	6985.4
MID ATLANTIC:								
NEW JERSEY	4343.2	212.2	4555.4	57973.5	427.8	24333.0	82734.3	87289.7
NEW YORK	13660.8	40324.9	53985.7	171517.1	117379.1	50417.0	339313.2	393298.9
PENNSYLVANIA	6245.8	3405.6	9651.4	60744.6	5394.4	26250.0	92389.0	102040.4
EAST NORTH CENTRAL:								
ILLINOIS	8071.2	21589.2	29660.4	88142.5	43477.8	16748.0	148368.3	178028.7
INDIANA	1981.5	886.7	2868.2	34364.6	1596.3	11779.0	47739.9	50608.1
MICHIGAN	2893.0	4672.7	7565.7	61237.7	12627.3	25292.0	99157.0	106722.7
OHIO	4932.3	12992.7	17925.0	67415.0	24129.3	25879.0	117423.3	135348.3
WISCONSIN	2157.7	1153.0	3310.7	27872.5	4180.0	12909.0	44961.5	48272.2
WEST NORTH CENTRAL:								
IOWA	1615.3	1319.7	2935.0	20320.4	3698.3	6728.0	30746.7	33681.7
KANSAS	2012.4	715.9	2728.3	19640.5	1443.1	4062.0	25145.6	27873.9
MINNESOTA	1667.6	1992.0	3059.6	20847.2	4858.0	7561.0	33266.2	36925.8
MISSOURI	3205.0	3526.2	6731.2	31647.6	4162.8	8036.0	43846.4	50577.6
NEBRASKA	1092.6	1416.1	2508.7	11778.9	3083.8	2154.0	17016.7	19525.4
NORTH DAKOTA	386.0	574.3	960.3	4150.4	752.7	1237.0	6140.1	7100.4
SOUTH DAKOTA	768.5	442.3	1210.8	4498.7	699.7	1306.0	6504.4	7715.2
SOUTH ATLANTIC:								
DELAWARE	429.4	51.1	480.5	5845.3	139.9	1425.0	7410.2	7890.7
DISTRICT OF COLUMBIA	7271.5	181.9	7453.4	11026.6	34.1	3796.0	14856.7	22310.1
FLORIDA	5890.8	12895.0	18785.8	77908.8	28185.0	14168.0	120261.8	139047.6
GEORGIA	4166.4	821.3	4987.7	55282.0	888.7	7085.0	63255.7	68243.4
MARYLAND	4739.3	162.0	4901.3	34730.1	96.0	11388.0	46214.1	51115.4
NORTH CAROLINA	2344.1	3454.5	5798.6	37060.9	7439.5	5867.0	50367.4	56166.0
SOUTH CAROLINA	1327.9	2401.5	3729.4	21043.8	3339.5	2736.0	27119.3	30848.7
VIRGINIA	5456.2	21943.6	27399.8	36151.4	12445.4	5489.0	54085.8	81485.6
WEST VIRGINIA	1032.1	110.5	1142.6	11671.8	277.5	1993.0	13942.3	15084.9
EAST SOUTH CENTRAL:								
ALABAMA	2524.6	165.3	2689.9	23768.3	173.7	6172.0	30114.0	32803.9
KENTUCKY	1331.6	6629.1	7960.7	15632.1	9161.9	5065.0	29859.0	37819.7
MISSISSIPPI	1315.8	1151.5	2467.3	18956.9	2123.5	3734.0	24814.4	27281.7
TENNESSEE	1231.4	82.4	1313.8	13966.7	138.6	14520.0	28625.3	29939.1
WEST SOUTH CENTRAL:								
ARKANSAS	1647.5	1416.5	3064.0	15723.9	2852.5	2255.0	20831.4	23895.4
LOUISIANA	1843.9	3420.8	5264.7	30485.5	9041.2	5704.0	45230.7	50495.4
OKLAHOMA	2607.4	7060.3	9667.7	24547.5	5896.7	2562.0	33006.2	42673.9
TEXAS	9473.2	13794.7	23267.9	113000.5	17866.3	14106.0	144972.8	168240.7
ROCKY MOUNTAIN:								
ARIZONA	2236.6	3775.6	6012.2	20840.5	4854.4	3312.0	29006.9	35019.1
COLORADO	2303.5	3801.2	6104.7	19998.1	3764.8	4403.0	28165.9	34270.6
IDAHO	513.0	211.1	724.1	7747.2	362.9	1162.0	9272.1	9996.2
MONTANA	455.6	270.2	725.8	5254.1	366.8	1656.0	7276.9	8002.7
NEVADA	755.3	368.3	1123.6	8860.1	622.7	1159.0	10641.8	11765.4
NEW MEXICO	1438.9	2719.8	4158.7	10297.7	2217.2	1535.0	14049.9	18208.6
UTAH	1581.0	2425.3	4006.3	6966.7	1137.7	2105.0	10209.4	14215.7
WYOMING	728.0	173.5	901.5	5495.9	295.5	658.0	6449.4	7350.9
FAR WEST:								
ALASKA	686.8	1187.3	1874.1	3242.8	851.7	602.0	4696.5	6570.6
CALIFORNIA	17544.1	16340.5	33884.6	175208.5	24902.5	50142.0	250253.0	284137.6
HAWAII	791.6	0.0	791.6	5366.7	0.0	1747.0	7113.7	7905.3
OREGON	1455.4	410.6	1866.0	15161.8	742.4	4328.0	20232.2	22098.2
WASHINGTON	1998.3	3018.1	5016.4	19730.9	4549.9	4728.0	29008.8	34025.2

Table G.3.7

Expenditures On Electricity In Thousand Dollars, 1972, By State

Use By Sector

REGION AND STATE	HOUSEHOLD USE	BUSINESS USE	FEDERAL GOVERNMENT USE	STATE & LOCAL GOVERNMENT USE	TOTAL USE
NEW ENGLAND:					
CONNECTICUT	200493.0	206555.5	1752.2	33719.3	442520.0
MAINE	57742.0	52570.7	1784.6	11095.7	123193.0
MASSACHUSETTS	321822.0	351206.3	6178.5	65206.2	744413.0
NEW HAMPSHIRE	50243.0	41365.8	456.5	6454.7	98520.0
RHODE ISLAND	49191.0	54179.4	1733.3	10096.3	115200.0
VERMONT	34928.0	25410.5	1144.8	5840.6	67324.0
MID ATLANTIC:					
NEW JERSEY	414898.0	536985.3	4555.4	82734.3	1039173.0
NEW YORK	895238.0	1135328.1	53985.7	339313.2	2423865.0
PENNSYLVANIA	691009.0	919696.6	9651.4	92389.0	1712746.0
EAST NORTH CENTRAL:					
ILLINOIS	644784.0	791742.3	29660.4	148368.3	1614555.0
INDIANA	303987.0	387128.0	2868.2	47739.9	741723.0
MICHIGAN	461322.0	611695.3	7565.7	99157.0	1179740.0
OHIO	568960.0	833901.7	17925.0	117423.3	1538210.0
WISCONSIN	256539.0	276445.8	3310.7	44961.5	581257.0
WEST NORTH CENTRAL:					
IOWA	187588.0	161111.4	2935.0	30746.7	382381.0
KANSAS	126880.0	133315.1	2728.3	25145.6	288069.0
MINNESOTA	222627.0	225592.2	3659.6	33266.2	485145.0
MISSOURI	286116.0	278324.4	6731.2	43846.4	615018.0
NEBRASKA	86002.0	69491.5	2508.7	17016.7	175019.0
NORTH DAKOTA	38874.0	26067.6	960.3	6140.1	72042.0
SOUTH DAKOTA	42281.0	24145.8	1210.8	6504.4	74142.0
SOUTH ATLANTIC:					
DELAWARE	39343.0	62905.3	480.5	7410.2	110139.0
DISTRICT OF COLUMBIA	36902.0	58725.0	7453.4	14856.7	117937.0
FLORIDA	609606.0	409849.4	18785.8	120261.8	1158503.0
GEORGIA	266073.0	281189.6	4987.7	63255.7	615506.0
MARYLAND	202722.0	289340.6	4901.3	46214.1	543178.0
NORTH CAROLINA	325452.0	312598.1	5798.6	50367.4	694216.0
SOUTH CAROLINA	165716.0	178904.2	3729.4	27119.3	375469.0
VIRGINIA	266591.0	221642.4	27399.8	54085.8	569719.0
WEST VIRGINIA	89888.0	136581.0	1142.6	13942.3	241554.0
EAST SOUTH CENTRAL:					
ALABAMA	205947.0	256666.1	2689.9	30114.0	495417.0
KENTUCKY	159439.0	253722.3	7960.7	29859.0	450981.0
MISSISSIPPI	126438.0	121366.3	2467.3	24814.4	275086.0
TENNESSEE	259821.0	308887.9	1313.8	28625.3	598648.0
WEST SOUTH CENTRAL:					
ARKANSAS	113642.0	117909.6	3064.0	20831.4	255447.0
LOUISIANA	236994.0	224585.6	5264.7	45230.7	512075.0
OKLAHOMA	168668.0	131870.1	9667.7	33006.2	343212.0
TEXAS	728228.0	760513.3	23267.9	144972.8	1656982.0
ROCKY MOUNTAIN:					
ARIZONA	130208.0	150320.9	6012.2	29006.9	315548.0
COLORADO	105670.0	112956.4	6104.7	28165.9	252897.0
IDAHO	45328.0	64048.7	724.1	9272.1	119373.0
MONTANA	36880.0	47448.3	725.8	7276.9	92331.0
NEVADA	36746.0	44071.6	1123.6	10641.8	92583.0
NEW MEXICO	42085.0	54648.4	4158.7	14049.9	114942.0
UTAH	43944.0	52114.3	4006.3	10209.4	110274.0
WYOMING	16738.0	32137.1	901.5	6449.4	56226.0
FAR WEST:					
ALASKA	18725.0	15663.3	1874.1	4696.5	40959.0
CALIFORNIA	932442.0	1197703.4	33884.6	250253.0	2414283.0
HAWAII	42317.0	58274.7	791.6	7113.7	108497.0
OREGON	139451.0	116604.7	1866.0	20232.2	278154.0
WASHINGTON	196305.0	166348.9	5016.4	29008.8	396679.0

Table G.3.8

Expenditures On Electricity In Thousand Dollars, 1972, By Region

Distribution Of Use, By Sector And Function

DISTRIBUTION OF BUSINESS USE BY FUNCTION

REGION	COMMERCIAL USE	INDUSTRIAL USE	RAILROADS AND RAILWAYS	INTER-DEPARTMENTAL	TOTAL BUSINESS USE
NEW ENGLAND	385918.20	340800.00	650.00	3920.00	731288.19
MID ATLANTIC	1288277.00	1228720.00	72695.00	2318.00	2592010.01
EAST NORTH CENTRAL	1169082.09	1720751.00	7302.00	3778.00	2900913.10
WEST NORTH CENTRAL	443754.00	470968.00	237.00	3089.00	918048.00
SOUTH ATLANTIC	943820.60	1000036.00	2988.00	4891.00	1951735.60
EAST SOUTH CENTRAL	226839.60	712357.00	0.00	1446.00	940642.60
WEST SOUTH CENTRAL	586557.60	641829.00	165.00	6327.00	1234878.59
ROCKY MOUNTAIN	324466.70	228659.00	439.00	4181.00	557745.70
FAR WEST	906054.00	639771.00	824.00	7946.00	1554595.01
TOTAL	6274769.90	6983890.98	85300.00	37896.00	13381856.70

DISTRIBUTION OF GOVERNMENT USE, BY FUNCTION

REGION	FEDERAL GOVERNMENT			STATE AND LOCAL GOVERNMENT				ALL GOVERNMENT
	Commercial Use	Other Public Authorities	Total Federal Government	Commercial Use	Other Public Authorities	Street & Highway Lighting	Total State & Local Government	Total Use
NEW ENGLAND	7758.40	5291.50	13049.90	83245.30	9629.50	39538.00	132412.80	145462.70
MID ATLANTIC	24249.80	43942.70	68192.50	290235.20	123201.30	101000.00	514436.50	582629.00
EAST NORTH CENTRAL	20035.70	41294.30	61330.00	279032.30	86010.70	92607.00	457650.00	518980.00
WEST NORTH CENTRAL	10747.40	9986.50	20733.90	112883.70	18698.40	31084.00	162666.10	183400.00
SOUTH ATLANTIC	32657.70	42021.40	74679.10	290720.70	52845.60	53947.00	397513.30	472192.40
EAST SOUTH CENTRAL	6403.40	8028.30	14431.70	72324.00	11597.70	29491.00	113412.70	127844.40
WEST SOUTH CENTRAL	15572.00	25692.30	41264.30	183757.40	35656.70	24627.00	244041.10	285305.40
ROCKY MOUNTAIN	10011.90	13745.00	23756.90	85460.30	13622.00	15990.00	115072.30	138829.20
FAR WEST	22476.20	20956.50	43432.70	218710.70	31046.50	61547.00	311304.20	354736.90
TOTAL	149912.50	210958.50	360871.01	1616369.62	382308.39	449831.00	2448509.04	2809379.96

USE BY SECTOR

REGION	HOUSEHOLD USE	BUSINESS USE	FEDERAL GOVERNMENT USE	STATE & LOCAL GOVERNMENT USE	TOTAL USE
NEW ENGLAND	714419.00	731288.19	13049.90	132412.80	1591170.00
MID ATLANTIC	2001145.00	2592010.01	68192.50	514436.50	5175784.01
EAST NORTH CENTRAL	2235592.01	2900913.10	61330.00	457650.00	5655485.02
WEST NORTH CENTRAL	990368.00	918048.00	20733.90	162666.10	2091815.99
SOUTH ATLANTIC	2002293.00	1951735.60	74679.10	397513.30	4426220.99
EAST SOUTH CENTRAL	751645.00	940642.60	14431.70	113412.70	1820132.01
WEST SOUTH CENTRAL	1247532.00	1234878.59	41264.30	244041.10	2767716.01
ROCKY MOUNTAIN	457599.00	557745.70	23756.90	115072.30	1154174.00
FAR WEST	1329240.00	1554595.01	43432.70	311304.20	3238571.99
TOTAL	11729833.00	13381856.70	360871.01	2448509.04	27921070.20

Appendix H

Coal

Coal – Overview

Coal quantities were based on data in Crump and Readling [7], the National Coal Association [23] and the Little Report [20]. A primary series on prices was based on data from [23] and Edison Electric Institute [10], with additional information from [15] and [18] used to extend that primary series. The product of quantities and prices yielded expenditures.

Coal - Quantities

Crump and Readling [7] present data on bituminous coal and lignite consumed in household-commercial use, industrial use and in electric power production. The latter category comprised the major use of coal in 1972, accounting for 64 percent of total consumption shown in [7]. Crump and Readling also list anthracite coal consumption, classifying it under miscellaneous use.

The data in [7] pose some problems of aggregation, because (1) the residential and commercial sectors are combined, and (2) because in a number of cases, data on consumption refers to the sum for two or more states. The first problem is relatively minor, because the residential-commercial category accounts for only two percent of all use. Further, the Little Report [20] presents a breakdown between residential and commercial use of coal by major census region, with all use in the northeast, north central and southern regions attributed to the residential subcategory, and the bulk of use (90%) in the west attributed to the commercial subcategory.

These distributions were accepted as applicable to the individual states in the regions. The second problem was solved directly for electric power use of coal by drawing on National Coal Association data [23], which lists coal consumption by electric utilities by individual states. For that use, the distribution within a grouping of states in [23] was applied to [7]. Then, the distribution of industrial use within sets of individual states was estimated by averaging the distributions that held for (1) the use of coal in power production, and (2) the use of petroleum in industrial production. This procedure attempted to account both for relative concentrations of coal use and of industry use of fuel. A similar averaging process was applied for residential-commercial use, here applying the relative use of petroleum heating fuels in conjunction with the electric power distribution of coal use.

These procedures involve a somewhat shaky expedient, because there were often marked disparities between the two distributions. On the other hand, most of the aggregated cases involved relatively low levels of use, so that errors should be a minor component of total consumption.

Table H.1.1 presents the distribution of bituminous coal use by state for household, commercial, and industrial use, and of anthracite coal use; the data are from [7], disaggregated between the household-commercial sector and some sets of states by applying the procedures described above. [1]

Table H.1.2 presents the regional totals for the categories of Table H.1.1.

---

[1] Data for 26 individual states appeared; for the remaining states, totals were given for the following groupings: (1) Maine, New Hampshire, Rhode Island and Vermont; (2) Kansas and Nebraska; (3) North and South Dakota; (4) Delaware, District of Columbia and Maryland; (5) Florida and Georgia; (6) Alabama and Mississippi; (7) Arkansas, Louisiana, Oklahoma and Texas; (8) Arizona and Nevada; (9) Idaho and Montana; and (10) Oregon and Washington.

The National Coal Association data on electric utility use of
coal ([23] table 2) were now explicitly compared to the data from [7],
and because the comparison showed a fair amount of consistency, the two
series were combined to yield a final set of estimates.

The use of coal by electric utilities in [23] includes anthracite
use, where [7] does not. Further, the data in [7] do not show a breakdown of anthracite between categories of use by state. However, for the
United States as a whole, this distribution was given:

household-commercial:	.500
industrial:	.268
electric utilities:	.232
total	1.000

It was assumed that this national distribution applied to every state;
since Pennsylvania accounted for the bulk of anthracite coal consumption
(71%), it seemed plausible that the U.S. distribution held in approximate
fashion for Pennsylvania, and that deviations elsewhere had minor impact.

Table H.1.3 shows the electric utility use of all coal as listed in
[23]; the corresponding series for bituminous coal, only, from [7]; the
inferred use of anthracite coal by electric utilities (obtained by applying
the national distribution); the total of the second and third column, yielding
all coal use by electric utilities for [7] ; and finally, the average of
the [23] and [7] data, treated as the final series. There was one
exception; since [23] did not present data on Hawaii and Alaska, the values
appearing in [7] for those states are employed as final estimates.
Table H.1.4 presents the regional analogue of Table H.1.3.

Tables H.1.3 and H.1.4 show generally good correspondence between the [23] and [7] series, although the total for [7] is above that for [23] even prior to the addition of anthracite coal use. That addition does bring the two series more closely together for the northeast, where the bulk of anthracite consumption occurs.

Table H.1.5 distributes the remaining anthracite coal quantities to the residential and industrial categories, by state. (There was no commercial consumption of coal in the states where anthracite use occurred.) The table also presents the final series for electric utility use, and then the total for all uses of coal. Table H.1.6 presents the corresponding regional totals.

Coal - Prices

Most of the basic data employed in developing price series for coal use appear in Table H.2.1, in units both of cents per million BTU, and in dollars per ton.

Relatively detailed information on price paid for coal by electric utilities appears in both Edison Electric Institute ([10], table 43S,51) and National Coal Association series ([23], table 2,53-54). Those price series are compared in Table H.2.1, which also contains available data on residential prices paid for coal as listed in [18], and the scale factors of BTU per pound of coal allowing conversion from price per ton to price per million BTU. Those scale factors appear in [10]; similar values appear in [23], with small deviations from the corresponding figures in [10]. The values from [10] were used in unit conversions here.

The prices for electric utility use show generally good correspondence, with an occasional major discrepancy between the [23] and [10] series. Thus, prices for Massachusetts, North Dakota, the District of Columbia, Montana and Wyoming are markedly divergent, while those for South Dakota, Tennessee and Colorado differ by about 10 percent between the two series. Remaining pairs are close or coincident in value.

Prices for residential use ranged from 2.4 to 7.2 times the price in electric utility use, comparing prices from [8] to those from [23]. The average for this ratio was 3.35, with the average obtained over the 22 states with entries appearing in both series.

The data in Table H.2.1 were used to develop a final set of prices for each use by the following procedures. Gaps in the electric utility series were filled in by assigning values on the basis of prices that held for other states in the region. For example, Arkansas and Louisiana prices were set equal to that of Texas. Then the [23] and [10] series for electric utility use were averaged to obtain a final set of estimates for that use.

Industrial prices were set at five percent above electric utility prices, based on data in Foster Associates ([15], 227). The coverage in that source was limited, consisting of coal prices in industrial use for individual cities in 14 states. Those values were compared to the corresponding electric utility prices in [23], and the average of the ratio of industrial price to electric utility price turned out to be 1.05. (There was considerable variation in this ratio between states.)

The residential price was related to the electric utility price
(from [23]) by regression equation, with the estimated result:
$P_{RES.} = \$15$ per ton $+ 1.6\ P_{EL.UT.}$, where P denotes price in dollars
per ton, RES is residential use and EL.UT is electric utility use. The
r^2 for the equation was .50. Given that equation, the unit conversion
factors (from tons to BTU), and the electric utility price estimates, a
set of residential price estimates was generated.

Finally, price for commercial use was obtained by assuming it fell
midway between prices for industrial and residential use. Given the very
small commercial use, this seemed an economic approach. Results are presented in Table H.2.2.

In developing these estimates, the price for electric utility use was
the base price used in generating the price for other uses. That base price
involved a mix of bituminous and anthracite coal, and this mix varied somewhat between classes of use, a variation not accounted for by the price
estimating procedures employed here. However, errors introduced should be
trivial, given the minor share of anthracite coal in consumption. In [7],
the BTU per pound of anthracite is shown as 1.07 that per pound of bituminous
coal; on the other hand, the 1972 price of Pennsylvania anthracite was 1.31
times that of Pennsylvania bituminous coal ([22], 72 and 124). This suggests
a net cost per BTU about 20 percent higher for anthracite than for bituminous
coal (1.31/1.06 = 1.23), perhaps a factor accounting for the great decline
in anthracite use. But these price data may overstate price differentials
in practice, since the listed values are F.O.B. mine prices; delivered plant
prices may be much closer in practice. An indication that such occurs is
to be found in ([23], 49, footnote 26) where the _lowest_ listed coal price
to a Pennsylvania electric utility occurs for anthracite coal.[2]

[2] The price is $6.30 per ton in contrast to a statewide average price of
$9.40 per ton.

This bit of evidence reinforces the conclusion that further attempts
at refinement of price estimates here would be unproductive.

Expenditures On Coal

The product of the quantities in Table H.1.5 and the corresponding
prices in Table H.2.2 (converted to dollars per million BTU) give expenditures in units of thousand dollars. These results are shown for states
in Table H.3.1, while the regional sums over states appear in Table H.3.2.
Comparing that table to Table H.1.6 it can be seen that the total quantity
of coal consumed of 12330.9 trillion BTU was purchased at a price of 5.07
billion dollars. Consumption and expenditures were distributed by functional
categories of use as follows:

	Fraction Of Total Quantity Consumed	Fraction Of Total Expenditures
Residential Use	.0250	.0791
Commercial Use	.0015	.0028
Industrial Use	.3443	.3396
Electric Utility Use	.6292	.5785
Total	1.0000	1.0000

Coal Use By Sectors

Given the small quantities of commercial use, it seems reasonable to
make the simplifying (but plausible) assumption that all commercial use is
by the business sector. Again treating all electrical utility use as
private sector consumption, and identifying industrial use as wholly private
in character, the allocation of use to sectors is quite straightforward. Residential use, of course, is treated as coincident with the household sector,
and all other categories of use fall in the business sector.

Table H.1.1

Consumption Of Coal In Billion BTU, 1972, By State

Use By Function (Other Than Electric Utility Use)

REGION AND STATE	BITUMINOUS COAL			ANTHRACITE COAL (all uses)
	Residential Use	Commercial Use	Industrial Use	
NEW ENGLAND:				
CONNECTICUT	0.0	0.0	1500.0	200.0
MAINE	0.0	0.0	200.0	200.0
MASSACHUSETTS	400.0	0.0	2900.0	1100.0
NEW HAMPSHIRE	200.0	0.0	500.0	200.0
RHODE ISLAND	0.0	0.0	100.0	100.0
VERMONT	0.0	0.0	0.0	400.0
MID ATLANTIC:				
NEW JERSEY	100.0	0.0	1100.0	6800.0
NEW YORK	1400.0	0.0	200000.0	23900.0
PENNSYLVANIA	12200.0	0.0	779600.0	109800.0
EAST NORTH CENTRAL:				
ILLINOIS	38600.0	0.0	226800.0	1100.0
INDIANA	23100.0	0.0	536600.0	1300.0
MICHIGAN	17700.0	0.0	354800.0	2100.0
OHIO	33700.0	0.0	663200.0	3900.0
WISCONSIN	21400.0	0.0	90200.0	200.0
WEST NORTH CENTRAL:				
IOWA	2100.0	0.0	39500.0	0.0
KANSAS	500.0	0.0	3600.0	0.0
MINNESOTA	8300.0	0.0	45300.0	300.0
MISSOURI	2600.0	0.0	54500.0	0.0
NEBRASKA	1000.0	0.0	4300.0	0.0
NORTH DAKOTA	1600.0	0.0	8100.0	0.0
SOUTH DAKOTA	2000.0	0.0	3000.0	0.0
SOUTH ATLANTIC:				
DELAWARE	400.0	0.0	27500.0	500.0
DISTRICT OF COLUMBIA	100.0	0.0	2800.0	0.0
FLORIDA	700.0	0.0	4700.0	0.0
GEORGIA	1000.0	0.0	6200.0	0.0
MARYLAND	1000.0	0.0	94900.0	1900.0
NORTH CAROLINA	10100.0	0.0	38800.0	0.0
SOUTH CAROLINA	5800.0	0.0	33300.0	0.0
VIRGINIA	11300.0	0.0	74100.0	200.0
WEST VIRGINIA	7400.0	0.0	257300.0	0.0
EAST SOUTH CENTRAL:				
ALABAMA	1800.0	0.0	227500.0	0.0
KENTUCKY	8700.0	0.0	98400.0	0.0
MISSISSIPPI	1600.0	0.0	60200.0	0.0
TENNESSEE	12300.0	0.0	55800.0	0.0
WEST SOUTH CENTRAL:				
ARKANSAS	0.0	0.0	1300.0	0.0
LOUISIANA	0.0	0.0	4200.0	0.0
OKLAHOMA	0.0	0.0	2100.0	0.0
TEXAS	100.0	0.0	17600.0	0.0
ROCKY MOUNTAIN:				
ARIZONA	0.0	0.0	1900.0	0.0
COLORADO	600.0	5800.0	44400.0	0.0
IDAHO	0.0	1400.0	2100.0	0.0
MONTANA	400.0	3900.0	6600.0	0.0
NEVADA	0.0	0.0	0.0	0.0
NEW MEXICO	0.0	0.0	200.0	0.0
UTAH	500.0	4100.0	61500.0	0.0
WYOMING	100.0	1000.0	5700.0	0.0
FAR WEST:				
ALASKA	100.0	600.0	11300.0	0.0
CALIFORNIA	0.0	100.0	48400.0	0.0
HAWAII	0.0	0.0	0.0	0.0
OREGON	100.0	700.0	2600.0	0.0
WASHINGTON	100.0	900.0	2900.0	0.0

Table H.1.2

Consumption Of Coal, 1972, In Billion BTU, By Region

Use By Function (Other Than Electric Utility Use)

REGION	BITUMINOUS COAL			ANTHRACITE COAL (all uses)
	Residential Use	Commercial Use	Industrial Use	
NEW ENGLAND	600.00	0.00	5200.00	2200.00
MID ATLANTIC	13700.00	0.00	980700.00	140500.00
EAST NORTH CENTRAL	134500.00	0.00	1871600.00	8600.00
WEST NORTH CENTRAL	18100.00	0.00	158300.00	300.00
SOUTH ATLANTIC	37800.00	0.00	539600.00	2600.00
EAST SOUTH CENTRAL	24400.00	0.00	441900.00	0.00
WEST SOUTH CENTRAL	100.00	0.00	25200.00	0.00
ROCKY MOUNTAIN	1600.00	16200.00	122400.00	0.00
FAR WEST	300.00	2300.00	65200.00	0.00
TOTAL	231100.00	18500.00	4210099.99	154200.00

Table H.1.3

Consumption Of Coal, 1972, In Billion BTU, By State

Use By Electric Utilities: Comparison Of Alternative Series

| REGION | NATL. COAL ASSN. | CRUMP AND READLING | | | FINAL SERIES |
	All Coal Use	Bituminous Coal Use	Anthracite Coal Use	All Coal Use	Average
NEW ENGLAND:					
CONNECTICUT	1715.7	2100.0	53.6	2153.6	1934.7
MAINE	0.0	0.0	53.6	53.6	26.8
MASSACHUSETTS	1787.6	2000.0	294.8	2294.8	2041.2
NEW HAMPSHIRE	29873.0	24700.0	53.6	24753.6	27313.3
RHODE ISLAND	0.0	0.0	26.8	26.8	13.4
VERMONT	1050.0	1000.0	107.2	1107.2	1078.6
MID ATLANTIC:					
NEW JERSEY	28004.8	24700.0	1822.4	26522.4	27263.6
NEW YORK	149181.0	135400.0	6405.2	141805.2	145493.1
PENNSYLVANIA	847160.0	783000.0	29426.4	812426.4	829793.2
EAST NORTH CENTRAL:					
ILLINOIS	610368.7	666300.0	294.8	666594.8	638481.8
INDIANA	525183.9	541900.0	348.4	542248.4	533716.1
MICHIGAN	491643.5	456300.0	562.8	456862.8	474253.2
OHIO	901091.0	897500.0	1045.2	898545.2	899818.1
WISCONSIN	238143.5	233500.0	53.6	233553.6	235848.6
WEST NORTH CENTRAL:					
IOWA	108672.6	119000.0	0.0	119000.0	113836.3
KANSAS	10077.8	9800.0	0.0	9800.0	9938.9
MINNESOTA	119539.0	140200.0	80.4	140280.4	129909.7
MISSOURI	283395.4	293500.0	0.0	293500.0	288447.7
NEBRASKA	27982.1	27100.0	0.0	27100.0	27541.0
NORTH DAKOTA	65400.9	107700.0	0.0	107700.0	86550.5
SOUTH DAKOTA	4919.5	8100.0	0.0	8100.0	6509.7
SOUTH ATLANTIC:					
DELAWARE	22638.7	19000.0	134.0	19134.0	20886.4
DISTRICT OF COLUMBIA	4628.8	3900.0	0.0	3900.0	4264.4
FLORIDA	123604.6	118900.0	0.0	118900.0	121252.3
GEORGIA	250198.4	240500.0	0.0	240500.0	245349.2
MARYLAND	111423.4	104500.0	509.2	105009.2	108216.3
NORTH CAROLINA	448057.1	419100.0	0.0	419100.0	433578.6
SOUTH CAROLINA	136134.3	127300.0	0.0	127300.0	131717.2
VIRGINIA	120519.8	113700.0	53.6	113753.6	117136.7
WEST VIRGINIA	461375.0	442400.0	0.0	442400.0	451887.5
EAST SOUTH CENTRAL:					
ALABAMA	380599.1	378000.0	0.0	378000.0	379299.6
KENTUCKY	472564.8	498300.0	0.0	498300.0	485432.4
MISSISSIPPI	12600.1	12900.0	0.0	12900.0	12750.1
TENNESSEE	317764.4	383300.0	0.0	383300.0	350532.2
WEST SOUTH CENTRAL:					
ARKANSAS	0.0	0.0	0.0	0.0	0.0
LOUISIANA	0.0	0.0	0.0	0.0	0.0
OKLAHOMA	32.6	100.0	0.0	100.0	66.3
TEXAS	25060.0	50600.0	0.0	50600.0	37830.0
ROCKY MOUNTAIN:					
ARIZONA	7246.1	8500.0	0.0	8500.0	7873.0
COLORADO	72582.2	76000.0	0.0	76000.0	74291.1
IDAHO	0.0	0.0	0.0	0.0	0.0
MONTANA	11917.8	17200.0	0.0	17200.0	14558.9
NEVADA	67078.7	2400.0	0.0	2400.0	34739.4
NEW MEXICO	124841.9	153000.0	0.0	153000.0	138920.9
UTAH	13788.5	13200.0	0.0	13200.0	13494.2
WYOMING	75112.3	101700.0	0.0	101700.0	88406.2
FAR WEST:					
ALASKA	0.0	6000.0	0.0	6000.0	6000.0
CALIFORNIA	0.0	0.0	0.0	0.0	0.0
HAWAII	0.0	0.0	0.0	0.0	0.0
OREGON	0.0	0.0	0.0	0.0	0.0
WASHINGTON	0.0	0.0	0.0	0.0	0.0

Table H.1.4

Consumption of Coal, 1972, In Billion BTU, By Region

Use By Electric Utilities: Comparison Of Alternative Series

| REGION | NATL. COAL ASSN. | CRUMP AND READLING | | | FINAL SERIES |
	All Coal Use	Bituminous Coal Use	Anthracite Coal Use	All Coal Use	Average
NEW ENGLAND	34426.30	29800.00	589.60	30389.60	32408.00
MID ATLANTIC	1024345.80	943100.00	37654.00	980754.00	1002549.90
EAST NORTH CENTRAL	2766430.60	2795500.01	2304.80	2797804.77	2782117.80
WEST NORTH CENTRAL	619987.29	705400.00	80.40	705480.40	662733.81
SOUTH ATLANTIC	1678580.10	1589300.00	696.80	1589996.80	1634288.62
EAST SOUTH CENTRAL	1183528.41	1272500.01	0.00	1272500.01	1228014.30
WEST SOUTH CENTRAL	25092.60	50700.00	0.00	50700.00	37896.30
ROCKY MOUNTAIN	372567.50	372000.00	0.00	372000.00	372283.70
FAR WEST	0.00	6000.00	0.00	6000.00	6000.00
TOTAL	7704958.69	7764300.03	41325.60	7805625.65	7758292.33

Table H.1.5

Consumption Of Coal, 1972, In Billion BTU, By State

Use By Function, All Categories Of Use

REGION AND STATE	RESIDENTIAL USE	COMMERCIAL USE	INDUSTRIAL USE	ELECTRIC UTILITY USE	TOTAL USE
NEW ENGLAND:					
CONNECTICUT	100.0	0.0	1546.4	1934.7	3581.1
MAINE	100.0	0.0	246.4	26.8	373.2
MASSACHUSETTS	950.0	0.0	3155.2	2041.2	6146.4
NEW HAMPSHIRE	300.0	0.0	546.4	27313.3	28159.7
RHODE ISLAND	50.0	0.0	123.2	13.4	186.6
VERMONT	200.0	0.0	92.8	1078.6	1371.4
MID ATLANTIC:					
NEW JERSEY	3500.0	0.0	2677.6	27263.6	33441.2
NEW YORK	13350.0	0.0	205544.8	145493.1	364387.9
PENNSYLVANIA	67100.0	0.0	805073.6	829793.2	1701966.8
EAST NORTH CENTRAL:					
ILLINOIS	39150.0	0.0	227055.2	638481.8	904687.0
INDIANA	23750.0	0.0	536901.6	533716.1	1094367.7
MICHIGAN	18750.0	0.0	355287.2	474253.2	848290.4
OHIO	35650.0	0.0	664104.8	899818.1	1599572.9
WISCONSIN	21500.0	0.0	90246.4	235848.6	347595.0
WEST NORTH CENTRAL:					
IOWA	2100.0	0.0	39500.0	113836.3	155436.3
KANSAS	500.0	0.0	3600.0	9938.9	14038.9
MINNESOTA	8450.0	0.0	45369.6	129909.7	183729.3
MISSOURI	2600.0	0.0	54500.0	288447.7	345547.7
NEBRASKA	1000.0	0.0	4300.0	27541.0	32841.1
NORTH DAKOTA	1600.0	0.0	8100.0	86550.5	96250.4
SOUTH DAKOTA	2000.0	0.0	3000.0	6509.7	11509.8
SOUTH ATLANTIC:					
DELAWARE	650.0	0.0	27616.0	20886.4	49152.4
DISTRICT OF COLUMBIA	100.0	0.0	2800.0	4264.4	7164.4
FLORIDA	700.0	0.0	4700.0	121252.3	126652.3
GEORGIA	1000.0	0.0	6200.0	245349.2	252549.2
MARYLAND	1950.0	0.0	95340.8	108216.3	205507.1
NORTH CAROLINA	10100.0	0.0	38800.0	433578.6	482478.6
SOUTH CAROLINA	5800.0	0.0	33300.0	131717.2	170817.1
VIRGINIA	11400.0	0.0	74146.4	117136.7	202683.1
WEST VIRGINIA	7400.0	0.0	257300.0	451887.5	716587.5
EAST SOUTH CENTRAL:					
ALABAMA	1800.0	0.0	227500.0	379299.6	608599.6
KENTUCKY	8700.0	0.0	98400.0	485432.4	592532.4
MISSISSIPPI	1600.0	0.0	60200.0	12750.1	74550.0
TENNESSEE	12300.0	0.0	55800.0	350532.2	418632.2
WEST SOUTH CENTRAL:					
ARKANSAS	0.0	0.0	1300.0	0.0	1300.0
LOUISIANA	0.0	0.0	4200.0	0.0	4200.0
OKLAHOMA	0.0	0.0	2100.0	66.3	2166.3
TEXAS	100.0	0.0	17600.0	37830.0	55530.0
ROCKY MOUNTAIN:					
ARIZONA	0.0	0.0	1900.0	7873.0	9773.1
COLORADO	600.0	5800.0	44400.0	74291.1	125091.1
IDAHO	0.0	1400.0	2100.0	0.0	3500.0
MONTANA	400.0	3900.0	6600.0	14558.9	25458.9
NEVADA	0.0	0.0	0.0	34739.4	34739.4
NEW MEXICO	0.0	0.0	200.0	138920.9	139120.9
UTAH	500.0	4100.0	61500.0	13494.2	79594.3
WYOMING	100.0	1000.0	5700.0	88406.2	95206.2
FAR WEST:					
ALASKA	100.0	600.0	11300.0	6000.0	18000.0
CALIFORNIA	0.0	100.0	48400.0	0.0	48500.0
HAWAII	0.0	0.0	0.0	0.0	0.0
OREGON	100.0	700.0	2600.0	0.0	3400.0
WASHINGTON	100.0	900.0	2900.0	0.0	3900.0

Table H.1.6

Consumption Of Coal, 1972, In Billion BTU, By Region

Use By Function, All Categories Of Use

REGION	RESIDENTIAL USE	COMMERCIAL USE	INDUSTRIAL USE	ELECTRIC UTILITY USE	TOTAL USE
NEW ENGLAND	1700.00	0.00	5710.40	32408.00	39818.40
MID ATLANTIC	83950.00	0.00	1013296.00	1002549.90	2099795.90
EAST NORTH CENTRAL	138800.00	0.00	1873595.21	2782117.80	4794512.99
WEST NORTH CENTRAL	18250.00	0.00	158369.60	662733.81	839353.50
SOUTH ATLANTIC	39100.00	0.00	540203.21	1634288.62	2213591.69
EAST SOUTH CENTRAL	24400.00	0.00	441900.00	1228014.30	1694314.20
WEST SOUTH CENTRAL	100.00	0.00	25200.00	37896.30	63196.30
ROCKY MOUNTAIN	1600.00	16200.00	122400.00	372283.70	512483.90
FAR WEST	300.00	2300.00	65200.00	6000.00	73800.00
TOTAL	308200.00	18500.00	4245874.43	7758292.33	12330866.90

Table H.2.1

Coal Prices In Cents Per Million BTU, And In Dollars Per Ton, 1972, By State

Use By Function: Comparison Of Alternative Series, Data From National Coal Assn. (NCA), Edison Electric Institute (EEI)
And Independent National Gas Assn. of America (INGAA)

REGION AND STATE	PRICES PAID BY ELECTRIC UTILITIES				PRICES IN RESIDENTIAL USE (INGAA) $ Per Ton	BTU PER POUND (EEI)
	CENTS PER MILLION BTU		DOLLARS PER TON			
	EEI	NCA	EEI	NCA		
NEW ENGLAND:						
CONNECTICUT	61.10	60.30	14.03	11.37	0.00	11472.0
MAINE	0.00 [a]	0.00	0.00	0.00	0.00	0.0
MASSACHUSETTS	45.40	63.10	13.15	14.81	46.00	14500.0
NEW HAMPSHIRE	47.90	47.90	13.03	0.00	0.00	13591.0
RHODE ISLAND	56.70	0.00	16.46	0.00	45.00	14500.0
VERMONT	61.90	60.70	16.18	16.08	0.00	13077.0
MID ATLANTIC:						
NEW JERSEY	64.40	64.30	16.26	16.07	38.00	12626.0
NEW YORK	51.50	51.50	12.60	12.18	36.95	12227.0
PENNSYLVANIA	40.00	39.70	9.89	9.40	22.00	12354.0
EAST NORTH CENTRAL:						
ILLINOIS	38.50	38.00	7.94	7.67	30.50	10303.0
INDIANA	31.40	32.40	6.87	6.97	31.10	10929.0
MICHIGAN	44.60	44.70	10.88	10.92	32.72	12184.0
OHIO	37.80	37.80	8.53	8.53	37.25	11275.0
WISCONSIN	46.50	47.60	10.74	10.60	36.00	11546.0
WEST NORTH CENTRAL:						
IOWA	39.00	39.40	8.04	8.00	23.40	10319.0
KANSAS	32.20	32.10	7.78	8.01	19.42	12071.0
MINNESOTA	40.80	41.80	7.61	7.65	31.50	9329.0
MISSOURI	29.20	31.70	6.41	6.84	23.90	10980.0
NEBRASKA	43.00	43.00	9.87	9.28	0.00	11487.0
NORTH DAKOTA	26.60	15.70	3.65	2.03	0.00	6863.0
SOUTH DAKOTA	42.90	39.50	7.27	6.40	0.00	8479.0
SOUTH ATLANTIC:						
DELAWARE	53.90	53.30	13.46	13.22	0.00	12477.0
DISTRICT OF COLUMBIA	53.90	66.00	13.46	15.93	0.00	12477.0
FLORIDA	42.50	42.30	9.61	9.61	0.00	11311.0
GEORGIA	44.70	44.60	10.56	10.35	0.00	11800.0
MARYLAND	53.90	53.50	13.46	12.89	32.58	12477.0
NORTH CAROLINA	44.30	44.30	10.60	10.70	30.94	11954.0
SOUTH CAROLINA	47.00	46.90	11.46	11.37	28.35	12195.0
VIRGINIA	43.40	43.40	10.86	10.54	32.85	12507.0
WEST VIRGINIA	35.40	34.90	8.30	8.08	0.00	11736.0
EAST SOUTH CENTRAL:						
ALABAMA	38.00	37.00	8.80	8.37	0.00	11585.0
KENTUCKY	28.40	27.80	6.13	5.99	27.00	10802.0
MISSISSIPPI	36.30	36.20	8.72	8.70	0.00	12008.0
TENNESSEE	36.00	33.80	7.95	7.48	25.00	11050.0
WEST SOUTH CENTRAL:						
ARKANSAS	0.00	0.00	0.00	0.00	0.00	0.0
LOUISIANA	0.00	0.00	0.00	0.00	0.00	0.0
OKLAHOMA	19.40	19.50	4.82	0.00	15.50	12438.0
TEXAS	21.60	21.00	3.02	2.94	0.00	7000.0
ROCKY MOUNTAIN:						
ARIZONA	31.80	31.60	6.62	5.98	0.00	10411.0
COLORADO	30.00	27.60	6.39	4.40	22.05	10640.0
IDAHO	0.00	0.00	0.00	0.00	23.00	0.0
MONTANA	26.00	21.00	3.38	3.22	23.10	6500.0
NEVADA	29.70	29.90	6.67	6.36	0.00	11248.0
NEW MEXICO	15.30	15.00	2.76	2.55	0.00	9089.0
UTAH	29.10	29.40	7.10	7.03	18.00	12187.0
WYOMING	17.10	22.70	2.82	4.11	0.00	8257.0
FAR WEST:						
ALASKA	67.50	0.00	11.74	0.00	0.00	8700.0
CALIFORNIA	0.00	0.00	0.00	0.00	0.00	0.0
HAWAII	0.00	0.00	0.00	0.00	0.00	0.0
OREGON	17.40	0.00	3.92	0.00	0.00	11288.0
WASHINGTON	17.40	0.00	3.92	0.00	34.85	11288.0

[a] Zero indicates no use of coal listed in source.

Table H.2.2

Coal Prices In Cents Per Million BTU, 1972, By State

Use By Function

REGION AND STATE	ELECTRIC UTILITY USE	INDUSTRIAL USE	COMMERCIAL USE	RESIDENTIAL USE
NEW ENGLAND:				
CONNECTICUT	60.70	63.73	113.12	162.50
MAINE	61.30	64.36	109.85	155.33
MASSACHUSETTS	54.25	56.96	97.74	138.52
NEW HAMPSHIRE	47.90	50.29	91.06	131.82
RHODE ISLAND	56.70	59.53	100.99	142.44
VERMONT	61.30	64.36	109.90	155.43
MID ATLANTIC:				
NEW JERSEY	64.35	67.57	114.96	162.36
NEW YORK	51.50	54.07	98.91	143.74
PENNSYLVANIA	39.85	41.84	83.16	124.47
EAST NORTH CENTRAL:				
ILLINOIS	38.25	40.16	87.08	133.99
INDIANA	31.90	33.50	76.58	119.66
MICHIGAN	44.65	46.88	89.94	133.00
OHIO	37.80	39.69	83.34	127.00
WISCONSIN	47.05	49.40	94.82	140.24
WEST NORTH CENTRAL:				
IOWA	39.20	41.16	88.28	135.40
KANSAS	32.15	33.76	73.66	113.57
MINNESOTA	41.30	43.36	94.92	146.47
MISSOURI	30.45	31.97	74.50	117.03
NEBRASKA	43.00	45.15	89.62	134.09
NORTH DAKOTA	21.15	22.21	82.66	143.12
SOUTH DAKOTA	41.20	43.26	98.82	154.37
SOUTH ATLANTIC:				
DELAWARE	53.60	56.28	101.08	145.87
DISTRICT OF COLUMBIA	59.95	62.95	109.49	156.03
FLORIDA	42.40	44.52	89.33	134.15
GEORGIA	44.65	46.88	90.94	135.00
MARYLAND	53.70	56.39	101.21	146.03
NORTH CAROLINA	44.30	46.51	90.07	133.62
SOUTH CAROLINA	46.95	49.30	92.96	136.62
VIRGINIA	43.40	45.57	87.49	129.41
WEST VIRGINIA	35.15	36.91	78.53	120.15
EAST SOUTH CENTRAL:				
ALABAMA	37.50	39.38	82.06	124.74
KENTUCKY	28.10	29.50	71.95	114.39
MISSISSIPPI	36.25	38.06	79.26	120.46
TENNESSEE	34.90	36.65	80.18	123.71
WEST SOUTH CENTRAL:				
ARKANSAS	21.30	22.36	81.79	141.22
LOUISIANA	21.30	22.36	81.79	141.22
OKLAHOMA	19.45	20.42	55.92	91.42
TEXAS	21.30	22.36	81.79	141.22
ROCKY MOUNTAIN:				
ARIZONA	31.70	33.28	78.02	122.76
COLORADO	28.80	30.24	73.40	116.57
IDAHO	23.50	24.67	88.83	152.98
MONTANA	23.50	24.67	88.83	152.98
NEVADA	29.80	31.29	72.82	114.36
NEW MEXICO	15.15	15.91	61.33	106.76
UTAH	29.25	30.71	69.53	108.34
WYOMING	19.90	20.89	71.78	122.67
FAR WEST:				
ALASKA	67.50	70.88	132.54	194.21
CALIFORNIA	22.00a	23.10	62.48	101.87
HAWAII	0.00	0.00	0.00	0.00
OREGON	17.40	18.27	56.28	94.28
WASHINGTON	17.40	18.27	56.28	94.28

a Zero indicates no consumption in any use.

Table H.3.1

Expenditures On Coal In Thousand Dollars, 1972, By State

Use By Function

REGION AND STATE	RESIDENTIAL USE	COMMERCIAL USE	INDUSTRIAL USE	ELECTRIC UTILITY USE	TOTAL USE
NEW ENGLAND:					
CONNECTICUT	162.5	0.0	985.5	1174.3	2322.4
MAINE	155.3	0.0	158.6	16.4	330.3
MASSACHUSETTS	1315.9	0.0	1797.2	1107.4	4220.5
NEW HAMPSHIRE	395.5	0.0	274.8	13083.1	13753.3
RHODE ISLAND	71.2	0.0	73.3	7.6	152.2
VERMONT	310.9	0.0	59.7	661.2	1031.8
MID ATLANTIC:					
NEW JERSEY	5682.6	0.0	1809.3	17544.1	25036.0
NEW YORK	19189.3	0.0	111138.1	74928.9	205256.3
PENNSYLVANIA	83519.4	0.0	336842.8	330672.6	751034.8
EAST NORTH CENTRAL:					
ILLINOIS	52457.1	0.0	91185.4	244219.3	387861.7
INDIANA	28419.2	0.0	179862.0	170255.5	378536.7
MICHIGAN	24937.5	0.0	166558.6	211754.0	403250.2
OHIO	45275.5	0.0	263583.2	340131.2	648989.9
WISCONSIN	30151.6	0.0	44581.7	110966.7	185700.1
WEST NORTH CENTRAL:					
IOWA	2843.4	0.0	16258.2	44623.8	63725.4
KANSAS	567.9	0.0	1215.4	3195.4	4978.6
MINNESOTA	12376.7	0.0	19672.3	53652.7	85701.7
MISSOURI	3042.8	0.0	17423.6	87832.3	108298.8
NEBRASKA	1340.9	0.0	1941.5	11842.7	15125.0
NORTH DAKOTA	2289.9	0.0	1799.0	18305.4	22394.4
SOUTH DAKOTA	3087.4	0.0	1297.8	2682.0	7067.2
SOUTH ATLANTIC:					
DELAWARE	948.2	0.0	15542.3	11195.1	27685.5
DISTRICT OF COLUMBIA	156.0	0.0	1762.6	2556.5	4475.1
FLORIDA	939.1	0.0	2092.4	51411.0	54442.5
GEORGIA	1350.0	0.0	2906.6	109548.4	113805.0
MARYLAND	2847.6	0.0	53762.7	58112.2	114722.4
NORTH CAROLINA	13495.6	0.0	18045.9	192075.3	223616.8
SOUTH CAROLINA	7924.0	0.0	16416.9	61841.2	86182.1
VIRGINIA	14752.7	0.0	33788.5	50837.3	99378.6
WEST VIRGINIA	8891.1	0.0	94969.4	158838.5	262699.0
EAST SOUTH CENTRAL:					
ALABAMA	2245.3	0.0	89589.5	142237.3	234072.2
KENTUCKY	9951.9	0.0	29028.0	136406.5	175386.4
MISSISSIPPI	1927.4	0.0	22912.1	4621.9	29461.4
TENNESSEE	15216.3	0.0	20450.7	122335.7	158002.8
WEST SOUTH CENTRAL:					
ARKANSAS	0.0	0.0	290.7	0.0	290.7
LOUISIANA	0.0	0.0	939.1	0.0	939.1
OKLAHOMA	0.0	0.0	428.8	12.9	441.7
TEXAS	141.2	0.0	3935.4	8057.8	12134.4
ROCKY MOUNTAIN:					
ARIZONA	0.0	0.0	632.3	2495.8	3128.1
COLORADO	699.4	4257.2	13426.6	21395.8	39779.0
IDAHO	0.0	1243.6	518.1	0.0	1761.7
MONTANA	611.9	3464.4	1628.2	3421.3	9125.9
NEVADA	0.0	0.0	0.0	10352.3	10352.3
NEW MEXICO	0.0	0.0	31.8	21046.5	21078.3
UTAH	541.7	2850.7	18886.7	3947.1	26226.1
WYOMING	122.7	717.8	1190.7	17592.8	19624.0
FAR WEST:					
ALASKA	194.2	795.2	8009.4	4050.0	13048.9
CALIFORNIA	0.0	62.5	11180.4	0.0	11242.9
HAWAII	0.0	0.0	0.0	0.0	0.0
OREGON	94.3	394.0	475.0	0.0	963.3
WASHINGTON	94.3	506.5	529.8	0.0	1130.6

Table H.3.2

Expenditures On Coal In Thousand Dollars, 1972, By Region

Use By Function

REGION	RESIDENTIAL USE	COMMERCIAL USE	INDUSTRIAL USE	ELECTRIC UTILITY USE	TOTAL USE
NEW ENGLAND	2411.30	0.00	3349.10	16050.00	21810.50
MID ATLANTIC	108391.30	0.00	449790.19	423145.60	981327.09
EAST NORTH CENTRAL	181240.90	0.00	745770.91	1077326.70	2004338.60
WEST NORTH CENTRAL	25549.00	0.00	59607.80	222134.30	307291.10
SOUTH ATLANTIC	51304.30	0.00	239287.30	696415.50	987007.00
EAST SOUTH CENTRAL	29340.90	0.00	161980.30	405601.40	596922.80
WEST SOUTH CENTRAL	141.20	0.00	5594.00	8070.70	13805.90
ROCKY MOUNTAIN	1975.70	12553.70	36314.40	80251.60	131075.40
FAR WEST	382.80	1758.20	20194.60	4050.00	26385.70
TOTAL	400737.39	14291.90	1721888.61	2933045.92	5069964.08

Appendix I

Hydroelectric and Nuclear Power

The Edison Electric Institute Statistical Yearbook ([10], Table 135, 21) presents Federal Power Commission data on electric generation by type of prime mover driving the generator, classified under hydropower, nuclear power, conventional steam and internal combustion power. The latter two categories cover power from coal, oil and gas. Table I.1.1 presents this data for states, in units of million kilowatt-hours. Table I.1.2 shows the fraction of total power generation furnished by each source, by state. Table I.1.3 presents the regional values corresponding to the state data in the two preceding tables.

For the U.S. as a whole in 1972, hydropower accounted for roughly 15 percent of total electric power production, and nuclear power for 3 percent. Considerable variation in proportions occur between states and regions, with hydropower use particularly high in the west, and nuclear power in New England. States with more than half their electricity generated by hydropower included Vermont, South Dakota, Idaho, Montana, Oregon and Washington; in most of these cases, almost all generation was derived from hydropower. Other states with more than one-quarter of their electricity generated by hydropower included Maine, New York, North Dakota, Arizona, Utah and California. Connecticut had the greatest reliance on nuclear power (almost one-third). Other states deriving more than 10 percent of electric generation from nuclear power included New Jersey, Illinois, Wisconsin, Minnesota, and South Carolina.

Given these data, it seemed useful to attempt to account for the fuel

equivalent quantity and value of both hydropower and nuclear power, and the

remainder of this appendix describes the procedures employed in that reckoning.

After the work was completed, a review of the procedures suggested an under-

estimate of about 10 percent had probably occurred; but this, in turn, could

be rationalized as an inadvertant but acceptable way of accounting for likely

efficiency differences between energy sources, so the initial estimates were

retained.

The initial estimates were developed in the following steps. Total

electric utility generation was listed as 1,747.3 billion kilowatt-hours in

1972, which contrasts with energy sales of 1,577.7 billion kilowatt-hours

([10], Table 225,33). The latter figure is .903 the former, and it was

assumed the difference between the two reflected power station use and losses,

so that the generation figure was initially interpreted as gross kilowatt-

hours, and the sales figure as net kilowatt-hours.

The National Coal Association ([23] Table 8, 111-113) presents data on

BTU of fuel needed to generate one net kilowatt-hour. For the U.S. as a

whole, in 1971, these BTU values were:

Coal	-	10,252
Oil	-	10,884
Gas	-	10,847

The weighted average of these figures was 10,520 BTU, and given that a kilo-

watt-hour is equivalent to 3,412 BTU ([7], p. 2) it follows that input is

3.083 times that of output in BTU in electric power production, i.e., two-

thirds of BTU content is "lost" in the transformation from fuel to electricity.

Combining these estimates, it followed that the "fuel-equivalent input" of hydropower and nuclear power was 2.77 BTU per kilowatt-hour generated, i.e., .903 times 3.083 is 2.77.   Since a kilowatt-hour corresponds to 3,412 BTU, it follows that 2.77 times 3.412 yields a scale factor of 9.45, which converts million kilowatt-hours to billion BTU of fuel equivalent input.

The fuel-equivalent input in effect is the estimate of the fuel that would be used to generate an equivalent amount of electricity if hydropower and nuclear power were replaced by fossil fuel.

Crump and Readling ([7], P.4) show a small amount of aggregate U.S. hydropower and nuclear power used in industry, but do not distribute the 3,389 million kilowatt hours involved to individual states.   It was assumed that this usage was furnished solely by hydropower and that it occurred in proportion to state electric power use; this led to an estimate of industrial use as .012 of electric utility use, for each state.

Table I.1.4 shows the fuel input equivalents obtained by applying these scale factors, by state, in terms of billion BTU equivalents for electric generation use of hydropower, nuclear power, and their total; the industrial use of hydropower; and the grand total of these uses. Table I.1.5 shows the regional totals of the BTU equivalents, with a U.S. grand total of 3,122.0 trillion BTU for all uses.

A similar estimating procedure is employed by the Bureau of Mines in ascribing BTU on the basis of kilowatt-hours produced to hydropower and nuclear power ([43], 1973 edition, table 16, p. 37). The conversion factors employed are listed in (]7], 82) as the following, in BTU per kilowatt-hour:

Hydropower: 10,660
Nuclear Power: 10,379

However, the losses between production and sales are not accounted for by the Bureau of Mines, and this lack of accounting seems defensible if most of the losses are transmission losses, which in fact is the case. Fuel equivalent input would best be measured at point of use by the utility, rather than at point of end use of electricity. Hence, in retrospect, the procedures employed here appeared to involve an underestimate of about 10 percent. But it seemed a reasonable hypothesis that hydroelectric and nuclear power are employed because they are "better" than alternative sources of energy. They may be more "efficient" in the sense of furnishing the same kilowatt-hours at lower levels of input (BTU) or they may be cheaper, in the sense of being lower-priced. In either event, an ex post reduction in cost of about 10 percent seems eminently reasonable. Hence, the apparent underestimate of BTU could be reinterpreted as an inadvertant, but acceptable way of accounting for somewhat greater efficiency of hydropower and nuclear power, carrying out that adjustment at the input level, rather than in terms of lower prices.

Prices, in fact, were generally estimated as the value per million BTU of energy furnished by fossil fuels, although there were some downward adjustments to account for "best" alternative fuel supplies. Table I.2.1 presents those price estimates, with most of the entries consisting of the composite average of the cost of all fossil fuel per million BTU consumed in electric generation, as listed in ([10], Table 435, 41). Where hydropower and nuclear power furnished more than 20 percent of a state's generation input, the composite fuel price was checked against (1) the price for other states in the region, (2) the lowest price for fossil fuel as among coal, oil and natural gas, and (3) the average price of electricity paid by all consumers in the state. This check led to a reduction of the price estimate in several cases. For example, the composite price for the state of Washington was 44.4 cents per million BTU, which is above the U.S. average composite price of 41.1 cents per million BTU, in contrast to an Oregon composite price of 17.6 cents per million BTU. In this instance, the Washington input of fossil fuel furnished a miniscule portion of total power generation, and the Washington price for electricity was well below the U.S. average; hence, the much lower Oregon composite fuel price was assumed applicable to Washington.

As a check on procedures here, estimated fuel prices were related to electricity prices for the 32 states with hydro and nuclear power accounting for less than 20 percent of generation. The resultant equation was:

$$P_{FUEL} = -.0139 + .0745 \, P_{EL.}, \quad \bar{R}^2 = .41,$$

where P_{FUEL} is composite fuel price and P_{EL} is average price of electricity to all consumers. Then the electricity price for each of the excluded states was inserted into this equation and a price estimate derived and compared to the initial set of prices for the excluded states, including those for which the composite price had been reduced on the basis of inspection. Good agreement emerged for the individual state comparisons; the average for the initial estimates was 39.7 cents per million BTU, and that for the regression results was 38.4 cents per million BTU. Because the initial estimates accounted for a variety of factors they were retained and employed in the final step of the accounting process, which estimated the money value of the

fuel equivalent input of hydropower and nuclear power. Here the prices
of Table I.2.1 were multiplied by the corresponding state quantities of
Table I.1.4 to yield the state expenditure equivalents (or substitution
costs) of Table I.3.1. Regional results are shown in Table I.3.2, with
a U.S. grand total of $1.059 billion as the estimated value of the hydro-
power and nuclear power input, with roughly three-quarters of input and
value accounted for by hydropower, and one-quarter by nuclear power.

Obviously, the cost approach employed here must beg some
questions, because in a strict accounting framework, "fuel" costs for
hydropower and nuclear power may be substantially different from those
shown here. In the case of hydropower, there is a substitution of capital
for fuel, since the fuel "input" (water) is essentially free; similar
substitutions probably occur in nuclear power production, so that the
price of uranium may not bear much relation to the price employed here.
Again, it will be easy to question the ex post rationale for the ten percent
reduction in BTU (and hence, in costs) relative to the Bureau of Mines estimate. Yet the substitution cost estimates for inputs, and the "shadow price"
estimates for unit-value of inputs, seem good enough for the purposes of
this report.

Table I.1.1

Consumption Of Hydroelectric And Nuclear Power, Scale Factors, 1972, By State

Millions Of Kilowatt-Hours Generated In Electricity Production: Distribution By Type Of
    Prime Mover Driving The Generator

REGION AND STATE	KILOWATT-HOURS IN MILLIONS				
	Hydro-Power	Nuclear Steam	Conventional Steam	Internal Combustion	Total
NEW ENGLAND:					
CONNECTICUT	559.0	7777.0	15609.0	10.0	23955.0
MAINE	1769.0	54.0	2909.0	76.0	4808.0
MASSACHUSETTS	786.0	1500.0	29039.0	288.0	31613.0
NEW HAMPSHIRE	1094.0	0.0	4121.0	0.0	5215.0
RHODE ISLAND	6.0	0.0	1263.0	21.0	1290.0
VERMONT	873.0	169.0	149.0	14.0	1205.0
MID ATLANTIC:					
NEW JERSEY	0.0	4356.0	30327.0	0.0	34459.0
NEW YORK	27542.0	6465.0	67884.0	249.0	102140.0
PENNSYLVANIA	1533.0	289.0	95978.0	56.0	97856.0
EAST NORTH CENTRAL:					
ILLINOIS	133.0	13067.0	69811.0	403.0	83414.0
INDIANA	385.0	0.0	53757.0	86.0	54228.0
MICHIGAN	1645.0	2125.0	56675.0	664.0	61109.0
OHIO	9.0	0.0	92252.0	301.0	92562.0
WISCONSIN	2107.0	3294.0	25042.0	54.0	30497.0
WEST NORTH CENTRAL:					
IOWA	993.0	0.0	14138.0	514.0	15645.0
KANSAS	4.0	0.0	16155.0	798.0	16957.0
MINNESOTA	859.0	3558.0	15475.0	277.0	20169.0
MISSOURI	612.0	0.0	31995.0	409.0	33016.0
NEBRASKA	1372.0	0.0	6708.0	358.0	8438.0
NORTH DAKOTA	3095.0	0.0	5491.0	4.0	8590.0
SOUTH DAKOTA	7390.0	0.0	670.0	35.0	8095.0
SOUTH ATLANTIC:					
DELAWARE	0.0	0.0	5391.0	9.0	5400.0
DISTRICT OF COLUMBIA	1.0	0.0	2735.0	0.0	2736.0
FLORIDA	238.0	66.0	66658.0	423.0	67385.0
GEORGIA	3332.0	0.0	30203.0	1.0	33536.0
MARYLAND	2283.0	0.0	24968.0	99.0	27350.0
NORTH CAROLINA	6429.0	0.0	51150.0	12.0	57591.0
SOUTH CAROLINA	3301.0	4829.0	17262.0	0.0	25392.0
VIRGINIA	1362.0	448.0	28416.0	25.0	30251.0
WEST VIRGINIA	534.0	0.0	48466.0	0.0	49000.0
EAST SOUTH CENTRAL:					
ALABAMA	10208.0	0.0	39550.0	0.0	49758.0
KENTUCKY	3819.0	0.0	49891.0	0.0	53710.0
MISSISSIPPI	0.0	0.0	12132.0	9.0	12141.0
TENNESSEE	11133.0	0.0	40690.0	0.0	51823.0
WEST SOUTH CENTRAL:					
ARKANSAS	1644.0	0.0	9521.0	18.0	11183.0
LOUISIANA	0.0	0.0	38992.0	356.0	39348.0
OKLAHOMA	1447.0	0.0	25309.0	262.0	27018.0
TEXAS	830.0	0.0	129560.0	352.0	130742.0
ROCKY MOUNTAIN:					
ARIZONA	6771.0	0.0	9268.0	11.0	16050.0
COLORADO	1242.0	0.0	12063.0	141.0	13446.0
IDAHO	7844.0	0.0	0.0	0.0	7844.0
MONTANA	9444.0	0.0	1245.0	0.0	10689.0
NEVADA	1563.0	0.0	11430.0	11.0	13004.0
NEW MEXICO	20.0	0.0	18131.0	61.0	18212.0
UTAH	1220.0	0.0	2123.0	22.0	3365.0
WYOMING	1172.0	0.0	7059.0	6.0	8237.0
FAR WEST:					
ALASKA	346.0	0.0	1114.0	157.0	1617.0
CALIFORNIA	31802.0	3115.0	90342.0	15.0	125274.0
HAWAII	22.0	0.0	4687.0	69.0	4778.0
OREGON	36469.0	0.0	55.0	0.0	36524.0
WASHINGTON	75716.0	2919.0	23.0	0.0	78658.0

Table I.1.2

Consumption Of Hydroelectric And Nuclear Power, Seale Factors, 1972, By State

Fraction Of Total Kilowatt-Hours Generated In Electricity Production: Distribution
   By Type Of Prime Mover Driving The Generator

REGION AND STATE	FRACTION OF TOTAL KILOWATT-HOURS OBTAINED FROM PRIME MOVERS			
	Hydro-Power	Nuclear Steam	Conventional Steam	Internal Combustion
NEW ENGLAND:				
CONNECTICUT	0.0233	0.3247	0.6516	0.0004
MAINE	0.3679	0.0112	0.6050	0.0158
MASSACHUSETTS	0.0249	0.0474	0.9186	0.0091
NEW HAMPSHIRE	0.2098	0.0000	0.7902	0.0000
RHODE ISLAND	0.0047	0.0000	0.9791	0.0163
VERMONT	0.7245	0.1402	0.1237	0.0116
MID ATLANTIC:				
NEW JERSEY	0.0000	0.1264	0.8801	0.0000
NEW YORK	0.2696	0.0633	0.6646	0.0024
PENNSYLVANIA	0.0157	0.0030	0.9808	0.0006
EAST NORTH CENTRAL:				
ILLINOIS	0.0016	0.1567	0.8369	0.0048
INDIANA	0.0071	0.0000	0.9913	0.0016
MICHIGAN	0.0269	0.0348	0.9274	0.0109
OHIO	0.0001	0.0000	0.9967	0.0033
WISCONSIN	0.0691	0.1080	0.8211	0.0018
WEST NORTH CENTRAL:				
IOWA	0.0635	0.0000	0.9037	0.0329
KANSAS	0.0002	0.0000	0.9527	0.0471
MINNESOTA	0.0426	0.1764	0.7673	0.0137
MISSOURI	0.0185	0.0000	0.9691	0.0124
NEBRASKA	0.1626	0.0000	0.7950	0.0424
NORTH DAKOTA	0.3603	0.0000	0.6392	0.0005
SOUTH DAKOTA	0.9129	0.0000	0.0828	0.0043
SOUTH ATLANTIC:				
DELAWARE	0.0000	0.0000	0.9983	0.0017
DISTRICT OF COLUMBIA	0.0004	0.0000	0.9996	0.0000
FLORIDA	0.0035	0.0010	0.9892	0.0063
GEORGIA	0.0994	0.0000	0.9006	0.0000
MARYLAND	0.0835	0.0000	0.9129	0.0036
NORTH CAROLINA	0.1116	0.0000	0.8882	0.0002
SOUTH CAROLINA	0.1300	0.1902	0.6798	0.0000
VIRGINIA	0.0450	0.0148	0.9393	0.0008
WEST VIRGINIA	0.0109	0.0000	0.9891	0.0000
EAST SOUTH CENTRAL:				
ALABAMA	0.2052	0.0000	0.7948	0.0000
KENTUCKY	0.0711	0.0000	0.9289	0.0000
MISSISSIPPI	0.0000	0.0000	0.9993	0.0007
TENNESSEE	0.2148	0.0000	0.7852	0.0000
WEST SOUTH CENTRAL:				
ARKANSAS	0.1470	0.0000	0.8514	0.0016
LOUISIANA	0.0000	0.0000	0.9910	0.0090
OKLAHOMA	0.0536	0.0000	0.9367	0.0097
TEXAS	0.0063	0.0000	0.9910	0.0027
ROCKY MOUNTAIN:				
ARIZONA	0.4219	0.0000	0.5774	0.0007
COLORADO	0.0924	0.0000	0.8971	0.0105
IDAHO	1.0000	0.0000	0.0000	0.0000
MONTANA	0.8835	0.0000	0.1165	0.0000
NEVADA	0.1202	0.0000	0.8790	0.0008
NEW MEXICO	0.0011	0.0000	0.9956	0.0033
UTAH	0.3626	0.0000	0.6309	0.0065
WYOMING	0.1423	0.0000	0.8570	0.0007
FAR WEST:				
ALASKA	0.2140	0.0000	0.6889	0.0971
CALIFORNIA	0.2539	0.0249	0.7212	0.0001
HAWAII	0.0046	0.0000	0.9810	0.0144
OREGON	0.9985	0.0000	0.0015	0.0000
WASHINGTON	0.9626	0.0371	0.0003	0.0000

Table I.1.3

Consumption Of Hydroelectric And Nuclear Power, 1972, Scale Factors, By Region

Electricity Generation in Millions Of Kilowatt Hours Generated And
   As Fraction Of Total Generation: Distribution By Type Of Prime Mover Driving
        The Generator

KILOWATT-HOURS IN MILLIONS

REGION	HYDRO-POWER	NUCLEAR	CONVENTIONAL STEAM	INTERNAL COMBUSTION	TOTAL
NEW ENGLAND	5087.00	9500.00	53090.00	409.00	68086.00
MID ATLANTIC	29075.00	11110.00	194189.00	305.00	234455.00
EAST NORTH CENTRAL	4279.00	18486.00	297537.00	1508.00	321810.00
WEST NORTH CENTRAL	14325.00	3558.00	90632.00	2395.00	110910.00
SOUTH ATLANTIC	17480.00	5343.00	275249.00	569.00	298641.00
EAST SOUTH CENTRAL	25160.00	0.00	142263.00	9.00	167432.00
WEST SOUTH CENTRAL	3921.00	0.00	203382.00	988.00	208291.00
ROCKY MOUNTAIN	29276.00	0.00	61319.00	252.00	90847.00
FAR WEST	144355.00	6034.00	96221.00	241.00	246851.00
TOTAL	272958.00	54031.00	1413882.00	6676.00	1747323.00

FRACTION OF TOTAL KILLOWATT-HOURS

	HYDRO-POWER	NUCLEAR STEAM	CONVENTIONAL STEAM	INTERNAL COMBUSTION
NEW ENGLAND	0.0747	0.1395	0.7797	0.0060
MID ATLANTIC	0.1240	0.0474	0.8283	0.0013
EAST NORTH CENTRAL	0.0133	0.0574	0.9246	0.0047
WEST NORTH CENTRAL	0.1292	0.0321	0.8172	0.0216
SOUTH ATLANTIC	0.0585	0.0179	0.9217	0.0019
EAST SOUTH CENTRAL	0.1503	0.0000	0.8497	0.0001
WEST SOUTH CENTRAL	0.0188	0.0000	0.9764	0.0047
ROCKY MOUNTAIN	0.3223	0.0000	0.6750	0.0028
FAR WEST	0.5848	0.0244	0.3898	0.0010
UNITED STATES	0.1562	0.0309	0.8092	0.0038

Table I.1.4

Consumption Of Hydropower And Nuclear Power In Billion BTU Of Fuel Equivalent, 1972, By State

Use By Function And Source Of Power

REGION AND STATE	ELECTRICITY GENERATION			INDUSTRIAL USE	TOTAL USE
	Hydro-Power	Nuclear Power	Total	(Hydro-Power)	
NEW ENGLAND:					
CONNECTICUT	5282.6	73492.7	78775.2	65.5	78840.7
MAINE	16717.1	510.3	17227.4	207.3	17434.6
MASSACHUSETTS	7427.7	14175.0	21602.7	92.1	21694.8
NEW HAMPSHIRE	10338.3	0.0	10338.3	128.2	10466.5
RHODE ISLAND	56.7	0.0	56.7	0.7	57.4
VERMONT	8249.9	1597.0	9846.9	102.3	9949.2
MID ATLANTIC:					
NEW JERSEY	0.0	41164.2	41164.2	0.0	41164.2
NEW YORK	260271.9	61094.3	321366.2	3227.4	324593.5
PENNSYLVANIA	14486.9	2731.1	17217.9	179.6	17397.5
EAST NORTH CENTRAL:					
ILLINOIS	1256.9	123483.2	124740.0	15.6	124755.6
INDIANA	3638.3	0.0	3638.3	45.1	3683.4
MICHIGAN	15545.3	20081.2	35626.5	192.8	35819.3
OHIO	85.1	0.0	85.1	1.1	86.1
WISCONSIN	19911.2	31128.3	51039.4	246.9	51286.3
WEST NORTH CENTRAL:					
IOWA	9383.9	0.0	9383.9	116.4	9500.2
KANSAS	37.8	0.0	37.8	0.5	38.3
MINNESOTA	8117.6	33623.1	41740.7	100.7	41841.3
MISSOURI	5783.4	0.0	5783.4	71.7	5855.1
NEBRASKA	12965.4	0.0	12965.4	160.8	13126.2
NORTH DAKOTA	29247.8	0.0	29247.8	362.7	29610.4
SOUTH DAKOTA	69835.5	0.0	69835.5	866.0	70701.5
SOUTH ATLANTIC:					
DELAWARE	0.0	0.0	0.0	0.0	0.0
DISTRICT OF COLUMBIA	9.5	0.0	9.5	0.1	9.6
FLORIDA	2249.1	623.7	2872.8	27.9	2900.7
GEORGIA	31487.4	0.0	31487.4	390.4	31877.8
MARYLAND	21574.4	0.0	21574.4	267.5	21841.9
NORTH CAROLINA	60754.1	0.0	60754.1	753.4	61507.4
SOUTH CAROLINA	31194.5	45634.1	76828.5	386.8	77215.3
VIRGINIA	12870.9	4233.6	17104.5	159.6	17264.1
WEST VIRGINIA	5046.3	0.0	5046.3	62.6	5108.9
EAST SOUTH CENTRAL:					
ALABAMA	96465.6	0.0	96465.6	1196.2	97661.8
KENTUCKY	36089.6	0.0	36089.6	447.5	36537.1
MISSISSIPPI	0.0	0.0	0.0	0.0	0.0
TENNESSEE	105206.9	0.0	105206.9	1304.6	106511.4
WEST SOUTH CENTRAL:					
ARKANSAS	15535.8	0.0	15535.8	192.6	15728.4
LOUISIANA	0.0	0.0	0.0	0.0	0.0
OKLAHOMA	13674.2	0.0	13674.2	169.6	13843.7
TEXAS	7843.5	0.0	7843.5	97.3	7940.8
ROCKY MOUNTAIN:					
ARIZONA	63986.0	0.0	63986.0	793.4	64779.4
COLORADO	11736.9	0.0	11736.9	145.5	11882.4
IDAHO	74125.8	0.0	74125.8	919.2	75045.0
MONTANA	89245.8	0.0	89245.8	1106.6	90352.4
NEVADA	14770.4	0.0	14770.4	183.2	14953.5
NEW MEXICO	189.0	0.0	189.0	2.3	191.3
UTAH	11529.0	0.0	11529.0	143.0	11672.0
WYOMING	11075.4	0.0	11075.4	137.3	11212.7
FAR WEST:					
ALASKA	3269.7	0.0	3269.7	40.5	3310.2
CALIFORNIA	300528.9	29436.8	329965.7	3726.6	333692.2
HAWAII	207.9	0.0	207.9	2.6	210.5
OREGON	344632.1	0.0	344632.1	4273.4	348905.5
WASHINGTON	715516.2	27584.6	743100.7	8872.4	751973.2

Table I.1.5

Consumption Of Hydropower And Nuclear Power In Billion BTU Of Fuel Equivalent, 1972, By Region

Use By Function And Source Of Power

REGION	ELECTRICITY GENERATION			INDUSTRIAL USE	TOTAL USE
	Hydro-Power	Nuclear Power	Total	(Hydro-Power)	
NEW ENGLAND	48072.30	89775.00	137847.20	596.10	138443.20
MID ATLANTIC	274758.80	104989.60	379748.30	3407.00	383155.20
EAST NORTH CENTRAL	40436.80	174692.70	215129.30	501.50	215630.70
WEST NORTH CENTRAL	135371.40	33623.10	168994.50	1678.80	170673.00
SOUTH ATLANTIC	165186.20	50491.40	215677.50	2048.30	217725.70
EAST SOUTH CENTRAL	237762.10	0.00	237762.10	2948.30	240710.30
WEST SOUTH CENTRAL	37053.50	0.00	37053.50	459.50	37512.90
ROCKY MOUNTAIN	276658.30	0.00	276658.30	3430.50	280088.70
FAR WEST	1364154.80	57021.40	1421176.10	16915.50	1438091.60
TOTAL	2579454.22	510593.21	3090046.79	31985.50	3122031.32

Table I.2.1

Hydropower And Nuclear Power Fuel Equivalent Prices, In Dollars
Per Million BTU, 1972, By State

Price As Substitution Cost Of Alternative Fuels In Electricity Generation

REGION AND STATE	PRICE	REGION AND STATE	PRICE
NEW ENGLAND:		EAST SOUTH CENTRAL:	
CONNECTICUT	0.626	ALABAMA	0.383
MAINE	0.345	KENTUCKY	0.285
MASSACHUSETTS	0.576	MISSISSIPPI	0.370
NEW HAMPSHIRE	0.448	TENNESSEE	0.358
RHODE ISLAND	0.572	WEST SOUTH CENTRAL:	
VERMONT	0.619	ARKANSAS	0.405
MID ATLANTIC:		LOUISIANA	0.259
NEW JERSEY	0.644	OKLAHOMA	0.246
NEW YORK	0.578	TEXAS	0.242
PENNSYLVANIA	0.453	ROCKY MOUNTAIN:	
EAST NORTH CENTRAL:		ARIZONA	0.318
ILLINOIS	0.428	COLORADO	0.298
INDIANA	0.321	IDAHO	0.182
MICHIGAN	0.488	MONTANA	0.262
OHIO	0.388	NEVADA	0.361
WISCONSIN	0.469	NEW MEXICO	0.201
WEST NORTH CENTRAL:		UTAH	0.426
IOWA	0.384	WYOMING	0.182
KANSAS	0.273	FAR WEST:	
MINNESOTA	0.408	ALASKA	0.675
MISSOURI	0.298	CALIFORNIA	0.378
NEBRASKA	0.391	HAWAII	0.534
NORTH DAKOTA	0.268	OREGON	0.176
SOUTH DAKOTA	0.429	WASHINGTON	0.176
SOUTH ATLANTIC:			
DELAWARE	0.539		
DISTRICT OF COLUMBIA	0.539		
FLORIDA	0.448		
GEORGIA	0.449		
MARYLAND	0.539		
NORTH CAROLINA	0.457		
SOUTH CAROLINA	0.490		
VIRGINIA	0.441		
WEST VIRGINIA	0.354		

Table I.3.1

Value Of Hydropower And Nuclear Power In Fuel Equivalent Terms,
In Thousand Dollars, 1972, By State

Use By Function And Source Of Power

REGION AND STATE	ELECTRICITY GENERATION			INDUSTRIAL USE	TOTAL USE
	Hydro-Power	Nuclear Power	Total	(Hydro-Power)	
NEW ENGLAND:					
CONNECTICUT	3306.9	46006.4	49313.3	41.0	49354.3
MAINE	5767.4	176.1	5943.4	71.5	6015.0
MASSACHUSETTS	4278.4	8164.8	12443.2	53.1	12496.2
NEW HAMPSHIRE	4631.6	0.0	4631.6	57.4	4689.0
RHODE ISLAND	32.4	0.0	32.4	0.4	32.8
VERMONT	5106.7	988.6	6095.2	63.3	6158.6
MID ATLANTIC:					
NEW JERSEY	0.0	26509.7	26509.7	0.0	26509.7
NEW YORK	150437.2	35312.5	185749.6	1865.4	187615.1
PENNSYLVANIA	6562.5	1237.2	7799.7	81.4	7881.1
EAST NORTH CENTRAL:					
ILLINOIS	537.9	52850.8	53388.7	6.7	53395.4
INDIANA	1167.9	0.0	1167.9	14.5	1182.4
MICHIGAN	7586.1	9799.6	17385.7	94.1	17479.8
OHIO	33.0	0.0	33.0	0.4	33.4
WISCONSIN	9338.3	14599.2	23937.5	115.8	24053.3
WEST NORTH CENTRAL:					
IOWA	3603.4	0.0	3603.4	44.7	3648.1
KANSAS	10.3	0.0	10.3	0.1	10.4
MINNESOTA	3312.0	13718.2	17030.2	41.1	17071.3
MISSOURI	1723.5	0.0	1723.5	21.4	1744.8
NEBRASKA	5069.5	0.0	5069.5	62.9	5132.3
NORTH DAKOTA	7838.4	0.0	7838.4	97.2	7935.6
SOUTH DAKOTA	29959.4	0.0	29959.4	371.5	30330.9
SOUTH ATLANTIC:					
DELAWARE	0.0	0.0	0.0	0.0	0.0
DISTRICT OF COLUMBIA	5.1	0.0	5.1	0.1	5.2
FLORIDA	1007.6	279.4	1287.0	12.5	1299.5
GEORGIA	14137.8	0.0	14137.8	175.3	14313.2
MARYLAND	11628.6	0.0	11628.6	144.2	11772.8
NORTH CAROLINA	27764.6	0.0	27764.6	344.3	28108.9
SOUTH CAROLINA	15285.3	22360.7	37646.0	189.5	37835.5
VIRGINIA	5676.1	1867.0	7543.1	70.4	7613.5
WEST VIRGINIA	1786.4	0.0	1786.4	22.2	1808.5
EAST SOUTH CENTRAL:					
ALABAMA	36946.3	0.0	36946.3	458.1	37404.5
KENTUCKY	10285.5	0.0	10285.5	127.5	10413.1
MISSISSIPPI	0.0	0.0	0.0	0.0	0.0
TENNESSEE	37664.1	0.0	37664.1	467.0	38131.1
WEST SOUTH CENTRAL:					
ARKANSAS	6292.0	0.0	6292.0	78.0	6370.0
LOUISIANA	0.0	0.0	0.0	0.0	0.0
OKLAHOMA	3363.8	0.0	3363.8	41.7	3405.6
TEXAS	1898.1	0.0	1898.1	23.5	1921.7
ROCKY MOUNTAIN:					
ARIZONA	20347.5	0.0	20347.5	252.3	20599.8
COLORADO	3497.6	0.0	3497.6	43.4	3541.0
IDAHO	13490.9	0.0	13490.9	167.3	13658.2
MONTANA	23382.4	0.0	23382.4	289.9	23672.3
NEVADA	5332.1	0.0	5332.1	66.1	5398.2
NEW MEXICO	38.0	0.0	38.0	0.5	38.5
UTAH	4911.4	0.0	4911.4	60.9	4972.3
WYOMING	2015.7	0.0	2015.7	25.0	2040.7
FAR WEST:					
ALASKA	2207.0	0.0	2207.0	27.4	2234.4
CALIFORNIA	113599.9	11127.1	124727.0	1408.6	126135.7
HAWAII	111.0	0.0	111.0	1.4	112.4
OREGON	60655.2	0.0	60655.2	752.1	61407.4
WASHINGTON	125930.9	4854.9	130785.7	1561.5	132347.3

Table I.3.2

Value Of Hydropower And Nuclear Power In Fuel Equivalent Terms, In Thousand Dollars, 1972, By Region

Use By Function And Source Of Power

REGION	ELECTRICITY GENERATION			INDUSTRIAL USE (Hydro-Power)	TOTAL USE
	Hydro-Power	Nuclear Power	Total		
NEW ENGLAND	23123.40	55335.90	78459.10	286.70	78745.90
MID ATLANTIC	156999.70	63059.40	220059.00	1946.80	222005.90
EAST NORTH CENTRAL	18663.20	77249.60	95912.80	231.50	96144.30
WEST NORTH CENTRAL	51516.50	13718.20	65234.70	638.90	65873.40
SOUTH ATLANTIC	77291.50	24507.10	101798.60	958.50	102757.10
EAST SOUTH CENTRAL	84895.90	0.00	84895.90	1052.60	85948.70
WEST SOUTH CENTRAL	11553.90	0.00	11553.90	143.20	11697.30
ROCKY MOUNTAIN	73015.60	0.00	73015.60	905.40	73921.00
FAR WEST	302504.00	15982.00	318485.90	3751.00	322237.20
TOTAL	799563.71	249852.20	1049415.50	9914.60	1059330.81

Sources For Tables - Part I

Chapter 1

Table 1   Column 1 from column 5, Table 87; column 2 from column 6, Table 125; column 3 from column 5, Table 146; column 4 from column 6, Table 174; column 5 is sum of preceding columns.

Table 2   Column 1 from column 5, Table 90; column 2 from column 6, Table 127; column 3 from column 5, Table 148; column 4 from column 6, Table 175; column 5 is sum of preceding columns.

Table 3   Aggregated from Tables 1 and 2.

Table 4   Obtained from Table 1 by dividing state entries by corresponding state populations (Table 196).

Table 5   Obtained from Table 2 by dividing state entries by corresponding state populations (Table 196).

Table 6   Obtained from Table 3 by dividing regional entries by corresponding regional populations (aggregated from Table 196).

Table 7   Obtained from Table 1 by dividing columns 1 through 4, in turn, by column 5 (total).

Table 8   Obtained from Table 2 by dividing columns 1 through 4, in turn, by column 5 (total).

Table 9   Obtained from Table 3 by dividing columns 1 through 4, in turn, by column 5 (total).

Table 10   Column 1 obtained from column 1, Table 87; column 2 from column 1, Table 126; column 3 from column 1, Table 146; column 4 from column 1, Table 174; column 5 is sum of preceding columns.

Table 11   Column 1 obtained from column 1, Table 90; column 2 from column 1, Table 128; column 3 from column 1, Table 148; column 4 from column 1, Table 175; column 5 is sum of preceding columns.

Table 12   Aggregated from Tables 10 and 11.

Table 13   Obtained from Table 10 by dividing state entries by corresponding state populations (Table 196).

Table 14   Obtained from Table 11 by dividing state entries by corresponding state populations (Table 196).

Table 15   Obtained from Table 12 by dividing regional entries by corresponding regional populations.

Table 16   Obtained from Table 10 by dividing columns 1 through 4, in turn, by column 5 (total).

Table 17 Obtained from Table 11 by dividing columns 1 through 4, in turn, by column 5 (total).

Table 18 Obtained from Table 12 by dividing columns 1 through 4, in turn, by column 5 (total).

Table 19 Obtained by summing columns for specific sectors from Table 87 (petroleum), Table 126 (natural gas), Table 146 (electricity) and Table 174 (coal, hydropower and nuclear power).

Table 20 Obtained by summing columns for specific sectors from Table 90 (petroleum), Table 128 (natural gas) Table 148 (electricity) and Table 175 (coal, hydropower and nuclear power).

Table 21 Aggregated from Tables 19 and 20.

Table 22 Obtained from Table 19 by dividing state entries by corresponding state populations (Table 196).

Table 23 Obtained from Table 20 by dividing state entries by corresponding state populations (Table 196).

Table 24 Obtained from Table 21 by dividing regional entries by corresponding regional populations.

Table 25 Column 1 (net business use) obtained by subtracting column 2 from column 2, Table 19 (business use); column 2 (energy production use) obtained from column 6, Table 78 (petroleum) plus column 2, Table 118 (natural gas) plus column 7, Table 147 (electricity) plus column 4, Table 174 (coal, hydropower and nuclear power); column 3 from sum of columns 1, 3 and 4, Table 19; column 4 from sum of columns 1 and 3; column 5 from sum of columns 2 and 4.

Table 26 Column 1 (net business use) obtained by subtracting column 2 from column 2, Table 20 (business use); column 2 (energy production use) obtained from column 6, Table 82 (petroleum) plus column 2, Table 121 (natural gas) plus column 7, Table 149 (electricity) plus column 4, Table 175 (coal, hydropower and nuclear power); column 3 from sum of columns 1, 3 and 4, Table 20; column 4 from sum of columns 1 and 3; column 5 from sum of columns 2 and 4.

Table 27 Aggregated from Tables 25 and 26.

Table 28 Obtained from Table 25 by dividing state entries by corresponding state populations (Table 196).

Table 29   Obtained from Table 26 by dividing state entries by corresponding state populations (Table 196).

Table 30   Obtained from Table 27 by dividing regional entries by corresponding regional populations.

Table 31   Obtained from Tables 19 and 25 by dividing component column
entries by corresponding totals. Columns 1, 4 and 5 from columns 1,
3 and 4, respectively, Table 19 divided by total (column 5); columns 2
and 3 from columns 1 and 2, respectively, Table 25, divided by total
(column 5).

Table 32   Obtained from Tables 20 and 26 by dividing component column
entries by corresponding totals. Columns 1, 4 and 5 from columns 1,
3 and 4, respectively, Table 20 divided by total (column 5); columns 2
and 3 from columns 1 and 2, respectively, Table 26, divided by total
(column 5).

Table 33   Obtained from Tables 21 and 27 by dividing component column
entries by corresponding totals. Columns 1, 4 and 5 from columns 1, 3
and 4, respectively, Table 21 divided by total (column 5); columns 2
and 3 from columns 1 and 2, respectively, Table 27, divided by total
(column 5).

Table 34   Energy expenditures per capita from Table 13; per capita income
from Survey of Current Business, August, 1974, Table 22, 33; energy
expenditures per capita divided by corresponding per capita income
to yield state fractions of Table 34.

Table 35   Obtained by combining component columns classified by function
from Tables 75 through 78 (petroleum), Tables 116 through 118 (natural
gas), Table 147 (electricity) and Table 174 (coal, hydropower and
nuclear power). Column 1 (residential) obtained by sum of following:
column 1, Table 76; column 1, Table 78; column 1, Table 116; column 1,
Table 147; and column 1, Table 174. Column 2 (commercial) obtained
by sum of following: columns 2, 5 and 6, Table 76; column 7, Table 78;
column 5, Table 116; column 2, Table 147 and column 2, Table 174.
Column 3 (industrial) obtained by sum of following: column 3, Table 76;
column 2, Table 78; column 4, Table 117; column 3, Table 147; column 3,
Table 174. Column 4 (transportation) obtained by sum of following:
Table 75, column 9; Table 77, column 8; and Table 147, column 6.
Column 5 (non-electric utility) obtained by sum of following: columns
3 and 4, Table 78; columns 4, 5 and 6, Table 118; column 7, Table 147.
Column 6 (electric utility) obtained by sum of following: column 5,
Table 78; column 3, Table 118; and column 4, Table 174. Column 7
(municipal-institutional) obtained by sum of following: column 1,
Table 118; and columns 4 and 5, Table 147. Column 8 is sum of preceding
columns.

Table 36   Obtained by combining component columns from Tables 79 through
   82 (petroleum), Tables 119 through 121 (natural gas), Table 149
   (electricity) and Table 175 (coal, hydropower and nuclear power).
   Column 1 (residential) obtained by sum of following: column 1,
   Table 80; column 1, Table 82; column 1, Table 119; column 1, Table 149;
   and column 1, Table 175. Column 2 (commercial) obtained by sum of
   following: columns 2, 5 and 6, Table 80; column 7, Table 82; column 5,
   Table 119; column 2, Table 149; and column 2, Table 175. Column 3
   (industrial) obtained by sum of following: column 3, Table 80; column 2,
   Table 82; column 4, Table 120; column 3, Table 149; and column 3,
   Table 175. Column 4 (transportation) obtained by sum of following:
   column 9, Table 79; column 8, Table 81; and column 6, Table 149.
   Column 5 (non-electric utility) obtained by sum of following: columns 3
   and 4, Table 82; columns 4, 5 and 6, Table 121; and column 7, Table 149.
   Column 6 (electric utility) obtained by sum of following: column 5,
   Table 182; column 3, Table 121 and column 4, Table 175. Column 7
   (municipal-institutional) obtained by sum of following: column 1, Table 121;
   and columns 4 and 5, Table 149. Column 8 is sum of preceding columns.

Table 37   Aggregated from Tables 35 and 36.

Table 38   Obtained from Table 35 by dividing state entries by corresponding
   state populations (Table 196).

Table 39   Obtained from Table 36 by dividing state entries by corresponding
   state populations (Table 196).

Table 40   Obtained from Table 37 by dividing regional entries by corresponding regional populations.

Table 41   Obtained by dividing Table 38 entries by corresponding U.S.
   entry in Table 40 and multiplying result by 100.

Table 42   Obtained by dividing Table 39 entries by corresponding U.S. entry
   in Table 40 and multiplying result by 100.

Table 43   Obtained by dividing Table 40 entries by corresponding U.S. entry
   in that table and multiplying result by 100.

Table 44   Columns 1 through 5, respectively, from residential use Tables
   76, 78, 116, 147 and 174, each divided by corresponding state populations
   (Table 196). Column 6 is sum of preceding columns.

Table 45   Columns 1 through 5, respectively, from residential use in
   Tables 80, 82, 119, 149 and 175, each divided by corresponding state
   populations (Table 196). Column 6 is sum of preceding columns.

Table 46. Obtained by forming regional aggregates of state data cited in
   source notes for Tables 44 and 45, followed by dividing each aggregate,
   in turn, by corresponding regional population.

Table 47   Columns 1 through 5, respectively, from commercial use in
    Table 76 (columns 2, 5 and 6), Table 78 (column 7), and Tables 116,
    147 and 174, each divided by corresponding state populations (Table 196).
    Column 6 is sum of preceding columns.

Table 48   Columns 1 through 5, respectively, from commercial use in
    Table 80 (columns 2, 5 and 6), Table 82 (column 7) and Tables 119, 149
    and 175, each divided by corresponding state populations (Table 196).
    Column 6 is sum of preceding columns.

Table 49   Obtained by forming regional aggregates of state data cited in
    source notes for Tables 47 and 48, followed by dividing each aggregate,
    in turn, by corresponding regional population.

Table 50   Columns 1 through 5, respectively, from industrial use in
    Tables 76, 78, 117, 147, and 174, each divided by corresponding state
    populations (Table 196).   Column 6 is sum of preceding columns.

Table 51   Columns 1 through 5, respectively, from industrial use in
    Tables 80, 82, 120, 149 and 175, each divided by corresponding state
    populations (Table 196).   Column 6 is sum of preceding columns.

Table 52   Obtained by forming regional aggregates of state data cited
    in source notes for Tables 50 and 51, followed by dividing each aggregate,
    in turn, by corresponding regional population.

Table 53   Column 1 from column 1, Table 75; column 2 from column 9 minus
    column 1, Table 75; column 3 from column 8, Table 77; column 4 from
    column 6, Table 147; each then divided by corresponding state populations
    (Table 196).   Column 5 is sum of preceding columns.

Table 54   Column 1 from column 1, Table 79; column 2 from column 9 minus
    column 1, Table 79; column 3 from column 8, Table 81; column 4 from
    column 6, Table 149; each then divided by corresponding state populations
    (Table 196).   Column 5 is sum of preceding columns.

Table 55   Obtained by forming regional aggregates of state data cited in
    source notes for Tables 53 and 54, followed by dividing each aggregate,
    in turn, by corresponding regional population.

Table 56   Regional consumption aggregates were formed from state entries
    showing electric utility use by specific energy source, in Tables 78,
    118 and 174.   Then regional aggregates were divided by corresponding
    regional populations.   Similarly, regional expenditure aggregates were
    formed from state entries in Tables 82, 121 and 175.   Again, regional
    aggregates were divided by corresponding regional population.

Table 57   Regional consumption aggregates were formed from state entries showing municipal-institutional use by specific energy source, in Tables 118 and 147 (columns 4 and 5). Then regional aggregates were divided by corresponding regional populations. Similarly, regional expenditure aggregates were formed from state entries in Tables 121 and 149 (columns 4 and 5). Again, regional aggregates were divided by corresponding regional populations.

Table 58   From Table 50, by dividing each column, in turn, by total.

Table 59   From Table 52, upper section, by dividing each column, in turn, by total.

Table 60   From Table 53 by dividing each column, in turn, by total.

Table 61   From Table 54, upper section, by dividing each column, in turn, by total.

Table 62   From Table 56, upper section, by dividing each column, in turn, by total.

Table 63   Obtained by dividing expenditures by quantities. Sector entries for expenditures in Table 20 divided by corresponding sector entries for quantities in Table 19.

Table 64   Sector entries for expenditures in Table 21 divided by corresponding sector entries for quantities in that table.

Table 65   Obtained by dividing expenditures by quantities. Function entries for expenditures in Table 36 divided by corresponding function entries for quantities in Table 35.

Table 66   Function entries for expenditures in Table 37 divided by corresponding function entries for quantities in that table.

Table 67   Natural gas entries from Table 144, columns 1 and 3, respectively; electricity entries from Table 166, columns 1 and 3, respectively; coal, hydropower and nuclear power entries from Table 191, columns 1 and 3, respectively.

Table 68   From columns 4 through 6, Table 113.

Table 69   Column 1 from division of entries in column 1, Table 79 by corresponding entries in column 1, Table 75. Column 2 as follows: expenditures formed by column 2 minus column 1, Table 79 plus column 1, Table 81; quantities formed by column 2 minus column 1, Table 75 plus column 1, Table 77; then expenditures were divided by corresponding quantities to yield prices. Column 3 as follows: expenditures formed by sum of column 1, Table 80 plus column 1, Table 82; quantities formed by column 1, Table 76 plus column 1, Table 78; then expenditures were divided by corresponding quantities to yield prices.

Table 70   Expenditures and quantities derived corresponding to each
column, then expenditures divided by corresponding quantities gave
prices. For column 1, expenditures from column 9 minus column 2,
Table 79, quantities from column 9 minus column 2, Table 75; for
column 2, expenditures from column 8 minus column 1, Table 81,
quantities from column 8 minus column 1, Table 77; for column 3,
expenditures from column 7 minus column 1, Table 80, quantities
from column 7 minus column 1, Table 76; for column 4, expenditures
from column 8 minus columns 1 and 5, Table 82, quantities from
column 8 minus columns 1 and 5, Table 78; for column 5 expenditures
from column 5, Table 82, quantities from column 5, Table 78.

Table 71   Upper section: petroleum prices from column 4, Table 115;
natural gas prices from column 1, Table 145; electricity prices from
column 1, Table 167; coal, hydropower and nuclear power prices from
column 1, Table 192; last column obtained by weighting previous columns
by fraction of BTU each energy source furnished consumption by households.
Weights were--petroleum: .61869, natural gas: .28037, electricity: .08579,
coal, etc: .01515. Lower section obtained by dividing entries in upper
section by U.S. value and multiplying by 100.

Table 72   Upper section: petroleum prices from column 6, Table 115;
natural gas prices from column 3, Table 145; electricity prices from
column 3, Table 167; coal, etc. prices from column 3, Table 192; last
column obtained by weighting previous columns by fraction of BTU each
energy source furnished consumption by households. Weights were--
petroleum: .40174, natural gas: .31358, electricity: .07355; coal, etc.:
.21113. Lower section obtained by dividing entries in upper section
by U.S. value and multiplying by 100.

Table 73   First two columns obtained from Tables 67 and 68 weighting prices
for each energy source by U.S. weights for the source (see source notes
for Tables 71 and 72). Last two columns obtained by dividing by corresponding U.S. price and multiplying by 100; thus, column 3 obtained by
dividing column 1 by U.S. price in last column of Table 71; column 4
obtained by dividing column 2 by U.S. price in last column of Table 72.

Table 74   Columns 1 and 3 from last column, Table 71, columns 2 and 4
from last column, Table 72; results checked by forming regional averages
and indexes from state data of Table 73, weighting by relative population
(Table 196).

Chapter 2

Table 75   All entries obtained from Appendix A, scaled by 5.248 (million
BTU per barrel), scale factor listed in [7]. Column 1 from column 1,
Table A.1.4; column 2 from column 1, Table A.1.5; column 3 from column 2,
Table A.1.5; column 4 from sum of columns 7, 10 and 11, Table A.1.4;
column 5 from sum of columns 8 and 9, Table A.1.4; column 6 from column 4,
Table A.1.5; column 7 from column 5, Table A.1.5; column 8 from column 6,
Table A.1.5; column 9 is sum of columns 2 through 5 and also sum of columns 6
through 8.

Table 76   Column 1 from column 1, Table B.1.28; column 2 from column 2, Table B.1.25 minus column 5, Table B.1.28 (all commercial minus government commercial yields business commercial); column 3 from column 3, Table B.1.25; column 4 from column 2, Table B.1.28; columns 5 and 6 from columns 4 and 5, respectively, Table B.1.28; column 7 is sum of columns 1, 4, 5 and 6.

Table 77   Columns 1, 2 and 3 from columns 1, 2 and 3, respectively, Table D.1.12; column 4 from sum of column 2, Table D.1.11 (civilian highway) and column 1, Table D.1.1, scaled by 5.825 (scale factor converting thousand barrels to billion BTU, from [7]), the latter item accounting for military use of distillates; column 5 from column 3, Table D.1.11; column 6 from sum of column 5, Table D.1.11 (civilian vessel bunkering) plus column 2, Table D.1.1 times 6.287 (scale factor converting thousand barrels to billion BTU, from [7]), the latter item accounting for military use of residual fuel oils; column 7 from column 4, Table D.1.11; column 8 is sum of columns 1 through 3, equal to sum of columns 4 through 7.

Table 78   Column 1 from column 5, Table E.1.11; columns 2, 3 and 4 from columns 1, 2 and 3, respectively, Table E.1.11; column 5 from column 1, Table C.1.4; column 6 from sum of columns 3, 4 and 5; column 7 from column 5, Table E.1.11; column 8 is sum of columns 1, 2, 6 and 7.

Table 79   Obtained by multiplying quantities by corresponding prices in Appendix A. Results in thousands of dollars correspond to results in millions of dollars in Appendix A. Column 1 corresponds to column 1, Table A.3.1; column 2 corresponds to column 2, Table A.3.3; column 3 corresponds to column 2, Table A.3.3; column 4 corresponds to the sum of columns 1, 4 and 5, Table A.3.2; column 5 corresponds to the sum of columns 2 and 3, Table A.3.2; columns 6, 7 and 8 correspond to columns 4, 5 and 6, Table A.3.3; column 9 is sum of columns 2 through 5 (sectors) equal to sum of columns 6 through 8 (functions).

Table 80   Columns 1, 2, 3, 5 and 6 directly from Table B.3.8; column 4 is sum of columns 2 and 3; column 7 is sum of columns 1, 4, 5 and 6.

Table 81   Obtained by multiplying quantities by corresponding prices in Appendix D. Results correspond to results in Appendix D which are rounded to one less decimal place. Columns 1, 2, and 3 correspond to Table D.3.4; column 4 corresponds to column 2, Table D.3.3 plus column 1, Table D.3.1 (civilian highway plus military distillates); column 5 to column 3, Table D.3.3; column 6 corresponds to column 5, Table D.3.3 plus column 2, Table D.3.1 (vessel bunkering plus military residuals); column 7 to column 4, Table D.3.3; column 8 is sum of columns 1 through 3 and of 4 through 7.

Table 82   Obtained by multiplying prices by corresponding prices in appendixes C and E. Column 5 from column 3, Table C.3.1; all other columns correspond to entries in Table E.3.2, listed to one more decimal place.

Table 83   Aggregated from Tables 75 **and** 79.

Table 84   Aggregated from Tables 76 and 80.

Table 85   Aggregated from Tables 77 and 81.

Table 86   Aggregated from Tables 78 and 82.

Table 87   Obtained by combining specific sector entries in Tables 75 through 78.   Column 1 (household) from column 2, Table 75 plus column 1, Table 76 plus column 1, Table 77 plus column 1, Table 78; column 2 (business) from column 3, Table 75 plus column 4, Table 76, plus column 2, Table 77 plus columns 2, 6 and 7, Table 78; column 3 (federal government) from column 4, Table 75 plus column 5, Table 76 plus column 3, Table 77; column 4 (state and local government) from column 5, Table 75 plus column 6, Table 76; column 5 (all) is sum of preceding columns.

Table 88   Obtained by dividing Table 87 entries by corresponding state populations (Table 196).

Table 89   Obtained by dividing Table 88 entries by corresponding U.S. values listed in Table 94 and then multiplying by 100 to put in index terms (percentages).

Table 90   Obtained by combining specific sector entries in Tables 79 through 82.   Column 1 (household) from column 2, Table 79 plus column 1, Table 80 plus column 1, Table 81 plus column 1, Table 82; column 2 (business) from column 3, Table 79 plus column 4, Table 80 plus column 2, Table 81 plus columns 2, 6 and 7, Table 82; column 3 (federal government) from column 4, Table 79 plus column 5, Table 80 plus column 3, Table 81; column 4 (state and local government) from column 5, Table 79 plus column 6, Table 80; column 5 (all) is sum of preceding columns.

Table 91   Obtained by dividing Table 90 entries by corresponding state populations (Table 196).

Table 92   Obtained by dividing Table 91 entries by corresponding U.S. values listed in Table 95, and then multiplying by 100 to put in index terms (percentages).

Table 93   Aggregated from Tables 87 and 90.

Table 94   BTU per capita obtained by dividing Table 93 consumption entries by corresponding regional populations (aggregated from Table 196).   Index of consumption obtained by dividing BTU per capita by corresponding U.S. value in upper part of Table 94, and then multiplying by 100.

Table 95   Expenditures per capita obtained by dividing Table 93 expenditures entries by corresponding regional populations (aggregated from Table 196).   Index of expenditures obtained by dividing expenditures per capita by corresponding U.S. value in upper part of Table 95, and then multiplying by 100.

Table 96   Column 1 from column 1, Table 75; column 2 from subtraction
of column 1 from column 5, Table 87; column 3 from column 5, Table 87;
column 4 from column 1, Table 79; column 5 from subtraction of column 1
from column 5, Table 90; column 6 from column 5, Table 90; column 7
from column 1 divided by column 3; column 8 from column 4 divided by
column 6.

Table 97   First four columns from household entries in Tables 79 through
82, divided by corresponding state populations (Table 196); last three
columns obtained by dividing columns 1 through 3, in turn, by column 4.

Table 98   First five columns from business entries in Tables 79 through
82, divided by corresponding state populations (Table 196); last four
columns obtained by dividing columns 1 through 4, in turn, by column 5.

Table 99   Obtained from detailed information in Tables 80 and 82, divided
by corresponding state populations (Table 196). Column 1 from column 3,
Table 80; column 2 from column 2, Table 82; column 3 from sum of column 1
and column 2; column 4 from column 2, Table 80; column 5 from column 7,
Table 82; column 6 from sum of column 4 and column 5; in all columns,
listed entries obtained by dividing source entries by corresponding
state populations.

Table 100   Columns 1 through 5 obtained by dividing amounts of expenditures
from Tables 79 through 81 by corresponding state populations (Table 196).
Aggregate expenditures for column 1 from column 4, Table 79 plus column 3,
Table 81; for column 2 from Table 80; for column 3 from Table 79; and for
column 4 from Table 80. Column 5 equals sum of preceding columns.
Fractions of columns 6 through 9 obtained by dividing column 5 into the
following, in turn: columns 1 plus 2; columns 3 plus 4; columns 1 plus
3; and columns 2 plus 4.

Table 101   First 6 columns aggregated from corresponding columns of Table 96;
column 7 obtained by division of column 1 by column 3; column 8 obtained
by division of column 4 by column 6.

Table 102   Regional analogue to Tables 97 and 100. Dollars per capita
obtained by aggregating amounts of expenditures from Tables 79 through
82, and then dividing regional totals by corresponding regional populations. Given dollars per capita, fractions of use obtained by dividing
component columns by totals.

Table 103   Regional analogue to Tables 98 and 99. Dollars per capita obtained
by aggregating amounts of expenditures from Tables 79 through 82,
and then dividing regional totals by corresponding regional populations.
Given dollars per capita, fractions of use obtained by dividing component
columns by totals.

Table 104 Summarizes Tables 75-82. Column 1 from sum of column 9,
Table 75 and column 8, Table 77; column 2 from column 7, Table 76;
column 3 from sum of columns 1, 2 and 7, Table 78; column 4 from column 6,
Table 78; column 5 from sum of column 9, Table 79 plus column 8, Table 81;
column 6 from column 7, Table 80; column 7 from sum of columns 1, 2 and 7,
Table 82; column 8 from column 6, Table 82.

Table 105 From division of component columns in Table 104 by corresponding
sum (grand totals) as listed in Table 96. Columns 1 through 4 from
columns 1 through 4, respectively, of Table 104, each divided by column 3
of Table 96; columns 5 through 8 from columns 5 through 8, respectively,
of Table 104, each divided by column 6 of Table 96.

Table 106 Consumption and expenditures aggregated from Table 104. Fractions
obtained by dividing components in upper part of table by corresponding
totals, as listed in Table 101.

Table 107 From entries in Tables 79 and 81 divided by corresponding state
populations (Table 196). Column 1 from column 1, Table 79; column 2 from
column 6 minus column 1, Table 79 plus column 4, Table 81; column 3 from
column 7, Table 79 plus column 5, Table 81; column 4 from column 7,
Table 81; column 5 from column 8, Table 79 plus column 6, Table 81;
column 6 from sum of preceding columns; all source entries divided by
state population.

Table 108 From corresponding entries in Table 82 divided by corresponding
state population

Table 109 From aggregate expenditures in Tables 83 and 85 for transportation,
and from aggregate expenditures in Table 86 for energy production, all
entries divided by corresponding regional populations.

Table 110 Column 1 from column 1, Table A.2.1; columns 2 and 3 from columns
1 and 3, respectively, Table B.2.1; column 4 from column 2, Table C.3.1.

Table 111 Corresponds to Table 110 entries divided by corresponding entries
in Table 112, and multiplied by 100. Round-off differences reflect greater
number of decimal places employed in practice, e.g., compare column 5,
Table A.2.4 and column 1, Table A.2.1.

Table 112 For upper part of table: column 1 from simple average of entries
in column 5, Table A.2.4; columns 2 and 3 from simple averages of entries
in columns 1 and 3, Table B.2.1, respectively; column 4 from simple
average of entries in column 2, Table C.3.1. For bottom part of table,
regional entries of upper part divided by U.S. value, and result multiplied by 100.

Table 113 First three columns obtained by division of expenditures in
Table 90 by corresponding consumption in Table 87. Column 1 from column 1,
Table 90 divided by column 1, Table 87; column 2 from column 5 minus column
1, Table 90, divided by column 5 minus column 1, Table 87; column 3 from
column 5, Table 90 divided by column 5, Table 87. Last three columns
obtained by first deriving prices for components of each category and

then weighting component prices by U.S. price weights. Column 4,
household components and U.S. weights were: passenger car and motorcycle
gasoline, 66793; all other transportation use, 00978; all other petroleum
products, .32229. Column 5, non-household use components and U.S.
weights were: gasoline, .22761; all other transportation fuels, .27927;
heating fuels, .09101; all other, except use by electric utilities,
.21934; electric utility use, .18277. Column 6 obtained by weighting
column 4 by .42798 and column 5 by .57202, equal to their national
shares, and summing. Component prices obtained by appropriate division
of expenditures in Tables 79 through 82 by corresponding quantities
in Tables 75 through 78.

Table 114   Obtained by dividing Table 113 entries by corresponding U.S.
values in Table 115 and then multiplying by 100.

Table 115   First three columns obtained by dividing aggregate of regional
expenditures by corresponding regional quantities consumed from Tables 83
through 86. Last three columns obtained by weighting corresponding state
entries in columns 4 through 6, Table 113 by population. State populations
as fraction of region population used as regional weights to obtain regional
prices; state populations as fraction of U.S. population used as weights
to obtain national price. See Table 196 for state shares of regional and
U.S. populations.

Chapter 3

Table 116   Column 1 from column 6, Table F.1.18; columns 2 through 5 from
F.1.19.

Table 117   Column 1 from column 1 plus column 2 minus columns 3, 4 and 5,
Table F.1.21; columns 2 and 3 from columns 4 and 5, respectively, Table
F.1.21; column 4 equals column 1 plus column 2 minus column 3, Table
F.1.21. In obtaining the industrial sum (column 4), use attributable
to energy production (column 3, Table F.1.21) is removed. Then business
use is obtained by removing industrial use by government.

Table 118   Column 1 from column 1, Table F.1.23; column 2 is total listed
in column 7, Table F.1.23; column 3 from columns 2 plus 3 of Table F.1.23;
columns 4, 5 and 6 from columns 4, 5 and 6, respectively, Table F.1.23.

Table 119   Column 1 from column 6, Table F.3.13; columns 2 through 5 from
Table F.3.14.

Table 120   Column 1 from column 1 plus column 2 minus columns 3, 4, and 5,
Table F.3.16; columns 2 and 3 from columns 4 and 5, respectively,
Table F.3.16; column 4 equals column 1 plus column 2 minus column 3,
Table F.3.16.

Table 121   Column 1 from column 1, Table F.3.18; column 2 from column 6,
Table F.3.18; column 3 from columns 2 plus 3, Table F.3.18; columns 4, 5,
6 from columns 4, 5, 6, respectively, Table F.3.18.

Table 122   Aggregated from Tables 116 and 119.

Table 123   Aggregated from Tables 117 and 120.

Table 124   Aggregated from Tables 118 and 121.

Table 125   Columns 1 and 2 from columns 1 and 5, respectively, Table 116;
    column 3 from column 4, Table 117; column 4 from column 2, Table 118;
    column 5 from column 1, Table 118; column 6 from sum of preceding columns.

Table 126   Sector sums from Tables 116 through 118. Column 1 equals
    column 1, Table 116; column 2 from sum of column 2, Table 116 plus column
    1, Table 117 plus column 2, Table 118; column 3 from sum of column 3,
    Table 116 plus column 2, Table 117; column 4 from sum of column 4,
    Table 116 plus column 3, Table 117 plus column 1, Table 118; column 5
    is sum of preceding columns.

Table 127   Columns 1 and 2 from columns 1 and 5, respectively, Table 119;
    column 3 from column 4, Table 120; column 4 from column 2, Table 121;
    column 5 from column 1, Table 121; column 6 from sum of preceding columns.

Table 128   Sector sums from Tables 119 through 121. Column 1 equals
    column 1, Table 119; column 2 from sum of column 2, Table 119 plus column 1,
    Table 120 plus column 2, Table 121; column 3 from sum of columns 3, Table
    119 plus column 2, Table 120; column 4 from sum of column 4, Table 119
    plus column 3, Table 120 plus column 1, Table 121; column 5 is sum of
    preceding columns.

Table 129   Aggregated from Tables 125 and 127.

Table 130   Aggregated from Tables 126 and 128.

Table 131   Obtained from Table 125 by dividing entries by corresponding
    state populations (Table 196).

Table 132   Obtained from Table 126 by dividing entries by corresponding
    state populations (Table 196).

Table 133   Obtained from Table 127 by dividing entries by corresponding
    state populations (Table 196).

Table 134   Obtained from Table 128 by dividing entries by corresponding
    state populations (Table 196).

Table 135   Obtained from Table 129 by dividing entries by corresponding
    regional populations.

Table 136   Obtained from Table 130 by dividing entries by corresponding
    regional populations.

Table 137   Obtained from corresponding entries in Table 131 divided by
    U.S. values in Table 135, with results multiplied by 100.

Table 138   Obtained from corresponding entries in Table 133 divided by U.S. values in Table 135, with results multiplied by 100.

Table 139   Obtained from Table 135 by dividing regional by U.S. values, and multiplying results by 100.

Table 140   Obtained by dividing expenditures in Table 127 by corresponding quantities in Table 125.

Table 141   Obtained by dividing expenditures in Table 128 by corresponding quantities in Table 126.

Table 142   Obtained by dividing expenditures in lower part of Table 129 by corresponding quantities in upper part of that table.

Table 143   Obtained by dividing expenditures in lower part of Table 130 by corresponding quantities in upper part of that table.

Table 144   Columns 1 and 2 obtained by dividing expenditures, columns 1 and 6, Table 127 by corresponding quantities, columns 1 and 6, Table 125; column 3 obtained by weighting prices in Table 140 by U.S. quantity weights, as follows--residential: .24847, "net" commercial: .04576, industrial: .38444, energy production: .30697, other use: .01436, corresponding to U.S. quantities in Table 129, upper part. Price indexes of columns 4 through 6 obtained by dividing columns 1 through 3 by corresponding U.S. values in Table 145, and multiplying by 100.

Table 145   First three columns obtained from corresponding columns of Table 144 by weighting state prices by state shares of region's population to obtain regional prices, and by state shares of U.S. population to obtain U.S. prices (see Table 196 for weights). Division of regional values by corresponding U.S. values and multiplication by 100 gave last three columns.

Chapter 4

Table 146   Reproduced from Table G.1.10.

Table 147   Reproduced from Table G.1.1.

Table 148   Reproduced from Table G.3.7.

Table 149   Reproduced from Table G.3.1.

Table 150   Aggregated from Tables 146 and 148.

Table 151   Aggregated from Tables 147 and 149.

Table 152   Obtained by dividing Table 146 entries by corresponding state populations (Table 196).

713

Table 153   Obtained by dividing Table 147 entries by corresponding
state populations (Table 196).

Table 154   Obtained by dividing Table 148 entries by corresponding state
populations (Table 196).

Table 155   Obtained by dividing Table 149 entries by corresponding state
populations (Table 196).

Table 156   Obtained by dividing Table 150 entries by corresponding
regional populations.

Table 157   Obtained by dividing Table 151 entries by corresponding regional
populations.

Table 158   Obtained by dividing Table 152 entries by corresponding U.S.
values in Table 156, and then multiplying by 100.

Table 159   Obtained by dividing Table 153 entries by corresponding U.S.
values in Table 157, and then multiplying by 100.

Table 160   Obtained by dividing Table 154 entries by corresponding U.S.
values in Table 156, and then multiplying by 100.

Table 161   Obtained by dividing Table 155 entries by corresponding U.S.
values in Table 157, and then multiplying by 100.

Table 162   Obtained by dividing regional values of Table 156 by corresponding U.S. values, and then multiplying by 100.

Table 163   Obtained by dividing regional values of Table 157 by corresponding U.S. values, and then multiplying by 100.

Table 164   Reproduced from Table G.2.1.

Table 165   Reproduced from Table G.2.2.

Table 166   Columns 1 and 2 from columns 1 and 8, respectively, of Table 164;
column 3 obtained by weighting prices for specific functional uses by
U.S. fractions of use, as follows--residential: .32416, commercial: .22936,
industrial: .40530, street and highway lighting: .00773, and "all other":
.03345. (Last category covers other public authorities, railroads and
railways, and interdepartmental use.) These weights can be derived from
Table 151. Price indexes of column 4 through 6 obtained by dividing
columns 1 through 3 by corresponding U.S. values in Table 167, and multiplying by 100.

Table 167   First three columns obtained from corresponding columns
of Table 166 by weighting state prices by state shares of region's
population to obtain regional prices, and by state shares of U.S.
population to obtain U.S. prices. (See Table 196 for weights.)
Dividing regional values by corresponding U.S. values and multiplying by 100 gave last three columns.

Chapter 5

Table 168   Reproduced from Table H.1.5.

Table 169   Reproduced from Table H.3.1.

Table 170   Aggregated from Tables 168 and 169.

Table 171   Obtained from Table I.1.4; columns 1 through 4 obtained from
columns 4, 1, 2 and 5, respectively, of Table I.1.4.

Table 172   Obtained from Table I.3.1; columns 1 through 4 obtained from
columns 4, 1, 2 and 5, respectively of Table I.3.1.

Table 173   Aggregated from Tables 171 and 172.

Table 174   Obtained by summing entries from corresponding columns of
Tables 168 and 171.

Table 175   Obtained by summing entries from corresponding columns of
Tables 169 and 172.

Table 176   Aggregated from Tables 174 and 175.

Table 177   Obtained by dividing energy source totals by corresponding state
populations (Table 196); energy source totals for column 1 obtained from
column 5, Table 168; for column 2 from sum of columns 1 and 2, Table 171;
and for column 3 from column 3, Table 171; column 4 is sum of preceding
columns.

Table 178   Obtained by dividing energy source totals by corresponding state
populations (Table 196); energy source totals for column 1 obtained
from column 5, Table 169; for column 2 from sum of columns 1 and 2,
Table 172; and for column 3 from column 3, Table 172; column 4 is sum
of preceding columns.

Table 179   Obtained by dividing energy source totals by corresponding
regional populations; energy source totals for column 1 obtained from
column 5, Table 170; for column 2 from sum of columns 1 and 2, Table 173;
and for column 3 from column 3, Table 173; column 4 is sum of preceding
columns.

Table 180   Obtained by summing corresponding category entries in Tables 168
and 171 and dividing totals by corresponding state populations (Table 196).

Table 181   Obtained by summing corresponding entries in Tables 169 and 172 and dividing totals by corresponding state populations (Table 196).

Table 182   Obtained by summing corresponding entries in Tables 170 and 173 and dividing totals by corresponding regional populations.

Table 183   Obtained by dividing Table 177 entries by corresponding U.S. values in Table 179 and then multiplying by 100.

Table 184   Obtained by dividing Table 178 entries by corresponding U.S. values in Table 179 and then multiplying by 100.

Table 185   Obtained by dividing regional values of Table 179 by corresponding U.S. values, and then multiplying by 100.

Table 186   Obtained by dividing Table 180 entries by corresponding U.S. values in Table 182 and than multiplying by 100.

Table 187   Obtained by dividing Table 181 entries by corresponding U.S. values in Table 182 and then multiplying by 100.

Table 188   Obtained by dividing regional values of Table 182 by corresponding U.S. values and then multiplying by 100.

Table 189   Columns 1 through 4 obtained from Table H.2.2, with listing in reverse order, i.e., columns 1, 2, 3 and 4 from columns 4, 3, 2 and 1, respectively, of Table H.2.2. Column 5 from Table I.2.1.

Table 190   Columns 1 through 4 obtained by dividing regional expenditures by corresponding regional quantities in Table 170. Column 5 obtained by dividing regional expenditures by corresponding quantities in column 4, Table 173.

Table 191   Column 1 from column 1, Table 189; column 2 from division of total expenditures by total quantities, with total expenditures obtained from column 6, Table 175 and total quantities from column 6, Table 174; column 3 obtained by weighting prices for specific uses by U.S. fractions of use, as follows--coal residential: .01994, coal commercial: .00120, coal industrial: .27476, coal electric utility: .50206, and hydropower-nuclear power: .20204. These weights can be derived from Tables 170, 173 and 176. Price indexes of columns 4 through 6 obtained by dividing columns 1 through 3 by corresponding U.S. values in Table 192, and multiplying by 100.

Table 192   First three columns obtained from corresponding columns of Table 191 by weighting state prices by state shares of region's population to obtain regional prices, and by state shares of U.S. population to obtain U.S. prices. (See Table 196 for weights.) Dividing regional values by corresponding U.S. values and multiplying by 100 gave last three columns.

Chapter 6

Table 193   Dependent variables are per capita residential use of
petroleum products, natural gas and electricity, by state, respectively obtained from BTU entries in Tables 76, 78, 127 and 147,
divided by the corresponding state population from Table 196.
Independent variables include the logs of petroleum products price,
natural gas price and electricity price in residential use, as
respectively listed in column 3, Table 69, and in columns 1 and 3,
Table 67.   The fraction of state population located in metropolitan
areas (fraction SMSA population) was obtained from U.S. Bureau of
the Census, Census of Population: 1970, Number of Inhabitants,
Final Report PC(1)-A1, p. 32.   For the log of state population
growth, 1960-1970, 1970 population was divided by 1960 population
and the ratio was then multiplied by 100; the population data were
obtained from U.S. Bureau of the Census, Current Population Reports,
Series P-25, No. 520, July, 1974, p. 21.   Climate data were obtained
from U.S. Bureau of the Census, Statistical Abstract, 1975, with
annual heating degree days from Table 332, p. 197, and summer and
winter temperature from July and January temperatures, respectively,
in Table 322, page 187.   Log "real" disposable income was per capita
personal income deflated for estimated price level differences by
region and population size of locale.   The initial data series employed
was per capita disposable income as listed in Survey of Current Business,
August, 1975, Table 2, p. 11. (Disposable income is personal income
minus taxes.)   Data cited in Irving Hoch, "City Size Effects, Trends,
and Policies," Science, September, 1976, 856-863, yielded the following
scale factors: (1) a price level for the South that was seven percent
below that in the North, and a price level for Alaska and Hawaii that
was 25 percent above that in the North, (conterminous U.S.), and (2)
a price level increment of six percent per order of magnitude of SMSA
population, so that an SMSA with 10 million population would have a
price level 1.06 times that of an SMSA of one million population, in
turn having a price level 1.06 times that of an SMSA of 100,000
population.   It was also estimated that for that last population size,
the SMSA price level would be 1.06 times that in non-SMSA areas.   Then
the distribution of population by SMSA size was obtained from The 1970
Census of Population, PC(1)-A1, Table 41, p. 1-210.   The size classes
and the assigned price level deflator for each class, based on assumed
class mid points, were:

Population in 000	Deflator Relative to Non-SMSA
0 - < 250	1.060
250 - < 500	1.085
500 - < 1,000	1.103
1,000 - < 2,500	1.120
2,500 - < 9,000	1.154
≥ 9,000	1.200

Then a weighted deflator was obtained for each state, based on
the proportion of population in each size class. (If a state had no
metropolitan population, its deflator was 1.00.) The deflator was
then divided into the initial per capita income figure cited above,
and the resulting deflated variable was called "real" disposable
income.

A dummy variable was defined for each of the nine census regions;
if a state falls in a given region, the dummy variable for that region
takes on a value of 1.0, and if a state does not fall in the region,
the dummy variable takes on a value of 0.0.

Table 194   Was obtained employing the data of Table 193, and eliminating
variables that were not statistically significant at the 10% level
by means of a step-wise procedure. Alternative combinations were
examined, so that a variable eliminated at one step might re-enter
the equation at a later step if other variables had been deleted.

Table 195   Dependent variables are industrial consumption of specific
energy source relative to manufacturing employment; industrial use of
petroleum products in BTU was obtained from Tables 76 and 78, natural
gas BTU from Table 125, electricity BTU from Table 147, andccoal-hydroelec-
tric power use from Table 174. The BTU data were divided by corresponding state manufacturing employment from U.S. Bureau of the Census,
Annual Survey of Manufactures, 1973, M73 (A5)-6, Washington, 1976.
Prices for industrial use of energy were obtained by dividing expenditures by corresponding quantities from tables listed above; the industrial
expenditures for petroleum, natural gas, electricity and coal plus hydroelectric power were respectively obtained from Tables 80 and 82;
Table 127; Table 149; and Table 175. The sources for independent variables
(population, income, climate and regional variables) are those cited
in Table 193.

Part II

Table 196   Column 1 refers to population as of July 1, 1972 and was
obtained from U.S. Bureau of the Census, Current Population Reports,
Series p-25, No. 520, July, 1974, p. 21; column 2 was obtained by dividing
each state population by the population of the region in which it is
located; column 3 was obtained by dividing state population by total
U.S. population and multiplying by 100. The use of fractions for column
2 and of percentages for column 3 was done to facilitate the joint
presentation of significant digits for the two series.

Appendixes

<u>Table A.1.1</u>   Columns 1 through 4 derived from several tables on
  civilian highway use in [48]. Column 5 from [42] for U.S. and
  regional aggregates. State distribution based on [48] and on
  confidential series whose citation was not permitted. Column 6
  from [48] after check using data from [5] and [46]. Column 7
  from [39], [43] and previous columns. Column 7 total obtained
  as residual by subtracting sum of previous columns from U.S.
  total in [43]. Then total distributed to states in same proportions as distillate fuel, from [39].

<u>Table A.1.2</u>   Aggregated from Table A.1.1.

<u>Table A.1.3</u>   Columns 1 and 2 from column 1, Table A.1.1, distributed
  by applying data from [21] and [47]. Columns 3, 4, and 5 from
  column 5, Table A.1.1, distributed by applying data from [42],
  [45], [46], [48] and confidential series. Columns 6 and 7 from
  column 7, Table A.1.1, distributed on basis of data in [39] and
  [42].

<u>Table A.1.4</u>   Rearrangement of data presented in Tables A.1.1 and A.1.3.
  Columns 1, 2, 4, 6, 9, 10, and 11 from Table A.1.3. Columns 3, 5, 7,
  and 8 from Table A.1.1.

<u>Table A.1.5</u>   Alternative summations from Table A.1.4.

<u>Table A.1.6</u>   Aggregated from Table A.1.3.

<u>Table A.1.7</u>   Aggregated from Table A.1.4.

<u>Table A.1.8</u>   Aggregated from Table A.1.5.

<u>Table A.1.9</u>   Derived from data in [48].

<u>Table A.1.10</u> Regional values are weighted averages of state data of
  Table A.1.9.

<u>Table A.2.1</u>   Column 1: base data for table. Data sources for conterminous
  U.S.: [24] and [25]. Hawaii and Alaska values based on [38]. Premium
  gasoline differential based on information in [24] and [26]. Distribution
  between regular and premium based on confidential series. Taxes per
  gallon from [25] and [48]. Columns 2-6 derived by adding or subtracting
  from base data (col. 1) amounts to account for 1) aviation gasoline
  differential, 2) tax differences, 3) bulk discounts. Sources drawn on
  include [12], [25], [26], [27], and [48].

Table A.2.2   Developed from column 1 of Table A.2.1 in same fashion as other columns of Table A.2.1 (see source description), with additional information from [6] and [30].

Table A.2.3   Weighted averages obtained by dividing expenditures (Table A.3.4) by corresponding quantities (Table A.1.7).

Table A.2.4   Presents components employed in deriving column 1 of Table A.2.1. See source information in Table A.2.1.

Table A.3.1   Data in Table A.1.4 multiplied by corresponding column entries in Table A.2.1.

Table A.3.2   Data in Table A.1.4 multiplied by corresponding column entries in Table A.2.2.

Table A.3.3   From appropriate additions of columns in Table A.3.1 and A.3.2. Household from sum of columns 1, 2 and 3 in Table A.3.1; business from sum of columns 4, 5 and 6 in Table A.3.1; government from sum of columns in Table A.3.2; highway from sum of columns 1, 4 and 5 in Table A.3.1 and columns 1, 2 and 4 in Table A.3.2; aviation from sum of columns 2 and 6 in Table A.3.1 and 3 and 5 in Table A.3.2; marine from column 3 of Table A.3.1.

Table A.3.4   Aggregated from Tables A.3.1 and A.3.2.

Table A.3.5   Aggregated from Table A.3.3.

Table A.3.6   Obtained from quantities in Table A.1.4 multiplied by federal tax rate as modified by adjustment to rate by type of use as shown in table in text: "Components of Gasoline Prices per Gallon."

Table A.3.7   Sum of Component columns in Table A.3.6.

Table A.3.8   Obtained from quantities in Table A.1.4 multiplied by state and local tax rates (from Table A.2.4 minus the four cent federal tax), modified by adjustment to rates by type of use as shown in table in text: "Components of Gasoline Prices per Gallon."

Table A.3.9   From corresponding columns on quantities in Table A.1.4 times non-highway tax rates listed in [48].

Table A.3.10 Totals of Tables A.3.8 and A.3.9, respectively, appear as columns 1 and 2; their total, in turn, equals column 3.

Table A.3.11 Aggregated from Tables A.3.6 and A.3.7.

Table A.3.12 Aggregated from Tables A.3.8, A.3.9 and A.3.10.

Table A.3.13   By function from Table A.3.7 plus Table A.3.10; by sector from Tables A.3.6, A.3.8 and A.3.9. Total from sum of component columns in table.

Table A.3.14   Aggregated from Table A.3.13.

Table A.3.15   This study state and local taxes from Table A.3.10; local taxes based on difference between state tax rates in [48] and the state plus local tax rates employed here (Table A.2.4). This study private sector federal taxes from highway taxes in Table A.3.7 minus federal highway and military highway in Table A.3.6. Corresponding state and federal taxes from [48].

Table A.3.16   Aggregated from Table A.3.15.

Table B.1.1   Data obtained from [39].

Table B.1.2   First two columns obtained as sums from corresponding columns of Table B.1.1; third column from [39]; fourth column [40].

Table B.1.3   Aggregated from Tables B.1.1 and B.1.2.

Table B.1.4   From Table B.1.2, converting units from thousand barrels to million BTU by applying scale factors in [7].

Table B.1.5   Aggregated from Table B.1.4.

Table B.1.6   Developed from data in [20], [31], and [45], 1974. U.S. industrial use as share of total based on data in [45]; regional distribution from [20]; allocation to states based on [31].

Table B.1.7   Totals (first two columns) from Table B.1.1 applying scale factors in [7]; distribution between industrial and non-industrial use by first allocating No. 6 fuel oil to estimated industrial use; if former exceeded latter, residual applied to non-industrial use; if latter exceeded former, deficit accounted for by No. 5 fuel oil.

Table B.1.8   Aggregated from Table B.1.7.

Table B.1.9   Column 1 from column 4 entries divided by regional average; in similar fashion, column 2 from column 5, and column 3 from column 6. Sources for column 4-6: office employment from [34], [36], [37], [45]; school enrollment and employment from [45]; hospital employment from [36] and [45].

Table B.1.10   Commercial use as fraction of residual oil use estimated
for regions from data in [20] and [39]; distributed to states by
application of Table B.1.9.

Table B.1.11   Control total from Table B.1.4, industrial total from
Table B.1.6, commercial total from Table B.1.10, residential use
from [20] and [39].

Table B.1.12   Aggregated from Tables B.1.10 and B.1.11.

Table B.1.13   Primary sources of data: [36] and [45]; additional
information from [34] and [37].

Table B.1.14   From application of Table B.1.13 to Table B.1.12.

Table B.1.15   Aggregated from Table B.1.14.

Table B.1.16   Obtained by combining Tables B.1.7 and B.1.14 in a step-
wise fashion, with No. 5 fuel oil allocated first to household use,
then to government, next to business commercial use and finally to
industrial use. This completes the process initiated in Table B.1.7.

Table B.1.17   Obtained by combining Tables B.1.7 and B.1.14 in a step-
wise fashion, with No. 6 fuel oil allocated first to industrial use,
then to business commercial use, then to government and finally to
household use. This completes the process initiated in Table B.1.7.

Table B.1.18   Aggregated from Tables B.1.16 and B.1.17.

Table B.1.19   Commercial use as fraction of distillates plus kerosine use
estimated for regions from data in [20] and [39], distributed to states
by application of Table B.1.9.

Table B.1.20   Commercial use of Table B.1.19 distributed to sectors by
applying Table B.1.13; all kerosine use treated as component of household
consumption, so that residential consumption of Table B.1.19 minus
kerosine from Table B.1.4 yields household distillates in Table B.1.20.

Table B.1.21   Aggregated from Tables B.1.19 and B.1.20.

Table B.1.22   LPG column in Table B.1.4 distributed on basis of information in [20].

Table B.1.23   Commercial categories of Table B.1.22 distributed to sectors
by applying scale factors of Table B.1.13.

Table B.1.24   Aggregated from Tables B.1.22 and B.1.23.

Table B.1.25   Obtained as sum of corresponding columns from Tables
    B.1.11, B.1.19, and B.1.22.

Table B.1.26   Obtained as sum of corresponding columns from Tables
    B.1.10, B.1.19 and B.1.22.

Table B.1.27   Aggregated from Tables B.1.25 and B.1.26.

Table B.1.28   Obtained as sum of corresponding columns from Tables
    B.1.14, B.1.20 and B.1.23.

Table B.1.29   Aggregated from Table B.1.28.

Table B.2.1   No. 2 fuel oil price based on data in [3], [16], [18] and
    Table A.2.4; No. 6 fuel oil price based on [2], [3], [15], [16], [43] and
    No. 2 fuel oil price estimates.

Table B.2.2   From Table B.2.1 scaled by unit conversion factors from [7]
    and level of use scale factors from [15] and [16].

Table B.2.3   Specific distillates as fraction of total from Table B.1.1;
    definition of distillates follows [39]; prices of distillates scaled
    from No. 2 price (Table B.2.1) on basis of data in [24] and [25].

Table B.2.4   Government fractions from Table B.1.14; LPG price estimates
    from [43] and [16] for regional scale factors which were multiplied
    by state prices in Table B.2.1.

Table B.2.5   All commercial level based on information in [15] and [16];
    kerosine price differential from [16] and [43]; No. 5 fuel oil price
    differential from [24] and [25]; other fuels from Tables B.2.1 through
    B.2.4; unit conversion factors from [7].

Table B.3.1   Derived from quantities in Tables B.1.16 and B.2.4 (govern-
    ment) multiplied by prices in Table B.2.5, as modified to account for
    level of use.   (Prices were scaled based on data in [15] and [16].

Table B.3.2   Derived from quantities in Tables B.1.17 and B.2.4 (govern-
    ment) multiplied by prices in Table B.2.5, as modified to account
    for level of use.

Table B.3.3   Derived from quantities in Table B.1.20 multiplied by
    prices in Table B.2.5, as modified to account for level of use.

Table B.3.4 Derived from quantities in Table B.1.23 multiplied by prices
    in Table B.2.5, as modified to account for level of use.

Table B.3.5   Aggregated from Tables B.3.1 and B.3.2.

Table B.3.6   Aggregated from Tables B.3.3 and B.3.4.

Table B.3.7   Column 1 from Table B.3.1; column 2 from Table B.3.2;
column 3 is sum of first two columns; columns 4 and 5 from Table B.3.3;
column 6 from Table B.3.4; column 7 is sum of columns 3 through 6.

Table B.3.8   Sector sums from Tables B.3.1, B.3.2, B.3.3 and B.3.4,
combining corresponding sector values from each of those tables.

Table B.3.9   Aggregated from Tables B.3.7 and B.3.8.

Table C.1.1   Columns 1 through 4 from [39] Tables 13 and 13a; remaining
columns derived from columns 3 and 4.

Table C.1.2   Aggregated from Table C.1.1.

Table C.1.3   Derived from Table C.1.1 using scale factors from [7].

Table C.1.4   BOM data from Table C.1.3, "total burned" (column 2), and
NCA data from [23].

Table C.1.5   Aggregated from Table C.1.4.

Table C.2.1   Columns 1-3 obtained from price data of Appendix B,
Table B.2.5, in particular, weighting by residual-distillates distribution implicit in Table C.1.1. Column 4 from [23].

Table C.2.2   Obtained by summing entries in Table C.2.1 and dividing by
number of cases per region.

Table C.3.1   Column 1 from column 1, Table C.1.4; most entries in column 2
obtained directly by averaging column 3 and column 4 in Table C.2.1;
exceptions included five states with zero entries and four with very
low values in column 4 (Me., N.H., Vt., and Utah). The four low value
cases were augmented by adding .3 to the amounts in column 4, which made
them roughly consistent with other state values in their respective
regions. The zero cases in column 4 were filled in by multiplying the
column 3 entries by .92, the average ratio that held for the non-zero
cases. Given these substitutions, column 3 and the revised column 4
entries were averaged to obtain column 2 of Table C.3.1. Column 3
obtained by multiplying column 1 by column 2.

Table C.3.2   Column 1 obtained by summing column 1 of Table C.3.1; column 2
obtained by summing column 3 of Table C.3.1; column 3 obtained by dividing
column 2 by column 1.

<u>Table D.1.1</u>   Data obtained from [39].

<u>Table D.1.2</u>   Aggregated from Table D.1.1.

<u>Table D.1.3</u>   Column 1 from [39], column 2 from [40], column 4 from [48]. Other columns derived from columns 1, 2 and 4.

<u>Table D.1.4</u>   Column 1 from column 2 of Table D.1.3 divided by column 1 of Table D.1.3; column 2 lists estimates developed on basis of internal evidence (see text); column 3 from column 2 of Table D.1.3 minus column 2 of this table; column 4 from column 3 of Table D.1.3 minus column 2 of this table.

<u>Table D.1.5</u>   Aggregated from Tables D.1.3 and D.1.4.

<u>Table D.1.6</u>   From data in [42] and a confidential series on state use, adjusted to account for later revisions.

<u>Table D.1.7</u>   From [42] applying state distributions based on military use of distillates, as shown in Table D.1.1.

<u>Table D.1.8</u>   Aggregated from Tables D.1.6 and D.1.7.

<u>Table D.1.9</u>   Data obtained from [39].

<u>Table D.1.10</u>   Aggregated from Table D.1.9.

<u>Table D.1.11</u>   Column 1 from Table D.1.1, column 2 from Tables D.1.3 (diesel) and D.1.4 (LPG), column 3 from Tables D.1.6 and D.1.7, columns 4 and 5 from Table D.1.9; all entries except aviation fuel were scaled by scale factors in [7]; in the case of aviation jet fuel, a weighted scale factor was employed for each P.A.D. district (see text).

<u>Table D.1.12</u>   Column 1, household, from Table D.1.9, column 4; column 2, business, from Tables D.1.3, D.1.4, D.1.6 and D.1.9 for highway diesel, highway LPG, civilian aviation, railroad and business vessel bunkering use; column 3, federal government, from Tables D.1.1 and D.1.7, military use of distillates and residuals and military aviation. Entries scaled by scale factors from [7] and set of scale factors developed for aviation use.

<u>Table D.1.13</u>   Aggregated from Tables D.1.11 and D.1.12.

<u>Table D.2.1</u>   Data on taxes from Table A.2.5 and [48]; data on prices based on Tables A.2.1, B.2.1 and B.2.5 and information in [24].

Table D.2.2   For aviation jet fuel, national average prices obtained from [19] and [26]; scaled to state levels applying relative values from Table B.2.5. For railroad fuel, national average price obtained from [4]; also scaled to state levels applying Table B.2.5.

Table D.2.3   Based on data from [26] applied to Table B.2.1 and adjusted to level of use.

Table D.3.1   Columns 1 and 2 (military use) derived as the products of corresponding columns in Tables D.1.1 and D.2.3; in similar fashion, column 3 (highway diesel use) derived from Tables D.1.3 and D.2.1; column 4 (highway LPG use) derived from Tables D.1.4 and D.2.1; column 5 (civilian aviation jet fuel) from Tables D.1.6 and D.2.2; and column 6 (military aviation jet fuel) from Tables D.1.7 and D.2.2.

Table D.3.2   Columns 1 and 2 (railroad use) derived as the products of corresponding columns in Tables D.1.9 and D.2.2; columns 3 through 5 (vessel bunkering) derived as the products of corresponding columns in Tables D.1.9 and D.2.3.

Table D.3.3   Derived from appropriate sum of columns in Tables D.3.1 and D.3.2; in all cases columns for given function appear under sub-headings of the function.

Table D.3.4   Derived from appropriate sum of columns in Tables D.3.1 and D.3.2; household appears under vessel bunkering, distillates; federal government is the sum of military use of distillates and residuals, and of military aviation; business covers all remaining categories.

Table D.3.5   Aggregated from Tables D.3.1 and D.3.2.

Table D.3.6   Aggregated from Tables D.3.3 and D.3.4.

Table E.1.1   Data obtained from [39] and [40].

Table E.1.2   Aggregated from Table E.1.1.

Table E.1.3   Data obtained from [39], [40] and [42]. Original data for columns 3 and 4 appeared in form of aggregates for groupings of states; distributed to individual states on basis of distribution in column 2. Conversion to barrel equivalents carried out using scale factors from [7] and [42].

Table E.1.4   Aggregated from Table E.1.3.

Table E.1.5   Data obtained from [39], [40] and Table D.1.4.

Table E.1.6   Aggregated from Table E.1.5.

Table E.1.7   From Table E.1.1, scaled by scale factors from [7].

Table E.1.8   From Table E.1.3, scaled by scale factors from [7].

Table E.1.9   From Table E.1.5, scaled by scale factors in [7].

Table E.1.10   Aggregated from Tables E.1.7, E.1.8 and E.1.9.

Table E.1.11   Column 1 from Table E.1.7, columns 2 through 4 from
    Table E.1.8, columns 5 through 7 from Table E.1.9 and column 8 as
    sum of subtotals of table.

Table E.1.12   Aggregated from Table E.1.11.

Table E.2.1   From base data in Table B.2.5, adjusted for level of use;
    additional information drawn on included that in [17] and [26].

Table E.3.1   From multiplication of corresponding columns of quantity
    data (Tables E.1.1, E.1.3 and E.1.5) by price data (Table E.2.1).
    Household kerosine use assumed to equal half of miscellaneous kerosine
    use, with price set at 1.15 kerosine price in business use.

Table E.3.2   Aggregated from Table E.3.1.

Table F.1.1   Data obtained from [1] and [43]; [43] units converted from
    million cubic feet to BTU using state conversion factors listed in [1].

Table F.1.2   Aggregated from Table F.1.1

Table F.1.3   Data obtained from [1], [7] and [43].

Table F.1.4   Application of data in Table F.1.3.

Table F.1.5   Aggregated from tables F.1.3 and F.1.4.

Table F.1.6   Data obtained from [1] and [43]; [43] units converted from
    million cubic feet to BTU using state conversion factors listed in [1].

Table F.1.7   Aggregated from Table F.1.6.

Table F.1.8   Data obtained from [1], [23] and [43].

Table F.1.9   Aggregated from Table F.1.8.

Table F.1.10   Data obtained from [1].

Table F.1.11   Aggregated from Table F.1.10.

Table F.1.12   Data obtained from [1].

Table F.1.13   Aggregated from Table F.1.12.

Table F.1.14   Derived from data in [33].

Table F.1.15   Columns 1 through 3 from Table B.1.9; columns 4 through 11 reproduced from Table B.1.13.

Table F.1.16   From application of first three columns of Table F.1.15 to data in [20].

Table F.1.17   Aggregated from Table F.1.16.

Table F.1.18   Initial data from [43] revised on basis of series of inferences developed primarily from information in [20], and employing data in [33]. Columns 1 and 5 from Table F.1.1, column 2 based on data in Table F.1.14, column 3 from Table F.1.16, column 4 obtained by subtracting columns 2 and 3 from column 1 and column 6 obtained by adding column 2 to column 5.

Table F.1.19   Obtained by distributing entries in Table F.1.16 to sectors on basis of scale factors in columns 4 through 11 in Table F.1.15.

Table F.1.20   Aggregated from Tables F.1.18 and F.1.19.

Table F.1.21   Column 1 obtained from columns 1 and 5 of Table F.1.3, using column 5 entries for first five regions, and column 1 entries for last four regions; column 2 obtained from Table F.1.18, column 4; column 3 from data in [1], distributed from regions to states on basis of oil company use of petroleum products by state, Table E.1.8, column 5; columns 4 and 5 based on data in [41]; and column 6 from [43].

Table F.1.22   Aggregated from Table F.1.21

Table F.1.23   Column 1 from Table F.1.6, column 2; column 2 from Table F.1.8, column 1 minus column 3, this table; column 3 from Table F.1.6, column 4 minus column 3; column 4 from Table F.1.21, column 3; column 5 from Table F.1.6, column 1; column 6 from Table F.1.21, column 6; column 7 is sum of other columns.

Table F.1.24   Aggregated from Table F.1.23.

Table F.2.1   Data obtained from [1] and [43] by division of state expenditures by state quantities.

Table F.2.2   Data obtained from [1] and [43] by division of regional expenditures by regional quantities.

Table F.2.3   Data obtained from [1] and [43] by division of state expenditures by state quantities.

Table F.2.4   Data obtained from [1] and [43] by division of regional expenditures by regional quantities.

Table F.2.5   Data obtained from [1] and [43] by division of state expenditures by state quantities.

Table F.2.6   Data obtained from [1] and [43] by division of regional expenditures by regional quantities.

Table F.2.7   Data obtained directly from [23], and from [1] and [43] by division of state expenditures by state quantities.

Table F.2.8   Data obtained directly from [23], and from [1] and [43] by division of regional expenditures by regional quantities.

Table F.2.9   Data obtained from [1] by division of state expenditures by state quantities.

Table F.2.10 Data obtained from [1] by division of regional expenditures by regional quantities.

Table F.2.11 Data obtained from [1] by division of state expenditures by state quantities.

Table F.2.12 Data obtained from [1] by division of regional expenditures by regional quantities.

Table F.3.1   Data obtained from [1] and [43].

Table F.3.2   Aggregated from Table F.3.1.

Table F.3.3   Data obtained from [1] and [43].

Table F.3.4   Aggregated from Table F.3.3.

Table F.3.5   Data obtained from [1] and [43].

Table F.3.6   Aggregated from Table F.3.4.

Table F.3.7   Data obtained from [1], [23] and [43].

Table F.3.8   Aggregated from Table F.3.7.

Table F.3.9   Data obtained from [1].

Table F.3.10 Aggregated from Table F.3.9.

Table F.3.11 Data obtained from [1].

Table F.3.12 Aggregated from Table F.3.11

Table F.3.13 Corresponds to Table F.1.18; initial data from [43], revised
   on basis of [20] and [33]. Columns 1 and 5 from Table F.3.1; columns
   2, 3 and 4 from corresponding columns in Table F.1.18, each multiplied
   by commercial price (BOM) as listed in Table F.2.1, column 4. Column 6
   obtained by sum of columns 2 and 5.

Table F.3.14 Corresponds to Table F.1.19; obtained by multiplying entries
   in Table F.1.19 by commercial prices (BOM) as listed in Table F.2.1,
   column 4.

Table F.3.15 Aggregated from Tables F.3.13 and F.3.14.

Table F.3.16 Corresponds to Table F.1.21. Column 1 obtained from
   columns 1 and 4 of Table F.3.3, using column 4 entries for first five
   regions, and column 1 entries for last four regions; column 2 from
   Table F.3.13, column 4; columns 3, 4 and 5 obtained by multiplying
   corresponding quantities of Table F.1.21 by industrial prices obtained
   by dividing entries in column 1 of Table F.3.16 by corresponding entries
   in column 1 of Table F.1.21; column 6 from [43].

Table F.3.17 Aggregated from Table F.3.16.

Table F.3.18 Corresponds to Table F.1.23. Column 1 from Table F.3.5,
   column 2; column 2 from Table F.3.7, column 1 minus column 3, this
   table; column 3 from Table F.3.5, column 4 minus column 3; column 4
   from Table F.3.16, column 3; column 5 from Table F.3.5, column 1;
   column 6 from Table F.3.16, column 6; column 7 equals sum of previous
   columns.

Table F.3.19 Aggregated from Table F.3.18.

Table G.1.1 Developed from data in [10], converted to BTU using scale
   factors from [7].

Table G.1.2 Aggregated from Table G.1.1.

Table G.1.3 Based on data in [20] and Table B.1.9 state scale factors.

Table G.1.4 From column 2, Table G.1.1 times row fractions in Table G.1.3.

Table G.1.5   Derived from Table G.1.4 by applying scale factors of
Table B.1.13, and then summing subsector entries to yield sector totals.

Table G.1.6   Aggregated from Tables G.1.4 and G.1.5.

Table G.1.7   Columns 1 and 2 (fractions) obtained from Table B.1.13,
columns 2 and 3, by summing those columns and dividing the sum into
each component, in turn. Columns 3 and 4 obtained by multiplying
columns 1 and 2, respectively, by column 5, Table G.1.1.

Table G.1.8   Column 1 from column 1, Table G.1.5; columns 2, 3 and 4 from
columns 3, 6 and 7, respectively, of Table G.1.1; column 5 is sum of
preceding columns.

Table G.1.9   Column 1 from column 2, Table G.1.5; column 2 from column 3,
Table G.1.7; column 3 from sum of column 1 and 2; column 4 from column 3,
Table G.1.5; column 5 from column 4, Table G.1.7; column 6 from column 4,
Table G.1.1; column 6 from column 4, Table G.1.1; column 7 from sum of
columns 4, 5 and 6; column 8 from sum of columns 3 and 7.

Table G.1.10   Column 1 from column 1, Table G.1.1; column 2 from column 5,
Table G.1.8; column 3 from column 3, Table G.1.9; column 4 from column 7,
Table G.1.9; column 5 from sum of preceding columns.

Table G.1.11   Aggregated from Tables G.1.8, G.1.9 and G.1.10.

Table G.2.1   Obtained by dividing state expenditures of Table G.3.1 by
corresponding quantities of Table G.1.1. Original data from [10].

Table G.2.2   Obtained by dividing regional expenditures of Table G.3.2
by corresponding quantities of Table G.1.2.

Table G.3.1   Obtained from [10].

Table G.3.2   Aggregated from Table G.3.1.

Table G.3.3   Corresponds to Table G.1.5. Obtained by multiplying Table G.1.5
entries by corresponding prices in Table G.2.1, column 2.

Table G.3.4   Aggregated from Table G.3.3.

Table G.3.5   Corresponds to Table G.1.8. Column 1 from column 1, Table G.1.8
times corresponding prices in Table G.2.1, column 2; columns 2, 3 and 4
from columns 3, 6 and 7, respectively, of Table G.3.1.

Table G.3.6   Corresponds to Table G.1.9. Columns 1 and 4 from corresponding
entries in Table G.1.9 times corresponding prices in Table G.2.1,
column 2; columns 2 and 5 from column 5, Table G.3.1 times corresponding
fractions in columns 1 and 2, Table G.1.7; column 6 from column 4,
Table G.3.1; column 3 is sum of columns 1 and 2; column 7 is sum of
columns 4 through 6.

Table G.3.7   Corresponds to Table G.1.10. Column 1 from column 1, Table G.3.1; column 2 from last column, Table G.3.5; column 3 from column 3, Table G.3.6; column 4 from last column, Table G.3.6; and column 5 equals sum of preceding columns.

Table G.3.8   Aggregated from Tables G.3.5, G.3.6 and G.3.7.

Table H.1.1   Primary data source was [7]; disaggregation from groupings of states based on data in [20] and [23].

Table H.1.2   Aggregated from Table H.1.1.

Table H.1.3   Column 1 from [23], columns 2 through 4 from [7], column 5 obtained as average of columns 1 and 4, except for Alaska entry, which was from [7].

Table H.1.4   Aggregated from Table H.1.3.

Table H.1.5   Column 1 from column 1 plus .5 of column 4, Table H.1.1; column 2 from column 2, Table H.1.1; column 3 from column 3 plus .268 of column 4, Table H.1.1; column 4 from column 4, Table H.1.3; column 5 is sum of preceding columns.

Table H.1.6   Aggregated from Table H.1.5.

Table H.2.1   Price data from [10], [18] and [23]. Conversion from price per ton to price per million BTU based on scale factors in [10].

Table H.2.2   Column 1 (electric utility use) obtained by averaging columns 1 and 2, Table H.2.1; column 2 equals column 1 times 1.05; column 3 equals average of column 2 and column 4; column 4 obtained by regression equation relating column 5 to column 4 in Table H.2.1, and then scaling by scale factors from [10].

Table H.3.1   Product of quantities of Table H.1.5 by prices of Table H.2.2 (in dollars per million BTU).

Table H.3.2   Aggregated from Table H.3.1.

Table I.1.1   Data from [10], drawing on FPC data.

Table I.1.2   Derived from Table I.1.1 by dividing each column entry by corresponding total in column 5 of Table I.1.1.

Table I.1.3   Kilowatt-hours by aggregation of Table I.1.1; fractions by division of aggregate subtotals by aggregate total.

Table I.1.4   Fuel equivalent scale factors derived from data in [7], [10] and [23], and applied to Table I.1.1.   Industrial use set at .012 electric utility use in each state, based on data in [7].

Table I.1.5   Aggregated from Table I.1.4.

Table I.2.1   Based on composite average of cost of all fossil fuel per million BTU, from [10], modified in some cases after check for reasonableness of estimate.   (See text.)

Table I.3.1   Derived as product of quantities from Table I.1.4 and prices from Table I.2.1.

Table I.3.2   Aggregated from Table I.3.1.

List Of References For
Part II

[1]   American Gas Association, 1972 Gas Facts (Arlington, Virginia, 1973).

[2]   American Petroleum Institute, Basic Petroleum Data Book (Washington, October 1973, looseleaf; supplements, 1976).

[3]   American Petroleum Institute, Petroleum Facts and Figures (Washington, 1971).

[4]   Association of American Railways, Public Information Office, Washington, D.C., telephone conversation, April 28, 1977.

[5]   Boating Industry Association, Chicago Illinois, telephone conversation, December 1975.

[6]   Myran Bollinger, Defense Supply Agency and S. Roberts, GSA Motor Equipment Division, telephone conversation, June 1976.

[7]   Lulie H. Crump and Charles L. Readling, Fuel and Energy Data, United States By States and Region, U.S. Bureau of Mines Information Circular 8647 (1974).

[8]   Joel Darmstadter, Resources for the Future, conversation, September 3, 1976.

[9]   James M. Diehl, Fuel Oil Sales, Bureau of Mines, telephone conversations, August 26 and 30, 1976.

[10] Edison Electric Institute, Statistical Yearbook of the Electric Utility Industry for 1972 (New York, 1973).

[11] Edison Electric Institute, Glossary of Electric Utility Terms, (New York, 1976).

References (2)

[12] Walter Faison, Aviation Plans section, Federal Aviation Administration, telephone conversation, June, 1976.

[13] Leonard Fanelli, Bureau of Mines, suggested the hypothesis in a telephone conversation, July, 1976.

[14] Annette Fleming, American Gas Association, telephone conversation, July 11, 1977.

[15] Foster Associates, Energy Prices 1960-73 (Cambridge: Ballinger Pub. Co., 1974, 259pp).

[16] Foster Associates, Prospective Regional Markets For Coal Conversion Plant Products Projected to 1980 and 1985, Vol. III Current and Projected Demand, Supply and Price of Energy In the United States. Schedules, prepared for the Office of Coal Research (1974).

[17] E. K. Grigsby, E. W. Mills, D. C. Collins, "Refiners Facing Future for 5.3 Billion/Year Investments" in Oil and Gas Journal (May 7, 1973).

[18] Independent National Gas Association of America, Comparison of Seasonal Househeating Costs For Gas, Fuel Oil, Coal and Electricity, 1971 Season (Washington), and "1972 Season" unpublished.

[19] Joseph Kull, Civil Aeronautics Board, telephone conversation, June 12, 1976.

[20] Arthur D. Little Inc., for Federal Energy Administration, Project Independence, Energy Conservation, Vol. I, Residential and Commercial Energy Use Patterns, 1970-1990. (Washington, D.C., 1974).

References (3)

[21] Motor Vehicle Manufacturers Association, <u>1975 Automobile Facts
      and Figures</u> (Detroit, Michigan).

[22] National Coal Association, <u>Bituminous Coal Data 1973 Edition</u>
      (Washington, 1974).

[23] National Coal Association, <u>Steam-Electric Plant Factors, 1973
      Edition</u> (Washington, 1974).

[24] <u>The Oil and Gas Journal</u> (Tulsa, Oklahoma, weekly).

[25] <u>Platt's Oil Price Handbook and Oilmanac Annual</u>, 1972 Edition
      (New York, New York).

[26] <u>Platt's Oilgram: Daily Price Service</u> (New York, New York, daily)

[27] John Reith, American Trucking Association, telephone conversation,
      January, 1976.

[28] Nancy Simon, Input-Output Division, Bureau of Economic Analysis,
      U.S. Department of Commerce, telephone conversation,
      September 3, 1976.

[29] Stanford Research Institute, <u>Patterns of Energy Consumption in the</u>
      United States, prepared for the Office of Science and Technology
      (Washington, D.C. 1973).

[30] Joseph Ullman and Kent Bramlett, Federal Highway Administration,
      telephone conversations, June, 1976.

[31] U.S. Bureau of the Census, <u>Annual Survey of Manufactures, 1973</u>
      <u>Statistics for States, Standard Metropolitan Statistical Areas,</u>
      <u>Large Industrial Counties and Selected Cities</u>, (Washington, 1976).

References (4)

[32] U.S. Bureau of the Census, Census of Housing: 1960, Vol. I,
     States and Small Areas, U.S. Summary, Final Report,
     (Washington, 1963).

[33] U.S. Bureau of the Census, Census of Housing: 1970, Detailed Housing
     Characteristics, Final Report, HC(1)-B1 U.S. Summary (Washington,
     1972).

[34] U.S. Bureau of the Census, Census of Population: 1970, General
     Social and Economic Characteristics Final Report PC(1)-C1,
     U.S. Summary (Washington, 1972).

[35] U.S. Bureau of the Census, Current Population Reports, Series P-25
     No. 560 (Washington, July 1974).

[36] U.S. Bureau of the Census, Public Employment in 1972 (Washington,
     1973).

[37] U.S. Bureau of Labor Statistics, Employment and Earnings, May 1973,
     "State and Area Employment" Table B-7 (Washington).

[38] U.S. Bureau of Labor Statistics, "News Release USDL-72-240, 1972."

[39] U.S. Bureau of Mines, Mineral Industry Surveys, Fuel Oil Sales Annual,
     Sales of Fuel Oil and Kerosene in 1972 (Washington).

[40] U.S. Bureau of Mines, Mineral Industry Surveys, Liquified Petroleum
     Gas Sales, Annual, Sale of Liquified Petroleum Gases and Ethane in
     1973 (Washington).

[41] U.S. Bureau of Mines, Mineral Industry Surveys; Main Line Natural Gas
     Sales to Industrial Users: 1974 (Washington, 1976).

References (5)

[42] U.S. Bureau of Mines, <u>Minerals Industry Surveys, Petroleum Statement Annual, Crude Petroleum, Petroleum Products and Natural Gas Liquids: 1972</u> (Washington).

[43] U.S. Bureau of Mines, <u>Minerals Yearbook, Vol. I</u>, (Washington) annual.

[44] U.S. Department of Commerce, <u>Survey of Current Business,</u> monthly.

[45] U.S. Department of Commerce, <u>U.S. Statistical Abstract</u>.

[46] U.S. Department of Transportation, Office of Policy, Plans, and International Affairs, <u>Summary of National Transportation Statistics, Final Report</u> No. DOT-TSC-OST-75-18 (June, 1975).

[47] U.S. Federal Highway Administration, <u>Nationwide Personal Study 1969</u> Reports 1 and 7 (Washington).

[48] U.S. Federal Highway Administration, <u>1972 Highway Statistics</u> (Washington, 1974).